Mercedes-Benz 190, 190E & 190D

Service and Repair Manual

Steve Rendle and Spencer Drayton

(3450-352-1AB1)

Models covered

Mercedes Benz 190,190E and 190D Saloon models with 4- and 6-cylinder petrol engines, and 4- and 5-cylinder diesel engines.
1797 cc, 1996 cc, 2298 cc and 2597 cc petrol engines.
1997 cc and 2497 cc (normally-aspirated and turbocharged) diesel engines

Does not cover 2.3-16, 2.5-16 or 2.5-16 Evolution models

ABCDE
FGHIJ
KLMNO
PQR

A book in the **Haynes Service and Repair Manual Series**

ISBN **1 85960 450 1**

British Library Cataloguing in Publication Data
A catalogue record for this book is available from the British Library.

Printed by **J H Haynes & Co Ltd, Sparkford, Nr Yeovil, Somerset BA22 7JJ, England**

Haynes Publishing
Sparkford, Nr Yeovil, Somerset BA22 7JJ, England

Haynes North America, Inc
861 Lawrence Drive, Newbury Park, California 91320, USA

Editions Haynes S.A.
Tour Aurore - La Défense 2, 18 Place des Reflets,
92975 PARIS LA DEFENSE Cedex, France

Haynes Publishing Nordiska AB
Box 1504, 751 45 UPPSALA, Sweden

Contents

LIVING WITH YOUR MERCEDES-BENZ 190

Introduction	Page **0•4**
Safety First!	Page **0•5**

Roadside Repairs

If your car won't start	Page **0•6**
Jump starting	Page **0•7**
Wheel changing	Page **0•8**
Identifying leaks	Page **0•9**
Towing	Page **0•9**

Weekly Checks

Introduction	Page **0•10**
Underbonnet check points	Page **0•10**
Engine oil level	Page **0•11**
Brake fluid level	Page **0•12**
Power steering fluid level	Page **0•12**
Coolant level	Page **0•13**
Washer fluid level	Page **0•13**
Wiper blades	Page **0•13**
Tyre condition and pressure	Page **0•14**
Battery	Page **0•15**
Bulbs and fuses	Page **0•15**

Lubricants, fluids and tyre pressures	Page **0•16**

MAINTENANCE

Routine Maintenance and Servicing

Mercedes 190 petrol models	Page **1A•1**
Maintenance schedule	Page **1A•4**
Maintenance procedures	Page **1A•7**
Mercedes 190 diesel models	Page **1B•1**
Maintenance schedule	Page **1B•3**
Maintenance procedures	Page **1B•5**

Contents

REPAIRS AND OVERHAUL

Engine and Associated Systems

Four-cylinder petrol engine in-car repair procedures Page 2A•1
Six-cylinder petrol engine in-car repair procedures Page 2B•1
Diesel engine in-car repair procedures Page 2C•1
Engine removal and general engine overhaul procedures Page 2D•1
Cooling, heating and ventilation systems Page 3•1
Carburettor fuel system Page 4A•1
Bosch CIS-E (KE-Jetronic) fuel injection system Page 4B•1
Diesel fuel injection system Page 4C•1
Exhaust and emission control systems Page 4D•1
Starting and charging systems Page 5A•1
Ignition system - 4-cylinder petrol engine Page 5B•1
Ignition system - 6-cylinder petrol engine Page 5C•1
Preheating system - diesel engine Page 5D•1

Transmission

Clutch Page 6•1
Manual transmission Page 7A•1
Automatic transmission Page 7B•0
Final drive, driveshafts and propeller shaft Page 8•1

Brakes and Suspension

Braking system Page 9•1
Suspension and steering Page 10•1

Body equipment

Bodywork Page 11•1
Body electrical system Page 12•1

Wiring Diagrams

Wiring Diagrams Page 12•16

REFERENCE

Dimensions and Weights Page REF•1
Conversion Factors Page REF•2
Buying Spare Parts and Vehicle Identification Page REF•3
General Repair Procedures Page REF•4
Jacking and Vehicle Support Page REF•5
Radio/cassette unit Anti-theft System Page REF•5
Tools and Working Facilities Page REF•6
MOT Test Checks Page REF•8
Fault Finding Page REF•12
Glossary of Technical Terms Page REF•20

Index

Index Page REF•24

The Mercedes Benz 190 was launched in Europe at the end of 1982 and introduced into the UK in September of the following year. All cars featured traditional, solid, practical Mercedes design and engineering combined with first class build quality. Only Saloon models were available, but with a choice of 1.8 litre, 2.0 litre, 2.3 litre, and 2.6 litre petrol engines, or 2.0 litre and 2.5 litre diesel engines, the latter available as normally aspirated and turbocharged variants.

All engines are derived from the well-proven engines which have appeared in many Mercedes-Benz vehicles. The engine is of four-cylinder (2.0 and 2.3 litre petrol engine), five-cylinder (2.5 litre diesel engine) or six-cylinder (2.6 litre petrol) overhead camshaft design, mounted longitudinally with the transmission mounted on its rear. Both manual and automatic transmissions were available.

All models have fully-independent suspension at both the front and rear.

A wide range of standard and optional equipment is available within the range to suit most tastes, including central locking, electric windows, an electric sunroof, an anti-lock braking system, and an air bag. An air conditioning system and traction control systems are available as options on certain models.

Provided that regular servicing is carried out in accordance with the manufacturer's recommendations, the vehicle should prove reliable and very economical. The engine compartment is well-designed, and most of the items requiring frequent attention are easily accessible.

Mercedes-Benz 190

Your Mercedes 190 Series manual

The aim of this manual is to help you get the best value from your vehicle. It can do so in several ways. It can help you decide what work must be done (even should you choose to get it done by a garage). It will also provide information on routine maintenance and servicing, and give a logical course of action and diagnosis when random faults occur. However, it is hoped that you will use the manual by tackling the work yourself. On simpler jobs it may even be quicker than booking the car into a garage and going there twice, to leave and collect it. Perhaps most important, a lot of money can be saved by avoiding the costs a garage must charge to cover its labour and overheads.

The manual has drawings and descriptions to show the function of the various components so that their layout can be understood. Tasks are described and photographed in a clear step-by-step sequence.

Acknowledgements

Thanks are due to Champion Spark Plug, who supplied the illustrations showing spark plug conditions, Sykes-Pickavant Limited, who provided some of the workshop tools, and to all those people at Sparkford who helped in the production of this manual. Thanks are also due to Mr J.K Foster of Bishops Lydeard who provided his vehicle.

We take great pride in the accuracy of information given in this manual, but vehicle manufacturers make alterations and design changes during the production run of a particular vehicle of which they do not inform us. No liability can be accepted by the authors or publishers for loss, damage or injury caused by any errors in, or omissions from, the information given.

Working on your car can be dangerous. This page shows just some of the potential risks and hazards, with the aim of creating a safety-conscious attitude.

General hazards

Scalding

• Don't remove the radiator or expansion tank cap while the engine is hot.

• Engine oil, automatic transmission fluid or power steering fluid may also be dangerously hot if the engine has recently been running.

Burning

• Beware of burns from the exhaust system and from any part of the engine. Brake discs and drums can also be extremely hot immediately after use.

Crushing

• When working under or near a raised vehicle, always supplement the jack with axle stands, or use drive-on ramps. ***Never venture under a car which is only supported by a jack.***

• Take care if loosening or tightening high-torque nuts when the vehicle is on stands. Initial loosening and final tightening should be done with the wheels on the ground.

Fire

• Fuel is highly flammable; fuel vapour is explosive.

• Don't let fuel spill onto a hot engine.

• Do not smoke or allow naked lights (including pilot lights) anywhere near a vehicle being worked on. Also beware of creating sparks (electrically or by use of tools).

• Fuel vapour is heavier than air, so don't work on the fuel system with the vehicle over an inspection pit.

• Another cause of fire is an electrical overload or short-circuit. Take care when repairing or modifying the vehicle wiring.

• Keep a fire extinguisher handy, of a type suitable for use on fuel and electrical fires.

Electric shock

• Ignition HT voltage can be dangerous, especially to people with heart problems or a pacemaker. Don't work on or near the ignition system with the engine running or the ignition switched on.

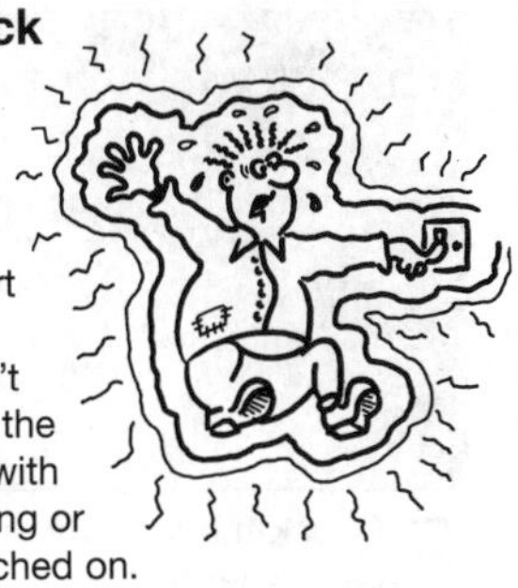

• Mains voltage is also dangerous. Make sure that any mains-operated equipment is correctly earthed. Mains power points should be protected by a residual current device (RCD) circuit breaker.

Fume or gas intoxication

• Exhaust fumes are poisonous; they often contain carbon monoxide, which is rapidly fatal if inhaled. Never run the engine in a confined space such as a garage with the doors shut.

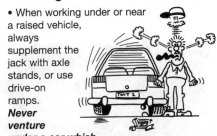

• Fuel vapour is also poisonous, as are the vapours from some cleaning solvents and paint thinners.

Poisonous or irritant substances

• Avoid skin contact with battery acid and with any fuel, fluid or lubricant, especially antifreeze, brake hydraulic fluid and Diesel fuel. Don't syphon them by mouth. If such a substance is swallowed or gets into the eyes, seek medical advice.

• Prolonged contact with used engine oil can cause skin cancer. Wear gloves or use a barrier cream if necessary. Change out of oil-soaked clothes and do not keep oily rags in your pocket.

• Air conditioning refrigerant forms a poisonous gas if exposed to a naked flame (including a cigarette). It can also cause skin burns on contact.

Asbestos

• Asbestos dust can cause cancer if inhaled or swallowed. Asbestos may be found in gaskets and in brake and clutch linings. When dealing with such components it is safest to assume that they contain asbestos.

Special hazards

Hydrofluoric acid

• This extremely corrosive acid is formed when certain types of synthetic rubber, found in some O-rings, oil seals, fuel hoses etc, are exposed to temperatures above 400°C. The rubber changes into a charred or sticky substance containing the acid. *Once formed, the acid remains dangerous for years. If it gets onto the skin, it may be necessary to amputate the limb concerned.*

• When dealing with a vehicle which has suffered a fire, or with components salvaged from such a vehicle, wear protective gloves and discard them after use.

The battery

• Batteries contain sulphuric acid, which attacks clothing, eyes and skin. Take care when topping-up or carrying the battery.

• The hydrogen gas given off by the battery is highly explosive. Never cause a spark or allow a naked light nearby. Be careful when connecting and disconnecting battery chargers or jump leads.

Air bags

• Air bags can cause injury if they go off accidentally. Take care when removing the steering wheel and/or facia. Special storage instructions may apply.

Diesel injection equipment

• Diesel injection pumps supply fuel at very high pressure. Take care when working on the fuel injectors and fuel pipes.

Warning: Never expose the hands, face or any other part of the body to injector spray; the fuel can penetrate the skin with potentially fatal results.

Remember...

DO

• Do use eye protection when using power tools, and when working under the vehicle.

• Do wear gloves or use barrier cream to protect your hands when necessary.

• Do get someone to check periodically that all is well when working alone on the vehicle.

• Do keep loose clothing and long hair well out of the way of moving mechanical parts.

• Do remove rings, wristwatch etc, before working on the vehicle – especially the electrical system.

• Do ensure that any lifting or jacking equipment has a safe working load rating adequate for the job.

DON'T

• Don't attempt to lift a heavy component which may be beyond your capability – get assistance.

• Don't rush to finish a job, or take unverified short cuts.

• Don't use ill-fitting tools which may slip and cause injury.

• Don't leave tools or parts lying around where someone can trip over them. Mop up oil and fuel spills at once.

• Don't allow children or pets to play in or near a vehicle being worked on.

The following pages are intended to help in dealing with common roadside emergencies and breakdowns. You will find more detailed fault finding information at the back of the manual, and repair information in the main chapters.

If your car won't start and the starter motor doesn't turn

- ☐ If it's a model with automatic transmission, make sure the selector is in 'P' or 'N'.
- ☐ Open the bonnet and make sure that the battery terminals are clean and tight.
- ☐ Switch on the headlights and try to start the engine. If the headlights go very dim when you're trying to start, the battery is probably flat. Get out of trouble by jump starting (see next page) using a friend's car.

If your car won't start even though the starter motor turns as normal

- ☐ Is there fuel in the tank?
- ☐ Is there moisture on electrical components under the bonnet? Switch off the ignition, then wipe off any obvious dampness with a dry cloth. Spray a water-repellent aerosol product (WD-40 or equivalent) on ignition and fuel system electrical connectors like those shown in the photos. Pay special attention to the ignition coil wiring connector and HT leads. (Note that diesel engines don't normally suffer from damp.)

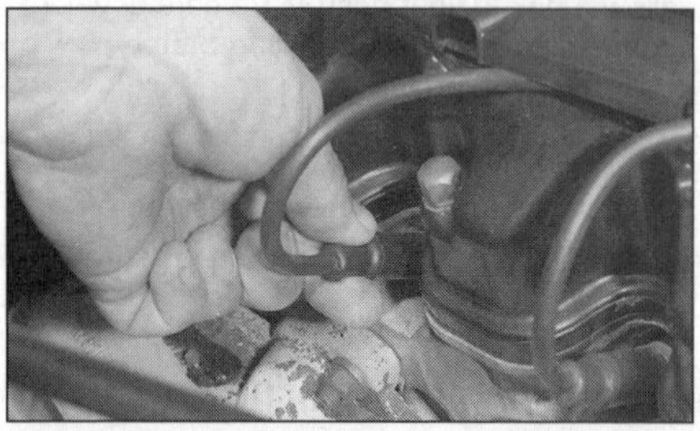

A Check that the spark plug HT leads are securely connected by pushing them onto the plugs (4-cylinder petrol model shown).

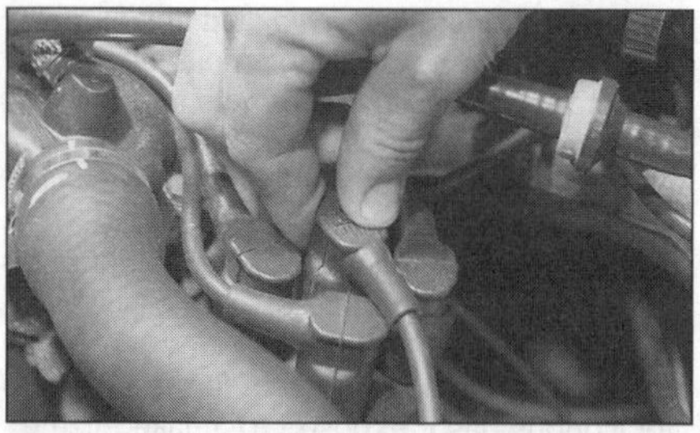

B Check that the HT leads are securely connected to the distributor (4-cylinder petrol model shown).

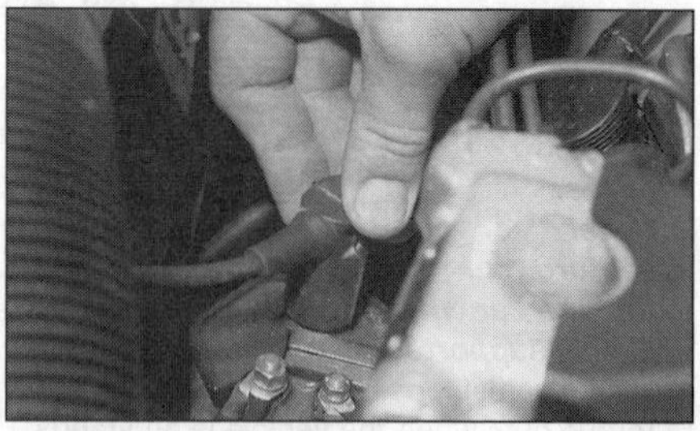

C Check that the HT lead and wiring connectors are securely connected to the ignition HT coil (4-cylinder petrol model shown).

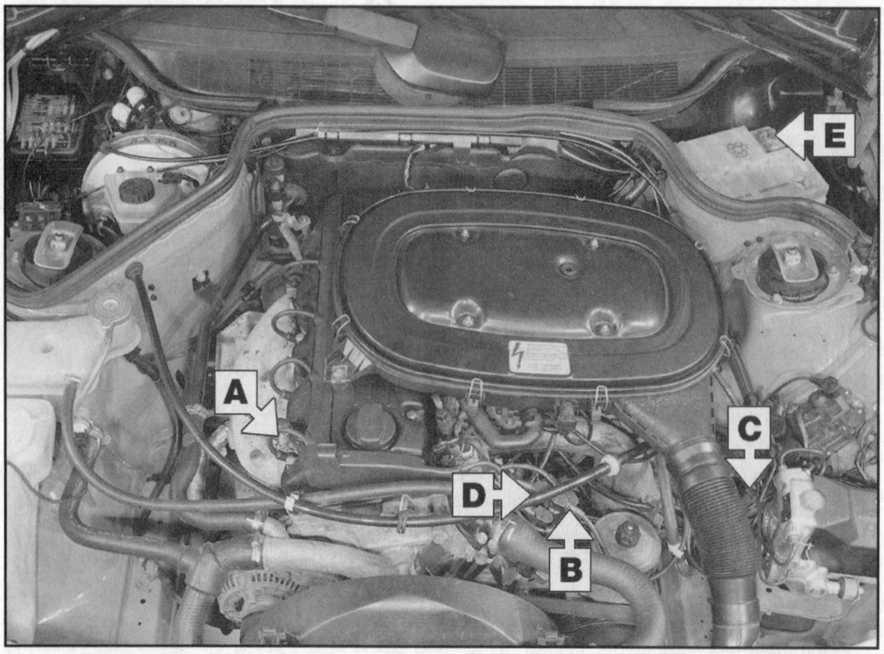

Check that electrical connections are secure (with the ignition switched off) and spray them with a water dispersant spray like WD-40 if you suspect a problem due to damp

D Check that all HT connections are clean, and spray them with a water dispersant spray like WD-40 if you suspect that damp may be causing a problem.

E Check the security and condition of the battery terminals.

Jump starting

HAYNES HiNT ***Jump starting will get you out of trouble, but you must correct whatever made the battery go flat in the first place. There are three possibilities:***

1) The battery has been drained by repeated attempts to start, or by leaving the lights on.
2) The charging system is not working properly (alternator drivebelt slack or broken, alternator wiring fault or alternator itself faulty).
3) The battery itself is at fault (electrolyte low, or battery worn out).

When jump-starting a car using a booster battery, observe the following precautions:

✔ Before connecting the booster battery, make sure that the ignition is switched off.

✔ Ensure that all electrical equipment (lights, heater, wipers, etc) is switched off.

✔ Take note of any special precautions printed on the battery case.

✔ Make sure that the booster battery is the same voltage as the discharged one in the vehicle.

✔ If the battery is being jump-started from the battery in another vehicle, the two vehicles MUST NOT TOUCH each other.

✔ Make sure that the transmission is in neutral (or PARK, in the case of automatic transmission).

1 Connect one end of the red jump lead to the positive (+) terminal of the flat battery

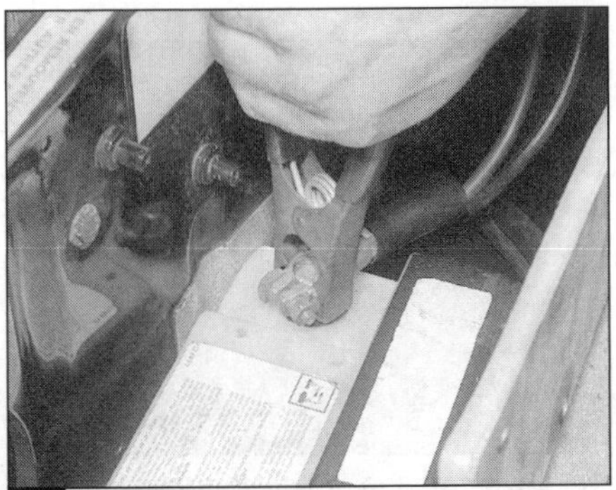

2 Connect the other end of the red lead to the positive (+) terminal of the booster battery

3 Connect one end of the black jump lead to the negative (-) terminal of the booster battery

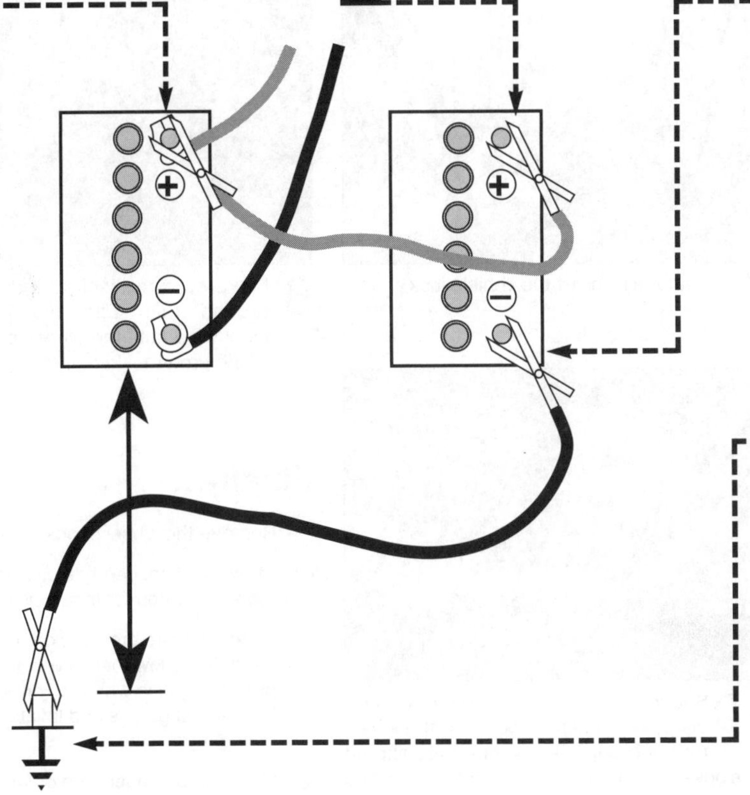

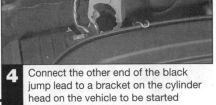

4 Connect the other end of the black jump lead to a bracket on the cylinder head on the vehicle to be started

5 Make sure that the jump leads will not come into contact with the fan, drivebelts or other moving parts of the engine

6 Start the engine using the booster battery, then with the engine running at idle speed, disconnect the jump leads in the reverse order of connection

Wheel changing

- ☐ When a puncture occurs, stop as soon as it is safe to do so.
- ☐ Park on firm level ground, if possible, and well out of the way of other traffic.
- ☐ Use hazard warning lights if necessary.
- ☐ If you have one, use a warning triangle to alert other drivers of your presence.
- ☐ Apply the handbrake and engage first or reverse gear (or Park on models with automatic transmission.
- ☐ Chock the wheel diagonally opposite the one being removed – a couple of large stones will do for this.
- ☐ If the ground is soft, use a flat piece of wood to spread the load under the jack.

1 The spare wheel and tools are stored in the luggage compartment. Lift up the carpet, then unscrew and remove the tool kit container.

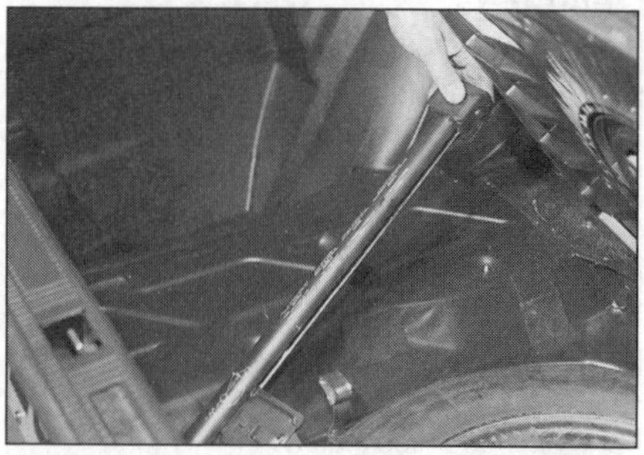

2 Unclip the jack from the mountings on the luggage compartment floor.

3 Remove the spare wheel from its recess.

4 Lever off the wheel trim/hub cap (as applicable) . . .

5 . . . then slacken each wheel bolt by half a turn. Where anti-theft wheel bolts are fitted, a special adaptor will be required.

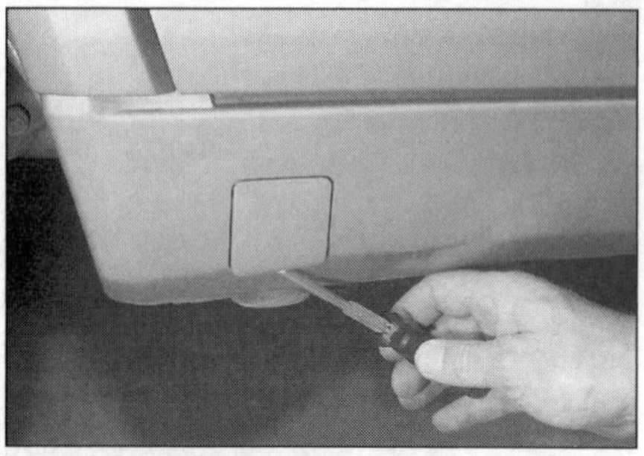

6 Unclip/remove the relevant access cover from the sill . . .

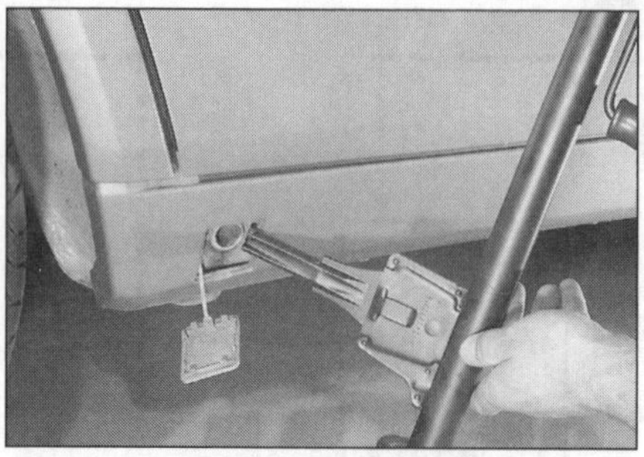

7 . . . and fully insert the vehicle jack.

8 Make sure the jack is located on firm ground then turn the jack handle clockwise until the wheel is raised clear of the ground.

9 Unscrew the wheel bolts and remove the wheel. Fit the spare wheel and screw in the bolts. Lightly tighten the bolts with the wheelbrace then lower the vehicle to the ground.

10 Securely tighten the wheel bolts in a diagonal sequence then refit the wheel trim/hub cap. The wheel bolts should be slackened and retightened to the specified torque at the earliest possible opportunity.

Finally...

- ☐ Remove the wheel chocks.
- ☐ Stow the damaged tyre or wheel, jack and tools in the correct locations in the car.
- ☐ Check the tyre pressure on the wheel just fitted. If it is low, or if you don't have a pressure gauge with you, drive slowly to the nearest garage and inflate the tyre to the right pressure.
- ☐ Have the damaged tyre or wheel repaired as soon as possible.

Identifying leaks

Puddles on the garage floor or drive, or obvious wetness under the bonnet or underneath the car, suggest a leak that needs investigating. It can sometimes be difficult to decide where the leak is coming from, especially if the engine bay is very dirty already. Leaking oil or fluid can also be blown rearwards by the passage of air under the car, giving a false impression of where the problem lies.

Warning: Most automotive oils and fluids are poisonous. Wash them off skin, and change out of contaminated clothing, without delay.

HAYNES HiNT ***The smell of a fluid leaking from the car may provide a clue to what's leaking. Some fluids are distinctively coloured. It may help to clean the car and to park it over some clean paper as an aid to locating the source of the leak. Remember that some leaks may only occur while the engine is running.***

Sump oil

Engine oil may leak from the drain plug...

Oil from filter

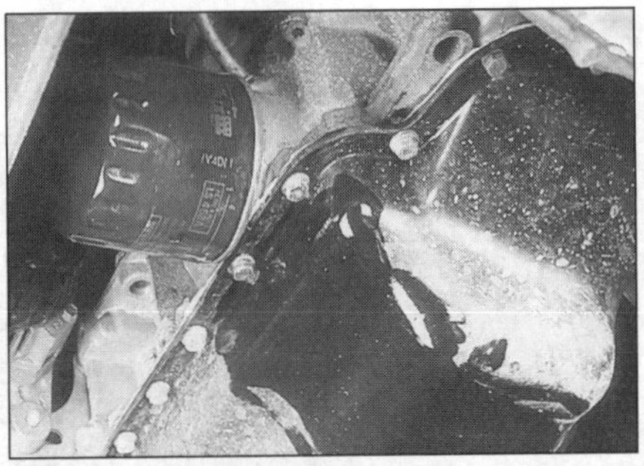

...or from the base of the oil filter.

Gearbox oil

Gearbox oil can leak from the seals at the inboard ends of the driveshafts.

Antifreeze

Leaking antifreeze often leaves a crystalline deposit like this.

Brake fluid

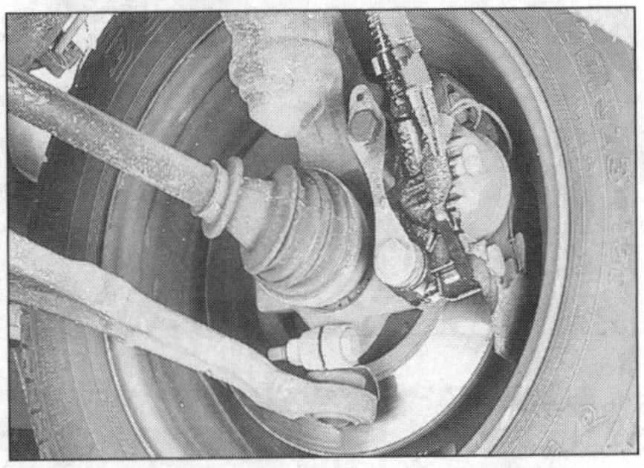

A leak occurring at a wheel is almost certainly brake fluid.

Power steering fluid

Power steering fluid may leak from the pipe connectors on the steering rack.

Towing

When all else fails, you may find yourself having to get a tow home – or of course you may be helping somebody else. Long-distance recovery should only be done by a garage or breakdown service. For shorter distances, DIY towing using another car is easy enough, but observe the following points:

☐ Use a proper tow-rope – they are not expensive. The vehicle being towed must display an 'ON TOW' sign in its rear window.

☐ Always turn the ignition key to the 'on' position when the vehicle is being towed, so that the steering lock is released, and that the direction indicator and brake lights will work.

☐ Towing eyes are provided at the front and rear of the vehicle, on the right-hand side. Do not attach the tow-rope to anything else.

☐ Before being towed, release the handbrake and select neutral on the transmission.

☐ Note that greater-than-usual pedal pressure will be required to operate the brakes, since the vacuum servo unit is only operational with the engine running.

☐ On models with power steering, greater-than-usual steering effort will also be required.

☐ The driver of the car being towed must keep the tow-rope taut at all times to avoid snatching.

☐ Make sure that both drivers know the route before setting off.

☐ Only drive at moderate speeds and keep the distance towed to a minimum. Drive smoothly and allow plenty of time for slowing down at junctions.

☐ On models with automatic transmission, special precautions apply. If in doubt, do not tow, or transmission damage may result.

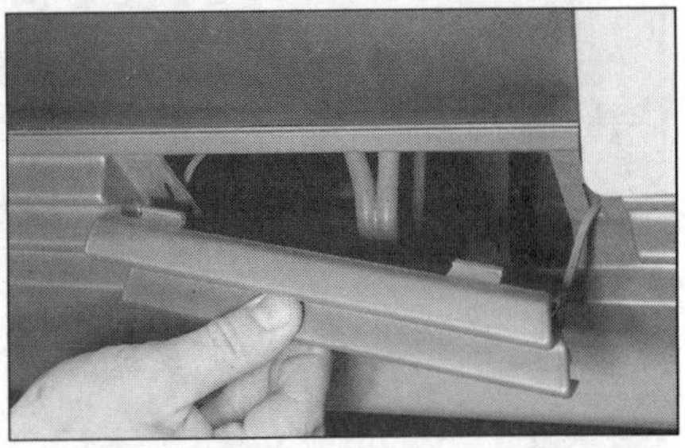

Unclip the flap in the front valence to expose the front towing eye.

Introduction

There are some very simple checks which need only take a few minutes to carry out, but which could save you a lot of inconvenience and expense.

These "Weekly checks" require no great skill or special tools, and the small amount of time they take to perform could prove to be very well spent, for example;

☐ Keeping an eye on tyre condition and pressures, will not only help to stop them wearing out prematurely, but could also save your life.

☐ Many breakdowns are caused by electrical problems. Battery-related faults are particularly common, and a quick check on a regular basis will often prevent the majority of these.

☐ If your car develops a brake fluid leak, the first time you might know about it is when your brakes don't work properly. Checking the level regularly will give advance warning of this kind of problem.

☐ If the oil or coolant levels run low, the cost of repairing any engine damage will be far greater than fixing the leak, for example.

Underbonnet check points

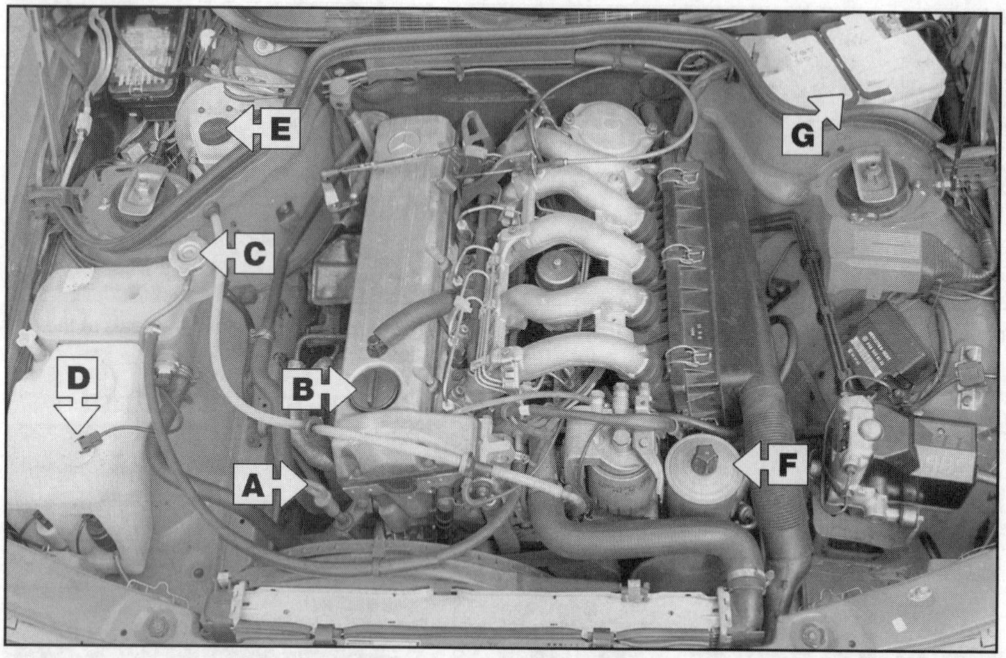

◀ **5-cylinder diesel engine (2.5 litre non-turbo diesel shown)**

A *Engine oil dipstick*
B *Engine oil filler cap*
C *Coolant expansion tank*
D *Screen washer fluid reservoir*
E *Brake and clutch fluid reservoir*
F *Power steering fluid reservoir*
G *Battery*

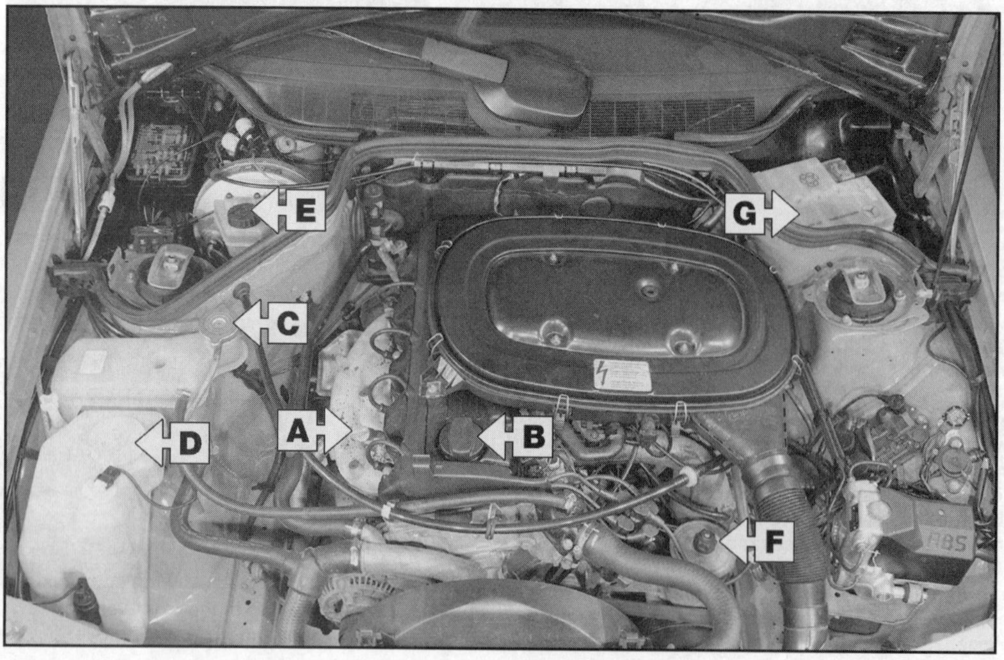

◀ **4-cylinder petrol engine (2.0 litre shown)**

A *Engine oil dipstick*
B *Engine oil filler cap*
C *Coolant expansion tank*
D *Screen washer fluid reservoir*
E *Brake and clutch fluid reservoir*
F *Power steering fluid reservoir*
G *Battery*

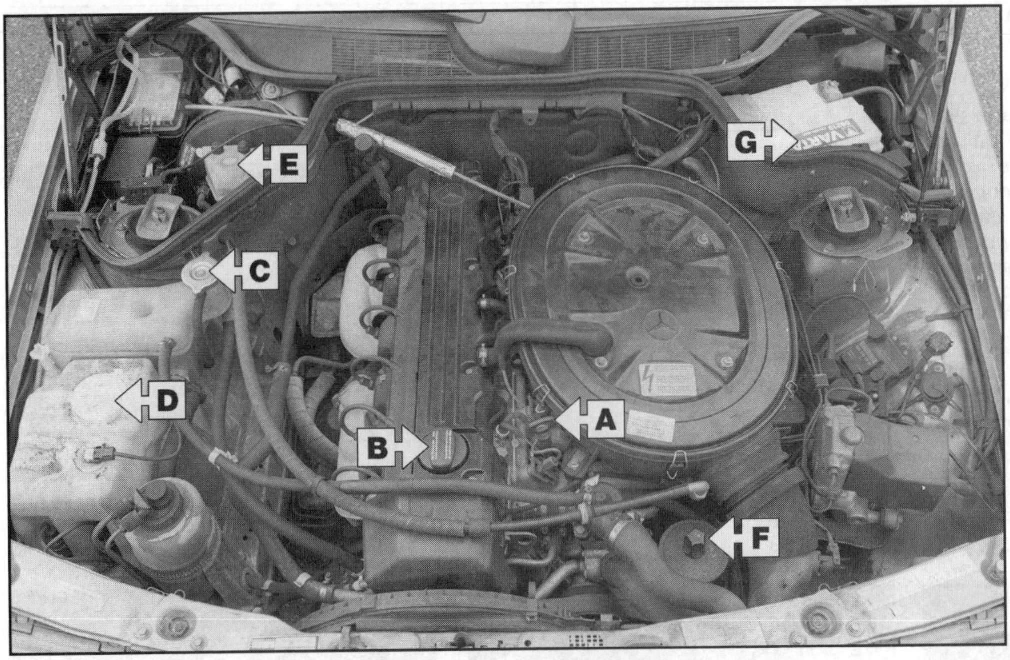

◀ 6-cylinder petrol engine (2.6 litre shown)

A *Engine oil dipstick*
B *Engine oil filler cap*
C *Coolant expansion tank*
D *Screen washer fluid reservoir*
E *Brake and clutch fluid reservoir*
F *Power steering fluid reservoir*
G *Battery*

Engine oil level

Before you start

✔ Make sure that your car is on level ground.
✔ Check the oil level before the car is driven, or at least 5 minutes after the engine has been switched off.

HAYNES HiNT ***If the oil level is checked immediately after driving the vehicle, some of the oil will remain in the upper engine components, resulting in an inaccurate reading on the dipstick!***

The correct oil

Modern engines place great demands on their oil. It is very important that the correct oil for your car is used (See "Lubricants, fluids and tyre pressures").

Car care

- If you have to add oil frequently, you should check whether you have any oil leaks. Place some clean paper under the car overnight, and check for stains in the morning. If there are no leaks, the engine may be burning oil *(see "Fault finding").*
- Always maintain the level between the upper and lower dipstick marks (see photo 3). If the level is too low severe engine damage may occur. Oil seal failure may result if the engine is overfilled by adding too much oil.

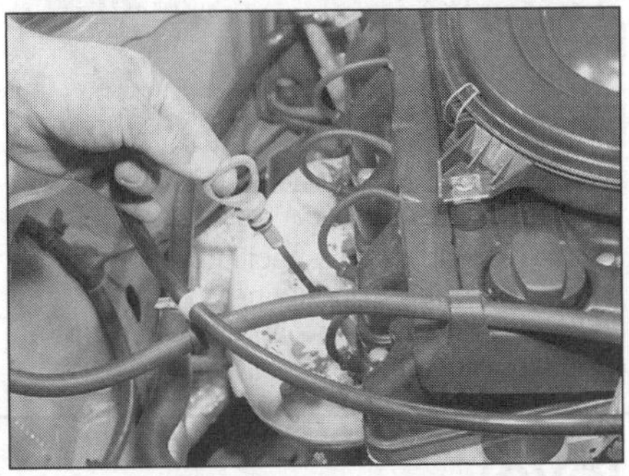

1 The engine oil dipstick and filler cap are both located towards the front of the engine (see *"Underbonnet check points"* on pages 0•10 for exact location). Pull out the dipstick.

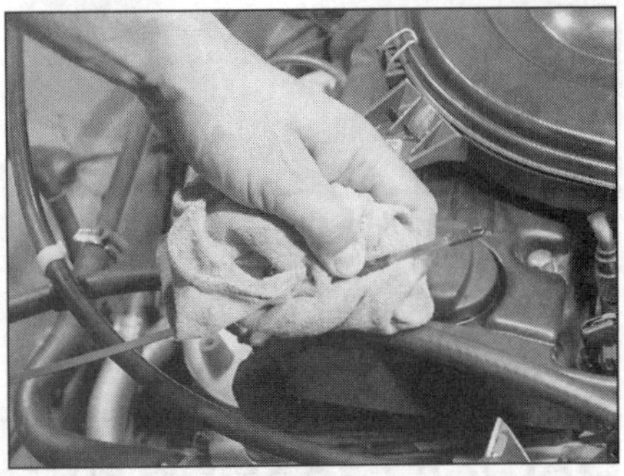

2 Wipe it with a clean rag. Push it back into its tube, then remove it again and hold it vertically, with the handle uppermost.

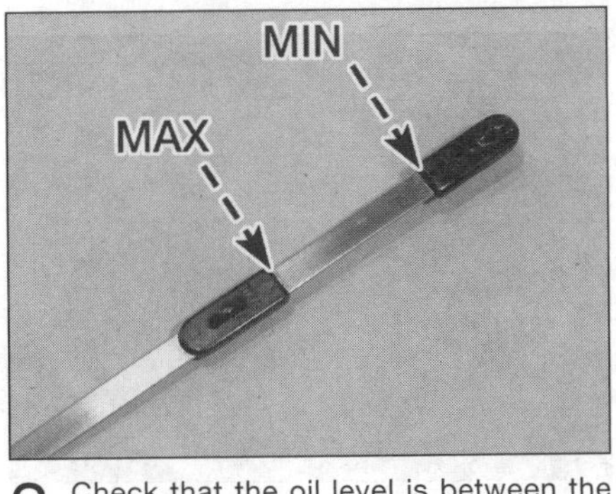

3 Check that the oil level is between the 'MIN' and 'MAX' markings on the dipstick.

4 If topping-up is required, use oil of the correct grade for your engine (see *"Lubricants and Fluids"*). Use a funnel to avoid spillage and do not overfill.

Brake fluid level

> **HAYNES HiNT**
> ***• Make sure that your car is on level ground.***
> ***• The fluid level in the reservoir will drop slightly as the brake pads wear down, but the fluid level must never be allowed to drop below the "MIN" mark.***

Warning:

- ***Brake fluid can harm your eyes and will damage painted surfaces, so use extreme caution when handling and pouring it.***
- ***Do not use fluid that has been standing open for some time, as it absorbs moisture from the air, which can cause a dangerous loss of braking effectiveness.***

Safety first!

- If the reservoir requires repeated topping-up this is an indication of a fluid leak somewhere in the system, which should be investigated immediately.
- If a leak is suspected, the car should not be driven until the braking system has been checked. Never take any risks where brakes are concerned.

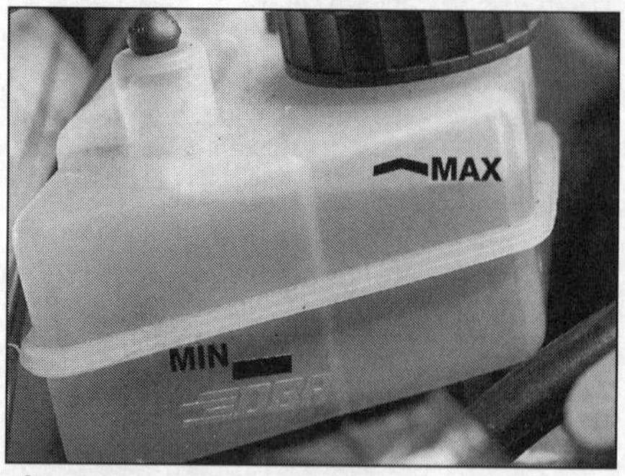

1 The 'MAX' and 'MIN' level markings are moulded on the side of the brake fluid reservoir.

2 If topping up is required, first remove any grime from around the filler cap, using a clean rag then unscrew the filler cap.

3 Before adding fluid, check that the reservoir filter (where fitted) is clean and free of debris.

4 Top up to the 'MAX' level marking using brake fluid of the specified grade from a newly opened container. Wipe off any spillage immediately - brake fluid is an effective paint stripper.

5 Test the operation of the dashboard-mounted brake fluid level warning light by depressing each of the rubber test buttons in turn.

Power steering fluid level

Before you start:

- ✔ Park the vehicle on level ground.
- ✔ Set the steering wheel straight-ahead.
- ✔ The engine should be turned off.

> **HAYNES HiNT**
> ***For the check to be accurate, the steering must not be turned once the engine has been stopped.***

Safety first!

- The need for frequent topping-up indicates a leak, which should be investigated immediately.

1 The reservoir is an integral part of the power steering pump. Wipe clean the reservoir then unscrew the retaining nut and remove the reservoir cover.

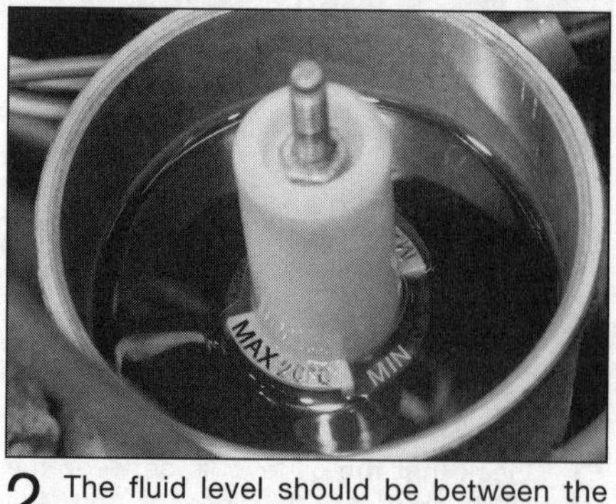

2 The fluid level should be between the upper (MAX) and lower (MIN) level marks on the plastic tube which is fitted to the reservoir cover stud.

3 When topping-up, use the specified type of fluid and do not overfill the reservoir. When the level is correct, securely refit the cap.

Coolant level

Warning: DO NOT attempt to remove the expansion tank pressure cap when the engine is hot, as there is a very great risk of scalding. Do not leave open containers of coolant about, as it is poisonous.

Car care

- Adding coolant should not be necessary on a regular basis. If frequent topping-up is required, it is likely there is a leak. Check the radiator, all hoses and joint faces for signs of staining or wetness, and rectify as necessary.

- It is important that antifreeze is used in the cooling system all year round, not just during the winter months. Don't top-up with water alone, as the antifreeze will become too diluted.

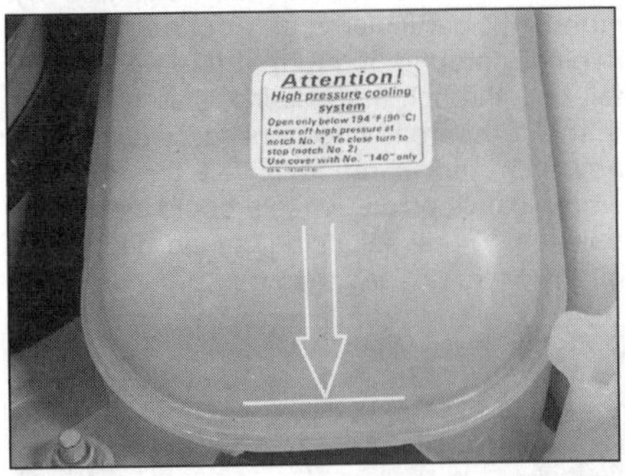

1 The coolant level varies with the temperature of the engine. When the engine is cold, the coolant level should be up to the level marking on the side of the expansion tank. When the engine is hot, the level may rise slightly above the mark.

2 If topping up is necessary, **wait until the engine is cold**. Slowly unscrew the expansion tank cap, to release any pressure present in the cooling system, and remove it.

3 Add a mixture of water and antifreeze to the expansion tank until the coolant level is up to the level marking. Refit the cap and tighten it securely.

Wiper blades

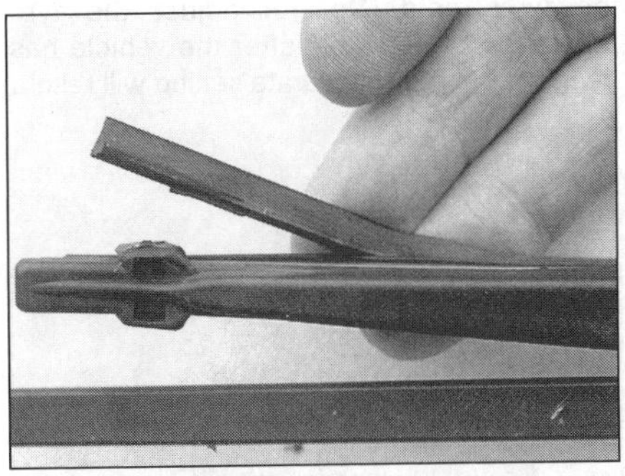

1 Check the condition of the wiper blades; if they are cracked or show any signs of deterioration, or if the glass swept area is smeared, renew them. Wiper blades should be renewed annually.

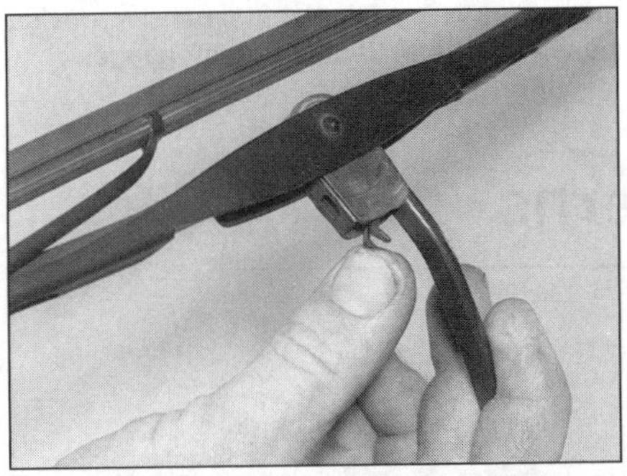

2 To remove a windscreen wiper blade, pull the arm fully away from the screen until it locks. Swivel the blade through 90°, then depress the locking clip at the base of the mounting block.

3 Slide the blade from the arm. Don't forget to check the tailgate wiper blade as well (where applicable).

Washer fluid level

Screenwash additives not only keep the winscreen clean during foul weather, they also prevent the washer system freezing in cold weather - which is when you are likely to need it most. Don't top up using plain water as the screenwash will become too diluted, and will freeze during cold weather. ***On no account use coolant antifreeze in the washer system - this could discolour or damage paintwork.***

1 The screen/headlight washer fluid reservoir is located in the front right-hand corner of the engine compartment. The level is visible through the reservoir body. If topping up is necessary, open up the cap and add water and a screenwash additive in the quantities recommended by the manufacturer.

Tyre condition and pressure

It is very important that tyres are in good condition, and at the correct pressure - having a tyre failure at any speed is highly dangerous. Tyre wear is influenced by driving style - harsh braking and acceleration, or fast cornering, will all produce more rapid tyre wear. As a general rule, the front tyres wear out faster than the rears. Interchanging the tyres from front to rear ("rotating" the tyres) may result in more even wear. However, if this is completely effective, you may have the expense of replacing all four tyres at once!

Remove any nails or stones embedded in the tread before they penetrate the tyre to cause deflation. If removal of a nail does reveal that the tyre has been punctured, refit the nail so that its point of penetration is marked. Then immediately change the wheel, and have the tyre repaired by a tyre dealer.

Regularly check the tyres for damage in the form of cuts or bulges, especially in the sidewalls. Periodically remove the wheels, and clean any dirt or mud from the inside and outside surfaces. Examine the wheel rims for signs of rusting, corrosion or other damage. Light alloy wheels are easily damaged by "kerbing" whilst parking; steel wheels may also become dented or buckled. A new wheel is very often the only way to overcome severe damage.

New tyres should be balanced when they are fitted, but it may become necessary to re-balance them as they wear, or if the balance weights fitted to the wheel rim should fall off. Unbalanced tyres will wear more quickly, as will the steering and suspension components. Wheel imbalance is normally signified by vibration, particularly at a certain speed (typically around 50 mph). If this vibration is felt only through the steering, then it is likely that just the front wheels need balancing. If, however, the vibration is felt through the whole car, the rear wheels could be out of balance. Wheel balancing should be carried out by a tyre dealer or garage.

1 ***Tread Depth - visual check***
The original tyres have tread wear safety bands (B), which will appear when the tread depth reaches approximately 1.6 mm. The band positions are indicated by a triangular mark on the tyre sidewall (A).

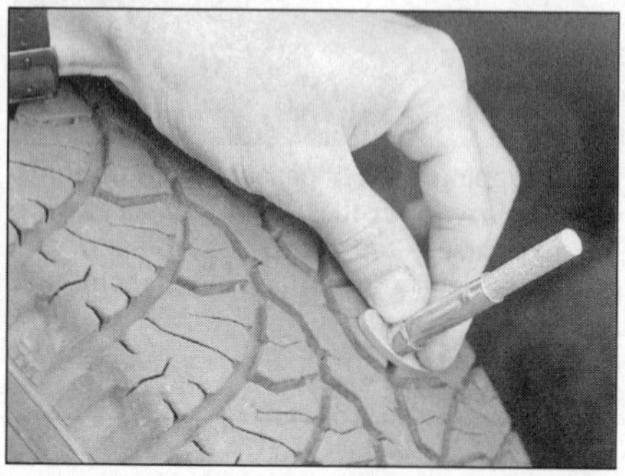

2 ***Tread Depth - manual check***
Alternatively, tread wear can be monitored with a simple, inexpensive device known as a tread depth indicator gauge.

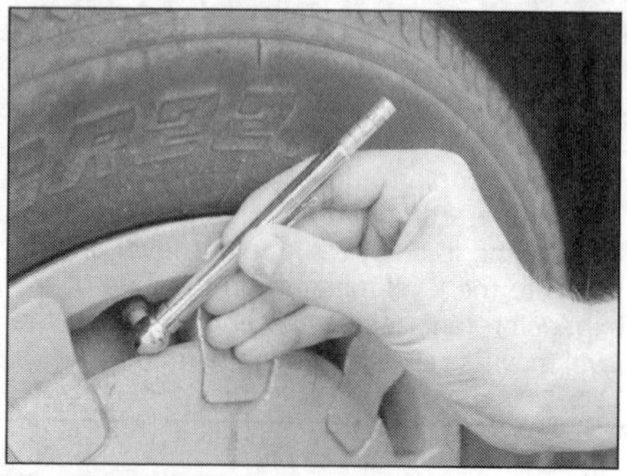

3 ***Tyre Pressure Check***
Check the tyre pressures regularly with the tyres cold. Do not adjust the tyre pressures immediately after the vehicle has been used, or an inaccurate setting will result.

Tyre tread wear patterns

Shoulder Wear

Underinflation (wear on both sides)
Under-inflation will cause overheating of the tyre, because the tyre will flex too much, and the tread will not sit correctly on the road surface. This will cause a loss of grip and excessive wear, not to mention the danger of sudden tyre failure due to heat build-up.
Check and adjust pressures
Incorrect wheel camber (wear on one side)
Repair or renew suspension parts
Hard cornering
Reduce speed!

Centre Wear

Overinflation
Over-inflation will cause rapid wear of the centre part of the tyre tread, coupled with reduced grip, harsher ride, and the danger of shock damage occurring in the tyre casing.
Check and adjust pressures

If you sometimes have to inflate your car's tyres to the higher pressures specified for maximum load or sustained high speed, don't forget to reduce the pressures to normal afterwards.

Uneven Wear

Front tyres may wear unevenly as a result of wheel misalignment. Most tyre dealers and garages can check and adjust the wheel alignment (or "tracking") for a modest charge.
Incorrect camber or castor
Repair or renew suspension parts
Malfunctioning suspension
Repair or renew suspension parts
Unbalanced wheel
Balance tyres
Incorrect toe setting
Adjust front wheel alignment
Note: *The feathered edge of the tread which typifies toe wear is best checked by feel.*

Battery

Caution: *Before carrying out any work on the vehicle battery, read the precautions given in "Safety first" at the start of this manual.*

✔ Make sure that the battery tray is in good condition, and that the clamp is tight. Corrosion on the tray, retaining clamp and the battery itself can be removed with a solution of water and baking soda. Thoroughly rinse all cleaned areas with water. Any metal parts damaged by corrosion should be covered with a zinc-based primer, then painted.

✔ Periodically (approximately every three months), check the charge condition of the battery as described in Chapter 5A.

✔ If the battery is flat, and you need to jump start your vehicle, see ***Roadside Repairs***.

1 The battery is located in the right-hand rear bulkhead area of the engine compartment. The exterior of the battery should be inspected periodically for damage such as a cracked case or cover.

2 Check the tightness of the battery cable clamps to ensure good electrical connections. You should not be able to move them. Also check each cable for cracks and frayed conductors.

HAYNES HiNT

Battery corrosion can be kept to a minimum by applying a layer of petroleum jelly to the clamps and terminals after they are reconnected.

3 If corrosion (white, fluffy deposits) is evident, remove the cables from the battery terminals, clean them with a small wire brush, then refit them. Automotive stores sell a useful tool for cleaning the battery post and terminals.

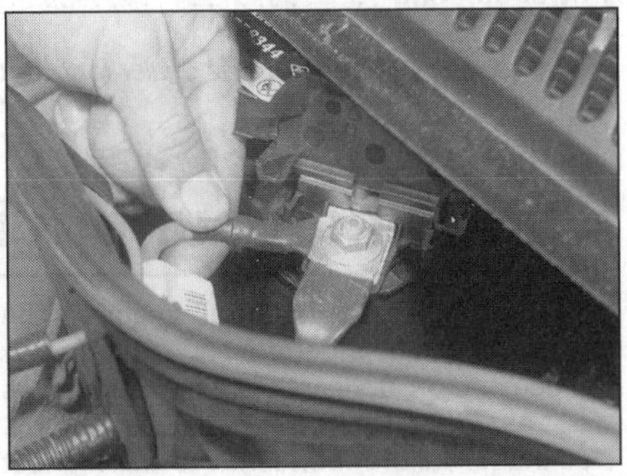

4 Note that the battery positive lead terminal can be disconnected by unscrewing the nut located under the plastic cover.

Bulbs and fuses

✔ Check all external lights and the horn. Refer to the appropriate Sections of Chapter 12 for details if any of the circuits are found to be inoperative.

✔ Visually check all accessible wiring connectors, harnesses and retaining clips for security, and for signs of chafing or damage.

HAYNES HiNT ***If you need to check your brake lights and indicators unaided, back up to a wall or garage door and operate the lights. The reflected light should show if they are working properly.***

1 If a single indicator light, stop light or headlight has failed, it is likely that a bulb has blown and will need to be replaced. Refer to Chapter 12 for details. If both stop lights have failed, it is possible that the switch has failed (see Chapter 9).

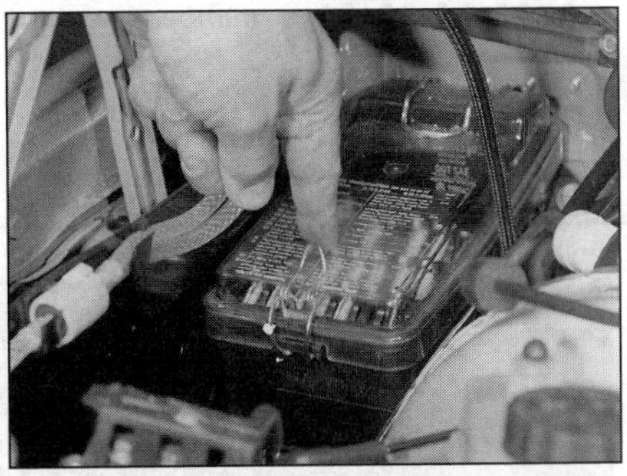

2 If more than one indicator light or tail light has failed it is likely that either a fuse has blown or that there is a fault in the circuit (see Chapter 12). The fuses are located behind in the fusebox in the rear corner of the engine compartment.

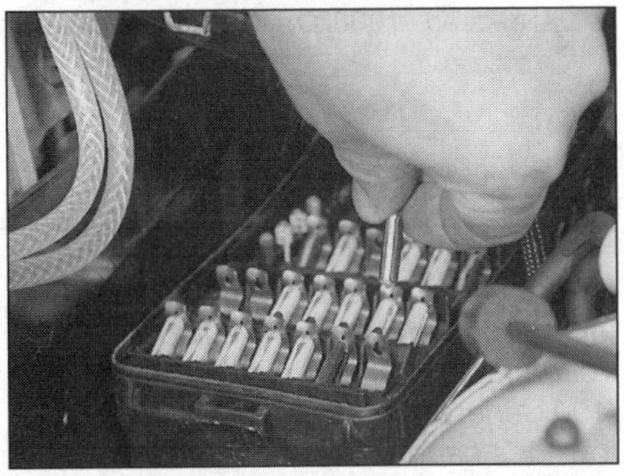

3 To replace a blown fuse, simply pull it out and fit a new fuse of the correct rating (see Chapter 12). If the fuse blows again, it is important that you find out why - a complete checking procedure is given in Chapter 12.

Lubricants and fluids

Engine (petrol)	Multigrade engine oil, viscosity SAE 10W/40 to 15W/50, to CCMC G4 or API SG* *(Duckhams QXR, QS, Hypergrade Plus, Hypergrade or 10W-40 Motor Oil)*
Engine (diesel)	Multigrade engine oil, viscosity SAE 10W/40 to 15W/50, to CCMC PD2 or API CE* *(Duckhams Diesel, QXR, QS, Hypergrade Plus, Hypergrade or 10W-40 Motor Oil)*
Carburettor damper oil	Automatic transmission fluid (ATF)* *(Duckhams Unimatic)*
Cooling system	Ethylene glycol based antifreeze* *(Duckhams Antifreeze and Summer Coolant)*
Manual transmission	Automatic transmission fluid (ATF)* *(Duckhams Unimatic)*
Automatic transmission	Automatic transmission fluid (ATF)* *(Duckhams Unimatic)*
Final drive unit	Hypoid gear oil SAE 90 or 85W90* *(Duckhams Hypoid 80W-90S, or Duckhams Hypoid 90DL if limited slip differential is fitted)*
Braking system	Hydraulic fluid to SAE J1703F or DOT 4* *(Duckhams Univeral Brake and Clutch Fuid)*
Power steering	Mercedes-Benz Lenkgetriebeol (000 989 88 03) **only**

**Refer to your Mercedes-Benz dealer for brand name and type recommendations*

Choosing your engine oil

Oils perform vital tasks in all engines. The higher the engine's performance, the greater the demand on lubricants to minimise wear as well as optimise power and economy. Duckhams tailors lubricants to the highest technical standards, meeting and exceeding the demands of all modern engines.

HOW ENGINE OIL WORKS

• Beating friction

Without oil, the surfaces inside your engine which rub together will heat, fuse and quickly cause engine seizure. Oil, and its special additives, forms a molecular barrier between moving parts, to stop wear and minimise heat build-up.

• Cooling hot spots

Oil cools parts that the engine's water-based coolant cannot reach, bathing the combustion chamber and pistons, where temperatures may exceed 1000°C. The oil assists in transferring the heat to the engine cooling system. Heat in the oil is also lost by air flow over the sump, and via any auxiliary oil cooler.

• Cleaning the inner engine

Oil washes away combustion by-products (mainly carbon) on pistons and cylinders, transporting them to the oil filter, and holding the smallest particles in suspension until they are flushed out by an oil change. Duckhams oils undergo extensive tests in the laboratory, and on the road.

OIL CARE — FOLLOW THE CODE

OIL BANK LINE 0800 66 33 66

Note: It is antisocial and illegal to dump oil down the drain. To find the location of your local oil recycling bank, call this number free.

Engine oil types

Mineral oils are the "traditional" oils, generally suited to older engines and cars not used in harsh conditions. *Duckhams Hypergrade Plus* and *Hypergrade* are well suited for use in most popular family cars.

Diesel oils such as *Duckhams Diesel* are specially formulated for Diesel engines, including turbocharged models and 4x4s.

Synthetic oils are the state-of-the-art in lubricants, offering ultimate protection, but at a fairly high price. One such is *Duckhams QS*, for use in ultra-high performance engines.

Semi-synthetic oils offer high performance engine protection, but at less cost than full synthetic oils. *Duckhams QXR* is an ideal choice for hot hatches and hard-driven cars.

For help with technical queries on lubricants, call Duckhams Oils on 0181 290 8207

DUCKHAMS

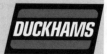

Tyre pressures

At the time of writing, Mercedes-Benz do not provide a definitive list of recommended tyre pressures for all 190 Series models. Refer to your owner's handbook, or the the information appearing inside the fuel filler flap ***(see illustration).*** *If there is still any doubt, refer to a Mercedes-Benz dealer for the most up-to-date information*

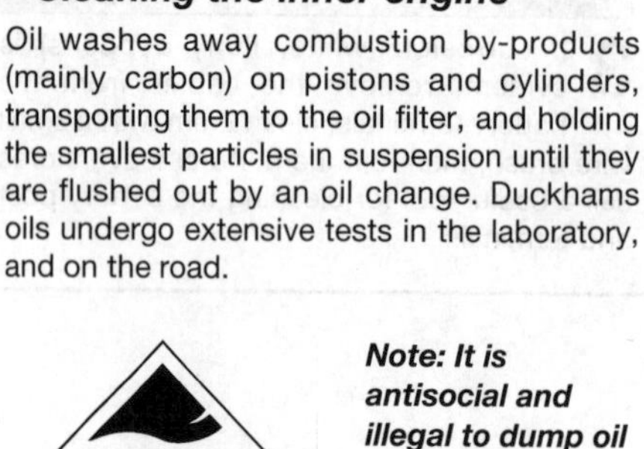

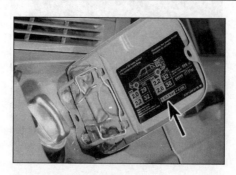

Chapter 1 Part A
Routine maintenance and servicing - petrol engine models

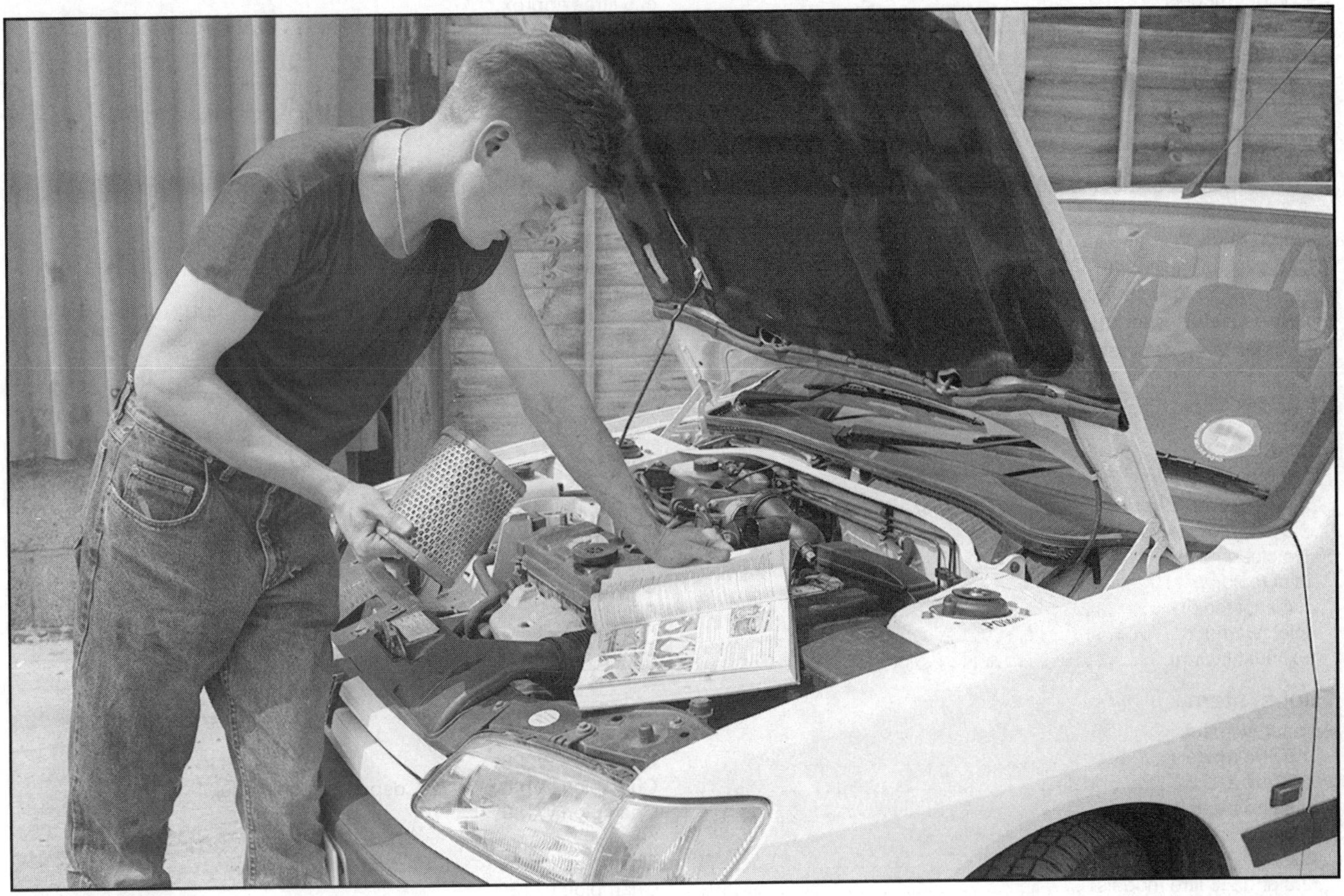

Contents

Air conditioning system check 9
Air cleaner filter element - renewal 30
Automatic transmission fluid level check 6
Automatic transmission fluid and filter - renewal 32
Auxiliary drivebelt(s) - check, renewal and adjustment 8
Brake fluid renewal 35
Carburettor damper oil level check - Stromberg carburettor 10
Charcoal canister renewal - models with an evaporative emission control system 34
Clutch - operation check 27
Clutch friction plate - check for wear 33
Coolant renewal 36
Driveshafts and driveshaft gaiters - condition check 13
Engine idle speed and mixture settings - check and adjustment 11
Engine oil and filter renewal 3
Exhaust system and mountings - condition and security check 17
Final drive unit oil - level check and renewal 19
Front brake pad check 14
Front hub bearings - check 26
Fuel filter renewal 31
Headlight beam - adjustment 23
Ignition system - condition check and timing adjustment 29
Introduction 1
Lubricate all hinges and locks, and the electric aerial 22
Manual transmission oil level check 18
Parking brake - operation check 16
Propeller shaft rubber couplings - condition check 20
Rear brake pad check 15
Regular maintenance 2
Road test 25
Seat belt check 21
Spark plug renewal 4
Steering and suspension components - condition and security check 12
Throttle linkage lubrication 5
Underbonnet/underbody components and hoses - check for leaks 7
Valve clearances (pre-1984 models) - check and adjustment 28
Windscreen/headlight washer system(s) - condition check 24

Lubricants and fluids

Refer to "*Weekly checks*"

Capacities

Engine oil (including filter)

4-cylinder models	5.0 litres
6-cylinder models	6.0 litres
Cooling system	
4-cylinder models	8.5 litres approx.
6-cylinder models	9.0 litres approx.
Transmission	
Manual transmission (approximate):	
4-speed unit	1.3 litres
5-speed unit	1.5 litres
Automatic transmission (approximate):	
All models except 2.3 and 2.6 litre models	6.6 litres
2.3 and 2.6 litre models	7.1 litres
Final drive unit*	
All models (approximate)	0.7 litres

**On some later 2.0 litre models the final drive unit capacity has been increased to 1.1 litres*

Power-assisted steering	
All models (approximate)	1.0 litres
Fuel tank	
All models (approximate)	55 litres

Engine

Oil filter:	
All except 2.0 litre models up to September 1984	Champion C113
2.0 litre models up to September 1984	Champion X106
Valve clearances:	
Inlet (cold)	0.15 mm
Exhaust (cold)	0.30 mm
Inlet (warm)	0.20 mm
Exhaust (warm)	0.35 mm

Fuel system

Air filter element:	
1.8 litre models	Champion W228
2.0 litre and 2.3 litre models	Champion W148 or W228, depending on model
2.6 litre models	Champion W189
Fuel filter:	
1.8 and 2.0 litre models	Champion L210
2.3 and 2.6 litre models	Champion L212
Idle mixture (CO)*	
Carburettor models:	
Without catalytic converter	1.0 ± 0.5%
With catalytic converter	2.0 ± 0.5%
Fuel injection models:	
Without catalytic converter	1.0 ± 0.5%
With catalytic converter	No figure specified by manufacturers
Idle speed:	
Carburettor models:	
Models without idle speed control	800 ± 50 rpm
Models with idle speed control	700 to 800 rpm
Models with air conditioning	720 to 820 rpm
Fuel injection models:	
1.8 litre engine	700 to 800 rpm
2.0 litre engine:	
Models up to 8/89	700 to 800 rpm
Models from 9/89	720 to 820 rpm
2.3 litre engine:	
Models up to 8/89	700 to 800 rpm
Models from 9/89 to 5/90	720 to 820 rpm
Models from 6/90	700 to 800 rpm
2.6 litre engine	650 to 750 rpm

**No CO figures available for fuel injection Cat models.*

Cooling system

Antifreeze mixture:	
50% antifreeze	Protection down to -37°C (-35°F)
55% antifreeze	Protection down to -45°C (-49°F)

Note: *Refer to antifreeze manufacturer for latest recommendations.*

Ignition system

Ignition timing	Refer to Chapter 5 Part B or C
Spark plugs:	
Type:	
4-cylinder models	Champion S9YCC
6-cylinder models	Champion S10YCC
Electrode gap	0.8 mm

**The spark plug gap quoted is that recommended by Champion for their specified plugs listed above. If spark plugs of any other type are to be fitted, refer to their manufacturer's recommendations.*

Brakes

Front brake pad friction material, minimum thickness	2.0 mm
Rear brake pad friction material, minimum thickness	2.0 mm

Torque wrench settings

	Nm	lbf ft
Oil filter through-bolt (4-cylinder engines)	25	18
Oil filter housing cover (6-cylinder engines)	25	18
Brake caliper bleed screws	7	5
Engine oil drain plug:		
4-cylinder engines	30	22
6-cylinder engines	25	18
Auxiliary drivebelt tensioner bolt:		
4-cylinder engines:		
19 mm AF bolt	75	55
17 mm AF bolt	80	59
6-cylinder engines	75	55
Manual transmission oil drain and level/filler plugs	60	44
Automatic transmission fluid drain plugs (main and torque converter)	14	10
Roadwheel bolts	110	81
Spark plugs:		
4-cylinder engines	15	11
6-cylinder engines	15	11

Degrees of difficulty

Easy, suitable for novice with little experience	**Fairly easy,** suitable for beginner with some experience	**Fairly difficult,** suitable for competent DIY mechanic	**Difficult,** suitable for experienced DIY mechanic	**Very difficult,** suitable for expert DIY or professional

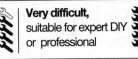

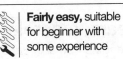

1 The maintenance intervals in this manual are provided with the assumption that you, not the dealer, will be carrying out the work. These are the minimum maintenance intervals recommended by us for vehicles driven daily. If you wish to keep your vehicle in peak condition at all times, you may wish to perform some of these procedures more often. We encourage frequent maintenance, because it enhances the efficiency, performance and resale value of your vehicle.
2 If the vehicle is driven in very dusty areas, used to tow a trailer, spends long periods with the engine idling, is driven frequently at slow speeds (eg: in heavy traffic) or is used mainly for short journeys, then *more frequent* maintenance intervals are recommended.
3 When the vehicle is new, it should be serviced by a factory-authorised dealer service department, in order to preserve the factory warranty.

Every 250 miles (400 km) or weekly

☐ *Refer to "Weekly checks"*

Every 6000 miles

Note: *Frequent oil and filter changes are good for the engine. We recommend changing the oil at the mileage specified here, or at least twice a year if the mileage covered is less.*

☐ Renew the engine oil and filter (Section 3)

Every 12 000 miles

☐ Renew the spark plugs (Section 4)
☐ Lubricate the throttle linkage (Section 5)
☐ Check the automatic transmission fluid level (Section 6)
☐ Check the underbonnet/underbody components and hoses for fluid leaks (Section 7)
☐ Check the auxiliary drivebelt(s) (Section 8)
☐ Check the air conditioning system refrigerant level (Section 9)
☐ Check the carburettor piston damper oil level (Stromberg carburettor) (Section 10)
☐ Check the engine idle speed and mixture settings (Section 11)
☐ Check the steering and suspension components (Section 12)
☐ Check the driveshafts and driveshaft gaiters (Section 13)
☐ Check the front brake pads (Section 14)
☐ Check the rear brake pads (Section 15)
☐ Check the parking brake operation (Section 16)
☐ Check the exhaust system and mountings (Section 17)
☐ Check the manual transmission oil level (Section 18)
☐ Check the final drive unit oil level (Section 19)
☐ Check the propeller shaft rubber couplings (Section 20)
☐ Check the seat belts (Section 21)
☐ Lubricate all hinges and locks, and the electric aerial (Section 22)
☐ Check the headlight beam adjustment (Section 23)
☐ Check the windscreen/headlight washer system(s) (Section 24)
☐ Road test (Section 25)
☐ Check the front hub bearings - (Section 26)
☐ Check the clutch (Section 27)
☐ Check the valve clearances (pre-1984 models) (Section 28)
☐ Check the ignition system and timing adjustment (Section 29)

Every 36 000 miles

☐ Renew the air cleaner filter element - renewal (Section 30)
☐ Renew the fuel filter (Section 31)
☐ Renew the automatic transmission fluid and filter (Section 32)
☐ Check the clutch friction plate for wear (Section 33)

Every 72 000 miles or 4 years - whichever comes sooner

☐ Renew the charcoal canister (models with an evaporative loss emission control system) (Section 34)

Every 12 months, regardless of mileage

☐ Renew the brake fluid (Section 35)

Every 3 years, regardless of mileage

☐ Renew the engine coolant (Section 36)

Underbonnet view of a 4-cylinder, 1.8 litre petrol model with automatic transmission

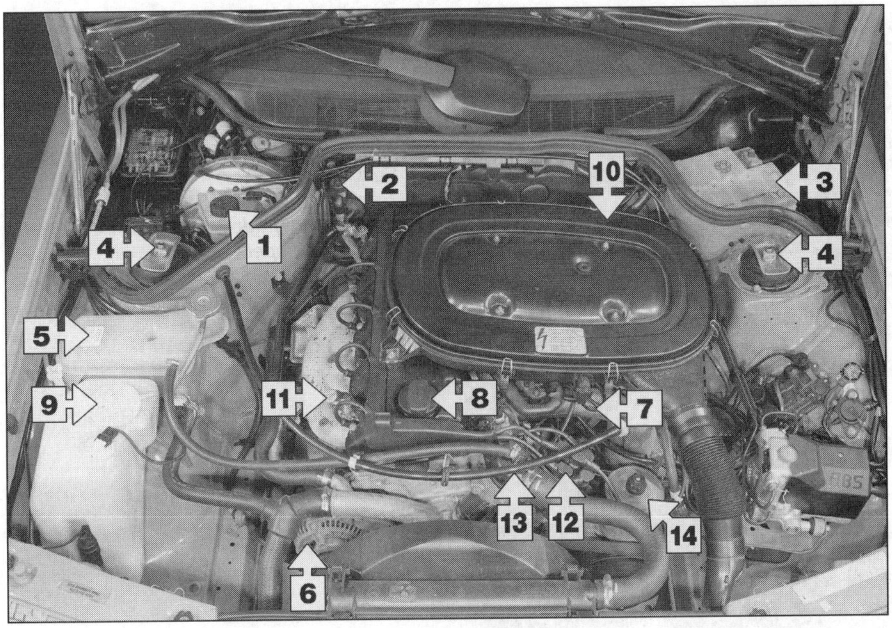

1 Brake fluid reservoir
2 Automatic transmission fluid filler/dipstick
3 Battery
4 Suspension strut upper mounting
5 Coolant expansion tank filler
6 Alternator
7 Inlet manifold
8 Engine oil filler cap
9 Screen wash filler
10 Air cleaner
11 Engine oil dipstick
12 Distributor
13 Thermostat housing
14 Power steering fluid reservoir

Underbonnet view of a 6-cylinder, 2.6 litre petrol model

1 Brake fluid reservoir
2 Automatic transmission fluid filler/dipstick
3 Battery
4 Suspension strut upper mounting
5 Coolant expansion tank filler
6 Ignition module
7 Exhaust manifolds
8 Engine oil filler cap
9 Screen wash filler
10 Air cleaner
11 Engine oil dipstick
12 Distributor
13 Thermostat housing
14 Power steering fluid reservoir

Typical front underbody view

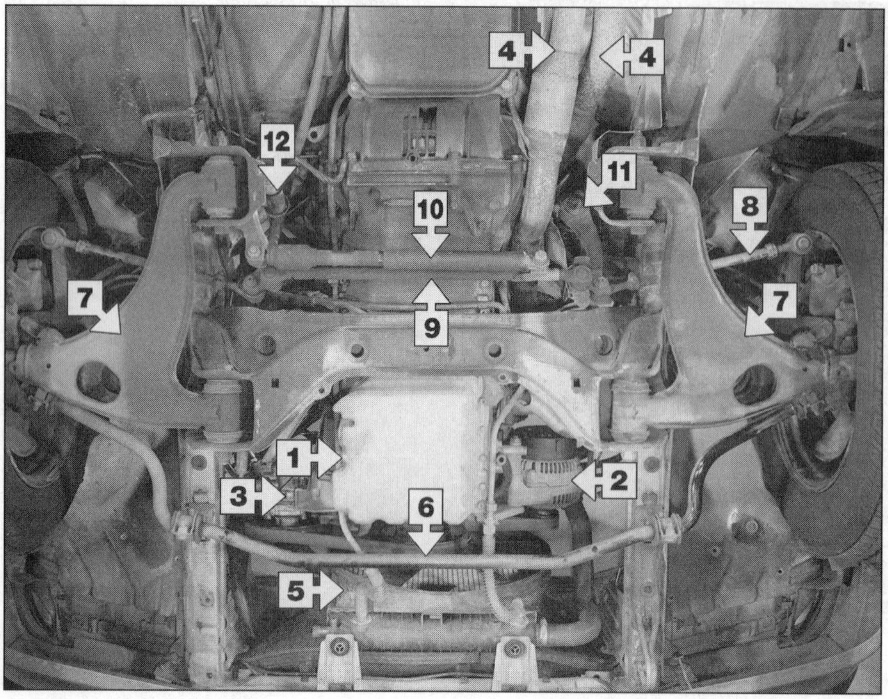

1 Engine oil drain plug
2 Alternator
3 Power steering pump
4 Exhaust front pipe
5 Radiator
6 Anti-roll bar
7 Suspension lower arm
8 Track rod
9 Steering drag link
10 Steering damper
11 Steering box
12 Steering intermediate arm

Typical rear underbody view

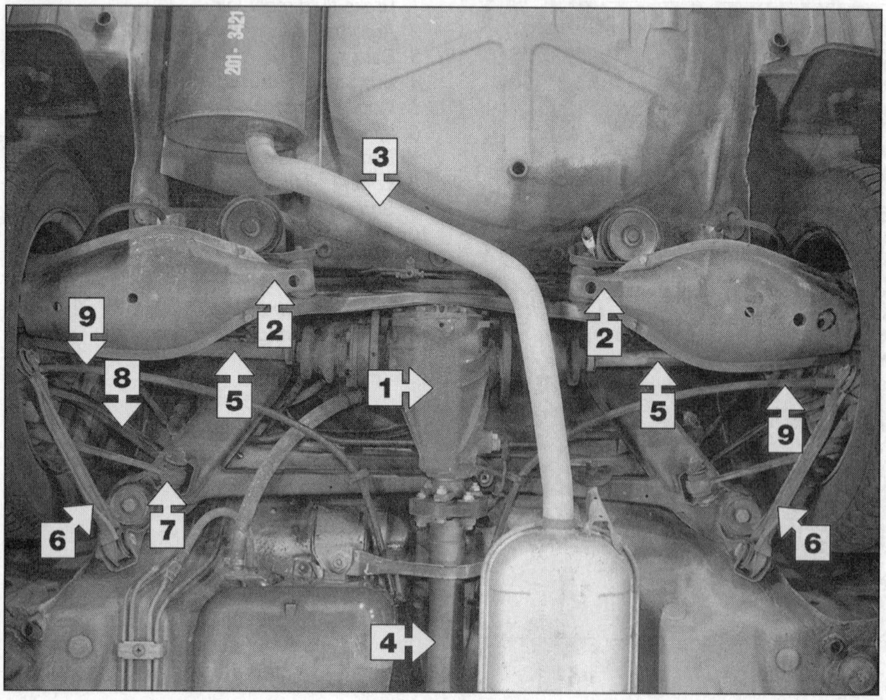

1 Final drive unit
2 Suspension lower arm
3 Exhaust system
4 Propeller shaft
5 Driveshaft
6 Thrust control arm
7 Track control arm
8 Torque control arm
9 Parking brake cable

1 Introduction

1 This Chapter is designed to help the home mechanic maintain his/her vehicle for safety, economy, long life and peak performance.
2 The Chapter contains a maintenance schedule, followed by Sections dealing specifically with each task in the schedule. Visual checks, adjustments, component renewal and other helpful items are included. Refer to the accompanying illustrations of the engine compartment and the underside of the vehicle for the locations of the various components.
3 Servicing your vehicle in accordance with the above recommendations and the following Sections will provide a planned maintenance programme, which should result in a long and reliable service life. This is a comprehensive plan, so maintaining some items but not others at the specified service intervals, will not produce the same results.
4 As you service your vehicle, you will discover that many of the procedures can - and should - be grouped together, because of the particular procedure being performed, or because of the proximity of two otherwise-unrelated components to one another. For example, if the vehicle is raised for any reason, the exhaust can be inspected at the same time as the suspension and steering components.
5 The first step in this maintenance programme is to prepare yourself before the actual work begins. Read through all the Sections relevant to the work to be carried out, then make a list and gather all the parts and tools required. If a problem is encountered, seek advice from a parts specialist, or a dealer service department.

2 Regular maintenance

1 If, from the time the vehicle is new, the routine maintenance schedule is followed closely, and frequent checks are made of fluid levels and high-wear items, as suggested throughout this manual, the engine will be kept in relatively good running condition, and the need for additional work will be minimised.
2 It is possible that there will be times when the engine is running poorly due to the lack of regular maintenance. This is even more likely if a used vehicle, which has not received regular and frequent maintenance checks, is purchased. In such cases, additional work may need to be carried out, outside of the regular maintenance intervals.
3 If engine wear is suspected, a compression test (refer to the relevant Part of Chapter 2) will provide valuable information regarding the overall performance of the main internal components. Such a test can be used as a basis to decide on the extent of the work to be carried out. If, for example, a compression test indicates serious internal engine wear, conventional maintenance as described in this Chapter will not greatly improve the performance of the engine, and may prove a waste of time and money, unless extensive overhaul work is carried out first.
4 The following series of operations are those most often required to improve the performance of a generally poor-running engine:

Primary operations

a) Clean, inspect and test the battery (See "Weekly checks").
b) Check all the engine-related fluids (See "Weekly checks").
c) Check the condition and tension of the auxiliary drivebelt (Section 8).
d) Renew the spark plugs (Section 4).
e) Check the condition of the air filter, and renew if necessary (Section 30).
f) Check the fuel filter (Section 31).
g) Check the condition of all hoses, and check for fluid leaks (Section 7).

5 If the above operations do not prove fully effective, carry out the following secondary operations:

Secondary operations

All items listed under "*Primary operations*", plus the following:

a) Check the charging system (see relevant Part of Chapter 5).
b) Check the ignition system (see relevant Part of Chapter 5).
c) Check the fuel system (see relevant Part of Chapter 4).

1A

Every 6000 miles

3 Engine oil and filter renewal

1 Frequent oil and filter changes are the most important preventative maintenance procedures which can be undertaken by the DIY owner. As engine oil ages, it becomes diluted and contaminated, which leads to premature engine wear.
2 Before starting this procedure, gather together all the necessary tools and materials. Also make sure that you have plenty of clean rags and newspapers handy, to mop up any spills. Ideally, the engine oil should be warm, as it will drain better, and more built-up sludge will be removed with it. Take care, however, not to touch the exhaust or any other hot parts of the engine when working under the vehicle. To avoid any possibility of scalding, and to protect yourself from possible skin irritants and other harmful contaminants in used engine oils, it is advisable to wear gloves when carrying out this work. Access to the underside of the vehicle will be greatly improved if it can be raised on a lift, driven onto ramps, or jacked up and supported on axle stands (see *"Jacking and Vehicle Support"*). Whichever method is chosen, make sure that the vehicle remains level, or if it is at an angle, so that the drain plug is at the lowest point. Where necessary remove the splash guard from under the engine.
3 Working in the engine compartment, locate the oil filter/housing at the left-hand rear corner of the engine, behind the inlet manifold.
4 Place a wad of rag around the bottom of the housing to absorb any spilt oil.
5 Proceed as follows according to engine type.

4-cylinder engines

Models with element-type oil filter

Note: *New oil filter housing cover and through-bolt O-rings will be required on refitting, and a new sump drain plug sealing ring will be required.*

6 Unscrew the through-bolt, then withdraw the bolt, complete with the oil filter housing cover. Recover the O-rings from the through-bolt and the cover, and discard them - new O-rings must be used on refitting **(see illustration)**.
7 Lift the oil filter element out from the

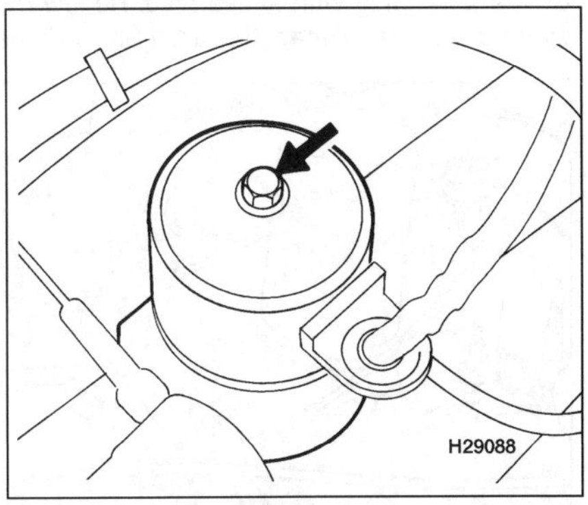

3.6 Oil filter housing cover through-bolt arrowed - 4-cylinder models with element-type filter

3.7 Lift out the oil filter element using the handle provided - 4-cylinder models with element-type filter

housing (using the handle provided), and discard it **(see illustration)**.

8 Working under the vehicle, slacken the sump drain plug about half a turn. Position the draining container under the drain plug, then remove the plug completely. If possible, try to keep the plug pressed into the sump while unscrewing it by hand the last couple of turns.

HAYNES HiNT

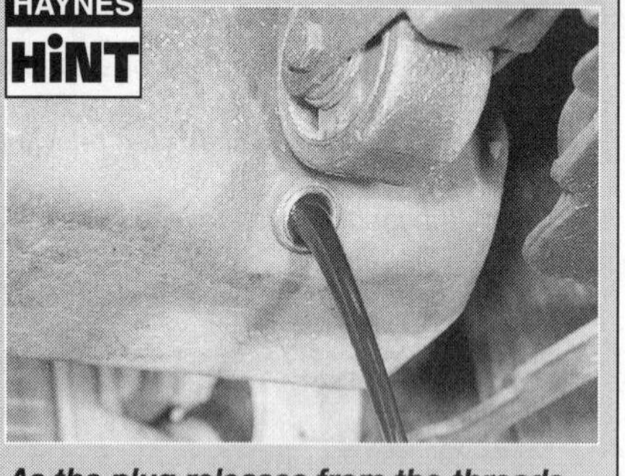

As the plug releases from the threads, move it away sharply so the stream of oil issuing from the sump runs into the container, not up your sleeve

9 Recover the sealing ring from the drain plug.

10 Allow some time for the old oil to drain, noting that it may be necessary to reposition the container as the oil flow slows to a trickle.

11 After all the old oil has drained out, wipe off the drain plug with a clean rag. Renew the sealing washer. Clean the area around the drain plug opening, then refit and tighten the plug.

12 Remove the old oil and all tools from under the car, then lower the car to the ground (if applicable).

13 Wipe out the oil filter housing and cover, using a clean rag, then fit a new oil filter element to the housing (with the handle at the top). Fit new O-rings to the housing cover and the through-bolt **(see illustration)**.

14 Refit the cover, and tighten the through-bolt to the specified torque.

15 Remove the dipstick then unscrew the oil filler cap from the cylinder head cover. Fill the engine, using the correct grade and type of oil (see *"Weekly checks"*). An oil can spout or funnel may help to reduce spillage. Pour in half the specified quantity of oil first, then wait a few minutes for the oil to fall to the sump. Continue adding oil a small quantity at a time until the level is up to the lower mark on the dipstick. Finally, bring the level up to the upper mark on the dipstick. Insert the dipstick, and refit the filler cap.

16 Start the engine and run it for a few minutes; check for leaks around the oil filter housing and the sump drain plug. Note that there may be a delay of a few seconds before the oil pressure warning light goes out when the engine is first started, as the oil circulates through the engine oil galleries and the new oil filter, before the pressure builds up.

17 Switch off the engine, and wait a few minutes for the oil to settle in the sump once more. With the new oil circulated and the filter completely full, recheck the level on the dipstick, and add more oil as necessary.

18 Where applicable, refit the engine undershield.

19 Dispose of the used engine oil safely, with reference to *"General repair procedures"* in the Reference Section of this manual.

Models with cartridge-type oil filter

Note: *A new sump drain plug sealing ring will be required on refitting.*

20 Using an oil filter removal tool if necessary, slacken the filter initially, then unscrew it by hand the rest of the way - be prepared for oil spillage **(see illustration)**. Empty the oil in the old filter into a suitable container.

21 Use a clean rag to remove all oil and dirt from the filter sealing area on the engine. Check the old filter to make sure that the rubber sealing ring has not stuck to the engine. If it has, carefully remove it.

22 Apply a light coating of engine oil to the sealing ring on the new filter, then screw it onto the housing. Tighten the filter firmly by hand only - **do not** use any tools.

23 Proceed as described previously for models with an element-type filter, in paragraphs 8 to 19, ignoring paragraphs 13 and 14.

6-cylinder engines

Note: *A new sump drain plug sealing ring will be required on refitting.*

24 Using an oil filter removal tool if necessary, slacken the filter initially, then unscrew it by hand the rest of the way - be prepared for oil spillage. Empty the oil in the old filter into a suitable container.

25 Use a clean rag to remove all oil and dirt from the filter sealing area on the engine. Check the old filter to make sure that the rubber sealing ring has not stuck to the engine. If it has, carefully remove it.

26 Apply a light coating of engine oil to the sealing ring on the new filter, then screw it onto the housing **(see illustration)**. Tighten the filter firmly by hand only - **do not** use any tools.

27 Proceed as described previously for 4-cylinder engines, in paragraphs 8 to 19, ignoring paragraphs 13 and 14 **(see illustration)**.

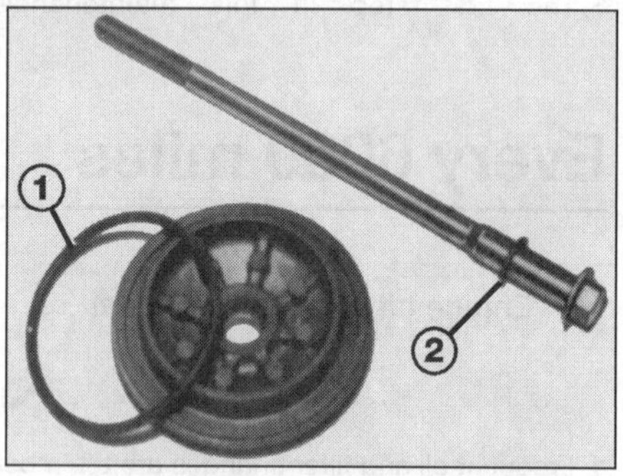

3.13 Fit new O-rings to the housing cover (1) and the through-bolt (2) - 4-cylinder models with element-type filter

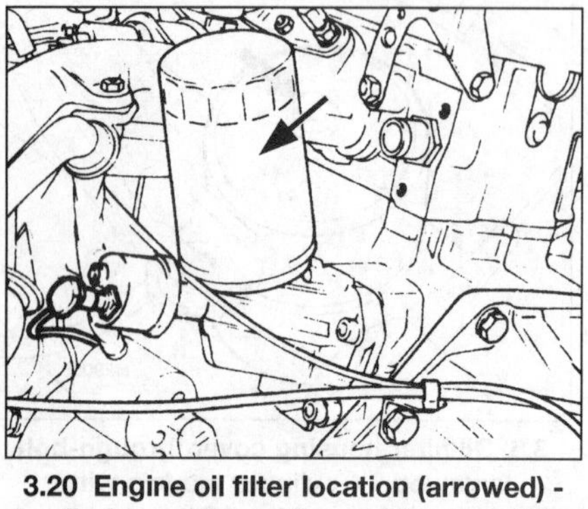

3.20 Engine oil filter location (arrowed) - 4-cylinder models with cartridge-type filter

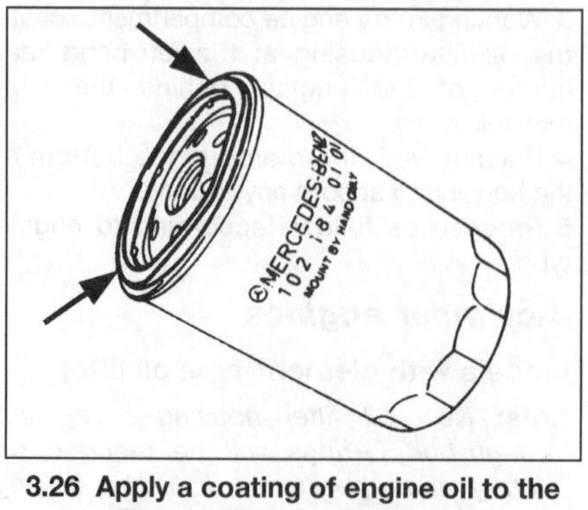

3.26 Apply a coating of engine oil to the filter sealing ring (arrowed)

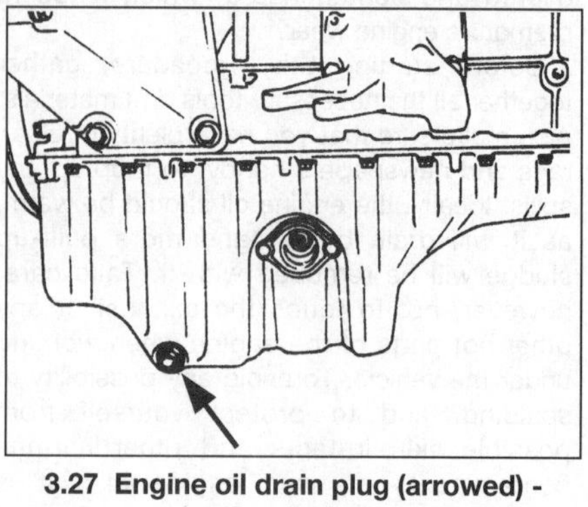

3.27 Engine oil drain plug (arrowed) - 6-cylinder

Every 12 000 miles

4 Spark plug renewal

1 The correct functioning of the spark plugs is vital for the correct running and efficiency of the engine. It is essential that the plugs fitted are appropriate for the engine (a suitable type is specified at the beginning of this Chapter). If this type is used and the engine is in good condition, the spark plugs should not need attention between scheduled replacement intervals. Spark plug cleaning is rarely necessary, and should not be attempted unless specialised equipment is available, as damage can easily be caused to the firing ends.

2 If the marks on the original-equipment spark plug (HT) leads cannot be seen, label the leads to correspond to the cylinder the lead serves (No 1 cylinder is at the timing chain end of the engine). Pull the leads from the plugs by gripping the end fitting, not the lead, otherwise the lead connection may be fractured **(see illustration)**.

3 It is advisable to remove the dirt from the spark plug recesses using a clean brush, vacuum cleaner or compressed air before removing the plugs, to prevent dirt dropping into the cylinders **(see illustration)**.

4 Unscrew the plugs using a spark plug spanner, suitable box spanner or a deep socket and extension bar. Keep the socket aligned with the spark plug - if it is forcibly moved to one side, the ceramic insulator may be broken off **(see illustration)**. As each plug is removed, examine it as follows.

5 Examination of the spark plugs will give a good indication of the condition of the engine. If the insulator nose of the spark plug is clean and white, with no deposits, this is indicative of a weak mixture or a plug of the wrong temperature grade (a 'hot' plug transfers heat away from the electrode slowly, a 'cold' plug transfers heat away quickly).

6 If the tip and insulator nose are covered with hard black-looking deposits, then this indicates that the mixture is too rich. Should the plug be black and oily, then it is likely that the engine is fairly worn, as well as the mixture being too rich.

7 If the insulator nose is covered with light tan to greyish-brown deposits, then the mixture is correct and it is likely that the engine is in good condition.

8 The spark plug electrode gap is of considerable importance as, if it is too large or too small, the size of the spark and its efficiency will be seriously impaired. The gap should be measured using a feeler gauge and set to the value given in the Specifications at the beginning of this Chapter.

9 To set the gap, bend the outer plug electrode in the required direction, until the correct gap is achieved. The centre electrode should never be bent, as this may crack the insulator and cause plug failure, if nothing worse. If using feeler blades, the gap is correct when the appropriate-size blade is a firm sliding fit **(see illustration)**.

10 Special spark plug electrode gap adjusting tools are available from most motor accessory shops, or from some spark plug manufacturers **(see illustration)**.

11 Before fitting the spark plugs **(see Haynes Hint)**, check that the threaded connector sleeves are tight, and that the plug exterior surfaces and threads are clean.

12 Remove the rubber hose (if used), and tighten the plug to the specified torque using the spark plug socket and a torque wrench. Refit the remaining spark plugs in the same manner.

13 Connect the HT leads in their correct order, and refit any components removed for access.

HAYNES HiNT

It is often difficult to insert spark plugs into their holes without cross-threading them. To avoid this possibility, fit a short length of 5/16 inch internal diameter rubber hose (arrowed) over the end of the spark plug. The flexible hose acts as a universal joint to help align the plug with the plug hole. Should the plug begin to cross-thread, the hose will slip on the spark plug, preventing thread damage to the cylinder head

4.2 Pull the HT leads from the spark plugs

4.3 Brush away dirt from the spark plug recess

4.4 Removing a spark plug

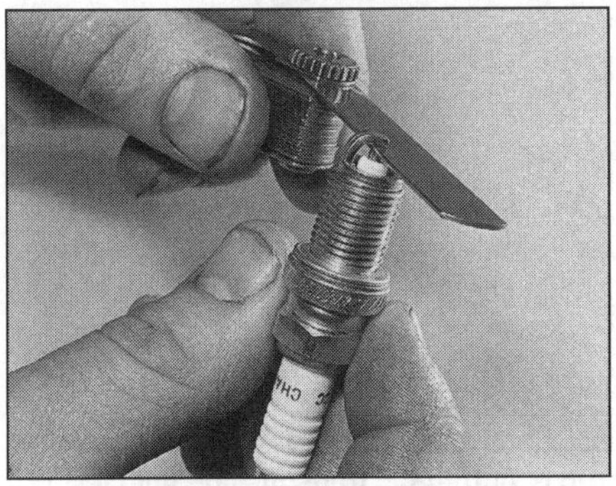

4.8 Measuring the spark plug electrode gap, using a feeler blade

4.10 Set the spark plug gap by carefully bending the electrode, using an adjusting tool

5.2 Lubricating the throttle linkage

6.4a Release the locking lever . . .

6.4b . . . and pull out the dipstick . . .

5 Throttle linkage lubrication

1 Inspect the throttle linkage components for wear or damage, and renew any worn components. Brush away dirt using a soft brush or cloth.

2 Lubricate all the moving parts of the throttle linkage and, where applicable, the kickdown and/or cruise control linkage, using light oil or grease **(see illustration)**. Note that on some models it will be necessary to remove the air cleaner (see Chapter 4) for access to the throttle linkage components.

6 Automatic transmission fluid level check

1 In order to check the automatic transmission fluid level, the transmission must be at operating temperature (fluid temperature 80°C). Operating temperature is reached after driving for approximately 10 miles. **Do not** attempt to check the fluid level when the transmission is cold.

2 With the transmission at operating temperature, ensure that the vehicle is parked on level ground.

3 With the engine running at idle speed, ensure that the transmission selector lever is in position 'P', and apply the parking brake.

4 Release the locking lever, and pull the transmission fluid level dipstick from the dipstick tube. Wipe the dipstick with a lint-free cloth, then re-insert it **(see illustrations)**.

5 Pull out the dipstick once more, and read off the fluid level. The level should be between the 'MIN' and 'MAX' marks **(see illustration)**.

6 If topping up is necessary, top up through the dipstick tube, using fluid of the specified type (see *'Recommended Lubricants and Fluids'*). **Do not** overfill the transmission - the fluid level must not be above the 'MAX' mark.

7 On completion, re-insert the dipstick tube, and re-check the fluid level. Ensure that the locking lever is engaged when finally refitting the dipstick.

7 Underbonnet/underbody components and hoses - check for leaks

1 Visually inspect the engine joint faces, gaskets and seals for any signs of water or oil leaks. Pay particular attention to the areas around the camshaft cover, cylinder head, oil filter and sump joint faces **(see illustration)**. Bear in mind that, over a period of time, some very slight seepage from these areas is to be expected - what you are really looking for is any indication of a serious leak. Should a leak be found, renew the offending gasket or oil seal by referring to the appropriate Chapters in this manual.

2 Also check the security and condition of all the engine-related pipes and hoses. Ensure that all cable ties or securing clips are in place and in good condition. Clips which are broken or missing can lead to chafing of the hoses, pipes or wiring, which could cause more serious problems in the future.

3 Carefully check the radiator hoses and heater hoses along their entire length. Renew any hose which is cracked, swollen or deteriorated. Cracks will show up better if the hose is squeezed. Pay close attention to the hose clips that secure the hoses to the cooling system components. Hose clips can pinch and puncture hoses, resulting in cooling system leaks.

4 Inspect all the cooling system components (hoses, joint faces etc.) for leaks. A leak in the cooling system will usually show up as white- or rust-coloured deposits on the area adjoining the leak **(see Haynes Hint)**. Where any

HAYNES HiNT

A leak in the cooling system will usually show up as white- or rust-coloured deposits on the area adjoining the leak

6.4c . . . then wipe the dipstick

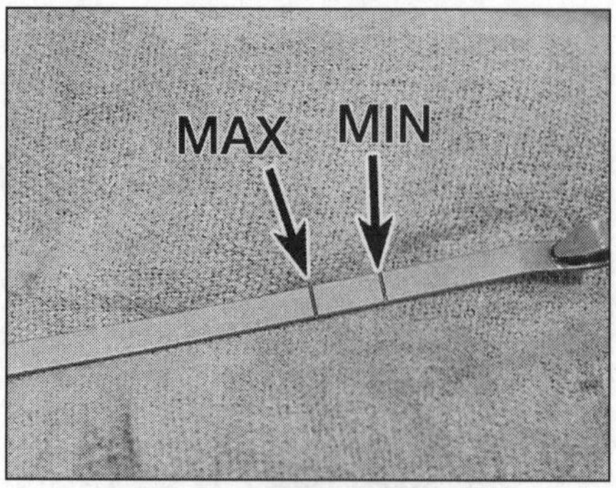

6.5 Automatic transmission fluid level dipstick markings

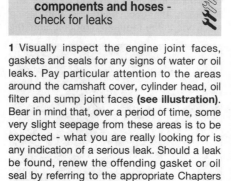

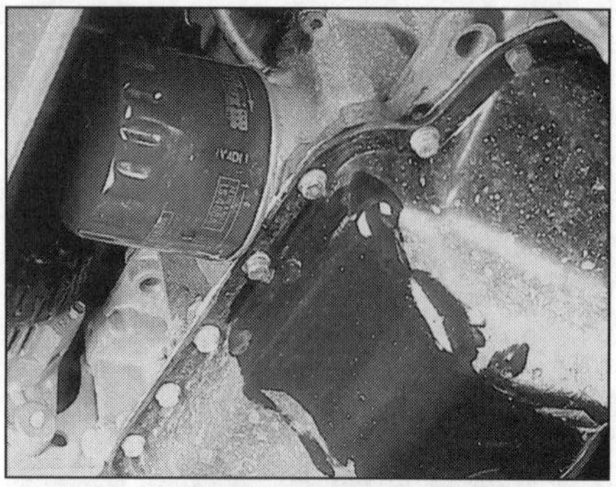

7.1 Visually inspect the area around the oil filter and sump joint faces for signs of leakage

problems of this nature are found on system components, renew the component or gasket with reference to Chapter 3.

5 Where applicable, inspect the automatic transmission fluid cooler hoses for leaks or deterioration.

6 With the vehicle raised, inspect the petrol tank and filler neck for punctures, cracks and other damage. The connection between the filler neck and tank is especially critical. Sometimes a rubber filler neck or connecting hose will leak due to loose retaining clamps or deteriorated rubber.

7 Carefully check all rubber hoses and metal fuel lines leading away from the petrol tank. Check for loose connections, deteriorated hoses, crimped lines, and other damage. Pay particular attention to the vent pipes and hoses, which often loop up around the filler neck and can become blocked or crimped. Follow the lines to the front of the vehicle, carefully inspecting them all the way. Renew damaged Sections as necessary.

8 Closely inspect the metal brake pipes which run along the vehicle underbody. If they show signs of excessive corrosion or damage they must be renewed.

9 From within the engine compartment, check the security of all fuel hose attachments and pipe unions, and inspect the fuel hoses and vacuum hoses for kinks, chafing and deterioration.

10 Where applicable, check the condition of the power steering fluid hoses and pipes.

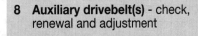

8 Auxiliary drivebelt(s) - check, renewal and adjustment

Drivebelt checking - general

1 Due to their function and construction, the belts are prone to failure after a period of time, and should be inspected periodically to prevent problems.

8.6 Slacken the tensioner bolt (1) and turn the adjuster nut (2) - 4-cylinder engine with single drivebelt

2 The number of belts used on a particular vehicle depends on the accessories fitted. Drivebelts are used to drive the coolant pump, alternator, power steering/suspension hydraulic pump, air conditioning compressor and air injection pump.

3 To improve access for belt inspection, if desired, remove the viscous cooling fan and cowl as described in Chapter 3.

4 With the engine stopped, using your fingers (and a torch if necessary), move along the belts, checking for cracks and separation of the belt plies. Also check for fraying and glazing, which gives the belt a shiny appearance. Both sides of the belts should be inspected, which means the belt will have to be twisted to check the underside. If necessary turn the engine using a socket on the crankshaft pulley hub bolt so that the whole of the belt can be inspected.

4-cylinder engines with single drivebelt - drivebelt renewal

5 Remove the cooling fan blades and shroud, as described in Chapter 3.

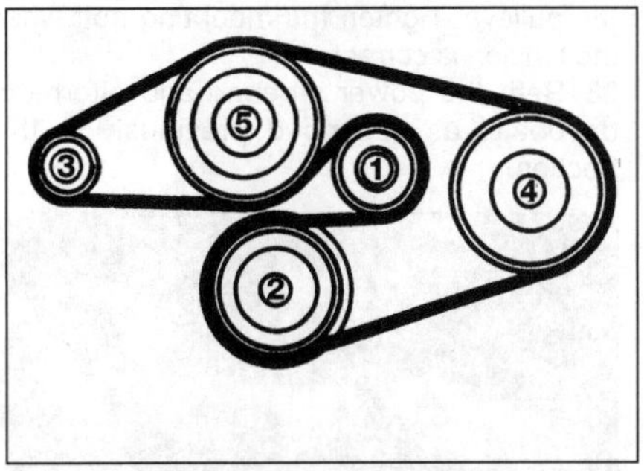

8.8b Auxiliary drivebelt - 4-cylinder engine with power steering but without air conditioning (single drivebelt)

Fit belt round pulleys in order shown
1. *Tensioner pulley*
2. *Crankshaft pulley*
3. *Alternator pulley*
4. *Power steering pump pulley*
5. *Coolant pump pulley*

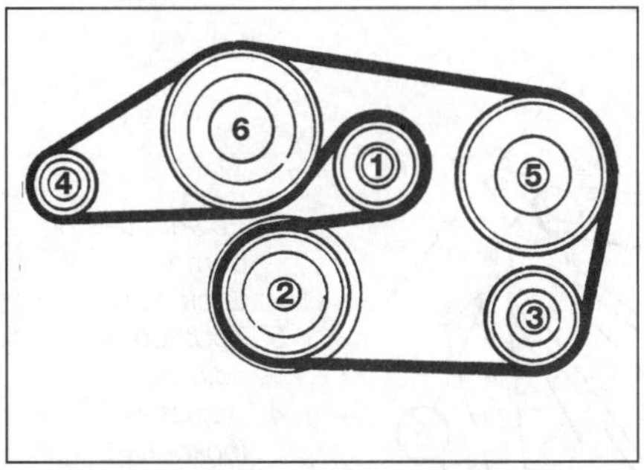

8.8c Auxiliary drivebelt - 4-cylinder engine with power steering and air conditioning (single drivebelt)

Fit belt round pulleys in order shown
1. *Tensioner pulley*
2. *Crankshaft pulley*
3. *Air conditioning compressor pulley*
4. *Alternator pulley*
5. *Power steering pump pulley*
6. *Coolant pump pulley*

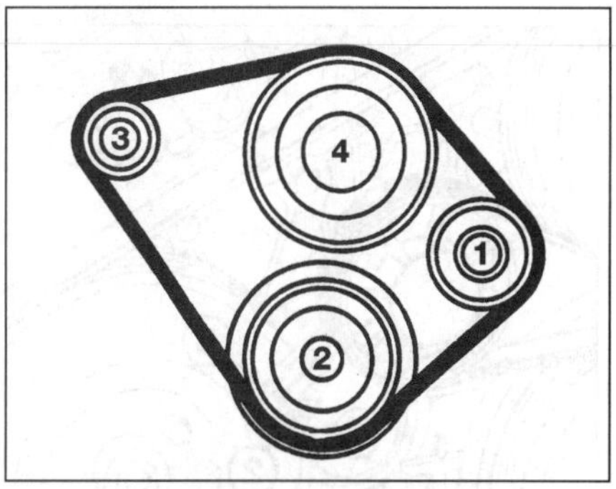

8.8a Auxiliary drivebelt - 4-cylinder engine without power steering (single drivebelt)

Fit belt round pulleys in order shown
1. *Tensioner pulley*
2. *Crankshaft pulley*
3. *Alternator pulley*
4. *Coolant pump pulley*

6 Slacken the tensioner bolt by a quarter- to half-a-turn (remove the plastic cover to expose the bolt where necessary) **(see illustration)**.

7 Slacken the adjuster nut (anti-clockwise) to back off the adjuster until the belt can be removed from the pulleys.

8 Fit the new belt round the pulleys, starting with the tensioner pulley, and proceeding in the order shown **(see illustrations)**. Check that the belt is correctly seated on the pulleys.

9 Tension the belt as follows.

Models with graduated scale on tensioner

10 On vehicle without power steering, turn the adjuster nut clockwise until the tip of the tensioner pointer is aligned with the 5th graduation (from the left, looking at the scale from the front of the engine compartment) on the scale **(see illustration)**.

11 On models with power steering, turn the adjuster nut clockwise until the tip of the tensioner pointer is positioned between the 8th and 9th graduations (from the left, looking at the scale from the front of the engine compartment) on the scale.

12 Tighten the tensioner bolt to the specified torque, and refit the cover, where applicable.

8.10 Turn the adjuster nut (1) until the tip of the pointer (2) is aligned with the 5th graduation on the scale (3) - 4-cylinder engine (single drivebelt)

8.14 Turn the adjuster nut (1) until the tip of the pointer (2) is aligned with the thick line (3) on the scale - 4-cylinder engine (single drivebelt)

8.18 Slacken the upper (2) and lower (1) alternator mounting nuts – 4-cylinder engine (multiple drivebelts)

8.19 Alternator adjuster arm bolt (1) and adjuster bolt (2) – 4-cylinder engine (multiple drivebelts)

13 Refit the cooling fan blades and shroud as described in Chapter 3.

Models with single thick mark (and cast triangle) on tensioner scale

14 Turn the adjuster nut clockwise until the tip of the tensioner pointer is aligned with the thick line (at the thicker end of the triangle) on the scale **(see illustration).**

15 Tighten the tensioner bolt to the specified torque, and refit the cover where applicable.

16 Refit the cooling fan blades and shroud as described in Chapter 3.

4-cylinder engines with multiple drivebelts - drivebelt renewal

Alternator/coolant pump drivebelt

17 If necessary to improve access, remove the engine undershield with reference to Chapter 11.

18 Slacken the upper and lower alternator mounting nuts, and the bolt securing the adjuster arm to the timing chain cover **(see illustration).**

19 Turn the adjuster bolt to move the alternator towards the engine until the drivebelt can be slipped from the pulleys **(see illustration).**

20 Fit the new belt around the pulleys, then turn the adjuster bolt to tension the belt until it is just possible to deflect the belt by approximately 12.0 mm under moderate finger pressure midway between the crankshaft pulley and the alternator pulley.

21 Hold the adjuster bolt in position, then tighten the upper and lower alternator mounting nuts, then the adjuster arm bolt, in that order.

22 Recheck the belt tension after running the engine for several minutes then, where applicable, refit the engine undershield.

Power steering pump drivebelt

23 Remove the alternator drivebelt as described previously in this Section.

24 Working at the rear of the power steering pump mounting bracket, slacken the adjuster lockbolt furthest from the engine, and the two mounting bolts nearest to the engine **(see illustration).**

25 Turn the toothed adjuster bolt using an open-ended spanner to move the pump towards the engine, then slip the drivebelt off the pulleys.

26 Fit the new belt over the pulleys, then turn the adjuster bolt until it is just possible to deflect the drivebelt by approximately 12.0 mm under moderate finger pressure midway between the two pulleys.

27 Tighten the adjuster lockbolt, followed by the two mounting bolts.

28 Refit the alternator drivebelt as described previously in this Section.

29 Recheck the tension of the belts after running the engine for several minutes then, where applicable, refit the engine undershield.

Air conditioning compressor drivebelt

30 Remove the alternator drivebelt and the power steering drivebelt as described previously in this Section.

31 Slacken the compressor mounting bolt, unscrew the tensioner bolt to move the compressor in towards the engine, and slip the drivebelt off the pulleys **(see illustration).**

32 Fit the new belt over the pulleys, and tighten the tensioning bolt until it is just possible to deflect the belt by 10.0 mm under moderate thumb pressure midway between the pulleys. Tighten the mounting bolt when the tension is correct.

33 Refit the power steering and alternator drivebelts as described previously in this Section.

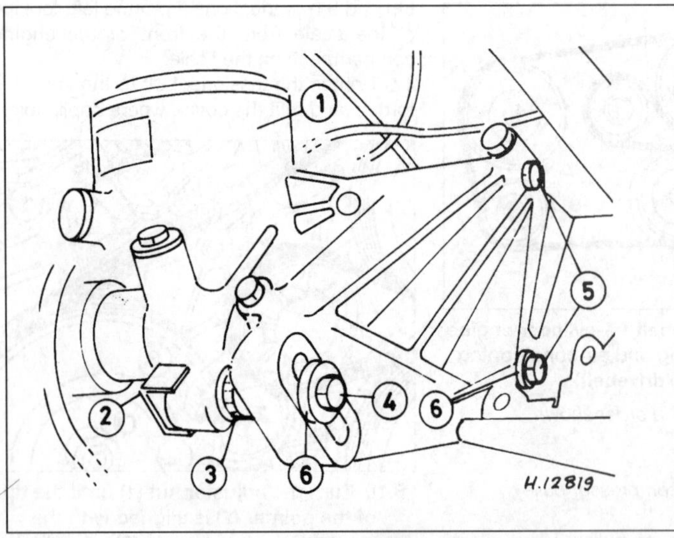

1 Power steering pump
2 Locking nut
3 Toothed adjuster
4 Adjuster lockbolt
5 Mounting bolts
6 Washers

8.24 Power steering pump mounting details – 4-cylinder engine (multiple drivebelts)

8.31 Air conditioning compressor mounting details – 4-cylinder engines (multiple drivebelts)

1 Mounting bolt 2 Tensioner bolt

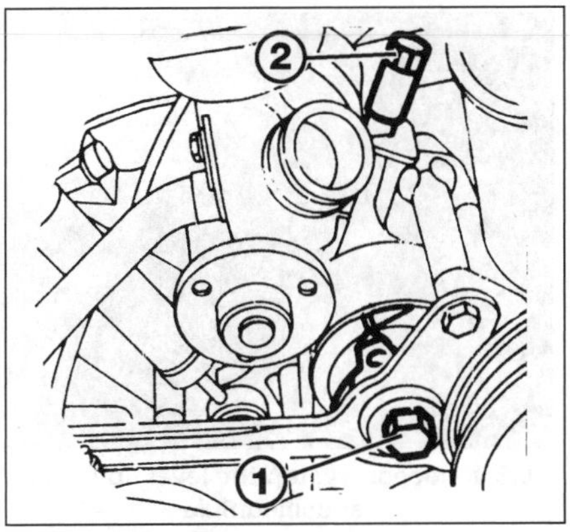

8.36 Slacken the tensioner bolt (1) and turn the adjuster nut (2) - 6-cylinder engine

34 Recheck the tension of the belts after running the engine for several minutes then, where applicable, refit the engine undershield.

6-cylinder engines - drivebelt renewal

35 Remove the cooling fan blades and shroud, as described in Chapter 3.

36 Slacken the tensioner bolt by a quarter- to half-a-turn (remove the plastic cover to expose the bolt, where necessary) **(see illustration)**.

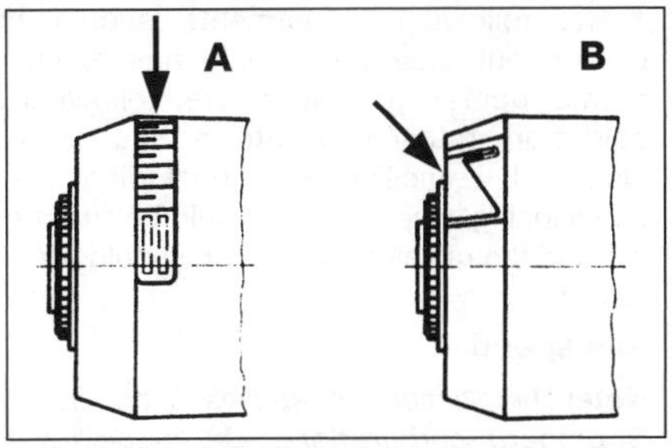

8.40 Alternative drivebelt adjuster types - 6-cylinder engines

A Adjuster with graduated scale
B Adjuster with cast triangle

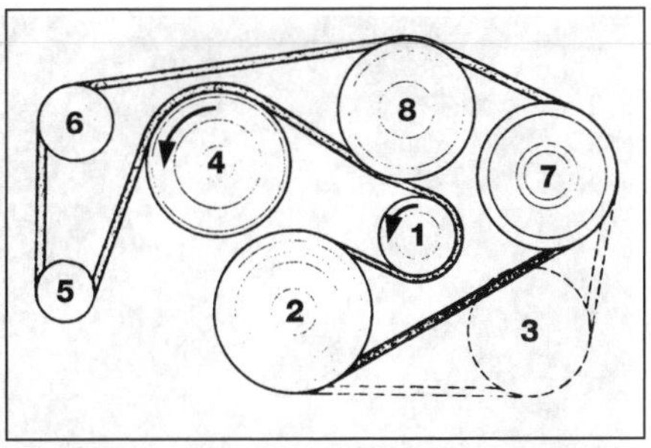

8.38a Auxiliary drivebelt - 6-cylinder engines without air injection pump

Fit belt round pulleys in order shown
1 Tensioner pulley
2 Crankshaft pulley
3 Air conditioning compressor pulley
4 Cooling fan pulley
5 Alternator pulley
6 Idler pulley
7 Power steering pump pulley
8 Coolant pump pulley

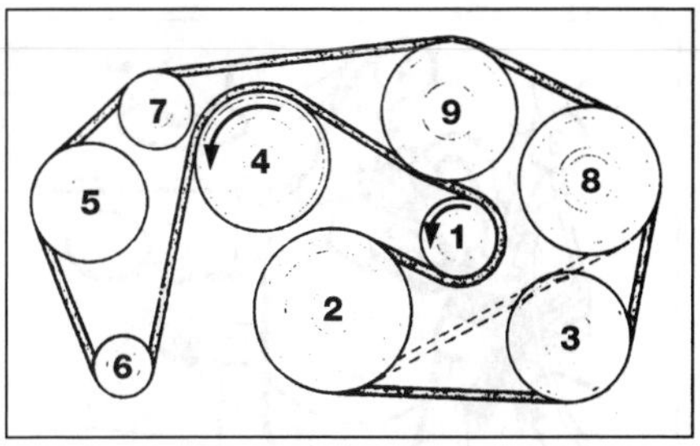

8.38b Auxiliary drivebelt - 6-cylinder engines with air injection pump

Fit belt round pulleys in order shown
1 Tensioner pulley
2 Crankshaft pulley
3 Air conditioning compressor pulley
4 Cooling fan pulley
5 Air injection pump pulley
6 Alternator pulley
7 Idler pulley
8 Power steering pump pulley
9 Coolant pump pulley

37 Slacken the adjuster nut (anti-clockwise) to back off the adjuster until the belt can be removed from the pulleys.

38 Fit the new belt round the pulleys, starting with the idler pulley, and proceeding in the order shown **(see illustrations)**. Check that the belt is correctly seated on the pulleys.

39 Tension the belt as follows.

Models with graduated scale on adjuster

40 Move the tensioner pointer until it aligns with the right-hand end (looking at the scale from the front of the engine compartment) of the scale **(see illustration)**.

41 On models without air conditioning, turn the adjuster nut clockwise until the tip of the tensioner pointer is aligned with the 5th graduation on the scale.

42 On models with air conditioning, turn the adjuster nut clockwise until the tip of the tensioner pointer is aligned with the 7th graduation on the scale.

43 Tighten the tensioner bolt to the specified torque, and refit the cover where applicable.

44 Refit the cooling fan blades and shroud as described in Chapter 3.

Models with single thick mark (and cast triangle) on tensioner scale

45 Move the tensioner pointer until the tip of the pointer aligns with the right-hand, narrowest end (looking at the scale from the front of the engine compartment) of the triangle on the scale.

46 Turn the adjuster nut clockwise until the tip of the tensioner pointer is aligned with the thick line (at the thicker end of the triangle) on the scale **(see illustration)**.

1A

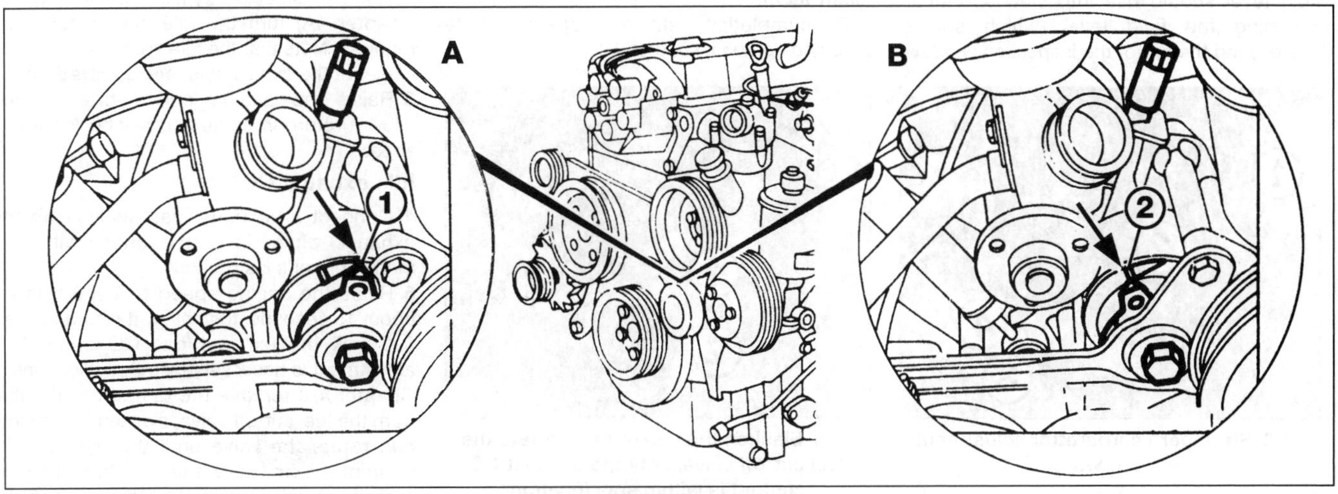

8.46 Auxiliary drivebelt adjustment - 6-cylinder engine

A Tensioner pointer (1) aligned with right-hand end of arrow (arrowed) on scale - belt slack
B Tensioner pointer (1) aligned with thick line (arrowed) on scale - belt tensioned

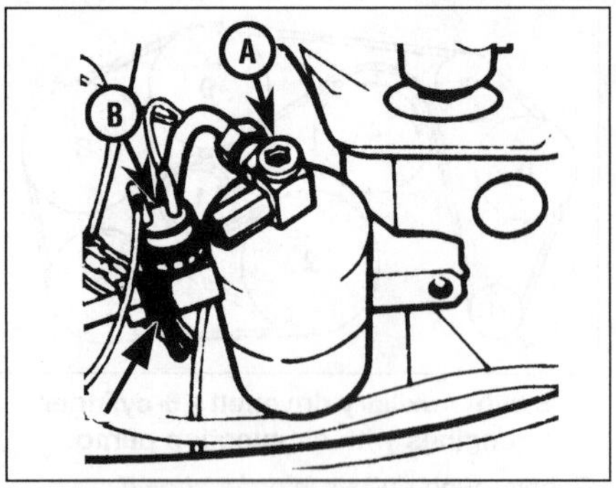

9.4 Air conditioning dehydrator unit

A Inspection window
B Pressure switch wiring connector

47 Tighten the tensioner bolt to the specified torque, and refit the cover where applicable.

48 Refit the cooling fan blades and shroud as described in Chapter 3.

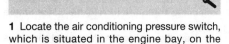

9 Air conditioning system check

1 Locate the air conditioning pressure switch, which is situated in the engine bay, on the side of the dehydrator unit.

2 With the engine and ignition switched off, unplug the wiring from the top of the pressure switch at the connector.

3 Start the engine, allow it to idle and turn on the air conditioning at the control panel.

4 Carefully wipe clean the inspection window on the top of the dehydrator unit **(see illustration)**.

5 Reconnect the pressure switch wiring, whilst observing the inspection window. This will cause the electromagnetic clutch to engage and as this happens, the refrigerant fluid level should rise into view. Continue watching the fluid level, which should rise beyond the top of the inspection window, until only bubble-free fluid can be seen flowing.

6 If the fluid level appears to be too low, or there is a pressure drop within the refrigeration system, the pressure switch will prevent the electromagnetic clutch from engaging and the air conditioning will not function. Under these circumstances, the vehicle should be taken to a Mercedes dealer or air conditioning specialist for diagnosis and/or re-charging. Do not attempt to by-pass the pressure switch in an attempt to restore operation, as serious component damage may result.

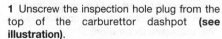

11.2 Stromberg carburettor adjustment screws

1 Choke lever connecting rod
2 Fast idle adjusting screw
3 Throttle lever
4 Idle speed adjusting screw

10.1 Unscrew the inspection hole plug from the top of the carburettor dashpot

10 Carburettor damper oil level check - Stromberg carburettor

1 Unscrew the inspection hole plug from the top of the carburettor dashpot **(see illustration)**.

2 Check that the level of the damper oil just reaches the lower edge of the inspection hole.

3 If necessary, top the level up with fluid of the grade listed in the Specifications **(see illustration)**.

4 On completion, refit the inspection hole plug and tighten it securely.

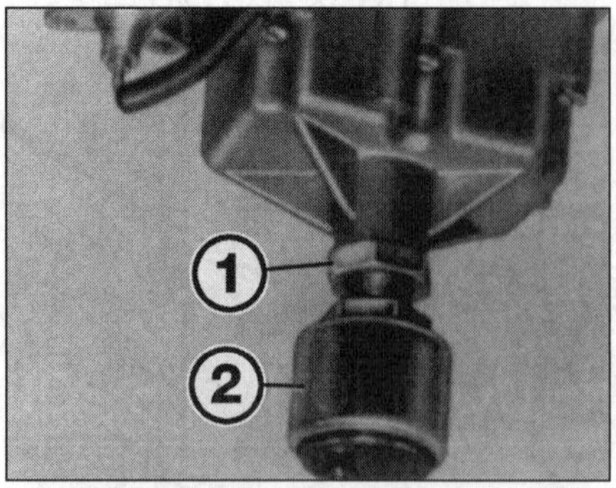

11.6 Slacken the locknut and rotate the fuel cut-off valve, until the exhaust CO content is within specification

1 Locknut
2 Fuel cut-off valve

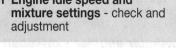

10.3 If necessary, top the level up with the specified fluid

11 Engine idle speed and mixture settings - check and adjustment

Models with carburettors

Note: *The information given is this Section is not applicable to vehicles fitted with catalytic converters.*

1 The following adjustments should be carried out after the engine has reached normal operating temperature, following a cold start, rather than after a long run. All electrical ancilliaries, (including air conditioning, where fitted) should be switched off, and the radiator cooling fan should not be running.

Idle speed

Note: *This Section only applies to models with Stromberg carburettors. On models with Pierburg carburettors, the idle speed is controlled electronically and cannot be adjusted manually.*

2 Connect a tachometer to the engine and monitor the engine speed at idle. If adjustment is necessary (see Specifications in Chapter 4A) turn the idle speed screw as required. Note that the idle speed screw is the longer of the two screws **(see illustration)**.

3 Raise the engine speed briefly, then allow it return to settle and re-check the idle speed.

Idle exhaust CO

4 Connect an exhaust gas analyser to the exhaust pipe, in accordance with the manufacturer's instructions.

5 Raise the engine speed to 2000 rpm for about 15 seconds, then allow it return to idle.

6 Check the exhaust gas CO content. If adjustment is necessary (see Specifications in Chapter 4A) remove the tamperproof collar from the fuel cut-off valve, slacken the locknut and rotate the valve until the exhaust CO content is within specification **(see illustration)**. Note that screwing in the valve will weaken the mixture, and screwing it out richens the mixture. Only rotate the valve half a turn at a time, between measurements.

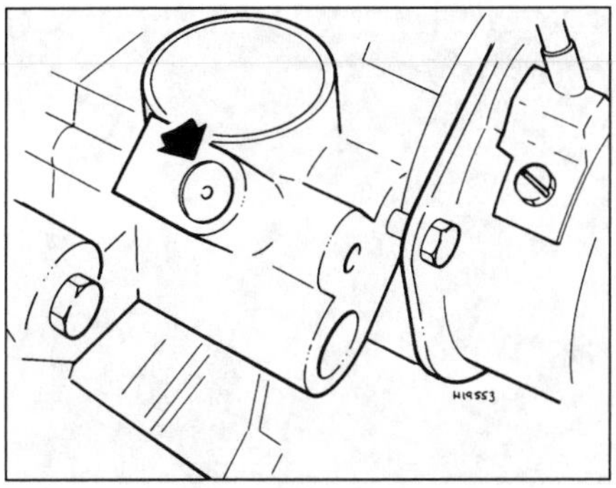

11.13 Remove the tamperproof plug (arrowed) from the auxiliary air adjusting screw

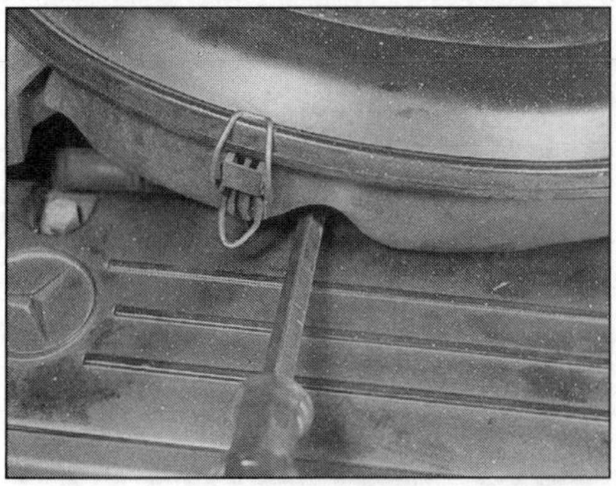
11.18 The idle speed adjustment screw is accessible via a recess in the underside of the air cleaner assembly

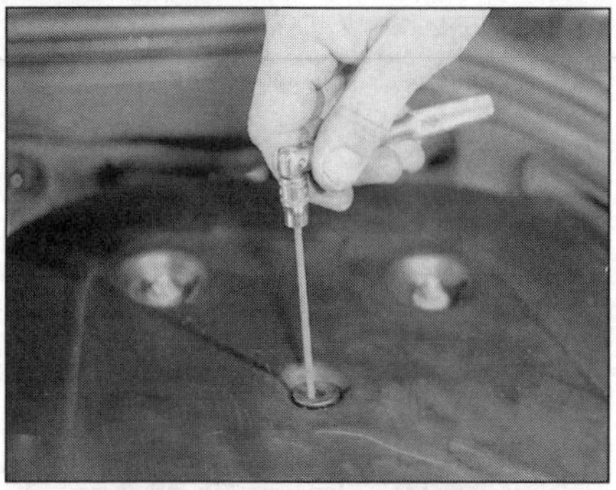
11.23 Insert an Allen key (or long hex bit) into the mixture adjustment screw tube

Fast idle speed

Note: *This Section only applies to models with Stromberg carburettors*.

7 Start the engine and allow it to idle. Ensure that the idle speed and exhaust CO content are correct, as described previously.

8 Hold the throttle open by hand, to an engine speed of about 2500 rpm. At the same time, insert a small screwdriver into the slot on the side of the choke housing, exposed by the removal of the plastic cover, and move the drive lever towards the engine until a noticeable stop is felt - do not try to force the lever beyond this point.

9 Whilst holding the drive lever with the screwdriver, release the throttle - the engine should now settle at a fast idle.

10 Check the fast idle speed with a tachometer. If adjustment is necessary (see Specifications in Chapter 4A) turn the idle speed screw as required. Note that the fast idle speed screw is the shorter of the two screws **(refer to illustration 11.2)**

11 On completion, open the throttle briefly to disengage the fast idle mechanism and allow the engine speed to return to a normal idle.

Fast idle exhaust CO

Note: *This Section only applies to models with Sromberg carburettors.*

12 Connect an exhaust gas analyser to the exhaust pipe, in accordance with the manufacturer's instructions.

13 With the engine set to run at a fast idle, as described previously, Check the exhaust gas CO content. If adjustment is necessary (see Specifications in Chapter 4A), remove the tamperproof plug from the auxiliary air adjusting screw and turn it until the exhaust CO content is within the specification **(see illustration)**. Note that screwing in the screw will richen the mixture, and screwing it out weakens the mixture. Only rotate the screw half a turn at a time, between measurements.

14 On completion, open the throttle briefly to disengage the fast idle mechanism and allow the engine speed to return to a normal idle.

Models with fuel injection

Note: *The following adjustments should be carried out when the engine has just reached normal operating temperature after starting from cold, rather than after a long drive. Ideally, the adjustments should be completed before the engine temperture exceeds 100ºC, or before the auxiliary cooling fan cuts in. On later models fitted with a rotary idle actuator, the idle speed is controlled electronically and adjustment without specialised test equipment is not possible. Vehicles so equipped should be taken to a Mercedes dealer or a Bosch fuel injection specialist for adjsustment.*

15 When carrying out the adjustment, the air cleaner should be in position, with all vacuum and breather hoses connected. The instrument pack tachometer is sufficiently accurate to allow idle speed adjustment.

16 Connect an exhaust gas analyser to the exhaust tailpipe/sample pipe, in accordance with the manufacturer's instructions.

17 Start the engine and allow it to idle. On vehicles with automatic transmission, select 'PARK'. Ensure that all ancillaries are switched off, including the air conditioning (where fitted).

18 The idle speed adjustment screw is accessible via a recess in the underside of the air cleaner assembly **(see illustration).**

19 Turn the idle speed adjustment screw until the idle speed is within the limits given in the Specifications. Accelerate the engine briefly, then allow it to idle again.

20 Re-check the idle speed and adjust if necessary. Switch off the engine on completion.

21 To adjust the exhaust gas CO content, remove the air cleaner assembly and prise out the tamperproof plug. Refit the air cleaner assembly.

22 Start the engine and accelerate it to roughly 2000 rpm. Maintain this speed for about 10 seconds, then allow it to return to idle.

23 Check the CO reading on the exhaust gas analyser. If it is not as specified, insert an Allen key into the mixture adjustment screw tube **(see illustration)**. Engage the end of the Allen key with the adjustment device and hold it down against the spring pressure, until the adjustment device engages with the adjustment screw.

24 Turn the adjustment screw as required to correct the exhaust gas CO content; clockwise enrichens the mixture and anticlockwise weakens it.

25 Re-check the exhaust gas CO content after accelerating the engine, as described from paragraph 8 onwards, and continue adjusting the mixture as required. Only turn the adustment screw through half a turn at a time, between measurements.

26 On completion, disconnect all test instruments and fit a new tamperproof plug to the mixture adjustment screw tube.

12 Steering and suspension components - condition and security check

Front suspension and steering check

1 Raise the front of the vehicle, and securely support it on axle stands.

2 Visually inspect the balljoint dust covers for splits, chafing or deterioration **(see illustration).** Any wear of these components will cause loss of lubricant, together with dirt and water entry, resulting in rapid

12.2 Visually inspect the balljoint dust covers for splits, chafing or deterioration

12.4 Grasp the roadwheel at the 12 o'clock and 6 o'clock positions, and try to rock it

12.9 The efficiency of the suspension strut/shock absorber may be checked by bouncing the vehicle at each corner

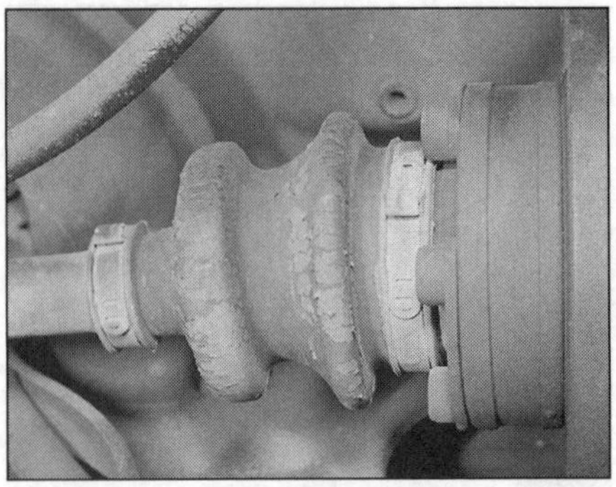

13.1 Inspect the condition of the CV joint rubber gaiters, checking for signs of cracking or splitting

deterioration of the balljoints. Also check that the steering box mountings are tightened to the specified torque settings (see Chapter 10).

3 On vehicles with power steering, check the fluid hoses for chafing or deterioration, and the pipe and hose unions for fluid leaks. Also check for signs of fluid leakage under pressure from the steering box, which would indicate failed fluid seals within the steering box.

4 Grasp the roadwheel at the 12 o'clock and 6 o'clock positions, and try to rock it **(see illustration)**. Very slight free play may be felt, but if the movement is appreciable, further investigation is necessary to determine the source. Continue rocking the wheel while an assistant depresses the footbrake. If the movement is now eliminated or significantly reduced, it is likely that the hub bearings are at fault. If the free play is still evident with the footbrake depressed, then there is wear in the suspension joints or mountings. Note that the front hub bearings are adjustable (See Chapter 10).

5 Now grasp the wheel at the 9 o'clock and 3 o'clock positions, and try to rock it as before. Any movement felt now may again be caused by wear in the hub bearings or the steering track-rod balljoints. If the inner or outer balljoint is worn, the visual movement will be obvious.

6 Using a large screwdriver or flat bar, check for wear in the suspension mounting bushes by levering between the relevant suspension component and its attachment point. Some movement is to be expected as the mountings are made of rubber, but excessive wear should be obvious. Also check the condition of any visible rubber bushes, looking for splits, cracks or contamination of the rubber.

7 With the car standing on its wheels, have an assistant turn the steering wheel back and forth about an eighth of a turn each way. There should be very little lost movement between the steering wheel and roadwheels. If this is not the case, closely observe the linkage joints and mountings previously described, but in addition, check the steering column universal joint/coupling for wear, and the steering box itself.

Suspension strut/shock absorber check

8 Check for any signs of fluid leakage around the suspension strut/shock absorber body, or from the rubber gaiter around the piston rod. Should any fluid be noticed, the suspension strut/shock absorber is defective internally, and should be renewed. **Note:** *Suspension struts/shock absorbers should always be renewed in pairs on the same axle.*

9 The efficiency of the suspension strut/shock absorber may be checked by bouncing the vehicle at each corner **(see illustration)**. Generally speaking, the body will return to its normal position and stop after being depressed. If it rises and returns on a rebound, the suspension strut/shock absorber is probably suspect. Examine also the suspension strut/shock absorber upper and lower mountings for any signs of wear.

13 Driveshafts and driveshaft gaiters - condition check

1 With the vehicle raised and securely supported on stands, slowly rotate the rear roadwheel. Inspect the condition of the outer constant velocity (CV) joint rubber gaiters, squeezing the gaiters to open out the folds. Check for signs of cracking, splits or deterioration of the rubber, which may allow the grease to escape, and lead to water and grit entry into the joint **(see illustration)**. Also check the security and condition of the retaining clips. Repeat these checks on the inner CV joints. If any damage or deterioration is found, the gaiters should be renewed (see Chapter 8).

2 At the same time, check the general condition of the CV joints themselves by first holding the driveshaft and attempting to rotate the wheel. Repeat this check by holding the inner joint and attempting to rotate the driveshaft. Any appreciable movement indicates wear in the joints, wear in the driveshaft splines, or a loose driveshaft retaining nut.

14 Front brake pad check

1 Firmly apply the parking brake, then jack up the front of the car and support it securely on axle stands. Remove the front roadwheels.

2 A quick check of the brake pads can be carried out by viewing through the inspection aperture, at the front of the caliper **(see Haynes Hint)**. The depth of friction material remaining on the pads can be seen, but note that only one of the pads wil be fully visible.

3 For a comprehensive check, the brake pads should be removed and cleaned. The operation of the caliper can then also be checked, and the condition of the brake disc itself can be fully examined on both sides. Refer to Chapter 9 for further information.

4 If friction material on any of the pads is worn to, or below, the specified thickness, then *all four front brake pads must be renewed as a set, to ensure that the braking performance remains consistent.*

Warning: Do not swap brake pads around in an attempt to compensate for uneven wear. The braking performance of the vehicle will be seriousy impaired.

HAYNES HiNT

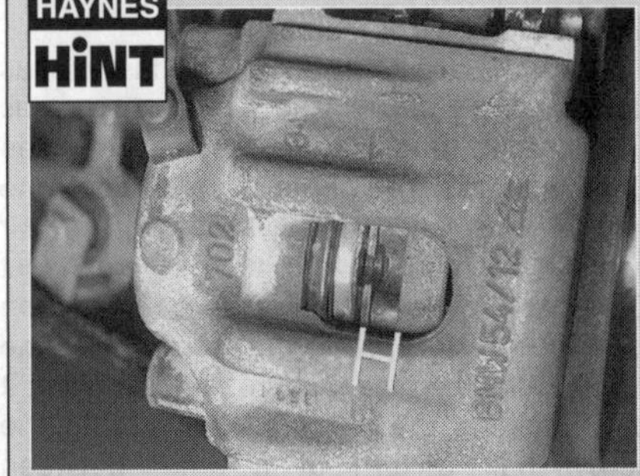

A quick check of the brake pads can be carried out by viewing through the inspection aperture, at the front of the caliper

15 Rear brake pad check

1 Chock the front wheels, then jack up the rear of the vehicle and support it on axle stands. Remove the rear roadwheels.

2 For a quick check, the thickness of friction material remaining on each brake pad can be measured through the top of the caliper body. If any pad's friction material is worn to the specified thickness or less, then *all four front brake pads must be renewed as a set, to ensure that the braking performance remains consistent.*

3 For a comprehensive check, the brake pads should be removed and cleaned. This will permit the operation of the caliper to be checked, and the condition of the brake disc itself to be fully examined on both sides. Refer to Chapter 9 for further information.

Warning: Do not swap brake pads around in an attempt to compensate for uneven wear. The braking performance of the vehicle will be seriousy impaired.

16 Parking brake - operation check

1 Applying normal moderate pressure, fully apply the parking brake whilst counting the number of 'clicks' of the ratchet mechanism. If adjustment is correct, there should be approximately 7 or 8 clicks before the parking brake is fully applied. If there are less than 4 clicks or more than 11 clicks, adjustment will be necessary; refer to Chapter 9 for a description of the adjustment procedure.

17 Exhaust system and mountings - condition and security check

1 With the engine cold (at least an hour after the vehicle has been driven), check the complete exhaust system from the engine to the end of the tailpipe. The exhaust system is

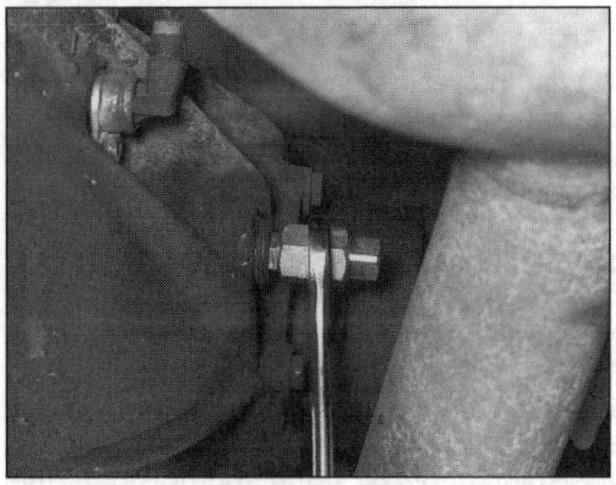

19.2 Location of the final drive unit filler/level plug

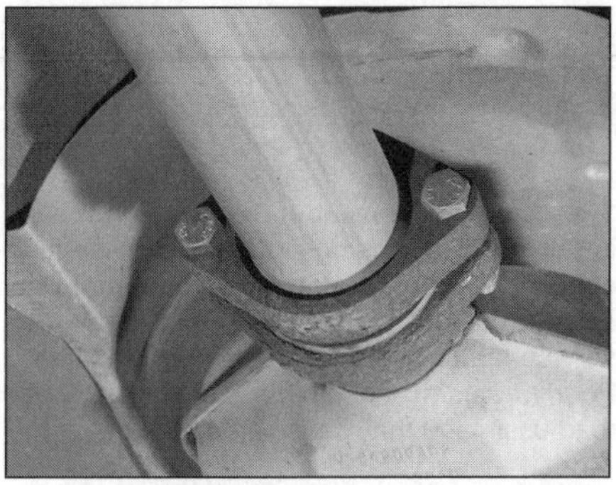

17.2 Check the security of the exhaust system joints

most easily checked with the vehicle raised on a hoist, or suitably supported on axle stands, so that the exhaust components are readily visible and accessible.

2 Check the exhaust pipes and connections for evidence of leaks, severe corrosion and damage. Make sure that all brackets and mountings are in good condition, and that all relevant nuts and bolts are tight **(see illustration)**. Leakage at any of the joints or in other parts of the system will usually show up as a black sooty stain in the vicinity of the leak.

3 Rattles and other noises can often be traced to the exhaust system, especially the brackets and mountings. Try to move the pipes and silencers. If the components are able to come into contact with the body or suspension parts, secure the system with new mountings. Otherwise separate the joints (if possible) and twist the pipes as necessary to provide additional clearance.

18 Manual transmission oil level check

Note: *A hexagonal key, or a suitable alternative (see text) will be required to unscrew the transmission level/filler plug.*

1 Place a suitable container beneath the transmission level/filler plug, located on the right-hand side of the transmission. A hexagonal key should be used to unscrew the plug, but a tool can be improvised using a

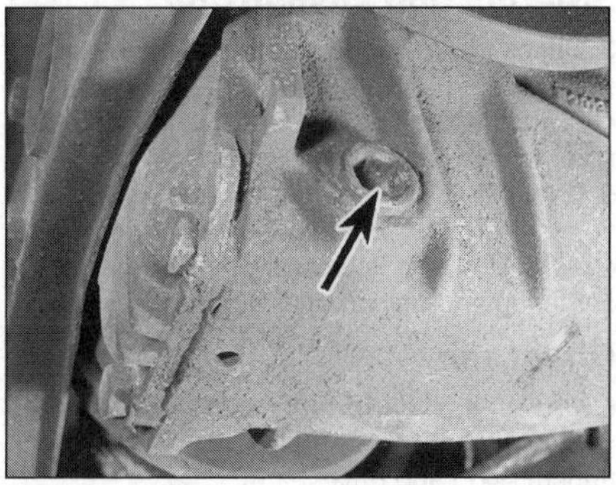

19.10 Location of the final drive unit drain plug

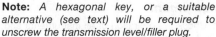

18.1 Using a long nut and a spanner to unscrew the transmission fluid level/filler plug

long nut, or a length of hexagonal bar, and a spanner **(see illustration)**.

2 The fluid level should just be up to the bottom of the level/filler plug hole.

3 If necessary, top up the level until fluid just begins to run out of the level/filler plug hole.

4 When the level is correct, refit the plug, and tighten securely.

19 Final drive unit oil - level check and renewal

Level check

1 Either position the vehicle over a well-ventilated inspection pit, or jack up the front and rear of the vehicle and support it on axle stands. The vehicle **must** be level, if the results of this check are to be accurate.

2 Clean the area around the filler/level plug on the left-hand side of the final drive unit, then slacken and remove the plug from the housing **(see illustration)**.

3 The oil level should be up to the lower edge of the filler/level plug aperture. Check that this is the case using a clean piece of wire, bent into a right-angle.

4 If necessary, top-up until the oil level is correct. Fill the final drive until oil starts to flow out and allow excess oil to drain.

5 Once the final drive unit oil level is correct, refit the filler/level plug and tighten it securely. Lower the vehicle to the ground.

6 Note that frequent need for topping-up indicates a leakage, possibly through an oil seal. The cause should be investigated and rectified.

Draining and refilling

7 The draining process will be simplified if the vehicle is taken on a short drive; this will allow the oil to heat up, reducing its viscosity.

9 Either position the vehicle over a well-ventilated inspection pit, or jack up the front and rear of the vehicle and support it on axle stands.

9 Clean the area around the filler/level plug, on the left-hand side of the final drive unit, then slacken and remove the plug from the housing.

10 Slacken and remove the drain plug, located towards the rear of the final drive unit, on the right hand side **(see illustration)**. Allow the oil to drain into a container. On completion, clean the plug and fit a new seal. Refit the plug and tighten it securely

11 Refill the differential via the filler/level plug with correct quantity of new oil. On completion, check the oil level as described in the previous sub-Section.

20 Propeller shaft rubber coupling - condition check

1 Chock the front wheels, then jack up the rear of the vehicle and support it on axle stands.

2 Carefully check the propeller shaft front and rear rubber couplings for signs of damage and deterioration. Look for deterioration in the form of splitting, cracking or perishing. Damage may also be caused by oil or grease contamination.

3 If either of the couplings require renewal, refer Chapter 8 for a description of the renewal procedure.

21 Seat belt check

1 Carefully examine the seat belt webbing for cuts or any signs of serious fraying or deterioration. If the seat belt is of the retractable type, pull the belt all the way out, and examine the full extent of the webbing.

2 Fasten and unfasten the belt, ensuring that the locking mechanism holds securely and releases properly when intended. If the belt is of the retractable type, check also that the retracting mechanism operates correctly when the belt is released.

3 Check the security of all seat belt mountings and attachments which are accessible, without removing any trim or other components, from inside the vehicle.

22 Lubricate all hinges and locks, and the electric aerial

1 Lubricate the hinges of the bonnet, doors and tailgate with a light general-purpose oil. Similarly, lubricate all latches, locks and lock strikers. At the same time, check the security and operation of all the locks, adjusting them if necessary (see Chapter 11).

2 Lightly lubricate the bonnet release mechanism and cable with a suitable grease.

3 If an electric aerial is fitted, extend the aerial and remove all traces of dirt from its mast. Lubricate the aerial mast with a light general-purpose oil and retract the aerial.

4 On models with a sunroof, slide the roof fully back and clean the sunroof guide rails. Apply a smear of fresh multi-purpose grease to the rails and close the sunroof.

23 Headlight beam - adjustment

1 Accurate adjustment of the headlight beam is only possible using optical beam-setting equipment, and this work should therefore be carried out by a Mercedes-Benz dealer or service station with the necessary facilities. Poorly adjusted headlights can dazzle other road users and may cause an accident.

24 Windscreen/headlight washer system(s) - condition check

1 Check that each of the washer jet nozzles are clear and that each nozzle provides a strong jet of washer fluid. The headlight jets should be aimed to spray at a point slightly above the centre of the screen/headlight. On the windscreen washer nozzles where there are two jets, aim one of the jets slightly above then centre of the screen and aim the other just below to ensure complete coverage of the screen. If necessary, adjust the jets using a pin. Bear in mind that, when the vehicle is being driven, the air flow over the bonnet and windscreen will tend to force the water jets downwards, so adjust them to allow for this.

2 Mercedes-Benz recommend that the windscreen wiper blades should be renewed at this interval, regardless of their apparent condition (see *"Weekly checks"*).

25 Road test

Instruments and electrical equipment

1 Check the operation of all instruments and electrical equipment.

2 Make sure that all instruments read correctly, and switch on all electrical equipment in turn, to check that it functions properly.

Steering and suspension

3 Check for any abnormalities in the steering, suspension, handling or road "feel".

4 Drive the vehicle, and check that there are no unusual vibrations or noises.

5 Check that the steering feels positive, with no excessive "sloppiness", or roughness, and check for any suspension noises when cornering and driving over bumps.

Drivetrain

6 Check the performance of the engine, clutch (where applicable), gearbox/transmission and driveshafts.

7 Listen for any unusual noises from the engine, clutch and gearbox/transmission.

8 Make sure that the engine runs smoothly when idling, and that there is no hesitation when accelerating.

9 Check that, where applicable, the clutch action is smooth and progressive, that the drive is taken up smoothly, and that the pedal travel is not excessive. Also listen for any noises when the clutch pedal is depressed.

10 On manual gearbox models, check that all gears can be engaged smoothly without noise, and that the gear lever action is not abnormally vague or "notchy".

11 On automatic transmission models, make sure that all gearchanges occur smoothly, without snatching, and without an increase in engine speed between changes. Check that all the gear positions can be selected with the vehicle at rest. If any problems are found, they should be referred to a Mercedes-Benz dealer.

Check the operation and performance of the braking system

12 Make sure that the vehicle does not pull to one side when braking, and that the wheels do not lock prematurely when braking hard.

14 Check that there is no vibration through the steering when braking.

15 Check that the parking brake operates correctly without excessive movement of the lever, and that it holds the vehicle stationary on a slope.

16 Test the operation of the brake servo unit as follows. With the engine off, depress the footbrake four or five times to exhaust the vacuum. Hold the brake pedal depressed, then start the engine. As the engine starts, there should be a noticeable "give" in the brake pedal as vacuum builds up. Allow the engine to run for at least two minutes, and then switch it off. If the brake pedal is depressed now, it should be possible to detect a slight 'hiss' from the servo as the pedal is depressed. After about four or five applications, no further hissing should be heard, and the pedal should feel considerably harder.

26 Front hub bearings - check

1 With the vehicle parked on a level surface, apply the parking brake and select first gear (manual transmission) or 'PARK' (automatic transmission). Jack up the front of the vehicle and support it securely on axle stands.

2 Grasp the first front roadwheel at the 12 o'clock and 6 o'clock positions, and try to rock it. Very slight free play may be felt, but if the movement is appreciable, further investigation is necessary to determine the source. Continue rocking the wheel while an assistant depresses the footbrake. If the movement is now eliminated or significantly reduced, it is likely that the hub bearings are

at fault. If the free play is still evident with the footbrake depressed, then there is wear in the suspension joints or mountings.
3 Now grasp the wheel at the 9 o'clock and 3 o'clock positions, and try to rock it as before. Any movement felt now may again be caused by wear in the hub bearings or the steering track-rod balljoints. If the inner or outer balljoint is worn, the visual movement will be obvious.
4 Repeat the operation at the other front road wheel. If the hub bearings are in need of adjustment, refer to Chapter 10 for a complete description of this procedure.

27 Clutch - operation check

1 Check that, where applicable, the clutch action is smooth and progressive, that the drive is taken up smoothly, and that the pedal travel is not excessive. Also listen for any noises when the clutch pedal is depressed.
2 Check that all gears can be engaged smoothly without noise.
3 Check the clutch release hydraulic components for leaks (see Chapter 6).

28 Valve clearances (pre-1984 models) - check and adjustment

Note: *Valve clearance adjustment is only necessary on engines without hydraulic tappets - those manufactured before October 1984. Checking and adjustment may be carried out with the engine cold or warm.*
1 Remove the camshaft cover as described in Chapter 2A.
2 Disconnect the LT wiring plug at the ignition system electronic control unit (see Chapter 5B).
3 Using a suitable socket or spanner, turn the engine by means of the crankshaft vibration damper/pulley bolt, in the normal direction of rotation, until the No 1 cylinder inlet and exhaust lobes on the camshaft are pointing downwards, away from the rocker arms.
4 Using a feeler blade of thickness equal to the specified valve clearance, check that the blade is a tight sliding fit between the valve stem and rocker arm **(see illustration)**. Note that the inlet valves are on the inlet manifold side of the cylinder head, and the exhaust valves are on the exhaust manifold side – the clearances are different for inlet and exhaust valves.
5 If adjustment is required, slacken the locknut, turn the rocker arm adjusting screw until the correct clearance is obtained, then tighten the locknut while holding the adjusting screw.
6 When both valves for No 1 cylinder have

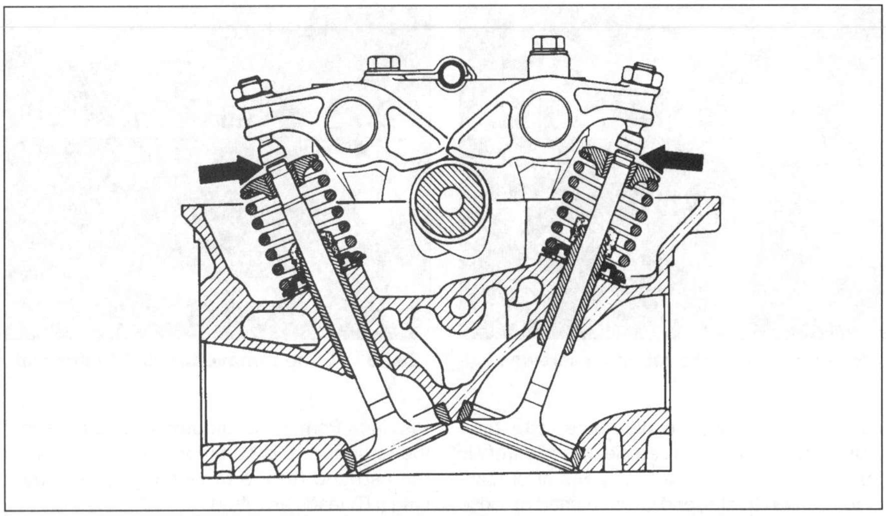

28.4 Check the valve clearance between the valve stems and rockers with the cam lobes pointing downwards

been adjusted, turn the crankshaft until the cam lobes for the next pair of valves (No 2 cylinder) are pointing downwards, and adjust these valves in the same way. Repeat the procedure for cylinders 3 and 4.
7 On completion, refit the camshaft cover as described in Chapter 2A.

29 Ignition system - condition check and timing adjustment

1 The ignition system components should be checked carefully for damage or deterioration to avoid starting and running problems.

General component check

2 The spark plug HT leads should be checked whenever new plugs are fitted.
3 Pull the lead from the first spark plug by gripping the end fitting, not the lead, otherwise the lead connection may be fractured **(see illustrations)**.
4 Check inside the HT lead end fitting for signs of corrosion, which will look like a white crusty powder. Push the end fitting back onto the spark plug, ensuring that it is a tight fit on the plug. If not, remove the lead again, and use pliers to carefully crimp the metal connector inside the end fitting until it fits securely on the end of the spark plug.
5 Using a clean rag, wipe the entire length of the lead to remove any built-up dirt and grease. Once the lead is clean, check for burns, cracks and other damage. Do not bend the lead excessively, or pull the lead lengthwise – the conductor inside is fragile and may break.
6 Disconnect the other end of the lead from the distributor cap **(see illustration)**. Again, pull only on the end fitting. Check for corrosion and a tight fit in the same manner as the spark plug end. If an ohmmeter is available, check the resistance of the lead by connecting the meter between the spark plug end of the lead and the segment inside the distributor cap. Refit the lead securely on completion.
7 Check the remaining leads one at a time in the same way.
8 If new spark plug (HT) leads are required, purchase a set for your specific car and engine.
9 Unscrew the retaining screws, or release the

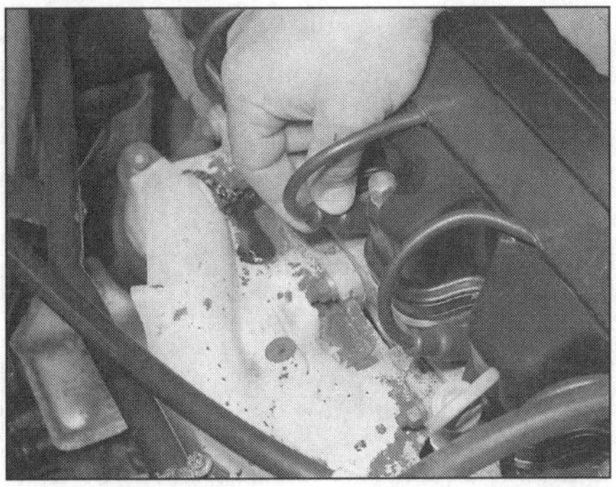

29.3 Pulling an HT lead from a spark plug

29.6 Disconnecting an HT lead from the distributor cap

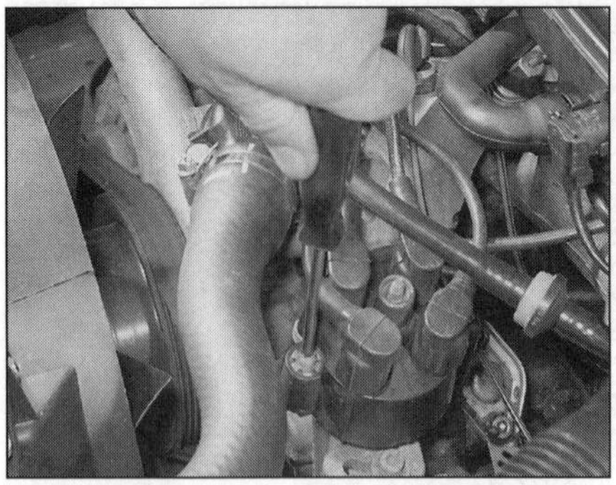

29.9a Unscrew the retaining screws . . .

29.9b . . . and remove the distributor cap

29.9c Check the carbon brush (arrowed) in the distributor cap

clips, and remove the distributor cap **(see illustrations)**. Wipe the cap clean, and carefully inspect it inside and out for signs of cracks, black carbon tracks, and worn, burned or loose contacts. Check that the carbon brush inside the centre of the cap is unworn, free to move against spring pressure, and making good contact with the rotor arm **(see illustration)**. Also inspect the cap seal for signs of wear or damage, and renew if necessary. Remove the rotor arm from the distributor shaft and inspect the rotor arm. It is common practice to renew the cap and rotor arm whenever new spark plug (HT) leads are fitted.

10 Do not simultaneously remove all the leads from the old cap, or firing order confusion may occur. When refitting, ensure that the rotor arm is securely pressed onto the shaft and, where applicable, tighten the cap retaining screws securely.

11 Even with the ignition system is first class condition, some engines may still occasionally experience poor starting attributable to damp ignition components. To disperse moisture, a water-dispersant aerosol can be very effective.

Ignition timing – checking and adjustment

12 Refer to Chapter 5B or 5C, as applicable.

Every 36 000 miles

30 Air cleaner filter element - renewal

Removal

1 Unscrew and remove the retaining nuts from the air cleaner upper cover. Work around the upper cover and prise open each of the tensioning clips **(see illustrations)**.

2 Lift off the air cleaner cover, then detach the crankcase breather hose (where applicable) and remove the air filter element **(see illustration)**.

Refitting

3 Fit the new filter by following the removal procedure in reverse, ensuring that the filter element is fitted the correct way up, according to the markings on its upper surface.

31 Fuel filter renewal

Warning: Petrol is extremely flammable - great care must be taken when working on any part of the fuel system. Keep the area well ventilated - open all available doors an windows to create a through-draught. Do not smoke, or allow any naked flames or uncovered light bulbs near the work area. Note that gas powered domestic appliances with pilot flames, such as heaters, boilers and tumble-dryers, also present a fire hazard - bear this in mind if you are working in an area where such appliances are installed. Always keep a suitable fire extinguisher close to the work area and familiarise yourself with its operation before starting work. Wear eye protection when working on fuel systems and wash off any fuel spilt on bare skin immediately with soap and plenty of water. Note that fuel vapour is just as dangerous as liquid fuel; a vessel that has been emptied of liquid fuel will still contain vapour and could be potentially explosive.

Caution: When working with fuel system components, pay particular attention to cleanliness - dirt entering the fuel system may cause blockages which could lead to poor running or even failure.

Removal

1 The fuel filter is mounted in the fuel supply line, adjacent to the fuel tank. Access is from the underside of the vehicle.

2 Refer to Chapter 4B, and depressurise the fuel system. Disconnect the battery negative lead and position it away from the terminal.

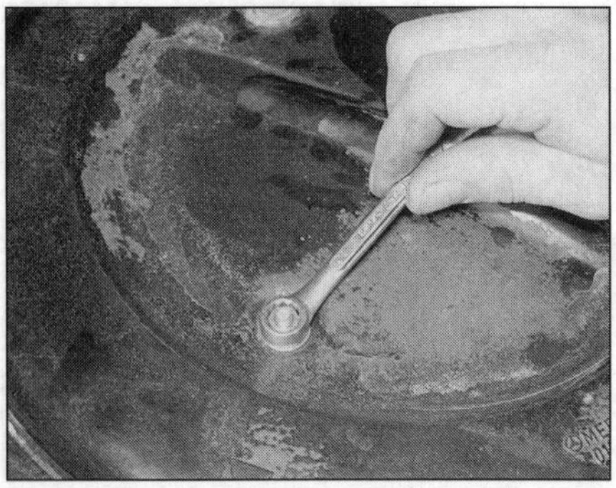

30.1a Unscrew the nuts . . .

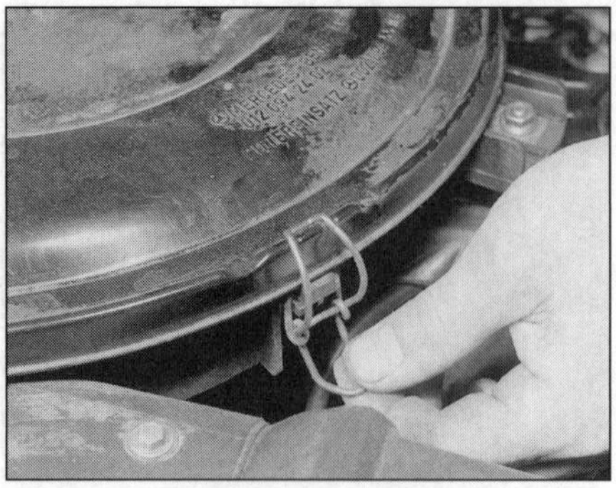

30.1b . . . and prise open the tensioning clips

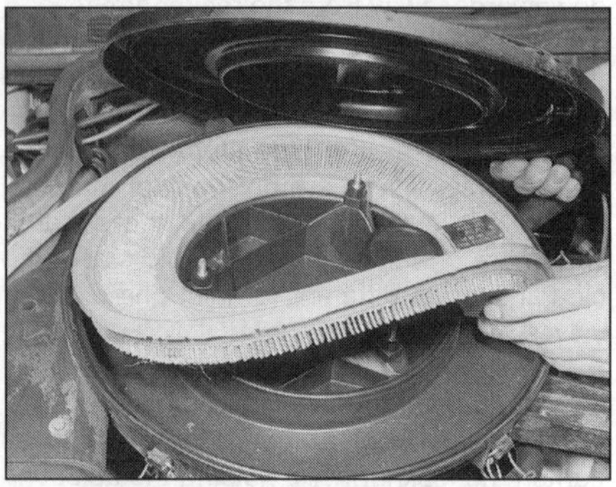

30.2 Remove the filter element – carburettor model shown

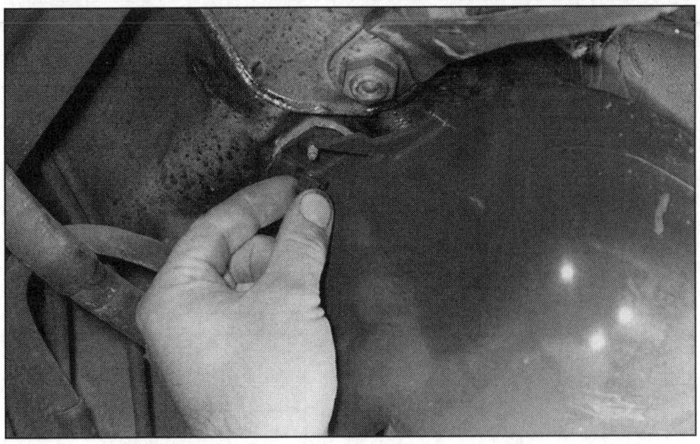

31.4 Removing the cover from the fuel pump

31.6 Fuel filter fuel line unions (A) and retaining strap screw (B)

3 With the vehicle parked on a level surface, apply the parking brake and chock the front roadwheels. Raise the rear of the vehicle and support it securely on axle stands (see "*Jacking and Vehicle Support*").

4 Remove the screws and lower the protective cover away from the fuel pump(s), filter and accumulator **(see illustration)**.

5 Pinch off the flexible fuel supply hose to the fuel pump and the fuel delivery hose from the fuel filter using proprietary hose clamps. Do not use G-clamps or mole grips as these may damage the hoses internally.

6 Slacken the unions and disconnect the fuel lines from either side of the filter unit **(see illustration)**. Where banjo bolt unions are used, recover the sealing washers and discard them - new items must be used on reassembly. Be prepared for some fuel loss, position a small container underneath the filter and pad the surrounding area with absorbent rags.

7 Slacken and remove the screw, release the retaining strap and lower the filter away from its mounting bracket **(see illustration).** Note that on later models, the bracket is held by two screws and also supports the fuel pump(s).

8 If the bracket cannot be lowered sufficiently to remove the fuel filter, where applicable, unscrew the banjo unions, and disconnect the fuel pipe from the fuel pump and the accumulator - again, be prepared for fuel spillage, and recover the sealing washers. Once the fuel pipe has been removed, it should be possible to lower the filter for removal.

Refitting

9 Refitting is a reversal of removal, noting the following points:

a) The arrow marking on the side of the filter unit casing must point in the direction of fuel flow, towards the engine, when fitted.

b) Ensure that the filter retaining clip is correctly positioned over the anti-corrosion plastic sleeving, on the filter casing.

c) Fit new sealing washers where banjo bolt unions are used.

10 On completion, start the vehicle and check around the disturbed components for leaks. Note that the fuel pump has to purge the system of air, so the engine may take a little longer than usual to start.

32 Automatic transmission fluid and filter - renewal

1 This operation should not be attempted unless clean, dust-free conditions can be achieved.

2 Jack up the vehicle, and support securely on axle stands (see '*Jacking and Vehicle Support*'), ensuring that the vehicle remains level.

3 Where applicable, remove the body undershield for access to the transmission.

4 Move the transmission selector lever to position 'P'.

5 Wipe clean the transmission fluid pan, particularly the area around the drain plug, the pan-to-transmission securing bolts, and the pan-to-transmission joint.

6 Place a suitable container beneath the transmission drain plug, then unscrew the drain plug, using an Allen key or hexagon bit, and allow the fluid to drain into the container **(see illustration)**. Refit the drain plug when all the fluid has drained.

7 Using a socket on the crankshaft pulley hub bolt (it may be necessary to remove the cooling fan cowl for access on some models - see Chapter 3), turn the crankshaft until the torque converter drain plug becomes visible through the aperture in the transmission casing **(see illustration)**.

8 Reposition the container beneath the torque converter drain plug, then unscrew the drain plug and allow the fluid to drain into the container. Refit the drain plug when all the fluid has drained.

9 Unscrew the fluid pan securing bolts, then remove the clamp plates, and lower the fluid pan from the transmission **(see illustration)**. Tap the pan gently using a soft-faced mallet if it is stuck. Recover the rubber seal.

1A

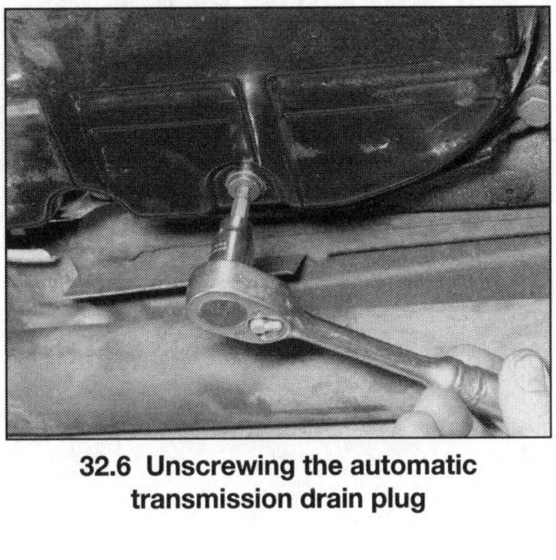

32.6 Unscrewing the automatic transmission drain plug

32.7 Torque converter drain plug (arrowed)

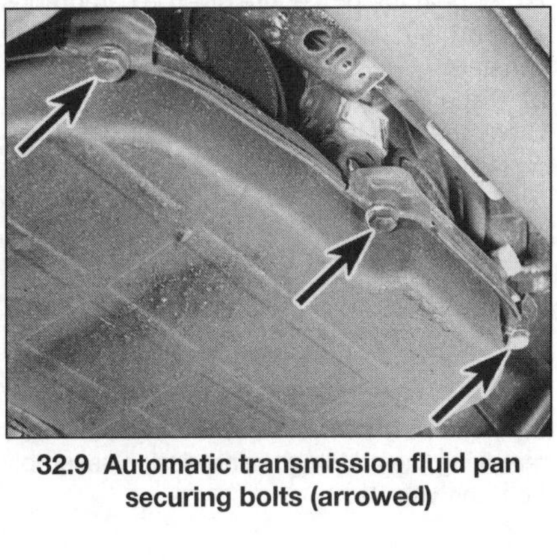

32.9 Automatic transmission fluid pan securing bolts (arrowed)

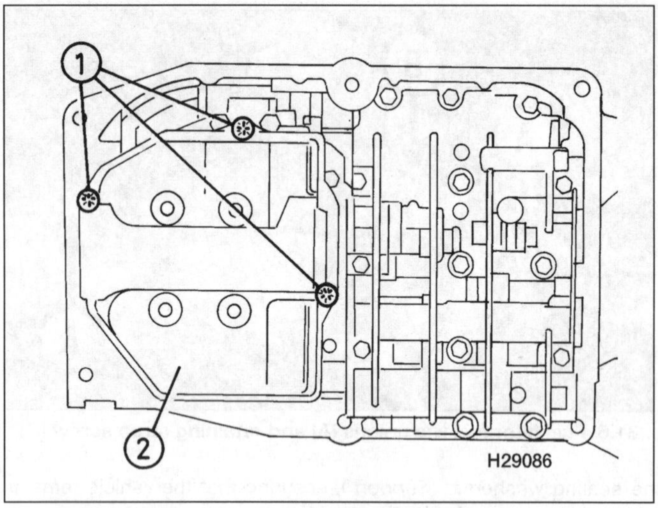

32.10 Unscrew the securing bolts (1) and withdraw the filter screen (2)

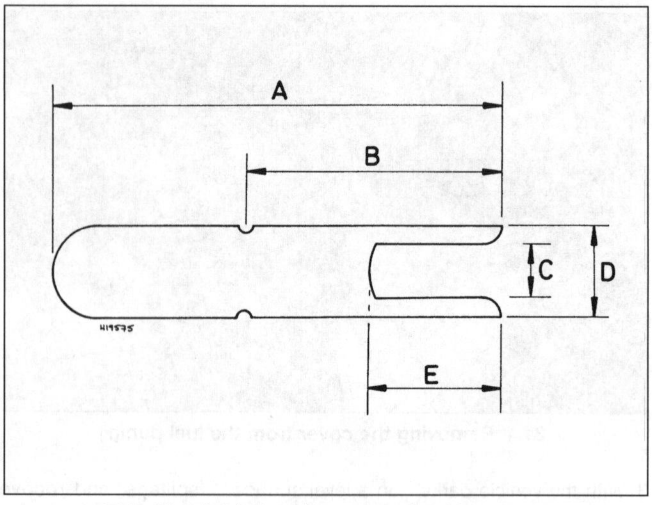

33.2 Clutch friction disc wear checking gauge

A 55.0 mm B 26.0 mm C 7.0 mm D 14.0 mm E 12.0 mm

10 Unscrew the securing screws, and withdraw the filter screen **(see illustration)**.

11 Thoroughly clean the fluid pan inside and outside using a clean lint-free cloth.

12 Fit a new filter screen, and tighten the securing screws.

13 Offer the fluid pan into position, and refit the clamp plates and securing bolts. Tighten the securing bolts to the specified torque.

14 Where applicable, refit the underbody shield.

15 Lower the vehicle to the ground, then release the locking lever, and withdraw the fluid level dipstick.

16 Initially fill the transmission with 4.0 litres of the specified fluid (see "*Recommended Lubricants and Fluids*") through the dipstick tube. Start the engine, and allow it to idle with the selector lever in the position "P".

17 Continue adding fluid until the level is 12.0 mm below the lower ("MIN") mark on the dipstick (see Section 6 of this Chapter).

18 Move the selector lever through all the gear positions, pausing for a few seconds in each position, then return the lever to the 'P' position.

19 Re-check the fluid level as described in paragraph 17.

20 Repeat the procedure given in paragraphs 18 and 17 until the fluid level remains constant.

21 Take the vehicle for a short drive, and check the fluid level as described in Section 6 of this Chapter.

33 Clutch friction plate - check for wear

1 Provision is made for assessing the wear of the clutch friction disc linings without removing the clutch or transmission assembly from the vehicle.

2 The check is carried out from below the clutch slave cylinder, and requires the use of a special checking gauge, which can easily be made from a strip of scrap metal or tin-plate to the dimensions shown **(see illustration)**.

3 After fabricating the checking tool, proceed as follows.

4 Apply the parking brake, then jack up the front of the vehicle, and support securely on axle stands (see *'Jacking and Vehicle Support'*).

5 Insert the forked end of the gauge into the machined slot between the slave cylinder flange and the bellhousing.

6 Push the gauge into the slot until the forked end contacts the slave cylinder pushrod.

7 If the two notches on the checking gauge are not visible, the friction disc linings are in a satisfactory condition. If the two notches are visible, the driven plate linings have reached their wear limit, and the clutch assembly must be renewed **(see illustrations)**.

8 On completion of the check, remove the gauge and lower the vehicle to the ground.

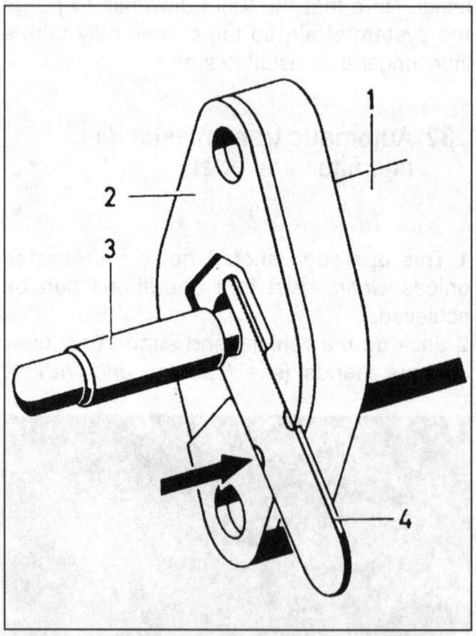

33.7a Checking clutch friction disc wear - linings in satisfactory condition

1 Slave cylinder
2 Slave cylinder shim
3 Pushrod
4 Checking gauge
Arrow indicates notches on gauge not visible

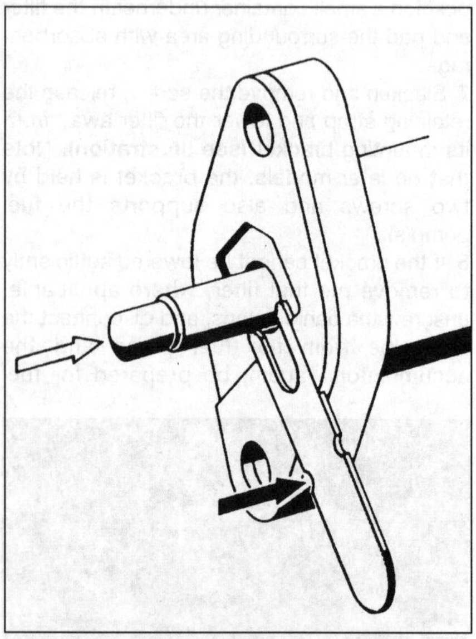

33.7b Checking clutch friction disc wear - linings worn

Light arrow — *Pushrod movement as wear takes place*
Dark arrow — *Notches on gauge visible*

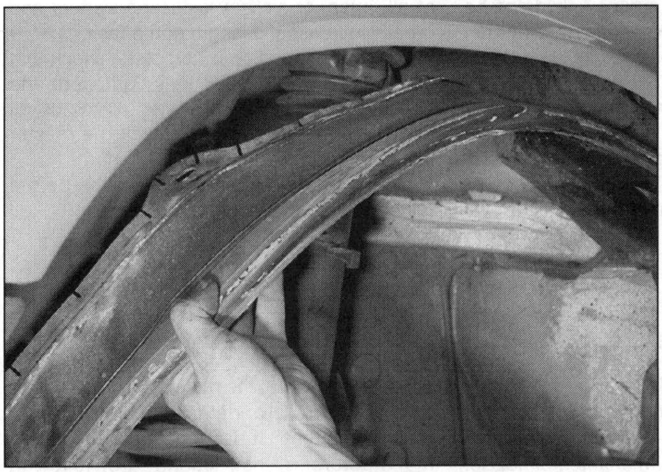

34.2 Removing the wheelarch liner

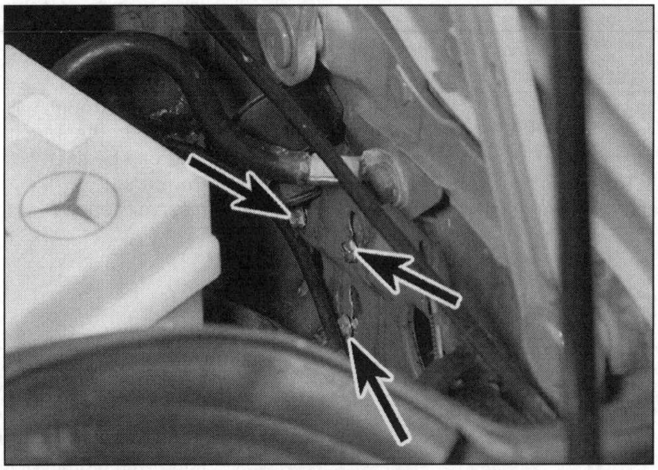

34.3 Charcoal canister mounting bracket securing screws (arrowed)

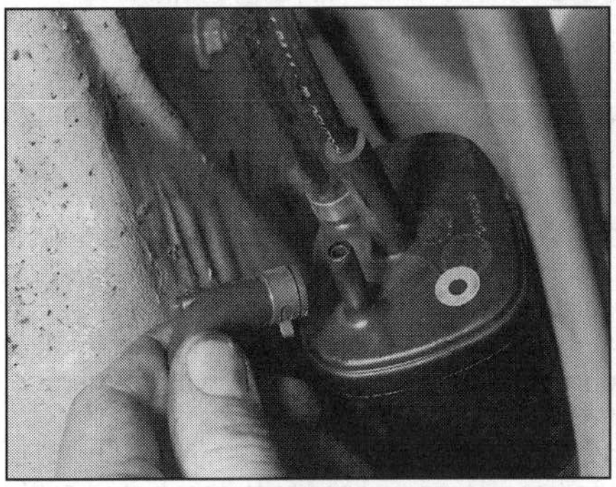

34.4a Disconnect the lower hose from the canister . . .

34.4b . . . then withdraw the canister

34.5 Make sure that the canister bracket screws (arrowed) line up with the holes in the wing panel

Every 72 000 miles or 4 years

34 Charcoal canister renewal - models with an evaporative emission system

Removal

1 Park the vehicle on a level surface and apply the parking brake. Jack up the front of the vehicle and remove the front left-hand road wheel - refer to "*Jacking and Vehicle support*' in the Reference chapter of this manual for guidance.

2 Remove the nuts from the mounting studs and lower the liner away from the inside of the left hand wheelarch **(see illustrations)**.

3 Working on the at the left-hand wing panel in the engine compartment, loosen the three screws securing the charcoal canister mounting bracket to the wing panel **(see illustration)**. There is no need to remove the screws, as the holes in the wing are elongated.

4 Disconnect the lower hose from the canister, then manipulate the canister, complete with the mounting bracket out from under the wheelarch **(see illustrations)**. Disconnect the remaining hoses before withdrawing the canister from under the wheelarch.

Refitting

5 Refitting is a reversal of removal **(see illustration)**.

Every 12 months (regardless of mileage)

35 Brake fluid renewal

Warning: Brake hydraulic fluid can harm your eyes and damage painted surfaces, so use extreme caution when handling and pouring it. Do not use fluid that has been standing open for some time, as it absorbs moisture from the air. Excess moisture can cause a dangerous loss of braking effectiveness.

1 The brake fluid renewal procedure is very similar to the hydraulic system bleeding procedure, described at the beginning of Chapter 9, except that the brake fluid reservoir should be emptied by siphoning, using a clean poultry baster or similar before starting. Note that the procedure is different for vehicles equipped with ABS/ASR. Allowance must also be made for the old fluid to be expelled, when bleeding a Section of the hydraulic circuit.

2 Working as described in Chapter 9, open the first bleed screw in the sequence, and pump the brake pedal gently until nearly all the old fluid has been emptied from the master cylinder reservoir.

HAYNES HiNT *Old hydraulic fluid is invariably much darker in colour than the new, making it easy to distinguish the two.*

3 Top-up to the "MAX" level with new fluid, and continue pumping until only the new fluid remains in the reservoir, and new fluid can be seen emerging from the bleed screw. Tighten the screw, and top the reservoir level up to the "MAX" level line.

4 Work through all the remaining bleed screws in the specified sequence until new fluid can be seen flowing from each of them. Be careful to keep the master cylinder reservoir topped-up to above the "MIN" level at all times, or air may enter the system and greatly increase the length of the task.

5 When the operation is complete, check that all bleed screws are securely tightened, and that their dust caps are refitted. Wash off all traces of spilt fluid, and recheck the master cylinder reservoir fluid level.

6 Check the operation of the brakes before taking the car on the road.

Every 3 years

36 Coolant renewal

Cooling system draining

Warning: Wait until the engine is cold before starting this procedure. Do not allow antifreeze to come in contact with your skin, or with the painted surfaces of the vehicle. Rinse off spills immediately with plenty of water. Never leave antifreeze lying around in an open container, or in a puddle in the driveway or on the garage floor. Children and pets are attracted by its sweet smell, but antifreeze can be fatal if ingested.

1 After allowing the engine to cool completely, cover the expansion tank cap with a wad of rag, and slowly turn the cap anti-clockwise to relieve the pressure in the cooling system (a hissing sound will normally be heard) **(see illustration)**. Wait until any pressure remaining in the system is released, then continue to turn the cap until it can be removed.

2 Position a suitable container beneath the radiator, then fit a length of rubber hose to the drain nozzle **(see illustration)**. Open the drain plug (underneath the nozzle) by turning it with a large screwdriver and allow the coolant to drain through the hose, into the container.

3 Re-position the container so that it lies beneath the engine block drain plug, which is located on the right-hand side of the cylinder block **(see illustration)**. (Certain engines are fitted with a drain plug with an integral nozzle, to which a length of rubber hose can be connected.) Open the drain plug by turning it with an open ended spanner and allow the coolant to drain into the container.

4 Once all the coolant has drained, remove the drain hoses and close the cylinder block and radiator drain plugs.

Cooling system flushing

5 If coolant renewal has been neglected, or if the antifreeze mixture has become diluted then, in time, the cooling system may gradually lose efficiency, as the coolant passages become restricted due to rust, scale deposits, and other sediment. The cooling system efficiency can be restored by flushing the system clean.

6 The radiator should be flushed independently of the engine, to avoid unnecessary contamination.

Radiator flushing

7 To flush the radiator disconnect the top and bottom hoses and any other relevant hoses from the radiator, with reference to Chapter 3.

8 Insert a garden hose into the radiator top inlet. Direct a flow of clean water through the radiator, and continue flushing until clean water emerges from the radiator bottom outlet.

9 If after a reasonable period, the water still does not run clear, the radiator can be flushed with a good proprietary cooling system cleaning agent. It is important that their manufacturer's instructions are followed carefully. If the contamination is particularly bad, insert the hose in the radiator bottom outlet, and reverse-flush the radiator.

Engine flushing

10 To flush the engine, remove the thermostat as described in Chapter 3, then temporarily refit the thermostat cover. Adjust the heater control to the maximum setting.

11 With the top and bottom hoses disconnected from the radiator, insert a garden hose into the radiator top hose. Direct a clean flow of water through the engine, and continue flushing until clean water emerges from the radiator bottom hose.

12 On completion of flushing, refit the thermostat and reconnect the hoses with reference to Chapter 3.

Cooling system refilling

13 Before attempting to fill the cooling system, make sure that all hoses and clips are in good condition, and that the clips are tight. Note that an antifreeze mixture must be used all year round, to prevent corrosion of the engine components (see following sub-Section).

14 Remove the expansion tank filler cap, and fill the system by slowly pouring the coolant into the expansion tank to prevent airlocks from forming.

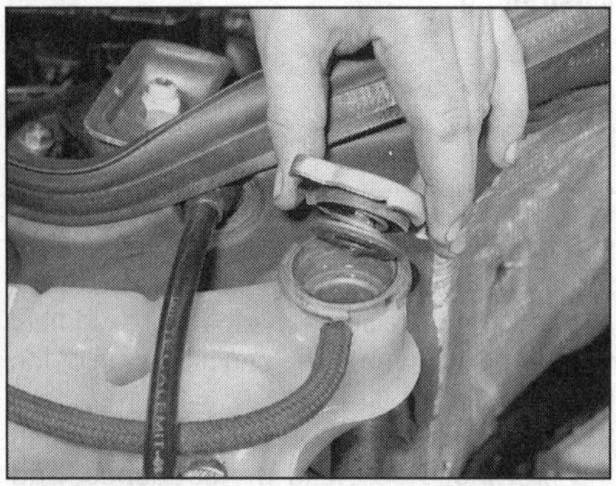

36.1 Relieve the pressure in the cooling system by removing the expansion tank cap

36.2 Radiator drain nozzle (arrowed)

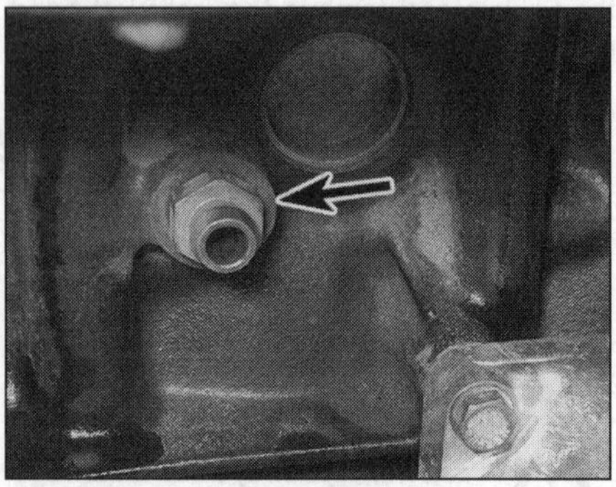

36.3 Engine block drain nozzle (arrowed)

15 If the coolant is being renewed, begin by pouring in a couple of litres of water, followed by the correct quantity of antifreeze, then top-up with more water **(see illustrations)**.

16 Once the level in the expansion tank starts to rise, squeeze the radiator top and bottom hoses to help expel any trapped air in the system. Once all the air is expelled, top-up the coolant level to the "MAX" mark. Refit the expansion tank cap securely.

17 On 6-cylinder SOHC models, unscrew the plug from the coolant sensor housing, on the upper surface of the cylinder head. As soon as coolant starts to flow out, refit the plug and tighten it. If none flows out, pour coolant into the hole vacated by the plug until it begins to flow back out. Refit the plug and tighten it securely. This removes any airlocks in the cooling system that might inhibit the operation of the coolant sensor(s).

18 Start the engine and run it until the thermostat opens - the radiator top hose will begin to heat up as coolant flows through it ot the radiator when this happens.

19 Check for leaks, particularly around disturbed components. Check the coolant level in the expansion tank, and top-up if necessary. Note that the system must be cold before an accurate level is indicated in the expansion tank. If the expansion tank cap is removed while the engine is still warm, cover the cap with a thick cloth, and unscrew the cap slowly to gradually relieve the system pressure (a hissing sound will normally be heard). Wait until any pressure remaining in the system is released, then continue to turn the cap until it can be removed.

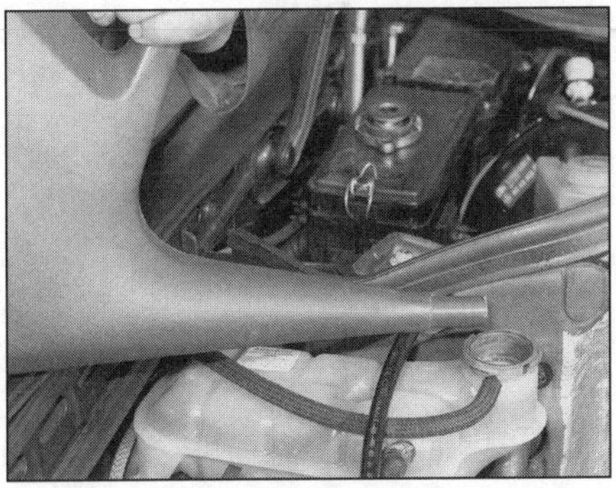

36.15a If the coolant is being renewed, begin by pouring in a couple of litres of water . . .

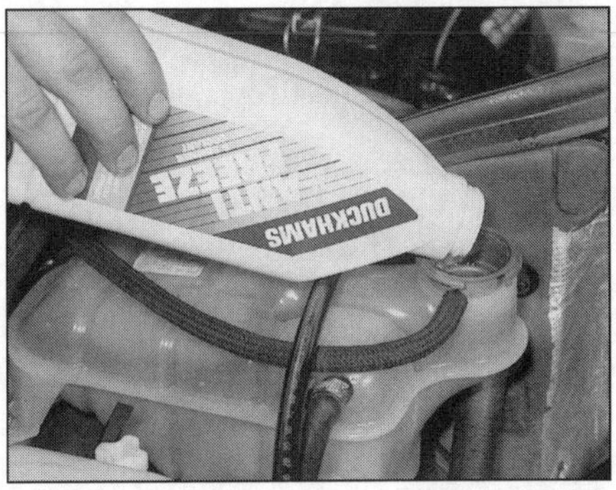

36.15b . . . followed by the correct quantity of antifreeze, then top-up with more water

Antifreeze mixture

20 The antifreeze should always be renewed at the specified intervals. This is necessary not only to maintain the antifreeze properties, but also to prevent corrosion which would otherwise occur as the corrosion inhibitors become progressively less effective.

21 Always use an ethylene-glycol based antifreeze which is suitable for use in mixed-metal cooling systems. The quantity of antifreeze and levels of protection are indicated in the Specifications.

22 Before adding antifreeze, the cooling system should be completely drained, preferably flushed, and all hoses checked for condition and security.

23 After filling with antifreeze, a label should be attached to the expansion tank, stating the type and concentration of antifreeze used, and the date installed. Any subsequent topping-up should be made with the same type and concentration of antifreeze.

24 Do not use engine antifreeze in the windscreen/tailgate washer system, as it will cause damage to the vehicle paintwork. A screenwash additive should be added to the washer system in the quantities stated on the bottle.

Notes

Chapter 1 Part B
Routine maintenance & servicing - diesel engine models

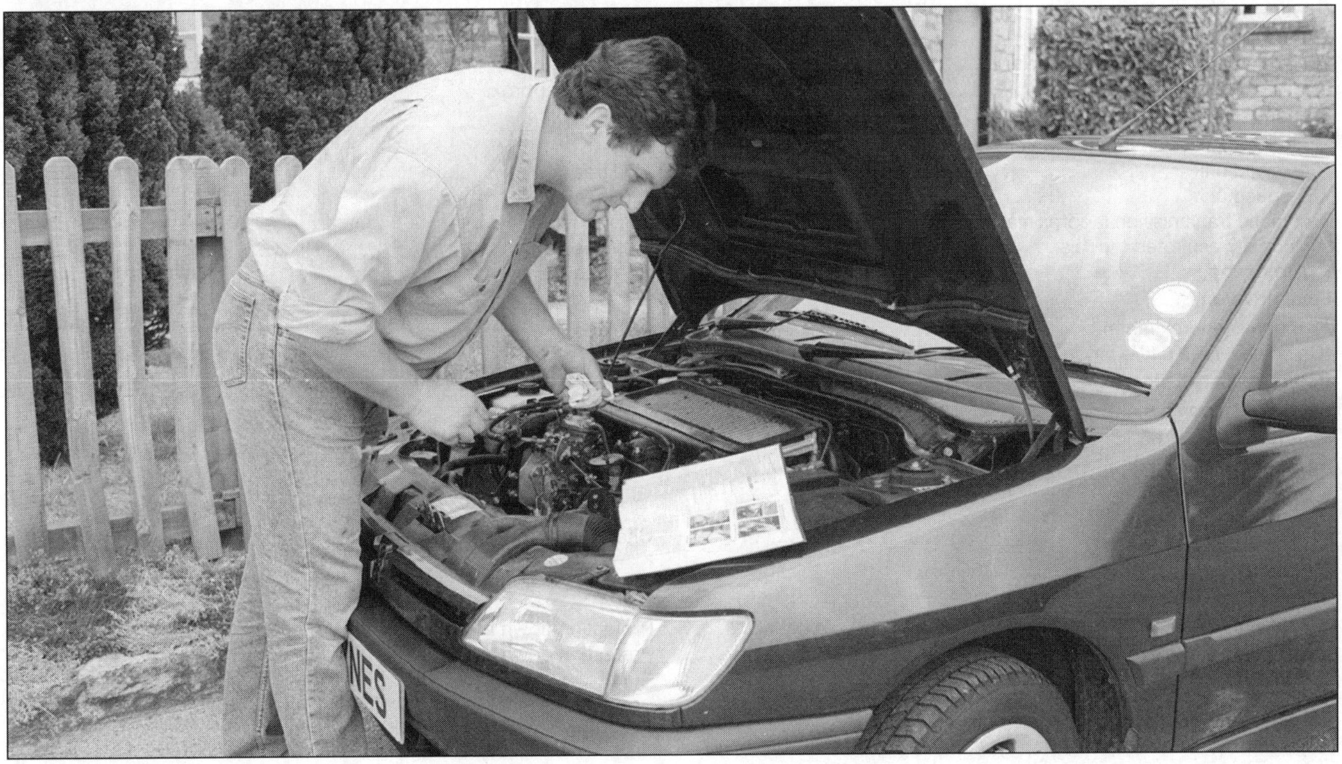

1B

Contents

Air conditioning system - refrigerant level check ... 8
Air filter element - renewal ... 26
Automatic transmission fluid - level check ... 5
Automatic transmission fluid and filter - renewal ... 28
Auxiliary drivebelt(s) - condition check, renewal and adjustment ... 7
Brake fluid renewal ... 30
Clutch - operation check ... 25
Clutch friction plate - check for wear ... 29
Coolant renewal ... 31
Driveshafts and driveshaft gaiters - condition check ... 11
Engine idle speed - check and adjustment ... 9
Engine oil and filter renewal ... 3
Exhaust system and mountings - condition and security check ... 15
Final drive unit oil - level check and renewal ... 17
Front brake pad check ... 12
Front hub bearings - check ... 24
Fuel filter and pre-filter - renewal ... 27
Headlight beam alignment - adjustment ... 21
Hinges, locks and electric aerial - lubrication ... 20
Introduction ... 1
Manual transmission oil - level check and renewal ... 16
Parking brake - operation check ... 14
Propeller shaft rubber couplings - condition and security check ... 18
Rear brake pad check ... 13
Regular maintenance ... 2
Road test ... 23
Seat belts - operation and condition check ... 19
Steering and suspension components - condition and security check ... 10
Throttle linkage - lubrication ... 4
Underbonnet/underbody components and hoses - check for fluid leaks ... 6
Windscreen/headlight washer system(s) - condition check ... 22

Degrees of difficulty

Easy, suitable for novice with little experience	**Fairly easy,** suitable for beginner with some experience	**Fairly difficult,** suitable for competent DIY mechanic	**Difficult,** suitable for experienced DIY mechanic	**Very difficult,** suitable for expert DIY or professional

Lubricants and fluids

Refer to "*Weekly checks*"

Capacities

Engine oil (including oil filter)	
2.0 litre models	6.0 litres
2.5 litre models:	
Normally-aspirated	6.5 litres
Turbo	7.0 litres
Cooling system	
2.0 litre normally-aspirated models	8.5 litres approx.
2.5 litre normally-aspirated models	9.0 litres approx.
2.5 litre turbocharged models	10.0 litres approx.
Transmission	
Manual transmission (approximate):	
4-speed unit	1.3 litres
5-speed unit	1.5 litres
Automatic transmission (approximate):	
Normally-aspirated models	6.6 litres
Turbo models	7.1 litres
Final drive unit*	
All models (approximate)	0.7 litres

**On some later 2.0 litre models the final drive unit capacity has been increased to 1.1 litres*

Power-assisted steering	
All models (approximate)	1.0 litres
Fuel tank	
All models (approximate)	55 litres

Engine

Oil filter	Champion X103

Cooling system

Antifreeze mixture:	
50% antifreeze	Protection down to -37°C (-35°F)
55% antifreeze	Protection down to -45°C (-49°F)

Note: *Refer to antifreeze manufacturer for latest recommendations.*

Fuel system

Adjustments	
Maximum no-load engine speed	5150 ± 50 rpm
Idle speed:	
4-cylinder engines with pneumatic idle speed increase	750 ± 50 rpm
4-cylinder engines with electronic idle speed control (ELR)	720 ± 20 rpm
5-cylinder engines with pneumatic idle speed increase	700 ± 50 rpm
5-cylinder engines with electronic idle speed control (ELR)	680 ± 20 rpm
General	
Air filter element:	
Normally-aspirated models	Champion U563
Turbo models	Champion U625
Fuel filter	Champion L104 or L116, depending on model

Preheating system

Glow plugs	Champion CH 68 or CH 156 depending on model

Brakes

Front and rear brake pad friction material, minimum thickness	2.0 mm

Torque wrench settings

	Nm	lbf ft
Engine oil filter housing cover nuts	25	18
Engine oil filter return pipe	25	18
Brake caliper bleed screw	7	5
Engine oil drain plug:		
M12 plug	30	22
M14 plug	25	18
Auxiliary drivebelt tensioner lever bolt	10	7
Manual transmission oil drain and level/filler plugs	60	44
Automatic transmission fluid drain plugs (main and torque converter)14	10	
Roadwheel bolts	110	81

The maintenance intervals in this manual are provided with the assumption that you, not the dealer, will be carrying out the work. These are the minimum maintenance intervals recommended by us for vehicles driven daily. If you wish to keep your vehicle in peak condition at all times, you may wish to perform some of these procedures more often. We encourage frequent maintenance, because it enhances the efficiency, performance and resale value of your vehicle.

If the vehicle is driven in dusty areas, used to tow a trailer, or driven frequently at slow speeds (idling in traffic) or mainly for short journeys, more frequent maintenance intervals are recommended.

When the vehicle is new, it should be serviced by a factory-authorised dealer service department, in order to preserve the factory warranty.

Every 250 miles (400 km) or weekly

- ☐ Refer to "*Weekly checks*"

Every 6000 miles

Note: *Frequent oil and filter changes are good for the engine. We recommend changing the oil at the mileage specified here, or at least twice a year if the mileage covered is less.*

- ☐ Renew the engine oil and filter (Section 3)

Every 12 000 miles

- ☐ Lubricate the throttle linkage (Section 4)
- ☐ Check the automatic transmission fluid level (Section 5)
- ☐ Check the underbonnet/underbody components and hoses for fluid leaks (Section 6)
- ☐ Check the condition of the auxiliary drivebelt(s) and adjust/renew if necessary (Section 7)
- ☐ Check the air conditioning system refrigerant level (Section 8)
- ☐ Check the engine idle speed and adjust if necessary (Section 9)
- ☐ Check the condition and security of the steering and suspension components (Section 10)
- ☐ Check the condition of the driveshafts and driveshaft gaiters (Section 11)
- ☐ Check the front brake pad (Section 12)
- ☐ Check the rear brake pad (Section 13)
- ☐ Check the operation of the parking brake (Section 14)
- ☐ Check the condition and security of the exhaust system and mountings (Section 15)
- ☐ Check the manual transmission oil level and renew (Section 16)
- ☐ Check the final drive unit oil level and renew (Section 17)
- ☐ Check the condition and security of the propeller shaft rubber couplings (Section 18)
- ☐ Check the operation and condition of the seat belts (Section 19)
- ☐ Lubricate all hinges and locks and the electric aerial (Section 20)
- ☐ Adjust the headlight beam alignment (Section 21)
- ☐ Check the condition of the windscreen/headlight washer system(s) (Section 22)
- ☐ Carry out a road test (Section 23)
- ☐ Adjust the front hub bearings (Section 24)
- ☐ Check the operation of the clutch (Section 25)

Every 36 000 miles

- ☐ Renew the air filter element (Section 26)
- ☐ Renew the fuel filter and pre-filter (Section 27)
- ☐ Renew the automatic transmission fluid and filter (Section 28)
- ☐ Check the clutch friction plate for wear (Section 29)

Every 12 months, regardless of mileage

- ☐ Renew the brake fluid (Section 30)

Every 3 years, regardless of mileage

- ☐ Renew the coolant (Section 31)

Underbonnet view of 5-cylinder, 2.5 litre non-turbo diesel model

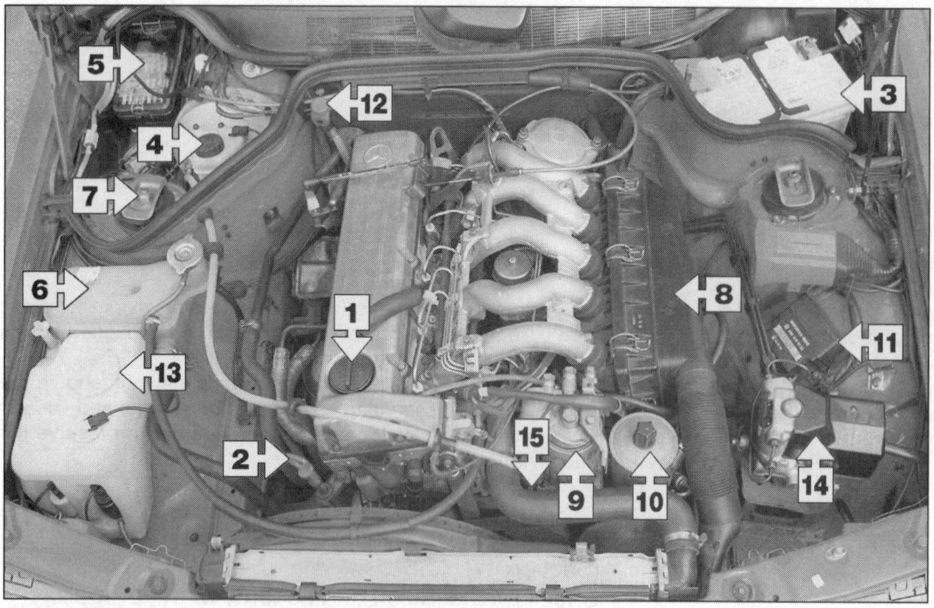

1 Engine oil filler cap
2 Engine oil level dipstick
3 Battery
4 Brake and clutch fluid reservoir
5 Fuse/relay box
6 Coolant expansion tank
7 Suspension strut upper mounting
8 Air filter housing
9 Fuel filter
10 Power steering fluid reservoir
11 Glow plug control unit
12 Automatic transmission fluid dipstick/filler neck
13 Washer fluid reservoir
14 Anti-lock braking system (ABS) hydraulic unit
15 Brake servo vacuum pump

Typical front underbody view

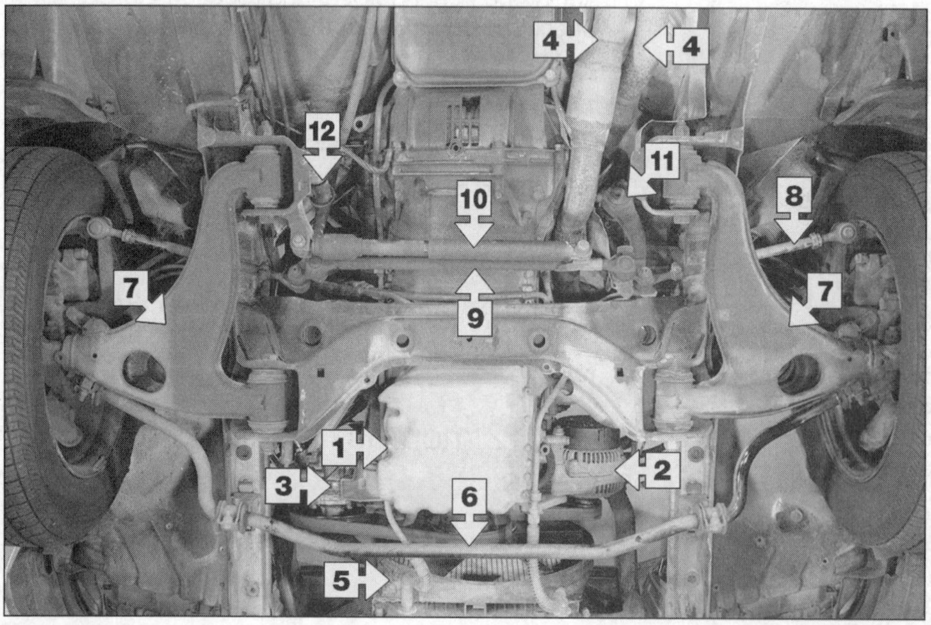

1 Engine oil drain plug
2 Alternator
3 Power steering pump
4 Exhaust front pipe
5 Radiator
6 Anti-roll bar
7 Suspension lower arm
8 Track rod
9 Steering drag link
10 Steering damper
11 Steering box
12 Steering intermediate arm

Typical rear underbody view

1 Final drive unit
2 Suspension lower arm
3 Exhaust system
4 Propeller shaft
5 Driveshaft
6 Thrust control arm
7 Track control arm
8 Torque control arm
9 Parking brake cable

1 Introduction

This Chapter is designed to help the home mechanic maintain his/her vehicle for safety, economy, long life and peak performance.

The Chapter contains a maintenance schedule, followed by Sections dealing specifically with each task in the schedule. Visual checks, adjustments, component renewal and other helpful items are included. Refer to the accompanying illustrations of the engine compartment and the underside of the vehicle for the locations of the various components.

Servicing your vehicle in accordance with the above recommendations and the following Sections will provide a planned maintenance programme, which should result in a long and reliable service life. This is a comprehensive plan, so maintaining some items but not others at the specified service intervals, will not produce the same results.

As you service your vehicle, you will discover that many of the procedures can - and should - be grouped together, because of the particular procedure being performed, or because of the proximity of two otherwise-unrelated components to one another. For example, if the vehicle is raised for any reason, the exhaust can be inspected at the same time as the suspension and steering components.

The first step in this maintenance programme is to prepare yourself before the actual work begins. Read through all the Sections relevant to the work to be carried out, then make a list and gather all the parts and tools required. If a problem is encountered, seek advice from a parts specialist, or a dealer service department.

2 Regular maintenance

1 If, from the time the vehicle is new, the routine maintenance schedule is followed closely, and frequent checks are made of fluid levels and high-wear items, as suggested throughout this manual, the engine will be kept in relatively good running condition, and the need for additional work will be minimised.

2 It is possible that there will be times when the engine is running poorly due to the lack of regular maintenance. This is even more likely if a used vehicle, which has not received regular and frequent maintenance checks, is purchased. In such cases, additional work may need to be carried out, outside of the regular maintenance intervals.

3 If engine wear is suspected, a compression test (refer to the relevant Part of Chapter 2) will provide valuable information regarding the overall performance of the main internal components. Such a test can be used as a basis to decide on the extent of the work to be carried out. If, for example, a compression test indicates serious internal engine wear, conventional maintenance as described in this Chapter will not greatly improve the performance of the engine, and may prove a waste of time and money, unless extensive overhaul work is carried out first.

4 The following series of operations are those most often required to improve the performance of a generally poor-running engine:

Primary operations

a) Clean, inspect and test the battery (See "Weekly checks").
b) Check all the engine-related fluids (See "Weekly checks").
c) Check the condition and tension of the auxiliary drivebelt (Section 7).
d) Check the condition of the air filter element, and renew if necessary (Section 26).
e) Check the fuel filter and pre-filter (Section 27).
f) Check the condition of all hoses, and check for fluid leaks (Section 6).

5 If the above operations do not prove fully effective, carry out the following secondary operations:

Secondary operations

All items listed under "*Primary operations*", plus the following:

a) Check the charging system (see relevant Part of Chapter 5).
c) Check the fuel system (see relevant Part of Chapter 4).
b) Check the preheating system (see relevant Part of Chapter 5).

3.5 Pull off the retaining clip (1) and pull the weatherstrip from the bulkhead

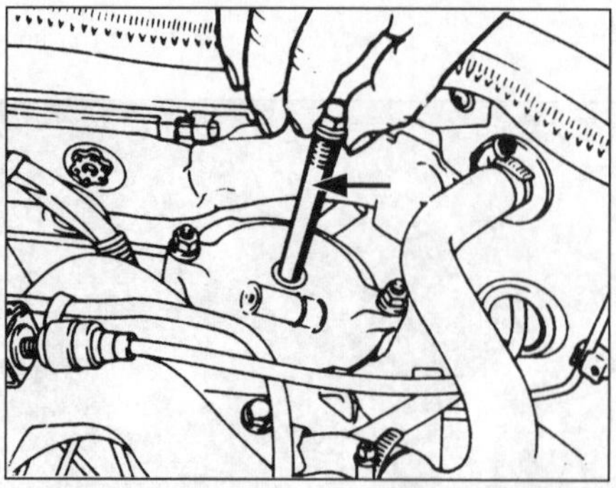
3.6 Unscrew the oil return pipe (arrowed)

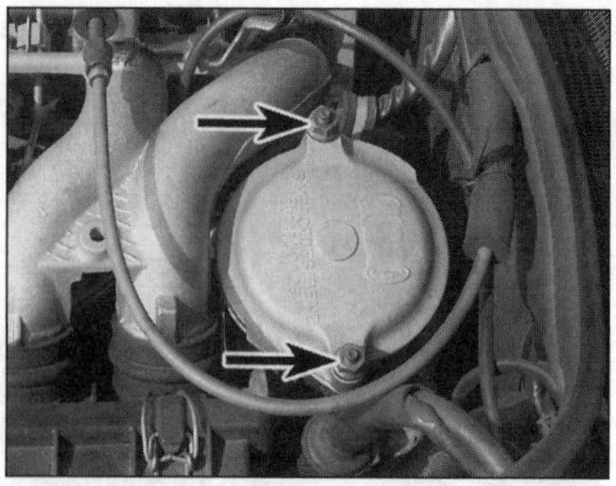
3.7 Unscrew the oil filter housing cover securing nuts (arrowed)

Every 6000 miles

3 Engine oil and filter renewal

Note: *A new oil filter housing cover O-ring and, where applicable, a new oil return pipe O-ring will be required on refitting. A new oil drain plug sealing ring will be required.*

1 Frequent oil and filter changes are the most important preventative maintenance procedures which can be undertaken by the DIY owner. As engine oil ages, it becomes diluted and contaminated, which leads to premature engine wear.

2 Before starting this procedure, gather together all the necessary tools and materials. Also make sure that you have plenty of clean rags and newspapers handy, to mop up any spills. Ideally, the engine oil should be warm, as it will drain better, and more built-up sludge will be removed with it. Take care, however, not to touch the exhaust or any other hot parts of the engine when working under the vehicle. To avoid any possibility of scalding, and to protect yourself from possible skin irritants and other harmful contaminants in used engine oils, it is advisable to wear gloves when carrying out this work. Access to the underside of the vehicle will be greatly improved if it can be raised on a lift, driven onto ramps, or jacked up and supported on axle stands (see *"Jacking and vehicle support"*). Whichever method is chosen, make sure that the vehicle remains level, or if it is at an angle, so that the drain plug is at the lowest point. Where necessary remove the splash guard from under the engine.

3 Working in the engine compartment, locate the oil filter/housing at the left-hand rear corner of the engine, behind the inlet manifold.

4 Place a wad of rag around the bottom of the housing to absorb any spilt oil.

5 Where applicable, pull off the retaining clip, or remove the screw (as applicable), and pull the rubber weatherstrip from the bulkhead at the rear of the engine compartment, to improve access to the oil filter housing **(see illustration)**.

6 On models with an oil return pipe protruding from the centre of the oil filter housing cover, unscrew the oil return pipe, and withdraw it from the housing/cover assembly **(see illustration)**. Where applicable, recover the O-ring from the top of the pipe and discard it - a new O-ring must be used on refitting.

7 Unscrew the two securing nuts, then lift out the oil filter housing cover **(see illustration)**. Recover the O-ring from the cover and discard it - a new O-ring must be used on refitting.

8 Working under the vehicle, slacken the sump drain plug about half a turn **(see illustration)**. Position the draining container under the drain plug, then remove the plug completely. If possible, try to keep the plug pressed into the sump while unscrewing it by hand the last couple of turns **(see Haynes Hint)**.

9 Recover the sealing ring from the drain plug.

10 Allow some time for the old oil to drain, noting that it may be necessary to reposition the container as the oil flow slows to a trickle.

11 After all the oil has drained, wipe off the drain plug with a clean rag. Renew the sealing washer. Clean the area around the drain plug opening, then refit and tighten the plug.

12 Remove the old oil and all tools from under the car, then lower the car to the ground (if applicable).

13 Lift the oil filter element from the housing, using the handle provided **(see illustration)**.

14 Wipe out the oil filter housing and cover, using a clean rag. Check the oil return pipe (either separate, or part of the cover) for blockage - it should be possible to blow

HAYNES HiNT

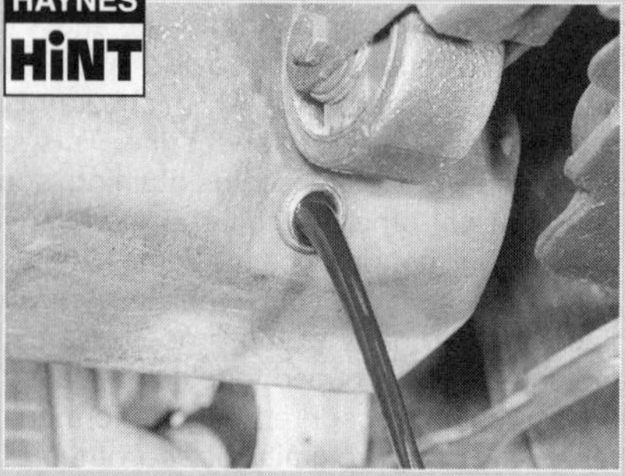

As the plug releases from the threads, move it away sharply so that the stream of oil issuing from the sump runs into the container, not up your sleeve!

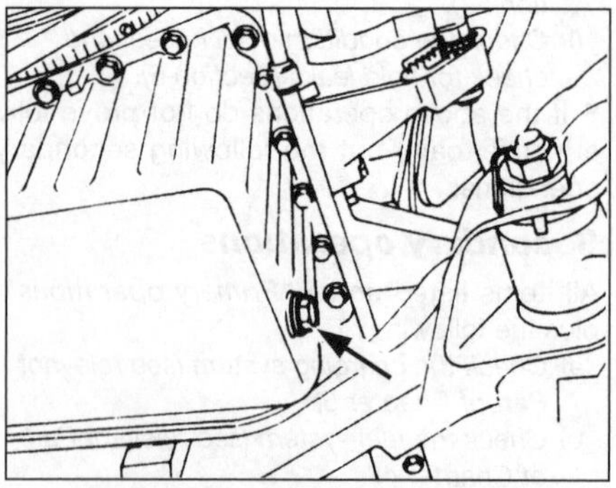
3.8 Sump drain plug (arrowed)

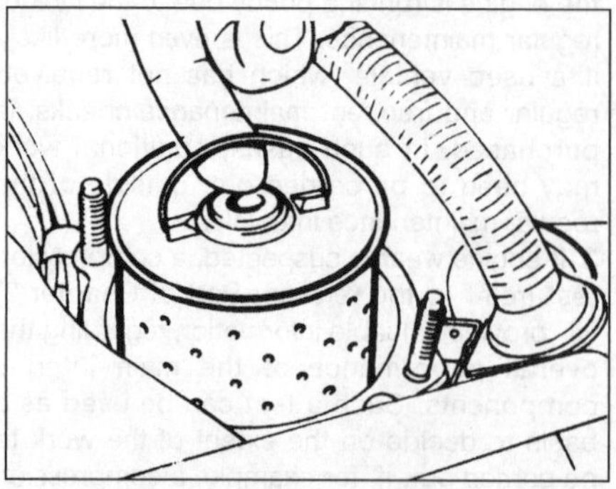
3.13 Lift out the oil filter element using the handle provided

through the small hole in the top of the pipe, and feel air escaping from the bottom of the pipe **(see illustration)**. Clean the pipe, and blow through with compressed air if necessary.

Warning: Wear eye protection when using compressed air.

15 Fit a new O-ring to the oil filter housing cover **(see illustration)**.

16 Fit a new oil filter element to the housing (with the handle at the top), then refit the cover, and tighten the securing nuts to the specified torque.

17 Where applicable, fit a new O-ring to the top of the oil return pipe, then refit the return pipe, and tighten to the specified torque.

18 Remove the dipstick then unscrew the oil filler cap from the cylinder head cover. Fill the engine, using the correct grade and type of oil (see *"Lubricants and fluids"*). An oil can spout or funnel may help to reduce spillage. Pour in half the specified quantity of oil first, then wait a few minutes for the oil to fall to the sump. Continue adding oil a small quantity at a time until the level is up to the lower mark on the dipstick. Finally, bring the level up to the upper mark on the dipstick. Insert the dipstick, and refit the filler cap.

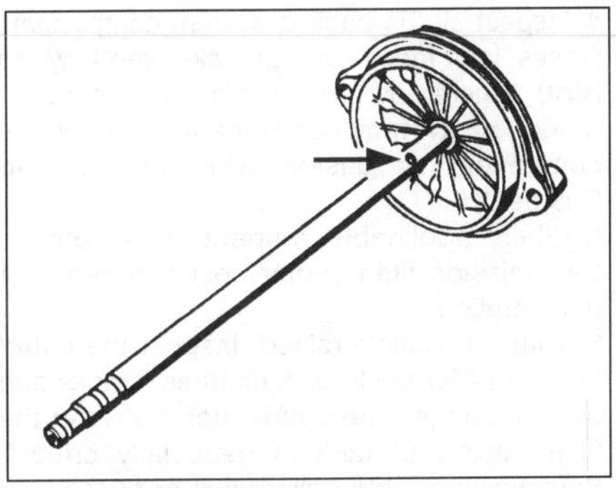

3.14 Check the small hole (arrowed) in the top of the oil return pipe for blockage

19 Start the engine and run it for a few minutes; check for leaks around the oil filter housing and the sump drain plug. Note that there may be a delay of a few seconds before the oil pressure warning light goes out when the engine is first started, as the oil circulates through the engine oil galleries and the new oil filter, before the pressure builds up.

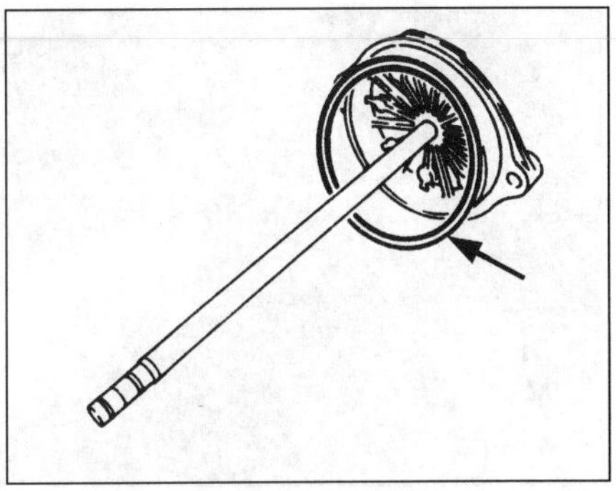

3.15 Fit a new O-ring (arrowed) to the oil filter housing cover

20 Switch off the engine, and wait a few minutes for the oil to settle in the sump once more. With the new oil circulated and the filter completely full, recheck the level on the dipstick, and add more oil as necessary.

21 Where applicable, refit the engine undershield.

22 Dispose of the used engine oil safely, with reference to *"General repair procedures"* in the Reference section of this manual.

Every 12 000 miles

4 Throttle linkage - lubrication

1 Inspect the throttle linkage components for wear or damage, and renew any worn components. Brush away dirt using a soft brush or cloth.

2 Lubricate all the moving parts of the throttle linkage and, where applicable, the kickdown and/or cruise control linkage, using light oil or grease.

5 Automatic transmission fluid - level check

1 In order to check the automatic transmission fluid level, the transmission must be at operating temperature (fluid temperature 80°C). Operating temperature is reached after driving for approximately 10 miles. **Do not** attempt to check the fluid level on a cold transmission.

2 With the transmission at operating temperature, ensure that the vehicle is parked on level ground.

3 With the engine running at idle speed, ensure that the transmission selector lever is in position "P", and apply the parking brake.

4 Release the locking lever, and pull the transmission fluid level dipstick from the dipstick tube. Wipe the dipstick with a lint-free cloth, then re-insert it **(see illustrations)**.

5 Pull out the dipstick once more, and read off the fluid level. The level should be between the "MIN" and "MAX" marks **(see illustration)**.

6 If topping up is necessary, top-up through the dipstick tube, using fluid of the specified type (see *"Lubricants and fluids"*). **Do not** overfill the transmission - the fluid level must not be above the "MAX" mark.

7 On completion, re-insert the dipstick tube, and re-check the fluid level. Ensure that the locking lever is engaged when finally refitting the dipstick.

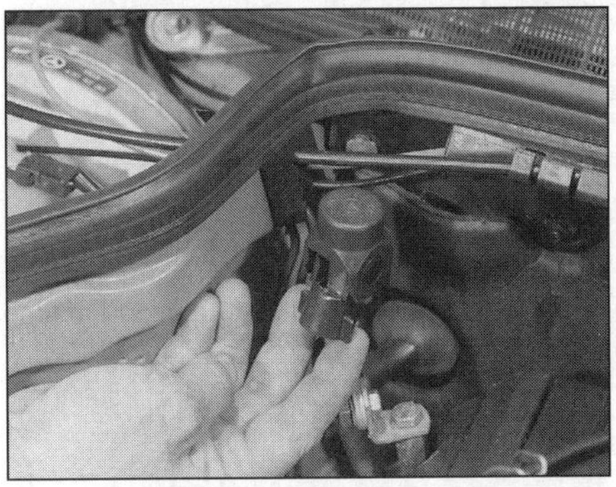

5.4a Release the locking lever . . .

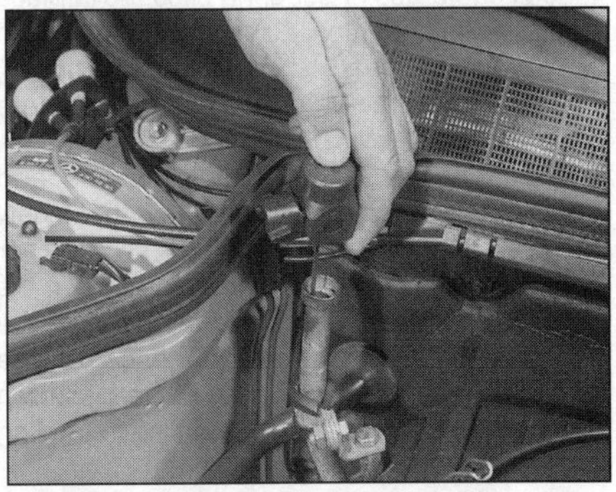

5.4b . . . and pull out the dipstick . . .

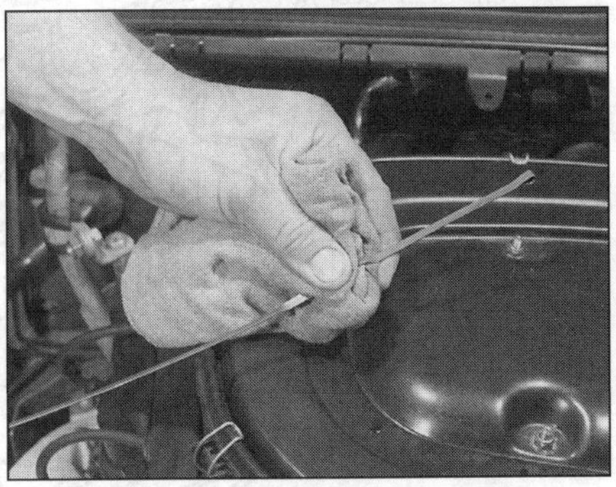

5.4c . . . then wipe the dipstick

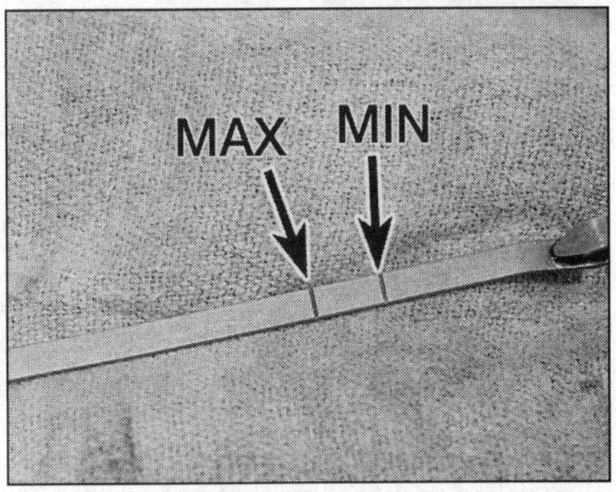

5.5 Automatic transmission fluid level dipstick markings

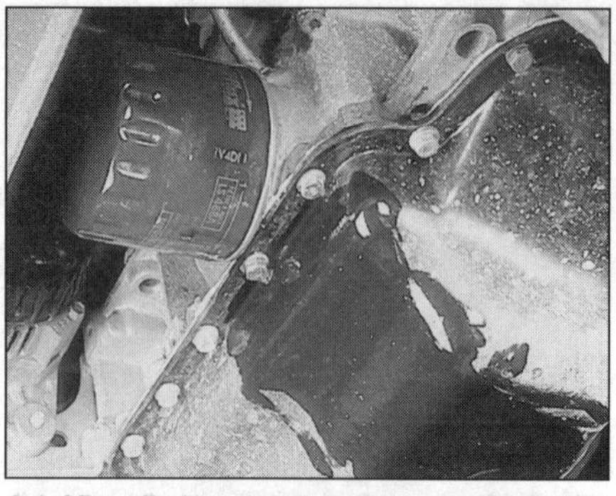

6.1 Visually inspect the area around the oil filter and sump joint faces for signs of leakage

6 Underbonnet/underbody components and hoses - check for fluid leaks

1 Visually inspect the engine joint faces, gaskets and seals for any signs of water or oil leaks. Pay particular attention to the areas around the camshaft cover, cylinder head, oil filter and sump joint faces. Bear in mind that, over a period of time, some very slight seepage from these areas is to be expected - what you are really looking for is any indication of a serious leak **(see illustration)**. Should a leak be found, renew the offending gasket or oil seal by referring to the appropriate Chapters in this manual.

2 Also check the security and condition of all the engine-related pipes and hoses. Ensure that all cable-ties or securing clips are in place and in good condition. Clips which are broken or missing can lead to chafing of the hoses, pipes or wiring, which could cause more serious problems in the future.

3 Carefully check the radiator hoses and heater hoses along their entire length. Renew any hose which is cracked, swollen or deteriorated. Cracks will show up better if the hose is squeezed. Pay close attention to the hose clips that secure the hoses to the cooling system components. Hose clips can pinch and puncture hoses, resulting in cooling system leaks.

HAYNES HiNT

A leak in the cooling system will usually show up as white- or rust-coloured deposits on the area adjoining the leak

4 Inspect all the cooling system components (hoses, joint faces etc.) for leaks **(see Haynes Hint)**. Where any problems of this nature are found on system components, renew the component or gasket with reference to Chapter 3.

5 Where applicable, inspect the automatic transmission fluid cooler hoses for leaks or deterioration.

6 With the vehicle raised, inspect the petrol tank and filler neck for punctures, cracks and other damage. The connection between the filler neck and tank is especially critical. Sometimes a rubber filler neck or connecting hose will leak due to loose retaining clamps or deteriorated rubber.

7 Carefully check all rubber hoses and metal fuel lines leading to and from the petrol tank. Check for loose connections, deteriorated hoses, crimped lines, and other damage. Pay particular attention to the vent pipes and hoses, which often loop up around the filler neck and can become blocked or crimped. Follow the lines to the front of the vehicle, carefully inspecting them all the way. Renew damaged sections as necessary.

8 Closely inspect the metal brake pipes which run along the vehicle underbody. If they show signs of excessive corrosion or damage they must be renewed.

9 From within the engine compartment, check the security of all fuel hose attachments and pipe unions, and inspect the fuel hoses and vacuum hoses for kinks, chafing and deterioration.

10 Where applicable, check the condition of the power steering fluid hoses and pipes.

7 Auxiliary drivebelt(s) - condition check, renewal and adjustment

Drivebelt checking - general

1 Due to their function and construction, the belts are prone to failure after a period of time, and should be inspected periodically to prevent problems.

2 The number of belts used on a particular vehicle depends on the accessories fitted. Drivebelts are used to drive the coolant pump, alternator, power steering/suspension hydraulic pump, air conditioning compressor and air injection pump.

3 To improve access for belt inspection, where possible, remove the viscous cooling fan and cowl as described in Chapter 3.

4 With the engine stopped, using your fingers (and a torch if necessary), move along the belts, checking for cracks and separation of the belt plies. Also check for fraying and glazing, which gives the belt a shiny appearance. Both sides of the belts should be inspected, which means the belt will have to be twisted to check the underside. If necessary turn the engine using a spanner or socket on the crankshaft pulley bolt so that the whole of the belt can be inspected.

Drivebelt renewal

5 Remove the cooling fan blades and shroud, as described in Chapter 3. On models with a one-piece cooling fan shroud, the complete radiator/fan shroud assembly must be removed.

6 Unscrew the nut from the end of the tensioner lever bolt **(see illustration)**.

7 Insert a suitable lever (approximately 12.0 mm diameter, and 300 mm long - eg, the wheel trim lever in the vehicle tool kit) into the hole in the tensioner lever, and press the lever anti-clockwise until the lever bolt can be slid back towards the inlet manifold.

8 Release the tensioner spring by pivoting the lever clockwise.

9 Push the idler pulley back, and withdraw the belt from the pulleys.

10 Fit the new belt as follows.

11 Raise the idler pulley slightly, and hold in position during the following procedure.

1 Tensioner lever nut
2 Tensioner lever bolt
3 Tensioner lever
4 Tensioner spring

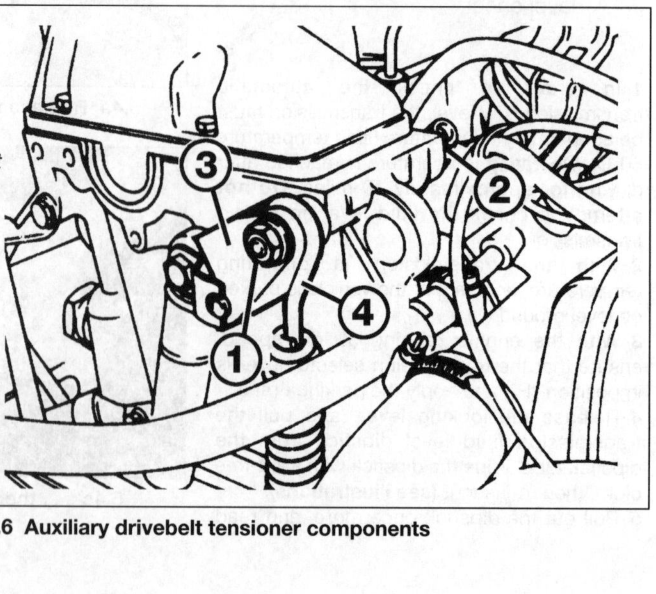

7.6 Auxiliary drivebelt tensioner components

7.12 Form a loop in the belt and slide it between the coolant pump and crankshaft pulleys

7.13 Turn the coolant pump anti-clockwise until the belt rides up onto the idler pulley

7.14a Slide the belt over the idler pulley and crankshaft pulley, then fit it around the remaining pulleys

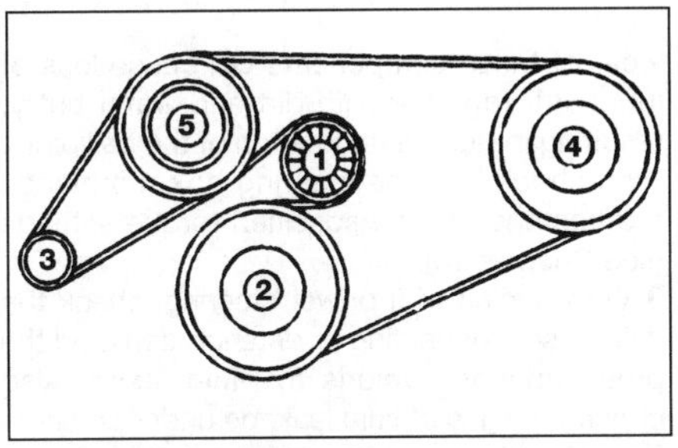

7.14b Auxiliary drivebelt - models without air conditioning

Fit belt round pulleys in order shown
1 *Tensioner pulley*
2 *Crankshaft pulley*
3 *Alternator pulley*
4 *Power steering pump pulley*
5 *Coolant pump pulley*

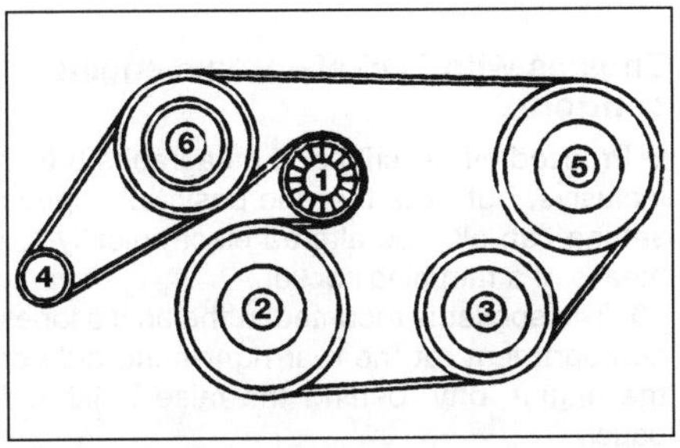

7.14c Auxiliary drivebelt - models with air conditioning, but without idler pulley

Fit belt round pulleys in order shown
1 *Tensioner pulley*
2 *Crankshaft pulley*
3 *Air conditioning compressor pulley*
4 *Alternator pulley*
5 *Power steering pump pulley*
6 *Coolant pump pulley*

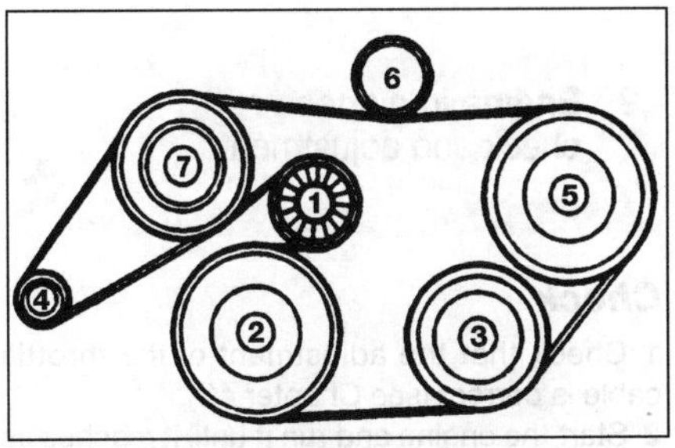

7.14d Auxiliary drivebelt - models with air conditioning and idler pulley

Fit belt round pulleys in order shown
1 *Tensioner pulley*
2 *Crankshaft pulley*
3 *Air conditioning compressor pulley*
4 *Alternator pulley*
5 *Power steering pump pulley*
6 *Idler pulley*
7 *Coolant pump pulley*

12 Form a loop in the belt, with the drive ribs on the outside, then slide the belt between the coolant pump and crankshaft pulleys **(see illustration)**.
13 Using the left hand, press the belt firmly into contact with the coolant pump pulley, then turn the coolant pump pulley anti-clockwise until the belt rides up onto the idler pulley **(see illustration)**.
14 Slide the belt over the idler pulley and the crankshaft pulley, then open out the remainder of the belt, and fit it around the remaining pulleys in the order shown **(see illustrations)**.
15 Release the idler pulley.
16 Press the tensioner lever as necessary to enable the lever bolt to be pushed into position.
17 Push the bolt back through the lever, checking that the tensioner spring locates correctly.
18 Refit the nut to the tensioner lever bolt, and tighten to the specified torque whilst counterholding the bolt.
19 Refit the cooling fan blades and shroud, and where applicable the radiator, as described in Chapter 3.

8 Air conditioning system - refrigerant level check

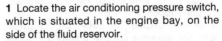

1 Locate the air conditioning pressure switch, which is situated in the engine bay, on the side of the fluid reservoir.
2 With the engine and ignition switched off, unplug the wiring from the top of the pressure switch at the connector.
3 Start the engine, allow it to idle and turn on the air conditioning at the control panel.
4 Carefully wipe clean the inspection window on the side of the fluid reservoir **(see illustration)**.
5 Reconnect the pressure switch wiring, whilst observing the inspection window. This will cause the electromagnetic clutch to engage and as this happens, the refrigerant fluid level should rise into view. Continue watching the fluid level, which should rise beyond the top of the inspection window, until only bubble-free fluid can be seen flowing.
6 If the fluid level appears to be too low, or there is a pressure drop within the refrigeration system, the pressure switch will prevent the electromagnetic clutch from engaging and the air conditioning will not function. Under these circumstances, the vehicle should be taken to a Mercedes dealer or air conditioning specialist for diagnosis and/or re-charging. Do not attempt to by-pass the pressure switch in an attempt to restore operation, as serious component damage may result.

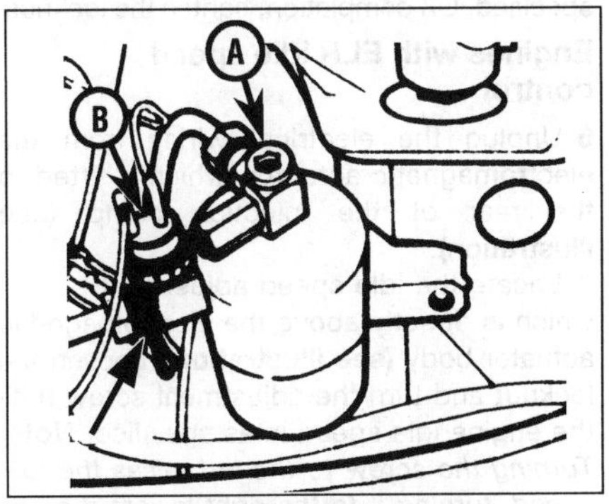

8. 4 Air conditioning dehydrator unit

A *Inspection window*
B *Pressure switch wiring connector*

1B

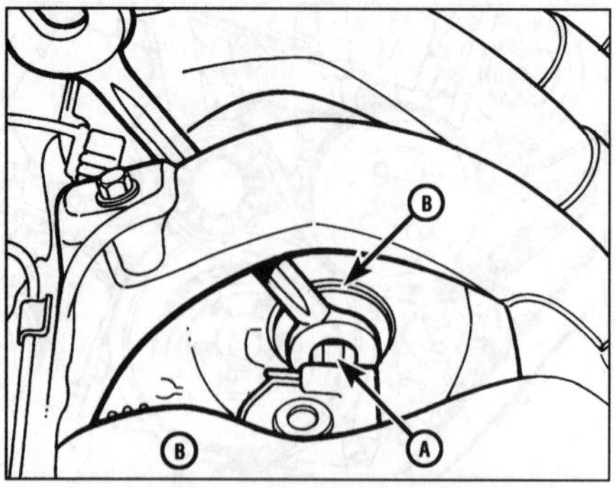

9.4 Loosen the locknut (A) and turn the vacuum unit (B) to adjust the idle speed – engines with pneumatic idle speed increase

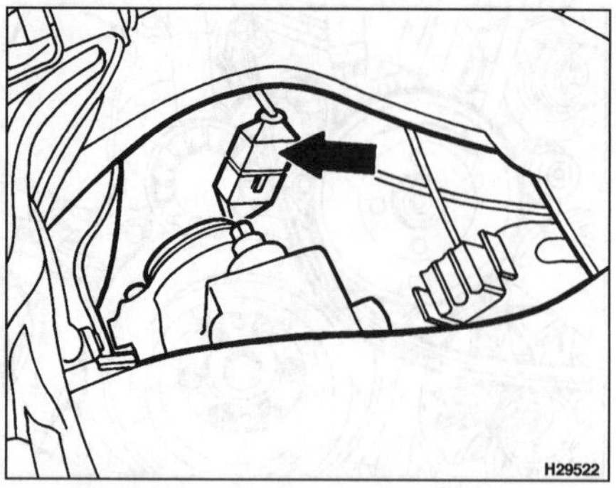

9.6 Unplug the electrical connector (arrowed) from the electromagnetic actuator – engines with ELR idle sped control

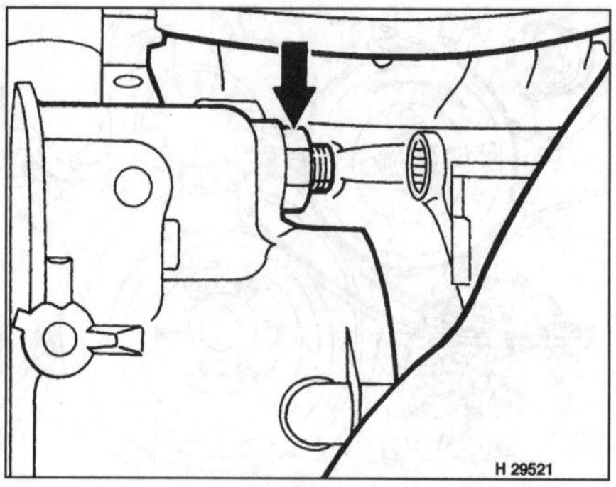

9.7 Idle speed adjustment screw (arrowed) – engines with ELR idle speed control

9 Engine idle speed - check and adjustment

Check

1 Check that the adjustment of the throttle cable is correct (see Chapter 4C).

2 Start the engine and run it until it reaches its normal operating temperature. With the parking brake applied and the transmission in neutral, allow the engine to idle. Check that all electrical consumers are switched off (including the air conditioning, where applicable).

3 Using a diesel engine tachometer, check that the engine idle speed is as quoted in the *Specifications*. If adjustment is necessary, proceed to the next sub-section.

Adjustment

Engines with pneumatic idle speed increase

4 Loosen the locknut on the top of the idle speed vacuum unit, which is fitted to the rear of the injection pump **(see illustration)**.

5 Using an open-ended spanner, gradually turn the vacuum unit, until the idle speed is as specified. On completion, tighten the locknut.

Engines with ELR idle speed control

6 Unplug the electrical wiring from the electromagnetic actuator, which is fitted to the rear of the injection pump **(see illustration)**.

7 Locate the idle speed adjustment screw, which is directly above the electromagnetic actuator body **(see illustration)**. Loosen the locknut and turn the adjustment screw until the engine idle speed is as specified. **Note:** *Turning the screw to the left raises the idle speed, turning it to the right lowers the idle speed.*

8 On completion, tighten the locknut and reconnect the actuator wiring.

Engines with EDS electronic engine control

9 Proceed as described in paragraphs 6 to 8 inclusive, but note that the basic idle speed setting can also be altered electronically, by means of a trimming socket.

10 The socket is mounted in the accessories compartment, at the rear right-hand side of the engine bay, behind the false bulkhead panel.

11 The position of the resistive plug can be altered by pulling it from the trimming socket, rotating it and refitting it - the positions are indicated by numbers, ranging from 1 to 7, marked on the rear of the resistive plug.

12 Position No 1 equates to roughly 600 rpm, and position No 7 equates roughly to 700 rpm.

10 Steering and suspension components - condition and security check

Front suspension and steering check

1 Raise the front of the vehicle, and securely support it on axle stands (see *"Jacking and vehicle support"*).

2 Visually inspect the balljoint dust covers and the steering linkage gaiters for splits, chafing or deterioration **(see illustration)**. Any wear of these components will cause loss of lubricant, together with dirt and water entry, resulting in rapid deterioration of the balljoints. Also check that the steering box mountings are tightened to the specified torque settings (see Chapter 10).

3 On vehicles with power steering, check the fluid hoses for chafing or deterioration, and the pipe and hose unions for fluid leaks. Also check for signs of fluid leakage under pressure from the steering box, which would indicate failed fluid seals within the steering box.

4 Grasp the roadwheel at the 12 o'clock and 6 o'clock positions, and try to rock it **(see illustration)**. Very slight free play may be felt, but if the movement is appreciable, further investigation is necessary to determine the source. Continue rocking the wheel while an assistant depresses the footbrake. If the movement is now eliminated or significantly reduced, it is likely that the hub bearings are at fault. If the free play is still evident with the footbrake depressed, then there is wear in the suspension joints or mountings. Note that the front hub bearings are adjustable (See Chapter 10).

5 Now grasp the wheel at the 9 o'clock and 3 o'clock positions, and try to rock it as before. Any movement felt now may again be caused by wear in the hub bearings or the steering track-rod balljoints. If the inner or outer balljoint is worn, the visual movement will be obvious.

10.2 Visually inspect the balljoint dust covers for splits, chafing or deterioration

10.4 Grasp the roadwheel at the 12 o'clock and 6 o'clock positions, and try to rock it

6 Using a large screwdriver or flat bar, check for wear in the suspension mounting bushes by levering between the relevant suspension component and its attachment point. Some movement is to be expected as the mountings are made of rubber, but excessive wear should be obvious. Also check the condition of any visible rubber bushes, looking for splits, cracks or contamination of the rubber.
7 With the car standing on its wheels, have an assistant turn the steering wheel back and forth about an eighth of a turn each way. There should be very little lost movement between the steering wheel and roadwheels. If this is not the case, closely observe the linkage joints and mountings previously described, but in addition, check the steering column universal joint/coupling for wear, and the steering box itself.

Suspension strut/shock absorber check

8 Check for any signs of fluid leakage around the suspension strut/shock absorber body, or from the rubber gaiter around the piston rod. Should any fluid be noticed, the suspension strut/shock absorber is defective internally, and should be renewed. **Note:** *Suspension strut inserts/shock absorbers should always be renewed in pairs on the same axle - never renew single shock absorbers, as the vehicles' handling and braking characteristics could be seriously affected.*
9 The efficiency of the suspension strut/shock absorber may be checked by bouncing the vehicle at each corner **(see illustration)**. Generally speaking, after being depressed once, the body should rise to its normal position and stop, without oscillation. If it rises and returns on a rebound, the suspension strut/shock absorber is probably in need of renewal. Examine also the suspension strut/shock absorber upper and lower mountings for any signs of wear.

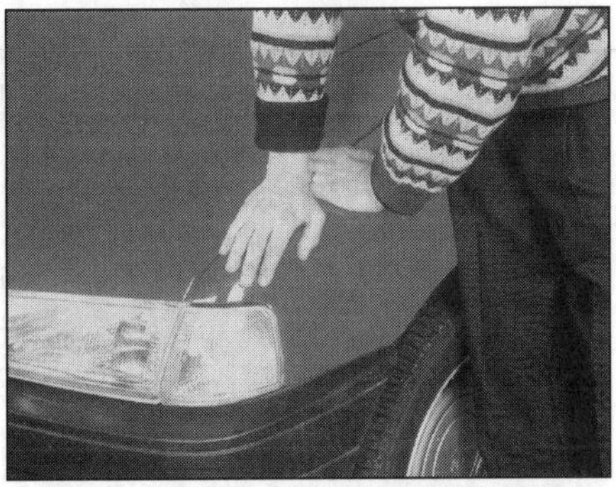

10.9 The efficiency of the suspension strut/shock absorber may be checked by bouncing the vehicle at each corner

11 Driveshafts and driveshaft gaiter - condition check

1 With the vehicle raised and securely supported on stands, slowly rotate the rear roadwheel. Inspect the condition of the outer constant velocity (CV) joint rubber gaiters, squeezing the gaiters to open out the folds **(see illustration)**. Check for signs of cracking, splits or deterioration of the rubber, which may allow the grease to escape, and lead to water and grit entry into the joint. Also check the security and condition of the retaining clips. Repeat these checks on the inner CV joints. If any damage or deterioration is found, the gaiters should be renewed (see Chapter 8).

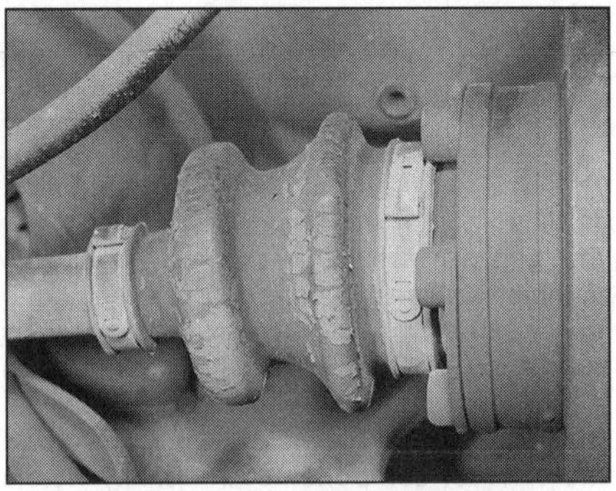

11.1 Inspect the condition of the CV joint rubber gaiters, checking for signs of cracking or splitting

2 At the same time, check the general condition of the CV joints themselves by first holding the driveshaft and attempting to rotate the wheel. Repeat this check by holding the inner joint and attempting to rotate the driveshaft. Any appreciable movement indicates wear in the joints, wear in the driveshaft splines, or a loose driveshaft retaining nut.

12 Front brake pad check

1 Firmly apply the parking brake, then jack up the front of the car and support it securely on axle stands (see *"Jacking and vehicle support"*). Remove the front roadwheels.
2 A quick check of the brake pads can be carried out by viewing through the inspection aperture, at the front of the caliper **(see Haynes Hint)**. The depth of friction material remaining on the pads can be seen, but note that only one of the pads will be fully visible.
3 For a comprehensive check, the brake pads should be removed and cleaned. The operation of the caliper can then also be checked, and the condition of the brake disc itself can be fully examined on both sides. Refer to Chapter 9 for further information.
4 If friction material on any of the pads is worn to, or below, the specified thickness, then *all four front brake pads must be renewed as a set, to ensure that the braking performance remains consistent.*

Warning: Do not swap brake pads around, in an attempt to compensate for uneven wear. The braking performance of the vehicle will be seriously impaired.

HAYNES HiNT

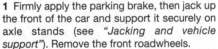

A quick check of the brake pads can be carried out by viewing through the inspection aperture, at the front of the caliper

13 Rear brake pad check

1 Chock the front wheels, then jack up the rear of the vehicle and support it on axle stands (see *"Jacking and vehicle support"*). Remove the rear roadwheels.
2 For a quick check, the thickness of friction material remaining on each brake pad can be measured through the top of the caliper body. If any pad's friction material is worn to the specified thickness or less, then *all four front brake pads must be renewed as a set, to ensure that the braking performance remains consistent.*
3 For a comprehensive check, the brake pads should be removed and cleaned. This will permit the operation of the caliper to be checked, and the condition of the brake disc itself to be fully examined on both sides. Refer to Chapter 9 for further information.

Warning: Do not swap brake pads around, in an attempt to compensate for uneven wear. The braking performance of the vehicle will be seriously impaired.

14 Parking brake - operation check

1 Applying normal moderate pressure, fully apply the parking brake whilst counting the number of 'clicks' of the ratchet mechanism. If adjustment is correct, there should be approximately 7 or 8 clicks before the parking brake is fully applied. If there are less than 4 clicks or more than 11 clicks, adjustment will be necessary; refer to Chapter 9 for a description of the adjustment procedure.

15 Exhaust system and mountings - condition and security check

1 With the engine cold (at least an hour after the vehicle has been driven), check the complete exhaust system from the engine to the end of the tailpipe. The exhaust system is most easily checked with the vehicle raised on a hoist, or suitably supported on axle stands (see *"Jacking and vehicle support"*), so that the exhaust components are readily visible and accessible.
2 Check the exhaust pipes and connections for evidence of leaks, severe corrosion and damage. Make sure that all brackets and mountings are in good condition, and that all relevant nuts and bolts are tight. Leakage at any of the joints or in other parts of the system will usually show up as a black sooty stain in the vicinity of the leak **(see illustration)**.
3 Rattles and other noises can often be traced to the exhaust system, especially the brackets and mountings. Try to move the pipes and silencers. If the components are able to come into contact with the body or suspension parts, secure the system with new mountings. Otherwise separate the joints (if possible) and twist the pipes as necessary to provide additional clearance.

16 Manual transmission oil - level check and renewal

Note: *A hexagonal key, or a suitable alternative (see text) will be required to unscrew the transmission level/filler plug.*
1 Place a suitable container beneath the transmission level/filler plug, located on the right-hand side of the transmission. A hexagonal key should be used to unscrew the plug, but a tool can be improvised using a long nut, or a length of hexagonal bar, and a spanner **(see illustration)**.
2 The fluid level should just be up to the bottom of the level/filler plug hole.
3 If necessary, top-up the level until fluid just begins to run out of the level/filler plug hole.
4 When the level is correct, refit the plug, and tighten securely.

17 Final drive unit oil - level check and renewal

Level check

1 Either position the vehicle over a well-ventilated inspection pit, or jack up the front and rear of the vehicle and support it on axle stands (see *"Jacking and vehicle support"*). The vehicle **must** be level, if the results of this check are to be accurate.
2 Clean the area around the filler/level plug on the left-hand side of the final drive unit, then slacken and remove the plug from the housing **(see illustration)**.
3 The oil level should be up to the lower edge of the filler/level plug aperture. Check that this is the case using a clean piece of wire, bent into a right-angle.
4 If necessary, top-up using the specified type of lubricant until the oil level is correct. Fill the final drive until oil starts to flow out and allow excess oil to drain.
5 Once the final drive unit oil level is correct, refit the filler/level plug and tighten it securely. Lower the vehicle to the ground.
6 Note that frequent need for topping-up indicates a leakage, possibly through an oil seal. The cause should be investigated and rectified.

Draining and refilling

7 The draining process will be simplified if the vehicle is taken on a short drive; this will allow the oil to heat up, reducing its viscosity.
8 Either position the vehicle over a well-ventilated inspection pit, or jack up the front and rear of the vehicle and support it on axle stands (see *"Jacking and vehicle support"*).
9 Clean the area around the filler/level plug, on the left-hand side of the final drive unit, then slacken and remove the plug from the housing.
10 Slacken and remove the drain plug, located towards the rear of the final drive unit, on the right hand side **(see illustration)**. Allow the oil to drain into a container. On completion, clean the plug and fit a new seal. Refit the plug and tighten it securely
11 Refill the differential via the filler/level plug with correct quantity of new oil of the specified grade. On completion, check the oil level as described in the previous sub-Section.

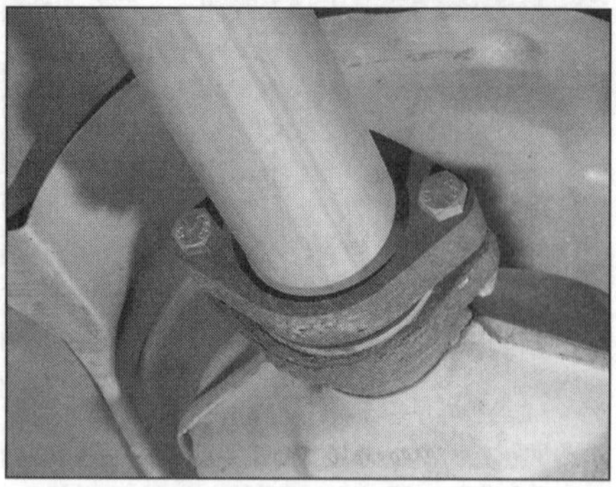

15.2 Check the security of the exhaust system joints

16.1 Using a long nut and a spanner to unscrew the transmission fluid level/filler plug

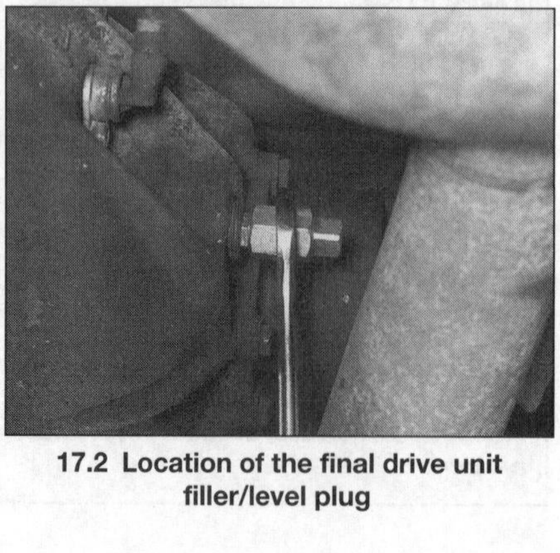

17.2 Location of the final drive unit filler/level plug

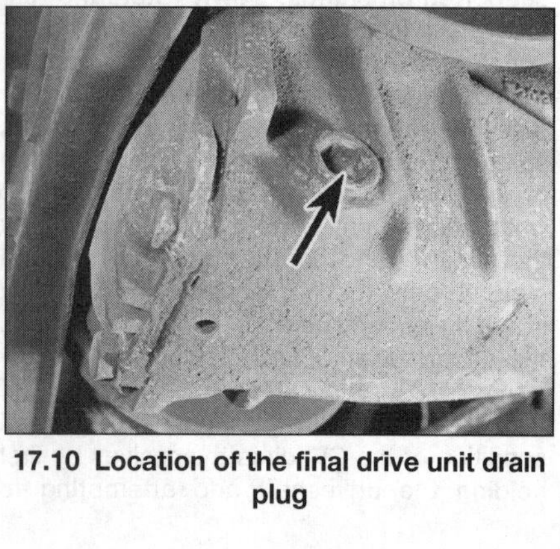

17.10 Location of the final drive unit drain plug

18 Propeller shaft rubber couplings - condition and security check

1 Chock the front wheels, then jack up the rear of the vehicle and support it on axle stands (see *"Jacking and vehicle support"*).
2 Carefully check the propeller shaft front and rear rubber couplings for signs of damage and deterioration. Look for deterioration in the form of splitting, cracking or perishing. Damage may also be caused by oil or grease contamination.
3 If either of the couplings require renewal, refer Chapter 8 for a description of the renewal procedure.

19 Seat belts - operation and condition check

1 Carefully examine the seat belt webbing for cuts or any signs of serious fraying or deterioration. If the seat belt is of the retractable type, pull the belt all the way out, and examine the full extent of the webbing.

2 Fasten and unfasten the belt, ensuring that the locking mechanism holds securely and releases properly when intended. If the belt is of the retractable type, check also that the retracting mechanism operates correctly when the belt is released.
3 Check the security of all seat belt mountings and attachments which are accessible, without removing any trim or other components, from inside the vehicle.

20 Hinges, locks and electric aerial - lubrication

1 Lubricate the hinges of the bonnet, doors and tailgate with a light general-purpose oil. Similarly, lubricate all latches, locks and lock strikers. At the same time, check the security and operation of all the locks, adjusting them if necessary (see Chapter 11).
2 Lightly lubricate the bonnet release mechanism and cable with a suitable grease.
3 If an electric aerial is fitted, extend the aerial and remove all traces of dirt from its mast. Lubricate the aerial mast with a light general-purpose oil and retract the aerial.
4 On models with a sunroof, slide the roof fully back and clean the sunroof guide rails. Apply a smear of fresh multi-purpose grease to the rails and close the sunroof.

21 Headlight beam alignment - adjustment

1 Accurate adjustment of the headlight beam is only possible using optical beam-setting equipment, and this work should therefore be carried out by a Mercedes-Benz dealer or service station with the necessary facilities. Poorly adjusted headlights can dazzle other road users and may cause an accident.

22 Windscreen/headlight washer system(s) - condition check

1 Check that each of the washer jet nozzles are clear and that each nozzle provides a strong jet of washer fluid. The headlight jets should be aimed to spray at a point slightly above the centre of the screen/headlight. On the windscreen washer nozzles where there are two jets, aim one of the jets slightly above then centre of the screen and aim the other just below to ensure complete coverage of the screen. If necessary, adjust the jets using a pin.
2 Mercedes-Benz recommend that the windscreen wiper blades should be renewed at this interval, regardless of their apparent condition (see "*Weekly checks*").

23 Road test

Instruments and electrical equipment

1 Check the operation of all instruments and electrical equipment.
2 Make sure that all instruments read correctly, and switch on all electrical equipment in turn, to check that it functions properly.

Steering and suspension

3 Check for any abnormalities in the steering, suspension, handling or road "feel".
4 Drive the vehicle, and check that there are no unusual vibrations or noises.
5 Check that the steering feels positive, with no excessive "sloppiness", or roughness, and check for any suspension noises when cornering and driving over bumps.

Drivetrain

6 Check the performance of the engine, clutch (where applicable), gearbox/ transmission and driveshafts.
7 Listen for any unusual noises from the engine, clutch and gearbox/transmission.
8 Make sure that the engine runs smoothly when idling, and that there is no hesitation when accelerating.
9 Check that, where applicable, the clutch action is smooth and progressive, that the drive is taken up smoothly, and that the pedal travel is not excessive. Also listen for any noises when the clutch pedal is depressed.
10 On manual gearbox models, check that all gears can be engaged smoothly without noise, and that the gear lever action is not abnormally vague or "notchy".
11 On automatic transmission models, make sure that all gearchanges occur smoothly, without snatching, and without an increase in engine speed between changes. Check that all the gear positions can be selected with the vehicle at rest. If any problems are found, they should be referred to a Mercedes-Benz dealer.

Check the operation and performance of the braking system

12 Make sure that the vehicle does not pull to one side when braking, and that the wheels do not lock prematurely when braking hard.
13 Check that there is no vibration through the steering when braking.
14 Check that the parking brake operates correctly without excessive movement of the lever, and that it holds the vehicle stationary on a slope.
15 Test the operation of the brake servo unit as follows. With the engine off, depress the footbrake four or five times to exhaust the vacuum. Hold the brake pedal depressed, then start the engine. As the engine starts, there should be a noticeable "give" in the brake pedal as vacuum builds up. Allow the engine to run for at least two minutes, and then switch it off. If the brake pedal is depressed now, it should be possible to detect a hiss from the servo as the pedal is depressed. After about four or five applications, no further hissing should be heard, and the pedal should feel considerably harder.

24 Front hub bearings - check

1 With the vehicle parked on a level surface, apply the parking brake and select first gear (manual transmission) or 'PARK' (automatic transmission). Jack up the front of the vehicle and support it securely on axle stands (see *"Jacking and vehicle support"*).
2 Grasp the first front roadwheel at the 12 o'clock and 6 o'clock positions, and try to rock it. Very slight free play may be felt, but if the movement is appreciable, further investigation is necessary to determine the source. Continue rocking the wheel while an assistant depresses the footbrake. If the movement is now eliminated or significantly reduced, it is likely that the hub bearings are at fault. If the free play is still evident with the footbrake depressed, then there is wear in the suspension joints or mountings.
3 Now grasp the wheel at the 9 o'clock and 3 o'clock positions, and try to rock it as before. Any movement felt now may again be caused by wear in the hub bearings or the steering track-rod balljoints. If the inner or outer balljoint is worn, the visual movement will be obvious.
4 Repeat the operation at the other front roadwheel. If the hub bearings are in need of adjustment, refer to Chapter 10 for a complete description of this procedure.

25 Clutch - operation check

1 Check that, where applicable, the clutch action is smooth and progressive, that the drive is taken up smoothly, and that the pedal travel is not excessive. Also listen for any noises when the clutch pedal is depressed.
2 Check that all gears can be engaged smoothly without noise.
3 Check the clutch release hydraulic components for leaks (see Chapter 6).

Every 36 000 miles

26 Air filter element - renewal

Turbo-diesel engines

1 Unscrew and remove the securing nuts from the air cleaner cover.
2 Lift off the air cleaner cover, together with the packing material. Cover the inlet orifice at the centre of the air cleaner base, to prevent dirt from entering the air flow meter and /or turbocharger.
3 Remove the filter element from the air cleaner.
4 Brush out all traces of dirt and debris from inside the air cleaner. Take care to prevent debris from falling down the inlet orifice.
5 Lay a new filter element in position, paying attention to the orientation markings on its edge.
6 Refit the packing material and cover, then screw on the retaining nuts and tighten them securely.

Normally-aspirated engines

7 Slacken the hose clip and detach the ducting from the front of the air cleaner. Where applicable, unclip the small hose from the air cleaner cover **(see illustrations)**.
8 Prise open the spring catches and release the air cleaner cover **(see illustration)**.
9 Release the filter element from the air cleaner cover **(see illustration)**.
10 Brush out all traces of dirt and debris from inside the air cleaner.
11 Lay a new filter element in position in the air cleaner cover, with the folds of the filter element facing into the cover. Press the rubber seal firmly into the channel that runs around the inside edge of the air cleaner cover.
12 Fit the cover, together with the filter element, over the fixed section of the air cleaner cover. Secure the cover in position with the spring clips.
13 Reconnect the ducting to the front of the air cleaner cover, noting that the orientation arrow marked on the ducting must face the engine. Tighten the hose clip securely.

27 Fuel filter and pre-filter - renewal

1 Disconnect the battery negative cable and position it away from the terminal.
2 To minimise fuel spillage, position a small container underneath the filter canister and pad the surrounding area with absorbent rags.
3 Support the fuel filter with one hand, then slacken and remove the banjo bolt at from the top of the fuel filter housing. Recover both O-ring seals and discard them - new items must be used on refitting **(see illustration)**.
4 Remove the filter canister from the engine bay, keeping the mating face upwards to minimise fuel spillage.
5 With the filter removed, check that the restriction orifice in the fuel return line, on the mating surface of the filter housing is clean and free from blockage.
6 Take the new filter canister and moisten the rubber seal with a little clean fuel.
7 Offer the filter up to the housing, then insert the banjo bolt (using new O-ring seals) and tighten it securely.
8 The pre-filter is positioned to the left hand side of the fuel injection pump. Clamp off the fuel supply hose from the fuel tank downstream of the pre-filter, then slacken the clips and detach the fuel hoses from either side of the pre-filter. Fit the new unit in its place and tighten the hose clips securely.
9 Restore the battery connection, then start and run the engine at idle and check around the fuel filter for fuel leaks. **Note:** *The fuel pump is self priming, but it may take a few seconds of cranking before the engine starts.*
10 Raise the engine speed to about 2000 rpm several times, then allow the engine to idle again. This should bleed the air bubbles from the filter canister, but if the engine idle is at all rough or hesitant, repeat the action until the fuel system clears itself.

26.7a Detach the ducting from the front of the air cleaner . . .

26.7b . . . and unclip the small hose from the air cleaner cover – normally-aspirated engines

26.8 Prise open the spring catches . . .

26.9 . . . and remove the element from the air cleaner cover – normally-aspirated engines

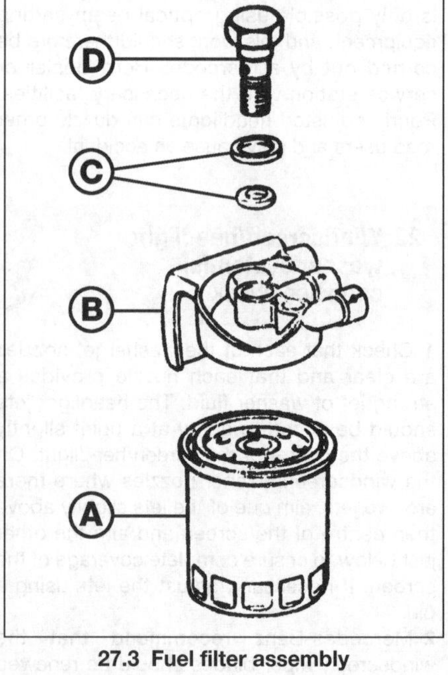

27.3 Fuel filter assembly

A Fuel filter canister
B Filter housing
C Sealing washers
D Banjo bolt

28.6 Unscrewing the automatic transmission drain plug

28.7 Torque converter drain plug (arrowed)

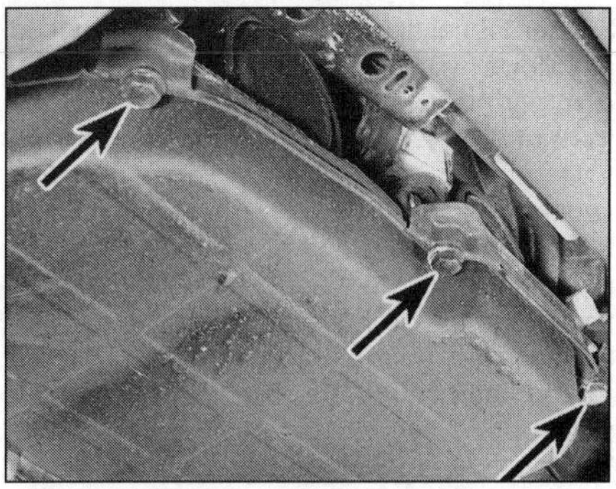

28.9 Automatic transmission fluid pan securing bolts (arrowed)

28 Automatic transmission fluid and filter - renewal

1 This operation should not be attempted unless clean, dust-free conditions can be achieved.
2 Jack up the vehicle, and support securely on axle stands (see *"Jacking and vehicle support"*), ensuring that the vehicle remains level.
3 Where applicable, remove the body undershield for access to the transmission.
4 Move the transmission selector lever to position "P".
5 Wipe clean the transmission fluid pan, particularly the area around the drain plug, the pan-to-transmission securing bolts, and the pan-to-transmission joint.
6 Place a suitable container beneath the transmission drain plug, then unscrew the drain plug, using an Allen key or hexagon bit, and allow the fluid to drain into the container **(see illustration)**. Refit the drain plug when all the fluid has drained.
7 Using a socket on the crankshaft pulley hub bolt (it may be necessary to remove the cooling fan cowl for access on some models - see Chapter 3), turn the crankshaft until the torque converter drain plug becomes visible through the aperture in the transmission casing **(see illustration)**.
8 Reposition the container beneath the torque converter drain plug, then unscrew the drain plug and allow the fluid to drain into the container. Refit the drain plug when all the fluid has drained.
9 Unscrew the fluid pan securing bolts, then remove the clamp plates, and lower the fluid pan from the transmission **(see illustration)**. Tap the pan gently using a soft-faced mallet if it is stuck. Recover the rubber seal.
10 Unscrew the securing screws, and withdraw the filter screen **(see illustration)**.
11 Thoroughly clean the fluid pan inside and outside using a clean lint-free cloth.
12 Fit a new filter screen, and tighten the securing screws.
13 Offer the fluid pan into position, and refit the clamp plates and securing bolts. Tighten the securing bolts to the specified torque.
14 Where applicable, refit the underbody shield.
15 Lower the vehicle to the ground, then release the locking lever, and withdraw the fluid level dipstick.
16 Initially fill the transmission with 4.0 litres of the specified fluid (see "*Lubricants and fluids*") through the dipstick tube. Start the engine, and allow it to idle with the selector lever in the position "P".
17 Continue adding fluid until the level is 12.0 mm below the lower ("MIN") mark on the dipstick (see Section 5).
18 Move the selector lever through all the gear positions, pausing for a few seconds in each position, then return the lever to the "P" position.
19 Re-check the fluid level as described in paragraph 17.
20 Repeat the procedure given in paragraphs 17 and 18 until the fluid level remains constant.
21 Take the vehicle for a short drive, and check the fluid level as described in Section 5.

29 Clutch friction plate - check for wear

1 Provision is made for assessing the wear of the clutch friction plate linings without removing the clutch or transmission assembly from the vehicle.
2 The check is carried out from below the clutch slave cylinder, and requires the use of a special checking gauge, which can easily be made from a strip of scrap metal or tin-plate, to the dimensions shown **(see illustration)**.

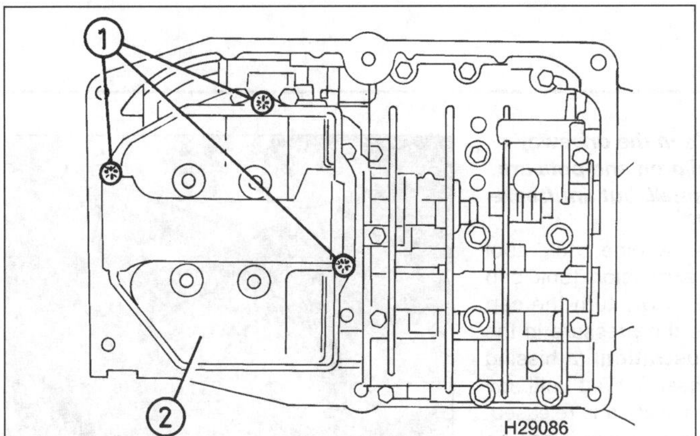

28.10 Unscrew the securing screws (1) and withdraw the filter screen (2)

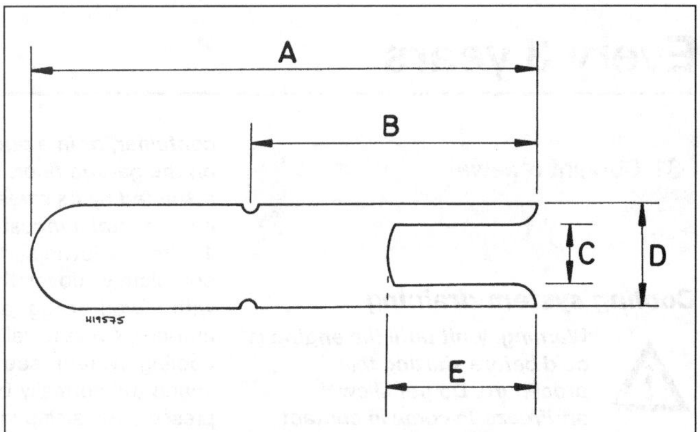

29.2 Clutch friction plate wear checking gauge
A 55.0 mm B 26.0 mm C 7.0 mm D 14.0 mm E 12.0 mm

3 After fabricating the checking tool, proceed as follows.

4 Apply the parking brake, then jack up the front of the vehicle, and support securely on axle stands (see *"Jacking and vehicle support"*).

5 Insert the forked end of the gauge into the machined slot between the slave cylinder flange and the bellhousing.

6 Push the gauge into the slot until the forked end contacts the slave cylinder pushrod.

7 If the two notches on the checking gauge are not visible, the friction plate linings are in a satisfactory condition. If the two notches are visible, the driven plate linings have reached their wear limit, and the clutch assembly must be renewed **(see illustrations)**.

8 On completion of the check, remove the gauge and lower the vehicle to the ground.

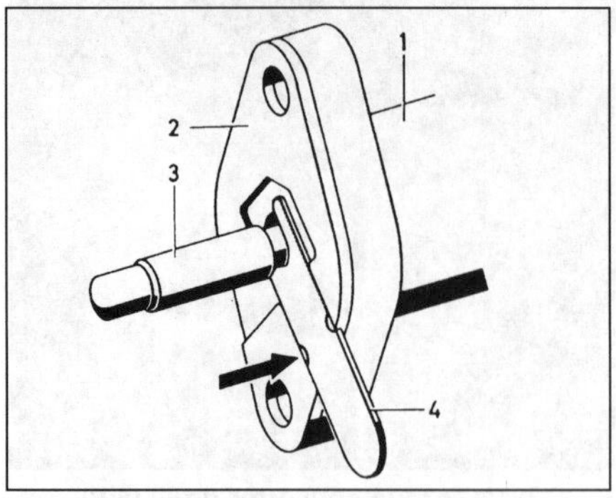

29.7a Checking clutch friction plate wear - linings in satisfactory condition

1 Slave cylinder
2 Slave cylinder shim
3 Pushrod
4 Checking gauge
Arrow indicates notches on gauge not visible

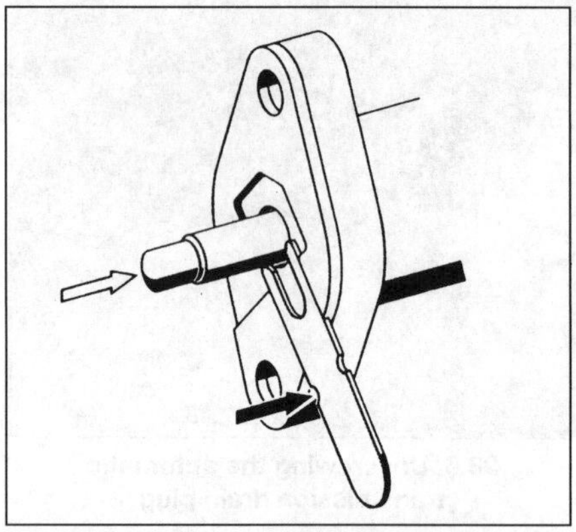

29.7b Checking clutch friction plate wear - linings worn

Light arrow — *Pushrod movement as wear takes place*
Dark arrow — *Notches on gauge visible*

Every 12 months

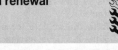

30 Brake fluid renewal

Warning: Brake hydraulic fluid can harm your eyes and damage painted surfaces, so use extreme caution when handling and pouring it. Do not use fluid that has been standing open for some time, as it absorbs moisture from the air. Excess moisture can cause a dangerous loss of braking effectiveness.

1 The brake fluid renewal procedure is very similar to the hydraulic system bleeding procedure, described at the beginning of Chapter 9, except that the brake fluid reservoir should be emptied by siphoning, using a clean poultry baster or similar before starting. Allowance must also be made for the old fluid to be expelled, when bleeding a section of the hydraulic circuit.

2 Working as described in Chapter 9, open the first bleed screw in the sequence, and pump the brake pedal gently until nearly all the old fluid has been emptied from the master cylinder reservoir. Note that the procedure is different for vehicles equipped with ABS/ASR.

3 Top-up to the "MAX" level with new fluid, and continue pumping until only the new fluid remains in the reservoir, and new fluid can be seen emerging from the bleed screw. Tighten the screw, and top the reservoir level up to the "MAX" level line.

> **HAYNES HiNT** ***Old hydraulic fluid is invariably much darker in colour than the new, making it easy to distinguish the two.***

4 Work through all the remaining bleed screws in the sequence until new fluid can be seen at all of them. Be careful to keep the master cylinder reservoir topped-up to above the "MIN" level at all times, or air may enter the system and greatly increase the length of the task.

5 When the operation is complete, check that all bleed screws are securely tightened, and that their dust caps are refitted. Wash off all traces of spilt fluid, and recheck the master cylinder reservoir fluid level.

6 Check the operation of the brakes before taking the car on the road.

Every 3 years

31 Coolant renewal

Cooling system draining

Warning: Wait until the engine is cold before starting this procedure. Do not allow antifreeze to come in contact with your skin, or with the painted surfaces of the vehicle. Rinse off spills immediately with plenty of water. Never leave antifreeze lying around in an open container, or in a puddle in the driveway or on the garage floor. Children and pets are attracted by its sweet smell, but antifreeze can be fatal if ingested.

1 After allowing the engine to cool completely, cover the expansion tank cap with a wad of rag, and slowly turn the cap anti-clockwise to relieve the pressure in the cooling system **(see illustration)** (a hissing sound will normally be heard). Wait until any pressure remaining in the system is released, then continue to turn the cap until it can be removed.

2 Position a suitable container beneath the radiator, then fit a length of rubber hose to the

31.1 Relieve the pressure in the cooling system by removing the expansion tank cap

31.2 Radiator drain nozzle (arrowed)

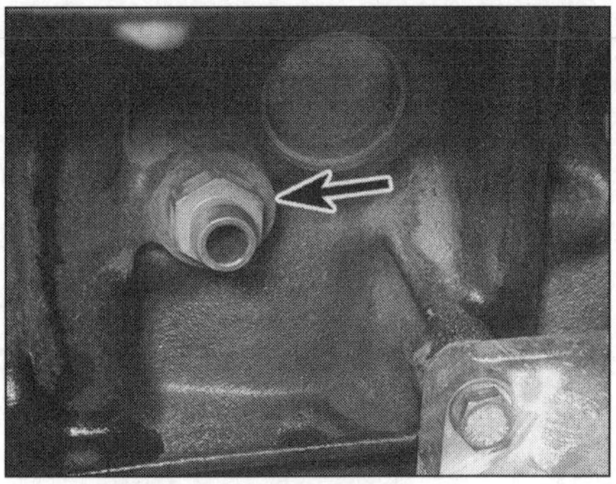

31.3 Engine block drain nozzle (arrowed)

drain nozzle **(see illustration)**. Open the drain plug (underneath the nozzle) by turning it with a large screwdriver and allow the coolant to drain through the hose, into the container.

3 Re-position the container so that it lies beneath the engine block drain plug, which is located on the right hand side of the cylinder block **(see illustration)**. (Certain engines are fitted with a drain plug with an integral nozzle, to which a length of rubber hose can be connected). Open the drain plug by turning it with an open ended spanner and allow the coolant to drain into the container.

4 Once all the coolant has drained, remove the drain hoses and close the cylinder block and radiator drain plugs.

Cooling system flushing

5 If coolant renewal has been neglected, or if the antifreeze mixture has become diluted, then in time, the cooling system may gradually lose efficiency, as the coolant passages become restricted due to rust, scale deposits, and other sediment. The cooling system efficiency can be restored by flushing the system clean.

6 The radiator should be flushed independently of the engine, to avoid unnecessary contamination.

Radiator flushing

7 To flush the radiator disconnect the top and bottom hoses and any other relevant hoses from the radiator, with reference to Chapter 3.

8 Insert a garden hose into the radiator top inlet. Direct a flow of clean water through the radiator, and continue flushing until clean water emerges from the radiator bottom outlet.

9 If after a reasonable period, the water still does not run clear, the radiator can be flushed with a good proprietary cooling system cleaning agent. It is important that their manufacturer's instructions are followed carefully. If the contamination is particularly bad, insert the hose in the radiator bottom outlet, and reverse-flush the radiator.

Engine flushing

10 To flush the engine, remove the thermostat as described in Chapter 3, then temporarily refit the thermostat cover. Adjust the heater control to the maximum setting.

11 With the top and bottom hoses disconnected from the radiator, insert a garden hose into the radiator top hose. Direct a clean flow of water through the engine, and continue flushing until clean water emerges from the radiator bottom hose.

12 On completion of flushing, refit the thermostat and reconnect the hoses with reference to Chapter 3.

Cooling system refilling

13 Before attempting to fill the cooling system, make sure that all hoses and clips are in good condition, and that the clips are tight. Note that an antifreeze mixture must be used all year round, to prevent corrosion of the engine components (see following sub-Section).

14 Remove the expansion tank filler cap, and fill the system by slowly pouring the coolant into the expansion tank to prevent airlocks from forming.

15 If the coolant is being renewed, begin by pouring in a couple of litres of water, followed by the correct quantity of antifreeze, then top-up with more water **(see illustrations)**.

16 Once the level in the expansion tank starts to rise, squeeze the radiator top and bottom hoses to help expel any trapped air in the system. Once all the air is expelled, top-up the coolant level to the "MAX" mark. Refit the expansion tank cap securely.

17 Where applicable, unscrew the plug from the coolant sensor housing, on the upper surface of the cylinder head. As soon as coolant starts to flow out, refit the plug and tighten it. If none flows out, pour coolant into the hole vacated by the plug until it begins to flow back out. Refit the plug and tighten it securely. This removes any airlocks in the cooling system that might inhibit the operation of the coolant sensor(s).

18 Start the engine and run it until the thermostat opens - the radiator top hose will begin to heat up as coolant flows through it of the radiator when this happens.

19 Check for leaks, particularly around disturbed components. Check the coolant level in the expansion tank, and top-up if necessary. Note that the system must be cold before an accurate level is indicated in the expansion tank. If the expansion tank cap is removed while the engine is still warm, cover the cap with a thick cloth, and unscrew the cap slowly to gradually relieve the system pressure (a hissing sound will normally be heard). Wait until any pressure remaining in the system is released, then continue to turn the cap until it can be removed.

Antifreeze mixture

20 The antifreeze should always be renewed at the specified intervals. This is necessary not only to maintain the antifreeze properties, but also to prevent corrosion which would otherwise occur as the corrosion inhibitors become progressively less effective.

21 Always use an ethylene-glycol based antifreeze which is suitable for use in mixed-metal cooling systems. The quantity of antifreeze and levels of protection are indicated in the *Specifications*.

22 Before adding antifreeze, the cooling system should be completely drained, preferably flushed, and all hoses checked for condition and security.

23 After filling with antifreeze, a label should be attached to the expansion tank, stating the type and concentration of antifreeze used, and the date installed. Any subsequent topping-up should be made with the same type and concentration of antifreeze.

24 Do not use engine antifreeze in the windscreen/tailgate washer system, as it will cause damage to the vehicle paintwork. A screenwash additive should be added to the washer system in the quantities stated on the bottle.

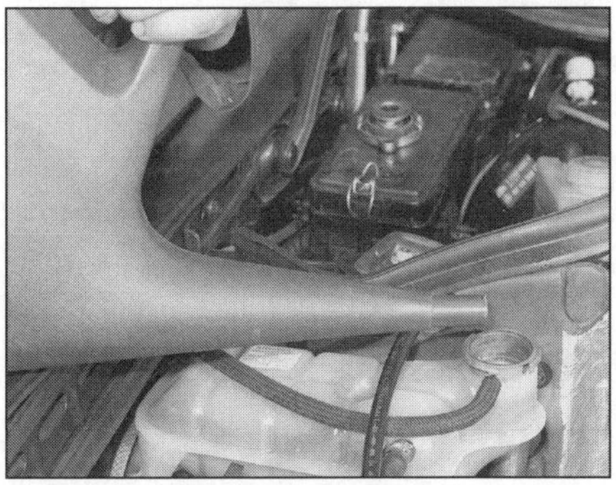

31.15a If the coolant is being renewed, begin by pouring in a couple of litres of water . . .

31.15b . . . followed by the correct quantity of antifreeze, then top-up with more water

1B

Notes

Chapter 2 Part A
Four-cylinder petrol engine in-car repair procedures

Contents

Auxiliary shaft - removal, inspection and refitting ... 9
Camshaft cover - removal and refitting ... 4
Compression test - description and interpretation ... 2
Crankshaft oil seals - renewal ... 15
Crankshaft pulley/vibration damper and hub - removal and refitting ... 5
Crankshaft spigot bearing - renewal ... 16
Cylinder head - removal, inspection and refitting ... 11
Engine assembly and valve timing marks - general information and usage ... 3
Engine oil and filter renewal ... See Chapter 1A
Engine oil level check ... See *"Weekly checks"*
Engine/transmission mountings - inspection and renewal ... 17
Flywheel/driveplate - removal, inspection and refitting ... 14
General information ... 1
Oil pump - removal, inspection and refitting ... 13
Rocker gear, valve lifters and camshaft - general information, removal, inspection and refitting ... 10
Sump - removal and refitting ... 12
Timing chain - inspection and renewal ... 7
Timing chain cover - removal and refitting ... 6
Timing chain tensioner, sprockets and guides - removal, inspection and refitting ... 8
Valve clearance adjustment ... See Chapter 1A

Degrees of difficulty

Easy, suitable for novice with little experience	**Fairly easy,** suitable for beginner with some experience	**Fairly difficult,** suitable for competent DIY mechanic	**Difficult,** suitable for experienced DIY mechanic	**Very difficult,** suitable for expert DIY or professional

Specifications

General

Engine code:	
1.8 litre engine	102.910
2.0 litre carburettor engine	102.924
2.0 litre fuel injection engine	102.962
2.3 litre engine	102.985
Displacement:	
1.8 litre engine	1797 cc
2.0 litre engines	1996 cc
2.3 litre engine	2298 cc
Bore:	
1.8 and 2.0 litre engines	89.0 mm
2.3 litre engine	95.5 mm
Stroke:	
1.8 litre engines	72.2 mm
2.0 litre and 2.3 litre engines	80.2 mm
Direction of engine rotation	Clockwise (viewed from front of vehicle)
No 1 cylinder location	Timing chain end
Firing order	1-3-4-2
Compression pressures:	
Minimum compression pressure (all engines)	8.5 bars (approx)
Maximum difference between cylinders	1.5 bars
Compression ratio:	
1.8 litre engine	9.0:1
2.0 litre engines	9.1:1
2.3 litre engine	9.0:1

Camshaft

Endfloat:	
New engine	0.070 to 0.150 mm
Wear limit	0.180 mm
Camshaft bearing running clearance:	
New engine	0.050 to 0.091 mm
Wear limit	0.110 mm

Cylinder head bolts

Maximum length	122.0 mm

Lubrication system

Minimum oil pressure:	
At idle speed	0.3 bar
At 3000 rpm	3.0 bars

Flywheel/driveplate bolts

Minimum diameter	8.0 mm
Maximum length	22.5 mm

Torque wrench settings

Torque wrench settings	Nm	lbf ft
Camshaft cover bolts	15	11
Crankshaft pulley/vibration damper-to-hub bolts	25	18
Crankshaft pulley/vibration damper hub bolt	300	221
Timing chain cover bolts	25	18
Auxiliary drivebelt tensioner mounting bolt (M12)	80	59
Auxiliary drivebelt tensioner pulley bolt	28	21
Auxiliary drivebelt tensioner damper strut bolts	10	7
Camshaft sprocket bolt	80	59
Timing chain tensioner cover nut	70	52
Timing chain tensioner body-to-cylinder block	15	11
Auxiliary shaft clamp bolt	5	4
Camshaft bearing cap bolts	21	15
Cylinder head bolts:		
M12 bolts:		
Stage 1	55	41
Stage 2	Angle-tighten through a further 90°	
Stage 3	Angle-tighten through a further 90°	
M8 bolts	25	18
Engine-to-transmission bolts:		
Manual transmission:		
M10 x 40 mm bolts	55	41
M10 x 90 mm bolts	45	33
Automatic transmission:		
M10 bolts	55	41
M12 bolts	65	48
Sump bolts:		
M6 bolts	10	7
M8 bolts	25	18
Oil drain plug	25	18
Oil pressure relief valve plug	30	22
Oil pump cover bolts	10	7
Flywheel/driveplate bolts:		
Stage 1:		
Standard flywheel	30	22
"Dual-mass" flywheel	40	30
Stage 2	Angle-tighten through a further 90 to 100°	
Crankshaft rear oil seal housing bolts	10	7
Engine mounting-to-engine mounting bracket bolts	25	18
Left- and right-hand engine mounting-to-crossmember bolts	40	30
Left- and right-hand engine mounting bracket bolts	25	18
Rear engine/transmission mounting-to-transmission nut	65	48
Rear engine/transmission mounting-to-crossmember bolts	25	18
Rear engine/transmission mounting crossmember-to-underbody bolts	35	26
Rear engine/transmission mounting adjuster bolt	30	22
Engine mounting damper securing bolts	10	7
Engine movement stop securing bolts	25	18
Engine movement stop adjuster bolt	130	96
Big-end bearing cap nuts:		
Stage 1	30	22
Stage 2	Angle-tighten through a further 90 to 100°	
Main bearing cap bolts:		
M12 bolts	90	66
M11 bolts:		
Stage 1	55	41
Stage 2	Angle-tighten through a further 90 to 100°	
Cylinder block coolant drain plug	30	22

1 General information

How to use this Chapter

This Part of Chapter 2 describes the repair procedures that can reasonably be carried out on the engine while it remains in the vehicle. If the engine has been removed from the vehicle and is being dismantled as described in Part D, any preliminary dismantling procedures can be ignored.

Note that, while it may be possible physically to overhaul items such as the piston/connecting rod assemblies while the engine is in the car, such tasks are not usually carried out as separate operations. Usually, several additional procedures are required (not to mention the cleaning of components and oilways); for this reason, all such tasks are classed as major overhaul procedures, and are described in Part D of this Chapter.

Part D describes the removal of the engine/transmission from the car, and the full overhaul procedures that can then be carried out.

Engine description

The engine is of four-cylinder in-line single overhead camshaft design, mounted in-line ("north-south") with the transmission at the front of the vehicle.

The crankshaft is supported in five main bearings within the cast iron cylinder block. Crankshaft endfloat is controlled by thrustwashers fitted on either side of the centre main bearing.

The connecting rods are attached to the crankshaft by horizontally-split big-end bearings, and to the pistons by interference-fit gudgeon pins. The alloy pistons are fitted with three piston rings: two compression and one oil control.

The camshaft is driven from the crankshaft sprocket by a single- or double-row chain (depending on engine type). The chain also drives the auxiliary shaft, which is used to drive the distributor, and also the fuel pump on carburettor models.

The camshaft is supported in five bearings in the aluminium alloy cylinder head, and actuates the valves via rocker arms. On early models, the valve clearances are adjusted manually, using adjuster screws on the rocker arms. On later models, the valves are operated via hydraulic valve lifters, mounted in the rocker arms, and no regular manual adjustment is required.

The gear-type oil pump is driven directly from the crankshaft, and is located in the timing chain cover.

Repair operations possible with the engine in the vehicle

The following operations can be carried out without having to remove the engine from the vehicle:

a) Removal and refitting of the cylinder head.
b) Removal and refitting of the timing chain and sprockets.
c) Removal and refitting of the camshaft.
d) Removal and refitting of the sump.
e) Removal and refitting of the big-end bearings, connecting rods, and pistons.*
f) Removal and refitting of the oil pump.
g) Renewal of the engine/transmission mountings.
h) Removal and refitting of the flywheel/driveplate.

** Although it is possible to remove these components with the engine in place, for reasons of access and cleanliness it is recommended that the engine is removed.*

2 Compression test - description and interpretation

1 When engine performance is down, or if misfiring occurs which cannot be attributed to the ignition or fuel systems, a compression test can provide diagnostic clues as to the engine's condition. If the test is performed regularly, it can give warning of trouble before any other symptoms become apparent.

2 The engine must be fully warmed-up to normal operating temperature, the battery must be fully charged, and all the spark plugs must be removed (Chapter 1A). The aid of an assistant will also be required.

3 Disable the ignition system by disconnecting the distributor wiring plug. On engines with fuel injection, remove the fuel pump relay, to ensure that no fuel is injected as the engine is cranked (on carburettor engines, the fuel cut-off solenoid wiring plug can be disconnected to prevent fuel build-up).

4 Fit a compression tester to the No 1 cylinder spark plug hole - the type of tester which screws into the plug thread is to be preferred.

5 Have the assistant hold the throttle wide open, and crank the engine on the starter motor. After one or two revolutions, the compression pressure should build up to a maximum figure, and then stabilise. Record the highest reading obtained.

6 Repeat the test on the remaining cylinders, recording the pressure in each **(see illustration)**.

7 All cylinders should produce very similar pressures; a difference of more than 1.5 bars between any two cylinders indicates a fault. Note that the compression should build up quickly in a healthy engine; low compression on the first stroke, followed by gradually-increasing pressure on successive strokes, indicates worn piston rings. A low compression reading on the first stroke, which does not build up during successive strokes, indicates leaking valves or a blown head gasket (a cracked head could also be the cause). Deposits on the undersides of the valve heads can also cause low compression.

8 Mercedes recommended values for compression pressures are given in the Specifications.

9 If the pressure in any cylinder is low, carry out the following test to isolate the cause. Introduce a teaspoonful of clean oil into that cylinder through its spark plug hole, and repeat the test.

10 If the addition of oil temporarily improves the compression pressure, this indicates that bore or piston wear is responsible for the pressure loss. No improvement suggests that leaking or burnt valves, or a blown head gasket, may be to blame.

11 A low reading from two adjacent cylinders is almost certainly due to the head gasket having blown between them; the presence of coolant in the engine oil will confirm this.

12 If one cylinder is about 20 percent lower than the others and the engine has a slightly rough idle, a worn camshaft lobe could be the cause.

13 If the compression reading is unusually high, the combustion chambers are probably coated with carbon deposits. If this is the case, the cylinder head should be removed and decarbonised.

14 On completion of the test, refit the spark plugs (Chapter 1A), reconnect the distributor wiring plug, and refit the fuel pump relay, where applicable.

3 Engine assembly and valve timing marks - general information and usage

1 Top Dead Centre (TDC) is the highest point in the cylinder that each piston reaches as it travels up and down when the crankshaft turns. Each piston reaches TDC at the end of the compression stroke and again at the end of the exhaust stroke, but TDC generally refers to piston position on the compression stroke. No 1 piston is at the timing chain end of the engine.

2 Positioning No 1 piston at TDC is an essential part of many procedures, such as timing chain removal and camshaft removal.

3 Note the position of the terminal for No 1 cylinder HT lead on the distributor cap. If the terminal is not marked, follow the HT lead

2.6 Compression tester fitted to spark plug hole

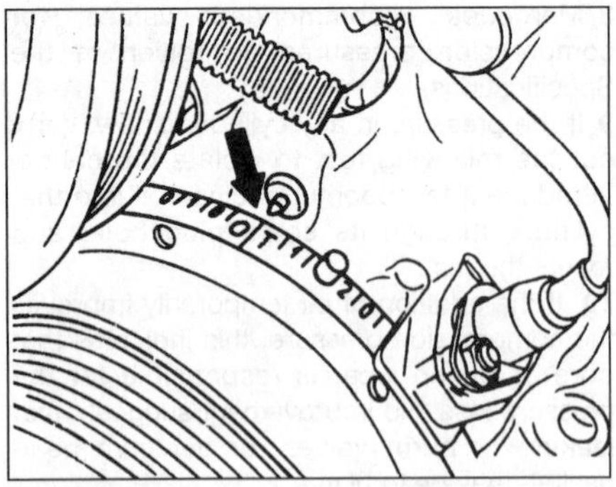

3.5a TDC ("O/T") mark on crankshaft pulley/vibration damper aligned with pointer

from the No 1 cylinder spark plug to the cap (No 1 cylinder is at the timing chain end of the engine).

4 Remove the camshaft cover as described in Section 4.

5 Using a suitable socket on the crankshaft pulley/vibration damper hub bolt (on some models, it may be necessary to remove the cooling fan shroud for access, as described in Chapter 3), turn the crankshaft clockwise until the following marks are aligned **(see illustrations)**.

a) The TDC ("O/T") mark on the crankshaft pulley/vibration damper is aligned with the pointer on the timing chain cover.

b) The TDC groove in the flange at the front of the camshaft is aligned with the upper face of the cylinder head.

c) The distributor rotor arm is aligned with the notch in the rim of the distributor body (it may be necessary to lift the distributor dust shield to view the notch).

3.5b Camshaft TDC groove (arrowed) aligned with upper face of cylinder head

6 When the marks are aligned as described in paragraph 5, No 1 piston is at TDC on the firing stroke. If the timing chain is to be removed, do not turn the camshaft or the crankshaft until the chain has been refitted.

4 Camshaft cover - removal and refitting

Removal

Note: *The camshaft cover should be removed complete with the ignition HT leads and the distributor cap. Do not attempt to remove the HT lead covers from the camshaft cover. A new gasket and/or seal(s) may be required on refitting.*

1 Disconnect the battery negative lead.

2 Remove the air cleaner as described in Chapter 4.

3 Where applicable, disconnect the breather hose(s) from the camshaft cover. Similarly, where applicable, release any hoses and/or wiring from the clips on the camshaft cover, noting their locations, and move them to one side **(see illustrations)**.

4 Check to ensure that the spark plug HT leads are numbered, and if not mark the leads to ensure correct refitting (No 1 cylinder is at the timing chain end of the engine). Disconnect the HT leads from the spark plugs.

5 Unclip the HT lead covers from the camshaft cover, and move the HT leads, complete with the covers, clear of the top of the engine **(see illustration)**. Lay the HT leads and covers on the distributor side of the engine.

6 On models with automatic transmission, unbolt the transmission dipstick tube from the bracket on the rear camshaft cover securing bolt, then unscrew the securing bolts, and lift the camshaft cover from the cylinder head **(see illustrations)**. If the cover is stuck, try rocking by hand, and if necessary tap carefully with a soft-faced mallet - take care, as the cover is easily damaged.

7 Recover the gasket and, where applicable, recover the sealing disk(s), complete with seals, from the cut-out(s) in the front and/or rear of the cover.

4.3a Disconnect the breather hose . . .

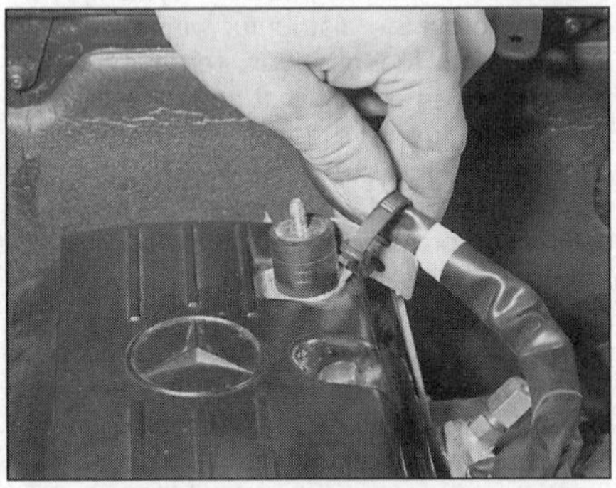

4.3b . . . and release the wiring from the clips on the camshaft cover

4.5 Unclip the HT lead covers from the camshaft cover

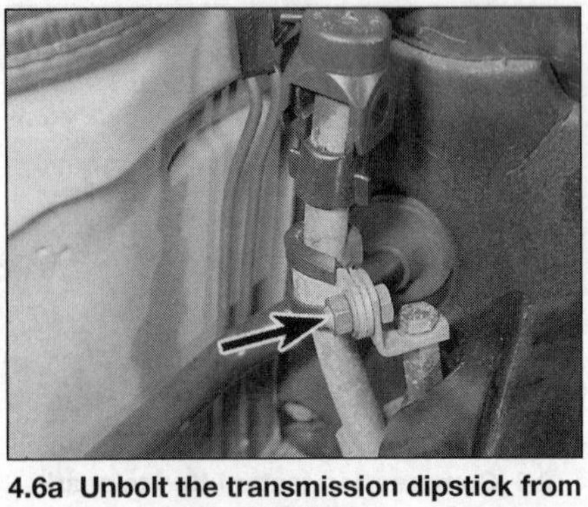

4.6a Unbolt the transmission dipstick from the bracket . . .

4.6b . . . then unscrew the securing bolts . . .

4.6c . . . and lift off the camshaft cover

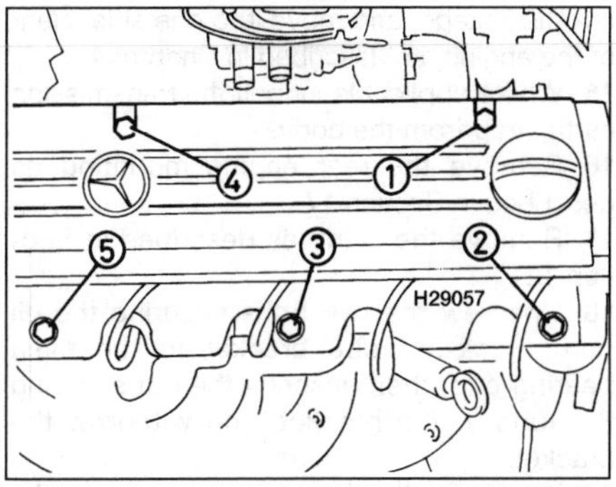

4.11 Camshaft cover bolt tightening sequence

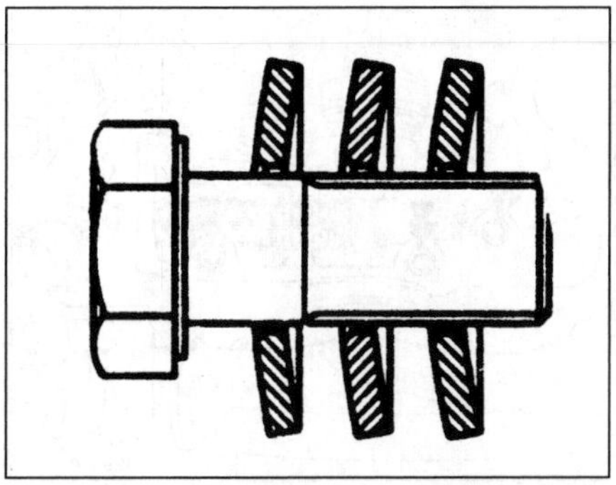

5.14 The convex side of the crankshaft pulley/vibration damper hub washers must face the bolt head

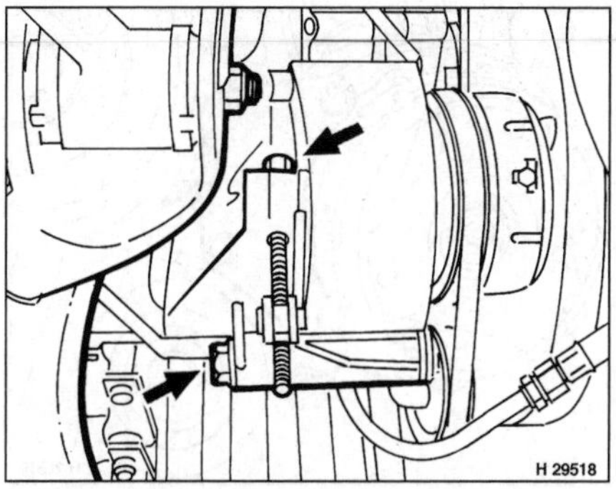

6.8 Air conditioning compressor drivebelt tensioner strut securing bolts (arrowed)

Refitting

8 Examine the condition of the gasket and, where applicable, the seals on the sealing disk(s), and renew if necessary. The seal(s) in the sealing disk(s) must be correctly located, and the seam on the seal should run straight (ie: no curves) around the full circumference of the disk.

9 Locate the gasket in the grooves in the camshaft cover, starting at the front and rear.

10 Lay the cover in position on the cylinder head, ensuring that the gasket locates correctly, then refit the securing bolts.

11 Tighten the bolts progressively, in the order shown, to the specified torque **(see illustration)**.

12 Refit the HT leads and covers to the camshaft cover, and reconnect the HT leads, ensuring that the leads are reconnected to the correct spark plugs.

13 Where applicable, reconnect the breather hose(s), and clip any wiring and hoses into position.

14 Refit the air cleaner.

15 Reconnect the battery negative lead.

16 Start the engine, and check for oil leaks around the edge of the cover.

5 Crankshaft pulley/vibration damper and hub - removal and refitting

Crankshaft pulley/vibration damper

Removal

1 To improve access, remove the cooling fan blades and cowl assembly as described in Chapter 3.

2 Remove the auxiliary drivebelt as described in Chapter 1A.

3 Unscrew the securing bolts, and remove the pulley/vibration damper from the hub. If necessary, counterhold the pulley/vibration damper using a socket on the hub securing bolt.

Refitting

4 Refitting is a reversal of removal, but refit the auxiliary drivebelt as described in Chapter 1A, and refit the cooling fan blades and cowl as described in Chapter 3.

Hub

Removal

Warning: The hub securing bolt is very tight. A tool will be required to counterhold the hub as the bolt is unscrewed. Do not attempt the job using inferior or poorly-improvised tools, as injury or damage may result.

Note: *A puller may be required to remove the hub. A torque wrench capable of providing 300 Nm (221 lbf ft) of torque will be required on refitting.*

5 Remove the crankshaft pulley/vibration damper as described previously in this Section.

6 Make up a tool to hold the hub. A suitable tool can be fabricated using two lengths of steel bar, joined by a large pivot bolt. Bolt the holding tool to the hub using the pulley/vibration damper bolts.

7 Using a socket and a long swing-bar, loosen the hub bolt. Note that the bolt is very tight.

8 Unscrew the hub bolt, and remove the spring washers.

9 Where applicable, unscrew the lower mounting bolt from the auxiliary belt tensioner damper strut, and pivot the strut away from the hub.

10 Using a suitable puller, pull the hub from the front of the crankshaft.

11 Where applicable, recover the Woodruff key from the front of the crankshaft.

Refitting

12 Where applicable, refit the Woodruff key to the groove in the crankshaft.

13 Align the groove in the hub with the key, and slide the hub onto the end of the crankshaft.

14 Oil the spring washers, then refit them with the convex side of each washer facing the hub bolt head **(see illustration)**.

15 Oil the bolt threads, then refit the hub securing bolt.

16 Bolt the holding tool to the hub, as during removal, then tighten the hub securing bolt to the specified torque. Take care to avoid injury and/or damage.

17 Refit the crankshaft pulley/vibration damper as described previously in this Section.

6 Timing chain cover - removal and refitting

Removal

Note: *New gaskets or new sealant (as applicable) will be required on refitting. A new oil supply tube O-ring may be required, and it is advisable to fit a new crankshaft front oil seal.*

1 Drain the engine oil and the cooling system as described in Chapter 1A.

2 Remove the air cleaner assembly as described in Chapter 4.

3 Remove the radiator as described in Chapter 3.

4 Where applicable, remove the self-levelling suspension system hydraulic pump, as described in Chapter 10. Note that the pump can be moved to one side, leaving the hydraulic lines connected.

5 Remove the camshaft cover as described in Section 4.

6 Remove the coolant pump as described in Chapter 3.

7 Remove the auxiliary drivebelt(s) as described in Chapter 1A.

8 On models with air conditioning, unscrew the securing bolts, and remove the air conditioning compressor drivebelt tensioner strut **(see illustration)**.

9 On models fitted with air conditioning, unbolt the compressor mounting bracket from the engine, then unscrew the securing bolts, and move the compressor to one side, leaving

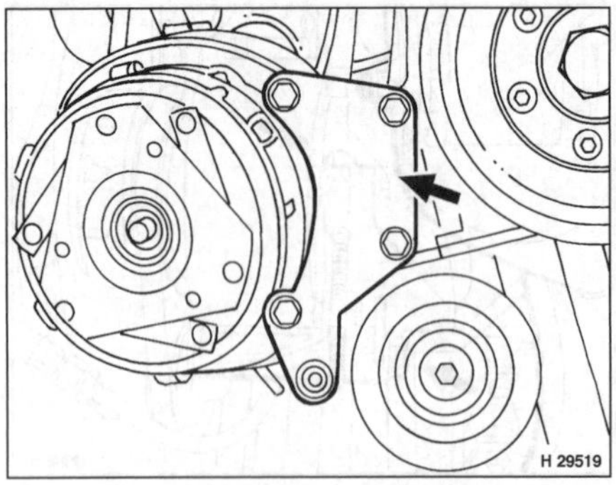

6.9 Unbolt the air conditioning compressor mounting bracket (arrowed)

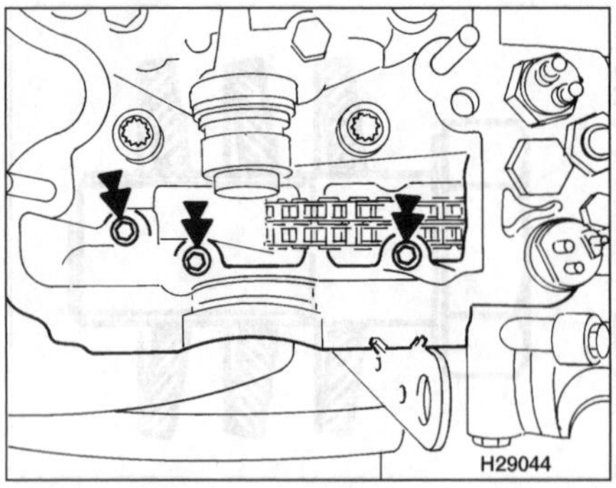

6.19 Cylinder head-to-timing chain cover bolts (arrowed)

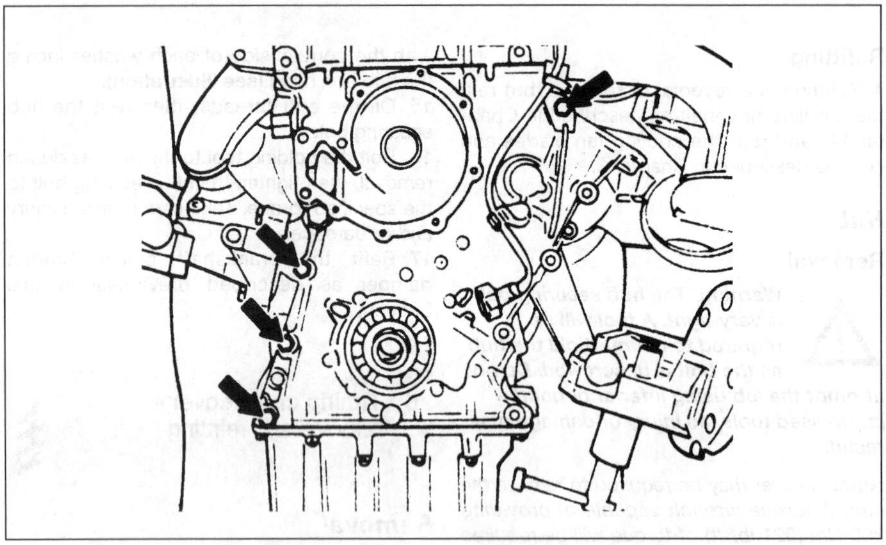

6.20 Remove the remaining bolts (arrowed) securing the timing chain cover

the refrigerant lines connected **(see illustration)**. Ensure that the compressor is adequately supported, and take care not to strain the refrigerant lines.

Warning: Do not attempt to disconnect the air conditioning refrigerent lines - refer to Chapter 3 for precautions to be observed when working on models fitted with air conditioning.

10 Turn the engine (clockwise) to bring No 1 piston to TDC, ensuring that crankshaft and camshaft timing marks are correctly aligned as described in Section 3.

11 Remove the crankshaft pulley/ vibration damper and hub, as described in Section 5.

12 Remove the distributor as described in Chapter 5.

13 Where applicable, remove the TDC sensor as described in Chapter 4.

14 Disconnect the throttle cable from the throttle linkage, and move it to one side, clear of the engine, as described in Chapter 4.

15 Where applicable, unbolt the transmission earth strap from the body.

16 Remove the rear engine mounting as described in Section 17.

17 Remove the sump as described in Section 12.

18 Unscrew the two bolts securing the oil pump pick-up tube bracket to the main bearing cap, then unscrew the nut securing the tube to the bracket, and withdraw the bracket.

19 Working in the timing chain housing at the top of the cylinder head, unscrew the three bolts securing the cylinder head to the timing chain cover **(see illustration)**.

20 Remove the remaining bolts securing the timing chain cover to the cylinder block (note the locations of the bolts, as they vary in length), then withdraw the cover from its dowels, and remove it complete with the oil pick-up tube **(see illustration)**. Take care not to damage the cylinder head gasket.

21 If not already done, remove the Woodruff key from the front of the crankshaft.

22 Slide the spacing ring from the front of the crankshaft. If the ring is tight, lever it gently.

Refitting

23 Carefully check the condition of the cylinder head gasket at its mating face with the timing chain cover. If there is any sign of damage, the gasket must be renewed as described during the cylinder head removal and refitting procedure in Section 11.

24 Thoroughly clean all traces of old gasket or sealant from the mating faces of the cylinder block and the timing chain cover. Note that the cover may be fitted using gaskets or sealant.

25 The crankshaft front oil seal, located in the timing chain cover, should be renewed as a matter of course. Prise out the old seal using a screwdriver, then place the new seal in position and tap it into the housing in the cover using a hammer, a block of wood, and the old seal **(see illustrations)**.

26 Check the condition of the oil supply tube O-ring at the rear of the oil pump, and renew if

6.25a Prise out the crankshaft oil seal . . .

6.25b . . . fit a new seal . . .

6.25c . . . and tap it squarely into the housing

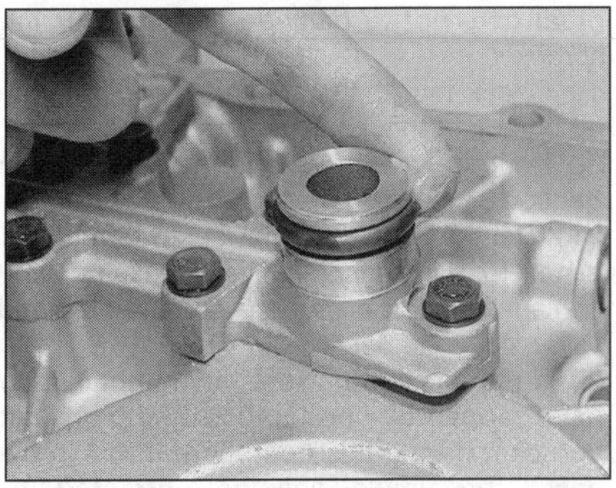

6.26 Lubricate the oil supply tube O-ring with a little grease

necessary. Lubricate the O-ring with a little grease **(see illustration)**.

27 Place the new gasket in position, or apply sealant to the mating faces on the cylinder block **(see illustration)**.

> **HAYNES HiNT** *If gaskets are used, apply a little grease to hold them in position.*

28 Where applicable, cut the gasket at the points shown, to remove the crosspieces. Note that the centre segment at the top of the gasket must be left in position **(see illustration)**.

29 Offer the timing chain cover into position over the locating dowels. If necessary, turn the oil pump inner rotor (located in the timing chain cover), so that the drive lugs align with the cut-outs in the oil pump drive sleeve on the crankshaft.

30 Refit the timing chain cover bolts which are not used to secure any other components,

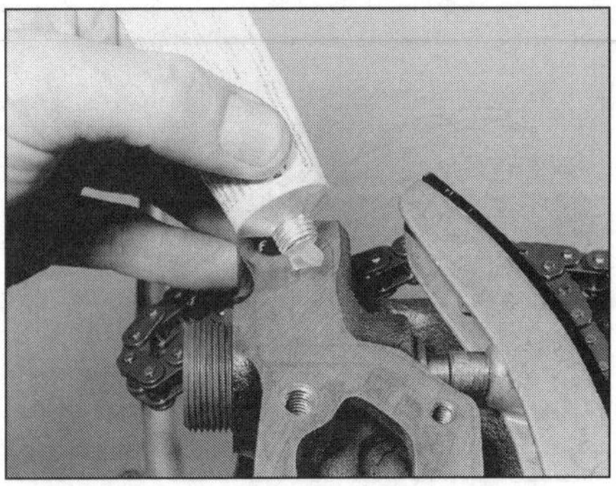

6.27 Applying sealant to the timing chain cover mating face on the cylinder block

and tighten them finger-tight only at this stage. Ensure that the bolts are fitted to their correct locations, as noted before removal.

Note: *When refitting components during the following procedure, do not fully tighten any bolts which are also used to secure the timing chain cover.*

31 Refit the oil pick-up pipe bracket, and tighten the securing nut and bolts.

32 Carefully slide the spacer ring into position on the front of the crankshaft, taking care not to damage the crankshaft oil seal in the cover **(see illustration)**, then refit the Woodruff key.

33 Where applicable, refit the air conditioning compressor and its mounting bracket.

34 Refit the three bolts securing the cylinder head to the timing chain cover, but do not fully tighten them at this stage.

35 Progressively tighten all of the front timing chain cover securing bolts to the specified torque in a diagonal sequence (including those which secure other components) - ensure that all bolts are tightened.

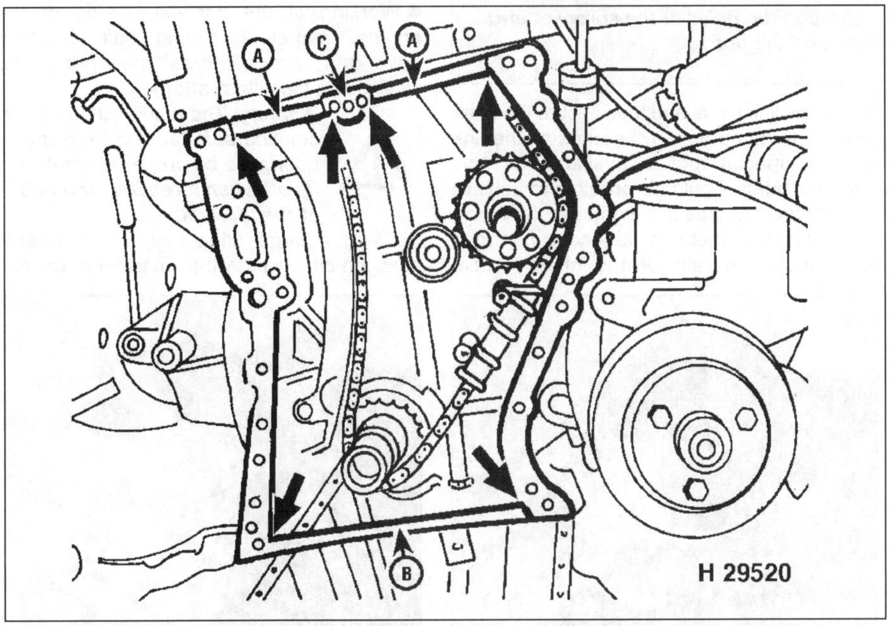

6.28 Cut the gaskets at the points arrowed to remove the crosspieces
A Upper crosspieces B Lower crosspiece C Centre segment

36 Refit the sump as described in Section 12.

37 Refit the rear engine mounting as described in Section 17.

38 Where applicable, refit the bolt securing the transmission earth strap to the body.

39 Reconnect and if necessary adjust the throttle cable as described in Chapter 4.

40 Refit the TDC sensor, and adjust its position if necessary, as described in Chapter 4.

41 Refit the distributor as described in Chapter 5.

42 Refit the crankshaft pulley/vibration damper as described in Section 5.

43 Refit and tension the auxiliary drivebelt(s) as described in Chapter 1A.

44 Refit the coolant pump as described in Chapter 3.

45 Where applicable, refit the self-levelling suspension system hydraulic pump, as described in Chapter 10.

46 Refit the camshaft cover as described in Section 4.

47 Refit the radiator as described in Chapter 3.

48 Refit the air cleaner, and reconnect the battery negative lead.

49 Refill the cooling system, and refill the engine with oil, as described in Chapter 1A.

7 Timing chain - inspection and renewal

Inspection

1 Remove the air cleaner assembly as described in Chapter 4.

2 Remove the camshaft cover as described in Section 4.

3 Using a socket on the crankshaft pulley/vibration damper hub bolt, turn the engine so that the whole length of the chain can be progressively viewed at the camshaft sprocket.

4 The chain should be renewed if the sprocket is worn or if the chain is worn (indicated by excessive lateral play between the links, and excessive noise in operation). It is wise to renew the chain in any case if the

6.32 Slide the spacer ring onto the front of the crankshaft

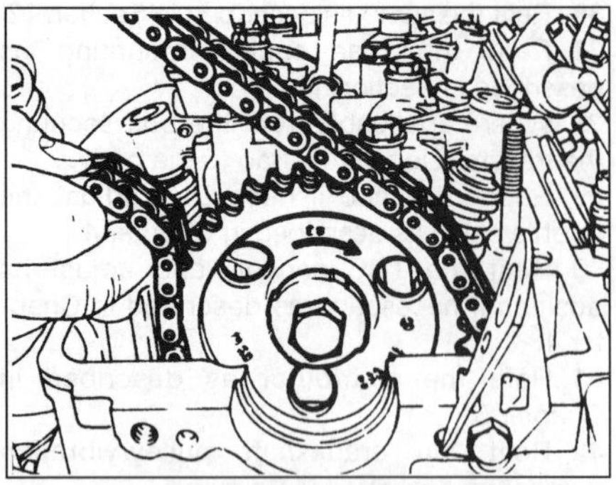

7.14 Keep tension on the new chain whilst feeding the chain round the sprockets and guides

engine is to be dismantled for overhaul. Note that the rollers on a very badly worn chain may be slightly grooved. To avoid future problems, if there is any doubt at all about the condition of the chain, renew it.

Renewal

Note: *Removal of the timing chain using the following procedure entails the use of a portable electric grinder to cut through one of the chain links. Ensure that such a tool is available, as well as a new chain and new connecting link before proceeding.*

5 Disconnect the battery negative lead.

6 If not already done, proceed as described in paragraphs 1 and 2.

7 Remove the spark plugs as described in Chapter 1A.

8 Remove the timing chain tensioner as described in Section 8.

9 Cover the camshaft and the chain opening in the timing cover with clean rags, but keep the rags clear of the camshaft sprocket upper section.

10 Using a grinder, grind off the protruding lugs of one of the chain links at the top of the sprocket - take great care not to damage the sprocket.

11 Pull off the chain link plate, then push the link out towards the rear of the chain.

12 Remove the rags, taking care not to allow any swarf to drop down into the timing chain housing.

13 Using the new link, connect one end of the new timing chain to the tail end of the old chain, in such a way that, as the engine is turned (clockwise), the new chain will be drawn down, around the sprockets and guides, then up the other side. Fit the link from the rear of the sprocket, and ensure that the link is pushed firmly into position - do not fit the link plate to secure the link at this stage.

14 It is now necessary to feed the new chain around the sprockets and guides. During this procedure it is essential to observe the following points **(see illustration)**.

a) *Keep tension on the new chain, ensuring that the links remain engaged with the camshaft sprocket, otherwise the valve timing will be lost.*

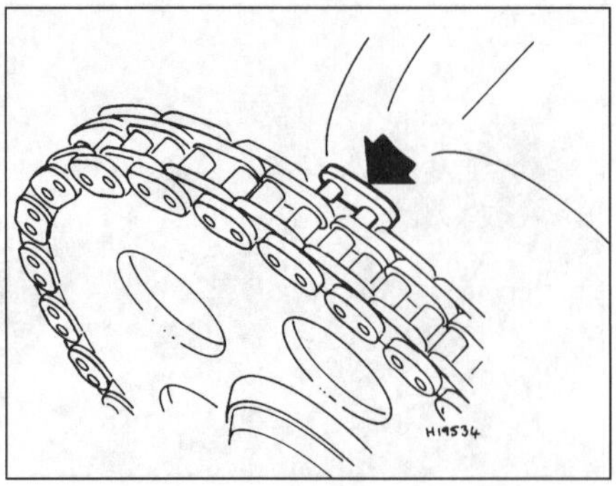

7.17 Refitting a timing chain link (arrowed) from the rear of the chain

b) *Pull up on the old chain to prevent it dropping off the crankshaft sprocket, or jamming in the guides.*

15 Using a suitable socket on the crankshaft pulley/vibration damper hub bolt, slowly turn the crankshaft clockwise, whilst observing the points made in the preceding paragraph.

16 When the end of the new chain appears, remove the link (ensuring that tension is kept on the new chain, and that the chain links remain engaged with the sprockets), and disconnect the new chain from the old chain. Remove the old chain.

17 Engage the new chain with the camshaft sprocket, then join the two ends of the chain with the connecting link, inserted from the rear of the sprocket **(see illustration)**.

> **HAYNES HiNT** ***Temporarily secure the ends of the new chain to the camshaft sprocket using wire or cable-ties passed through the holes in the sprocket and around the chain.***

18 Fit the link plate, and then secure the plate to the link by flattening the ends of the link pins. A special tool is available for this purpose, but it should be possible to achieve a satisfactory result using a hammer, with a block of metal (or a second hammer) to support the rear of the chain - *take great care not to damage the chain or the sprocket.*

19 Check that the chain link is secure, with no burring of the metal, or loose swarf.

20 Refit the chain tensioner as described in Section 8.

21 Turn the engine (clockwise) to bring No 1 piston to TDC, ensuring that crankshaft and camshaft timing marks are correctly aligned as described in Section 3.

22 It is possible that the timing chain may have slipped by one tooth on the camshaft sprocket during this operation. If this is the case, the timing can be corrected by removing the camshaft sprocket (see Section 8), and altering the position of the camshaft and sprocket by one tooth in relation to the chain.

23 Refit the spark plugs.

24 Refit the camshaft cover as described in Section 4, then refit the air cleaner assembly.

25 Reconnect the battery negative lead.

8 Timing chain tensioner, sprockets and guides - removal, inspection and refitting

Tensioner

Removal

Note: *A new tensioner cover nut sealing ring will be required on refitting.*

1 Disconnect the battery negative lead.

2 Remove the auxiliary drivebelt(s) as described in Chapter 1A.

3 To improve access, remove the alternator as described in Chapter 5.

4 Working at the right-hand side of the engine, unscrew the timing chain tensioner cover nut, and withdraw the spring and sealing ring **(see illustrations)**.

> ***Warning: The cover nut is under considerable tension from the spring, so be prepared for it to fly off when it reaches the end of the threads.***

5 Using a large Allen key, or a suitable hexagon bit, unscrew the tensioner body, and

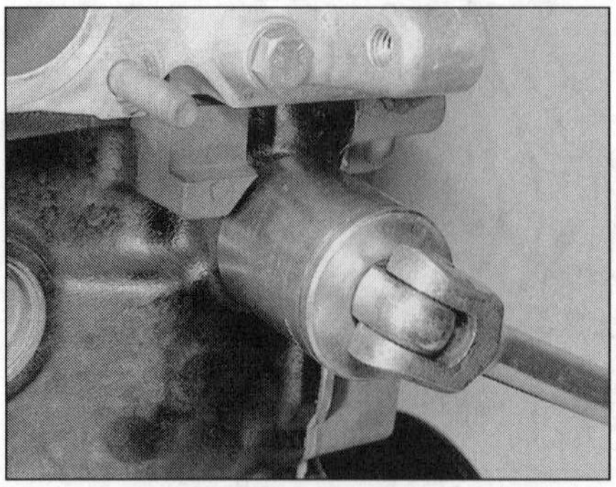

8.4a Unscrew the timing chain tensioner cover nut . . .

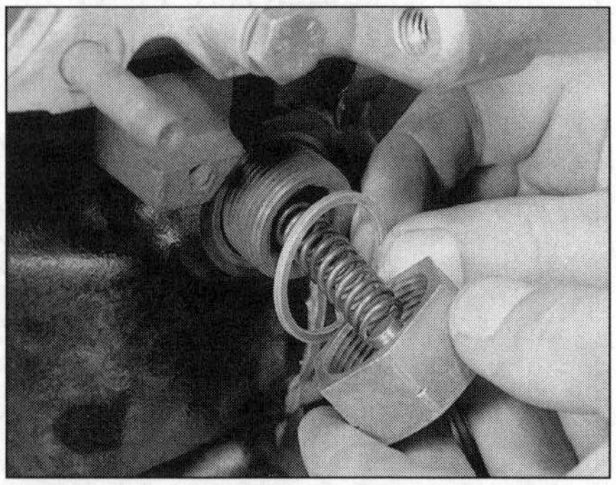

8.4b . . . and withdraw the spring and sealing ring

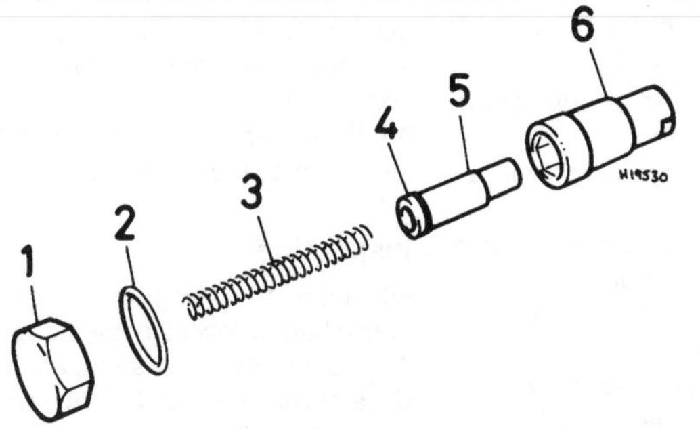

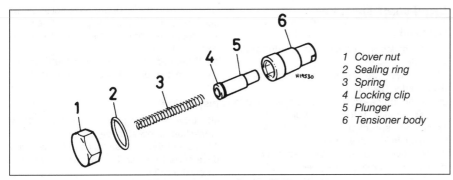

1 Cover nut
2 Sealing ring
3 Spring
4 Locking clip
5 Plunger
6 Tensioner body

8.5 Timing chain tensioner components

remove it from the cylinder block **(see illustration)**.

6 Press the tensioner plunger and the locking clip out of the tensioner body **(see illustration)**.

Inspection

7 Thoroughly clean the tensioner components, and examine the plunger and the tensioner body for signs of damage or wear.

8 Check the condition of the locking clip, and the tensioner spring, and renew if necessary. If in any doubt as to the condition of the spring, renew it.

Refitting

9 Screw the chain tensioner body into the cylinder block, and tighten to the specified torque.

10 Push the plunger, complete with the locking clip, into the tensioner body, until the plunger reaches the detent in the tensioner body **(see illustration)**. Note that the smaller end of the plunger fits against the tensioner rail.

11 Position the spring and a new sealing ring on the cover nut, then push the cover nut into position, and screw it onto the end of the tensioner body. Take care not to cross-thread the cover nut.

12 Tighten the tensioner cover nut to the specified torque.

13 Refit the alternator (Chapter 5).

14 Refit the auxiliary drivebelt(s) as described in Chapter 1A.

15 Reconnect the battery negative lead.

Camshaft sprocket

Removal

16 Remove the air cleaner assembly as described in Chapter 4.

17 Remove the cooling fan blades and shroud, as described in Chapter 3.

18 Where applicable, remove the self-levelling suspension system hydraulic pump, as described in Chapter 10. Note that the pump can be moved to one side, leaving the hydraulic lines connected.

19 Remove the camshaft cover as described in Section 4.

20 Turn the engine to position No 1 piston at TDC, ensuring that crankshaft and camshaft timing marks are correctly aligned as described in Section 3.

21 Remove the timing chain tensioner as described previously in this Section.

22 Using quick-drying paint or a suitable scriber, make reference marks on the camshaft sprocket, and on an adjacent timing chain link, to aid refitting.

23 Counterhold the camshaft using a spanner on the camshaft rear flange flats, then unscrew the camshaft sprocket bolt. Remove the bolt and the washer **(see illustrations)**.

24 Withdraw the sprocket from the camshaft (complete with the hydraulic pump drive sleeve on models with self-levelling suspension), noting which way round it is fitted, and unhook the sprocket from the

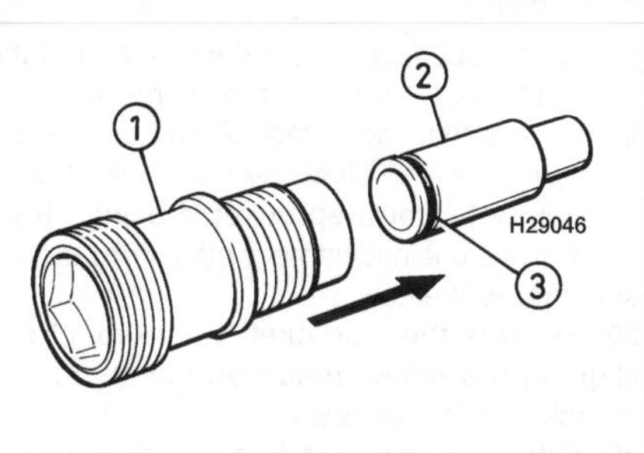

8.6 Press the tensioner plunger out of the body

1 Tensioner bod 2 Plunger 3 Locking clip

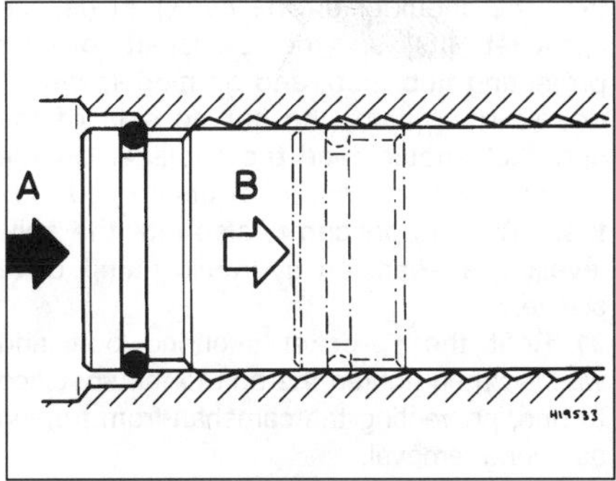

8.10 Tensioner plunger assembly position

A Initial detent when fitting plunger
B Direction of plunger removal and refitting to tensioner body

timing chain **(see illustration)**. Keep tension on the chain, and support the chain in the top of the housing, to prevent it from dropping off the crankshaft or auxiliary shaft sprockets.

25 Recover the Woodruff key and, where applicable, the spacer from the end of the camshaft if they are loose.

Inspection

26 Examine the teeth on the sprocket for wear. Each tooth forms an inverted "V". If worn, the side of each tooth under tension will be slightly concave in shape when compared with the other side of the tooth (ie: the teeth will have a "hooked" appearance). If the teeth appear worn, the sprocket must be renewed.

8.23a Counterhold the camshaft using a spanner on the rear flange flats . . .

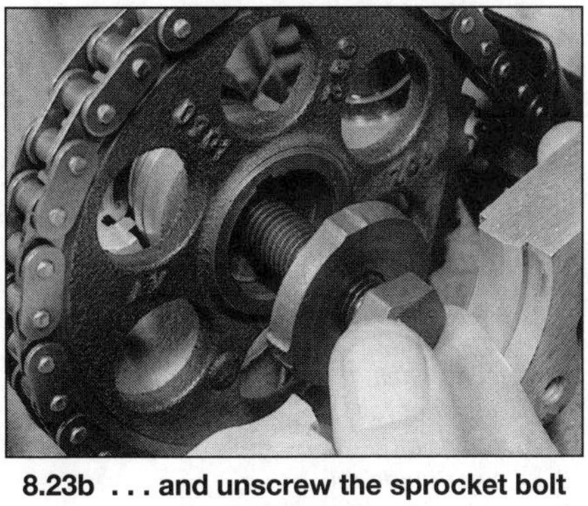

8.23b . . . and unscrew the sprocket bolt and washer

8.24 Remove the sprocket from the camshaft

Refitting

27 Where applicable, refit the spacer and the Woodruff key to the end of the camshaft.

28 Ensure that the camshaft and crankshaft timing marks are still aligned, as described in Section 3. If a new sprocket is being fitted, transfer the chain alignment mark from the old sprocket to the new.

29 Engage the sprocket with the chain, aligning the marks made on the chain and sprocket before removal.

30 Offer the sprocket into position on the camshaft, ensuring that it is fitted the correct way round, as noted before removal. Note that on models with a single-row chain, the greater projecting hub of the sprocket should face the shoulder on the camshaft (ie: the sprocket fits on the camshaft greater projecting hub first), and on models with a double-row chain, the curved side of the sprocket should face the shoulder on the camshaft (ie: the sprocket fits curved side first). Where applicable, also refit the self-levelling suspension hydraulic pump drive sleeve.

31 Refit the sprocket securing bolt and washer, then tighten the bolt to the specified torque, preventing the camshaft from turning as during removal.

32 Refit the timing chain tensioner, as described previously in this Section.

33 Using a suitable socket on the crankshaft pulley/vibration damper hub bolt, turn the engine through two full turns clockwise, and check that the crankshaft and camshaft timing marks are still correctly aligned as described in Section 3. If not, it is likely that the timing chain has slipped by one tooth on the camshaft sprocket, in which case the sprocket must be removed again, and the position of the chain altered.

34 Refit the camshaft cover as described in Section 4.

35 Where applicable, refit the self-levelling suspension hydraulic pump with reference to Chapter 10.

36 Refit the cooling fan blades and shroud as described in Chapter 3.

37 Refit the air cleaner assembly as described in Chapter 4.

8.42 Withdraw the oil pump drive collar from the front of the crankshaft

Crankshaft sprocket

Removal

Note: *A puller may be required to remove the sprocket.*

38 Remove the timing chain cover as described in Section 6.

39 Using quick-drying paint or a suitable scriber, make reference marks on the crankshaft sprocket, and on an adjacent timing chain link, to aid refitting.

40 Remove the camshaft sprocket as described previously in this Section.

41 On later engines, it will be necessary to remove the timing chain tensioner rail to enable the chain to be unhooked from the crankshaft sprocket. Where applicable, remove the tensioner rail as described later in this Section.

42 Withdraw the oil pump drive collar from the front of the crankshaft **(see illustration)**. If the collar is tight, it can be pulled off with the crankshaft sprocket later in the procedure.

43 Unhook the timing chain from the crankshaft sprocket.

44 Withdraw the crankshaft sprocket from the front of the crankshaft. If the sprocket is tight, it may be possible to lever it off using two large screwdrivers positioned either side of the sprocket. Alternatively, remove the sprocket (and the oil pump drive collar, where applicable) using a suitable puller. Note which way round the sprocket is fitted to ensure correct refitting.

45 Where applicable, recover the Woodruff key from the end of the crankshaft if it is loose.

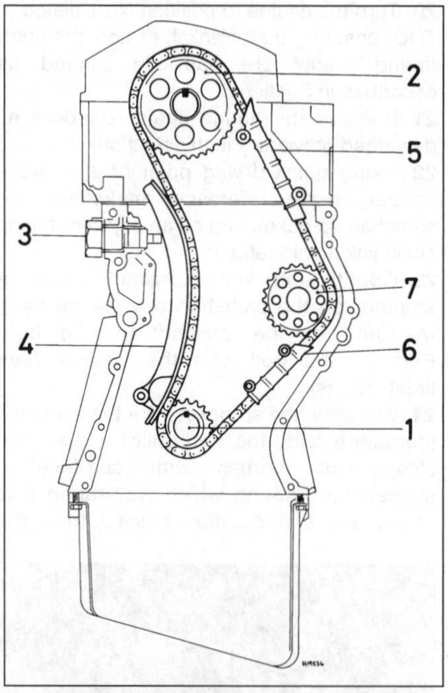

8.58a Timing chain and associated components - models with single-row timing chain

1 *Crankshaft sprocket*
2 *Camshaft sprocket*
3 *Timing chain tensioner*
4 *Tensioner rail*
5 *Upper guide rail*
6 *Lower guide rail*
7 *Auxiliary shaft sprocket*

Inspection

46 Refer to paragraph 26 for details of crankshaft sprocket inspection.

47 Inspect the drive surfaces of the oil pump drive collar for wear. If heavy wear is evident, renew the collar.

Refitting

48 Where applicable, refit the Woodruff key to the end of the crankshaft.

49 If a new sprocket is being fitted, transfer the chain alignment mark from the old sprocket to the new.

50 Tap the sprocket onto the front of the crankshaft, using a metal tube if necessary. Ensure that the sprocket engages with the Woodruff key, or the locating pin in the crankshaft, as applicable.

51 Refit the oil pump drive collar.

52 Engage the timing chain with the crankshaft sprocket, ensuring that the marks made on the sprocket and the chain before removal are aligned.

53 Where applicable, refit the timing chain tensioner rail as described later in this Section.

54 Refit the camshaft sprocket as described previously in this Section.

55 Refit the timing chain cover as described in Section 6.

Auxiliary shaft sprocket

56 The sprocket is integral with the auxiliary shaft. Removal and refitting details for the auxiliary shaft are given in Section 9.

Guide rails

Lower guide rail - models with single-row timing chain

57 Remove the timing chain cover as described in Section 6.

58 Pull the chain guide from the locating lugs **(see illustrations)**.

8.58b Removing the lower guide rail - model with single-row timing chain

8.74a Use a slide hammer, adapter, and a suitable bolt . . .

59 Examine the rail for signs of excessive wear, damage or cracks, and renew if necessary.
60 To refit, simply push the guide rail into position, ensuring that it is securely located.
61 Refit the timing chain cover as described in Section 6.

Lower guide rail - models with double-row timing chain

62 Remove the auxiliary shaft as described in Section 9.
63 Unhook the timing chain from the crankshaft sprocket.
64 Pull the crankshaft sprocket forwards on the end of the crankshaft to provide sufficient clearance for the guide rail to be removed. If the sprocket is tight, it may be possible to lever it off using two large screwdrivers positioned either side of the sprocket. Alternatively, remove the sprocket (and the oil pump drive collar, where applicable) using a suitable puller.
65 Pull the chain guide from the locating lugs.
66 Examine the rail for signs of excessive wear, damage or cracks, and renew if necessary.
67 To refit, simply push the guide rail into position, ensuring that it is securely located.
68 Tap the sprocket onto the front of the crankshaft, using a metal tube if necessary. Ensure that the sprocket engages with the Woodruff key, or the locating pin in the crankshaft, as applicable.
69 Where applicable, refit the oil pump drive collar.

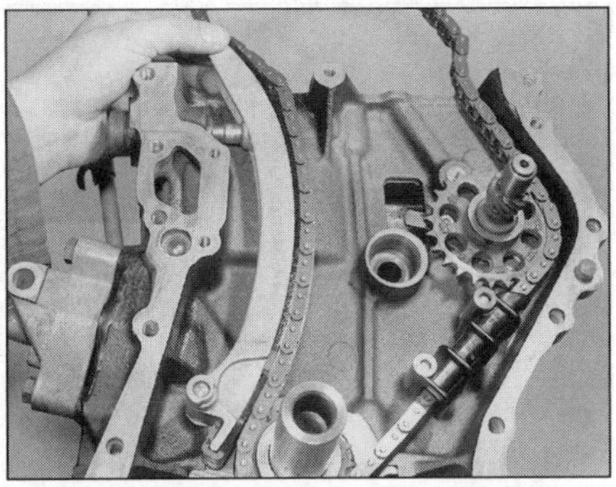

8.83 Withdrawing the tensioner rail - model with single-row timing chain

8.74b . . . to remove the upper guide rail locating pin

70 Engage the timing chain with the crankshaft sprocket, ensuring that the marks made on the sprocket and the chain before removal are aligned.
71 Refit the auxiliary shaft as described in Section 9.

Upper guide rail

Note: *A suitable slide hammer and adapter will be required for this operation. Sealant will be required to coat the ends of the guide rail locating pins on refitting.*
72 Remove the camshaft sprocket as described previously in this Section.
73 Screw a suitable bolt into one of the guide rail locating pins (accessible from the front of the cylinder head).
74 Engage a slide hammer and suitable adapter with the bolt, and use the slide hammer to remove the guide rail locating pin **(see illustrations)**.
75 Repeat the procedure for the remaining locating pin, ensuring that the guide rail does not slide down the timing chain into the housing as the pin is removed.
76 Withdraw the guide rail from the cylinder head **(see illustration)**.
77 Examine the rail for signs of excessive wear, damage or cracks, and renew if necessary.
78 Offer the guide rail into position in the housing, then position the locating pins in their holes in the cylinder head, and tap them into position sufficiently to retain the guide rail.
79 Apply sealant to the outer collar of each locating pin, where it seats in the cylinder

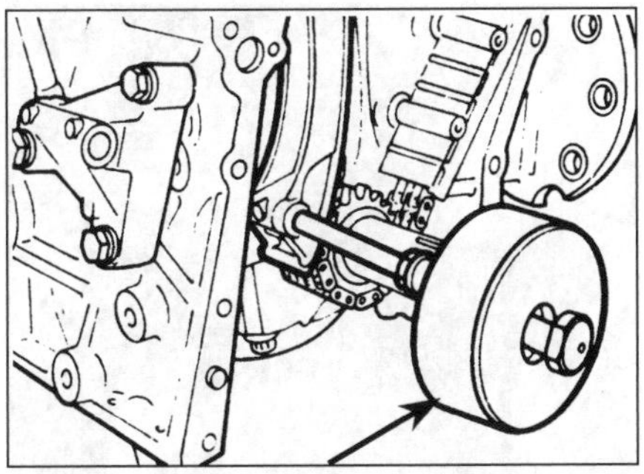

8.91 Using a slide hammer (arrowed) to remove the tensioner rail pivot pin - models with double-row timing chain

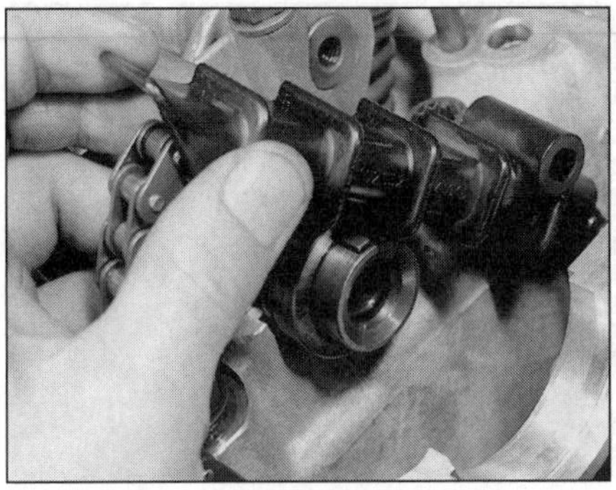

8.76 Withdrawing the upper guide rail from the cylinder head

head, then tap the pins fully into the cylinder head. Ensure that the locating lug on the guide rail engages with the groove in the upper locating pin.
80 Refit the camshaft sprocket as described previously in this Section.

Tensioner rail - models with single-row timing chain

Removal

81 Remove the timing chain cover as described in Section 6.
82 Remove the camshaft sprocket as described previously in this Section.
83 Pivot the tensioner rail as required, to enable it to be withdrawn from the pivot pin **(see illustration)**.

Inspection

84 Examine the rail for signs of excessive wear, damage or cracks, and renew if necessary.

Refitting

85 Push the rail into position, ensuring that it locates correctly over the pivot pin.
86 Refit the camshaft sprocket as described previously in this Section.
87 Refit the timing chain cover as described in Section 6.

Tensioner rail - models with double-row timing chain

Removal

Note: *A suitable slide hammer and adapter will be required for this operation. A new tensioner rail pivot pin will be required on refitting.*
88 Remove the timing chain cover as described in Section 6.
89 Remove the camshaft sprocket as described previously in this Section.
90 Drill a small hole (eg: 5.8 mm) in the end of the tensioner rail pivot pin, then cut a thread approximately 10 mm deep in the end of the pin using a suitable tap (eg: M6).
91 Screw a small bolt into the end of the pivot pin, then attach a slide hammer with suitable adapter to the bolt, and use the slide hammer to remove the pivot pin **(see illustration)**.

9.7a Unscrew the auxiliary shaft clamp bolt . . .

9.7b . . . and withdraw the clamp

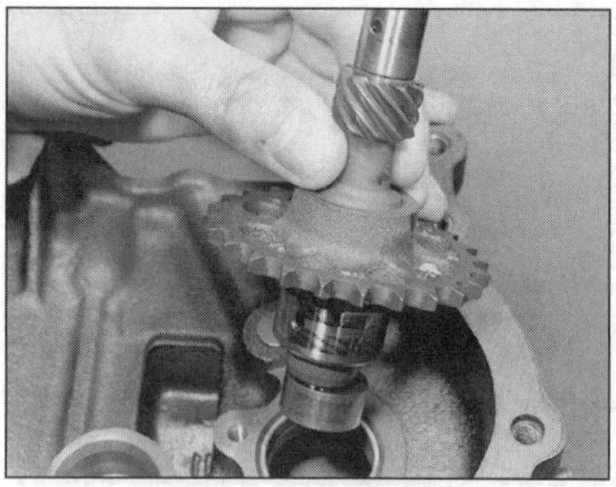

9.8 Withdrawing the auxiliary shaft

92 Withdraw the tensioner rail.

Inspection

93 Examine the rail for signs of excessive wear, damage or cracks, and renew if necessary.

Refitting

94 Offer the tensioner rail into position, ensuring that it is correctly located, then tap the new pivot pin into position using a hammer and punch.

95 Refit the camshaft sprocket as described previously in this Section.

96 Refit the timing chain cover as described in Section 6.

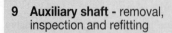

9 Auxiliary shaft - removal, inspection and refitting

Removal

1 Remove the timing chain cover as described in Section 6.

2 On carburettor models, remove the fuel pump as described in Chapter 4A.

3 Remove the camshaft sprocket as described in Section 8.

4 Using quick-drying paint or a suitable scriber, make reference marks on the crankshaft sprocket, and on an adjacent timing chain link, to aid refitting.

5 On models with a single-row timing chain, pull off the lower chain guide rail.

6 If necessary, turn the auxiliary shaft until the shaft clamp bolt can be reached through one of the holes in the sprocket.

7 Working through the hole in the sprocket, unscrew the clamp bolt, then withdraw the auxiliary shaft clamp **(see illustrations)**.

8 Disengage the timing chain from the sprocket, then withdraw the auxiliary shaft from the cylinder block **(see illustration)**.

Inspection

9 Inspect the surfaces of the shaft for signs of damage and wear (particularly on the fuel pump and/or distributor drive surfaces, as applicable), and renew the shaft if necessary.

10 Examine the teeth on the sprocket for wear. Each tooth forms an inverted "V". If worn, the side of each tooth under tension will be slightly concave in shape when compared with the other side of the tooth (ie: the teeth will have a "hooked" appearance). If the teeth appear worn, the complete auxiliary shaft must be renewed.

Refitting

11 Slide the auxiliary shaft into position in the cylinder block, then refit the clamp, and tighten the clamp bolt to the specified torque.

12 Engage the timing chain with the auxiliary shaft sprocket.

13 Where applicable, refit the lower chain guide rail.

14 Ensure that the marks made on the timing chain and the crankshaft sprocket before removal are aligned, then refit the camshaft sprocket as described in Section 8.

15 On carburettor models, refit the fuel pump as described in Chapter 4A.

16 Refit the timing chain cover as described in Section 6.

10 Rocker gear, valve lifters and camshaft - general information, removal, inspection and refitting

General information

1 The rocker gear is integral with the camshaft bearing caps. The rocker arms are mounted on individual short rocker shafts which are an interference-fit in the camshaft bearing caps. One exhaust and one inlet rocker arm is fitted to each bearing cap.

2 The hydraulic valve lifters are fitted to the rocker arms, and are supplied with oil via drillings in the rocker arms.

Removal

3 Remove the air cleaner assembly as described in Chapter 4.

4 Remove the camshaft cover as described in Section 4.

5 Remove the camshaft sprocket as described in Section 8.

6 On models with manually-adjustable valve clearances, slacken the locknuts, and unscrew the rocker arm adjuster screws as far as possible.

7 Check the rocker arms and the camshaft bearing caps for identification marks. The bearing caps are normally numbered 1 to 4 from the camshaft sprocket end of the cylinder head, on the exhaust manifold side of the bearing caps **(see illustration)**. A corresponding mark is cast into the cylinder head beneath the camshaft. If any of the bearing caps are not marked, make suitable marks using a pin-punch.

8 Progressively unscrew the camshaft bearing cap bolts, working in a diagonal sequence, noting the locations of the oil spray pipe brackets.

9 Lift off the oil spray pipe **(see illustration)**.

10.7 Camshaft bearing cap identification number (arrowed)

10.9 Lift off the oil spray pipe

10.10 Lifting off a camshaft bearing cap/rocker assembly

10.11 Remove the valve lifter contact pads

10 Lift off the camshaft bearing cap/rocker assemblies **(see illustration)**. Note that the bearing caps locate on dowels - if they are stuck, tap gently using a soft-faced mallet.

11 On models with hydraulic valve lifters, remove the valve lifter contact pads from the tops of the valve stems, keeping them in strict order **(see illustration)**. The components must not be mixed up.

> **HAYNES HiNT** *On models with hydraulic valve lifters, keep the contact pads in a compartmentalised box, with eight compartments, numbered 1 to 4 for the inlet valves, and 1 to 4 for the exhaust valves.*

12 Carefully lift the camshaft from the cylinder head.

Dismantling, inspection and reassembly

Camshaft

13 Examine the camshaft bearings and cam lobes for any sign of scoring, wear grooves or pitting, and if apparent, renew the camshaft. Any damage of this nature may be attributable to a blocked oil passage either in the cylinder head, rocker assemblies or the oil spray pipe, and careful examination should be carried out to determine the cause. If the camshaft is renewed, all the rocker arms must be renewed at the same time.

Rocker gear

14 With the camshaft bearing caps removed, the rocker arms can be removed from the bearing caps by drawing out the short rocker shafts. Before removing the rocker arms, check them for identification marks, and if none are present, make suitable marks to ensure that the arms are fitted in their original locations (mark the rocker arms 1 to 4 for the inlet valves, and 1 to 4 for the exhaust valves) - do not mix the components up. Also note which way round the rocker arms are fitted on the shafts.

15 Ideally, the manufacturer's tool, consisting of a slide hammer and special adapter, should be used to remove the rocker shafts. An alternative method is to screw a suitable long bolt (M8), with a washer, into the rocker shaft, then strike the washer with a hammer away from the bearing cap, to draw out the shaft - take great care not to damage the components **(see illustration)**. With the shaft removed, the rocker arm can be withdrawn. The components should be stored in order, eg: in a compartmentalised box.

16 On models with manually-adjustable valve clearances, check the ends of the adjusters which contact the valve stems for wear, and check the fit of the rocker arms on their shafts. If there is any sign of wear or damage, it is advisable to renew the components as a complete set.

17 On models with hydraulic valve lifters, check the valve lifter contact pads for wear, and check the fit of the rocker arms on their shafts. Again, if there is any sign of wear or damage, it is advisable to renew the components as a complete set.

18 Thoroughly clean the components before refitting.

19 Lubricate the rocker arm and shaft contact surfaces, then refit the shaft and the rocker arm to the relevant camshaft bearing cap, noting the following points.

a) *If the original components are being refitted, ensure that all components are refitted to their original locations.*
b) *Ensure that each rocker arm is fitted the correct way round on the shaft, as noted before removal.*
c) *Ensure that the groove for the camshaft bearing cap securing bolt in each rocker shaft is aligned with the bolt hole in the bearing cap.*
d) *If the manufacturer's tools are not available, use the long bolt and washer used during removal to tap each rocker shaft into position in the bearing cap.*

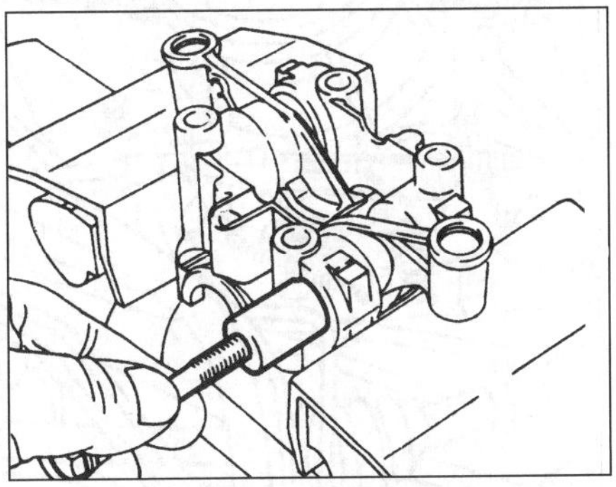

10.15 Using an M8 bolt to withdraw a rocker shaft from the bearing cap assembly

Hydraulic valve lifters

20 To remove a valve lifter from a rocker arm, insert a suitable mandrel through the aperture in the top of the rocker arm, and push the valve lifter from the arm.

21 Withdraw the spacer washer from the top of the valve lifter housing in the rocker arm **(see illustration)**.

22 Ensure that the valve lifters and spacer washers are kept in order so that they can be refitted in their original locations.

23 Inspect the valve lifters and spacer washers for obvious signs of wear or damage, and renew if necessary.

24 The design and construction of the hydraulic valve lifters is such that the amount of free-play or clearance that they can compensate for is limited. This is mainly due to the compactness of the units. To keep the free-play or clearance to a minimum, and to allow the valve lifters to stay within their operating limits, the spacer washers are available in a number of thicknesses.

25 Under normal operating conditions, the valve lifters will automatically adjust to take up the clearance between the rocker arm and the valve stem, and no problems will occur.

26 If, however, component wear becomes excessive, or the valve train becomes noisy in operation after renewal of the camshaft, rocker arms, valves, or any of the valve lifters themselves, it is possible that the operating clearance has now become outside the operating limits of the valve lifters. In this case, it will be necessary to change the spacer washer for one of a different thickness.

27 To determine the required thickness of the spacer washer, a Mercedes-Benz special dial gauge tool and clamp is required, and the work should be entrusted to a dealer.

28 It is advisable to refit the valve lifters with the rocker arms already in position on the

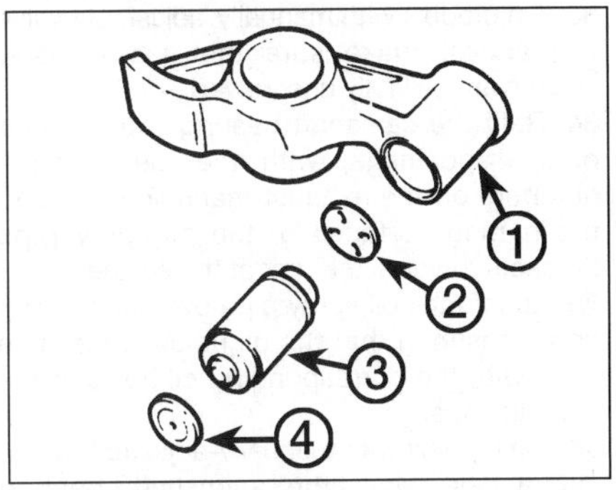

10.21 Rocker arm/valve lifter assembly

1 *Rocker arm*
2 *Spacer washer*
3 *Valve lifter*
4 *Contact pad*

2A

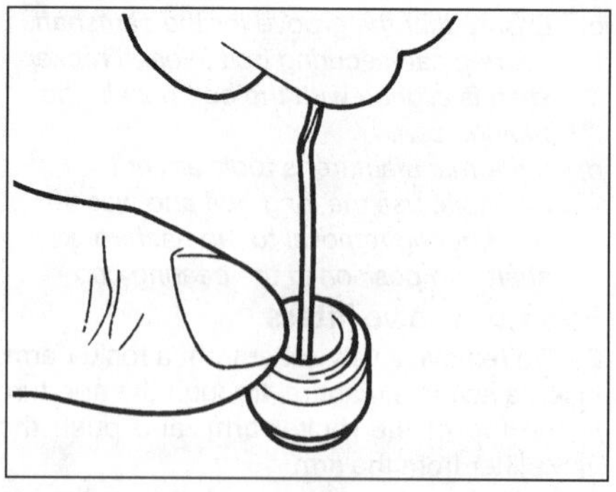

10.29 Push the valve lifter ball valve off its seat using a thin piece of wire

10.31a Lubricate the camshaft thoroughly

10.31b Align the camshaft groove (arrowed) with the top face of the cylinder head

rocker shafts. This will reduce the time taken for assembly, and will reduce the possibility of the oil draining from the valve lifters once they have been primed during the following procedure.

29 Prior to refitting, each valve lifter must be filled with engine oil. To do this, hold the unit vertically, and fill the supply chamber with clean engine oil. Using a thin piece of wire, inserted down through the supply chamber, push the ball valve off its seat so that oil can enter the operating chamber **(see illustration)**. At the same time, push the plunger upwards to its stop. Repeat this procedure several times until no more oil can be added.

30 Insert the spacer washer into the housing in the rocker arm, with the oil slots facing the valve lifter, then insert the valve lifter. Push the valve lifter up into contact with the snap-ring. The camshaft bearing cap/rocker assemblies can now be refitted to the engine.

Refitting

31 Lubricate the camshaft, and the bearings in the bearing caps and the cylinder head with clean engine oil, then lay the camshaft in position on the cylinder head. Turn the camshaft so that the timing mark is aligned with the top face of the cylinder head - see Section 3 **(see illustrations)**.

32 On models with hydraulic valve lifters, refit the valve lifter contact pads to their original valve stems.

33 On models with manually-adjustable valve clearances, make sure that the adjuster screws are still fully unscrewed.

34 Refit the camshaft bearing caps in their original positions, with the identification numbers on the exhaust manifold side, and the mating surfaces of the oil spray pipe brackets towards the rear of the engine.

35 Locate the oil spray pipe over the bearing caps, ensuring that the oil holes in the pipe align with the corresponding oil holes in the bearing caps.

36 On models with manually-adjustable valve clearances, refit the camshaft bearing cap bolts, and tighten the bolts progressively, in a diagonal sequence, to the specified torque.

37 On models with hydraulic valve lifters, proceed as follows.

a) *Turn the camshaft so that the cam lobes for No 1 cylinder are pointing down (ie: away from the rocker arm) - so that the valve lifters are not under load when the bearing cap bolts are tightened.*
b) *Refit No1 bearing cap bolts, and tighten the bolts progressively to the specified torque.*
c) *Repeat steps a) and b), for No 3 bearing cap, No 4 bearing cap, and finally No 2 bearing cap, turning the camshaft so that the relevant cam lobes are pointing down before tightening the bolts in each case.*

38 If not already done, turn the camshaft so that the timing mark is aligned with the top face of the cylinder head, then check that the crankshaft timing mark is still aligned, with No 1 piston at TDC (see Section 3).

39 Refit the camshaft sprocket as described in Section 8.

40 On models with manually-adjustable valve clearances, adjust the valve clearances as described in Chapter 1A.

41 Refit the camshaft cover as described in Section 4.

42 Refit the air cleaner assembly.

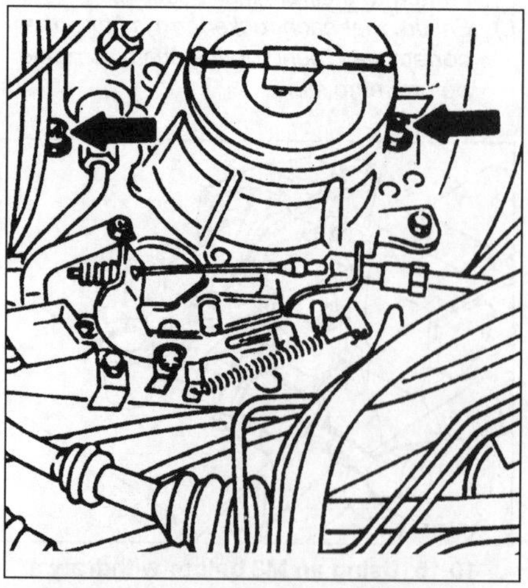

11.11 Inlet manifold mounting strut bolts (arrowed) - fuel injection engine

11 Cylinder head - removal, inspection and refitting

Removal

Note: *A new cylinder head gasket will be required on refitting, and new cylinder head bolts may be required - see text. The new gasket will be supplied in a sealed wrapper - do not remove the wrapper until the gasket is about to be fitted.*

1 Ensure that the engine is cold before attempting to remove the cylinder head, and note that the cylinder head is removed complete with the inlet and exhaust manifolds.

2 Disconnect the battery negative lead.

3 Raise the bonnet to the fully open position, as described in Chapter 11.

4 Drain the cooling system as described in Chapter 1A.

5 Remove the air cleaner assembly as described in Chapter 4.

6 Remove the camshaft sprocket and the timing chain upper guide rail, as described in Section 8.

7 Remove the auxiliary drivebelt as described in Chapter 1A.

8 Disconnect the exhaust front pipes from the exhaust manifold, with reference to Chapter 4.

9 Unscrew the nut securing the dipstick guide tube to the exhaust manifold, and pull out the dipstick. Plug the dipstick tube to prevent dirt entry.

10 Disconnect the throttle cable from the throttle linkage, and move it clear of the working area as described in Chapter 4.

11 Unbolt the mounting strut from the inlet manifold. On carburettor engines, unscrew the single bolt securing the strut to the manifold. On fuel injection engines, unscrew the two bolts and, working below the manifold, unhook the throttle valve return spring **(see illustration)**.

12 Disconnect the coolant hoses from the front and rear of the cylinder head **(see illustration)**.

13 Working around the cylinder head and manifolds, disconnect the wiring plugs from the switches and sensors mounted in the cylinder head and inlet manifold/carburettor (as applicable), noting their locations to aid refitting **(see illustration)**.

14 Similarly, disconnect any vacuum lines from the vacuum valves mounted on the cylinder head and inlet manifold/carburettor (as applicable).

15 Unscrew the union nut, and disconnect the brake servo vacuum hose from the inlet manifold.

16 On models with fuel injection, depressurise the fuel system as described in Chapter 4.

17 Disconnect fuel supply and return lines from the carburettor or from the fuel pressure regulator and fuel distributor (fuel injection models), as applicable. Where applicable, counterhold the unions when unscrewing the union nuts. Plug or cover the open ends of the pipes and unions to reduce fuel spillage and to prevent dirt entry.

18 On models fitted with air conditioning, unbolt the air conditioning pipe brackets from the cylinder head.

19 On automatic transmission models, disconnect the control pressure cable from the throttle linkage, with reference to Chapter 7B, and unscrew the bolt securing the automatic transmission fluid dipstick tube to the cylinder head.

20 Slacken the hose clip securing the coolant pump bypass hose to the thermostat housing.

21 Disconnect the radiator top hose from the thermostat housing.

22 Where applicable, unbolt and remove the EGR pipe, which connects the EGR valve to the inlet manifold.

23 Where applicable, check around the emission control system components, and disconnect any relevant hoses, unbolt valves, etc, to allow removal of the cylinder head. Note the location and routing of all hoses to aid refitting.

24 Make a final check to ensure that all relevant hoses, pipes and wires have been disconnected (or the brackets/clips unbolted) to allow cylinder head removal.

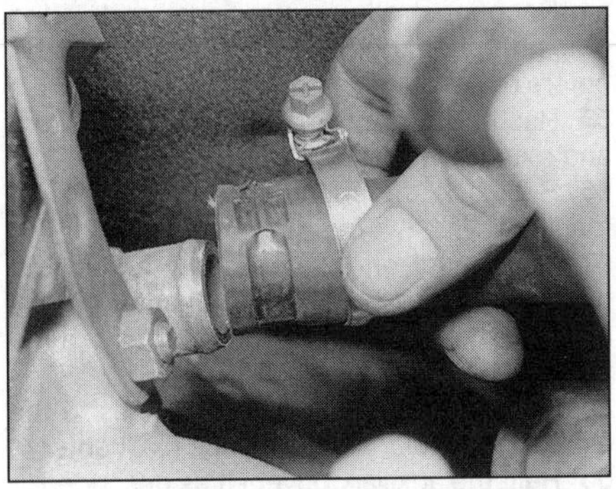

11.12 Disconnecting the heater coolant hose from the cylinder head

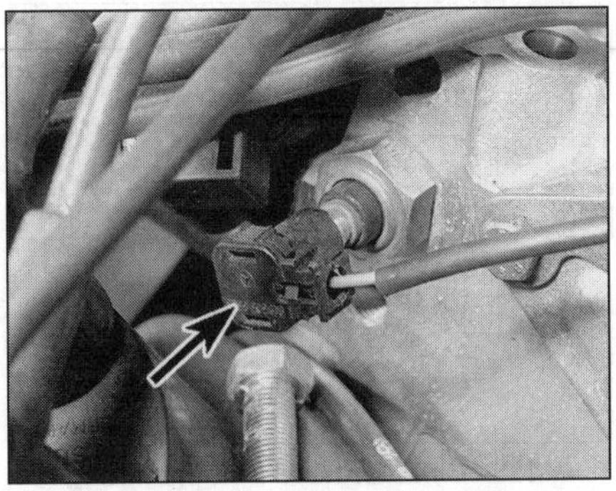

11.13 Disconnect the coolant temperature sensor wiring plug (arrowed)

25 Working in the timing chain housing at the top of the cylinder head, unscrew the three bolts securing the cylinder head to the timing chain cover **(see illustration)**.

26 Progressively loosen the cylinder head bolts, working in the reverse order to that shown in illustration 11.44 **(see illustration)**.

27 Remove the cylinder head bolts.

28 Release the cylinder head from the cylinder block and locating dowels by rocking it. Do not prise between the mating faces of the cylinder head and block, as this may damage the gasket faces.

29 Ideally, an assistant will now be required to help lift the cylinder head from the block - take care as the cylinder head is heavy.

30 Recover the cylinder head gasket.

Inspection

31 Refer to Chapter 2D for details of cylinder head dismantling and reassembly. If desired, the manifolds can be removed with reference to Chapter 4.

32 The mating faces of the cylinder head and block must be perfectly clean before refitting the head. Use a scraper to remove all traces of gasket and carbon, and also clean the tops of the pistons. Take particular care with the aluminium cylinder head, as the soft metal is easily damaged. Also make sure that debris is not allowed to enter the oil and water passages. Using adhesive tape and paper, seal the water, oil and bolt holes in the cylinder block. To prevent carbon entering the gap between the pistons and bores, smear a little grease in the gap. After cleaning each piston, rotate the crankshaft so that the piston moves **down** the bore, then wipe out the grease and carbon with a cloth rag.

33 Check the block and head for nicks, deep scratches and other damage. If very slight, they may be removed from the cylinder block carefully with a file. More serious damage may be repaired by machining, but this is a specialist job.

34 If warpage of the cylinder head is suspected, use a straight-edge to check it for distortion, with reference to Chapter 2D.

35 Clean out the bolt holes in the block using a pipe cleaner or thin rag and a screwdriver. Make sure that all oil and water is removed, otherwise there is a possibility of the block being cracked by hydraulic pressure when the bolts are tightened.

36 Examine the bolt threads and the threads in the cylinder block for damage. If necessary, use the correct size tap to chase out the threads in the block.

37 The manufacturers recommend that the cylinder head bolts are measured, to determine whether renewal is necessary; however, some owners may wish to renew all the bolts as a matter of course.

38 Measure the length of each bolt from the base of the head to the end of the shank **(see illustration)**. If the bolt length is greater than the maximum specified, the bolts should be renewed.

11.25 Two of the three cylinder head-to-timing chain cover bolts (arrowed)

11.26 Unscrewing a cylinder head bolt

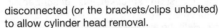

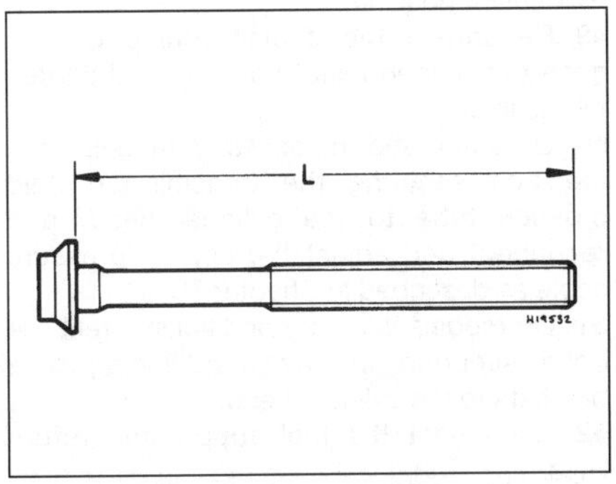

11.38 Cylinder head bolt length measuring

L Maximum permissible length = 122.0 mm

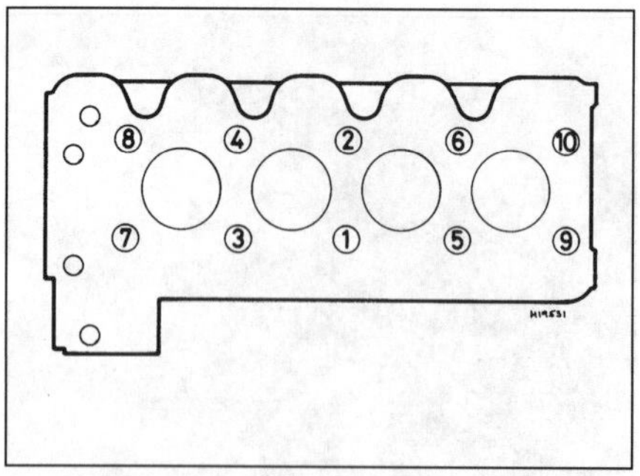

11.44 Cylinder head bolt tightening sequence - 4-cylinder petrol engines

Refitting

Note: *A new cylinder head gasket will be required on refitting. The new gasket will be supplied in a sealed wrapper - do not remove the wrapper until the gasket is about to be fitted.*

39 Where applicable, refit the manifolds with reference to Chapter 4.

40 Check that the camshaft and crankshaft timing marks are still aligned with No 1 piston at TDC, as described in Section 3.

41 Fit the gasket over the dowels in the cylinder block, ensuring that it is fitted the correct way round.

42 Lower the cylinder head onto the block.

43 Oil the threads and the contact faces of the cylinder head bolts, then insert them and screw them into the cylinder block by hand.

44 Tighten the cylinder head bolts in the order shown **(see illustration)**. Tighten the bolts in the stages given in the Specifications - ie: tighten all bolts to the Stage 1 torque, then tighten all bolts to the Stage 2 torque, and so on.

45 Refit and tighten the three bolts securing the cylinder head to the timing chain cover.

46 Where applicable, reconnect any emission control system hoses, and/or refit components removed to enable removal of the cylinder head. Make sure that the hoses are located and routed as noted before removal.

47 Where applicable, refit the EGR pipe which connects the EGR valve to the inlet manifold.

48 Reconnect the radiator top hose to the thermostat housing.

49 Reconnect the coolant pump bypass hose to the thermostat housing, and tighten the hose clip.

50 On automatic transmission models, refit the bolt securing the transmission fluid dipstick tube to the cylinder head, and reconnect and adjust the control pressure cable as described in Chapter 7B.

51 On models with air conditioning, refit the bolts securing the air conditioning pipe brackets to the cylinder head.

52 Reconnect the fuel supply and return lines.

53 Reconnect the brake servo vacuum hose, and tighten the union nut.

54 Reconnect all vacuum lines, and wiring plugs to their correct locations, as noted before removal.

55 Reconnect the coolant hoses to the front and rear of the cylinder head.

56 Refit the mounting strut to the inlet manifold.

57 Reconnect and if necessary adjust the throttle cable, as described in Chapter 4.

58 Refit the nut securing the dipstick guide tube, then refit the dipstick.

59 Reconnect the exhaust front pipes to the exhaust manifold, with reference to Chapter 4.

60 Refit the auxiliary drivebelt as described in Chapter 1A.

61 Refit the timing chain upper guide rail and the camshaft sprocket, as described in Section 8.

62 Refit the air cleaner assembly.

63 Make a final check to ensure that all components have been refitted, and all hoses, pipes and wiring have been correctly reconnected.

64 Refill the cooling system as described in Chapter 1A.

65 Reconnect the battery negative lead, then run the engine and check for leaks.

12 Sump - removal and refitting

Note: *A suitable hoist and lifting tackle will be required for this operation. A new sump gasket will be required on refitting, and new exhaust clamp nuts will be required.*

Removal

1 Disconnect the battery negative lead.

2 Remove the air cleaner assembly as described in Chapter 4.

3 Remove the engine undershield as described in Chapter 11.

4 Remove the front anti-roll bar as described in Chapter 10.

5 Drain the engine oil with reference to Chapter 1A.

6 Where applicable, disconnect the wiring from the oil level sensor mounted in the sump.

7 Pull out the engine oil level dipstick, and cover or plug the dipstick tube to prevent dirt entry.

8 Unclip the cooling fan shroud, and lay it in position over the fan blades as described in Chapter 3.

9 On models with automatic transmission, disconnect the transmission fluid cooler lines from the transmission. Be prepared for fluid spillage, and cover or plug the open ends of the fluid lines, and the openings in the transmission to prevent dirt entry and further fluid loss.

10 Where applicable, unscrew the two bolts securing the engine mounting damper to the body member on the left-hand side of the vehicle.

11 Where applicable, remove the engine movement stop, as described in Section 17.

12 Unscrew the bolts securing the exhaust mounting bracket to the transmission, then slacken the U-bolt nuts securing the bracket to the exhaust system, and pivot the bracket down, away from the transmission.

13 Disconnect the exhaust front pipes from the manifold, with reference to Chapter 4.

14 Unscrew the two lower engine-to-transmission bolts.

15 Disconnect the steering drag link at one end, with reference to Chapter 10.

16 Where applicable, unscrew the securing bolts, and remove the sump bracing plate. Note that on some models, the bracing plate is integral with the sump.

17 Attach a hoist and suitable lifting tackle to the engine lifting brackets, and raise the hoist to just take the weight of the engine.

18 Working on each side of the vehicle in turn, unscrew the bolts securing the left- and right-hand engine mountings to the front crossmember.

19 Carefully lift the engine sufficiently for access to the sump securing bolts. It is wise to place thin sheets of card or board between the engine and the bulkhead, and between the engine and the radiator, to protect against damage when the engine tilts as it is lifted.

20 Working progressively, in a diagonal sequence, unscrew and remove the sump securing bolts. Note the locations of the bolts to aid refitting, as various lengths of bolts may used. Also note the locations of any brackets and/or clips secured by the bolts.

21 Lower the sump from under the vehicle, and recover the gasket.

Refitting

22 Commence refitting by cleaning the remains of the gasket from the sump and cylinder block, and wipe dry.

23 Position a new gasket on the sump, then lift the sump into position, and insert the bolts in their original locations.

24 Tighten the bolts progressively to the specified torque.

25 On models with a separate sump bracing plate, cut off the projecting webs of the sump gasket, at the flywheel end of the engine.

26 Carefully lower the engine into position, then refit and tighten the lower engine mounting bolts to the specified torque.

27 Disconnect the lifting tackle from the engine lifting brackets, and withdraw the hoist.

28 Where applicable, refit and adjust the engine movement stop as described in Section 17.

29 Where applicable, refit the sump bracing plate, and tighten the securing bolts.

30 Reconnect the steering drag link, with reference to Chapter 10.

31 Refit the two lower engine-to-transmission bolts, and tighten them to the specified torque.

32 Reconnect the exhaust front pipes to the manifold, with reference to Chapter 4.

33 Refit the bolts securing the exhaust

mounting bracket to the transmission, then reposition the bracket on the exhaust, and tighten the U-bolt nuts.
34 Where applicable, refit and tighten the bolts securing the engine mounting damper to the body member.
35 On models with automatic transmission, reconnect the transmission fluid cooler lines to the transmission.
36 Refit the cooling fan shroud (Chapter 3).
37 Where applicable, reconnect the oil level sensor wiring.
38 Refit the front anti-roll bar as described in Chapter 10.
39 Ensure that the oil drain plug has been refitted and tightened, then refit the engine undershield.
40 Refit the air cleaner assembly.
41 Lower the vehicle to the ground, and refill the engine with the correct grade and quantity of oil (see *"Weekly checks"* and Chapter 1A).
42 Reconnect the battery negative lead.
43 On models with automatic transmission, check the transmission fluid level and top up if necessary as described in Chapter 1A.

13 Oil pump - removal, inspection and refitting

Note: *A new oil pick-up pipe gasket, and a new oil supply pipe O-ring will be required on refitting.*

Removal

1 The oil pump is driven directly from the end of the crankshaft, and is located in the timing chain cover.
2 Remove the timing chain cover as described in Section 6.
3 Unscrew the securing bolts, and remove the oil pick-up pipe **(see illustration)**. Recover the gasket.
4 Unscrew the securing bolts, and withdraw the oil pump cover **(see illustration)**.
5 Lift out the oil pump inner and outer rotors, noting which way round they are fitted **(see illustrations)**.
6 Unscrew the oil pressure relief valve plug from the side of the timing chain cover, then withdraw the sealing ring, spring and plunger **(see illustrations)**.

Inspection

7 Thoroughly clean all components.
8 Check for scoring or wear ridges on the pump inner and outer rotors, the rotor teeth, the pump cover and the pump housing in the timing chain cover. If the rotors are worn, they can be renewed as a rotor set. If the pump housing or pump cover are worn, it will be necessary to fit a new timing chain cover. A new timing chain cover will incorporate a complete new oil pump.
9 Remove the O-ring from the oil supply pipe at the rear of the pump, and discard it **(see illustration)**.

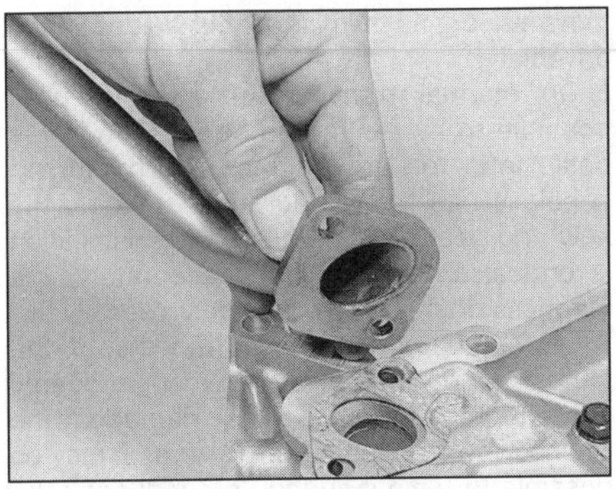

13.3 Remove the oil pick-up pipe

13.4 Remove the oil pump cover

13.5a Lift out the oil pump inner . . .

13.5b . . . and outer rotors

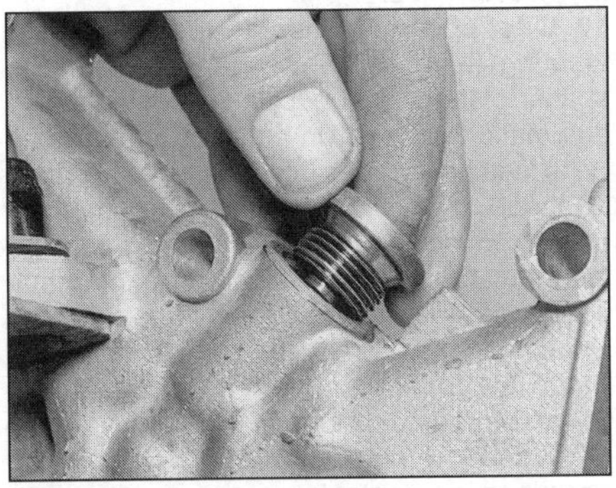

13.6a Unscrew the oil pressure relief valve plug . . .

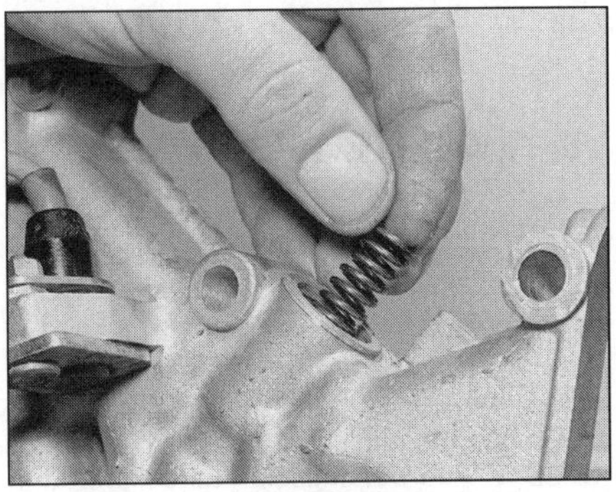

13.6b . . . and withdraw the spring . . .

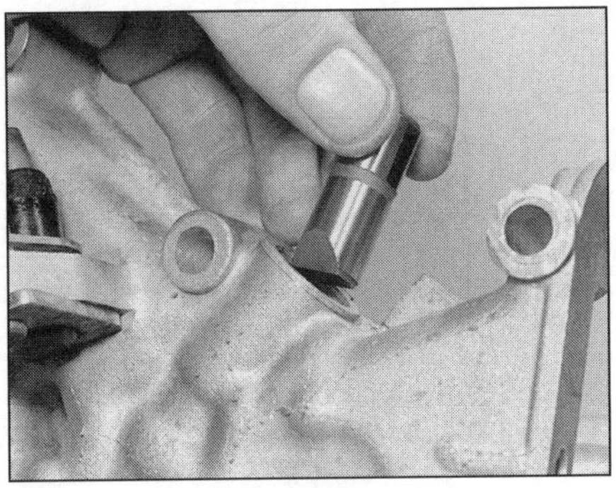

13.6c . . . and plunger

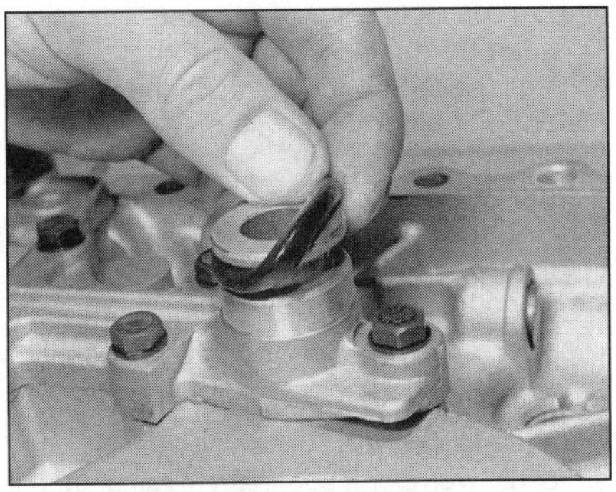

13.9 Remove the O-ring from the oil supply pipe

2A

13.10 Inject clean engine oil into the space between the rotors

Refitting

10 Refit the pump outer and inner rotors, then inject clean engine oil into the space between the two rotors **(see illustration)**.

11 Refit the pump cover, and tighten the securing bolts to the specified torque.

12 Fit a new oil pick-up pipe gasket, with the rounded offset edge of the gasket towards the top of the timing chain cover.

13 Fit the pick-up pipe and secure it with the two bolts.

14 Fit a new O-ring to the oil supply tube at the rear of the pump.

15 Lubricate the oil pressure relief valve plunger with clean engine oil, then refit the plunger, spring, sealing ring and plug. Tighten the plug to the specified torque.

16 Refit the timing chain cover as described in Section 6.

14 Flywheel/driveplate - removal, inspection and refitting

Removal

Note: *New flywheel/driveplate securing bolts may be required on refitting.*

1 Remove the engine as described in Chapter 2D, or the transmission as described in Chapter 7.

2 Where applicable, remove the clutch as described in Chapter 6.

3 In order to unscrew the securing bolts, the flywheel/driveplate must be locked in position. This can be done by bolting a toothed tool (engage the tooth with the starter ring gear) to the cylinder block using one of the engine-to-transmission bolts.

4 Progressively unscrew the securing bolts, then withdraw the flywheel/driveplate from the crankshaft. Note that the flywheel/driveplate locates on dowels. Recover the spacer discs on models with automatic transmission.

Inspection

5 If the teeth on the flywheel starter ring gear are badly worn, or if some are missing, then it will be necessary to renew the complete driveplate on models with automatic transmission, as the ring gear is welded to the driveplate.

6 On manual transmission models, it is possible to renew the ring gear. The job is best left to an engine reconditioning specialist, as the temperature to which the new ring gear must be heated for installation is critical and, if not done accurately, the hardness of the teeth will be destroyed.

7 On manual transmission models, if the clutch mating face of the flywheel is deeply scored, cracked or otherwise damaged, the flywheel must be renewed. However, it may be possible to have it surface-ground; seek the advice of an engine reconditioning specialist.

8 The manufacturers recommend that the flywheel/driveplate securing bolts are measured, to determine whether renewal is necessary; however, some owners may wish to renew all the bolts as a matter of course.

9 Measure the length of each bolt from the base of the head to the end of the shank **(see illustration)**. If the bolt length is greater than the maximum specified, the bolts should be renewed.

10 Similarly, measure the diameter across the bolt shank, between the underside of the head, and the start of the bolt threads, and renew the bolts if the diameter is less than the minimum specified.

Refitting

11 Commence refitting by cleaning the mating faces of the crankshaft and flywheel/driveplate.

12 Offer up the flywheel to the crankshaft, locating it on the dowel (ensure that the spacer plates are in position on models with automatic transmission), then fit the securing bolts (see paragraphs 8 to 10).

13 Lock the flywheel using the method employed during removal, then tighten the securing bolts progressively in a diagonal sequence in the stages given in the Specifications - ie: tighten all bolts to the Stage 1 torque, then tighten all bolts to the Stage 2 torque, and so on.

14 Where applicable, refit the clutch as described in Chapter 6.

15 Refit the engine as described in Chapter 2D, or the transmission as described in Chapter 7.

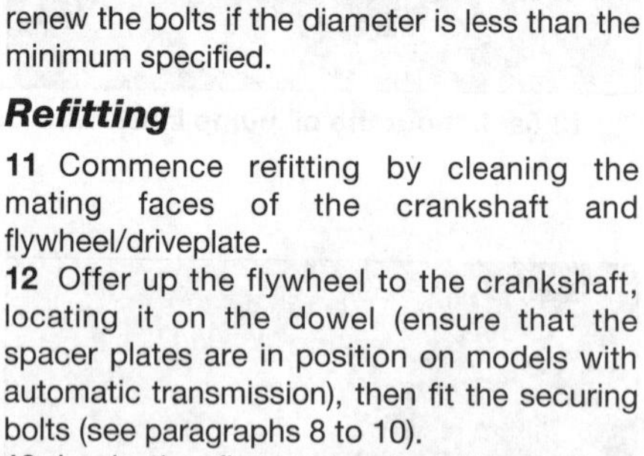

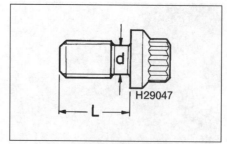

14.9 Flywheel/driveplate bolt measurement

d Minimum diameter = 8.0 mm
L Maximum length = 22.5 mm

15 Crankshaft oil seals - renewal

Front oil seal

1 Remove the crankshaft pulley/vibration damper and hub as described in Section 5.

2 Measure and note the fitted depth of the oil seal.

3 Pull the oil seal from the housing using a hooked instrument. Alternatively, drill a small hole in the oil seal, and use a self-tapping screw and a pair of pliers to remove it.

4 Examine the spacer ring at the front of the crankshaft for scoring or wear, and renew it if necessary. If the ring is tight, lever it gently.

5 Clean the oil seal housing, and the crankshaft spacer ring.

6 Dip the new oil seal in clean engine oil, and press it into the housing (open end first) to the previously-noted depth, using a suitable tube or socket. A piece of thin plastic or tape wound around the front of the spacer ring is useful to prevent damage to the oil seal as it is fitted.

7 Where applicable, remove the plastic or tape from the spacer ring.

8 Refit the crankshaft pulley/vibration damper and hub as described in Section 5.

Rear oil seal

9 Remove the flywheel/driveplate as described in Section 14.

10 Proceed as described in paragraphs 2 and 3.

11 Examine the oil seal contact surface on the crankshaft for signs of damage. If excessive wear is evident, the crankshaft must be renewed.

12 Clean the oil seal housing and the contact surface on the crankshaft flange.

13 Dip the new oil seal in clean engine oil, and press it into the housing (open end first) to the previously-noted depth, using a suitable tube or socket. A piece of thin plastic or tape wound around the rear of the crankshaft flange is useful to prevent damage to the oil seal as it is fitted. Note that the seal must be fitted exactly at right-angles to the crankshaft flange to provide satisfactory sealing.

14 Where applicable, remove the plastic or tape from the crankshaft.

15 Refit the flywheel/driveplate as described in Section 14.

16 Crankshaft spigot bearing - renewal

Note: *A slide hammer and suitable adapter will be required for this operation.*

1 On manual transmission models, a ball or needle roller bearing assembly is fitted to the end of the crankshaft to support the end of the transmission input shaft.

2 To renew the bearing, proceed as follows.
3 Remove the clutch as described in Chapter 6.
4 Using a slide hammer fitted with a suitable adapter, withdraw the bearing and its retaining ring, from the end of the crankshaft.
5 Thoroughly clean the bearing housing in the end of the crankshaft.
6 The manufacturers recommend that the bearing is coated with Mercedes-Benz adhesive before fitting.
7 Tap the new bearing into position, up to the stop, using a tube or socket on the bearing outer race.
8 Tap the retaining ring into position using the tube or socket, until it is flush with the end of the crankshaft.
9 Refit the clutch as described in Chapter 6.

17 Engine/transmission mountings - inspection and renewal

General

1 Three engine/transmission mountings are used, one on either side of the engine, and one under the rear of the transmission **(see illustration)**. Additionally, on some models, an engine movement stop is fitted at the front of the engine, between the sump and the crossmember. Some models also have an engine mounting damper fitted at the left-hand side of the engine.

Inspection

2 If improved access is required, raise the front of the vehicle and support it securely on axle stands (see *"Jacking and Vehicle Support"*).
3 Check the condition of the mounting rubber to see if it is cracked, hardened or separated from the metal at any point. Renew the mounting if any such damage or deterioration is evident.
4 Check that all the mounting fasteners are securely tightened.
5 Using a large screwdriver or metal bar, check for wear in the mounting by carefully levering against it to check for free-play. Where this is not possible, enlist the aid of an assistant to move the engine/transmission back and forth, or from side-to-side, while you observe the mounting. While some free-play is to be expected, even from new components, excessive wear should be obvious. If excessive free-play is found, check first that the fasteners are correctly secured, then renew any worn components as required.
6 The engine movement stop is adjustable, and when checking the engine mountings, the adjustment of the stop should be checked as described later in this Section.
7 To check the condition of the engine mounting damper, remove the damper as described later in this Section, then move the damper piston through a full stroke, and then through short strokes. In both cases, the resistance felt should be smooth and continuous. If the resistance is jerky or uneven, or if there is any visible sign of wear or damage to the damper, renewal is necessary.

Renewal

Left- and right-hand engine mountings

8 If not already done, raise the front of the vehicle and support it securely on axle stands (see *"Jacking and Vehicle Support"*).
9 Support the engine, either using a hoist and lifting tackle connected to the engine lifting brackets, or by positioning a jack and interposed block of wood under the sump. Ensure that the engine is adequately supported before proceeding.
10 Remove the engine undershield as described in Chapter 11.
11 Where applicable, unscrew and remove the adjusting bolt from the engine movement stop (see paragraph 30).
12 On models fitted with an engine mounting damper, unscrew the two bolts securing the lower end of the damper to the front crossmember.
13 Unscrew the bolts securing the left- and right-hand engine mountings to the front crossmember.
14 Unclip the cooling fan shroud, and lay it in position over the fan blades as described in Chapter 3.
15 Attach an engine hoist and lifting tackle to the front engine lifting bracket, then carefully raise the hoist to lift the engine.
16 Where applicable, remove the heat shield from the right-hand engine mounting.
17 Unscrew the bolts securing the engine mountings to the engine mounting brackets, then withdraw the mountings.
18 If desired, the engine mounting brackets can now be unbolted from the cylinder block.
19 Refitting is a reversal of removal, bearing in mind the following points.
a) Tighten all fixings to the specified torque.
b) When refitting the engine movement stop bolt, adjust the stop as described later in this Section.

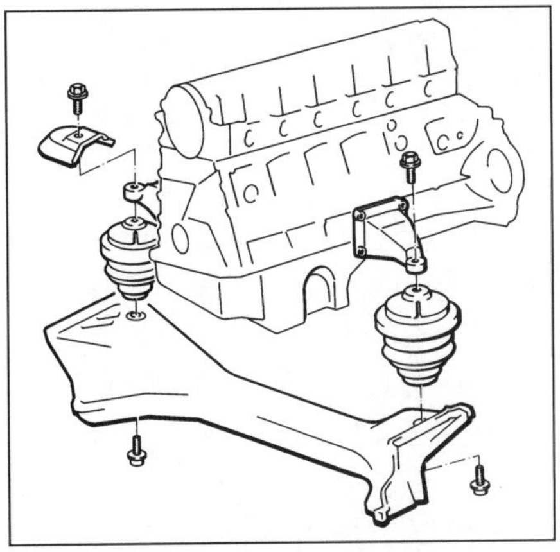

17.1 Front engine mountings

Rear engine/transmission mounting

20 If not already done, raise the front of the vehicle and support it securely on axle stands (see *"Jacking and Vehicle Support"*).
21 If necessary, remove the engine undershield as described in Chapter 11.
22 Support the transmission using a jack and interposed block of wood.
23 Where applicable, unscrew the mounting adjuster screw.
24 Unscrew the bolts securing the mounting crossmember to the underbody, then unscrew the two bolts securing the crossmember to the mounting, and withdraw the crossmember.
25 Unscrew the nut securing the mounting to the transmission, and withdraw the mounting.
26 Refitting is a reversal of removal, bearing in mind the following points.
a) Tighten all fixings to the specified torque.
b) Before tightening the mounting adjuster screw, adjust the engine movement stop as described later in this Section.

Engine movement stop

27 If not already done, raise the front of the vehicle and support it securely on axle stands (see *"Jacking and Vehicle Support"*).
28 If necessary, remove the engine undershield as described in Chapter 11.
29 Turn the steering onto full lock in one direction.
30 Unscrew and remove the movement stop adjuster bolt.
31 Unscrew the two securing bolts, and remove the movement stop.
32 Commence refitting by offering the movement stop into position and tightening the securing bolts to the specified torque.
33 Lower the vehicle to the ground, so that it rests on its wheels.
34 Fit the adjusting bolt, but do not tighten it at this stage.
35 Slacken the rear engine/transmission adjuster screw fully.
36 Ideally, the Mercedes-Benz special tool should be used to set the stop rubber, but a suitable alternative can be improvised using two strips of metal plate, approximately 3.0 mm thick. Slide tool or metal plates either side of the stop rubber **(see illustration)**.

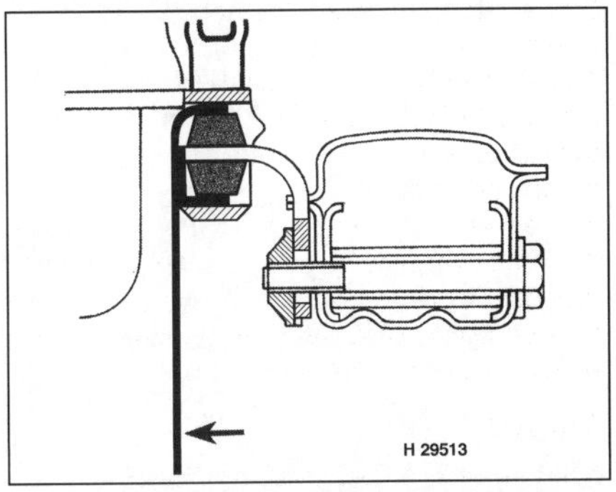

17.36 Using the Mercedez-Benz special tool (arrowed) to adjust the engine movement stop

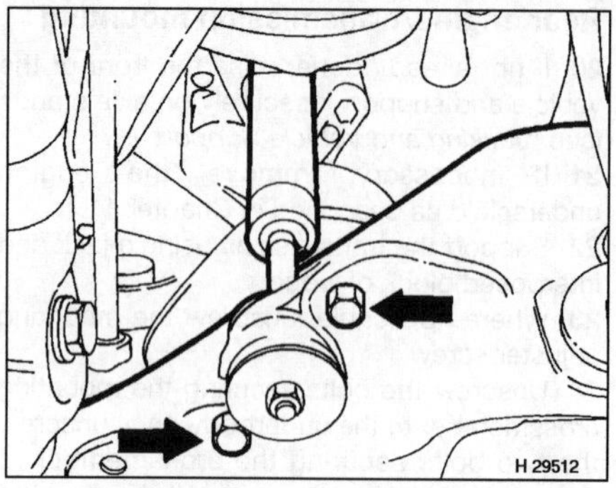

17.42 Engine mounting damper-to-front crossmember bolts (arrowed)

37 Grasp the engine, and move the engine/transmission assembly by hand, by shaking from side-to-side.

38 Tighten the rear engine/transmission mounting adjuster screw to the specified torque.

39 Tighten the engine stop adjuster bolt to the specified torque.

40 Where applicable, refit the engine undershield.

Engine mounting damper

41 The engine mounting damper is bolted between the engine mounting bracket and the front crossmember.

42 Unscrew the two bolts securing the lower end of the damper to the front crossmember **(see illustration)**.

43 Unscrew the bolt securing the upper end of the damper to the engine mounting bracket.

44 Compress the strut as necessary to allow it to be manipulated out from the engine mounting.

45 If the damper rubbers are unbolted from the damper, note their locations and orientation so that they can be refitted correctly.

46 Refitting is a reversal of removal.

Chapter 2 Part B
Six-cylinder petrol engine in-car repair procedures

Contents

Camshaft cover - removal and refitting 4
Compression test - description and interpretation 2
Crankshaft pulley/vibration damper and hub - removal and refitting 5
Crankshaft spigot bearing - renewal 15
Cylinder head - removal, inspection and refitting 10
Engine assembly and valve timing marks - general information and usage 3
Engine oil and filter renewal .... See Chapter 1A
Engine oil level check .... See *"Weekly checks"*
Engine/transmission mountings - inspection and renewal 16
Flywheel/driveplate - removal, inspection and refitting 13
General information 1
Oil pump and drive chain - removal, inspection and refitting 12
Oil seals - renewal 14
Rocker gear, valve lifters and camshaft - general information, removal, inspection and refitting 9
Sump - removal and refitting 11
Timing chain - inspection and renewal 7
Timing chain covers - removal and refitting 6
Timing chain tensioner, sprockets and guides - removal, inspection and refitting 8

Degrees of difficulty

Easy, suitable for novice with little experience	**Fairly easy,** suitable for beginner with some experience	**Fairly difficult,** suitable for competent DIY mechanic	**Difficult,** suitable for experienced DIY mechanic	**Very difficult,** suitable for expert DIY or professional

2B

Specifications

General

Engine code	103.942
Displacement	2597 cc
Bore	82.9 mm
Stroke	80.2 mm
Direction of engine rotation	Clockwise (viewed from front of vehicle)
No 1 cylinder location	Timing chain end
Firing order	1-5-3-6-2-4
Compression pressures:	
Minimum compression pressure	8.5 bars (approx)
Maximum difference between cylinders	1.5 bars
Compression ratio (all engines)	9.2:1

Camshaft

Endfloat:	
New engine	0.030 to 0.110 mm
Wear limit	0.150 mm
Camshaft bearing running clearance:	
New engine	0.040 to 0.082 mm
Wear limit	0.100 mm

Cylinder head bolts

Maximum length	108.4 mm

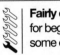

Lubrication system

Minimum oil pressure:	
At idle speed	0.3 bar
At 3000 rpm	3.0 bars

Flywheel/driveplate bolts

Minimum diameter	8.0 mm
Maximum length	22.5 mm

Torque wrench settings

	Nm	lbf ft
Camshaft cover bolts	15	11
Crankshaft pulley/vibration damper bolts	23	17
Crankshaft pulley/vibration damper hub bolt	300	221
Cooling fan bracket bolts	21	15
Rotor arm drive sleeve-to-camshaft bolt:		
M7 bolt	16	12
M8 bolt	21	15
Upper timing chain cover bolts	21	15
Lower timing chain cover bolts:		
M6 bolts	9	7
M8 bolts	21	15
Auxiliary drivebelt tensioner mounting bolt (M12)	75	55
Auxiliary drivebelt idler pulley bolts	30	22
Auxiliary drivebelt tensioner pulley bolt	30	22
Camshaft sprocket bolt	16	12
Timing chain tensioner cover nut	50	37
Timing chain tensioner threaded ring-to-housing	30	22
Camshaft bearing cap bolts	21	15
Cylinder head bolts:		
Stage 1	70	52
Stage 2	Angle-tighten through a further 90°	
Stage 3	Angle-tighten through a further 90°	
Engine-to-transmission bolts:		
Manual transmission:		
M10 x 40 mm bolts	55	41
M10 x 90 mm bolts	45	33
Automatic transmission:		
M10 bolts	55	41
M12 bolts	65	48
Sump bolts:		
M6 bolts	10	7
M8 bolts	25	18
Oil drain plug	25	18
Oil pressure relief valve plug	50	37
Oil pump sprocket bolt	32	24
Oil pump securing bolts	25	18
Flywheel/driveplate bolts:		
Stage 1:		
Standard flywheel	30	22
"Dual-mass" flywheel	40	30
Stage 2	Angle-tighten through a further 90 to 100°	
Crankshaft rear oil seal housing bolts	10	7
Engine mounting-to-engine mounting bracket bolts	25	18
Left- and right-hand engine mounting-to-crossmember bolts	40	30
Left- and right-hand engine mounting bracket bolts	25	18
Rear engine/transmission mounting-to-transmission nut	65	48
Rear engine/transmission mounting-to-crossmember bolts	25	18
Rear engine/transmission mounting crossmember-to-underbody bolts	35	26
Rear engine/transmission mounting adjuster bolt	30	22
Engine mounting damper securing bolts	10	7
Engine movement stop securing bolts	25	18
Engine movement stop adjuster bolt	130	96
Big-end bearing cap nuts:		
Stage 1	30	22
Stage 2	Angle-tighten through a further 90 to 100°	
Main bearing cap bolts:		
Stage 1	55	41
Stage 2	Angle-tighten through a further 90 to 100°	
Cylinder block coolant drain plug	30	22

1 General information

How to use this Chapter

This Part of Chapter 2 describes the repair procedures that can reasonably be carried out on the engine while it remains in the vehicle. If the engine has been removed from the vehicle and is being dismantled as described in Part D, any preliminary dismantling procedures can be ignored.

Note that, while it may be possible physically to overhaul items such as the piston/connecting rod assemblies while the engine is in the car, such tasks are not usually carried out as separate operations. Usually, several additional procedures are required (not to mention the cleaning of components and oilways); for this reason, all such tasks are classed as major overhaul procedures, and are described in Part D of this Chapter.

Part D describes the removal of the engine/transmission from the car, and the full overhaul procedures that can then be carried out.

Engine description

The engine is of six-cylinder in-line single overhead camshaft design, mounted in-line ("north-south") with the transmission at the front of the vehicle.

The crankshaft is supported in seven main bearings within the cast iron cylinder block. Crankshaft endfloat is controlled by thrustwashers fitted on either side of No 5 main bearing.

The connecting rods are attached to the crankshaft by horizontally-split big-end bearings, and to the pistons by fully-floating gudgeon pins retained by circlips. The alloy pistons are fitted with three piston rings: two compression and one oil control.

The camshaft is driven from the crankshaft sprocket by a single-row chain.

The camshaft is supported in seven bearings in the aluminium alloy cylinder head, and actuates the valves via rocker arms. The rocker arms are operated via hydraulic valve lifters.

The oil pump is chain-driven from the front of the crankshaft.

Repair operations possible with the engine in the vehicle

The following operations can be carried out without having to remove the engine from the vehicle:

a) *Removal and refitting of the cylinder head.*
b) *Removal and refitting of the timing chain and sprockets.*
c) *Removal and refitting of the camshaft.*
d) *Removal and refitting of the sump.*
e) *Removal and refitting of the big-end bearings, connecting rods, and pistons*.*
f) *Removal and refitting of the oil pump.*
g) *Renewal of the engine/transmission mountings.*
h) *Removal and refitting of the flywheel/driveplate.*

** Although it is possible to remove these components with the engine in place, for reasons of access and cleanliness it is recommended that the engine is removed.*

2 Compression test - description and interpretation

The procedure is identical to that described in Chapter 2A, for four-cylinder petrol engines.

3 Engine assembly and valve timing marks - general information and usage

1 Top Dead Centre (TDC) is the highest point in the cylinder that each piston reaches as it travels up and down when the crankshaft turns. Each piston reaches TDC at the end of the compression stroke and again at the end of the exhaust stroke, but TDC generally refers to piston position on the compression stroke. No 1 piston is at the timing chain end of the engine.

2 Positioning No 1 piston at TDC is an essential part of many procedures, such as timing chain removal and camshaft removal.

3 Note the position of the terminal for No 1 cylinder HT lead on the distributor cap. If the terminal is not marked, follow the HT lead from the No 1 cylinder spark plug to the cap (No 1 cylinder is at the timing chain end of the engine).

4 Remove the camshaft cover as described in Section 4.

5 Using a suitable socket on the crankshaft pulley/vibration damper hub bolt (on some models, it may be necessary to remove the cooling fan cowl and blades for access), turn the crankshaft clockwise until the following marks are aligned **(see illustrations)**.

a) *The TDC ("O/T") mark on the crankshaft pulley/vibration damper is aligned with the edge of the crankshaft position sensor mounting bracket.*
b) *The TDC pin or hole (depending on engine type) in the flange at the front of the camshaft is aligned with the raised rib on the front camshaft bearing cap.*
c) *The distributor rotor arm is aligned with the No 1 cylinder HT lead terminal in the distributor cap (it will be necessary to remove the distributor cap to check this - see Chapter 5C).*

6 When the marks are aligned as described in paragraph 5, No 1 piston is at TDC on the firing stroke. If the timing chain is to be removed, do not turn the camshaft or the crankshaft until the chain has been refitted.

2B

4 Camshaft cover - removal and refitting

Removal

Note: *A new gasket may be required on refitting.*

1 Disconnect the battery negative lead.

2 Raise the bonnet to the fully open position.

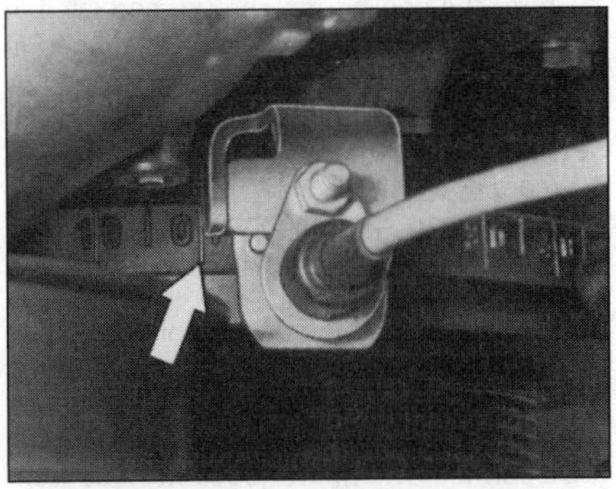

3.5a TDC ("O/T") mark (arrowed) on crankshaft pulley/vibration damper aligned with the edge of the crankshaft position sensor mounting bracket

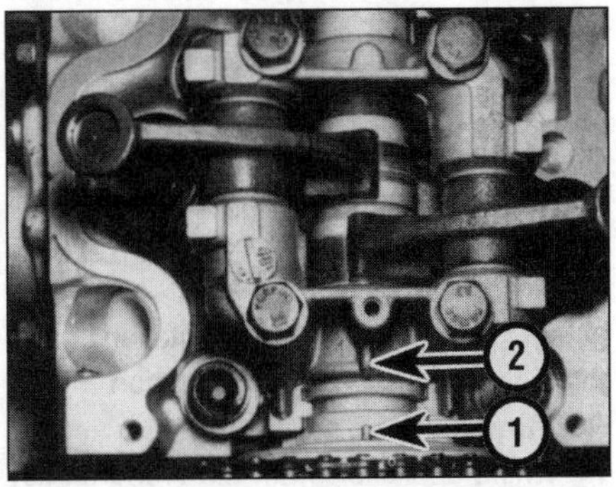

3.5b TDC pin (1) on camshaft aligned with raised rib (2) on camshaft bearing cap

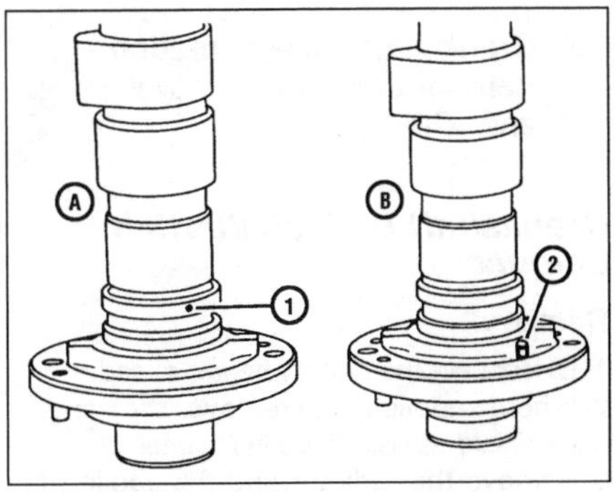

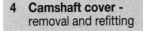

3.5c Camshaft TDC indicators

A *Later type camshaft with TDC hole (1)*
B *Early type camshaft with TDC pin (2)*

3 Release the securing clips, and pull the plastic cover from the top of the distributor cap **(see illustration)**.
4 Pull the HT leads from the spark plugs, making sure that they are identified to ensure correct refitting.
5 Using a screwdriver, carefully lever the HT lead housing from the camshaft cover, and place it to one side (leave the leads attached to the housing). There is no need to disconnect the HT leads from the distributor cap, unless this is required for later work. If the HT leads are disconnected from the distributor cap, ensure that they are identified so that they can be correctly reconnected.
6 Disconnect the camshaft cover breather hose from the air cleaner assembly.
7 Disconnect the small breather hose from the camshaft cover.
8 Unscrew the eight camshaft cover securing bolts, and recover the washers.
9 Lift the camshaft cover from the cylinder head. If the cover is stuck, try rocking by hand, and if necessary tap carefully with a soft-faced mallet - take care, as the cover is easily damaged.
10 Recover the gasket.

Refitting

11 Examine the condition of the gasket, and renew if necessary.
12 Locate the gasket in the grooves in the camshaft cover, starting at the front and rear.
13 Lay the cover in position on the cylinder head, ensuring that the gasket locates correctly, then refit the securing bolts.
14 Tighten the bolts progressively to the specified torque.
15 Reconnect the breather hoses.
16 Clip the HT lead housing into position on the camshaft cover, then reconnect the HT leads to the spark plugs, and where applicable to the distributor cap, ensuring that they are correctly reconnected, as noted before removal.
17 Refit the plastic cover to the distributor cap.
18 Reconnect the battery negative lead.

5 Crankshaft pulley/vibration damper and hub - removal and refitting

Crankshaft pulley/vibration damper

Removal

1 Disconnect the battery negative lead.
2 Where applicable, remove the engine undershield as described in Chapter 11.
3 Remove the radiator and the cooling fan blades as described in Chapter 3.
4 Slacken the cooling fan pulley bolts, then remove the auxiliary drivebelt as described in Chapter 1A.

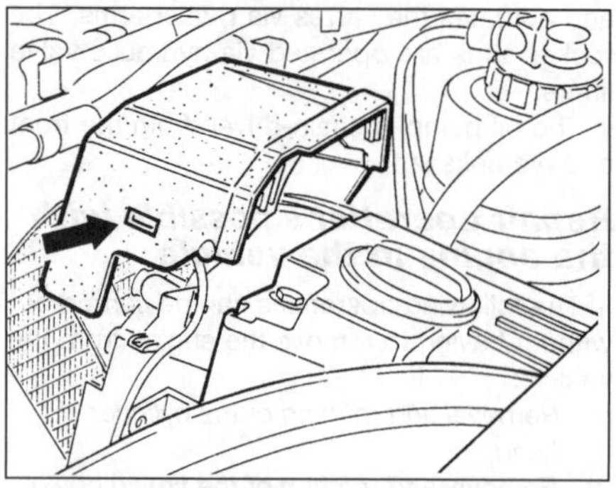

4.3 Release the clips (arrowed) and pull the plastic cover from the distributor

5 Remove the bolts, and withdraw the cooling fan pulley.
6 Unscrew the securing bolts, and remove the pulley/vibration damper from the hub. If necessary, counterhold the pulley/vibration damper using a socket on the hub securing bolt.

Refitting

7 Refitting is a reversal of removal, but refit the auxiliary drivebelt as described in Chapter 1A, and refit the cooling fan blades and the radiator as described in Chapter 3.

Hub

Removal

Warning: The hub securing bolt is very tight. A tool will be required to counterhold the hub as the bolt is unscrewed. Do not attempt the job using inferior or poorly-improvised tools, a injury or damage may result.

Note: *A torque wrench capable of providing 300 Nm (221 lbf ft) of torque will be required on refitting. Also note that the hub must be heated to a temperature of approximately 50° C to enable it to be refitted. A puller may be required to remove the hub.*

8 Remove the crankshaft pulley/vibration damper as described previously in this Section.
9 Make up a tool to hold the hub. A suitable tool can be fabricated using two lengths of steel bar, joined by a large pivot bolt. Bolt the holding tool to the hub using the pulley/vibration damper-to-hub bolts.
10 Using a socket and a long swing-bar, loosen the hub bolt. Note that the bolt is very tight.
11 Unscrew the hub bolt, and remove the spring washers.
12 Using a suitable puller, pull the hub from the front of the crankshaft.
13 Where applicable, recover the Woodruff key from the front of the crankshaft.

Refitting

14 Where applicable, refit the Woodruff key to the groove in the crankshaft.
15 The hub must now be heated to a temperature of approximately 50°C to enable it to slide onto the crankshaft.

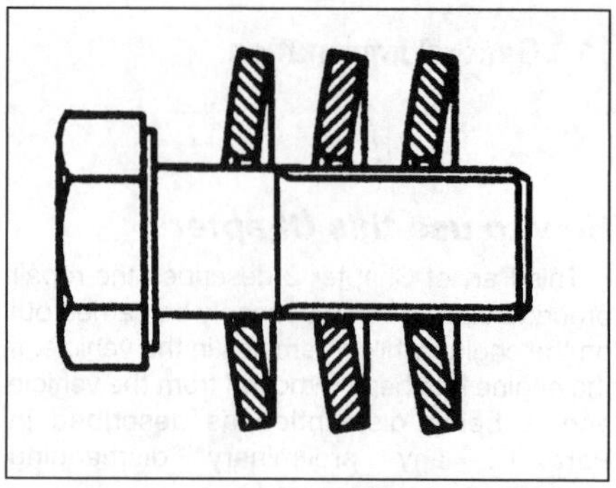

5.17 Fit the spring washers with the convex side of each washer facing the hub bolt head

16 Once the hub is at the appropriate temperature (it should be possible to achieve satisfactory results by immersing the hub for some time in very hot water), align the groove in the hub with the key, and slide the hub onto the end of the crankshaft.
17 Oil the spring washers, then refit them with the convex side of each washer facing the hub bolt head **(see illustration)**.
18 Oil the bolt threads, then refit the hub securing bolt.
19 Bolt the holding tool to the hub, as during removal, then tighten the hub securing bolt to the specified torque. Take care to avoid injury and/or damage.
20 Refit the crankshaft pulley/vibration damper as described previously in this Section.

6 Timing chain covers - removal and refitting

Upper cover

Note: *Suitable sealant, a new timing chain cover seal (see text) and a new coolant pipe O-ring will be required on refitting. It is advisable to renew the camshaft oil seal on refitting.*

Removal

1 Unclip the cooling fan shroud, and lay it in position over the fan blades as described in Chapter 3.
2 Remove the camshaft cover as described in Section 4.
3 Where applicable, unclip the cover from the distributor cap. Disconnect the coil HT lead from the distributor cap, then unscrew the three securing screws, and remove the distributor cap. Lay the distributor cap to one side, complete with the HT leads and housing.
4 Partially drain the cooling system as described in Chapter 1A.
5 Disconnect the heater coolant hose from the pipe running across the front of the cylinder head.
6 Unscrew the securing bolt(s), then pull the coolant pipe from the coolant pump, and

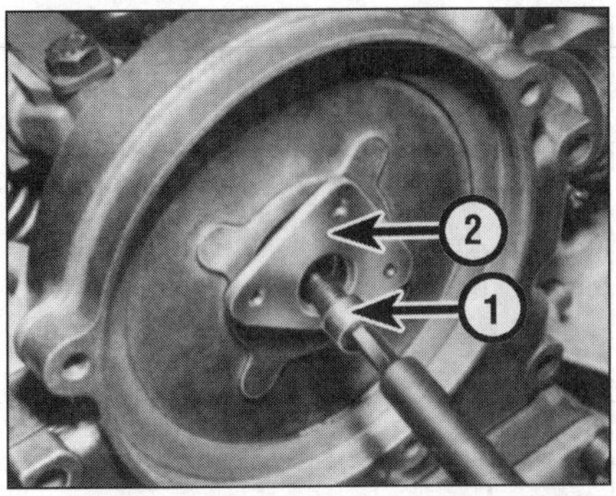

6.8 Unscrew the rotor arm drive sleeve securing bolt (1) and remove the drive sleeve (2)

withdraw the pipe. Recover the O-ring from the coolant pump end of the pipe.

7 Unscrew the three securing screws, and remove the distributor rotor arm.

8 Unscrew the securing bolt, and remove the rotor arm drive sleeve **(see illustration)**. Unclip the plastic cover from the front of the upper timing chain cover.

9 Unscrew the upper timing chain cover securing bolts, then remove the cover. The cover is fitted using sealant, and is located on dowels, so it will probably be necessary to tap the cover from behind using a plastic mallet, to free it from the cylinder head.

10 Recover the gasket from the groove in the top of the lower timing chain cover.

Refitting

11 Commence refitting by thoroughly cleaning the mating faces of the upper and lower timing chain covers, and the cylinder head. Clean away all traces of old sealant.

12 It is advisable to renew the camshaft oil seal in the timing chain cover as follows.

a) *Prise out the old oil seal using a screwdriver.*

b) *Clean the oil seal seating face in the timing chain cover.*

c) *Tap the new seal (dry) into position using a suitable tube or socket until the seal is flush with the outer face of the cover.*

13 A piece of thin plastic or tape wound around the front edge of the camshaft flange is useful to prevent damage to the oil seal as the cover is fitted.

14 Apply a little sealant to the joints between the lower timing chain cover and the cylinder head, then position a new gasket in the groove in the top of the lower timing chain cover **(see illustration)**.

15 Apply sealant to the cylinder head mating face of the upper timing chain cover.

16 Coat the lips of the camshaft oil seal with clean engine oil, then slide the cover into position over the camshaft, ensuring that the cover engages with the cylinder head dowels. Take great care not to damage the oil seal lips as the cover is fitted.

17 Fit the cover securing bolts, then tighten the bolts, starting with the bottom two, to the specified torque.

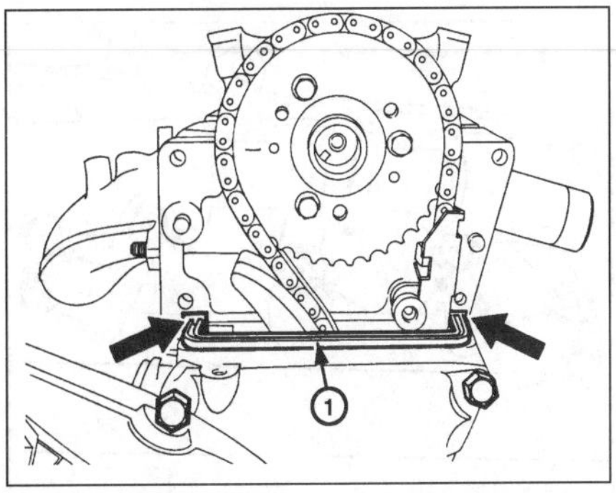

6.14 Apply sealant (arrowed) to the lower timing chain cover-to-cylinder head joints, then fit a new gasket (1)

18 Carefully wipe away any excess sealant using a lint-free rag.

19 Where applicable, remove the plastic or tape from the camshaft.

20 Where applicable, refit the cover to the front of the upper timing chain cover, then refit the rotor arm drive sleeve, ensuring that the groove in the sleeve engages with the lug on the camshaft. Refit the drive sleeve securing bolt, and tighten to the specified torque.

21 Refit the rotor arm, and tighten the securing screws.

22 Refit the coolant pipe to the coolant pump, using a new O-ring, then tighten the pipe securing bolt(s).

23 Reconnect the coolant hose to the pipe.

24 Refit the distributor cap, and reconnect the coil HT lead.

25 Refit the camshaft cover as described in Section 4.

26 Refit the cooling fan shroud, with reference to Chapter 3.

27 Refill the cooling system as described in Chapter 1A.

Lower cover

Note: *Suitable sealant, a new cooling fan bracket bolt seal (see text), and a new coolant pipe O-ring will be required on refitting. It is advisable to renew the crankshaft front oil seal.*

Removal

28 Disconnect the battery negative lead.

29 Raise the bonnet to the fully open position.

30 Where applicable, remove the engine undershield, as described in Chapter 11.

31 Remove the air cleaner assembly as described in Chapter 4.

32 Remove the radiator, and the cooling fan blades, as described in Chapter 3.

33 Slacken the cooling fan clutch, coolant pump, and power steering/self-levelling suspension pump pulley securing bolts, then remove the auxiliary drivebelt as described in Chapter 1A.

34 Unscrew the securing bolts, and remove the belt pulleys.

35 Remove the crankshaft pulley/vibration damper and hub as described in Section 5.

36 Unscrew the securing bolt(s), then pull the coolant pipe, which runs across the front of the cylinder head, from the coolant pump. Recover the O-ring from the end of the pipe. Move the pipe to one side, clear of the working area.

37 Unscrew the nut, and withdraw the bolt from the front of the engine lifting bracket at the front of the cylinder head **(see illustration)**.

38 On models with self-levelling suspension, loosen the hose clip, and disconnect the hydraulic fluid hose from the pipe at the front left-hand side of the cylinder head. Be prepared for fluid spillage, and plug the open ends of the pipe and hose to prevent dirt ingress and further fluid spillage.

39 Remove the upper timing chain cover as described previously in this Section.

40 Slacken the central bolt securing the power steering/self-levelling suspension pump bracket, then unscrew the remaining three bracket securing bolts (counterhold the nut at the rear of the bolt, where applicable) **(see illustration)**. Recover the washers.

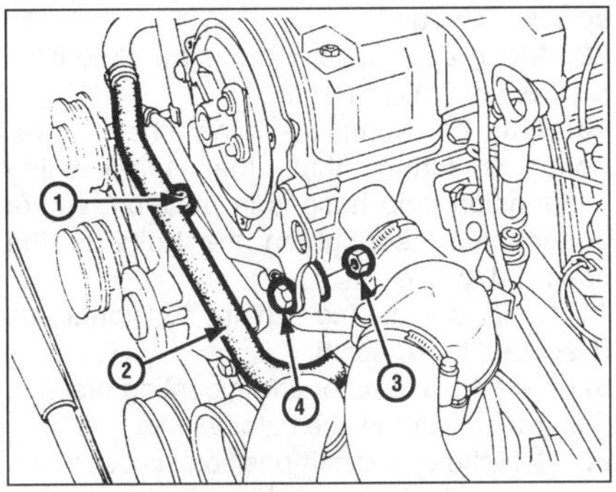

6.37 Coolant pipe and engine lifting bracket details

1. *Coolant pipe securing bolt*
2. *Coolant pipe*
3. *Nut*
4. *Bolt*

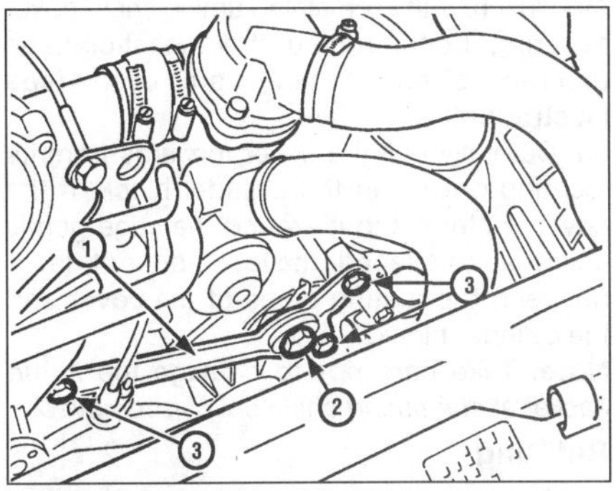

6.40 Power steering/self-levelling suspension pump mounting bracket

1. *Mounting bracket*
2. *Central bolt*
3. *Securing bolts*

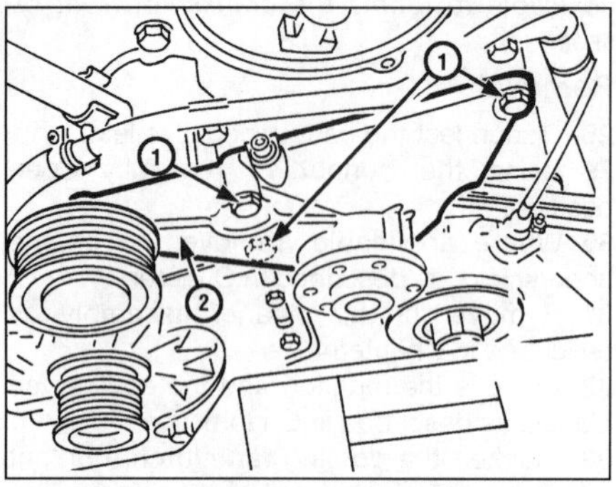

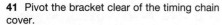

6.43 Unscrew the securing bolts (1) and remove the cooling fan pulley bracket (2)

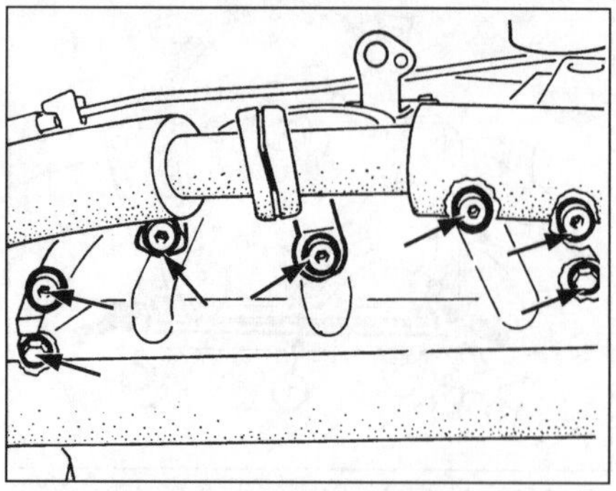

6.48 Unscrew the bolts (arrowed) securing the sump to the timing chain cover

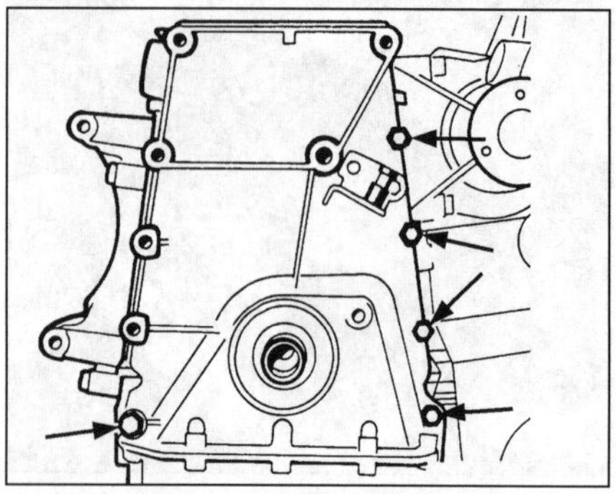

6.49 Unscrew the remaining timing chain cover securing bolts (arrowed)

41 Pivot the bracket clear of the timing chain cover.

42 Unscrew the two bolts securing the power steering/self-levelling suspension pump to the mounting bracket, then pivot the pump away from the engine.

43 Unscrew the securing bolts, and remove the cooling fan pulley bracket from the front of the timing chain cover **(see illustration)**.

44 Unscrew the securing nut, and remove the crankshaft position sensor from the bracket on the front of the timing chain cover. Where applicable, release the wiring from any securing clips, and move the sensor to one side, clear of the working area.

45 Disconnect the alternator wiring connector.

46 Unscrew the four bolts securing the alternator mounting bracket to the engine and the alternator, then remove the mounting bracket and the alternator.

47 Remove the timing chain tensioner as described in Section 8.

48 Working underneath the vehicle, unscrew the bolts securing the sump to the timing chain cover **(see illustration)**. Note the bolt locations, as different sizes of bolts are used. On models with self-levelling suspension, move the fluid hose (secured to the sump by the sump-to-timing chain cover bolts) to one side.

49 Unscrew the remaining timing chain cover securing bolts, noting their locations, as different sizes of bolts are used **(see illustration)**.

50 Carefully pull the cover forwards from its locating dowels in the cylinder block. If the cover is stuck, tap it around the edge gently using a soft-faced mallet - do not lever between the mating faces of the cover and the cylinder block.

Note: *Take care not to damage the sump gasket as the timing chain cover is removed.*

Refitting

51 Commence refitting by thoroughly cleaning the mating faces of the lower timing chain cover, and the cylinder block, and the upper timing chain cover. Clean away all traces of old sealant.

52 Carefully check the condition of the sump gasket. If the gasket has been damaged during the removal procedure, the sump should be removed in order to renew the gasket, as described in Section 11.

53 It is advisable to renew the crankshaft oil seal in the timing chain cover as follows.

a) *Prise out the old oil seal using a screwdriver.*
b) *Clean the oil seal seating face in the timing chain cover.*
c) *Tap the new seal (dry) into position using a suitable tube or socket until the seal seats on the shoulder in the cover.*

54 A piece of thin plastic or tape wound around the front edge of the crankshaft flange is useful to prevent damage to the oil seal as the cover is fitted.

55 Renew the seal located in the lower cooling fan bracket securing bolt location in the timing chain cover.

56 Apply sealant to the cylinder block mating face of the timing chain cover.

57 Coat the lips of the crankshaft oil seal with clean engine oil, then slide the cover into position over the crankshaft, ensuring that the cover engages with the cylinder block dowels. Take great care not to damage the oil seal lips as the cover is fitted.

58 Fit the cover securing bolts shown in illustration 6.49, ensuring that the bolts are refitted to their correct locations as noted before removal, then tighten the bolts to the specified torque.

59 Where applicable, remove the tape from the front of the crankshaft.

60 Refit the sump-to-timing chain cover bolts, ensuring that the self-levelling suspension fluid hose is in position, where applicable, then tighten the bolts to the specified torque.

61 Refit the timing chain tensioner as described in Section 8.

62 Refit the alternator and mounting bracket, then reconnect the alternator wiring.

63 Refit the crankshaft position sensor to the bracket on the timing chain cover, and tighten the securing nut. **Note:** *If a new timing chain cover has been fitted, the position of the crankshaft position sensor must be checked with reference to Chapter 4.*

64 Refit the cooling fan bracket, and tighten the securing bolts to the specified torque.

65 Pivot the power steering/self-levelling suspension pump into position on the mounting bracket, then refit and tighten the securing bolts.

66 Apply sealant to both sides of the timing chain cover bolt location in the power steering/self-levelling suspension pump bracket.

67 Pivot the power steering/self-levelling suspension pump bracket into position, then refit and tighten the securing bolts, ensuring that the washers are in place. Tighten the central bolt.

68 Refit the upper timing chain cover as described previously in this Section.

69 Where applicable, reconnect the self-levelling suspension fluid hose to the pipe at the front of the cylinder head.

70 Refit the bolt and nut to the engine lifting bracket.

71 Reconnect the coolant pipe to the coolant pump, using a new O-ring, then refit the securing bolt(s).

72 Refit the crankshaft pulley/vibration damper and hub as described in Section 5.

73 Refit the auxiliary drivebelt pulleys, and refit the securing bolts.

74 Refit the auxiliary drivebelt as described in Chapter 1A, then tighten the pulley securing bolts.

75 Refit the cooling fan blades and the radiator as described in Chapter 3.

76 Refit the air cleaner assembly.

77 Where applicable, refit the engine undershield.

78 Refill the cooling system as described in Chapter 1A.

79 Check and if necessary top-up the engine oil level and, where applicable, the power steering/self-levelling suspension fluid level, as described in *"Weekly checks"*.

80 Reconnect the battery negative lead.

7 Timing chain - inspection and renewal

Inspection

1 Remove the upper timing chain cover as described in Section 6.

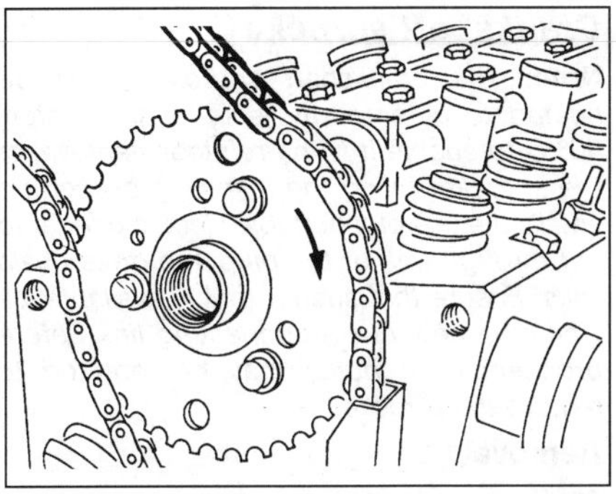

7.13 Feed the new timing chain around the sprockets, keeping tension on the chain

2 Using a socket on the crankshaft pulley/vibration damper hub bolt, turn the engine so that the whole length of the chain can be progressively viewed at the camshaft sprocket.

3 The chain should be renewed if the sprocket is worn or if the chain is worn (indicated by excessive lateral play between the links, and excessive noise in operation). It is wise to renew the chain in any case if the engine is to be dismantled for overhaul. Note that the rollers on a very badly worn chain may be slightly grooved. To avoid future problems, if there is any doubt at all about the condition of the chain, renew it.

Renewal

Note: *Removal of the timing chain using the following procedure entails the use of a portable electric grinder to cut through one of the chain links. Ensure that such a tool is available, as well as a new chain and new connecting link before proceeding.*

4 Disconnect the battery negative lead.

5 If not already done, remove the upper timing chain cover as described in Section 6.

6 Remove the timing chain tensioner, as described in Section 8.

7 Remove the spark plugs, with reference to Chapter 1A.

8 Cover the camshaft and the chain opening in the timing cover with clean rags, but keep the rags clear of the camshaft sprocket upper section.

9 Using a grinder, grind off the protruding lugs of one of the chain links at the top of the sprocket - take great care not to damage the sprocket.

10 Pull off the chain link plate, then push the link out towards the rear of the chain.

11 Remove the rags, taking care not to allow any swarf to drop down into the timing chain housing.

12 Using the new link, connect one end of the new timing chain to the tail end of the old chain, in such a way that as the engine is turned (clockwise), the new chain will be drawn down, around the sprockets and guides, then up the other side. Fit the link from the rear of the sprocket, and ensure that the link is pushed firmly into position - do not fit the link plate to secure the link at this stage.

13 It is now necessary to feed the new chain around the sprockets and guides. During this procedure it is essential to observe the following points **(see illustration)**.

a) Keep tension on the new chain, ensuring that the links remain engaged with the camshaft sprocket, otherwise the valve timing will be lost.

b) Pull up on the old chain to prevent it dropping off the crankshaft sprocket, or jamming in the guides.

14 Using a suitable socket on the crankshaft pulley/vibration damper hub bolt, slowly turn the crankshaft clockwise, whilst observing the points made in the preceding paragraph.

15 When the end of the new chain appears, remove the link (ensuring that tension is kept on the new chain, and that the chain links remain engaged with the sprockets), and disconnect the new chain from the old chain. Remove the old chain.

16 Engage the new chain with the camshaft sprocket, then join the two ends of the chain with the connecting link, inserted from the rear of the sprocket.

HAYNES HiNT ***Temporarily secure the ends of the new chain to the camshaft sprocket using wire or cable-ties passed through the holes in the sprocket and around the chain.***

17 Fit the link plate, and then secure the plate to the link by flattening the ends of the link pins. A special tool is available for this purpose, but it should be possible to achieve a satisfactory result using a hammer, with a block of metal (or a second hammer) to support the rear of the chain - *take great care not to damage the chain or the sprocket.*

18 Check that the chain link is secure, with no burring of the metal, or loose swarf.

19 Refit the chain tensioner as described in Section 8.

20 Turn the engine (clockwise) to bring No 1 piston to TDC, ensuring that crankshaft and camshaft timing marks are correctly aligned as described in Section 3.

21 It is possible that the timing chain may have slipped by one tooth on the camshaft sprocket during this operation. If this is the case, the timing can be corrected by removing the camshaft sprocket (see Section 8), and altering the position of the camshaft and sprocket by one tooth in relation to the chain.

22 Refit the spark plugs as described in Chapter 1A.

23 Refit the upper timing chain cover as described in Section 6.

24 Reconnect the battery negative lead.

8 Timing chain tensioner, sprockets and guides - removal, inspection and refitting

Tensioner

Removal

Note: *A new cover nut sealing ring will be required on refitting.*

1 Disconnect the battery negative lead.

2 Raise the bonnet to the fully open position.

3 Working at the right-hand side of the engine, unscrew the timing chain tensioner cover nut, and withdraw the spring and sealing ring **(see illustration)**.

Warning: The cover nut is under considerable tension from the spring, so be prepared for it to fly off when it reaches the end of the threads.

2B

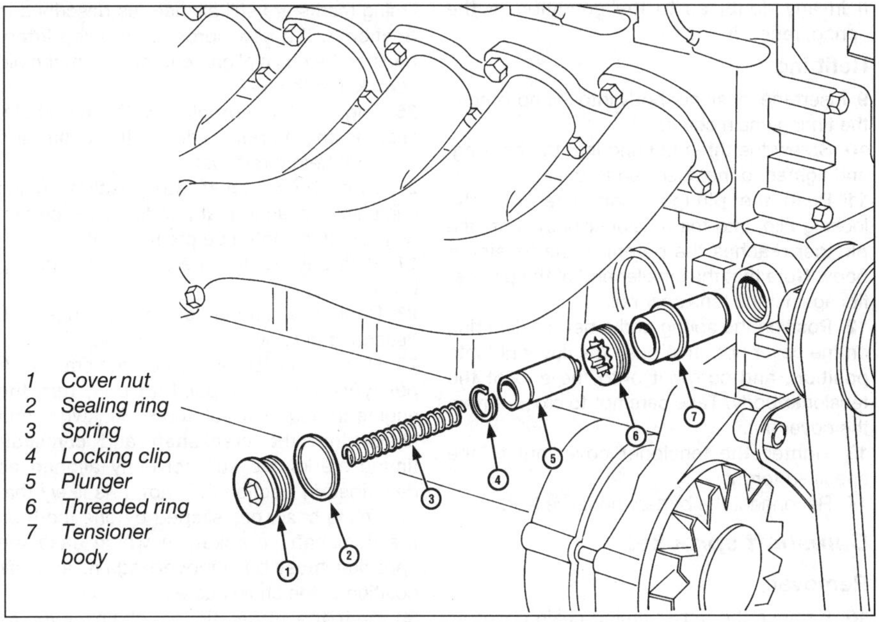

8.3 Timing chain tensioner components

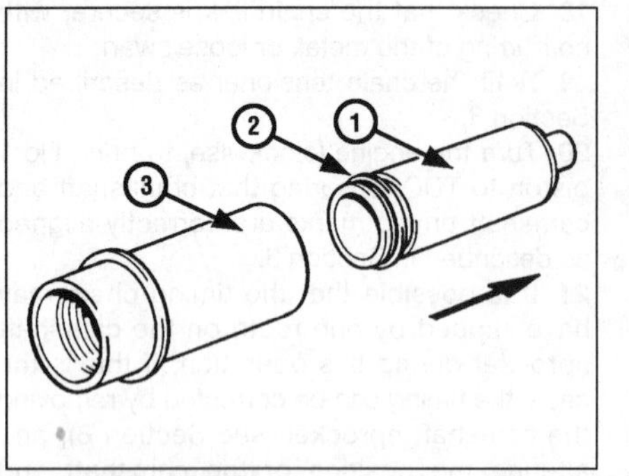

8.6 Press the tensioner plunger (1) and locking clip (2) out of the tensioner body (3) in the direction of the arrow

4 Using a large Allen key or a suitable hexagon bit, unscrew the tensioner threaded ring, and withdraw it from the housing.
5 Withdraw the tensioner plunger/body assembly from the housing.

> **HAYNES HiNT** ***The tensioner plunger/body assembly can be withdrawn using an M8 bolt. Note that the bolt cannot be screwed into the assembly, but the bolt can be engaged with the aperture in the top of the body, and used to "hook" the assembly out.***

6 Press the tensioner plunger and the locking clip out of the tensioner body **(see illustration)**.

Inspection

7 Thoroughly clean the tensioner components, and examine the plunger and the tensioner body for signs of damage or wear.
8 Check the condition of the locking clip, and the tensioner spring, and renew if necessary. If in any doubt as to the condition of the spring, renew it.

Refitting

9 Insert the tensioner body into the housing in the timing chain cover.
10 Screw the threaded ring into the housing, and tighten to the specified torque.
11 Push the plunger, complete with the locking clip, into the tensioner body, until the plunger reaches the detent in the tensioner body. Note that the smaller end of the plunger fits against the tensioner rail.
12 Position the spring and a new sealing ring on the cover nut, then push the cover nut into position, and screw it onto the end of the tensioner body. Take care not to cross-thread the cover nut.
13 Tighten the tensioner cover nut to the specified torque.
14 Reconnect the battery negative lead.

Camshaft sprocket

Removal

15 Remove the upper timing chain cover as described in Section 6.
16 Turn the engine to position No 1 piston at TDC, ensuring that crankshaft and camshaft timing marks are correctly aligned as described in Section 3.
17 Remove the timing chain tensioner as described previously in this Section.
18 Using quick-drying paint or a suitable scriber, make reference marks on the camshaft sprocket, and on an adjacent timing chain link, to aid refitting. Similarly, make alignment marks between the end of the camshaft and the camshaft sprocket.
19 Unscrew the three camshaft sprocket securing bolts.
20 Withdraw the sprocket from the camshaft, noting which way round it is fitted, and unhook the sprocket from the timing chain. Keep tension on the chain, and support the chain in the top of the housing, to prevent it from dropping off the crankshaft sprocket.
21 Where applicable, recover the Woodruff key from the end of the camshaft.

Inspection

Note: *Various modifications have been made to the camshaft sprocket during production. If a sprocket is to be renewed, it is strongly recommended that a Mercedes-Benz dealer is consulted to ensure that the correct new sprocket is obtained.*
22 Examine the teeth on the sprocket for wear. Each tooth forms an inverted "V". If worn, the side of each tooth under tension will be slightly concave in shape when compared with the other side of the tooth (ie: the teeth will have a "hooked" appearance). If the teeth appear worn, the sprocket must be renewed.

Refitting

23 Where applicable, refit the Woodruff key to the end of the camshaft.
24 Ensure that the camshaft and crankshaft timing marks are still aligned, as described in Section 3. If a new sprocket is being fitted, transfer the chain alignment mark from the old sprocket to the new.
25 Engage the sprocket with the chain, aligning the marks made on the chain and sprocket before removal.
26 Offer the sprocket into position on the camshaft, ensuring that it is fitted the correct way round, as noted before removal.
27 Refit and tighten the sprocket securing bolts.
28 Refit the timing chain tensioner as described previously in this Section.
29 Using a suitable socket on the crankshaft pulley/vibration damper hub bolt, turn the engine through two full turns clockwise, and check that the crankshaft and camshaft timing marks are still correctly aligned as described in Section 3. If not, it is likely that the timing chain has slipped by one tooth on the camshaft sprocket, in which case the sprocket must be removed again, and the position of the chain altered.
30 Refit the upper timing chain cover as described in Section 6.

Crankshaft sprocket

Note: *The crankshaft sprocket must be heated to a temperature of approximately 50° C to enable it to be refitted. Removal of the sprocket using the following procedure entails the use of a portable electric grinder to cut through one of the oil pump drive chain links. Ensure that such a tool is available, as well as a new chain connecting link before proceeding. A puller may be required to remove the sprocket.*

Removal

31 Remove the timing chain tensioner rail, as described later in this Section.
32 Cover the opening in the sump using clean rags.
33 Pull the oil pump drive chain tensioner rail and spring from the lug on the cylinder block - note the orientation of the spring to aid correct refitting **(see illustration)**. Recover the bush.
34 Using a grinder, grind off the protruding lugs of one of the oil pump drive chain links at the top of the sprocket - take great care not to damage the sprocket.
35 Support the chain (**do not** allow the chain to drop off the oil pump drive gear), then pull off the chain link plate, and push the link out towards the rear of the chain.
36 Remove the rags, taking care not to allow any swarf to drop down into the sump.
37 Support the chain using wire or string to keep it engaged with the oil pump drive gear.
38 Make alignment marks on the camshaft sprocket and timing chain, then lift the timing chain from the sprocket.
39 Remove the crankshaft sprocket from the front of the crankshaft, using a suitable puller. Alternatively, it may be possible to lever it off using two large screwdrivers positioned either side of the sprocket. Note which way round the sprocket is fitted to ensure correct refitting.
40 Where applicable, recover the Woodruff key from the end of the crankshaft if it is loose.

Inspection

41 Refer to paragraph 22 for details of crankshaft sprocket inspection.

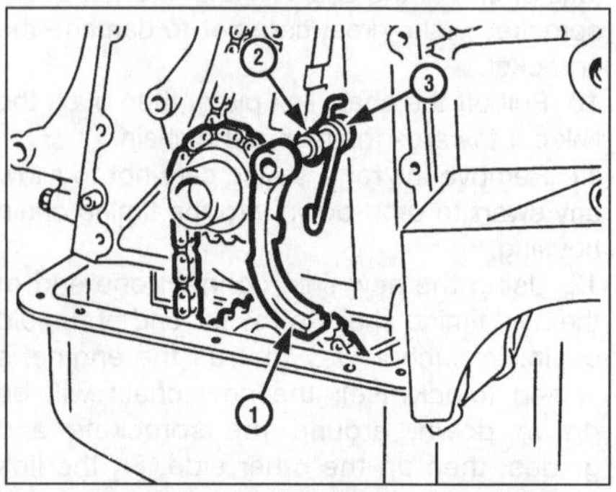

8.33 Pull the oil pump drive chain tensioner rail (1), bush (2) and spring (3) from the lug on the cylinder block

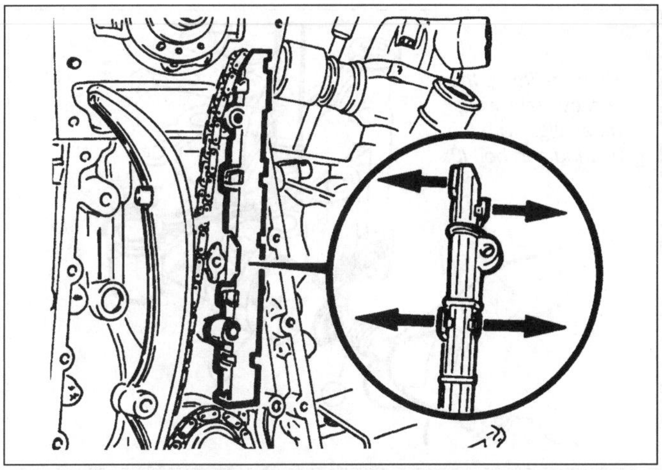

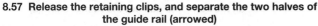

8.57 Release the retaining clips, and separate the two halves of the guide rail (arrowed)

8.67 Make alignment marks (arrowed) on the timing chain and sprocket, then withdraw the tensioner rail (1)

Refitting

42 Where applicable, refit the Woodruff key to the end of the crankshaft.

43 If a new sprocket is being fitted, transfer the chain alignment mark from the old sprocket to the new.

44 The crankshaft sprocket must now be heated to a temperature of approximately 50° C to enable it to slide onto the crankshaft.

45 Once the sprocket is at the appropriate temperature (it should be possible to achieve satisfactory results by immersing the sprocket for some time in very hot water), align the groove in the sprocket with the key, and slide the sprocket onto the end of the crankshaft. Ensure that the sprocket is fitted the correct way round as noted before removal.

46 Fit the timing chain around the camshaft sprocket, ensuring that the marks made on the sprocket and chain before removal are aligned.

47 Fit the timing chain around the crankshaft sprocket, again ensuring that the marks made on the sprocket and the chain before removal are aligned.

48 Lay the two ends of the oil pump drive chain onto the crankshaft sprocket then, using a new link, reconnect the two ends of the chain. Fit the link from the rear of the sprocket, and ensure that the link is pushed firmly into position.

49 Fit the chain link plate, and then secure the plate to the link by flattening the ends of the link pins. A special tool is available for this purpose, but it should be possible to achieve a satisfactory result using a hammer, with a block of metal (or a second hammer) to support the rear of the chain - *take great care not to damage the chain or the sprocket.*

50 Check that the chain link is secure, with no burring of the metal, or loose swarf.

51 Refit the oil pump drive chain tensioner rail bush, spring, and then the tensioner rail. Ensure that the spring is orientated as noted before removal.

52 Refit the timing chain tensioner rail as described later in this Section.

Guide rail

Removal

53 Turn the engine to position No 1 piston at TDC, ensuring that crankshaft and camshaft timing marks are correctly aligned as described in Section 3.

54 Remove the lower timing chain cover as described in Section 6.

55 Make alignment marks on the timing chain and the camshaft sprocket.

56 Remove the camshaft sprocket as described previously in this Section.

57 Using a screwdriver, carefully release the retaining clips, and withdraw the outer section of the guide rail from the inner section **(see illustration)**. Take care, as the clips are easily broken.

58 Pull the chain forwards sufficiently to enable the inner section of the guide to be withdrawn from the lugs on the cylinder block.

Inspection

59 Examine the rail for signs of excessive wear, damage or cracks, and renew if necessary. Examine the inner section-to-outer section clip for any signs of damage, and renew the assembly if there is any doubt as to the condition of the clips, or if the plastic has become brittle.

Refitting

60 Push the inner section of the rail into position on the cylinder block lugs.

61 Lay the chain in position in the rail inner section, then refit the outer section, and secure in position with the clips. Ensure that the clips engage securely, and take care not to break them.

62 Refit the camshaft sprocket as described previously in this Section, ensuring that the marks made on the timing chain and sprocket before removal are aligned.

63 Refit the lower timing chain cover as described in Section 6.

Tensioner rail

Removal

64 Turn the engine to position No 1 piston at TDC, ensuring that crankshaft and camshaft timing marks are correctly aligned as described in Section 3.

65 Remove the lower timing chain cover as described in Section 6.

66 Make alignment marks on the timing chain and the crankshaft sprocket.

67 Pivot the tensioner rail as required, to enable it to be withdrawn from the pivot pin **(see illustration)**.

Inspection

68 Examine the rail for signs of excessive wear, damage or cracks, and renew if necessary.

Refitting

69 Push the rail into position, ensuring that it locates correctly over the pivot pin.

70 Ensure that the crankshaft and camshaft timing marks are still aligned with No 1 piston at TDC, as described in Section 3.

71 Ensure that the marks made on the timing chain and crankshaft sprocket before removal are aligned.

72 Refit the lower timing chain cover as described in Section 6.

9 Rocker gear, valve lifters and camshaft - general information, removal, inspection and refitting

General information

1 The rocker gear is integral with the camshaft bearing caps. The rocker arms are mounted on individual short rocker shafts which are an interference-fit in the camshaft bearing caps. One exhaust and one inlet rocker arm is fitted to each bearing cap assembly.

9.7 No 1 camshaft bearing cap bolts (arrowed)

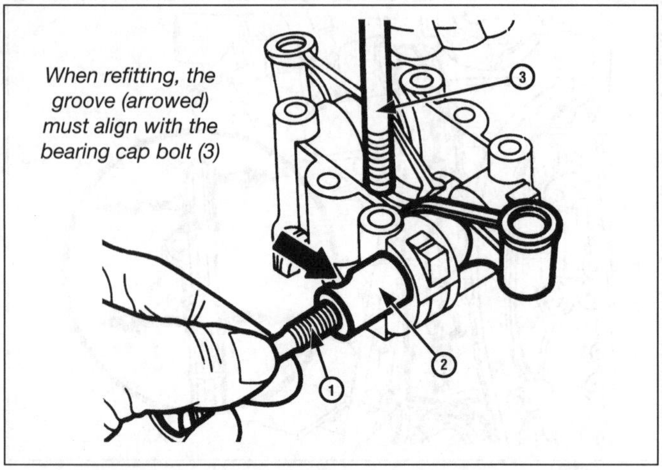
When refitting, the groove (arrowed) must align with the bearing cap bolt (3)
1
2
3

9.13 Use an M8 bolt (1) to pull out the rocker shaft (2)

2 The hydraulic valve lifters are fitted to the rocker arms, and are supplied with oil via drillings in the rocker arms.

Removal

Warning: A number of modifications have been made to the camshaft, rocker gear components and oil spray pipe during production. Certain combinations of old and new components are not compatible, and damage may result if incompatible components are mixed. In view of this, it is strongly recommended that a Mercedes-Benz dealer is consulted if any components are to be renewed, to ensure that the correct new parts are obtained.

3 Remove the air cleaner assembly as described in Chapter 4.

4 Remove the camshaft sprocket as described in Section 8.

5 Unscrew the securing bolts, and remove the oil spray pipe from the top of the camshaft bearing caps. Note that the pipe may be secured by two or three bolts, depending on model. Where applicable, recover the retaining plate from the central securing bolt.

6 Check the rocker arms and the camshaft bearing caps for identification marks. The bearing caps are normally numbered 1 to 6 from the camshaft sprocket end of the cylinder head, on the exhaust manifold side of the bearing caps. A corresponding mark is cast into the cylinder head beneath the camshaft. If any of the bearing caps are not marked, make suitable marks using a pin-punch.

7 Progressively unscrew the camshaft bearing cap bolts (each bearing cap is secured by four bolts), working in a diagonal sequence **(see illustration)**.

8 Lift off the camshaft bearing cap/rocker assemblies. Note that the bearing caps locate on dowels - if they are stuck, tap gently using a soft-faced mallet.

9 Remove the valve lifter contact pads from the tops of the valve stems, keeping them in strict order. The components must not be mixed up.

> **HAYNES HiNT** ***Keep the contact pads in a compartmentalised box, with twelve compartments, numbered 1 to 6 for the inlet valves, and 1 to 6 for the exhaust valves.***

10 Carefully lift the camshaft from the cylinder head. Where applicable, recover the endfloat control thrustwasher from the front bearing location.

Dismantling, inspection and reassembly

Camshaft

11 Examine the camshaft bearings and cam lobes for any sign of scoring, wear grooves or pitting, and if apparent, renew the camshaft. Any damage of this nature may be attributable to a blocked oil passage either in the cylinder head, rocker assemblies or the oil spray pipe, and careful examination should be carried out to determine the cause. If the camshaft is renewed, all the rocker arms must be renewed at the same time.

Rocker gear

12 With the camshaft bearing caps removed, the rocker arms can be removed from the bearing caps by drawing out the short rocker shafts. Before removing the rocker arms, check them for identification marks, and if none are present, make suitable marks to ensure that the arms are fitted in their original locations (mark the rocker arms 1 to 6 for the inlet valves, and 1 to 7 for the exhaust valves) - do not mix the components up. Also note which way round the rocker arms are fitted on the shafts.

13 Screw an M8 bolt into the rocker shaft, then use the bolt to pull out the rocker shaft by hand. With the shaft removed, the rocker arm can be withdrawn. The components can be stored in the compartmentalised box used to store the valve lifter contact pads **(see illustration)**.

14 Check the valve lifter contact pads for wear, and check the fit of the rocker arms on their shafts. If there is any sign of wear or damage, it advisable to renew the components as a complete set.

15 Thoroughly clean the components before refitting.

16 Lubricate the rocker arm and shaft contact surfaces, then refit the shaft and the rocker arm to the relevant camshaft bearing cap, noting the following points.

a) If the original components are being refitted, ensure that all components are refitted to their original locations.

b) Ensure that each rocker arm is fitted the correct way round on the shaft, as noted before removal.

c) Ensure that the groove for the camshaft bearing cap securing bolt in each rocker shaft is aligned with the bolt hole in the bearing cap.

d) Use the M8 bolt used during removal to push each rocker shaft into position in the bearing cap.

Valve lifters

17 To remove a valve lifter from a rocker arm, insert a suitable mandrel through the aperture in the top of the rocker arm, and push the valve lifter from the arm **(see illustration)**.

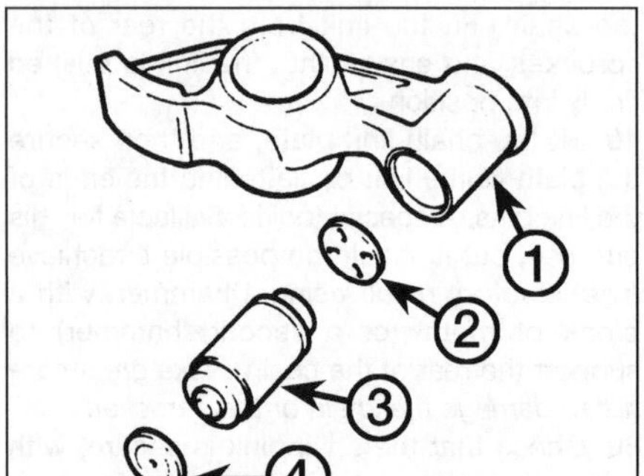
1
2
3
4

9.17 Rocker arm/valve lifter assembly

1 Rocker arm	*3 Valve lifter*
2 Spacer washer	*4 Contact pad*

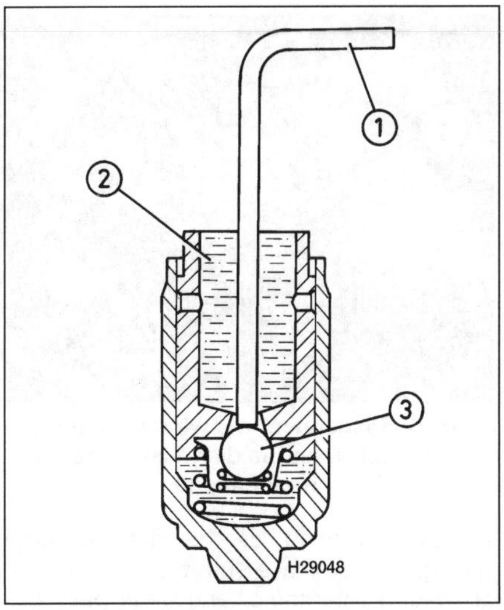

9.21 Checking the operation of the valve lifter

1 1.5 mm diameter wire
2 Oil supply chamber
3 Ball valve

18 Withdraw the spacer washer from the top of the valve lifter housing in the rocker arm.
19 Ensure that the valve lifters and spacer washers are kept in order so that they can be refitted in their original locations.
20 Inspect the valve lifters and spacer washers for obvious signs of wear or damage, and renew if necessary.
21 The operation of the valve lifters can be checked as follows **(see illustration)**.
a) *Hold the valve lifter in the vertical position.*
b) *Fill the oil supply chamber in the top of the valve lifter with clean engine oil.*
c) *Insert a thin piece of wire (diameter 1.5 mm) through the hole in the centre of the lifter, and press down on the ball valve as far as the stop, then release the ball valve. Repeat this procedure until the working chamber at the base of the lifter is filled with oil.*
d) *Press down firmly on the top of the lifter piston, using a blunt instrument such as a wooden hammer handle, for approximately 10 seconds.*
e) *If the lifter piston move down, the complete lifter assembly should be renewed.*

22 The design and construction of the hydraulic valve lifters is such that the amount of free-play or clearance, that they can compensate for is limited. This is mainly due to the compactness of the units. To keep the free-play or clearance to a minimum, and to allow the valve lifters to stay within their operating limits, the spacer washers are available in a number of thicknesses.
23 Under normal operating conditions, the valve lifters will automatically adjust to take up the clearance between the rocker arm and the valve stem, and no problems will occur.
24 If, however, component wear becomes excessive, or the valve train becomes noisy in operation after renewal of the camshaft, rocker arms, valves, or any of the valve lifters themselves, it is possible that the operating clearance has now become outside the operating limits of the valve lifters. In this case, it will be necessary to change the spacer washer for one of a different thickness.
25 To determine the required thickness of the spacer washer, a Mercedes-Benz special dial gauge tool and clamp is required, and the work should be entrusted to a dealer.
26 It is advisable to refit the valve lifters with the rocker arms already in position on the rocker shafts. This will reduce the time taken for assembly, and will reduce the possibility of the oil draining from the valve lifters once they have been primed during the following procedure.
27 Prior to refitting, each valve lifter must be filled with engine oil. To do this, hold the unit vertically, and fill the supply chamber with clean engine oil **(see illustration 9.21)**. Using a thin piece of wire, inserted down through the supply chamber, push the ball valve off its seat so that oil can enter the operating chamber. At the same time, push the plunger upwards to its stop. Repeat this procedure several times until no more oil can be added.
28 Insert the spacer washer into the housing in the rocker arm, with the oil slots facing the valve lifter, then insert the valve lifter. Push the valve lifter up into contact with the snap-ring. The camshaft bearing cap/rocker assemblies can now be refitted to the engine.

Refitting

29 Ensure that the endfloat control thrustwasher is correctly located at the front bearing location.
30 Lubricate the camshaft, and the bearings in the bearing caps and the cylinder head with clean engine oil, then lay the camshaft in position on the cylinder head. Turn the camshaft so that the TDC pin or hole in the flange at the front of the camshaft is pointing vertically upwards - see Section 3.
31 Refit the valve lifter contact pads to their original valve stems.
32 Refit the camshaft bearing caps in their original positions, with the identification numbers on the exhaust manifold side.
33 Refit the camshaft bearing cap bolts, and tighten the bolts progressively, in a diagonal sequence, to the specified torque.
34 Check the condition of the oil spray pipe, paying particular attention to the oil spray holes. If the holes are mis-shaped or damaged, renew the oil spray pipe.
35 Check that the crankshaft and camshaft timing marks are still aligned, with No 1 piston at TDC (see Section 3), then refit the camshaft sprocket as described in Section 8.
36 Refit the air cleaner assembly.

10 Cylinder head - removal, inspection and refitting

Removal

Note: *A hoist and suitable lifting tackle and a suitable slide hammer and adapter will be required for this operation. A new cylinder head gasket will be required on refitting. New cylinder head bolts may be required - see text.*

1 Ensure that the engine is cold before attempting to remove the cylinder head, and note that the cylinder head is removed complete with the inlet and exhaust manifolds.
2 Disconnect the battery negative lead.
3 Raise the bonnet to the fully open position.
4 Drain the cooling system as described in Chapter 1A.
5 Remove the camshaft sprocket as described in Section 8.
6 Screw a suitable bolt into the upper timing chain guide rail locating pin (accessible from the front of the cylinder head).
7 Engage a slide hammer and suitable adapter with the bolt, and use the slide hammer to remove the guide rail locating pin **(see illustration)**.
8 Unscrew the bolt securing the dipstick tube bracket to the cylinder head.
9 Unbolt and remove the two inlet manifold support brackets **(see illustration)**.

10.7 Using a slide hammer to remove the upper guide rail locating pin

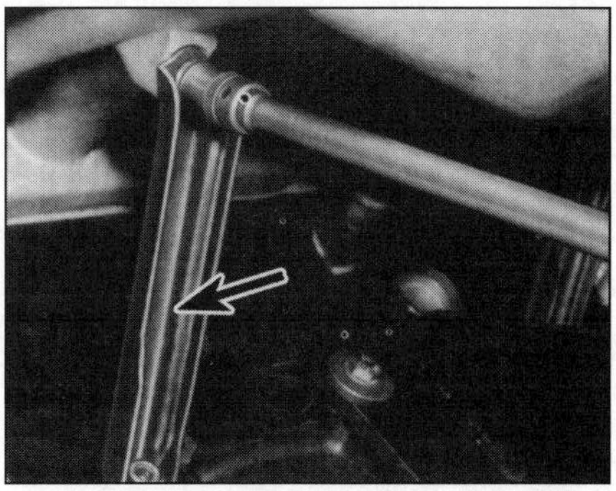

10.9 Unbolt the inlet manifold support brackets (arrowed)

10.10 Loosen the hose clip (arrowed) securing the coolant pump hose to the cylinder head

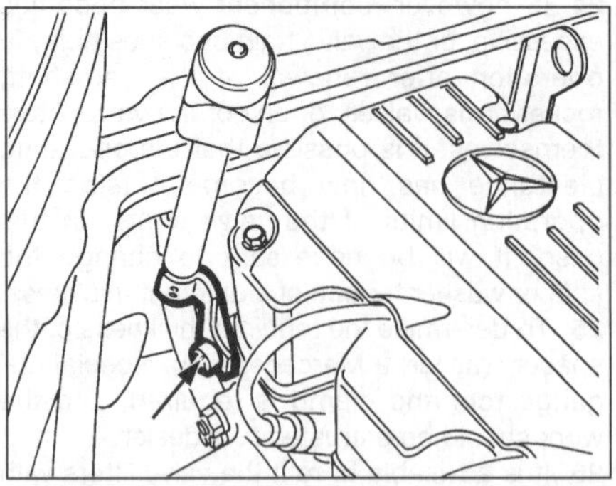

10.12 Automatic transmission fluid level dipstick-to-cylinder head bolt (arrowed)

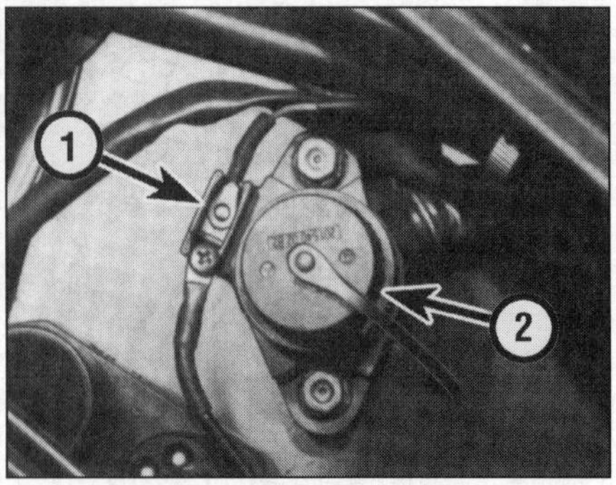

10.19 Disconnect the wire(s) from the terminal (1) on the diagnostic socket mounting (2)

10 Loosen the clip securing the short coolant pump hose to the cylinder head **(see illustration)**.

11 Similarly, disconnect the heater coolant return hose from the pipe at the rear of the cylinder head.

12 On models with automatic transmission, unscrew the bolt securing the transmission fluid level dipstick tube to the cylinder head **(see illustration)**.

13 Depressurise the fuel system as described in Chapter 4, then unscrew the unions, and disconnect the fuel feed and return lines. Counterhold the union on the fuel pressure regulator when unscrewing the union nut. Be prepared for fuel spillage, and take adequate fire precautions.

14 Disconnect the throttle cable from the throttle linkage as described in Chapter 4.

15 On models with automatic transmission, disconnect the control pressure cable from the throttle linkage as described in Chapter 7.

16 Work around the cylinder head, and disconnect all the engine wiring harness connectors, noting their locations to aid refitting.

17 Release the engine wiring harness from any brackets and clips on the engine.

18 Disconnect the wiring plugs and the vacuum hose from the ignition control unit.

19 Unscrew the securing screw, and disconnect the wire(s) from the terminal on the diagnostic socket mounting **(see illustration)**.

20 Unbolt the diagnostic socket, then disconnect the grey wiring connector from the left-hand side of the socket.

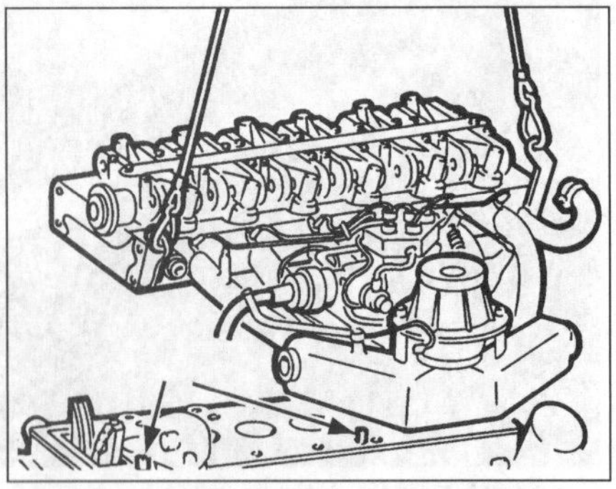

10.26 Lifting off the cylinder head - locating dowels arrowed

21 Disconnect the exhaust front sections from the manifold with reference to Chapter 4.

22 Make a final check to ensure that all relevant hoses and wires have been disconnected to allow cylinder head removal.

23 Progressively loosen the cylinder head bolts, working in the reverse order to that shown in illustration 10.42.

24 Remove the cylinder head bolts.

25 Attach a hoist and lifting tackle to the engine lifting brackets on the cylinder head. Raise the hoist to just take the weight of the cylinder head.

26 Release the cylinder head from the cylinder block and locating dowels by rocking it. Do not prise between the mating faces of the cylinder head and block, as this may damage the gasket faces **(see illustration)**.

27 Carefully lift the cylinder head, complete with manifolds, from the block, and manoeuvre it out from the engine compartment.

28 Recover the cylinder head gasket.

Inspection

29 Refer to Chapter 2D for details of cylinder head dismantling and reassembly. If desired, the manifolds can be removed with reference to Chapter 4.

30 The mating faces of the cylinder head and block must be perfectly clean before refitting the head. Use a scraper to remove all traces of gasket and carbon, and also clean the tops of the pistons. Take particular care with the cylinder head, as the metal is easily damaged. Also make sure that debris is not allowed to enter the oil and water passages. Using adhesive tape and paper, seal the water, oil and bolt holes in the cylinder block. To prevent carbon entering the gap between the pistons and bores, smear a little grease in the gap. After cleaning each piston, rotate the crankshaft so that the piston moves **down** the bore, then wipe out the grease and carbon with a cloth rag.

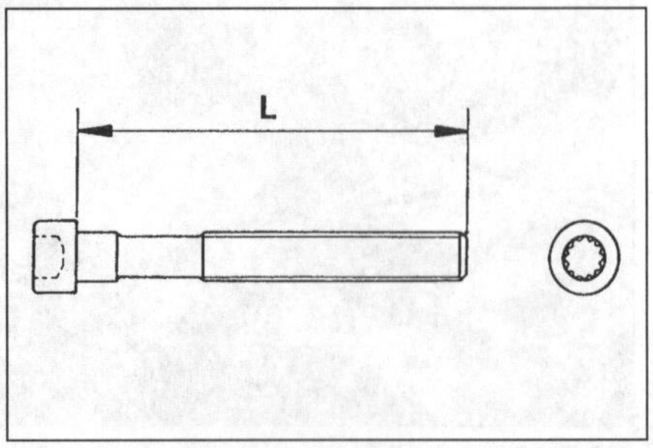

10.36 Cylinder head bolt measurement
L Maximum length = 108.4 mm

31 Check the block and head for nicks, deep scratches and other damage. If very slight, they may be removed from the cylinder block carefully with a file. More serious damage may be repaired by machining, but this is a specialist job.

32 If warpage of the cylinder head is suspected, use a straight-edge to check it for distortion, with reference to Chapter 2D.

33 Clean out the bolt holes in the block using a pipe cleaner or thin rag and a screwdriver. Make sure that all oil and water is removed, otherwise there is a possibility of the block being cracked by hydraulic pressure when the bolts are tightened.

34 Examine the bolt threads and the threads in the cylinder block for damage. If necessary, use the correct size tap to chase out the threads in the block.

35 The manufacturers recommend that the cylinder head bolts are measured, to determine whether renewal is necessary; however, some owners may wish to renew all the bolts as a matter of course.

36 Measure the length of each bolt from the base of the head to the end of the shank **(see illustration)**. If the bolt length is greater than the maximum specified, the bolts should be renewed.

Refitting

37 Where applicable, refit the manifolds with reference to Chapter 4.

38 Check that the camshaft and crankshaft timing marks are still aligned with No 1 piston at TDC, as described in Section 3.

39 Fit the gasket over the dowels in the cylinder block, ensuring that it is fitted the correct way round.

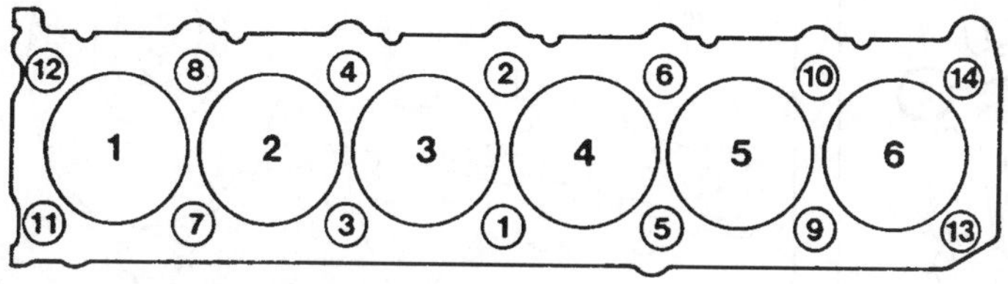

10.42 Cylinder head bolt tightening sequence - 6-cylinder petrol engines

40 Support the cylinder head using the hoist and lifting tackle, then lower the cylinder head onto the block.

41 Oil the threads and the contact faces of the cylinder head bolts, then insert them and screw them into the cylinder block by hand.

42 Tighten the cylinder head bolts in the order shown **(see illustration)**. Tighten the bolts in the stages given in the Specifications - ie: tighten all bolts to the Stage 1 torque, then tighten all bolts to the Stage 2 torque, and so on.

43 Reconnect the exhaust front section to the manifold with reference to Chapter 4.

44 Reconnect all vacuum lines, and wiring plugs to their correct locations, as noted before removal. Clip the engine wiring harness into position on the engine using the appropriate clips and brackets.

45 On models with automatic transmission, reconnect the control pressure cable to the throttle linkage with reference to Chapter 7.

46 Reconnect the throttle cable to the throttle linkage with reference to Chapter 4.

47 Reconnect the fuel lines and tighten the unions.

48 Where applicable, refit the bolt securing the automatic transmission fluid level dipstick tube to the cylinder head.

49 Reconnect the heater coolant hose to the pipe at the rear of the cylinder head, and reconnect the coolant hose to the coolant pump.

50 Refit the two inlet manifold support brackets.

51 Refit the bolt securing the dipstick tube bracket to the cylinder head.

52 Ensure that the timing chain guide rail is correctly positioned, then tap the guide rail locating pin into position using a hammer and punch. Ensure that the threaded end of the pin faces forwards - ie: the thread should be visible when the pin is fitted.

53 Refit the camshaft sprocket as described in Section 8.

54 Refill the cooling system as described in Chapter 1A.

55 Reconnect the battery negative lead, and lower the bonnet.

11 Sump - removal and refitting

Removal

Note: *A suitable hoist and lifting tackle will be required for this operation. A new sump gasket will be required on refitting, and new exhaust clamp nuts will be required.*

1 Disconnect the battery negative lead.

2 Remove the air cleaner assembly as described in Chapter 4.

3 Unclip the cooling fan shroud, and lay it in position over the fan blades as described in Chapter 3.

4 Remove the engine undershield as described in Chapter 11.

5 Remove the front anti-roll bar as described in Chapter 10. Note that the anti-roll bar can be left in position under the vehicle, provided that the mounting bolts have been removed.

6 Drain the engine oil with reference to Chapter 1A.

7 Where applicable, disconnect the wiring from the oil level sensor mounted in the sump.

8 Disconnect the wiring from the oil pressure warning light switch.

9 On models with automatic transmission, unscrew the securing bolts, and release the transmission fluid cooler lines from the sump.

10 Similarly, on models with self-levelling suspension, unscrew the securing bolt, and release the hydraulic fluid line from the sump.

11 Disconnect the exhaust front sections from the exhaust manifold, with reference to Chapter 4.

12 Where applicable, working under the vehicle, unscrew the clamp nuts, and release the exhaust system from the bracket on the transmission.

13 Insert a metal or thick card plate between the rear of the engine and the engine compartment bulkhead, to protect the bulkhead and the brake pipes during the following procedure **(see illustration)**.

14 Disconnect the steering drag link on the left-hand side, and the steering damper on the right-hand side, with reference to Chapter 10.

15 Attach a hoist and suitable lifting tackle to the engine lifting brackets, and raise the hoist to just take the weight of the engine.

16 Working on each side of the vehicle in turn, unscrew the lower engine mounting bolts from the left- and right-hand engine mountings.

17 Carefully lift the engine sufficiently for access to the sump securing bolts.

18 Working progressively, in a diagonal sequence, unscrew and remove the sump securing bolts **(see illustration)**. Note the

11.13 Insert a plate (arrowed) at the rear of the engine to protect the bulkhead

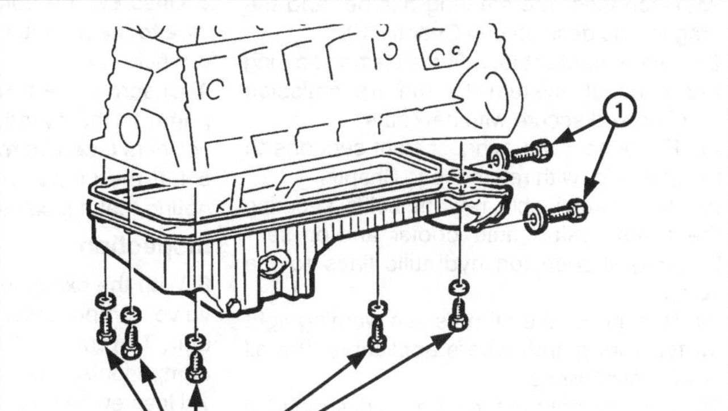

11.18 Unscrew the sump securing bolts
1 Sump-to-transmission bolts 2 Sump-to-cylinder block bolts

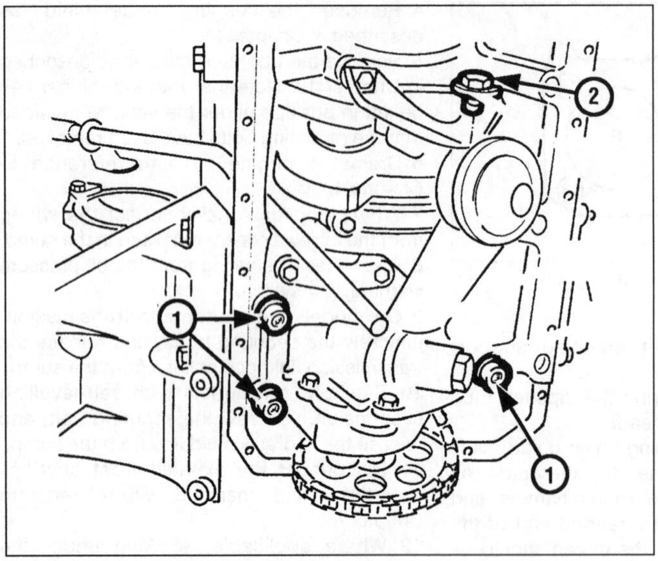

12.4 Oil pump mounting details

1 Oil pump securing bolts
2 Oil pick-up pipe-to-mounting bracket bolt

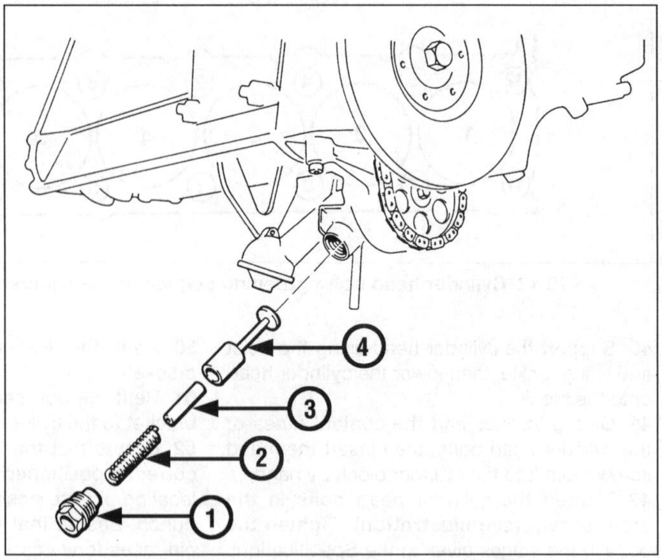

12.7 Oil pressure relief valve components

1 Plug
2 Spring
3 Guide pin
4 Piston

locations of the bolts to aid refitting, as various lengths of bolts may used.

19 Lower the sump from under the vehicle, and recover the gasket.

Refitting

20 Commence refitting by cleaning the remains of the gasket from the sump and cylinder block, and wipe dry.

21 Position a new gasket on the sump, then lift the sump into position, and insert the bolts in their original locations.

22 Tighten the bolts progressively to the specified torque.

23 Carefully lower the engine into position, then refit and tighten the lower engine mounting bolts to the specified torque.

24 Disconnect the lifting tackle from the engine lifting brackets, and withdraw the hoist.

25 Reconnect the steering damper and the drag link as described in Chapter 10.

26 Where applicable, refit the clamp securing the exhaust system to the transmission bracket, and secure with new nuts.

27 Reconnect the exhaust front sections to the manifold, with reference to Chapter 4.

28 Where applicable, refit the bolt(s) securing the transmission fluid cooler and/or self-levelling suspension hydraulic lines to the sump.

29 Reconnect the oil pressure warning light switch wiring and, where applicable, the oil level sensor wiring.

30 Refit the front anti-roll bar as described in Chapter 10.

31 Ensure that the oil drain plug has been refitted and tightened, then refit the engine undershield.

32 Refit the cooling fan shroud.

33 Refit the air cleaner assembly.

34 Lower the vehicle to the ground, and refill the engine with the correct grade and quantity of oil (see *"Weekly checks"* and Chapter 1A).

35 Reconnect the battery negative lead.

12 Oil pump and drive chain - removal, inspection and refitting

Oil pump

Removal

1 Remove the sump as described in Section 11.

2 Unscrew the oil pump sprocket securing bolt, and recover the washer. Withdraw the oil pump sprocket, complete with the drive chain, from the oil pump shaft.

3 Unscrew the bolt securing the oil pick-up pipe to the mounting bracket, and recover the washer.

4 Unscrew the three bolts securing the oil pump to the cylinder block, and recover the washers **(see illustration)**.

5 Lift the oil pump from the cylinder block, noting that it locates on two dowels.

Inspection

6 With the exception of the oil pressure relief valve components, the oil pump is a sealed unit. To remove the oil pressure relief valve components, proceed as follows.

7 Unscrew the relief valve plug. Take care, as the plug will be pushed out by the spring pressure when it reaches the end of the threads **(see illustration)**.

8 Withdraw the spring, guide pin and piston.

9 Thoroughly clean all components, and examine them for wear and damage. If there is any sign of excessive wear or damage, renew the appropriate component(s) - pay particular attention to the spring.

10 Refit the components using a reversal of the removal procedure, and tighten the plug to the specified torque.

Refitting

11 Refitting is a reversal of removal, bearing in mind the following points.

a) *Prime the oil pump by filling it with clean engine oil.*
b) *Ensure that the pump locates correctly on the dowels.*
c) *Tighten the pump securing bolts to the specified torque.*
d) *Fit the pump sprocket with the convex side of the sprocket facing the pump.*
e) *Tighten the pump sprocket securing bolt to the specified torque.*
f) *Refit the sump as described in Section 11.*

Drive chain - renewal

Note: *Removal of the oil pump drive chain using the following procedure entails the use of a portable electric grinder to cut through one of the chain links. Ensure that such a tool is available, as well as a new chain and new connecting link before proceeding. The oil pump sprocket should be renewed whenever the chain is renewed.*

12 Remove the sump as described in Section 11.

13 Slacken the oil pump sprocket securing bolt.

14 Using a grinder, grind off the protruding lugs of one of the chain links at the bottom of the sprocket - take great care not to damage the sprocket.

15 Pull off the chain link plate, then push the

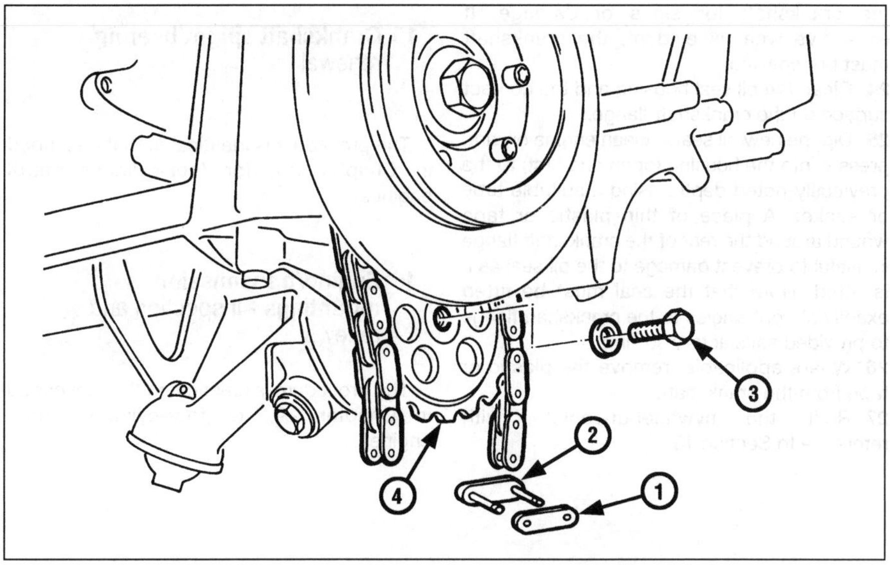

12.15 Renewing the oil pump drive chain
1 Chain link plate 2 Chain link 3 Oil pump sprocket bolt 4 Oil pump sprocket

link out towards the rear of the chain **(see illustration)**.

16 Unscrew the oil pump sprocket securing bolt, and recover the washer, then withdraw the sprocket from the pump shaft.

17 Fit the new sprocket to the pump shaft, with the convex side of the sprocket facing the pump.

18 Using the new link, connect one end of the new chain to the tail end of the old chain, in such a way that as the engine is turned (clockwise), the new chain will be drawn up, around the crankshaft sprocket, then down the other side. Fit the link from the rear of the sprocket, and ensure that the link is pushed firmly into position - do not fit the link plate to secure the link at this stage.

19 It is now necessary to feed the new chain around the crankshaft sprocket. During this procedure it is essential to observe the following points.

a) *Keep tension on the new chain, ensuring that the links of the chains remain engaged with the crankshaft sprocket.*
b) *Pull down on the old chain as it appears from the timing chain cover to prevent it dropping off the crankshaft sprocket, or jamming in the casing.*

20 Using a suitable socket on the crankshaft pulley/vibration damper hub bolt, slowly turn the crankshaft clockwise, whilst observing the points made in the preceding paragraph.

21 When the end of the new chain appears, remove the link (ensuring that tension is kept on the new chain, and that the chain links remain engaged with the crankshaft sprocket), and disconnect the new chain from the old chain. Remove the old chain.

22 Engage the new chain with the oil pump sprocket, then join the two ends of the chain with the connecting link, inserted from the rear of the sprocket.

HAYNES HiNT ***Temporarily secure the ends of the new chain to the oil pump sprocket using wire or cable-ties passed through the holes in the sprocket and around the chain.***

23 Fit the link plate, and then secure the plate to the link by flattening the ends of the link pins. A special tool is available for this purpose, but it should be possible to achieve a satisfactory result using a hammer, with a block of metal (or a second hammer) to support the rear of the chain - *take great care not to damage the chain or the sprocket.*

24 Check that the chain link is secure, with no burring of the metal, or loose swarf.

25 Tighten the oil pump sprocket bolt to the specified torque.

26 Refit the sump as described in Section 11.

13 Flywheel/driveplate - removal, inspection and refitting

The procedure is identical to that described in Chapter 2A, for four-cylinder petrol engines.

14 Oil seals - renewal

Camshaft front oil seal

1 Unclip the cooling fan shroud, and lay it in position over the fan blades as described in Chapter 3.

2 Where applicable, unclip the cover from the distributor cap. Disconnect the coil HT lead from the distributor cap, then unscrew the three securing screws, and remove the distributor cap. Lay the distributor cap to one side, complete with the HT leads and housing.

3 Unscrew the three securing screws, and remove the distributor rotor arm.

4 Unscrew the securing bolt, and remove the rotor arm drive sleeve **(see illustration 6.8)**. Where applicable, unclip the cover from the front of the upper timing chain cover.

5 Carefully prise out the old oil seal using a screwdriver. Alternatively, drill a small hole in the oil seal, and use a self-tapping screw and a pair of pliers to remove it. Take care not to damage the seal housing.

6 Thoroughly clean the oil seal housing and the front edge of the camshaft.

7 A piece of thin plastic or tape wound around the front edge of the camshaft flange is useful to prevent damage as the new oil seal is fitted.

8 Carefully tap the new (dry) oil seal into position in the housing using a suitable tube or socket until the seal is flush with the outer face of the timing chain cover.

9 Where applicable, remove the plastic or tape from the front of the camshaft.

10 Where applicable, refit the cover to the front of the upper timing chain cover, then refit the rotor arm drive sleeve, ensuring that the groove in the sleeve engages with the lug on the camshaft. Refit the drive sleeve securing bolt, and tighten to the specified torque.

11 Refit the rotor arm, and tighten the securing screws.

12 Refit the distributor cap, and reconnect the coil HT lead.

13 Refit the cooling fan shroud.

Crankshaft front oil seal

14 Remove the crankshaft pulley/vibration damper and hub as described in Section 5.

15 Measure and note the fitted depth of the oil seal.

16 Pull the oil seal from the housing using a hooked instrument or a screwdriver - protect the crankshaft using a wad of rag **(see illustration)**. Alternatively, drill a small hole in the oil seal, and use a self-tapping screw and a pair of pliers to remove it.

17 Clean the oil seal housing.

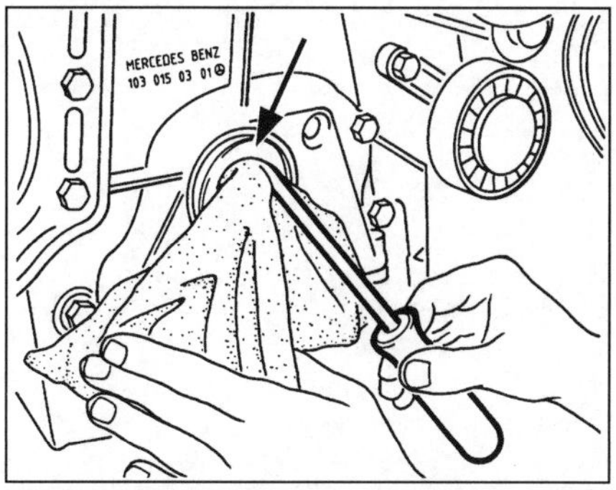

14.16 Levering out the crankshaft front oil seal (arrowed). Note rag used to protect crankshaft

18 Dip the new oil seal in clean engine oil, and press it into the housing (open end first) to the previously-noted depth, using a suitable tube or socket. A piece of thin plastic or tape wound around the front of the crankshaft is useful to prevent damage to the oil seal as it is fitted.
19 Where applicable, remove the plastic or tape from the crankshaft.
20 Refit the crankshaft pulley/vibration damper and hub as described in Section 5.

Crankshaft rear oil seal

21 Remove the flywheel/driveplate with reference to Section 13.
22 Proceed as described in paragraphs 15 and 16.
23 Examine the oil seal contact surface on the crankshaft for signs of damage. If excessive wear is evident, the crankshaft must be renewed.
24 Clean the oil seal housing and the contact surface on the crankshaft flange.
25 Dip the new oil seal in clean engine oil, and press it into the housing (open end first) to the previously-noted depth, using a suitable tube or socket. A piece of thin plastic or tape wound around the rear of the crankshaft flange is useful to prevent damage to the oil seal as it is fitted. Note that the seal must be fitted exactly at right-angles to the crankshaft flange to provided satisfactory sealing.
26 Where applicable, remove the plastic or tape from the crankshaft.
27 Refit the flywheel/driveplate with reference to Section 13.

15 Crankshaft spigot bearing - renewal

The procedure is identical to that described in Chapter 2A, for four-cylinder petrol engines.

16 Engine/transmission mountings - inspection and renewal

The procedure is identical to that described in Chapter 2A, for four-cylinder petrol engines.

Chapter 2 Part C
Diesel engine in-car repair procedures

Contents

Camshaft and valve lifters - removal, inspection and refitting 9
Camshaft cover - removal and refitting 4
Compression and leakdown tests - description and interpretation . 2
Crankshaft oil seals - renewal 14
Crankshaft pulley/vibration damper and hub - removal and refitting 5
Crankshaft spigot bearing - renewal 15
Cylinder head - removal, inspection and refitting 10
Engine assembly and valve timing marks - general information and usage 3
Engine oil and filter renewal ..... See Chapter 1B
Engine oil cooler - removal and refitting 17
Engine oil level check ..... See *"Weekly checks"*
Engine/transmission mountings - inspection and renewal 16
Flywheel/driveplate - removal, inspection and refitting 13
General information 1
Oil pump and drive chain - removal, inspection and refitting 12
Sump - removal and refitting 11
Timing chain - inspection and renewal 7
Timing chain cover - removal and refitting 6
Timing chain tensioner, sprockets and guides - removal, inspection and refitting 8

Degrees of difficulty

Easy, suitable for novice with little experience	**Fairly easy,** suitable for beginner with some experience	**Fairly difficult,** suitable for competent DIY mechanic	**Difficult,** suitable for experienced DIY mechanic	**Very difficult,** suitable for expert DIY or professional

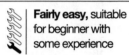

2C

Specifications

General

Engine code:	
2.0 litre (4-cylinder) engine	601.911
2.5 litre (5-cylinder) engine:	
Non-Turbo	602.911
Turbo	602.961
Displacement:	
2.0 litre engine	1997 cc
2.5 litre engine	2497 cc
Bore (all engines)	87.0 mm
Stroke (all engines)	84.0 mm
Direction of engine rotation	Clockwise (viewed from front of vehicle)
No 1 cylinder location	Timing chain end
Firing order:	
2.0 litre (4-cylinder) engine	1-3-4-2
2.5 litre (5-cylinder) engine	1-2-4-5-3
Compression pressures:	
Minimum compression pressure	18.0 bars (approx)
Maximum difference between cylinders	3.0 bars
Compression ratio (all engines)	22.0:1

Camshaft

Endfloat:	
New engine	0.030 to 0.100 mm
Wear limit	0.150 mm
Camshaft bearing running clearance:	
New engine	0.050 to 0.091 mm
Wear limit	0.150 mm

Valve lifters

Maximum clearance between cam lobe and valve lifter (see Section 9)	0.40 mm

Cylinder head bolts

Maximum length:	
M10 x 80 mm bolts	83.6 mm
M10 x 102 mm bolts	105.6 mm
M10 x 115 mm bolts	118.6 mm

Lubrication system

Minimum oil pressure:	
At idle speed	0.3 bar
At 3000 rpm	3.0 bars

Flywheel/driveplate bolts

Minimum diameter	8.0 mm
Maximum length	22.5 mm

Torque wrench settings

Torque wrench settings	Nm	lbf ft
Camshaft cover bolts	10	7
Crankshaft pulley/vibration damper-to-hub bolts	25	18
Crankshaft pulley/vibration damper hub bolt (see Section 5):		
Bolt with spring washers	320	236
Bolt with conical washer:		
Stage 1	200	148
Stage 2	Angle-tighten through a further 90°	
Timing chain cover bolts:		
M6 bolts	10	7
M8 bolts	25	18
Cooling fan pulley bolts		
Hexagon head bolt	10	7
Torx head bolt	14	10
Auxiliary drivebelt tensioner securing bolt	10	7
Auxiliary drivebelt tensioner pivot pin	100	74
Auxiliary drivebelt idler pulley bolt	25	18
Auxiliary drivebelt tensioner damper strut bolts:		
Upper bolt	25	18
Lower bolt	20	15
Self-levelling suspension hydraulic pump drive sleeve bolt:		
Hexagon head bolt	25	18
Splined bolt:		
Stage 1	25	18
Stage 2	Angle-tighten through a further 90°	
Camshaft sprocket bolt:		
M10 hexagonal head bolt	65	48
M11 splined bolt:		
Stage 1	25	18
Stage 2	Angle-tighten through a further 90°	
Timing chain tensioner cover plug	40	30
Timing chain tensioner body-to-cylinder block	80	59
Camshaft bearing cap bolts	25	18
Cylinder head-to-timing chain cover bolts	25	18
Fuel filter securing bolts	25	18
Cylinder head bolts:		
Stage 1	15	11
Stage 2	35	26
Stage 3	Angle-tighten through a further 90°	
Stage 4	Wait for 10 minutes	
Stage 5	Angle-tighten through a further 90°	
Engine-to-transmission bolts:		
Manual transmission:		
M10 x 40 mm bolts	55	41
M10 x 90 mm bolts	45	33
Automatic transmission:		
M10 bolts	55	41
M12 bolts	65	48
Sump auxiliary section bolts	10	7

Torque wrench settings

	Nm	lbf ft
Sump bolts:		
M6 bolts	10	7
M8 bolts	25	18
Oil drain plug:		
M12 plug	30	22
M14 plug	25	18
Oil pressure relief valve plug	50	37
Oil pump sprocket bolt	32	24
Oil pump securing bolts	25	18
Oil baffle plate bolts	25	18
Flywheel/driveplate bolts:		
Stage 1:		
Standard flywheel	30	22
"Dual-mass" flywheel	40	30
Stage 2	Angle-tighten through a further 90 to 100°	
Crankshaft rear oil seal housing bolts	10	7
Engine mounting-to-engine mounting bracket bolts	25	18
Left- and right-hand engine mounting-to-crossmember bolts	40	30
Left- and right-hand engine mounting bracket bolts	25	18
Rear engine/transmission mounting-to-transmission nut	65	48
Rear engine/transmission mounting-to-crossmember bolts	25	18
Rear engine/transmission mounting crossmember-to-underbody bolts	35	26
Rear engine/transmission mounting adjuster bolt	30	22
Engine mounting damper securing bolts	10	7
Engine movement stop securing bolts	25	18
Engine movement stop adjuster bolt	130	96
Big-end bearing cap nuts:		
Stage 1:		
Models built up to November 1990	30	22
Models built from December 1990	40	30
Stage 2	Angle-tighten through a further 90 to 100°	
Main bearing cap bolts:		
M11 bolts:		
Stage 1	55	41
Stage 2	Angle-tighten through a further 90 to 100°	
M12 bolts	90	66
Cylinder block coolant drain plug	30	22

1 General information

How to use this Chapter

This Part of Chapter 2 describes the repair procedures that can reasonably be carried out on the engine while it remains in the vehicle. If the engine has been removed from the vehicle and is being dismantled as described in Part D, any preliminary dismantling procedures can be ignored.

Note that, while it may be possible physically to overhaul items such as the piston/connecting rod assemblies while the engine is in the car, such tasks are not usually carried out as separate operations. Usually, several additional procedures are required (not to mention the cleaning of components and oilways); for this reason, all such tasks are classed as major overhaul procedures, and are described in Part D of this Chapter.

Part D describes the removal of the engine/ transmission from the car, and the full overhaul procedures that can then be carried out.

Engine description

4- and 5-cylinder diesel engines are available, but both engines are fundamentally similar, the only significant difference being the number of cylinders.

The engines are of in-line single overhead camshaft design, mounted in-line ("north-south") with the transmission at the front of the vehicle.

On 4-cylinder engines, then crankshaft is supported in five main bearing within the cast iron cylinder block. Crankshaft endfloat is controlled by thrustwashers fitted on either side of No 3 main bearing. Similarly, on 5-cylinder engines the crankshaft is supported in six main bearings, and the endfloat thrustwashers are fitted either side of No 4 bearing location.

The connecting rods are attached to the crankshaft by horizontally-split big-end bearings, and to the pistons by fully-floating gudgeon pins retained by circlips. The alloy pistons are fitted with three piston rings; two compression and one oil control.

The camshaft is driven from the crankshaft sprocket by a double-row chain. The timing chain also drives the fuel injection pump.

The camshaft is supported in bearings in the cylinder head, and actuates the valves directly, via hydraulic valve lifters.

The oil pump is chain-driven from the front of the crankshaft.

Repair operations possible with the engine in the vehicle

The following operations can be carried out without having to remove the engine from the vehicle:

a) Removal and refitting of the cylinder head.
b) Removal and refitting of the timing chain and sprockets.
c) Removal and refitting of the camshaft.
d) Removal and refitting of the sump.
e) Removal and refitting of the big-end bearings, connecting rods, and pistons.*
f) Removal and refitting of the oil pump.
g) Renewal of the engine/transmission mountings.
h) Removal and refitting of the flywheel/driveplate.

** Although it is possible to remove these components with the engine in place, for reasons of access and cleanliness it is recommended that the engine is removed.*

2 Compression and leakdown tests - description and interpretation

Compression test

Note: *A compression tester designed for diesel engines must be used for this test.*

1 When engine performance is down, or if misfiring occurs which cannot be attributed to the ignition or fuel systems, a compression test can provide diagnostic clues as to the engine's condition. If the test is performed regularly, it can give warning of trouble before any other symptoms become apparent.

2 A compression tester specifically intended for diesel engines must be used, because of the higher pressures involved. The tester is connected to an adapter which screws into the glow plug or injector hole. On these engines, an adapter suitable for use in the injector holes is preferable. It is unlikely to be worthwhile buying such a tester for occasional use, but it may be possible to borrow or hire one - if not, have the test performed by a garage.

3 Unless specific instructions to the contrary are supplied with the tester, observe the following points.

a) The battery must be in a good state of charge, the air filter must be clean, and the engine should be at normal operating temperature.

b) All the injectors or glow plugs should be removed before starting the test.

c) The stop solenoid must be disconnected, to prevent the engine from running or fuel from being discharged.

4 There is no need to hold the accelerator pedal down during the test, because the diesel engine air inlet is not throttled.

5 Crank the engine on the starter motor. After one or two revolutions, the compression pressure should build up to a maximum figure, and then stabilise. Record the highest reading obtained.

6 Repeat the test on the remaining cylinders, recording the pressure in each.

7 The cause of poor compression is less easy to establish on a diesel engine than on a petrol one. The effect of introducing oil into the cylinders ("wet" testing) is not conclusive, because there is a risk that the oil will sit in the swirl chamber or in the recess in the piston crown instead of passing to the rings. However, the following can be used as a rough guide to diagnosis.

8 All cylinders should produce very similar pressures; a difference of more than 3.0 bars between any two cylinders indicates a fault. Note that the compression should build up quickly in a healthy engine; low compression on the first stroke, followed by gradually-increasing pressure on successive strokes, indicates worn piston rings. A low compression reading on the first stroke, which does not build up during successive strokes, indicates leaking valves or a blown head gasket (a cracked head could also be the cause). Deposits on the undersides of the valve heads can also cause low compression.

9 A low reading from two adjacent cylinders is almost certainly due to the head gasket having blown between them; the presence of coolant in the engine oil will confirm this.

10 If the compression reading is unusually high, the combustion chambers are probably coated with carbon deposits. If this is the case, the cylinder head should be removed and decarbonised.

11 Mercedes recommended values for compression pressures are given in the Specifications.

12 On completion of the test, refit the injectors or the glow plugs, and reconnect the stop solenoid.

Leakdown test

13 A leakdown test measures the rate at which compressed air fed into the cylinder is lost. It is an alternative to a compression test, and in many ways is better, since the escaping air provides easy identification of where a pressure loss is occurring (piston rings, valves or head gasket).

14 The equipment needed for leakdown testing is unlikely to be available to the home mechanic. If poor compression is suspected, have the test performed by a suitably-equipped garage.

3 Engine assembly and valve timing marks - general information and usage

Warning: When turning the engine, do not turn the engine using the camshaft sprocket bolt, and do not turn the engine backwards (ie: anti-clockwise).

1 Top Dead Centre (TDC) is the highest point in the cylinder that each piston reaches as it travels up and down when the crankshaft turns. Each piston reaches TDC at the end of the compression stroke and again at the end of the exhaust stroke, but TDC generally refers to piston position on the compression stroke. No 1 piston is at the timing chain end of the engine.

2 Positioning No 1 piston at TDC is an essential part of many procedures, such as timing chain removal and camshaft removal.

3 Remove the camshaft cover as described in Section 4.

4 Using a suitable socket on the crankshaft pulley/vibration damper hub bolt (on some models, it may be necessary to remove the cooling fan cowl and blades for access), turn the crankshaft clockwise until the following marks are aligned **(see illustrations)**.

a) The TDC ("O/T") mark on the crankshaft pulley/vibration damper is aligned with the pointer on the timing chain cover.

b) The TDC notch in the flange at the front of the camshaft is aligned with the raised rib on the front camshaft bearing cap.

3.4a TDC ("O/T") mark on crankshaft pulley/vibration damper aligned with pointer on timing chain cover

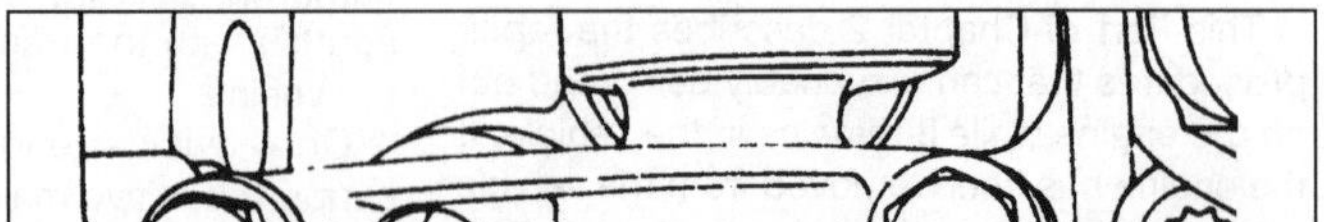

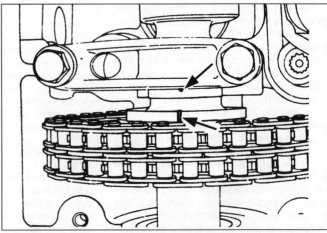

3.4b TDC notch in camshaft flange aligned with raised rib on camshaft bearing cap

5 When the marks are aligned as described in paragraph 4, No 1 piston is at TDC on the firing stroke. If the timing chain is to be removed, do not turn the camshaft or the crankshaft until the chain has been refitted.

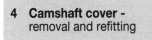

4 Camshaft cover - removal and refitting

Removal

Note: *A new gasket may be required on refitting.*

1 Disconnect the battery negative lead.

2 Raise the bonnet to the fully open position, as described in Chapter 11.

3 On Turbo engines, where applicable, disconnect and remove the turbocharger-to-inlet manifold air trunking, to allow sufficient clearance to remove the camshaft cover.

4 Disconnect the breather hose from the camshaft cover.

5 Where applicable, disconnect the throttle/kickdown cable operating lever, which runs across the top of the camshaft cover. If the lever adjuster bolt is removed, make alignment marks between the two sections of the lever before removing the bolt.

6 Unscrew the camshaft cover securing bolts and, where applicable, recover the washers.

7 Lift the camshaft cover from the cylinder head. If the cover is stuck, try rocking by hand, and if necessary tap carefully with a soft-faced mallet - take care, as the cover is easily damaged.

8 Recover the gasket.

Refitting

9 Examine the condition of the gasket, and renew if necessary.

10 Locate the gasket in the grooves in the camshaft cover, starting at the front and rear.

11 Lay the cover in position on the cylinder head, ensuring that the gasket locates correctly, then refit the securing bolts.

12 Tighten the bolts progressively to the specified torque.

13 Reconnect the breather hose.

14 Where applicable, refit the turbocharger-to-inlet manifold trunking.

15 Reconnect the battery negative lead, and lower the bonnet.

5 Crankshaft pulley/vibration damper and hub - removal and refitting

General

1 4-cylinder engines do not have a vibration damper, whilst 5-cylinder engines have a one-piece crankshaft pulley/vibration damper. The removal and refitting procedure for both types is similar.

Crankshaft pulley/vibration damper

Removal

2 Disconnect the battery negative lead.

3 Raise the bonnet to the fully open position, as described in Chapter 11.

4 Remove the radiator as described in Chapter 3.

5 Remove the auxiliary drivebelt as described in Chapter 1B.

6 Unscrew the securing bolts, and withdraw the crankshaft pulley/vibration damper. If necessary, counterhold the pulley/vibration damper using a socket or spanner on the pulley/vibration damper hub securing bolt.

Refitting

7 Refitting is a reversal of removal, but refit the auxiliary drivebelt as described in Chapter 1B, and refit the radiator as described in Chapter 3.

Hub

Removal

Warning: The hub securing bolt is very tight. A tool will be required to counterhold the hub as the bolt is unscrewed. Do not attempt the job using inferior or poorly-improvised tools, an injury or damage may result.

Note: *A torque wrench capable of providing the appropriate torque (see Specifications) will be required on refitting. A puller may be required to remove the hub.*

8 Remove the crankshaft pulley/vibration damper as described previously in this Section.

9 Make up a tool to hold the hub. A suitable tool can be fabricated using two lengths of steel bar, joined by a large pivot bolt. Bolt the holding tool to the hub using the pulley/vibration damper-to-hub bolts **(see illustration)**.

10 Using a socket and a long swing-bar, loosen the hub bolt. Note that the bolt is very tight.

11 Unscrew the hub bolt, and remove the four spring washers, or the large conical washer, as applicable.

12 Withdraw the hub from the front of the crankshaft. If necessary use a suitable puller.

Refitting

13 Align the hole in the hub with the locating pin in the crankshaft flange, and slide the hub onto the end of the crankshaft.

14 On models with spring washers fitted under the hub bolt head, oil the spring washers, then refit them with the convex side of each washer facing the hub bolt head **(see illustration)**.

15 On models with a conical washer under the hub bolt head, refit the washer with the larger diameter against the hub.

16 Oil the bolt threads, then refit the hub securing bolt.

17 Bolt the holding tool to the hub, as during removal, then tighten the hub securing bolt to the specified torque. Note the different torques for the two different types of bolt. Take care to avoid injury and/or damage.

18 Refit the crankshaft pulley/vibration damper as described previously in this Section.

6 Timing chain cover - removal and refitting

Removal

Note: *A hoist and lifting tackle will be required for this operation. Suitable sealant will be required on refitting, and it is advisable to renew the crankshaft front oil seal.*

1 Disconnect the battery negative lead.

2 Raise the bonnet to the fully open position, as described in Chapter 11.

3 Remove the engine undershield, with reference to Chapter 11.

4 Remove the radiator and the cooling fan drive assembly as described in Chapter 3.

5 Remove the crankshaft pulley/vibration damper and hub as described in Section 5.

6 Remove the auxiliary drivebelt tensioner as follows.

a) *Pull off the plastic cover, unscrew the securing bolt, and remove the auxiliary drivebelt idler pulley.*

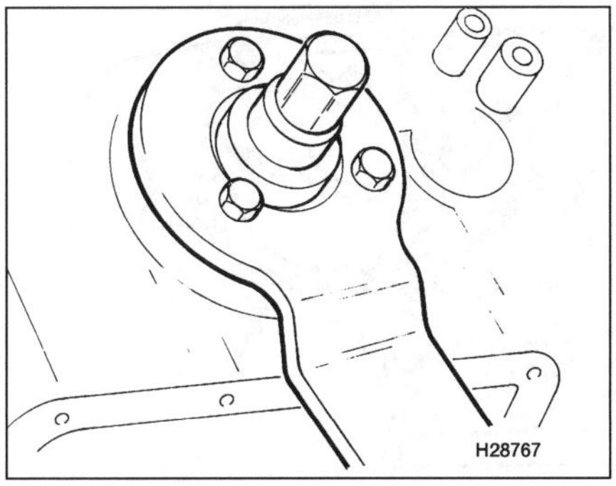

5.9 Special tool used to hold crankshaft pulley/vibration damper hub

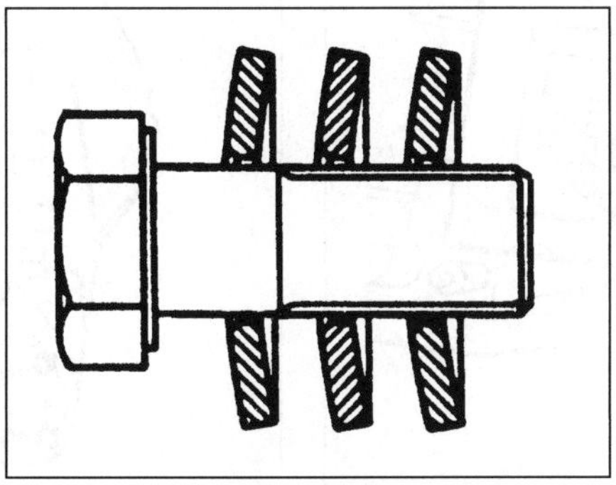

5.14 The convex side of the crankshaft pulley/vibration damper hub washers must face the bolt head

2C

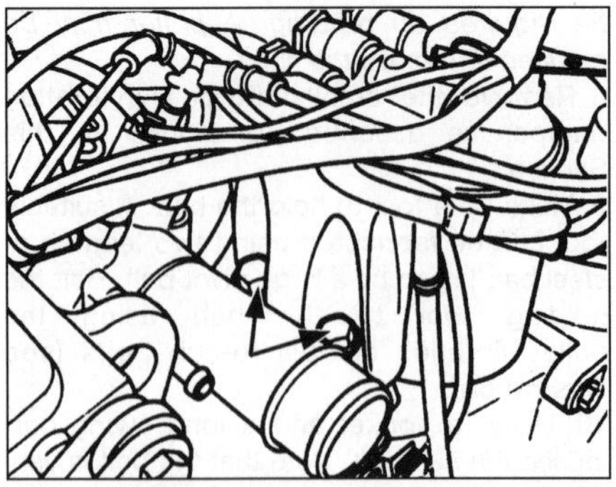

6.14 Where applicable, unscrew the two bolts (arrowed) from the front of the fuel filter/thermostat assembly

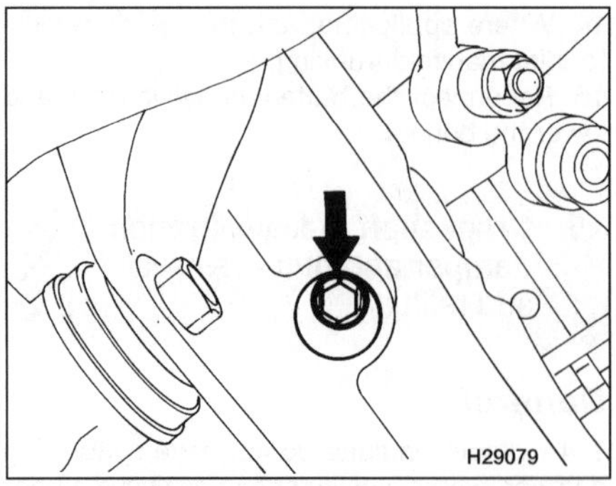

6.21 Left-hand lower engine mounting bolt (arrowed)

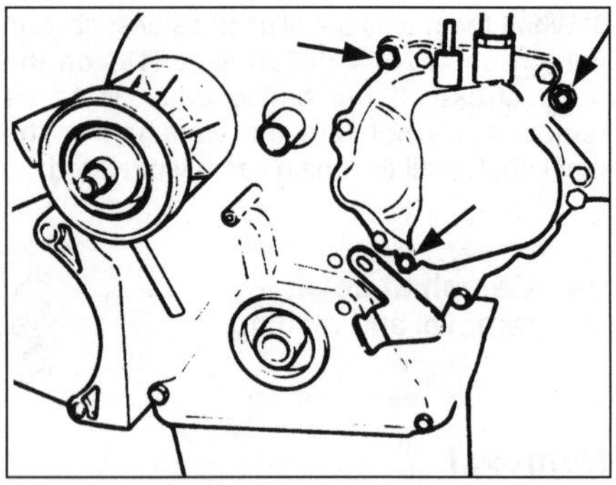

6.25 Counterhold the nuts and unscrew the three fuel injection pump mounting bolts (arrowed)

b) Unscrew the securing bolts, and remove the cooling fan pulley.
c) Unscrew the securing bolts, and withdraw the tensioner damper strut. Recover any spacers and/or brackets from the bolts noting their locations.
d) Using a pair of pliers, unhook the tension spring, noting its orientation to aid refitting.
e) Where applicable, pull off the plastic cover, then unscrew the tensioner securing bolt and, slide off the spacer sleeve (if applicable).
f) Withdraw the tensioner, and recover the spacer (where applicable).

7 Remove the brake vacuum pump as described in Chapter 9.
8 Remove the power steering/self-levelling suspension pump as described in Chapter 10.
9 Where applicable, remove the self-levelling suspension hydraulic pump from the front of the cylinder head, as described in Chapter 10.
10 Remove the alternator as described in Chapter 5.
11 Drain the engine oil as described in Chapter 1B.
12 Remove the camshaft cover with reference to Section 4.
13 On models with air conditioning, place a cardboard or similar shield in front of the condenser to prevent damage during the following procedure.
14 Where applicable, unscrew the two bolts from the front of the fuel filter/thermostat assembly **(see illustration)**.
15 Unbolt the engine oil level dipstick tube from the cylinder head.
16 Unscrew the securing bolts, and remove the alternator mounting bracket, noting the bolt locations.
17 Where applicable, mark the position of the crankshaft position sensor mounting bracket on the timing chain cover, then unbolt the sensor mounting bracket. Move the bracket to one side, clear of the working area.
18 Where applicable, unscrew the adjuster bolt and the two securing bolts, and remove the engine movement stop, with reference to Section 16.
19 Where applicable, unscrew the two securing bolts, and disconnect the lower end of the engine mounting damper from the left-hand side of the crossmember.
20 Attach a hoist and suitable lifting tackle to the front engine lifting bracket.
21 Working under the vehicle, unscrew the two lower engine mounting bolts (one on each side of the vehicle) **(see illustration)**.
22 Raise the hoist to lift the engine sufficiently for access to the sump-to-timing chain cover bolts.
23 Unscrew and remove the sump-to-timing chain cover bolts, and loosen the remaining sump bolts.
24 Lower the engine until it is again supported by the engine mountings.
25 Counterhold the nuts, and unscrew the three fuel injection pump mounting bolts from the timing chain cover **(see illustration).** Recover the nuts.
26 Working through the aperture at the top of the cylinder head, unscrew the two bolts securing the cylinder head to the timing chain cover **(see illustration)**.
27 Progressively unscrew the remaining timing chain cover securing bolts, noting their locations **(see illustration)**.
28 Carefully pull the cover forwards from the cylinder block. If the cover is stuck, tap it around the edge gently using a soft-faced mallet - do not lever between the mating faces of the cover and the cylinder block. **Note:** *Take care not to damage the cylinder head and sump gaskets as the timing chain cover is removed.*

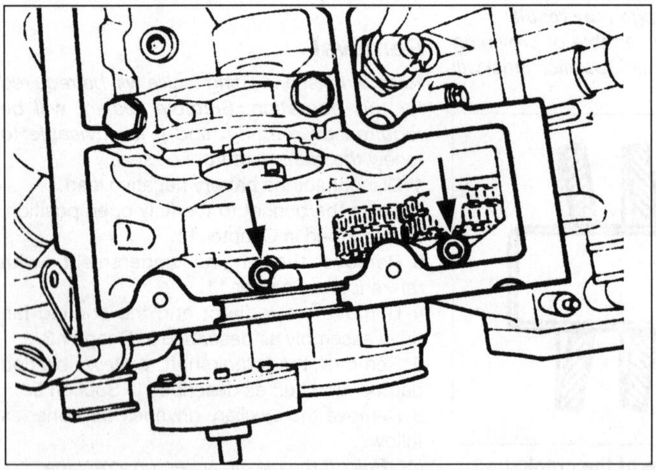

6.26 Unscrew the two bolts (arrowed) securing the cylinder head to the timing chain cover

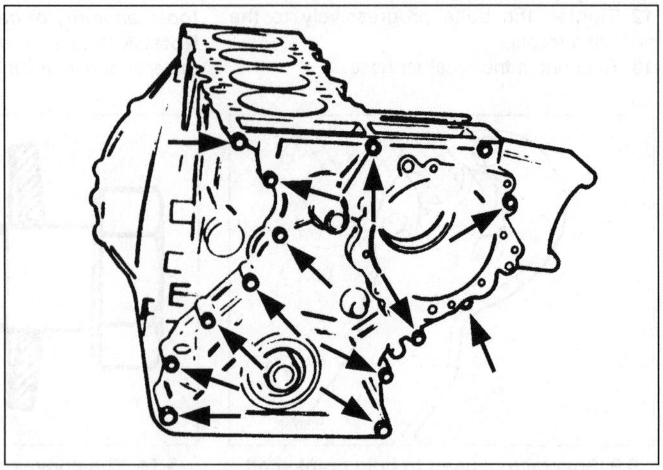

6.27 Unscrew the remaining timing chain cover securing bolts (arrowed)

Refitting

29 Commence refitting by thoroughly cleaning the mating faces of the timing chain cover, the cylinder block, and the cylinder head. Clean away all traces of old sealant.
30 Carefully check the condition of the cylinder head gasket. If the gasket has been damaged during the removal procedure, the cylinder head should be removed in order to renew the gasket, as described in Section 10.
31 Similarly, carefully check the condition of the sump gasket. If the gasket has been damaged during the removal procedure, the sump should be removed in order to renew the gasket, as described in Section 11.
32 It is advisable to renew the crankshaft oil seal in the in the cover as follows.
a) *Prise out the old oil seal using a screwdriver.*
b) *Clean the oil seal seating face in the timing chain cover.*
c) *Tap the new seal (dry) into position using a suitable tube or socket until the seal seats on the shoulder in the cover.*
33 A piece of thin plastic or tape wound around the front edge of the crankshaft flange is useful to prevent damage to the oil seal as the cover is fitted.
34 Apply sealant to the cylinder block mating face of the timing chain cover.
35 Coat the lips of the crankshaft oil seal with clean engine oil, then slide the cover into position over the crankshaft. Take great care not to damage the oil seal lips, or the cylinder head and sump gaskets as the cover is fitted.
36 Refit the timing chain cover-to-cylinder block securing bolts, then tighten them progressively to the specified torque.
37 Refit the cylinder head-to-timing chain cover bolts, and tighten them to the specified torque.
38 Where applicable, remove the tape from the front of the crankshaft.
39 Refit and tighten the fuel injection pump mounting bolts and nuts.
40 Raise the hoist to lift the engine sufficiently to enable the sump-to-timing chain cover bolts to be refitted.
41 Refit the sump-to-timing chain cover bolts, and tighten all the sump bolts progressively to the specified torque.
42 Lower the engine back onto the engine mountings, then refit and tighten the lower engine mounting bolts.
43 Where applicable, refit the two bolts securing the engine mounting damper to the crossmember, and tighten them to the specified torque.
44 Where applicable, refit and adjust the engine movement stop as described in Section 16.
45 Where applicable, refit the crankshaft position sensor mounting bracket, ensuring that the bracket is aligned with the marks made before removal.
46 Refit the alternator mounting bracket, ensuring that the bolts are refitted to their correct locations.
47 Refit the bolt securing the dipstick to the cylinder head.
48 Where applicable, refit the fuel filter/thermostat assembly bolts.
49 Where applicable, remove the shield from the air conditioning condenser.
50 Refit the camshaft cover with reference to Section 4.
51 Refit the alternator with reference to Chapter 5.
52 Where applicable, refit the self-levelling suspension hydraulic pump to the cylinder head with reference to Chapter 10.
53 Refit the power steering/self-levelling suspension pump as described in Chapter 10.
54 Refit the brake vacuum pump as described in Chapter 9.
55 Refit the auxiliary drivebelt tensioner using a reversal of the procedure described in paragraph 6.
56 Refit the crankshaft pulley/vibration damper and hub as described in Section 5.
57 Refit the cooling fan drive assembly and the radiator as described in Chapter 3.
58 Refit the engine undershield.
59 Refill the engine with the correct grade and quantity of oil, as described in Chapter 1B.
60 Reconnect the battery negative lead and lower the bonnet.

7 Timing chain - inspection and renewal

Inspection

1 Remove the camshaft cover as described in Section 4.
2 Using a socket on the crankshaft pulley/vibration damper hub bolt, turn the engine so that the whole length of the chain can be progressively viewed at the camshaft sprocket.
3 The chain should be renewed if the sprocket is worn or if the chain is worn (indicated by excessive lateral play between the links, and excessive noise in operation). It is wise to renew the chain in any case if the engine is to be dismantled for overhaul. Note that the rollers on a very badly worn chain may be slightly grooved. To avoid future problems, if there is any doubt at all about the condition of the chain, renew it.

Renewal

Note: *Removal of the timing chain using the following procedure entails the use of a portable electric grinder to cut through one of the chain links. Ensure that such a tool is available, as well as a new chain and new connecting link before proceeding.*
4 Disconnect the battery negative lead.
5 If not already done, remove the camshaft cover as described in Section 4.
6 Remove the fuel injectors as described in Chapter 4.
7 Remove the cooling fan and shroud, as described in Chapter 3.
8 Remove the timing chain tensioner as described in Section 8.
9 Cover the camshaft and the chain opening in the timing cover with clean rags, but keep the rags clear of the camshaft sprocket.
10 Using a grinder, grind off the protruding lugs of one of the chain links at the camshaft sprocket - take great care not to damage the sprocket.
11 Pull off the chain link plate, then push the link out towards the rear of the chain.
12 Remove the rags, taking care not to allow any swarf to drop down into the timing chain housing.
13 Using the new link, connect one end of the new timing chain to the tail end of the old chain, in such a way that as the engine is turned (clockwise), the new chain will be drawn down, around the sprockets and guides, then up the other side. Fit the link from the rear of the sprocket, and ensure that the link is pushed firmly into position - do not fit the link plate to secure the link at this stage.
14 It is now necessary to feed the new chain around the sprockets and guides. During this procedure it is essential to observe the following points.
a) *Keep tension on the new chain, ensuring that the links remain engaged with the camshaft sprocket, otherwise the valve timing will be lost.*
b) *Pull up on the old chain to prevent it dropping off the crankshaft sprocket, or jamming in the guides.*
15 Using a suitable socket on the crankshaft pulley/vibration damper hub bolt, slowly turn the crankshaft clockwise, whilst observing the points made in the preceding paragraph.
16 When the end of the new chain appears, remove the link (ensuring that tension is kept on the new chain, and that the chain links remain engaged with the sprockets), and disconnect the new chain from the old chain. Remove the old chain.
17 Engage the new chain with the camshaft sprocket, then join the two ends of the chain with the connecting link, inserted from the rear of the sprocket **(see illustration)**.

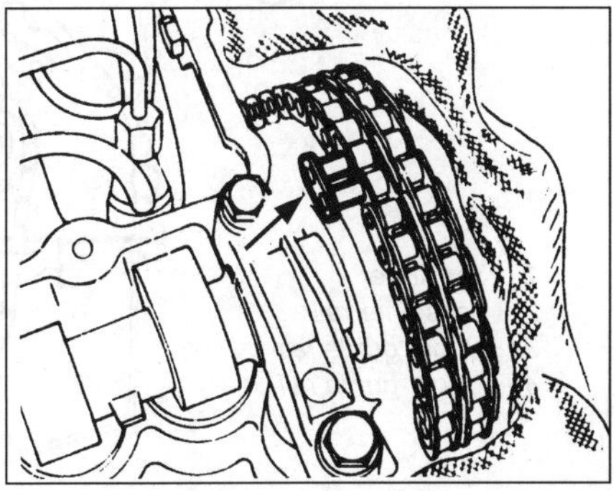

7.17 Push the chain link (arrowed) in from the rear of the chain

HAYNES HiNT ***Temporarily secure the ends of the new chain to the camshaft sprocket using wire or cable-ties passed through the holes in the sprocket and around the chain.***

18 Fit the link plate, and then secure the plate to the link by flattening the ends of the link pins. A special tool is available for this purpose, but it should be possible to achieve a satisfactory result using a hammer, with a block of metal (or a second hammer) to support the rear of the chain - *take great care not to damage the chain or the sprocket.*
19 Check that the chain link is secure, with no burring of the metal, or loose swarf.
20 Refit the timing chain tensioner as described in Section 8.
21 Turn the engine (clockwise) to bring No 1 piston to TDC, ensuring that crankshaft and camshaft timing marks are correctly aligned as described in Section 3.
22 It is possible that the timing chain may have slipped by one tooth on the camshaft sprocket during this operation. If this is the case, the timing can be corrected by removing the camshaft sprocket (see Section 8), and altering the position of the camshaft and sprocket by one tooth in relation to the chain. In this case, also check the fuel injection pump timing as described in Chapter 4.
23 Refit the cooling fan and shroud as described in Chapter 3.
24 Refit the fuel injectors as described in Chapter 4.
25 Refit the camshaft cover, with reference to Section 4.
26 Reconnect the battery negative lead.

8 Timing chain tensioner, sprockets and guides - removal, inspection and refitting

Tensioner

Removal

1 Working at the right-hand side of the engine, unscrew the tensioner body (**do not** unscrew the tensioner cover plug) from the cylinder head **(see illustrations)**. Recover the sealing ring.

Inspection

2 Do not attempt to dismantle the tensioner assembly. If it is suspected that the tensioner is worn or faulty, the complete unit should be renewed.

Refitting

3 Before refitting the tensioner, the unit must be primed with oil as follows.
a) *Place the tensioner, with the plunger facing downwards in a container of engine oil. The oil level should be up to the level of the cover plug.*
b) *Press slowly down on the assembly (a hydraulic press may be required to achieve sufficient pressure) between seven and ten times until the plunger reaches the stop.*
c) *Once the tensioner has been primed, it should be possible to compress the tensioner slowly, evenly, and with little effort.*

4 Screw the tensioner into position in the cylinder head, and tighten to the specified torque.

Camshaft sprocket

Removal

5 Remove the auxiliary drivebelt as described in Chapter 1B.
6 Remove the camshaft cover as described in Section 4.
7 Remove the timing chain tensioner as described previously in this Section.
8 Where applicable, remove the self-levelling suspension hydraulic pump from the front of the cylinder head, as described in Chapter 10. Recover the O-ring and spacer plate, then unscrew the securing bolt and withdraw the pump drive sleeve from the front of the camshaft.
9 Turn the engine to position No 1 piston at TDC, ensuring that crankshaft and camshaft timing marks are correctly aligned as described in Section 3. Make alignment marks on the camshaft sprocket and the timing chain.
10 The camshaft sprocket bolt must now be slackened. The camshaft must be prevented from turning as the sprocket bolt is loosened, and this can be achieved by using a screwdriver to hold the sprocket stationary by means of the holes in the sprocket - take care not to damage surrounding components.
11 Unscrew the sprocket securing bolt, and recover the washer.
12 Withdraw the sprocket from the camshaft, noting which way round it is fitted to ensure correct refitting.

Inspection

13 Examine the teeth on the sprocket for wear. Each tooth forms an inverted "V". If worn, the side of each tooth under tension will be slightly concave in shape when compared with the other side of the tooth (ie: the teeth will have a "hooked" appearance). If the teeth appear worn, the sprocket must be renewed.

Refitting

14 Ensure that the camshaft and crankshaft timing marks are still aligned, as described in

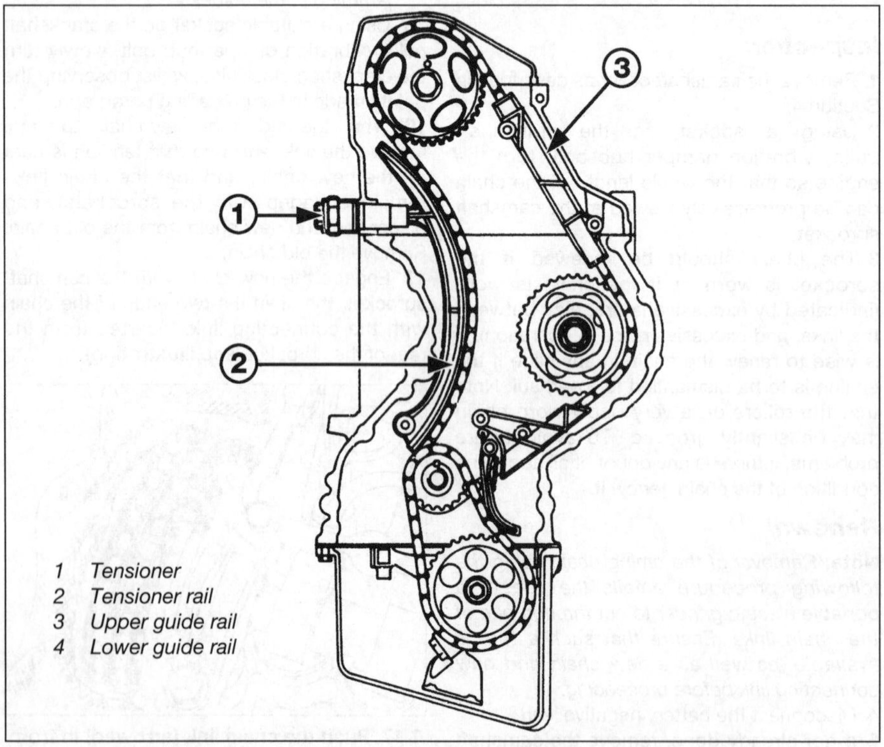

8.1a Timing chain tensioner and guide components

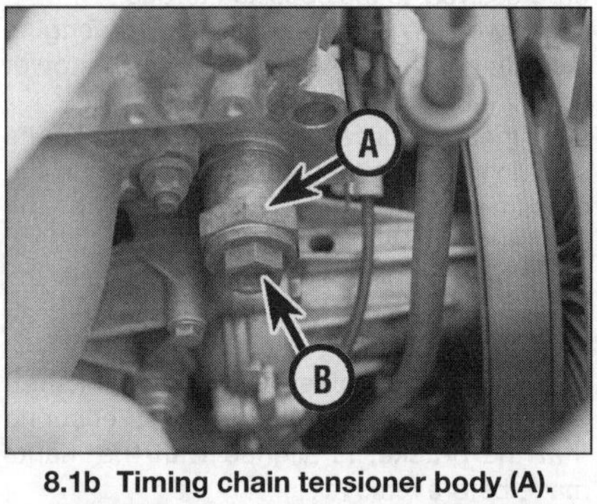

8.1b Timing chain tensioner body (A). DO NOT unscrew the cover plug (B)

Section 3. If a new sprocket is being fitted, copy the chain alignment mark from the old sprocket to the new.

15 Engage the sprocket with the chain, aligning the marks made on the chain and sprocket before removal.

16 Offer the sprocket into position on the camshaft, ensuring that it is fitted the correct way round, as noted before removal. Make sure that the locating pin on the camshaft flange engages with the hole in the sprocket.

17 Refit the securing bolt and washer, and tighten the bolt to the specified torque, holding the sprocket as during removal.

18 Where applicable, refit the self-levelling suspension hydraulic pump drive sleeve to the front of the camshaft, and tighten the securing bolt to the specified torque. Refit the spacer plate and the O-ring (check, and renew if necessary), then refit the hydraulic pump with reference to Chapter 10.

19 Refit the timing chain tensioner as described previously in this Section.

20 Using a socket on the crankshaft pulley/vibration damper hub bolts, turn the crankshaft through one complete revolution, and check that the crankshaft and camshaft timing marks are still aligned with No 1 piston at TDC, as described in Section 3.

Warning: Do not turn the engine by means of the camshaft sprocket bolt.

21 Refit the camshaft cover as described in Section 4.

22 Refit the auxiliary drivebelt as described in Chapter 1B.

Crankshaft sprocket

Note: *A puller may be required to remove the sprocket.*

Removal

23 Remove the timing chain cover as described in Section 6.

24 Remove the sump as described in Section 11.

25 Remove the camshaft sprocket as described previously in this Section. Allow the timing chain to hang down into the timing chain housing so that it disengages from the crankshaft sprocket.

26 Pull the oil pump drive chain tensioner rail and spring from the lug on the cylinder block - note the orientation of the spring to aid correct refitting.

27 Unscrew the securing bolt and remove the oil pump drive sprocket, complete with the chain, from the oil pump shaft. Recover the washer.

28 Make alignment marks on the timing chain and the crankshaft sprocket.

29 Remove the crankshaft sprocket from the front of the crankshaft, using a suitable puller. Alternatively, it may be possible to lever it off using two large screwdrivers positioned either side of the sprocket. Note which way round the sprocket is fitted to ensure correct refitting.

30 Recover the Woodruff key if it is loose.

Inspection

31 Refer to paragraph 13.

Refitting

32 Where applicable, refit the Woodruff key to the end of the crankshaft.

33 If a new sprocket is being fitted, transfer the chain alignment mark from the old sprocket to the new.

34 Engage the timing chain with the crankshaft sprocket and the camshaft sprocket, ensuring that the marks made before removal are aligned, then refit the camshaft sprocket, as described previously in this Section.

35 Refit the oil pump sprocket and chain (the convex side of the sprocket should face the oil pump). Tighten the securing bolt to the specified torque, ensuring that the washer is in place.

36 Refit the oil pump drive chain tensioner rail bush, spring, and then the tensioner rail. Ensure that the spring is orientated as noted before removal.

37 Refit the sump as described in Section 11.

38 Refit the timing chain cover as described in Section 6.

Fuel injection pump sprocket

39 The procedure is described as part in Chapter 4.

Tensioner rail

Removal

40 Remove the cylinder head as described in Section 10.

41 Remove the timing chain cover as described in Section 6.

42 Remove the timing chain tensioner as described previously in this Section.

43 Pull the tensioner rail from its locating lugs.

Inspection

44 Examine the tensioner rail for signs of excessive wear, damage or cracks, and renew if necessary.

Refitting

45 Push the tensioner rail into position, ensuring that it engages correctly with the locating lugs.

46 Refit the timing chain tensioner as described previously in this Section.

47 Refit the timing chain cover as described in Section 6.

48 Refit the cylinder head as described in Section 10.

Upper guide rail

Note: *A suitable slide hammer and adapter will be required for this operation, and suitable sealant will be required to coat the guide rail locating pins on refitting.*

Removal

49 Remove the camshaft sprocket as described previously in this Section.

50 Screw a suitable bolt into one of the guide rail locating pins (accessible from the front of the cylinder head).

51 Engage a slide hammer and suitable adapter with the bolt, and use the slide hammer to remove the guide rail locating pin **(see illustrations)**.

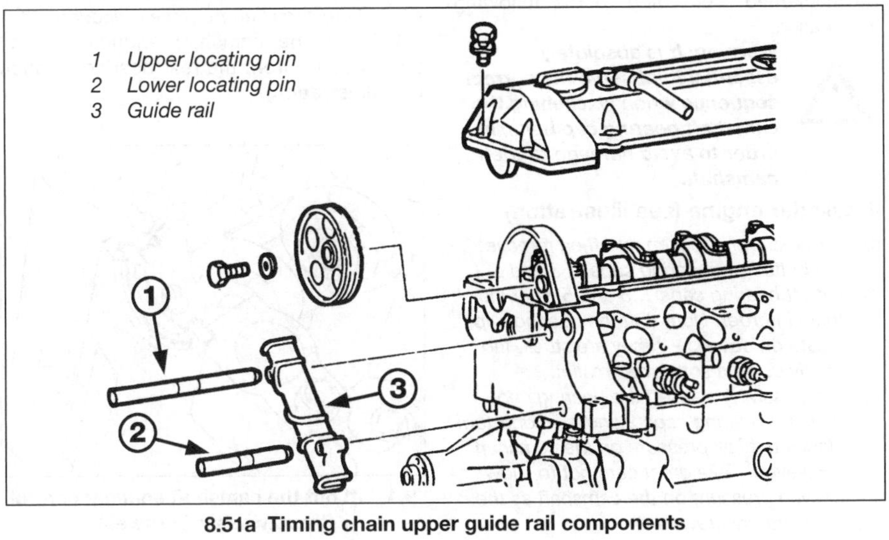

8.51a Timing chain upper guide rail components

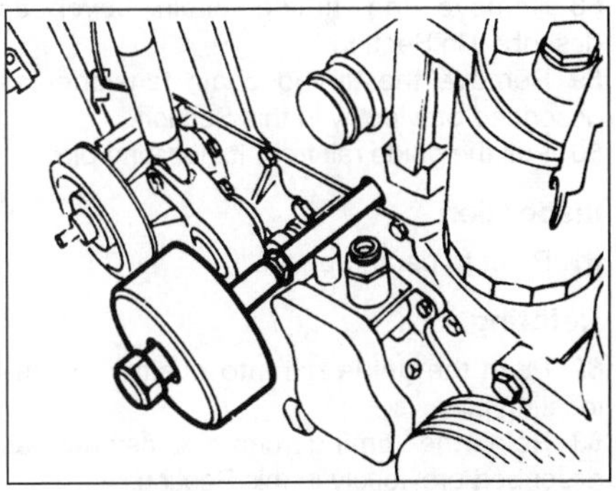

8.51b Using a slide hammer to extract an upper guide rail locating pin

2C

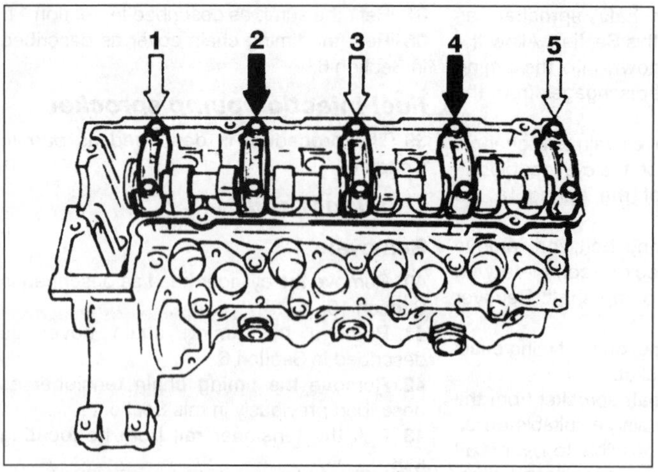

9.3a Camshaft bearing cap loosening sequence - 4-cylinder engine
Remove bearing caps 1, 3 and 5 (light arrows), then slacken the bolts for bearing caps 2 and 4 (dark arrows) in one-turn stages

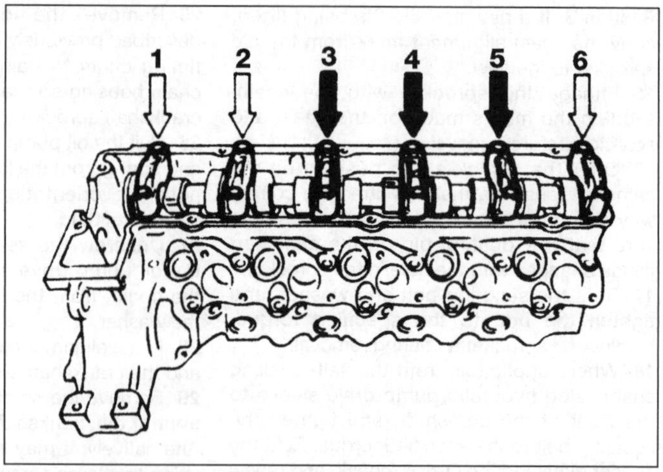

9.3b Camshaft bearing cap loosening sequence - 5-cylinder engine
Remove bearing caps 1, 2 and 6 (light arrows), then slacken the bolts for bearing caps 3, 4 and 5 (dark arrows) in one-turn stages

52 Repeat the procedure for the remaining locating pin, ensuring that the guide rail does not slide down the timing chain into the housing as the pin is removed.
53 Withdraw the guide rail from the cylinder head.

Inspection

54 Refer to paragraph 44.

Refitting

55 Offer the guide rail into position in the housing, then position the locating pins in their holes in the cylinder head, and tap them into position sufficiently to retain the guide rail.
56 Apply sealant to the outer collar of each locating pin, where it seats in the cylinder head, then tap the pins fully into the cylinder head..
57 Refit the camshaft sprocket as described previously in this Section.

Lower guide rail

Removal

58 Remove the timing chain cover as described in Section 6.
59 Remove the timing chain tensioner as described previously in this Section.
60 Pull the guide rail from its locating pin.

Inspection

61 Refer to paragraph 44.

Refitting

62 Push the guide rail into position on the locating pin.
63 Refit the timing chain tensioner as described previously in this Section.
64 Refit the timing chain cover as described in Section 6.

9 Camshaft and valve lifters - removal, inspection and refitting

Removal

Note: *If desired, before removing the camshaft, the condition of the valve lifters can be checked as described in paragraphs 10 to 18. A new camshaft endfloat control thrustwasher may be required on refitting (see Chapter 2D).*
1 Remove the camshaft sprocket as described in Section 8.
2 The camshaft bearing caps are numbered from the timing chain end of the engine. Check the bearing caps to ensure that marks are present, and if necessary make suitable marks using quick-drying paint or a centre-punch.
3 The camshaft bearing cap bolts must now be slackened, according to the following information.

Warning: It is absolutely essential to observe the correct sequence when slackening the camshaft bearing cap bolts, in order to avoid damage to the camshaft.

4-cylinder engine (see illustration)

a) *Progressively slacken and then remove the bolts from bearing caps 1, 3 and 5.*
b) *Lift off bearing caps 1, 3 and 5, keeping them in order. Note that the bearing caps locate on dowels - if they are stuck, tap gently using a soft-faced mallet.*
c) *Progressively slacken the bearing cap bolts for bearing caps 2 and 4, in one-turn stages until all pressure on the camshaft is relieved. Take great care not to allow uneven pressure on the camshaft as the bolts are unscrewed.*
d) *Fully unscrew the remaining bearing cap bolts, and lift off the bearing caps (2 and 4), again keeping them in order.*
e) *Lift the camshaft from the cylinder head.*

5-cylinder engine (see illustration)

a) *Progressively slacken and then remove the bolts from bearing caps 1, 2 and 6.*
b) *Lift off bearing caps 1, 2 and 6, keeping them in order. Note that the bearing caps locate on dowels - if they are stuck, tap gently using a soft-faced mallet.*
c) *Progressively slacken the bearing cap bolts for bearing caps 3, 4 and 5, in one-turn stages until all pressure on the camshaft is relieved. Take great care not to allow uneven pressure on the camshaft as the bolts are unscrewed.*
d) *Fully unscrew the remaining bearing cap bolts, and lift off the caps (3, 4 and 5), again keeping them in order.*
e) *Lift the camshaft from the cylinder head.*

4 Lift out the camshaft endfloat control thrustwasher from the rear bearing location **(see illustration)**.

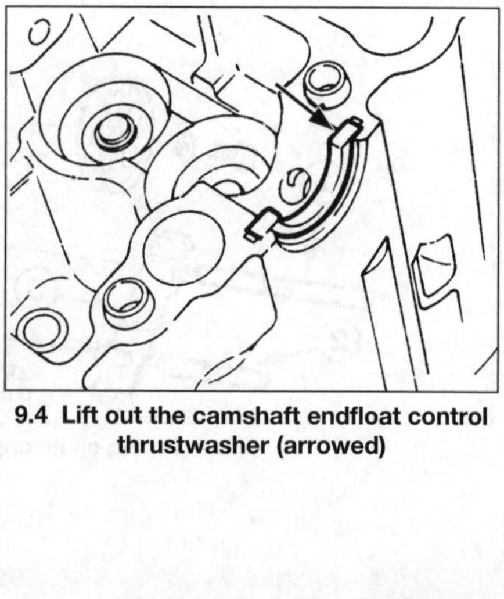

9.4 Lift out the camshaft endfloat control thrustwasher (arrowed)

5 Withdraw the hydraulic valve lifters from the bores in the cylinder head. This is most easily done using a suction valve-grinding tool - push the tool onto the top of the valve lifter, and pull out the valve lifter - **do not** use a magnet to remove the lifters, as this may cause damage to the cam lobe contact faces. Identify the lifters for location, and store them upright in a container of clean engine oil to prevent the oil from draining from inside the lifters.

> **HAYNES HiNT** ***Store each valve lifter in a labelled plastic cup filled with oil.***

Inspection

Camshaft

6 Examine the camshaft bearings and cam lobes for any sign of scoring, wear grooves or pitting, and if apparent, renew the camshaft. Any damage of this nature may be attributable to a blocked oil passage in the cylinder head, and careful examination should be carried out to determine the cause.

Valve lifters - checking with valve lifters removed

7 Inspect the valve lifters and spacer washers for obvious signs of wear or damage, and renew if necessary.

8 The operation of the valve lifters can be checked as follows.

a) Press down firmly on the top of each valve lifter piston, using a blunt instrument such as a wooden hammer handle, for approximately 10 seconds.

b) Note how far the piston moves when depressed.

c) Repeat the operation for all the valve lifters in turn.

d) If any one valve lifter piston can be depressed more easily than the others, renew the relevant lifter.

9 Check the valve lifter bores in the cylinder head for wear and scoring. If any serious damage or wear is evident, the cylinder head must be renewed.

Valve lifters - checking with valve lifters *in situ*

10 Run the engine until it reaches normal operating temperature.

11 Check the engine oil level, ensuring that the engine has not been overfilled.

12 Remove the camshaft cover as described in Section 4 - take care as the engine will be hot!

13 Turn the engine to position No 1 piston at TDC, ensuring that crankshaft and camshaft timing marks are correctly aligned as described in Section 3.

14 Ensure that the valves are fully closed - ie: the cam lobes are pointing upwards, then, using a soft metal or strong wooden rod, push down lightly on the top of the No 1 valve lifter at the front of the cylinder head **(see illustration)**.

15 Keep the valve lifter pressed down, and measure the clearance between the top of the valve lifter and the camshaft lobe, using a feeler blade.

16 If the clearance is greater than specified, the valve lifter should be renewed. Note that it is possible to dismantle the valve lifters for further checking, but this is best entrusted to a Mercedes-Benz dealer or a suitably-qualified engineer.

17 Turn the crankshaft using a socket on the crankshaft pulley/vibration damper hub bolt, and repeat the checking procedure for the remaining valve lifters. Each clearance must be checked with the relevant valve fully closed - ie: the cam lobe pointing upwards.

> ***Warning: When turning the engine, do not turn the engine using the camshaft sprocket bolt, and do not turn the engine backwards (ie: anti-clockwise).***

18 When all the valve lifters have been checked, refit the camshaft cover with reference to Section 4.

Refitting

19 Lubricate the external surfaces of the valve lifters with clean engine oil, then refit the lifters to their original locations in the cylinder head. Check that the lifters slide freely in their bores.

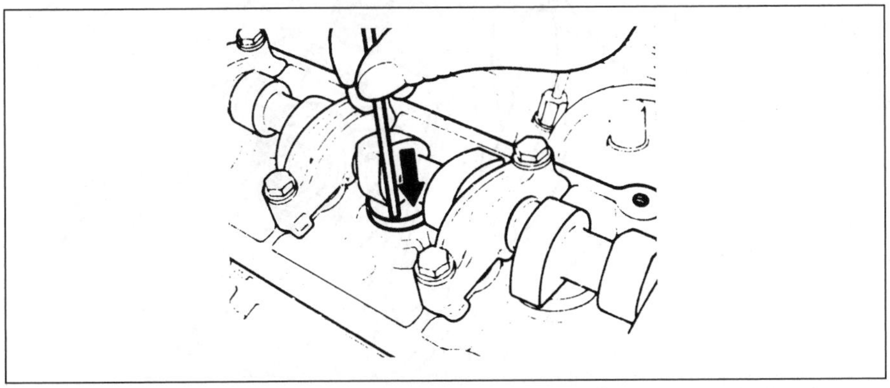

9.14 Pressing a valve lifter down to check the clearance between the lifter and the cam lobe

20 Check the condition of the camshaft endfloat control thrustwasher (see Chapter 2D), and if necessary renew. Refit the washer to the rear bearing location.

21 Lubricate the camshaft and the bearing locations in the cylinder head with clean engine oil, then lay the camshaft in position on the cylinder head. The timing notch in the flange at the front of the camshaft should point vertically upwards.

22 Lay the bearing caps in position over the camshaft and tighten the securing bolts according to the following information, ensuring that the bearing caps are fitted to their original locations.

> ***Warning: It is absolutely essential to observe the correct sequence when tightening the camshaft bearing cap bolts, in order to avoid damage to the camshaft.***

4-cylinder engine

a) Fit bearing caps 2 and 4, then fit the bolts, and tighten them progressively in one-turn stages to the specified torque. Take care not to allow uneven pressure on the camshaft as the bolts are tightened.

b) Fit bearing caps 1, 3 and 5, and tighten the bolts to the specified torque.

5-cylinder engine

a) Fit bearing caps 3, 4 and 5, then fit the bolts, and tighten them progressively in one-turn stages to the specified torque. Take care not to allow uneven pressure on the camshaft as the bolts are tightened.

b) Fit bearing caps 1, 2 and 6, and tighten the bolts to the specified torque.

23 Refit the camshaft sprocket as described in Section 8.

2C

10 Cylinder head - removal, inspection and refitting

Removal

Note: *A suitable hoist and lifting tackle, and a slide hammer and adapter will be required for this operation. A new cylinder head gasket and a new coolant elbow O-ring will be required on refitting. New cylinder head bolts may be required - see text.*

1 Ensure that the engine is cold before attempting to remove the cylinder head, and note that the cylinder head is removed complete with the exhaust manifold.

2 Disconnect the battery negative lead.

3 Raise the bonnet to the fully open position as described in Chapter 11.

4 Drain the engine oil and the coolant as described in Chapter 1B.

5 Remove the camshaft as described in Section 9.

6 Remove the fuel injectors as described in Chapter 4.

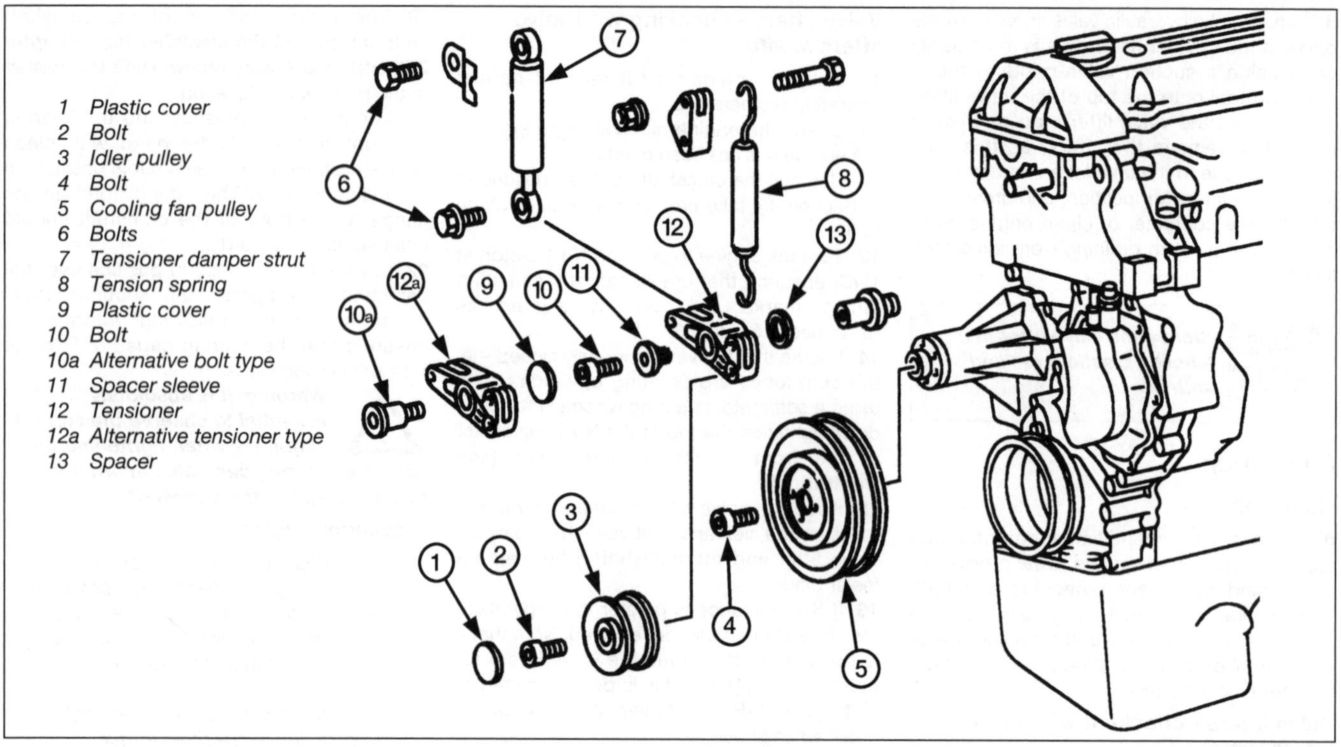

10.8 Auxiliary drivebelt tensioner components

7 Remove the radiator as described in Chapter 3.

8 Remove the auxiliary drivebelt tensioner as follows **(see illustration)**.

a) Pull off the plastic cover, unscrew the securing bolt, and remove the auxiliary drivebelt idler pulley.

b) Unscrew the securing bolts, and remove the cooling fan pulley.

c) Unscrew the securing bolts, and withdraw the tensioner damper strut. Recover any spacers and/or brackets from the bolts noting their locations.

d) Using a pair of pliers, unhook the tension spring, noting its orientation to aid refitting.

e) Where applicable, pull off the plastic cover, then unscrew the tensioner securing bolt and, slide off the spacer sleeve (if applicable).

f) Withdraw the tensioner, and recover the spacer (where applicable).

9 On non-Turbo models, remove the air cleaner cover, inlet hose and air filter element, as described in Chapter 4.

10 On Turbo models, carry out the following operations.

a) Remove the turbocharger inlet air hose.

b) Unbolt the turbocharger support bracket.

c) Unscrew the union nut, and disconnect the turbocharger oil return pipe from the cylinder block.

11 Place a wad of rag beneath the fuel line connections at the fuel filter, then unscrew the union nuts, and disconnect the fuel lines, noting their locations to aid refitting **(see illustration)**. Plug the open ends of the unions and pipes to prevent dirt entry and further fuel loss.

12 Unbolt the fuel filter from the cylinder head, and remove the filter.

13 Unbolt the engine oil level dipstick tube from the cylinder head.

14 On models with exhaust gas recirculation, disconnect the hose from the exhaust gas recirculation valve **(see illustration)**.

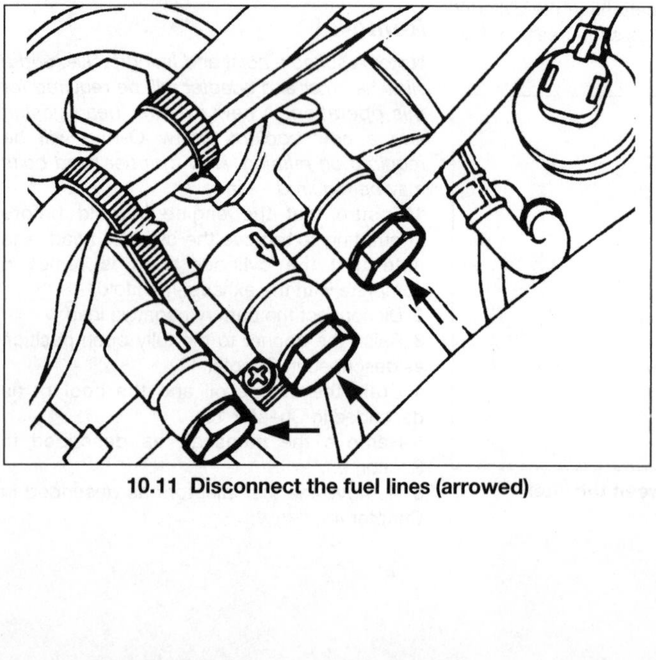

10.11 Disconnect the fuel lines (arrowed)

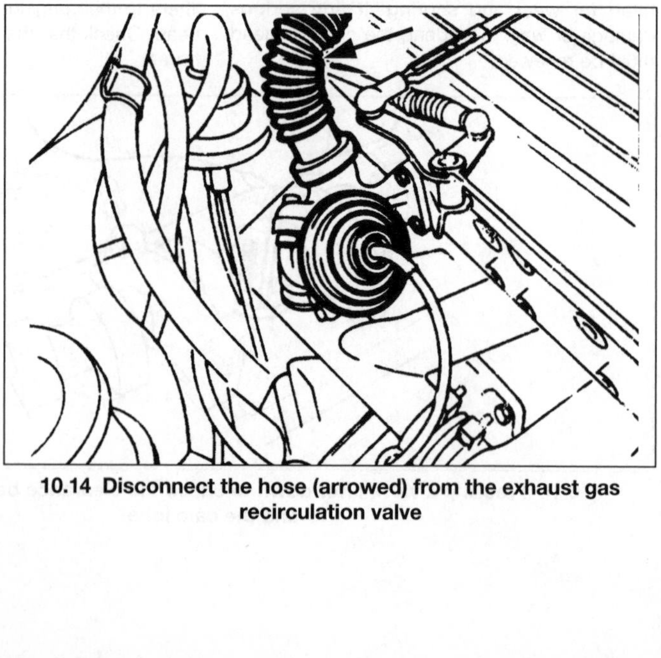

10.14 Disconnect the hose (arrowed) from the exhaust gas recirculation valve

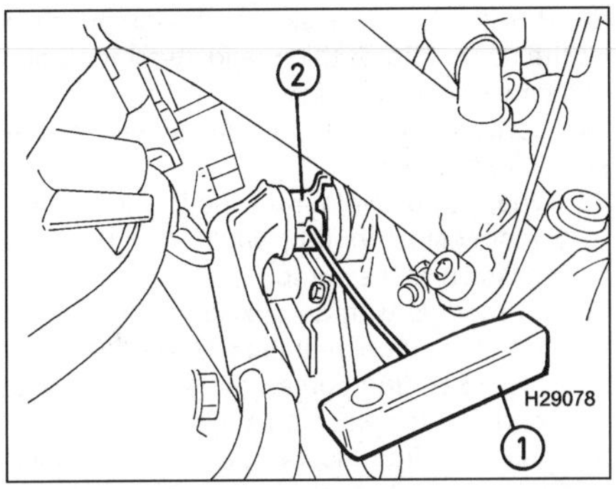

10.17 Use a hooked instrument (1) to pull the locking clip (2) from the coolant elbow connection

15 Working under the vehicle, unscrew the bolts securing the exhaust mounting bracket to the transmission, then unscrew the bolts securing the mounting bracket to the exhaust system.

16 Disconnect the exhaust front section from the manifold with reference to Chapter 4.

17 Using a suitable hooked instrument or a bent piece of wire, pull the locking clip from the coolant elbow connection to the oil cooler assembly **(see illustration)**.

18 Unscrew the elbow from the oil filter assembly, then pull the elbow from the connector.

19 Unscrew the securing nuts, and disconnect the wiring connector bar from the glow plugs.

20 Remove the inlet manifold as described in Chapter 4.

21 Remove the upper timing chain guide as described in Section 8.

22 Working in the timing chain housing, unscrew the two bolts securing the cylinder head to the timing chain cover.

23 Make a final check to ensure that all relevant hoses and wires have been disconnected to allow cylinder head removal.

24 Progressively loosen the cylinder head bolts, working in the reverse order to that shown in illustration 10.43a or 10.43b.

25 Remove the cylinder head bolts, noting their locations, as different lengths of bolts are used.

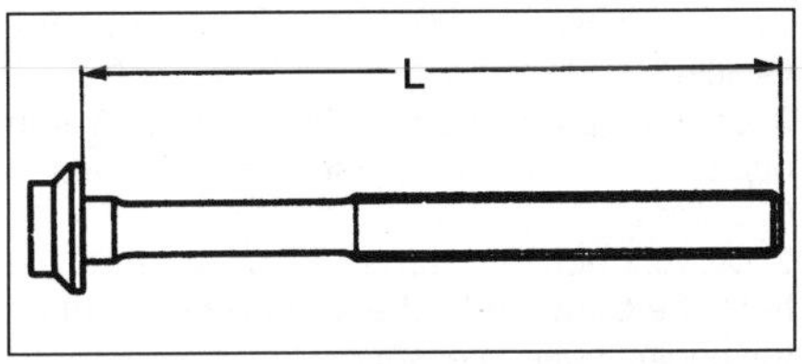

10.37 Measure the length (L) of the cylinder head bolts

See Specifications for maximum length

26 Attach a hoist and lifting tackle to the lifting bracket at the front left of the cylinder head, and the rear right of the exhaust manifold. Raise the hoist to just take the weight of the cylinder head.

27 Release the cylinder head from the cylinder block and locating dowels by rocking it. Do not prise between the mating faces of the cylinder head and block, as this may damage the gasket faces.

28 Carefully lift the cylinder head, complete with exhaust manifold, from the block, and manoeuvre it out from the engine compartment.

29 Recover the cylinder head gasket.

Inspection

30 Refer to Chapter 2D for details of cylinder head dismantling and reassembly. If desired, the exhaust manifold can be removed with reference to Chapter 4.

31 The mating faces of the cylinder head and block must be perfectly clean before refitting the head. Use a scraper to remove all traces of gasket and carbon, and also clean the tops of the pistons. Take particular care with the cylinder head, as the metal is easily damaged. Also make sure that debris is not allowed to enter the oil and water passages. Using adhesive tape and paper, seal the water, oil and bolt holes in the cylinder block. To prevent carbon entering the gap between the pistons and bores, smear a little grease in the gap. After cleaning each piston, rotate the crankshaft so that the piston moves **down** the bore, then wipe out the grease and carbon with a cloth rag.

32 Check the block and head for nicks, deep scratches and other damage. If very slight, they may be removed from the cylinder block carefully with a file. More serious damage may be repaired by machining, but this is a specialist job.

33 If warpage of the cylinder head is suspected, use a straight-edge to check it for distortion, with reference to Chapter 2D.

34 Clean out the bolt holes in the block using a pipe cleaner or thin rag and a screwdriver. Make sure that all oil and water is removed, otherwise there is a possibility of the block being cracked by hydraulic pressure when the bolts are tightened.

35 Examine the bolt threads and the threads in the cylinder block for damage. If necessary, use the correct size tap to chase out the threads in the block.

36 The manufacturers recommend that the cylinder head bolts are measured, to determine whether renewal is necessary; however, some owners may wish to renew all the bolts as a matter of course.

37 Measure the length of each bolt from the base of the head to the end of the shank **(see illustration)**. If the bolt length is greater than the maximum specified, the bolts should be renewed.

Refitting

38 Where applicable, refit the exhaust manifold with reference to Chapter 4.

39 Check that the camshaft and crankshaft timing marks are still aligned with No 1 piston at TDC, as described in Section 3.

40 Fit the gasket over the dowels in the cylinder block, ensuring that it is fitted the correct way round.

41 Support the cylinder head using the hoist and lifting tackle, then lower the cylinder head onto the block.

42 Oil the threads and the cylinder head contact faces of the cylinder head bolts (see paragraphs 36 and 37), then insert them and screw them into the cylinder block by hand. Ensure that the bolts are fitted to their correct locations as noted before removal.

43 Tighten the cylinder head bolts in the order shown **(see illustrations)**. Tighten the bolts in the stages given in the Specifications

2C

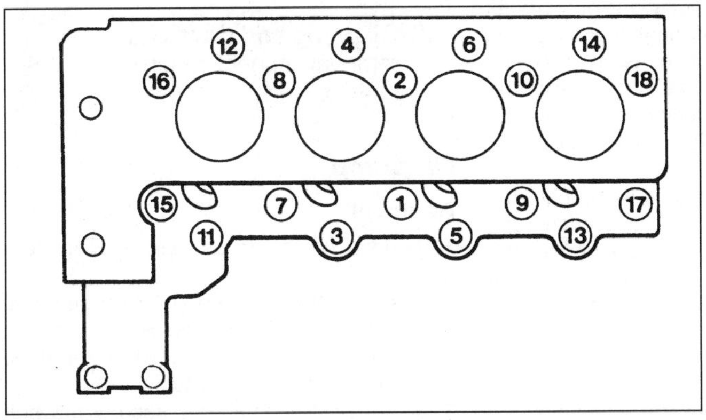

10.43a Cylinder head bolt tightening sequence - 4-cylinder diesel engines

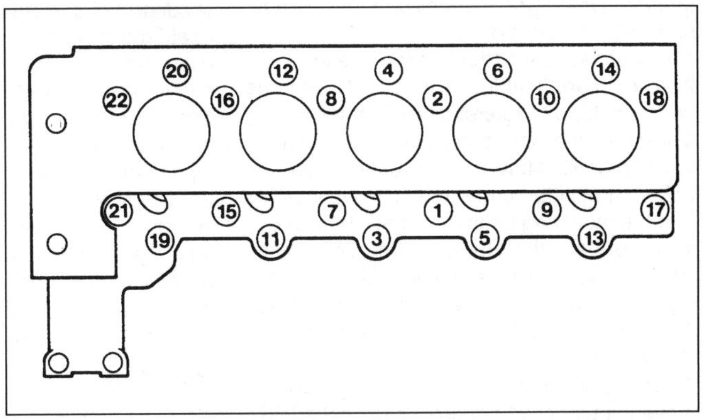

10.43b Cylinder head bolt tightening sequence - 5-cylinder diesel engines

- ie: tighten all bolts to the Stage 1 torque, then tighten all bolts to the Stage 2 torque, and so on.

44 Refit and tighten the bolts securing the cylinder head to the timing chain cover.

45 Refit the upper timing chain guide rail as described in Section 8.

46 Refit the inlet manifold as described in Chapter 4.

47 Reconnect the wires to the glow plugs, and tighten the securing nuts.

48 Refit the coolant elbow to the oil cooler assembly, using a new O-ring. Lubricate the O-ring with clean coolant before fitting. Refit the locking clip.

49 Reconnect the exhaust front section to the manifold with reference to Chapter 4.

50 Refit the exhaust-to-transmission mounting bracket, and tighten the securing bolts, ensuring that the exhaust system is mounted free from stress.

51 Further refitting is a reversal of removal, bearing in mind the following points.

a) *Ensure that the fuel lines are correctly reconnected to the fuel filter, as noted before removal.*
b) *Refit the auxiliary drivebelt tensioner using a reversal of the procedure described in paragraph 8.*
c) *Refit the radiator with reference to Chapter 3.*
d) *Refit the fuel injectors as described in Chapter 4.*
e) *Refit the camshaft as described in Section 9.*
f) *Refill the cooling system and refill the engine with oil as described in Chapter 1B.*

11 Sump - removal and refitting

Removal

Note: *A suitable hoist and lifting tackle will be required for this operation. A new sump gasket, and a new sump auxiliary section gasket (where applicable) will be required on refitting. New front suspension crossmember bolts will be required.*

1 Disconnect the battery negative lead.

2 Where applicable, remove the engine undershield, with reference to Chapter 11.

3 Remove the front anti-roll bar as described in Chapter 10. Note that the anti-roll bar can be left in position under the vehicle, provided that the mounting bolts have been removed.

4 Disconnect the steering drag link on the left-hand side, and the steering damper on the right-hand side, with reference to Chapter 10.

5 Drain the engine oil with reference to Chapter 1B.

6 Where applicable, remove the engine movement stop with reference to Section 16.

7 Where applicable, unscrew the two bolts securing the engine mounting damper to the body member on the left-hand side of the vehicle.

8 Unclip the cooling fan shroud, and lay it in position over the fan blades as described in Chapter 3.

9 Disconnect the starter motor earth strap from the body and, where applicable, unbolt the engine speed sensor.

10 Where applicable, disconnect the wiring from the engine oil level sensor.

11 Disconnect the engine oil cooler hoses from the rigid pipes. Plug or clamp the open ends of the hoses, and plug the pipes to prevent dirt entry.

12 Attach an engine hoist and lifting tackle to the front engine lifting eye.

13 Unbolt the left- and right-hand engine mountings from the crossmember, with reference to Section 16.

14 Carefully raise the engine as far as possible, until the rear of the cylinder head touches the engine compartment bulkhead. Take care not to damage any of the components in the engine compartment.

15 Remove the front suspension coil springs, as described in Chapter 10.

16 Remove the steering column-to-coupling upper clamp bolt, and disconnect the steering column from the coupling, with reference to Chapter 10.

17 Support the front suspension crossmember using a jack and a suitable large block of wood, then unscrew the four securing bolts (unbolt the plastic covers for access to the rear bolts), and lower the crossmember assembly until it is supported by the shock absorbers - see *"Front lower arm - removal and refitting"* in Chapter 10. Discard the crossmember securing bolts - new bolts must be used on refitting, and take care not to strain any pipes, hoses or wiring as the crossmember is lowered.

18 On models with an auxiliary section bolted to the right-hand side of the sump, unscrew the securing bolts, and remove the sump side section. Recover the washers and the gasket.

19 Where applicable, unscrew the two lower engine-to-transmission bolts, which secure the transmission to the sump.

20 Working progressively, in a diagonal sequence, unscrew and remove the sump securing bolts. Note the locations of the bolts to aid refitting, as various lengths of bolts may used. Also note the locations of any brackets secured by the bolts (note that some of the bolts may already have been removed in order to release the transmission fluid and oil cooler pipes from the sump).

21 Lower the sump forwards from under the vehicle, and recover the gasket. If necessary, turn the crankshaft using a socket on the pulley/vibration damper hub bolt to move the crankshaft webs, allowing clearance for the sump to be withdrawn.

Refitting

22 Commence refitting by cleaning the remains of the gasket from the sump and cylinder block, and wipe dry.

23 Position a new gasket on the sump, then lift the sump into position, and insert the bolts in their original locations.

24 Tighten the bolts progressively to the specified torque.

25 Where applicable, refit the lower engine-to-transmission bolts, which secure the transmission to the sump.

26 On models with an auxiliary side section bolted to the sump, refit the side section using a new gasket, and tighten the securing bolts, ensuring that the washers are in place.

27 Raise the front suspension crossmember, and secure it in position using new bolts, as described in *"Front lower arm - removal and refitting"* in Chapter 10. Tighten the bolts to the specified torque.

28 Reconnect the steering column to the coupling, ensuring that the column and coupling are correctly aligned, as described in Chapter 10.

29 Refit the front suspension coil springs as described in Chapter 10.

30 Carefully lower the engine into position, and refit the engine mounting bolts. Tighten the bolts to the specified torque. Disconnect the lifting tackle and hoist.

31 Reconnect the engine oil cooler hoses to the rigid pipes, and tighten the clamp bolts.

32 Where applicable, reconnect the wiring to the engine oil level sensor.

33 Reconnect the starter motor earth strap to the body and, where applicable, refit the engine speed sensor.

34 Refit the cooling fan shroud as described in Chapter 3.

35 Refit and adjust the engine movement damper as described in Section 16.

36 Reconnect the steering drag link and the steering damper, with reference to Chapter 10.

37 Refit the front anti-roll bar as described in Chapter 10.

38 Ensure that the engine oil drain plug has been tightened, then refit the engine undershield.

39 Reconnect the battery negative lead, then fill the engine with oil and, where applicable, check the automatic transmission fluid level as described in Chapter 1B.

12 Oil pump and drive chain - removal, inspection and refitting

Oil pump

Removal

1 Remove the sump as described in Section 11.

2 Unscrew the oil pump sprocket securing bolt, and recover the washer. Withdraw the oil pump sprocket, complete with the drive chain, from the oil pump shaft.

3 On 5-cylinder engines, unscrew the bolt securing the oil pick-up pipe to the support bracket.

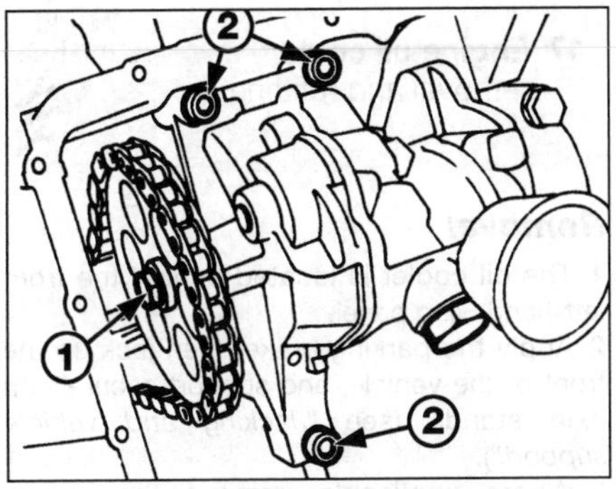

12.4 Oil pump sprocket bolt (1) and oil pump securing bolts (2)

4 Unscrew the three bolts securing the oil pump to the cylinder block, and recover the washers **(see illustration)**. Where applicable, unscrew the securing bolts, and withdraw the oil pump baffle plate.

5 Lift the oil pump from the cylinder block, noting that it locates on two dowels.

Inspection

6 With the exception of the oil pressure relief valve components, the oil pump is a sealed unit. To remove the oil pressure relief valve components, proceed as follows.

7 Unscrew the relief valve plug. Take care, as the plug will be pushed out by the spring pressure when it reaches the end of the threads.

8 Withdraw the spring, guide pin and piston **(see illustration)**.

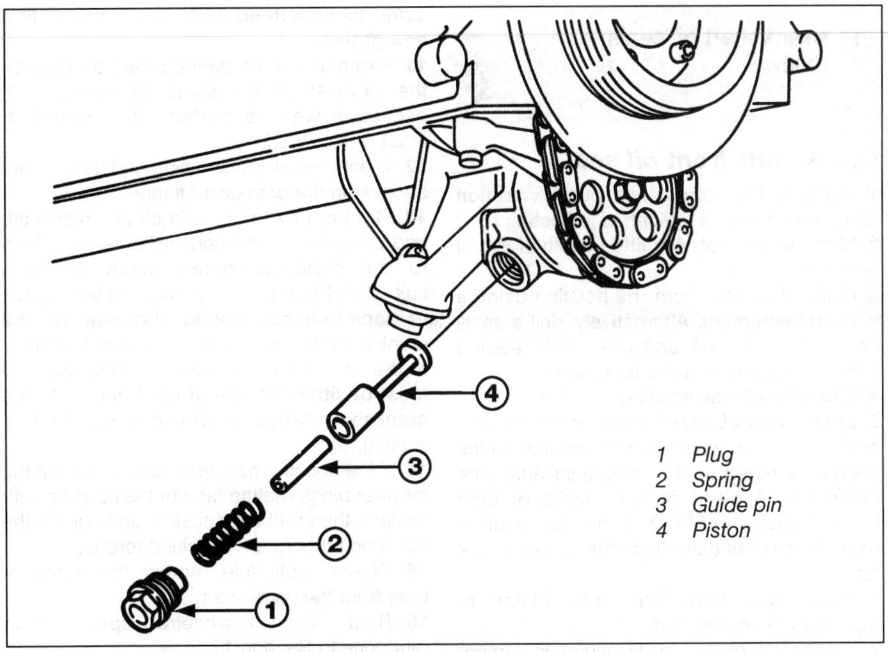

12.8 Oil pressure relief valve components

9 Thoroughly clean all components, and examine them for wear and damage. If there is any sign of excessive wear or damage, renew the appropriate component(s) - pay particular attention to the spring.

10 Refit the components using a reversal of the removal procedure, and tighten the plug to the specified torque.

11 On models with an oil baffle plate fitted to the cylinder block, when the oil pump is removed, it is advisable to remove and clean the baffle plate. Simply unbolt the baffle plate, clean it, and refit.

Refitting

12 Refitting is a reversal of removal, bearing in mind the following points.

a) Prime the oil pump by filling it with clean engine oil.

b) Ensure that the pump locates correctly on the dowels.

c) Tighten the pump securing bolts to the specified torque.

d) Fit the pump sprocket with the convex side of the sprocket facing the pump.

e) Tighten the pump sprocket securing bolt to the specified torque.

f) Refit the sump as described in Section 11.

Drive chain - renewal

Note: *Removal of the oil pump drive chain using the following procedure entails the use of a portable electric grinder to cut through one of the chain links. Ensure that such a tool is available, as well as a new chain and new connecting link before proceeding. The oil pump sprocket should be renewed whenever the chain is renewed.*

13 Remove the sump as described in Section 11.

14 Slacken the oil pump sprocket securing bolt.

15 Using a grinder, grind off the protruding lugs of one of the chain links at the bottom of the sprocket - take great care not to damage the sprocket.

16 Pull off the chain link plate, then push the link out towards the rear of the chain.

17 Unscrew the oil pump sprocket securing bolt, and recover the washer, then withdraw the sprocket from the pump shaft.

18 Using the new link, connect one end of the new chain to the tail end of the old chain, in such a way that as the engine is turned (clockwise), the new chain will be drawn up, around the crankshaft sprocket, then down the other side. Fit the link from the rear of the sprocket, and ensure that the link is pushed firmly into position - do not fit the link plate to secure the link at this stage.

19 It is now necessary to feed the new chain around the crankshaft sprocket. During this procedure it is essential to observe the following points.

a) Keep tension on the new chain, ensuring that the links of the chains remain engaged with the crankshaft sprocket.

b) Pull down on the old chain as it appears from the timing chain cover to prevent it dropping off the crankshaft sprocket, or jamming in the casing.

20 Using a suitable socket on the crankshaft pulley/vibration damper hub bolt, slowly turn the crankshaft clockwise, whilst observing the points made in the preceding paragraph.

21 When the end of the new chain appears, remove the link (ensuring that tension is kept on the new chain, and that the chain links remain engaged with the crankshaft sprocket), and disconnect the new chain from the old chain. Remove the old chain.

22 Join the two ends of the chain with the connecting link, inserted from the rear of the sprocket.

23 Fit the link plate, and then secure the plate to the link by flattening the ends of the link pins. A special tool is available for this purpose, but it should be possible to achieve a satisfactory result using a hammer, with a block of metal (or a second hammer) to support the rear of the chain - *take great care not to damage the chain or the sprocket.*

24 Check that the chain link is secure, with no burring of the metal, or loose swarf.

25 Engage the chain with the new oil pump sprocket.

26 Fit the new sprocket to the pump shaft, with the convex side of the sprocket facing the pump.

27 Tighten the oil pump sprocket bolt to the specified torque.

28 Refit the sump as described in Section 11.

13 Flywheel/driveplate - removal, inspection and refitting

The procedure is identical to that described in Chapter 2A, for four-cylinder petrol engines.

14 Crankshaft oil seals - renewal

Crankshaft front oil seal

1 Remove the crankshaft pulley/vibration damper and hub as described in Section 5.
2 Measure and note the fitted depth of the oil seal.
3 Pull the oil seal from the housing using a hooked instrument. Alternatively, drill a small hole in the oil seal, and use a self-tapping screw and a pair of pliers to remove it.
4 Clean the oil seal housing.
5 Dip the new oil seal in clean engine oil, and press it into the housing (open end first) to the previously-noted depth, using a suitable tube or socket. A piece of thin plastic or tape wound around the front of the crankshaft is useful to prevent damage to the oil seal as it is fitted.
6 Where applicable, remove the plastic or tape from the crankshaft.
7 Refit the crankshaft pulley/vibration damper and hub as described in Section 5.

Crankshaft rear oil seal

8 Remove the flywheel/driveplate with reference to Section 13.
9 Proceed as described in paragraphs 2 and 3.
10 If it is not possible to lever out the oil seal, the housing can be unbolted from the rear of the cylinder block, and the seal can be tapped out of the housing. Note that it will necessary to unscrew the sump bolts which secure the sump to the rear oil seal housing - take care not to damage the sump gasket as the housing is removed. If necessary, remove the sump as described in Section 11, and fit a new gasket.
11 Examine the oil seal contact surface on the crankshaft for signs of damage. If excessive wear is evident, the crankshaft must be renewed.
12 Clean the oil seal housing and the contact surface on the crankshaft flange.
13 Dip the new oil seal in clean engine oil, and press it into the housing (open end first) to the previously-noted depth, using a suitable tube or socket. A piece of thin plastic or tape wound around the rear of the crankshaft flange is useful to prevent damage to the oil seal as it is fitted. Note that the seal must be fitted exactly at right-angles to the crankshaft flange to provided satisfactory sealing.
14 If the housing has been removed, coat the cylinder block mating face of the housing with sealant, then refit the housing, and tighten the securing bolts to the specified torque.
15 Where applicable, remove the plastic or tape from the crankshaft.
16 Refit the flywheel/driveplate with reference to Section 13.

15 Crankshaft spigot bearing - renewal

The procedure is identical to that described in Chapter 2A, for four-cylinder petrol engines.

16 Engine/transmission mountings - inspection and renewal

The procedure is identical to that described in Chapter 2A, for four-cylinder petrol engines.

17 Engine oil cooler - removal and refitting

Removal

1 The oil cooler is located behind the front left-hand wing panel.
2 Apply the parking brake, then jack up the front of the vehicle, and support securely on axle stands (see *"Jacking and vehicle support"*).
3 Where applicable, remove the engine undershield, with reference to Chapter 11 if necessary.
4 Unscrew the securing screws and nuts, and withdraw the wheelarch liners from the left-hand wheelarch.
5 Place a suitable container beneath the wheel arch to catch escaping oil, then reach up behind the front wing panel, and unscrew the oil pipe unions from the top of the oil cooler. Be prepared for oil spillage.
6 Unscrew the two bolts and two nuts securing the oil cooler support frame to the vehicle body.
7 Lower the support frame, complete with the oil cooler, from under the wheelarch.
8 Release the securing clips, and withdraw the oil cooler from the support frame.

Refitting

9 Before refitting, it is advisable to clean the oil cooler fins, using a soft brush or compressed air.
10 Refitting is a reversal of removal, but when refitting the assembly into the wheelarch, ensure that the lugs at the top of the oil cooler engage with the mounting rubbers on the body.

Chapter 2 Part D
Engine removal and general engine overhaul procedures

Contents

Crankshaft - inspection . . . 15
Crankshaft - refitting and main bearing running clearance check . . 19
Crankshaft - removal . . . 12
Cylinder block/crankcase - cleaning and inspection . . . 13
Cylinder head - dismantling . . . 8
Cylinder head - reassembly . . . 10
Cylinder head and valves - cleaning and inspection . . . 9
Diesel engines - removal and refitting . . . 6
Engine - initial start-up after overhaul . . . 21
Engine overhaul - dismantling sequence . . . 7
Engine overhaul - general information . . . 2
Engine overhaul - reassembly sequence . . . 17
Engine removal - methods and precautions . . . 3
Four-cylinder petrol engines - removal and refitting . . . 4
General information . . . 1
Main and big-end bearings, and bearing cap bolts - inspection . . . 16
Piston rings - refitting . . . 18
Piston/connecting rod assembly - cleaning and inspection . . . 14
Piston/connecting rod assembly - refitting and big-end bearing running clearance check . . . 20
Piston/connecting rod assembly - removal . . . 11
Six-cylinder petrol engines - removal and refitting . . . 5

Degrees of difficulty

Easy, suitable for novice with little experience	**Fairly easy,** suitable for beginner with some experience	**Fairly difficult,** suitable for competent DIY mechanic	**Difficult,** suitable for experienced DIY mechanic	**Very difficult,** suitable for expert DIY or professional

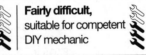

Specifications

Cylinder head

Maximum gasket face distortion:	
4-cylinder petrol engines:	
Longitudinal	0.15 mm
Transverse	0.05 mm
All engines except 4-cylinder petrol engines:	
Longitudinal	0.08 mm
Transverse	0 mm
Minimum height after machining:	
4-cylinder petrol engines	97.8 mm
6-cylinder petrol engines*	89.5 mm
Diesel engines	142.4 mm
Swirl chamber protrusion (diesel engines)	7.6 to 8.1 mm
Maximum valve recess below cylinder head sealing face (wear limit):	
4-cylinder petrol engines:	
1.8 and 2.0 litre engines:	
Inlet	2.3 mm
Exhaust	0.9 mm
2.3 litre engines:	
Inlet	1.7 mm
Exhaust	0.9 mm
6-cylinder petrol engines:	
Inlet	1.7 mm
Exhaust	1.5 mm
Diesel engines (inlet and exhaust valves)	0.7 mm

***Note:** *The total thickness of metal removed from the cylinder head and cylinder block mating faces combined must not exceed 0.5 mm.*

Valves*

Valve head diameter:	
4-cylinder petrol engines:	
Inlet:	
2.0 litre engines	42.90 to 43.10 mm
2.3 litre engine	45.90 to 46.19 mm
Exhaust	38.90 to 39.10 mm
6-cylinder petrol engines:	
Inlet	40.0 mm
Exhaust	35.0 mm
Diesel engines:	
Inlet	37.90 to 38.10 mm
Exhaust	34.90 to 35.10 mm
Valve stem diameter:	
Petrol engines:	
Inlet	7.955 to 7.970 mm
Exhaust	8.938 to 8.960 mm
Diesel engines:	
Inlet	7.955 to 7.970 mm
Exhaust	8.945 to 8.960 mm

***Note:** *No information was available for 1.8 litre engines at the time of writing.*

Valve springs*

Free length:	
4-cylinder petrol engines	49.0 mm
6-cylinder petrol engines	No figure specified by manufacturer
Diesel engines:	
Springs with yellow/green or violet/green colour marking	50.8 mm
Springs with yellow/blue or violet/blue colour marking	50.0 mm

***Note:** *No information was available for 1.8 litre engines at the time of writing.*

Cylinder block

Cylinder bore diameter:	
4-cylinder petrol engines:	
1.8 and 2.0 litre engines:	
Standard 0	88.998 to 89.008 mm
Standard 1	89.009 to 89.018 mm
Standard 2	89.019 to 89.028 mm
Standard A	89.000 to 89.006 mm
Standard X	89.007 to 89.012 mm
Standard B	89.013 to 89.018 mm
Oversize + 0.5	Grades as above + 0.500 mm
Oversize + 1.0	Grades as above + 0.500 mm
2.3 litre engine:	
Standard 0	95.498 to 95.508 mm
Standard 1	95.509 to 95.518 mm
Standard 2	95.519 to 95.528 mm
Standard A	95.500 to 95.506 mm
Standard X	95.507 to 95.512 mm
Standard B	95.513 to 95.518 mm
Oversize + 0.5	Grades as above + 0.500 mm
Oversize + 1.0	Grades as above + 0.500 mm
6-cylinder petrol engines:	
Standard 0	82.898 to 82.908 mm
Standard 1	82.908 to 82.918 mm
Standard 2	82.918 to 82.928 mm
Standard A	82.900 to 82.906 mm
Standard X	82.906 to 82.912 mm
Standard B	82.912 to 82.918 mm
Oversize + 0.5 mm	Grades as above + 0.500 mm
Oversize + 1.0 mm	Grades as above + 1.000 mm
Diesel engines:	
Standard grade A	87.000 to 87.006 mm
Standard grade X	87.006 to 87.012 mm
Standard grade B	87.012 to 87.018 mm
Oversize + 0.7 mm	Grades as above + 0.700 mm
Maximum cylinder bore ovality:	
Petrol engines	0.05 mm
Diesel engines	0.07 mm

Maximum cylinder bore taper:	
Petrol engines	0.05 mm
Diesel engines	0.07 mm
Minimum cylinder block height:	
4-cylinder petrol engines	292.35 mm
6-cylinder petrol engines	281.95 mm
Diesel engines	299.62 mm
Maximum gasket face distortion:	
4-cylinder petrol engines	No information available at time of writing
6-cylinder petrol engines:	
Longitudinal	0.100 mm
Transverse	0.05 mm
Diesel engines	0.03 mm

Pistons

Piston diameter:	
4-cylinder petrol engines:	
1.8 and 2.0 litre engines:	
Standard 0	88.968 to 88.982 mm
Standard 1	88.978 to 88.992 mm
Standard 2	88.988 to 89.002 mm
Standard A	88.973 to 88.979 mm
Standard X	88.978 to 88.986 mm
Standard B	88.985 to 88.991 mm
Oversize + 0.5	Grades as above + 0.500 mm
Oversize + 1.0	Grades as above + 0.500 mm
2.3 litre engine:	
Standard 0	95.469 to 95.481 mm
Standard 1	95.479 to 95.491 mm
Standard 2	95.489 to 95.501 mm
Standard A	95.473 to 95.479 mm
Standard X	95.478 to 95.486 mm
Standard B	95.485 to 95.491 mm
Oversize + 0.5	Grades as above + 0.500 mm
Oversize + 1.0	Grades as above + 0.500 mm
6-cylinder petrol engines:	
Standard 0	82.868 to 82.882 mm
Standard 1	82.878 to 82.892 mm
Standard 2	82.888 to 82.902 mm
Standard A	82.873 to 82.879 mm
Standard X	82.878 to 82.886 mm
Standard B	82.885 to 82.891 mm
Oversize + 0.5 mm	Grades as above + 0.500 mm
Oversize + 1.0 mm	Grades as above + 1.000 mm
Diesel engines:	
Standard grade A	86.970 to 86.976 mm
Standard grade X	86.975 to 86.983 mm
Standard grade B	86.982 to 86.988 mm
Oversize + 0.7 mm	Grades as above + 0.700 mm
Piston protrusion (diesel engines):	
Minimum	0.735 mm
Maximum	0.965 mm

Piston rings*

End gaps:	
4-cylinder petrol engines:	
Top compression ring	0.30 to 1.00 mm
Second compression ring	0.25 to 0.80 mm
Oil control ring	0.25 to 0.80 mm
6-cylinder petrol engines:	
Top compression ring	0.015 to 0.050 mm
Second compression ring	0.020 to 0.040 mm
Oil control ring	0.010 to 0.045 mm
Diesel engines:	
Top compression ring	0.090 to 0.20 mm
Second compression ring	0.050 to 0.15 mm
Oil control ring	0.030 to 0.10 mm

***Note:** *No information was available for 1.8 litre engines at the time of writing.*

Crankshaft

Endfloat:	
4-cylinder petrol engines	0.300 mm
6-cylinder petrol engines	0.100 to 0.240 mm
Diesel engines	0.300 mm
Endfloat thrustwasher thicknesses (all engines)	2.15, 2.20, 2.25, 2.35 and 2.40 mm
Main bearing journal diameters:	
4-cylinder petrol engines:	
Standard code blue	57.960 to 57.965 mm
Standard code yellow	57.955 to 57.960 mm
Standard code red	57.950 to 57.955 mm
Standard 1 code blue	57.945 to 57.950 mm
Standard 1 code yellow	57.940 to 57.945 mm
Standard 1 code red	57.935 to 57.940 mm
Undersize 1	57.705 to 57.715 mm
Undersize 2	57.455 to 57.465 mm
Undersize 3	57.205 to 57.215 mm
Undersize 4	56.955 to 56.965 mm
6-cylinder petrol engines	No information available at time of writing
Diesel engines:	
Standard	57.959 to 57.965 mm
Undersize 1	57.700 to 57.715 mm
Undersize 2	57.450 to 57.465 mm
Undersize 3	57.200 to 57.215 mm
Undersize 4	56.959 to 56.965 mm
Main bearing running clearance	0.025 to 0.070 mm
Big-end bearing journal diameters:	
4-cylinder petrol engines:	
Standard	47.955 to 47.965 mm
Undersize 1	47.705 to 47.715 mm
Undersize 2	47.455 to 47.465 mm
Undersize 3	47.205 to 47.215 mm
Undersize 4	46.955 to 46.965 mm
6-cylinder petrol engines	No information available at time of writing
Diesel engines:	
Standard	47.950 to 47.965 mm
Undersize 1	47.700 to 47.715 mm
Undersize 2	47.450 to 47.650 mm
Undersize 3	47.200 to 47.215 mm
Undersize 4	46.950 to 46.965 mm
Big-end bearing running clearance	0.030 to 0.070 mm
Radial play of crankshaft in bearings:	
4-cylinder petrol engines	0.070 mm
6-cylinder petrol engines	0.030 to 0.05 mm
Diesel engines	0.080 mm
Radial play of big-end bearings on crankshaft:	
4-cylinder petrol engines	0.070 mm
6-cylinder petrol engines	0.030 to 0.060 mm
Diesel engines	0.080 mm

Big-end bearing cap bolts

Minimum diameter - 2.0 and 2.3 litre petrol engines (see Section 16)	8.0 mm
Maximum length - all except 2.0 and 2.3 litre petrol engines (see Section 16)	52.9 mm

Torque wrench settings

4-cylinder petrol engines

Refer to Chapter 2A Specifications

6-cylinder petrol engines

Refer to Chapter 2B Specifications

Diesel engines

Refer to Chapter 2C Specifications

1 General information

Included in this Part of Chapter 2 are details of removing the engine from the car and general overhaul procedures for the cylinder head, cylinder block/crankcase and all other engine internal components.

The information given ranges from advice concerning preparation for an overhaul and the purchase of replacement parts, to detailed step-by-step procedures covering removal, inspection, renovation and refitting of engine internal components.

After Section 7, all instructions are based on the assumption that the engine has been removed from the car. For information concerning in-car engine repair, as well as the removal and refitting of those external components necessary for full overhaul, refer to Part A, B or C of this Chapter, as applicable, and to Section 7. Ignore any preliminary dismantling operations described in Parts A, B or C that are no longer relevant once the engine has been removed from the car.

Apart from torque wrench settings, which are given at the beginning of Parts A, B and C, all specifications relating to engine overhaul are at the beginning of this Part of Chapter 2.

2 Engine overhaul - general information

1 It is not always easy to determine when, or if, an engine should be completely overhauled, as a number of factors must be considered.

2 High mileage is not necessarily an indication that an overhaul is needed, while low mileage does not preclude the need for an overhaul. Frequency of servicing is probably the most important consideration. An engine which has had regular and frequent oil and filter changes, as well as other required maintenance, should give many thousands of miles of reliable service. Conversely, a neglected engine may require an overhaul very early in its life.

3 Excessive oil consumption is an indication that piston rings, valve seals and/or valve guides are in need of attention. Make sure that oil leaks are not responsible before deciding that the rings and/or guides are worn. Perform a compression test, as described in Part A, B or C of this Chapter (as applicable), to determine the likely cause of the problem.

4 Check the oil pressure with a gauge fitted in place of the oil pressure switch, and compare it with that specified in earlier parts of this Chapter. If it is extremely low, the main and big-end bearings, and/or the oil pump, are probably worn out.

5 Loss of power, rough running, knocking or metallic engine noises, excessive valve gear noise, and high fuel consumption may also point to the need for an overhaul, especially if they are all present at the same time. If a complete service does not remedy the situation, major mechanical work is the only solution.

6 A full engine overhaul involves restoring all internal parts to the specification of a new engine. During a complete overhaul, the pistons and the piston rings are renewed, and the cylinder bores are reconditioned. New main and big-end bearings are generally fitted; if necessary, the crankshaft may be reground, to compensate for wear in the journals. The valves are also serviced as well, since they are usually in less-than-perfect condition at this point. Always pay careful attention to the condition of the oil pump when overhauling the engine, and renew it if there is any doubt as to its serviceability. The end result should be an as-new engine that will give many trouble-free miles. **Note:** *Critical cooling system components such as the hoses, thermostat and coolant pump should be renewed when an engine is overhauled. The radiator should be checked carefully, to ensure that it is not clogged or leaking. Also, it is a good idea to renew the oil pump whenever the engine is overhauled.*

7 Before beginning the engine overhaul, read through the entire procedure, to familiarise yourself with the scope and requirements of the job. Overhauling an engine is not difficult if you follow carefully all of the instructions, have the necessary tools and equipment, and pay close attention to all specifications. It can, however, be time-consuming. Plan on the car being off the road for a minimum of two weeks, especially if parts must be taken to an engineering works for repair or reconditioning. Check on the availability of parts and make sure that any necessary special tools and equipment are obtained in advance. Most work can be done with typical hand tools, although a number of precision measuring tools are required for inspecting parts to determine if they must be renewed. Often the engineering works will handle the inspection of parts and offer advice concerning reconditioning and renewal. **Note:** *Always wait until the engine has been completely dismantled, and until all components (especially the cylinder block/crankcase and the crankshaft) have been inspected, before deciding what service and repair operations must be performed by an engineering works. The condition of these components will be the major factor to consider when determining whether to overhaul the original engine, or to buy a reconditioned unit. Do not, therefore, purchase parts or have overhaul work done on other components until they have been thoroughly inspected. As a general rule, time is the primary cost of an overhaul, so it does not pay to fit worn or sub-standard parts.*

8 As a final note, to ensure maximum life and minimum trouble from a reconditioned engine, everything must be assembled with care, in a spotlessly-clean environment.

3 Engine removal - methods and precautions

1 If you have decided that the engine must be removed for overhaul or major repair work, several preliminary steps should be taken.

2 Locating a suitable place to work is extremely important. Adequate work space, along with storage space for the car, will be needed. If a workshop or garage is not available, at the very least, a flat, level, clean work surface is required.

3 Cleaning the engine compartment and engine/transmission before beginning the removal procedure will help keep tools clean and organised.

4 An engine hoist or A-frame will also be necessary. Make sure the equipment is rated in excess of the weight of the engine. Safety is of primary importance, considering the potential hazards involved in lifting the engine/transmission out of the car.

5 If this is the first time you have removed an engine, an assistant should ideally be available. Advice and aid from someone more experienced would also be helpful. There are many instances when one person cannot simultaneously perform all of the operations required when lifting the engine out of the vehicle.

6 Plan the operation ahead of time. Before starting work, arrange for the hire of or obtain all of the tools and equipment you will need. Some of the equipment necessary to perform engine/transmission removal and installation safely and with relative ease (in addition to an engine hoist) is as follows: a heavy duty trolley jack, complete sets of spanners and sockets (see *"Tools and working Facilities"*), wooden blocks, and plenty of rags and cleaning solvent for mopping up spilled oil, coolant and fuel. If the hoist must be hired, make sure that you arrange for it in advance, and perform all of the operations possible without it beforehand. This will save you money and time.

7 Plan for the car to be out of use for quite a while. An engineering works will be required to perform some of the work which the do-it-yourselfer cannot accomplish without special equipment. These places often have a busy schedule, so it would be a good idea to consult them before removing the engine, in order to accurately estimate the amount of time required to rebuild or repair components that may need work.

8 Always be extremely careful when removing and refitting the engine/transmission. Serious injury can result from careless actions. Plan ahead and take your time, and a job of this nature, although major, can be accomplished successfully.

9 On all models, the engine and transmission are removed as an assembly by lifting the assembly out from above the vehicle.

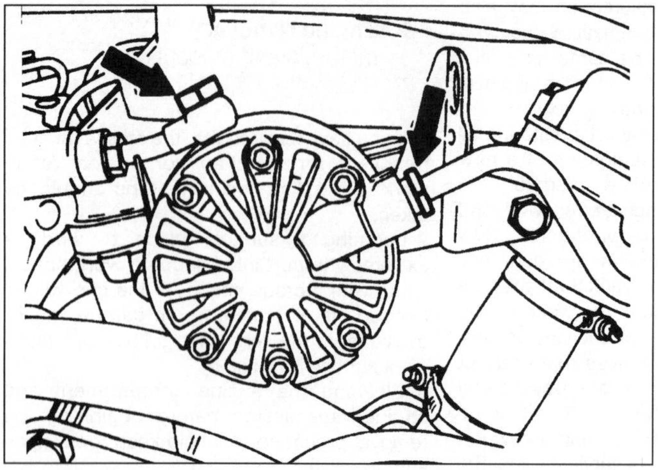

4.7 Disconnect the hydraulic fluid pipes (arrowed) from the self-levelling suspension hydraulic pump

4.9a Unscrew the securing bolt (arrowed) and withdraw the auxiliary drivebelt tensioner - models without hydraulic damper strut

4 Four-cylinder petrol engines - removal and refitting

Removal

Note: *A suitable hoist and lifting tackle will be required for this operation.*

1 Remove the transmission as described in Chapter 7.

2 Where applicable, remove the engine undershield with reference to Chapter 11.

3 Drain the engine oil and the coolant as described in Chapter 1A.

4 Remove the air cleaner assembly as described in Chapter 4.

5 Remove the radiator and the cooling fan assembly as described in Chapter 3.

6 On models with air conditioning, place a large sheet of cardboard, or a similar protector in front of the air conditioning condenser to prevent damage during the following procedure.

7 Where applicable, unscrew the union nuts, and disconnect the hydraulic fluid pipes from the self-levelling suspension hydraulic pump at the front of the cylinder head **(see illustration)**. Be prepared for fluid spillage, and plug the open ends of the pump and the pipes.

8 On models fitted with air conditioning, remove the auxiliary drivebelt as described in Chapter 1, and disconnect the wiring plug from the air conditioning compressor.

9 Unbolt the auxiliary drivebelt tensioner components, and remove them from the front of the engine as follows according to type. Note the location and orientation of all components to ensure correct refitting **(see illustrations)**.

a) ***On models without a hydraulic damper strut****, unscrew the securing bolt, and withdraw the tensioner.*

b) ***On models with a hydraulic damper strut mounted below the tensioner****, unscrew the bolt securing the lower end of the damper strut, and the two bolts securing the tensioner bracket, then unscrew the bolt from the centre of the tensioner, and withdraw the components.*

c) ***On models with a hydraulic damper strut mounted above the tensioner****, unbolt the power steering pump pulley, then unbolt the tensioner pulley. Unbolt the end of the damper strut from the tensioner bracket, counterholding the bolt using a spanner if necessary. Unbolt the damper strut from the alternator mounting*

4.9b Auxiliary drivebelt tensioner components - models with hydraulic damper strut mounted below tensioner

1 Damper strut lower bolt
2 Tensioner bracket bolts
3 Tensioner centre bolt

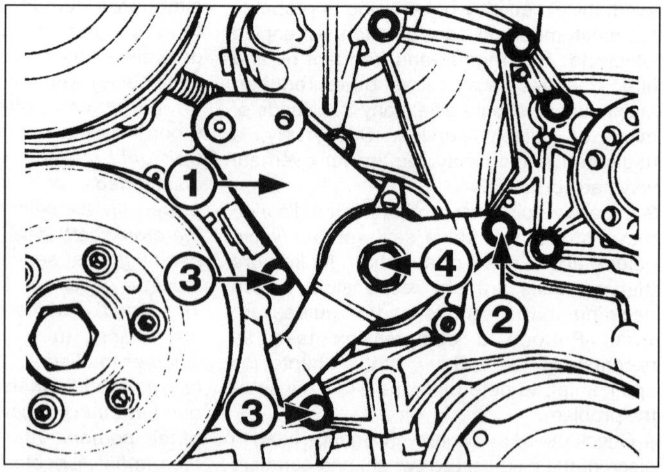

4.9c Auxiliary drivebelt tensioner components - models with hydraulic damper strut mounted above tensioner

1 Tensioner assembly
2 Tensioner-to-power steering pump bracket bolt
3 Tensioner bracket-to-timing chain cover bolts
4 Tensioner centre bolt

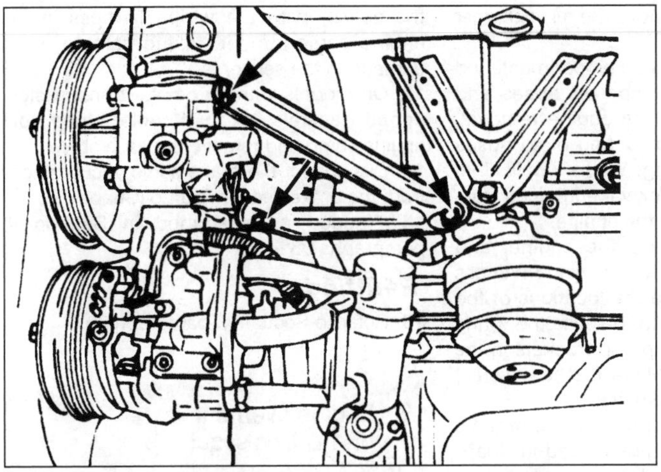

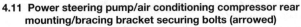

4.11 Power steering pump/air conditioning compressor rear mounting/bracing bracket securing bolts (arrowed)

4.24 Insert a sheet of card (arrowed) or similar at the rear of the engine

bracket, and recover the washer, where applicable. Counterhold the bolt securing the tensioner assembly to the power steering pump bracket, and unscrew the nut from behind the bracket. Unscrew the two bolts securing the tensioner bracket to the timing chain cover. Unscrew the bolt from the centre of the tensioner, then remove the tensioner/bracket assembly.

10 Unbolt the power steering pump pulley.

11 Unbolt the rear mounting/bracing bracket from the power steering pump, air conditioning compressor (where applicable), and the cylinder block, and withdraw the bracket **(see illustration)**.

12 Unbolt the power steering pump (with reference to Chapter 10 if necessary), and move it to one side, clear of the working area, leaving the hoses connected.

13 Similarly, on models with air conditioning, unbolt the air conditioning compressor (with reference to Chapter 3 if necessary), and move it to one side, clear of the working area, leaving the refrigerent lines connected.

14 Where applicable, unbolt the bracket, and release the pipe/hose assembly from the front left-hand corner of the cylinder head.

15 Disconnect the alternator wiring plug.

16 Work around the engine, and disconnect the wiring connectors from all relevant components and connectors. Note the locations and routing of all connections to aid refitting. Unbolt or unclip all relevant wires and wiring harnesses from any clips or brackets on the engine.

17 Similarly, disconnect all vacuum lines, noting their locations and routing.

18 Disconnect the throttle cable from the throttle linkage, with reference to Chapter 4 if necessary, then release the cable from any brackets on the engine, and move it to one side.

19 On models with fuel injection, depressurise the fuel system as described in Chapter 4B.

20 Where applicable, unscrew the union nuts, then disconnect the fuel feed and return lines from the carburettor/fuel distributor/pressure regulator. Where necessary counterhold the unions. Be prepared for fuel spillage, and plug the open ends of the fuel lines and unions.

21 Disconnect the heater coolant hose from the rear left-hand corner of the cylinder head.

22 Unscrew the union, and disconnect the brake servo vacuum hose from the inlet manifold.

23 If not already done, connect a hoist and lifting tackle to the engine lifting brackets on the cylinder head, and adjust the lifting tackle to just take the weight of the engine. Note that the hoist must be able to lift the engine sufficiently high to clear the front of the vehicle.

24 Again, if not already done, insert a sheet of card or a similar shield between the rear of the cylinder head and the engine compartment bulkhead to prevent damage to the bulkhead as the engine is lifted **(see illustration)**.

25 Make a final check to ensure that all relevant hoses, pipes and wires have been disconnected to facilitate engine removal.

26 If not already done, unscrew the two lower engine mounting bolts. Where applicable, also unbolt the engine mounting damper on the left-hand side of the vehicle.

27 Raise the hoist, and if necessary adjust the lifting tackle to enable the engine to be lifted out vertically.

28 Lift the assembly out slowly, and take care not to damage surrounding components in the engine compartment.

Refitting

29 Refitting is a reversal of removal, bearing in mind the following points.

a) *Tighten all fixings to the appropriate torque, where specified.*
b) *Ensure that all wiring, hoses and brackets are positioned and routed as noted before removal.*
c) *Reconnect and if necessary adjust the throttle cable with reference to Chapter 4.*
d) *Where applicable, refit the auxiliary drivebelt with reference to Chapter 1.*
e) *Refit the radiator and the cooling fan assembly with reference to Chapter 3.*
f) *Refit the transmission as described in Chapter 7.*
g) *On completion, refill the engine with oil, and refill the cooling system as described in Chapter 1A.*

5 Six-cylinder petrol engines - removal and refitting

2D

Removal

Note: *A suitable hoist and lifting tackle will be required for this operation.*

1 Proceed as described in Section 4, paragraphs 1 to 6.

2 Unscrew the power steering fluid reservoir cap, and draw off as much fluid as possible, using a large syringe, such as a poultry baster. Refit the filler cap once the reservoir has been emptied.

3 Where applicable unscrew the union(s) and disconnect the fluid lines from the power steering/self-levelling suspension hydraulic pump. Release the fluid lines from any clamps and/or brackets on the engine.

4 Where applicable, unbolt the air conditioning compressor from the engine with reference to Chapter 3, and support it in the engine compartment, clear of the engine, leaving the refrigerent lines connected.

5 Depressurise the fuel system as described in Chapter 4.

6 Unscrew the union nuts, and disconnect the fuel supply and return lines. Where applicable, counterhold the unions. Disconnect the return line from the pressure regulator and disconnect the supply line from the fuel distributor, or the supply pipe, as applicable.

7 Disconnect the throttle cable from the throttle linkage as described in Chapter 4. Release the cable from any brackets on the engine, and move it to one side.
8 Work around the engine compartment, and disconnect all relevant coolant hoses and vacuum lines, to facilitate engine removal. Note the locations and routing of all hoses and pipes to aid refitting.
9 Similarly, work around the engine, and disconnect all relevant engine wiring harness connectors. Again, note the locations of the connectors to aid refitting. Release the wiring harness from any clips or brackets in the engine compartment.
10 Where applicable, unbolt the engine speed sensor from the flywheel end of the engine, and release wiring from clips. Leave the sensor with the wiring harness in the engine compartment, taking care to avoid damage to the sensor.
11 Where applicable, disconnect the knock sensor wiring connector from the ignition module on the left-hand wing panel, then release the wiring harness from the securing clips, and lay the harness across the engine.
12 On models with automatic transmission, unbolt the transmission fluid cooler pipes from the engine sump, and remove the assembly.
13 Proceed as described in Section 4, paragraphs 21 to 28.

Refitting

14 Refer to Section 4, paragraph 29.

6 Diesel engines - removal and refitting

Removal

Note: *A suitable hoist and lifting tackle will be required for this operation.*
1 Proceed as described in Section 4, paragraphs 1 to 8, noting that there is no need to remove the air cleaner.
2 On non-Turbo models, remove the air inlet trunking, then release the securing clips, and remove the air cleaner cover and the filter element **(see illustration).**
3 On Turbo models, remove the turbocharger inlet trunking.
4 Work around the engine compartment, and disconnect all relevant coolant hoses and vacuum lines, to facilitate engine removal. Note the locations and routing of all hoses and pipes to aid refitting. Where applicable, release the hoses and/or vacuum lines from any clips or brackets on the engine.
5 Similarly, work around the engine, and disconnect all relevant engine wiring harness connectors. Again, note the locations of the connectors to aid refitting. Release the wiring harness(es) from any clips or brackets in the engine compartment. Move the harness(es) clear to enable engine removal.
6 On models with air conditioning, remove the auxiliary drivebelt as described in Chapter 1. Unbolt the air conditioning compressor from the engine with reference to Chapter 3, and support it in the engine compartment, clear of the engine, leaving the refrigerent lines connected.
7 Unscrew the union nuts, and disconnect the fuel supply and return lines from the fuel filter and/or the fuel injection pump, as applicable. Where applicable, counterhold the unions.
8 Disconnect the throttle cable from the throttle linkage as described in Chapter 4. Release the cable from any brackets on the engine, and move it clear of the engine.
9 Unscrew the power steering fluid reservoir cap, and draw off as much fluid as possible, using a large syringe, such as a poultry baster. Refit the filler cap once the reservoir has been emptied.
10 Where applicable unscrew the union(s) and disconnect the fluid lines from the power steering/self-levelling suspension hydraulic pump. Release the fluid lines from any clamps and/or brackets on the engine.
11 Where applicable, remove the wheel arch liners from the front left-hand wheel arch, then unscrew the unions and disconnect the oil pipes from the oil cooler located under the wheel arch (refer to Chapter 2D for further details).
12 Where applicable, unbolt the engine speed sensor from the flywheel end of the engine, and release wiring from clips. Leave the sensor with the wiring harness in the engine compartment, taking care to avoid damage to the sensor.
13 On models with automatic transmission, unbolt transmission fluid cooler pipes from engine sump and remove the assembly.
14 Disconnect the brake servo vacuum hose from the brake vacuum pump (Chapter 9).
15 Proceed as described in Section 4, paragraphs 23 to 28.

Refitting

16 Refer to Section 4, paragraph 29.

7 Engine overhaul - dismantling sequence

1 It is much easier to dismantle and work on the engine if it is mounted on a portable engine stand. These stands can often be hired from a tool hire shop. Before the engine is mounted on a stand, the flywheel/driveplate should be removed, so that the stand bolts can be tightened into the end of the cylinder block/crankcase.
2 If a stand is not available, it is possible to dismantle the engine with it blocked up on a sturdy workbench, or on the floor. Be extra-careful not to tip or drop the engine when working without a stand.
3 If you are going to obtain a reconditioned engine, all the external components must be removed first, to be transferred to the replacement engine (just as they will if you are doing a complete engine overhaul yourself). These components include the following **(see illustrations)**.

a) *Ancillary unit mounting brackets (oil filter, alternator, power steering pump, engine mountings, crankcase breather housing, etc.)*
b) *Thermostat and housing (Chapter 3).*
c) *Dipstick tube.*
d) *All electrical switches and sensors.*
e) *Inlet and exhaust manifolds - where applicable (Chapter 4).*
f) *Ignition coils and spark plugs - as applicable (Chapter 4).*

6.2 Remove the air cleaner cover and filter element

7.3a Removing the oil filter housing . . .

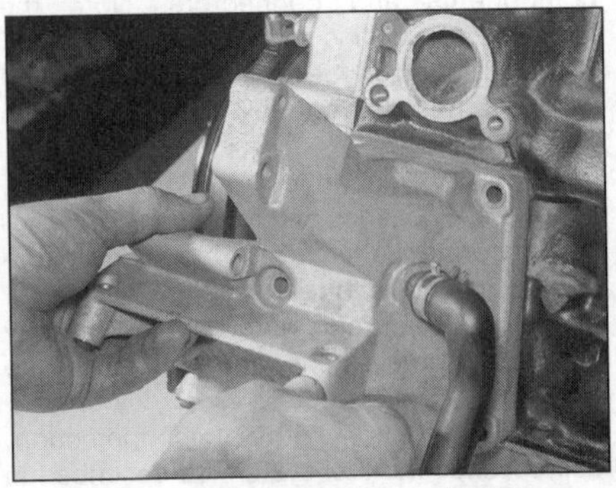
7.3b . . . and the crankcase breather housing

Note: *When removing the external components from the engine, pay close attention to details that may be helpful or important during refitting. Note the fitted position of gaskets, seals, spacers, pins, washers, bolts, and other small items.*

4 If you are obtaining a "short" engine (which consists of the engine cylinder block/crankcase, crankshaft, pistons and connecting rods all assembled), then the cylinder head, sump, oil pump, and timing chain will have to be removed also.

5 If you are planning a complete overhaul, the engine can be dismantled, and the internal components removed, in the order given below, referring to Part A, B or C of this Chapter unless otherwise stated.

a) Inlet and exhaust manifolds - where applicable (Chapter 4).
b) Timing chain, sprockets and tensioner.
c) Cylinder head.
d) Flywheel/driveplate.
e) Sump.
f) Oil pump.
g) Piston/connecting rod assemblies (Section 11).
h) Crankshaft (Section 12).

6 Before beginning the dismantling and overhaul procedures, make sure that you have all of the correct tools necessary. Refer to *"Tools and working facilities"* for further information.

8 Cylinder head - dismantling

Note: *New and reconditioned cylinder heads are available from the manufacturer, and from engine overhaul specialists. Be aware that some specialist tools are required for the dismantling and inspection procedures, and new components may not be readily available. It may therefore be more practical and economical for the home mechanic to purchase a reconditioned head, rather than dismantle, inspect and recondition the original head. A valve spring compressor tool will be required for this operation.*

8.6a Compress the valve spring . . .

8.6b . . . and remove the split collets . . .

8.6c . . . followed by the spring cap . . .

8.6d . . . and the spring

Four-cylinder petrol engines

1 Remove the cylinder head as described in Part A of this Chapter

2 Remove the inlet and exhaust manifolds as described in Chapter 4.

3 Remove the rocker gear, valve lifters and camshaft as described in Part A of this Chapter.

4 If desired, unscrew the spark plugs from the cylinder head.

5 Where applicable, unbolt the thermostat housing from the cylinder head.

6 Using a valve spring compressor, compress the spring on each valve in turn until the split collets can be removed. Release the compressor, and lift off the spring cap and spring **(see illustrations)**. If, when the valve spring compressor is screwed down, the spring cap refuses to free and expose the split collets, gently tap the top of the tool, directly over the spring cap, with a light hammer. This will free the retainer.

7 Using a pair of pliers, carefully extract the valve stem oil seal from the top of the guide, then lift off the spring seat **(see illustrations)**.

8 Withdraw the valve through the combustion chamber **(see illustration)**.

9 It is essential that each valve is stored together with its collets, cap, spring, and spring seat. The valves should also be kept in their correct sequence, unless they are so badly worn that they are to be renewed. If they are going to be kept and used again, place each valve assembly in a labelled polythene bag or similar small

8.7a Remove the valve stem oil seal . . .

8.7b . . . and the spring seat

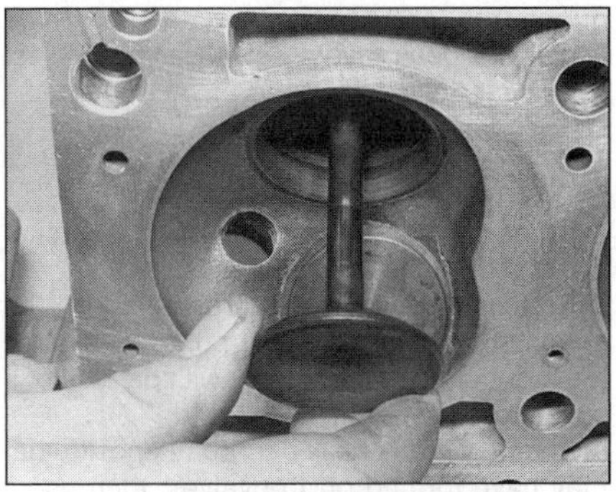
8.8 Withdraw the valve through the combustion chamber

8.9 Store the valve components in a labelled bag

container **(see illustration)**. Label each bag No 1 inlet, No 1 exhaust, No 2 inlet, No 2 exhaust, etc, noting that No 1 valve is nearest to the timing chain end of the engine.

Six-cylinder petrol engines

10 Remove the cylinder head as described in Part B of this Chapter.
11 Remove the inlet and exhaust manifolds as described in Chapter 4.
12 Remove the rocker gear, valve lifters and camshaft as described in Part B of this Chapter.
13 Proceed as described in paragraphs 4 to 9.

Diesel engines

14 Remove the cylinder head as described in Part C of this Chapter.
15 Remove the exhaust manifold as described in Chapter 4.
16 If desired, remove the glow plugs as described in Chapter 5.
17 Proceed as described in paragraphs 5 to 9.

9 Cylinder head and valves - cleaning and inspection

1 Thorough cleaning of the cylinder head and valve components, followed by a detailed inspection, will enable you to decide how much valve service work must be carried out during the engine overhaul. **Note:** *If the engine has been severely overheated, it is best to assume that the cylinder head is warped - check carefully for signs of this.*

Cleaning

2 Scrape away all traces of old gasket material from the cylinder head.
3 Scrape away the carbon from the combustion chambers and ports, then wash the cylinder head thoroughly with paraffin or a suitable solvent.
4 Scrape off any heavy carbon deposits that may have formed on the valves, then use a power-operated wire brush to remove deposits from the valve heads and stems.

Inspection

Note: *Be sure to perform all the following inspection procedures before concluding that the services of a machine shop or engine overhaul specialist are required. Make a list of all items that require attention.*

Cylinder head

5 Inspect the head very carefully for cracks, evidence of coolant leakage, and other damage. If cracks are found, a new cylinder head should be obtained.
6 Use a straight-edge and feeler blade to check that the cylinder head gasket surface is not distorted **(see illustration)**. If it is, it may be possible to have it machined, provided that the cylinder head is not reduced to less than the specified height. Note also that on diesel engines, the swirl chamber protrusion must be checked whenever the cylinder head surface is machined - see paragraphs 11 to 13.
7 Examine the valve seats in each of the combustion chambers. If they are severely pitted, cracked, or burned, they will need to be renewed or re-cut by an engine overhaul specialist. If they are only slightly pitted, this can be removed by grinding-in the valve heads and seats with fine valve-grinding compound, as described later in this Section. If the valve seats are re-cut, check that the valve recess dimensions, measured between the plane of the cylinder head sealing face and the centre of the valve head, are maintained within the specified limits.
8 Check the valve guides for wear by inserting the relevant valve, and checking for side-to-side motion of the valve. A very small amount of movement is acceptable. If the movement seems excessive, remove the valve. Measure the valve stem diameter (see later in this Section), and renew the valve if it is worn. If the valve stem is not worn, the wear must be in the valve guide, and the guide must be reamed or renewed, and corresponding oversize (stem) valves fitted. The reaming and renewal of valve guides should be entrusted to a Mercedes-Benz dealer or engine overhaul specialist, who will have the necessary tools available.
9 If reaming or renewing the valve guides, the valve seats should be re-cut or re-ground only *after* the guides have been reamed or renewed.
10 Examine the camshaft bearing surfaces in the cylinder head and the bearing caps for signs of wear or damage. If the bearings are excessively worn, it may be possible to have the cylinder head/bearing cap assembly rebored in order to fit a camshaft with oversize bearings. Consult a Mercedes-Benz dealer, or an engine overhaul specialist for further advice.

Swirl chambers - diesel engines

11 When inspecting the cylinder head, the swirl chamber protrusion should be checked - this is particularly important if the cylinder head face has been machined. If the swirl chamber protrusion is too great, the pistons may hit the swirl chambers when the engine is running, causing expensive damage.
12 Measure the protrusion of the swirl chamber from the sealing face of the cylinder head **(see illustration)**. If the protrusion is greater than the specified maximum, the protrusion can be altered by removing the swirl chamber, and fitting sealing spacers of varying thickness to achieve the specified protrusion. If the cylinder head has been machined, thicker spacers must be fitted, the increased thickness corresponding to the amount of metal removed from the cylinder head.
13 Removal and refitting of the swirl chambers, and fitting of the appropriate spacers should be entrusted to a Mercedes-Benz dealer, or an engine overhaul specialist, due to the special tools required.

Valves

Warning: The exhaust valves on 4-cylinder petrol engines and diesel engines are filled with sodium to improve their heat transfer. Sodium-filled valves may also be used on certain other engines. Sodium is a highly reactive metal, which will ignite or explode spontaneously on contact with water (including water vapour in the air). These valves must NOT be disposed of as ordinary scrap. Seek advice from a Mercedes-Benz dealer or your local authority when disposing of the valves.

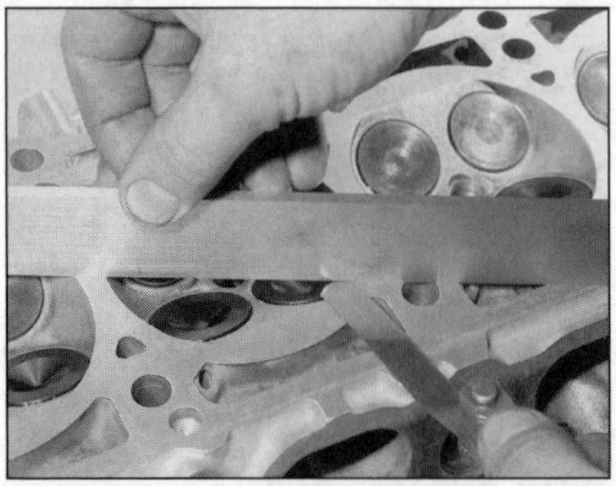

9.6 Use a straight-edge and feeler blade to check the cylinder head gasket face for distortion

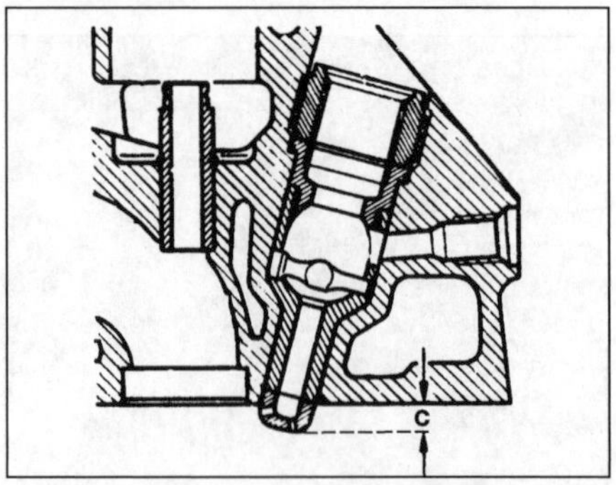

9.12 Measure the swirl chamber protrusion (c) - diesel engines

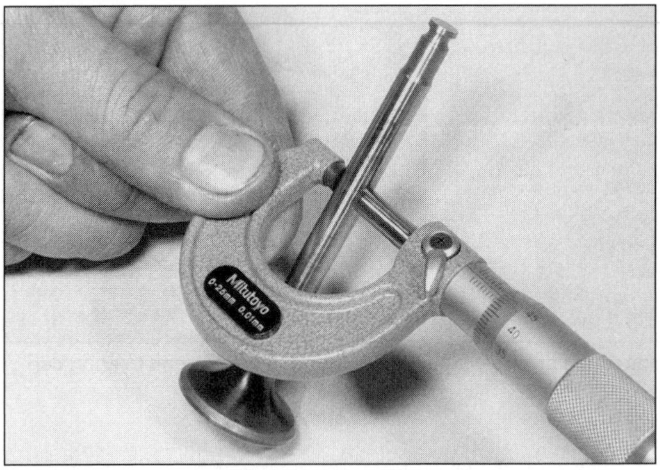

9.15 Measuring a valve stem diameter

9.18 Using a suction valve-grinding tool to grind in a valve

14 Examine the head of each valve for pitting, burning, cracks, and general wear. Check the valve stem for scoring and wear ridges. Rotate the valve, and check for any obvious indication that it is bent. Look for pits or excessive wear on the tip of each valve stem. Renew any valve that shows any such signs of wear or damage.

15 If the valve appears satisfactory at this stage, measure the valve stem diameter at several points using a micrometer **(see illustration)**. Any significant difference in the readings obtained indicates wear of the valve stem. Should any of these conditions be apparent, the valve(s) must be renewed.

16 If the valves are in satisfactory condition, they should be ground (lapped) into their respective seats, to ensure a smooth, gas-tight seal. If the seat is only lightly pitted, or if it has been re-cut, fine grinding compound *only* should be used to produce the required finish. Coarse valve-grinding compound should *not* be used, unless a seat is badly burned or deeply pitted. If this is the case, the cylinder head and valves should be inspected by an expert, to decide whether seat re-cutting, or even the renewal of the valve or seat insert (where possible) is required.

17 Valve grinding is carried out as follows. Place the cylinder head upside-down on a bench.

18 Smear a trace of (the appropriate grade of) valve-grinding compound on the seat face, and press a suction grinding tool onto the valve head **(see illustration)**. With a semi-rotary action, grind the valve head to its seat, lifting the valve occasionally to redistribute the grinding compound. A light spring placed under the valve head will greatly ease this operation.

19 If coarse grinding compound is being used, work only until a dull, matt even surface is produced on both the valve seat and the valve, then wipe off the used compound, and repeat the process with fine compound. When a smooth unbroken ring of light grey matt finish is produced on both the valve and seat, the grinding operation is complete. *Do not* grind-in the valves any further than absolutely necessary, or the seat will be prematurely sunk into the cylinder head.

20 When all the valves have been ground-in, carefully wash off *all* traces of grinding compound using paraffin or a suitable solvent, before reassembling the cylinder head.

Valve components

21 Examine the valve springs for signs of damage and discoloration. Check the free-length of the springs against the Specifications, and if necessary renew the springs. Where no figure is specified, if possible compare the length of the relevant valve spring with that of a new component.

22 Stand each spring on a flat surface, and check it for squareness. If any of the springs are damaged, distorted or have lost their tension, obtain a complete new set of springs. It is normal to renew the valve springs as a matter of course if a major overhaul is being carried out.

23 Renew the valve stem oil seals regardless of their apparent condition.

Rocker gear/valve lifters

24 Examine the contact surfaces for wear or scoring. If excessive wear is evident, the component(s) should be renewed. Refer to Part, A, B or C of this Chapter for further details.

10 Cylinder head - reassembly

Note: *New valve stem oil seals should be fitted, and a valve spring compressor tool will be required for this operation.*

Four-cylinder petrol engines

1 Lubricate the stems of the valves, and insert the valves into their original locations. If new valves are being fitted, insert them into the locations to which they have been ground.

2 Refit the spring seat.

3 Working on the first valve, dip the new valve stem seal in fresh engine oil. New seals are normally supplied with protective sleeves which should be fitted to the tops of the valve stems to prevent the collet grooves from damaging the oil seals. If no sleeves are supplied, wind a little thin tape round the top of the valve stems to protect the seals. Carefully locate the seal over the valve and onto the guide. Take care not to damage the seal as it is passed over the valve stem. Use a suitable socket or tube to press the seal firmly onto the guide.

4 Locate the valve spring on top of the seat, then refit the spring cap.

5 Fit the compressor tool, then compress the valve spring, and locate the split collets in the recess in the valve stem. Release the compressor, then repeat the procedure on the remaining valves.

> HAYNES HiNT — ***Use a little dab of grease to hold the collets in position on the valve stem while the spring compressor is released.***

6 With all the valves installed, support the cylinder head on blocks of wood and, using a hammer and interposed block of wood, tap the end of each valve stem to settle the components.

7 Where applicable, refit the thermostat housing to the cylinder head.

8 Where applicable, refit the spark plugs.

9 Refit the rocker gear, valve lifters and camshaft as described in Part A of this Chapter.

10 Refit the inlet and exhaust manifolds as described in Chapter 4.

11 Refit the cylinder head as described in Part A of this Chapter.

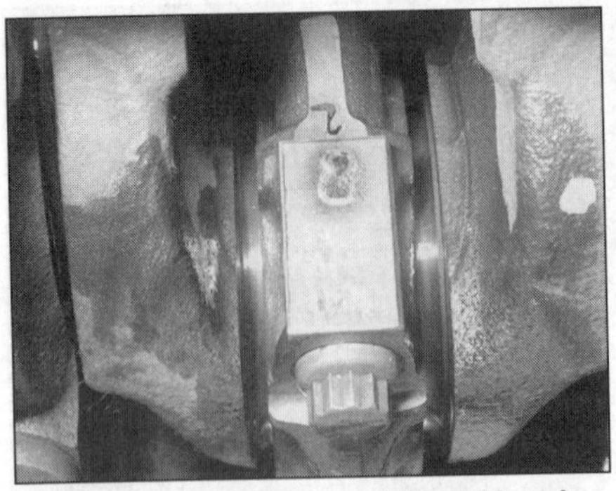

11.3 Connecting rod and big-end bearing cap identification markings

11.4 Piston crown direction arrow

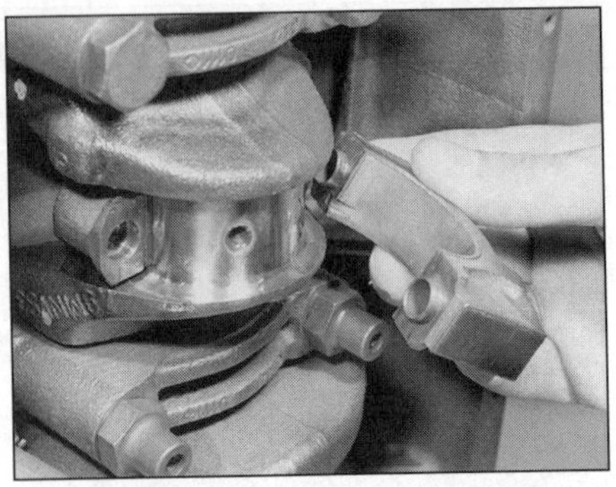

11.6 Removing a big-end bearing cap

Six-cylinder petrol engines

12 Proceed as described in paragraphs 1 to 8.
13 Refit the rocker gear, valve lifters and camshaft as described in Part B of this Chapter.
14 Refit the inlet and exhaust manifolds as described in Chapter 4.
15 Refit the cylinder head as described in Part B of this Chapter.

Diesel engines

16 Proceed as described in paragraphs 1 to 7.
17 Where applicable, refit the glow plugs as described in Chapter 5.
18 Refit the exhaust manifold as described in Chapter 4.
19 Refit the cylinder head as described in Part C of this Chapter.

11 Piston/connecting rod assembly - removal

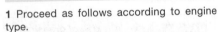

1 Proceed as follows according to engine type.

a) ***On 4-cylinder petrol engines**, remove the cylinder head and sump as described in Part A of this Chapter.*
b) ***On 6-cylinder petrol engines**, remove the cylinder head, sump and oil pump, as described in Part B of this Chapter.*
c) ***On diesel engines**, remove the cylinder head, sump, oil pump and, where applicable, the oil baffle plate, as described in Part C of this Chapter.*

2 If there is a pronounced wear ridge at the top of any bore, it may be necessary to remove it with a scraper or ridge reamer, to avoid piston damage during removal. Such a ridge indicates excessive wear of the cylinder bore.
3 Check the connecting rods and big-end caps for identification marks. Both rods and caps should be marked with the cylinder number on the inlet manifold side of each assembly **(see illustration)**. Note that No 1 cylinder is at the timing chain end of the engine. If no marks are present, using a hammer and centre-punch, paint or similar, mark each connecting rod and big-end bearing cap with its respective cylinder number on the flat machined surface provided - note on which side of the connecting rods the marks are made.
4 Similarly, check the piston crowns for a direction marking. An arrow on each piston crown should point towards the timing chain end of the engine **(see illustration)**. On some engines, this mark may be obscured by carbon build-up, in which case the piston crown should be cleaned to check for a mark. In some cases, the direction arrow may have worn off, in which case a suitable mark should be made on the piston crown using a scriber - do not deeply score the piston crown, but ensure that the mark is easily visible.
5 Turn the crankshaft to bring piston Nos 1 and 4 (4-cylinder engines), No 1 (5-cylinder engine), or Nos 1 and 6 (6-cylinder engines), as applicable, to BDC (bottom dead centre).
6 Unscrew the bolts from No 1 piston big-end bearing cap. Take off the cap, and recover the bottom half bearing shell **(see illustration)**. If the bearing shells are to be re-used, tape the cap and the shell together.
7 Using a hammer handle, push the piston up through the bore, and remove it from the top of the cylinder block (where applicable, take care not to damage the piston cooling oil spay jets in the cylinder block as the piston/connecting rod assembly is removed). Recover the bearing shell, and tape it to the connecting rod for safe-keeping.
8 Loosely refit the big-end cap to the connecting rod, and secure with the bolts - this will help to keep the components in their correct order.
9 Where applicable, remove No 4 piston assembly (4-cylinder engines), or No 6 piston assembly (6-cylinder engines), in the same way.
10 Turn the crankshaft as necessary to bring the remaining pistons to BDC, and remove them in the same way.

12 Crankshaft - removal

1 Proceed as follows according to engine type.

a) ***On 4-cylinder engines**, remove the sump, the timing chain cover, timing chain, and the flywheel/driveplate, as described in Part A of this Chapter. If desired, also remove the crankshaft sprocket.*
b) ***On 6-cylinder petrol engines**, remove the sump, oil pump, lower timing chain cover, timing chain, and the flywheel/driveplate, as described in Part B of this Chapter. If desired, also remove the crankshaft sprocket.*
c) ***On diesel engines**, remove the sump, oil pump, oil baffle plate (where applicable), timing chain cover, timing chain, and the flywheel/driveplate, as described in Part C of this Chapter. If desired, also remove the crankshaft sprocket.*

2 Unbolt the crankshaft rear oil seal housing from the cylinder block. Recover the gasket **(see illustration)**.
3 Remove the pistons and connecting rods, as described in Section 11. If no work is to be done on the pistons and connecting rods, there is no need to remove the cylinder head, or to push the pistons out of the cylinder

12.2 Crankshaft rear oil seal housing securing bolts (arrowed) - 4-cylinder petrol engine shown

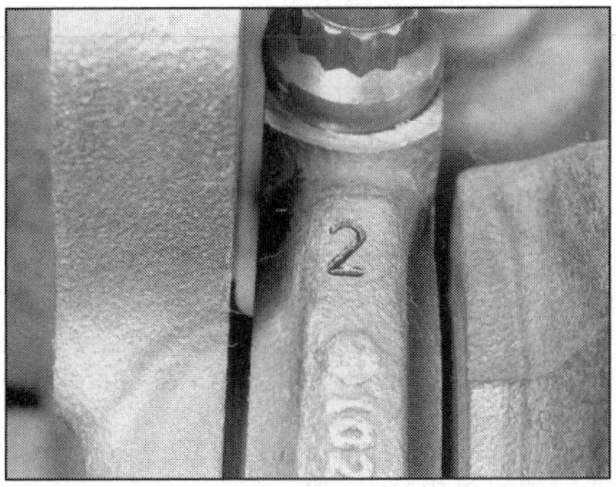

12.5 Main bearing cap identification marking

12.6 Removing a main bearing cap

12.7 Recover the thrustwashers (arrowed) from the bearing cap . . .

bores. The pistons should just be pushed far enough up the bores so that they are positioned clear of the crankshaft journals.

Warning: If the pistons are pushed up the bores, and the cylinder head is still fitted, take care not to force the pistons into the open valves.

4 Check the crankshaft endfloat as described in Section 15, then proceed as follows.

5 On 4-cylinder engines, the crankshaft bearing caps should be numbered 1 to 5 from the timing chain end of the engine. Similarly, on the 5-cylinder engine, the bearing caps should be numbered 1 to 6, and on 6-cylinder engines, the bearing caps should be numbered 1 to 7 **(see illustration)**. If the bearing caps are not marked, mark them accordingly using a centre-punch. Note the orientation of the markings to ensure correct refitting.

6 Slacken and remove the main bearing cap retaining bolts, and lift off each bearing cap **(see illustration)**. Recover the lower bearing shells, and tape them to their respective caps for safe-keeping. Where applicable, note the location and orientation of the oil pick-up pipe support bracket, secured by the bearing cap bolts.

7 Recover the lower endfloat control thrustwasher halves from either side of the appropriate bearing cap, noting their positions, as follows **(see illustration)**.

a) ***4-cylinder engines*** *- centre (No 3) main bearing cap.*
b) ***5-cylinder engine*** *- No 4 main bearing cap.*
c) ***6-cylinder engines*** *- No 5 main bearing cap.*

8 Lift out the crankshaft. Take care as the crankshaft is heavy

9 Recover the upper bearing shells from the cylinder block, and tape them to their respective caps for safe-keeping. Similarly, recover the upper thrustwasher halves, noting their orientation **(see illustration)**.

13 Cylinder block/crankcase - cleaning and inspection

Cleaning

1 Remove all external components and electrical switches/sensors from the block. For complete cleaning, the core plugs should be removed. Drill a small hole in the plugs, then insert a self-tapping screw into the hole. Pull out the plugs by pulling on the screw with a pair of grips, or by using a slide hammer.

2 Scrape all traces of gasket from the cylinder block/crankcase, taking care not to damage the gasket/sealing surfaces.

3 Remove all oil gallery plugs (where fitted). The plugs are usually very tight - they may have to be drilled out, and the holes re-tapped. Use new plugs when the engine is reassembled.

4 If any of the castings are extremely dirty, all should be steam-cleaned.

5 After the castings have been steam-cleaned, clean all oil holes and oil galleries one more time. Flush all internal passages with warm water until the water runs clear. Dry thoroughly, and apply a light film of oil to all mating surfaces, to prevent rusting. Also oil the cylinder bores. If you have access to compressed air, use it to speed up the drying process, and to blow out all the oil holes and galleries.

Warning: Wear eye protection when using compressed air!

6 If the castings are not very dirty, you can do an adequate cleaning job with soapy water, as hot as you can stand, and a stiff brush. Take plenty of time, and do a thorough job. Regardless of the cleaning method used, be sure to clean all oil holes and galleries very thoroughly, and to dry all components well. Protect the cylinder bores as described above, to prevent rusting.

7 Where applicable, it is advisable to remove the piston oil spray jets from the cylinder block and clean them. To remove a jet, unscrew the securing bolt, recover the sealing ring (where applicable), and withdraw the jet from the cylinder block **(see illustration)**. Renew any jets which show signs of damage. Check the oil spray hole and oil passages for blockage.

8 All threaded holes must be clean, to ensure accurate torque readings during reassembly. To clean the threads, run the correct-size tap into each of the holes to remove rust, corrosion, thread sealant or sludge, and to restore damaged threads **(see illustration)**. If possible, use compressed air to clear the holes of debris produced by this operation.

12.9 . . . and from the cylinder block

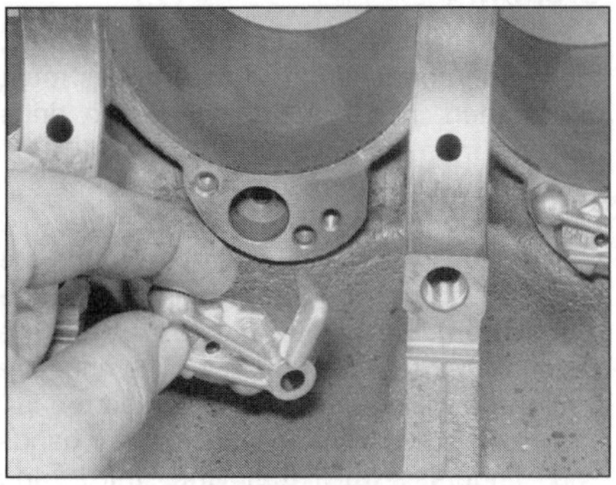

13.7 Removing a piston oil spray jet from the cylinder block

13.8 Clean damaged threads using a tap

HAYNES HiNT *A good alternative is to inject aerosol-applied water-dispersant lubricant into each hole, using the long spout usually supplied.*

Warning: ***Wear eye protection when cleaning out these holes in this way!***

9 Ensure that all threaded holes in the cylinder block are dry.

10 After coating the mating surfaces of the new core plugs with suitable sealant, fit them to the cylinder block. Make sure that they are driven in straight and seated correctly, or leakage could result.

HAYNES HiNT *A large socket with an outside diameter which will just fit into the core plug can be used to drive core plugs into position.*

11 Apply suitable sealant to the new oil gallery plugs, and insert them into the holes in the block. Tighten them securely.

12 If the engine is not going to be reassembled right away, cover it with a large plastic bag to keep it clean; protect all mating surfaces and the cylinder bores as described above, to prevent rusting.

Inspection

Note: *Certain diesel engines may be fitted with dry cylinder liners. Where fitted, it is possible to renew the cylinder liners to compensate for cylinder bore wear, instead of carrying out conventional cylinder block reboring. It is also possible to fit liners to most cylinder blocks not originally fitted with liners, provided that the block is machined accordingly. Cylinder liner removal and refitting must be carried out by a Mercedes-Benz dealer or an engine reconditioning specialist, as special tools and a press are required.*

13 Visually check the castings for cracks and corrosion. Look for stripped threads in the threaded holes. If there has been any history of internal water leakage, it may be worthwhile having an engine overhaul specialist check the cylinder block/crankcase with special equipment. If defects are found, have them repaired if possible, or renew the assembly.

14 Check each cylinder bore for scuffing and scoring. Check for signs of a wear ridge at the top of the cylinder, indicating that the bore is excessively worn.

15 If the necessary measuring equipment is available, measure the bore diameter of each cylinder at the top (just under the wear ridge), centre, and bottom of the cylinder bore, parallel to the crankshaft axis.

16 Next, measure the bore diameter at the same three locations, at right-angles to the crankshaft axis. Compare the results with the figures given in the Specifications. If there is any doubt about the condition of the cylinder bores, seek the advice of a Mercedes-Benz dealer or suitable engine reconditioning specialist.

17 If the cylinder bore wear exceeds the permitted tolerances, or if the cylinder walls are badly scored or scuffed, then the cylinders will have to be rebored by a suitably-qualified specialist, and new oversize pistons will have to be fitted. A Mercedes-Benz dealer or engineering workshop will normally be able to supply suitable oversize pistons when carrying out the reboring work. Note that the piston and bore size grades are stamped on the piston crowns, and on the adjacent cylinder head mating face of the cylinder block.

18 Inspect the upper surface of the cylinder block for damage. Use a straight-edge and feeler blade to check that the cylinder head gasket surface is not distorted. If it is, it may be possible to have it machined, provided that the cylinder block is not reduced to less than the specified height. Note also that, on diesel engines, the piston protrusion must be checked whenever the cylinder head surface is machined - see paragraph 19.

Piston protrusion - diesel engines

19 When inspecting the cylinder block, the piston protrusion should be checked - this is particularly important if the cylinder head face has been machined. If the piston protrusion is too great, the pistons may hit the swirl chambers when the engine is running, causing expensive damage.

20 Measure the protrusion of the piston from the sealing face of the cylinder head (a dial gauge should be used if possible). If the protrusion is greater than the specified maximum, consult a Mercedes-Benz dealer or an engine reconditioning specialist for advice - it is likely that the cylinder block will have to be renewed.

14 Piston/connecting rod assembly - cleaning and inspection

Cleaning

1 Before the inspection process can begin, the piston/connecting rod assemblies must be cleaned, and the original piston rings removed from the pistons.

2 Carefully expand the old rings over the top of the pistons. The use of two or three old feeler blades will be helpful in preventing the rings dropping into empty grooves **(see illustration)**. Be careful not to scratch the piston with the ends of the ring. The rings are brittle, and will snap if they are spread too far. They are also very sharp - protect your hands and fingers. Note that the third ring incorporates an expander. Keep each set of rings with its piston if the old rings are to be re-used. Note which way up each ring is fitted to ensure correct refitting.

3 Scrape away all traces of carbon from the top of the piston. A hand-held wire brush (or a piece of fine emery cloth) can be used, once the majority of the deposits have been scraped away.

4 Remove the carbon from the ring grooves in the piston, using an old ring. Break the ring in half to do this (be careful not to cut your fingers - piston rings are sharp). Be careful to remove only the carbon deposits - do not remove any metal, and do not nick or scratch the sides of the ring grooves.

5 Once the deposits have been removed, clean the piston/connecting rod assembly with paraffin or a suitable solvent, and dry thoroughly. Make sure that the oil return holes in the ring grooves are clear.

Inspection

6 If the pistons and cylinder bores are not damaged or worn excessively, and if the cylinder block does not need to be rebored, the original pistons can be refitted. Measure the piston diameters, and check that they are within limits for the corresponding bore diameters. If the piston-to-bore clearance is excessive, the block will have to be rebored, and new pistons and rings fitted. Normal piston wear shows up as even vertical wear on the piston thrust surfaces, and slight looseness of the top ring in its groove. New piston rings should always be used when the engine is reassembled. Note that the piston and bore size grades are stamped on the piston crowns, and on the adjacent cylinder head mating face of the cylinder block.

7 Carefully inspect each piston for cracks around the skirt, around the gudgeon pin holes, and at the piston ring "lands" (between the ring grooves).

8 Look for scoring and scuffing on the piston skirt, holes in the piston crown, and burned areas at the edge of the crown. If the skirt is scored or scuffed, the engine may have been suffering from overheating, and/or abnormal combustion which caused excessively high operating temperatures. The cooling and lubrication systems should be checked thoroughly. Scorch marks on the sides of the pistons show that blow-by has occurred. A

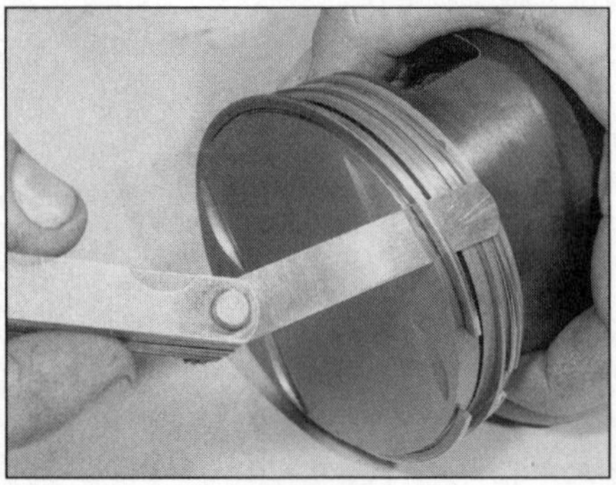

14.2 Using a feeler blade to help remove a piston ring

14.13a Prise out the circlips . . .

hole in the piston crown, or burned areas at the edge of the piston crown, indicates that abnormal combustion (pre-ignition, knocking, or detonation) has been occurring. If any of the above problems exist, the causes must be investigated and corrected, or the damage will occur again. The causes may include incorrect ignition/injection pump timing, inlet air leaks or incorrect air/fuel mixture (petrol engines), or a faulty fuel injector (diesel engines).

9 Corrosion of the piston, in the form of pitting, indicates that coolant has been leaking into the combustion chamber and/or the crankcase. Again, the cause must be corrected, or the problem may persist in the rebuilt engine.

10 New pistons can be purchased from a Mercedes-Benz dealer.

11 Examine each connecting rod carefully for signs of damage, such as cracks around the big-end and small-end bearings. Check that the rod is not bent or distorted. Damage is highly unlikely, unless the engine has been seized or badly overheated. Detailed checking of the connecting rod assembly can only be carried out by a Mercedes-Benz dealer or engine repair specialist with the necessary equipment.

12 The gudgeon pins are of the floating type, secured in position by two circlips. The pistons and connecting rods can be separated as follows.

13 Using a small flat-bladed screwdriver, prise out the circlips, and push out the gudgeon pin **(see illustrations)**. Hand

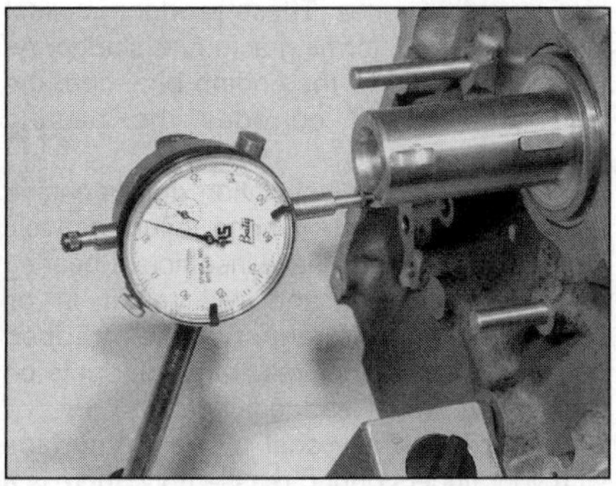

15.2 Checking crankshaft endfloat using a dial gauge

14.13b . . . and push out the gudgeon pin

pressure should be sufficient to remove the pin. Identify the piston and rod to ensure correct reassembly. Discard the circlips - new ones ***must*** be used on refitting.

14 Examine the gudgeon pin and connecting rod small-end bearing for signs of wear or damage. It should be possible to push the gudgeon pin through the connecting rod bush by hand, without noticeable play. Wear can be cured by renewing both the pin and bush. Bush renewal, however, is a specialist job - press facilities are required, and the new bush must be reamed accurately.

15 The connecting rods themselves should not be in need of renewal, unless seizure or some other major mechanical failure has occurred. Check the alignment of the connecting rods visually, and if the rods are not straight, take them to an engine overhaul specialist for a more detailed check.

16 Examine all components, and obtain any new parts from your Mercedes-Benz dealer. If new pistons are purchased, they will be supplied complete with gudgeon pins and circlips. Circlips can also be purchased individually.

17 Position the piston in relation to the connecting rod as follows according to engine type **(see illustration)**.

a) ***On petrol engines****, the small oil bore in the top of the connecting rod, and the arrow on the piston crown must point towards the timing chain end of the engine.*

b) ***On diesel engines****, the cut-outs for the bearing shell locating tabs in the connecting rod and the bearing cap must be on the fuel injection pump side of the engine, and the arrow on the piston crown must point towards the timing chain end of the engine.*

15.3 Checking crankshaft endfloat using a feeler blade

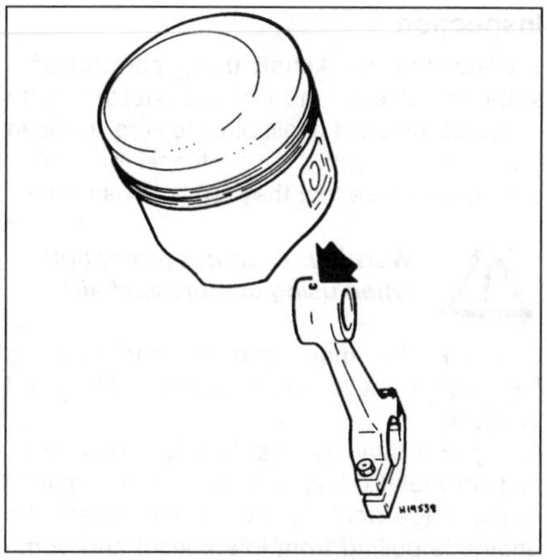

14.17 The small oil bore hole (arrowed) must be offset towards the timing chain end of the engine - petrol engines

18 Apply a smear of clean engine oil to the gudgeon pin. Slide it into the piston and through the connecting rod small-end. Check that the piston pivots freely on the rod, then secure the gudgeon pin in position with two new circlips. Ensure that each circlip is correctly located in its groove in the piston.

15 Crankshaft - inspection

Checking crankshaft endfloat

1 If the crankshaft endfloat is to be checked, this must be done when the crankshaft is still installed in the cylinder block/crankcase, but is free to move (see Section 12).

2 Check the endfloat using a dial gauge in contact with the end of the crankshaft. Push the crankshaft fully one way, and then zero the gauge. Push the crankshaft fully the other way, and check the endfloat. The result can be compared with the specified amount, and will give an indication as to whether new thrustwasher halves are required **(see illustration)**. Note that all thrustwashers must be of the same thickness - refer to the Specifications for the thicknesses of thrustwashers available.

3 If a dial gauge is not available, feeler blades can be used. First push the crankshaft fully towards the flywheel end of the engine, then use feeler blades to measure the gap between the web of No 3 crankpin and the thrustwasher halves on 4-cylinder engines, between the web of No 4 crankpin and the thrustwasher halves on the 5-cylinder engine, or between the web of No 5 crankpin and the thrustwasher halves on 6-cylinder engines **(see illustration)**.

Inspection

4 Clean the crankshaft using paraffin or a suitable solvent, and dry it, preferably with compressed air if available. Be sure to clean the oil holes with a pipe cleaner or similar probe, to ensure that they are not obstructed.

Warning: Wear eye protection when using compressed air!

5 Check the main and big-end bearing journals for uneven wear, scoring, pitting and cracking.

6 Big-end bearing wear is accompanied by distinct metallic knocking when the engine is running (particularly noticeable when the engine is pulling from low speed) and some loss of oil pressure.

7 Main bearing wear is accompanied by severe engine vibration and rumble - getting progressively worse as engine speed increases - and again by loss of oil pressure.

8 Check the bearing journal for roughness by running a finger lightly over the bearing surface. Any roughness (which will be accompanied by obvious bearing wear) indicates that the crankshaft requires regrinding (where possible) or renewal.

9 If the crankshaft has been reground, check for burrs around the crankshaft oil holes (the holes are usually chamfered, so burrs should not be a problem unless regrinding has been carried out carelessly). Remove any burrs with a fine file or scraper, and thoroughly clean the oil holes as described previously.

10 Using a micrometer, measure the diameter of the main and big-end bearing journals, and compare the results with the Specifications **(see illustration)**. By measuring the diameter at a number of points around each journal's circumference, you will be able to determine whether or not the journal is out-of-round. Take the measurement at each end of the journal, near the webs, to determine if the journal is tapered.

11 Check the oil seal contact surfaces at each end of the crankshaft for wear and damage. If the seal has worn a deep groove in the surface of the crankshaft, consult an engine overhaul specialist; repair may be possible, but otherwise a new crankshaft will be required.

15.10 Measuring a big-end bearing journal diameter using a micrometer

12 If the crankshaft journals have not already been reground, it may be possible to have the crankshaft reconditioned, and to fit oversize shells (see Section 19). If no oversize shells are available and the crankshaft has worn beyond the specified limits, it will have to be renewed. Consult your Mercedes-Benz dealer or engine specialist for further information on parts availability.

16 Main and big-end bearings, and bearing cap bolts - inspection

Bearings

1 Even though the main and big-end bearings should be renewed during the engine overhaul, the old bearings should be retained for close examination, as they may reveal valuable information about the condition of the engine. The bearing shells are graded by thickness, the grade of each shell being indicated by the colour code marked on it.

2 Bearing failure can occur due to lack of lubrication, the presence of dirt or other foreign particles, overloading the engine, or corrosion **(see illustration)**. Regardless of the cause of bearing failure, the cause must be corrected (where applicable) before the engine is reassembled, to prevent it from happening again.

3 When examining the bearing shells, remove them from the cylinder block/crankcase, the connecting rods and the connecting rod big-end bearing caps. Lay them out on a clean surface in the same general position as their location in the engine. This will enable you to match any bearing problems with the corresponding crankshaft journal. *Do not* touch any shell's bearing surface with your fingers while checking it, or the delicate surface may be scratched.

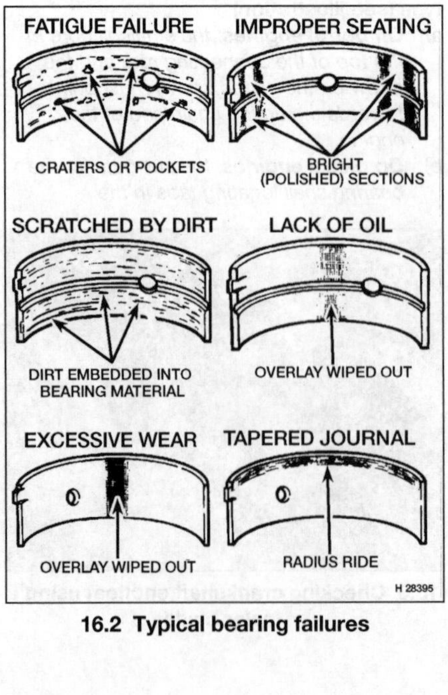

16.2 Typical bearing failures

4 Dirt and other foreign matter gets into the engine in a variety of ways. It may be left in the engine during assembly, or it may pass through filters or the crankcase ventilation system. It may get into the oil, and from there into the bearings. Metal chips from machining operations and normal engine wear are often present. Abrasives are sometimes left in engine components after reconditioning, especially when parts are not thoroughly cleaned using the proper cleaning methods. Whatever the source, these foreign objects often end up embedded in the soft bearing material, and are easily recognised. Large particles will not embed in the bearing, and will score or gouge the bearing and journal. The best prevention for this cause of bearing failure is to clean all parts thoroughly, and keep everything spotlessly-clean during engine assembly. Frequent and regular engine oil and filter changes are also recommended.

5 Lack of lubrication (or lubrication breakdown) has a number of interrelated causes. Excessive heat (which thins the oil), overloading (which squeezes the oil from the bearing face) and oil leakage (from excessive bearing clearances, worn oil pump or high engine speeds) all contribute to lubrication breakdown. Blocked oil passages, which usually are the result of misaligned oil holes in a bearing shell, will also oil-starve a bearing, and destroy it. When lack of lubrication is the cause of bearing failure, the bearing material is wiped or extruded from the steel backing of the bearing. Temperatures may increase to the point where the steel backing turns blue from overheating.

6 Driving habits can have a definite effect on bearing life. Full-throttle, low-speed operation (labouring the engine) puts very high loads on bearings, tending to squeeze out the oil film. These loads cause the bearings to flex, which produces fine cracks in the bearing face (fatigue failure). Eventually, the bearing material will loosen in pieces, and tear away from the steel backing.

7 Short-distance driving leads to corrosion of bearings, because insufficient engine heat is produced to drive off the condensed water and corrosive gases. These products collect in the engine oil, forming acid and sludge. As the oil is carried to the engine bearings, the acid attacks and corrodes the bearing material.

8 Incorrect bearing installation during engine assembly will lead to bearing failure as well. Tight-fitting bearings leave insufficient bearing running clearance, and will result in oil starvation. Dirt or foreign particles trapped behind a bearing shell result in high spots on the bearing, which lead to failure.

9 *Do not* touch any shell's bearing surface with your fingers during reassembly; there is a risk of scratching the delicate surface, or of depositing particles of dirt on it.

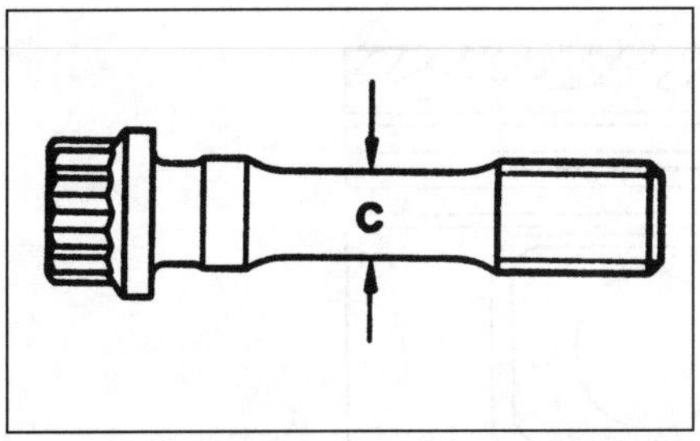

16.14 Measure the diameter of the big-end bearing cap bolts at the narrowest section (c) - 4-cylinder petrol engines

10 As mentioned at the beginning of this Section, the bearing shells should be renewed as a matter of course during engine overhaul; to do otherwise is false economy. Refer to Section 19 for details of bearing shell selection.

Main bearing cap bolts

11 The manufacturers make no recommendation to inspect the main bearing cap bolts, however, as a precautionary measure, we recommended that new main bearing cap bolts are used on all engines, although this is at the discretion of the individual owner

Big-end bearing cap bolts

12 The manufacturers recommend that the big-end bearing cap bolts are measured to determine whether renewal is necessary, however, some owners may wish to renew all the bolts as a matter of course. It is strongly recommended that the bolts are renewed when reassembling the engine.

13 Press or tap the bolts out from the connecting rods.

14 On 4-cylinder petrol engines, measure the diameter of the bolts at the narrowest section **(see illustration)**. If the diameter is less than the minimum specified (see Specifications), the bolts should be renewed.

15 On all except 4-cylinder petrol engines, measure the length of each bolt from the base of the head to the end of the shank. If the bolt length is greater than the maximum specified (see Specifications), the bolts should be renewed.

17 Engine overhaul - reassembly sequence

1 Before reassembly begins, ensure that all new parts have been obtained, and that all necessary tools are available. Read through the entire procedure to familiarise yourself with the work involved, and to ensure that all items necessary for reassembly of the engine are at hand. In addition to all normal tools and materials, thread-locking compound will be needed. A suitable tube of liquid sealant will also be required for the joint faces that are fitted without gaskets.

2 In order to save time and avoid problems, engine reassembly can be carried out in the following order, referring to Part A, B, or C of this Chapter unless otherwise stated. Where applicable, use new gaskets and seals when refitting the various components **(see illustrations)**.

a) Crankshaft (Section 19).
b) Piston/connecting rod assemblies (Section 20).
c) Oil pump.
d) Sump.
e) Flywheel/driveplate.
f) Cylinder head.
g) Timing chain, tensioner and sprockets.
h) Engine external components.

3 At this stage, all engine components should be absolutely clean and dry, with all faults repaired. The components should be laid out (or in individual containers) on a completely clean work surface.

18 Piston rings - refitting

1 Before fitting new piston rings, the ring end gaps must be checked as follows.

2 Lay out the piston/connecting rod assemblies and the new piston ring sets, so that the ring sets will be matched with the same piston and cylinder during the end gap measurement and subsequent engine reassembly.

3 Insert the top ring into the first cylinder, and push it down the bore using the top of the piston. This will ensure that the ring remains square with the cylinder walls. Position the ring near the bottom of the cylinder bore, at the lower limit of ring travel. Note that the top and second compression rings are different. The second ring is easily identified by the step on its lower surface.

4 Measure the end gap using feeler blades.

5 Repeat the procedure with the ring at the top of the cylinder bore, at the upper limit of its travel **(see illustration)**, and compare the measurements with the figures given in the Specifications.

6 If the gap is too small (unlikely if genuine Mercedes-Benz parts are used), it must be enlarged, or the ring ends may contact each other during engine operation, causing serious damage. Ideally, new piston rings providing the correct end gap should be fitted. As a last resort, the end gap can be increased by filing the ring ends very carefully with a fine file. Mount the file in a vice equipped with soft jaws, slip the ring over the file with the ends contacting the file face, and slowly move the ring to remove material from the ends. Take care, as piston rings are sharp, and are easily broken.

7 With new piston rings, it is unlikely that the end gap will be too large. If the gaps are too large, check that you have the correct rings for your engine and for the particular cylinder bore size.

8 Repeat the checking procedure for each ring in the first cylinder, and then for the rings in the remaining cylinders. Remember to keep rings, pistons and cylinders matched up.

9 Once the ring end gaps have been checked and if necessary corrected, the rings can be fitted to the pistons.

10 Fit the piston rings using the same technique as for removal. Fit the bottom (oil control) ring first, and work up. When fitting the oil control ring, first insert the wire expander, then fit the ring with its gap positioned 180° from the protruding wire ends of the expander. Ensure that the rings are fitted the correct way up - the top surface of

2D

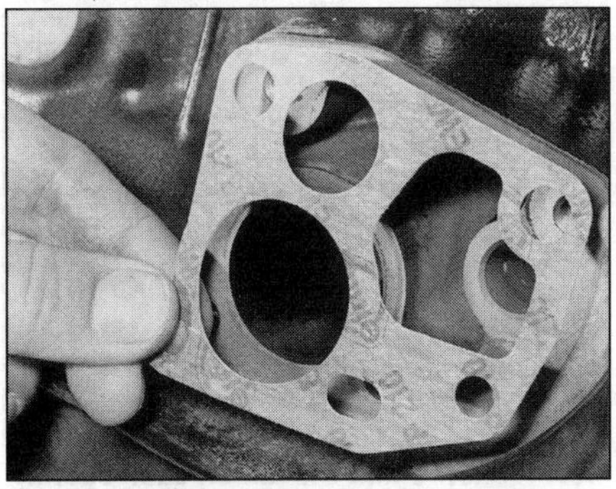

17.2a Use a new gasket when refitting the oil filter housing

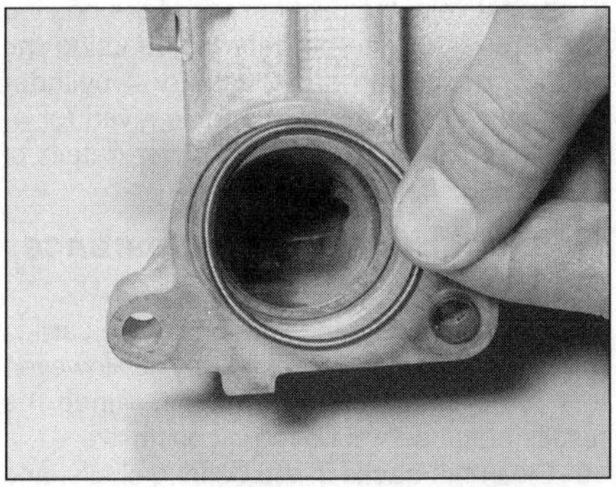

17.2b Use a new O-ring when refitting the coolant pump

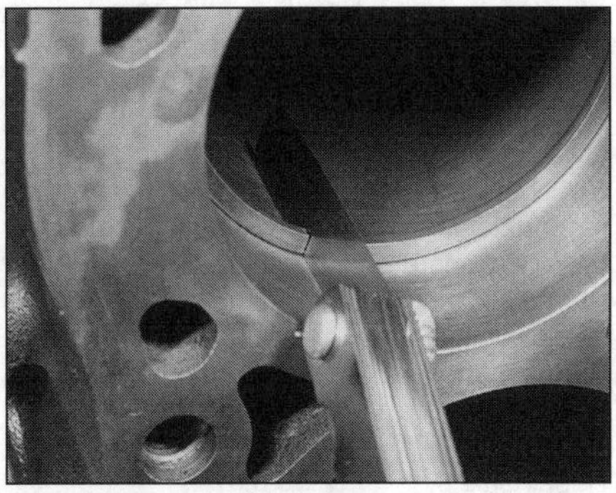

18.5 Measuring a piston ring end-gap

18.10a Fitting the oil control ring expander

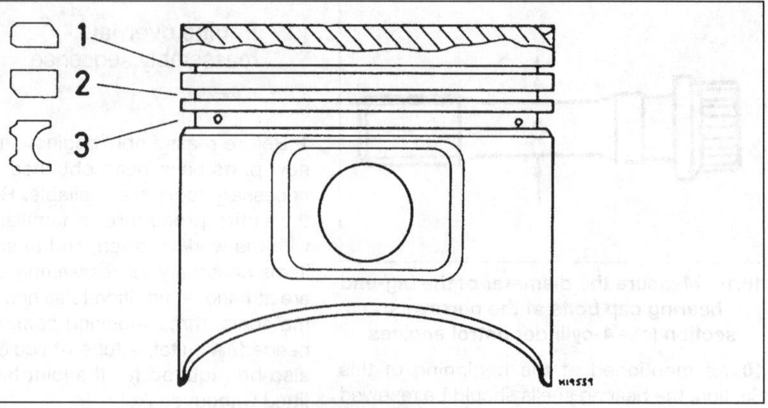

18.10b Piston ring orientation

1 Top compression ring 2 Middle compression ring 3 Oil control ring

the rings is normally marked "TOP" **(see illustrations)**. Arrange the gaps of the top and second compression rings 120° either side of the oil control ring gap, but make sure that none of the rings gaps are positioned over the gudgeon pin hole. **Note:** *Always follow any instructions supplied with the new piston ring sets - different manufacturers may specify different procedures. Do not mix up the top and second compression rings, as they have different cross-sections.*

19 Crankshaft - refitting and main bearing running clearance check

Selection of new bearing shells

Four-cylinder petrol engines

1 To determine the thickness of the new bearing shells required, the bearing diameter, crankshaft journal diameter, and bearing running clearance must be measured. The appropriate bearing thickness can then be calculated as shown in the following example.

Bearing diameter	62.51 mm
Minus crankshaft journal diameter	- 57.95 mm
Equals	4.55 mm
Minus bearing running clearance	- 0.04 mm
Equals	4.51 mm
Divided by 2 to find the thickness required for each shell	
Equals	2.25 mm

2 If it is determined that upper and lower bearing shells of different thicknesses are required, the thicker bearing shell should always be fitted to the bearing cap.

3 A Mercedes-Benz dealer or an engine reconditioning specialist will be able to supply the appropriate bearing shells required. Refer to the following table for details of the bearing shells available.

Bearing shells	Bearing shell thickness
Standard	2.25 mm
Repair size 1	2.37 mm
Repair size 2	2.50 mm
Repair size 3	2.62 mm
Repair size 4	2.75 mm

Six-cylinder petrol engines

4 The thickness of the new bearing shells required can be determined using the method described previously for 4-cylinder petrol engines. At the time of writing, no information was available regarding the availability of bearing shells for 6-cylinder petrol engines. A Mercedes-Benz dealer or an engine reconditioning specialist should be able to offer advice, and will be able to supply the appropriate bearings.

Diesel engines

5 The bearing shells are colour-coded. Three different bearing shell thicknesses are available, colour-coded blue, yellow and red.

6 Colour code markings appear on the crankshaft, either on the crankshaft cheeks, or on the counterweights, next to the crankshaft journals. Marks also appear on the cylinder block - these marks take the form of punch marks on the sump mating face of the cylinder block, next to the bearing locations.

7 To eliminate the need to measure the bearing running clearance, select new bearing shells in accordance with the following table.

Crankshaft colour code	Punch markings on cylinder block		
	1 dot	2 dots	3 dots
Blue	Blue	Yellow	Yellow
Yellow	Blue	Yellow	Red
Red	Yellow	Yellow	Red

8 Alternatively, the thicknesses of the bearing shells required can be determined using the method described previously for 4-cylinder petrol engines. Refer to the table given for 4-cylinder engines in paragraph 3 for details of the bearing shells available.

Main bearing running clearance check

9 The running clearance check can be carried out using the original bearing shells. However, it is preferable to use a new set, since the results obtained will be more conclusive.

10 Clean the backs of the bearing shells, and the bearing locations in both the cylinder block/crankcase and the main bearing caps.

11 Press the bearing shells into their locations, ensuring that the tab on each shell engages in the notch in the cylinder block/crankcase or bearing cap **(see illustration)**. Take care not to touch any shell's bearing surface with your fingers. If the original bearing shells are being used for the check, ensure that they are refitted in their original locations. Note that the bearings shells with oil grooves fit in the cylinder block, and the plain bearing shells fit in the bearing caps.

12 The clearance can be checked in either of two ways.

13 One method (which will be difficult to achieve without a range of internal micrometers or internal/external expanding calipers) is to refit the main bearing caps to the cylinder block/crankcase, with bearing shells in place. With the original cap retaining bolts tightened to the specified torque, measure the internal diameter of each assembled pair of bearing shells. If the diameter of each corresponding crankshaft journal is measured and then subtracted from the bearing internal diameter, the result will be the main bearing running clearance.

14 The second (and more accurate) method is to use a product known as "Plastigauge". This consists of a fine thread of perfectly-

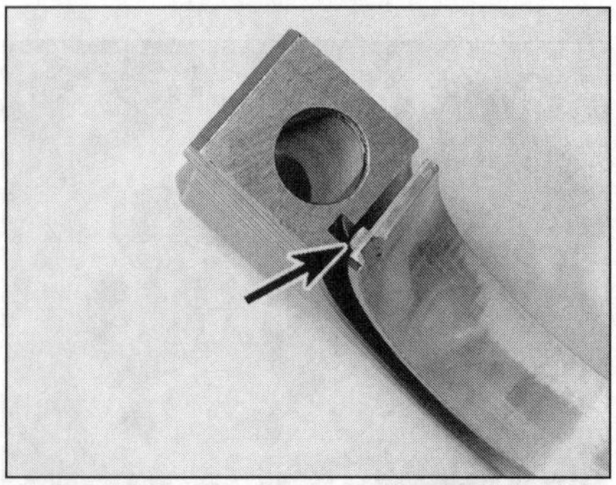

19.11 Ensure that the tab on each bearing shell (arrowed) engages with the notch in the cap

19.16 Plastigauge in place on crankshaft main bearing journal

19.19 Measure the width of the deformed Plastigauge using the scale on the card

round plastic, which is compressed between the bearing shell and the journal. When the shell is removed, the plastic is deformed, and can be measured with a special card gauge supplied with the kit. The running clearance is determined from this gauge. Enquiries at one of the larger specialist motor factors should produce the name of a stockist in your area. The procedure for using Plastigauge is as follows.

15 With the main bearing upper shells in place, carefully lay the crankshaft in position. Do not use any lubricant; the crankshaft journals and bearing shells must be perfectly clean and dry.

16 Cut several lengths of the appropriate-size Plastigauge (they should be slightly shorter than the width of the main bearings), and place one length on each crankshaft journal axis **(see illustration)**.

17 With the main bearing lower shells in position, refit the main bearing caps. Starting with the centre main bearing and working outwards, tighten the original main bearing cap bolts progressively to their specified torque. Take care not to disturb the Plastigauge, and *do not* rotate the crankshaft at any time during this operation.

18 Remove the main bearing cap bolts and carefully lift off the caps, keeping them in order. Again, take great care not to disturb the Plastigauge or rotate the crankshaft. If any of the bearing caps are difficult to remove, free them by carefully tapping them with a soft-faced mallet.

19 Compare the width of the crushed Plastigauge on each journal to the scale printed on the Plastigauge envelope, to obtain the main bearing running clearance **(see illustration)**. Compare the clearance measured with that given in the Specifications at the start of this Chapter.

20 If the clearance is significantly different from that expected, the bearing shells may be the wrong size (or excessively worn, if the original shells are being re-used). Before deciding that different-size shells are required, make sure that no dirt or oil was trapped between the bearing shells and the caps or block when the clearance was measured. If the Plastigauge was wider at one end than at the other, the crankshaft journal may be tapered.

21 If the clearance is not as specified, use the reading obtained, along with the shell thicknesses quoted in the Specifications, to calculate the necessary grade of bearing shells required. When calculating the bearing clearance required, bear in mind that it is always better to have the running clearance towards the lower end of the specified range, to allow for wear in use.

22 Where necessary, obtain the required grades of bearing shell, and repeat the running clearance checking procedure as described above.

23 On completion, carefully scrape away all traces of the Plastigauge material from the crankshaft and bearing shells. Use your fingernail, or a wooden or plastic scraper which is unlikely to score the bearing surfaces.

Final crankshaft refitting

Note: *It is strongly recommended that new main bearing cap bolts are used when finally refitting the crankshaft. Suitable sealant may be required when refitting the crankshaft rear oil seal housing.*

24 Carefully lift the crankshaft out of the cylinder block once more.

25 Where applicable, ensure that the oil spray jets are fitted to the bearing locations in the cylinder block.

26 Place the bearing shells in their locations as described earlier. If new shells are being fitted, ensure that all traces of protective grease are cleaned off using paraffin. Wipe dry the shells and connecting rods with a lint-free cloth. Liberally lubricate each bearing shell in the cylinder block/crankcase and cap with clean engine oil.

27 Similarly, fit the upper thrustwasher halves to the appropriate bearing location in the cylinder block as follows.

a) ***4-cylinder engines*** *- centre (No 3) main bearing.*
b) ***5-cylinder engine*** *- No 4 main bearing.*
c) ***6-cylinder engines*** *- No 5 main bearing.*

Ensure that the oil grooves in the thrustwasher halves face out towards the crankshaft journals.

> **HAYNES HiNT** ***Use a little grease to hold the thrustwasher halves in position.***

28 Lower the crankshaft into position.

29 Lubricate the lower bearing shells in the main bearing caps with clean engine oil. Make sure that the locating lugs on the shells engage with the corresponding recesses in the caps.

30 Fit the main bearing caps to their correct locations, ensuring that they are fitted the correct way round. Ensure that the thrustwasher halves are in place on the appropriate bearing cap (see paragraph 27) **(see illustrations)**.

31 Lightly lubricate the bolt threads, then fit the main bearing cap bolts, using new bolts if required (see Section 16 - it is strongly recommended that new bolts are used on all engines). Where applicable, ensure that the oil pick-up pipe support bracket is in place on the relevant bolts, as noted before removal. Tighten the bolts by hand only at this stage.

32 Progressively tighten the main bearing cap bolts to the specified torque, starting with the centre bearing cap, and working outwards. Where applicable, observe the two tightening stages given in the Specifications

2D

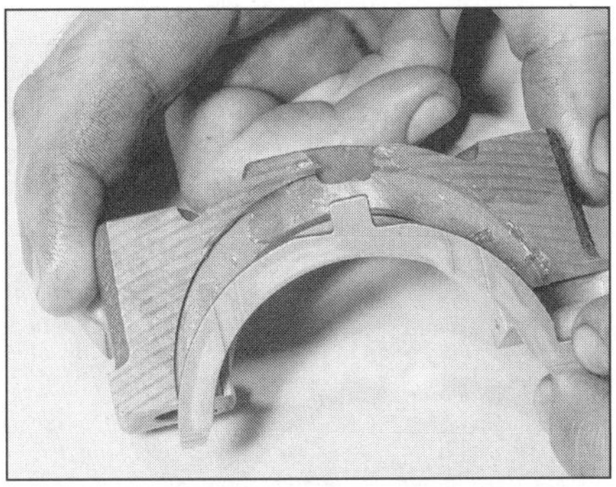

19.30a Fitting a thrustwasher half to a main bearing cap (use a little grease to hold the washer in position)

19.30b Fitting a main bearing cap

19.32a Tighten the main bearing cap bolts to the specified torque . . .

(see illustrations). If the bolts are angle-tightened, it is recommended that an angle-measuring gauge is used during this stage of the tightening, to ensure accuracy. If a gauge is not available, use a dab of white paint to make alignment marks between the bolt and bearing cap prior to tightening; the marks can then be used to check that the bolt has been rotated sufficiently during tightening.

33 Check that the crankshaft rotates freely.

34 Fit a new crankshaft rear oil seal to the housing, then refit the housing, using a new gasket, or suitable sealant, as applicable **(see illustrations)**.

35 Refit the piston/connecting rod assemblies as described in Section 20.

36 Proceed as follows according to engine type.

a) ***On 4-cylinder petrol engines**, where applicable refit the crankshaft sprocket, then refit the timing chain, timing chain cover, sump, and the flywheel/driveplate, as described in Part A of this Chapter.*

b) ***On 6-cylinder petrol engines**, where applicable refit the crankshaft sprocket, then refit the timing chain, lower timing chain cover, oil pump, sump, and the flywheel/driveplate, as described in Part B of this Chapter.*

c) ***On diesel engines**, where applicable refit the crankshaft sprocket, then refit the timing chain, timing chain cover, oil pump, oil baffle plate (where applicable), sump, and the flywheel/driveplate, as described in Part C of this Chapter.*

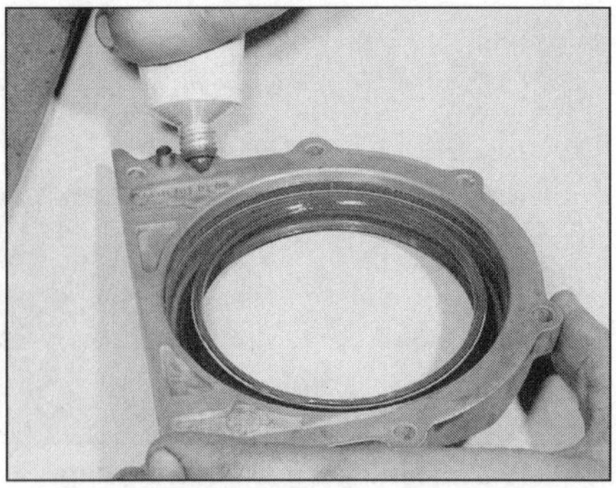

19.34a Applying sealant to the crankshaft rear oil seal housing

19.32b . . . then through the specified angle

20 Piston/connecting rod assembly - refitting and big-end bearing running clearance check

Selection of new bearing shells

Four-cylinder petrol engines

1 To determine the thickness of the new bearing shells required, the bearing diameter, crankshaft journal diameter, and bearing running clearance must be measured. The appropriate bearing thickness can be calculated as shown in the example for selection of new crankshaft bearing shells in Section 19.

2 A Mercedes-Benz dealer or an engine reconditioning specialist will be able to supply the appropriate bearing shells required. Refer to the following table for details of the bearing shells available.

Bearing shells	Bearing shell thickness
Standard	1.80 mm
Repair size 1	1.92 mm
Repair size 2	2.05 mm
Repair size 3	2.18 mm
Repair size 4	2.30 mm

Six-cylinder petrol engines

3 The thickness of the new bearing shells required can be determined using the method described previously for new crankshaft bearing shells on 4-cylinder petrol engines in Section 19. At the time of writing, no information was available regarding the availability of bearing shells for 6-cylinder petrol engines. A Mercedes-Benz dealer or an engine reconditioning specialist should be able to offer advice, and will be able to supply the appropriate bearings.

19.34b Tighten the crankshaft rear oil seal housing bolts to the specified torque

Diesel engines

4 The thickness of the new bearing shells required can be determined using the method described previously for new crankshaft bearing shells on 4-cylinder petrol engines in Section 19.

5 A Mercedes-Benz dealer or an engine reconditioning specialist will be able to supply the appropriate bearing shells required. Refer to the table given in paragraph 2 for 4-cylinder petrol engines for details of the bearing shells available.

Big-end bearing running clearance check

6 Clean the backs of the bearing shells, and the bearing locations in both the connecting rod and bearing cap.

7 Press the bearing shells into their locations, ensuring that the tab on each shell engages in the notch in the connecting rod and cap. Take care not to touch any shell's bearing surface with your fingers. If the original bearing shells are being used for the check, ensure that they are refitted in their original locations. The clearance can be checked in either of two ways.

8 One method is to refit the big-end bearing cap to the connecting rod, using the marks made or noted on removal to ensure that they are fitted the correct way around, with the bearing shells in place. With the original cap retaining bolts and nuts correctly tightened, use an internal micrometer or vernier caliper to measure the internal diameter of each assembled pair of bearing shells. If the diameter of each corresponding crankshaft journal is measured and then subtracted from the bearing internal diameter, the result will be the big-end bearing running clearance.

9 The second, and more accurate method is to use Plastigauge (see Section 19).

10 Ensure that the bearing shells are correctly fitted. Place a strand of Plastigauge on each (cleaned) crankpin journal.

11 Refit the (clean) piston/connecting rod assemblies to the crankshaft, and refit the big-end bearing caps, using the marks made or noted on removal to ensure that they are fitted the correct way around.

12 Refit the bearing cap nuts, and tighten the nuts to the specified torque in the two stages given in the Specifications. Take care not to disturb the Plastigauge, nor rotate the connecting rod during the tightening sequence.

13 Dismantle the assemblies without rotating the connecting rods. Use the scale printed on the Plastigauge envelope to obtain the big-end bearing running clearance.

14 If the clearance is significantly different from that expected, the bearing shells may be

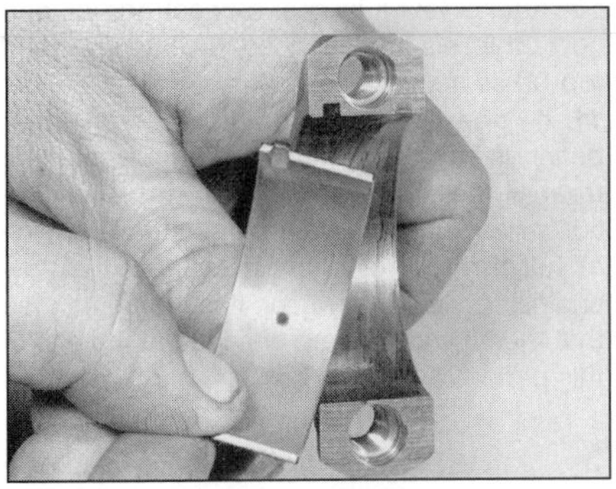

20.17 Fitting a big-end bearing shell to a connecting rod

the wrong size (or excessively worn, if the original shells are being re-used). Make sure that no dirt or oil was trapped between the bearing shells and the caps or block when the clearance was measured. If the Plastigauge was wider at one end than at the other, the crankshaft journal may be tapered.

15 On completion, carefully scrape away all traces of the Plastigauge material from the crankshaft and bearing shells. Use your fingernail, or some other object which is unlikely to score the bearing surfaces.

Final piston/connecting rod refitting

Note: *It is strongly recommended that new big-end bearing cap bolts are used when finally refitting the piston/connecting rod assemblies. A piston ring compressor tool will be required for this operation.*

16 Note that the following procedure assumes that the main bearing caps are in place (see Section 19).

17 Ensure that the bearing shells are correctly fitted as described earlier. If new shells are being fitted, ensure that all traces of the protective grease are cleaned off using paraffin **(see illustration)**. Wipe dry the shells and connecting rods with a lint-free cloth.

18 Lubricate the cylinder bores, the pistons, and piston rings, then lay out each piston/connecting rod assembly in its respective position.

19 Start with assembly No 1. Make sure that the piston rings are still spaced as described in Section 18, then clamp them in position with a piston ring compressor.

20 Insert the piston/connecting rod assembly into the top of cylinder No 1. Ensure that the arrow on the piston crown points towards the timing chain end of the engine, and that the identifying marks on the connecting rods and big-end caps are positioned as noted before removal. Using a block of wood or hammer handle against the piston crown, tap the assembly into the cylinder until the piston crown is flush with the top of the cylinder **(see illustration)**. Where applicable, take great care not to damage the piston cooling oil spray jets as the piston/connecting rod assemblies are refitted.

21 Ensure that the bearing shell is still correctly installed. Liberally lubricate the crankpin and both bearing shells. Taking care not to mark the cylinder bores, pull the piston/connecting rod assembly down the bore and onto the crankpin. Refit the big-end bearing cap. Note that the bearing shell locating tabs must abut each other.

22 Lightly lubricate the bolt threads, then screw the big-end bearing cap bolts by hand into position in the connecting rods, using new bolts if required (see Section 16 - it is strongly recommended that new bolts are used on all engines).

23 Progressively tighten the bolts to the specified torque. Where applicable, observe the two tightening stages given in the Specifications **(see illustration)**. If the bolts are angle-tightened, it is recommended that an angle-measuring gauge is used during this stage of the tightening, to ensure accuracy. If a gauge is not available, use a dab of white paint to make alignment marks between the bolt and bearing cap prior to tightening; the marks can then be used to check that the bolt has been rotated sufficiently during tightening.

24 Once the bearing cap bolts have been correctly tightened, rotate the crankshaft. Check that it turns freely; some stiffness is to be expected if new components have been fitted, but there should be no signs of binding or tight spots.

25 Refit the remaining piston/connecting rod assemblies in the same way.

26 Proceed as follows according to engine type.

a) ***On 4-cylinder petrol engines****, refit the sump and the cylinder head as described in Part A of this Chapter.*

b) ***On 6-cylinder petrol engines****, refit the oil pump, sump and cylinder head, as described in Part B of this Chapter.*

c) ***On diesel engines****, refit the oil pump, oil baffle plate (where applicable), the sump and cylinder head, as described in Part C of this Chapter.*

21 Engine - initial start-up after overhaul

1 With the engine refitted in the vehicle, double-check the engine oil and coolant levels. Make a final check that everything has been reconnected, and that there are no tools or rags left in the engine compartment.

Petrol engines

2 Remove the spark plugs, then disable the fuel system (models with fuel injection) and ignition system by removing the fuel pump relay, and disconnecting the coil HT lead, or the Direct Ignition module wiring plug (Chapter 5).

3 Turn the engine on the starter until the oil pressure warning light goes out, then refit the spark plugs, refit the fuel pump relay (where applicable) and reconnect the coil HT lead or ignition module plug, as applicable.

20.20 Tapping a piston/connecting rod assembly into the cylinder bore

20.23 Angle-tightening a big-end bearing cap bolt

Diesel engines

4 Disconnect the wiring from the stop solenoid on the fuel injection pump (Chapter 4), then turn the engine on the starter until the oil pressure warning light goes out. Reconnect the wire to the stop solenoid.

5 Prime the fuel system (Chapter 4).

6 Fully depress the accelerator pedal, turn the ignition key to position "2", and wait for the preheating warning light to go out.

All engines

7 Start the engine, noting that this may take a little longer than usual, due to the fuel system components having been disturbed.

8 While the engine is idling, check for fuel, water and oil leaks. Don't be alarmed if there are some odd smells and smoke from parts getting hot and burning off oil deposits.

9 Assuming all is well, keep the engine idling until hot water is felt circulating through the top hose, then switch off the engine.

10 After a few minutes, recheck the oil and coolant levels as described in Chapter 1, and top-up as necessary.

11 If new pistons, rings or crankshaft bearings have been fitted, the engine must be treated as new, and run-in for the first 500 miles (800 km). *Do not* operate the engine at full-throttle, or allow it to labour at low engine speeds in any gear. It is recommended that the oil and filter are changed at the end of this period.

Chapter 3
Cooling, heating and ventilation systems

Contents

Air conditioning system - general information and precautions 9
Air conditioning system refrigerant level check ....See Chapter 1
Coolant level check ....See *"Weekly checks"*
Coolant pump - removal and refitting 7
Coolant renewal ....See Chapter 1
Cooling fan - removal and refitting 5
Cooling system electrical switches - removal and refitting 6
Cooling system hoses - disconnection and renewal 2
General information and precautions 1
Heater/ventilation components - removal and refitting 8
Radiator - removal, inspection and refitting 3
Thermostat - removal, testing and refitting 4

Degrees of difficulty

Easy, suitable for novice with little experience	**Fairly easy,** suitable for beginner with some experience	**Fairly difficult,** suitable for competent DIY mechanic	**Difficult,** suitable for experienced DIY mechanic	**Very difficult,** suitable for expert DIY or professional

Specifications

System type

4 cylinder petrol engines	Pressurised, with crossflow or downflow radiator, auxiliary belt-driven electromagnetically-coupled cooling fan, centrifugal water pump driven by auxiliary belt, bypass thermostat and remote expansion tank.
6 cylinder petrol engines	Pressurised, with crossflow or downflow radiator, auxiliary belt-driven, thermostatically controlled thermo-viscous coupled cooling fan, centrifugal water pump driven by auxiliary belt, bypass thermostat, remote expansion tank and overflow tank.
Diesel engines	Pressurised, with crossflow or downflow radiator, auxiliary belt-driven, thermostatically controlled thermo-viscous or electromagnetically-coupled cooling fan, centrifugal water pump driven by auxiliary belt, bypass thermostat, remote expansion tank and overflow tank.

General

Pressure cap opening pressure:	
Models up to 1987	1.2 bar
Models from 1987 onwards	1.4 bar
Maximum coolant temperature:	
Models up to 1987	125°C
Models from 1987 onwards	129°C
Electromagnetically-coupled cooling fan thermo-switch:	
Switch on temperature	102°C max
Switch off temperature	98°C

Thermostat

Petrol engines:	
Opening commences	87± 2°C
Fully open	102°C
Non-turbo diesel engines:	
Opening commences	85 ± 2°C
Fully open	94°C
Turbo-diesel engines:	
Opening commences	80 ± 2°C
Fully open	100°C

Coolant

Type	Soft water and Mercedes approved antifreeze	
Water/antifreeze mixture ratio:*		
Protection to -37°C	50% water, 50% antifreeze by volume	
Protection to -45°C	45% water, 55% antifreeze by volume	

***Note:** *Do not use coolant that is greater than 55% antifreeze by volume, as this will impair the heat dissipation and anti-freezing qualities.*

Cooling system capacity:	
4-cylinder petrol engines:	
With automatic heating system	8.5 litres
With air conditioning/climate control	9.5 litres
6-cylinder petrol engines:	
With automatic heating system	9.0 litres
With air conditioning/climate control	9.5 litres
4-cylinder 2.0 litre diesel engines:	
With automatic heating system	8.5 litres
With air conditioning/climate control	9.0 litres
5-cylinder 2.5 litre normally-aspirated diesel engines:	
With automatic heating system	9.0 litres
With air conditioning/climate control	9.5 litres
5-cylinder 2.5 litre turbo-diesel engines (all models)	9.0 litres

Torque wrench settings

Torque wrench settings	Nm	lbf ft
Coolant pump to crankcase/timing cover:		
4-cylinder petrol engine	10	8
6-cylinder petrol engine	23	17
Diesel engine	10	8
Coolant pump to housing (diesel engine)	10	8
Coolant pump belt pulley:		
4-cylinder petrol engine	15	11
6-cylinder petrol engine	10	8
Diesel engine	15	11
Cooling fan to electromagnetic/viscous coupling:		
4-cylinder petrol engine	25	18
6-cylinder petrol engine	10	8
4-cylinder diesel engine	25	18
5-cylinder diesel engine	10	8
Viscous fan coupling to coolant pump/bearing body	45	33
Electromagnetic coupling to coolant pump/support bracket	6	4
Radiator drain plug	2	1
Thermostat housing cover:		
4-cylinder petrol engine:		
With metal thermostat housing	10	8
With plastic thermostat housing	8	6
6-cylinder petrol engine	6	4
Diesel engine	10	8
Thermostat housing to cylinder head (4 cylinder petrol engine only)	20	15
Alternator mounting bracket bolts	45	33
Cylinder block drain plug	30	22
Automatic transmission fluid cooler unions	20	15

1 General information and precautions

The cooling system is of the pressurised, pump-assisted thermo-syphon type, comprising a radiator, coolant pump, thermostat, electromagnetic cooling fan, expansion tank and associated hoses.

One of two types of radiator are used, depending on model. On cars fitted with air conditioning, the radiator is a light alloy crossflow type with plastic coolant compartments at each side. On cars without air conditioning, the radiator is a light alloy gravity flow type with plastic coolant compartments at the top and bottom. On cars also equipped with automatic transmission, a transmission fluid cooler is incorporated in either the right-hand side or bottom coolant compartment accordingly.

The thermostat is of the twin-valve type incorporating a main valve, which opens at a predetermined temperature to allow coolant flow to the radiator, and a bypass valve, which is open when the main valve is closed to allow coolant circulation through the engine and heater.

The impeller-type coolant pump is located on the front of the engine and is belt-driven from the crankshaft pulley.

The electromagnetic cooling fan is mounted on the coolant pump spindle, and operates in conjunction with a temperature-sensitive switch located in the cylinder head. When the engine coolant reaches a predetermined temperature, the electromagnetic coupling is energized and the fan is rigidly locked to the pump pulley. At lower temperatures, the coupling is released and the fan is allowed to freewheel, turning only under the influence of bearing friction or the inrush of air when the car is moving forwards.

The plastic expansion tank is located on the right-hand side of the engine compartment. and collects the coolant which is displaced from the system as it expands due to the rise in temperature. The displaced coolant is returned to the radiator as the system cools.

3.2a Slacken the clips and disconnect the top hose . . .

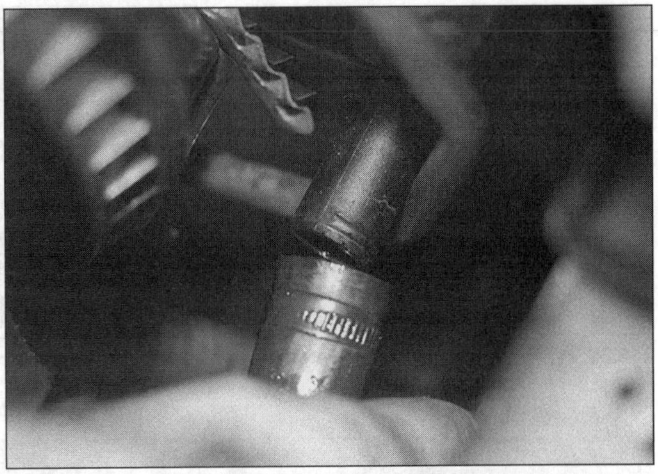

3.2b . . . and bottom hoses from the radiator stubs (6-cylinder petrol engine shown)

Precautions

Warning: Do not attempt to remove the expansion tank pressure cap, or to disturb any part of the cooling system, while the engine is hot, as there is a high risk of scalding. If the expansion tank pressure cap must be removed before the engine and radiator have fully cooled (even though this is not recommended), the pressure in the cooling system must first be relieved. Cover the cap with a thick layer of cloth, to avoid scalding, and slowly unscrew the pressure cap until a hissing sound is heard. When the hissing stops, indicating that the pressure has reduced, slowly unscrew the pressure cap until it can be removed; if more hissing sounds are heard, wait until they have stopped before unscrewing the cap completely. At all times, keep your face well away from the pressure cap opening, and protect your hands.

Warning: Do not allow antifreeze to come into contact with your skin, or with the painted surfaces of the vehicle. Rinse off spills immediately, with plenty of water. Never leave antifreeze lying around in an open container, or in a puddle in the driveway or on the garage floor. Children and pets are attracted by its sweet smell, but antifreeze can be fatal if ingested.

Warning: If the engine is hot, the electric cooling fan may start rotating even if the engine and ignition are switched off. Be careful to keep your hands, hair, and any loose clothing well clear when working in the engine compartment.

2 Cooling system hoses - disconnection and renewal

1 The number, routing and pattern of hoses will vary according to model, but the same basic procedure applies. Before commencing work, make sure that the new hoses are to hand, along with new hose clips if needed. It is good practice to renew the hose clips at the same time as the hoses.

2 Drain the cooling system, as described in Chapter 1, saving the coolant if it is fit for re-use. Squirt a little penetrating oil onto the hose clips if they are corroded.

3 Release the hose clips from the hose concerned. Three types of clip are used; worm-drive, spring and "sardine-can". The worm-drive clip is released by turning its screw anti-clockwise. The spring clip is released by squeezing its tags together with pliers, at the same time working the clip away from the hose stub. The "sardine-can" clips are not re-usable, and are best cut off with snips or side cutters.

4 Unclip any wires, cables or other hoses which may be attached to the hose being removed. Make notes for reference when reassembling if necessary.

5 Release the hose from its stubs with a twisting motion. Be careful not to damage the stubs on delicate components such as the radiator, or thermostat housings. If the hose is stuck fast, the best course is often to cut it off using a sharp knife, but again be careful not to damage the stubs.

6 Before fitting the new hose, smear the stubs with washing-up liquid or a suitable rubber lubricant to aid fitting. Do not use oil or grease, which may attack the rubber.

7 Fit the hose clips over the ends of the hose, then fit the hose over its stubs. Work the hose into position. When satisfied, locate and tighten the hose clips.

8 Refill the cooling system as described in Chapter 1. Run the engine, and check that there are no leaks.

9 Recheck the tightness of the hose clips on any new hoses after a few hundred miles.

10 Top-up the coolant level if necessary (see "*Weekly checks*").

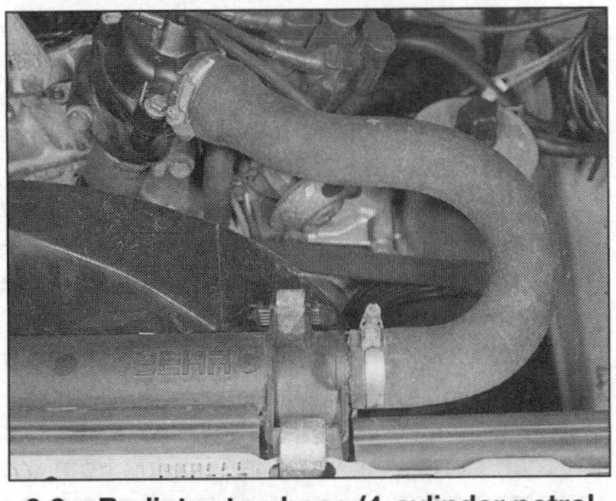

3.2c Radiator top hose (4-cylinder petrol engine shown)

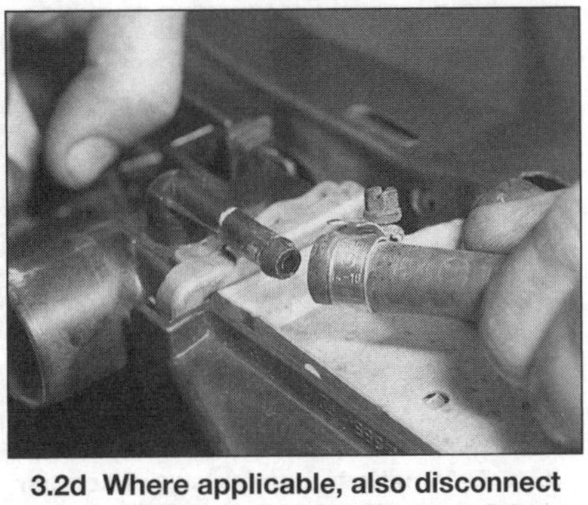

3.2d Where applicable, also disconnect the overflow hose from the top of the radiator

3 Radiator - removal, inspection and refitting

Removal

1 Refer to Chapter 1 and drain the cooling system.

2 Slacken the clips and disconnect the top, bottom and where applicable, overflow hoses from the radiator **(see illustrations)**.

3

3.3a Prise out the fan shroud retaining spring clips . . .

3.3b . . . then disengage the shroud from the radiator and place it over the fan blades

3.3c On models with a split fan cowl, remove the locking pin (arrowed) . . .

3.3d . . . then detach the cowl ring by rotating it to the left and place it over the fan blades

3.3e Prise off the spring clips . . .

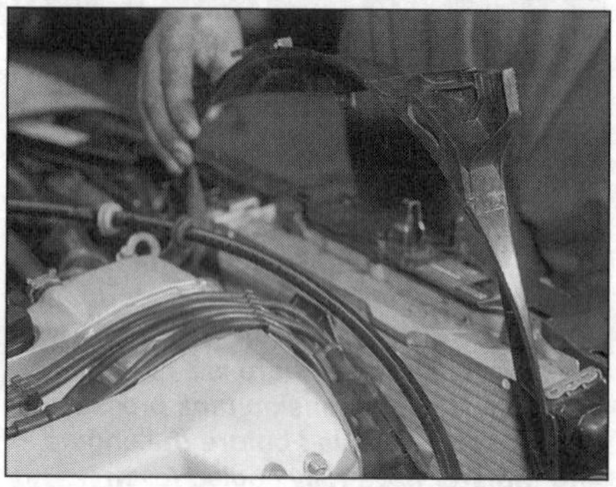

3.3f . . . then release the fan cowl from the radiator and remove it from the engine bay

3.4a Remove the screws . . .

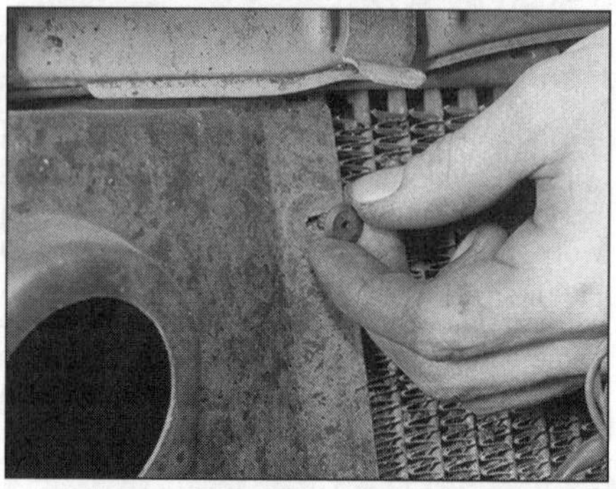

3.4b . . . and the expander bodies . . .

3.4c . . . located at the top and bottom of the side panels (4-cylinder engine shown)

3.5a Disconnect the hoses from the automatic transmission fluid cooler (6-cylinder petrol engine shown)

3.5b Automatic transmission fluid cooler unions (arrowed) (4-cylinder petrol engine shown)

3 Carefully prise out the retaining spring clips securing the top of the fan shroud to the radiator. Disengage the shroud from the radiator and place it over the fan blades **(see illustrations)**.

4 On cars without air conditioning, unscrew the plastic expander screws securing the side panels to the radiator and remove the expander body **(see illustrations)**.

5 On automatic transmission models, clamp the transmission fluid cooler hoses using self-grip wrenches with protected jaws or similar tools and unscrew the hose unions from the radiator bottom or side compartments, as applicable **(see illustrations)**. Carefully withdraw and cover the hoses.

3.6a Prise out the metal . . .

3.6b . . . and where applicable, the plastic spring clips (arrowed)

3.7a Lift the radiator from the engine bay (6-cylinder petrol engine with air conditioning shown)

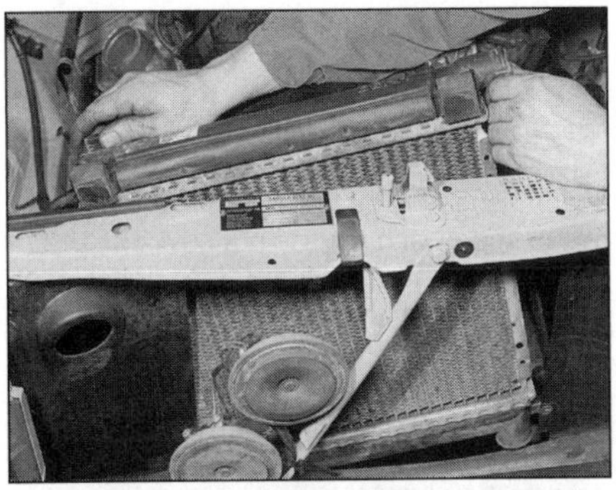
3.7b Removing the radiator (4-cylinder petrol engine without air conditioning shown)

3.9 Ensure that the radiator lower mountings engage with the rubber grommets (arrowed)

4.3 Slacken the clip and detach the coolant hose from the thermostat cover (4-cylinder petrol engine shown)

4.4 Remove the thermostat cover from the housing

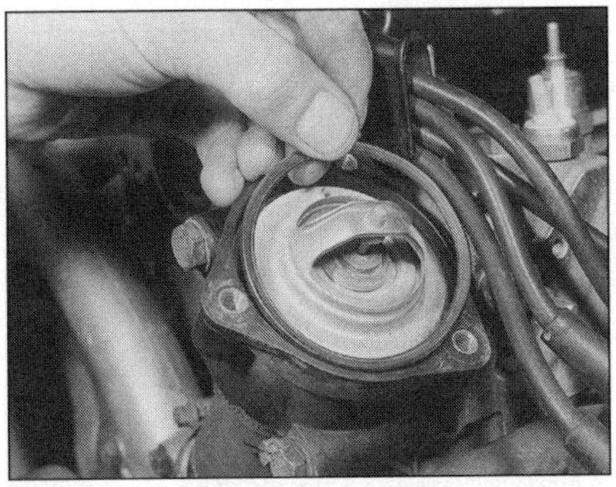
4.5a Recover the seal . . .

4.5b . . . then lift the thermostat from its housing

6 Carefully prise out the retaining spring clips securing the top of the radiator to the body panel **(see illustrations)**.

7 Lift the radiator upwards to disengage the lower mounting lugs and remove it from the car **(see illustration)**.

Inspection

8 Carefully examine the radiator for signs of leaks, corrosion of the alloy core, or damage to the plastic side, top or bottom compartments. Should the radiator require attention, this work should be left to a specialist due to the nature of its construction. Clear the radiator core of flies, small leaves or other debris by brushing or hosing. Check the condition of all hoses, clips, mountings and retaining spring clips and renew as necessary.

Refitting

9 Refitting the radiator is the reverse sequence to removal, but ensure that the lower mounting lugs properly engage with their rubber grommets **(see illustration)**. After fitting, fill the cooling system as described in Chapter 1. On automatic transmission models, check the transmission fluid level as described in Chapter 1.

4 Thermostat - removal, testing and refitting

Removal

1 The thermostat is located in a housing which is bolted to the side of the coolant pump.

2 Disconnect the battery negative cable and position it away from the terminal. Drain the cooling system as described in Chapter 1.

3 Slacken the clip and detach the coolant hose from the thermostat cover **(see illustration)**.

4 Unscrew the securing bolts, and remove the thermostat cover from the housing. If the cover is stuck to the housing, tap it gently, or carefully rock it back and forth to free it - do not lever between the mating faces **(see illustration)**.

5 Recover the seal, then lift the thermostat from its housing, noting its orientation **(see illustrations)**.

Testing

6 A rough test of the thermostat may be made by suspending it with a piece of string in a container full of water. Heat the water to bring it to the boil - the thermostat must open by the time the water boils. If not, renew it.

7 If a thermometer is available, the precise opening temperature of the thermostat may be determined; compare with the figures given in the *Specifications*. The opening temperature is also marked on the thermostat.

8 Note that a thermostat which fails to close completely as the water cools must also be considered faulty, and should be renewed.

Refitting

9 Commence refitting by thoroughly cleaning the mating faces of the cover and the housing.

10 Refit the thermostat to the housing, noting that the spring loaded side faces into the housing. Note that on diesel engined models, the recess on the thermostat rim must be aligned with the rib on the housing cover. On petrol engined models, position the thermostat such that the air bleed valve is at the highest point in the housing.

11 Lay a new seal in position on the housing, ensuring that it is correctly seated.

12 Fit the cover to the thermostat housing, then refit the securing bolts, and tighten to the specified torque.

13 Reconnect the coolant hose to the thermostat cover.

14 Refill the cooling system as described in Chapter 1.

5 Cooling fan - removal and refitting

Thermo-viscous coupled fan

Removal

Note: *On petrol models, this procedure involves the use of a special tool, which is required to lock the cooling fan pulley to the fan bearing bracket. If the tool cannot be borrowed or hired from a dealer, a substitute can be fabricated from a length of 4 mm diameter rod. On diesel engined models, it is recommended that the correct Mercedes locking tool is obtained, to avoid damaging the fan pulley and its associated components.*

1 Disconnect the battery negative cable and position it away from the terminal. Refer to Chapter 1 and remove the auxiliary drivebelt.

2 Remove the screws and detach the plastic panels from above and below the radiator. Where applicable, release the coolant hose from the clip on the upper panel.

3 On models with a one-piece fan shroud, prise off the metal spring clips, then detach the shroud from the radiator. Pass the shroud over the fan and allow it to rest between the engine and the fan blades - refer to Section 3.

4 On models with a split fan shroud, remove the locking pin and rotate the shroud ring to the left, to disengage it from the fan shroud. Pass the shroud ring over the fan and allow it to rest between the engine and the fan blades - refer to Section 3.

5 Prise off the metal spring clips, then detach the fan shroud from the radiator and remove it from the engine bay, followed by the shroud ring.

6 On petrol engined models, turn the cooling fan pulley until the locking hole on its rear surface lines up with the recess in the fan bearing bracket. Insert the special tool (see paragraph 1) so that the pulley is locked to the bearing bracket and no rotation is possible **(see illustration)**.

7 On diesel engined models, the fan pulley shaft should be counter-held with a special Mercedes tool, which grips the edge of the fan pulley with the auxiliary belt still in place. Due to the high torque to which the viscous clutch assembly centre bolt is tightened, the use of improvised tools is not advised.

8 Slacken and withdraw the bolts, then detach the fan blade assembly from the viscous clutch unit. On models with a one-piece fan shroud, remove the shroud from the engine bay **(see illustration)**.

9 Slacken and withdraw the centre bolt, then detach the clutch assembly from the pulley shaft. If required, remove the bolts and detach the pulley from the shaft **(see illustrations)**.

5.6 Cooling fan pulley shaft locked using home made tool (arrowed) - fan, coupling and pulley removed for clarity

5.8 Slacken and withdraw the bolts and detach the fan blade assembly from the viscous clutch unit

5.9a Slacken and withdraw the centre bolt . . .

5.9b . . . then detach the clutch assembly from the pulley shaft

5.9c If required, remove the bolts, recover the washer . . .

5.9d . . . and detach the pulley from the shaft

5.10 **Ensure that the coupling centre bolt is tightened to the specified torque**

5.13 **Undo the centre retaining bolt and remove the fan from the pump spindle**

5.14 **Slacken and withdraw the bolts (arrowed), then remove the coolant pump pulley from its spindle**

5.15a Location of coupling left hand securing bolts (arrowed) - early models

1 Coupling body 2 Wiring connector

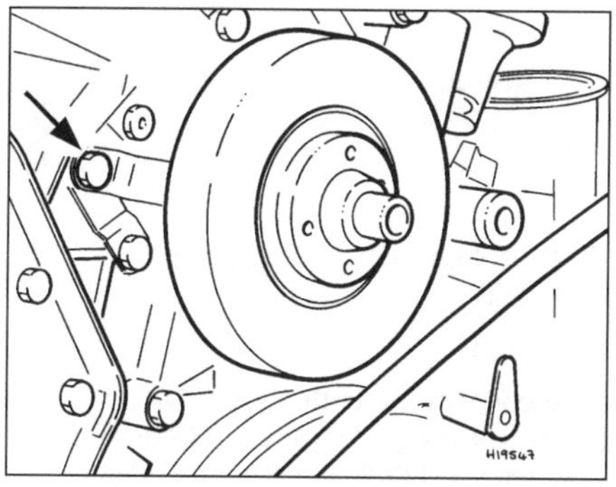

5.15b Location of coupling bracket securing bolt (arrowed) - early models

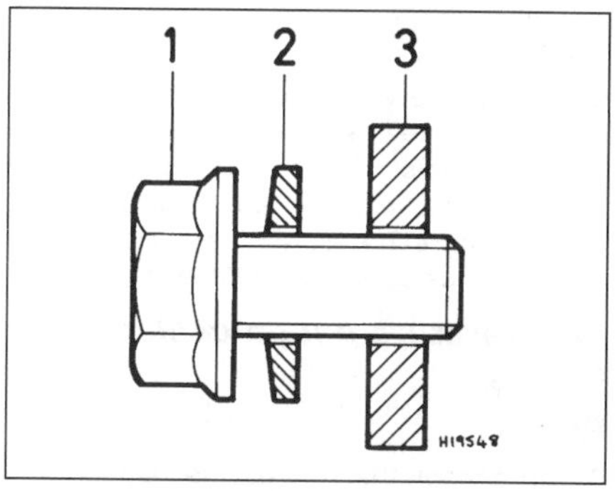

5.17 Fan retaining bolt, washer and spacer arrangement

1 Bolt 2 Dished washer 3 Spacer

Refitting

10 Refitting is a reversal of removal. Ensure that all bolts are tightened to the specified torque **(see illustration)**.

Electromagnetically coupled fan

Removal

11 Disconnect the battery negative cable and position it away from the terminal. On 4-cylinder petrol engined models, carry out the following:

a) Refer to Chapter 1 and drain the cooling system.
b) Refer to Section 3 and remove the radiator.
c) Refer to Chapter 4 and remove the air cleaner.

12 Refer to Chapter 1 and remove the auxiliary drivebelt from the cooling pump pulley.

13 Undo the centre retaining bolt and remove the fan from the pump spindle **(see illustration)**.

14 Slacken and withdraw the bolts, then remove the coolant pump pulley from its spindle **(see illustration)**.

15 On early models with multiple auxiliary drivebelts, undo the three bolts securing the coupling body to the coolant pump and pump bracket. Withdraw the coupling, unplug the wiring at the connector and remove the unit from the engine **(see illustrations)**.

16 On later models with a single ribbed auxiliary drivebelt, undo the bolts at the rear of the coupling body that secure it to the mounting plate. Withdraw the coupling, unplug the wiring at the connector and remove the unit from the engine.

Refitting

17 Refitting is a reversal of removal. Ensure that the arrangement of the washers on the fan retaining bolt is as shown in the illustration **(see illustration)** and tighten all fixings to the correct torque where specified.

6 Cooling system electrical switches - removal and refitting

Note: *Procedures for the removal and refitting of the coolant sensors associated with the fuelling and ignition systems are detailed in the relevant Part of Chapter 4.*

Coolant level sensor

Removal

1 The sensor is mounted in the side of the coolant expansion tank **(see illustration)**. Ensure that the engine is cold, then refer to Chapter 1 and partially drain the cooling system, so that only the expansion tank is emptied.

2 Ensure that the ignition is switched off, then unplug the wiring from the coolant level switch at the connector.

3 Remove the circlip and withdraw the sensor from the expansion tank. Recover the O-ring seal if it is loose.

4 Connect a continuity tester, or a workshop multimeter, set to measure resistance across the sensor terminals. With the float held at the top of its travel, the contacts should be open circuit. If the float is allowed to hang at the bottom of its travel, the contacts should close, indicated by a short circuit.

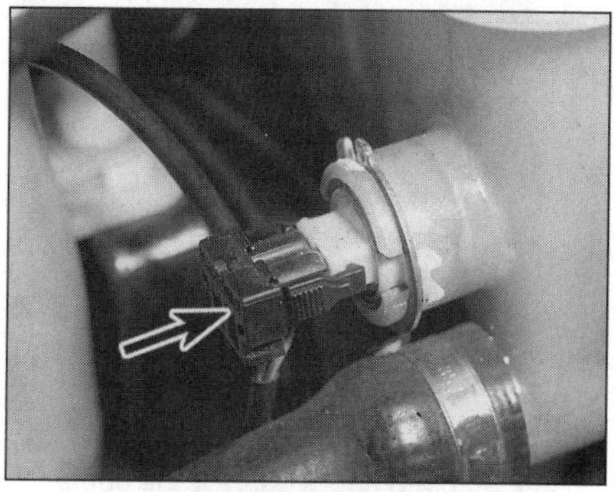

6.1 Coolant level sensor location (arrowed)

7.3a Slacken the hose clips (arrowed) . . .

7.3b . . . then detach the bypass hose from the coolant pump and remove the thermostat housing from the engine

7.4 Disconnect the radiator bottom hose and heater return hose from the coolant pump

Refitting

5 Refit the level sensor by following the removal procedure in reverse, noting the following points:

a) Fit a new O-ring seal to the sensor body.
b) On completion, top-up the cooling system as described in Chapter 1.

Temperature gauge coolant sensor

Removal

6 The sensor that drives the temperature gauge is threaded into the upper surface of the cylinder head, on the left hand side of the engine. Do not confuse it with the fuelling/ ignition system coolant temperature sensor, which is mounted nearby.

7 Ensure that the engine is cold, then refer to Chapter 1 and partially drain the cooling system.

8 Ensure that the ignition is switched off, then unplug the wiring from the sensor at the connector.

9 Unscrew the sensor from the cylinder head and recover the sealing ring.

Refitting

10 Refitting is a reversal of removal, noting the following points:

a) Use a new sealing ring.
b) On completion, top-up the cooling system with respect to Chapter 1.

7 Coolant pump - removal and refitting

4-cylinder petrol engined models

Removal

1 Disconnect the battery negative cable and position it away from the terminal. Refer to Chapter 1 and drain the cooling system.

2 With reference to Section 5, remove the cooling fan and auxiliary belt pulley from the coolant pump.

3 Remove the thermostat as described in Section 4, then unbolt the thermostat housing from the cylinder head. Slacken the hose clips, detach the bypass hose from the coolant pump and remove the thermostat housing from the engine **(see illustrations)**.

4 Slacken the hose clips and disconnect the radiator bottom hose and heater return hose from the ports on the coolant pump **(see illustration)**. Similarly, disconnect the auxiliary hose from the left hand side of the pump.

5 On early models with multiple auxiliary drivebelts, refer to Section 5 and remove the electromagnetic coupling from the coolant pump spindle.

6 On later models with a single, ribbed auxiliary drivebelt, unplug the wiring from the electromagnetic coupling at the connector and release the cable from the retaining clips - refer to Section 5 for details.

7 Refer to Chapter 5A and remove the alternator. Unbolt the alternator mounting bracket from the coolant pump.

8 Slacken and withdraw the coolant pump retaining bolts, then lift off the coolant pump **(see illustrations)**. Make a careful note of the fitted location of each bolt, as they are of different lengths.

Refitting

9 Carefully clean the coolant pump and cylinder block mating surfaces, removing all traces of the old gasket. Take care to avoid scoring the surfaces as this will cause leakage. Similarly, clean the mating surfaces of the thermostat housing and the cylinder head.

10 Refit the coolant pump by following the removal procedure in reverse, noting these points **(see illustration)**:

a) Use new gaskets and tighten all bolts to the correct torque, where specified.
b) Refit the electromagnetic coupling with reference to Section 5.
c) Refit and tension the auxiliary drivebelt(s) with reference to Chapter 1.
d) On completion, refill the cooling system with reference to Chapter 1.

7.8a Slacken and withdraw the coolant pump retaining bolts (left hand side bolts arrowed) . . .

7.8b . . . then lift off the coolant pump

7.10 Use a new gasket on refitting

7.17a Disconnect the heater return pipe from the coolant pump . . .

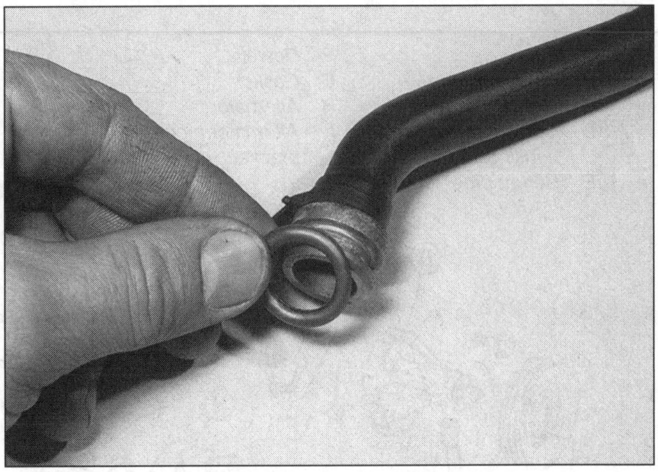

7.17b . . . and recover the O-ring seal

6-cylinder petrol engined models

Removal

11 Disconnect the battery negative cable and position it away from the terminal. Refer to Chapter 1 and drain the cooling system.

12 Refer to Chapter 1 and remove the auxiliary drivebelt and tensioner.

13 With reference to Chapter 10, unbolt the power steering pump from the engine, leaving the hydraulic hoses connected and position it away from the work area.

14 Refer to Chapter 4 and remove the air cleaner and inlet scoop moulding.

15 Access to the coolant pump may be improved by removing the distributor (see Chapter 5C) and the auxiliary belt cover panel.

16 Where applicable on early models, undo the six securing bolts and move the air conditioning compressor to one side, with the refrigerant hoses still attached.

17 Slacken and withdraw the bolt, then disconnect the heater return pipe from the coolant pump. Recover the O-ring seal **(see illustrations)**. Release the pipe from the retaining clip on the cooling fan bearing bracket.

18 On vehicles with an oil cooler, unbolt the coolant pipe union from the side of the coolant pump and recover the O-ring seal. Release the coolant pipe retaining bracket from the inlet manifold support strut by removing the screw.

19 Refer to Section 4 and remove the thermostat.

20 Slacken the clips and disconnect the cylinder head and radiator top hoses from the coolant pump **(see illustrations)**.

21 Slacken and withdraw the four retaining bolts, then lift the coolant pump away from the engine **(see illustration)**. Recover the two dowel sleeves and the sealing ring.

Refitting

22 Carefully clean the coolant pump and cylinder block mating surfaces, removing all traces of the old gasket. Take care to avoid scoring the surfaces as this will cause leakage.

23 Refitting is a reversal of removal, noting the following points:

a) Access to the rearmost coolant pump retaining bolts is limited. Insert them using a rod and magnet, or a magnetic hex bit and extension bar.

b) Tighten all bolts to the correct torque, where specified.

c) Renew the heater return hose-to-coolant pump seal, the coolant pump-to-cylinder block seal and the thermostat to housing seal.

d) Refit and tension the auxiliary drivebelt(s) with reference to Chapter 1.

e) On completion, refill the cooling system with reference to Chapter 1.

Diesel engined models

Removal

24 Disconnect the battery negative cable and position it away from the terminal. Refer to Chapter 1 and drain the cooling system.

25 On models with an electromagnetically-coupled cooling fan, refer to Chapter 1 and remove the auxiliary drivebelt and tensioner.

26 Refer to Section 5 and remove the viscous or electromagnetically-coupled (as applicable) cooling fan from the coolant pump.

27 On models with a viscous-coupled cooling fan, remove the auxiliary drivebelt as described in Chapter 1, then undo the bolts and remove the pulley from the coolant pump.

28 Slacken the clips and disconnect all the

7.20a Disconnect the radiator . . .

7.20b . . . and cylinder head hoses (arrowed) from the coolant pump

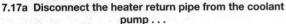

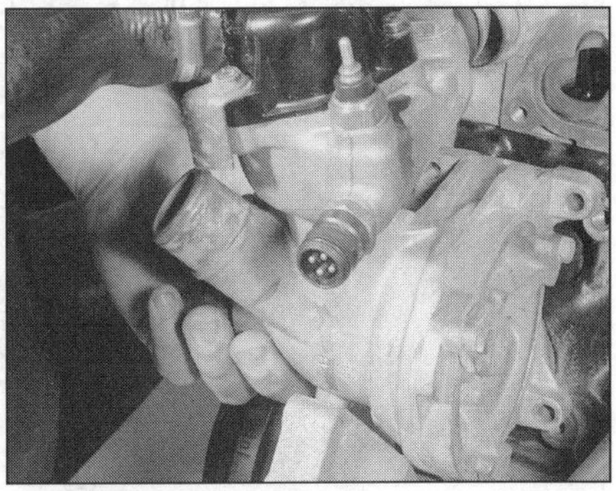

7.21 Slacken and withdraw the bolts, then remove the coolant pump from the engine

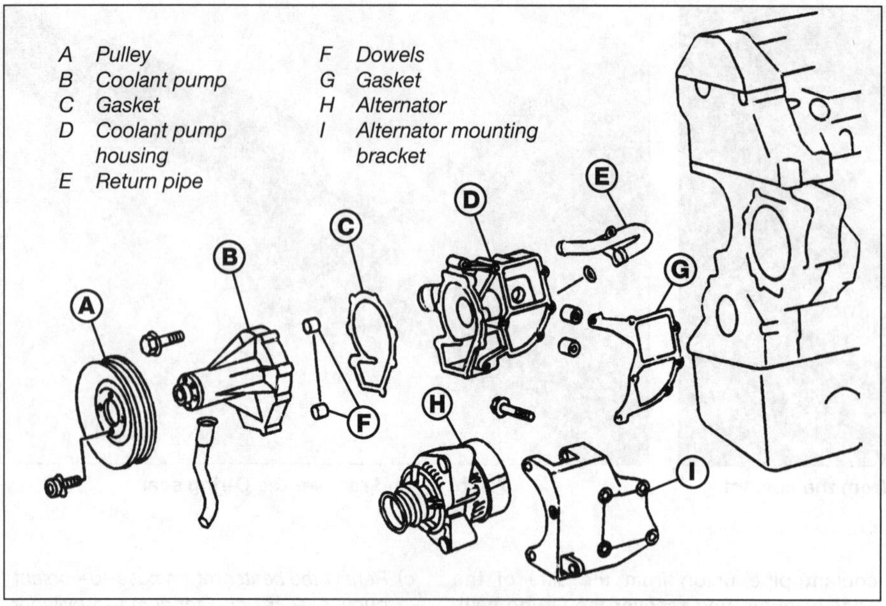

7.28 Coolant pump assembly (diesel engined models)

hoses from the coolant pump housing **(see illustration)**. Unbolt the heater return pipe from the pump at the union and recover the O-ring seal.

29 With reference to Chapter 5A, remove the alternator, then unbolt the alternator mounting bracket from the engine.

30 Unbolt the coolant pump hosing and remove it, together with the coolant pump itself, from the engine block. Recover the gasket.

31 Unbolt the coolant pump from the housing and recover the gasket.

Refitting

32 Carefully clean the coolant pump and cylinder block mating surfaces, removing all traces of the old gasket. Take care to avoid scoring the surfaces as this will cause leakage.

33 Refitting is a reversal of removal, noting the following points:

a) Use new gaskets and tighten all bolts to the correct torque, where specified.

b) Refit the electromagnetic/viscous coupled cooling fan with reference to Section 5.

c) Refit and tension the auxiliary drivebelt(s) with reference to Chapter 1.

d) On completion, refill the cooling system with reference to Chapter 1.

8 Heater/ventilation components - removal and refitting

Note: *This Section is only applicable to models equipped with the standard automatic heating system - it does not cover models fitted with air conditioning; see Section 9 for further details.*

Heater unit

Removal

1 Drain the cooling system as described in Chapter 1.

2 Remove the facia as described in Chapter 11.

3 Release the cable retaining tie on the left-hand side of the heater unit, and undo the screw on the wiring terminal.

4 Disconnect the wiring plug at the rear of the blower motor switch **(see illustration)**.

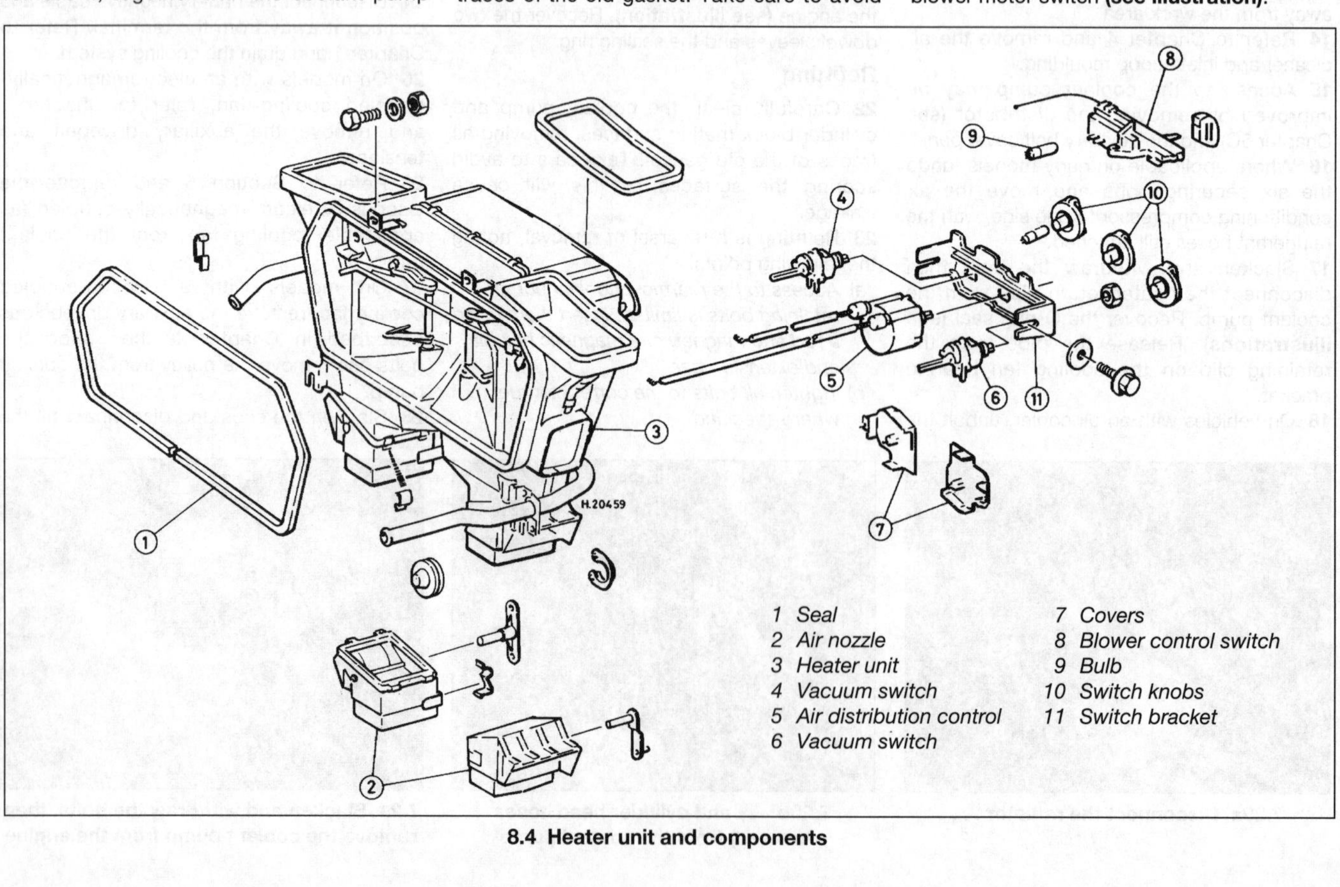

8.4 Heater unit and components

5 Disconnect the vacuum lines and illumination bulb wiring at the rear of the heater controls.

6 Disconnect the heater feed hose at the rear of the cylinder head.

7 Place a container beneath the engine, under the disconnected feed hose.

8 Disconnect the heater return hose at the thermostat housing. Using compressed air from a foot pump, blow the residual coolant out of the heater matrix by inserting the foot pump hose into the heater return hose. The coolant will be forced out of the feed hose into the container.

9 Undo the two bolts and separate the return flow pipe at the matrix flange joint **(see illustration)**.

10 Pull off the right-hand air duct at the heater unit below the return flow pipe.

11 Undo the two bolts and separate the feed flow pipe at the matrix flange joint on the other side of the heater.

12 Pull off the left-hand air duct at the heater unit below the feed flow pipe.

13 Force off the feed flow pipe holder at the bulkhead on the left-hand side.

14 Unscrew the mounting bracket nut below the feed flow pipe holder.

15 Unscrew the right-hand mounting bracket nut below the return flow pipe.

16 Unscrew the two mounting nuts at the top of the heater unit.

17 Disconnect the control cable at the blower motor slide switch.

18 Disconnect the control cable at the main air flap on the side of the heater unit.

19 Withdraw the heater unit from the mounting studs, lift the unit upwards and remove it from the car.

Refitting

20 Refitting is the reverse sequence to removal. When connecting the blower control cable, connect and secure the cable at the slide switch, then move the switch to blower position 'MAX'. Connect the control cable end to the main air flap lever, open the main air flap up to its stop, then clip the outer cable into position.

21 On completion, refill the cooling system as described in Chapter 1.

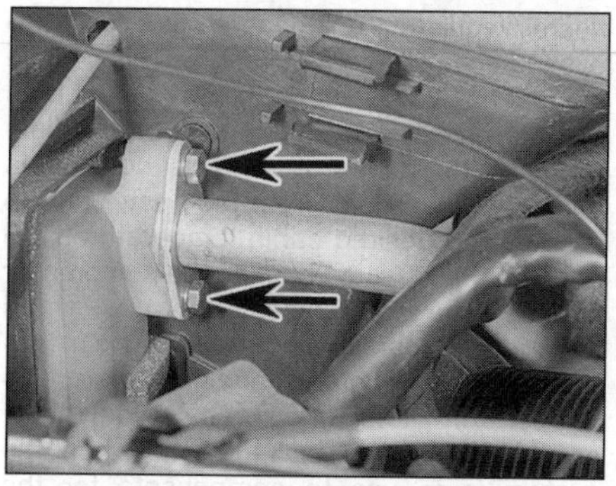

8.9 Undo the return flow pipe bolts (arrowed)

Heater matrix

Removal

22 Remove the heater unit as described earlier in this Section.

23 Undo the screws on the heater unit air inlet.

24 Carefully prise off all the retaining clips along the top, on both sides, and on the bottom of the heater unit.

25 Force the connecting linkage out of the left- and right-hand demister flap arms.

26 Push back the lock on the left-hand demister flap, while at the same time pulling off the connecting linkage lever.

27 Pull off the gaskets on the left- and right-hand demister nozzle connections.

28 Push off the connecting levers of the mixed air flaps on the left- and right-hand levers.

29 Prise the left- and right-hand mixed air flap connecting lever ball heads off the ball sockets.

30 Separate the two halves of the heater unit and remove the mixed air flaps.

31 Undo the matrix frame retaining screws. Remove the frame and take out the matrix.

Refitting

32 Refitting is the reverse sequence to removal.

Heater blower motor

Removal

33 Remove the air inlet cover over the plenum chamber as described in Chapter 12.

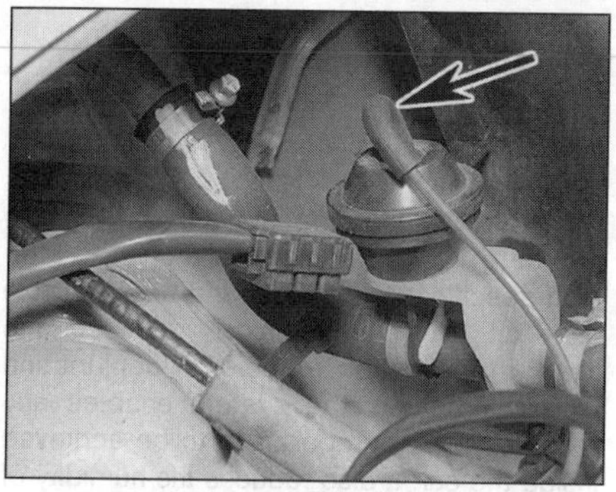

8.34 Disconnect the vacuum hose (arrowed)

34 Disconnect the vacuum hose at the heater valve **(see illustration)**.

35 Undo the two screws on the blower motor cover **(see illustration)**.

36 Lift the rubber sealing strip off the inner bulkhead wall and undo the two bulkhead retaining screws each side **(see illustration)**.

37 Move the bulkhead wall upwards and forwards, then remove the blower motor cover.

38 Remove the cable-ties and disconnect the blower motor wiring plug.

39 Undo the blower motor retaining bolts and remove the motor sideways out of the housing **(see illustration)**.

Refitting

40 Refitting is the reverse sequence to removal.

Heater valve

Removal

41 Remove the air inlet cover over the plenum chamber as described in Chapter 12.

42 Remove the expansion tank pressure cap slowly to release any residual pressure in the cooling system.

43 Disconnect the vacuum hose at the heater valve, located adjacent to the heater blower motor in the plenum chamber.

44 Disconnect the coolant hoses and remove the heater valve from its bracket.

Refitting

45 Refitting is the reverse sequence to removal, but note that the side of the valve marked 'water inlet' must be towards the engine. Top-up the cooling system on completion.

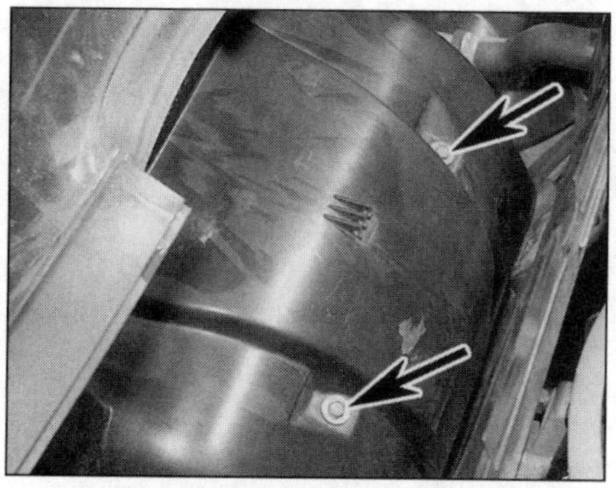

8.35 Undo the blower motor cover screws (arrowed)

8.36 Inner bulkhead retaining screws (arrowed)

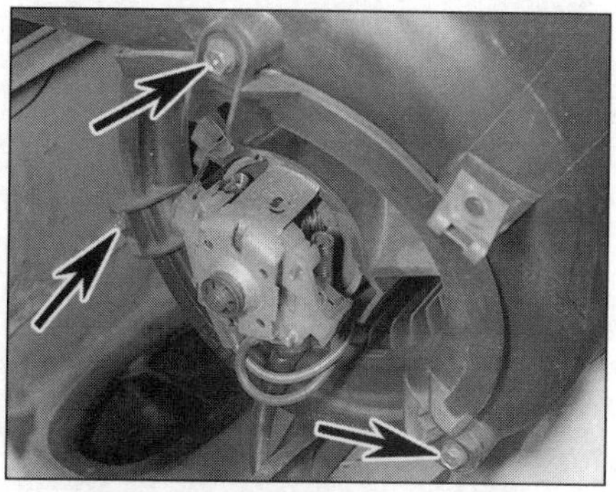

8.39 Blower motor retaining bolts (arrowed)

9 Air conditioning system - general information and precautions

An air conditioning system is fitted as standard equipment on later high-specification models, and was available as an optional extra on some lower-specification models. In conjunction with the heater, the system enables any reasonable air temperature to be achieved inside the car, it also reduces the humidity of the incoming air, aiding demisting even when cooling is not required.

The refrigeration circuit of the air conditioning system functions in a similar way to a domestic refrigerator. A compressor, belt-driven from the crankshaft pulley, draws refrigerant in its gaseous state from an evaporator. The refrigerant heats up as a result of being compressed, but is then passed through a condenser (mounted in front of the engine radiator) where it loses heat and enters its liquid state. After dehydration, the refrigerant is passed through an evaporator (mounted alongside the heater/ventilation unit) where it is allowed to expand and reverts to being gas. This change of state has the effect of absorbing heat from the air passing over the evaporator fins, reducing its temperature. This cool air is mixed with warm air from the heater unit to achieve the desired cabin temperature. The refrigerant is directed back to the compressor and the cycle is then repeated.

Various subsidiary controls and sensors protect the system against excessive temperature and pressures. Additionally, engine idle speed is increased when the system is in use to compensate for the additional load imposed by the compressor. Electronic sensors detect the rotational speed differential between the engine and the compressor - if this becomes too great (due to a malfunctioning compressor), the compressor clutch is disengaged, to preserve the drivebelt.

Although the refrigerant is not itself toxic, in the presence of a naked flame (or a lighted cigarette) it forms a highly toxic gas.

Do not allow refrigerant lines to be exposed to temperatures in excess of 110°C (230°F), for example during welding or paint drying operations.

Do not operate the air conditioning system if it is known to be short of refrigerant, or component damage may result.

Note: *The air conditioning electronic control system can only be tested using dedicated equipment. For this reason, it is recommended that problems with the operation of the air conditioning system are referred to a Mercedes dealer for diagnosis. A description of the refrigerant level checking procedure is given in Chapter 1.*

Warning: The refrigeration circuit contains pressurised liquid refrigerant. The refrigerant is potentially dangerous, and should only be handled by qualified persons. Refrigerant that is allowed to come into contact with the skin will cause severe frostbite. It is not itself poisonous, but in the presence of a naked flame (including a cigarette), it forms a poisonous gas. Uncontrolled discharging of the refrigerant is dangerous and is also extremely damaging to the environment. For these reasons, disconnection of any part of the system without specialised knowledge and equipment is not recommended.

Chapter 4 Part A
Carburettor fuel system

Contents

Air cleaner air temperature control system - testing and component renewal 3
Air cleaner assembly and filter element - removal and refitting 2
Carburettor - removal and refitting 10
Fuel gauge sender unit - removal and refitting 5
Fuel pump - removal and refitting 4
Fuel tank - removal and refitting 6
General information and precautions 1
Idle speed and mixture adjustment . . . . . See Chapter 1A
Inlet manifold - removal and refitting 11
Inlet manifold pre-heater - removal and refitting 12
Pierburg 2E-E carburettor fuel system - general information and component renewal 9
Stromberg 175 CDT carburettor - general information and component renewal 8
Throttle cable - removal, refitting and adjustment 7

Degrees of difficulty

Easy, suitable for novice with little experience	**Fairly easy,** suitable for beginner with some experience	**Fairly difficult,** suitable for competent DIY mechanic	**Difficult,** suitable for experienced DIY mechanic	**Very difficult,** suitable for expert DIY or professional

Specifications

Fuel pump

Type	Mechanical, driven by eccentric lobe on intermediate shaft via a pushrod
Delivery pressure (at cranking speed)	0.20 - 0.40 bar
Delivery rate (at cranking speed)	0.15 litre per 10 seconds

Stromberg 175 CDT carburettor data

Description	Variable choke, constant depression side-draught
Main jet	100
Jet needle	UC
Float needle valve	2.25 mm
Float level	18 -19 mm

Pierburg 2E-E carburettor data

Description	Twin choke down-draught, with electronic mixture and idle speed control. Closed-loop fuelling control on catalyst-equipped models.
Venturi diameter:	
Primary	23 mm
Secondary	29 mm
Barrel diameter:	
Primary	29 mm
Secondary	34 mm
Main jet:	
Primary	X 110
Secondary	X 135
Air correction jet:	
Primary	92.5
Secondary	70
Idle jet	X 50
Idle air jet	5
Float needle valve	2.5
Float height setting	26.5 - 28.5 mm

Coolant sensor

Resistance:	
20°C	2.2 to 2.8 kΩ
80°C	0.29 to 0.37 kΩ

Recommended fuel

Minimum octane rating:	
Pierburg 2E-E carburettor:	
Vehicles without catalytic converter (RÜF engines)	95 RON unleaded* or 98 RON leaded
Vehicles with catalytic converter (KAT engines)	95 RON unleaded
Stromberg 175 CDT	95 RON unleaded* or 98 RON leaded

* *With ignition timing adjustment*

Torque wrench settings

	Nm	lbf ft
Fuel tank retaining nuts	20	15
Fuel level sender retaining nut	40	30

1 General information and precautions

General information

On all carburettor variants, the major components of the fuel system include either a Stromberg or Pierburg carburettor, the fuel tank, a mechanical fuel pump, metal and rubber supply and return fuel hoses, an air cleaner assembly and a cartridge type fuel filter, mounted in the fuel tank.

The fuel tank is mounted towards the front of the luggage compartment, inside the vehicle.

Fuel is drawn from the tank, through the filter canister, by the fuel pump. It is fed via a supply hose to the carburettor float chamber, where a float and needle valve mechanism regulates the level of fuel held in the chamber. Surplus fuel is directed back to the fuel tank by a fuel return hose.

The air cleaner is mounted either over the camshaft cover, or directly over the carburettor inlet (depending on model) and contains a replaceable paper and gauze filter cartridge. All variants have a thermostatically controlled flap valve, mounted in the air cleaner assembly. This optimises the temperature of the inlet air entering the carburettor, by automatically blending air at ambient temperature with hot air, drawn from around the exhaust manifold.

The type of carburettor fitted depends on the age of the vehicle and the intended market. A Stromberg CDT 175 carburettor or a Pierburg 2E-E carburettor may be fitted.

On the Stromberg CDT 175 carburettor, cold start fuelling and fast idle are controlled by a thermo-delay valve. This contains an electrically heated bi-metallic strip which controls the supply of vacuum to the choke pull-down diaphragm. When the engine is started from cold, the thermo-delay valve interrupts the supply of vacuum to the diaphragm and the choke is held closed. As the bi-metallic strip in the delay valve is heated by current supplied from the ignition switch, the vacuum supply to the pull-down diaphragm is gradually reinstated and the choke opens, returning the idle speed and fuel mixture to normal. Also fitted is an electromagnetic fuel cut-off valve; this prevents run-on when the engine ignition is switched off, and also serves to limit maximum engine speed by closing when the crankshaft speed exceeds a pre-determined threshold.

Vehicles specified for certain markets are equipped with Pierburg 2E-E electronically-controlled carburettors. Idle speed and fuelling (mixture) are controlled by a throttle valve actuator and a choke actuator respectively. The engine operating parameters are monitored by a series of sensors and the overall system is managed by an electronic control unit (ECU). At engine speeds above idle, fuelling is controlled by the choke actuator altering the position of the choke flap and hence the amount of air entering the engine. At engine speeds at or near idle, the choke actuator controls fuelling by altering the position of a needle within an idle air correction jet; this either enriches or weakens the mixture entering the engine via the idle jet. Engine idle speed is monitored by the ECU and compared with a set of "mapped" values stored in memory. Idle speed is maintained at an optimum for all operating conditions by the ECU, which controls the position of the throttle valve via the throttle valve actuator. Closed-loop position control is achieved by means of a throttle valve potentiometer. Secondary functions carried out by the two actuators include deceleration fuel cut-off, maximum engine speed limitation and anti-run on fuel cut-off.

Precautions

Many of the operations described in this Chapter involve the disconnection of fuel lines, which may cause an amount of fuel spillage. Before commencing work, refer to the *Warning* and *Caution* below as well as the information in *"Safety First!"* at the beginning of this manual.

Warning: Petrol is extremely flammable - great care must be taken when working on any part of the fuel system. Keep the area well ventilated - open all available doors and windows to create a through-draught. Do not smoke, or allow any naked flames or uncovered light bulbs near the work area. Note that gas powered domestic appliances with pilot flames, such as heaters, boilers and tumble-dryers, also present a fire hazard - bear this in mind if you are working in an area where such appliances are present. Always keep a suitable fire extinguisher close to the work area and familiarise yourself with its operation before starting work. Wear eye protection when working on fuel systems and wash off any fuel spilt on bare skin immediately with soap and plenty of water. Note that fuel vapour is just as dangerous as liquid fuel; a vessel that has been emptied of liquid fuel will still contain vapour and could be potentially explosive.

Caution: When working with fuel system components, pay particular attention to cleanliness - dirt entering the fuel system may cause blockages which will lead to poor running.

2 Air cleaner assembly and filter element - removal and refitting

Removal

1 Detach the inlet ducting that runs from the air cleaner to the front of the engine bay.
2 Detach the warm air ducting from the base of the inlet air pre-heating flap valve.
3 On models with a Stromberg carburettor,

2.3a Slacken the hose clips at the carburettor . . .

2.3b . . . and the air cleaner . . .

2.3c . . . and remove the inlet ducting - Stromberg carburettor

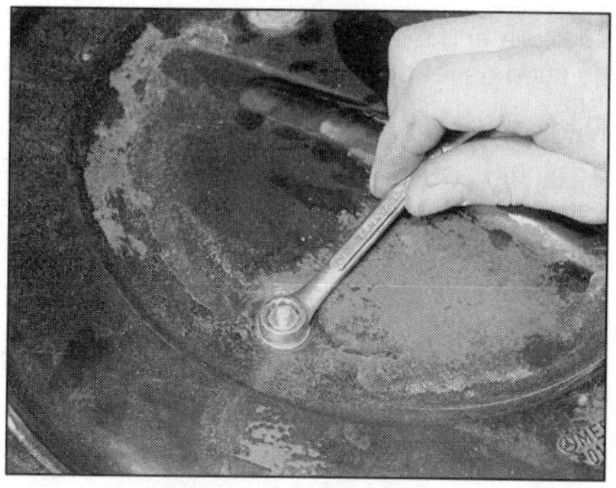

2.6a Undo the nuts . . .

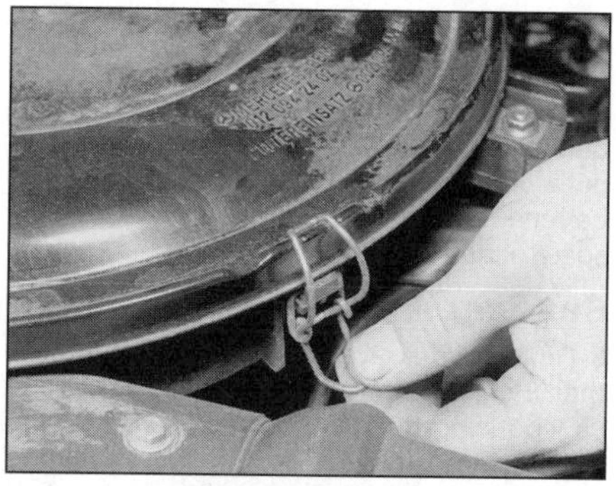

2.6b . . . release the clips and lift off the air cleaner cover

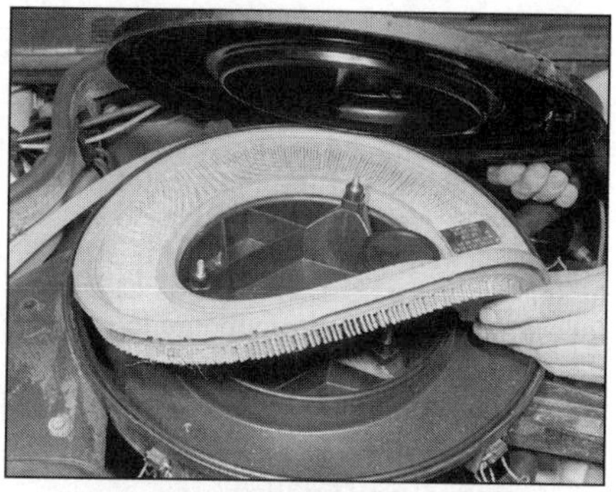

2.6c Remove the filter element

slacken the clips and remove the ducting from the air cleaner to the carburettor **(see illustrations)**.

4 On models with a Pierburg carburettor, remove the nut that secures the inlet ducting to the camshaft cover.

5 Pull off the crankcase ventilation hose from the port on the underside of the lower half of the air cleaner.

6 Undo the nuts, release the clips, and lift off the air cleaner cover. Remove the filter element. Remove the securing screws/nuts and lift off the lower section of the air cleaner **(see illustrations)**. On models with Pierburg carburettors, recover the rubber seal.

7 On later models with Stromberg carburettors and air cleaners with external clip fastenings, unscrew the nuts and disengage the lower section of the air cleaner from the clips.

Refitting

8 Refitting is a reversal of removal. Ensure that the air filter element is fitted the correct way up, according to the markings on its upper surface. Tighten all fixings to the correct torque, where specified.

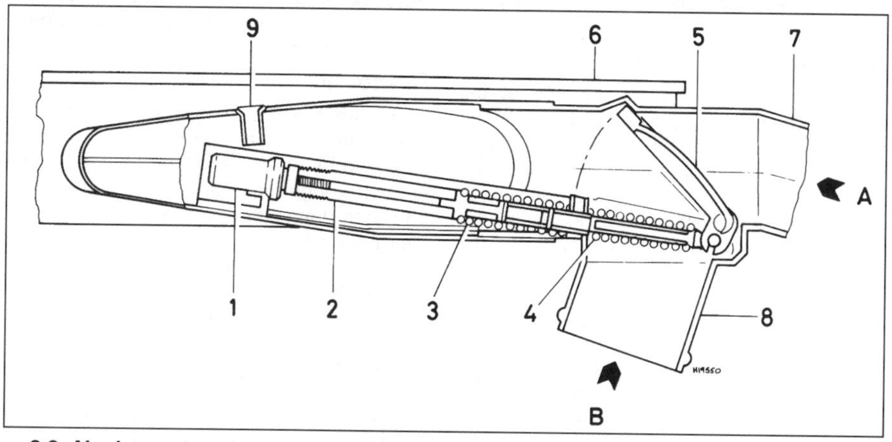

3.2 Air cleaner temperature control system - shown in fully open position (cold start conditions)

1 Thermostat
2 Control rod
3 Main compression spring
4 Secondary compression spring
5 Flap valve
6 Air cleaner
7 Air inlet duct
8 Air inlet duct
9 Thermostat compensating air supply duct
A Cold inlet air
B Hot inlet air

3 Air cleaner air temperature control system - testing and component renewal

4A

Testing

1 Pull off the ducting that runs from the air cleaner inlet to the front of the engine compartment.

2 Remove the screws and detach the pre-heater flap valve from the air cleaner air inlet. Detach the warm air ducting from the base of the valve **(see illustration)**.

3 Direct a stream of warm air over the thermostat, at the rear of the valve housing and observe the flap valve through the inlet, at the front of the housing. The thermostat should move the flap valve and close off the warm air inlet when its temperature exceeds 30°C. If this is not the case, renew the thermostat as described in the following sub-section.

Thermostat renewal

4 With the flap valve housing removed from the air cleaner inlet, carefully prise the

4.3 Removing the fuel pump

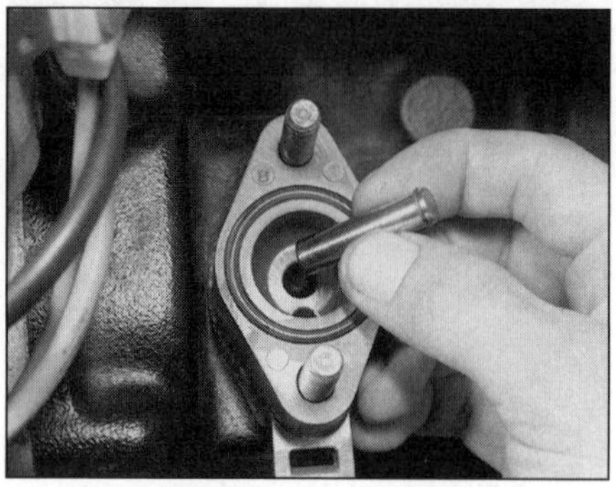

4.4a Withdraw the pushrod . . .

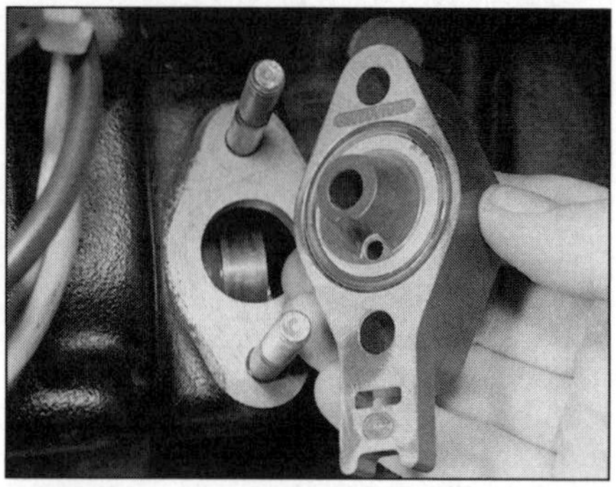

4.4b . . . and then lift off the insulating block

thermostat from its mounting and detach it from the pushrod.

5 To fit the new thermostat, first push the control rod and its spring back into the housing, then press the thermostat into its mounting. Release the pushrod, ensuring that it engages with the end of the thermostat.

6 Refit the valve housing to the air cleaner by following the removal procedure in reverse, then refit the inlet ducting.

4 Fuel pump - removal and refitting

Removal

Note: *This procedure involves the disconnection of fuel lines - refer to the precautions given in Section 1, and in "Safety first!" at the beginning of this manual before proceeding.*

1 Disconnect the battery negative cable and position it away from the terminal.

2 Position a small container underneath the fuel pump and pad the surrounding area with absorbent rags. Slacken the clips and disconnect the fuel supply and return hoses from the fuel pump. Label each hose for position, to aid correct refitting later.

3 Remove the securing nuts and washers, then lift off the fuel pump **(see illustration)**. Be prepared for fuel spillage, and take adequate fire precautions.

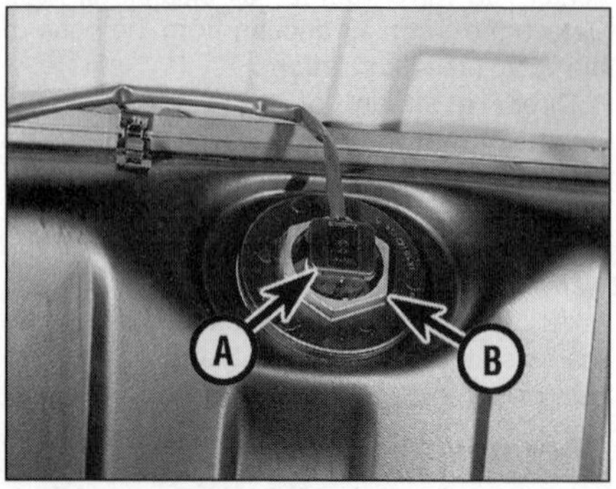

5.4 Fuel gauge sender unit
A Wiring connector B Retaining nut

4 Withdraw the pushrod and then lift off the insulating block **(see illustrations)**.

5 Inspect the O-ring seal in the insulating block. If it shows signs of damage or deterioration, the entire insulating block must be renewed, as the seals are not available as spare parts.

Refitting

6 Refitting is a reversal of removal, but note that the pushrod must be inserted with the circlip facing the fuel pump. Ensure that the pushrod can move freely in the insulating block aperture, before refitting the fuel pump.

5 Fuel gauge sender unit - removal and refitting

Warning: Observe the precautions in Section 1 before working on any component in the fuel system. The following procedure must be carried out in a well ventilated area, to avoid the build-up of hazardous fumes.

Removal

1 If the full tank is full, at least 8 litres of fuel must be pumped or siphoned out of the tank before commencing work, to avoid spillage. This is particularly important if the sender unit is thought to be faulty and you are unsure of the amount of fuel left in the tank. Ideally, the operation should be carried out with the fuel tank empty.

2 Disconnect the battery negative lead and position it away from the terminal.

3 Remove the load space floor carpet, then extract the clip fixings and pull back the fuel tank cover panel for access to the fuel tank - refer to Chapter 11 for more detail.

4 Unplug the wiring connector from the top of the gauge sender unit **(see illustration)**. Secure the connector with string or wire, to prevent from slipping down behind the tank.

5 Unscrew the large retaining nut and lift the sender unit from the tank - allow it to drain for a few seconds before removing it completely.

6 Recover the sealing rings from the tank aperture and discard them - new items must be used on refitting.

Refitting

7 Refitting is a reversal of removal, noting the following points:

a) If fitting a new sender unit, remove the protective tape and extract the locking pin before attempting to fit the unit to the tank.
b) Renew the tank aperture sealing rings.
c) Tighten the sender unit retaining nut securely.
d) Ensure that the sender unit wiring plug is securely reconnected.
e) Test drive the vehicle and then check around the area of sender unit for signs of fuel leakage, before refitting the trim panels.

6 Fuel tank - removal and refitting

Warning: The following procedure must be carried out in a well ventilated area, to avoid the build-up of hazardous fumes.

Removal

1 The fuel tank must be emptied before the operation can be started. This is best achieved by waiting until the tank is almost empty through the course of normal driving, and then draining out the remainder via the filler neck either by siphoning or by using a hand pump.

2 Park the vehicle on a level surface and chock the front roadwheels. Raise the rear of the vehicle, and support it securely on axle stands (see *"Jacking and vehicle support"*).

Warning: The use of an inspection pit is not advised; petrol vapours are heavier than air and can quickly build up on the floor of the pit, causing a potential hazard.

3 Disconnect the battery negative lead and position it away from the terminal.

4 From under the vehicle, disconnect the fuel supply, return and vent hoses from the ports on the underside of the fuel tank. Carefully label each hose to aid refitting later. Plug the open ends of the ports and hoses to minimise leakage and prevent the ingress of dirt.

5 Release the large rubber closing grommet from the fuel tank ports.

6 Working in the luggage compartment, extract the retaining clips and peel back the carpet. Release the press-studs and retaining clips, then remove the fuel tank cover panel **(see illustrations)**.

7 With reference to Section 5, unplug the wiring from the fuel gauge sender unit at the connector. Release the wiring from its clips.

8 Undo the fuel tank securing nuts, lift the tank slightly and then pull out the drain hose. Note the routing of the drain hose to ensure correct refitting. Separate the filler neck from the bodywork and recover the sealing ring(s) and sleeves **(see illustration)**.

9 Lift the tank upwards for clearance, then pull it towards the rear of the vehicle and remove it from the luggage compartment. Recover the padding strips if they are loose.

10 Unscrew and remove the fuel strainer from the tank, recovering the O-ring seal. Wash out all traces of sediment, using clean fuel. Refit the strainer, using a new O-ring seal and tighten it securely.

11 If the fuel tank is contaminated with sediment or water, remove the gauge sender unit as described in Section 5, and swill the tank out with a quantity clean fuel. If the tank is severely corroded or shows signs of leakage, it should either be repaired by a specialist or renewed.

Warning: Do not attempt to repair the tank yourself by welding, soldering or brazing. The tank will contain an explosive mixture of air and fuel vapour, even when emptied of liquid fuel.

Refitting

12 Refit the fuel tank by following the removal procedure in reverse, noting the following points:

a) Tighten all fixings to the correct torque, where specified.

b) Ensure that the padding strips are correctly refitted.

c) Ensure that the fuel tank drain hose is correctly routed, as noted before removal.

d) Ensure that the sender unit wiring plug is securely reconnected.

e) Test drive the vehicle and then check around the area of all disturbed components for signs of fuel leakage.

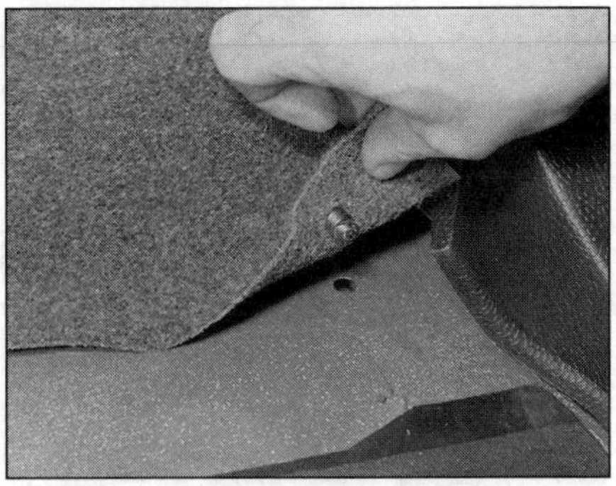

6.6a Release the press-studs . . .

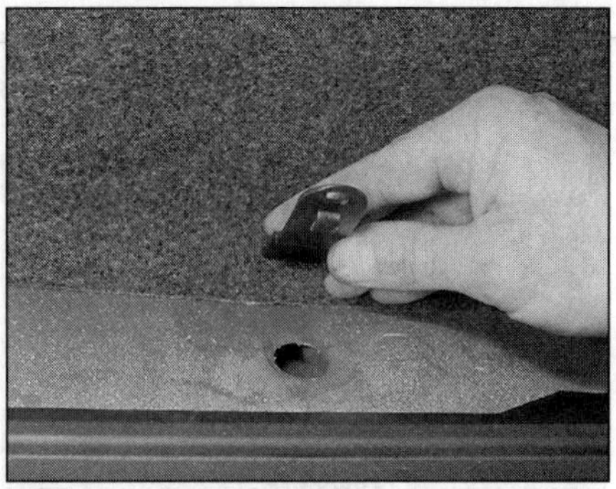

6.6b . . . and retaining clips from the fuel tank cover panel

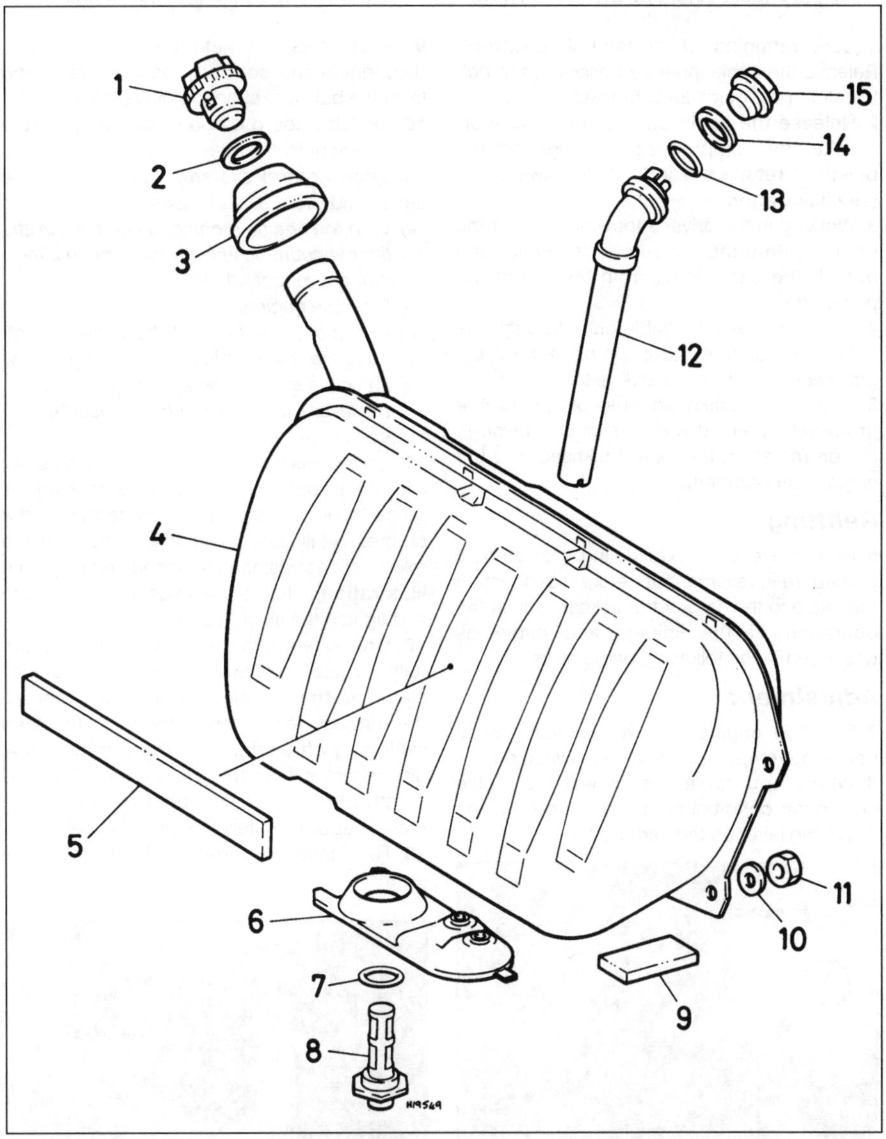

6.8 Fuel tank and associated components

1 Filler cap
2 Sealing ring
3 Sealing sleeve
4 Fuel tank
5 Rear padding strip
6 Closing grommet
7 Strainer seal
8 Strainer
9 Bottom padding strip
10 Washer
11 Nut
12 Fuel gauge sender unit
13 O-ring
14 O-ring
15 Sender unit nut

7 Throttle cable - removal, refitting and adjustment

Removal

1 Working in the engine compartment, disconnect the throttle cable inner from the carburettor guide lever by prising out the

4A

7.1 Disconnect the throttle cable inner from the carburettor guide lever by prising out the square retaining block (arrowed)

square retaining block **(see illustration)**. Release the cable inner by passing it through the slot in the guide lever bracket.

2 Release the cable outer from its support bracket by compressing the lugs on the plastic retainer and withdrawing it **(see illustration)**.

3 Working in the driver's footwell, unhook the return spring, then prise off the circlip, and detach the cable inner from the top of the pedal arm.

4 Carefully press the cable outer through the bulkhead grommet. **Note:** *Do not remove the grommet from the inner bulkhead.*

5 At the outer bulkhead, prise out the rubber grommet, then draw the cable through the grommet on the inner bulkhead into the engine compartment.

Refitting

6 Refit the cable by following the removal procedure in reverse, but before reconnecting the cable to the carburettor linkage, adjust the operation of the linkage and cable as described in the following paragraphs.

Adjustment

7 Run the engine until it reaches normal operating temperature and then switch off.

8 Where applicable, disconnect the cruise control/air conditioning control rod from the operating lever on the carburettor.

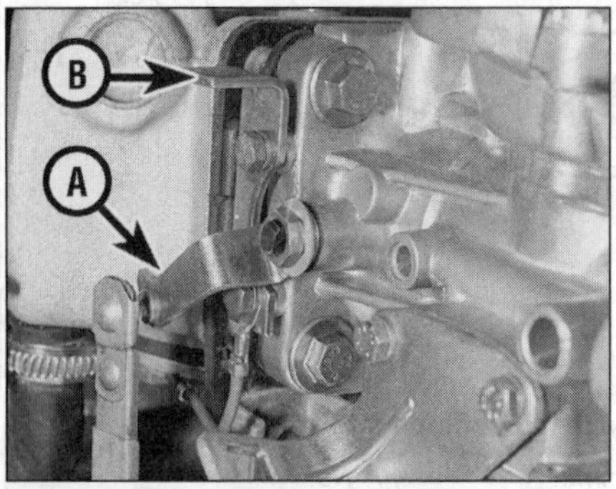

7.16a The throttle lever on the carburettor should be in contact with the full throttle stop plate

A Throttle lever B Full throttle stop plate

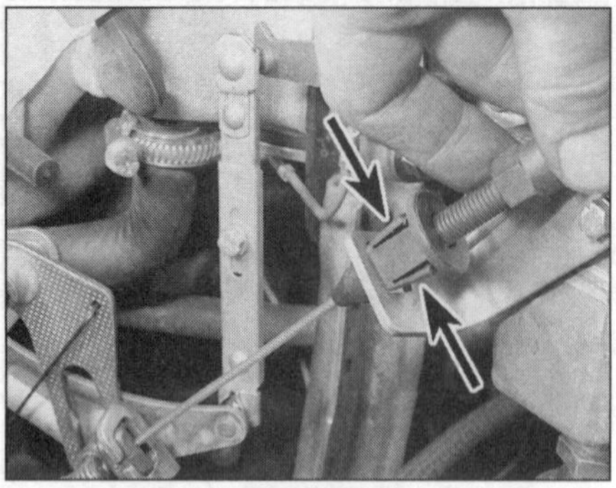

7.2 Release the cable outer from its support bracket by compressing the lugs (arrowed) on the plastic retainer

9 On vehicles with automatic transmission, disconnect the control pressure cable end from the ball socket on the guide lever.

10 On Stromberg carburettor models fitted with a vacuum throttle lifter unit (part of the emission control system), start the engine again, and proceed as follows.

a) With the engine running, pinch the throttle lifter vacuum hose (with the throttle lifter plunger retracted).

b) Stop the engine.

c) Check that the throttle linkage lever is not touching the throttle lifter adjusting screw.

d) If necessary, turn the adjusting nut until the lever is just clear of the adjusting screw.

11 On models with the Stromberg carburettor, with the throttle cable disconnected from the guide lever, loosen the clamp screw on the progressive linkage. Move the linkage until the roller rests against the idle speed end stop **(see illustration)**. Hold the linkage in this position and tighten the clamp screw.

12 On models with the Pierburg carburettor, fully retract the throttle actuator plunger by clamping the vacuum supply hose, running the engine for a few seconds and then switching off again. With the throttle cable disconnected from the guide lever, adjust the length of the idle travel control rod so that there is approximately 0.5 mm of travel.

13 Reconnect the throttle cable to the guide lever.

7.16b Adjustment nut (arrowed) at the support bracket

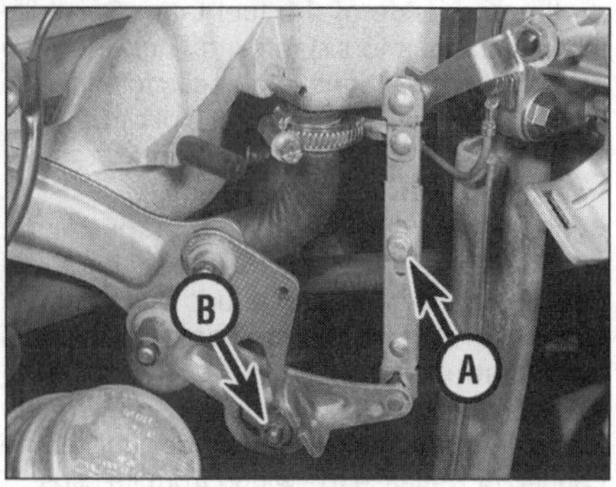

7.11 Progressive linkage arrangement

A Connecting rod clamp screw B Roller

14 On models with an adjustable full throttle stop mounted in the driver's footwell, behind the pedal, turn the throttle stop pin to the left, and pull it out slightly.

15 Have an assistant fully depress the throttle pedal, on vehicles with manual transmission, or just far enough to reach (but not operate) the kickdown switch, on vehicles with automatic transmission.

16 The throttle lever on the carburettor should now be in contact with the full throttle stop plate on the side of the carburettor. On models without a throttle stop behind the pedal, turn the adjustment nut at the support bracket to achieve this, if necessary **(see illustrations)**.

17 Release the throttle pedal again, allowing the linkage roller to rest against the idle speed stop on the guide lever. On models with an adjustable full throttle stop mounted in the driver's footwell, behind the pedal, lock the full throttle stop pin by turning to the right, taking care not to move the pin in or out.

18 In this position, the nipple on the end of the throttle cable (at the guide lever) should be resting against the compression spring with no free-play. Adjust the adjusting nut at the throttle pedal end of the cable to achieve this, if necessary - the adjusting nut is accessible from the driver's footwell **(see illustration)**.

19 Where applicable, remove the clamp from the throttle actuator plunger vacuum supply hose.

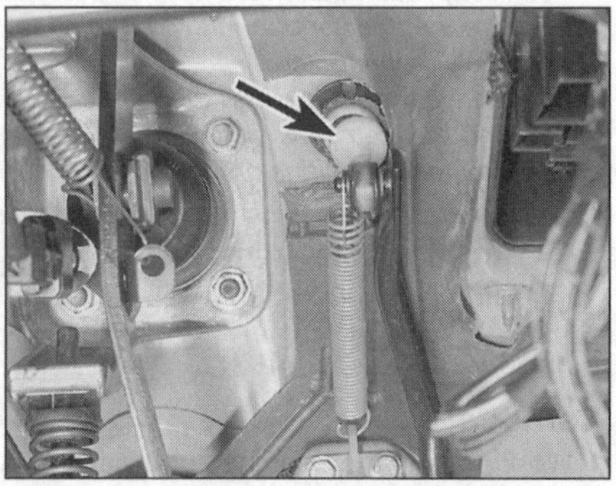

7.18 Accelerator cable idle adjustment nut (arrowed), at the accelerator pedal

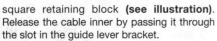

20 Where applicable, reconnect and adjust the cruise control/air conditioning control rod, as described in Chapter 12.

21 On vehicles with automatic transmission, reconnect the control pressure cable and adjust its operation with reference to Chapter 7B.

8 Stromberg 175 CDT carburettor - general information and component renewal

General information

1 Before condemning the carburettor, check first that the ignition timing is correctly adjusted, and that the spark plugs are correctly gapped and in good condition. Also check that the throttle cable and choke control mechanisms are correctly adjusted, and that the air cleaner filter element is clean - see the relevant Sections of this Chapter and Chapter 1A for guidance. If the engine is running roughly, check the valve clearances (where applicable) and the cylinder compression pressures, as described in Chapters 1A and 2A.

2 If, after eliminating all other possibilities, the carburettor appears to be faulty, check the price and availability of spares and service kits for the carburettor, before deciding how to proceed. Renewing the carburettor as a complete unit may prove to be more economical than attempting to repair the existing one.

3 Carburettor service kits generally contain those components which either wear out with normal use or are destroyed during the dismantling process, e.g. gaskets, washers, seals, jets, diaphragms, etc. Check with the supplier that the correct kit for your carburettor is available, before taking anything apart. Note that in the majority of cases, it will be sufficient to dismantle the carburettor and clean out the jets and passages with carburettor cleaning fluid.

4 The remainder of this section deals with the repair/renewal of the major sub-assemblies within the carburettor.

Component renewal

Air piston diaphragm

5 Remove the screws and lift off the carburettor dashpot cover, complete with the piston damper **(see illustration)**. Recover the gasket and discard it - a new item must be used on reassembly.

6 Slacken and withdraw the screws and lift the dashpot from the carburettor body. Note that the thermo-delay valve is secured by one of these screws **(see illustrations)**.

7 Withdraw the piston return spring, then remove the piston, diaphragm and jet needle from the carburettor body - these components lift out as one assembly **(see illustrations)**.

8 Examine the piston diaphragm carefully - hold it in front of a light source to highlight pinholes. If it is perished, split or holed, the function of the carburettor will be seriously impaired. Renew the diaphragm as follows: grasp the piston firmly and undo the diaphragm securing screws **(see illustration)**. Lift off the washer and detach the diaphragm from the piston.

9 Lay a new diaphragm in position on the piston, ensuring that the lug on the underside of the diaphragm hub engages with the recess in the top surface of the piston.

10 Fit the washer in place over the diaphragm, then insert and tighten the retaining screws.

11 Refit the piston assembly to the carburettor body, such that the lug on the diaphragm outer collar engages with the recess in the carburettor body **(see illustration)**. When correctly fitted, the air

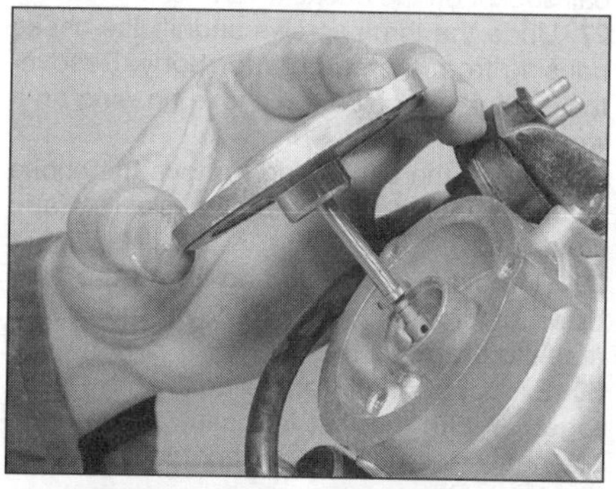

8.5 Remove the screws and lift off the carburettor dashpot cover, complete with the piston damper

8.6a Slacken and withdraw the screws and lift the dashpot from the carburettor body

8.6b Note that the thermo-delay valve is secured by one of the dashpot screws

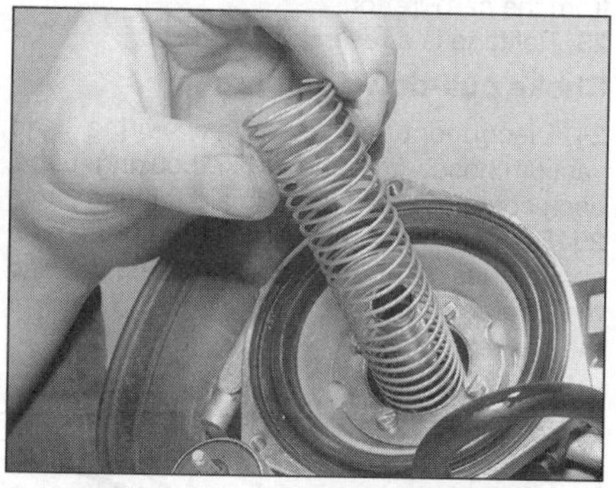

8.7a Withdraw the piston return spring . . .

8.7b . . . piston, diaphragm and jet needle from the carburettor body

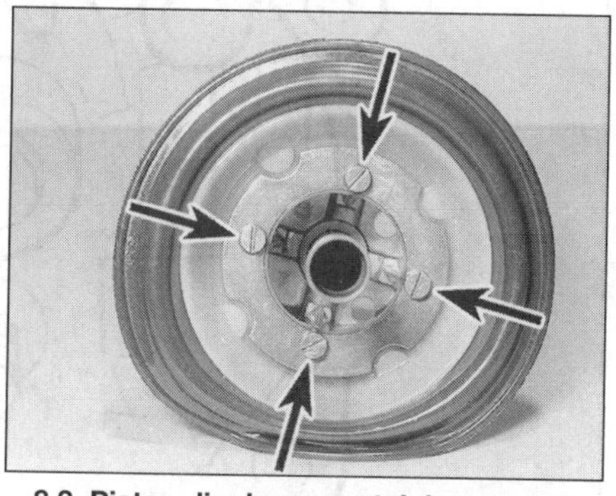

8.8 Piston diaphragm retaining screws (arrowed)

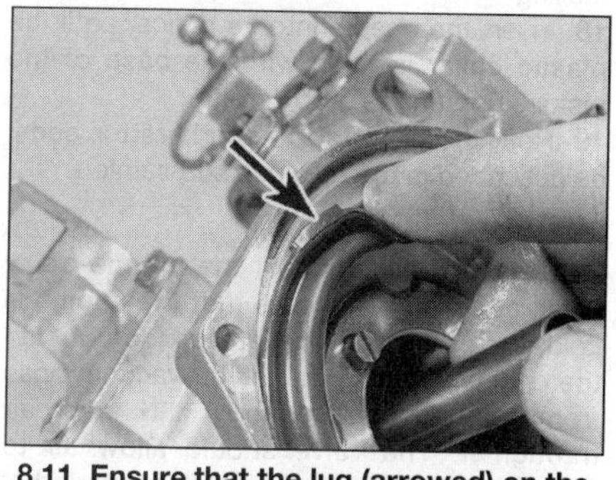

8.11 Ensure that the lug (arrowed) on the diaphragm outer collar engages with the recess in the carburettor body

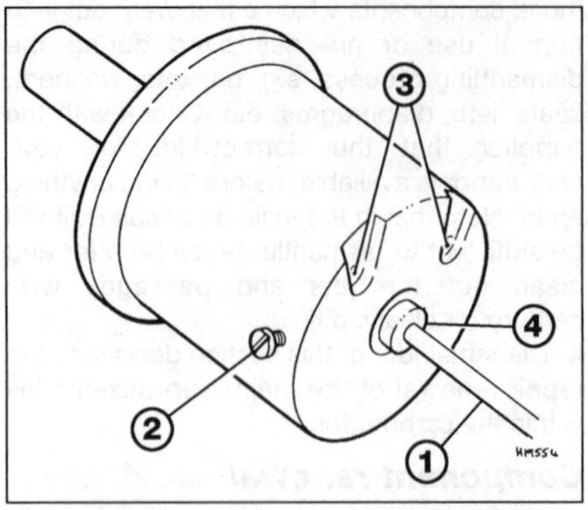

8.16 Piston and jet needle assembly

1 Jet needle *3 Air ports*
2 Grub screw *4 Plastic collar*

drillings on the bottom of the piston should face the engine.

12 Refit the piston return spring, then lower the dashpot into position. Insert and tighten the screws, remembering that one secures the thermo-delay valve. **Note:** *To avoid displacing the diaphragm, do not rotate the dashpot when fitting it in position over the piston.*

13 Refit the dashpot cover and piston damper using a new gasket, then insert and tighten the screws.

14 Unscrew the damper filler plug, then top-up the damper with the specified grade and quantity of oil, so that the level is just below the bottom of the filler plug orifice. Refit and tighten the filler plug.

Jet needle

15 Remove the piston assembly from the carburettor, as described in the previous sub-section.

16 Slacken the grub screw on the side of the piston and withdraw the jet needle **(see illustration)**.

17 Examine the jet needle closely. If is coated with gum or dirt, clean it carefully with carburettor cleaning fluid; take great care to avoid distorting the needle. If a significant wear ridge has formed on the side of the needle, it should be renewed as this will have an adverse effect on the idle and part-throttle fuelling.

18 Insert the needle into its orifice, until the plastic collar is flush with the base of the piston. Tighten the grub screw.

19 Refit the piston to the carburettor body, as described in the previous sub-section.

Thermo-delay valve

20 Test the operation of the thermo-delay valve as follows - ensure that the engine is cold, then switch on the ignition (do not start the engine). Unplug the longer vacuum hose from the carburettor body and suck air through it. The valve should allow air to flow through it initially, then after a period of between 5 and 15 seconds from switch on, it should close. If the valve allows air to flow

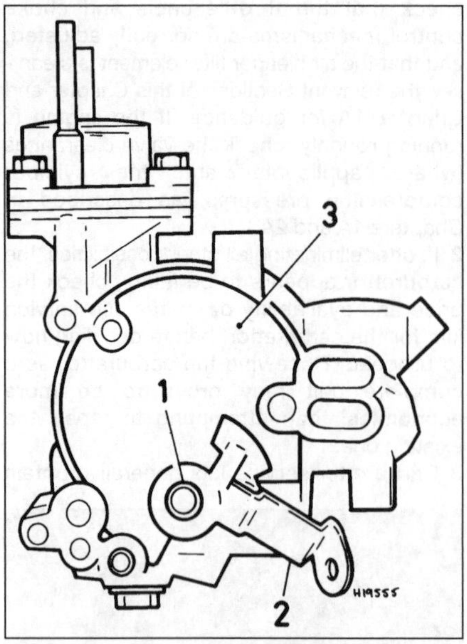

8.28 Choke lever circlip (1), choke lever (2) and dirt guard (3)

constantly, or not at all, then it is probably faulty and should be renewed.

21 Pull the short, curved vacuum hose from the port on the base of the thermo-delay valve; label the port to aid correct refitting later. Unplug the wiring from the valve at the connector.

22 Remove the screw and detach the valve from the carburettor.

23 Refitting is a reversal of removal.

Choke pull-down diaphragm

24 Disconnect all electrical wiring and vacuum hoses from the choke housing. Label each connector and hose to aid refitting later.

25 Remove the screws and lift the bi-metallic spring housing off the choke housing, leaving the coolant hoses connected to it. Recover the gasket.

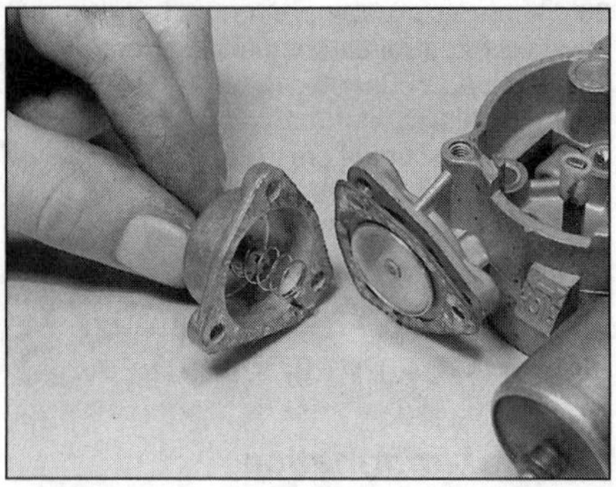

8.29 Lifting off the pull-down diaphragm cover

26 Disengage the connecting rod from the ball socket on the choke lever.

27 Undo the three screws and lift the choke housing from the carburettor body. Recover the gasket and place the choke housing on a work bench.

28 Extract the circlip and remove the choke lever, followed by the dirt guard **(see illustration)**.

29 Remove the screws and lift off the pull-down diaphragm cover. Recover the gasket **(see illustration)**.

30 Extract the circlip and slide the drive lever, together with the fast idle cam, forwards to disengage the pull-down diaphragm rod **(see illustration)**.

31 Withdraw the pull-down diaphragm and rod from the choke housing.

32 Examine the pull-down diaphragm closely for signs of perishing or holes. Renew it if necessary.

33 Reassemble the choke housing as follows. Fit the pull-down diaphragm and rod into the housing, then fit the spring and cover, using a new gasket. Tighten the securing screws.

34 Engage the choke drive lever with the end of the pull-down diaphragm rod and refit the circlip.

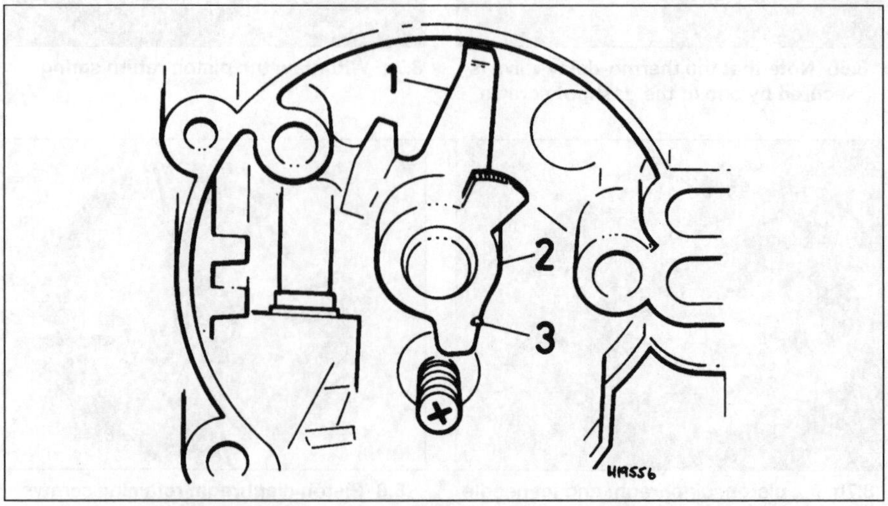

8.30 Automatic choke drive lever (1), fast idle cam (2) and spring (3)

35 Refit the choke lever without the dirt guard, at this stage, to enable the following checks to be carried out.

36 Push the pull-down diaphragm rod upwards to its stop, and push the drive lever to the left so that it rests against the pull-down rod (ie: the fast idle position). The choke lever should now be resting in the centre of the second highest step on the fast idle cam. Carefully bend the drive lever arm to achieve this, if required.

37 Now push the drive lever fully to the left, against its stop (ie: the engine starting position). The choke lever should now be resting on the highest step of the fast idle cam, for a distance of at least 0.5 mm **(see illustration)**. Again, carefully bend the drive lever arm to achieve this, if required.

38 Finally, check that with the drive lever pushed fully to the right (ie: the normal idle position), the choke lever no longer rests on the stepped segment of the fast idle cam.

39 With the choke operating correctly, remove the choke lever, fit the dirt guard, then refit the choke lever. Secure the lever with the circlip.

40 Refit the choke housing to the carburettor, using a new gasket, then insert and tighten the securing screws.

41 Place a new gasket on the choke housing, then refit the bi-metallic spring housing, ensuring that the spring lug engages with the choke drive lever **(see illustration)**. Line up the assembly markings on both housings, then insert and tighten the securing screws.

42 Refit the connecting rod to the choke lever ball socket.

43 Reconnect the electrical wiring and vacuum hoses, using the notes made during dismantling.

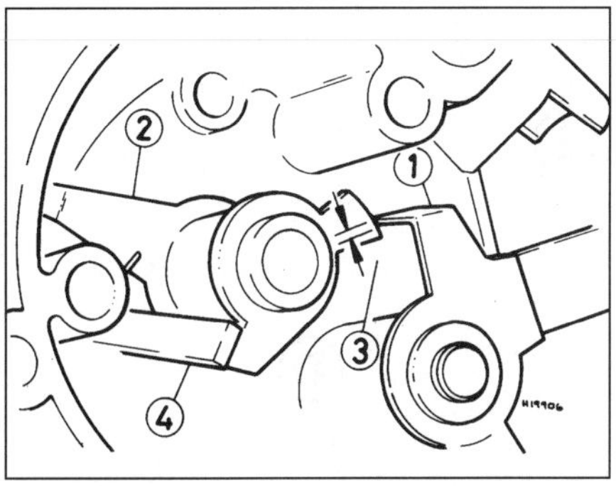

8.37 Choke lever set in cold start position

1 Choke lever *3 Fast idle cam*
2 Drive lever *4 Drive lever arm*
Arrows indicate choke lever resting on highest step of fast idle cam for a distance of 0.5 mm

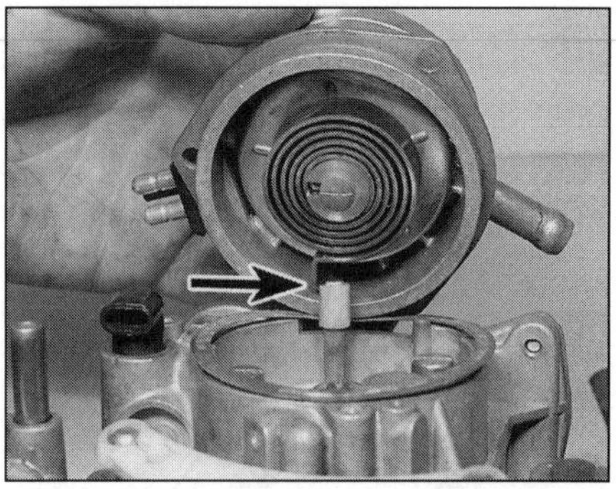

8.41 Fit the bi-metallic spring housing with the spring end (arrowed) behind the drive lever

9 Pierburg 2E-E carburettor fuel system - general information and component renewal

General information

1 Before condemning the carburettor, check first that the ignition timing is correctly adjusted, and that the spark plugs are correctly gapped and in good condition. Also check that the throttle cable and choke control mechanisms are correctly adjusted, and that the air cleaner filter element is clean - see the relevant Sections of this Chapter and Chapter 1A for guidance. If the engine is running roughly, check the valve clearances (where applicable) and the cylinder compression pressures, as described in Chapters 1A and 2A.

2 If, after eliminating all other possibilities, the carburettor appears to be faulty, check the price and availability of spares and service kits for the carburettor, before deciding how to proceed. Renewing the carburettor as a complete unit may prove to be more economical than attempting to repair the existing one.

3 Carburettor service kits generally contain those components which either wear out with normal use or are destroyed during the dismantling process, e.g. gaskets, washers, seals, jets, diaphragms, etc. Check with the supplier that the correct kit for your carburettor is available, before taking anything apart. Note that in the majority of cases, it will be sufficient to dismantle the carburettor and clean out the jets and passages with carburettor cleaning fluid.

4 The remainder of this section deals with the repair/renewal of the major sub-assemblies within the carburettor control system.

Component renewal

Choke actuator

5 Remove the air cleaner as described in Section 2.

6 Unplug the wiring from the actuator at the connector.

7 Remove the screw and lift off the retaining ring **(see illustration)**.

8 Disconnect the link rod from the choke lever, then rotate the actuator body to disengage the locking pin and withdraw the actuator from the carburettor.

9 Refitting is a reversal of removal.

Throttle valve actuator

10 Remove the air cleaner as described in Section 2.

11 Unplug the wiring from the actuator at the connector. Detach the vacuum hose from the port on the side of the actuator.

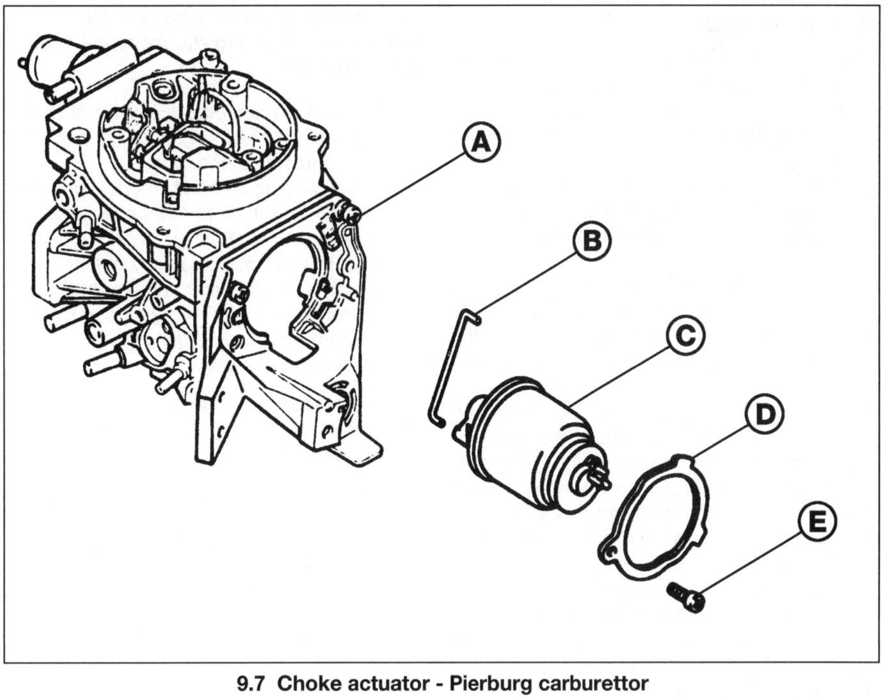

9.7 Choke actuator - Pierburg carburettor

A Carburettor body *B Link rod* *C Actuator body* *D Retaining ring* *E Screw*

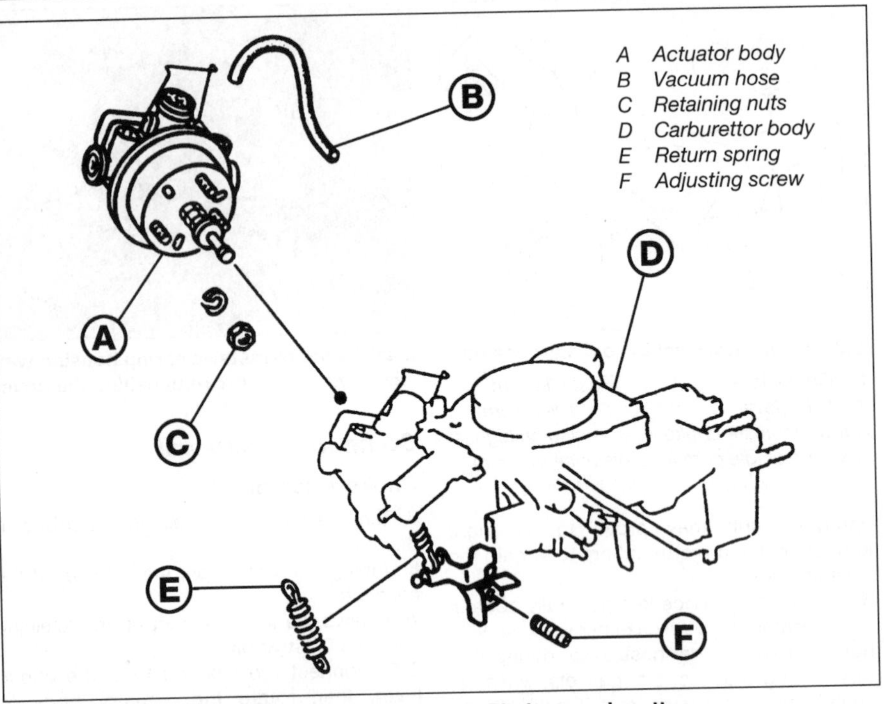

9.12 Throttle valve actuator - Pierburg carburettor

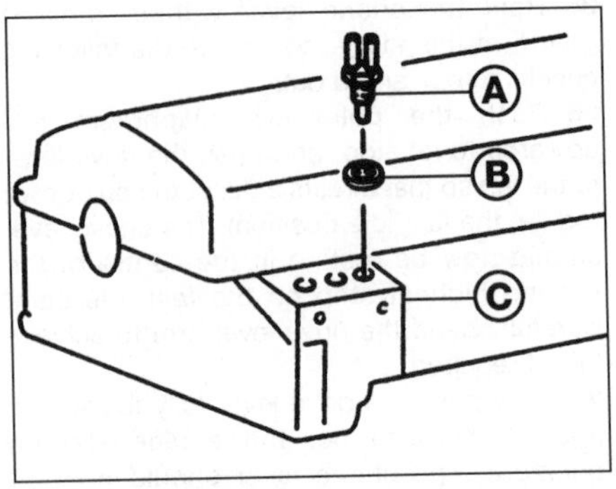

9.15 Coolant sensor location

A Coolant sensor
B Sealing ring
C Cylinder head boss

12 Remove the three retaining nuts and recover the washers **(see illustration)**.

13 Withdraw the actuator from the carburettor.

14 Refitting is a reversal of removal, but note that the clearance between the actuator plunger and the stop screw on the throttle lever must be between 1.5 and 2.5 mm.

Coolant sensor

15 The coolant sensor is located on the cylinder head, at the front (auxiliary drivebelt) end of the engine **(see illustration)**.

16 Unplug the wiring from the sensor at the connector.

17 Ensure that the engine has cooled completely, then briefly remove the expansion tank/radiator cap, to relieve the pressure in the cooling system.

18 Unscrew the coolant sensor from the cylinder head, and recover the sealing ring. Be prepared for some coolant leakage - pad the surrounding area with plenty of absorbent rags.

19 The coolant sensor can be tested by heating it a vessel of water alongside a thermometer. Using an ohmmeter, measure the electrical resistance of the sensor at a number of different temperatures as it heats up and compare your results with the data in the *Specifications*.

20 Refit the coolant sensor by following the removal procedure in reverse. On completion, start the engine and check the area surrounding the sensor for leaks.

Electronic control unit

Caution: Electronic Control Units (ECUs) contain components that are sensitive to the levels of static electricity generated by a person during normal activity. Once the multiway harness connector has been unplugged, the exposed ECU connector pins can freely conduct stray static electricity to these components, damaging or even destroying them - the damage will be invisible and may not manifest itself immediately. Expensive repairs can be avoided by observing the following basic handling rules:

a) Handle a disconnected ECU by its case only; do not allow fingers or tools to come into contact with the pins.
b) When carrying an ECU around, "ground" yourself from time to time, by touching a metal object such as an unpainted water pipe, this will discharge any potentially damaging static that may have built up.
c) Do not leave the ECU unplugged from its connector for any longer than is absolutely necessary.

21 The electronic control unit is located at the rear of the engine compartment, on the right-hand side of the bulkhead behind a cover panel.

22 Disconnect the battery negative cable and position it away from the terminal.

23 Prise out the clips and remove the cover panel.

24 Depress the metal clips on the control unit, then unplug the multiway connector. Pull the connector out squarely, to avoid bending the contact pins inside.

25 Remove the screws and lift out the control unit.

26 Refitting is a reversal of removal.

10 Carburettor - removal and refitting

Removal

1 Ensure that the engine has cooled completely before starting work. Disconnect the battery negative lead and position it away from the terminal.

2 Refer to Section 2 and remove the air cleaner.

3 Seal off the fuel supply and return hoses to the carburettor, using proprietary hose clamps (not G-clamps), then slacken the clips and disconnect the hoses from the carburettor. Be prepared for some fuel loss - position a container under the hoses and pad the surrounding area with absorbent rags.

4 Briefly loosen the coolant expansion tank cap to relieve the pressure in the cooling system. Seal off the coolant hoses to the choke housing using proprietary hose clamps (not G-clamps), then slacken the clips and disconnect the hoses from the carburettor **(see illustration)**. Be prepared for coolant spillage - position a container under the hoses and pad the surrounding area with absorbent rags. **Note:** *If suitable hose clamps are not available, refer to Chapter 1A and partially drain the cooling system before disconnecting the hoses.*

10.4 Disconnect the coolant hoses (arrowed) from the carburettor - Stromberg carburettor shown

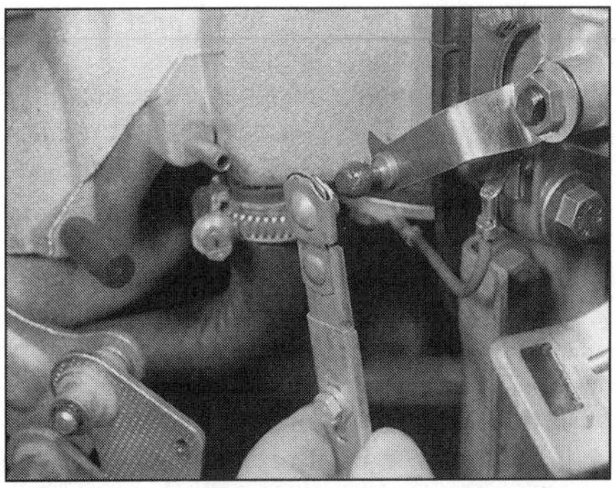

10.5 Disconnecting the throttle operating rod from the throttle lever - Stromberg carburettor shown

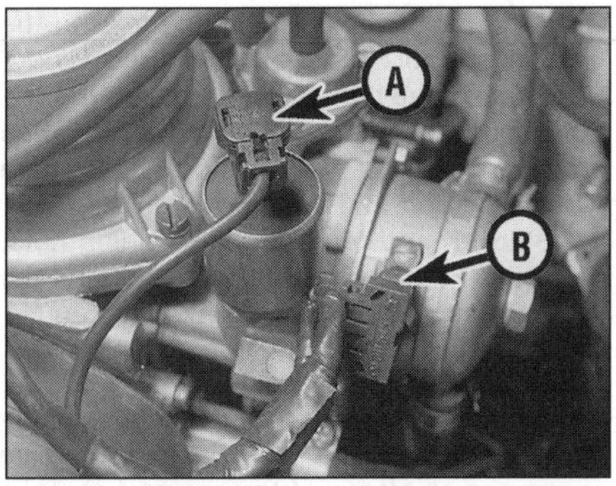

10.8a Disconnect the wiring connectors from the vent valve solenoid (A), the choke housing (B) . . .

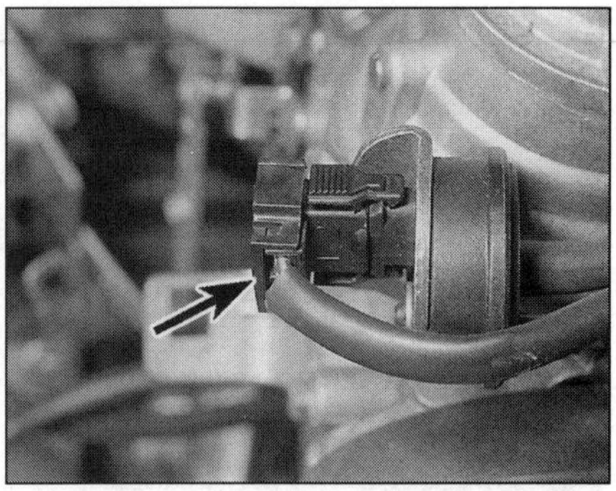

10.8b . . . the thermotime delay valve (arrowed) . . .

10.8c . . . and the fuel shut-off valve (arrowed)

10.8d Earth cable securing bolt (arrowed)

5 With reference to Section 7, disconnect the throttle cable from the carburettor. Alternatively, where applicable, disconnect the throttle operating rod from the throttle lever **(see illustration)**.

6 Where applicable, disconnect the cruise control/air conditioning control rod from the operating lever on the carburettor.

7 On vehicles with automatic transmission, where applicable, refer to Chapter 7B and disconnect the control pressure cable from the carburettor.

8 Work around the carburettor and unplug all wiring connectors, labelling each one carefully to aid refitting later. In addition, remove the screw and disconnect the earth cable from the carburettor **(see illustrations)**.

9 Make a note of the connection point of each of the vacuum hoses on the carburettor, then disconnect them.

10 Unbolt the inlet manifold support strut (where fitted). Slacken and remove the carburettor-to-inlet manifold bolts, then lift off the carburettor. Recover the adapter plate and gasket.

Refitting

11 Refit the carburettor by following the removal procedure in reverse, noting the following points:

a) Do not re-use old gaskets, always fit new items.

b) Tighten the adapter plate securing screws to the specified torque.

c) Refit the fuel supply and return hoses in accordance with the arrowed markings on the carburettor.

d) Refit all wiring connectors and vacuum hoses according to the notes made during removal.

e) Reconnect the coolant hoses to the choke housing and top-up the cooling system as required.

f) Where applicable, reconnect the cruise control/air conditioning control rod to the carburettor with reference to Chapter 12.

g) On vehicles with automatic transmission, reconnect the control pressure cable to the carburettor with reference to Chapter 7B.

h) Check and if necessary top-up the carburettor damper oil level, as described in Chapter 1A.

i) On completion, check the idle and fast idle engine speed and exhaust CO content, as described in Chapter 1A.

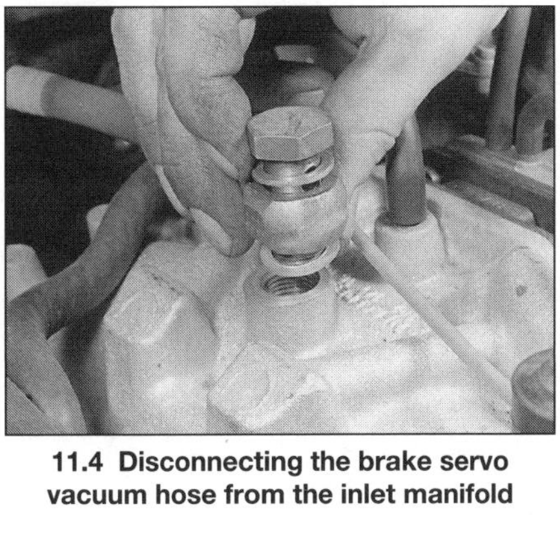

11.4 Disconnecting the brake servo vacuum hose from the inlet manifold

11 Inlet manifold - removal and refitting

Removal

1 Disconnect the battery negative lead and position it away from the terminal.

2 Refer to Chapter 1A and drain the cooling system.

3 Remove the carburettor as described in Section 10.

4 Disconnect the brake servo vacuum hose from the inlet manifold - unscrew the banjo union bolt, and recover the washers **(see illustration)**.

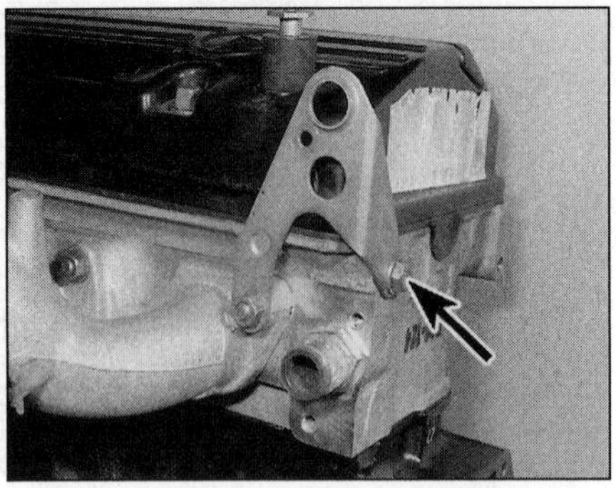

11.10 Unscrew the bolt (arrowed) securing the engine lifting bracket

5 Disconnect the vacuum hoses for the crankcase emission system, automatic transmission, central locking and the EGR valve (as applicable) from the inlet manifold. Make a careful note of each hose location, to avoid confusion when refitting.

6 Slacken the clips and pull the coolant hoses from the ports on the inlet manifold.

7 Where applicable, release the wiring harness from the securing clips. Disconnect the wiring from the inlet manifold pre-heater at the connector - refer to Section 12 for details.

8 Unscrew the securing bolts, and remove the manifold support strut.

9 Where applicable, unbolt the throttle linkage support bracket from the cylinder head, and move the assembly to one side.

10 Unscrew the bolt securing the engine lifting bracket to the cylinder head **(see illustration)**.

11 Slacken and remove the retaining nuts, then lift off the engine lifting bracket and the inlet manifold. Recover the gasket.

Refitting

12 Carefully clean the mating surfaces of the cylinder head and the inlet manifold - be sure to remove all traces of the old gasket. Take care to avoid pitting or scratching the mating surfaces, as this could lead to leakage. Check both surfaces for distortion using a straight edge, before progressing any further - refer to Chapter 2D for greater detail.

13 Lay a new gasket on the cylinder head manifold studs, then offer the inlet manifold into position.

14 The remainder of the refitting process is a reversal of removal, noting the following points:

a) *Tighten the manifold retaining nuts to the specified torque.*
b) *Refill the cooling system with the correct quantity and mixture of water and antifreeze, as described in Chapter 1A.*
c) *Reconnect the wiring to the inlet manifold pre-heater - see Section 12.*
d) *On completion, check and if necessary adjust the idle engine speed and exhaust CO content, as described in Chapter 1A.*

12 Inlet manifold pre-heater - removal and refitting

Removal

1 Disconnect the battery negative lead and position it away from the terminal.

2 Unplug the wiring from the inlet manifold pre-heater at the connector.

3 Where applicable, unbolt and remove the inlet manifold support strut.

4 Remove the securing screws and lower the pre-heater from the manifold. Recover the insulating ring and rubber sealing ring.

Refitting

5 Fit a new rubber sealing ring to the pre-heater, then fit the insulating ring.

6 Offer up the heater to the inlet manifold, then insert and tighten the securing screws.

7 Reinstate the wiring connector, then fit the manifold support strut.

8 Reconnect the battery negative cable.

Chapter 4 Part B
Bosch CIS-E (KE-Jetronic) fuel injection system

Contents

Air cleaner and filter element - removal and refitting 3
Bosch KE-Jetronic fuel injection system components - removal and refitting 10
Fuel accumulator - removal and refitting 8
Fuel filter - removal and refitting .... See Chapter 1A
Fuel gauge sender unit - removal and refitting 5
Fuel injection system - depressurisation 2
Fuel pump(s) - removal and refitting 4
Fuel tank - removal and refitting 6
General information and precautions 1
Idle speed and exhaust CO content adjustments ..... See Chapter 1A
Inlet manifold - removal and refitting 11
Throttle body - removal and refitting 9
Throttle cable - removal, refitting and adjustment 7

Degrees of difficulty

Easy, suitable for novice with little experience	**Fairly easy,** suitable for beginner with some experience	**Fairly difficult,** suitable for competent DIY mechanic	**Difficult,** suitable for experienced DIY mechanic	**Very difficult,** suitable for expert DIY or professional

Specifications

General

System type	Bosch CIS-E electronically controlled, continuous fuel injection system
System operating fuel pressure	5.3 to 5.5 bar

Fuel pump

Type	Self-priming, 12V electric roller-cell
Delivery rate	1.5 litre/min (minimum)
Delivery pressure	2 - 4 bar

Fuel injectors

Type	Mechanical
Opening pressure:	
Up to 08/1988:	
New injectors	3.5 - 4.1 bar
Used injectors	3.0 bar (minimum)
From 09/1988 onwards:	
New injectors	3.7 to 4.3 bar
Used injectors	3.2 bar (minimum)

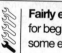

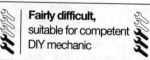

Sensors and actuators

Note: *All values are approximate and are intended for indication only.*

Coolant temperature sensor

Type	NTC (negative temperature coefficient)
Electrical resistance:	
At 80°C	325 W
At 40°C	1200 W
At 0°C	6000 W

Thermo-time switch

Heater coil electrical resistance	93 W
Duration (length of time contacts are closed):	
At -20°C	12.0 seconds
At 0°C	1.5 seconds
At 3°C	0.5 seconds

Air flow sensor potentiometer

Supply voltage	7 - 9 V
Wiper voltage variation:	
Engine off	0.25 - 0.5 V
Full scale deflection	7.0 - 9.0 V

Torque wrench settings

	Nm	lbf ft
Fuel gauge sender unit	40	30
Throttle body securing screws	25	18
Fuel line unions	10	7
Fuel tank strainer	40	30
Fuel tank bolts	20	15
Lambda sensor	55	41

1 General information and precautions

The fuel tank is mounted upright, in a central position behind the rear seats. The tank is fabricated from sheet steel, although later models may be fitted with a plastic tank. A fuel level sender unit is mounted on the top of the tank, which can be renewed without removing the fuel tank from the vehicle.

The fuel pump is of the electric, roller-cell type and is mounted under the floor pan at the rear of the vehicle. The pump motor is cooled by the fuel, in which both the pump and the pump motor are permanently immersed. The pump contains a non-return valve, which prevents the fuel supply line from emptying when the engine is switched off and also isolates the fuel tank from the rest of the fuel system. The pump also contains a pressure relief valve, to prevent excessive fuel pressure build-up in the event of a restriction occurring.

The fuel accumulator is mounted adjacent to the fuel pump, in-line with the fuel supply line. Its primary function is to maintain fuel supply line pressure for a period of time after the engine has been switched off. This helps to prevent the formation of fuel vapour locks, improving hot starting performance. In addition, the fuel accumulator acts as a damper, reducing the noise caused by the hydraulic pulsations that can occur in the fuel lines as the fuel injectors open and close.

A cartridge type fuel filter is mounted close to the fuel accumulator, downstream of the fuel pump. This prevents dirt and debris from the tank entering the fuel system.

Fuel metering is performed by the fuel distributor unit, which regulates the amount of fuel reaching the injectors mechanically, based on the deflection of an inlet air flow sensor. This basic mixture is adjusted dynamically by an electro-hydraulic pressure actuator, under the control of an electronic control unit (ECU). In this manner, the fuelling can be fine-tuned in response to information received from sensors mounted on and around the engine. This results in improved fuel consumption and engine performance, as well as a reduction in the production of harmful exhaust gas emissions.

As the accuracy of the fuel metering depends heavily on fuel supply pressure; the system is fitted with a primary fuel pressure regulator, which controls the supply to the fuel distributor unit. In addition, differential pressure valves within the distributor unit ensure that the fuel supply presented to the metering slits remains constant under all operating conditions.

Effective starting at low ambient temperatures is achieved by means of a cold start valve and an auxiliary air device. The cold start valve is an electrically operated injector, mounted in the inlet manifold, which sprays additional fuel into the stream of inlet air to enrichen the mixture. A thermo-time switch controls the amount of time for which the cold start valve remains open. The auxiliary air device is a valve which allows air to bypass the throttle valve, hence raising the idle speed. An internal bi-metallic strip and heater coil controls both the amount of valve opening and the length of time for which it remains open. The auxiliary air device only operates during cold starting and warm-up.

Later variants are fitted with a rotary idle actuator. This component replaces the auxiliary air device and is driven electronically by the ECU. It provides engine idle speed stabilisation during all operating conditions, including fast idle during warm-up, and idle speed control under load, e.g. when the power steering, or air conditioning are actuated.

Models fitted with a catalytic converter employ closed-loop fuelling. This is achieved by monitoring signals from a Lambda sensor, mounted in the exhaust system and adapting the fuel mixture to maintain the optimum air:fuel ratio.

Precautions

Many of the operations described in this Chapter involve the disconnection of fuel lines, which may cause an amount of fuel spillage. Before commencing work, refer to the *Warning* and *Caution* below as well as the information in *"Safety first !"* at the beginning of this manual.

Residual fuel pressure always remain in the fuel system, long after the engine has been switched off. This pressure must be relieved in a controlled manner before work can commence on any component in the fuel system - refer to Section 2 for details.

In the interests of personal safety and equipment protection, many of the procedures in this Chapter suggest that the negative lead be removed from the battery terminal. This firstly eliminates the possibility of accidental short circuits being caused as the vehicle is being worked upon, and secondly prevents damage to electronic components (eg sensors, actuators, ECU's) which are particularly sensitive to the power surges caused by disconnection or reconnection of the wiring harness whilst they are still "live".

Warning: Petrol is extremely flammable - great care must be taken when working on any part of the fuel system. Keep the area well ventilated - open all available doors and windows to create a through-draught. Do not smoke, or allow any naked flames or uncovered light bulbs near the work area. Note that gas powered domestic appliances with pilot flames, such as heaters, boilers and tumble-dryers, also present a fire hazard - bear this in mind if you are working in an area where such appliances are installed. Always keep a suitable fire extinguisher close to the work area and familiarise yourself with its operation before starting work. Wear eye protection when working on fuel systems and wash off any fuel spilt on bare skin immediately with soap and plenty of water. Note that fuel vapour is just as dangerous as liquid fuel; a vessel that has been emptied of liquid fuel will still contain vapour and could be potentially explosive.

3.1a Unscrew the retaining nuts . . .

Caution: When working with fuel system components, pay particular attention to cleanliness - dirt entering the fuel system may cause blockages which could lead to poor running or even failure.

2 Fuel injection system - depressurisation

Warning: Observe the precautions in Section 1 before working on any component in the fuel system.

Warning: The following procedure will merely relieve the pressure in the fuel system - remember that fuel will still be present in the system components and take precautions accordingly before disconnecting any of them.

1 The fuel system referred to in this Section is defined as the fuel pump, the fuel accumulator, the fuel filter, the fuel injectors, the fuel pressure regulator, the fuel distributor and the metal pipes and flexible hoses of the fuel lines between these components.

2 All the previously-mentioned components contain fuel which will be under pressure while the engine is running and/or while the ignition is switched on. The pressure will remain for some time after the ignition has been switched off and must be relieved before any of these components are disturbed for servicing work. Ideally, the engine should be allowed to cool completely before work commences.

3 Refer to Chapter 12 and locate the fuel pump relay. Remove the relay from its housing, then crank the engine for a few seconds on the starter motor. The engine may fire and run for a while, but continue cranking until it stops. The fuel injectors should have opened enough times during cranking to considerably reduce the line fuel pressure.

4 Disconnect the battery negative terminal. Briefly remove the fuel filler cap, to relieve the pressure in the fuel tank, then refit the cap.

5 Place a suitable container beneath the relevant connection/union to be disconnected, and have a large, absorbent rag ready to soak up any escaping fuel not caught by the container.

6 Slowly loosen the connection or union nut (as applicable) to avoid a sudden release of pressure, and position the rag around the connection to catch any fuel spray which may be expelled. Once the pressure has been released, disconnect the fuel line and insert plugs to minimise fuel loss and prevent the entry of dirt into the fuel system.

3 Air cleaner and filter element - removal and refitting

Air filter element

Removal

1 Unscrew and remove the retaining nuts from the air cleaner upper cover. Work around the upper cover and prise open each of the tensioning clips **(see illustrations)**.

2 Lift off the air cleaner cover, then detach the crankcase breather hose (where applicable) and remove the air filter element **(see illustration)**.

Refitting

3 Fit the new filter by following the removal procedure in reverse, ensuring that the filter element is fitted the correct way up, according to the markings on its upper surface.

Air cleaner assembly

Removal

4 Remove the screw (where fitted) and detach the inlet ducting that runs from the air cleaner to the air scoop at the front of the engine bay **(see illustration)**.

5 Where applicable, pull off the crankcase breather hose from the port on the side of the air cleaner.

6 Where applicable, ensure that the ignition is switched off, then unplug the wiring from the inlet air temperature sensor(s) on the side of the air cleaner.

7 Where applicable, unscrew and remove the mounting nuts that secure the lower part of

3.1b . . . and prise open the tensioning clips

3.2 Lift off the air cleaner cover and remove the filter element

3.4 Detach the inlet ducting from the air cleaner

3.7a Unscrew the nuts securing the lower part of the air cleaner at the front . . .

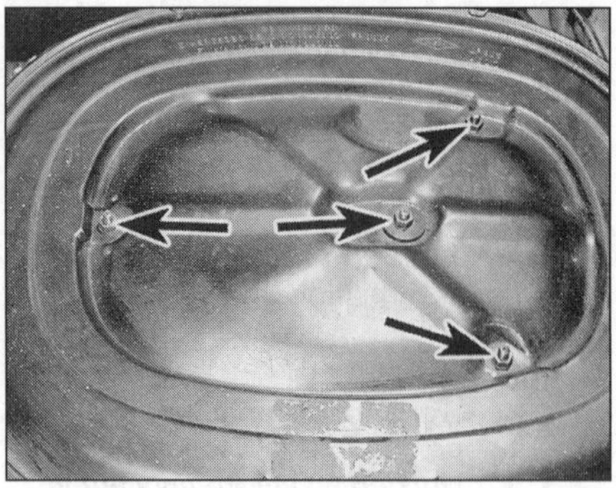

3.7b . . . side . . .

3.7c . . . and rear

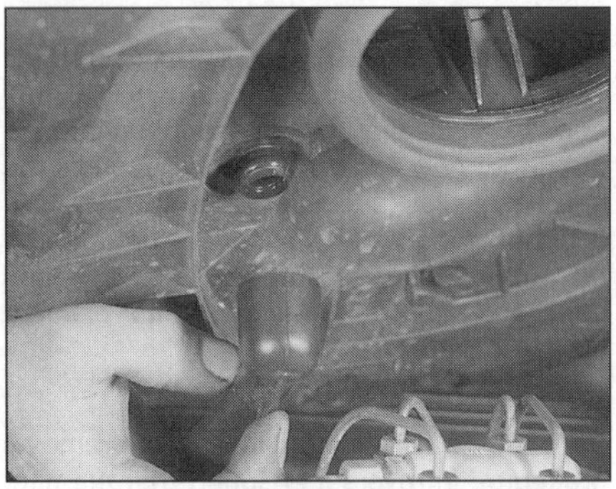

3.8 Lift off the air cleaner and disconnect the breather hose

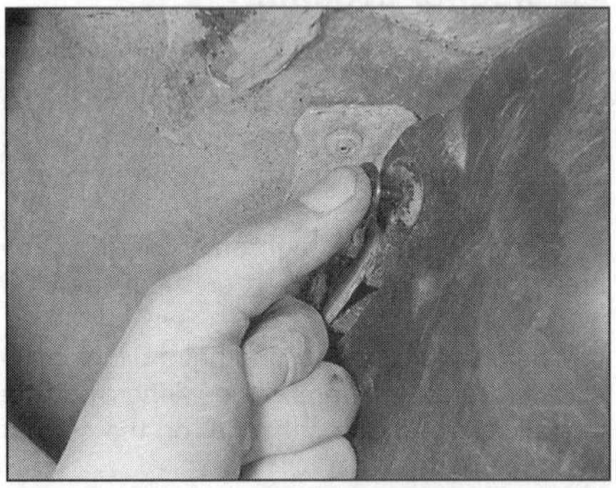

4.5a Remove the clips . . .

the air cleaner to the inlet manifold/fuel distributor unit **(see illustrations)**.

8 Unclip the air cleaner cover, remove the retaining nuts and lift out the filter element, with reference to the previous sub-section. Remove the securing screws/nuts, then lift off the lower section of the air cleaner, and disconnect the breather hose, where applicable **(see illustration)**. Recover the rubber seal.

Refitting

9 Refitting is a reversal of removal, but ensure that the rubber seal between the air cleaner and the fuel distributor is securely seated.

4 Fuel pump(s) - removal and refitting

Removal

Warning: Observe the precautions in Section 1 before working on any component in the fuel system.

1 The fuel pump is mounted on the underside of the floorpan, at the rear of the vehicle, adjacent to the fuel filter.

2 Refer to Section 2 and depressurise the fuel system.

3 Disconnect the battery negative lead and position it away from the terminal.

4 With the vehicle parked on a level surface, apply the parking brake and chock the front roadwheels. Raise the rear of the vehicle and support it securely on axle stands (see *"Jacking and vehicle support"*).

5 Remove the screws or clips, and lower the protective cover away from the fuel pump, filter and accumulator **(see illustrations)**.

6 Unplug the electrical wiring from the fuel pump at the connectors **(see illustration)**. Label each connector carefully to avoid confusion during refitting.

7 Pinch off the flexible fuel supply hose to the *pump* and the fuel delivery hose from the fuel *filter* using proprietary hose clamps. Do not use G-clamps as these may damage the hoses internally.

Caution: Do not clamp the hose at the elbow, as this may cause it to collapse, restricting the fuel flow. Only clamp the hose on a straight section.

TOOL TiP ***If you don't have access to hose clamps, fit two 13 mm sockets over the jaws of a pair of mole grips and use these to clamp the hose. The rounded sides of the sockets will prevent the wall of the hose being damaged.***

8 Slacken the unions and disconnect the fuel lines from the front and rear of the fuel pump.

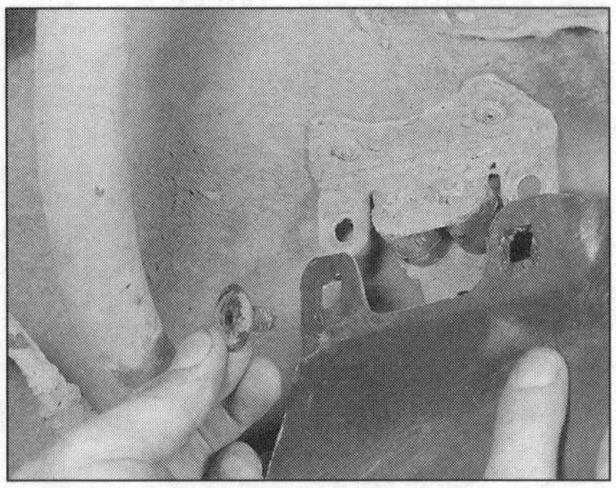

4.5b . . . and lower the cover from the fuel pump, filter and accumulator

4.5c Fuel filter (A), fuel pump (B) and fuel accumulator (C)

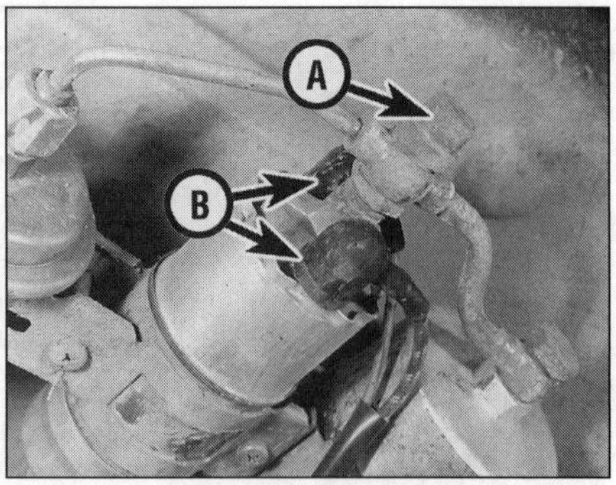

4.6 Fuel pump banjo union bolt (A) and electrical connections (B)

4.9 Slacken and remove the screw(s) to release the filter retaining strap

7.1a Prise out the square retaining block (arrowed) . . .

7.1b . . . and release the throttle cable inner by passing it through the slot in the guide lever bracket

Where banjo bolt unions are used, recover the sealing washers and discard them - new items must be used on reassembly. Be prepared for an amount of fuel loss, position a small container underneath the pump and pad the surrounding area with absorbent rags.

9 Slacken and remove the screw(s), release the retaining strap and lower the pump away from its mounting bracket **(see illustration)**.

10 If the mounting bracket cannot be lowered sufficiently to remove the pump, where applicable, unscrew the banjo unions, and disconnect the fuel pipe from the fuel accumulator and the filter - again, be prepared for fuel spillage, and recover the sealing washers. Once the fuel pipe has been removed, it should be possible to lower the pump for removal.

Refitting

11 Refitting is a reversal of removal, noting the following points:

a) *Where applicable, ensure that the anti-corrosion plastic sleeving is correctly positioned, to prevent metal-to-metal contact between the pump and the retaining strap.*

b) *Fit new sealing washers when reconnecting the banjo bolt unions.*

12 On completion, start the engine and check around the disturbed components for leaks. Note that the fuel pump has to purge the system of air, so the engine may take a little longer than usual to start.

7.2 Compress the lugs (arrowed) on the plastic retainer to release the outer cable

5 Fuel gauge sender unit - removal and refitting

Refer to the information given in Chapter 4A.

6 Fuel tank - removal and refitting

Refer to the information given in Chapter 4A, but before commencing the removal procedure, depressurise the fuel system as described in Section 2.

7 Throttle cable - removal, refitting and adjustment

Removal

1 Working in the engine compartment, disconnect the throttle cable inner from the guide lever by prising out the square retaining block. Release the cable inner by passing it through the slot in the guide lever bracket **(see illustrations)**.

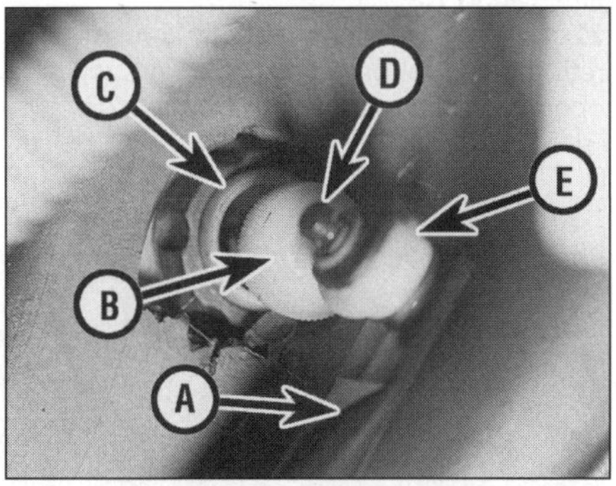

7.3 Throttle pedal and cable arrangement

A Top of throttle pedal
B Idle stop adjustment nut
C Grommet
D Lug for return spring
E End of accelerator pedal

2 Release the cable outer from its support bracket by compressing the lugs on the plastic retainer and withdrawing it **(see illustration)**.

3 Working in the driver's footwell, unhook the return spring then, where applicable prise off the circlip, and detach the cable inner from the top of the pedal arm **(see illustration)**.

4 Carefully press the cable outer through the bulkhead grommet. **Note:** *Do not remove the grommet from the inner bulkhead.*

5 At the outer bulkhead, prise out the rubber grommet, then draw the cable through the grommet on the inner bulkhead into the engine compartment.

Refitting

6 Refit the cable by following the removal procedure in reverse, but before reconnecting the cable to the throttle linkage, adjust the operation of the linkage and cable as described in the following paragraphs **(see illustration)**.

Adjustment

Note: *On vehicles fitted with ASR traction control, accurate adjustment of the throttle*

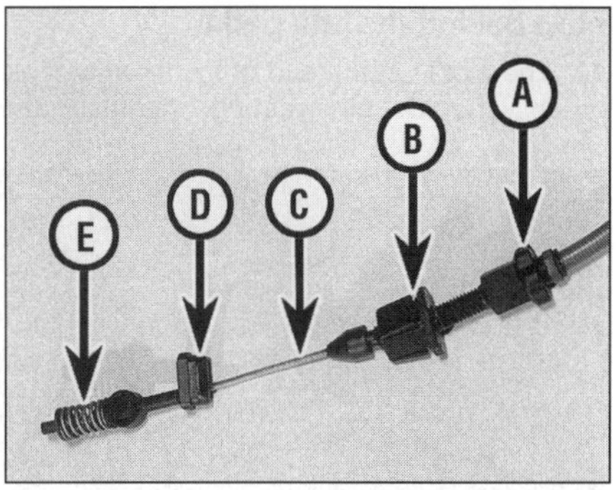

7.6 Details of throttle cable assembly - throttle linkage end

A Full throttle stop adjustment knob
B Plastic retainer
C Cable inner
D Retaining block
E Compression spring

4B

7.10 Move the guide lever until the roller rests against the idle speed end stop (arrowed)

linkage is a very complex procedure. It is recommended that this operation is carried out by a Mercedes-Benz dealer or Bosch fuel injection specialist.

7 Check that the throttle cable and linkage operate smoothly, without any stiffness or binding. Check that the cable is not kinked at any point along its length and lubricate the linkage if required.

8 At the throttle body, disconnect the throttle cable inner from the guide lever by releasing the square retainer from the lever. Pass the cable inner through the slot on the side of the lever.

9 Prise the end of the connecting lever from the ball joint socket on the guide lever. (The connecting lever is the flat, adjustable lever that joins the guide lever to the throttle lever).

10 Move the guide lever until the roller rests against the idle speed end stop **(see illustration)**. With the linkage in this position, slacken the clamp screw and adjust the length of the connecting lever, if required, to enable it to be fitted to the guide lever ball socket free of tension.

11 Reconnect the accelerator cable inner to the guide lever. On models with automatic transmission, disconnect the control pressure cable from the guide lever.

Models with adjustable full throttle stop behind throttle pedal

12 The nipple at the end of the throttle cable inner should be resting against the compression spring with no free-play. In addition, the guide lever must operate the idle microswitch by resting against its actuating lever. Turn the adjustment nut at the support bracket to achieve this, if necessary **(see illustrations)**.

13 Release the full throttle stop in the driver's footwell by turning the stop pin to the left, and pulling it out slightly.

14 Slowly move the throttle pedal into the full throttle position until the throttle valve lever is resting against the full throttle stop on the throttle body, then release the throttle pedal.

15 Lock the full throttle stop pin by turning to the right, taking care not to move the pin in or out.

16 Repeat the checks described in paragraphs 7 to 15, and re-adjust if necessary.

17 On vehicles with automatic transmission, refit the control pressure cable and adjust its operation, with reference to Chapter 7B.

Models without adjustable full throttle stop behind throttle pedal

18 Have an assistant fully depress the accelerator pedal on vehicles with manual transmission, or just far enough to reach (but not operate) the kickdown switch, on vehicles with automatic transmission.

19 The throttle lever should now be in contact with the full throttle stop on the throttle body. Turn the adjustment nut at the support bracket to achieve this, if necessary **(see illustration 7.12c)**.

20 Release the accelerator pedal again, allowing the linkage roller to rest against the idle speed stop on the guide lever.

21 In this position, the nipple at the end of the accelerator cable inner should be resting against the compression spring with no free-play. In addition, the guide lever must operate the idle microswitch by resting against its actuating lever **(see illustrations 7.12a and 7.12b)**.Turn the adjusting nut at the accelerator pedal end of the cable to achieve this, if necessary - the adjusting nut is accessible from the driver's footwell **(refer to illustration 7.3)**.

22 On vehicles with automatic transmission, refit the control pressure cable and adjust its operation, with reference to Chapter 7B.

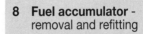

8 Fuel accumulator - removal and refitting

Warning: Observe the precautions in Section 1 before working on any component in the fuel system.

Removal

1 The fuel accumulator is mounted in the fuel supply line, adjacent to the fuel filter **(see illustration 4.5c)**. Access is from the underside of the vehicle.

2 Refer to Section 2 and depressurise the fuel system.

3 Disconnect the battery negative lead and position it away from the terminal.

4 With the vehicle parked on a level surface, apply the parking brake and chock the front roadwheels. Raise the rear of the vehicle and support it securely on axle stands (see *"Jacking and vehicle support"*).

5 Remove the screws and lower the protective cover away from the fuel pump, filter and accumulator.

6 Pinch off the flexible fuel supply hose to the fuel pump and the fuel delivery hose from the fuel filter using proprietary hose clamps. Do not use G-clamps or mole grips as these may damage the hoses internally.

7 Slacken the unions and disconnect the fuel lines from the front and rear of the accumulator unit. Where banjo bolt unions are used, recover the sealing washers and discard them - new items must be used on reassembly. Be prepared for some of fuel loss, position a small container underneath the filter and pad the surrounding area with absorbent rags.

8 Slacken and remove the screws, release the retaining strap and lower the accumulator away from its mounting bracket.

9 If the mounting bracket cannot be lowered sufficiently to remove the accumulator, where applicable, unscrew the banjo unions, and disconnect the fuel pipe from the fuel pump and the filter - again, be prepared for fuel spillage, and recover the sealing washers.

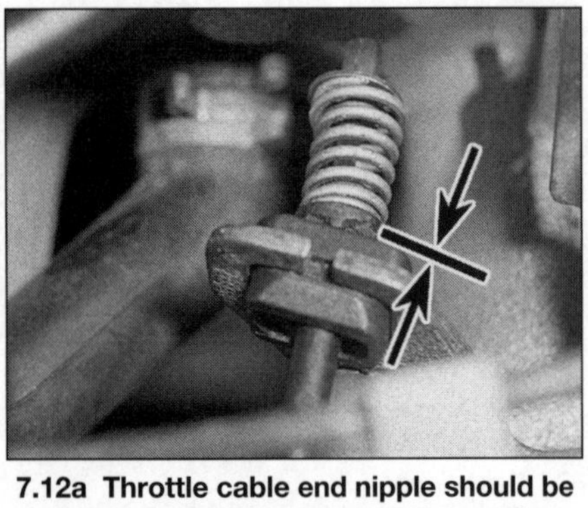

7.12a Throttle cable end nipple should be resting against the compression spring with no freeplay

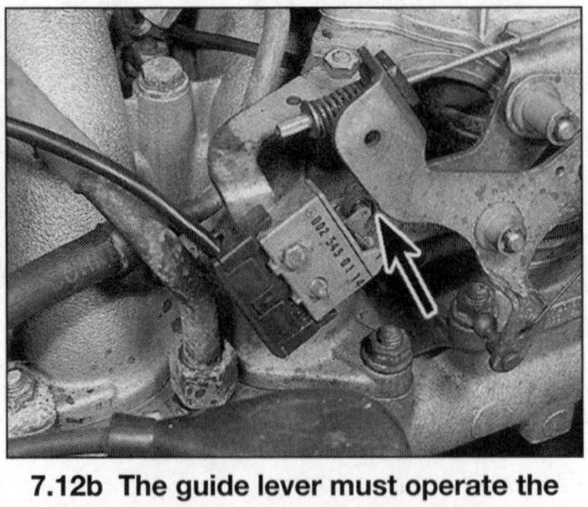

7.12b The guide lever must operate the idle microswitch by resting against the actuating lever (arrowed)

7.12c Full throttle stop adjustment nut (arrowed) at the support bracket

9.9 Slacken the large hose clip (arrowed) on the rubber connecting sleeve

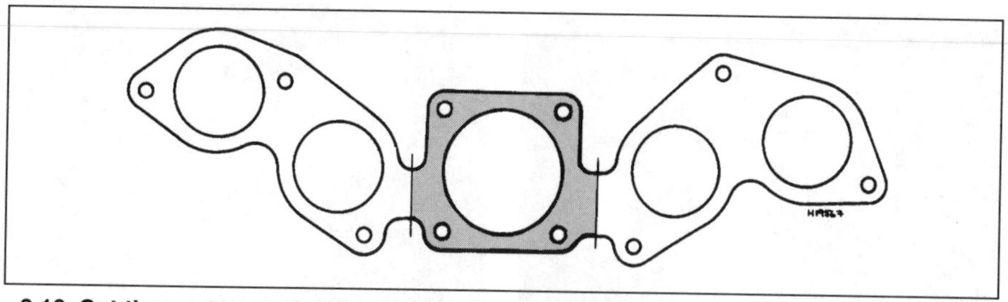

9.16 Cut the centre section from a new inlet manifold gasket and lay it in position over the throttle body contact area

Once the fuel pipe has been removed, it should be possible to lower the accumulator for removal.

Refitting

10 Refitting is a reversal of removal, but fit new sealing washers where banjo bolt unions are used.

11 On completion, start the vehicle and check around the disturbed components for leaks. Note that the fuel pump has to purge the system of air, so the engine may take a little longer than usual to start.

9 Throttle body - removal and refitting

Removal

1 On 6-cylinder engine models, depressurise the fuel system with reference to Section 2.

2 Disconnect the battery negative lead and position it away from the terminal.

3 Remove the air cleaner assembly as described in Section 3.

4 Where applicable, unbolt the throttle linkage bracket on the air flow sensor and move it to one side.

5 Disconnect the linkage return spring(s) on the throttle body and the linkage connecting rod. Where applicable, disconnect the cruise control actuator linkage from the throttle valve lever.

6 Disconnect the vacuum hose(s) at the throttle body. Label each hose carefully to avoid confusion during refitting.

7 Unplug the throttle valve switch wiring at the harness connector.

8 Unscrew the nuts securing the throttle body to the inlet manifold.

9 Slacken the large hose clip on the rubber connecting sleeve between the throttle body and the airflow sensor **(see illustration)**.

10 On 6-cylinder engine models, it will be necessary to remove the entire fuel distributor unit from the inlet manifold - refer to Section 10 for details, then proceed to paragraph 14. On 4-cylinder engine models, proceed as described in paragraphs 11 to 13 inclusive.

11 Unscrew the two nuts securing the airflow sensor to its rubber mountings at the throttle linkage end.

12 Unscrew the fuel return line union nut at the rear of the fuel pressure regulator, and disconnect the return line. Be prepared for fuel spillage.

13 Carefully lift the airflow sensor up just enough to allow the throttle body to be removed.

14 Unscrew the securing bolts, and lift the throttle body from the inlet manifold.

15 On 6-cylinder engine models, recover the throttle body gasket. On 4-cylinder engine models, using a sharp blade, cut out and remove the inlet manifold gasket centre section, at the throttle body contact area. Take care to avoid scoring the mating surface.

Refitting

16 Refit the throttle body by following the removal procedure in reverse, noting the following points **(see illustration)**.

a) If the throttle body is to be renewed, a new throttle switch must be also be fitted as the two components are matched.

b) On 6-cylinder engine models, use a new throttle body gasket.

c) On 4-cylinder engine models, cut the centre section from a new inlet manifold gasket and lay it in position over the throttle body contact area.

d) Tighten the throttle body securing bolts to the specified torque.

e) Ensure that the vacuum hoses are refitted correctly, according to the notes made during removal.

f) On completion, check and if necessary adjust the engine idle speed, as described in Chapter 1A.

10 Bosch KE-Jetronic fuel injection system components - removal and refitting

Warning: Observe the precautions in Section 1 before working on any component in the fuel system.

Note: *After disturbing any of the fuel system components, it is advisable to have a Mercedes-Benz dealer or Bosch fuel injection specialist carry out a diagnostic check. This is to ensure that any fault codes that may have been stored in the memory of the fuel system electronic control unit are erased, before bringing the vehicle back into service.*

Fuel distributor

Removal

1 Depressurise the fuel system with reference to Section 2. Disconnect the battery negative lead and position it away from the terminal.

2 Remove the air cleaner assembly as described in Section 3.

3 Undo the injector fuel line unions, at the fuel distributor and at the injectors themselves. Ensure that the injector body is counter-held with a spanner, as the union nuts are slackened.

4 At the fuel distributor, undo the fuel line unions for the cold start valve, pressure regulator and the fuel supply pipe.

5 Unplug the wiring harness from the electro-hydraulic pressure actuator at the multiway connector, on the side of the fuel distributor.

6 Slacken and withdraw the three retaining screws from the top of the fuel distributor, then lift the unit upwards whilst twisting from side to side, to separate it from the air flow sensor **(see illustrations)**. Recover the O-ring seal.

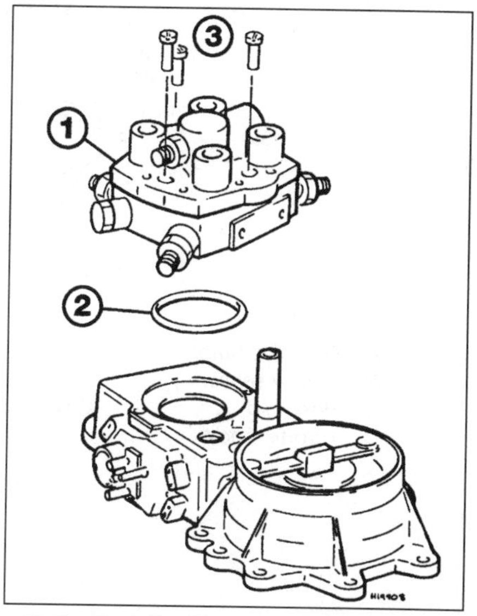

10.6a Fuel distributor-to-airflow sensor assembly details (4-cylinder engine shown)

1 Fuel distributor
2 O-ring seal
3 Retaining screws

4B

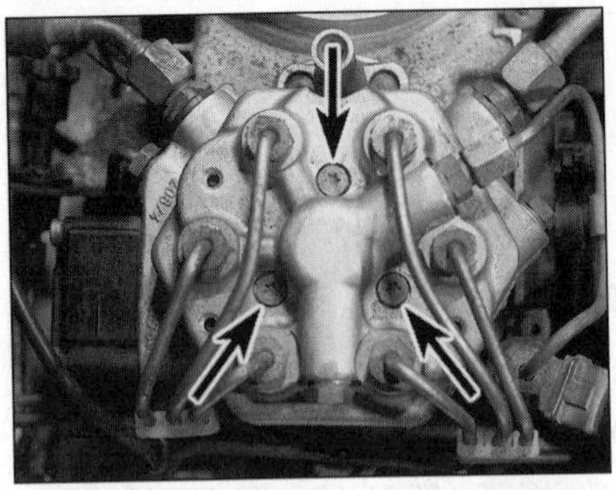

10.6b Fuel distributor-to-airflow sensor screws (arrowed) - 6-cylinder engine shown

10.10 Throttle linkage support bracket bolts (arrowed)

10.11 Airflow sensor wiring connector (arrowed)

Refitting

7 Refitting is a reversal of the removal procedure, but note that a new O-ring seal must be fitted between the fuel distributor and the air flow sensor. Tighten all fixings and unions to the correct torque, where specified.

8 On completion, start the engine and check around the disturbed components for leakage, then check and if necessary adjust the engine idle speed and exhaust gas CO content, as described in Chapter 1A.

Air flow sensor

Removal

9 Refer to the relevant paragraphs elsewhere in this Section, and remove the fuel distributor and fuel pressure regulator.

10 Unscrew the bolts and move the throttle linkage support bracket to one side **(see illustration)**.

11 Unplug the wiring harness from the airflow sensor at the multiway connector **(see illustration)**.

12 With reference to Section 9, separate the throttle body from the base of the airflow sensor assembly **(see illustration)**.

13 Unscrew the nuts that secure the airflow sensor to its rubber mountings and brackets **(see illustration)**.

14 Lift the unit away from the throttle body, disconnect the idle speed air hose and remove the airflow sensor from the car.

15 The rubber air guide moulding may be separated from the sensor body, after removing the retaining screws. Note, however, that the screws are of different lengths and must be refitted in their original positions, on reassembly.

Refitting

16 Refitting is a reversal of the removal procedure. Tighten all fixings and unions to the correct torque, where specified.

17 On completion, start the engine and check around the disturbed components for leakage, then check and if necessary adjust the engine idle speed and exhaust gas CO content, as described in Chapter 1A.

Air injection pump (6-cylinder engine models only)

Removal

18 Disconnect the battery negative lead and position it away from the terminal.

19 With reference to Chapter 1, relieve the tension from the auxiliary drivebelt and slip the belt off the air injection pump pulley.

20 Unplug the wiring for the electromagnetic clutch at the connector.

21 Slacken the clip and disconnect the air hose from the port at the rear of the pump.

22 Unscrew the upper and lower mounting bolts, then lift the pump away from the engine.

Refitting

23 Refitting is a reversal of removal. On completion, refer to Chapter 1 and tension the auxiliary drivebelt.

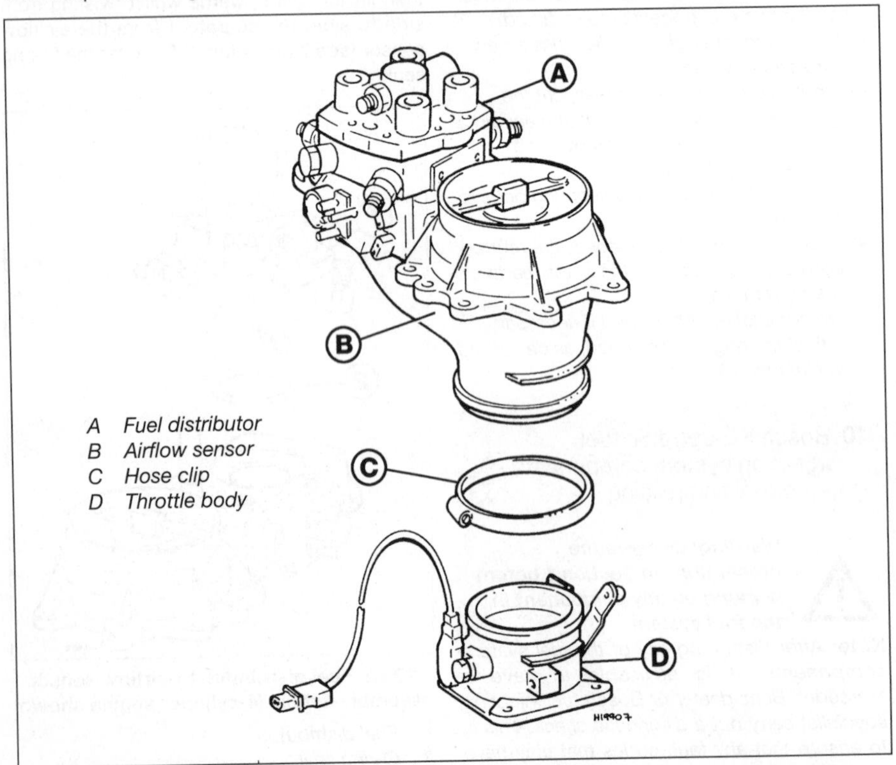

10.12 Airflow sensor-to-throttle body assembly details (4-cylinder engine shown)

10.13 Airflow sensor-to-rubber mounting retaining nuts (arrowed)

Cold start valve

Removal

24 Depressurise the fuel system with reference to Section 2. Disconnect the battery negative cable and position it away from the terminal.

25 Unplug the wiring from the cold start valve at the connector, which is located on the inlet manifold, close to the cylinder head mating surface **(see illustration)**.

26 Slacken and unscrew the fuel line union nut, then disconnect the fuel line from the valve and the fuel distributor **(see illustration)**. Be prepared for fuel spillage, and take adequate fire precautions.

27 Undo the two Allen screws and lift out the cold start valve. Recover the gasket.

Refitting

28 Refitting is a reversal of removal.

Coolant temperature sensor

Removal

29 Refer to Chapter 3 and partially drain the cooling system. Ensure that the ignition is switched off.

30 The coolant sensor is screwed into the upper surface of the cylinder head on the left-hand side of the engine. Do not confuse it with the temperature gauge sender unit.

31 Unplug the wiring from the sensor at the connector.

32 Unscrew the sensor from the housing and recover the O-ring seal.

Refitting

33 Refitting is a reversal of removal. On completion, top-up the cooling system.

Throttle switch

Removal

34 The throttle switch can be detached after removing the throttle body - refer to Section 9 for details. Note that once disturbed, the switch must be matched to the throttle body and this is a job that should ideally be entrusted to a Mercedes-Benz dealer or Bosch fuel injection specialist.

Electronic control unit (ECU)

Removal

Caution: Electronic Control Units (ECUs) contain components that are sensitive to the levels of static electricity generated by a person during normal activity. Once the multiway harness connector has been unplugged, the exposed ECU connector pins can freely conduct stray static electricity to these components, damaging or even destroying them - the damage will be invisible and may not manifest itself immediately. Expensive repairs can be avoided by observing the following basic handling rules:

a) Handle a disconnected ECU by its case only; do not allow fingers or tools to come into contact with the pins.

b) When carrying an ECU around, "ground" yourself from time to time, by touching a metal object such as an unpainted water pipe, this will discharge any potentially damaging static that may have built up.

c) Do not leave the ECU unplugged from its connector for any longer than is absolutely necessary.

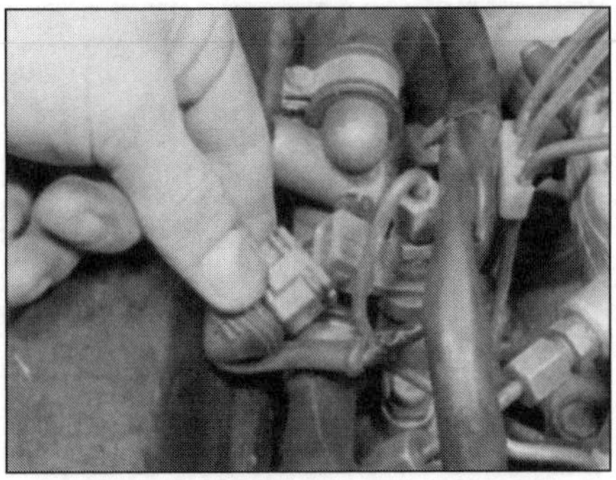

10.25 Disconnecting the wiring plug from the cold start valve

35 The ECU is located in the compartment behind the engine bay bulkhead, adjacent to the battery.

36 Disconnect the battery negative lead and position it away from the terminal. On certain models, it will be necessary to remove the battery (see Chapter 5A) to give sufficient clearance to remove the ECU.

37 To unplug the multiway connector, first depress the spring tab at the cable end of the connector block, lift the block at the cable end then disengage the lug at the opposite end of the block.

38 Depress the locking clip, then remove the screws (where applicable) and lift the ECU up and out of its mountings **(see illustrations)**. Note that on certain models with ABS, it will be necessary to first remove the ABS ECU - refer to Chapter 9 for details.

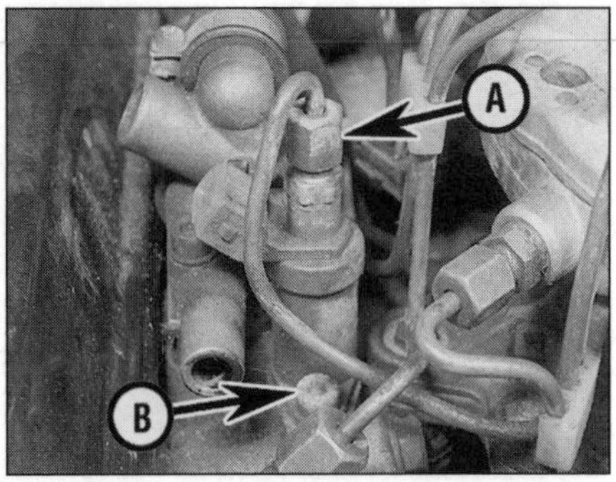

10.26 Cold start valve fuel line union nut (A) and front valve securing screw (B)

Refitting

39 Refitting is a reversal of removal.

Fuel injectors

Removal

40 Depressurise the fuel system as described in Section 2. Disconnect the battery negative lead and position it away from the terminal.

41 Remove the air cleaner assembly as described in Section 3 and, where necessary, disconnect the hoses at the camshaft cover and the auxiliary air device to improve access **(see illustrations)**.

10.38a Depress the locking clip . . .

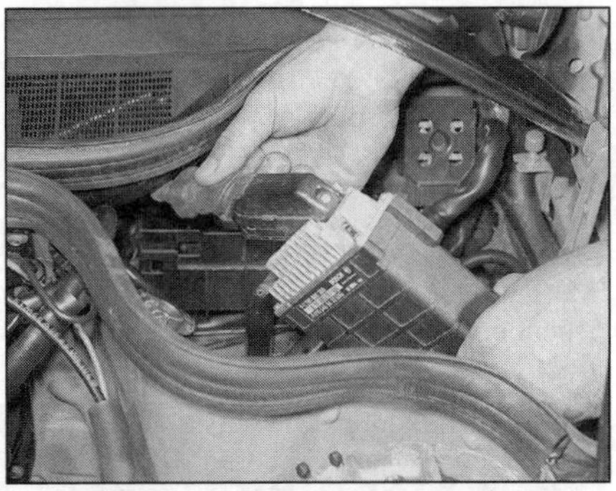

10.38b . . . then lift out the ECU and disconnect the wiring plug

10.41a Disconnect the hoses from the camshaft cover . . .

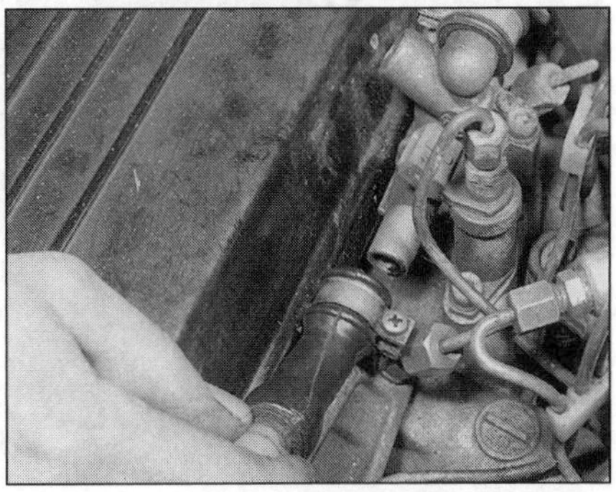

10.41b . . . and the auxiliary air device - 4-cylinder engine

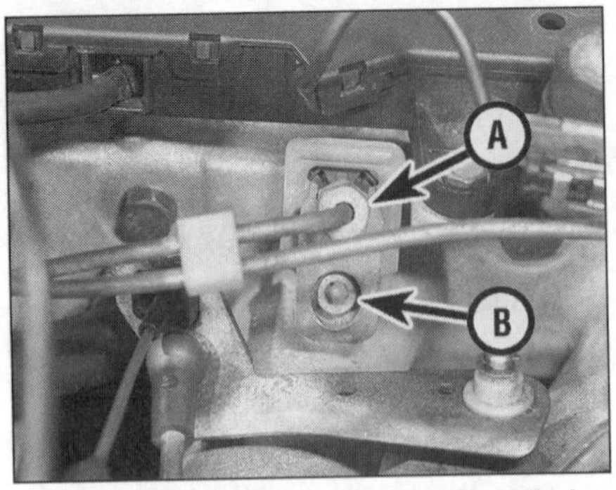

10.43a Fuel injector assembly - 6-cylinder engine

A Fuel line union nut
B Securing clip screw

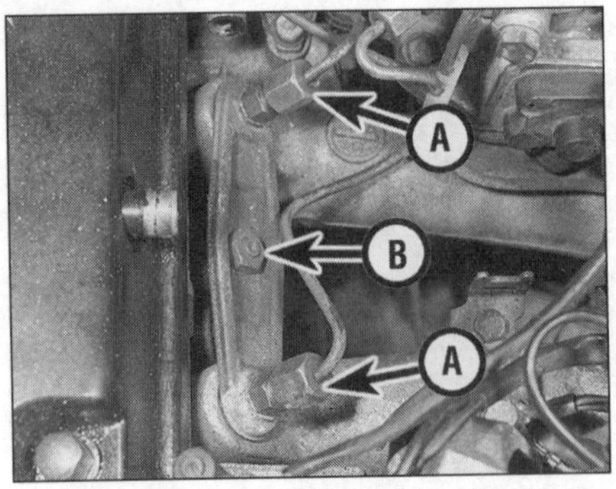

10.43b Fuel injector assembly - 4-cylinder engine

A Fuel line union nut
B Injector bridging piece nut

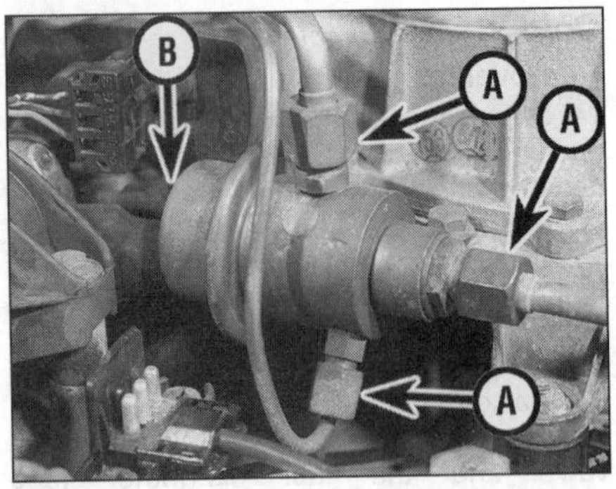

10.49 Fuel pressure regulator connections

A Fuel line unions
B Vacuum hose

42 Slacken the fuel line union nuts, at each fuel injector and the corresponding ports on the fuel distributor. Counter-hold the injector body with a spanner, as the union nuts are slackened. Move the fuel lines to one side.
43 On 4-cylinder engine models, slacken the centre nut then lift out the bridging piece between each pair of injectors. On 6-cylinder models, slacken and remove the screw, then remove the injector securing clip **(see illustrations)**.
44 Withdraw the injectors, recovering the seals.

Refitting

45 Refitting is a reversal of removal, but use new injector seals. Tighten the retaining screw(s) securely.

Fuel pressure regulator

Removal

46 Depressurise the fuel system as described in Section 2. Disconnect the battery negative lead and position it away from the terminal.
47 Remove the air cleaner assembly as described in Section 3.
48 Clamp off the flexible fuel lines leading to the pressure regulator, using proprietary hose clamps. Do not use G-clamps as these may damage the hoses internally.
49 Unscrew the fuel line unions and detach the fuel lines from the ports on the pressure regulator **(see illustration)**. Be prepared for fuel spillage. Where applicable, detach the vacuum hose from the rear of the pressure regulator.
50 Slacken and withdraw the clamp bolt, then remove the pressure regulator from the airflow sensor housing.

Refitting

51 Refit the fuel pressure regulator by following the removal procedure in reverse.

Auxiliary air device/rotary idle actuator

6-cylinder engines

52 Disconnect the battery negative lead and position it away from the terminal.
53 The rotary idle actuator is situated above the inlet manifold, in front of the fuel distributor.
54 Unplug the wiring from the actuator, at the connector.
55 Pull the air hoses from the actuator ports, noting their fitted positions to aid refitting.
56 Unscrew the bolts and remove the actuator from its mountings **(see illustration)**.
57 Refitting is a reversal of removal, but ensure that the air hoses are correctly reconnected as noted before removal.

4-cylinder engines

58 Disconnect the battery negative lead and position it away from the terminal.
59 The auxiliary air device is situated to the rear of the inlet manifold, adjacent to the engine compartment bulkhead.
60 Unplug the wiring from the auxiliary air device, at the connector **(see illustration)**.
61 Slacken the hose clip and pull the air hose from the port on the upper surface of the auxiliary air device.
62 Unscrew the bolts and remove the unit from its mountings.
63 Refitting is a reversal of removal.

Lambda sensor

Removal

64 The Lambda sensor is screwed into a boss on the exhaust system downpipe - access is from the underside of the vehicle.

10.56 Rotary idle actuator mounting bolts (arrowed) - 6-cylinder engine

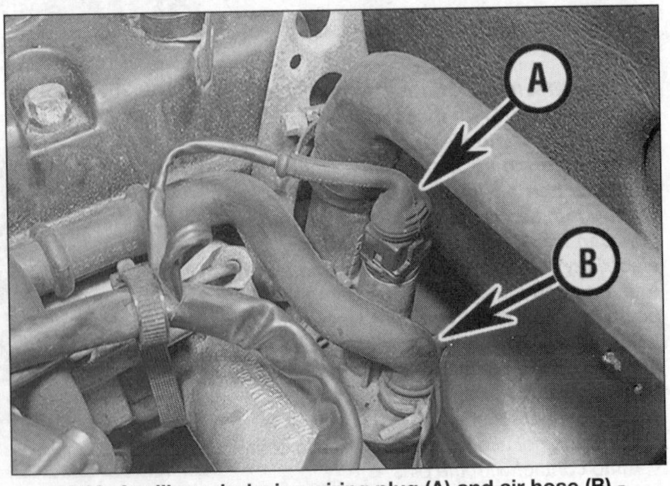

10.60 Auxiliary air device wiring plug (A) and air hose (B) - 4-cylinder engine

10.68 Unclip the metal shield (arrowed) from the Lambda sensor

65 Jack up the front of the car and support it on axle stands (see *"Jacking and vehicle support"*). Alternatively position the car over an inspection pit or on car ramps.

66 Ensure that the ignition is switched off and wait until the exhaust system has cooled completely, before starting work.

67 Working under the vehicle, disconnect the Lambda sensor wiring at the union on the floorpan. The union has a bayonet fitting - rotate it through a quarter of a turn anti-clockwise to disengage it. **Note:** *On later models the wiring connector is located inside the vehicle, under the drivers footwell carpet. Unplug the connector and then feed the wiring through the grommet in the floorpan.*

68 Unclip the metal shield then, using an open-ended spanner or a socket, unscrew the Lambda sensor from the downpipe **(see illustration)**. **Note:** *As a flying lead remains connected to the sensor after is has been disconnected, if the correct size spanner is not available, a slotted socket will be required to remove the sensor.* Take care to avoid damaging the wiring or the sensor tip, as it withdrawn.

Refitting

69 Apply a little anti-seize grease to the sensor threads - avoid contaminating the probe tip.

70 Refit the sensor to its housing, tightening it to the correct torque. Restore the harness connection.

11 Inlet manifold - removal and refitting

Removal

1 Disconnect the battery negative lead and position it away from the terminal.

2 Refer to Section 2 and depressurise the fuel system.

3 Refer to Section 7 and detach the throttle cable from the throttle guide lever. On models with automatic transmission, also detach the control pressure cable from the throttle linkage. On models with cruise control, disconnect the throttle control linkage at the throttle actuator unit.

4 Unbolt the wiring harness support rail from the inlet manifold, after unclipping the harness from it.

5 Remove the air cleaner assembly.

6 Refer to Section 10 and carry out the following.

a) Remove the cold start valve from the inlet manifold.

b) Remove the fuel distributor/airflow sensor unit.

c) Remove the throttle body.

7 On 6-cylinder engine models with cruise control, unbolt the throttle actuator unit, complete with its mounting bracket, from the inlet manifold.

8 Where applicable on 4-cylinder engine models, disconnect the hoses from the idle speed air distributor; labelling each hose carefully to avoid confusion during refitting.

9 Unscrew the union nut and disconnect the brake servo vacuum hose from the inlet manifold. Release the hose from its support bracket.

10 Where applicable, on 4-cylinder engine models, unbolt the engine lifting bracket from the manifold.

11 Disconnect the remaining wiring plugs and vacuum hoses from the manifold, labelling each one carefully to avoid confusion during refitting.

12 Unbolt and remove the support strut(s) from beneath the inlet manifold **(see illustration)**. Check nothing remains

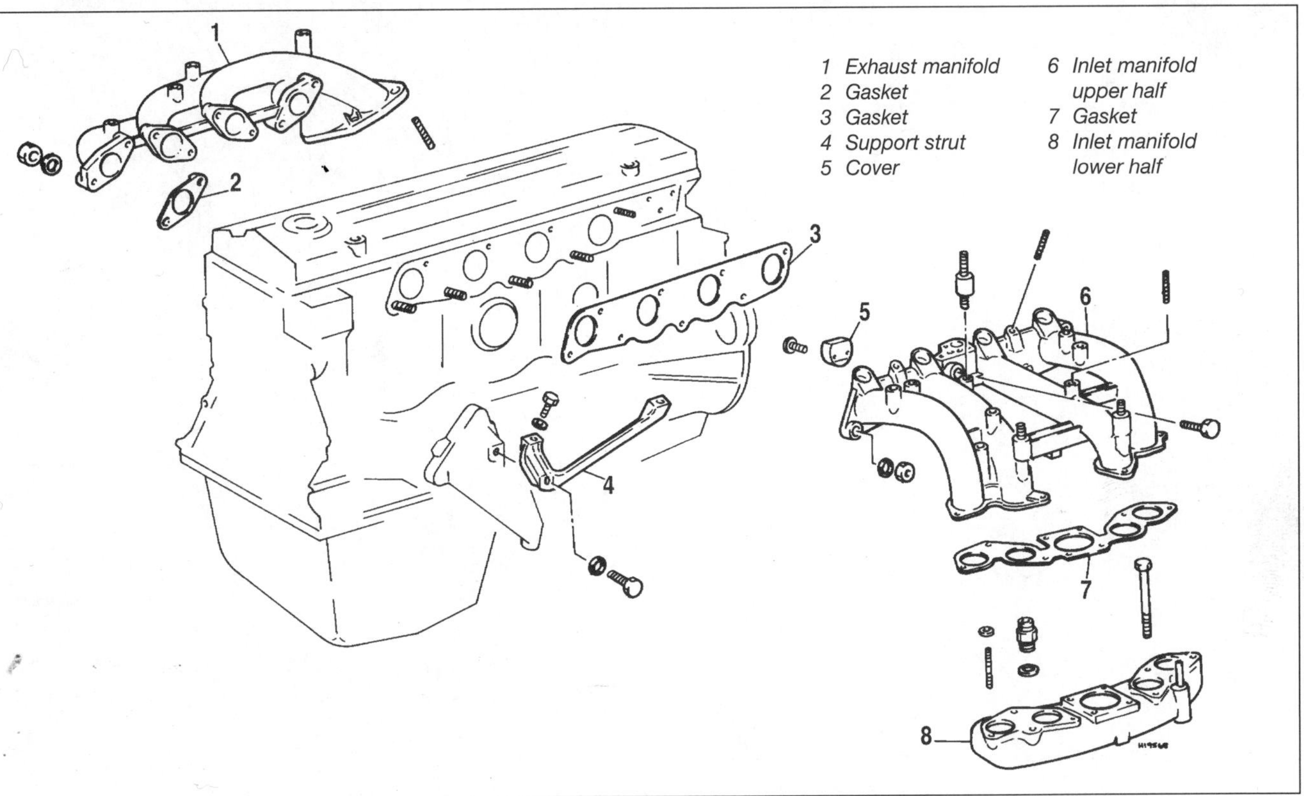

11.12 Inlet and exhaust manifold details - 4-cylinder engine

4B

connected to the manifold that might impede its removal.

13 Slacken and remove the retaining nuts and bolts, then lift the inlet manifold away from the cylinder head. Recover and discard the gasket.

14 Where applicable, the upper and lower sections of the manifold can be separated if required, after removing the securing bolts. Note that the gasket between the two sections must be renewed on reassembly (on 4-cylinder engine models, the throttle body shares this gasket).

15 Clean the mating surfaces of the cylinder head and the manifold, taking care to avoid scoring them. Ensure that all traces of the old gasket have been removed. If there is evidence of leakage, check both surfaces for distortion using a straight edge and feeler blade, as described in Chapter 2.

Refitting

16 Refitting is a reversal of removal, noting the following points.

a) *Ensure that both mating surfaces are completely clean, before laying the new gasket in position on the cylinder head studs.*

b) *Refer to Section 7 and adjust the throttle cable.*

c) *On models with automatic transmission, refer to Chapter 7B and adjust the operation of the control pressure cable.*

d) *Start the engine and check for leakage around the manifold.*

e) *Check and if necessary adjust the engine idle speed with reference to Chapter 1A.*

Chapter 4 Part C
Diesel fuel injection system

Contents

Air cleaner assembly - removal and refitting 2
Air filter element renewal . . . . . see Chapter 1B
ARA electronic anti-jerk control system - component removal and refitting 13
Electronic diesel engine control system (EDS) - component removal and refitting 14
ELR electronic idle speed control system - component removal and refitting 12
Engine idle speed - check and adjustment . . . . . see Chapter 1B
Engine overload protection system - component removal and refitting 15
Fuel filter renewal . . . . . see Chapter 1B
Fuel gauge sender unit - removal and refitting 4
Fuel injection pump - removal and refitting 7
Fuel injection pump timing device and sprocket - removal and refitting 8
Fuel injection pump start of delivery - general information, checking and adjustment 9
Fuel lift pump - removal and refitting 3
Fuel tank - removal and refitting 5
Fuel thermostat - removal and refitting 11
General information and precautions 1
Injectors and high pressure fuel lines - removal and refitting 10
Inlet manifold - removal and refitting 16
Throttle cable - removal and refitting 6

Degrees of difficulty

Easy, suitable for novice with little experience	**Fairly easy,** suitable for beginner with some experience	**Fairly difficult,** suitable for competent DIY mechanic	**Difficult,** suitable for experienced DIY mechanic	**Very difficult,** suitable for expert DIY or professional

Specifications

General

Maximum no-load engine speed	5150 ± 50 rpm
Engine idle speed:	
4-cylinder engines with pneumatic idle speed increase	750 ± 50 rpm
4-cylinder engines with electronic idle speed control (ELR)	720 ± 20 rpm
5 -cylinder engines with pneumatic idle speed increase	700 ± 50 rpm
5-cylinder engines with electronic idle speed control (ELR)	680 ± 20 rpm

Fuel injection pump

Injection pump start of delivery (test value)	15° AFTER TDC on cylinder No 1

Torque wrench settings

	Nm	lbf ft
Inlet manifold bolts	25	18
Injection pump to rear mounting bracket	25	18
Injection pump to front mounting bolts	25	18
Injection pump sprocket bolt	45	33
Injection pump inspection hole plug	35	26
Injector fuel pipe unions	15	11
Injectors	75	55

1 General information and precautions

General information

Normally-aspirated engines

The fuel system major components comprise a fuel tank, a fuel injection pump, engine compartment-mounted fuel pre-filter and canister-type main filter, fuel supply and return lines and one fuel injector per cylinder.

The injection pump is driven at half crankshaft speed by the timing chain. Fuel is drawn from the fuel tank, through the pre-filter and main filter by the injection pump, which then distributes the fuel under very high pressure to the injectors via separate delivery pipes.

The basic injection timing is set by the position of the injection pump on its mounting bracket. When the engine is running, the injection timing is advanced and retarded mechanically by the injection pump itself, and is influenced primarily by accelerator position and engine speed. The injection timing can be altered by means of a threaded adjustment device mounted on the side of the injection pump.

The injectors are spring-loaded mechanical valves, which open when the pressure of the fuel supplied to them exceeds a specific limit. Fuel is then sprayed from the injector nozzle into the cylinder via a pre-chamber (indirect injection).

The engine is stopped by means of a vacuum controlled shut-off module, mounted on the upper surface of the fuel injection pump. When the facia mounted ignition key is turned to the "OFF" position, a vacuum switch integral with the ignition lock assembly interrupts the supply of vacuum to the shut-off module, which in turn interrupts the supply of fuel to the injection pump, stopping the engine.

Engine idle speed is controlled primarily by a mechanical governor, integral with the injection pump. This mechanism uses the centrifugal force generated by a number of shaft-mounted rotating weights to alter the position of the injection pump control rod via a spring loaded lever. The mechanism may be pre-loaded by one or more actuators, which cause a steep rise in engine idle speed under load, e.g. when the power steering or air conditioning is operated, or when drive is engaged on models with automatic transmission, or under cold start conditions, when the engines mechanical resistance is high.

Models with air conditioning and automatic transmission are fitted with an electronic idle speed control system (ELR). This system employs an electronic control unit which monitors engine speed via a sensor mounted at the flywheel, and coolant temperature via a sensor screwed into the cylinder head. The ECU then compares the actual engine speed with a mapped value stored in memory. If the two are different, the ECU drives an electromagnetic actuator which mechanically pre-loads the injection pump governor to alter the engine idle speed accordingly.

An anti-jerk system (ARA) is fitted to certain models equipped with manual transmission. This system uses engine speed and coolant temperature information to eliminate the tendency for the vehicle to "jerk" during part-load acceleration and deceleration. Under these conditions, an electromagnetic actuator mounted on the side of the injection pump briefly reduces the amount of fuel supplied to the engine, reducing the torque developed and lessening the tendency to jerk. The overall operation is controlled by a dedicated electronic control unit.

Turbo-diesel engines

The operation of the fuel injection system is identical to that of the normally-aspirated engines. However, the idle speed control and anti-jerk systems are now managed by an Electronic Diesel Engine Control System (EDS), which also controls the inlet charge pressure (turbo-boost) and exhaust gas recirculation systems.

Precautions

Many of the operations described in this Chapter involve the disconnection of fuel lines, which may cause an amount of fuel spillage. Before commencing work, refer to the *Warnings* and *Caution* given below and the information in *"Safety First!"* at the beginning of this manual.

Caution: Under no circumstances should diesel fuel be allowed to come into contact with coolant hoses - wipe off accidental spillage immediately. Hoses that have been contaminated with fuel for an extended period should be renewed. Diesel fuel systems are particularly sensitive to contamination from dirt, air and water. Pay particular attention to cleanliness when working on any part of the fuel system, to prevent the ingress of dirt. Thoroughly clean the area around fuel unions before disconnecting them. Store dismantled components in sealed containers to prevent contamination and the formation of condensation. Only use lint-free cloths and clean fuel for component cleansing. Avoid using compressed air when cleaning components in situ.

Warning: When working on any part of the fuel system, avoid direct contact skin contact with diesel fue! - wear protective clothing and gloves when handling fuel system components. Ensure the work area is well ventilated to prevent the build up of diesel fuel vapour.

Warning: Fuel injectors operate at extremely high pressures and the jet of fuel produced at the nozzle is capable of piercing skin, with potentially fatal results. When working with pressurised injectors, take great to avoid exposing any part of the body to the fuel spray. It is recommended that any pressure testing of the fuel system components should be carried out by a diesel fuel injection specialist.

2 Air cleaner assembly - removal and refitting

Removal

1 Refer to Chapter 1B and remove the air filter element.

Turbo-diesel engines

2 On models with an inlet air temperature sensor mounted in the air cleaner, unplug the wiring from the sensor at the connector.

3 Unscrew the securing bolts and/or nuts, and lift the air cleaner casing from the body panel. Where applicable, disengage the air cleaner casing from the air intake tube.

4 Where applicable, loosen the hose clip, and disconnect the air trunking connecting the air cleaner casing to the airflow meter, then withdraw the air cleaner casing from the engine compartment **(see illustration)**.

Normally-aspirated engines

5 Where applicable, disconnect the vacuum line from the control flap actuator.

6 Unbolt the front and rear mounting brackets and release the air cleaner from them -

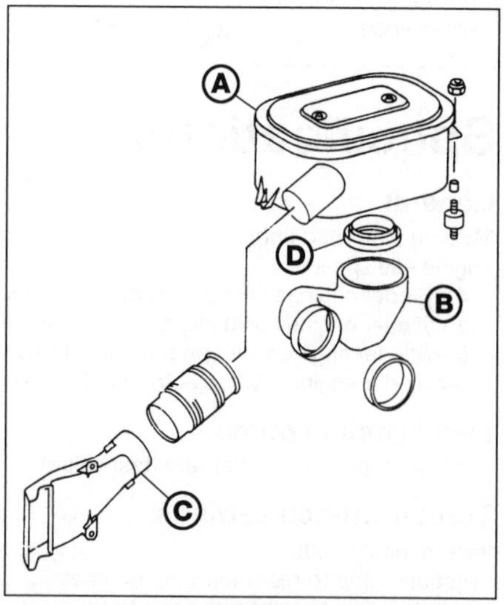

2.4 Air cleaner assembly - turbo-diesel engines

A Air cleaner
B Inlet elbow
C Inlet scoop
D Cup seal

recover the rubber mountings **(see illustration)**.

7 Lift the air cleaner away from the inlet manifold and recover the rubber sealing boots.

Refitting

8 Refitting is a reversal of removal. On completion, refit the air filter element with reference to Chapter 1B.

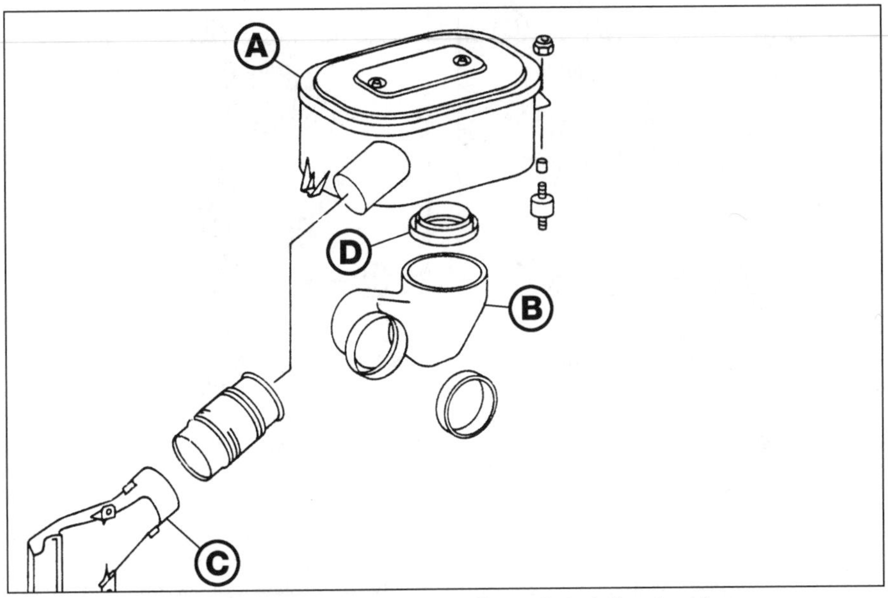

2.6 Air cleaner assembly - normally-aspirated diesel engines

A Retaining clips
B Air filter element
C Air ducting
D Inlet scoop
E Mounting brackets
F Rubber sealing boots

3 Fuel lift pump - removal and refitting

Removal

1 Disconnect the battery negative lead and position it away from the terminal.

2 Where necessary, on normally-aspirated engines, refer to Section 2 and remove the air cleaner.

3 Clamp off the fuel supply line using a proprietary hose clamp **(see illustration)**. Slacken the clip and detach the fuel line from the port at the rear of the lift pump. Be prepared for fuel loss - position a container underneath the pump and pad the surrounding area with absorbent rags.

4 Slacken the union at the top of the lift pump and disconnect the fuel supply line. Again be prepared for fuel loss.

5 When the lift pump is removed, there will be a small amount of engine oil loss - position a container underneath the pump in preparation for this.

6 Slacken and withdraw the retaining nuts then pull the lift pump away from the injection pump body. Recover the washers and the pump gasket.

Refitting

7 Refitting is a reversal of removal, noting the following points:

a) *If the pump is to be renewed, unscrew the fuel supply line union from the top of the pump and transfer it to the new unit.*
b) *Use a new gasket when refitting the lift pump to the injection pump.*
c) *On completion, tighten the lift pump retaining nuts securely.*

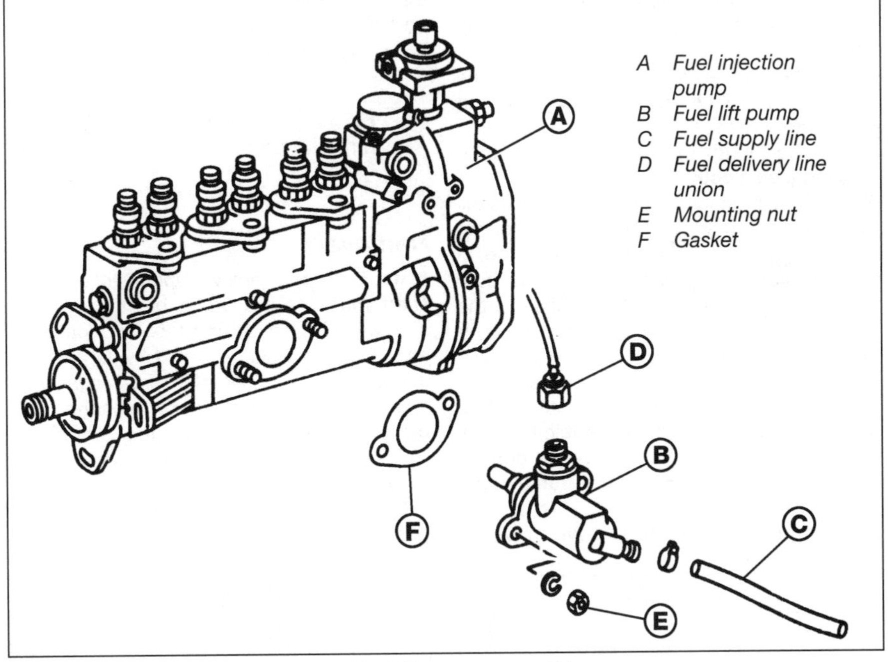

A Fuel injection pump
B Fuel lift pump
C Fuel supply line
D Fuel delivery line union
E Mounting nut
F Gasket

3.3 Fuel lift pump assembly

4 Fuel gauge sender unit - removal and refitting

Refer to the information given in Chapter 4A.

5 Fuel tank - removal and refitting

Refer to the information given in Chapter 4A.

6 Throttle cable - removal, refitting and adjustment

Removal and refitting

1 Refer to the information given in Chapter 4B. On completion, adjust the operation of the cable as described in the following sub-section.

Adjustment

2 Before attempting adjustment, check that the route taken by the cable avoids kinking, crushing or tight bends. Operate the throttle pedal through its full stroke and check that no resistance can be felt.

3 With the throttle linkage in the idle position, check that the spring plate at the end of the throttle cable is resting lightly against the

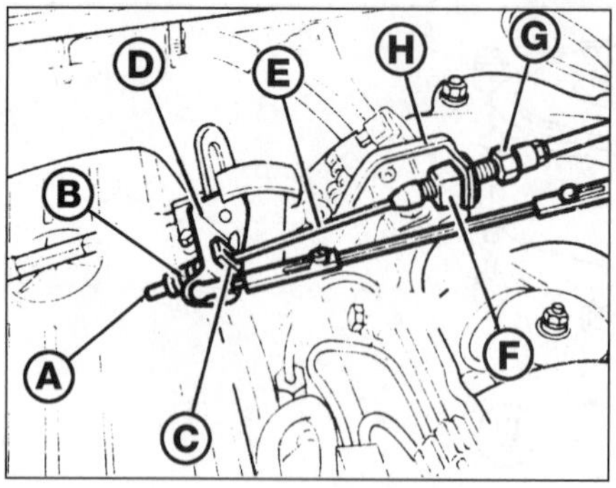

6.3 Throttle cable linkage

A End of throttle cable
B Compression spring
C Retaining block
D Guide lever
E Throttle cable inner
F Plastic retainer
G Adjustment nut
H Guide bracket

compression spring, without tension **(see illustration)**.

4 If this is not the case, remove the trim panel above the driver's footwell, to expose the hole in the bulkhead, where the throttle cable passes from the footwell into the engine compartment **(see illustration)**. Turn the adjuster at the bulkhead until the conditions in paragraph 3 are met.

5 With the relay lever in the idle position, the roller pivot should be resting against the end of the slotted section of the fulcrum lever. Adjust the length of the connecting rod if required **(see illustrations)**.

6 Pull the throttle control lever through its full travel. Check that the fuel injection pump control lever rests against the full load stop. In this position, also check that the relay lever pivot stops approximately 1 mm short of the end of the slotted section of the fulcrum lever **(see illustration)**.

7 If this not the case, slacken the locknut at the ball socket on the end of the connecting rod and reposition the socket within the relay lever slotted section to achieve the correct travel **(see illustration)**. On completion, tighten the locknut.

8 On models with automatic transmission,

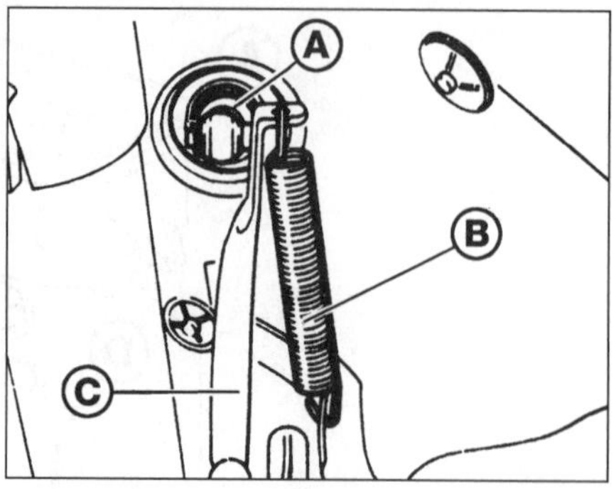

6.4 Cable adjustment knob at throttle pedal

A Adjustment knob
B Return spring
C Throttle pedal

refer to Chapter 7B and adjust the operation of the control pressure cable.

9 Have an assistant press the throttle pedal to the end of its travel, from inside the vehicle. Check that the fuel injection pump control lever rests against the full load stop. If required, turn the adjustment nut at the throttle guide bracket to achieve the correct travel **(refer to illustration 6.3)**.

10 On completion, repeat the operation described in paragraphs 3 and 4.

7 Fuel injection pump - removal and refitting

Removal

Note: *Following removal, the injection pump shaft must be locked in position using a specially shaped locking tool. Fabrication of an accurate substitute would be very difficult and its use could risk internal damage to the injection pump. For these reasons, it is recommended that a locking tool is borrowed from a Mercedes-Benz dealer or a Bosch diesel fuel injection system specialist.*

1 Disconnect the battery negative lead and position it away from the terminal.

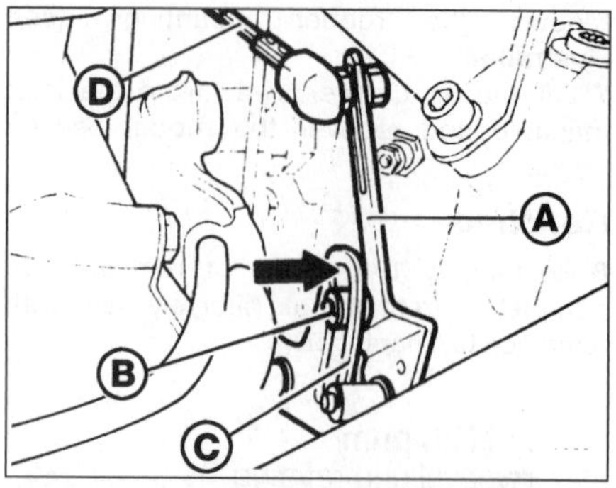

6.5a At idle, the roller pivot should be resting against the end (arrowed) of the slot in the fulcrum lever

A Relay lever
B Roller pivot
C Fulcrum lever
D Connecting rod

2 Where applicable, remove the engine undershield as described in Chapter 11.

3 Remove the auxiliary drivebelt tensioner as follows.

a) *Pull off the plastic cover, unscrew the securing bolt, and remove the auxiliary drivebelt idler pulley.*
b) *Unscrew the securing bolts, and remove the cooling fan pulley.*
c) *Unscrew the securing bolts, and withdraw the tensioner damper strut. Recover any spacers and/or brackets from the bolts noting their locations.*
d) *Using a pair of pliers, unhook the tension spring, noting its orientation to aid refitting.*
e) *Where applicable, pull off the plastic cover, then unscrew the tensioner securing bolt and slide off the spacer sleeve (if applicable).*
f) *Withdraw the tensioner and recover the spacer (where applicable).*

4 With reference to Chapter 3, remove the cooling fan and shroud.

5 Refer to Chapter 9 and remove the brake vacuum pump from the timing cover. Note that the gasket must be renewed on refitting.

6 If desired to improve access, remove the inlet manifold as described in Section 16.

7 Counterhold the crankshaft using a socket or spanner on the crankshaft pulley/vibration

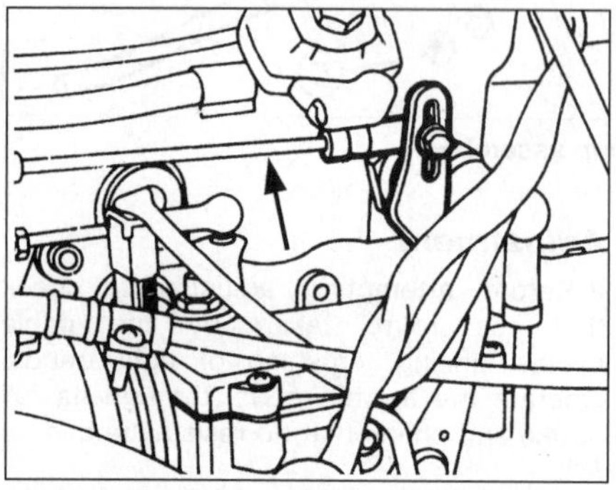

6.5b Adjust the length of the connecting rod (arrowed) if required

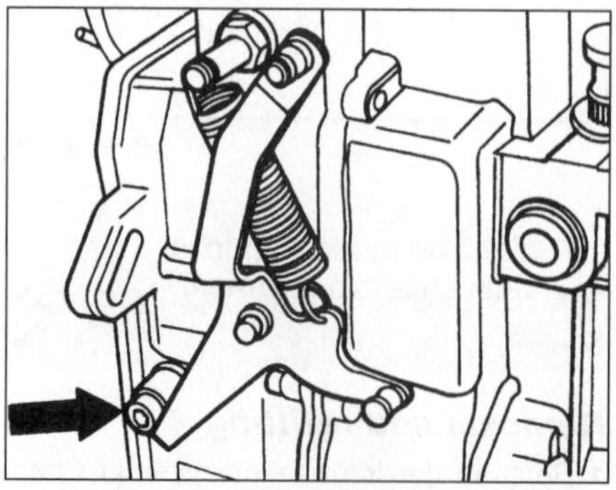

6.6 Check that the fuel injection pump control lever rests against the full load stop (arrowed)

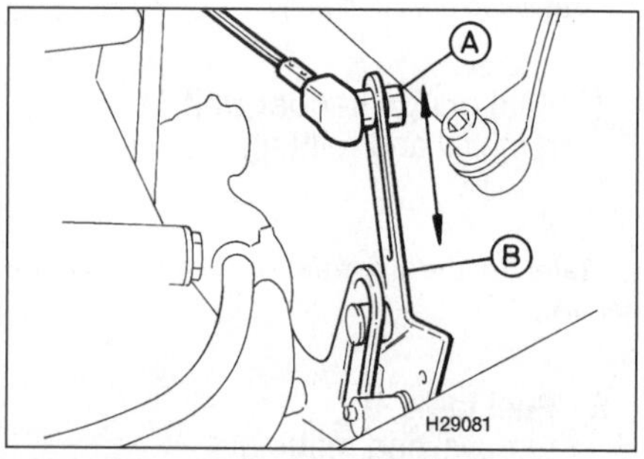

6.7 Slacken the locknut at the ball socket on the end of the connecting rod and reposition it

A Locknut B Relay lever

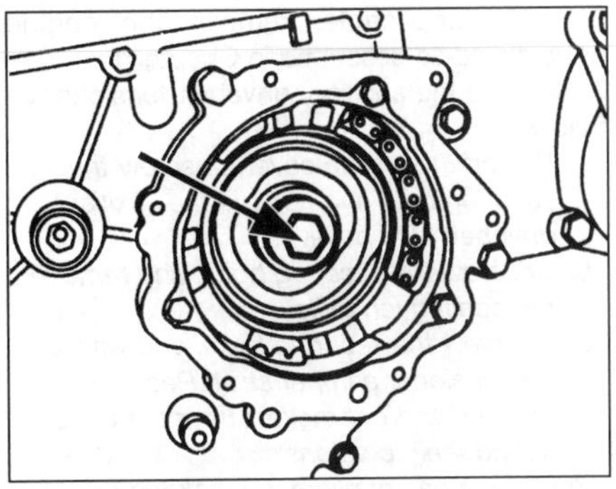

7.7 Slacken and remove the injection pump timing sprocket centre bolt (arrowed) - note that the bolt has a *LEFT-HAND THREAD*

damper hub bolt, then slacken and remove the injection pump sprocket centre bolt **(see illustration)**. **Note:** *The bolt has a LEFT-HAND THREAD.* Recover the washer.

8 Using a socket and wrench on the crankshaft pulley/vibration damper hub bolt, turn the crankshaft in its normal direction of rotation until the engine is set to 15° *AFTER* top dead centre on cylinder No 1. Use the pointer on the timing cover and the graduated markings on the vibration damper to achieve the correct alignment **(see illustration)**.

9 Refer to Chapter 2C and remove the timing chain tensioner **(see illustration)**.

10 Using a suitable open-ended spanner, or a wrench and crow's foot adapter, slacken the unions and detach the high pressure injector fuel lines from the injection pump. Be prepared for fuel loss - pad the surrounding area with absorbent rags **(see illustration)**.

11 Similarly, slacken and withdraw the banjo bolts, then disconnect the fuel supply, delivery and return hoses from the injection pump. Recover the seals and discard them - new items must be used on refitting. Clamp off the flexible section of the hoses to prevent further fuel loss.

12 Where applicable, remove the injection pump control lever damper strut.

13 Disconnect all vacuum hoses from the actuators on the top and rear of the injection pump, noting their locations to aid refitting later.

14 Similarly, disconnect all electrical wiring from the actuators and sensors on the top

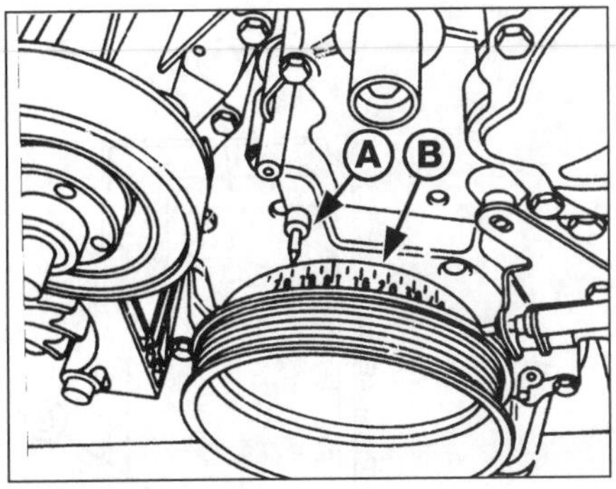

7.8 Set the engine to 15° *AFTER* top dead centre on cylinder No 1, using the pointer on the timing cover and the graduated markings on the vibration damper

A Pointer   B Graduated markings

and rear of the injection pump, noting the connector locations to aid refitting.

15 Detach the accelerator linkage from the injection pump control lever.

16 Mark the body of the injection pump in relation to the rear surface of its mounting flange, to allow approximate alignment during refitting.

17 When the injection pump is removed, it will be necessary to hold the sprocket (and timing device) in place in the timing chain casing, so that it cannot disengage from the timing chain, but in a manner which still allows it to rotate, if the engine is turned over by hand. On later models, a special retaining cage is fitted for this purpose.

18 On earlier models, not fitted with a sprocket retaining cage, have ready a length of metal tubing, of roughly the same outside diameter as the threaded section of the injection pump sprocket centre bolt.

19 Unscrew and withdraw the mounting bolts that secure the front of the injection pump to its mounting flange **(see illustration)**. Remove the bolt that secures the rear of the injection pump to the support bracket, then lift the injection pump away from its mountings. *At the same time,* support the pump sprocket (and timing device) to keep it in place. **Note:** ***DO NOT*** *allow the sprocket to disengage from the timing chain. Be prepared for an amount of engine oil loss as the injection pump is removed from its mounting flange.*

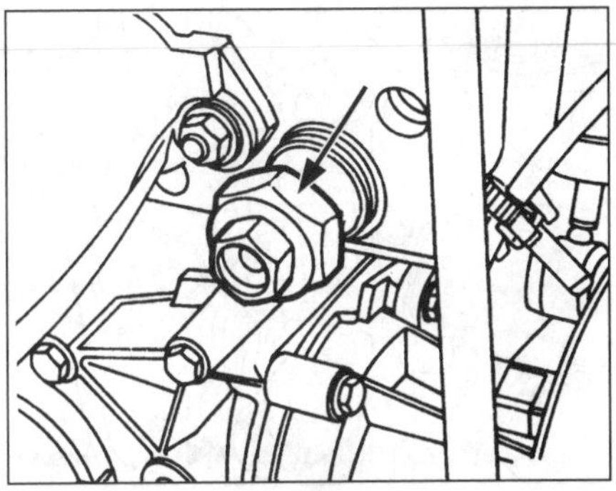

7.9 Remove the timing chain tensioner (arrowed)

20 Where applicable on earlier models not fitted with a sprocket retaining cage, slide the metal tubing through the sprocket centre hole. Pass a length of sturdy wire, or a large nylon cable-tie through the tubing, then secure it and the sprocket over the top of the timing chain casing.

21 Unbolt the fuel thermostat from the injection pump body and position it to one side **(see illustration)**. It should not be necessary to disconnect the fuel lines from the thermostat.

22 Cover all exposed fuel unions to minimise fuel loss and prevent the ingress of dirt **(see Tool Tip)**.

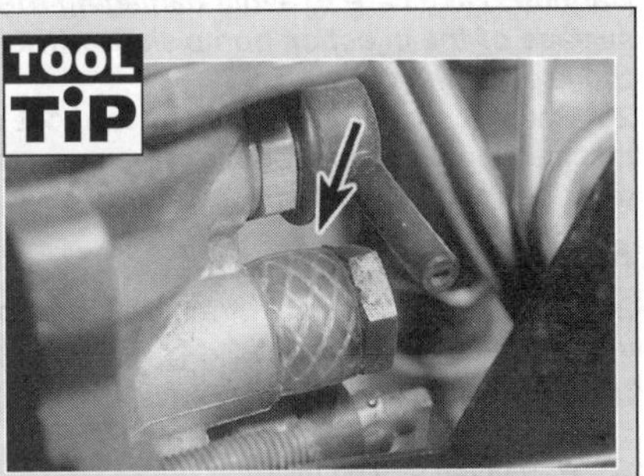

Fit a short length of hose over the banjo bolt so that the drillings are covered, then thread the bolt back into its injection pump port and finger tighten it

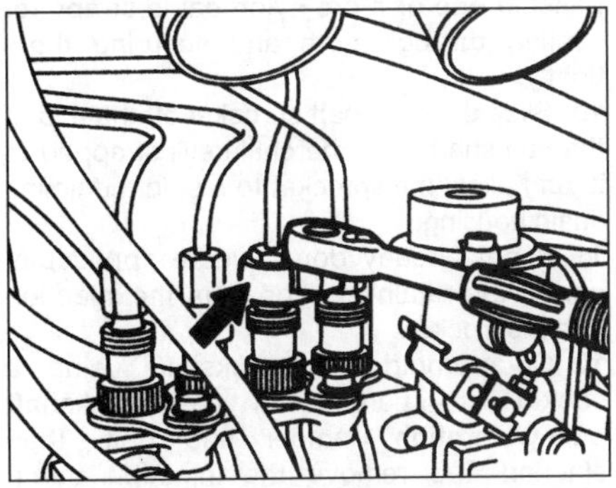

7.10 Slacken the unions and detach the high pressure injector fuel lines from the injection pump

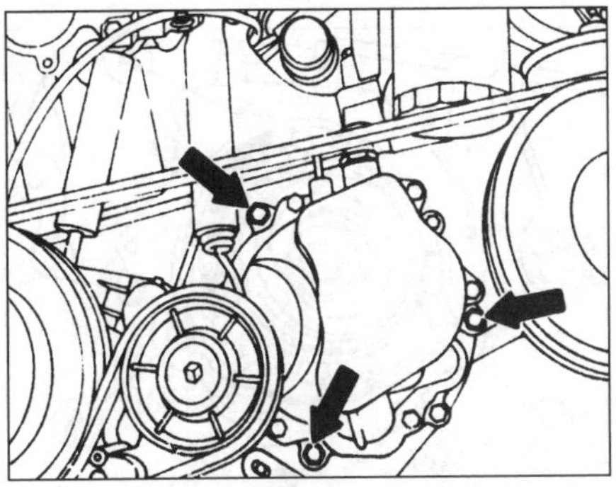

7.19 Unscrew and withdraw the mounting bolts (arrowed) that secure the front of the injection pump to its mounting flange

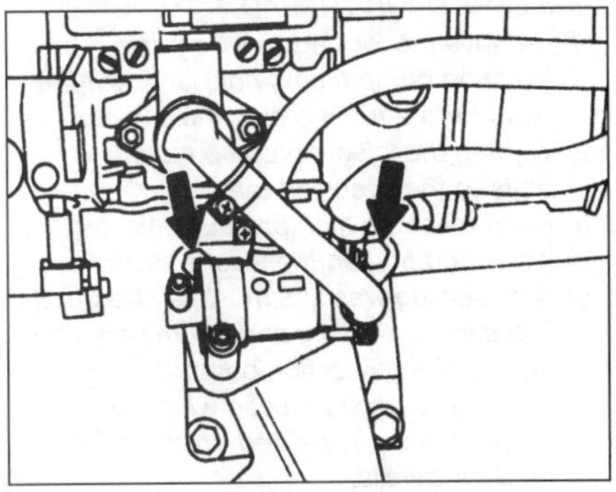

7.21 Undo the bolts (arrowed) and remove the fuel thermostat from the injection pump body

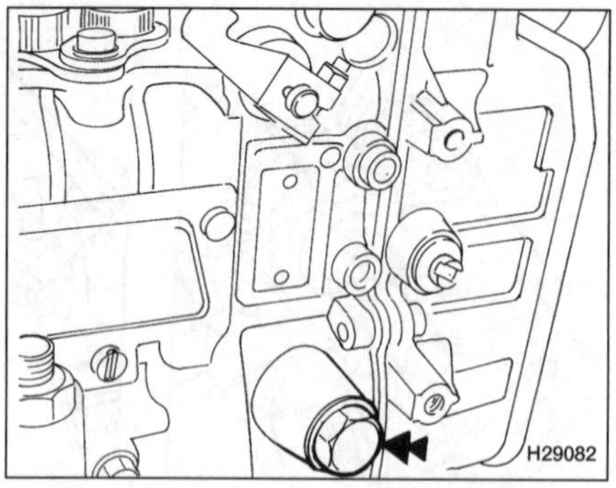

7.23 **Unbolt and remove the timing plug (arrowed) from the side of the pump body**

23 With the injection pump on a workbench, unbolt and remove the timing plug from the side of the pump body **(see illustration)**.

24 Using a suitable pair of grips, turn the injection pump shaft in its normal direction of rotation, whilst observing the movement of the governor body through the timing plug hole. Continue turning the shaft until the lug on the governor body lines up with the hole. At this point, the governor body must be locked to the injection pump body using the special Mercedes-Benz locking tool, to prevent further movement of the pump shaft (refer to the note at the beginning of this Section) **(see illustration)**.

Caution: Take care to avoid damaging the surface of the injection pump shaft with the jaws of the grips.

25 Recover the O-ring seal from the front of the injection pump and discard it - a new seal must be used on refitting.

Refitting

26 Refitting is a reversal of removal, bearing in mind the following points:

a) Fit a new O-ring seal to the injection pump mating face and lubricate it lightly with clean engine oil.

b) Ensure that the engine is still set to 15° AFTER top dead centre on cylinder No 1 before refitting the injection pump.

c) Counterhold the crankshaft, and tighten the injection pump sprocket bolt to the specified torque, noting that the bolt has a LEFT-HAND THREAD.

d) Remove the locking tool from the injection pump timing hole (and refit the plug) before turning over the engine.

e) Tighten the injection pump mounting bolts to the specified torque.

f) Reconnect the high pressure injector pipes and tighten the unions securely.

g) New sealing washers must be fitted to the fuel supply, delivery and return banjo bolt unions at the injection pump.

h) A new seal must be used when the vacuum pump is refitted - refer to Chapter 9 for details.

i) On completion, check and if necessary adjust the injection pump start of delivery with reference to Section 9.

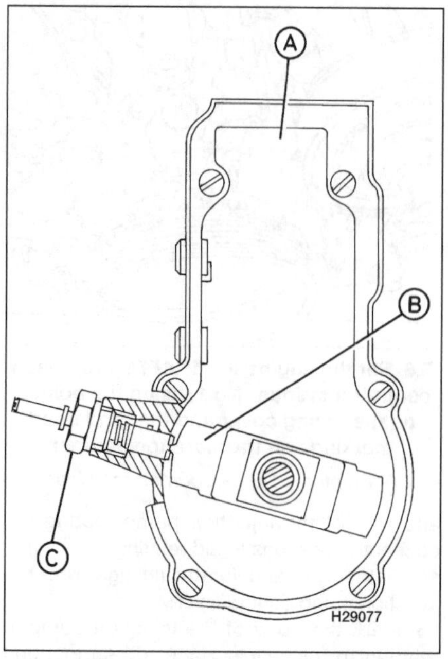

7.24 Turn the injection pump shaft until the lug on the governor body lines up with the inspection hole

A *Injection pump - viewed from rear*
B *Governor body*
C *Locking tool*

8 Fuel injection pump timing device and sprocket - removal and refitting

Removal

Note: *Following removal of the timing device and sprocket, the injection pump shaft must be locked in position using a specially shaped locking tool. Fabrication of an accurate substitute would be very difficult and its use could risk internal damage to the injection pump. For these reasons, it is recommend that a locking tool is borrowed from a Mercedes-Benz dealer or a Bosch diesel fuel injection system specialist.*

1 Disconnect the battery negative lead and position it away from the terminal.

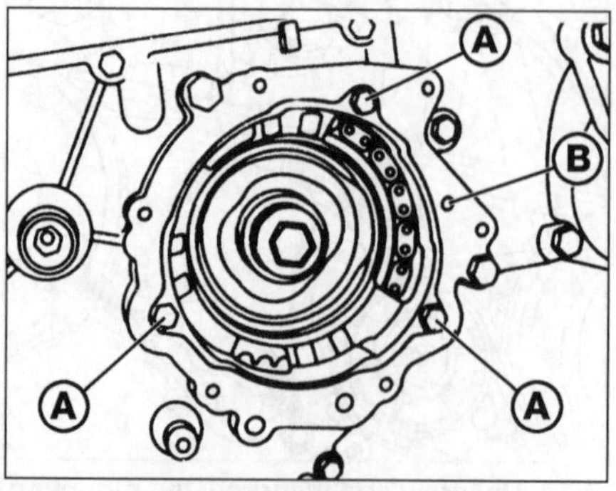

8.7 Sprocket retaining cage
A Mounting bolts B Locking pin

2 Where applicable, remove the engine undershield as described in Chapter 11.

3 Remove the auxiliary drivebelt tensioner as follows.

a) Pull off the plastic cover, unscrew the securing bolt, and remove the auxiliary drivebelt idler pulley.

b) Unscrew the securing bolts, and remove the cooling fan pulley.

c) Unscrew the securing bolts, and withdraw the tensioner damper strut. Recover any spacers and/or brackets from the bolts noting their locations.

d) Using a pair of pliers, unhook the tension spring, noting its orientation to aid refitting.

e) Where applicable, pull off the plastic cover, then unscrew the tensioner securing bolt and, slide off the spacer sleeve (if applicable).

f) Withdraw the tensioner, and recover the spacer (where applicable).

4 With reference to Chapter 3, remove the cooling fan and shroud.

5 Refer to Chapter 9 and remove the brake vacuum pump from the timing cover. Note that the gasket must be renewed on refitting.

6 Using a socket and wrench on the crankshaft pulley/vibration damper hub bolt, turn the crankshaft in its normal direction of rotation until the engine is set to 15° *AFTER* top dead centre on cylinder No 1. Use the pointer on the timing cover and the graduated markings on the vibration damper to achieve the correct alignment **(refer to illustration 7.9)**.

7 Where applicable, unbolt the retaining cage from the front of the injection pump sprocket **(see illustration)**. On later models, the cage is secured with a locking pin. Remove the pin by threading an M6 bolt into the end of it, then attach a slide hammer or impact puller to the bolt head and gradually draw the pin out.

8 Refer to Chapter 2C and carry out the following:

a) Remove the cylinder head cover.

b) Remove the timing chain tensioner.

c) Slacken and withdraw the securing bolt and washer for the camshaft sprocket.

9 Preserve the relationship between the camshaft sprocket and the timing chain by passing one or more nylon cable straps (or similar) through both and securing them tightly.

10 Slide the camshaft sprocket off the end of the camshaft, with the chain still strapped to it, and allow the sprocket to rest in the timing chain housing.

11 If not already done, where applicable, unbolt the retaining cage from the injection pump sprocket.

12 Counterhold the crankshaft using a socket or spanner on the crankshaft pulley/vibration damper hub bolt, then slacken and remove the injection pump sprocket centre bolt **(see illustration 7.7)**. **Note:** *The bolt has a LEFT-HAND THREAD.* Recover the washer.

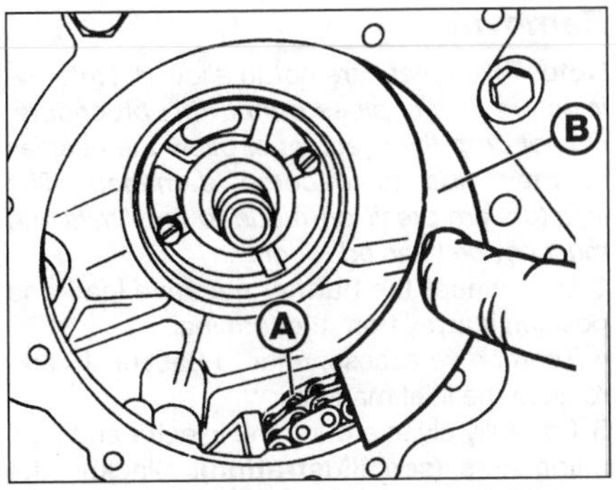

8.16 Expand the home-made tool, to push the timing chain off the sprocket teeth

A Timing chain B Home made tool

13 Using a socket and wrench on the crankshaft pulley/vibration damper hub bolt, turn the crankshaft in its normal direction of rotation until the engine is set to 15° *AFTER* top dead centre on cylinder No 1. Use the pointer on the timing cover and the graduated markings on the vibration damper to achieve the correct alignment **(see illustration 7.8)**.

14 At this point, mark the relationship between the injection pump sprocket and the timing chain using a small dab of paint - this will aid alignment during refitting.

15 The timing chain must now be pushed off the injection pump sprocket teeth, to allow the sprocket and timing device to be withdrawn. Fabricate a tool from a sheet of thin scrap metal for this purpose - cut out a rectangle measuring 140 mm by 70 mm (approx) and bend it into a partial circle, so that it is about the same shape as the injection pump sprocket.

16 Press the home-made tool against the front of the injection pump sprocket, then expand it, so that it pushes the timing chain off the sprocket teeth and retains it in that position **(see illustration)**.

17 With the chain now clear of the sprocket teeth, withdraw the timing device, together with the sprocket from the timing chain housing using a large pair of pliers or grips.

18 Unbolt and remove the timing plug from the side of pump body. Be prepared for fuel loss, and place a wad of rage beneath the plug hole to absorb any spilt fuel.

19 Using a suitable pair of grips, turn the injection pump shaft in its normal direction of rotation, whilst observing the movement of the governor body through the timing plug hole. Continue turning the shaft until the lug on the governor body lines up with the hole. At this point, the governor body must be locked to the injection pump body using the special Mercedes-Benz locking tool, to prevent further movement of the pump shaft - refer to the note at the beginning of this Section **(refer to illustration 7.24)**. This step must not be omitted, as it is the only means of ensuring the correct injection pump timing during reassembly.

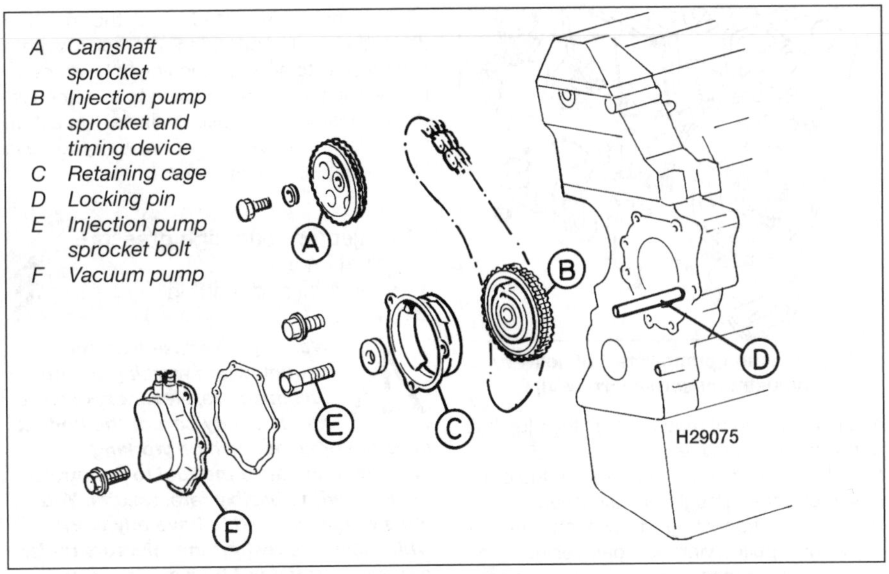

8.20 Injection pump sprocket and timing device assembly

Caution: Take care to avoid damaging the surface of the injection pump shaft with the jaws of the grips.

Refitting

20 Refitting is a reversal of removal, noting the following points **(see illustration)**:

a) Ensure that the engine is still set to 15° AFTER top dead centre on cylinder No 1 before refitting the sprocket and timing device to the injection pump shaft.

b) Use the paint marks made during removal to align the injection pump sprocket with the timing chain.

c) Counterhold the crankshaft and tighten the injection pump sprocket to the specified torque, noting that the bolt has a LEFT-HAND THREAD.

d) Remove the locking tool from the injection pump timing hole (and refit the plug) before turning over the engine.

e) Refer to Chapter 2C and refit the camshaft sprocket. To verify the camshaft timing, rotate the engine through one complete crankshaft revolution and check that the camshaft and crankshaft TDC markings line up correctly.

f) A new seal must be used when the brake vacuum pump is refitted - refer to Chapter 9 for details.

g) On completion, check and if necessary adjust the injection pump start of delivery with reference to Section 9.

9 **Fuel injection pump start of delivery** - general information, checking and adjustment

General information

1 To ensure that the injection pump delivers fuel to each cylinder at the correct time during the engine cycle, the "start of delivery" must be checked, and if necessary adjusted, if the injection pump, or any of its associated components, have been disturbed.

2 The injection pump has a timing inspection hole bored into its body. During normal operation this hole is closed off with a threaded metal plug. Start of delivery to cylinder No 1 is indicated when an alignment lug, mounted on the governor body inside the injection pump, passes directly behind the inspection hole.

3 When the lug is exactly aligned with the centre of the inspection hole, the position of the crankshaft can then be read off, using the pointer on the timing chain cover and the graduated markings on the crankshaft vibration damper. The relationship between the angle of the crankshaft and the injection pump at this point, provides an indirect "start of delivery" measurement.

4 Ideally, the measurement should be carried out electronically, using a sensor that screws into the injection pump inspection hole. However, as this equipment is only available to Mercedes-Benz dealers and Bosch diesel fuel injection specialists, an alternative method is described here. It should be noted however, that this method provides an *approximate* reading only, to allow the engine to be started - the vehicle **must** then be taken to a dealer or Bosch injection specialist at the *earliest* opportunity to have the reading accurately checked.

Checking

5 Disconnect the battery negative lead and position it away from the terminal.

6 Refer to Chapter 3 and remove the cooling fan and shroud, to improve access to crankshaft pulley and vibration damper.

7 Unbolt and remove the timing plug from the side of pump body. Be prepared for fuel loss,

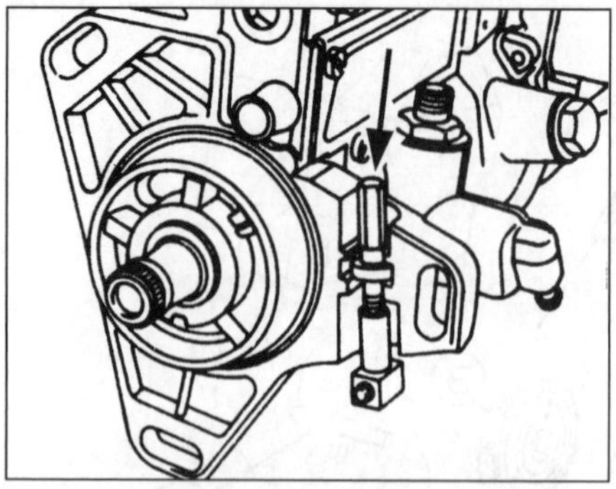

9.15 Injection pump "start of delivery" adjustment screw (arrowed)

and place a wad of rage beneath the plug hole to absorb any spilt fuel.

8 With a small mirror, observe the edge of the governor body through the inspection hole.

9 Using a socket and wrench on the crankshaft pulley/vibration damper hub bolt, turn over the engine in its normal direction of rotation, until the alignment lug on the edge of the governor body is exactly aligned with the centre of the inspection hole **(refer to illustration 7.24)**.

10 Prevent further engine rotation, then read off the crankshaft angle, using the pointer on the timing chain cover and the graduated markings on the vibration damper **(refer to illustration 7.8)**.

11 Compare the reading with the *Specifications* and adjust if required. Refit the inspection hole plug, observing the correct torque.

Adjustment

12 With reference to the previous sub-section, turn the crankshaft by hand until the engine is set to its nominal "start of delivery" test value - refer to the *Specifications* for the exact figure.

13 Slacken the three mounting bolts that secure the front of the injection pump to its mounting flange. Similarly, slacken the bolt that secures the rear of the injection pump to the support bracket (refer to Section 7 for details).

14 Unbolt and remove the timing plug from the side of pump body. Be prepared for fuel loss, and place a wad of rage beneath the plug hole to absorb any spilt fuel.

15 With a small mirror, observe the edge of the governor body through the inspection hole. Turn the delivery adjusting screw at the side of the injection pump until the alignment lug on the edge of the governor body is exactly aligned with the centre of the inspection hole **(see illustration)**. **Note:** *Turning the screw to the right retards the start of delivery, turning it to the left advances the start of delivery.*

16 When the alignment is correct, tighten the front and rear injection pump mounting bolts, observing the correct torque.

17 Refit the inspection hole plug and tighten it to the correct torque.

18 It should be noted that the method described here provides an *approximate* setting only, to allow the engine to be started - the vehicle must now be taken to a Mercedes-Benz dealer or Bosch diesel injection specialist at the *earliest* opportunity to have the reading accurately verified.

10 Injectors and high pressure fuel lines - removal and refitting

Warning: Exercise extreme caution when working on the fuel injectors. Never expose the hands or any part of the body to injector spray, as the high working pressure can cause the fuel to penetrate the skin, with possibly fatal results. You are strongly advised to have any work which involves testing the injectors under pressure carried out by a dealer or fuel injection specialist. Refer to the precautions given in Section 1 of this Chapter before proceeding.

General information

1 Injectors deteriorate with prolonged use and it is reasonable to expect them to need reconditioning or renewal after 60 000 miles (100 000 km) or so. Accurate testing, overhaul and calibration of the injectors must be left to a specialist. A defective injector which is causing knocking or smoking can be located without dismantling as follows.

2 Run the engine at a fast idle. Slacken each injector union in turn, placing rag around the union to catch spilt fuel and being careful not to expose the skin to any spray. When the union on the defective injector is slackened, the knocking or smoking will stop.

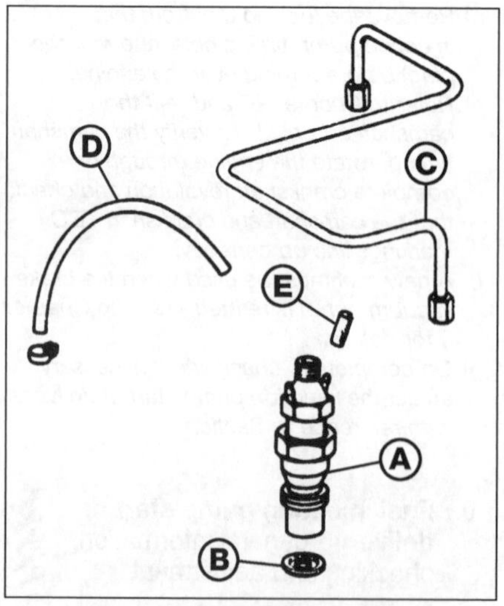

10.5 Fuel injector assembly

A Injector body
B Washer
C High pressure fuel pipe
D Bleed hose
E End cap

Removal

Note: *Take great care not to allow dirt into the injectors or fuel pipes during this procedure. Do not drop the injectors or allow the needles at their tips to become damaged. The injectors are precision-made to fine limits and must not be handled roughly.*

3 Disconnect the battery negative lead and position it away from the terminal.

4 To improve access, refer to Section 16 and remove the inlet manifold.

5 Carefully clean around the injector and pipe union nuts **(see illustration)**. Slacken the clip(s) (where applicable) and pull the bleed hose(s) from the injector.

6 Pad the area around the injector union with absorbent rags. Wipe clean the pipe unions, then slacken the union nut securing the relevant high pressure pipe to the top of the injector.

7 Slacken the relevant union nut securing the high pressure pipe to the top of the injection pump. As each pump union nut is slackened, retain the adapter on the pump with a suitable open-ended spanner to prevent it being unscrewed from the pump. With the union nuts undone, remove the injector pipes from the engine. Cover the injector and pipe unions to prevent the entry of dirt into the system **(see Tool Tip)**.

8 Unscrew the injector, using a deep socket or box spanner, and remove it from the cylinder head.

Warning: Unscrew the injector by the hexagonal section closest to the cylinder head. Do not unscrew it by the upper hexagonal section or the injector will fall apart.

9 Recover the washer, noting which way up it is fitted.

Refitting

10 Fit a new washer to the cylinder head, then screw the injector into position and tighten it to the specified torque.

11 Refit the injector pipes and tighten the union nuts securely. Position any clips attached to the pipes as noted before removal.

12 Reconnect the bleed hose(s) securely to

TOOL TiP

Cut the fingertips from an old rubber glove and secure them over the open unions with elastic bands to prevent the ingress of dirt

the injector and tighten the hose clips (where applicable).

13 Refit the inlet manifold with reference to Section 16.

14 Reconnect the battery negative lead, and check the running of the engine.

11 Fuel thermostat - removal and refitting

General information

1 The fuel thermostat is a bypass valve that directs the fuel supply around a heat exchanger, mounted in the cooling system, before it is supplied to the injection pump. This permits reliable starting and running in low ambient temperatures.

Removal

2 The fuel thermostat is bolted to a bracket, adjacent to the fuel injection pump, upstream of the fuel pre-filter.

3 Disconnect the battery negative lead and position it away from the terminal.

4 Clamp off the fuel hoses using proprietary hose clamps. Slacken the hose clips and detach the hoses from the ports on the thermostat. Be prepared for fuel spillage - pad the surrounding area with absorbent rags.

5 Slacken and withdraw the bolts and remove the thermostat from its mounting bracket.

Refitting

6 Refitting is a reversal of removal.

12 ELR electronic idle speed control system - component removal and refitting

Crankshaft speed sensor

Removal

1 Disconnect the battery negative lead and position it away from the terminal.

2 Unplug the crankshaft sensor wiring from the harness at the connector, which is located in the engine compartment, behind the battery.

3 The sensor is located at the mating surface between the cylinder block and the transmission bellhousing, above the starter motor aperture. Unscrew the retaining bolt and withdraw the sensor from the bellhousing. Recover the spacer, where fitted.

Refitting

4 Refit the crankshaft sensor by following the removal procedure in reverse. Where applicable, ensure that the spacer is fitted to the sensor probe before inserting it into the bellhousing.

Coolant temperature sensor

Removal

5 Refer to Chapter 1 and partially drain the cooling system. Ensure that the ignition is switched off.

6 The coolant sensor is screwed into the upper surface of the cylinder head on the left-hand side of the engine. Do not confuse it with the temperature gauge sender unit.

7 Unplug the wiring from the sensor at the connector.

8 Unscrew the sensor from the cylinder head, and recover the O-ring seal.

Refitting

9 Refitting is a reversal of removal. On completion, top-up the cooling system.

Electronic control unit

Removal

10 The ELR electronic control unit is located at the rear of the engine bay, behind the false bulkhead panel.

11 Disconnect the battery negative lead and position it away from the terminal.

12 Unplug the wiring from the control unit at the multiway connector.

13 Remove the securing screws and lift the unit away from the bulkhead.

Refitting

14 Refitting is a reversal of removal.

Electromagnetic actuator

Removal

15 The ELR electromagnetic actuator is bolted to the rear of the injection pump body. On vehicles equipped with ELR electronic idle speed control and ARA anti-jerk control, the ELR electromagnetic actuator is the upper of the two actuators **(see illustration)**.

16 Disconnect the battery negative lead and position it away from the terminal.

17 On normally-aspirated engines, refer to Section 2 and remove the complete air cleaner assembly.

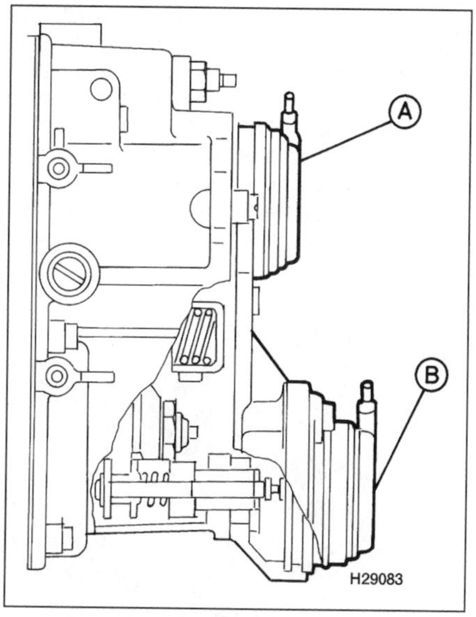

12.15 Rear of the injection pump (side view)

A ELR electromagnetic actuator
B ARA electromagnetic actuator

18 Unplug the wiring from the actuator at the connector.

19 Slacken and withdraw the two securing screws at the rear of the actuator. Lift off the associated brackets.

20 Remove the actuator body, recovering the O-ring seal, shim(s) (where applicable), and intermediate plate (where applicable).

Refitting

21 Refitting is a reversal of removal, noting the following points.

- *a) Transfer the shims to the new actuator, if the existing unit is to be renewed.*
- *b) Renew the O-ring seal.*
- *c) Ensure that the electrical connector is facing upwards when the actuator is refitted.*

13 ARA electronic anti-jerk control system - component removal and refitting

Electronic control unit

Removal

1 On models with ELR electronic idle speed control, the ARA function is managed by the ELR electronic control unit - refer to the information given in Section 12.

2 On models with a pneumatic idle speed control system, the ARA electronic control unit is located at the rear of the engine compartment, behind the false bulkhead panel.

3 Disconnect the battery negative lead and position it away from the terminal.

4 Unplug the wiring from the control unit at the multiway connector.

5 Remove the securing screws and lift the unit away from the bulkhead.

Refitting

6 Refitting is a reversal of removal.

Crankshaft speed sensor

7 Refer to the information given for the electronic idle speed control system in Section 12.

Coolant temperature sensor

8 Refer to the information given for the electronic idle speed control system in Section 12.

Electromagnetic actuator

Removal

9 The ARA electromagnetic actuator is bolted to the rear of the injection pump body. On vehicles equipped with ELR electronic idle speed control and ARA anti-jerk control, the ARA electromagnetic actuator is the lower of the two **(refer to illustration 12.15)**.

10 Disconnect the battery negative lead and position it away from the terminal.

11 On normally-aspirated engines, refer to Section 2 and remove the complete air cleaner assembly.

12 Unplug the wiring from the actuator at the connector.
13 Slacken and withdraw the two securing screws at the rear of the actuator. Lift off the associated brackets.
14 Remove the actuator body, recovering the O-ring seal and the pushrod.

Refitting

15 Refitting is a reversal of removal. Transfer the push rod to the new actuator, if the existing unit is to be renewed. Renew the O-ring seal.

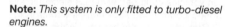

14 Electronic diesel engine control system (EDS) - component removal and refitting

Electronic control unit

Removal

1 The EDS electronic control unit is located at the rear of the engine compartment, behind the false bulkhead panel.
2 Disconnect the battery negative lead, and position it away from the terminal.
3 Unplug the wiring from the control unit at the multiway connector.
4 Remove the securing screws and lift the unit away from the bulkhead.

Refitting

5 Refitting is a reversal of removal.

Over-voltage protection relay

Removal

6 The relay is mounted on a base unit, adjacent to the EDS ECU - refer to the previous sub-Section. It contains fuses and diodes which protect the EDS system from current overload and high supply voltage peaks.
7 Disconnect the battery negative lead, and position it away from the terminal.
8 Carefully pull the relay from its base.

Refitting

9 Refitting is a reversal of removal.

Crankshaft speed sensor

10 Refer to the information given for the electronic idle speed control system in Section 12.

Coolant temperature sensor

11 Refer to the information given for the electronic idle speed control system in Section 12.

ELR electromagnetic actuator

12 Refer to the information given for the electronic idle speed control system in Section 12.

ELR vacuum solenoid valve

13 Refer to the information given in Chapter 4D.

Air flow meter

Removal

14 Disconnect the battery negative lead and position it away from the terminal. Remove the air cleaner assembly, as described in Section 2.
15 Unbolt the air cleaner support bracket from the air flow meter body.
16 Slacken the hose clips and detach the inlet elbow and ducting from either side of the air flow meter. Recover the sealing rings.
17 Unplug the wiring from the air flow meter at the connector.
18 Remove the securing nuts and bolts, then lift the air flow meter away from its mounting bracket.

Caution: Handle the air flow meter carefully - it is a delicate component.

Refitting

19 Refitting is a reversal of removal.

Intake air temperature sensor

20 The intake air temperature sensor is integral with the air flow meter - refer to the previous sub-Section.

15 Engine overload protection system - component removal and refitting

Note: *This system is only fitted to turbo-diesel engines.*

General information

1 The engine overload protection system is designed to limit the power produced by the engine in the event of the turbocharger pressure control valve failure. A pressure switch, mounted in the inlet manifold, monitors the inlet charge pressure and switches when the pressure exceeds a preset limit. This interrupts the operation of a solenoid valve, which in turn closes off the supply of vacuum to a diaphragm unit, mounted on the injection pump. The result is that the injection pump fuel delivery is immediately reduced to that of a normally-aspirated engine.
2 The only serviceable components are the pressure switch and the vacuum solenoid valve.

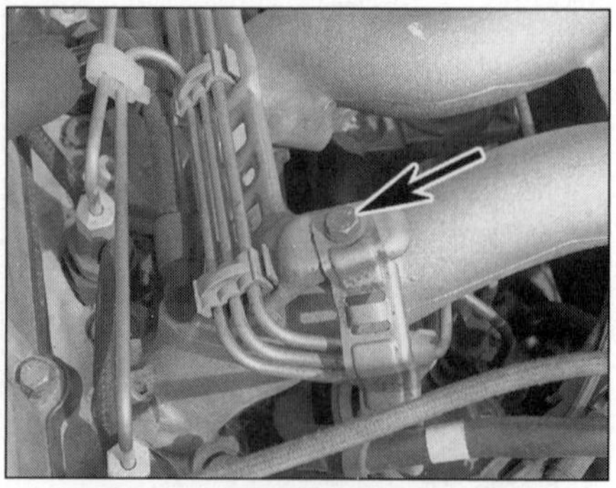

16.2 Unbolt the fuel pipe brackets (arrowed) from the manifold

Pressure switch

Removal

3 The switch is mounted on the side of the inlet manifold plenum chamber, adjacent to the washer fluid container.
4 Unplug the wiring from the switch at the connector.
5 Unscrew the switch from the manifold and recover the sealing ring.

Refitting

6 Refitting is a reversal of removal.

Vacuum solenoid valve

Removal

7 The vacuum solenoid valve is mounted at the rear of the engine compartment, on the front left-hand side of the false bulkhead panel.
8 Unplug the wiring from the switch at the connector.
9 Disconnect the vacuum hoses from the ports on the solenoid valve - make a *careful note* of their fitted positions to aid refitting later.
10 Undo the securing screw and lift off the solenoid valve.

Refitting

11 Refitting is a reversal of removal. Take great care to ensure that the vacuum hoses are refitted correctly, or engine performance could be seriously affected.

16 Inlet manifold - removal and refitting

Removal

Normally-aspirated diesel engines

1 Disconnect the battery negative lead and position it away from the terminal.
2 To improve access, refer to Section 2 and remove the air cleaner. Where applicable, also unbolt the fuel pipe brackets from the manifold **(see illustration)**.
3 Disconnect the ventilation hoses from the ports on the top of the manifold pipes **(see illustration)**.

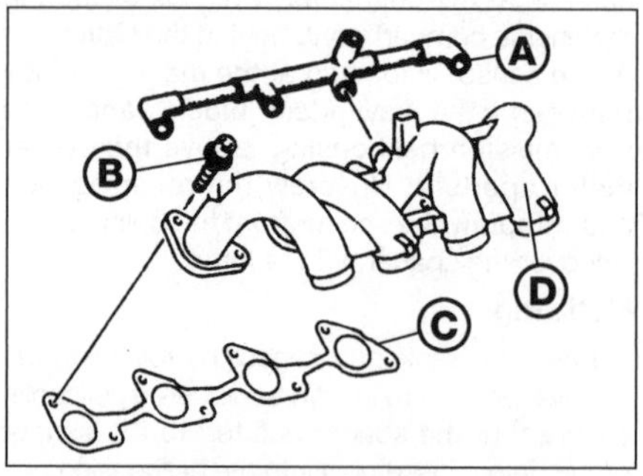

16.3 Inlet manifold assembly - normally-aspirated diesel engines

A Ventilation hose
B Manifold securing bolts
C Gasket
D Manifold casting

4 Work along the manifold and slacken each of the securing bolts until they can be withdrawn by hand.
5 Lift the manifold away from the cylinder head and recover the gasket.

Turbo-diesel engines

6 Disconnect the battery negative lead and position it away from the terminal.
7 Pull the vacuum hose from the port at the end of the plenum casting **(see illustration)**.
8 Unplug the wiring from the over-load protection pressure switch at the connector.
9 Unbolt the transverse section of the inlet ducting from the support bracket on the upper surface of the cylinder head. Remove the bolts and detach the ducting from the inlet manifold. Recover the gasket.
10 Work along the manifold and slacken each of the securing bolts until they can be withdrawn by hand.
11 Lift the manifold away from the cylinder head and recover the gasket.

Refitting

12 Refitting is a reversal of removal. Tighten the inlet manifold securing bolts to the specified torque.

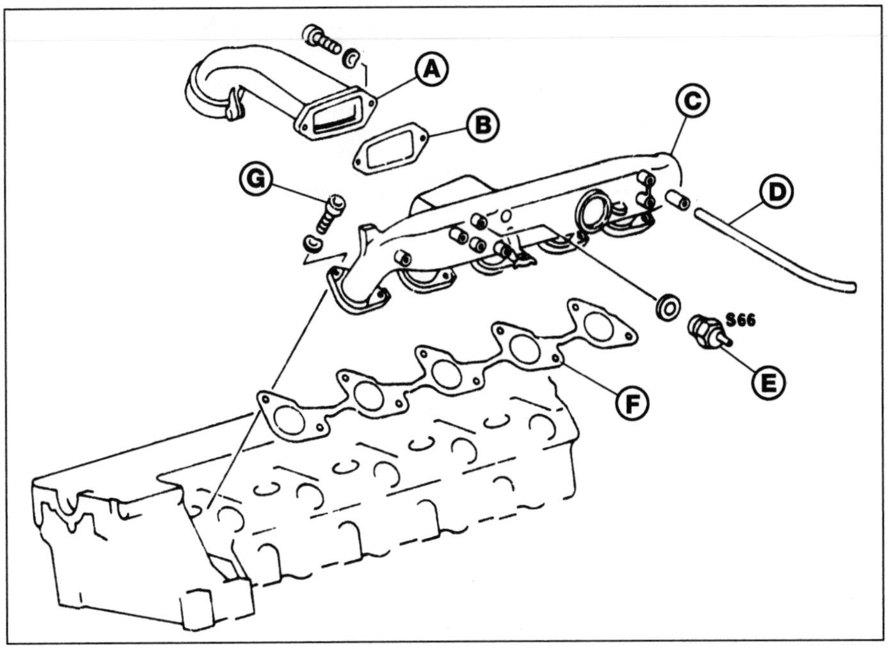

16.7 Inlet manifold assembly - turbo-diesel engines

A Inlet ducting
B Gasket
C Plenum casting
D Vacuum hose
E Pressure switch
F Gasket
G Inlet manifold-to-cylinder head bolts

Notes

Chapter 4 Part D
Exhaust and emission control systems

Contents

Air injection system - component removal and refitting 9
Catalytic converter - general information and precautions 8
Crankcase emission system - general information 3
Evaporative loss emission control system 2
Exhaust Gas Recirculation (EGR) system 5
Exhaust manifold - removal and refitting 4
Exhaust system - general information and component renewal 7
General information 1
Turbocharger - removal and refitting 6

Degrees of difficulty

Easy, suitable for novice with little experience	**Fairly easy,** suitable for beginner with some experience	**Fairly difficult,** suitable for competent DIY mechanic	**Difficult,** suitable for experienced DIY mechanic	**Very difficult,** suitable for expert DIY or professional

Specifications

Turbocharger

Type	Garrett T/TB 025 or KKK K14
Maximum boost pressure:	
All models up to 08/91	0.85 - 0.95 bar at 4000 rpm, full load.
All models from 09/91	0.75 - 0.85 bar at 4000 rpm, full load.
Charge pressure control valve opening pressure	0.95 bar.
Engine overload protection valve opening pressure	1.1 bar

Torque wrench settings

	Nm	lbf ft
EGR valve mounting bolts	25	18
Trap oxidiser/ intermediate pipe bolts	45	33
Exhaust downpipe to intermediate silencer nuts/bolts	20	15

1 General information

Emission control systems

All petrol engine models have the ability to use unleaded petrol and are controlled by engine management systems which are "tuned" to give the best compromise between driveability, fuel consumption and exhaust emission production. In addition, a number of systems are fitted to help to minimise other harmful emissions - a crankcase emission-control system which reduces the release of pollutants from the engine lubrication system is fitted to all models, catalytic converters are fitted to most models to reduce exhaust gas pollutants, and all models are fitted with an evaporative loss emission control system which reduces the release of gaseous hydrocarbons from the fuel tank. In addition, certain models are fitted with an Exhaust Gas Recirculation (EGR) and/or air injection system, which help to reduce the exhaust gas pollutants produced by partially burnt fuel.

All diesel-engined models are equipped with a crankcase emission control system. In addition, certain models are fitted with a catalytic converter and an Exhaust Gas Recirculation (EGR) system to reduce exhaust emissions.

Crankcase emission control

To reduce the emission of unburned hydrocarbons from the crankcase into the atmosphere, the engine is sealed, and the blow-by gases and oil vapour are drawn from inside the crankcase, through a wire mesh oil separator, into the inlet tract to be burned by the engine during normal combustion.

Under conditions of high manifold depression (idling, deceleration), the gases will be sucked positively out of the crankcase. Under conditions of low manifold depression (acceleration, full-throttle running) the gases are forced out of the crankcase by the (relatively) higher crankcase pressure.

Exhaust emission control - petrol models

To minimise the amount of pollutants which escape into the atmosphere, most models are fitted with a catalytic converter in the exhaust system. On all models with a factory-fitted catalytic converter, the fuelling system is of the closed-loop type, in which a Lambda sensor in the exhaust system provides the fuel injection system ECU with constant feedback, enabling the ECU to adjust the air/fuel mixture to optimise combustion.

The Lambda sensor has a heating element built-in, which is controlled by the ECU through the Lambda sensor relay, to quickly bring the sensor tip to its optimum operating temperature. The sensor tip is sensitive to oxygen, and relays a voltage signal to the ECU which varies according to the amount of oxygen in the exhaust gas. If the inlet air/fuel mixture is too rich, the exhaust gases are low in oxygen so the sensor sends a low voltage signal, the voltage increasing as the mixture weakens and the amount of oxygen rises in the exhaust gases. Peak conversion efficiency of all major pollutants occurs if the inlet air/fuel mixture is maintained at the chemically-correct ratio for the complete combustion of petrol of 14.7 parts (by weight) of air to 1 part of fuel (the "stoichiometric" ratio). The sensor output voltage alters in a large step at this point, the ECU using the signal change as a reference point and correcting the inlet air/fuel mixture accordingly by altering the fuel injector pulse width. Details of Lambda sensor removal and refitting are given in Chapter 4B.

On some models, air injection is employed to help reduce the production of gaseous hydrocarbons and carbon monoxide. A mechanical air pump, driven from the auxiliary drivebelt, forces air into the exhaust manifold where it mixes with the partially-burnt fuel particles. The oxygen-rich air combines with pollutants and allows further oxidation to take place, converting a proportion of the hydrocarbons and carbon monoxide into harmless carbon dioxide and water vapour.

An Exhaust Gas Recirculation (EGR) system is fitted to models in certain markets. This reduces the level of nitrogen oxides produced during combustion by introducing a proportion of the exhaust gas back into the inlet manifold, under certain engine operating conditions, via a plunger valve. The system is electro-pneumatically driven and is managed by a dedicated electronic control unit (ECU).

Exhaust emission control - diesel models

An oxidation catalyst is fitted in the line with the exhaust system on diesel-engined models, in some markets. This has the effect of removing a large proportion of the gaseous hydrocarbons and carbon monoxide present in the exhaust gas. In certain markets, a particulate trap incorporated into the silencer assembly helps to remove the solid hydrocarbons suspended in the exhaust gas.

Certain diesel engine models are fitted with an Exhaust Gas Recirculation (EGR) system. This reduces the level of nitrogen oxides produced during combustion by introducing a proportion of the exhaust gas back into the inlet manifold, under certain engine operating conditions, via a plunger valve. The system is electro-pneumatically driven and is managed by an electronic control unit (ECU).

Evaporative emission control - petrol models

To minimise the escape of hydrocarbons from the fuel system into the atmosphere, an evaporative loss emission control system is fitted to all petrol models. The fuel tank filler cap is sealed, and a charcoal canister (or canisters) mounted inside the left-hand wing collects the petrol vapours released from the fuel contained in the fuel tank (and on carburettor models, the float chamber).

The canister stores then fuel vapours until they can be drawn from the canister by manifold depression, via the purge valve into the throttle body (or carburettor), where they are then burned by the engine during normal combustion.

The flow of fuel vapour from the charcoal canister through the purge valve to the throttle body is controlled by a thermo-valve, which prevents the purge valve from opening until the coolant temperature exceeds a preset limit. This is to ensure that the engine runs correctly when it is cold, and to protect the catalytic converter from the effects of an over-rich mixture. In addition, because the purge valve is controlled by manifold vacuum, the charcoal canister is only purged when the engine is under load. This prevents an over-rich mixture from being supplied at idle, preserving idle speed stability and low speed driveability.

Exhaust systems

The exhaust system comprises the exhaust manifold, a number of silencer units and intermediate pipes (depending on model and specification), a catalytic converter (where fitted), a number of mounting brackets and rubber mountings.

The turbocharger fitted to turbo-diesel-engined models is oil cooled and has an integral charge pressure limiting valve. In the event of the charge pressure control valve failing, an engine overload protection valve (controlled by a switch mounted on the inlet manifold) opens, and limits the fuel supplied to the engine, via an actuator mounted on the fuel injection pump.

2 Evaporative loss emission control system

General information

1 The major components of the evaporative loss emission control system are the purge valve, the thermo-valve, one or two activated charcoal filter canisters (depending on model), and a series of connecting vacuum hoses.

2 The purge valve is clipped to the left-hand side of the bulkhead, at the rear of the engine compartment. The charcoal canister is mounted on a bracket inside the left-hand front wheel housing.

Charcoal canister

3 Refer to the information given in Chapter 1A.

Thermo-valve/purge valve

Removal

4 The thermo-valve is screwed into a housing, on the front left-hand side of the cylinder head.

5 Ensure that the engine is cold, then refer to Chapter 1 and partially drain the cooling system.

6 Disconnect the vacuum hoses, then unscrew the thermo-valve from the housing and recover the sealing ring.

Refitting

7 Refitting is a reversal of removal, but fit a new sealing ring to the thermo-valve.

3 Crankcase emission system - general information

The crankcase emission control system consists of a series of hoses which connect the crankcase vent to the camshaft cover vent and the air inlet, a pressure regulating valve (where applicable), and an oil separator unit.

The components of this system require no attention other than to check at regular intervals that the hose(s) are free of blockages and undamaged.

4 Exhaust manifold - removal and refitting

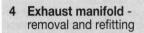

Removal

1 Jack up the front of the car and support it securely on axle stands (see *"Jacking and vehicle support"*).

2 Slacken the U-bolt nuts securing the exhaust downpipe(s) to the transmission-mounted support bracket **(see illustration)**.

3 Undo the bolts securing the bracket to the transmission, and move the bracket clear **(see illustration)**.

4 On 6-cylinder petrol engine models, unbolt and remove the heat shield from the underside of the manifolds.

5 Support the exhaust downpipe(s) on a trolley jack, then slacken and remove the bolts securing the exhaust downpipe(s) to the manifold(s).

6 Lower the jack to separate the downpipe/ manifold joint(s) and recover the gaskets.

7 Where applicable, refer to relevant part of Chapter 4 and remove the air cleaner to improve access.

8 Slacken and remove the nuts that secure the exhaust manifold to the cylinder head. Where applicable, unbolt the upper end of the dipstick tube from the engine, noting the position of the retaining clip **(see illustrations)**. On models with air injection, unbolt the air injection nozzle from the exhaust manifold and position the air pipe to one side.

9 On models with exhaust gas recirculation, unbolt the EGR valve and recirculation pipes from the exhaust manifold.

10 Withdraw the manifold(s) from the cylinder head studs and recover the gasket. Note that on 6-cylinder engine models, the exhaust manifold is split into two castings. Slacken the connecting pipe clips to allow the two sections to be separated on removal.

Refitting

11 Refitting is a reversal of removal, noting the following points.

a) *Thoroughly clean the mating surfaces of the manifold(s) and the cylinder, taking care not to gouge or score them.*

b) *On 6-cylinder petrol engines where individual gaskets are supplied for each exhaust port, the beaded surface of the gaskets should face the manifold mating surface. (Note that the gasket for cylinder No 6 has an extra hole).*

c) *Use new manifold securing nuts as a matter of course.*

4.2 Slacken the U-bolt nuts (arrowed) securing the exhaust downpipe(s) to the support bracket

4.3 Undo the bolts (arrowed) securing the bracket to the transmission

5 Exhaust Gas Recirculation (EGR) system

General information

1 Several different versions of the EGR control system have been fitted. The type of system fitted and its mode of operation will depend on the age of the vehicle, the engine type and the market for which the vehicle is specified.

2 In-depth coverage of each system type is beyond the scope of this manual, therefore the procedures described in this section are limited to the renewal of the major components which are common to each system.

Vacuum solenoid valve

Removal

3 The solenoid valve is located on the right-hand side of the engine compartment.

4 Ensure that the ignition is switched off, then unplug the wiring from the solenoid valve at the connector.

5 Make a careful note of the vacuum hose locations, to aid refitting, then pull the hoses from the ports on the solenoid valve.

6 Remove the screws and withdraw the valve from the engine compartment.

4.8a Unscrew the nut (arrowed) securing the dipstick tube to the engine

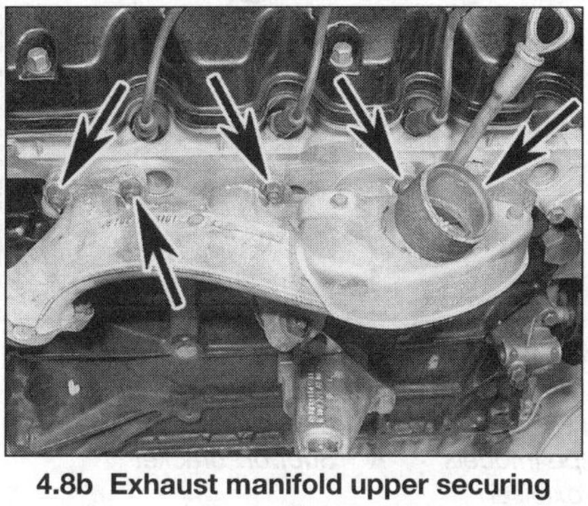

4.8b Exhaust manifold upper securing nuts (arrowed) . . .

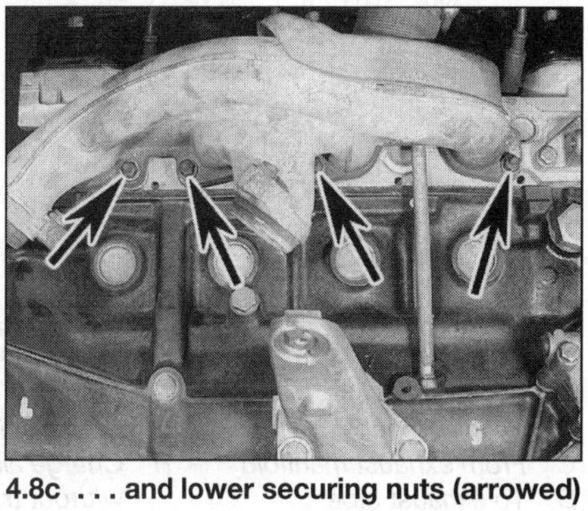

4.8c . . . and lower securing nuts (arrowed)

Refitting

7 Refitting is a reversal of removal, but ensure that the vacuum hoses are reconnected to the correct ports on the solenoid valve, as noted before removal.

EGR valve

Removal

8 Ensure that the engine has cooled completely before starting work.
9 Unplug the vacuum hose from the port on the top of the EGR valve.
10 Where applicable, undo the nuts and separate the recirculation pipe from the EGR valve flange. Recover the gasket.
11 Slacken and remove the nuts and lift the EGR valve from the exhaust manifold.

Refitting

12 Refitting is a reversal of removal. Ensure that the securing nuts are tightened to the correct torque.

6 Turbocharger - removal and refitting

General information

1 The turbocharger is mounted beneath the exhaust manifold. Lubrication is provided by a dedicated oil supply pipe that runs from a tapping on the cylinder head. Oil is returned to the sump via a return pipe that connects to the side of the cylinder block. The turbocharger unit has an integral wastegate valve and vacuum actuator diaphragm, which is used to limit the boost pressure applied to the inlet manifold.
2 The turbocharger internal components rotate at very high speed and as such are very sensitive to contamination; a great deal of damage can be caused by small particles of dirt, particularly if they strike the delicate turbine blades. Refer to the *Caution* and *Warning* notes given below before working on or removing the turbocharger unit.

Caution: Thoroughly clean the area around all oil pipe unions before disconnecting them, to prevent the ingress of dirt. Store dismantled components in a sealed container to prevent contamination. Cover the turbocharger air inlet ducts to prevent debris entering, and clean using lint-free cloths only.

Warning: Do not run the engine with the turbocharger air inlet hose disconnected; the depression at the inlet can build up very suddenly if the engine speed is raised, and there is a risk of foreign objects being sucked in and then ejected at very high speed.

Removal

3 Disconnect the battery negative lead and position it away from the terminal.
4 Where applicable, remove the engine undershield as described in Chapter 11.
5 Where necessary, refer to the relevant part of this Chapter and remove the air cleaner assembly. On vehicles fitted with a trap oxidiser, undo the screws and remove the heat shield from between the air cleaner and the trap oxidiser.
6 Slacken the clips and detach the air cleaner-to-turbocharger ducting **(see illustration)**.
7 Disconnect the vacuum hoses from the wastegate actuator diaphragm housing and where applicable, the EGR valve. Carefully note the hose locations and colour coding to aid correct refitting later.
8 Where applicable, slacken the clips, then detach and remove the corrugated hosing from the base of the EGR valve.
9 Where applicable, unscrew the nuts and remove the trap oxidiser from the exhaust manifold, together with its support bracket. **Note:** *On vehicles without a trap oxidiser, an intermediate pipe is fitted in its place.*
10 Slacken the clips and detach the turbocharger-to-inlet manifold ducting.
11 Unscrew the fixings and detach the mixer pipe (where fitted) at the base of the EGR valve from the turbocharger.
12 Loosen the unions and disconnect the oil supply and return pipes from the turbocharger unit - be prepared for oil spillage. Recover the sealing washers and discard them - new items must be used on refitting. Free the supply pipe from the clip on the inlet manifold.
13 Remove the nuts and disconnect the exhaust downpipe from the turbocharger outlet. Recover and discard the gasket - a new item must be used on refitting.
14 Slacken and withdraw the turbocharger-to-mounting bracket and strut bolts, lift the turbocharger unit away from the underside of the exhaust manifold.

Refitting

15 Refit the turbocharger by following the removal procedure in reverse, noting the following points.

a) Hand-tighten the exhaust downpipe nuts before tightening the turbocharger-to-mounting bracket bolts.
b) Apply high temperature grease to the threads and heads of the new intermediate pipe/trap oxidiser bolts, then fit and tighten them to the specified torque.
c) Tighten the exhaust downpipe nuts securely.
d) Prime the oil supply pipe and turbocharger oil inlet port with clean engine oil before reconnecting the unions and tightening them securely.
e) Tighten the oil return union securely.
f) Reconnect the wastegate actuator and EGR valve vacuum hoses according to the notes made during removal.
g) When the engine is initially started after refitting, allow the engine to idle for approximately one minute, to give the oil time to circulate around the turbine shaft bearings.

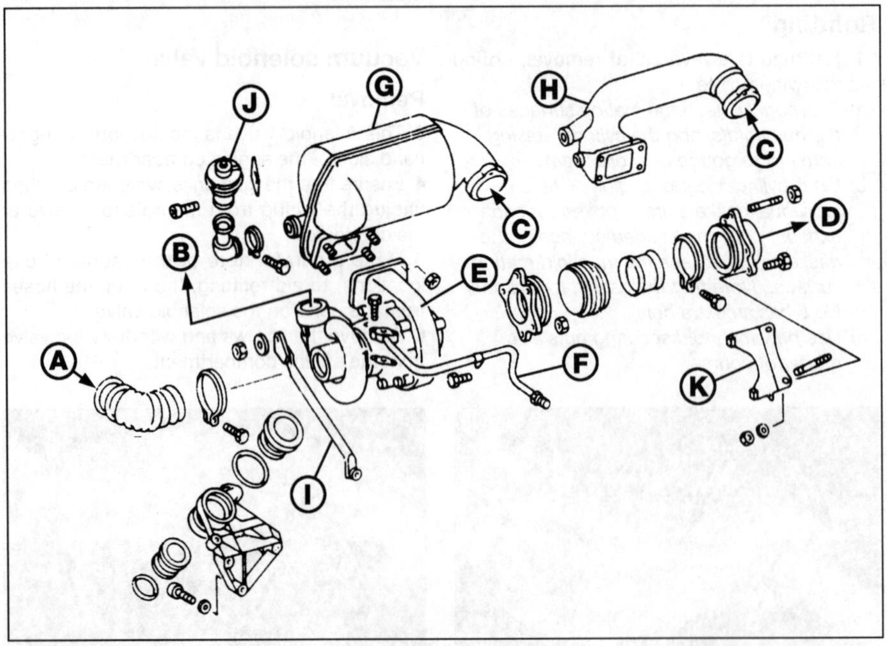

6.6 Turbocharger assembly

A From air cleaner
B To inlet manifold
C From exhaust manifold
D To exhaust pipe
E Turbocharger
F Oil pipe
G Trap oxidiser
H Charge air pipe (models without trap oxidiser)
I Support strut
J EGR valve
K Support bracket

7.7 Exhaust downpipe-to-intermediate silencer joint

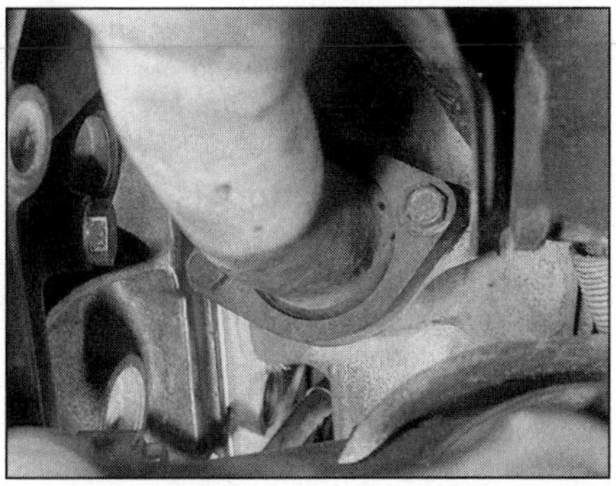

7.9 Exhaust downpipe-to-manifold joint

7.17 Exhaust system rear rubber mountings

7 Exhaust system - general information and component renewal

General information

1 On all models, the exhaust system is made up of three sections (excluding the exhaust manifolds) - the downpipe, which incorporates the catalytic converter (where fitted), the intermediate silencer, and the tail section which contains the rear silencer.

2 The exhaust system is suspended along its entire length by rubber mountings, which are secured to the underside of the vehicle by metal brackets. The downpipe is secured to the transmission by means of a bracket and U-bolts.

3 The connection between the exhaust manifold and the downpipe is a gasketed flange joint, secured with nuts or bolts. The connections between the downpipe, catalytic converter (where applicable) and the intermediate silencer are also flange joints and are fitted with sealing olives. A clamping ring, secured with a bolt is used to connect the intermediate silencer to the tail section.

Removal

4 Each exhaust section can be removed individually or, alternatively, the complete system can be removed as a unit.

5 Before removing any part of the system, first jack up the front or rear of the car, as applicable, and support it securely on axle stands (see *"Jacking and vehicle support"*). Alternatively, position the car over an inspection pit or on car ramps.

Downpipe

6 Place blocks of wood under the catalytic converter, or the lowest point of the downpipe, to act as a support. Where applicable, refer to Chapter 4B and remove the Lambda sensor from the exhaust pipe. Alternatively, if the downpipe is to be refitted, disconnect the Lambda sensor wiring connector.

7 Slacken and remove the nuts securing the downpipe or catalytic converter (as applicable) to the intermediate silencer **(see illustration)**. Remove the bolts and recover the sealing olive from the joint.

8 Slacken and withdraw the bolts that secure the downpipe bracket to the base of the transmission casing.

9 Undo the nuts or bolts (as applicable) and separate the downpipe from the exhaust manifold/turbocharger **(see illustration)**. Recover the gasket then withdraw the downpipe from underneath the vehicle.

Catalytic converter

10 Slacken and remove the nuts securing the downpipe to the catalytic converter. Remove the bolts and recover the sealing olive from the joint .

11 Slacken the catalytic converter to intermediate pipe clamping ring nut and bolt.

12 Free the catalytic converter from the intermediate pipe then withdraw it from underneath the vehicle.

Intermediate silencer

13 Slacken and clamping ring nut and bolt securing the downpipe or the catalytic converter (as applicable) to the intermediate silencer.

14 Slacken the clamping ring nut and bolt, and disconnect the tailpipe from the intermediate silencer.

15 Free the intermediate silencer, then withdraw it from underneath the vehicle.

Tailpipe

16 Slacken the clamping ring bolts and disengage the tailpipe from the intermediate silencer.

17 Unhook the tailpipe from its mounting rubbers and remove it from the vehicle **(see illustration)**. **Note:** *Where applicable, silencers in the tail section can be carefully cut from the exhaust system using a hacksaw and renewed individually; refer to a Mercedes-Benz dealer or an exhaust specialist for further advice.*

Complete system

18 Disconnect the downpipe from the manifold(s) as described previously in this Section. Where applicable, unplug the Lambda sensor wiring at the connector.

19 With the aid of an assistant, free the system from all its mounting rubbers and manoeuvre it out from underneath the vehicle.

Refitting

20 Each section is refitted by a reverse of the removal sequence, noting the following points.

a) Ensure that all traces of corrosion have been removed from the flanges and renew all necessary gaskets.

b) Inspect the rubber mountings for signs of damage or deterioration and renew as necessary.

c) Renew the sealing olive in the intermediate silencer-to-downpipe joint.

d) On joints which are secured by clamping rings, apply a smear of exhaust system jointing paste to the joint mating surfaces to ensure a gas-tight seal. Tighten the clamping ring nuts securely.

e) Prior to tightening the exhaust system fasteners, ensure that all rubber mountings are correctly located and that there is adequate clearance between the exhaust system and vehicle underbody.

4D

8 Catalytic converter - general information and precautions

The catalytic converter is a reliable and simple device, with no moving parts and as such requires no maintenance. There are, however, some facts of which an owner should be aware if the catalytic converter is to function properly for its full service life.

Petrol models

a) DO NOT use leaded petrol in a car equipped with a catalytic converter - the lead will coat the precious metals inside the casing, reducing their converting efficiency, and will eventually destroy the catalytic converter.

b) Always keep the ignition and fuel systems well-maintained in accordance with the manufacturer's schedule.

c) If the engine develops a misfire, do not drive the car at all (or at least as little as possible) until the fault is cured.

d) DO NOT push- or tow-start the car - this will soak the catalytic converter in unburned fuel, causing it to overheat when the engine does start.

e) DO NOT switch off the ignition at high engine speeds.

f) In some cases a sulphurous smell (like that of rotten eggs) may be noticed from the exhaust. This is common to many catalytic converter-equipped cars and once the car has covered a few thousand miles the problem should disappear. Low quality fuel with a high sulphur content will exacerbate this effect.

g) The catalytic converter, used on a well-maintained and well-driven car, should last for between 50 000 and 100 000 miles - if the converter is no longer effective it must be renewed.

Petrol and diesel models

a) DO NOT use fuel or engine oil additives - these may contain substances harmful to the catalytic converter.

b) DO NOT continue to use the car if the engine burns oil to the extent of leaving a visible trail of blue smoke.

c) Remember that the catalytic converter operates at very high temperatures and its external casing can take a while to cool down. DO NOT, therefore, park the car in dry undergrowth, over long grass, or over piles of dead leaves, after a long run.

d) Remember that the catalytic converter is FRAGILE - do not strike it with tools during servicing work.

9 Air injection system - component removal and refitting

At the time of writing, no information was available for removal and refitting of the air injection system components.

Chapter 5 Part A
Starting and charging systems

Contents

Alternator - brush holder/regulator module renewal 6
Alternator - removal and refitting 5
Alternator/charging system - testing in vehicle 4
Auxiliary drivebelt - removal, refitting and adjustment . . .see Chapter 1
Battery - condition check . . . . .see *"Weekly checks"*
Battery - removal and refitting 3
Battery - testing and charging 2
Electrical fault finding - general information . . . . .see Chapter 12
General information and precautions 1
Starter motor - overhaul 9
Starter motor - removal and refitting 8
Starting system - testing 7

Degrees of difficulty

Easy, suitable for novice with little experience	**Fairly easy,** suitable for beginner with some experience	**Fairly difficult,** suitable for competent DIY mechanic	**Difficult,** suitable for experienced DIY mechanic	**Very difficult,** suitable for expert DIY or professional

Specifications

General

System type	12-volt, negative earth

Battery

Rating:	
Petrol engined models	62 Ah
Diesel engined models	74 or 100 Ah, depending on market
Charge condition:	
Poor	12.5 volts
Normal	12.6 volts
Good	12.7 volts

Starter motor

Rating:	
4-cylinder petrol engined models	1.4 kW
6-cylinder petrol engined models	1.7 kW
Diesel engined models	2.2 kW

Alternator

Rating:	
4-cylinder petrol engined models	55 A/70 A
6-cylinder petrol engined models	70 A/90 A
Diesel engined models	55 A/70 A
Minimum brush length	5 mm

1 General information and precautions

General information

The engine electrical system consists mainly of the charging and starting systems. Because of their engine-related functions, these components are covered separately from the body electrical devices such as the lights, instruments, etc (which are covered in Chapter 12). On petrol engine models refer to Part B or C of this Chapter for information on the ignition system, and on diesel models refer to Part D for information on the pre-heating system.

The electrical system is of the 12-volt negative earth type.

The battery may be of the low maintenance or "maintenance-free" (sealed for life) type and is charged by the alternator, which is belt-driven from the crankshaft pulley.

The starter motor is of the pre-engaged type incorporating an integral solenoid. On starting, the solenoid moves the drive pinion into engagement with the flywheel ring gear before the starter motor is energised. Once the engine has started, a one-way clutch prevents the motor armature being driven by the engine until the pinion disengages from the flywheel.

Precautions

Further details of the various systems are given in the relevant Sections of this Chapter. While some repair procedures are given, the usual course of action is to renew the component concerned. The owner whose interest extends beyond mere component renewal is advised to obtain a copy of the *"Automobile Electrical & Electronic Systems Manual"*, available from the publishers of this manual.

It is necessary to take extra care when working on the electrical system to avoid damage to semi-conductor devices (diodes and transistors), and to avoid the risk of personal injury. In addition to the precautions given in *"Safety first!"* at the beginning of this manual, observe the following when working on the system.

Always remove rings, watches, etc before working on the electrical system. Even with the battery disconnected, capacitive discharge could occur if a component's live terminal is earthed through a metal object. This could cause a shock or nasty burn.

Do not reverse the battery connections. Components such as the alternator, electronic control units, or any other components having semi-conductor circuitry could be irreparably damaged.

If the engine is being started using jump leads and a slave battery, connect the batteries *positive-to-positive* and *negative-to-negative* (see *"Jump starting"*). This also applies when connecting a battery charger.

Never disconnect the battery terminals, the alternator, any electrical wiring or any test instruments when the engine is running.

Do not allow the engine to turn the alternator when the alternator is not connected.

Never "test" for alternator output by "flashing" the output lead to earth.

Never use an ohmmeter of the type incorporating a hand-cranked generator for circuit or continuity testing.

Always ensure that the battery negative lead is disconnected when working on the electrical system.

Before using electric-arc welding equipment on the car, disconnect the battery, alternator and components such as the fuel injection/ignition electronic control unit to protect them from the risk of damage.

Certain radio/cassette units fitted as standard equipment by the manufacturer are equipped with a built-in security code to deter thieves. If the power source to the unit is cut, the anti-theft system will activate. Even if the power source is immediately reconnected, the radio/cassette unit will not function until the correct security code has been entered. Therefore, if you do not know the correct security code for the radio/cassette unit **do not** disconnect the battery negative terminal of the battery or remove the radio/cassette unit from the vehicle. Refer to *"Radio/cassette unit anti-theft system precaution"* in the *Reference Section* of this manual for further information.

2 Battery - testing and charging

Standard and low maintenance battery - testing

1 If the vehicle covers a small annual mileage it is worthwhile checking the specific gravity of the electrolyte every three months to determine the state of charge of the battery. Use a hydrometer to make the check and compare the results with the following table.

	Ambient temperature above 25°C (77°F)	Ambient temperature below 25°C (77°F)
Fully charged	*1.210 to 1.230*	*1.270 to 1.290*
70% charged	*1.170 to 1.190*	*1.230 to 1.250*
Fully discharged	*1.050 to 1.070*	*1.110 to 1.130*

Note that the specific gravity readings assume an electrolyte temperature of 15°C (60°F); for every 10°C (18°F) below 15°C (60°F) subtract 0.007. For every 10°C (18°F) above 15°C (60°F) add 0.007.

2 If the battery condition is suspect, first check the specific gravity of electrolyte in each cell. A variation of 0.040 or more between any cells indicates loss of electrolyte or deterioration of the internal plates.

3 If the specific gravity variation is 0.040 or more, the battery should be renewed. If the cell variation is satisfactory but the battery is discharged, it should be charged as described later in this Section.

Maintenance-free battery - testing

4 In cases where a "sealed for life" maintenance-free battery is fitted, topping-up and testing of the electrolyte in each cell is not possible. The condition of the battery can therefore only be tested using a battery condition indicator or a voltmeter.

5 Certain models may be fitted with a maintenance-free battery, with a built-in charge condition indicator. The indicator is located in the top of the battery casing, and indicates the condition of the battery from its colour. If the indicator shows green, then the battery is in a good state of charge. If the indicator turns darker, eventually to black, then the battery requires charging, as described later in this Section. If the indicator shows clear/yellow, then the electrolyte level in the battery is too low to allow further use, and the battery should be renewed. **Do not** attempt to charge, load or jump start a battery when the indicator shows clear/yellow.

6 If testing the battery using a voltmeter, connect the voltmeter across the battery and compare the result with those given in the *Specifications* under "charge condition". The test is only accurate if the battery has not been subjected to any kind of charge for the previous six hours. If this is not the case, switch on the headlights for 30 seconds, then wait four to five minutes before testing the battery after switching off the headlights. All other electrical circuits must be switched off, so check that the doors and tailgate are fully shut when making the test.

7 If the voltage reading is less than 12.2 volts, then the battery is discharged, whilst a reading of 12.2 to 12.4 volts indicates a partially discharged condition.

8 If the battery is to be charged, remove it from the vehicle and charge it as described later in this Section.

Standard and low maintenance battery - charging

Note: *The following is intended as a guide only. Always refer to the manufacturer's recommendations (often printed on a label attached to the battery) before charging a battery.*

9 Charge the battery at a rate equivalent to 10% of the battery capacity (eg for a 45 Ah battery charge at 4.5 A) and continue to charge the battery at this rate until no further rise in specific gravity is noted over a four hour period.

10 Alternatively, a trickle charger charging at the rate of 1.5 amps can safely be used overnight.

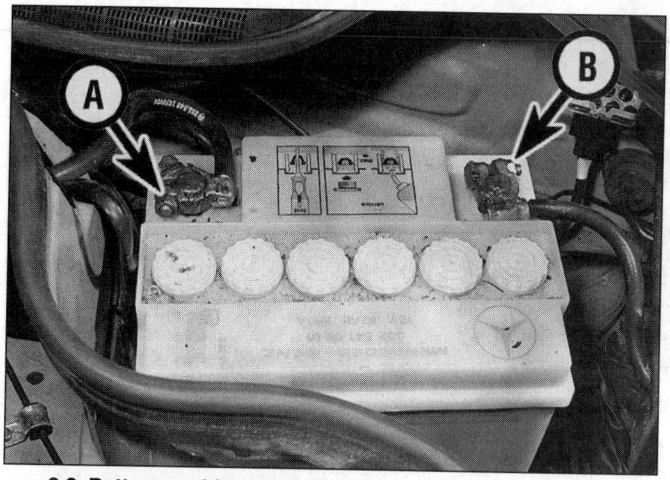

3.2 Battery positive terminal (A) and negative terminal (B)

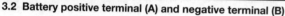

3.3 Battery clamp nut (arrowed)

11 Specially rapid "boost" charges which are claimed to restore the power of the battery in 1 to 2 hours are not recommended, as they can cause serious damage to the battery plates through overheating.

12 While charging the battery, note that the temperature of the electrolyte should never exceed 37.8°C (100°F).

Maintenance-free battery - charging

Note: *The following is intended as a guide only. Always refer to the manufacturer's recommendations (often printed on a label attached to the battery) before charging a battery.*

13 This battery type takes considerably longer to fully recharge than the standard type, the time taken being dependent on the extent of discharge, but it can take anything up to three days.

14 A constant voltage type charger is required, to be set, when connected, to 13.9 to 14.9 volts with a charger current below 25 amps. Using this method, the battery should be usable within three hours, giving a voltage reading of 12.5 volts, but this is for a partially discharged battery and, as mentioned, full charging can take considerably longer.

15 If the battery is to be charged from a fully discharged state (condition reading less than 12.2 volts), have it recharged by your Mercedes-Benz dealer or local automotive electrician, as the charge rate is higher and constant supervision during charging is necessary.

3 Battery - removal and refitting

Removal

1 Slacken the clamp screw and disconnect the battery negative cable from the terminal.

2 Unclip the plastic cover and disconnect the battery positive cable in the same manner **(see illustration)**.

3 At the base of the battery, slacken and withdraw the retaining nut, then lift off the clamping plate **(see illustration)**.

4 Remove the battery from the engine compartment. Take care, as the battery is heavy.

Refitting

5 Refit the battery by following the removal procedure in reverse. Tighten the battery clamping plate screw securely.

4 Alternator/charging system - testing in vehicle

Note: *Refer to the warnings given in "Safety first!" and in Section 1 of this Chapter before starting work.*

1 If the ignition warning light fails to illuminate when the ignition is switched on, first check the alternator wiring connections for security. If satisfactory, check that the warning light bulb has not blown, and that the bulbholder is secure in its location in the instrument panel. If the light still fails to illuminate, check the continuity of the warning light feed wire from the alternator to the bulbholder. If all is satisfactory, the alternator is at fault and should be renewed or taken to an auto-electrician for testing and repair.

2 If the ignition warning light illuminates when the engine is running, stop the engine and check that the drivebelt is correctly tensioned (see Chapter 1) and that the alternator connections are secure. If all is so far satisfactory, check the alternator brushes and slip rings as described in Section 6. If the fault persists, the alternator should be renewed, or taken to an auto-electrician for testing and repair.

3 If the alternator output is suspect even though the warning light functions correctly, the regulated voltage may be checked as follows.

4 Connect a voltmeter across the battery terminals and start the engine.

5 Increase the engine speed until the voltmeter reading remains steady; the reading should be approximately 12 to 13 volts, and no more than 14 volts.

6 Switch on as many electrical accessories (eg, the headlights, heated rear window and heater blower) as possible, and check that the alternator maintains the regulated voltage at around 13 to 14 volts.

7 If the regulated voltage is not as stated, the fault may be due to worn brushes, weak brush springs, a faulty voltage regulator, a faulty diode, a severed phase winding or worn or damaged slip rings. The brushes and slip rings may be checked (see Section 6), but if the fault persists, the alternator should be renewed or taken to an auto-electrician for testing and repair.

5A

5 Alternator - removal and refitting

1 On all models, the alternator is bolted to the right-hand side of the engine block and is driven by the auxiliary drivebelt.

2 The alternator can be removed from the top of the engine compartment, without raising the vehicle on most models. On certain high specification models, the size of the engine and the number of ancillaries mean that the alternator must be removed from the underside of the engine.

Removal

3 Disconnect the battery negative lead, and position it away from the terminal. Where applicable, jack up the front of the vehicle and support it securely on axle stands (see *"Jacking and vehicle support"*).

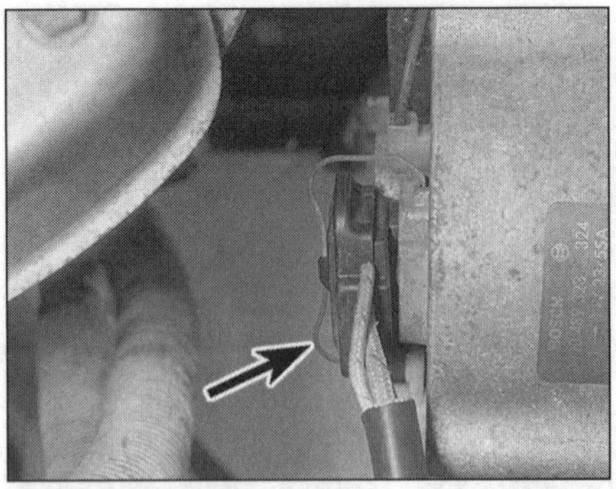

5.6 Release the locking clip (arrowed) and unplug the alternator wiring connector

4 Where applicable, remove the engine undershield as described in Chapter 11. If required, the inlet air ducting can also be removed to improve access - refer to Chapter 4 for details.

5 Remove the auxiliary drivebelt as described in Chapter 1.

6 On models with a conventional alternator, unscrew the four bolts and remove the rear plastic casing from the alternator. Release the locking clip and unplug the multiway cable connector **(see illustration)**.

7 On models equipped with a "compact" alternator, peel back the rubber cover, unscrew the nuts and disconnect the alternator wiring from the terminal posts **(see illustration)**.

8 Slacken and remove first the lower, then the upper mounting bolts, then lift the alternator away from its mounting bracket **(see illustration)**.

6.4a Remove the brush holder/voltage regulator module screws (arrowed), . . .

5.7 Wiring terminals (arrowed) - "compact" alternator

9 Refer to Section 6 if the removal of the brush holder/voltage regulator module is required.

Refitting

10 Refitting is a reversal of removal. Refer to Chapter 1 for details of refitting and tensioning the auxiliary drivebelt.

6 Alternator - brush holder/regulator module renewal

1 Remove the alternator, as described in Section 5.

2 Place the alternator on a clean work surface, with the pulley facing down.

3 On models equipped with a compact alternator, remove the retaining screws, then prise open the clips and lift the plastic cover from the rear of the alternator.

4 Slacken and withdraw the brush holder/voltage regulator module screws, then lift the module away from the alternator **(see illustrations)**.

5 Measure the free length of the brushes - take the measurement from the manufacturers emblem etched on the side of the brush, to the shallowest part of the curved end face of the brush. Check the measurement with the *Specifications* - renew the module if the brushes are worn below the minimum limit.

5.8 Alternator mounting bolts (arrowed)

6 Inspect the surfaces of the slip rings, at the end of the alternator shaft. If they appear excessively worn, burnt or pitted, then renewal must be considered - refer to an automobile electrical system specialist for further guidance.

7 Reassemble the alternator by following the dismantling procedure in reverse. On completion, refer to Section 5 and refit the alternator.

7 Starting system - testing

Note: *Refer to the precautions given in "Safety first!" and in Section 1 of this Chapter before starting work.*

1 If the starter motor fails to operate when the ignition key is turned to the appropriate position, the following possible causes may be to blame.

a) The battery is faulty.

b) The electrical connections between the switch, solenoid, battery and starter motor are somewhere failing to pass the necessary current from the battery through the starter to earth.

c) The solenoid is faulty.

d) The starter motor is mechanically or electrically defective.

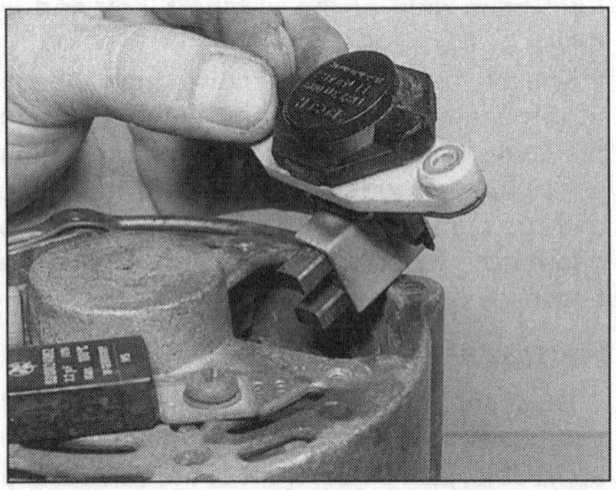

6.4b . . . then lift the module away from the alternator - conventional alternator

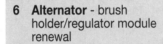

6.4c Remove the retaining screws . . .

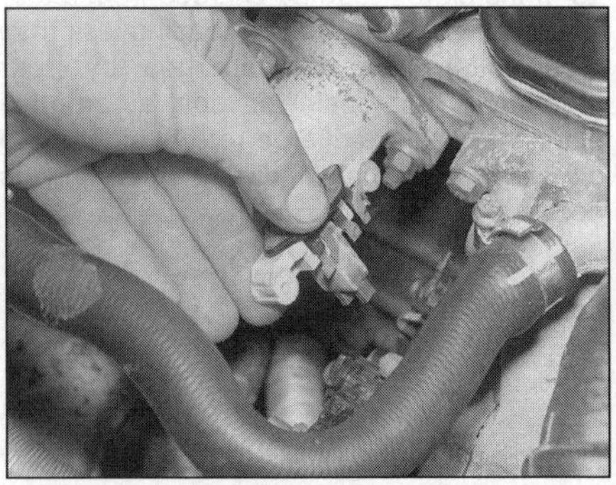

6.4d . . . then lift the module from the alternator - "compact" alternator

2 To check the battery, switch on the headlights. If they dim after a few seconds, this indicates that the battery is discharged - recharge (see Section 2) or renew the battery. If the headlights glow brightly, operate the ignition switch and observe the lights. If they dim, then this indicates that current is reaching the starter motor, therefore the fault must lie in the starter motor. If the lights continue to glow brightly (and no clicking sound can be heard from the starter motor solenoid), this indicates that there is a fault in the circuit or solenoid - see following paragraphs. If the starter motor turns slowly when operated, but the battery is in good condition, then this indicates that either the starter motor is faulty, or there is considerable resistance somewhere in the circuit.

3 If a fault in the circuit is suspected, disconnect the battery leads (including the earth connection to the body), the starter/solenoid wiring and the engine/transmission earth strap. Thoroughly clean the connections, and reconnect the leads and wiring, then use a voltmeter or test lamp to check that full battery voltage is available at the battery positive lead connection to the solenoid, and that the earth is sound. Smear petroleum jelly around the battery terminals to prevent corrosion - corroded connections are amongst the most frequent causes of electrical system faults.

4 If the battery and all connections are in good condition, check the circuit by disconnecting the wire from the solenoid blade terminal. Connect a voltmeter or test lamp between the wire end and a good earth (such as the battery negative terminal), and check that the wire is live when the ignition switch is turned to the "start" position. If it is, then the circuit is sound - if not the circuit wiring can be checked as described in Chapter 12.

5 The solenoid contacts can be checked by connecting a voltmeter or test lamp between the battery positive feed connection on the starter side of the solenoid, and earth. When the ignition switch is turned to the "start" position, there should be a reading or lighted bulb, as applicable. If there is no reading or lighted bulb, the solenoid is faulty and should be renewed.

6 If the circuit and solenoid are proved sound, the fault must lie in the starter motor. In this event, it may be possible to have the starter motor overhauled by a specialist, but check on the availability and cost of spares before proceeding, as it may prove more economical to obtain a new or exchange motor.

8.9 Guide the starter assembly out of the bellhousing aperture and lower it

8 Starter motor - removal and refitting

1 On all models, the starter motor is bolted to the transmission bellhousing, at the rear of the engine on the left-hand side. Access is easiest from the underside of the engine compartment. On diesel engined models fitted with an engine oil cooler, the removal procedure is more complex than for other models and involves lifting the whole engine assembly off its mountings with a hoist.

Removal

Petrol engined models, and diesel engined models without an engine oil cooler

2 Disconnect the battery negative lead and position it away from the terminal. Jack up the front of the vehicle and support it securely on axle stands (see *"Jacking and vehicle support"*).

3 Remove the engine undershield as described in Chapter 11.

4 Refer to the relevant part of Chapter 4 and remove the air cleaner assembly. To gain additional clearance, unbolt and remove the inlet manifold support strut.

5 Where applicable, unbolt the hose guide bracket from the underside of the sump casting and position the hose(s) to one side.

6 Where applicable unscrew and nut(s) and/or screw(s), and disconnect the wiring from the starter motor solenoid.

7 Turn the steering to full lock to ensure that the left-hand steering drop arm is positioned away from the starter motor.

8 Remove the nuts, then withdraw the upper and lower starter motor mounting bolts.

9 Guide the starter motor out of the bellhousing aperture and lower it from the engine compartment **(see illustration)**.

Diesel engined models with oil cooler

10 Proceed as described in paragraphs 1 to 4 inclusive.

11 Attach a hoist and lifting tackle to the engine lifting brackets. Raise the hoist to just take the weight of the engine assembly, then unscrew the bolts from the underside of the left- and right-hand engine mountings. Where applicable, also unbolt the engine mounting damper from the right-hand side of the vehicle - see Chapter 2D.

12 Continue raising the hoist until there is enough clearance to allow the starter motor to be withdrawn.

13 Remove the nuts, then withdraw the upper and lower starter motor mounting bolts.

14 Guide the starter motor out of the bellhousing aperture and lower it from the engine compartment.

Refitting

15 Refit the starter motor by following the removal procedure in reverse.

9 Starter motor - overhaul

If the starter motor is thought to be defective, it should be removed from the vehicle and taken to an auto-electrician for assessment. In the majority of cases, new starter motor brushes can be fitted at a reasonable cost. However, check the cost of repairs first, as it may prove more economical to purchase a new or exchange motor.

Notes

Chapter 5 Part B
Ignition system: 4-cylinder petrol engine

Contents

Distributor - removal and refitting 4
General information 1
HT Coil - removal and refitting 3
Ignition control system components - removal and refitting 7
Ignition system - testing 2
Ignition system - check ....see Chapter 1A
Ignition timing - checking and adjusting 6
Rotor arm - removal and refitting 5
Spark plugs - renewal ....see Chapter 1A

Degrees of difficulty

Easy, suitable for novice with little experience	**Fairly easy,** suitable for beginner with some experience	**Fairly difficult,** suitable for competent DIY mechanic	**Difficult,** suitable for experienced DIY mechanic	**Very difficult,** suitable for expert DIY or professional

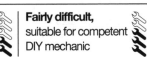

Specifications

System type

1.8 litre models	EZL
2.0 litre models with Stromberg carburettor	TSZ
2.0 litre models with Pierburg 2E-E carburettor	EZL
2.0 litre models with fuel injection:	
Later models	EZL
Early models without factory-fitted catalytic converter	TSZ
2.3 litre models with fuel injection:	
Later models	EZL
Early models without factory-fitted catalytic converter	TSZ

Ignition coil

Models with TSZ ignition:	
Primary winding resistance	0.5 to 0.9 Ω
Secondary winding resistance	6 to 16 kΩ
Models with EZL ignition:	
Primary winding resistance	0.3 to 0.6 Ω
Secondary winding resistance	8 to 13 kΩ

Distributor

Type	Breakerless, driven from crankshaft
Dwell angle	Governed by ignition control system
Sensor resistance (TSZ ignition only)	500 to 700 W
Ignition timing:*	
Models with EZL ignition and Pierburg 2E-E carburettor:	
At idle	11 to 15° BTDC
At 3200 rpm, vacuum applied, trimming plug in "S" position	38 to 42° BTDC
At 3200 rpm, vacuum applied, trimming plug in "N" position	38 to 42° BTDC
At 3200 rpm, no vacuum applied, trimming plug in "S" position	22 to 26° BTDC
At 3200 rpm, no vacuum applied, trimming plug in "N" position	15 to 19° BTDC
Models with EZL ignition and fuel injection:	
At idle	8 to 12° BTDC
At 3200 rpm, vacuum applied, trimming plug in "S" position	35 to 39° BTDC
At 3200 rpm, vacuum applied, trimming plug in "N" position	35 to 39° BTDC
At 3200 rpm, no vacuum applied, trimming plug in "S" position	23 to 27° BTDC
At 3200 rpm, no vacuum applied, trimming plug in "N" position	17 to 21° BTDC
Models with TSZ ignition and fuel injection:	
At idle, using leaded fuel, vacuum applied	12 to 18° BTDC
At idle, using unleaded fuel, vacuum applied	7 to 13° BTDC
Total advance at 4500 rpm, without vacuum, using leaded fuel	32° BTDC
Total advance at 4500 rpm, without vacuum, using unleaded fuel	27° BTDC
Vacuum advance at 4500 rpm	8 to 12° BTDC
Models with TSZ ignition and Stromberg carburettor:	
At idle, using leaded fuel, without vacuum	10 to 16° BTDC
Total advance at 4500 rpm, vacuum applied	40 to 44° BTDC
Vacuum advance at 4500 rpm	8 to 12° BTDC

*__Note:__ *These are typical figures - vehicles specified for different markets may have differing ignition advance characteristics.*

Spark plugs

All models	Champion S9YC/CC
Electrode gap	0.8 mm

Sensors

Crankshaft sensor resistance	680 to 1200 W
Coolant temperature sensor:	
Electrical resistance:	
At 80°C	325 W
At 40°C	1.2 kW
At 0°C	6 kW
Inlet air temperature sensor:	
Electrical resistance:	
At 80°C	325 W
At 40°C	1.2 kW
At 0°C	6 kW

Torque wrench settings

	Nm	lbf ft
Spark plugs	15	11

1 General information

Models with EZL ignition system

The EZL ignition system major components comprise the spark plugs (one per cylinder), HT leads, the distributor, an electronic ignition coil, and an Electronic Control Unit (ECU) together with its associated sensors, actuators and wiring. The component layout varies slightly between models, but the basic operation is the same.

The basic operation is as follows. The control unit supplies a voltage to the input stage of the ignition coil, which causes the primary windings in the coil to be energised. The supply voltage is periodically interrupted by the ECU, and this results in the collapse of primary magnetic field, which then induces a much larger voltage in the coil's secondary windings, called the HT voltage. This HT voltage is directed, by the distributor via the HT leads, to the spark plug in the cylinder currently on its ignition stroke. The spark plug electrodes form a gap small enough for the HT voltage to arc across, and the resulting spark ignites the fuel/air mixture in the cylinder. The timing of this sequence of events is critical and is regulated solely by the ECU.

The ECU calculates and controls the ignition timing and dwell angle primarily according to engine speed, crankshaft position and inlet manifold depression information, received from sensors mounted on and around the engine. Other parameters that affect ignition timing are throttle position (idle and full throttle positions are sensed via a changeover switch), inlet air temperature, and coolant temperature. Again, these are monitored via sensors mounted on the engine.

The basic ignition timing can be altered in fixed steps, to suit the type of fuel being used. This is achieved by means of a trimming socket, located in the engine compartment, close to the ignition system ECU - refer to Section 6 for details.

Models with TSZ ignition

The overall operation of the TSZ system is essentially the same as that of the EZL system, with the following differences.

Instead of deriving its timing from a crankshaft position sensor, the TSZ ignition system is triggered by a sensor mounted on the inside of the distributor body. This arrangement means that the basic ignition timing can be adjusted by rotating the distributor body in relation to the distributor shaft. Similarly, if the distributor has been removed, the ignition timing must be checked and if necessary reset.

Ignition advance is controlled partly by the electronic control unit and partly by a distributor-mounted vacuum module. The electronic control unit provides engine speed-related advance, and the vacuum module provides engine load-related advance, from a vacuum tapping on the carburettor/throttle body (as applicable).

On carburettor models, a thermo-switch and check valve provide additional ignition advance, via the vacuum advance module, during warm-up.

2 Ignition system - testing

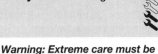

Warning: Extreme care must be taken when working on the system with the ignition switched on; it is possible to get a substantial electric shock from a vehicle's ignition system. Persons with cardiac pacemaker devices should keep well clear of the ignition circuits, components and test equipment. Always switch off the ignition before disconnecting or connecting any component, and when using a multi-meter to check resistances.

General

1 Most ignition system faults are likely to be due to loose or dirty connections or to "tracking" (unintentional earthing) of HT voltage due to dirt, dampness or damaged insulation, rather than by the failure of any of the system's components. **Always** check all wiring thoroughly before condemning an electrical component and work methodically to eliminate all other possibilities before deciding that a particular component is faulty.

2 The old practice of checking for a spark by holding the live end of an HT lead a short distance away from the engine is not recommended; not only is there a high risk of an electric shock, but the HT coil could be damaged. Similarly, **never** try to "diagnose" misfires by pulling off one HT lead at a time, as well as the risk of electric shock, the test may be invalid, as the ignition system fitted to later models has the capability to detect and temporarily disable HT lines that are open-circuit.

3 Problems with the system operation that cannot be pinpointed by following the guidelines in the following paragraphs should therefore be referred to a Mercedes-Benz dealer for assessment.

Engine will not start

4 If the engine either will not turn over at all, or only turns very slowly, check the battery and starter motor. Connect a voltmeter across the battery terminals (meter positive probe to battery positive terminal), disconnect the ignition coil HT lead from the distributor cap and earth it, then note the voltage reading obtained while turning over the engine on the starter for (no more than) ten seconds. If the reading obtained is less than approximately 9.5 volts, first check the battery, starter motor and charging systems (see Chapter 5A).

5 If the engine turns over at normal speed but will not start, check the HT circuit by connecting a timing light (following the manufacturer's instructions) and turning the engine over on the starter motor; if the light flashes, voltage is reaching the spark plugs, so these should be checked first. If the light does not flash, check the HT leads themselves followed by the distributor cap, carbon brush and rotor arm using the information given in Chapter 1A.

6 If there is a spark, check the fuel system for faults referring to the relevant part of Chapter 4 for further information.

7 If there is still no spark, then the problem may lie within the ignition control/engine management system. In these cases, the vehicle should be referred to a Mercedes-Benz dealer or automotive electrical specialist for assessment.

Engine misfires

8 An irregular misfire suggests either a loose connection or intermittent fault in the control system or primary circuit, or an HT fault on the coil side of the rotor arm (where applicable).

9 With the ignition switched off, check carefully through the system ensuring that all connections are clean and securely fastened. If the equipment is available, check the LT circuit as described previously.

10 Check that the HT coil, the distributor cap and the HT leads are clean and dry. Check the leads themselves and the spark plugs (by substitution, if necessary), then check the distributor cap, carbon brush and rotor arm as described in Chapter 1A.

11 Regular misfiring is almost certainly due to a fault in the distributor cap (where applicable), coil, HT leads or spark plugs. Use a timing light (paragraph 5 above) to check whether HT voltage is present at all leads.

12 If HT voltage is not present on one particular lead, the fault will be in that lead or in the distributor cap. If HT is present on all leads, the fault will be in the spark plugs; check and renew them if there is any doubt about their condition.

13 If no HT voltage is present, check the HT coil - the secondary windings may be breaking down under load.

3 HT coil - removal and refitting

Models with EZL ignition

1 Refer to the information given in Chapter 5C.

Models with TSZ ignition

Removal

2 Disconnect the battery negative lead, and position it away from the terminal.

3 Pull off the protective cap, then unplug the HT king lead from the centre terminal **(see illustrations)**.

4 Remove the nuts and disconnect the positive and negative LT leads from the terminal studs. Label each LT cable for position, to avoid confusion during refitting.

5 Slacken and withdraw the mounting screws, then lift the coil and mounting bracket away from the inner wing.

6 Observe the safety plug on the upper surface of the coil **(see illustration)**. If the oil

5B

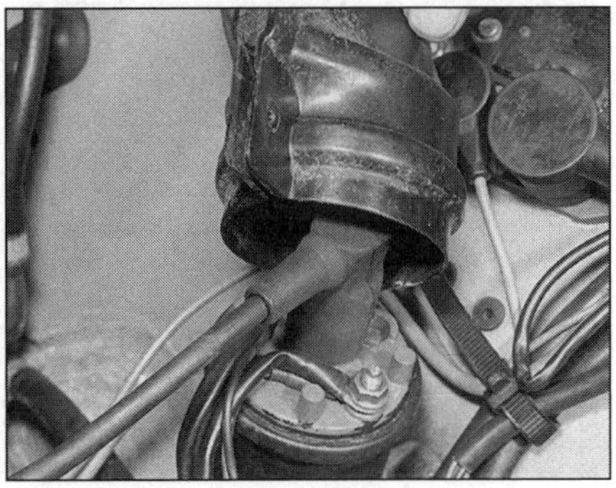

3.3a Pull off the protective cap . . .

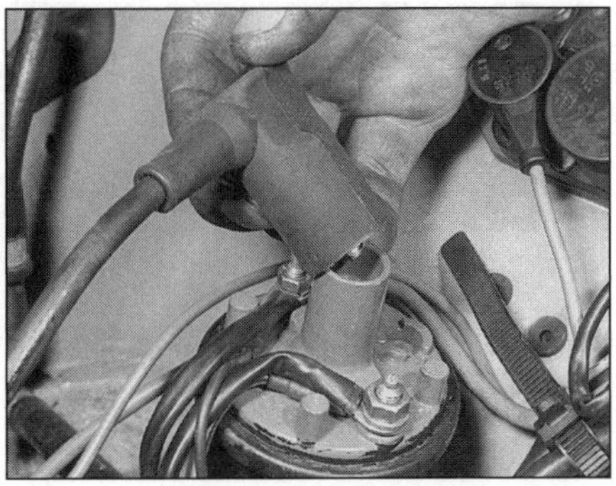

3.3b . . . then unplug the HT king lead from the centre terminal

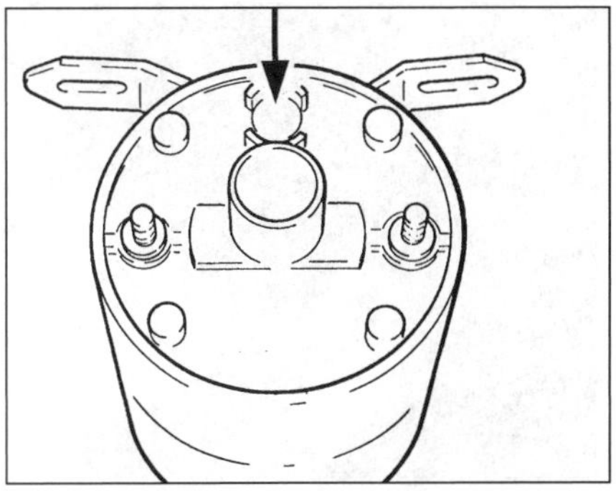

3.6 HT coil safety plug (arrowed)

coolant in the coil has overheated at some point, due to overloading or internal malfunction, the plug will have popped out. Under these circumstances, the coil must be renewed, but only after the fault has been identified and corrected.

Refitting

7 Refitting is a reversal of removal.

4 Distributor - removal and refitting

Models with EZL ignition

Note: *Unlike the TSZ breakerless system which is triggered by a sensor mounted inside the distributor, the EZL ignition system is triggered solely by the crankshaft position sensor - the sole function of the distributor is to direct HT voltage to the spark plugs. Because of this, the basic ignition timing setting cannot be altered by rotating the distributor body on its mountings. No adjustment of the ignition timing is required, therefore, after removal and refitting of the distributor.*

Removal

1 Disconnect the battery negative lead, and position it away from the terminal.

2 Loosen the securing screws, then remove the distributor cap and move it to one side.

3 Turn the crankshaft to bring No 1 piston to TDC, as described in Chapter 2A or 2B, as applicable. The distributor can now be removed and refitted without losing its alignment, provided that the engine is not rotated after the distributor body has been withdrawn from the crankcase.

4 Slacken and withdraw the clamp bolt, then lift the distributor body from the crankcase **(see illustration)**.

5 Check the condition of the O-ring oil seal (where fitted) - if it shows signs of deterioration or if there are signs of leakage, fit a new seal.

Refitting

6 If the engine has not been rotated from TDC on cylinder No 1 since the removal of the distributor, then proceed from paragraph 8. If the alignment of the engine has been lost, then proceed from paragraph 7.

4.4 Slackening the distributor clamp bolt

7 Remove No 1 spark plug with reference to Chapter 1A. Place a thumb over the spark plug hole, then turn the crankshaft (as described during *"Removal"*) until the following conditions are met **(see illustration)**.

a) *Pressure can be felt building up at the spark plug hole.*
b) *The TDC marking on the crankshaft vibration damper is exactly aligned with the pointer on the timing chain cover (see "Removal" for details).*

8 Insert the distributor into the crankcase and engage the end of the distributor shaft with the drive gear, such that:

a) *When the distributor body is flush with its mounting flange, the rotor arm is pointing directly at the alignment marking on the distributor body (temporarily remove the rotor arm, then remove the plastic shield to view the alignment marking)* ***(see illustrations)***.
b) *The clamp bolt hole on the mounting flange is aligned with the centre of the elongated slot mounting on the base of the distributor. Turn the distributor body to achieve this if necessary.*

Note: *The distributor drive gear is cut helically, so the rotor arm will tend to turn, as the distributor shaft is inserted. To compensate for this, turn the rotor arm to one side of the alignment marking, before inserting the distributor shaft.*

4.7 TDC marking on vibration damper aligned with pointer (arrowed) on timing chain cover

9 Fit the distributor clamp bolt and tighten it securely.

10 Fit the distributor cap, then insert and tighten the securing screws.

Models with TSZ ignition

Note: *Unlike the EZL breakerless system which is triggered by a crankshaft position sensor, the TSZ ignition system is triggered by a sensor mounted inside the distributor. Because of this, the basic ignition timing setting must be checked and adjusted, after removing and refitting the distributor.*

Removal

11 Proceed as described in paragraphs 1 to 3 inclusive.

12 Unplug the hose from the vacuum unit on the side of the distributor body.

13 Unplug the distributor sensor wiring, at the connector on the side of the distributor body.

14 Mark the relationship between the base of the distributor and the mounting flange on the engine, using a dab of paint or a scriber, to act as an alignment aid during refitting.

15 Slacken and remove the clamp bolt, then lift the distributor from the crankcase **(see illustration)**.

16 Check the condition of the O-ring oil seal (where fitted); if it shows signs of deterioration or if there are signs of leakage, fit a new seal.

4.8a Remove the plastic shield . . .

4.8b . . . to check that the rotor arm is pointing at the alignment marking

4.15 Distributor clamp bolt (arrowed)

4.17 Rotor arm pointing directly at the alignment marking (arrowed) on the distributor body

5.2 Pull the rotor arm from the end of the distributor shaft

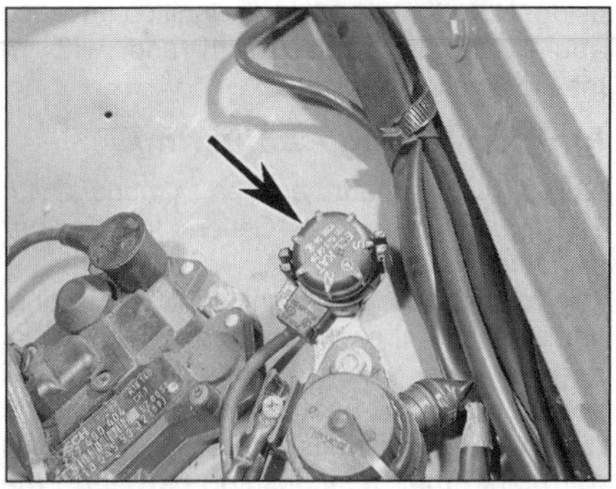

6.3 Ignition timing trimming plug (arrowed)

Refitting

17 Proceed as described in paragraphs 6 to 10 **(see illustration)**. Use the alignment marks made on the base of the distributor body and mounting flange during removal, to give an approximate ignition timing setting.

18 Reconnect the vacuum unit hose and the sensor wiring.

19 On completion, check and if necessary adjust the ignition timing with reference to Section 6.

5 Rotor arm - removal and refitting

Removal

1 Remove the securing screws and withdraw the distributor cap.

2 Pull the rotor arm from the end of the distributor shaft **(see illustration)**.

3 Check the condition of the rotor arm metal contact surfaces. If there are signs of corrosion, or severe pitting or wear, the rotor arm should be renewed. Similarly, if the plastic body is cracked or shows signs or tracking, then the rotor arm must be renewed.

Refitting

4 Push the rotor arm firmly onto the end of the distributor shaft, ensuring that the lug on the inside of the rotor arm engages with the corresponding recess in the end of the shaft.

5 Refit the distributor cap, and tighten the securing screws.

6 Ignition timing - checking and adjusting

General information

Models with EZL ignition

1 The EZL ignition system is triggered by an electronic signal generated by the crankshaft position sensor. The ignition control system then calculates the correct ignition timing and dwell angle primarily according to engine speed, crankshaft position and inlet manifold depression information, received from sensors mounted on and around the engine (refer to Sections 1 and 7 for details).

2 Unlike other breakerless ignition systems, which are triggered by a rotor mounted on the distributor shaft, the timing of the EZL ignition system cannot be adjusted by rotating the distributor body with respect to the distributor shaft.

3 The basic ignition timing can, however, be altered in fixed steps to suit the type of fuel being used. This is achieved by means of a trimming socket, located in the engine compartment, close to the ignition system ECU. The socket is fitted with a plug, which has a number of fixed value resistors built into it. The plug may be fitted to the socket in a number of different positions, indicated by markings on the upper surface of the plug **(see illustration)**. Moving the plug to another position connects a different resistor across the socket terminals - this is sensed electronically by the ignition system ECU, which advances or retards the ignition timing in steps of 3° to suit. Refer to the information given in Chapter 5C *"Ignition timing - checking and adjusting"* for greater detail.

4 It is possible to measure the ignition timing, using a stroboscopic lamp in the conventional manner, as described later in this section.

Models with TSZ ignition

5 The TSZ ignition system is triggered by a sensor mounted inside the distributor body. This arrangement means that the basic ignition timing can be adjusted by rotating the distributor body in relation to the distributor shaft. Similarly, if the distributor has been removed, the ignition timing must be checked and if necessary reset using the method described in the following paragraphs.

Ignition timing - checking

Note: *The engine should be at normal operating temperature to ensure correct results. Ideally the test should be completed before the coolant temperature exceeds 95°C, or before the radiator cooling fan cuts in.*

6 Connect a stroboscopic timing light to the engine in accordance with the manufacturer's instructions, so that it is triggered from the No 1 cylinder HT lead.

7 Start the engine and run it at idling speed. Direct the beam from the timing light at the pointer protruding from the timing chain cover. The stroboscopic effect should "freeze" the motion of the rotating crankshaft pulley/vibration damper and the graduated timing mark. If the mark appears to be moving back and forth, this may be due to erratic idling - check that all electrical accessories are switched off and that the radiator cooling fan is not running. The engine should be at normal operating temperature, but the idle speed may be become unstable if it is a particularly hot day and the engine has been idling for some time.

8 Read off the ignition timing by observing the position of the pointer on the timing chain cover in relation to the markings on the crankshaft pulley/vibration damper **(see illustration)**.

9 Compare your readings with the *Specifications*. On models with EZL ignition, if the ignition timing is retarded or advanced by exactly 3°, the trimming plug may be incorrectly set. Refer to the *Specifications* and check that the position of the trimming plug is correct for the type of fuel you are currently

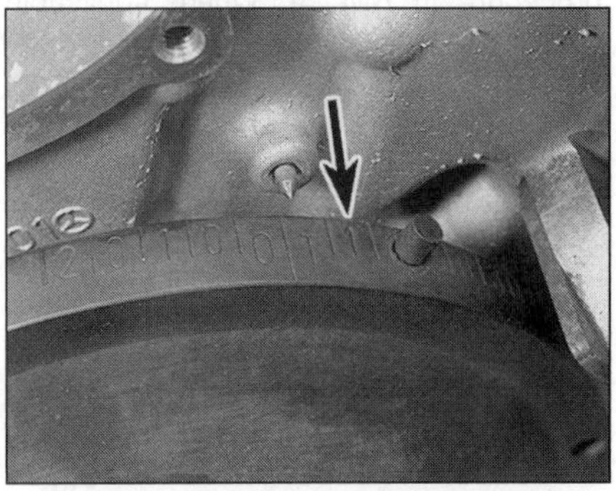

6.8 Observe the position of the pointer on the timing chain cover in relation to the markings (arrowed) on the crankshaft pulley/vibration damper

using. Note that the data for ignition advance above idle is quoted with and without manifold vacuum applied.

Ignition timing - adjusting

Note: *This procedure applies to models with TSZ ignition only - see "General Information" earlier in this section.*

10 To adjust the basic ignition timing setting, first switch off the ignition, to avoid the risk of a getting an electric shock from the HT voltage. Refer to Section 4 and slacken the distributor clamp bolt(s). **Note:** *It is good idea to mark the relationship between the distributor body and the engine with a dab of paint, before adjustment is attempted. This gives a reference point that can be reverted to if the timing setting is lost.*

11 Turn the distributor *by a small amount* clockwise to advance, or anti-clockwise to retard, the ignition timing. Tighten the bolts lightly and re-check the timing using the stroboscopic light, as described previously in this Section. Repeat this process, until the timing setting is correct, then tighten the distributor clamp bolt(s) securely and disconnect the stroboscopic light.

7 Ignition control system components - removal and refitting

Crankshaft speed sensor

Removal

1 Disconnect the battery negative lead, and position it away from the terminal.

2 Unplug the sensor wiring from the harness at the connector, which is located in the engine compartment, behind the battery.

3 The sensor is located at the mating surface between the cylinder block and the transmission bellhousing, above the starter motor aperture. Unscrew the retaining bolt and withdraw the sensor from the bellhousing. Recover the spacer, where fitted.

Refitting

4 Refit the sensor by following the removal procedure in reverse. Where applicable, ensure that the spacer is fitted to the sensor probe before inserting it into the bellhousing.

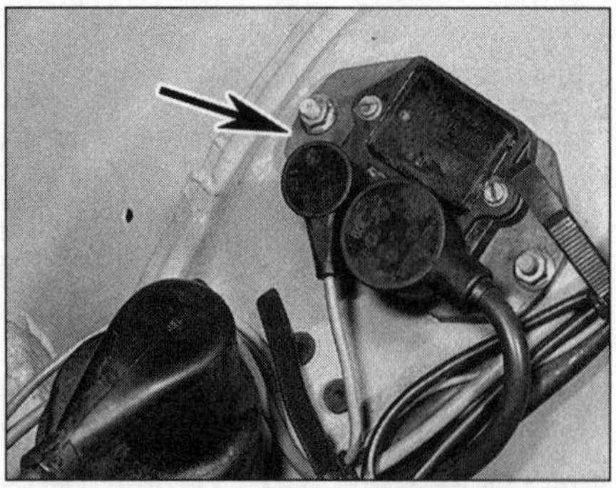

7.5a Location of the ignition system electronic control unit (arrowed) - model with TSZ ignition

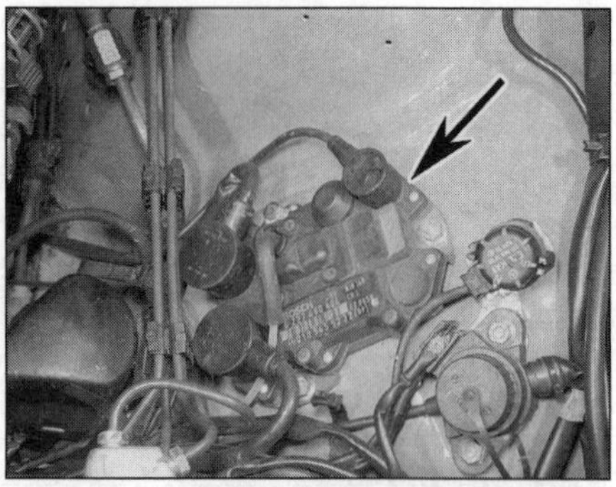

7.5b Location of the ignition system electronic control unit (arrowed) - model with EZL ignition

Electronic control unit

Removal

5 The ignition system electronic control unit is located on the left-hand side of the engine bay, on top of the inner wheel arch **(see illustrations).**

6 Disconnect the battery negative lead, and position it away from the terminal.

7 Unplug the multiway connectors from the control unit, labelling each one carefully to avoid confusion during refitting.

8 Disconnect the manifold vacuum hose from the port of the top of the control unit. Plug the port to prevent the entry of dirt.

9 Remove the securing nuts and lift the control unit away from the engine compartment. **Note:** *The underside of the control unit is coated with heat conducting paste to ensure adequate cooling - take care to avoid contaminating surrounding components with it. Do not remove the protective sheet.*

Refitting

10 Refitting is a reversal of removal. If the layer of conductive paste is contaminated, or has hardened with age, obtain a quantity of new paste from a Mercedes-Benz dealer and re-apply. Ensure that the protective sheet is correctly refitted.

Coolant temperature sensor

11 Where applicable, the ignition system shares a coolant temperature sensor with the fuel injection system - refer to the information given in the relevant part of Chapter 4.

Throttle position switch

12 The ignition system shares a throttle position switch with the fuel injection system - refer to the information given in the relevant part of Chapter 4.

Inlet air temperature sensor

Removal

13 The inlet air temperature sensor is located on the side of the air cleaner housing.

14 Ensure that the ignition is switched off, then unplug the sensor wiring at the connector.

15 The sensor is bayonet fit - squeeze the locating lugs, then turn it through a quarter-turn and withdraw it from the air cleaner housing. Recover the seal.

Refitting

16 Refitting is a reversal of removal.

TDC sensor

17 The TDC sensor is mounted on a bracket above the crankshaft vibration damper at the front of the engine. The alignment of the sensor within its bracket with respect to the edge of the vibration damper is critical to the correct operation of the ignition system, and entails a complex setting-up procedure. For this reason it is recommended that the

Chapter 5 Part C
Ignition system: 6-cylinder petrol engine

Contents

Distributor and rotor arm - removal and refitting 4
General information 1
HT coil - removal and refitting 3
Ignition control system components - removal and refitting 6
Ignition system - testing 2
Ignition system - check .... see Chapter 1A
Ignition timing - checking and adjusting 5
Spark plugs - renewal .... see Chapter 1A

Degrees of difficulty

Easy, suitable for novice with little experience	**Fairly easy,** suitable for beginner with some experience	**Fairly difficult,** suitable for competent DIY mechanic	**Difficult,** suitable for experienced DIY mechanic	**Very difficult,** suitable for expert DIY or professional

Specifications

General

Type	EZL

Ignition coil

Primary winding resistance	1.0 Ω minimum
Secondary winding resistance	8 to 13 kΩ

Distributor

Type	Breakerless, driven from camshaft
Dwell angle	Governed by ignition control system
Ignition timing:*	
At idle	7 to 11° BTDC
At 3200 rpm, vacuum applied, trimming plug in "S" position	25 to 29° BTDC
At 3200 rpm, vacuum applied, trimming plug in "N" position	19 to 23° BTDC
At 3200 rpm, no vacuum applied	40 to 44° BTDC

***Note:** *These are typical figures - vehicles specified for different markets will have differing ignition advance characteristics.*

Spark plugs

Type	Champion S10YCC
Electrode gap	0.8 mm

Sensors

Crankshaft speed sensor resistance	680 to 1200 Ω
Camshaft sensor resistance	900 to 1600 Ω
Coolant temperature sensor:	
Electrical resistance:	
At 80°C	325 Ω
At 40°C	1.2 kΩ
At 0°C	6 kΩ
Inlet air temperature sensor:	
Electrical resistance:	
At 80°C	325 Ω
At 40°C	1.2 kΩ
At 0°C	6 kΩ

Torque wrench settings

Torque wrench settings	Nm	lbf ft
Rotor arm screws	3	2
Distributor follower centre bolt:		
M8 bolt	20	15
M6 bolt	15	11
Knock sensor bolts	20	15
Spark plugs	15	11

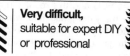

1 General information

The EZL ignition system major components comprise the spark plugs (one per cylinder), HT leads, the distributor, an electronic ignition coil, and an Electronic Control Unit (ECU) together with its associated sensors, actuators and wiring. The component layout varies slightly between models, but the basic operation is the same.

The basic operation is as follows. The control unit supplies a voltage to the input stage of the ignition coil which causes the primary windings in the coil to be energised. The supply voltage is periodically interrupted by the ECU and this results in the collapse of the primary magnetic field, which then induces a much larger voltage in the coil's secondary windings, called the HT voltage. This HT voltage is directed, by the distributor via the HT leads, to the spark plug in the cylinder currently on its ignition stroke. The spark plug electrodes form a gap small enough for the HT voltage to arc across, and the resulting spark ignites the fuel/air mixture in the cylinder. The timing of this sequence of events is critical and is regulated solely by the ECU.

The ECU calculates and controls the ignition timing and dwell angle primarily according to engine speed, crankshaft position and inlet manifold depression information, received from sensors mounted on and around the engine. Other parameters that affect ignition timing are throttle position (idle and full throttle positions are sensed via a changeover switch), inlet air temperature, and coolant temperature. Again, these are monitored via sensors mounted on the engine.

The basic ignition timing can be altered in fixed steps, to suit the type of fuel being used. This is achieved by means of a trimming socket, located in the engine compartment, close to the ignition system ECU - refer to Section 5 for details.

2 Ignition system - testing

Warning: Extreme care must be taken when working on the system with the ignition switched on; it is possible to get a substantial electric shock from a vehicle's ignition system. Persons with cardiac pacemaker devices should keep well clear of the ignition circuits, components and test equipment. Always switch off the ignition before disconnecting or connecting any component and when using a multi-meter to check resistances.

General

1 Most ignition system faults are likely to be due to loose or dirty connections or to "tracking" (unintentional earthing) of HT voltage due to dirt, dampness or damaged insulation, rather than by the failure of any of the system's components. **Always** check all wiring thoroughly before condemning an electrical component and work methodically to eliminate all other possibilities before deciding that a particular component is faulty.

2 The old practice of checking for a spark by holding the live end of an HT lead a short distance away from the engine is not recommended; not only is there a high risk of an electric shock, but the HT coil could be damaged. Similarly, **never** try to "diagnose" misfires by pulling off one HT lead at a time, as well as the risk of electric shock, the test may be invalid as the ignition system fitted to later models has the capability to detect and temporarily disable HT lines that are open circuit.

3 Problems with the system operation that cannot be pinpointed by following the guidelines in the following paragraphs should therefore be referred to a Mercedes-Benz dealer for assessment.

Engine will not start

4 If the engine either will not turn over at all, or only turns very slowly, check the battery and starter motor . Connect a voltmeter across the battery terminals (meter positive probe to battery positive terminal), disconnect the ignition coil HT lead from the distributor cap and earth it, then note the voltage reading obtained while turning over the engine on the starter for (no more than) ten seconds. If the reading obtained is less than approximately 9.5 volts, first check the battery, starter motor and charging systems (see Chapter 5A).

5 If the engine turns over at normal speed but will not start, check the HT circuit by connecting a timing light (following the manufacturer's instructions) and turning the engine over on the starter motor; if the light flashes, voltage is reaching the spark plugs, so these should be checked first. If the light does not flash, check the HT leads themselves followed by the distributor cap, carbon brush and rotor arm using the information given in Chapter 1A.

6 If there is a spark, check the fuel system for faults referring to the relevant part of Chapter 4 for further information.

7 If there is still no spark, the problem may lie within the ignition control/engine management system. In these cases, the vehicle should be referred to a Mercedes-Benz dealer or automotive electrical specialist for assessment.

Engine misfires

8 An irregular misfire suggests either a loose connection or intermittent fault in the control system or primary circuit, or an HT fault on the coil side of the rotor arm (where applicable).

9 With the ignition switched off, check carefully through the system, ensuring that all connections are clean and securely fastened. If the equipment is available, check the LT circuit as described above.

10 Check that the HT coil, the distributor cap and the HT leads are clean and dry. Check the leads themselves and the spark plugs (by substitution, if necessary), then check the distributor cap, carbon brush and rotor arm as described in Chapter 1A.

11 Regular misfiring is almost certainly due to a fault in the distributor cap, coil, HT leads or spark plugs. Use a timing light (paragraph 5 above) to check whether HT voltage is present at all leads.

12 If HT voltage is not present on one particular lead, the fault will be in that lead or in the distributor cap. If HT is present on all leads, the fault will be in the spark plugs; check and renew them if there is any doubt about their condition.

13 If no HT voltage is present, check the HT coil; the secondary windings may be breaking down under load.

3 HT coil - removal and refitting

Removal

1 Disconnect the battery negative lead and position it away from the terminal.

2 On all models, the coil is bolted to a bracket, at the front left-hand side of the engine compartment. Unclip and lift off the plastic cover **(see illustration)**.

3 Trace the HT king lead back from the distributor to the coil and unplug it from the coil terminal **(see illustration)**.

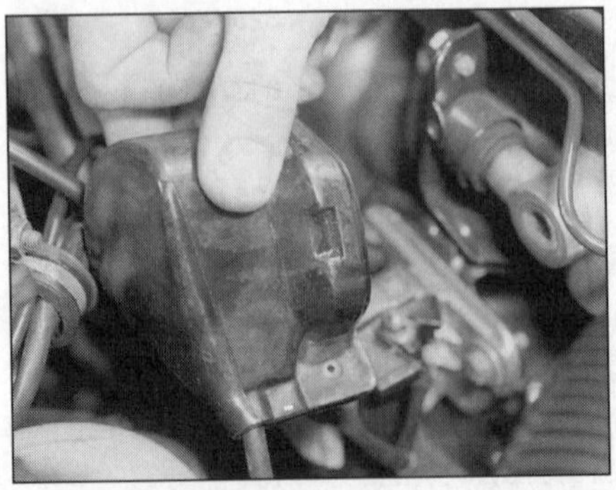

3.2 Unclip the plastic cover from the ignition coil

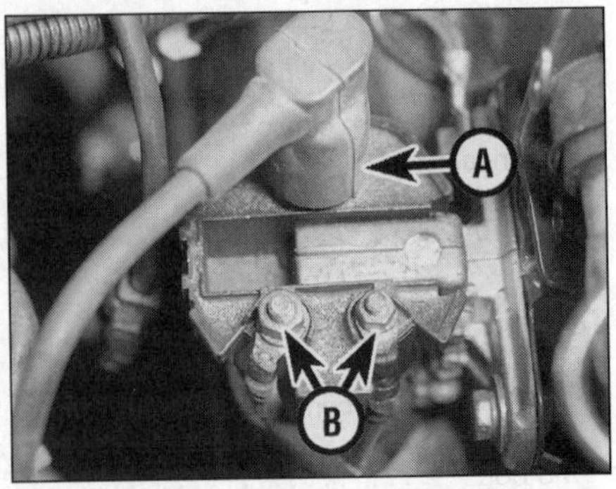

3.3 Ignition coil connections
A HT terminal B LT terminals

4.5 Lift the rotor arm off the follower

4.6 Unscrew the centre bolt and remove the follower

4.7 Lift off the plastic cover and O-ring seal

4 Unscrew the nuts and disconnect the positive and negative LT cables from the coil. Label the cables to avoid confusion during refitting.
5 Slacken and withdraw the bolts, then lift the coil away from its mounting bracket.

Refitting

6 Refitting is a reversal of removal.

4 Distributor and rotor arm - removal and refitting

Removal

1 The distributor is mounted longitudinally on the front of the cylinder head.
2 Unclip and remove the plastic cover.
3 Make a careful note of the firing order, then unplug the HT leads from the distributor cap (if required).
4 Slacken and withdraw the screws, then lift off the distributor cap.
5 Remove the screws and lift the rotor arm off the follower **(see illustration)**.
6 Unscrew the centre bolt and remove the follower from the end of the camshaft **(see illustration)**.
7 Lift off the plastic cover and O-ring seal **(see illustration)**. Renew the seal if it shows signs of wear or deterioration.

Refitting

8 Fit the plastic cover and O-ring seal in position.
9 Push the follower onto the end of the camshaft, engaging the slot on the follower hub with the locating pin that protrudes from the camshaft. Fit the centre bolt and tighten it to the specified torque.
10 Fit the rotor arm to the follower, then insert the retaining screws and tighten them to the specified torque.
11 Place the distributor cap in position over the rotor arm, taking care to avoid damaging the centre carbon brush. Insert and tighten the cap retaining screws.
12 Reconnect the spark plug HT leads to the distributor cap, ensuring that they are connected in the correct firing order - refer to the *Specifications* in Chapter 2B for details.
13 Note that because the ignition system is triggered by the crankshaft position sensor, the basic ignition timing setting will not be affected by the removal the distributor components, hence no adjustment is required.

5 Ignition timing - checking and adjusting

1 The EZL ignition system is triggered by an electronic signal generated by the crankshaft position sensor. The ignition control system then calculates the correct ignition timing and dwell angle primarily according to engine speed, crankshaft position and inlet manifold depression information, received from sensors mounted on and around the engine. Other parameters that affect ignition timing are throttle position, inlet air temperature, coolant temperature and on certain systems, engine knock. Again, these are monitored via sensors mounted on the engine (refer to Sections 1 and 6 for details).
2 Unlike other breakerless ignition systems, which are triggered by a rotor mounted on the distributor shaft, the timing of the EZL ignition system cannot be adjusted by rotating the distributor body with respect to the distributor shaft.
3 The basic ignition timing can, however, be altered to suit the type of fuel being used. This is achieved by means of a trimming socket, located in the engine compartment, close to the ignition system ECU. The socket is fitted with a plug, which has a number of fixed value resistors built into it. The plug may be fitted to the socket in a number of different positions, indicated by markings on the upper surface of the plug. Moving the plug to another position connects a different resistor across the socket terminals; this is sensed electronically by the ignition system ECU, which alters the ignition timing to suit. **(see illustration)**.
4 It is possible to measure the basic ignition timing, using a stroboscopic lamp in the conventional manner, as follows.

Note: *The engine should be at normal operating temperature to ensure correct results. Ideally the test should be completed before the coolant temperature exceeds 95°C, or before the radiator cooling fan cuts in.*
5 Connect the stroboscopic timing light to the engine in accordance with the manufacturer's instructions, so that it is triggering from the No 1 cylinder HT lead.
6 Start the engine and run it at idling speed. Direct the beam from timing light at the pointer protruding from the timing chain cover. The stroboscopic effect should "freeze" the motion of the rotating crankshaft pulley and the graduated timing mark. If the mark appears to be moving back and forth, this may be due erratic idling - check that all of the car's electrical accessories are switched off and that the radiator cooling fan is not running. The engine should be at normal operating temperature, but the idle speed may be become unstable if it is particularly hot day and the engine has been idling for some time.
7 Read off the ignition timing by observing the position of the pointer on the timing chain cover in relation to the markings on the crankshaft pulley.
8 Compare the readings with the *Specifications*. If the ignition timing is retarded or advanced by exactly 3°, the trimming plug may be incorrectly set. Refer to the *Specifications* and check that the position of the trimming plug is correct for the type of fuel

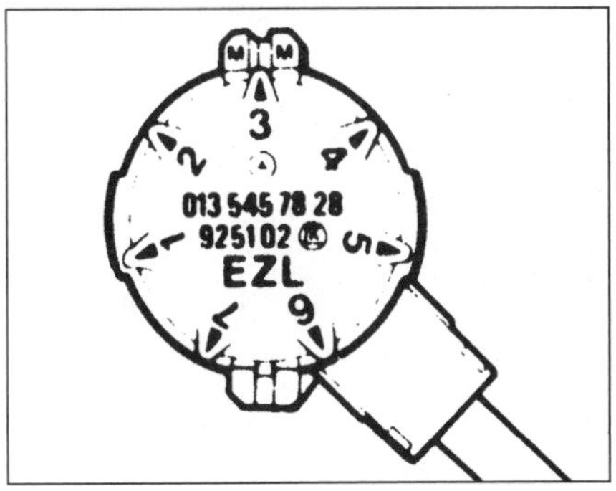

5.3 Ignition timing trimming socket shown in correct position for use with 95 RON unleaded premium fuel

6.5 Ignition electronic control unit

6.11 Coolant temperature sensor

you are currently using. Note that the data for ignition advance above idle is quoted with and without manifold vacuum applied.

6 Ignition control system components - removal and refitting

Note: *Disconnecting/removing sensors from the ignition control system may result in faults being registered in the memory of the ignition system electronic control unit. Certain faults cause the system to enter an "emergency running" mode which could affect the vehicles driveability. Therefore on completion of the repair work, it is advisable to have these faults "erased" by a Mercedes-Benz dealer at the earliest opportunity.*

Crankshaft speed sensor

Removal

1 Disconnect the battery negative lead and position it away from the terminal.

2 Unplug the crankshaft speed sensor wiring from the harness at the connector, which is located in the engine compartment, behind the battery.

3 Unscrew the retaining bolt and withdraw the sensor from the bellhousing. Recover the spacer, where fitted.

Refitting

4 Refit the crankshaft speed sensor by following the removal procedure in reverse. Where applicable, ensure that the spacer is fitted to the sensor probe before inserting it into the bellhousing.

ECU

Removal

5 The ignition system electronic control unit is located on the left-hand side of the engine compartment, on top of the inner wheel arch **(see illustration)**.

6 Disconnect the battery negative lead and position it away from the terminal.

7 Unplug the wiring for the crankshaft sensor and the knock sensors, at the connectors. Also unplug the two multiway connectors, labelling each one carefully to avoid confusion during refitting.

8 Disconnect the manifold vacuum hose from the port of the top of the control unit. Plug the port to prevent the entry of dirt.

9 Remove the securing nuts and lift the control unit away from the engine compartment. **Note:** *The underside of the control unit is coated with heat conducting paste to ensure adequate cooling - take care to avoid contaminating surrounding components with it. Do not remove the protective sheet.*

Refitting

10 Refitting is a reversal of removal. If the layer of conductive paste is contaminated, or has hardened with age, obtain a quantity of new paste from a Mercedes-Benz dealer and re-apply. Ensure that the protective sheet is correctly refitted.

Coolant temperature sensor

11 The ignition system shares a coolant temperature sensor with the fuel injection system - refer to the information given in Chapter 4B **(see illustration)**.

Throttle position switch

12 The ignition system shares a throttle position switch with the fuel injection system - refer to the information given in Chapter 4B.

TDC sensor

13 The TDC sensor is mounted on a bracket above the vibration damper at the front of the engine. The alignment of the sensor within its bracket with respect to the edge of the vibration damper is critical to the correct operation of the ignition system and entails a complex setting-procedure. For this reason it is recommended that the removal of this component is carried out by a Mercedes-Benz dealer.

Chapter 5 Part D
Preheating system: diesel engine

Contents

Coolant temperature sensor - removal and refitting 4
General information 1
Glow plug control unit - removal and refitting 2
Glow plugs - testing, removal and refitting 3

Degrees of difficulty

Easy, suitable for novice with little experience	**Fairly easy,** suitable for beginner with some experience	**Fairly difficult,** suitable for competent DIY mechanic	**Difficult,** suitable for experienced DIY mechanic	**Very difficult,** suitable for expert DIY or professional

Specifications

Glow plugs

Nominal operating voltage	11.5 V
Electrical resistance	0.75 to 1.5 Ω (approx., at operating temperature)
Current consumption	8 to 15A (per glow plug, after approx. 8 seconds of operation)

Torque wrench settings

	Nm	lbf ft
Glow plug	20	15
Glow plug terminal nuts	4	3

1 General information

To assist cold starting, diesel engine models are fitted with a pre-heating system, which comprises a number of glow plugs (one per cylinder), a glow plug control unit, a facia mounted warning lamp, a coolant temperature sensor (later models only) and the associated electrical wiring.

The glow plugs are miniature electric heating elements, encapsulated in a metal case with a probe at one end and electrical connection at the other. Each combustion chamber has one glow plug threaded into it. When the glow plug is energised, it heats up rapidly causing the temperature of the air charge drawn into each of the combustion chambers to rise. The glow plug probe is positioned directly in line with the incoming spray of fuel from the injectors. Hence the fuel passing over the glow plug probe is also heated, allowing its optimum combustion temperature to be achieved more readily. In addition, small particles of the fuel passing over the glow plugs are ignited and this helps to trigger the combustion process.

The duration of the pre-heating period is governed by the glow plug control unit. This device monitors the temperature of the air in the engine compartment, via an ambient air temperature sensor (early models), or via the temperature of the engine coolant (measured by a sensor threaded into the cylinder head - later models), and then alters the pre-heating time (the length for which the glow plugs are supplied with current) to suit the prevailing conditions.

A facia-mounted warning lamp informs the driver that pre-heating is taking place. The lamp extinguishes when sufficient pre-heating has taken place to allow the engine to be started, but power will still be supplied to the glow plugs for a further period until the engine is started. If no attempt is made to start the engine, the power supply to the glow plugs is switched off to prevent battery drain and glow plug burn-out. Note that on later models, the warning lamp will also illuminate during normal driving if a pre-heating system malfunction occurs.

Later models employ post-heating - after the engine has been started, the glow plugs continue to operate for a further period of time. This helps to improve fuel combustion whilst the engine is warming up, resulting in quieter, smoother running and reduced exhaust emissions. The duration of the post-heating period is dependant on the coolant temperature.

2 Glow plug control unit - removal and refitting

Removal

1 The glow plug control unit is located in the engine compartment, on the left-hand inner wing **(see illustration)**.
2 Disconnect the battery negative lead, and position it away from the terminal.
3 Prise the protective cap from the top of the control unit, to expose the fuse and electrical connections.
4 Disconnect the wiring harness from the control unit at the connectors.
5 Remove the retaining nuts lift the control unit away from the wing.

Refitting

6 Refitting is a reversal of removal.

3 Glow plugs - testing, removal and refitting

Testing

1 If the system malfunctions, testing is ultimately by substitution of known good units, but some preliminary checks may be made as described in the following paragraphs.
2 Connect a voltmeter or 12-volt test lamp between the glow plug supply cable, and a good earth point on the engine.
Caution: Make sure that the live connection is kept well clear of the engine and bodywork.
3 Have an assistant activate the pre-heating system by turning the ignition key to the second position, and check that battery voltage is applied to the glow plug electrical connection. **Note:** *The supply voltage will be less than battery voltage initially, but will rise and settle as the glow plug heats up. It will then drop to zero when the pre-heating period ends and the safety cut-out operates.*
4 If no supply voltage can be detected at the glow plug, then either the glow plug relay (where applicable) or the supply cable must be faulty.

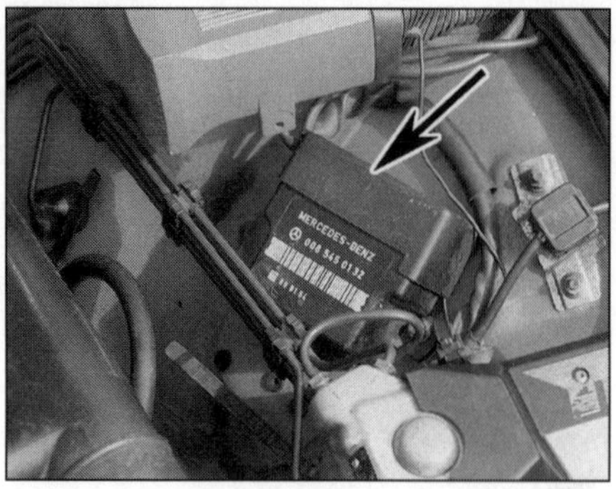

2.1 Glow plug control unit location (arrowed)

5 To locate a faulty glow plug, first operate the pre-heating system to allow the glow plugs to reach working temperature, then disconnect the battery negative cable and position it away from the terminal.
6 Refer to the next sub-Section and remove the supply cable from the glow plug terminal. Measure the electrical resistance between the glow plug terminal and the engine earth. A reading of anything more than a few Ohms indicates that the glow plug is defective.
7 If a suitable, heavy duty ammeter is available, connect it between the glow plug and its supply cable, and measure the steady state current consumption (ignore the initial current surge which will be about 50% higher). Compare the result with the *Specifications* - high current consumption (or no current draw at all) indicates a faulty glow plug.
8 As a final check, remove the glow plugs and inspect them visually, as described in the following paragraphs.

Removal

9 Disconnect the battery negative lead and position it away from the terminal.
10 Slacken the nuts at the glow plug terminal. Lift off the cable connector **(see illustration)**. Note that the nuts are captive in the cable connector.
11 Slacken and withdraw the glow plug **(see illustrations)**.

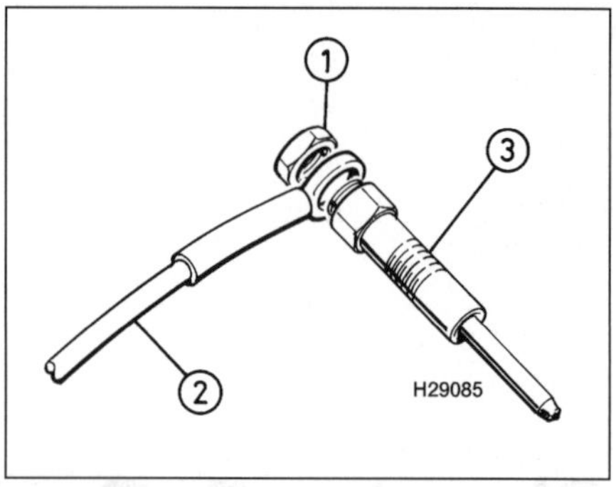

3.10 Glow plug and electrical connections
1 Terminal nut 2 Supply cable 3 Glow plug

12 Inspect the glow plug probe for signs of damage. A badly burned or charred probe is usually an indication of a faulty fuel injector; refer to Chapter 4C for greater detail.

Refitting

13 Refitting is a reversal of removal, but tighten the glow plug to the specified torque

4 Coolant temperature sensor - removal and refitting

Removal

1 The coolant temperature sensor is screwed into the side of the top of the coolant pump assembly.
2 Ensure that the engine has cooled completely before starting work. Disconnect the battery negative lead, and position it away from the terminal.
3 With reference to Chapter 1B, partially drain the cooling system.
4 Unplug the wiring from the sensor at the connector.
5 Unscrew the sensor from the coolant pump and recover the sealing washer.

Refitting

6 Refitting is a reversal of removal. On completion, refill the cooling system as described in Chapter 1B.

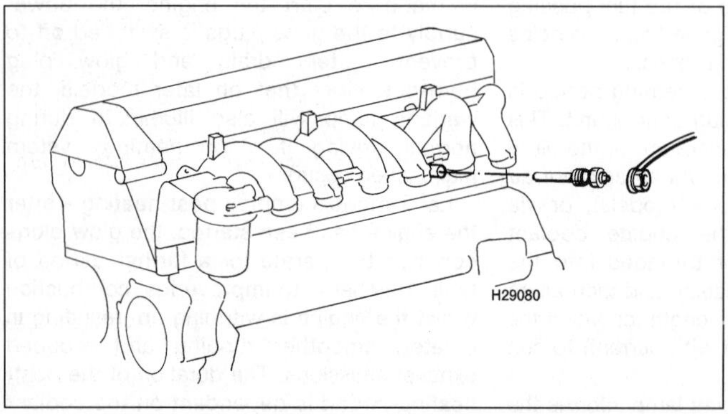

3.11a Glow plug location - normally-aspirated engines

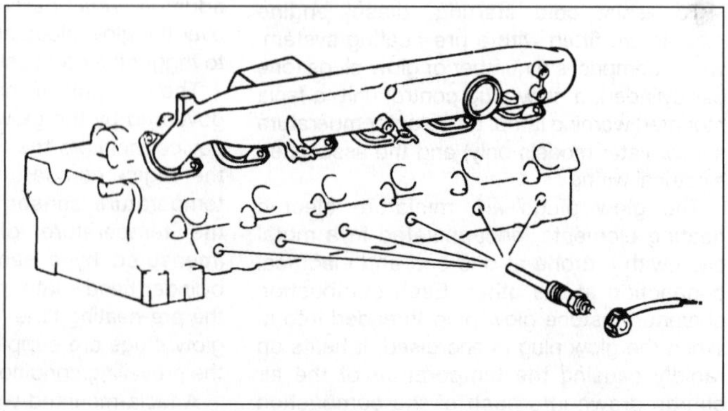

3.11b Glow plug location - turbo-diesel engines

Chapter 6
Clutch

Contents

Clutch assembly - removal, inspection and refitting 2
Clutch - operation check . . . . .See Chapter 1
Clutch fluid level check . . . . .See *"Weekly checks"*
Clutch friction plate - wear check . . . . .See Chapter 1
Clutch pedal - removal and refitting 7
Clutch release bearing and lever - removal, inspection and refitting 3
General information 1
Hydraulic master cylinder - removal, overhaul and refitting 5
Hydraulic slave cylinder - removal, overhaul and refitting 4
Hydraulic system - bleeding 6

Degrees of difficulty

Easy, suitable for novice with little experience	**Fairly easy,** suitable for beginner with some experience	**Fairly difficult,** suitable for competent DIY mechanic	**Difficult,** suitable for experienced DIY mechanic	**Very difficult,** suitable for expert DIY or professional

Specifications

Driveplate

Lining thickness:		
New	3.6 to 4.0 mm	
Wear limit	2.6 to 3.0 mm	

Torque wrench settings

	Nm	lbf ft
Clutch cover-to-flywheel bolts	25	18

1 General information

All models are fitted with a single dry plate clutch, which consists of five main components; friction plate, pressure plate, diaphragm spring, cover and release bearing.

The friction plate is free to slide along the splines of the transmission input shaft, and is held in position between the flywheel and the pressure plate, by the pressure exerted on the pressure plate by the diaphragm spring. Friction lining material is riveted to both sides of the friction plate, and cushioning springs between the friction surfaces help to absorb transmission shocks and ensure a smooth take-up of power as the clutch is engaged.

The diaphragm spring is mounted on pins, and is held in place in the cover by annular fulcrum rings.

The release bearing is located on a guide sleeve at the front of the transmission, and the bearing is free to slide on the sleeve, under the action of the release arm which pivots inside the clutch bellhousing.

The release mechanism is operated by the clutch pedal, using hydraulic pressure. The pedal acts on the hydraulic master cylinder pushrod, and a slave cylinder, mounted on the transmission bellhousing, operates the clutch release lever via a pushrod.

When the clutch pedal is depressed, the release arm pushes the release bearing forwards, to bear against the centre of the diaphragm spring, thus pushing the centre of the diaphragm spring inwards. The diaphragm spring acts against the fulcrum rings in the cover, and so as the centre of the spring is pushed in, the outside of the spring is pushed out, so allowing the pressure plate to move backwards away from the friction plate.

When the clutch pedal is released, the diaphragm spring forces the pressure plate into contact with the friction linings on the friction plate, and simultaneously pushes the friction plate forwards on its splines, forcing it against the flywheel. The friction plate is now firmly sandwiched between the pressure plate and the flywheel, and drive is taken up.

The clutch is self-adjusting. As wear takes place on the friction plate over a period of time, the pressure plate automatically moves closer to the friction plate to compensate.

2 Clutch assembly - removal, inspection and refitting

Warning: Dust created by clutch wear and deposited on the clutch components may contain asbestos, which is a health hazard. DO NOT blow it out with compressed air, or inhale any of it. DO NOT use petrol (or petroleum-based solvents) to clean off the dust. Brake system cleaner or methylated spirit should be used to flush the dust into a suitable receptacle. After the clutch components are wiped clean with rags, dispose of the contaminated rags and cleaner in a sealed, marked container.

Removal

1 Remove the transmission, as described in Chapter 7A.

2 If the original clutch is to be refitted, make alignment marks between the clutch cover and the flywheel, so that the clutch can be refitted in its original position.

3 Progressively unscrew the bolts securing

2.4 Removing the clutch cover from the flywheel

2.12 Fit the friction plate with the greater projecting side of the hub facing away from the flywheel

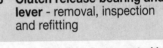

2.15 Using a clutch alignment tool to centralise the friction plate

the clutch cover to the flywheel, and recover the washers.

4 Withdraw the clutch cover from the flywheel **(see illustration)**. Be prepared to catch the clutch friction plate, which may drop out of the cover as it is withdrawn, and note which way round the friction plate is fitted - the two sides of the disc are normally marked "Engine side" and "Transmission side". The greater projecting side of the hub faces away from the flywheel.

Inspection

5 With the clutch assembly removed, clean off all traces of dust using a dry cloth. Although most friction plates now have asbestos-free linings, some do not, and it is wise to take suitable precautions; *asbestos dust is harmful, and must not be inhaled.*

6 Examine the linings of the friction plate for wear and loose rivets, and the disc for distortion, cracks, broken damping springs (where applicable) and worn splines. The surface of the friction linings may be highly glazed, but, as long as the friction material pattern can be clearly seen, this is satisfactory. If there is any sign of oil contamination, indicated by a continuous, or patchy, shiny black discolouration, the disc must be renewed. The source of the contamination must be traced and rectified before fitting new clutch components; typically, a leaking crankshaft rear oil seal or transmission input shaft oil seal - or both - will be to blame (renewal procedures are given in the relevant Part of Chapter 2, and Chapter 7A respectively). The disc must also be renewed if the lining thickness has worn down to, or just above, the level of the rivet heads. Note that the friction plate can be checked for wear with the clutch and transmission assemblies installed in the vehicle - see Chapter 1.

7 Check the machined faces of the flywheel and pressure plate. If either is grooved, or heavily scored, renewal is necessary. The pressure plate must also be renewed if any cracks are apparent, or if the diaphragm spring is damaged or its pressure suspect.

8 With the clutch removed, it is advisable to check the condition of the release bearing, as described in Section 3.

9 Check the spigot bearing in the end of the crankshaft. Make sure that it turns smoothly and quietly. If the transmission input shaft contact face on the bearing is worn or damaged, fit a new bearing, as described in the relevant Part of Chapter 2.

Refitting

10 If new clutch components are to be fitted, where applicable, ensure that all anti-corrosion preservative is cleaned from the friction material on the disc, and the contact surfaces of the pressure plate.

11 It is important to ensure that no oil or grease gets onto the friction plate linings, or the pressure plate and flywheel faces. It is advisable to refit the clutch assembly with clean hands, and to wipe down the pressure plate and flywheel faces with a clean rag before assembly begins.

12 Apply a smear of molybdenum disulphide grease to the splines of the friction plate hub, then offer the disc to the flywheel, with the greater projecting side of the hub facing away from the flywheel (most friction plates will have an "Engine side" marking which should face the flywheel) **(see illustration)**. Hold the friction plate against the flywheel while the cover/pressure plate assembly is offered into position.

13 Fit the clutch cover assembly, where applicable aligning the marks on the flywheel and clutch cover. Ensure that the clutch cover locates over the dowels on the flywheel. Insert the securing bolts and washers, and tighten them finger-tight, so that the friction plate is gripped, but can still be moved.

14 The friction plate must now be centralised, so that when the engine and transmission are mated, the transmission input shaft splines will pass through the splines in the friction plate hub.

15 Centralisation can be carried out by inserting a round bar or a long screwdriver through the hole in the centre of the friction plate, so that the end of the bar rests in the spigot bearing in the centre of the crankshaft. Where possible, use a blunt instrument, but if a screwdriver is used, wrap tape around the blade to prevent damage to the bearing surface. Moving the bar sideways or up and down as necessary, move the friction plate in whichever direction is necessary to achieve centralisation. With the bar removed, view the friction plate hub in relation to the hole in the centre of the crankshaft and the circle created by the ends of the diaphragm spring fingers. When the hub appears exactly in the centre, all is correct. Alternatively, if a suitable clutch alignment tool can be obtained, this will eliminate all the guesswork, and obviate the need for visual alignment **(see illustration)**.

16 Tighten the cover retaining bolts gradually in a diagonal sequence, to the specified torque. Remove the alignment tool.

17 Refit the transmission as described in Chapter 7A.

3 Clutch release bearing and lever - removal, inspection and refitting

Warning: Dust created by clutch wear and deposited on the clutch components may contain asbestos, which is a health hazard. DO NOT blow it out with compressed air, or inhale any of it. DO NOT use petrol (or petroleum-based solvents) to clean off the dust. Brake system cleaner or methylated spirit should be used to flush the dust into a suitable receptacle. After the clutch components are wiped clean with rags, dispose of the contaminated rags and cleaner in a sealed, marked container.

Release bearing

Removal

1 Remove the transmission, as described in Chapter 7A.

2 Rotate the bearing to disengage it from the release fork, then pull the bearing forwards, and slide it from the guide sleeve in the transmission bellhousing **(see illustration)**.

3.2 Removing the clutch release bearing

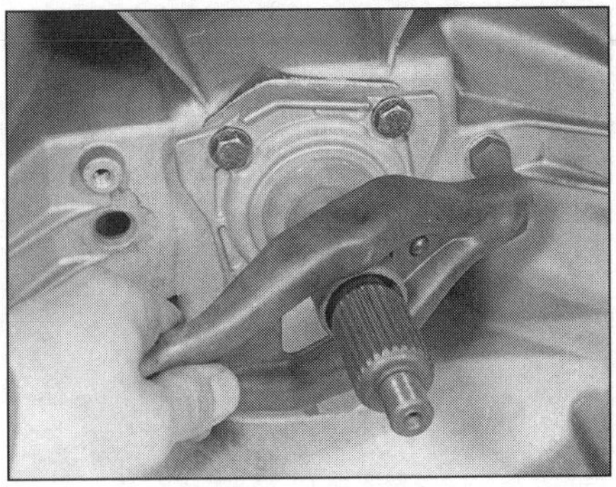
3.8 Removing the clutch release lever

3.11 Lightly grease the pivot pin and the guide sleeve (arrowed)

Inspection

3 Spin the release bearing, and check it for excessive roughness. Hold the outer race, and attempt to move it laterally against the inner race. If any excessive movement or roughness is evident, renew the bearing. If a new clutch has been fitted, it is wise to renew the release bearing as a matter of course.

Refitting

4 Clean and then lightly grease the release bearing contact surfaces on the release lever. Similarly, lightly grease the guide sleeve.
5 Slide the bearing into position on the guide sleeve, then rotate the bearing until it snaps into position in the release lever.
6 Refit the transmission as described in Chapter 7A.

Release lever

Removal

7 Remove the release bearing, as described previously in this Section.
8 Pull the slave cylinder end of the release lever forwards, then slide the lever sideways to release if from the pivot pin, and withdraw the lever over the guide sleeve **(see illustration)**.

Inspection

9 Inspect the release bearing, pivot and slave cylinder pushrod contact faces on the release lever for wear. Renew the lever if excessive wear is evident.
10 Check the condition of the release lever retaining spring clip, and the lever if necessary.

Refitting

11 Clean and then lightly grease the release bearing contact surfaces on the release lever, and the pivot pin. Similarly, lightly grease the guide sleeve **(see illustration)**.
12 Slide the release lever into position over the guide sleeve, then slide the end of the lever over the pivot pin, ensuring that the retaining spring clip engages around the rear of the pivot pin **(see illustration)**.
13 Refit the release bearing as described previously in this Section.

4 Hydraulic slave cylinder - removal, overhaul and refitting

Warning: Hydraulic fluid is poisonous; wash off immediately and thoroughly in the case of skin contact, and seek immediate medical advice if any fluid is swallowed or gets into the eyes. Certain types of hydraulic fluid are inflammable, and may ignite when allowed into contact with hot components; when servicing any hydraulic system, it is safest to assume that the fluid is inflammable, and to take precautions against the risk of fire as though it is petrol that is being handled. Hydraulic fluid is also an effective paint stripper, and will attack plastics; if any is spilt, it should be washed off immediately, using copious quantities of fresh water. Finally, it is hygroscopic (it absorbs moisture from the air) - old fluid may be contaminated and unfit for further use. When topping-up or renewing the fluid, always use the recommended type, and ensure that it comes from a freshly-opened sealed container.

Removal

1 Apply the parking brake, then jack up the front of the vehicle and support securely on axle stands (see *"Jacking and vehicle support"*).
2 Working on the right-hand side of the vehicle, place a suitable container beneath the slave cylinder, then unscrew the fluid pipe union, and disconnect the fluid pipe from the rear of the cylinder. Alternatively, if desired, the flexible hose can be disconnected from the rigid fluid pipe. Once the fluid has drained, plug the open ends of the pipe/hose and slave cylinder (as applicable) to prevent dirt ingress.
3 Unscrew the two bolts securing the slave cylinder to the transmission bellhousing, then withdraw the cylinder, complete with the pushrod **(see illustration)**. Recover the shim.

Overhaul

4 Using a screwdriver, carefully hook out the notched retaining ring, and withdraw the pushrod assembly.
5 Tap the cylinder on a block of wood to release the piston, then remove the piston and spring **(see illustrations)**.

6

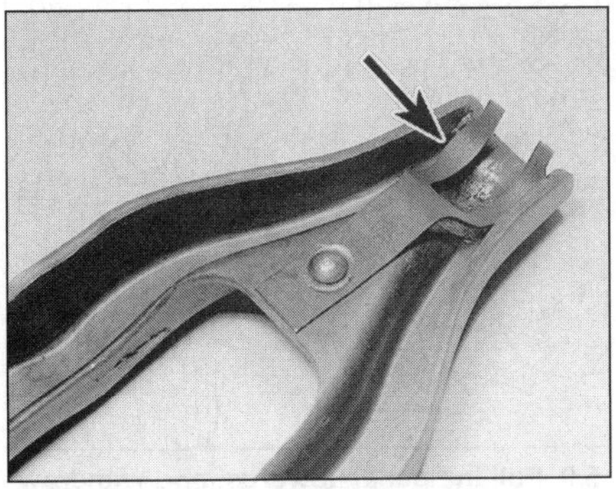
3.12 Ensure that the spring clip (arrowed) engages with the pivot pin

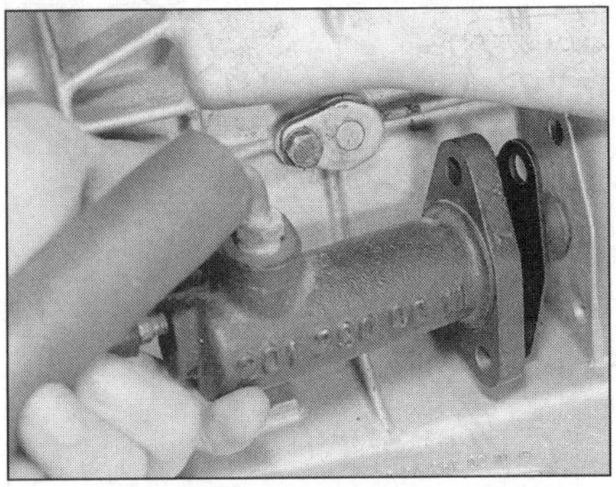
4.3 Removing the clutch slave cylinder from the transmission bellhousing

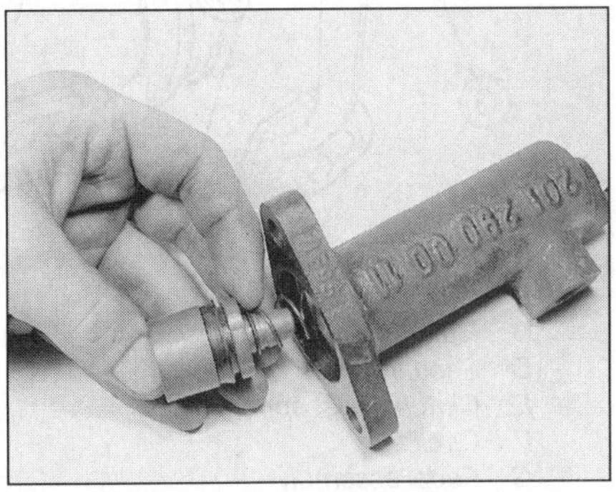
4.5a Remove the slave cylinder piston . . .

4.5b . . . followed by the spring

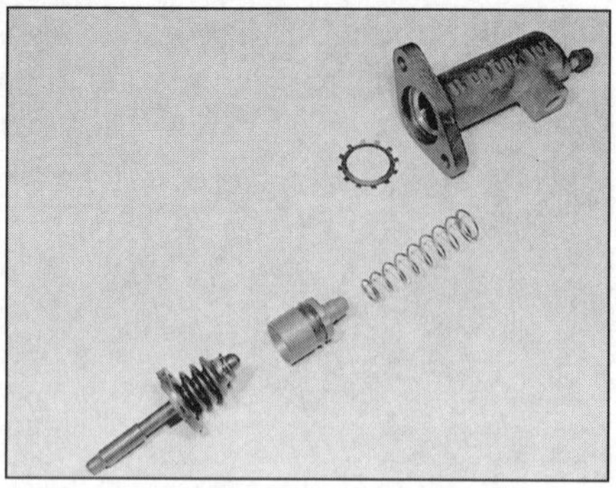

4.6 Clutch slave cylinder components

6 Wash all the parts in clean hydraulic fluid, then lay them out for inspection **(see illustration)**.

7 Examine the cylinder bore and piston carefully for signs of scoring or wear ridges. If these are apparent, renew the complete slave cylinder. If the condition of the components appears satisfactory, a repair kit containing new rubber seals should be obtained. Never re-use the old seals.

8 Remove the old seal from the piston, and fit the new one, using the fingers only. To ease fitting of the seal, lubricate with clean hydraulic fluid. Ensure that the sealing lip edge is towards the spring end of the piston.

9 Lubricate the cylinder bore and insert the spring, with the larger coils towards fluid union end of the cylinder.

10 Carefully insert the piston, engaging the protruding end into the centre of the spring.

11 If necessary, fit a new dust cover to the pushrod, then insert the pushrod assembly into the cylinder. The dust cover end of the pushrod should face the piston.

12 Press a new retaining ring into position, and push it in firmly to secure the pushrod assembly.

Refitting

13 Commence refitting by placing the shim in position, with the grooved side facing towards the bellhousing.

14 Offer the cylinder and pushrod to the bellhousing, ensuring that the pushrod engages with the spherical recess in the clutch release lever.

15 Refit and tighten the securing bolts.

16 Reconnect the pipe or hose, as applicable, then bleed the clutch hydraulic system as described in Section 6.

5 Hydraulic master cylinder - removal, overhaul and refitting

Warning: Hydraulic fluid is poisonous; wash off immediately and thoroughly in the case of skin contact, and seek immediate medical advice if any fluid is swallowed or gets into the eyes. Certain types of hydraulic fluid are inflammable, and may ignite when allowed into contact with hot components; when servicing any hydraulic system, it is safest to assume that the fluid is inflammable, and to take precautions against the risk of fire as though it is petrol that is being handled. Hydraulic fluid is also an effective paint stripper, and will attack plastics; if any is spilt, it should be washed off immediately, using copious quantities of fresh water. Finally, it is hygroscopic (it absorbs moisture from the air) - old fluid may be contaminated and unfit for further use. When topping-up or renewing the fluid, always use the recommended type, and ensure that it comes from a freshly-opened sealed container.

Removal

1 The clutch master cylinder is located inside the vehicle, attached to the clutch and brake pedal mounting bracket **(see illustration)**. Hydraulic fluid for the unit is supplied by a flexible rubber hose connected to the brake fluid reservoir in the engine compartment.

2 Disconnect the battery negative lead.

3 Remove the driver's side lower facia trim panel to gain access to the master cylinder and pedal assembly.

4 Pull back the floor carpet, and cover the floor beneath the pedals to protect against fluid spillage.

5 To reduce fluid loss, draw off as much fluid as possible from the appropriate chamber of the brake fluid reservoir, using a clean syringe, until the fluid level is below the level of the clutch master cylinder supply pipe.

6 Place a suitable container beneath the clutch master cylinder to catch any spilt fluid.

7 Unscrew the hydraulic pipe union on the clutch master cylinder, and carefully withdraw the pipe. Plug the open ends of the pipe and master cylinder to prevent dirt entry and further fluid loss.

8 Unscrew the two nuts securing the master cylinder to the pedal mounting bracket.

9 Pull the clutch pedal upwards, and withdraw the clutch assist spring seat, spring and washer from the pushrod **(see illustration)**.

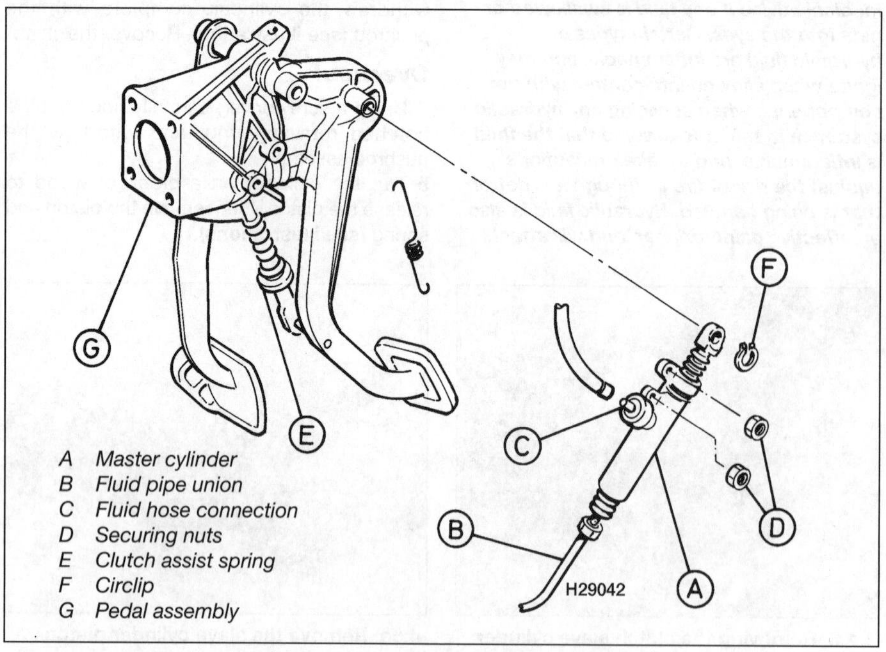

5.1 Clutch master cylinder and pedal assembly

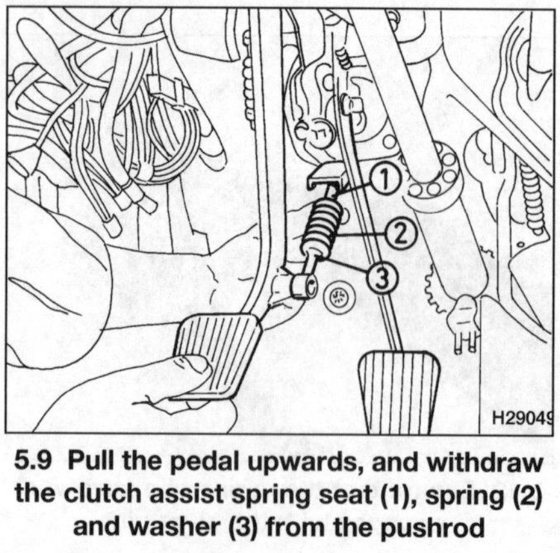

5.9 Pull the pedal upwards, and withdraw the clutch assist spring seat (1), spring (2) and washer (3) from the pushrod

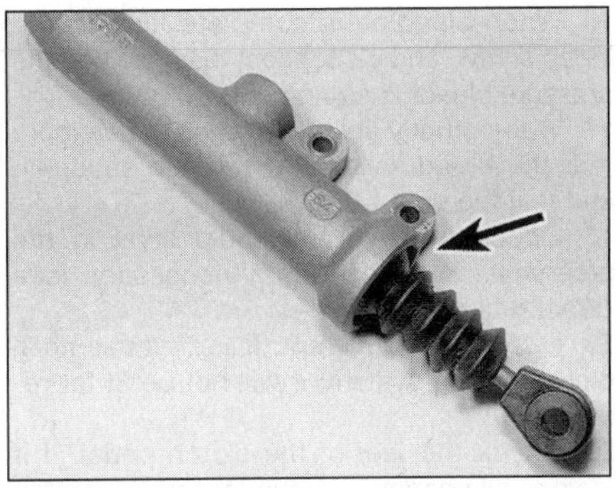

5.12 Ease off the dust cover (arrowed)

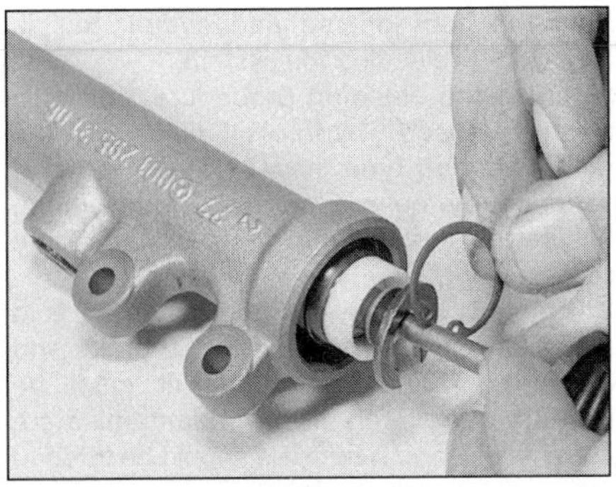

5.13a Remove the circlip . . .

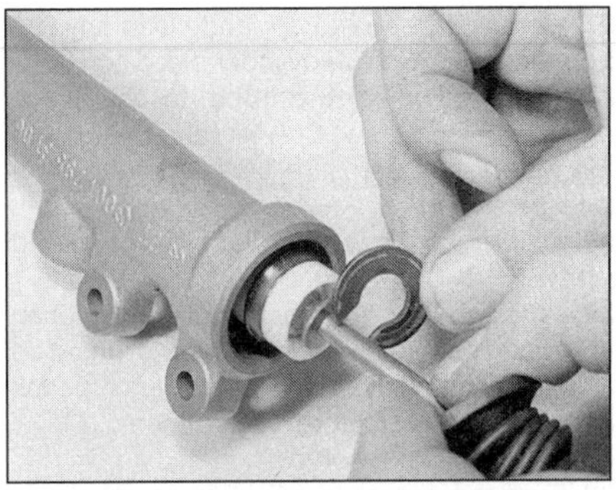

5.13b . . . and the retaining washer

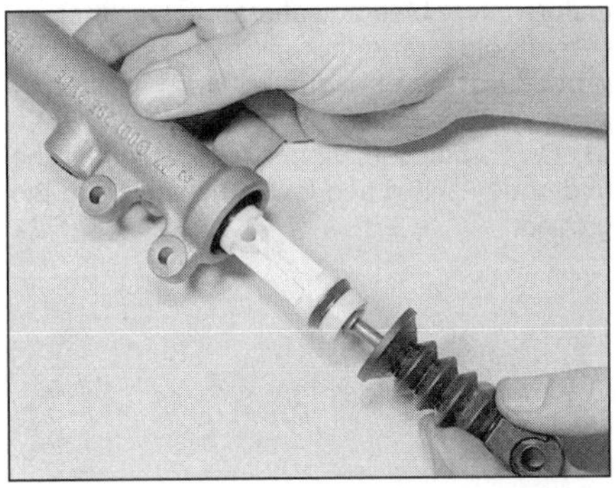

5.14a Withdraw the pushrod and piston assembly . . .

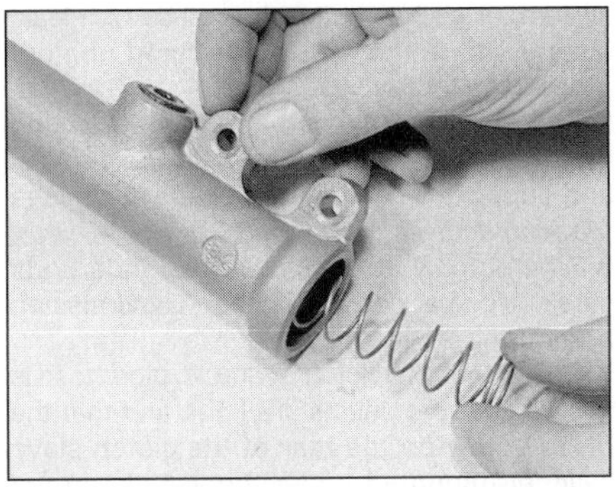

5.14b . . . followed by the piston spring

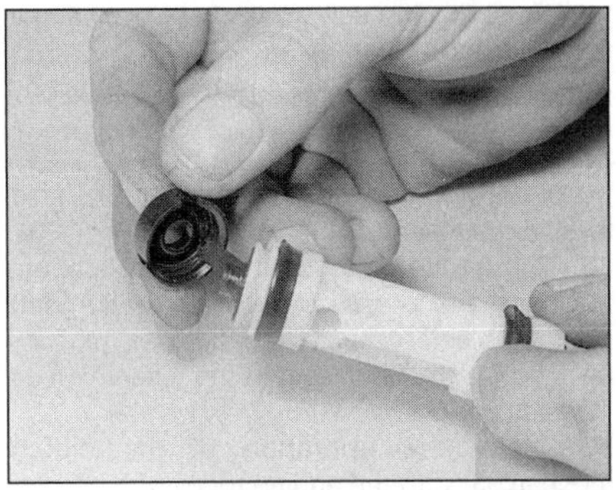

5.15 Remove the end cap and check valve from the piston

10 Using a screwdriver or a suitable pair of pliers, pull off the circlip securing the end of the master cylinder pushrod to the pedal

11 Disconnect the fluid hose from the master cylinder (again, be prepared for fluid spillage), then withdraw the assembly from the footwell.

Overhaul

12 Ease the dust cover on the pushrod away from the cylinder body to provide access to the circlip **(see illustration)**.

13 Using circlip pliers, extract the circlip, then remove the retaining washer **(see illustrations)**.

14 Withdraw the pushrod and piston assembly from the cylinder bore, followed by the piston spring **(see illustrations)**.

15 Remove the end cap and check valve from the end of the piston **(see illustration)**.

16 Wash all components in clean hydraulic fluid, then lay them out for inspection.

17 Examine the cylinder bore and piston carefully for signs of scoring or wear ridges. If these are evident, renew the complete master cylinder. If the condition of the components is satisfactory, a new set of rubber seals must be obtained. Never re-use the old seals.

18 Remove the old seals from the piston, and carefully fit the new ones, using the fingers only. To ease fitting of the seals, lubricate with clean hydraulic fluid. Ensure that the sealing lip of each seal is towards the spring end of the piston.

19 Lubricate the cylinder bore and the piston with hydraulic fluid, then insert the spring into the bore.

20 Place the check valve and end cap on the piston, and carefully enter the piston into the cylinder bore.

21 Fit the retaining washer over the pushrod, followed by the circlip.

22 Push the piston down the bore slightly, and engage the circlip in its groove. Ensure that the circlip is correctly seated.

23 Slide the dust cover into position, and locate its end under the edge of the cylinder.

Refitting

24 Refitting is a reversal of the removal procedure, bearing in mind the following points.

a) *Commence refitting by fitting the washer, clutch assist spring and spring seat onto the master cylinder pushrod, and inserting into the guide on the pedal bracket by depressing the clutch pedal.*

b) *Ensure that the master cylinder pushrod eye is fitted with the flanged side towards the pedal.*

c) *Do not refit the driver's side lower facia panel until the pushrod adjustment (paragraph 25 on) has been checked.*

d) *On completion, bleed the clutch hydraulic system as described in Section 6, then check the pushrod adjustment as described in the following paragraphs.*

Pushrod adjustment

Note: *Pressure-bleeding equipment (see Section 6), and the aid of an assistant will be required to carry out this operation.*

25 For access to the clutch slave cylinder, apply the parking brake, then jack up the front of the vehicle, and support securely on axle stands (see *"Jacking and vehicle support"*). Draw off half the fluid from the appropriate chamber of the brake fluid reservoir, using a clean syringe.

26 Insert several thin strips of metal (approximately 60.0 x 20.0 x 1.0 mm) between the upper clutch pedal stop, and the rubber buffer **(see illustration)**.

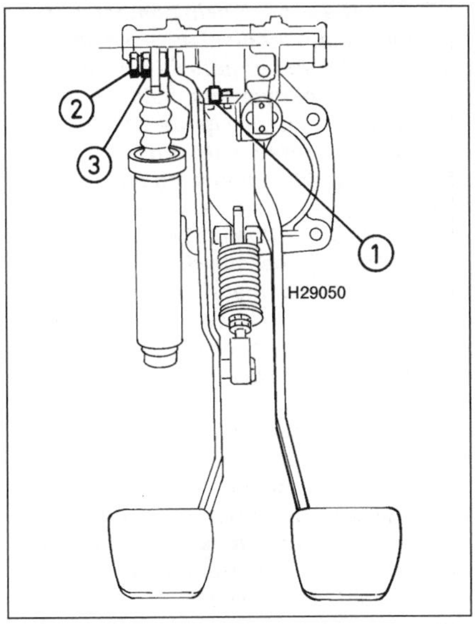

5.26 Clutch master cylinder pushrod adjustment

1 *Metal strips*
2 *Clamping screw*
3 *Adjusting screw*

6

27 Remove the dust cap, and clean any dirt from around the slave cylinder bleed screw.
28 Fit a spanner and tube to the slave cylinder bleed screw. Connect the free end of the tube to the pressure-bleeding equipment (see Section 6).
29 Using the spanner, slacken the bleed screw.
30 Working in the driver's footwell, slacken the clamp screw on the eccentric pushrod adjusting screw, at the top of the clutch pedal.
31 Have the assistant observe the fluid level in the brake fluid reservoir.
32 Turn the eccentric adjusting screw slowly until the fluid level in the reservoir rises, then turn the adjusting screw slowly back until the fluid level stops increasing.
33 Lock the adjusting screw in position by tightening the clamp screw.
34 Remove the metal strips from between the pedal stop and the rubber buffer. The fluid level in the reservoir should rise.
35 Tighten the bleed screw, and disconnect the hose and pressure-bleeding equipment. Refit the bleed screw dust cap.
36 Top-up the fluid level in the reservoir (see *"Weekly checks"*).
37 Check the operation of the clutch mechanism with the engine running.
38 On completion, refit the driver's side lower facia panel.

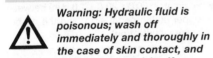

6 Hydraulic system - bleeding

Warning: Hydraulic fluid is poisonous; wash off immediately and thoroughly in the case of skin contact, and seek immediate medical advice if any fluid is swallowed or gets into the eyes. Certain types of hydraulic fluid are inflammable, and may ignite when allowed into contact with hot components; when servicing any hydraulic system, it is safest to assume that the fluid is inflammable, and to take precautions against the risk of fire as though it is petrol that is being handled. Hydraulic fluid is also an effective paint stripper, and will attack plastics; if any is spilt, it should be washed off immediately, using copious quantities of fresh water. Finally, it is hygroscopic (it absorbs moisture from the air) - old fluid may be contaminated and unfit for further use. When topping-up or renewing the fluid, always use the recommended type, and ensure that it comes from a freshly-opened sealed container.

Note: *Mercedes-Benz recommend that pressure-bleeding equipment is used to bleed the clutch hydraulic system.*

1 The correct operation of any hydraulic system is only possible after removing all air from the components and circuit; this is achieved by bleeding the system.
2 During the bleeding procedure, add only clean, unused hydraulic fluid of the recommended type; never re-use fluid that has already been bled from the system. Ensure that sufficient fluid is available before starting work.
3 If there is any possibility of incorrect fluid being already in the system, the brake and clutch components and circuit must be flushed completely with uncontaminated, correct fluid, and new seals should be fitted to the various components.
4 If hydraulic fluid has been lost from the system, or air has entered because of a leak, ensure that the fault is cured before proceeding further.
5 To improve access, apply the parking brake, then jack up the front of the vehicle, and support it securely on axle stands (see *"Jacking and vehicle support"*).
6 Where applicable, remove the underbody shield for access to the transmission bellhousing.
7 Check that the clutch hydraulic pipe/hose is secure, that the unions are tight, and that the bleed screw on the rear of the clutch slave cylinder (mounted under the vehicle on the right-hand side of the transmission) is closed. Remove the dust cap, and clean any dirt from around the bleed screw.
8 Note that the brake fluid reservoir feeds both the brake and clutch hydraulic systems.
9 It is recommended that pressure-bleeding equipment is used to bleed the system. Pressure-bleeding kits are usually operated by the reservoir of pressurised air contained in the spare tyre. However, note that it will probably be necessary to reduce the pressure to a lower level than normal; refer to the instructions supplied with the kit.
10 By connecting a pressurised, fluid-filled container to the brake fluid reservoir, bleeding can be carried out simply by opening the bleed screw on the clutch slave cylinder, and allowing the fluid to flow out until no more air bubbles can be seen in the expelled fluid.
11 This method has the advantage that the large reservoir of fluid provides an additional safeguard against air being drawn into the system during bleeding.
12 Collect a clean glass jar, a suitable length of plastic or rubber tubing which is a tight fit over the bleed screw, and a ring spanner to fit the screw.
13 Fit the spanner and tube to the slave cylinder bleed screw, place the other end of the tube in the jar, and pour in sufficient fluid to cover the end of the tube **(see illustration)**.
14 Connect the pressure-bleeding equipment to the brake fluid reservoir in accordance with the manufacturer's instructions.
15 Loosen the bleed screw using the spanner, and allow fluid to drain into the jar until no more air bubbles emerge.
16 When bleeding is complete, tighten the bleed screw, and disconnect the hose and the pressure bleeding equipment.
17 Wash off any spilt fluid, check once more that the bleed screw is tightened securely, and refit the dust cap.
18 Check the hydraulic fluid level in the reservoir, and top-up if necessary (see *"Weekly checks"*).
19 Discard any hydraulic fluid that has been bled from the system; it will not be fit for re-use.
20 Check the feel of the clutch pedal. If it feels at all spongy, air must still be present in the system, and further bleeding is required. Failure to bleed satisfactorily after a reasonable repetition of the bleeding procedure may be due to worn master or slave cylinder seals.
21 On completion, where applicable refit the underbody shield and lower the vehicle to the ground.

7 Clutch pedal - removal and refitting

Removal

1 Disconnect the battery negative lead.
2 Remove the driver's side lower facia trim panel to gain access to the master cylinder and pedal assembly.
3 Pull back the floor carpet, and cover the floor beneath the pedals to protect against fluid spillage.
4 To reduce fluid loss, draw off as much fluid as possible from the appropriate chamber of the brake fluid reservoir, using a clean syringe, until the fluid level is below the level of the clutch master cylinder supply pipe.
5 Place a suitable container beneath the clutch master cylinder to catch any spilt fluid.
6 Unscrew the hydraulic pipe union on the clutch master cylinder, and carefully withdraw the pipe. Plug the open ends of the pipe and master cylinder to prevent dirt entry and further fluid loss.

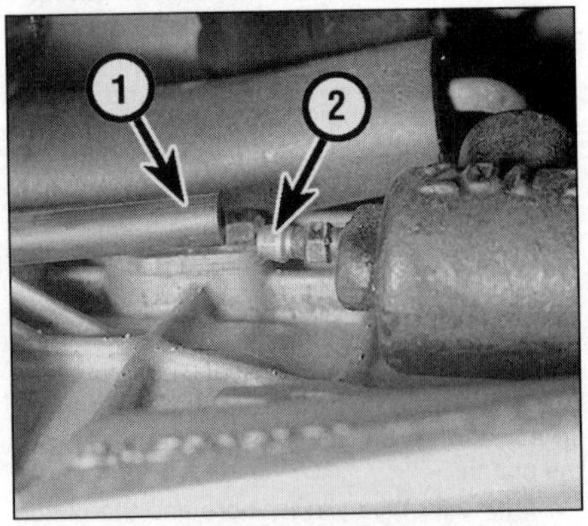

6.13 Fit a tube (1) to the slave cylinder bleed screw (2)

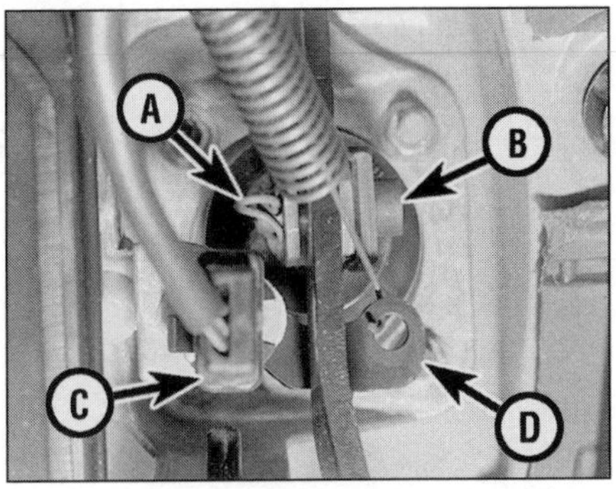

7.7 Brake pedal mounting details

A Clevis pin locking clip
B Clevis pin
C Stop light switch wiring plug
D Return spring bracket

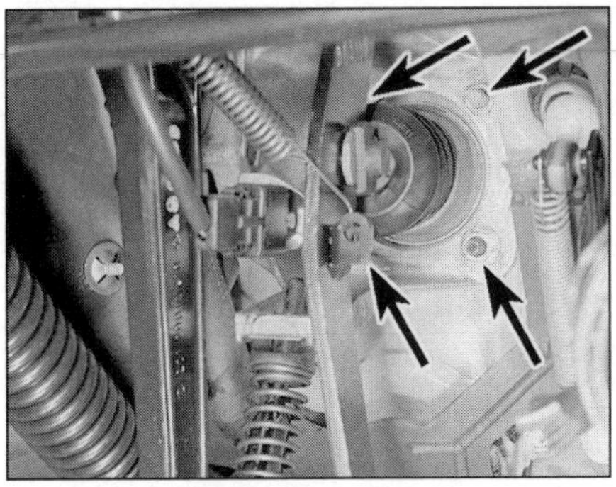

7.10a Pedal assembly securing nuts (arrowed) . . .

7.10b . . . and securing bolt (arrowed)

7 Carefully unhook the brake pedal return spring **(see illustration)**.

8 Disconnect the wiring plug from the stop light switch, then unclip the switch from the bracket on the pedal assembly.

9 Remove the locking clip from the brake pedal-to-servo pushrod clevis pin, then withdraw the clevis pin.

10 Unscrew the four nuts securing the pedal assembly to the front of the bulkhead (note that these nuts also secure the brake vacuum servo), and the single bolt securing the assembly to the top of the bulkhead **(see illustrations)**.

11 Pull the pedal assembly back from the bulkhead until the mounting bracket disengages from the studs, then lower the assembly, and disconnect the fluid hose from the clutch master cylinder (be prepared for fluid spillage).

12 Withdraw the assembly from under the facia.

13 Dismantling of the assembly is self-explanatory. Note the locations of all components to ensure correct refitting **(see illustration)**.

Refitting

14 Refitting is a reversal of removal, bearing in mind the following points.

a) Check the adjustment of the stop light switch as described in Chapter 9.

b) On completion, bleed the clutch hydraulic system as described in Section 6.

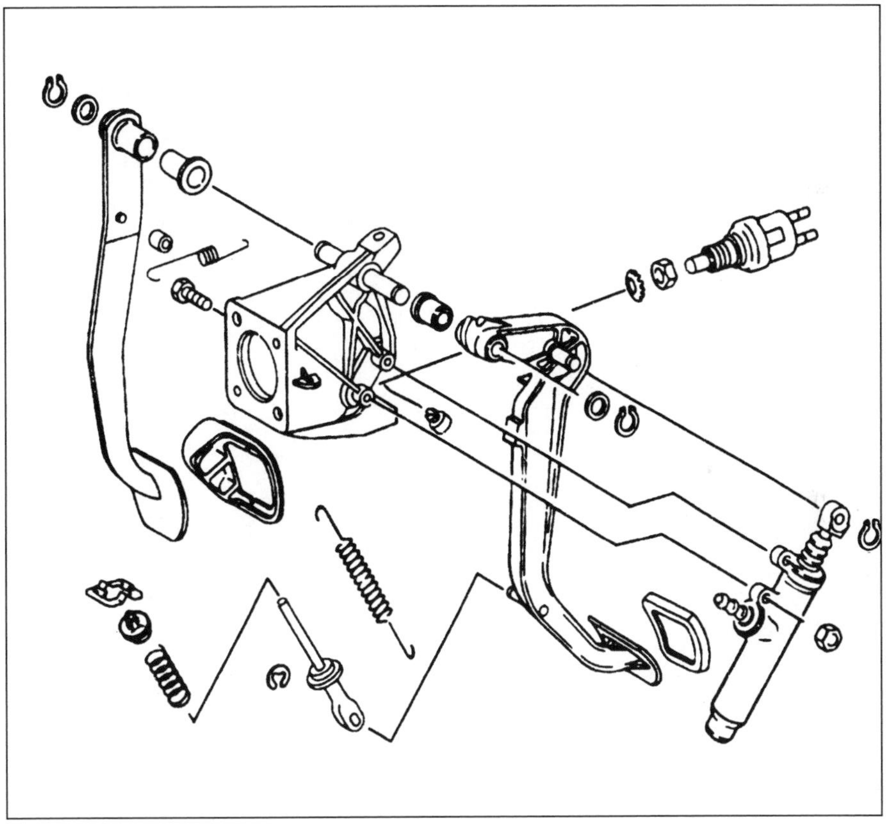

7.13 Exploded view of clutch and brake pedal assembly

6

Notes

Chapter 7 Part A
Manual transmission

Contents

Gearchange components - removal, refitting and adjustment 3
General information 1
Manual transmission - removal and refitting 6
Manual transmission oil - draining and refilling 2
Manual transmission oil level check ..... See Chapter 1
Manual transmission overhaul - general information 7
Oil seals - renewal 4
Reversing light switch - testing, removal and refitting 5

Degrees of difficulty

Easy, suitable for novice with little experience	**Fairly easy,** suitable for beginner with some experience	**Fairly difficult,** suitable for competent DIY mechanic	**Difficult,** suitable for experienced DIY mechanic	**Very difficult,** suitable for expert DIY or professional

Specifications

General

Transmission code:	
4-speed transmission	716.2
5-speed transmission	717.4

Transmission oil

Type	Mercedez-Benz approved manual transmission oil

Torque wrench settings

Torque wrench settings	Nm	lbf ft
Oil drain and level/filler plugs	60	44
Crossmember-to-vehicle floor bolts	45	33
Engine-to-transmission bolts:		
M10 bolts	55	41
M12 bolts	65	48
Transmission output flange nut	160	
Transmission input shaft end cover plate securing bolts	20	15

1 General information

Both 4-speed and 5-speed transmissions are available. The transmission is contained in a casing bolted to the rear of the engine.

Drive is transmitted from the crankshaft via the clutch to the input shaft, which has a splined extension to accept the clutch friction plate. The output shaft transmits the drive via the propeller shaft to the rear differential.

The input shaft runs in line with the output shaft. The input shaft and output shaft gears are in constant mesh with the layshaft gear cluster. Selection of gears is by sliding synchromesh hubs, which lock the appropriate output shaft gears to the output shaft.

Gear selection is via a floor-mounted lever and selector mechanism. The selector mechanism causes the appropriate selector fork to move its respective synchro-sleeve along the shaft, to lock the gear pinion to the synchro-hub. Since the synchro-hubs are splined to the output shaft, this locks the pinion to the shaft, so that drive can be transmitted. To ensure that gear-changing can be made quickly and quietly, a synchro-

2.1a Using a long nut and a spanner to unscrew the transmission fluid level/filler plug

mesh system is fitted to all forward gears, consisting of baulk rings and spring-loaded fingers, as well as the gear pinions and synchro-hubs. The synchro-mesh cones are formed on the mating faces of the baulk rings and gear pinions.

2 Manual transmission oil - draining and refilling

Note: *An hexagonal key, or a suitable alternative (see text) will be required to unscrew the transmission level/filler and drain plugs.*

1 Place a suitable container beneath the transmission drain plug, at the bottom of the casing, then unscrew the plug. Unscrew the level/filler plug, located on the right-hand side of the transmission, to assist draining. A hexagonal key should be used to unscrew the plugs, but a tool can be improvised using a long nut, or a length of hexagonal bar, and a spanner **(see illustrations)**.

2 Once all the oil has drained, refit and tighten the drain plug, using a new sealing ring where applicable.

3 Fill the transmission until oil runs from the level/filler plug hole. The level should just be up to the bottom of the level/filler plug hole.

4 When the level is correct, refit the plug, and tighten to the specified torque.

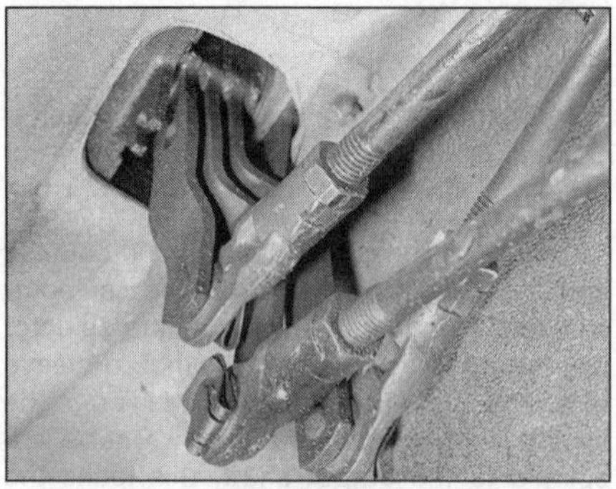

3.14 Prise off the securing clips and disconnect the gearchange rods from the gearchange lever assembly

2.1b Transmission fluid drain plug location (arrowed)

3 Gearchange components - removal, refitting and adjustment

Gearchange lever

Removal

1 Pull the gearchange lever gaiter from the centre console, and fold it up over the lever.

2 Using a screwdriver, lever the spring clip out of the holes in the gearchange lever tube, and remove the clip **(see illustration)**.

3 Pull the lever from the tube.

Refitting

4 Refitting is a reversal of removal, but ensure that the spring clip is correctly located.

Gearchange lever assembly

Removal

5 To improve access, apply the parking brake, then jack up the front of the vehicle and support it securely on axle stands (see *"Jacking and vehicle support"*).

6 Working under the vehicle, prise off the securing clips, and disconnect the gearchange rods from the gearchange lever assembly.

7 Working inside the vehicle, remove the cover from the centre console (see Chapter 11) to expose the gearchange lever assembly.

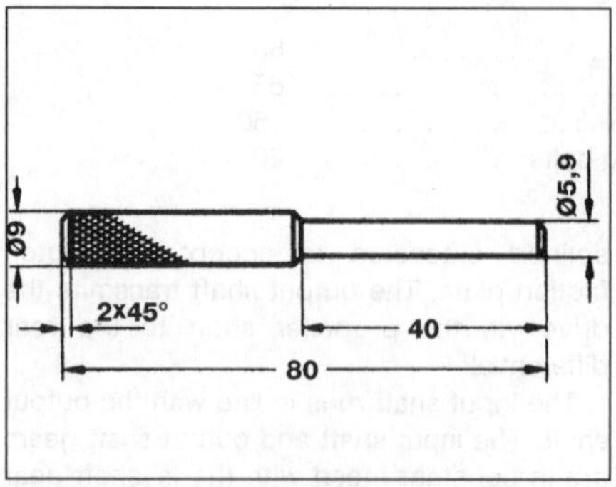

3.15 Gearchange linkage adjustment locating pin

All dimensions in mm

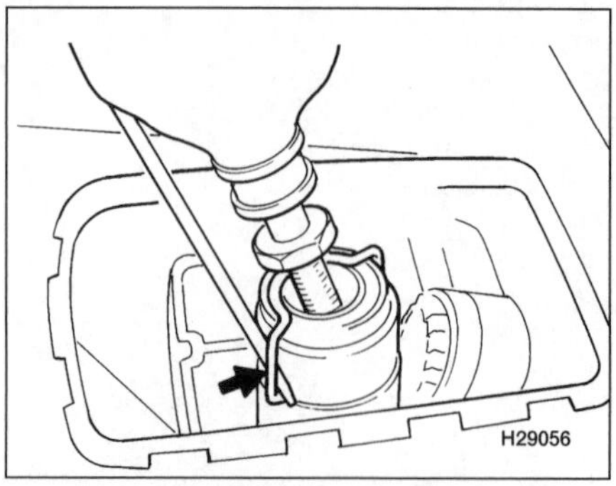

3.2 Lever the spring clip from the gearchange lever tube

8 Unclip the reversing light switch from the bracket.

9 Unscrew the gearchange lever assembly securing bolts.

10 Withdraw the assembly through the floor into the vehicle interior. Recover the gasket.

Refitting

11 Refitting is a reversal of removal, but make sure that the gearchange rod securing clips are securely refitted and, on completion, check the linkage adjustment as described in the following paragraphs.

Adjustment

Note: *To check the adjustment, it will be necessary to make up a suitable locating pin - see text.*

12 To improve access, apply the parking brake, then jack up the front of the vehicle and support it securely on axle stands (see *"Jacking and vehicle support"*).

13 Make sure that the transmission is in neutral.

14 Working under the vehicle, prise off the securing clips, and disconnect the gearchange rods from the gearchange lever assembly **(see illustration)**.

15 Make up a locating pin to the dimensions shown, ideally using steel bar **(see illustration)**.

16 Insert the locating pin through the bores provided in the gearchange levers **(see illustration)**.

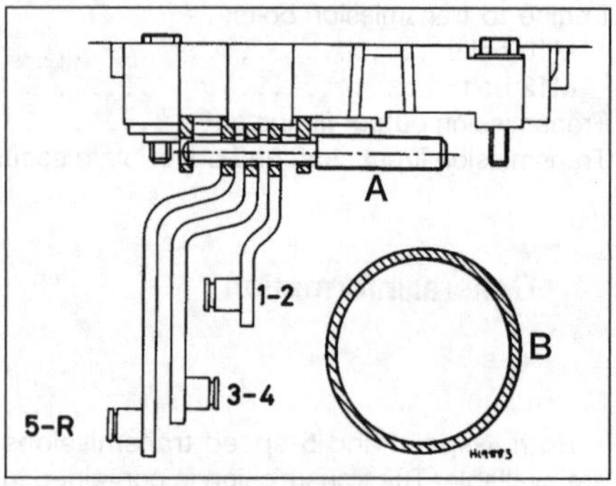

3.16 Locating pin in position in gearchange levers

A Locating pin B Propeller shaft

17 With the gearchange levers locked in position, it should be possible to slide the gearchange rods easily onto the gearchange lever pins. If necessary, adjust the position of the gearchange rod end fitting(s) until the rod(s) can be slid onto the lever pin(s), as follows.

a) Slacken the gearchange rod end fitting.
b) Turn the end fitting to adjust the length of the rod as required.
c) Tighten the locknut.

18 When the adjustment is satisfactory, refit the clips to secure the gearchange rods to the lever pins, then withdraw the locating pin.
19 Lower the vehicle to the ground, then start the engine, and check the operation of the gearchange linkage. Take the vehicle on a road test, and check that all gears can be engaged easily.

4 Oil seals - renewal

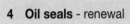

Input shaft oil seal

1 Remove the transmission as described in Section 6.
2 Remove the clutch release bearing and lever, with reference to Chapter 6.
3 Unscrew the securing bolts, and remove the cover plate from inside the transmission bellhousing **(see illustration)**.
4 Carefully slide the cover plate off, over the input shaft, and recover the spacer shim(s) **(see illustration)**.
5 Lever the oil seal from the cover plate using a screwdriver **(see illustration)**.
6 Thoroughly clean the oil seal housing in the cover plate.
7 Tap the new seal into position, using a suitable socket or tube, until the seal seats on the shoulder in the cover plate.
8 Hold the spacer shim(s) in position using a little grease, then slide the cover plate into position over the input shaft.
9 Apply sealant to the threads of the cover plate securing bolts, then refit the bolts and tighten to the specified torque.
10 Refit the clutch release lever and bearing, with reference to Chapter 6.
11 Refit the transmission as described in Section 6.

Output flange oil seal

Note: *A new transmission output flange securing nut will be required on refitting.*
12 Disconnect the propeller shaft from the transmission output flange, with reference to Chapter 8.
13 Ensure that the transmission is in neutral.
14 Bolt a suitable holding tool to the transmission output flange. A suitable tool can be made up using two pieces of flat bar, and bolts - engage the tool with two of the bolts holes in the output flange, and use it to counterhold the flange. Note that it must be possible to gain access to the output flange nut with the tool in place.
15 Counterhold the output flange, then unscrew the flange securing nut. Discard the nut, a new one must be used on refitting **(see illustration)**.
16 Pull the output flange from the shaft, using a suitable puller if necessary.
17 Prise the oil seal from the housing using a screwdriver.
18 Thoroughly clean the oil seal seat.
19 Tap the new seal into position, using a suitable socket or tube, until the outer face of the seal is flush with the end face of the housing.
20 Refit the output flange to the output shaft, and secure using a new nut. Tighten the nut to the specified torque.
21 Reconnect the propeller shaft to the output flange, with reference to Chapter 8.

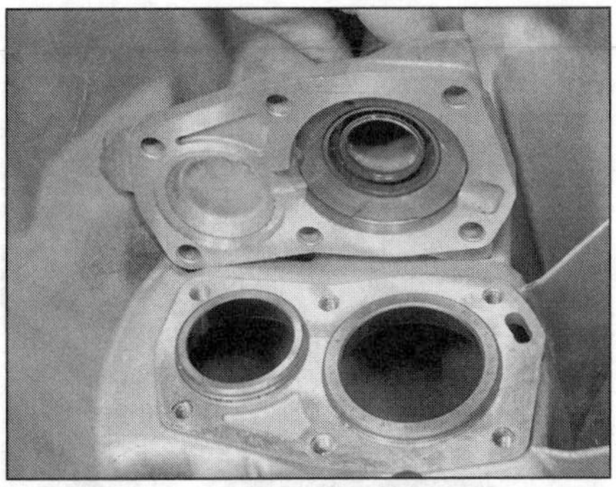

4.3 Removing the cover plate from the transmission bellhousing

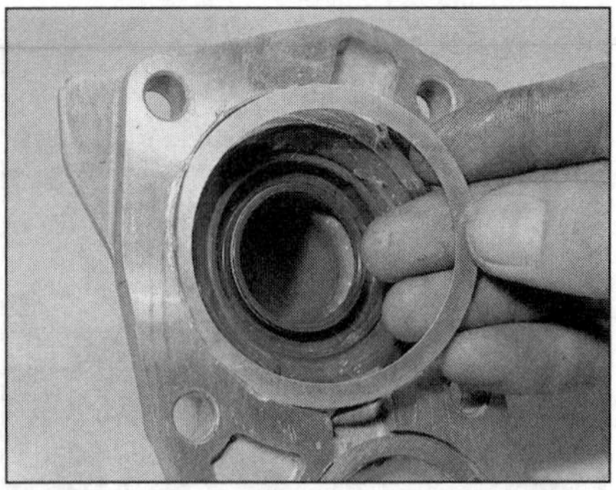

4.4 Recover the spacer shim(s)

5 Reversing light switch - testing, removal and refitting

Testing

1 The reversing light circuit is controlled by a plunger-type switch located at the rear of the gear selector lever assembly under the centre console. If a fault develops in the circuit, first ensure that the circuit fuse has not blown.
2 For access to the switch, working inside the vehicle, remove the cover from the centre console (see Chapter 11) to expose the gearchange lever assembly.
3 To test the switch, disconnect the wiring connector, and use a multimeter (set to the resistance function) or a battery-and-bulb test circuit to check that there is continuity between the switch terminals only when reverse gear is selected. If this is not the case, and there are no obvious breaks or other damage to the wires, the switch is faulty, and must be renewed.

Removal

4 Disconnect the battery negative lead.
5 Proceed as described in paragraph 2.
6 Unclip the switch from the mounting bracket, and disconnect the wiring plug.

Refitting

7 Refitting is a reversal of removal.

6 Manual transmission - removal and refitting

Removal

Note: *This is a difficult operation, due to the limited access to the engine-to-transmission bolts. It is suggested that the procedure is read through thoroughly before starting the operation. Suitable ratchet extensions may be required to reach some of the engine-to-transmission bolts.*
1 Raise the bonnet, and place a thin sheet of metal (approximately 300 mm square) at the

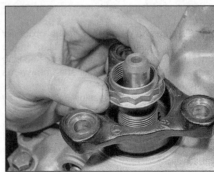

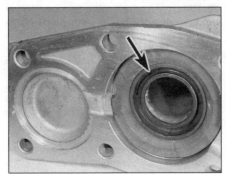

4.5 Input shaft oil seal location (arrowed) in cover plate

4.15 Removing the transmission output flange securing nut

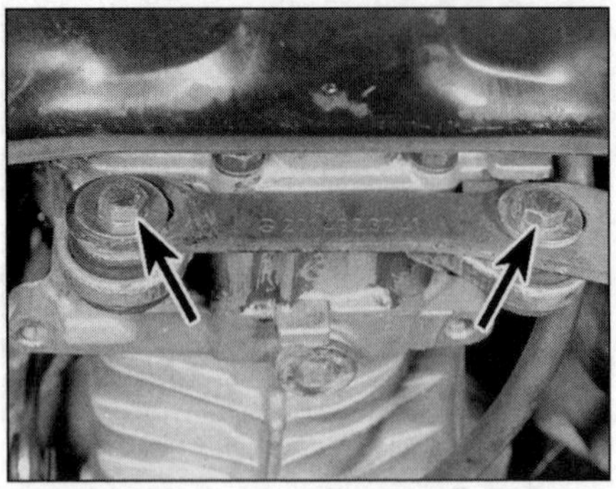

6.9 Exhaust mounting bracket-to-transmission bolts (arrowed)

6.13 Remove the rear engine/transmission support bracket

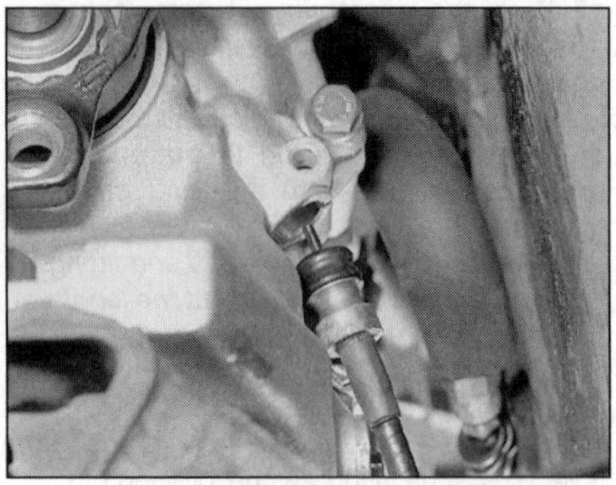

6.15 Disconnecting the speedometer cable from the transmission

rear of the engine compartment bulkhead, to protect the bulkhead insulation and the brake pipes during the following procedure.

2 Disconnect the battery negative lead.

3 On models fitted with an auxiliary heater, take care not to damage the coolant hose at the rear of the engine compartment during the following procedure. Unbolt the transmission oil level dipstick tube from the cylinder head.

4 Apply the parking brake, then jack up the vehicle and support securely on axle stands (see *"Jacking and vehicle support"*). The vehicle must be raised sufficiently to enable the transmission to be lowered and removed from under the vehicle. Where applicable, remove the engine undershield, with reference to Chapter 11.

5 Drain the transmission oil with reference to Section 2.

6 Place a small wooden block between the engine sump and the welded crossmember under the vehicle floor.

7 Remove the complete exhaust system as described in Chapter 4.

8 Where applicable, unbolt the exhaust heat shield from the vehicle floor for access to the propeller shaft intermediate bearing assembly.

9 Unbolt the exhaust mounting brackets from the vehicle floor (under the propeller shaft), and from the transmission, if not already done **(see illustration)**. Where applicable, unclip the wiring from the bracket on the transmission.

10 Disconnect the propeller shaft from the transmission flange with reference to Chapter 8.

11 Slacken the clamp nut at the propeller shaft intermediate bearing, then slacken (do not remove) the intermediate bearing securing nuts, and push the propeller shaft rearwards as far as possible.

12 Support the transmission using a trolley jack and interposed block of wood.

13 Unbolt the rear engine/transmission support bracket from the transmission and the vehicle floor, and remove the bracket **(see illustration)**.

14 If not already done, unbolt the exhaust mounting bracket from the rear of the transmission.

15 Unscrew the clamp bolt, and pull the speedometer cable from the transmission, with reference to Chapter 12 if necessary **(see illustration)**. Where applicable, release the cable-tie(s) securing the cable to the transmission.

16 Unbolt the clutch slave cylinder from the transmission, and carefully pull it, complete with the oil pipe, to the rear until the pushrod is clear of the transmission. Recover the plastic shim.

Note: *On some models, unbolting the slave cylinder leaving the oil pipe connected will not give sufficient clearance to remove the transmission. In this case, the oil hose must be disconnected from the slave cylinder pipe (and the oil drained), leaving the slave cylinder in position on the transmission. Place a suitable container beneath the oil hose/pipe connection to catch the oil which will be released, and plug or cover the open ends of the pipe and hose.*

17 Prise off the securing clips, and disconnect the gear selector rods from the gear selector levers under the vehicle floor.

18 Remove the starter motor as described in Chapter 5A.

19 Ensure that the transmission is adequately supported, then lower the assembly as far as possible, until the engine is resting on the block of wood inserted between the crossmember and the sump. Take care not to damage the brake pipes and any other components at the rear of the bulkhead, as the cylinder head may be forced into the bulkhead.

20 Unscrew all the engine-to-transmission bolts, leaving one bolt on either side of the transmission. Access to the upper bolts is very difficult, even with the assembly tilted, and several long ratchet extensions may be required. On some engines (particularly 6-cylinder engines), the top bolt cannot be reached from underneath, and access is most easily obtained, with a spanner, from the right-hand side as follows.

a) *Unbolt the heat shields from the area around the steering box for access to the exhaust manifold securing nuts.*
b) *Unscrew the securing nuts, and remove the (rear) exhaust manifold from the cylinder head. Recover the gasket(s).*

Note the locations of the earth strap, and any brackets secured by the engine-to-transmission bolts.

21 Once the upper engine-to-transmission bolts have been removed, raise the transmission until the engine/transmission assembly is level.

22 Unscrew the remaining two engine-to-transmission bolts, then pull the transmission rearwards to release the transmission input shaft from the clutch. Take care not to allow the weight of the transmission to hang on the clutch and input shaft, and take care not to damage the clutch slave cylinder and oil pipe during this procedure. If necessary, rotate the transmission to the left to enable the top of the bellhousing to clear the vehicle body.

23 Once the input shaft is clear of the clutch, lower the transmission from under the vehicle using the jack.

Refitting

24 Commence refitting by checking that the clutch friction disc is centralised as described in Chapter 6 (*"Clutch assembly - removal, inspection and refitting"*).

25 Before refitting the transmission, it is advisable to inspect and grease the clutch release mechanism as described in Chapter 6.

26 Also check the condition of the crankshaft spigot bearing, with reference to Chapter 2.

27 Lubricate the transmission input shaft splines with a little molybdenum disulphide grease.

28 Support the transmission using the trolley jack and block of wood, as during removal, then raise the transmission into position beneath the vehicle.

29 Lift the transmission into position, and if the clutch slave cylinder is still in position in the vehicle, lift the oil pipe over the transmission to ensure that it does not get trapped during the refitting procedure.

30 Slide the transmission forwards, ensuring that the input shaft engages with the clutch friction disc splines (where applicable, turn the transmission to the left to enable the bellhousing to clear the vehicle floor). It may be necessary to rock the engine and transmission slightly and/or turn the crankshaft slightly, to allow the input shaft to engage. Take care not to allow the weight of the transmission to hang on the input shaft.

31 Slide the transmission forwards until the bellhousing is firmly mated with the engine. Where applicable, turn the transmission to align the engine-to-transmission bolt holes in the engine and transmission.

32 Refit and tighten the engine-to-transmission bolts, ensuring that the earth strap and any brackets noted during removal are in place.

33 Further refitting is a reversal of removal, bearing in mind the following points.

a) *Where applicable, refit the exhaust manifold using a new gasket.*
b) *Where applicable, bleed the clutch hydraulic system as described in Chapter 6.*
c) *Reconnect the propeller shaft to the transmission flange with reference to Chapter 8.*
d) *Refit the exhaust system with reference to Chapter 4.*
e) *Refill the transmission with oil as described in Section 2.*

7 Manual transmission overhaul - general information

Overhauling a manual transmission is a difficult and involved job for the DIY home mechanic. In addition to dismantling and reassembling many small parts, clearances must be precisely measured and, if necessary, changed by selecting shims and spacers. Internal transmission components are also often difficult to obtain, and in many instances, extremely expensive. Because of this, if the transmission develops a fault or becomes noisy, the best course of action is to have the unit overhauled by a specialist repairer, or to obtain an exchange reconditioned unit. Be aware that some transmission repairs can be carried out with the transmission in the car.

Nevertheless, it is not impossible for the more experienced mechanic to overhaul the transmission, provided the special tools are available, and the job is done in a deliberate step-by-step manner, so that nothing is overlooked.

The tools necessary for an overhaul include internal and external circlip pliers, bearing pullers, a slide hammer, a set of pin punches, a dial test indicator, and possibly a hydraulic press. In addition, a large, sturdy workbench and a vice will be required.

During dismantling of the transmission, make careful notes of how each component is fitted, to make reassembly easier and more accurate.

Before dismantling the transmission, it will help if you have some idea what area is malfunctioning. Certain problems can be closely related to specific areas in the transmission, which can make component examination and replacement easier. Refer to the *"Fault finding"* Section at the end of this manual for more information.

Chapter 7 Part B
Automatic transmission

Contents

Automatic transmission - removal and refitting 6
Automatic transmission fluid drain and refill . . . . See Chapter 1
Automatic transmission fluid level check . . . . See Chapter 1
Automatic transmission overhaul - general information 7
Control pressure cable - adjustment 4
Gear selector lever - removal and refitting 2
Gear selector rod - adjustment, removal and refitting 3
General information 1
Starter inhibitor/reversing light switch - removal, refitting and adjustment 5

Degrees of difficulty

Easy, suitable for novice with little experience	**Fairly easy,** suitable for beginner with some experience	**Fairly difficult,** suitable for competent DIY mechanic	**Difficult,** suitable for experienced DIY mechanic	**Very difficult,** suitable for expert DIY or professional

Specifications

General

Transmission code	722.4	

Transmission fluid

Type	Mercedes-Benz approved automatic transmission fluid	

Torque wrench settings

Torque wrench settings	Nm	lbf ft
Crossmember-to-vehicle floor bolts	45	33
Transmission fluid drain plugs (main and torque converter)	14	10
Torque converter-to-driveplate bolts	42	31
Engine-to-transmission bolts:		
M10 bolts	55	41
M12 bolts	65	48

1 General information

A Mercedes-Benz five-speed automatic transmission is available as an option on all models covered by this manual.

The transmission comprises a torque converter, an epicyclic geartrain, and hydraulically-operated clutches and brakes.

The torque converter provides a fluid coupling between engine and transmission, which acts as a clutch, and also provides a degree of torque multiplication when accelerating.

The epicyclic geartrain provides either of the four forward or one reverse gear ratios, according to which of its component parts are held stationary or allowed to turn. The components of the geartrain are held or released by brakes and clutches which are activated by a hydraulic control unit. A fluid pump within the transmission provides the necessary hydraulic pressure to operate the brakes and clutches.

Driver control of the transmission is by a selector lever and a two-position switch. A control pressure cable, operated by movement of the accelerator pedal alters the hydraulic control pressure in the transmission, according to throttle position. The selector lever has a "drive" position, and a "hold" facility on 2nd and 3rd gear. The "drive" position ("D") provides automatic changing throughout the range of all forward gear ratios, and is the position selected for normal driving. An automatic kickdown facility shifts the transmission down a gear if the accelerator pedal is fully depressed. The "hold" facility is similar to the "drive" position, but limits the number of gear ratios available - ie, when the selector lever is in the "3" position, only the first three ratios can be selected; in the "2" position, only the first two can be selected, and so on. The lower ratio "hold" is useful when travelling down steep gradients, or for preventing unwanted selection of high gears on twisty roads. Two driving programs are provided for selection by the switch; "economy" or "standard". With the switch in the "economy" ("E") position, the vehicle will move away from a standstill in 2nd gear with a light throttle, or 1st gear with full throttle. With the switch in the "standard" ("S") position, the vehicle will always move away from a standstill in 2nd gear, and the gearchange points will occur at lower driving speeds.

Due to the complexity of the automatic transmission, any repair or overhaul work must be left to a Mercedes-Benz dealer with the necessary special equipment for fault diagnosis and repair. The contents of the following Sections are therefore confined to supplying general information, and any service information and instructions that can be used by the owner.

2 Gear selector lever - removal and refitting

Removal

1 Disconnect the battery negative lead.

2 Apply the parking brake, then jack up the front of the vehicle, and support securely on axle stands (see *"Jacking and vehicle support"*).

3 Working under the vehicle, prise off the metal retaining clip, and disconnect the gear selector lever from the selector rod **(see illustration)**.

4 Remove the cover from the centre console as described in Chapter 11. On later models, it may be necessary to remove the complete centre console assembly.

5 Disconnect the gear position indicator lighting cable from the light distributor, and/or pull the illumination bulb from the gear selector housing.

6 Disconnect the wiring plug from the "economy"/"standard" switch.

7 Unscrew the securing screws, then withdraw the gear selector lever from the vehicle floor **(see illustration)**. Recover the gasket.

Refitting

8 Examine the condition of the gasket, and renew if necessary.

9 Fit the gasket to the underside of the gear selector lever assembly, then insert the securing screws to locate the gasket.

10 Further refitting is a reversal of removal.

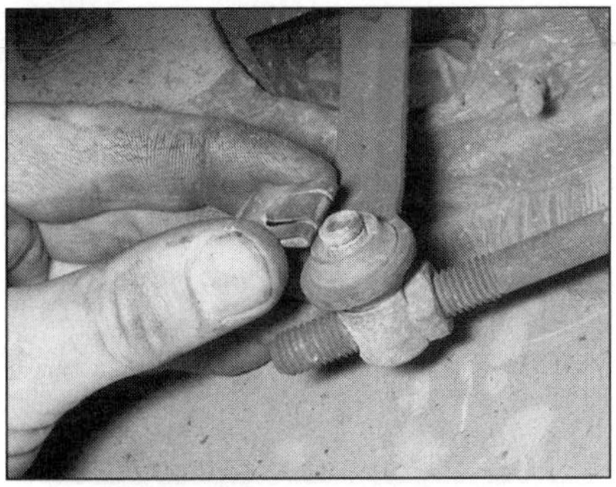

2.3 Prise off the clip securing the gear selector lever to the selector rod

3 Gear selector rod - adjustment, removal and refitting

Adjustment

1 For the following adjustment, the vehicle should be resting on its wheels.

2 Working under the vehicle, prise off the metal retaining clip, and disconnect the gear selector lever from the selector rod **(see illustration 2.3)**.

3 Move the selector lever on the transmission to position "N".

4 Slacken the locknut on the end of the selector rod **(see illustration)**.

5 Adjust the length of the selector rod by turning the end fitting until, with the selector rod reconnected to the gear selector lever, there is approximately 1.0 mm clearance between the driver's gear selector lever and the "N" stop on the gear selector gate.

6 When the adjustment is correct, secure the selector rod to the selector lever with the metal clip, then tighten the locknut.

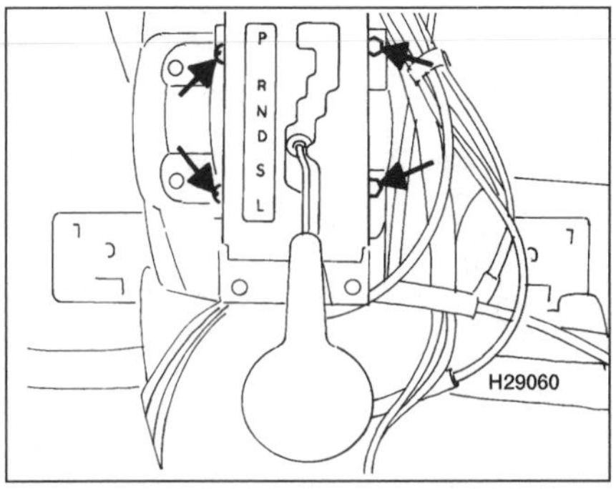

2.7 Unscrew the four gear selector lever securing screws (arrowed)

Removal

7 To improve access, apply the parking brake, then jack up the vehicle, and support securely on axle stands (see *"Jacking and vehicle support"*).

8 Prise the securing clips from the ends of the selector rod, at the selector lever and the transmission, then withdraw the rod from under the vehicle.

Refitting

9 Refitting is a reversal of removal.

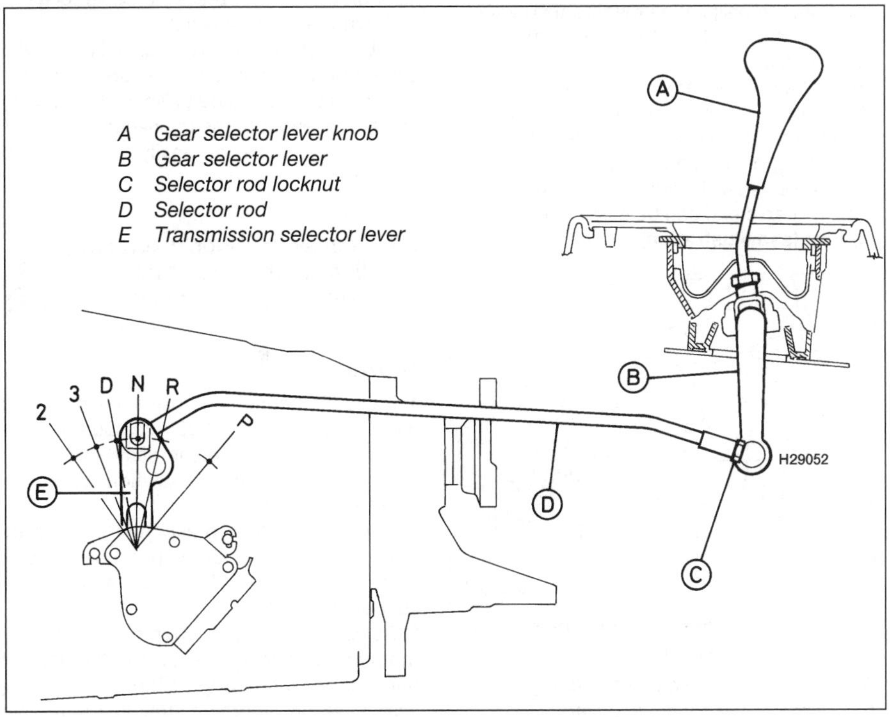

3.4 Gear selector rod adjustment

4 Control pressure cable - adjustment

Carburettor engines

1 Remove the air cleaner as described in Chapter 4, then check that the carburettor throttle valve lever is resting against the idle speed adjusting screw. If not, proceed as follows **(see illustration)**.

a) Start the engine.

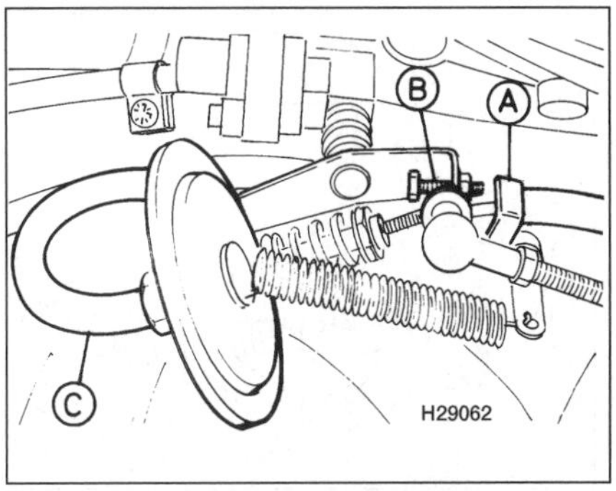

4.1 Control pressure cable adjustment - carburettor models

A Throttle valve lever
B Idle speed adjusting screw
C Vacuum hose

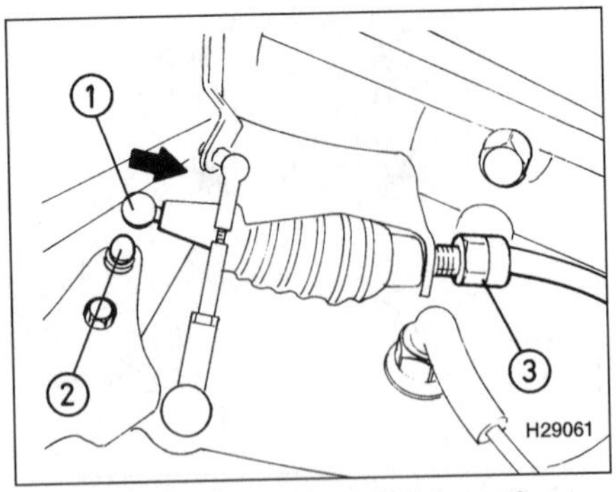

4.4 Pull the cable end (1) from the balljoint (2), then push in the direction of the arrow. If necessary, turn cable sheath adjuster (3) - carburettor models

b) Pinch the throttle valve actuator vacuum hose, so that the throttle valve lever rests against the idle speed adjusting screw.

c) Stop the engine.

2 Disconnect the control pressure cable end from the balljoint on the throttle linkage.

3 Push the inner cable back into the cable sheath (ie, push it towards the transmission), then pull it out again until slight resistance is felt.

4 At the point where resistance is just felt, it should be possible to fit the cable end back onto the throttle linkage balljoint. If the cable is too long or too short to achieve this, turn the cable sheath adjuster as necessary until the cable end can be easily refitted to the balljoint **(see illustration)**.

5 When the adjustment is correct, refit the air cleaner.

4-cylinder petrol fuel injection engines

Models with cable connecting plate

6 Remove the air cleaner as described in Chapter 4.

7 Loosen the clamp screw on the control pressure cable connecting plate **(see illustration)**.

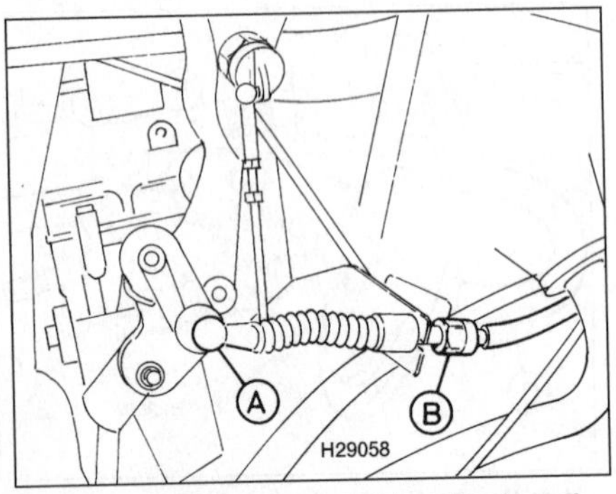

4.14 Control pressure cable adjustment - 4-cylinder petrol fuel injection engines with adjuster on cable sheath

A Cable end fitting
B Cable sheath adjuster

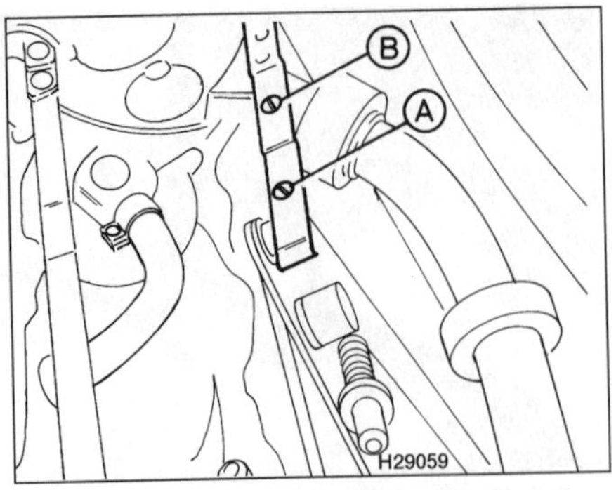

4.7 Control pressure cable adjustment - 4-cylinder petrol fuel injection engines with cable connecting plate

A Connecting plate
B Clamp screw

8 Extend the connecting plate, then retract the plate again until slight resistance is felt, and tighten the clamp screw.

9 Refit the air cleaner as described in Chapter 4.

Models with knurled adjuster wheel and pointer

10 Turn the adjuster wheel sufficiently to give approximately 1.0 mm of play between the cable end fitting and the spacer sleeve at the end of the adjuster.

11 Turn the adjuster wheel back until the tip of the adjuster pointer is positioned exactly above the groove in the centre of the adjuster wheel **(see illustration)**.

Models with adjuster on cable sheath

12 Disconnect the control pressure cable end from the balljoint on the throttle linkage.

13 Pull the cable forward until slight resistance is felt.

14 At the point where resistance is just felt, it should be possible to fit the cable end back onto the throttle linkage balljoint. If the cable is too long or too short to achieve this, turn the cable sheath adjuster as necessary until the cable end can be easily refitted to the balljoint **(see illustration)**.

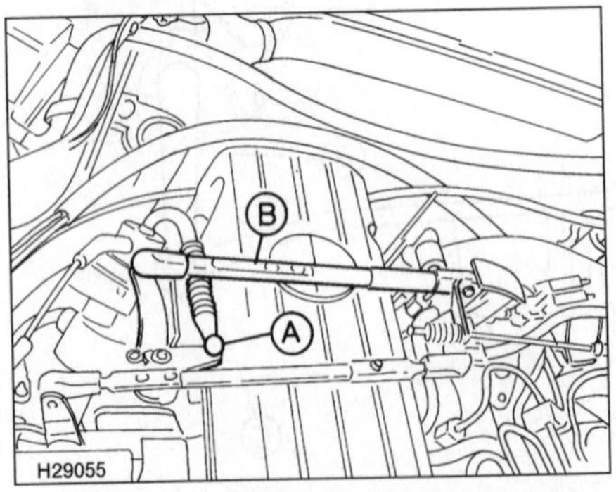

4.18 Control pressure cable adjustment - diesel engines

A Control pressure cable end fitting
B Throttle lever connecting plate

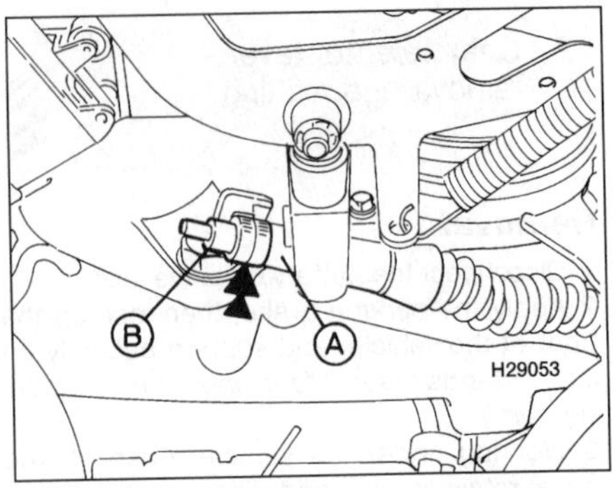

4.11 Control pressure cable adjustment - 4-cylinder petrol fuel injection engines with knurled adjuster wheel and pointer

A Adjuster wheel
B Spacer sleeve
Groove in adjuster wheel arrowed

6-cylinder petrol engines

Models with adjuster on cable sheath

15 Proceed as described in paragraphs 12 to 14.

Models with knurled adjuster wheel and pointer

16 Proceed as described in paragraphs 10 and 11.

Diesel engines

17 Disconnect the control pressure cable from the balljoint on the throttle linkage.

18 Loosen the clamping screw(s) on the throttle lever connecting plate, then pull the two sections of the plate apart as far as the stop **(see illustration)**.

19 Pull the control pressure cable forwards until slight resistance is felt.

20 At the point where resistance is just felt, it should be possible to fit the cable end back onto the throttle linkage balljoint. If necessary, adjust the length of the connecting plate until the cable end can be easily refitted to the balljoint.

5 Starter inhibitor/reversing light switch - removal, refitting and adjustment

Removal

1 Raise the bonnet, and place a thin sheet of metal (approximately 300 mm square) at the rear of the engine compartment bulkhead, to protect the bulkhead insulation during the following procedure.

2 Apply the parking brake, then jack up the front of the vehicle and support securely on axle stands (see *"Jacking and vehicle support"*).

3 Release the exhaust system from the rear mountings (with reference to Chapter 4 if necessary), then support the system using wire or string, approximately 500 mm lower than its normal fitted position.

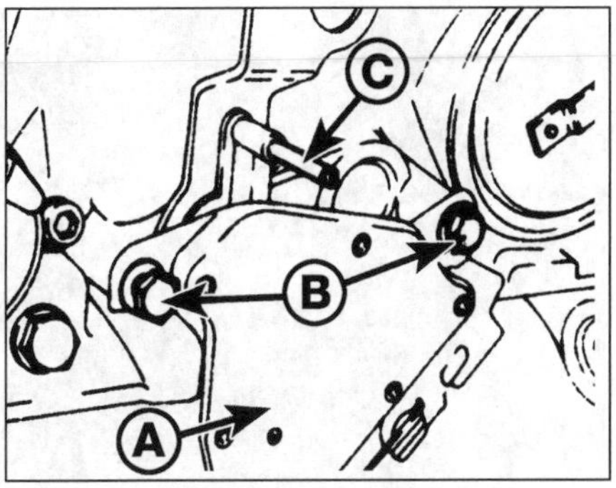

5.14 Starter inhibitor/reversing light switch adjustment

A Starter inhibitor/reversing light switch
B Switch securing screws
C 4.0 mm twist drill

4 On models fitted with an auxiliary heater, take care not to damage the coolant hose at the rear of the engine compartment during the following procedure.
5 Move the selector lever on the transmission to position "N".
6 Working under the vehicle, prise off the metal retaining clip, and disconnect the gear selector lever from the selector rod.
7 Unbolt the exhaust mounting bracket from the transmission and the exhaust system, and remove the bracket.
8 Place a trolley jack and interposed block of wood beneath the engine/transmission rear mounting bracket, and raise the jack to just take the weight of the transmission.
9 Unbolt the rear engine/transmission support bracket from the vehicle floor.
10 Carefully lower the jack to lower the rear of the transmission sufficiently for access to the starter inhibitor/reversing light switch. Take care not to damage the components at the rear of the engine compartment.
11 Release the clip securing the speedometer cable to the transmission.
12 Swivel the locking clip upwards, then pull the wiring connector from the starter inhibitor/reversing light switch.
13 Remove the two securing screws, and withdraw the switch from the transmission.

Refitting and adjustment

14 Locate the switch in position on the transmission, ensuring that the peg on the switch engages with the corresponding hole in the selector lever **(see illustration)**. Ensure that the selector lever is in position "N" (the positions are marked on the transmission casing).
15 Insert a 4.0 mm diameter twist drill or rod through the selector lever and switch peg until it engages with the locating hole in the switch housing.
16 Tighten the switch securing screws, then withdraw the drill or rod.
17 Reconnect the switch wiring connector, and secure with the locking clip.
18 Raise the jack, and refit the bolts securing the rear engine/transmission support bracket to the vehicle floor.
19 Refit the exhaust mounting bracket.
20 Clip the speedometer cable into position.
21 Reconnect the gear selector rod to the selector lever and secure with the retaining clip.
22 Reconnect the exhaust system to the rear mounting.
23 Lower the vehicle to the ground, and remove the metal protector from the engine compartment bulkhead.

6 Automatic transmission - removal and refitting

Removal

Note: *This is a difficult operation, due to the limited access to the engine-to-transmission bolts, and to the weight of the transmission assembly. It is suggested that the procedure is read through thoroughly before starting the operation. Suitable ratchet extensions may be required to reach some of the engine-to-transmission bolts.*
1 Raise the bonnet, and place a thin sheet of metal (approximately 300 mm square) at the rear of the engine compartment bulkhead, to protect the bulkhead insulation and the brake pipes during the following procedure.
2 Disconnect the battery negative lead.
3 On models fitted with an auxiliary heater, take care not to damage the coolant hose at the rear of the engine compartment during the following procedure. Unbolt the transmission fluid level dipstick tube from the cylinder head.
4 Disconnect the transmission control pressure cable from the throttle linkage on the inlet manifold.
5 Apply the parking brake, then jack up the vehicle and support securely on axle stands (see *"Jacking and vehicle support"*). The vehicle must be raised sufficiently to enable the transmission to be lowered and removed from under the vehicle. Where applicable, remove the engine undershield, with reference to Chapter 11.
6 Where applicable, unbolt the crossmember (located in front of the transmission sump) from the vehicle floor. Discard the securing bolts, new ones must be used on refitting.
7 Place a suitable container beneath the main transmission fluid drain plug, then unscrew the drain plug, and drain the transmission fluid (see Chapter 1).
8 Reposition the container beneath the torque converter aperture in the transmission casing. Using a socket on the crankshaft pulley/vibration damper hub, turn the crankshaft until the torque converter drain plug is aligned with the transmission aperture **(see illustration)**. Unscrew the drain plug, then drain the torque converter fluid.
9 Prise the plastic plug from the transmission bellhousing for access to the torque converter-to-driveplate bolts **(see illustration)**.
10 Unscrew the six torque converter-to-driveplate bolts, turning the crankshaft for access to each pair of bolts in turn.
11 Place a small wooden block between the engine sump and the welded crossmember under the vehicle floor.
12 Remove the complete exhaust system as described in Chapter 4.
13 Where applicable, unbolt the exhaust heat shield from the vehicle floor for access to the propeller shaft intermediate bearing assembly **(see illustration)**.

7B

6.8 Torque converter drain plug (arrowed) aligned with transmission aperture

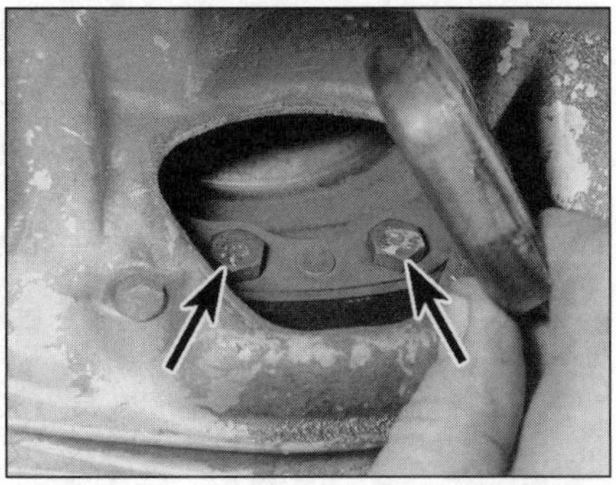

6.9 Prise out the plastic plug for access to the torque converter-to-driveplate bolts (arrowed)

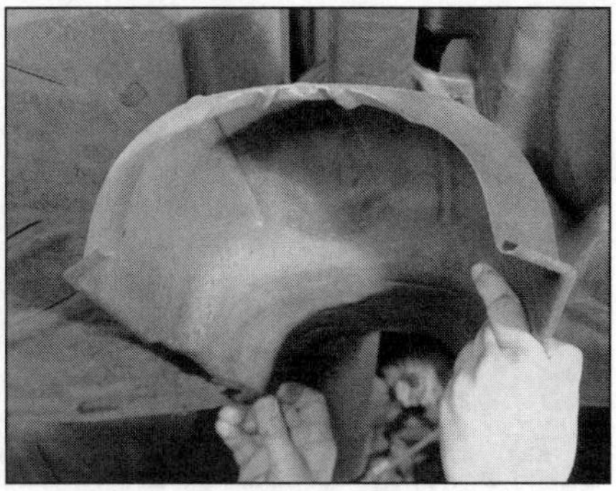

6.13 Remove the exhaust heat shield for access to the propeller shaft

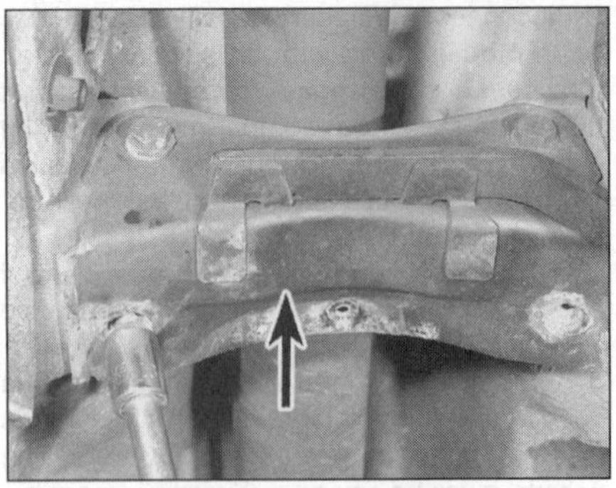

6.14 Unbolt the exhaust mounting bracket (arrowed) from the vehicle floor

6.16 Slacken the propeller shaft clamp nut (arrowed)

6.18 Unbolt the rear engine/transmission support bracket (arrowed)

14 Unbolt the exhaust mounting brackets from the vehicle floor (under the propeller shaft), and from the transmission, if not already done **(see illustration)**. Where applicable, unclip the wiring from the bracket on the transmission.

15 Disconnect the propeller shaft from the transmission flange with reference to Chapter 8.

16 Slacken the clamp nut at the propeller shaft intermediate bearing, then slacken (do not remove) the intermediate bearing securing nuts, and push the propeller shaft rearwards as far as possible **(see illustration)**.

17 Support the transmission using a trolley jack and large flat interposed block of wood under the transmission sump.

18 Unbolt the rear engine/transmission support bracket from the transmission and the vehicle floor, and remove the bracket **(see illustration)**.

19 Disconnect the wiring plug from the kickdown solenoid, at the rear right-hand corner of the transmission **(see illustration)**.

20 Unscrew the clamp bolt, and pull the speedometer cable from the transmission, with reference to Chapter 12 if necessary **(see illustrations)**. Where applicable, release the cable-tie(s) securing the cable to the transmission.

21 Release the starter inhibitor/reversing light switch wiring connector locking clip by pushing it upwards off the connector lug. Carefully prise off the switch wiring connector, using two screwdrivers **(see illustration)**.

22 Where applicable, unscrew the knurled locking ring, and disconnect the wiring plug from the left-hand side of the transmission **(see illustration)**.

23 Work around the transmission, and disconnect any remaining wiring connectors. Release the wiring from any clips and/or brackets on the transmission casing, and move the wiring clear of the transmission.

24 Disconnect the vacuum lines from the vacuum unit on the left-hand side of the transmission **(see illustration)**. Again, work around the transmission, and disconnect any remaining vacuum pipes. Release the pipes from any clips and/or brackets on the

6.19 Disconnect the wiring plug from the kickdown solenoid

6.20a Unscrew the clamp bolt . . .

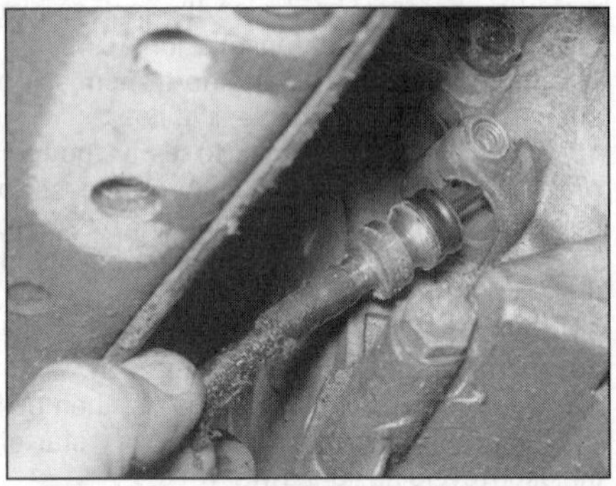

6.20b . . . and pull out the speedometer cable

6.21 Disconnect the starter inhibitor/reversing light switch wiring connector (arrowed)

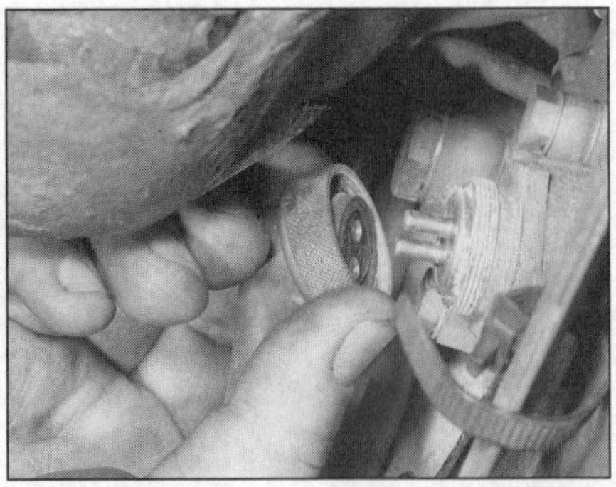

6.22 Unscrew the knurled locking ring and disconnect the wiring plug

6.24 Disconnect the vacuum lines from the vacuum unit (arrowed)

6.26 Disconnect the transmission fluid cooler pipes (arrowed)

transmission casing, and move the pipes clear of the transmission. Note that on some models, it may be necessary to disconnect certain vacuum pipes from the inlet manifold in the engine compartment to enable them to be moved clear of the transmission.

25 Prise off the securing clips, and disconnect the selector rod from the selector lever on the transmission, and the gear selector lever, with reference to Section 3 if necessary. Remove the selector rod.

26 Unscrew the union bolts and disconnect the transmission fluid cooler feed and return pipes from the transmission **(see illustration)**. Recover the sealing rings, and cover or plug the open ends of the pipes and transmission to prevent dirt entry and further fluid loss.

27 Unbolt the transmission fluid cooler pipes brackets from the transmission and engine (where applicable), and move the pipes clear to enable transmission removal.

28 Pull up the locking clip, and remove the transmission fluid level dipstick.

29 Unscrew the clamp bolt securing the transmission fluid dipstick tube/filler pipe to the transmission casing. Where applicable, unscrew the engine-to-transmission bolt, which secures the dipstick tube/filler pipe bracket to the transmission bellhousing.

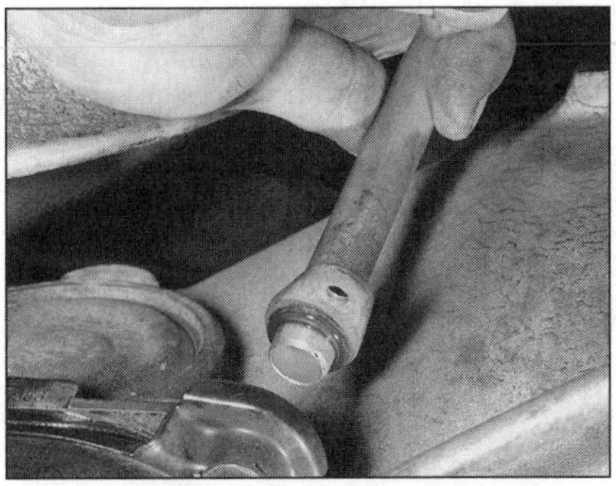

6.29 Withdraw the dipstick tube/filler pipe

Withdraw the dipstick tube/filler pipe from the transmission **(see illustration)**.

30 Remove the starter motor as described in Chapter 5A.

31 Ensure that the transmission is adequately supported, then lower the assembly as far as possible, until the engine is resting on the block of wood inserted between the crossmember and the sump. Take care not to damage the brake pipes and any other components at the rear of the bulkhead, as the cylinder head may be forced into the bulkhead.

32 Unscrew all the engine-to-transmission bolts, leaving one bolt on either side of the transmission. Access to the upper bolts is very difficult, even with the assembly tilted, and several long ratchet extensions may be required. On some engines (particularly 6-cylinder engines), the top bolt cannot be reached from underneath, and access is most easily obtained, with a spanner, from the right-hand side as follows.

a) *Unbolt the heat shields from the area around the steering box for access to the exhaust manifold securing nuts.*
b) *Unscrew the securing nuts, and remove the (rear) exhaust manifold from the cylinder head. Recover the gasket(s).*

Note the locations of the earth strap, and any brackets secured by the engine-to-transmission bolts **(see illustration)**.

33 Once the upper engine-to-transmission bolts have been removed, raise the transmission until the engine/transmission assembly is level.

34 On models with diesel engines, it is necessary to hold the torque converter in position as the transmission is withdrawn, otherwise there is a risk of it falling out (other models have a plastic retainer built into the bellhousing). The best way of holding the torque converter in position is to insert a suitable bar through the aperture in the bellhousing, into the torque converter oil drain hole (see paragraph 8).

35 Unscrew the remaining two engine-to-transmission bolts, then slide the transmission rearwards as far as possible, and lower the transmission from under the vehicle using the jack. Take great care not to allow the torque converter to fall out as the transmission is withdrawn.

Warning: The transmission is heavy!

36 To remove the torque converter, proceed as follows **(see illustration)**.

a) *Support the transmission on wooden blocks in a vertical position, with the bellhousing and torque converter pointing vertically upwards.*
b) *Using an 8.0 mm Allen key, turn the torque converter plastic holding pin through a quarter-turn anti-clockwise, then remove the holding pin (on models with diesel engines, remove the holding bar inserted during transmission removal).*
c) *Bolt two suitable lifting handles to the torque converter, using long bolts in the torque converter-to-driveplate bolt holes, and use the handles to lift the torque converter from the transmission. Pull*

6.32 Unscrew the engine-to-transmission bolts, noting the location of the earth strap

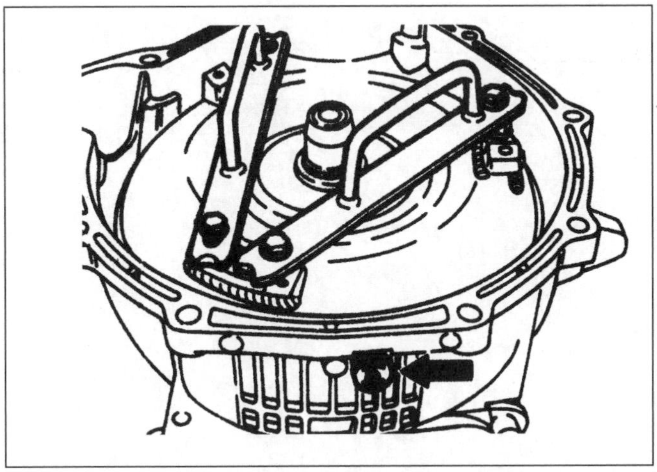

6.36 Lifting handles bolted to torque converter. Plastic holding pin arrowed

evenly on both handles. Alternatively, screw two long bolts into two of the torque converter-to-driveplate bolt holes, and use the bolts to lift out the torque converter. Be prepared for fluid spillage.

d) Store the torque converter in a safe place, where it cannot be damaged.

Refitting

37 Where applicable, refit the torque converter as follows.

a) Lightly grease the torque converter drive flange. Molykote grease is recommended.

b) Using the two bolts, manipulate the converter into position. Move the converter back and forth as it is fitted to ensure that the teeth mesh with the transmission input shaft.

c) Where applicable, fit the plastic holding pin, and turn it a quarter-turn clockwise to secure (on diesel engine models, re-engage the torque converter holding bar with the oil drain hole in the converter, as during removal).

d) Turn the torque converter until two of the torque converter-to-flywheel bolt holes are positioned at the bottom of the transmission bellhousing.

38 Support the transmission using the trolley jack and block of wood, as during removal, then raise the transmission into position beneath the vehicle.

39 Slide the transmission forwards until the bellhousing is firmly mated with the engine.

40 Refit and tighten the engine-to-transmission bolts, ensuring that the earth strap and any brackets noted during removal are in place.

41 Refit the torque converter-to-driveplate bolts, and tighten them to the specified torque. Turn the crankshaft as during removal for access to the bolts (where applicable, remove the holding tool from the torque converter, and refit the fluid drain plug).

42 Further refitting is a reversal of removal, bearing in mind the following points.

a) Use new sealing rings when connecting the transmission fluid cooler pipes.

b) Reconnect the propeller shaft as described in Chapter 8.

c) Where applicable, tighten fixings to the specified torque.

d) Ensure that all wires and vacuum lines are correctly reconnected and routed as noted before removal.

e) Refit the exhaust system with reference to Chapter 4.

f) Refill the transmission with fluid as described in Chapter 1.

g) On completion, check the adjustment of the control pressure cable as described in Section 4.

7 Automatic transmission overhaul - general information

In the event of a fault occurring with the transmission, it is first necessary to determine whether it is of an electrical, mechanical or hydraulic nature, and to do this special test equipment is required. It is therefore essential to have the work carried out by a Mercedes-Benz dealer if a transmission fault is suspected.

Do not remove the transmission from the vehicle for possible repair before professional fault diagnosis has been carried out, since most tests require the transmission to be in the vehicle.

Chapter 8
Final drive, driveshafts and propeller shaft

Contents

Driveshaft - removal and refitting 5
Driveshaft gaiters - renewal 6
Final drive unit - draining and refilling 2
Final drive unit - removal and refitting 3
Final drive unit oil level check . . . . See Chapter 1
Final drive unit oil seals - renewal 4
General information 1
Propeller shaft - removal and refitting 7
Propeller shaft rubber coupling - check and renewal 8
Propeller shaft support bearing - check and renewal 9
Propeller shaft universal joint - check and renewal 10

Degrees of difficulty

Easy, suitable for novice with little experience	**Fairly easy,** suitable for beginner with some experience	**Fairly difficult,** suitable for competent DIY mechanic	**Difficult,** suitable for experienced DIY mechanic	**Very difficult,** suitable for expert DIY or professional

Specifications

Final drive

Type	Unsprung, casing bolted to rear suspension crossmember

Driveshaft

Type	Steel shafts with ball-and-cage type constant velocity joints at each end

Propeller shaft

Type	Two-piece tubular shaft with centre bearing and universal joint. Rubber coupling at front and rear joints

Torque wrench settings

Torque wrench settings	Nm	lbf ft
Final drive unit		
Mounting bolts:		
Front bolts	45	33
Rear bolts	50	37
Driveshaft		
Shaft to final drive flange bolts	70	52
Driveshaft retaining nut	280 to 320	207 to 236
Propeller shaft		
Coupling bolt nuts:		
M10 bolts	45	33
M12 bolts	60	44
Sling bracket / seat belt anchor nuts	280	207
Support bearing bracket bolts	25	18
Threaded sleeve nut	30 to 40	22 to 30
Transmission rear mounting bracket:		
Bracket to body bolts	45	33
Bracket to transmission nut	70	52
Roadwheels		
Wheel bolts	110	81

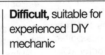

1 General information

Power is transmitted from the transmission to the rear axle by a two-piece propeller shaft, joined in front of the centre bearing by a "slip joint", a sliding, splined coupling. The slip joint allows slight fore-and-aft movement of the propeller shaft. The propeller shaft is attached to the flanges of the transmission and final drive unit by flexible rubber couplings, a vibration damper being fitted between the front coupling and the shaft. The middle of the propeller shaft is supported by the centre bearing which is bolted to the vehicle body. A universal joint is located at the rear of the centre bearing, to compensate for movement of the transmission and differential on their mountings and for any flexing of the chassis.

The final drive assembly includes the drive pinion, the ring gear, the differential and the output flanges. The drive pinion, which drives the ring gear, is also known as the differential input shaft and is connected to the propeller shaft via an input flange. The differential is bolted to the ring gear and drives the rear wheels through a pair of output flanges bolted to driveshafts with constant velocity (CV) joints at either end. The differential allows the wheels to turn at different speeds when cornering.

The driveshafts deliver power from the final drive unit output flanges to the rear wheels. The driveshafts are equipped with Constant Velocity (CV) joints at each end. The inner CV joints are bolted to the differential flanges. and the outer CV joints engage the splines of the wheel hubs, and are secured by a large nut.

Major repair work on the differential assembly components (drive pinion, ring-and-pinion, and differential) requires many special tools and a high degree of expertise, and therefore should not be attempted by the home mechanic. If major repairs become necessary, we recommend that they be performed by a Mercedes-Benz service department or other suitably equipped automotive engineer.

2 Final drive unit - draining and refilling

1 This operation is much quicker and more efficient if the car is first taken on a journey of sufficient length to warm the final drive unit up to normal operating temperature.

2 Park the car on level ground, switch off the ignition and apply the parking brake firmly. For improved access, jack up the rear of the car and support it securely on axle stands (see "*Jacking and vehicle support*"). Note that the car must be lowered to the ground and level, to ensure accuracy, when refilling and checking the oil level.

3 Wipe clean the area around the filler/level plug, which is situated on the left-hand side of the final drive unit **(see illustration)** and unscrew it.

4 Position a suitable container under the drain plug and unscrew the plug from the right-hand side of the housing **(see illustration)**.

5 Allow the oil to drain completely into the container. If the oil is hot, take precautions against scalding. Clean both the filler/level and the drain plugs, being especially careful to wipe any metallic particles off the magnetic inserts.

6 When the oil has finished draining, clean the drain plug threads and those of the transmission casing, and refit the drain plug. If the car was raised for the draining operation, now lower it to the ground.

7 Refilling the final drive unit is an extremely awkward operation. Above all, allow plenty of time for the oil level to settle properly before checking it. Note that the car must be parked on flat level ground when checking the oil level.

8 Refill the final drive unit with the exact amount of the specified type of oil then check the oil level as described in Chapter 1; if the correct amount was poured into the final drive unit and a large amount flows out on checking the level, refit the filler/level plug and take the car on a short journey so that the new oil is distributed fully around the final drive components, then check the level again on your return.

3 Final drive unit - removal and refitting

Note: *New propeller shaft rear coupling nuts, driveshaft joint bolts and final drive unit mounting bolt nuts will be required on refitting.*

Removal

1 Chock the front wheels. Jack up the rear of the vehicle and support it on axle stands (see "*Jacking and vehicle support*"). Remove both rear wheels.

2 On models with ABS, carry out the following operations:

a) *Drain the oil from the final drive unit, as described in Chapter 1.*

b) *Refer to Chapter 9 and remove the wheel speed sensor from the final drive casing.*

3 With reference to Chapter 4D, remove the nuts and lower the exhaust pipe heat shield away from the floorpan.

4 Using a 41 mm open-ended spanner, slacken the propeller shaft clamping nut, located just to the rear of the centre support bearing, approximately two turns. Use a second spanner to hold the propeller shaft stationary as the clamping nut is slackened.

5 Undo the two screws securing the propeller shaft centre support bearing to the underbody.

6 Undo the three nuts and remove the bolts securing the propeller shaft rear flexible coupling to the differential pinion flange.

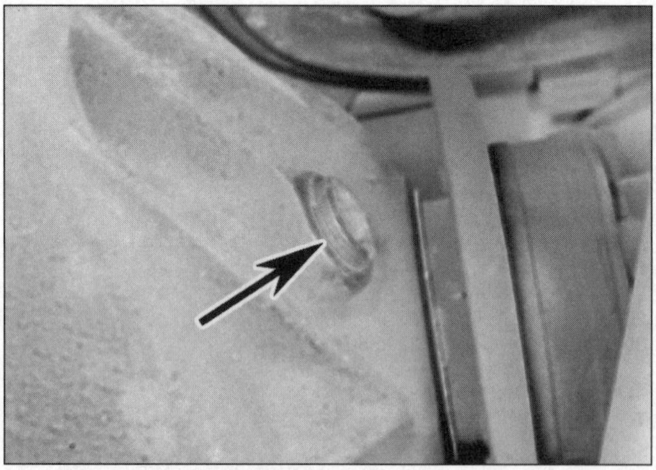

2.3 Final drive unit filler/level plug

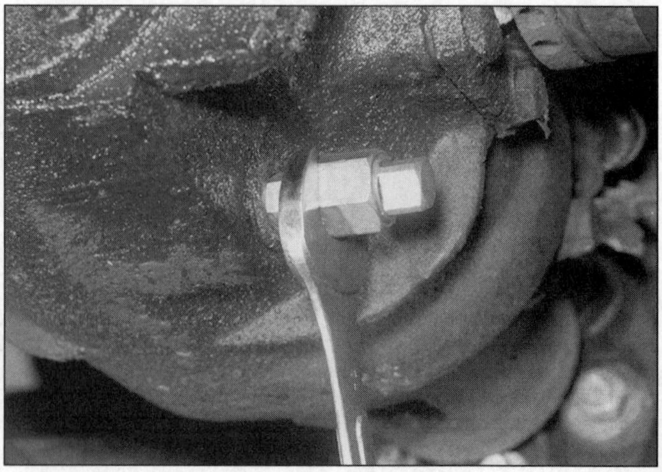

2.4 Final drive unit drain plug

7 Push the propeller shaft forwards as far as it will go to disengage the pinion flange centering sleeve. Move the disconnected propeller shaft to the side and support it using a length of wire tied to the parking brake cable.
8 Using a multi-toothed key or socket bit, unscrew the bolts securing both driveshaft inner constant velocity joints to the differential drive flanges. Remove the bolts and locking plates.
9 Push the driveshafts outwards to clear the drive flanges and tie them up, using a length of wire, to the rear suspension camber strut.
10 Place a jack beneath the final drive housing and just take the weight of the unit.
11 Undo the bolts at the rear securing the final drive housing to the subframe, and remove the bolts together with the locking plates **(see illustration)**.
12 Undo the nut and remove the socket-headed bolt securing the housing to the subframe at the front **(see illustration)**.
13 Lower the jack and remove the final drive housing from under the car.

Refitting

14 To refit the unit, position it centrally within the subframe and refit the front retaining bolt and nut finger-tight.
15 Refit the four rear retaining bolts and locking plates and tighten to the specified torque. Now tighten the front nut and bolt to the specified torque as well.
16 Engage the propeller shaft over the pinion flange centering sleeve, and secure the flexible coupling to the pinion flange with the three nuts and bolts.
17 Refit the two centre support bearing retaining bolts, but tighten them finger-tight only at this stage.
18 With the propeller shaft in position, tighten the clamping nut, then fully tighten the centre bearing retaining bolts to the specified torque.
19 Refit the exhaust heat shield.
20 Lightly lubricate the driveshaft inner constant velocity joint-to-differential drive flange bolt threads with light oil, refit the bolts and locking plates, and tighten to the specified torque.

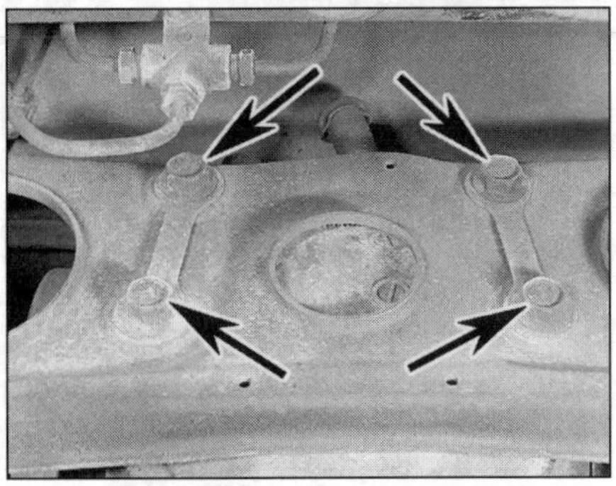

3.11 Final drive housing to subframe rear retaining bolts (arrowed)

21 On cars with ABS brakes, refit the rpm sender and secure with the retaining bolt, after first removing any metallic particles which may have collected on the sensor magnetic probe.
22 Unscrew the housing filler/level plug and refill or top-up the final drive oil to the level of the plug orifice, using the specified lubricant. Refit the plug and tighten securely.
23 Remove the stands and lower the car to the ground.

4 Final drive unit oil seals - renewal

Renewal of the final drive unit oil seals is a complex task, requiring the final drive unit to be partially dismantled. This operation should therefore be entrusted to a Mercedes-Benz dealer.

5 Driveshaft - removal and refitting

Note: *A new driveshaft retaining nut and bolts will be required on refitting.*

Removal

1 Remove the wheel trim/hub cap (as applicable) and, using a hammer and pointed-

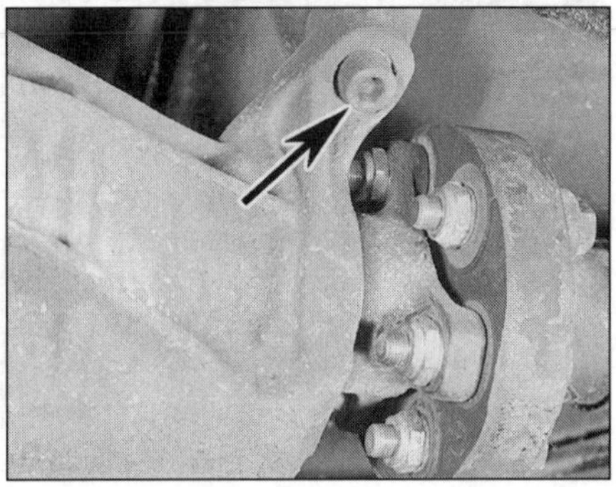

3.12 Final drive housing to subframe retaining bolt (arrowed)

nose chisel, carefully relieve the driveshaft retaining nut staking. Slacken the driveshaft retaining nut with the vehicle resting on its wheels. Also slacken the wheel bolts.
2 Chock the front wheels, then jack up the rear of the vehicle and support it on axle stands (see "*Jacking and vehicle support*").
3 Remove the relevant rear roadwheel. If the left-hand driveshaft is to be removed, note that it may be necessary to remove the exhaust system tailpipe to gain the relevant clearance required to manoeuvre the shaft out of position (see Chapter 4).
4 Slacken and remove the retaining bolts and plates securing the driveshaft to the final drive unit flange and support the driveshaft by tying it to the vehicle underbody using a piece of wire **(see illustration)**. **Note:** *Do not allow the driveshaft to hang under its own weight as the CV joint may be damaged.* Discard the bolts, new ones should be used on refitting.
5 Remove the driveshaft retaining nut and withdraw the driveshaft outer constant velocity joint from the hub assembly. If necessary, tap the joint out of the hub using a soft-faced mallet. If this fails to free it from the hub, the joint will have to be pressed out using a suitable tool which is bolted to the hub.
6 Remove the driveshaft from underneath the vehicle.

Refitting

7 Refitting is the reverse of removal noting the following points **(see illustrations)**.

5.4 Slacken and remove the retaining bolts and plates securing the driveshaft to the final drive unit flange

5.7a Lubricate the face and the threads of the new driveshaft nut with clean engine oil

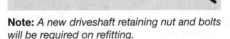

5.7b Tighten the driveshaft retaining nut to the specified torque . . .

5.7c . . . then stake it firmly into the driveshaft groove using a hammer and punch

a) Lubricate the threads and face of the new driveshaft nut and retaining bolts with clean engine oil prior to fitting.
b) Fit the new retaining bolts with the retaining plates and tighten them to the specified torque.
c) Tighten the driveshaft retaining nut to the specified torque and stake it firmly into the driveshaft groove using a hammer and punch. If necessary, lightly tighten the nut and then tighten and stake the nut once the vehicle is resting on its wheels .

6 Driveshaft gaiters - renewal

1 Remove the driveshaft as described in Section 5.
2 Clean the driveshaft and mount it in a vice.
3 Lever off the sealing cover from the end of the inner constant velocity (CV) joint **(see illustration)**.
4 Cut/release the two inner joint gaiter retaining clips and slide the gaiter along the driveshaft **(see illustration)**.
5 Wipe away excess grease and remove the inner joint circlip from the end of the driveshaft **(see illustration)**.
6 Securely support the joint inner member and tap the driveshaft out of position using a hammer and suitable drift. If the joint is a tight fit, a suitable puller will be required to draw off the joint. Do not dismantle the inner joint.

6.3 Remove the sealing cover from the end of the inner CV joint

7 With the joint removed, slide the gaiter off from the end of the driveshaft.
8 Release the outer joint gaiter retaining clips then slide the gaiter along the shaft and remove it.
9 Thoroughly clean the constant velocity joints using paraffin, or a suitable solvent, and dry thoroughly. Carry out a visual inspection as follows.
10 Move the inner splined driving member from side to side to expose each ball in turn at the top of its track. Examine the balls for cracks, flat spots or signs of surface pitting.
11 Inspect the ball tracks on the inner and outer members. If the tracks have widened, the balls will no longer be a tight fit. At the same time check the ball cage windows for wear or cracking between the windows. If necessary the dust covers can be removed from each joint assembly and renewed; on refitting ensure that the joint and cover mating surfaces are clean and dry and apply a smear of sealant to the cover surface to prevent leakage.
12 If on inspection any of the constant velocity joint components are found to be worn or damaged, it must be renewed. The inner joint is available separately but if the outer joint is worn it will be necessary to renew the complete joint and driveshaft assembly. If the joints are in satisfactory condition, obtain new gaiter repair kits which contain gaiters, retaining clips, an inner constant velocity joint circlip and the correct type and quantity of grease required.

6.4 Cut the retaining clips and disengage the inner gaiter from the joint

6.5 Remove the circlip and tap/pull the inner joint off the end of the driveshaft

13 Tape over the splines on the end of the driveshaft.
14 Slide the new outer gaiter onto the end of the driveshaft.
15 Pack the outer joint with the specified type of grease. Work the grease well into the bearing tracks whilst twisting the joint, and fill the rubber gaiter with any excess **(see illustration)**.
16 Ease the gaiter over the joint and ensure that the gaiter lips are correctly located on both the driveshaft and constant velocity joint. Lift the outer sealing lip of the gaiter to equalise air pressure within the gaiter **(see illustrations)**.

6.15 Pack the driveshaft outer joint with the grease supplied with the repair kit

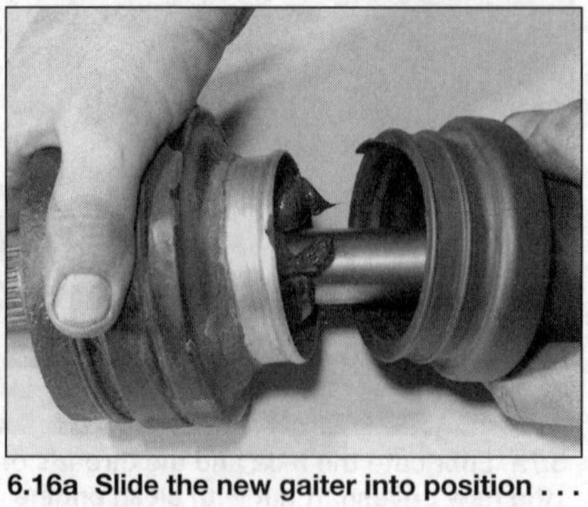

6.16a Slide the new gaiter into position . . .

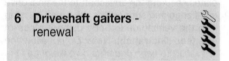

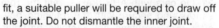

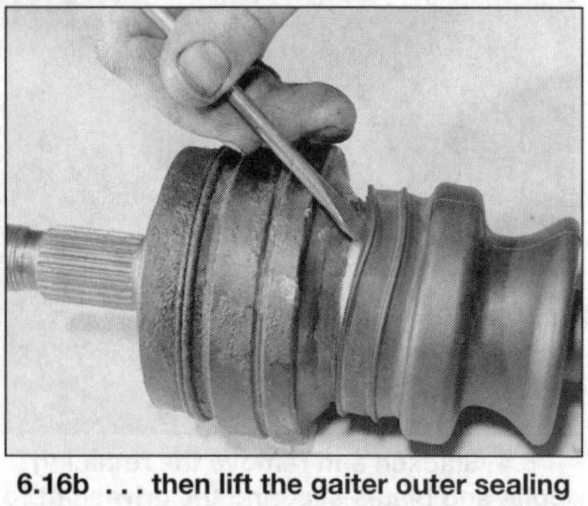

6.16b . . . then lift the gaiter outer sealing lip to equalise air pressure in the gaiter

6.17a Hook the retaining clip tightly around the gaiter . . .

6.17b . . . and remove any slack by compressing the raised section of the clip

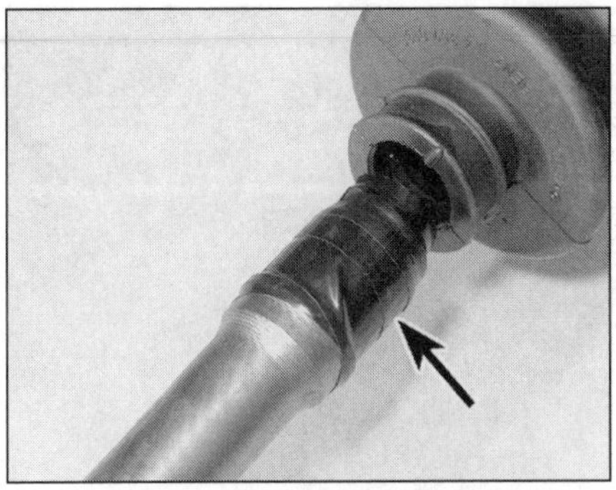

6.18 Slide on the new inner joint gaiter then remove the protective tape (arrowed) . . .

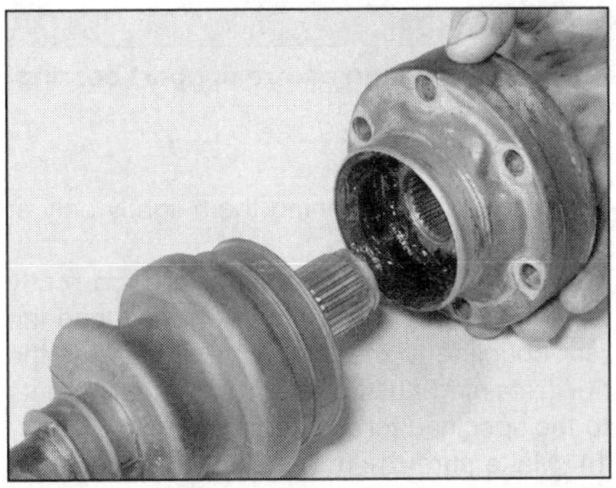

6.19 . . . and fit the inner joint assembly

6.20 Pack the inner joint with the special grease supplied

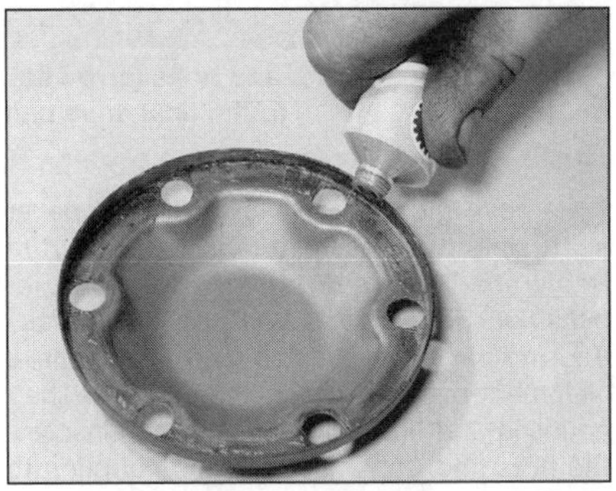

6.22 Ensure the sealing cover mating surface is clean and dry and apply a smear of sealant to it before fitting it to the inner joint

17 Fit the large metal retaining clip to the gaiter. Pull the clip as tight as possible and locate its hook in one of the slots. Remove all slack from the retaining clip by compressing the raised section of the clip using special pliers; if the special pliers are not available, **carefully** compress the clip using side-cutters taking care not to cut the clip. Secure the small retaining clip using the same procedure **(see illustrations)**.

18 Slide the new inner joint gaiter onto the driveshaft **(see illustration)**.

19 Remove the tape from the driveshaft splines and fit the inner constant velocity joint. Press the joint fully onto the shaft and secure it in position with a new circlip **(see illustration)**.

20 Work the grease supplied fully into the inner joint and fill the gaiter with any excess **(see illustration)**.

21 Ease the gaiter over the joint and ensure that the gaiter lips are correctly located on both the driveshaft and constant velocity joint. Lift the outer sealing lip of the gaiter to equalise air pressure within the gaiter, and secure it in position with the retaining clips (see paragraph 17).

22 Ensure that the inner joint and dust cover mating surfaces are clean and dry then apply a smear of sealant to the inner edge of the cover and press the cover fully onto the inner joint **(see illustration)**.

23 Check that both constant velocity joints are free to move easily then refit the driveshaft as described in Section 5.

7 Propeller shaft - removal and refitting

Note: *New propeller shaft front and rear coupling nuts will be required on refitting.*

Removal

1 Chock the front wheels. Jack up the rear of the vehicle and support it on axle stands (see "*Jacking and vehicle support*").

2 Unbolt and remove the exhaust system heatshield(s) **(see illustration)**. Unbolt and remove the support bracket which is fitted across the propeller shaft tunnel to allow the shaft to be lowered out of position.

3 Place a jack with a block of wood underneath the transmission and raise the jack so that it is supporting the weight of the unit.

4 Unscrew the nut securing the rear mounting bracket to the transmission and the bolts securing it to the body and remove the mounting bracket .

5 Using a large open-ended spanner, loosen the threaded sleeve nut, which is situated near the support bearing, through a couple of turns taking care not to damage the rubber gaiter.

6 Make alignment marks between the shaft coupling and transmission flange then slacken and remove the retaining nuts and bolts securing the flexible coupling to the transmission **(see illustration)**. Discard the nuts, new ones should be used on refitting.

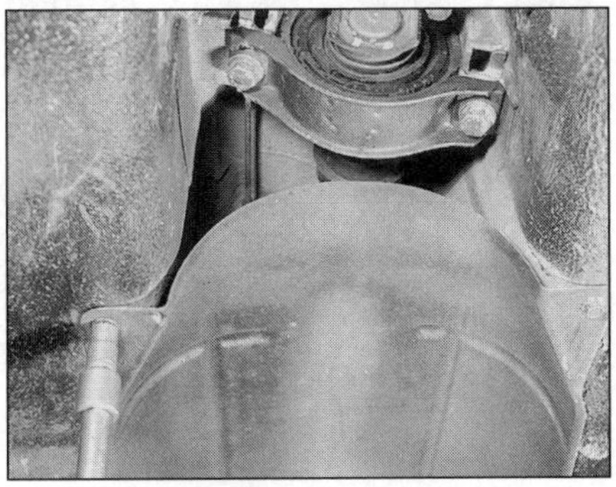

7.2 Unbolt and remove the exhaust system heatshield

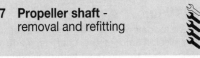

7.6 Remove the flexible coupling to the transmission flange nuts and bolts

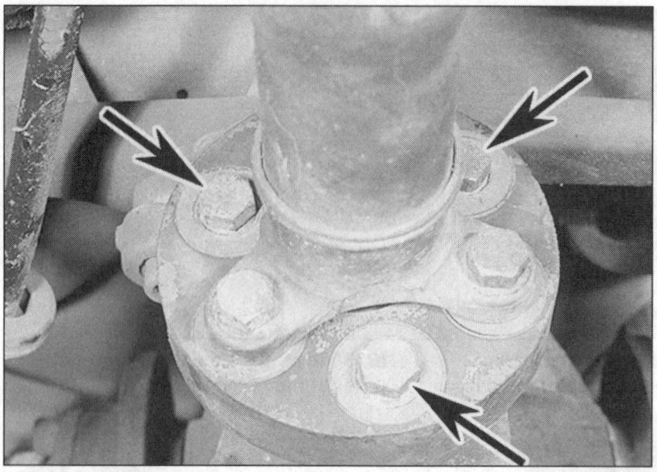

7.8 **Unscrew the nuts and bolts (arrowed) securing the coupling to the final drive unit**

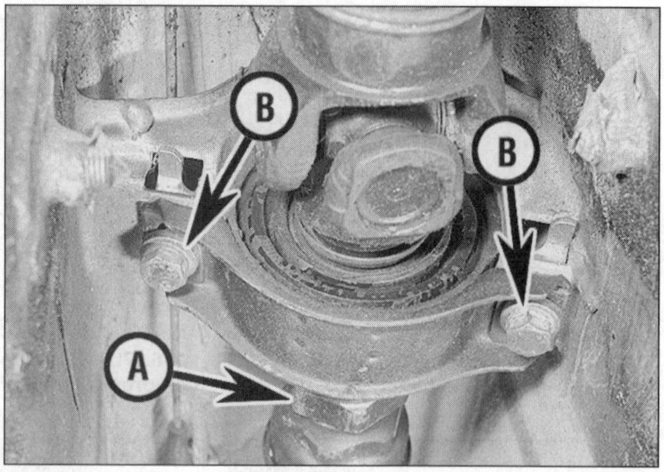

7.9a **Propeller shaft clamping nut (A) and centre support bearing bracket bolts (B)**

7 Remove the nuts and lower the propeller shaft sling bracket. **Note:** *On vehicles from September 1988 onwards, the sling bracket bolts/nuts double up as front seat belt fixings.*

8 Using paint or a suitable marker pen, make alignment marks between the propeller shaft coupling and final drive unit flange. Unscrew the nuts and bolts securing the coupling to the final drive unit and discard them; new ones must be used on refitting **(see illustration)**.

9 With the aid of an assistant, support the propeller shaft then unscrew the centre support bearing bracket retaining bolts. Slide the rear of the shaft forwards and disengage the shaft from the final drive unit. Free the front of the shaft from the transmission and remove the shaft assembly from underneath the vehicle **(see illustrations)**. **Note:** *Do not separate the two halves of the shaft without first making alignment marks. If the shafts are incorrectly joined, the propeller shaft assembly may become imbalanced, leading to noise and vibration during operation. On some models there are alignment marks already on the shaft; the raised mark on the front section must be positioned in between the two marks on the rear section universal joint.*

10 Inspect the rubber couplings, the support bearing and shaft universal joint as described in Sections 8, 9 and 10. Inspect the transmission flange locating pin and propeller shaft bush for signs of wear or damage and renew as necessary.

Refitting

11 On models where the shaft bush in the transmission end of the shaft is made of bronze lubricate the bush with molybdenum disulphide grease. Where the bush is not made of bronze use multi-purpose grease.

12 Manoeuvre the shaft into position, aligning the marks made prior to removal, and engage the shaft with the transmission and final drive unit flanges. With the marks correctly aligned, refit the support bracket retaining bolts, tightening them lightly only at this stage.

13 Making sure the marks are correctly aligned, insert the retaining bolts securing the rear coupling to the final drive unit and fit the new retaining nuts. Tighten the retaining nuts to the specified torque setting.

14 Make sure the front coupling is correctly aligned with the transmission flange and refit the coupling bolts. Fit the new retaining nuts and tighten them to the specified torque .

15 With both the front and rear couplings correctly tightened, tighten the centre bearing bracket bolts to the specified torque setting.

16 Tighten the threaded sleeve nut to the specified torque ensuring that the rubber gaiter remains correctly seated.

17 Refit the mounting bracket to the rear of the transmission and tighten its mounting bolts and nut to their specified torque settings.

18 Refit the exhaust system heatshield(s) and support brackets (as applicable) and lower the vehicle to the ground.

7.9b **Slide the rear of the shaft forwards and disengage the shaft from the final drive unit**

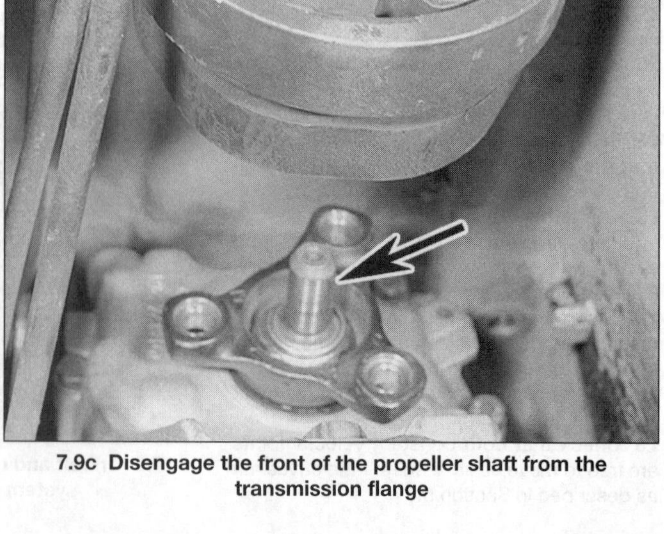

7.9c **Disengage the front of the propeller shaft from the transmission flange**

8.6a Refitting the vibration damper

8.6b On models where the bolt hole centres are positioned 40 mm out from the centre of the shaft, the damper should be fitted so that the raised pointer is positioned as shown

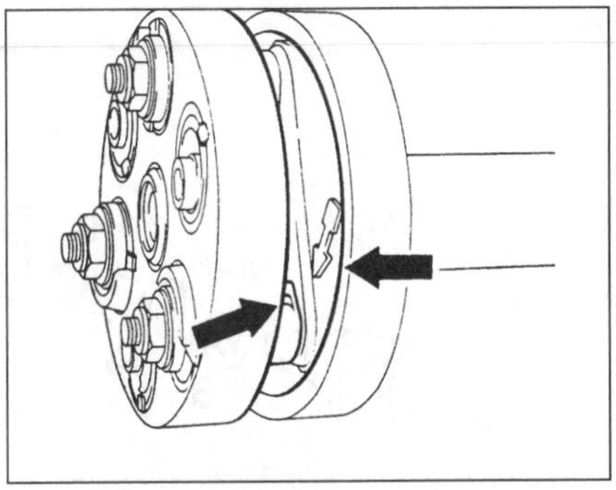

8.7a On models where the hole centres are 45 mm or more out from the centre, position the damper so that the arrow is pointing towards the raised lug on the flange (arrowed) - models up to 12/89

8 Propeller shaft rubber coupling - check and renewal

Check

1 Firmly apply the parking brake, then jack up the front of the vehicle and support it on axle stands (see "*Jacking and vehicle support*").

2 Closely examine the rubber couplings which link the propeller shaft to the transmission and final drive, looking for signs of damage such as cracking or splitting or for signs of general deterioration. If necessary, renew the coupling as follows.

Renewal

Note: *New propeller shaft coupling nuts will be required.*

3 Remove the propeller shaft as described in Section 7.

Front coupling

4 Make alignment marks between the coupling and vibration damper (where fitted) and propeller shaft.

5 Unscrew the retaining nuts then withdraw the bolts and remove the coupling from the propeller shaft. Inspect the vibration damper for signs of wear or damage and renew if necessary.

6 Position the vibration damper (where fitted) correctly in relation to the propeller shaft using the marks made prior to removal. On models where the bolt hole centres are positioned 40 mm out from the centre of the shaft (bolt hole centres diameter of 80 mm) the damper should be positioned so that its raised pointer is positioned as shown **(see illustrations)**.

7 On models where the hole centres are 45 mm or more out from the centre (diameter of 90 mm or more) position the damper so that its arrow is pointing towards the raised lug on the flange **(see illustrations)**.

8 Fit the new rubber coupling to the driveshaft ensuring that the side with the wording "DIESE SEITE ZUR GELENKWELLE" is facing towards the propeller shaft (where necessary) **(see illustration)**. Insert the retaining bolts then fit the new retaining nuts and tighten them to the specified torque.

9 Refit the propeller shaft as described in Section 7.

Rear coupling

10 Unscrew the retaining nuts then withdraw the bolts and remove the coupling from the propeller shaft.

11 Fit the new coupling, then fit the retaining bolts and new nuts, tightening them to the specified torque.

12 Refit the propeller shaft as described in Section 7.

9 Propeller shaft support bearing - check and renewal

Check

1 Wear in the support bearing will lead to noise and vibration when the vehicle is driven. The bearing is best checked with the propeller shaft removed (see Section 7).

2 Rotate the bearing and check that it turns smoothly with no sign of freeplay; if it's difficult to turn, or if it has a gritty feeling,

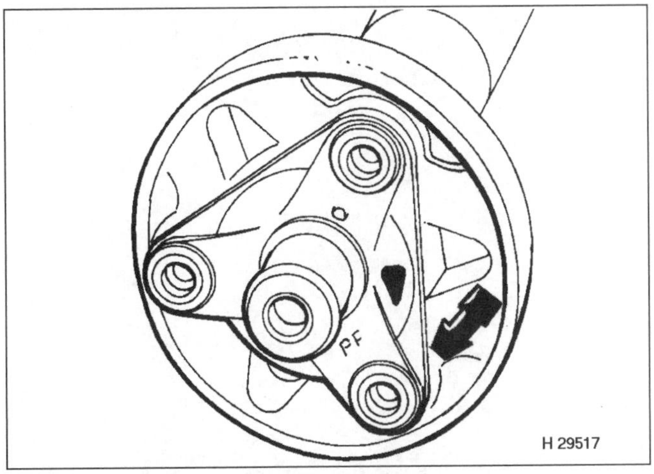

8.7b Vibration damper alignment arrow position - models from 01/90

8.8 Refit the rubber coupling, ensuring that the wording faces the damper/propeller shaft

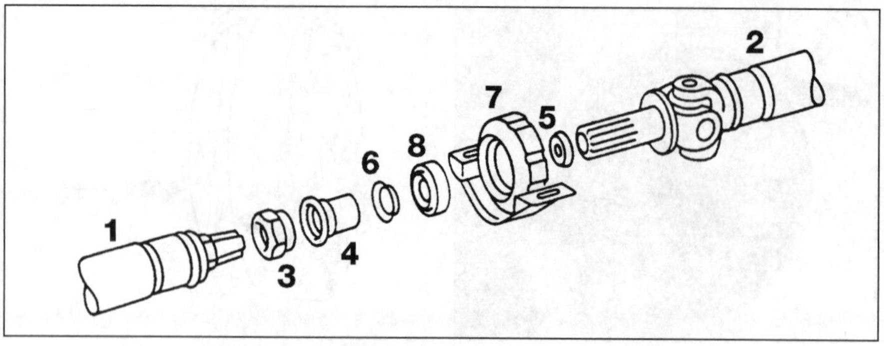

9.5 Propeller shaft centre bearing components

1 *Propeller shaft*
2 *Propeller shaft*
3 *Sleeve nut*
4 *Rubber gaiter*
5 *Protective cap*
6 *Protective cap*
7 *Centre mounting*
8 *Bearing*

renew it. Also inspect the rubber portion. If it's cracked or deteriorated, renew it.

Renewal

Note: *Bearing renewal requires the use of a puller and hydraulic press as well as suitable spacers. If access to suitable equipment cannot be gained entrust the task to your Mercedes-Benz dealer.*

3 Remove the propeller shaft as described in Section 7.

4 Make alignment marks between the front and rear sections of the propeller shaft noting that on some models there are alignment marks already on the shaft; the raised mark on the front section must be positioned in between the two marks on the rear section universal joint - see Section for details.

5 Release the rubber gaiter from the threaded sleeve nut then fully slacken the nut and separate the two shaft halves **(see illustration)**.

6 Remove the rubber gaiter from the rear section of the shaft.

7 Using a legged-puller, draw the centre mounting assembly **off** the end of the shaft, noting which way around the bracket is fitted. Recover the front and rear bearing covers.

8 Support the mounting bracket assembly and carefully press the bearing out of position using a tubular drift.

9 Inspect all components for signs of wear or damage and renew as necessary. Note that the bearing protective covers and the rubber gaiter should be renewed regardless of their apparent condition.

10 Support the mounting bracket securely and press the new bearing fully into position using a tubular drift which bears only on the bearing outer race.

11 Remove all traces of dirt from the propeller shaft and fit the new rear protective cap.

12 Ensure that the mounting bracket is positioned the correct way around and press the assembly fully onto the shaft using a tubular drift which bears only on the bearing inner race.

13 Fit the front protective cap to the shaft and install the new rubber gaiter, ensuring it is correctly located in the shaft groove.

14 Lubricate the propeller shaft splines with molybdenum disulphide grease. Carefully slide the two halves of the propeller shaft together making sure the alignment marks are correctly positioned (see paragraph 4).

15 Seat the rubber gaiter in the threaded sleeve nut groove and refit the propeller shaft as described in Section 7.

10 Propeller shaft universal joint - check and renewal

Check

1 Wear in the universal joint is characterised by vibration in the transmission, noise during acceleration, and metallic squeaking and grating sounds as the bearings disintegrate. The joint can be checked with the propeller shaft still fitted.

2 Hold the front half of the propeller shaft and try to turn the rear half of the shaft. Free play between the propeller shaft halves indicates excessive wear. If the axial movement is excessive, renew the propeller shaft.

Renewal

3 At the time of writing, no spare parts were available to enable renewal of the universal joints to be carried out. Therefore, if any joint shows signs of damage or wear the propeller shaft assembly must be renewed. Consult your Mercedes-Benz dealer for latest information on parts availability.

4 If renewal of the propeller shaft is necessary, it may be worthwhile seeking the advice of an automotive engineering specialist. They may be able to repair the original shaft assembly or supply a reconditioned shaft on an exchange basis.

Chapter 9
Braking system

Contents

Anti-lock braking system (ABS) - general information 17
Anti-lock braking system (ABS) components - removal and refitting ... 18
Brake pad wear check .... See Chapter 1
Braking system vacuum pump (diesel models) - testing, removal and refitting 19
Front brake caliper - removal, overhaul and refitting 8
Front brake disc - inspection, removal and refitting 6
Front brake pads - renewal 4
General information 1
Hydraulic fluid level check .... See "*Weekly checks*"
Hydraulic fluid renewal .... See Chapter 1
Hydraulic pipes and hoses - renewal 3
Hydraulic system - bleeding 2
Master cylinder - removal, overhaul and refitting 10
Parking brake - adjustment 13
Parking brake cables - removal and refitting 15
Parking brake shoes - removal and refitting 14
Rear brake caliper - removal, overhaul and refitting 9
Rear brake disc - inspection, removal and refitting 7
Rear brake pads - renewal 5
Stop-light switch - removal and refitting 16
Vacuum servo unit - testing, removal and refitting 11
Vacuum servo unit check valve - removal, testing and refitting 12

Degrees of difficulty

Easy, suitable for novice with little experience	**Fairly easy,** suitable for beginner with some experience	**Fairly difficult,** suitable for competent DIY mechanic	**Difficult,** suitable for experienced DIY mechanic	**Very difficult,** suitable for expert DIY or professional

Specifications

Front brakes

Disc diameter (all models)	262.0 mm
Disc thickness:	
2.0 litre petrol and normally aspirated diesel models:	
New	11.0 mm
Minimum (before repair)	9.5 mm
Minimum (limit)	9.0
2.3 and 2.6 litre petrol and turbo-diesel models :	
New	22.0 mm
Minimum (before repair)	20.4 mm
Minimum (limit)	19.4 mm
Maximum disc runout	0.12 mm
Brake pad friction material minimum thickness	2.0 mm
Pad wear indicator actuates at	3.5 mm
Caliper bore diameter	54.0 mm

Rear brakes

Disc diameter	258.0 mm
Disc thickness:	
New	9.0 mm
Minimum (before repair)	7.6 mm
Minimum (limit)	7.3 mm
Maximum disc runout	0.15 mm
Brake pad friction material minimum thickness	2.0 mm
Pad wear indicator actuates at	2.5 mm
Caliper bore diameter	34.98 to 35.03 mm

Parking brake

Type	Cable-operated brake shoes with drum machined into rear disc hub
Parking brake drum diameter	164 ± 0.2 mm
Brake shoe friction material thickness:	
New	2.65 mm
Minimum	1.00 mm

Master cylinder

Bore diameter:	
Primary circuit:	
2.6 litre petrol models	23.81 mm
All other models	22.22 mm
Secondary circuit:	
2.6 litre petrol models	19.05 mm
All other models	17.46 mm

Torque wrench settings

Torque wrench settings	Nm	lbf ft
ABS wheel sensor retaining bolts:		
Front sensor	22	16
Rear sensor	8	6
Brake disc retaining screw	10	7
Brake hose unions:		
Caliper unions	18	13
All other unions	15	11
Caliper bleed screws	7	5
Front brake caliper:		
Guide pin bolts	35	22
Mounting bracket bolts	115	85
Master cylinder mounting nuts	20	15
Rear brake caliper mounting bolts	50	37
Roadwheel bolts	110	81
Servo unit mounting nuts	15	15
Servo unit vacuum hose union nut	30	22

1 General information

The braking system is of the servo-assisted, dual-circuit hydraulic type. The layout is such that under normal circumstances, both circuits operate in unison. Should a hydraulic failure occur in one of the circuits, full braking force will still be available in the other circuit (operating on two diagonally-opposite roadwheels), albeit with increased pedal travel.

All models have disc brakes at the front and rear wheels as standard. An Anti-lock Braking System (ABS) is fitted as standard to all later models, and was offered as an option on some early models (refer to the appropriate section for further information on the operation of the ABS). **Note:** *On models equipped with electronic traction control (ASR) this function is also carried out by the ABS.*

The front disc brakes, on all models covered by this manual, are actuated by sliding single-piston type calipers. This design of caliper ensures that equal pressure is applied to each disc pad.

On all models, the rear disc brakes are actuated by fixed, opposed-piston calipers.

The parking brake provides an independent, mechanical means of applying the rear brakes. A drum and shoe arrangement is fitted in the centre of each rear brake disc. The parking brake is applied by a conventional hand lever, which in turn actuates the brake shoes via twin cables.

Note: *When servicing any part of the system, work carefully and methodically; also observe scrupulous cleanliness when overhauling any part of the hydraulic system. Always renew components (in axle sets, where applicable) if in doubt about their condition, and use only genuine Mercedes-Benz replacement parts, or at least those of known good quality. Note the warnings given in "Safety first" and at relevant points in this Chapter concerning the dangers of asbestos dust and hydraulic fluid.*

2 Hydraulic system - bleeding

Warning: Hydraulic fluid is poisonous; wash off immediately and thoroughly in the case of skin contact, and seek immediate medical advice if any fluid is swallowed or gets into the eyes.

Warning: Certain types of hydraulic fluid are flammable, and may ignite when brought into contact with hot components. Hence when servicing any part of the hydraulic system, it is safest to assume that the fluid is flammable, and to take precautions against the risk of fire as though it were petrol being handled.

Warning: Hydraulic fluid is also an effective paint stripper, and will attack plastics; if any is spilt, it should be washed off immediately, using copious quantities of fresh water.

Warning: Finally, brake fluid is hygroscopic, which means that if left in an open container, it will absorb moisture from the air. This has the effect of lowering the boiling point of the fluid, rendering it unfit for use. When topping-up or renewing the fluid, always use the recommended type, and ensure that it comes from a sealed, freshly opened container.

General

1 The correct operation of any hydraulic system is only possible after removing all air from the components and circuit; this is achieved by bleeding the system.

2 During the bleeding procedure, add only clean, unused hydraulic fluid of the recommended type; never re-use fluid that has already been bled from the system. Ensure that sufficient fluid is available before starting work.

3 If there is any possibility of incorrect fluid being already in the system, the brake components and circuit must be flushed completely with uncontaminated, correct fluid, and new seals should be fitted to the various components.
4 If hydraulic fluid has been lost from the system, or air has entered because of a leak, ensure that the fault is cured before continuing further.
5 Park the vehicle on level ground, switch off the engine and select first or reverse gear, then chock the wheels and release the parking brake.
6 Check that all pipes and hoses are secure, unions tight and bleed screws closed. Clean any dirt from around the bleed screws.
7 Unscrew the master cylinder reservoir cap, and top the master cylinder reservoir up to the "MAX" level line; refit the cap loosely, and remember to maintain the fluid level at least above the "MIN" level line throughout the procedure, or there is a risk of further air entering the system.
8 There are a number of one-man, do-it-yourself brake bleeding kits currently available from motor accessory shops. It is recommended that one of these kits is used whenever possible, as they greatly simplify the bleeding operation, and reduce the risk of expelled air and fluid being drawn back into the system. If such a kit is not available, the basic (two-man) method must be used, which is described in detail below.
9 If a kit is to be used, prepare the vehicle as described previously, and follow the kit manufacturer's instructions, as the procedure may vary slightly according to the type being used; generally, they are as outlined below in the relevant sub-section.
10 Whichever method is used, the same sequence must be followed (paragraphs 11 and 12) to ensure that the removal of all air from the system. On completion, test the operation of the braking system exhaustively, before bringing the vehicle back into service on the public highway.

Bleeding sequence

11 If the system has been only partially disconnected, and suitable precautions were taken to minimise fluid loss, it should be necessary only to bleed that part of the system.
12 If the complete system is to be bled, then it should be done working in the following sequence:

a) Right-hand rear brake.
b) Left-hand rear brake.
c) Right-hand front brake.
d) Left-hand front brake.

Note: *On models with traction control (ASR), if the hydraulic system linking the master cylinder, hydraulic unit, pressure pump and accumulator has been disturbed then the hydraulic unit reservoir must also be bled once the main braking system has been bled (see paragraph 32).*

Bleeding - basic (two-man) method

13 Collect a clean glass jar, a suitable length of plastic or rubber tubing which is a tight fit over the bleed screw, and a ring spanner to fit the screw. The help of an assistant will also be required.
14 Remove the dust cap from the first screw in the sequence. Fit the spanner and tube to the screw, place the other end of the tube in the jar, and pour in sufficient fluid to cover the end of the tube.
15 Ensure that the master cylinder reservoir fluid level is maintained at least above the "MIN" level line throughout the procedure.
16 Have the assistant fully depress the brake pedal several times to build up pressure, then maintain it on the final downstroke.
17 While pedal pressure is maintained, unscrew the bleed screw (approximately one turn) and allow the compressed fluid and air to flow into the jar. The assistant should maintain pedal pressure, following it down to the floor if necessary, and should not release it until instructed to do so. When the flow stops, tighten the bleed screw again, have the assistant release the pedal slowly, and recheck the reservoir fluid level.
18 Repeat the steps given in paragraphs 16 and 17 until the fluid emerging from the bleed screw is free from air bubbles. If the master cylinder has been drained and refilled, and air is being bled from the first screw in the sequence, allow approximately five seconds between cycles for the master cylinder passages to refill.
19 When no more air bubbles appear, tighten the bleed screw to the specified torque, remove the tube and spanner, and refit the dust cap. Do not overtighten the bleed screw.
20 Repeat the procedure on the remaining screws in the sequence, until all air is removed from the system and the brake pedal feels firm again.

Bleeding - using a one-way valve kit

21 As their name implies, these kits consist of a length of tubing with a one-way valve fitted, to prevent expelled air and fluid being drawn back into the system; some kits include a translucent container, which can be positioned so that the air bubbles can be more easily seen flowing from the end of the tube **(see illustration)**.
22 The kit is connected to the bleed screw, which is then opened. The user returns to the driver's seat, depresses the brake pedal with a smooth, steady stroke, and slowly releases it; this is repeated until the expelled fluid is clear of air bubbles.
23 Note that these kits simplify work so much that it is easy to forget the master cylinder reservoir fluid level; ensure that this is maintained at least above the "MIN" level line at all times.

Bleeding - using a pressure-bleeding kit

24 These kits are usually operated by the reservoir of pressurised air contained in the spare tyre. However, note that it will probably be necessary to reduce the pressure to a lower level than normal; refer to the instructions supplied with the kit. **Note:** *Mercedes-Benz specify that a pressure of 2 bar (29 psi) should not be exceeded.*
25 By connecting a pressurised, fluid-filled container to the master cylinder reservoir, bleeding can be carried out simply by opening each brake caliper bleed screw in turn (in the specified sequence), and allowing the fluid to flow out until no more air bubbles can be seen in the expelled fluid.
26 This method has the advantage that the large reservoir of fluid provides an additional safeguard against air being drawn into the system during bleeding.
27 Pressure-bleeding is particularly effective when bleeding "difficult" systems, or when bleeding the complete system at the time of routine fluid renewal.

All methods

28 When bleeding is complete, and firm pedal feel is restored, wash off any spilt fluid, tighten the bleed screws to the specified torque, and refit their dust caps.
29 Check the hydraulic fluid level in the master cylinder reservoir, and top-up if necessary (see "*Weekly checks*").
30 Discard any hydraulic fluid that has been bled from the system; it will not be fit for re-use.
31 Check the feel of the brake pedal. If it feels at all spongy, air must still be present in the system, and further bleeding is required. Failure to bleed satisfactorily after a reasonable repetition of the bleeding procedure may be due to worn master cylinder seals.

Bleeding the hydraulic unit - models equipped with traction control (ASR)

32 On models with traction control (ASR), if the hydraulic system linking the master cylinder, hydraulic unit, pressure pump and accumulator has been disturbed then the hydraulic unit pressure reservoir must also be bled once the main braking system has been bled as follows.

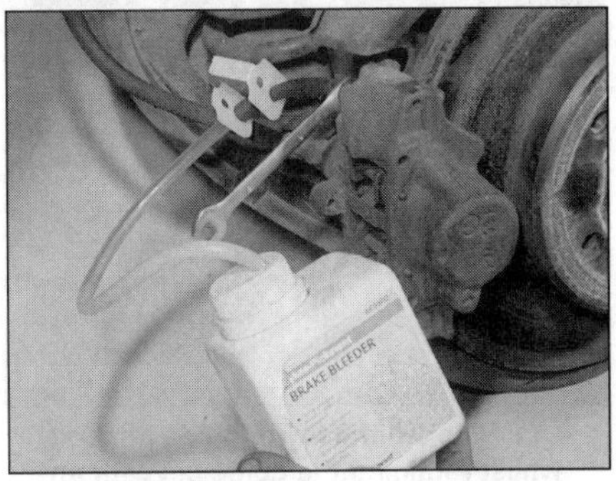

2.21 Bleeding a rear brake caliper

33 Remove the cover from the (ASR) hydraulic unit in the engine compartment to gain access to the pressure reservoir bleed screw (marked "SP").
34 Attach a plastic tube to the bleed screw and place the end of the tube into a container (see paragraphs 13 and 14).
35 Start the engine and allow it to idle.
36 Ensuring that the master cylinder reservoir fluid level is maintained at least above the "MIN" level, open up the bleed screw and allow fluid to flow from the reservoir until the fluid emerging from the bleed screw is free from air bubbles.
37 When no more air bubbles appear securely tighten the bleed screw. The pressure pump in the pressure pump should carry on running for approximately 30 seconds until full operating pressure is present in the reservoir; the pump can be heard running. Once the pump cuts out, switch the engine off and disconnect tube and spanner from the bleed screw.
38 Wash off any spilt fluid and refit the cover to the hydraulic unit.
39 Check the hydraulic fluid level in the master cylinder reservoir, and top-up if necessary (see "*Weekly checks*").

3 Hydraulic pipes and hoses - renewal

Note: *Before starting work, refer to the warnings at the beginning of Section 2.*

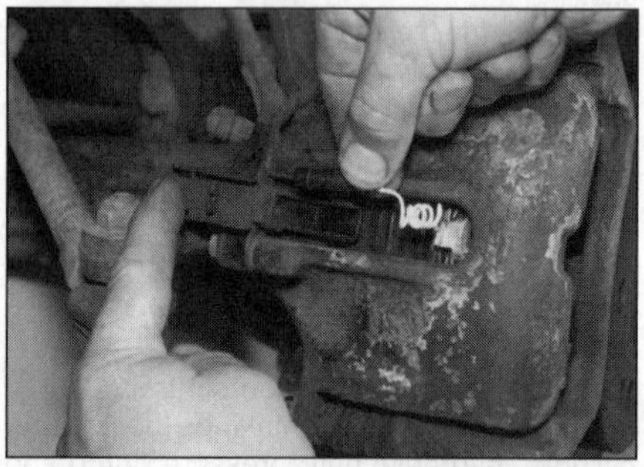

4.3 Unclip the cover and disconnect the wear sensor wiring connector

1 If any pipe or hose is to be renewed, minimise fluid loss by first removing the master cylinder reservoir cap, then tightening it down onto a piece of polythene to obtain an airtight seal. Alternatively, flexible hoses can be sealed, if required, using a proprietary brake hose clamp; metal brake pipe unions can be plugged (if care is taken not to allow dirt into the system) or capped immediately they are disconnected. Place a wad of rag under any union that is to be disconnected, to catch any spilt fluid.
2 If a flexible hose is to be disconnected, unscrew the brake pipe union nut before removing the spring clip which secures the hose to its mounting bracket .
3 To unscrew the union nuts, it is preferable to obtain a brake pipe spanner of the correct size; these are available from most large motor accessory shops. Failing this, a close-fitting open-ended spanner will be required, though if the nuts are tight or corroded, their flats may be rounded-off if the spanner slips. In such a case, a self-locking wrench is often the only way to unscrew a stubborn union, but it follows that the pipe and the damaged nuts must be renewed on reassembly. Always clean a union and surrounding area before disconnecting it; this helps to prevent the entry of dirt into the hydraulic system. If disconnecting a component with more than one union, make a careful note of the connections before disturbing any of them.
4 If a brake pipe is to be renewed, it can be obtained, cut to length and with the union nuts and end flares in place, from Mercedes-Benz dealers. All that is then necessary is to bend it to shape, following the line of the original, before fitting it to the car. Alternatively, most motor accessory shops can make up brake pipes from kits, but this requires very careful measurement of the original, to ensure that the replacement is of the correct length. The safest answer is usually to take the original to the shop as a pattern.
5 On refitting, do not overtighten the union nuts. It is not necessary to exercise brute force to obtain a sound joint.
6 Ensure that the pipes and hoses are correctly routed, with no kinks, and that they are secured in the clips or brackets provided. After fitting, remove the polythene from the reservoir, and bleed the hydraulic system as described in Section 2. Wash off any spilt fluid, and check carefully for fluid leaks.
7 Finally, test the operation of the braking system exhaustively, before bringing the vehicle back into service on the public highway.

4 Front brake pads - renewal

Warning: Renew both sets of front brake pads at the same time - never renew the pads on only one wheel, as uneven braking may result. Note that the dust created by wear of the pads may contain asbestos, which is a health hazard. Never blow it out with compressed air, and do not inhale any of it. An approved filtering mask should be worn when working on the brakes. DO NOT use petrol or petroleum-based solvents to clean brake parts; use brake cleaner or methylated spirit only.

Note: *New caliper guide pin bolts will be required on refitting.*

1 Apply the parking brake, then jack up the front of the vehicle and support it on axle stands (see "*Jacking and vehicle support*"). Remove the front roadwheels and continue as described under the relevant sub-heading.
2 Release the retaining clips and unclip the pad wear sensor wiring connector cover from the caliper aperture.
3 Disconnect the wear sensor connector from the caliper housing **(see illustration)**.
4 On pre-1985 models, remove the upper guide pin and pivot the caliper down.
5 On post-1985 models, slacken and remove the lower caliper guide pin bolt, using a slim open-ended spanner to prevent the guide pin itself from rotating **(see illustrations)**. Discard the guide pin bolt - a new bolt must be used on refitting.
6 Pivot the caliper away from the brake pads and mounting bracket. Remove the heat shield from the caliper piston, where applicable **(see illustration)**.
7 Withdraw the two brake pads from the caliper mounting bracket noting the correct

4.5a Slacken the lower guide pin bolt, whilst retaining the guide pin with an open-ended spanner . . .

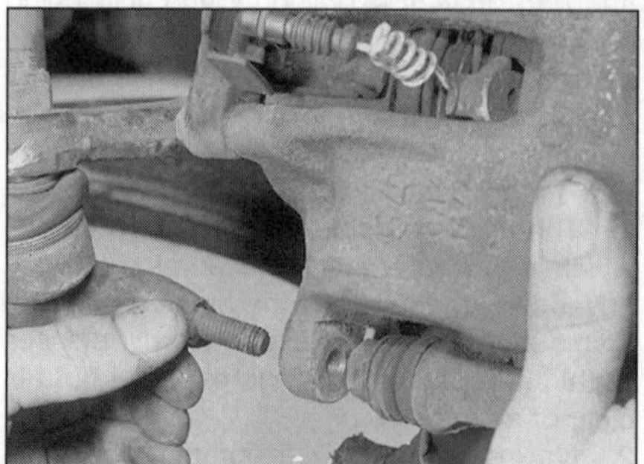

4.5b . . . then withdraw it from the caliper

4.6 Pivot the caliper away from the disc and remove the heat shield from the piston

4.7a Remove the inner . . .

4.7b . . . and outer pads from the caliper mounting bracket

4.14 On refitting, ensure that the pad with the wear sensor (arrowed) is fitted as the inner pad

fitted location of the wear sensor **(see illustrations)**.

8 First measure the thickness of each brake pad's friction material (excluding the metal backplate). If either pad is worn at any point to the specified minimum thickness or less, all four pads must be renewed. Also, the pads should be renewed if any of them are fouled with oil or grease. There is no satisfactory way of degreasing friction material, once contaminated. If any of the brake pads are worn unevenly, or are fouled with oil or grease, trace and rectify the cause before reassembly. Inspect the wear sensor for signs of damage and renew if necessary. New brake pad kits are available from Mercedes-Benz dealers.

9 If the brake pads are still serviceable, carefully clean them using a clean, fine wire brush or similar, paying particular attention to the sides and back of the metal backing. Clean out the grooves in the friction material (where applicable), and pick out any large embedded particles of dirt or debris. Carefully clean the pad locations in the caliper body/mounting bracket.

10 Prior to fitting the pads check the pins are free to slide easily in the caliper bracket, and are a reasonably tight fit. Ensure that the guide pin gaiters are undamaged. Remove all traces of locking compound from guide pin threads using a tap of the correct thread size and pitch.

HAYNES HiNT ***If a suitable tap is not available, clean out the holes using the old bolt with a slot cut in its threads.***

11 Brush the dust and dirt from the caliper and piston, but *do not* inhale it, as it may contain asbestos, which is a health hazard. Inspect the dust seal around the piston for damage, and the piston itself for evidence of fluid leaks, corrosion or damage. If any such deterioration is found, the caliper must be overhauled - refer to Section 8 for details.

12 If new brake pads are to be fitted, the caliper piston must be pushed back into the cylinder to make room for them. Either use a G-clamp or similar tool, or use suitable pieces of wood as levers. Provided that the master cylinder reservoir has not been overfilled with hydraulic fluid, there should be no spillage, but keep a careful watch on the fluid level while retracting the piston. If the fluid level rises above the "MAX" level line at any time, the surplus should be syphoned off or ejected through a plastic tube connected to the bleed screw (see Section 2).

Warning: Do not syphon the fluid by mouth, as it is poisonous; use a syringe or an old poultry baster.

13 Apply a smear of brake grease to the backing plate of each pad (Mercedes-Benz recommend the use of brake paste - number 001 989 10 51); do not apply excess grease or allow the grease to contact the friction material.

14 Clip the pad wear sensor (where removed) securely in position and fit the pads to the caliper mounting bracket ensuring that their friction material is against the brake disc. Note that the pad with the wear sensor should be fitted as the inner pad **(see illustration)**.

15 Clip the heat shield into position over the caliper piston then pivot the caliper down into position over the pads, passing the wear sensor wiring up through the caliper aperture **(see illustration)**.

16 Ensure that the pad anti-rattle springs are correctly positioned against the caliper housing then press down on the caliper and install the new guide pin bolt **(see illustration)**. Tighten the bolt to the specified torque setting while retaining the guide pin with an open-ended spanner.

17 Reconnect the wear sensor wiring connector to the caliper, making sure the excess wiring is wrapped neatly around the connector. Ensure that the connector is correctly fitted and clip the sensor cover into the caliper aperture.

18 Depress the brake pedal repeatedly, until the pads are pressed into firm contact with the brake disc, and normal (non-assisted) pedal pressure is restored.

19 Repeat the above procedure on the remaining front brake caliper.

20 Refit the roadwheels, then lower the vehicle to the ground and tighten the roadwheel bolts to the specified torque setting.

21 Check the hydraulic fluid level as described in "*Weekly checks*". Test the operation of the braking system exhaustively, before bringing the vehicle back into service on the public highway.

Warning: New pads will not give full braking efficiency until they have 'bedded in'. Be prepared for this - avoid hard braking as far as possible for the first hundred miles or so after pad renewal.

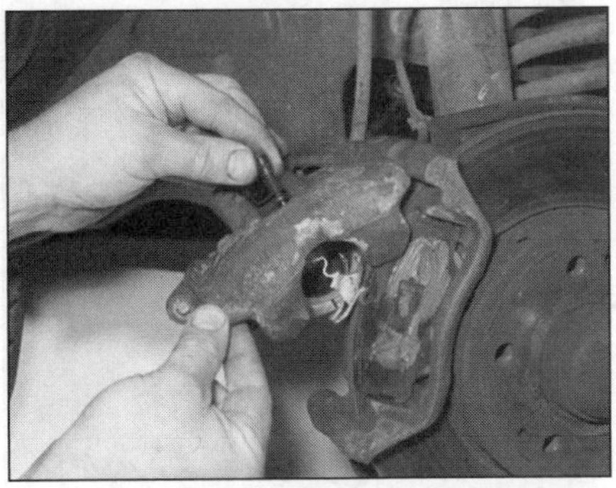

4.15 Pivot the caliper into position whilst passing the wear sensor wiring connector up through the caliper aperture

4.16 Insert the new guide pin bolt

5.2a On the rear brake, tap out the retaining pins . . .

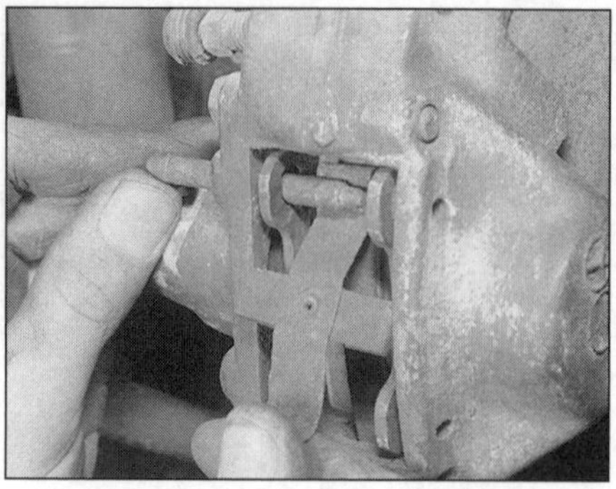

5.2b . . . and recover the anti-rattle spring

5.3a Withdraw the inner pad . . .

5 Rear brake pads - renewal

Warning: Renew both sets of rear brake pads at the same time - never renew the pads on only one wheel, as uneven braking may result. Note that the dust created by wear of the pads may contain asbestos, which is a health hazard. Never blow it out with compressed air, and do not inhale any of it. An approved filtering mask should be worn when working on the brakes. DO NOT use petrol or petroleum-based solvents to clean brake parts; use brake cleaner or methylated spirit only.

1 Where applicable, pull the pad wear sensor wiring connectors out from the caliper body, noting the correct routing of the wiring.

2 Using a hammer and suitable punch, carefully tap out the pad retaining pins and recover the anti-rattle spring **(see illustrations).**

3 Slide the pads out from the caliper body noting the correct fitted position of the wear sensors. Where necessary, recover the shims which are fitted between the pads and pistons **(see illustrations).**

4 Inspect the brake pads as described in Section 4. Renew the anti-rattle spring, pad retaining pins and shims (as applicable) if the pads are to be renewed.

5 Prior to fitting the pads, brush the dust and dirt from the caliper and pistons, but *do not* inhale it, as it is injurious to health. Inspect the dust seals around each piston for damage, and the pistons for evidence of fluid leaks, corrosion or damage. If any such deterioration is found, the caliper must be overhauled - refer to Section 8 for details.

6 If new brake pads are to be fitted, the caliper pistons must be pushed back into the cylinder to make room for them. Carefully prise the pistons back into position using a suitable piece of wood as a lever. Provided that the master cylinder reservoir has not been overfilled with hydraulic fluid, there should be no spillage, but keep a careful watch on the fluid level while retracting the piston. If the fluid level rises above the "MAX" level line at any time, the surplus should be syphoned off or ejected through a plastic tube connected to the bleed screw (see Section 2).

Warning: Do not syphon the fluid by mouth, as it is poisonous; use a syringe or an old poultry baster.

5.3b . . . and outer pad from the caliper

7 If the brake pad backing plates are equipped with damper pads which align with the caliper pistons, **do not** apply any lubricant to the pads. On pads where the backing plates are plain, apply a smear of brake grease to the backing plate edges of each pad (Mercedes-Benz recommend the use of brake paste - number 001 989 10 51); do not apply excess grease or allow the grease to contact the friction material **(see illustrations).**

8 Ensure that the wear sensors are clipped securely into the backing plate of each pad and (where fitted) fit the shims to the back of each pad.

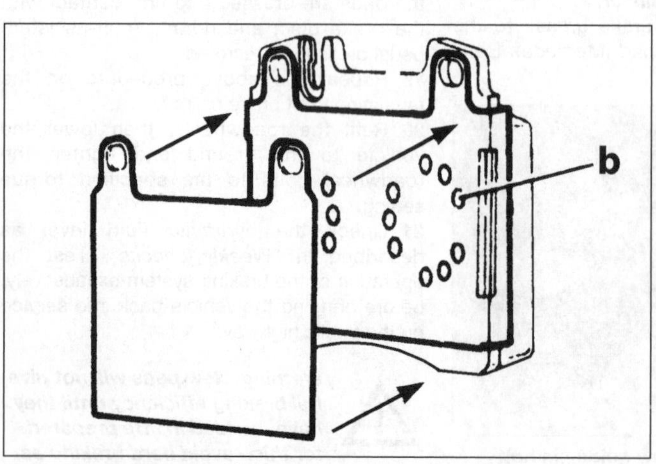

5.7a If the pad backing plates are equipped with damper pads (b) do not apply any lubricant to the pad

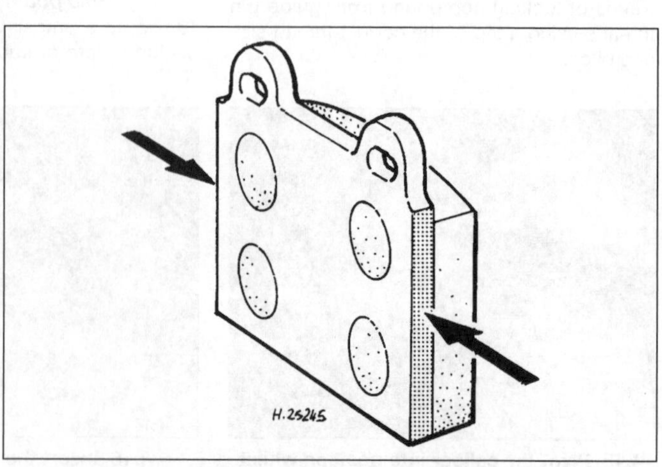

5.7b If the pad backing plates do not have damper pads apply lubricant to the edges of the backing plate (arrowed)

9 Slide the brake pads and (where fitted) shims into position in the caliper making sure the friction material of each pad is against the brake disc.
10 Fit the new anti-rattle spring to the top of the pads making sure it is fitted the right way up.
11 Slide in the pad retaining pins, making sure they go over the anti-rattle spring, and tap them fully into the caliper body.
12 Ensure that the wiring is correctly routed and connect the wear sensor connectors to the caliper body.
13 Depress the brake pedal repeatedly, until the pads are pressed into firm contact with the brake disc, and normal (non-assisted) pedal pressure is restored.
14 Repeat the above procedure on the remaining front brake caliper.
15 Refit the roadwheels, then lower the vehicle to the ground and tighten the roadwheel bolts to the specified torque setting.
16 Check the hydraulic fluid level as described in "*Weekly checks*". Test the operation of the braking system exhaustively, before bringing the vehicle back into service on the public highway.

Warning: New pads will not give full braking efficiency until they have bedded in. Be prepared for this, and avoid hard braking as far as possible for the first hundred miles or so after pad renewal.

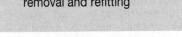

6 Front brake disc - inspection, removal and refitting

Note: *Before starting work, refer to the note at the beginning of Section 4 concerning the dangers of asbestos dust.*

Inspection

Note: *If either disc requires renewal, BOTH should be renewed at the same time, to ensure even and consistent braking. New brake pads should also be fitted.*
1 Apply the parking brake, then jack up the front of the car and support it on axle stands (see "*Jacking and vehicle support*"). Remove the appropriate front roadwheel.
2 Slowly rotate the brake disc so that the full area of both sides can be checked; remove the brake pads if better access is required to the inboard surface. Light scoring is normal in the area swept by the brake pads, but if heavy scoring or cracks are found, the disc must be renewed.
3 It is normal to find a lip of loose rust and brake dust around the disc's perimeter; this can be scraped off if required. However, if a lip of solid material has formed due to excessive wear of the brake pad swept area, then the disc thickness must be measured using a micrometer **(see illustration)**. Take measurements at several places around the disc, and at the inside and outside edges of the pad swept area; if the disc has worn at *any* point to the specified minimum thickness or less, the disc must be renewed.

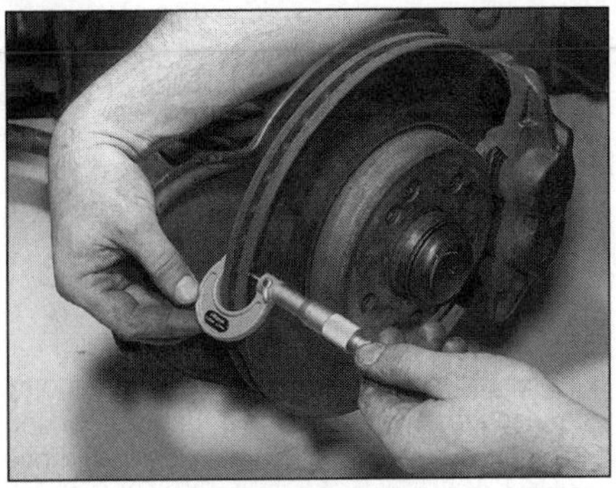

6.3 Using a micrometer to measure the brake disc thickness

6.4 Checking disc run-out with a dial gauge (rear disc shown - procedure for front disc similar)

4 If the disc is thought to be warped, it can be checked for run-out **(see illustration)**, but first eliminate wheel bearing play as the cause of the problem, with reference to Chapter 10.
5 To check the disc run-out, fit large, plain washers under the heads of two of the wheel bolts, then bolt them to the hub through the disc. Position the wheel bolts diagonally opposite each other, to ensure that the disc seats evenly, then tighten the bolts securely. Either use a dial gauge mounted on any convenient fixed point, while the disc is slowly rotated, or use feeler blades to measure (at several points all around the disc) the clearance between the disc and a fixed point, such as the caliper mounting bracket. If the measurements obtained are at the specified maximum or beyond, the disc is excessively warped, and must be renewed.
6 Check the disc for cracks, especially around the wheel bolt holes, and any other wear or damage, and renew if necessary.

Removal

Note: *New brake caliper mounting bolts and disc retaining screws will be required on refitting.*
7 Unscrew the two bolts securing the brake caliper mounting bracket to the swivel hub then slide the caliper assembly off the disc. Using a piece of wire or a nylon cable tie, attach the caliper to the front suspension coil spring, to avoid placing any strain on the hydraulic brake hose or the caliper wiring. Discard the bolts, new ones must be used on refitting **(see illustration)**.
8 Slacken and remove the screw securing the brake disc to the hub **(see illustration)**. Discard the screw as a new one should be used on refitting.
9 Remove the disc from the hub, noting the correct fitted location of its locating pins. If it is tight, lightly tap its rear face with a hide or plastic mallet.

Refitting

10 Prior to refitting remove all traces of old locking compound from the caliper bolt hole threads in the hub by running a tap of the correct thread size and pitch down them. Clean the disc retaining screw threads in the hub in the same way.

> **HAYNES HiNT** *If a suitable tap is not available, clean out the holes using an old bolt/screw with a slot cut in its threads*

11 Ensure that the mating surfaces of the disc and hub are clean and flat and that the disc locating pins are in position. If a new disc has been fitted, use a suitable solvent to wipe any preservative coating from the disc. Apply a thin coat of high temperature grease to the mating surface of the hub, but ensure

6.7 Unbolt the brake caliper from the steering knuckle . . .

6.8 . . . then undo the retaining screw and remove the brake disc

9

6.12 On refitting secure the disc in position with a new retaining screw

that the surface of the disc is not contaminated.

12 Fit the disc to the hub making sure it is correctly located with the pins. Fit the new disc retaining screw and tighten it to the specified torque setting **(see illustration)**.

13 Slide the caliper into position over the disc, making sure the pads pass either side of the disc.

14 Fit the new caliper mounting bracket bolts and tighten them to the specified torque setting.

15 Refit the roadwheel, then lower the vehicle to the ground and tighten the roadwheel bolts to the specified torque. On completion, repeatedly depress the brake pedal until normal (non-assisted) pedal pressure returns. Test the operation of the braking system exhaustively, before bringing the vehicle back into service on the public highway.

7 Rear brake disc - inspection, removal and refitting

Note: *Before starting work, refer to the note at the beginning of Section 5 concerning the dangers of asbestos dust.*

Inspection

Note: *If either disc requires renewal, BOTH should be renewed at the same time, to ensure even and consistent braking. New brake pads should be fitted also.*

1 Firmly chock the front wheels, then jack up the rear of the car and support it on axle stands (see "*Jacking and vehicle support*"). Remove the appropriate rear roadwheel.

2 Inspect the disc as described in Section 6.

Removal

3 Refer to Section 6 noting that there is only one disc locating pin. Ensure that the parking brake is fully released before trying to remove the disc. If the disc is still tight on the shoes with the brake fully released slacken the parking brake adjustment as described in Section 13.

Refitting

4 Refer to Section 6. On completion adjust the parking brake as described in Section 13. Test the operation of the braking system exhaustively, before bringing the vehicle back into service on the public highway.

8 Front brake caliper - removal, overhaul and refitting

Note: *Before starting work, refer to the note at the beginning of Section 2 concerning the dangers of hydraulic fluid, and to the warning at the beginning of Section 4 concerning the dangers of asbestos dust.*

Removal

Note: *New brake caliper guide pin bolts will be required on refitting.*

1 Apply the parking brake, then jack up the front of the vehicle and support it on axle stands (see "*Jacking and vehicle support*"). Remove the appropriate roadwheel.

2 Minimise fluid loss by first removing the master cylinder reservoir cap, and then tightening it down onto a piece of polythene, to obtain an airtight seal. Alternatively, use a brake hose clamp, a G-clamp or a similar tool to clamp the flexible hose.

3 Clean the area around the union, then loosen the brake hose union nut at the caliper.

4 Remove the brake pads as described in Section 4.

5 Slacken and remove the upper guide pin bolt then unscrew the caliper and remove it from the end of the brake hose **(see illustration)**.

Overhaul

6 With the caliper on the bench, wipe away all traces of dust and dirt, but *avoid inhaling the dust, as it is injurious to health.*

7 Withdraw the partially ejected piston from the caliper body, and remove the dust seal.

> **HAYNES HiNT**
>
> ***If the piston cannot be withdrawn by hand, it can be pushed out by applying compressed air to the brake hose union hole. Only low pressure should be required, such as that generated by a foot pump. Place a block of wood between the end of the piston and the caliper body to prevent damage to the piston, as it pops out of its bore - also take great care not to trap your fingers when this happens.***

8 Using a soft blunt instrument, such as the end of a pen cap, extract the piston hydraulic seal, taking great care not to damage the caliper bore **(see illustration)**.

9 Thoroughly clean all components, using only methylated spirit, isopropyl alcohol or clean hydraulic fluid as a cleaning medium. Never use mineral-based solvents such as petrol or paraffin, as they will attack the hydraulic system's rubber components. Dry the components immediately, using compressed air or a clean, lint-free cloth. Use compressed air to blow clear the fluid passages.

10 Check all components, and renew any that are worn or damaged. Check particularly the cylinder bore and piston; these should be renewed (note that this means the renewal of the complete body assembly) if they are scratched, worn or corroded in any way.

8.2 Use a brake hose clamp, a G-clamp or a similar tool to clamp the flexible hose

8.5 Removing the brake caliper

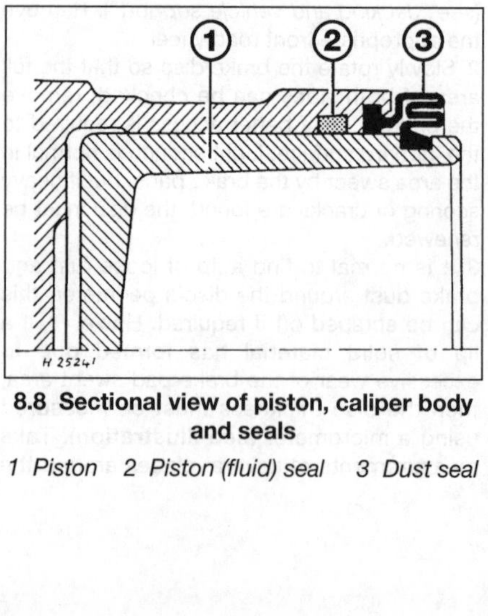

8.8 Sectional view of piston, caliper body and seals

1 Piston 2 Piston (fluid) seal 3 Dust seal

Similarly check the condition of the guide pins and their bushes; both pins should be undamaged and (when cleaned) a reasonably tight sliding fit in the bushes. If there is any doubt about the condition of any component, renew it.

11 If the assembly is fit for further use, obtain the appropriate repair kit; the components are available from Mercedes-Benz dealers in various combinations. All rubber seals should be renewed as a matter of course; these should never be re-used.

12 On reassembly, ensure that all components are clean and dry.

13 Soak the piston and the new piston (fluid) seal in clean hydraulic fluid. Smear clean fluid on the cylinder bore surface.

14 Fit the new piston (fluid) seal, using only your fingers (no tools) to manipulate it into the cylinder bore groove.

15 Fit the new dust seal to the rear of the piston and seat the outer lip of the seal in the caliper body groove. Carefully ease the piston squarely into the cylinder bore using a twisting motion. Press the piston fully into position and seat the inner lip of the dust seal in the piston groove.

16 If the guide pins are being renewed, lubricate the pin shafts with the special grease supplied in the repair kit and fit the gaiters to the pin grooves. Insert the pins into the caliper bracket and seat the gaiters correctly in the bracket grooves.

Refitting

17 Remove all traces of old locking compound from the caliper guide pin/bolt hole threads (as applicable) by running a tap of the correct thread size and pitch down them.

> **HAYNES HiNT** ***If a suitable tap is not available, clean out the holes using an old bolt with a slot cut in its threads***

18 Screw the caliper fully onto the flexible hose union.

19 Offer the caliper up to the mounting bracket and fit the new upper guide pin bolt, tightening it to the specified torque setting.

20 Tighten the brake hose union nut to the specified torque and remove the brake hose clamp or polythene (as applicable).

21 Refit the brake pads as described in Section 4 and bleed the hydraulic system as described in Section 2. Note that, providing the precautions described were taken to minimise brake fluid loss, it should only be necessary to bleed the relevant front brake.

22 Refit the roadwheel, then lower the vehicle to the ground and tighten the roadwheel bolts to the specified torque. On completion, check the hydraulic fluid level as described in *"Weekly checks"*. Test the operation of the braking system exhaustively, before bringing the vehicle back into service on the public highway.

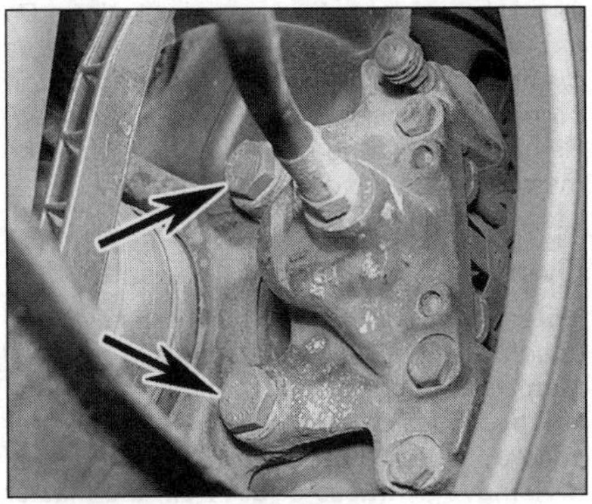

9.5 Slacken and remove the caliper mounting bolts (arrowed)

9 Rear brake caliper - removal, overhaul and refitting

Note: *Before starting work, refer to the note at the beginning of Section 2 concerning the dangers of hydraulic fluid, and to the warning at the beginning of Section 5 concerning the dangers of asbestos dust.*

Removal

Note: *New caliper mounting bolts will be required on refitting.*

1 Chock the front wheels, then jack up the rear of the vehicle and support on axle stands (see *"Jacking and vehicle support"*). Remove the relevant rear wheel.

2 Minimise fluid loss by first removing the master cylinder reservoir cap, and then tightening it down onto a piece of polythene, to obtain an airtight seal. Alternatively, use a proprietary brake hose clamp to seal off the flexible hose leading to the caliper. Do not use a G-clamp, or any other device with flat jaws, as this may pinch the hose, leading to premature failure.

3 Clean the area around the union, then loosen the brake hose union nut.

4 Remove the brake pads as described in Section 5.

5 Slacken and remove the caliper mounting bolts then unscrew the caliper from the end of the flexible hose and remove it from the vehicle **(see illustration)**. Discard the mounting bolts - they should be renewed whenever they are disturbed.

Caution: Never slacken the bolts securing the two halves of the caliper together. If the bolts are slackened and the caliper is body is dismantled, the assembly may leak after reassembly.

6 With the caliper on the bench, wipe away all traces of dust and dirt, but *avoid inhaling the dust, as it is injurious to health.*

7 Make identification markings between each piston and its relative bore in the caliper to avoid interchanging the pistons on reassembly.

> **HAYNES HiNT** ***Check that all the pistons move easily before withdrawing them completely. If any piston cannot be withdrawn by hand, insert a piece of wood (approximately 28 mm thick) into the caliper body and push out the pistons by applying compressed air to the brake hose union hole. Only low pressure should be required, such as that generated by a foot pump. Ensure that all pistons are pushed out simultaneously until they are in contact with the wood then remove the wood from the caliper. This avoids the possibility of having one piston left in the caliper, which will be very difficult to remove.***

8 Withdraw the partially ejected pistons from the caliper body, and remove the dust seals.

9 Using a small screwdriver, extract the piston hydraulic seal, taking great care not to damage the caliper bore.

Overhaul

10 Thoroughly clean all components, using only methylated spirit, isopropyl alcohol or clean hydraulic fluid as a cleaning medium. Never use mineral-based solvents such as petrol or paraffin, as they will attack the hydraulic system's rubber components. Dry the components immediately, using compressed air or a clean, lint-free cloth. Use compressed air to blow clear the fluid passages.

11 Check all components, and renew any that are worn or damaged. Check particularly the cylinder bore and piston; these should be renewed (note that this means the renewal of the complete body assembly) if they are scratched, worn or corroded in any way. If you have any doubts about the condition of a component, it is safest to renew it.

12 If the assembly is fit for further use, obtain the appropriate repair kit; the components are available from Mercedes-Benz dealers in various combinations. All rubber seals should be renewed as a matter of course; these should never be re-used.

13 On reassembly, ensure that all components are clean and dry and that each piston is refitted in its original bore.

14 Working on the first piston, soak it and the new piston (fluid) seal in clean hydraulic fluid. Smear clean fluid on the cylinder bore surface.

15 Fit the new piston (fluid) seal, using only your fingers (no tools) to manipulate

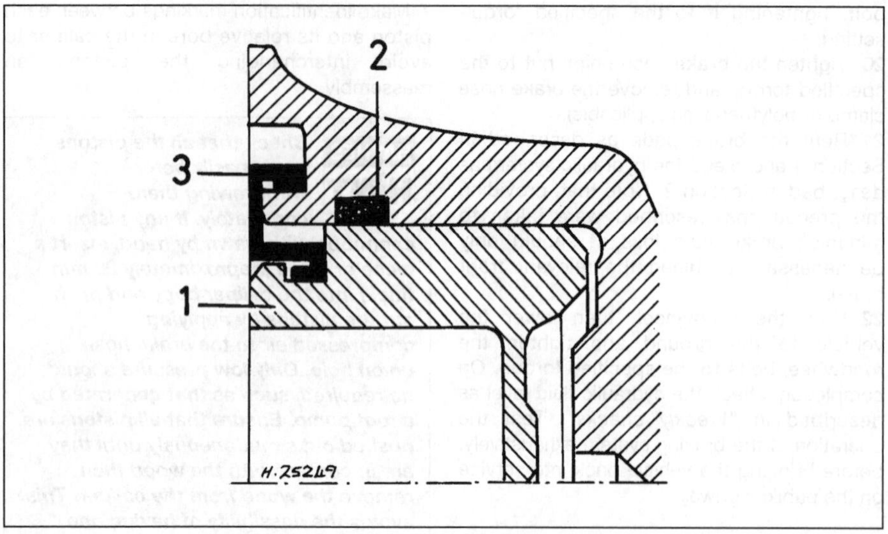

9.15 Rear brake caliper piston and dust seal arrangement

1 Piston 2 Piston seal 3 Dust cap

it into the cylinder bore groove **(see illustration)**.

16 Fit the new dust seal to the piston groove and carefully ease the piston squarely into its respective cylinder bore using a twisting motion. Press the piston fully into position and seat the outer lip of the dust seal in the caliper body.

17 Repeat the previous operations on the remaining piston(s).

18 Prior to pushing the pistons fully into the caliper, position each one so that its raised section will be positioned uppermost when the caliper is refitted. Mercedes-Benz dealers use a special gauge to ensure that the piston is correctly positioned **(see illustration)**. The raised section of the piston ensures the pad contacts the disc at a slight angle and reduces the possibility of the break squeal.

Refitting

19 Remove all traces of old locking compound from the caliper bolt hole threads by running a tap of the correct thread size and pitch down them.

> **HAYNES HiNT** ***If a suitable tap is not available, clean out the holes using an old bolt with a slot cut in its threads***

20 Screw the caliper fully onto the flexible hose union, using a new sealing washer where applicable.

21 Slide the caliper assembly into position then fit the new mounting bolts and tighten them to the specified torque.

22 Tighten the brake hose union nut to the specified torque and remove the brake hose clamp (or the polythene sheet from the fluid reservoir as applicable).

23 Refit the brake pads as described in Section 5 and bleed the hydraulic system as described in Section 2. Note that, providing the precautions described were taken to minimise brake fluid loss, it should only be necessary to bleed the relevant front brake.

24 Refit the roadwheel, then lower the vehicle to the ground and tighten the roadwheel bolts to the specified torque. On completion, check the hydraulic fluid level as described in "*Weekly checks*". Test the operation of the braking system exhaustively, before bringing the vehicle back into service on the public highway.

10 Master cylinder - removal, overhaul and refitting

Removal

Note: *Before starting work, refer to the warning at the beginning of Section 2 concerning the dangers of hydraulic fluid.*

1 Disconnect the battery negative terminal.

2 Disconnect the wiring connector from the brake fluid level sender unit.

3 Remove the master cylinder reservoir cap, and syphon the hydraulic fluid from the reservoir. Alternatively, open any convenient bleed screw in the system, and gently pump the brake pedal to expel the fluid through a plastic tube connected to the screw (see Section 2).

> ***Warning: Do not syphon the fluid by mouth, as it is poisonous; use a syringe or an old poultry baster***

4 Where necessary, disconnect the fluid hose(s) from the side of the reservoir and plug the hose end(s) to minimise fluid loss.

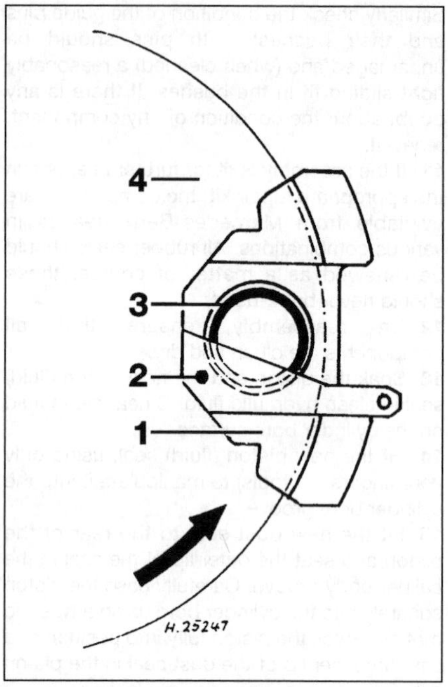

9.18 Correct positioning of piston in the rear brake caliper

1 Caliper 3 Piston
2 Special positioning tool 4 Disc

5 Carefully ease the fluid reservoir out from the top of the master cylinder. Recover the reservoir seals and plug the cylinder ports to prevent dirt entry.

6 Wipe clean the area around the brake pipe unions on the side of the master cylinder, and place absorbent rags beneath the pipe unions to catch any surplus fluid. Make a note of the correct fitted positions of the unions, then unscrew the union nuts and carefully withdraw the pipes. Plug or tape over the pipe ends and master cylinder orifices, to minimise the loss of brake fluid, and to prevent the entry of dirt into the system. Wash off any spilt fluid immediately with cold water.

7 Slacken and remove the two nuts and washers securing the master cylinder to the vacuum servo unit, then withdraw the unit forwards and away from servo unit. **Note:** *Do not tilt the master cylinder until it is disengaged from the servo unit pushrod otherwise the servo unit will be damaged.* Remove the sealing ring from the rear of the master cylinder.

Overhaul

Note: *Prior to dismantling the master cylinder, check the availability of spares from your Mercedes-Benz dealer noting that there are two possible types of master cylinder fitted.*

8 Remove all traces of dirt from the master cylinder body.

9 Remove the fluid reservoir mounting seals

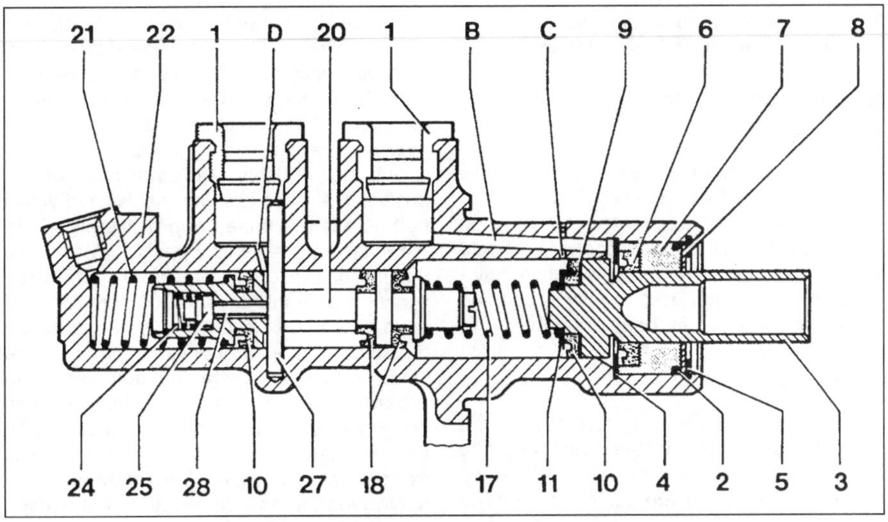

10.9 Cross-sectional view of master cylinder assembly - Teves model shown, others similar

1 *Mounting seals*
2 *Sealing ring*
3 *Primary piston*
4 *Stop washer*
5 *Circlip*
6 *Seal*
7 *Bush*
8 *Washer*
9 *Seal*
10 *Seal*
11 *Spring seat*
17 *Spring*
20 *Secondary piston*
21 *Spring*
22 *Cylinder body*
24 *Valve spring*
25 *Valve seal*
27 *Secondary piston pin*
28 *Valve pin*
B *Fluid supply bore*
C *Compensating bore*
D *Filling and compensating bore*

from the master cylinder, noting each seals correct fitted location **(see illustration)**.

10 Carefully grip the master cylinder body in a vice equipped with soft-jaws then using a suitable punch, press the piston into the cylinder until the secondary piston retaining pin can be withdrawn from the reservoir port.

11 Press the piston into the cylinder again and remove the piston retaining circlip from the master cylinder, along with its washer and sealing ring (where fitted).

12 Noting each component's correct fitted location, withdraw the primary piston assembly and spring from the cylinder.

13 Tap the master cylinder body on a clean wooden surface and withdraw the secondary piston assembly and spring from the master cylinder, noting which way around the piston assembly is fitted.

14 Thoroughly clean all components using only methylated spirit, isopropyl alcohol or clean hydraulic fluid as a cleaning medium. Never use mineral-based solvents such as petrol or paraffin which will attack the hydraulic system's rubber components. Dry the components immediately using compressed air or a clean, lint-free cloth.

15 Check all components and renew any that are worn or damaged. Check particularly the cylinder bores and pistons; the complete assembly should be renewed if these are scratched, worn or corroded. If there is any doubt about the condition of the assembly or of any of its components, renew it. Check that the fluid passages are clear.

16 If the assembly is fit for further use, obtain a repair kit from your Mercedes-Benz dealer. Renew all seals disturbed on dismantling as a matter of course; these should never be re-used.

17 Prior to reassembly, soak the piston assemblies and all new seals in clean hydraulic fluid. Smear clean fluid into the cylinder bore.

18 Fit the spring to the secondary piston assembly and insert the assembly into the master cylinder body, making sure the piston assembly is the correct way around. Fit the piston assembly using a twisting motion whilst ensuring that the piston seals do not become trapped as they enter the cylinder.

19 Ensure that the secondary piston slot is correctly positioned in relation to the master cylinder body then press the piston into position and secure it with the retaining pin.

20 Fit the new primary piston assembly as described in paragraph 18.

21 Where applicable, fit the new sealing ring to the end of the master cylinder then refit the washer and circlip. Make sure that the circlip is correctly located in the master cylinder groove.

22 Press the new fluid reservoir seals into the master cylinder ports.

Refitting

23 Remove all traces of dirt from the master cylinder and servo unit mating surfaces, and fit a new sealing ring to the rear of the master cylinder body.

24 Fit the master cylinder to the servo unit, ensuring that the servo unit pushrod enters the master cylinder bore centrally. Refit the master cylinder retaining nuts and tighten them to the specified torque.

25 Wipe clean the brake pipe unions, then refit them to the master cylinder ports and tighten them to the specified torque.

26 Ease the fluid reservoir into position in the master cylinder and (where necessary) reconnect the fluid hose(s).

27 Refill the master cylinder reservoir with new fluid, and bleed the complete hydraulic system as described in Section 2. Test the operation of the braking system exhaustively, before bringing the vehicle back into service on the public highway.

11 Vacuum servo unit - testing, removal and refitting

Testing

1 To test the operation of the servo unit, depress the footbrake several times with the engine off, to exhaust the vacuum from the servo. Now start the engine whilst keeping the pedal firmly depressed. There should be a noticeable "give" in the brake pedal as the engine starts and the vacuum builds up. Allow the engine to run for at least two minutes, then switch it off. If the brake pedal is now depressed it should feel normal, but further applications should result in the pedal feeling progressively firmer, with the pedal stroke decreasing on each application.

2 If the servo does not operate as described, first inspect the servo unit check valve as described in Section 12.

3 If the servo unit still fails to operate satisfactorily, the fault lies within the unit itself. Repairs to the unit are not possible - if faulty, the servo unit must be renewed.

Removal

Note: *New retaining nuts will be required on refitting.*

4 Remove the master cylinder as described in Section 10.

5 Unscrew the retaining nut and disconnect the vacuum hose from the servo unit; see Section 12.

6 Remove the driver's side lower facia panel as described in Chapter 11.

7 Remove the spring clip and slide out the clevis pin securing the brake pedal to the servo unit pushrod.

8 Slacken and remove the four servo unit retaining nuts, then return to the engine compartment and remove the servo unit from the vehicle.

Refitting

9 Prior to refitting, check the condition of the gasket which is glued to the rear of the servo unit. If the gasket shows signs of wear or damage, cut it off and stick a new one on.

10 Manoeuvre the servo unit into position in the engine compartment.
11 From inside the vehicle, ensure that the servo unit pushrod is correctly engaged with the brake pedal then fit the servo retaining nuts and tighten them to the specified torque.
12 Apply a smear of grease to the servo pushrod clevis pin and secure it in position with the spring clip.
13 Refit the driver's side lower facia panel (see Chapter 11).
14 Reconnect the vacuum hose to the servo and tighten its retaining nut to the specified torque.
15 Refit the master cylinder as described in Section 10. On completion, start the engine and check for air leaks at the vacuum hose-to-servo unit connection; check the operation of the braking system before using the vehicle on the road.

12 Vacuum servo unit check valve - removal, testing and refitting

Removal

1 Slacken the union nut and disconnect the vacuum hose from the servo unit **(see illustration)**.

12.1 Vacuum hose to servo unit union nut (arrowed)

2 Trace the hose back then disconnect it from the inlet manifold/pump connection (as applicable) and remove the hose and valve assembly from the engine compartment.

Testing

3 Examine the vacuum hose and check valve for signs of damage and renew if necessary.
4 The valve may be tested by blowing through the hose in both directions, air should flow through the valve in one direction only - when blown through from the servo unit end of the hose. Renew the hose assembly if this is not the case.

Refitting

5 Ensuring that the hose is correctly routed, securely reconnect it to the manifold/pump (as applicable). Connect the hose to the servo unit and tighten the union nut to the specified torque.
6 On completion, start the engine and check the valve to servo unit connection for signs of air leaks. Test the operation of the braking system exhaustively, before bringing the vehicle back into service on the public highway.

13 Parking brake - adjustment

1 Applying normal moderate pressure, fully apply the parking brake whilst counting the number of 'clicks' at the ratchet mechanism. If adjustment is correct, there should be approximately 7 or 8 clicks before the parking brake is fully applied. If there are less than 4 clicks or more than 11 clicks, adjust as follows.
2 Slacken and remove one wheel bolt from each of the rear wheels then chock the front wheels and jack up the rear of the vehicle, supporting it on axle stands (see "*Jacking and vehicle support*").
3 Locate the parking brake cable adjuster which is situated above the propeller shaft on the pivot assembly where the rear cables join. With the parking brake lever fully released, unscrew the cable adjuster to obtain maximum freeplay in the cables.
4 Starting on the left-hand rear wheel, position the wheel/disc so the vacated wheel bolt hole is positioned approximately 45° to the rear from the vertical position. Make sure the parking brake is fully released then insert a screwdriver in through the bolt hole and fully expand the parking brake shoes by rotating the adjuster knurled ring; looking through the wheel bolt hole rotate the adjuster in an upwards direction. When the wheel/disc can no longer be turned, back the knurled ring off by 5 or 6 teeth (notches) so that the wheel is free to rotate easily **(see illustrations)**.
5 Working on the right-hand rear wheel, adjust the brake as described in paragraph 4 noting that the adjuster should be rotated in a downwards direction to lock the disc/wheel.
6 With each set of shoes correctly adjusted, apply the parking brake lever firmly several times to settle the cable and brake components.
7 Adjust the parking brake cable using the cable adjuster until the brake is fully applied on the 7th click of the lever ratchet mechanism.
8 With the cable correctly adjusted, lower the vehicle to ground and refit the wheel bolts, tightening them to the specified torque. Test the operation of the parking brake exhaustively, before bringing the vehicle back into service on the public highway.

14 Parking brake shoes - removal and refitting

Removal

1 Remove the rear brake disc as described in Section 7, making a note of the correct

13.4a Position the wheel bolt hole as described in text and adjust the parking brake shoes . . .

13.4b . . . by rotating the adjuster ring (arrowed) with a flat-bladed screwdriver (shown with disc removed)

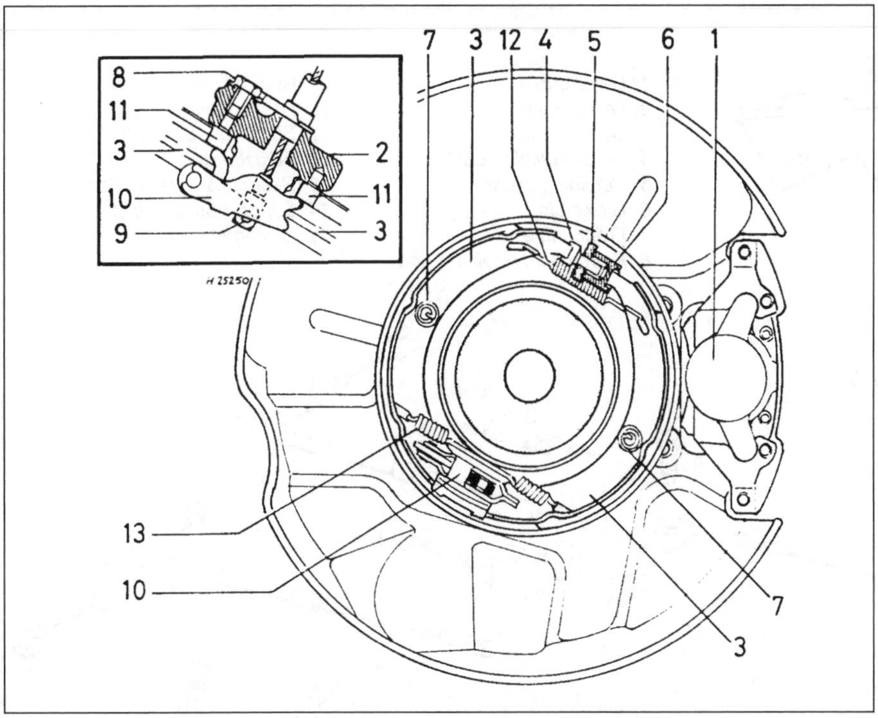

14.1 Layout of parking brake shoe components (left-hand side shown)

1 Brake caliper
2 Rear hub carrier
3 Parking brake shoes
4 Adjuster stud
5 Adjuster knurled ring
6 Adjuster body
7 Retaining spring
8 Cable retaining bolt
9 Cable pin
10 Expander mechanism
11 Locating bolts
12 Upper return spring
13 Lower return spring

fitted position of all components **(see illustration)**.

2 Using a pair of pliers, compress the shoe retaining springs then rotate them through 90° and remove them from the backplate. Access to the springs can be gained through the hub flange holes **(see illustration)**.

3 Carefully unhook and remove the parking brake shoe lower return spring, noting which way around the spring is fitted - it is not symmetrical **(see illustration)**.

4 Free the lower ends of the shoes from the expander mechanism and remove the assembly from the vehicle **(see illustration)**.

5 With the assembly on a bench, note each components correct fitted location then unhook the upper return spring and separate the shoes and adjuster assembly.

6 Inspect the parking brake shoes for signs of wear or contamination and renew if necessary. It is recommended that the return springs are renewed as a matter of course. Mercedes-Benz do not state any wear limit for the shoe friction material thickness, but shoes with anything less than 1.5 mm of friction material should be renewed.

7 Whilst the shoes are removed, clean and inspect the condition of the shoe adjuster and expander mechanisms, renew them if they show signs of wear or damage. If all is well, apply a fresh coat of brake grease (Mercedes-Benz recommend Molykote Paste U or G-Rapid) to the threads of the adjuster and sliding surfaces of the expander mechanism. Do not allow the grease to contact the shoe friction material.

14.2 Remove the retaining springs . . .

Refitting

8 Prior to installation, clean the backplate, and apply a thin smear of high-temperature brake grease (see paragraph 7) or anti-seize compound to all those surfaces of the backplate which bear on the shoes. Do not allow the lubricant to foul the friction material.

9 Assemble the shoes and the adjuster mechanism noting that the adjuster must be fitted with its knurled ring at the front of the adjuster. Fully retract the adjuster and fit the upper return spring.

10 Manoeuvre the assembly into position and engage the lower end of each shoe with the expander mechanism.

11 Fit the shoe lower return spring making sure it is fitted with its larger hooked end in the upper shoe **(see illustration)**.

12 Ensure that the shoes are correctly positioned and secure them in position with the retaining springs.

13 Check all components are correctly fitted and centralise the parking brake shoes.

14 Refit the brake disc as described in Section 7. Prior to refitting the roadwheel, adjust the parking brake as described in Section 13.

14.3 . . . then unhook the lower return spring, noting which way around it is fitted . . .

14.4 . . . and remove the parking brake shoe assembly from the vehicle

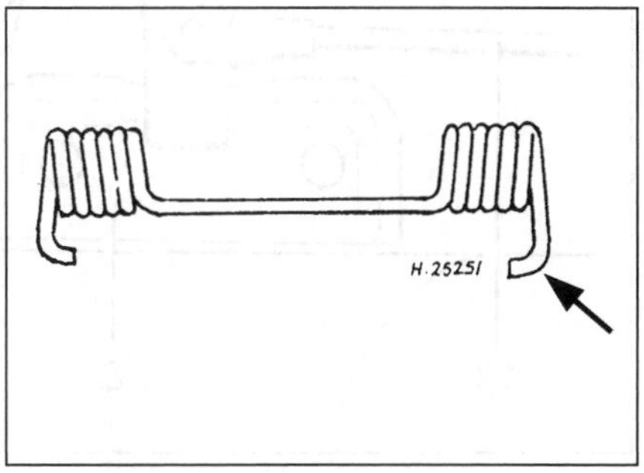

14.11 Ensure the lower return spring is fitted with its longer hook (arrowed) engaged with the upper parking brake shoe

9

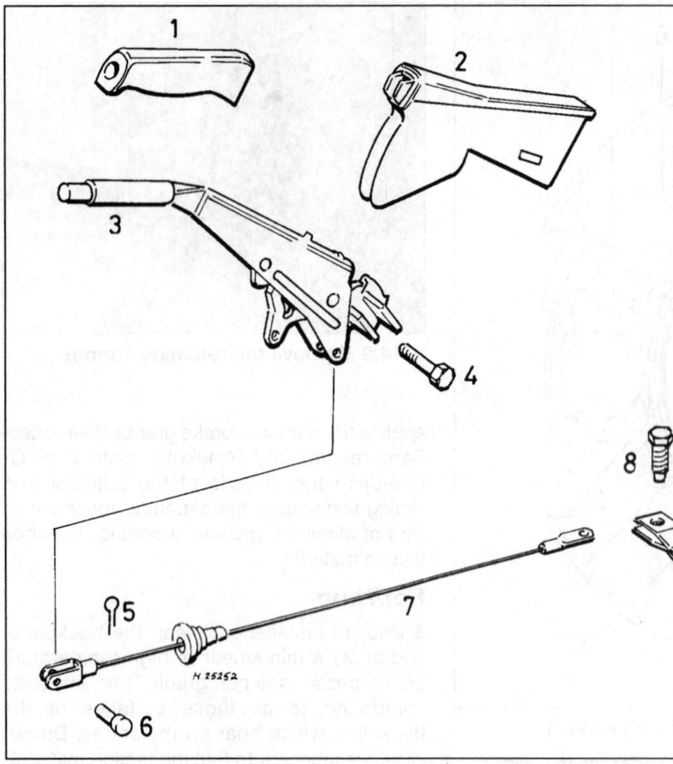

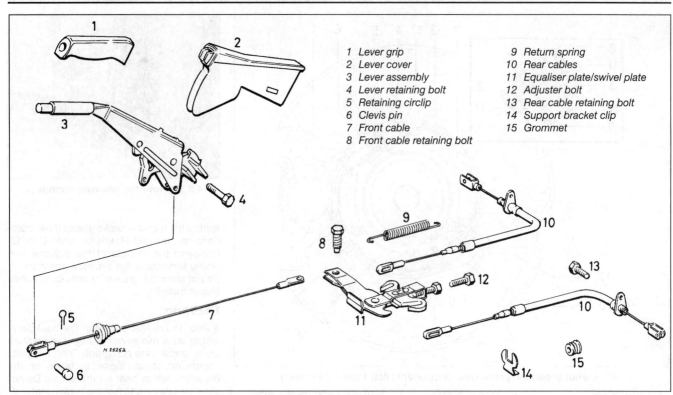

1 Lever grip
2 Lever cover
3 Lever assembly
4 Lever retaining bolt
5 Retaining circlip
6 Clevis pin
7 Front cable
8 Front cable retaining bolt
9 Return spring
10 Rear cables
11 Equaliser plate/swivel plate
12 Adjuster bolt
13 Rear cable retaining bolt
14 Support bracket clip
15 Grommet

15.2 Parking brake lever and cable arrangement

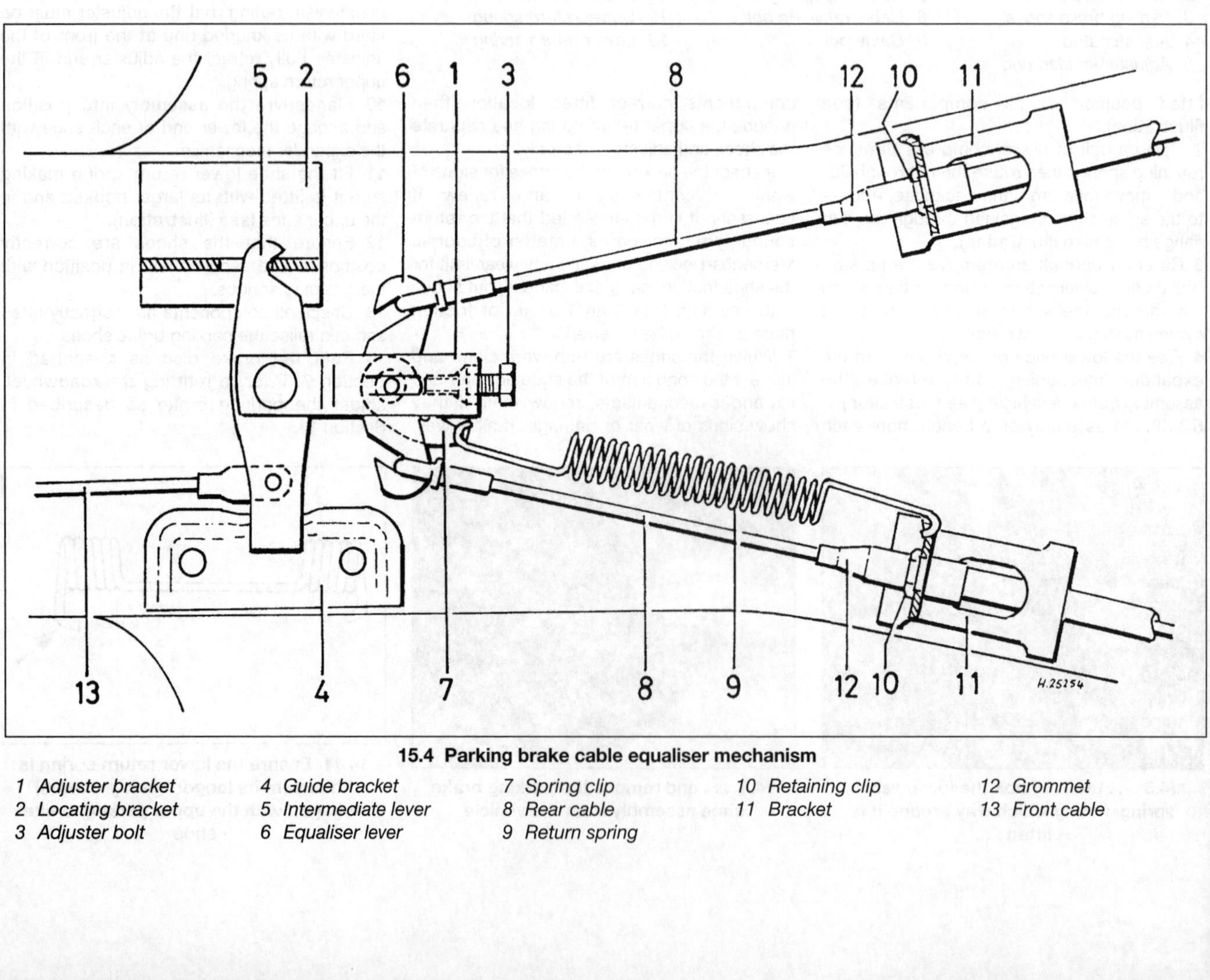

15.4 Parking brake cable equaliser mechanism

1 Adjuster bracket
2 Locating bracket
3 Adjuster bolt
4 Guide bracket
5 Intermediate lever
6 Equaliser lever
7 Spring clip
8 Rear cable
9 Return spring
10 Retaining clip
11 Bracket
12 Grommet
13 Front cable

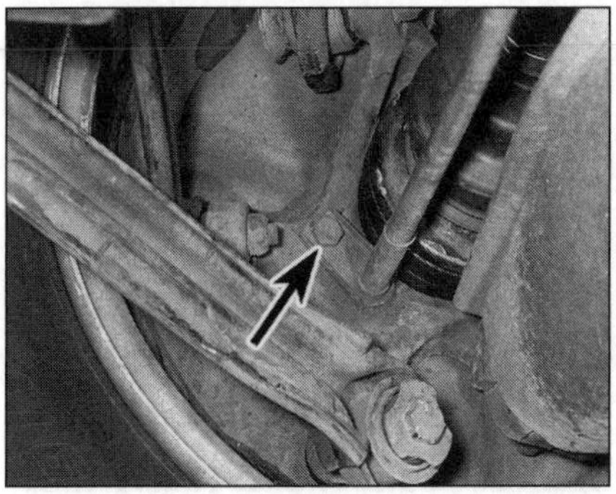

15.9 Parking brake rear cable to rear hub carrier bolt (arrowed)

15 Parking brake cables - removal and refitting

Front cable

Removal

Note: *A new cable-to-equaliser plate bolt will be required on refitting.*

1 Remove the driver's seat and centre console as described in Chapter 11.

2 Working at the base of the parking brake lever, extract the cotter pin, then withdraw the clevis pin and disconnect the cable from the lever **(see illustration)**.

3 Prise out the grommet, then pass the cable through the floorpan.

4 Working underneath the vehicle, unhook the return spring and remove it from the cable swivel plate **(see illustration)**.

5 Unscrew the bolt securing the rear of the front cable to the cable swivel plate. Discard the bolt, a new one should be used on refitting.

6 Working along the cable, noting its correct routing, and free it from all the relevant retaining clips and ties and remove it from the vehicle.

Refitting

7 Refitting is a reversal of the removal procedure, securing the cable to the cable swivel plate with a new bolt. On completion adjust the parking brake as described in Section 13.

Rear cable

Removal

Note: *A new cable-to-hub bolt will be required on refitting.*

8 Remove the relevant set of parking brake shoes as described in Section 14 and detach the expander mechanism from the end of the cable.

9 Unscrew the bolt securing the outer cable to the hub assembly and withdraw the cable from the rear of the backplate **(see illustration)**. Discard the bolt as a new one should be used on refitting.

10 Remove the fixings and lower the exhaust heat shield away from the floorpan.

15.12 Parking brake rear cable retaining clip (arrowed)

11 Unhook the return spring and remove it from the cable swivel plate.

12 Slide out the retaining clip securing the front end of the cable to its bracket then unhook the cable from the equaliser plate and remove it from underneath the vehicle **(see illustration)**.

Refitting

13 Refitting is a reversal of the removal procedure, securing the cable to the hub with a new bolt. On completion adjust the parking brake as described in Section 13.

16 Stop-light switch - removal and refitting

Removal

1 Remove the driver's side lower facia panel as described in Chapter 11.

2 Ensure that the ignition is switched off, then disconnect the wiring connector from the stop-light switch **(see illustration)**.

3 Depress the lug on the side of the switch body, then rotate the switch and withdraw it from the pedal mounting bracket .

Refitting

4 Fully extend the stop-light switch plunger from the switch body to reset the switch **(see illustration)**.

16.2 Disconnect the wiring connector (arrowed) from the stop-light switch

5 Fully depress the brake pedal and hold it in position then manoeuvre the switch into position. Rotate the switch until the locking lug clips into position. Slowly release the brake pedal and allow it to return to its stop. This will automatically adjust the stop-light switch.

6 Reconnect the wiring connector, and check the operation of the stop-lights. The stop-lights should illuminate after the brake pedal has travelled approximately 5 mm. If the switch is not functioning correctly, it is faulty and must be renewed; no other adjustment is possible.

7 On completion, refit the driver's side lower facia panel (see Chapter 11).

17 Anti-lock braking system (ABS) - general information

Note: *On models equipped with traction control, the ABS unit is a dual function unit and performs both the anti-lock braking system (ABS) and traction control (ASR) system functions.*

Models without traction control

1 ABS was fitted to most models as standard and available as an option on all others. The system comprises a hydraulic unit which contains the three hydraulic solenoid valves (one for each front brake and another for the rear brakes and the electrically driven return pump, the three roadwheel sensors; one for each wheel, and the electronic control unit (ECU). The purpose of the system is to prevent the wheel(s) locking during heavy braking and/or slippery road conditions. This is achieved by automatic release of the brake on the relevant wheel, followed by re-application of the brake. In the case of the rear wheels both brakes are applied at the same time.

2 The solenoids are controlled by the ECU, which itself receives signals from the four wheel sensors (front sensors are fitted to the hubs and the rear sensor is fitted to the final drive unit), which monitor the speed of rotation of each wheel. By comparing these

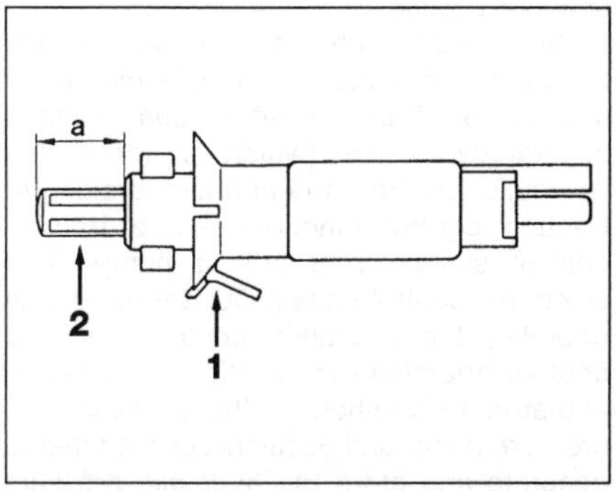

16.4 Stop-light switch retaining clip (1). On refitting fully extend the switch plunger (2) to the full extent of its travel (a)

signals, the ECU can determine the speed at which the vehicle is travelling. It can then use this speed to determine when a wheel is decelerating at an abnormal rate, compared to the speed of the vehicle, and therefore predicts when a wheel is about to lock. During normal operation, the system functions in the same way as a non-ABS braking system.

3 If the ECU senses that a wheel is about to lock, it operates the relevant solenoid valve in the hydraulic unit, which then isolates the relevant brake caliper(s) on the wheel(s) which is/are about to lock from the master cylinder, effectively sealing-in the hydraulic pressure.

4 If the speed of rotation of the wheel continues to decrease at an abnormal rate, the ECU switches on the electrically driven return pump operates and pumps the hydraulic fluid back into the master cylinder, releasing pressure on the brake caliper(s) so that the brake is released. Once the speed of rotation of the wheel returns to an acceptable rate, the pump stops; the solenoid valve opens, allowing the hydraulic master cylinder pressure to return to the caliper, which then re-applies the brake. This cycle can be carried out at up to 10 times a second.

5 The action of the solenoid valves and return pump creates pulses in the hydraulic circuit. When the ABS system is functioning, these pulses can be felt through the brake pedal.

6 The operation of the ABS system is entirely dependent on electrical signals. To prevent the system responding to any inaccurate signals, a built-in safety circuit monitors all signals received by the ECU. If an inaccurate signal or low battery voltage is detected, the ABS system is automatically shut down, and the warning light on the instrument panel is illuminated, to inform the driver that the ABS system is not operational. Normal braking should still be available, however.

7 If a fault does develop in the ABS system, the vehicle must be taken to a Mercedes-Benz dealer for fault diagnosis and repair.

Models with traction control (ASR)

8 On models also equipped with traction control (ASR), the hydraulic unit also performs the traction control function as well as the anti-lock braking.

9 On models with traction control, the hydraulic unit contains four solenoid valves (instead of three), a return pump and a changeover valve (which switches the hydraulic unit from the anti-lock braking to traction control function) and a traction control system pressurising pump. Two electronic control units (ECU) are fitted, one operates the hydraulic control unit and another operates the throttle valve position actuator. In addition to these changes, a pressure pump and accumulator are fitted to generate and store the hydraulic pressure needed to operate the braking side of the traction control system.

10 The braking side of the system works as described above, but each rear brake is now operated individually. An additional rear wheel sensor is fitted to the final drive unit and the hydraulic unit contains a solenoid valve for each rear brake.

11 The traction control system prevents the rear wheels from losing traction by either gently applying the brake or by closing the throttle valve, depending on the speed of the vehicle. In extreme cases a combination of both may be used.

12 On the braking side of the system, if a wheel is about to lose traction the hydraulic unit uses the hydraulic pressure stored in the accumulator to gently apply the brake on the relevant wheel. Once the risk of wheel spin has passed, the hydraulic unit allows the fluid to return to the accumulator and releases the brake, allowing the wheel to rotate freely again.

13 On the throttle side of the system, if traction is about to be lost, the second ECU operates the throttle valve actuator and closes the throttle valve, decreasing the engine power output. Once the risk of wheel spin has passed the actuator returns the throttle valve to its normal position and returns control of the throttle to the driver.

14 In the same way as the ABS, the vehicle must be taken to a Mercedes-Benz dealer for testing if a fault develops in the traction control (ASR) system.

Warning: Diagnosis of the faults within ABS/ASR systems requires access to dedicated test equipment. For safety reasons, owners are strongly advised against attempting to investigate complex problems with the ABS/ASR systems using standard workshop equipment.

18 Anti-lock braking system (ABS) components - removal and refitting

Warning: If any of the ABS system components have been disturbed or renewed, the operation of the system must be verified before the vehicle is brought back into service. This procedure must be carried out using dedicated test equipment and as such should be entrusted to a Mercedes Benz dealer.

Models without traction control

Hydraulic unit

Note: *Before starting work, refer to the note at the beginning of Section 2 concerning the dangers of hydraulic fluid.*

Removal

1 Disconnect the battery negative cable and position it away from the terminal.

2 Unscrew the master cylinder reservoir filler cap and top-up the reservoir to the "MAX" mark (see Chapter 1). Place a piece of polythene over the filler neck and securely refit the cap. This will minimise brake fluid loss during subsequent operations. As a precaution place absorbent rags beneath the hydraulic unit.

18.3 ABS hydraulic unit brake pipe unions (1) and wiring connector (2)

3 Wipe clean the area around the hydraulic unit brake pipe unions then make a note of how the pipes are arranged to use as a reference on refitting **(see illustration)**. Unscrew the union nuts and carefully withdraw the pipes. Plug or tape over the pipe ends and unit orifices to minimise the loss of brake fluid and to prevent the entry of dirt into the system. Wash off any spilt fluid immediately with cold water.

4 Undo the retaining screw and remove the relay cover from the unit to gain access to the wiring. Disconnect the wiring connector, free it from the hydraulic unit then undo the retaining bolt and disconnect the earth strap.

5 Slacken and remove the mounting nuts and release the hydraulic unit from its mounting bracket. If necessary, unscrew the rubber mounting bushes and remove them.

Note: *Do not attempt to dismantle the modulator block hydraulic assembly; overhaul of the unit is not possible.*

Refitting

6 Refitting is the reverse of the removal procedure noting the following points.

a) Examine the rubber mounting bushes for signs of wear or damage and renew if necessary.

b) Refit the brake pipes to their respective unions and tighten the union nuts to the specified torque.

c) Ensure that the wiring is correctly routed and the connector is firmly pressed into position.

d) On completion prior to refitting the battery, bleed the complete braking system as described in Section 2.

Electronic control unit (ECU)

Removal

7 The ABS electronic control unit (ECU) is located behind the plastic insulating cover which is fitted to the rear of the battery tray. Prior to removal, disconnect the battery negative lead.

8 Peel off the rubber seal and remove the cover from behind the battery. To further improve access, unclip the rubber sealing

18.9 ABS electronic control unit location

strip from the base of the windscreen then slide out the retaining clip and undo the retaining screws and remove the end section of the vent housing cover panel

9 Lift the wiring connector retaining clip and disconnect the connector then slide the ECU out of position and remove it from the vehicle **(see illustration)**.

Refitting

10 Refitting is the reverse of removal ensuring that the wiring connector is securely reconnected.

Front wheel sensor

Note: *New sensor retaining bolt(s) will be required on refitting,*

Removal

11 Chock the rear wheels, then firmly apply the parking brake, jack up the front of the vehicle and support on axle stands (see "*Jacking and vehicle support*"). Remove the appropriate front roadwheel.

12 Ensure that the ignition switch is turned off then trace the wiring back from the sensor to the connector. Unclip the wiring connector from its retaining clip and disconnect it from the main harness. Free the sensor wiring from any relevant retaining clips or ties, noting its correct routing, so that it is free to be removed.

13 Slacken and remove the bolt(s) securing the sensor to the steering knuckle, and remove the sensor and lead assembly from the vehicle **(see illustration)**. Examine the sensor sealing ring for signs of wear or damage and renew as necessary; Discard the retaining bolts, they must be renewed whenever they are disturbed.

Refitting

14 Prior to refitting, ensure that the mating surfaces of the sensor and steering knuckle are clean and dry and apply a thin coat of multi-purpose grease to them (Mercedes-Benz recommend the use of Molykote Longterm 2).

15 Ensure that the sensor tip and reluctor rings are clean and free from debris, and fit the sealing ring to the sensor.

16 Insert the sensor into the steering knuckle. Ensure that the sensor is correctly positioned then fit the new retaining bolt(s) and tighten to the specified torque.

17 Secure the wiring in position with all the necessary clips and ties making sure it is correctly routed. Ensure that the connector sealing ring is in good condition then connect the wiring and clip the connector into its retaining clip.

18 Refit the roadwheel, then lower the vehicle to the ground and tighten the roadwheel bolts to the specified torque.

Rear wheel sensor

Removal

Note: *A new sensor retaining bolt will be required on refitting.*

19 Chock the front wheels, then jack up the rear of the vehicle and support it on axle stands (see "*Jacking and vehicle support*").

20 To gain access to the sensor wiring connector, remove the rear seat as described in Chapter 11.

21 Ensure that the ignition switch is turned off then disconnect the sensor wiring from the connector. Free the wiring from its retaining clips so that it is free to be withdraw with the sensor.

22 From underneath the vehicle, ease the sensor wiring out from the floor and release it from any relevant retaining clips.

23 Unscrew the sensor retaining bolt and remove the sensor and sealing ring from the final drive unit **(see illustration)**. Renew the sealing ring if it shows signs of damage or deterioration and discard the retaining bolt, the bolt must be renewed whenever it is disturbed.

Refitting

24 Ensure that the sensor and final drive unit surfaces are clean and dry and fit the sealing ring to the sensor.

25 Ease the sensor into position then fit the new retaining bolt and tighten it to the specified torque setting.

26 Feed the wiring back up through the rubber grommet in the floor then, from inside the vehicle, connect it to the main harness. Ensure that the wiring is correctly routed and secure it in position with all the relevant clips.

27 Refit the rear seat and lower the vehicle to the ground.

Front reluctor rings

28 The front reluctor rings are fixed onto the rear of wheel hubs. Examine the rings for damage such as chipped or missing teeth. If renewal is necessary, the complete hub assembly must be renewed as described in Chapter 10.

Rear reluctor ring

29 The rear reluctor ring is an integral part of the final drive unit. With the sensor removed, examine the ring for signs of damage such as chipped or missing teeth, and renew as necessary. If renewal is necessary, the final drive unit will have to be overhauled by a Mercedes-Benz dealer or other suitable specialist.

Voltage protection relay

Removal

30 The voltage protection relay is located next to electronic control unit (ECU). Prior to removal ensure that the ignition is switched off.

31 Undo the retaining screw (where fitted) then unplug the relay and remove it from the engine compartment.

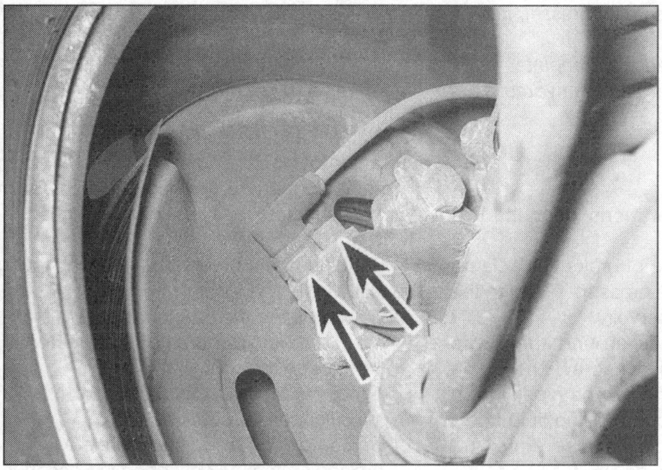

18.13 Front wheel sensor retaining bolts (arrowed)

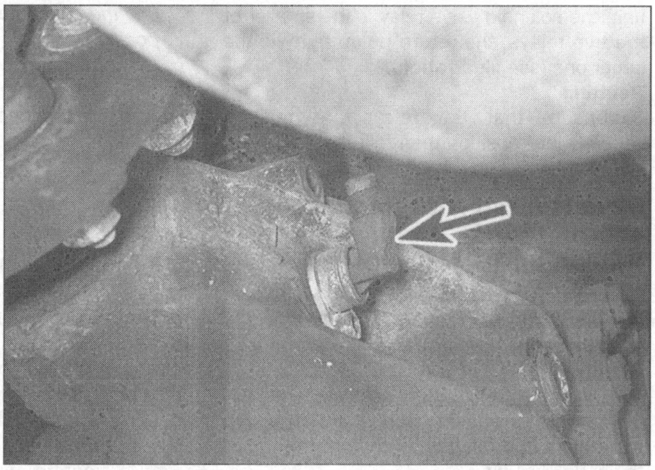

18.23 Rear wheel sensor is fitted to the side of the final drive unit

9

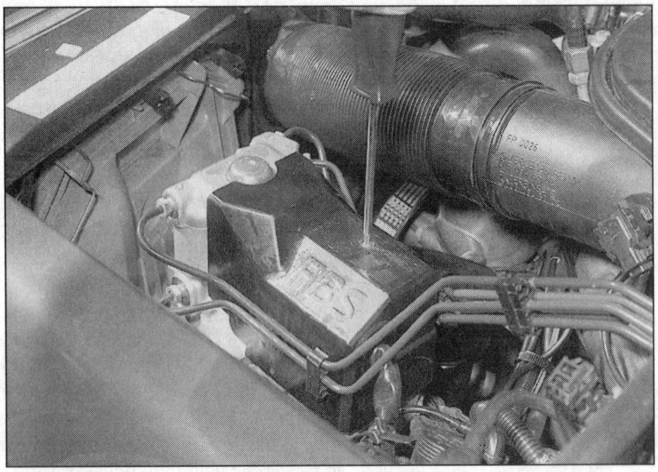

18.33a Slacken and remove the retaining screw . . .

18.33b . . . and lift off the relay cover from the hydraulic unit

18.34 ABS solenoid valve relay (1) and return pump relay (2)

Refitting

32 On refitting ensure that the relay and wiring connector terminals are clean and dry.

ABS relays

Removal

33 Undo the retaining screw and remove the relay cover from the top of the hydraulic unit **(see illustrations)**.

34 Ensure that the ignition is switched off and pull the relevant relay out from the control unit; the solenoid valve relay is the smaller of the two relays, the return pump relay is the larger one **(see illustration)**.

Refitting

35 Ensure that the relays are pushed securely into position then refit the cover and securely tighten its retaining screw.

Models fitted with traction control (ASR)

Hydraulic unit

Note: *Before starting work, refer to the note at the beginning of Section 2 concerning the dangers of hydraulic fluid.*

Removal

36 Disconnect the battery negative terminal.

37 Undo the retaining screw(s) then unclip the covers and remove them from the top of the hydraulic unit.

38 Attach a piece of hose to the hydraulic unit bleed screw (marked "SP") and place the end of the hose into a container. Depressurise the hydraulic unit by slackening the bleed screw and allowing the fluid to drain into the container.

39 Release the retaining clip and disconnect the wiring connector from the hydraulic unit.

40 Disconnect the hydraulic pipes from the unit as described in paragraphs 2 and 3.

41 Unscrew the retaining nut and detach the earth strap from the unit.

42 Slacken and remove the retaining bolts and lift the hydraulic unit out of position.

Note: *Do not attempt to dismantle the modulator block hydraulic assembly; overhaul of the unit is not possible.*

Refitting

43 Refitting is the reverse of the removal procedure noting the following points.

a) *Examine the rubber mounting bushes for signs of wear or damage and renew if necessary.*
b) *Refit the brake pipes to their respective unions and tighten the union nuts to the specified torque.*
c) *Ensure that the wiring is correctly routed and the connector is firmly pressed into position.*
d) *On completion, bleed the complete braking system (including the hydraulic unit) as described in Section 2.*

Pressure pump

Removal

44 Carry out the operations described in paragraphs 36 to 38.

45 To minimise the loss of brake fluid, clamp the hose connecting the pressure pump to the master cylinder fluid reservoir.

46 Wipe clean the area around the pump hose and pipe unions. Unscrew the union nut(s) and carefully withdraw the pipe(s) from the pump and also disconnect the fluid hose. Plug or tape over the pipe/hose ends and pump orifices to minimise the loss of brake fluid and to prevent the entry of dirt into the system. Wash off any spilt fluid immediately with cold water.

47 Disconnect the wiring connector from the pump then free the pump from its mounting bracket and remove it from the engine compartment.

Refitting

48 Refitting is a reverse of the removal sequence, noting the following points.

a) *Renew the pump mounting rubber if it shows signs of damage or deterioration.*
b) *On completion bleed the complete braking system as described in Section 2, not forgetting to bleed the hydraulic unit.*

Pressure accumulator

Removal

49 Carry out the operations described in paragraphs 36 to 38.

50 Working as described in paragraphs 2 and 3, disconnect the pressure accumulator pipes from the base of the hydraulic unit.

51 Firmly apply the parking brake then jack up the front of the vehicle and support it on axle stands (see "*Jacking and vehicle support*"). Remove the left-hand front roadwheel.

52 Undo the retaining screws and remove the wheelarch liner from underneath the left-hand wing.

53 Slacken and remove the nuts securing the accumulator to its mounting bracket then carefully manoeuvre the accumulator out of position complete with its hydraulic pipes.

Refitting

54 Refitting is the reverse of removal noting the following.

a) *When refitting the assembly, ensure that the hydraulic pipes are correctly routed up through the circular bracket.*
b) *Tighten the pipe union nuts to the specified torque setting.*
c) *On completion bleed the complete braking system as described in Section 2, not forgetting to bleed the hydraulic unit.*

Electronic control units (ECU)

55 Refer to paragraphs 7 to 10 noting that the hydraulic unit ECU is the rear of the two ECU's and the throttle valve position actuator ECU is the front ECU.

Front wheel sensor

56 Refer to paragraphs 11 to 18.

Rear wheel sensor

Note: *A new sensor retaining bolt and final drive unit mounting bolt nuts will be required on refitting. A sensor sealing ring will also be required.*

Removal

57 Chock the front wheels, then jack up the rear of the vehicle and support it on axle stands (see "*Jacking and vehicle support*").

58 Unscrew the retaining nuts and free the sensor wiring tray from the vehicle body.

59 Position a jack with a block of wood on its head underneath the final drive unit and raise the jack until it is supporting the weight of the final drive.

60 Undo the retaining nuts and withdraw the two rear mounting bolts from the final drive unit.

61 Slacken and remove the nut and withdraw the final drive unit front mounting bolt.

62 Carefully lower the final drive unit until the propeller shaft contacts the seat belt support bar or heatshield which is fitted across the body tunnel. Recover the washers and mounting rubbers from the final drive unit front mounting; renew the rubbers if they show signs of damage.

63 Slacken and remove the sensor retaining bolt and withdraw the sensor from the top of the final drive unit, along with its sealing ring. Renew the sealing ring.

64 Trace the sensor wiring back to the connector block and remove the cover. Rotate the retaining ring and disconnect the wiring connector from the block.

65 If both sensors are to be removed, make alignment marks between the sensor wires and connector. Unclip the cover from the rear of the connector then free the sensor terminal(s) and remove it from underneath the vehicle.

Refitting

66 Insert the sensor terminal(s) into the wiring connector, using the marks made on removal to ensure that they are correctly fitted, and clip the cover back into position. Reconnect the connector to the block, securing it in position with the retaining ring, and refit the cover.

67 Ensure that the sensor and final drive surfaces are clean and dry and fit a new sealing ring to the sensor.

68 Insert the sensor into the final drive unit, making sure it is correctly seated, then fit the new retaining bolt and tighten to the specified torque setting.

69 Ensure that the upper and lower front mounting rubber and washers are correctly positioned the carefully raise the final drive unit back into position.

70 Insert the final drive unit mounting bolts and fit the new nuts. Tighten the mounting bolts to the specified torque setting (see Chapter 8).

71 Ensure that the sensor wiring is correctly routed then refit the wiring tray and lower the vehicle to the ground.

Front reluctor rings

72 The front reluctor rings are fixed onto the rear of wheel hubs. Examine the rings for damage such as chipped or missing teeth. If renewal is necessary, the complete hub assembly must be renewed as described in Chapter 10.

Rear reluctor rings

73 The rear reluctor rings are an integral part of the final drive unit. If renewal is necessary, the final drive unit will have to be overhauled by a Mercedes-Benz dealer or other suitable specialist.

Voltage protection relay

74 Refer to paragraphs 30 to 32.

ASR relays

75 Refer to paragraphs 33 to 35.

19 Braking system vacuum pump (diesel models) - testing, removal and refitting

Testing

1 The operation of the braking system vacuum pump can be checked using a vacuum gauge.

2 Disconnect the vacuum pipe from the pump, and connect the gauge to the pump union using a suitable length of hose.

3 Start the engine and allow it to idle, then measure the vacuum created by the pump. As a guide, a minimum of approximately 500 mm Hg should be recorded. If the vacuum registered is significantly less than this, it is likely that the pump is faulty. However, seek the advice of a Mercedes-Benz dealer before condemning the pump.

Removal

4 Remove the cooling fan as described in Chapter 3.

5 Remove the auxiliary drivebelt as described in Chapter 1.

6 Slacken the union nut and disconnect the vacuum hose from the top of the pump which is mounted on the front of the cylinder block.

7 Slacken and remove the pump retaining bolts and remove it from the cylinder block. Recover the pump gasket and discard it.

Refitting

8 Refitting is the reverse of removal, using a new gasket and making sure the pump drive flange is correctly engaged.

Notes

Chapter 10
Suspension and steering

Contents

Front hub assembly - removal, overhaul and refitting 3
Front hub bearing - checking and adjustment 2
Front steering knuckle assembly - removal and refitting 4
Front suspension and steering check . . . . .See Chapter 1
Front suspension anti-roll bar - removal and refitting 8
Front suspension coil spring - removal and refitting 6
Front suspension lower arm - removal, overhaul and refitting 7
Front suspension shock absorber - removal, overhaul and refitting . . 5
General information 1
Power steering fluid level check . . . . .See *"Weekly checks"*
Power steering pump - removal and refitting 24
Power steering pump drivebelt check, adjustment and renewal . . . . .See Chapter 1
Power steering system - bleeding 25
Rear hub bearing - renewal 10
Rear hub carrier - removal and refitting 9
Rear suspension anti-roll bar - removal and refitting 15
Rear suspension anti-roll bar connecting link - removal and refitting . . 16
Rear suspension coil spring - removal and refitting 12
Rear suspension control arms - removal and refitting 13
Rear suspension lower arm - removal, overhaul and refitting 14
Rear suspension shock absorber - removal, testing and refitting . . 11
Steering box - removal, overhaul and refitting 21
Steering box drop arm - removal and refitting 22
Steering box lower seal - renewal 23
Steering column - removal, inspection and refitting 18
Steering column rubber coupling - removal and refitting 20
Steering damper - removal and refitting 26
Steering drag link - removal and refitting 27
Steering intermediate arm - removal and refitting 28
Steering lock/ignition switch - removal and refitting 19
Steering wheel - removal and refitting 17
Track rod - removal and refitting 30
Track rod balljoint - removal and refitting 29
Wheel alignment and steering angles - general information 31
Wheel and tyre maintenance and tyre pressure checks . . . . .See *"Weekly checks"*

Degrees of difficulty

Easy, suitable for novice with little experience	**Fairly easy,** suitable for beginner with some experience	**Fairly difficult,** suitable for competent DIY mechanic	**Difficult,** suitable for experienced DIY mechanic	**Very difficult,** suitable for expert DIY or professional

Specifications

Front suspension

Type	Independent, with coil springs and telescopic shock absorbers. Anti-roll bar fitted to most models

Rear suspension

Type	Independent, with coil springs and telescopic shock absorbers. Anti-roll bar fitted to most models

Steering

Type	Power-assisted steering box with drag link, intermediate arm and track rod arrangement. Steering damper fitted to track rod

Front hub bearing

Endfloat	0.01 to 0.02 mm

Wheel alignment and steering angles

Front wheel:	
Camber angle:	
Models up to October 1988	0° 0'
Models from October 1988	-0° 25'
Castor angle (wheel in the straight-ahead position):	
Models up to October 1988	10° 10'
Models from October 1988	10° 25'
Toe setting (total)	0° 20'
Rear wheel:	
Camber angle	-1° 30'
Toe setting (total)	0° 25'

Roadwheels

Type	Pressed steel or aluminium alloy (depending on model)
Size	6J x 15, 6.5J x 15 or 7J x 15

Tyres

Roadwheels size:	
6J x 15 wheels	185/65 R 15
6.5J x 15 wheels	195/65 R 15
7J x 15 wheels	205/60 R 15
Tyre pressures	Refer to "*Weekly checks*"

Torque wrench settings

	Nm	lbf ft
Front suspension		
Anti-roll bar:		
Mounting clamp nuts	20	15
Mounting bracket bolts	60	44
Hub nut clamp bolt	12	8
Lower arm:		
Balljoint clamp bolt nut	125	92
Pivot bolt nut	120	88
Shock absorber:		
Upper mounting to body nuts	20	15
Mid-mounting to steering knuckle nut:		
Models up to December 1984	75	55
Models from January 1985	110	81
Lower mounting to steering knuckle bolts (x2)	110	81
Mounting plate nut	60	44
Steering knuckle:		
Steering arm bolts	80	59
Rear suspension		
Anti-roll bar:		
Mounting clamp bolts	28	21
Connecting link:		
Upper nut	30	22
Lower bolt nut	20	15
Control arms:		
Pivot bolt nuts:		
M10 nuts	40	30
M12 nuts	70	52
Lower rear (track) arm balljoint nut	35	22
Lower arm:		
Inner pivot bolt	70	52
Outer pivot bolt	120	88
Shock absorber:		
Upper mounting nut	15	11
Upper mounting locknut	30	22
Lower mounting bolt nut	60	44
Steering		
Drag link balljoint nut	35	26
Drop arm clamp bolt	55	40
Intermediate arm pivot bolt	110	81
Power steering pump:		
Mounting bolts	25	18
Pulley bolts	30	22
Rubber coupling clamp bolts	25	18
Steering box mounting bolts	70 to 80	52 to 59
Steering column mounting nuts and bolts	20	15
Steering damper bolt nuts	40	30
Steering wheel bolt	80	59
Track rod:		
Balljoint nut	35	26
Inner balljoint clamp bolt	20	15
Outer balljoint clamping sleeve	50	37
Roadwheels		
Roadwheel bolts	110	81

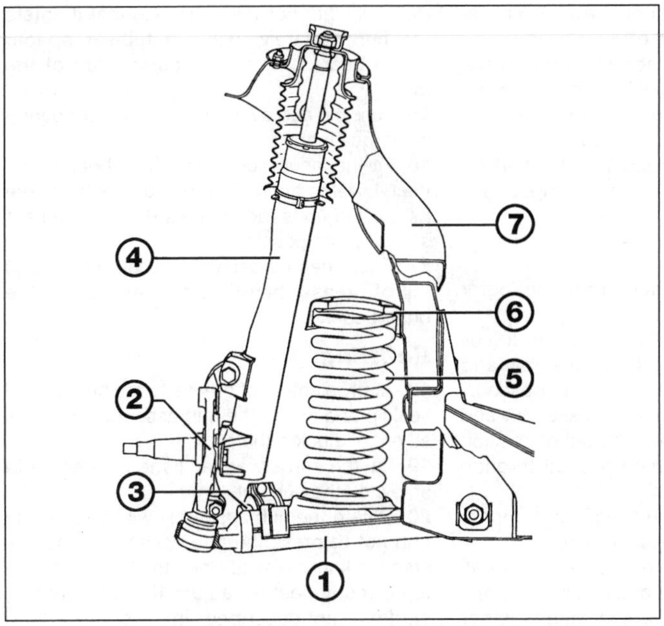

1.1 Cross-sectional view of the front suspension

1 *Lower arm*
2 *Steering knuckle*
3 *Anti-roll bar*
4 *Shock absorber*
5 *Coil spring*
6 *Spring seat*
7 *Body*

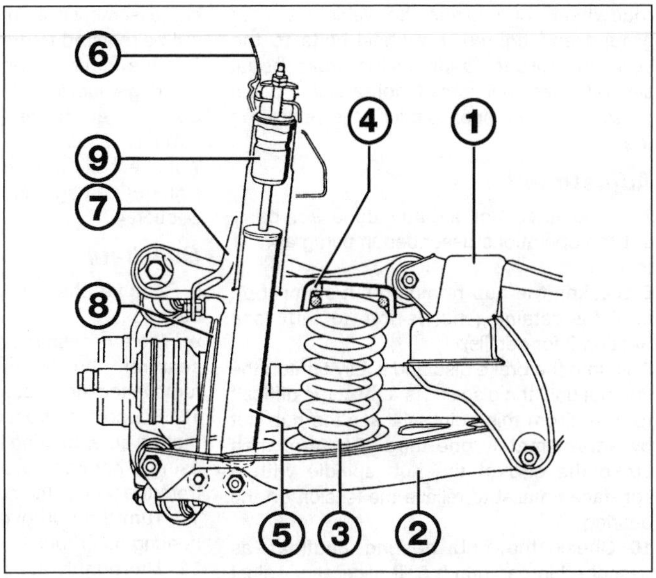

1.2 Cross-sectional view of the rear suspension - later model shown (early models similar)

1 *Subframe*
2 *Lower arm*
3 *Coil spring*
4 *Spring seat*
5 *Shock absorber*
6 *Body*
7 *Anti-roll bar*
8 *Connecting link*
9 *Rubber damper*

1 General information

The independent front suspension incorporates coil springs and telescopic shock absorbers **(see illustration)**. The shock absorbers are located by transverse lower suspension arms, which use rubber inner mounting bushes, and incorporate a balljoint at the outer ends. The front steering knuckles, which carry the brake calipers and the hub/disc assemblies, are bolted to the shock absorbers, and connected to the lower arms through balljoints. A front anti-roll bar is fitted to most models. The anti-roll bar is rubber-mounted and is connected to both lower arms by mounting clamps.

The independent rear suspension also incorporates coil springs and telescopic shock absorbers **(see illustration)**. The shock absorbers are located by transverse lower suspension arms, which use rubber mounting bushes. The hub assemblies are fastened to the lower arms and are joined to the rear subframe by the three control arms; two upper arms and a lower one. Coil springs are fitted between the lower arms and vehicle body. A rear anti-roll bar is fitted to most models. The anti-roll bar is rubber-mounted and is connected to both lower arms by connecting links.

The steering column is connected to the steering gear by an intermediate shaft and rubber coupling.

The steering box is mounted onto the bulkhead. The steering box is connected to one of the steering knuckles directly by a track rod and is connected to the other steering knuckle by a drag link, intermediate arm and track rod linkage. The track rod and drag link have a balljoint at each of their ends. The track rod balljoint ends are threaded to facilitate adjustment.

Power-assisted steering is standard on all models. The hydraulic steering system is powered by a belt-driven pump which is driven off the crankshaft pulley.

Note: *Many of the suspension and steering components are secured in position with self-locking nuts. Whenever a self-locking nut is disturbed, it must be discarded and a new nut fitted.*

2 Front hub bearing - checking and adjustment

Checking

1 Firmly apply the parking brake then jack up the front of the vehicle and support it on axle stands (see "*Jacking and vehicle support*"). Remove the relevant front roadwheel.

2 Using spacers, refit two of the wheel bolts, positioning them on opposite sides, and tightening them securely.

3 Tap the grease cap out from the centre of the hub. If the cap is damaged on removal, it must be renewed. Where necessary, remove the radio interference spring from the centre of the axle shaft.

4 Using a large, flat-bladed screwdriver, carefully lever the brake pads clear of the disc so that they will not affect the hub bearing free play.

5 Mount the dial gauge onto the front face of the hub/disc and position the gauge probe so that it is in contact with the end of the axle shaft. Zero the gauge scale, then grasp the disc at two opposite points and pull it in and out **(see illustration)**. Note the reading obtained on the gauge and check that the hub bearing endfloat is within the limits given in the *Specifications* at the start of this Chapter. If not adjust the bearing as described under the following sub-heading.

6 If all is well, remove the dial gauge then refit the radio interference spring (where fitted) and tap the grease cap into position. Refit the

2.5 Using a dial gauge to check the hub bearing endfloat adjustment

roadwheel then lower the vehicle to the ground and tighten the wheel bolts to the specified torque. Depress the brake pedal several times until normal, non-assisted pedal pressure returns prior to taking the vehicle on the road.

Adjustment

7 If you have not already done so, carry out the operations described in paragraphs 1 to 4.

8 Slacken the hub retaining nut clamp bolt until the retaining nut is free to turn (see Section 3 for details).

9 Rotate the brake disc and lightly tighten the hub nut until the disc starts to become difficult to turn. From this point, slacken the hub nut by approximately one-third of a turn, then strike the end of the hub spindle with a soft-faced mallet to relieve the tension on the bearing.

10 Check the hub bearing endfloat as described in paragraph 5. If necessary adjust the endfloat by rotating the hub nut as necessary. Once the endfloat is correctly set, tighten the hub nut clamp bolt to the specified torque.

11 Recheck the bearing endfloat then refit all disturbed components as described in paragraph 6.

3 Front hub assembly - removal, overhaul and refitting

Note: *The hub assembly should not be removed unless the bearings are to be renewed since the hub bearing inner race is a press-fit on the steering knuckle and removal of the hub will almost certainly damage the bearings. A press will be required to dismantle and rebuild the assembly; if such a tool is not available, a large bench vice and spacers (such as large sockets) will serve as an adequate substitute. The bearing's inner races are an interference fit on the hub; if the inner race remains on the hub when it is pressed out of the hub carrier, a knife-edged bearing puller will be required to remove it.*

Removal

1 Remove the front brake disc as described in Chapter 9. On models with ABS also remove the front wheel sensor.

2 Tap the grease cap out from the centre of the hub **(see illustration)**. If the cap is damaged on removal, it must be renewed.

3 Remove the radio interference spring (where fitted) from the centre of the axle shaft **(see illustration)**.

4 Slacken the hub nut clamp bolt then slacken and remove the hub nut from the axle **(see illustrations)**. Remove the thrustwasher (where fitted).

5 The front hub assembly can now be withdrawn from the steering knuckle. If the hub assembly is a tight-fit on the axle, a puller will be required to draw it off.

6 If the inner bearing race remains on the steering knuckle, a knife-edge type puller will be required to remove it. With the race removed, slide off the hub oil seal.

7 Inspect the steering knuckle axle shaft for signs of damage and renew if damaged (see Section 4).

Overhaul

8 Remove the inner race from the outer bearing.

9 Where necessary, carefully lever out the oil seal from the rear of the hub assembly and remove the inner race from the inner bearing.

10 Support the front of the hub assembly and tap the outer bearing inner race out of position using a hammer and punch passed through from the rear of the hub.

11 Turn the hub over and remove the inner bearing outer race in the same way.

12 Thoroughly clean the hub, removing all traces of dirt and grease, and polish away any burrs or raised edges which might hinder reassembly. Check for cracks or any other signs of wear or damage, and renew if necessary. On models with ABS ensure that the sensor ring is in good condition.

13 On reassembly, apply a light coating of grease (Mercedes-Benz recommend Castrol LMX) to the bearing outer race and hub contact surfaces. Also work the grease well into the inner race tracks.

14 Securely support the hub, and locate the inner bearing outer race in the hub. Press the race fully into position, ensuring that it enters the hub squarely, using a tubular spacer which bears only on the outer edge of the race.

15 Turn the hub over and fit the outer bearing inner race in the same way.

16 Fit the inner race to the inner bearing. Fit the oil seal to the rear of the hub, making sure its sealing lip is facing inwards, and press it squarely into position.

17 Pack the hub assembly about two thirds full of grease then fit the inner race to the outer bearing.

Refitting

18 Apply a smear of grease to the hub rear oil seal lip and locate the hub assembly onto the steering knuckle shaft.

19 Fit the thrustwasher (where fitted) and screw on the hub nut.

20 Rotate the hub assembly whilst using the hub nut to press the hub assembly onto the steering knuckle axle. Once the hub assembly is correctly seated, adjust the hub bearing endfloat as described in Section 2 and tighten the hub nut clamp bolt to the specified torque.

21 With the endfloat correctly set, remove the dial gauge.

22 Fit the radio interference spring (where fitted) to the centre of the axle shaft.

23 Fit the grease cap to the hub and tap it squarely into position.

24 Refit the brake disc and (where necessary) the ABS front wheel sensor as described in Chapter 9.

3.2 Remove the grease cap from the centre of the hub . . .

3.3 . . . and pull out the radio interference spring from the hub spindle

3.4a Slacken the clamp bolt . . .

3.4b . . . and unscrew the hub nut

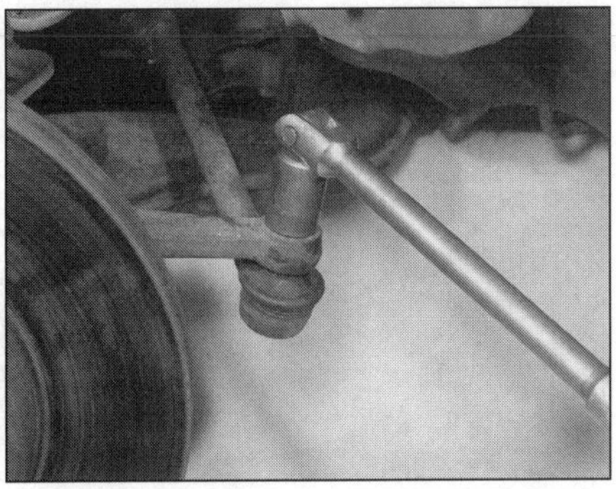

4.4 Unscrew the retaining nut and detach the track rod from the steering knuckle

4.9 Remove the lower arm balljoint clamp bolt and nut

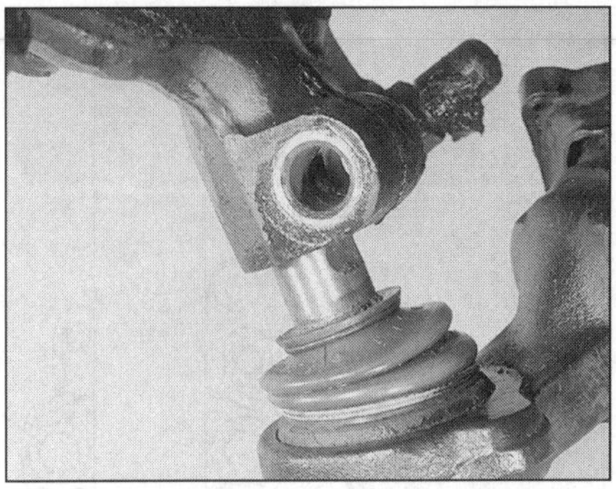

4.10 Free the steering knuckle from the lower arm balljoint

4 Front steering knuckle assembly - removal and refitting

Note: *New shock absorber to steering knuckle lower bolts and upper bolt nut, a steering rod balljoint nut and a lower arm balljoint clamp bolt nut will be required on refitting.*

Removal

1 Firmly apply the parking brake then jack up the front of the vehicle and support it on axle stands (see "*Jacking and vehicle support*"). Remove the relevant front roadwheel.

2 If the steering knuckle is to be renewed, remove the hub assembly as described in Section 3.

3 If the steering knuckle assembly is to be refitted, slacken and remove the two bolts securing the brake caliper mounting bracket to the knuckle then slide the caliper assembly off the disc. **Note:** *Discard the caliper bolts, new ones must be used on refitting.* Using a piece of wire or string, tie the caliper to the front suspension coil spring, to avoid placing any strain on the hydraulic brake hose. On models with ABS also remove the wheel sensor as described in Chapter 9.

4 Slacken and remove the nut securing the steering rod balljoint to the steering knuckle **(see illustration)**, and release the balljoint tapered shank using a universal balljoint separator.

5 On models equipped with ASD (automatic locking differential), if work is being carried out on the right-hand side, undo the retaining bolts and remove the wheel acceleration sensor.

Caution: The ASD sensor is sensitive to impacts and must not be dropped or knocked.

6 Whilst the steering knuckle is removed it will be necessary to support the lower arm. Do this by positioning a jack and block of wood underneath the arm and raising the jack to support the arm. Alternately, compress the coil spring using a suitable spring compressor.

7 Slacken and remove the two lower bolts securing the strut to the shock absorber.

8 Slacken and remove the nut and washer and withdraw the upper bolt securing the shock absorber to the steering knuckle.

9 Free the steering knuckle from the shock absorber then slacken and remove the lower arm balljoint clamp bolt and nut **(see illustration).**

10 Free the steering knuckle from the lower arm balljoint and remove it from the vehicle **(see illustration)**. Inspect the knuckle for signs of wear or damage and renew as necessary. Note that the steering arm can be renewed separately; the arm bolts must be renewed whenever they are disturbed.

Refitting

11 Prior to refitting, clean the threads of the steering knuckle lower bolt holes by running a tap of the correct thread size and pitch down them.

> **HAYNES HiNT** ***If a suitable tap is not available, clean out the holes using one of the old bolts with slots cut in its threads.***

12 Engage the knuckle with the lower arm balljoint stud. Insert the clamp bolt then fit the new nut and tighten it to the specified torque. To prevent corrosion, fill the steering knuckle clamp split with sealant.

13 Locate the knuckle correctly with the shock absorber, making sure the knuckle peg is correctly located in the hole.

14 Insert the steering knuckle upper retaining bolt and washers and fit the new nut. Fit the two new lower bolts securing the shock absorber to the knuckle. With all bolts loosely fitted, push firmly down on the steering knuckle axle to force the top of the knuckle into contact with the shock absorber. Hold the knuckle in this position and tighten the upper bolt nut to the specified torque setting, then tighten both the lower bolts to the specified torque.

15 Remove the jack/spring compressor (as applicable) and connect the steering rod balljoint to the knuckle. Fit a new nut to the balljoint and tighten it to the specified torque setting.

16 Fit the hub assembly as described in Section 3.

17 On models where the hub was not disturbed, remove all traces of locking compound (see paragraph 11) and slide the caliper into position over the disc, making sure the pads pass either side of the disc. Fit the new mounting bolts and tighten them to the specified torque setting (see Chapter 9).

18 Where necessary, refit the ASD sensor to the hub and securely tighten its retaining bolts.

19 Refit the roadwheel then lower the vehicle to the ground and tighten the wheel bolts to the specified torque.

5 Front suspension shock absorber - removal, overhaul and refitting

Note: *New shock absorber upper mounting nuts, a shock absorber to steering knuckle upper bolt nut and lower retaining bolts will be required on refitting.*

Removal

1 Chock the rear wheels, apply the parking brake, then jack up the front of the vehicle and support on axle stands (see "*Jacking and vehicle support*"). Remove the appropriate roadwheel.

2 Whilst the shock absorber is removed it will be necessary to support the lower arm. Do this by positioning a jack and block of wood underneath the arm and raising the jack to support the arm. Alternately, compress the coil spring using a suitable spring compressor (see Section 6).

3 Slacken and remove the two lower bolts securing the shock absorber to the steering knuckle then remove the nut and

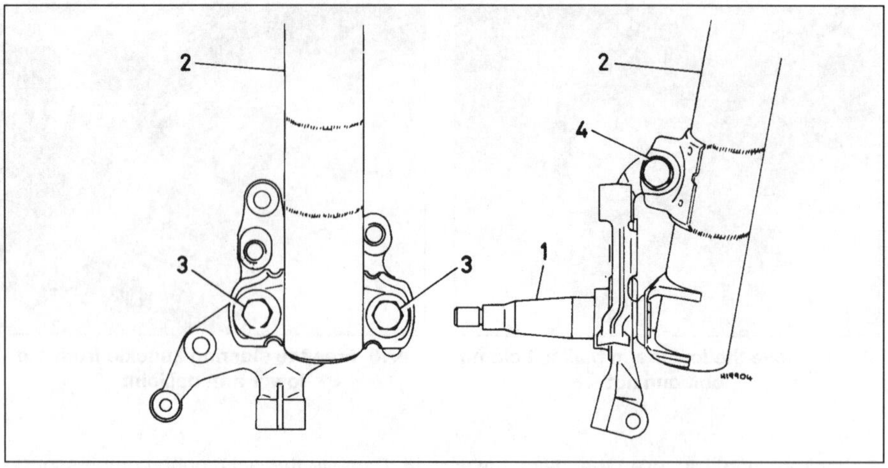

5.3 Front shock absorber to steering knuckle mounting details

1 *Steering knuckle* 2 *Shock absorber* 3 *Lower mounting bolts* 4 *Upper mounting nut and bolt*

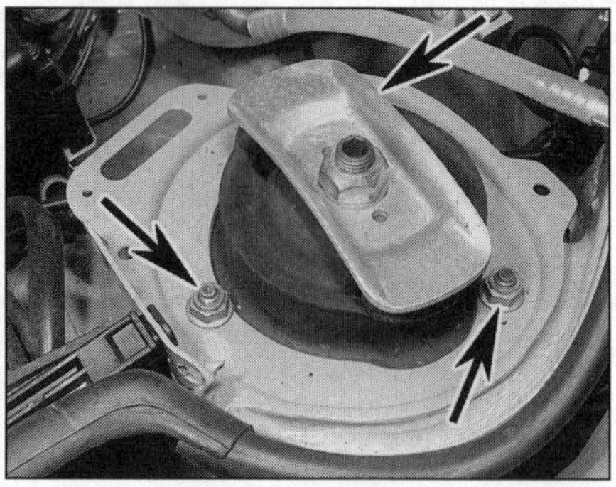

5.4 Unscrew the strut upper mounting nuts (arrowed)

washer and withdraw the upper bolt **(see illustration)**.

4 From within the engine compartment, unscrew the strut upper mounting nuts **(see illustration)** then carefully lower the strut assembly out from underneath the wing.

Overhaul

Note: *A new mounting plate nut will be required.*

5 With the strut removed from the car, clean away all external dirt, then mount it upright in a vice.

6 Slacken and remove the upper mounting plate nut whilst retaining the shock absorber piston with a suitable Allen key **(see illustration)**.

7 Remove the nut and washer and lift off the mounting plate and upper mounting assembly.

8 Remove the rubber bump stop from the piston then release the retaining clip and slide off the dust gaiter from the shock absorber **(see illustration)**.

9 Examine the shock absorber for signs of fluid leakage. Check the piston for signs of pitting along its entire length, and check the shock body for signs of damage. While holding it in an upright position, test the operation of the shock absorber by moving the piston through a full stroke, and then through short strokes of 50 to 100 mm. In both cases, the resistance felt should be smooth and continuous. If the resistance is jerky, or uneven, or if there is any visible sign of wear or damage to the shock absorber, renewal is necessary.

10 Inspect all other components for signs of damage or deterioration, and renew any that are suspect.

11 Fit the dust gaiter to the shock absorber. Make sure the lower end of gaiter is correctly positioned and secure it in position with the retaining clip.

12 Slide the rubber bump stop onto the shock absorber piston and fit the upper mounting.

13 Fit the upper mounting plate and washer and screw on the new nut. Retain the shock absorber piston and tighten the mounting plate nut to the specified torque.

14 Engage the upper end of the dust gaiter with the lip on the base of the upper mounting.

Refitting

15 Prior to refitting, clean the threads of the shock absorber to steering knuckle lower bolt holes by running a tap of the correct thread size and pitch down them.

HAYNES HiNT ***If a suitable tap is not available, clean out the holes using one of the old bolts with slots cut in its threads.***

16 Manoeuvre the shock absorber into position, and fit the new upper mounting nuts.

5.6 Slacken and remove the upper mounting plate nut whilst retaining the shock absorber piston with a suitable Allen key

17 Locate the knuckle correctly with the shock absorber, making sure the knuckle peg is correctly located in the hole.

18 Insert the steering knuckle upper retaining bolt and washers and fit the new nut. Fit the two new lower bolts securing the shock absorber to the knuckle. With all bolts loosely fitted, pull the shock absorber firmly upwards to force the top of the steering knuckle into contact with the shock absorber lug. Hold the shock absorber in this position and tighten the two lower bolts to the specified torque setting first, then tighten the upper bolt nut to the specified torque.

19 Remove the jack/spring compressor (as applicable) and tighten the upper mounting nuts to the specified torque.

20 Refit the roadwheel then lower the vehicle to the ground and tighten the wheel bolts to the specified torque.

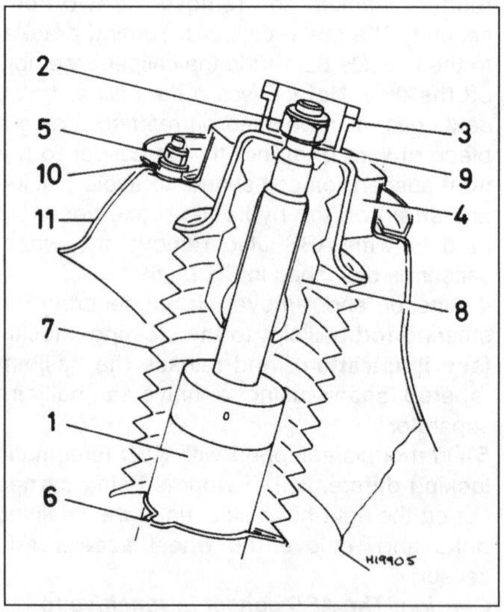

5.8 Front shock absorber components - assembly and mounting details

1 *Shock absorber*
2 *Upper mounting plate nut*
3 *Rebound stop*
4 *Upper mounting*
5 *Upper mounting nuts*
6 *Dust cover clip*
7 *Dust cover*
8 *Bump stop*
9 *Washer*
10 *Washer*
11 *Body turret*

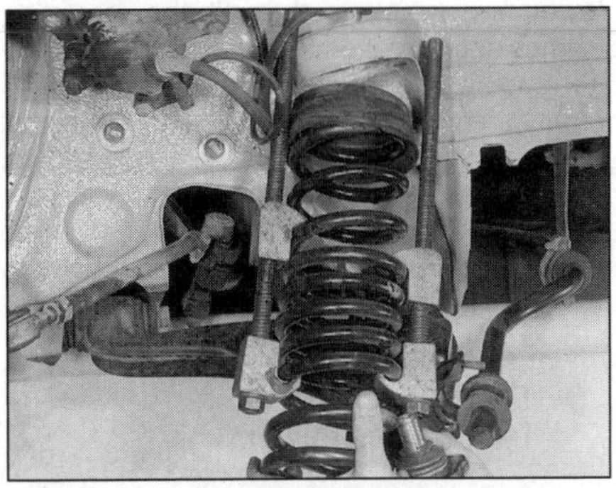

6.5 Remove the coil spring and upper spring seat, together with the spring compressors

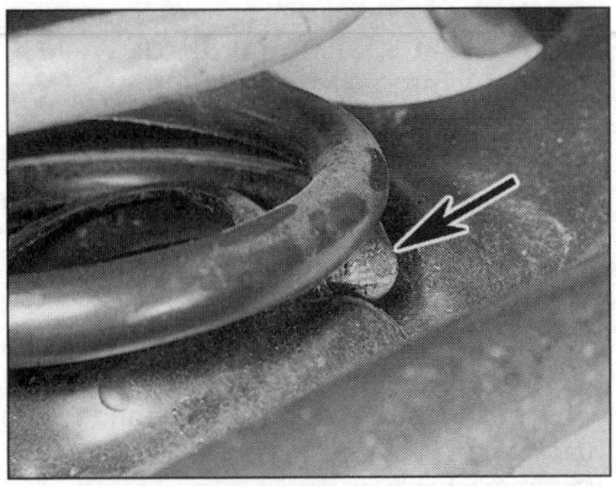

6.8a Locate the lower end of the spring correctly against the stop (arrowed) on the lower arm seat

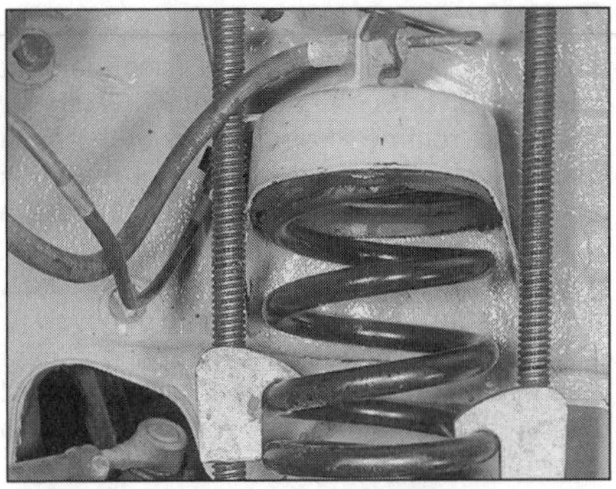

6.8b Align the upper spring seat with the body mounting and carefully raise the lower arm

6 Front suspension coil spring - removal and refitting

Note: *New shock absorber upper mounting nuts will be required on refitting.*

Removal

Warning: A suitable tool to hold the coil spring in compression must be obtained. Adjustable coil spring compressors are readily-available, and are recommended for this operation. Any attempt to remove the spring without such a tool is likely to result in damage or personal injury.

1 Chock the rear wheels, apply the parking brake, then jack up the front of the vehicle and support on axle stands (see "*Jacking and vehicle support*"). Remove the appropriate roadwheel.

2 Fit the spring compressor, and compress the coil spring until all tension is relieved from the spring seats.

3 Position a jack and block of wood beneath the lower arm and raise the jack head until the arm is securely supported.

4 Slacken and remove the shock absorber mounting upper mounting nuts.

5 Carefully lower the lower suspension arm until it is possible to the remove the coil spring and upper spring seat **(see illustration)**.

6 Inspect the coil spring for signs of wear or damage and renew if necessary. The upper spring seat should also be renewed if it is damaged or shows signs of deterioration.

Refitting

7 Ensure that the lower arm spring seat is clean then fit the upper spring seat to the coil spring and manoeuvre the spring into position.

8 Locate the lower end of the spring correctly against the stop on the lower arm seat. Align the upper spring seat with the body mounting and carefully raise the lower arm whilst also aligning the shock absorber upper mounting with the body **(see illustrations)**.

9 Check that the spring is correctly located then fit the new nuts to the shock absorber upper mounting and tighten them to the specified torque.

10 Remove the jack from beneath the lower arm then carefully release the spring compressor whilst making sure both its upper and lower ends are correctly located.

11 Refit the roadwheel then lower the vehicle to the ground and tighten the wheel bolts to the specified torque.

7 Front suspension lower arm - removal, overhaul and refitting

Note: *New lower arm pivot bolt nuts, a balljoint clamp bolt nut and anti-roll bar mounting clamp nuts will be required on refitting.*

Removal

1 Chock the rear wheels, apply the parking brake, then jack up the front of the vehicle and support on axle stands (see "*Jacking and vehicle support*"). Remove the appropriate roadwheel.

2 Undo the retaining screws and remove the plastic cover from beneath the engine/ transmission.

3 Slacken and remove the retaining nuts securing the anti-roll bar mounting clamp to the front of the lower arm and remove the mounting rubber.

4 Fit a spring compressor to the coil spring and compress the spring to relieve the tension from its upper and lower seats (see Section 6).

5 Position a jack and block of wood beneath the lower arm and raise the jack until it is supporting the weight of the arm.

6 Slacken and remove the nut and clamp bolt securing the lower arm balljoint to the steering knuckle. Carefully lower the arm slightly, freeing the balljoint from the knuckle clamp, until it is possible to withdraw the coil spring and spring seat.

7 Make alignment marks between the lower arm pivot bolt eccentric washers and the subframe. This will be necessary to ensure that the camber and castor angles remain correct on refitting.

8 Slacken and remove the lower arm pivot bolt nuts and remove the bolts and eccentric washers, noting which way around the bolts are inserted **(see illustration)**. The lower arm can then be removed from underneath the vehicle.

Overhaul

9 Thoroughly clean the lower arm and the area around the arm mountings, removing all traces of dirt and underseal if necessary, then check carefully for cracks, distortion or any other signs of wear or damage paying particular attention to the mounting bushes and balljoint. If either bush or the balljoint requires renewal, the lower arm should be taken to a Mercedes-Benz dealer or suitably equipped garage. A hydraulic press and suitable spacers are required to press the bushes or balljoint out of position and install the new ones.

10 Inspect the lower arm balljoint gaiter for signs of wear or damage and renew if necessary **(see illustration)**.

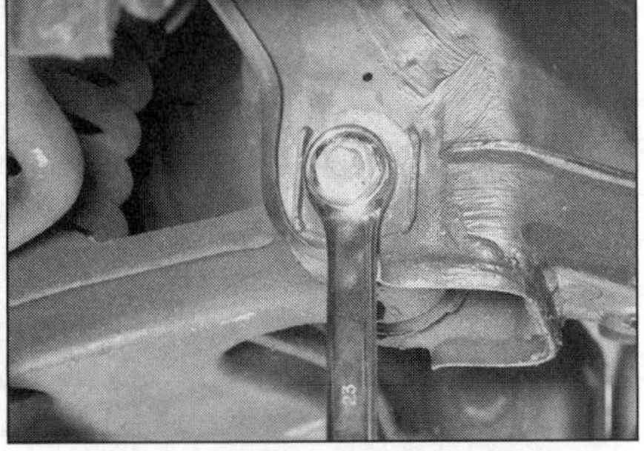

7.8 Remove the lower arm pivot bolt nuts and withdraw the bolts; note the orientation of the eccentric washers

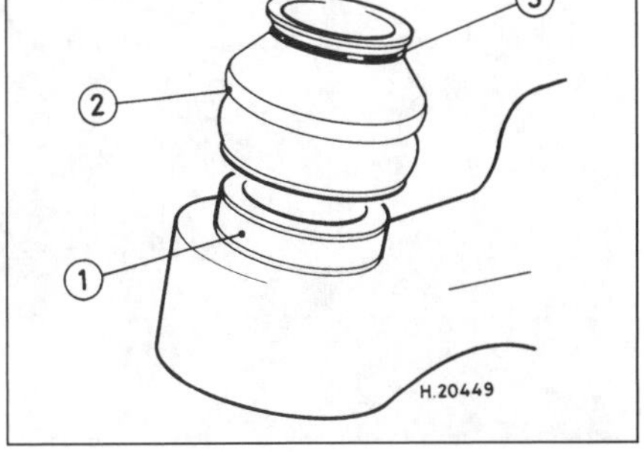

7.10 Suspension lower arm balljoint gaiter

1 Balljoint 2 Gaiter 3 Upper retaining clip

Refitting

11 Offer up the lower arm and insert the front and rear pivot bolts and eccentric washers. Insert the front bolt from the rear of the bush and the rear bolt from the front of the bush and ensure that the eccentric washers are correctly located on the subframe. Fit the new nuts, tightening them lightly only at this stage, and align the marks made prior to removal.

12 Ensure that the lower arm spring seat is clean then fit the upper spring seat to the coil spring and manoeuvre the spring into position.

13 Locate the lower end of the spring correctly against the stop on the lower arm seat. Align the upper spring seat with the body mounting and carefully raise the lower arm whilst also aligning the balljoint shank with the steering knuckle.

14 Check that the coil spring is correctly located then insert the lower arm balljoint clamp bolt. Ensure that the balljoint is correctly located then fit the new clamp bolt nut and tighten it to the specified torque setting. To prevent corrosion, fill the steering knuckle clamp split with sealant.

15 Slide the rubber mounting onto the end of the anti-roll bar and locate it in the lower arm clamp. Fit the mounting clamp and then screw on the new nuts and tighten them to the specified torque.

16 Remove the jack from beneath the lower arm then carefully release the spring compressor whilst making sure both its upper and lower ends are correctly located.

17 Refit the roadwheel then lower the vehicle to the ground and tighten the wheel bolts to the specified torque.

18 With the vehicle resting on its wheels, rock it to settle the lower arm in position. Ensure that the lower arm pivot bolt eccentric washers are correctly aligned with the marks made prior to removal, then tighten both the pivot bolt nuts to the specified torque and refit the engine undercover. **Note:** *It is recommended that the front steering angles and wheel alignment are checked at the earliest possible opportunity by a Mercedes-Benz dealer or other suitably equipped garage.*

8 Front suspension anti-roll bar - removal and refitting

Note: *New mounting clamp retaining nuts will be required on refitting.*

Removal

1 Chock the rear wheels, firmly apply the parking brake, then jack up the front of the vehicle and support on axle stands (see "*Jacking and vehicle support*"). Remove both front roadwheels.

2 Undo the retaining screws and remove the plastic undercover from beneath the engine/transmission.

3 Make alignment marks between the mounting bushes and anti-roll bar.

4 Unscrew the retaining nuts and remove the mounting clamps securing the anti-roll bar to the suspension lower arms **(see illustration)**.

5 Slacken and remove the nuts and bolts securing the mounting clamps to the body brackets and remove the clamps **(see illustration)**.

6 Free the anti-roll bar and manoeuvre it out from underneath the vehicle. If necessary, the mounting brackets can then be unbolted and removed from the vehicle body.

7 Inspect the mounting rubbers for signs of damage or deterioration and renew as necessary **(see illustration)**.

Refitting

8 Where necessary, refit the anti-roll bar mounting brackets to the vehicle body and tighten the retaining bolts to the specified torque.

9 Lubricate the mounting bushes with soapy water and slide them into position.

10 Align the mounting rubbers with the marks made prior to removal and manoeuvre the anti-roll bar into position.

11 Engage the mounting rubbers with the body brackets and refit the mounting clamps. Insert the clamp bolts and fit the new nuts, tightening them lightly only.

12 Locate the outer mounting rubbers in the lower arm brackets then fit the mounting clamps and screw on the new clamp nuts.

13 Ensure that the marks made prior to removal are correctly aligned then tighten all the clamp nuts to the specified torque setting.

14 Refit the plastic undercover.

15 Fit the roadwheels then lower the vehicle to the ground and tighten the wheel bolts to the specified torque.

9 Rear hub carrier - removal and refitting

Note: *A new driveshaft retaining nut and control arm and lower arm outer pivot bolt/balljoint nuts will be required on refitting.*

Removal

1 Remove the wheel trim or hub cap, then using a hammer and pointed-nose chisel, carefully relieve the driveshaft retaining nut staking (where applicable). Slacken the driveshaft retaining nut with the vehicle resting on its wheels. Also slacken the wheel bolts.

2 Chock the front wheels, then jack up the rear of the vehicle and support it on axle stands (see "*Jacking and vehicle support*").

3 Remove the relevant rear roadwheel.

4 With reference to Chapter 9 , carry out the following:

a) Remove the brake caliper
b) Remove the brake disc
c) Unhook the relevant rear parking brake cable from the equaliser bar.

5 Undo the retaining screws and remove the protective cover from the base of the suspension lower arm. Position a jack and block of wood underneath the lower arm and raise the jack until it is supporting the weight of the arm.

6 Slacken and remove the nut and pivot bolt securing the lower arm to the hub carrier.

7 Support the hub carrier assembly and slacken and remove the nuts and pivot bolts securing the upper and lower control arms to the hub carrier (see Section 13). **Note:** *To preserve the rear wheel alignment settings,*

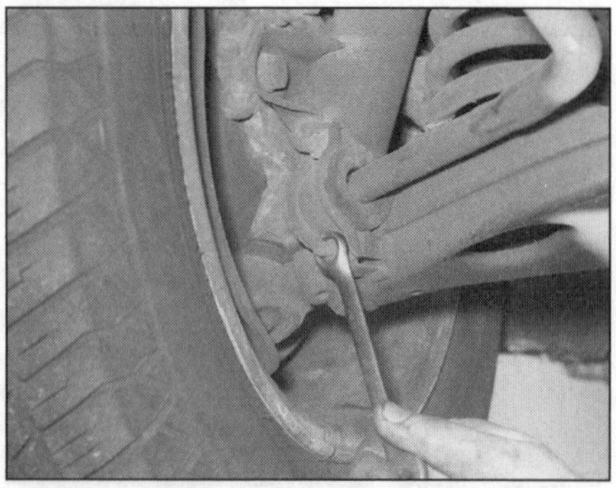

8.4 Unscrew the retaining nuts and remove the clamps securing the front anti-roll bar to the lower arms . . .

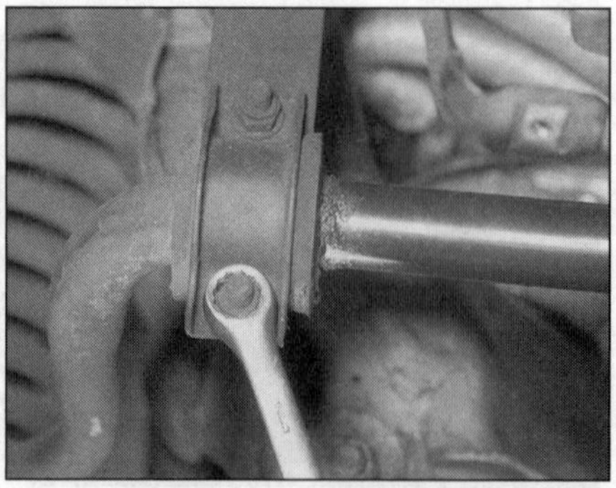

8.5 . . . and undo the nuts and bolts and remove the clamps securing it to the mounting brackets

8.7 Renewing an anti-roll bar mounting rubber

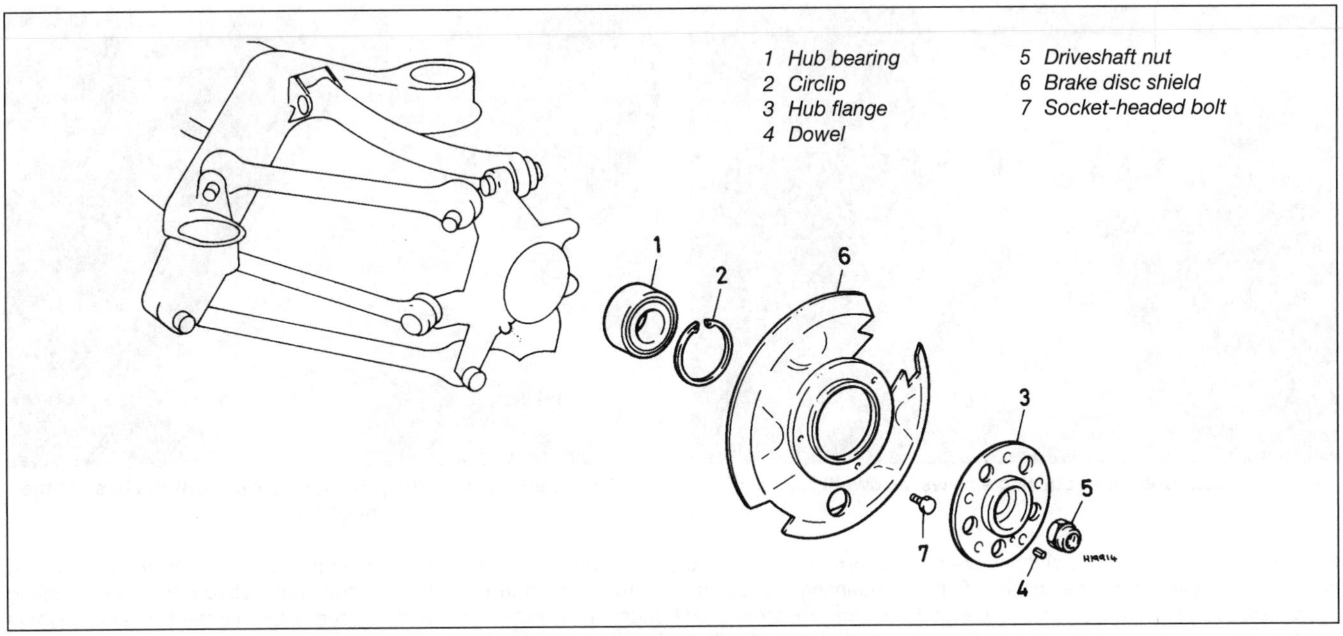

10.4 Rear hub and bearing components

mark the position of the eccentric screw and cam, before removing the upper and lower control arms.

8 Remove the driveshaft retaining nut completely and withdraw the hub assembly from the end of the driveshaft joint. If necessary, tap the joint out of the hub using a soft-faced mallet. If this fails to free it from the hub, the joint will have to be pressed out using a suitable tool which is bolted to the hub.

9 Remove the hub assembly and support the driveshaft by hanging it from the vehicle underbody using a piece of wire. **Note:** *Do not allow the driveshaft to hang under its own weight as the CV joint may be damaged.*

Refitting

10 Manoeuvre the hub assembly into position and engage it with the driveshaft joint.

11 Align the hub assembly with the control arms and (where necessary) insert the pivot bolts. Fit a new nut to each of the pivot bolts and the balljoint, tightening them lightly only at this stage.

12 Insert the lower arm pivot bolt and fit the new retaining nut, tightening it lightly only. **Note:** *To preserve the rear wheel alignment, observe the alignment markings made on the control arm eccentric screw and cam. If no marks were made during removal, position the screw at the centre of its range of adjustment.*

13 Lubricate the threads of the new driveshaft nut with clean engine oil and screw the nut onto the driveshaft end. Tighten the driveshaft retaining nut to the specified torque and stake it firmly into the driveshaft groove using a hammer and punch. If necessary, lightly tighten the nut and then tighten and stake the nut once the vehicle is resting on its wheels.

14 Refit the brake disc as described in Chapter 9.

15 Refit the roadwheel then lower the vehicle to the ground and tighten the wheel bolts to the specified torque.

16 With the vehicle resting on its wheels, rock it to settle the hub carrier in position then tighten the control arm and lower arm outer pivot bolt/balljoint nuts to their specified torque settings. Refit the protective cover to the lower arm and securely tighten its retaining screws. **Note:** *It is recommended that the rear wheel alignment is checked at the earliest possible opportunity by a Mercedes-Benz dealer or other suitably equipped garage.*

10 Rear hub bearing - renewal

Note: *A press and suitable tubular spacers will be required to dismantle and rebuild the assembly; if such a tool is not available, a large bench vice and spacers (such as large sockets) will serve as an adequate substitute. The bearing's inner races are an interference fit on the hub flange; if the inner race remains on the hub flange when it is pressed out of position, a knife-edged bearing puller will be required to remove it.*

1 Remove the rear hub carrier as described in Section 9.

2 Securely support the hub carrier and carefully press the hub flange out from the centre of the bearing. If the bearing inner race remains on the flange, remove it with a knife-edge bearing puller.

3 Remove the hub bearing retaining circlip from the hub carrier.

4 Support the hub carrier and press the hub bearing out of position using a suitable tubular spacer **(see illustration)**.

5 Thoroughly clean the hub carrier bore, removing all traces of dirt and grease and polish away any burrs or raised edges which might hinder reassembly. Renew the circlip if there is any doubt about its condition.

6 On reassembly, apply a light film of clean engine oil to the bearing outer race to aid installation.

7 Locate the bearing in the hub carrier and press it fully into position, ensuring that it enters the carrier squarely, using a suitable tubular spacer which bears only on the bearing outer race.

8 Secure the bearing in position with the circlip making sure it is correctly located in the hub carrier groove.

9 Securely support the bearing inner race and press the hub flange fully into the bearing.

10 Check the bearing rotates freely then refit the rear hub carrier as described in Section 9.

11 Rear suspension shock absorber - removal, testing and refitting

Note: *This procedure does not apply to models fitted with self-levelling rear suspension.*

Caution: A new shock absorber lower mounting bolt nut will be required on refitting.

Removal

2 Check the front wheels then jack up the rear of the vehicle and support it on axle stands (see "*Jacking and vehicle support*"). To improve access, remove the rear roadwheel.

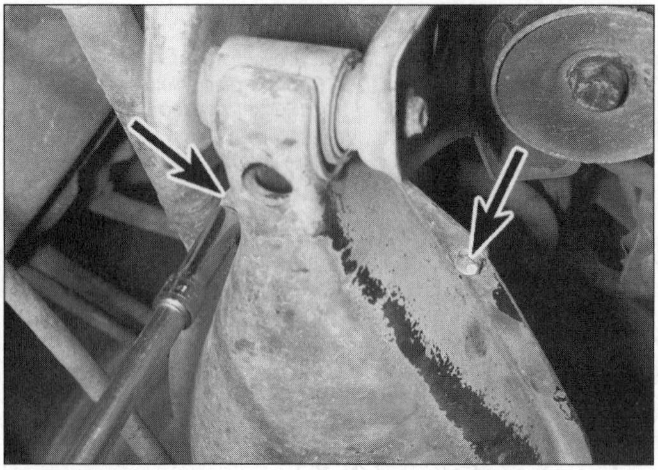

11.3a Undo the retaining screws (arrowed) . . .

11.3b . . . and remove the protective cover from the base of the lower arm

3 Undo the retaining screws and remove the protective cover from the base of the suspension lower arm. Position a jack and block of wood underneath the lower arm and raise the jack until it is supporting the weight of the arm **(see illustrations).**

4 Remove the luggage compartment side trim panel to gain access to the shock absorber upper mounting **(see illustrations).**

5 Retain the shock absorber upper mounting nut with an open-ended spanner and slacken and remove the locknut. Unscrew the upper mounting nut, taking care to ensure that the shock absorber body/piston rod does not rotate, and lift off the washer and rubber mounting **(see illustrations).**

Warning: Do not attempt to remove the shock absorber upper mounting nuts unless the lower arm is securely supported by the jack.

6 From underneath the vehicle, slacken and remove the shock absorber lower mounting bolt nut and withdraw the bolt and washers **(see illustration).**

7 Carefully lower the suspension arm slightly then manoeuvre the shock absorber out from underneath the wheelarch and recover the mounting rubber from its upper end. On later (December 1986 on) models also remove the spacer, which is fitted to the upper mounting rubbers then remove the dust cover from the

11.4a Remove the luggage compartment side trim panel . . .

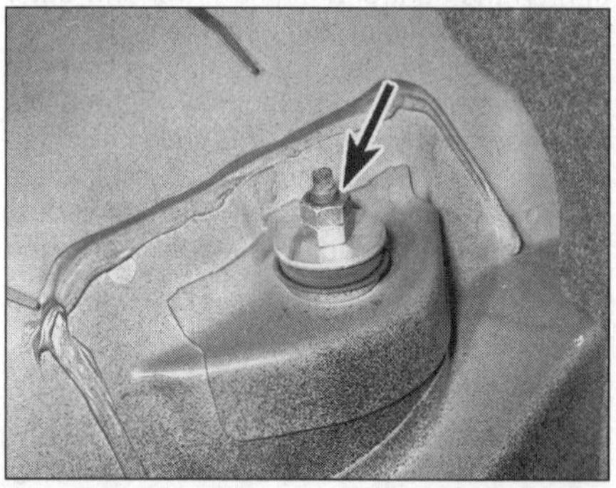

11.4b . . . to gain access to the rear shock absorber upper mounting (arrowed)

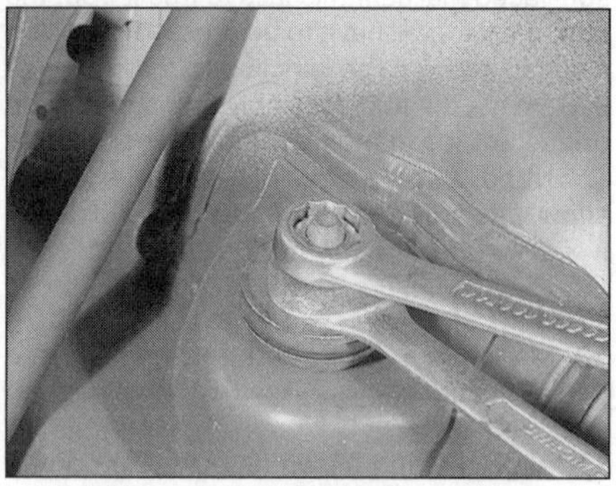

11.5a Remove the two nuts . . .

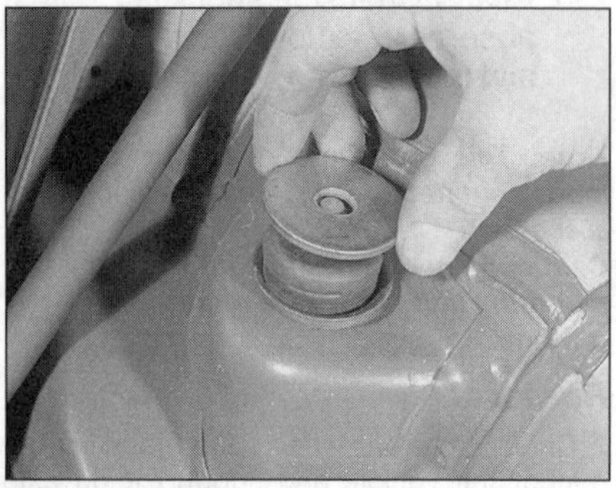

11.5b . . . the washer . . .

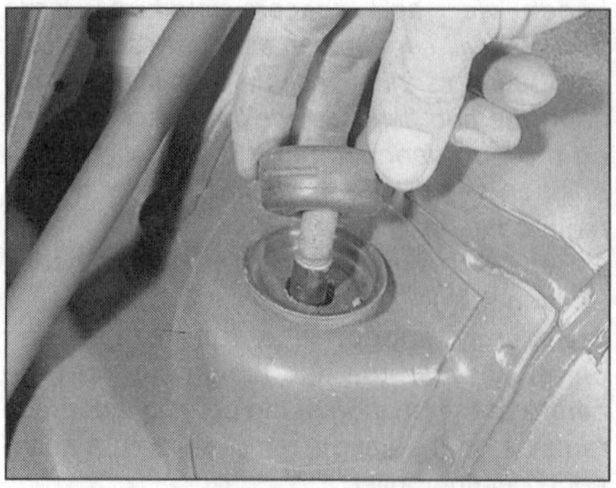

11.5c . . . and then the rubber mounting

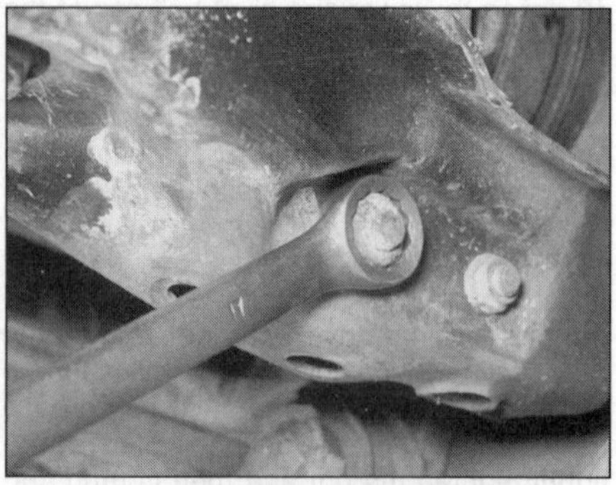

11.6 Unscrew the nut and withdraw the shock absorber lower mounting bolt

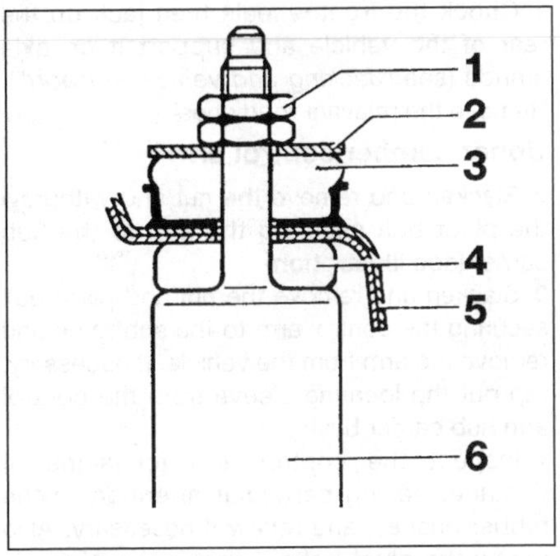

11.7a Rear shock absorber upper mounting components - early models

1 Locknut and mounting nut
2 Washer
3 Mounting rubber
4 Mounting rubber
5 Body
6 Shock absorber

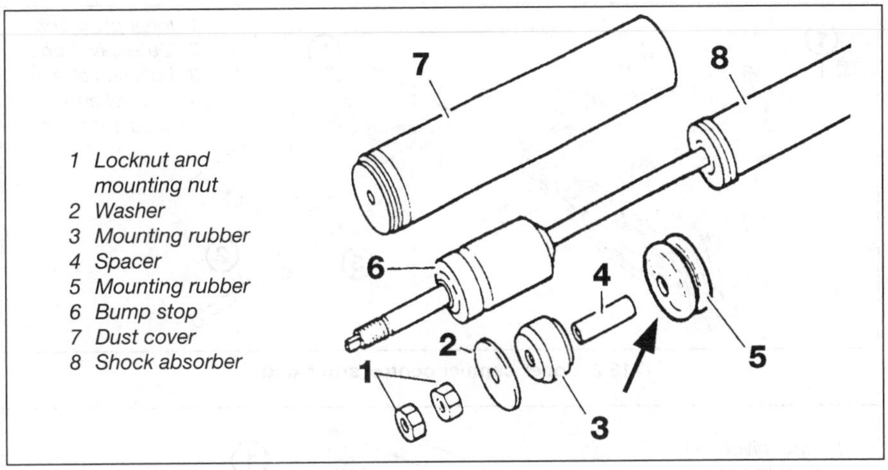

11.7b Rear shock absorber upper mounting components - later models

shock absorber and slide off the bump stop **(see illustrations).**

Testing

8 Examine the shock absorber for signs of fluid leakage. Check the piston for signs of pitting along its entire length, and check the body for signs of damage. While holding it in an upright position, test the operation of the shock absorber by moving the piston through a full stroke, and then through short strokes of 50 to 100 mm. In both cases, the resistance felt should be smooth and continuous. If the resistance is jerky, or uneven, or if there is any visible sign of wear or damage, renewal is necessary. Inspect all other components for signs of damage or deterioration, and renew any that are suspect.

Refitting

9 On later models slide the bump stop onto the shock absorber piston then refit the dust cover and spacer.

10 On all models, fit the lower of the mounting rubbers to the shock absorber and manoeuvre the shock absorber into position.

11 Engage the lower end of the shock absorber with the suspension arm and insert the mounting bolt. Fit a new nut to the bolt, tightening it lightly only at this stage.

12 Raise the lower suspension arm whilst ensuring that the shock absorber upper end locates correctly in the body.

13 From inside the luggage compartment, fit the upper mounting rubber and washer to the top of the shock absorber and screw on the upper mounting nut. Ensure that the mounting rubber is correctly located, then tighten the nut to the specified torque setting whilst ensuring that the shock absorber body/piston does not rotate. Hold the upper mounting nut stationary then refit the locknut and tighten it to the specified torque.

14 Refit the luggage compartment trim panel.

15 Refit the roadwheel then lower the vehicle to the ground and tighten the wheel bolts to the specified torque.

16 With the vehicle resting on its wheels, rock it to settle the shock absorber in position then tighten the lower mounting bolt nut to the specified torque setting. Refit the protective cover to the lower arm and securely tighten its retaining screws.

12 Rear suspension coil spring - removal and refitting

Warning: A suitable tool to hold the coil spring in compression must be obtained. Adjustable coil spring compressors are readily-available, and are recommended for this operation. Any attempt to remove the spring without such a tool is likely to result in damage or personal injury.

Note: *A new lower arm inner pivot bolt nut and anti-roll bar connecting link nut will be required on refitting.*

Removal

1 Chock the front wheels then jack up the rear of the vehicle and support it on axle stands (see "*Jacking and vehicle support*"). Remove the relevant roadwheel.

2 Fit the spring compressor, and compress the coil spring until all tension is relieved from the spring seats.

3 Undo the retaining screws and remove the protective cover from the base of the lower suspension arm. Position a jack and block of wood beneath the arm and raise the jack head until the arm is securely supported.

4 Slacken and remove the nut and withdraw the pivot bolt securing the lower suspension arm to the rear subframe. Also slacken and remove the nut and bolt securing the anti-roll bar connecting link to the lower arm.

5 Carefully lower the lower suspension arm until it is possible to remove the coil spring and upper spring seat.

6 Inspect the coil spring for signs of wear or damage and renew if necessary. The upper spring seat should also be renewed if it is damaged or shows signs of deterioration.

Refitting

7 Ensure that the lower arm spring seat is clean then fit the upper spring seat to the coil spring and manoeuvre the spring into position.

8 Locate the lower end of the spring correctly against the stop on the lower arm seat. Align the upper spring seat with the body mounting and carefully raise the lower arm whilst also aligning it with the subframe.

9 Check that the spring is correctly located then insert the lower arm pivot bolt. Fit a new nut to the pivot bolt tightening it lightly only at this stage. Refit the anti-roll bar connecting link bolt and tighten the new retaining nut to the specified torque.

10 Remove the jack from beneath the lower arm then carefully release the spring compressor whilst making sure both its upper and lower ends are correctly located.

11 Refit the roadwheel then lower the vehicle to the ground and tighten the wheel bolts to the specified torque.

12 With the vehicle resting on its wheels, rock it to settle the spring and lower arm in position then tighten the lower arm pivot bolt nut to the specified torque setting. Refit the protective cover to the lower arm and securely tighten its retaining screws.

13 Rear suspension control arms - removal and refitting

Note: *New pivot bolt nuts will be required on refitting. On the lower rear (track) control arm a new balljoint nut will also be required.*

Removal

Note: *If more than one control arm is to be removed at the same time, support the lower arm with a jack and block of wood.*

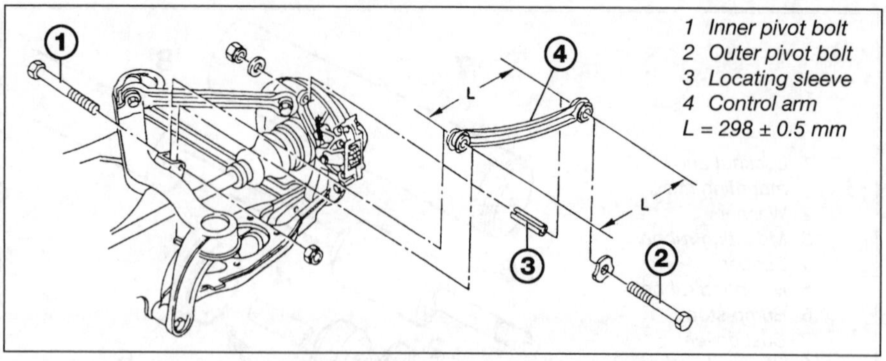

13.2 Upper camber control arm fixings

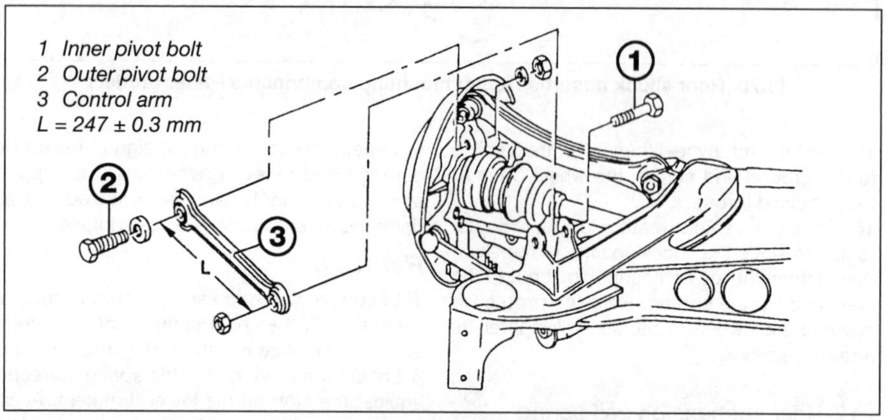

13.5 Upper torque control arm fixings

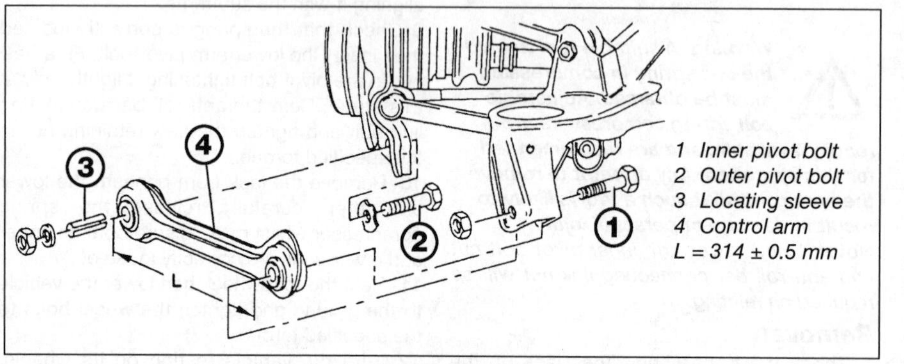

13.6 Lower thrust control arm fixings

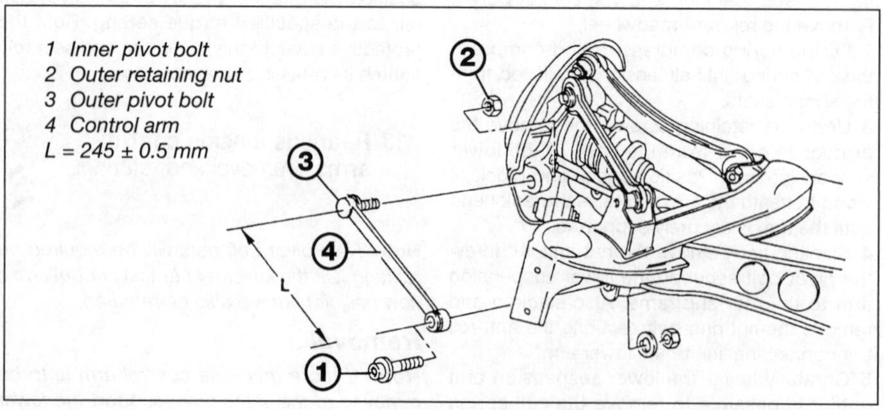

13.7 Lower track control arm fixings

1 Chock the front wheels then jack up the rear of the vehicle and support it on axle stands (see "*Jacking and vehicle support*"). Remove the relevant roadwheel.

Upper camber control arm

2 Slacken and remove the nut and withdraw the pivot bolt securing the arm to the hub carrier **(see illustration)**.

3 Slacken and remove the nut and pivot bolt securing the control arm to the subframe and remove the arm from the vehicle. If necessary, tap out the locating sleeve from the control arm hub carrier bush.

4 Inspect the control arm for signs of damage, paying particular attention to the rubber bushes, and renew if necessary. Also renew the pivot bolts if they show signs of wear.

Upper torque control arm

5 Remove the arm as described in paragraphs 2 to 4, ignoring the remark about the locating sleeve **(see illustration)**.

Lower thrust control arm

6 Remove the arm as described in paragraphs 2 to 4 **(see illustration)**.

Lower track control arm

7 Prior to removal, make alignment marks between the arm inner pivot bolt, the eccentric washers and the subframe. This will be necessary to ensure that the rear wheel toe setting remains correct on refitting **(see illustration)**.

8 Slacken and remove the nut and eccentric washer and withdraw the pivot bolt securing the arm to the subframe.

9 Unscrew the nut from the balljoint shank then free the balljoint from the hub carrier and remove the arm from the vehicle. If necessary, use a balljoint separator to free the balljoint shank from the carrier.

10 Inspect the control mounting bush for signs of damage or deterioration and check that the balljoint is free to move easily and that its gaiter is undamaged. Renew the control arm if necessary.

Refitting

Upper camber control arm

11 Where necessary, tap the locating sleeve back into position in the arm hub carrier bush.

12 Locate the arm in position and insert the pivot bolts. Fit the new nuts to the pivot bolts, tightening them lightly only at this stage.

13 Refit the rear roadwheel then lower the vehicle to ground and tighten the wheel bolts to the specified torque.

14 With the vehicle resting on its wheels, rock it to settle the control arm in position then tighten both pivot bolt nuts to the specified torque setting.

Upper torque control arm

15 Refit the arm as described in paragraphs 11 to 14.

Lower thrust control arm

16 Refit the arm as described in paragraphs 11 to 14.

Lower track control arm

17 Manoeuvre the arm into position then insert the inner pivot bolt, eccentric washer and fit the new retaining nut. Align the marks made prior to removal and lightly tighten the nut.

18 Fit the new retaining nut to the balljoint shank and tighten it to the specified torque setting.

19 Refit the rear roadwheel then lower the vehicle to ground and tighten the wheel bolts to the specified torque.

20 With the vehicle resting on its wheels, rock it to settle the control arm in position. Check that the marks on the subframe, pivot bolt and eccentric washer are still correctly aligned then tighten the pivot bolt nut to the specified torque setting. **Note:** *It is recommended that the rear wheel toe setting alignment is checked at the earliest possible opportunity.*

14 Rear suspension lower arm - removal, overhaul and refitting

Note: *New lower pivot bolt nuts, new shock absorber lower mounting bolt nut(s) and an anti-roll bar connecting link bolt nut will be required on refitting.*

Removal

1 Chock the rear wheels, apply the parking brake, then jack up the front of the vehicle and support on axle stands (see "*Jacking and vehicle support*"). Remove the appropriate roadwheel.

2 Undo the retaining screws/clips and remove the protective cover from the base of the lower arm.

3 Fit a spring compressor to the coil spring and compress the spring to relieve the tension from its upper and lower seats (see Section 12).

4 Slacken and remove the nut and bolt securing the anti-roll bar connecting link to the lower arm **(see illustration)**.

5 Position a jack (with a block if required) beneath the lower arm and raise the jack until it is supporting the weight of the arm.

6 Slacken and remove the shock absorber lower mounting bolt nut(s) and withdraw the bolt(s) and washers.

7 Unscrew the nut from the lower arm outer pivot bolt and withdraw the bolt. Carefully lower the arm slightly until it is possible to withdraw the coil spring and spring seat **(see illustrations)**.

8 Unscrew the nut then withdraw the inner pivot bolt and washers and remove the lower arm from underneath the vehicle **(see illustration)**.

Overhaul

9 Thoroughly clean the lower arm and the area around the arm mountings, removing all traces of dirt and underseal if necessary, then check carefully for cracks, distortion or any other signs of wear or damage paying particular attention to the mounting bushes. If either bush requires renewal, the lower arm should be taken to a Mercedes-Benz dealer or suitably equipped garage. A hydraulic press and suitable spacers are required to press the bushes out of position and install the new ones.

Refitting

10 Offer up the lower arm and insert the inner pivot bolt and washers. Fit the new nut to the bolt tightening it lightly only at this stage.

11 Ensure that the lower arm spring seat is clean then fit the upper spring seat to the coil spring and manoeuvre the spring into position.

12 Locate the lower end of the spring correctly against the stop on the lower arm seat. Align the upper spring seat with the body mounting and carefully raise the lower arm whilst also aligning it with the hub carrier, anti-roll bar link and the shock absorber.

13 Check that the coil spring is correctly located then insert the lower arm outer pivot bolt. Fit the new retaining nut to the bolt tightening it lightly only at this stage.

14 Align the lower end of the shock absorber with the arm and insert the mounting bolt(s). Fit a new nut(s) to the bolt(s), tightening it lightly only at this stage.

15 Insert the anti-roll bar connecting link bolt then fit the new retaining nut and tighten lightly.

16 Refit the rear roadwheel then lower the vehicle to ground and tighten the wheel bolts to the specified torque.

17 With the vehicle resting on its wheels, rock it to settle all disturbed components in position, then tighten the lower arm pivot bolts, shock absorber lower mounting bolts(s) and the anti-roll bar connecting link bolt to their specified torque settings. Refit the protective cover to the lower arm and securely tighten its retaining screws.

15 Rear suspension anti-roll bar - removal and refitting

Note: *New mounting clamp bolts and connecting link nuts will be required on refitting. If it is necessary to disturb the rear subframe assembly, new subframe mounting bolts and propeller shaft coupling nuts will also be required.*

Removal

1 Chock the front wheels then jack up the rear of the vehicle and support it on axle

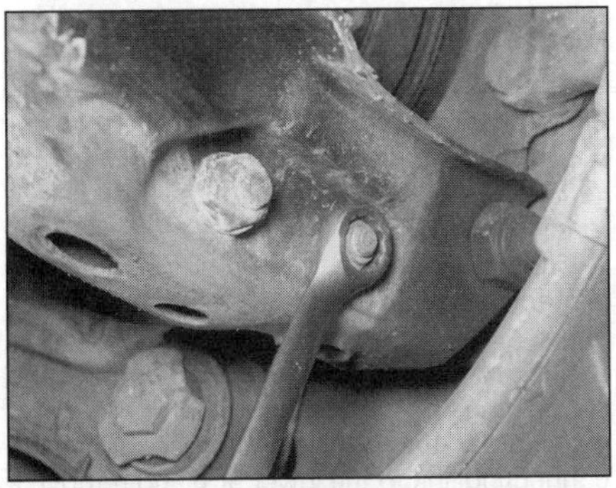

14.4 Unscrew the retaining nut and bolt and detach the anti-roll bar connecting link from the lower arm

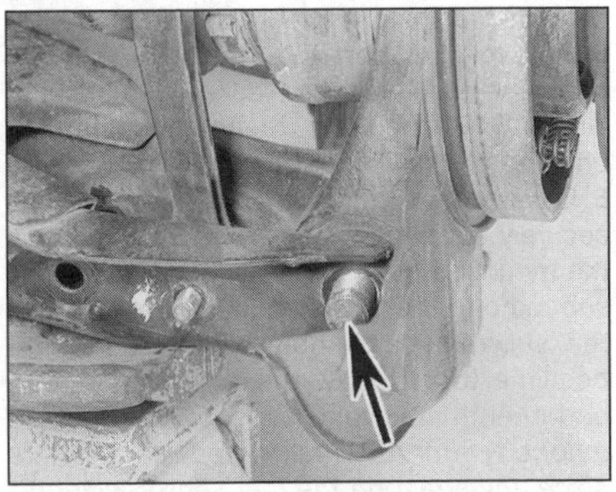

14.7a Remove the lower arm outer pivot bolt (arrowed)

14.7b Carefully lower the arm using the jack, until it is possible to withdraw the coil spring and spring seat

14.8 Unscrew the nut, withdraw the inner pivot bolt and washers and remove the lower arm from underneath the vehicle

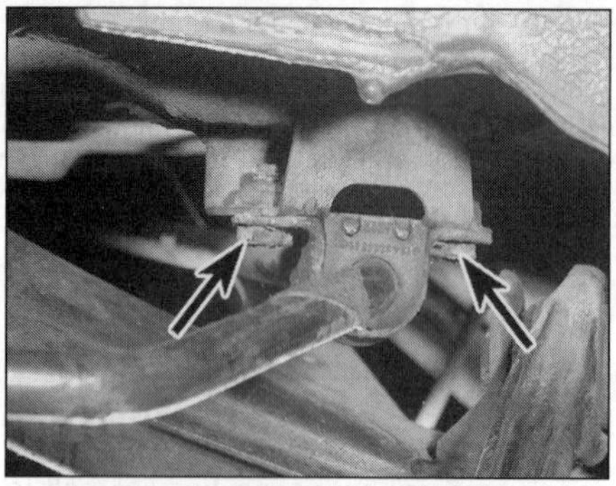

15.3 Rear anti-roll to body mounting clamp bolts (arrowed)

stands (see "*Jacking and vehicle support*"). To improve access, remove the rear roadwheels.

2 Slacken and remove the nut securing each connecting link to the anti-roll bar.

3 Make alignment marks between the mounting bushes and anti-roll bar then slacken the two anti-roll bar mounting clamp retaining bolts and remove the clamps **(see illustration)**. Remove the rubber mountings from the anti-roll bar, noting which way around they are fitted. Try and manoeuvre the anti-roll bar out of position from underneath the vehicle noting that it is likely that the following work will be required to gain the necessary clearance to remove the bar.

4 Referring to Chapter 8, disconnect the propeller shaft from the final drive unit and slacken the propeller shaft centre bearing bolts so the shaft assembly is free to move.

5 Securely support the weight of the rear subframe assembly on a jack, with a block of wood positioned on its head, positioned underneath the final drive unit.

6 Ensure that the subframe assembly is securely supported then slacken and remove the mounting bolts and washers securing the subframe to the vehicle body. Carefully lower the subframe assembly slightly until it is possible to withdraw the anti-roll bar from underneath the vehicle. **Note:** *On models quipped with ABS, take great care not to place any strain on the rear sensor wiring as the assembly is lowered. If necessary unbolt the sensor(s) from the final drive unit or disconnect the sensor wiring (see Chapter 9).*

Refitting

7 Manoeuvre the anti-roll bar into position and engage it with the connecting links.

8 Where necessary, raise the subframe assembly back into position then fit the new mounting bolts and washers and tighten them to the specified torque. Reconnect the propeller shaft to the final drive unit and tighten the centre mounting bolts as described in Chapter 8.

9 Fit the mounting rubbers to the anti-roll bar, positioning them so their splits are facing forwards, and align them with the marks made prior to removal. Locate the flat of each rubber against the vehicle body then refit the mounting clamps and screw in the new clamp bolts.

10 Fit the new nuts to the connecting links and tighten them to the specified torque setting then tighten the mounting clamp bolts to the specified torque setting.

11 Refit the rear roadwheels then lower the vehicle to the ground and tighten the wheel bolts to the specified torque settings.

16 Rear suspension anti-roll bar connecting link - removal and refitting

Note: *New connecting link nuts will be required on refitting.*

Removal

1 Chock the rear wheels, apply the parking brake, then jack up the front of the vehicle and support on axle stands (see "*Jacking and vehicle support*"). Remove the appropriate roadwheel.

2 Undo the retaining screws and remove the protective cover from the base of the lower arm.

3 Slacken and remove the nut securing the connecting link to the anti-roll bar.

4 Unscrew the nut and bolt securing the connecting link to the lower arm and remove it from the vehicle. Inspect the connecting link for signs of wear or damage and renew if necessary.

Refitting

5 Manoeuvre the connecting link into position and fit the connecting link lower retaining bolt.

6 Fit a new nut to the connecting link stud and tighten it to the specified torque then fit the new nut to the lower retaining bolt and tighten it to the specified torque.

7 Refit the protective cover to the lower arm and securely tighten its retaining screws.

8 Refit the roadwheel then lower the vehicle to the ground and tighten the wheel bolts to the specified torque.

17 Steering wheel - removal and refitting

Removal

Note: *A new steering wheel retaining bolt will be required on refitting.*

1 Set the front wheels in the straight-ahead position, and release the steering lock by inserting the ignition key.

Models not fitted with an airbag

2 Prise the Mercedes-Benz emblem/horn pad out from the centre of the wheel **(see illustration)**.

3 Slacken and remove the steering wheel retaining bolt **(see illustration)**.

4 If marks do not already exist, mark the steering wheel and steering column shaft in relation to each other, then lift the steering wheel off the column splines. If it is tight, tap it up near the centre, using the palm of your hand, or twist it from side to side, whilst pulling upwards to release it from the shaft splines.

5 Inspect the horn contacts and contact ring for signs of wear or damage and renew as necessary.

Models equipped with an airbag

6 Remove the airbag unit from the centre of the steering wheel as described in Chapter 12.

7 Remove the steering wheel as described above in paragraphs 3 to 5.

Refitting

Models not fitted with an airbag

8 Refitting is a reversal of removal, noting the following.

a) *Coat the steering wheel horn contact ring with a smear of petroleum jelly and engage the wheel with the column splines, aligning the marks made on removal.*

b) *Fit the new steering wheel retaining bolt and tighten it to the specified torque setting.*

Models equipped with an airbag

9 Refitting is the reverse of removal, noting the following points.

a) *If the contact unit has been rotated with the wheel removed, centralise it by*

17.2 Prise the Mercedes-Benz emblem/horn pad out from the centre of the wheel

17.3 Slacken and remove the steering wheel retaining bolt

pressing down on the contact unit and rotating its centre fully anti-clockwise. From this position rotate the centre back through three complete rotations in a clockwise direction.

b) Coat the steering wheel horn contact ring with a smear of petroleum jelly and refit the wheel, making sure the contact unit wiring is correctly routed.

c) Ensure that the locating peg at the top of the steering column engages correctly with the recess in the contact unit, as the steering wheel is refitted.

d) Engage the wheel with the column splines, aligning the marks made on removal, and tighten the steering wheel retaining bolt to the specified torque setting.

e) Refit the airbag unit as described in Chapter 12.

18 Steering column - removal, inspection and refitting

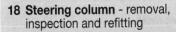

Pre April 1984 models

Removal

Note: *A new steering rubber coupling clamp bolt will be required on refitting.*

1 Remove the trim panel, under the facia on the drivers side.

2 Remove the steering wheel as described in Section 17.

3 With reference to Chapter 12, carry out the following:

a) Remove the instrument panel from the facia.

b) Remove the multi-function stalk switch from the steering column.

4 Jack the front of the car and support it securely on axle stands.

5 Working underneath the front of the car, at the point where the base of the steering column joins the steering gear, slacken and withdraw the upper of the two socket headed bolts **(see illustration)**. This ensures that the rubber coupling remains connected to the steering gear, not the steering column.

6 Remove the fixings and lift off the steering column shroud.

7 Refer to Section 19 and remove the steering lock/ignition switch assembly.

8 Remove the two nuts and withdraw the bolts that secure the upper end of steering column to the support crossmember **(see illustration)**.

9 Slacken and withdraw the bolt that secures the lower section of the steering column to the support bracket **(see illustration)**. Check that the threaded washer is pushed fully into the support bracket.

10 Prise the rubber guide sleeve from the bulkhead aperture then withdraw the steering column from the vehicle.

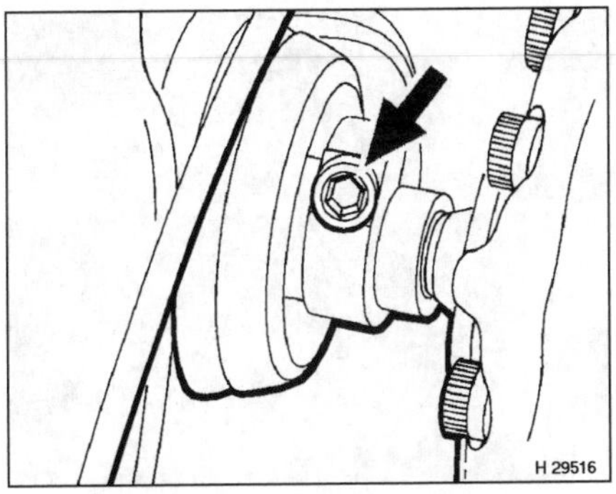

18.5 At the flexible rubber coupling, slacken and withdraw the upper of the two socket headed bolts (arrowed)

Refitting

11 Before refitting the steering column, the steering gear must be centered, with the road wheels in the dead-ahead position. To do this, unscrew the hex-headed plug from the steering gear (adjacent to the drop arm) **(see illustration)**. Slowly turn the steering gear by means of the steering spindle, whilst looking through the aperture exposed by the removal of the hex-headed plug. When the centering hole in the top of the piston (visible through the aperture) appears, the steering gear is correctly centered. Ideally, the gear should be locked in this position by means of a long bolt, filed to a point at its end. This will engage with the piston and preserve the alignment of the steering gear whilst it is fitted.

12 Lubricate the sealing ring at the base of the steering column lower shaft, then place the column and rubber guide sleeve in position in the car.

13 Insert and hand-tighten the column upper and lower mounting bolts; do not tighten them fully at this stage.

14 Refit the ignition switch/steering lock assembly as described in Section 19.

15 Engage the base of the column with the flexible rubber coupling at the top of the steering gear. Insert the new pinch bolt but do not tighten it fully at this stage.

16 Tighten the steering column upper and lower mounting bolts to the specified torque.

17 Tighten the flexible rubber coupling pinch bolt to the specified torque.

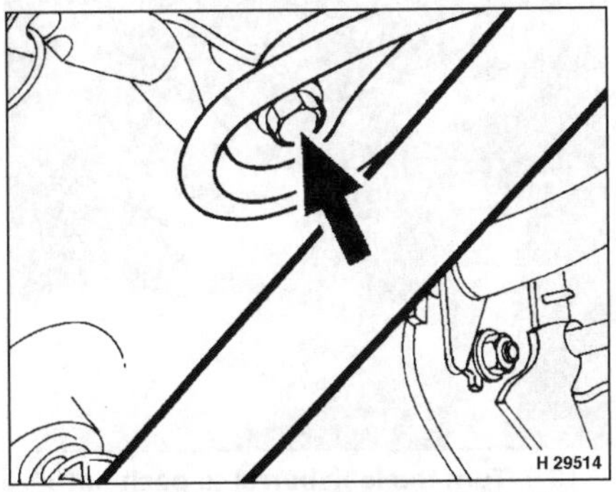

18.9 Slacken and withdraw the steering column lower mounting bolt (arrowed)

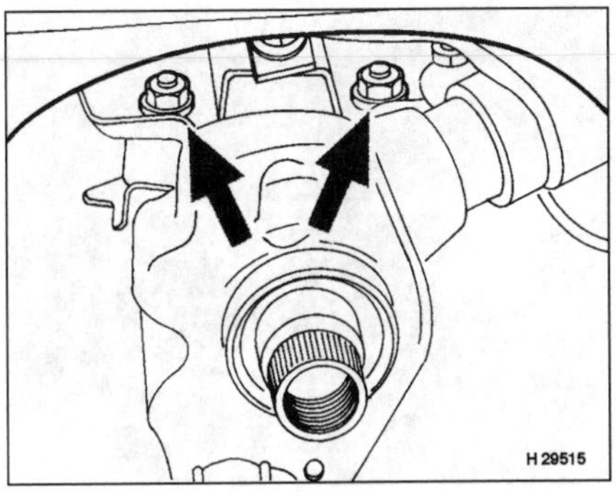

18.8 Remove the steering column upper mounting nuts and bolts (arrowed)

18 Remove the locking bolt (if used) from the steering gear and refit the hex-head plug in its place. The car can now be lowered to the ground.

19 Refit the steering column stalk switch and shroud panel.

20 Press the rubber guide sleeve into position in its aperture in the bulkhead.

21 Refit the instrument panel with reference to Chapter 12.

22 Refit the steering wheel with reference to Section 17.

23 Refit the trim panel to the underside of the facia.

Models from April 1984 onwards

Removal

Note: *A new steering rubber coupling clamp bolt will be required on refitting.*

24 Disconnect the battery negative terminal.

25 Remove the steering wheel as described in Section 17.

26 Remove the steering lock as described in Section 19.

27 Remove the instrument panel and steering column combination switch(es) as described in Chapter 12 and lift off the steering column shroud.

28 Working in the engine compartment, using paint or a suitable marker pen, make alignment marks between the lower end of the steering column and the rubber coupling. Note that on some models it will be necessary to unbolt the steering box heatshield(s) to gain access to the coupling.

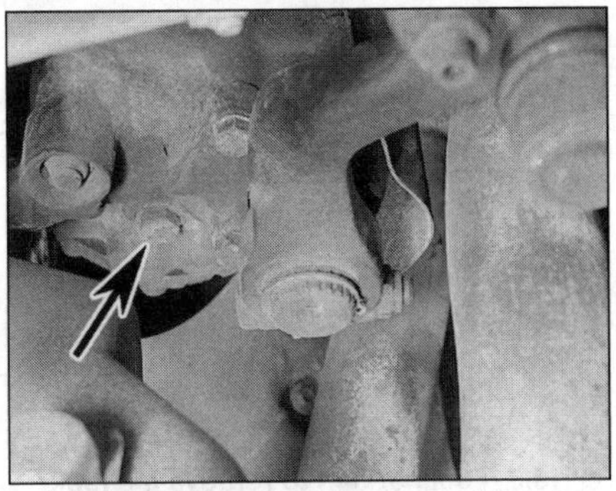

18.11 Unscrew the hex-headed plug from the steering gear

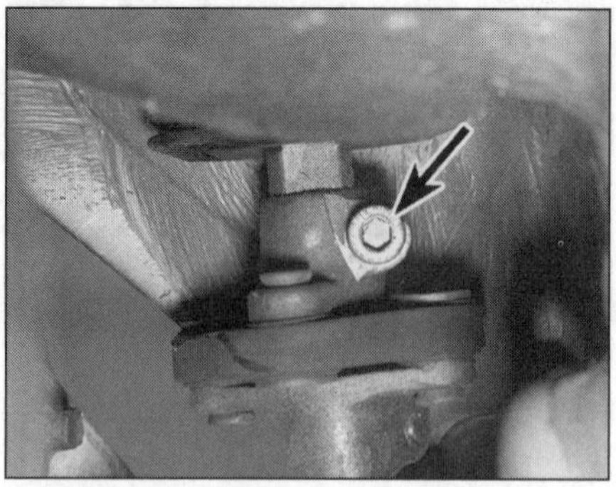

18.29 At the rubber coupling, slacken and remove the upper clamp bolt (arrowed)

18.30a Remove the steering column upper mounting bolts (arrowed) which are accessed via the instrument panel aperture . . .

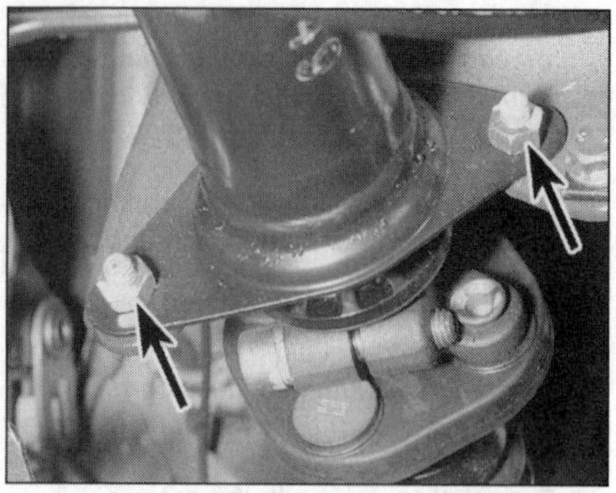

18.30b . . . and the lower mounting nuts

29 Slacken and remove the coupling upper clamp bolt, securing the coupling to the steering column **(see illustration)**.

30 Slacken and remove the steering column upper mounting bolts (which are accessed through the instrument panel aperture) and the lower mounting nuts **(see illustrations)**.

31 Free the steering column gaiter bush from the bulkhead and remove the column from the vehicle. Whilst the column is removed, inspect the rubber coupling and renew if necessary (see Section 20).

Inspection

32 The steering column incorporates a telescopic safety feature. In the event of a front-end crash, the shaft collapses and prevents the steering wheel injuring the driver. Before refitting the steering column, examine the column and mountings for signs of damage and deformation, and renew as necessary.

19.1 Remove the trim panel from around the steering lock/ignition switch (steering wheel removed for clarity)

33 Check the steering shaft for signs of free play in the column bushes. If any damage or wear is found on the steering column bushes, the column should be overhauled. Overhaul of the column is a complex task requiring several special tools and should be entrusted to a Mercedes-Benz dealer.

Refitting

34 Prior to refitting, lubricate the column lower bush with multi-purpose grease.

35 Aligning the marks made on removal, manoeuvre the steering column into position and engage it with the rubber coupling splines.

36 Ensure that the column gaiter bush is correctly located in the bulkhead then refit the steering column mounting nuts and bolts, tightening them to the specified torque.

37 Fit the new clamp bolt to the rubber coupling and tighten it to the specified torque.

38 Refit the combination switches and instrument panel as described in Chapter 12.

39 Refit the steering lock as described in Section 19.

40 Refit the steering wheel as described in Section 17.

19 Steering lock/ignition switch - removal and refitting

Lock cylinder

Removal

1 Using a small screwdriver, carefully prise off the trim panel from around the lock cylinder **(see illustration)**.

2 Insert the ignition key and turn the switch to position "I".

3 Bend a suitable length of 2.0 mm diameter wire (a piece of welding rod is ideal) into a U-shape, and file a 70° chamfer on each end, facing inwards **(see illustration)**.

4 Insert the releasing wire into the slots on each side of the lock barrel, and push the wire in to compress the lock cylinder detents.

5 Withdraw the lock barrel using the ignition key **(see illustration)**.

6 Remove the releasing wire and ignition key, then withdraw the lock barrel from its sleeve **(see illustration)**.

Refitting

7 To refit, insert the lock barrel into the steering lock body, with the raised section engaged in the lock body groove.

8 Position the sleeve over the lock barrel with its cutout towards the steering column.

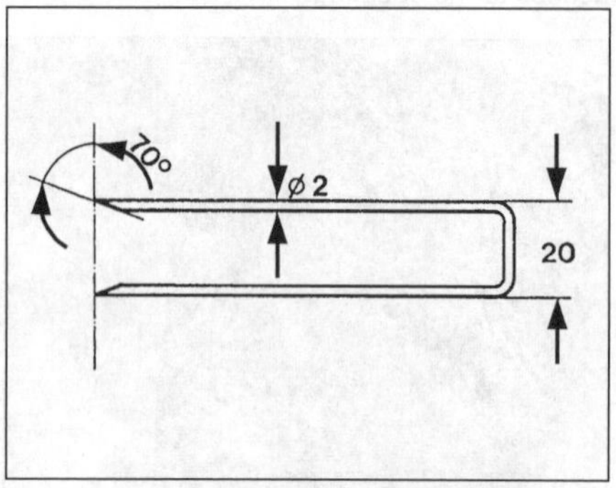

19.3 Tool needed to remove the lock cylinder (dimensions in mm)

19.5 Turn the lock barrel to position "I" then insert the releasing wire and withdraw the assembly from its housing

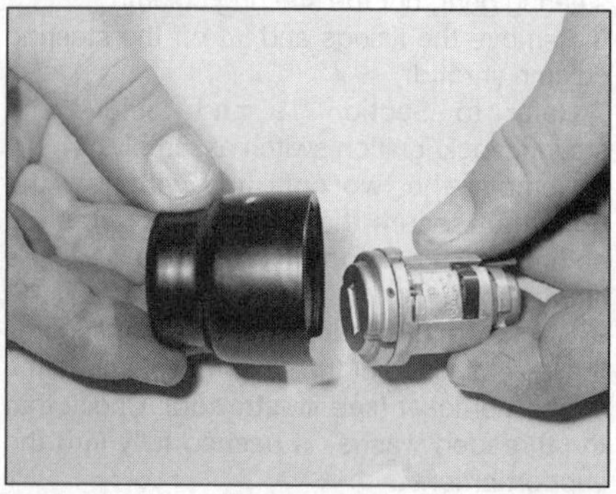

19.6 Remove the ignition key and separate the barrel and sleeve

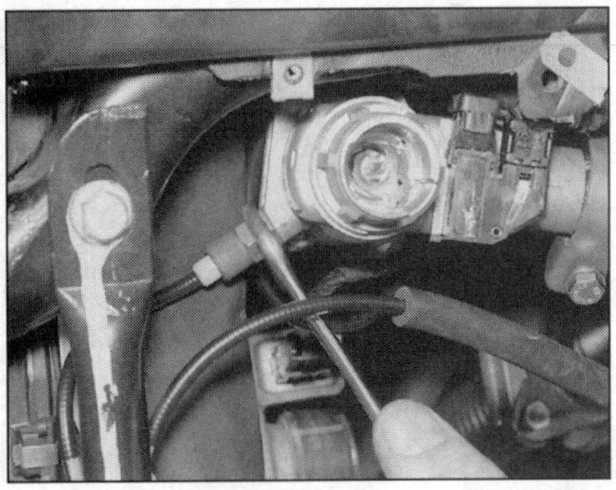

19.15 On models with automatic transmission, unscrew the nut and detach the interlock cable from the lock housing

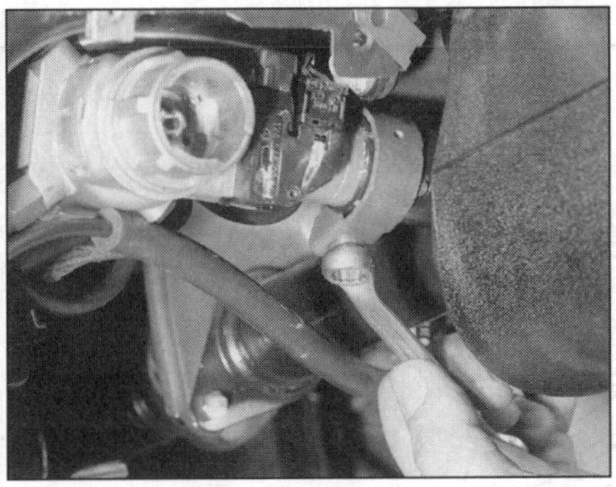

19.16a Slacken the clamp bolt . . .

19.16b . . . then depress the detent pin . . .

9 Insert the ignition key, turn it to position "I" and push both the lock barrel and cover fully into the steering lock body. **Note:** *The edge of the ignition key must point towards the mark on the cover while fitting, indicating that the cover detent is in correct alignment.*

10 Check the lock and lock barrel for correct operation, then refit the trim panel.

Complete switch assembly

Removal

11 Disconnect the battery negative terminal.

12 Remove the lock cylinder as described in paragraphs 1 to 6, noting that the switch must not be turned from the position "I"

13 Remove the driver's side lower facia panel as described in Chapter 11.

14 Disconnect the wiring connector(s) from the switch assembly, noting the wiring correct routing and fitting.

15 On diesel models, make alignment marks between the vacuum hoses and switch and disconnect the hoses from the side of the switch body. On models with automatic transmission, it will be necessary to unscrew the selector mechanism interlock cable from the lock assembly **(see illustration)**.

16 Slacken the switch clamp bolt then depress the detent pin and remove the switch assembly from the column **(see illustrations)**.

Refitting

17 Refitting is the reverse of removal, noting the following.

a) *Ensure that the switch remains in the position "I".*
b) *When refitting the switch to the column, ensure that the detent pin locks into position in the column hole and securely tighten the clamp bolt.*
c) *Ensure that the wiring is correctly routed and securely reconnected.*
d) *On diesel models ensure that the vacuum hoses are connected the right way around.*
e) *Prior to fitting the facia panel insert the lock cylinder and check the operation of the assembly.*

Ignition/starter wiring block

Removal

18 Remove the switch assembly as described in paragraphs 11 to 16

19 Undo the retaining screws and remove the wiring block from the rear of the switch **(see illustration)**.

Refitting

20 Fit the wiring block ensuring its locating lug is correctly engaged with the cutout in the switch body. Refit the retaining screws and tighten them securely.

21 Refit the switch assembly as described in paragraph 17.

20 Steering column rubber coupling - removal and refitting

Note: *New coupling clamp bolt(s) will be required on refitting.*

Removal

1 Remove the steering column as described in Section 18.

2 Make alignment marks between the coupling and the steering box pinion then unscrew the lower clamp bolt and remove the coupling from the vehicle.

3 Inspect the coupling rubber for signs of damage or deterioration and renew if necessary.

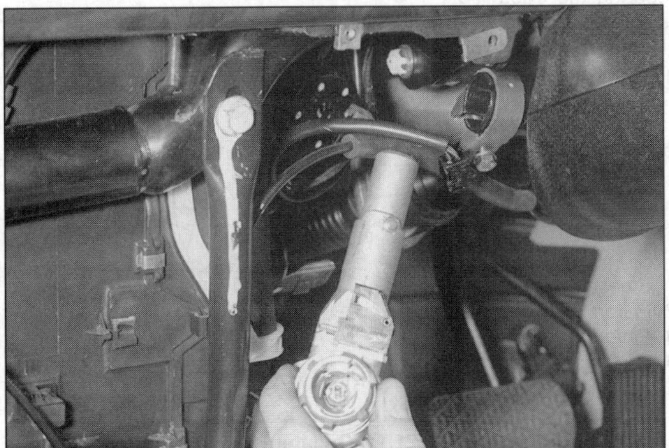

19.16c . . . and separate the lock housing from the steering column

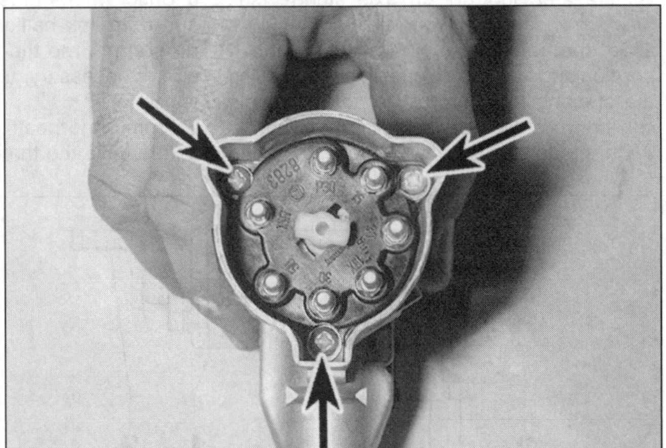

19.19 Ignition/starter wiring block retaining screws (arrowed)

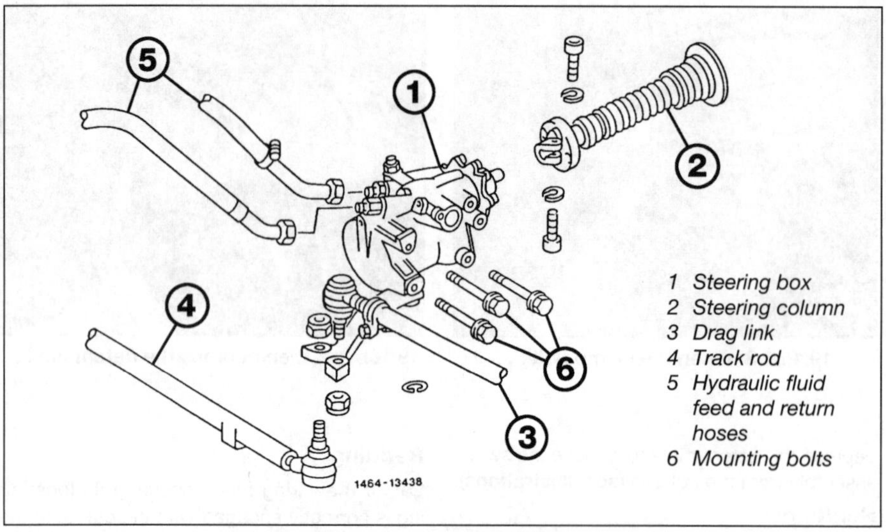

21.3a Steering box and associated components

21.3b Steering box hydraulic hose unions (arrowed)

Refitting

4 Align the marks made prior to removal and engage the coupling with the steering box splines.

5 Insert the new lower clamp bolt and tighten it to the specified torque.

6 Refit the steering column as described in Section 18.

21 Steering box - removal, overhaul and refitting

Note: *New steering box mounting bolts, drag link and track rod balljoint nuts and rubber coupling clamp bolts will be required on refitting.*

Removal

1 Chock the rear wheels, firmly apply the parking brake, then jack up the front of the vehicle and support on axle stands (see "*Jacking and vehicle support*").

2 Set the front wheel in the straight-ahead position and lock the column in position using the steering lock. **Note:** *Do not rotate the column whilst the steering box is removed.*

3 On models with power steering, using brake hose clamps, clamp both the supply and return hoses near the steering box to minimise fluid loss. Mark the unions to ensure that they are correctly positioned on reassembly, then slacken and remove the feed and return hose union nuts **(see illustrations)**. Be prepared for fluid spillage, and position a suitable container beneath the hoses whilst unscrewing the nuts. Plug the hose ends and steering box orifices, to prevent fluid leakage and to keep dirt out of the hydraulic system.

4 Using paint or a suitable marker pen, make alignment marks between the lower end of the steering column, rubber coupling and the steering box pinion. Note that on some models it will be necessary to unbolt the steering box heatshield(s) to gain access to the coupling.

5 Slacken and remove the clamp bolts, then slide the coupling upwards and onto the steering column to disengage it from the steering box pinion.

6 Unscrew the nuts securing the track rod and drag link balljoints to the steering box drop arm. Free the balljoints from the drop arm, if necessary, using a universal balljoint separator.

7 From underneath the wheelarch, slacken and remove the three steering box mounting bolts and manoeuvre the steering box out from underneath the vehicle.

Overhaul

8 Examine the steering box assembly for signs of wear or damage. If overhaul of the steering box assembly is necessary, the task must be entrusted to a Mercedes-Benz dealer. The only service item which is easily replaced is the steering box seal which can be renewed as described in Section 23.

Refitting

9 If a new steering box is being fitted it will be necessary position the steering pinion correctly prior to fitting the box.

10 On early (pre 1990) models, unscrew the plug and sealing ring from the side of the steering box then rotate the pinion until its centring hole is correctly aligned with the plug aperture. If the special tapered locking screw is available, screw it into position so that the steering box pinion is securely held **(see illustration)**.

11 On later (1990 on) models, align the index mark on the steering gear pinion with the mark on the steering box housing **(see illustration)**.

12 Manoeuvre the steering box assembly into position. Align the marks made on removal (original box) or ensure that the pinion remains correctly centred (new box) and engage the pinion with the rubber coupling.

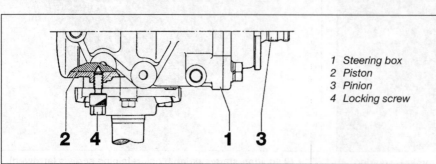

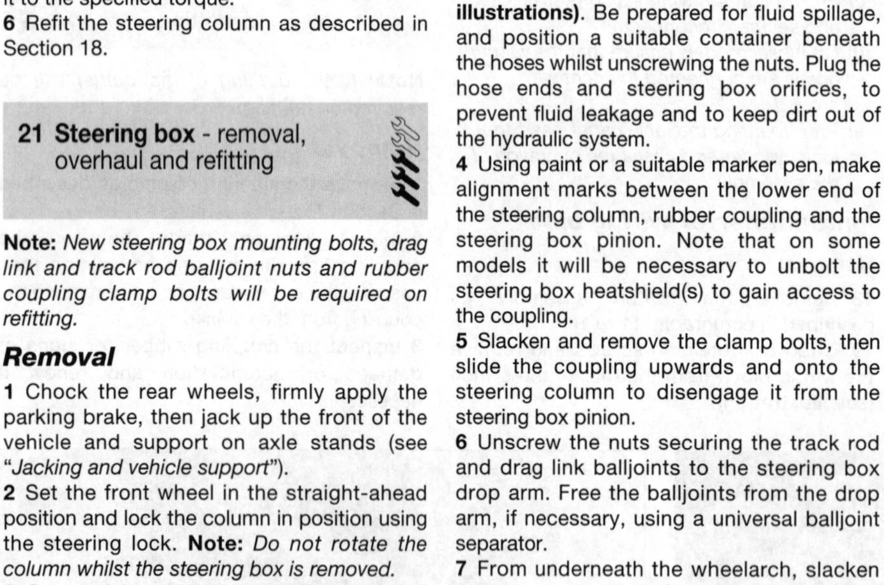

21.10 Steering box centring details - early (pre 1990) models

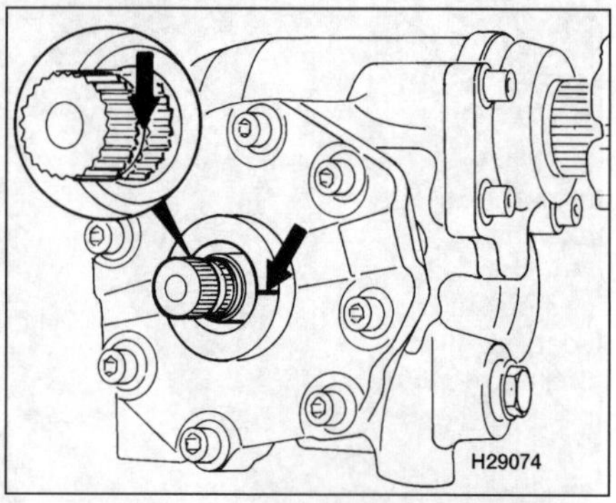

21.11 On later (1990 on) models align the mark on the steering gear pinion with the line on the housing to centre the assembly (arrowed)

13 Slide the rubber coupling fully into position then fit the new steering gear mounting bolts and tighten them to the specified torque.
14 On early models, where necessary, remove the centring bolt and refit the plug and sealing ring to the side of the steering box.
15 Fit the new coupling clamp bolts and tighten them to the specified torque.
16 Insert the drag link and track rod balljoints into the steering box drop arm then fit the new retaining nuts and tighten them to the specified torque.
17 On models with power steering, reconnect the fluid hoses to the steering box and tighten the union nuts securely. On completion, refill and bleed the hydraulic system as described in Section 25.

22 Steering box drop arm - removal and refitting

Note: *New drag link and track rod balljoint nuts and a drop arm clamp bolt nut will be required on refitting.*

Removal

1 Chock the rear wheels, firmly apply the parking brake, then jack up the front of the vehicle and support on axle stands (see *"Jacking and vehicle support"*).
2 Unscrew the nuts securing the track rod and drag link balljoints to the steering box drop arm. Free the balljoints from the drop arm, if necessary, using a universal balljoint separator.
3 Slacken and remove the drop arm clamp bolt and nut and remove the retaining circlip **(see illustration)**.
4 Prior to removal measure the distance between the top edge of the drop arm and the steering box housing and note this down. Also check that the pinion mark which aligns with the drop arm clamp split is clearly visible; if not make an alignment mark.
5 Using a universal puller, draw the drop arm off from the steering box pinion and remove it from underneath the vehicle. Whilst the arm is removed inspect the steering box lower seal for signs of leakage and renew if necessary.

Refitting

6 Remove all traces of old locking compound from the steering box pinion and drop arm and ensure that the splines are clean and dry.
7 Apply a smear of locking compound (Mercedes-Benz recommend the use of Loctite 270) to the splines of the drop arm.
8 Engage the drop arm with the steering box pinion splines ensuring that the index mark on the pinion is correctly aligned with the arm clamp split.
9 Press the drop arm onto the steering box until the distance between its upper edge and the housing is as was noted prior to removal.
10 Insert the drop arm clamp bolt then fit the

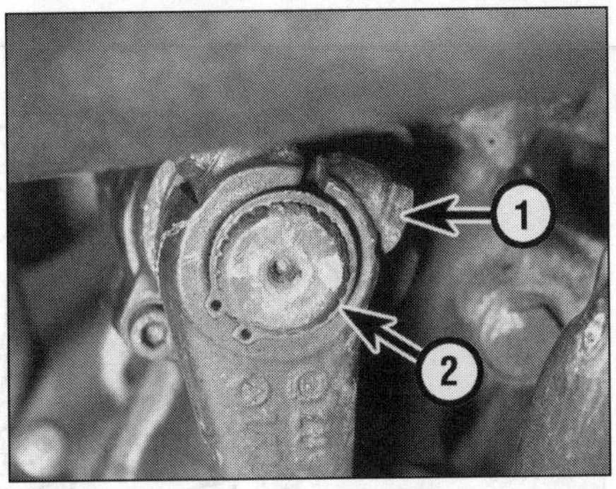

22.3 Steering box drop arm clamp bolt (1) and circlip (2)

new nut and tighten it to the specified torque setting. Secure the arm in position by fitting the circlip, making sure it is correctly located in the pinion groove.
11 Reconnect the balljoints to the drop arm, then fit the new retaining nuts and tighten them to the specified torque. Lower the vehicle to the ground.

23 Steering box lower seal - renewal

1 Remove the drop arm as described in Section 22.
2 Remove the upper circlip from the steering box pinion then carefully lever the seal out of position whilst taking great care to mark the pinion of housing.
3 Remove all trace of dirt from the housing and pinion and tape over the pinion splines.
4 Ease the new seal over the end of the steering box pinion and press it squarely into the steering box housing.
5 Remove the tape from the pinion splines then fit the upper circlip, making sure it is correctly located in the pinion groove.
6 Refit the drop arm as described in Section 22.

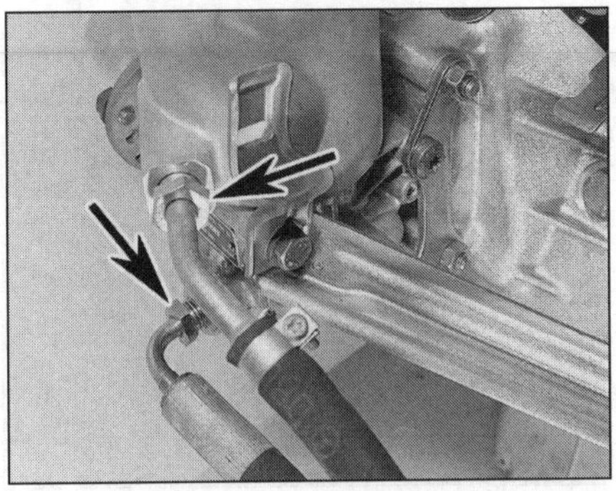

24.5 Unscrew the unions, then withdraw the delivery (A) and return (B) fluid pipes from the side of the pump

7 On models with power steering bleed the hydraulic system as described in Section 25.

24 Power steering pump - removal and refitting

Pre October 1984 models

Removal

1 Unscrew and remove the cap from the PAS pump fluid reservoir.
2 Unscrew the nut from the long stud at the centre of the reservoir, then remove the pressure spring from the stud.
3 Withdraw the filter cartridge from the reservoir.
4 Using a clean syringe or an old poultry baster, empty the PAS fluid from the reservoir.
5 Unscrew the unions, then withdraw the delivery and return fluid pipes from the side of the pump **(see illustration)** - be prepared for an amount of leakage. Plug or cover the exposed ports to prevent contamination.
6 At the rear of the pump mounting bracket, slacken the toothed adjuster bolt so that the pump move towards the engine, relieving the tension on the drive belt **(see illustration)**.

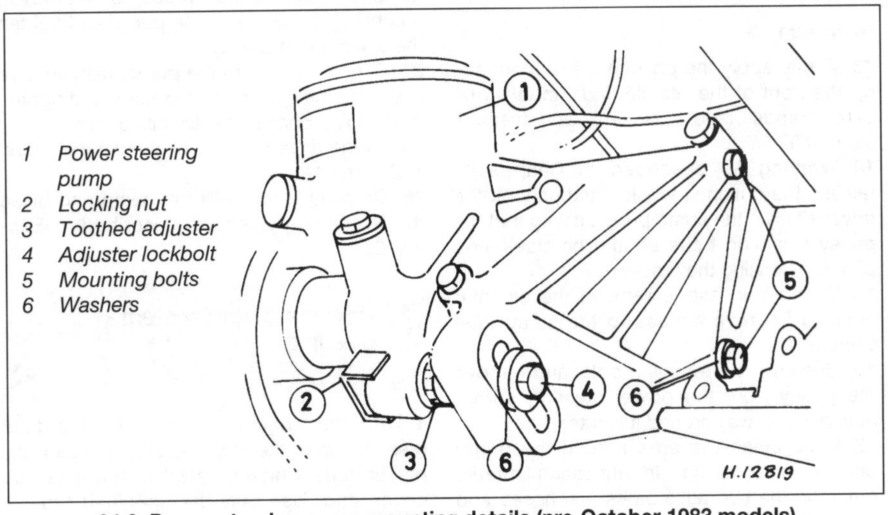

24.6 Power steering pump mounting details (pre-October 1983 models)

24.8 Undo the three bolts and remove the pulley from the pump shaft

7 Remove the drivebelt from the pump pulley.

8 Undo the three bolts and remove the pulley from the pump shaft **(see illustration)**.

9 Remove the two mounting bolts at the rear of the pump mounting bracket and recover the threaded retaining plate from the front **(see illustration)**.

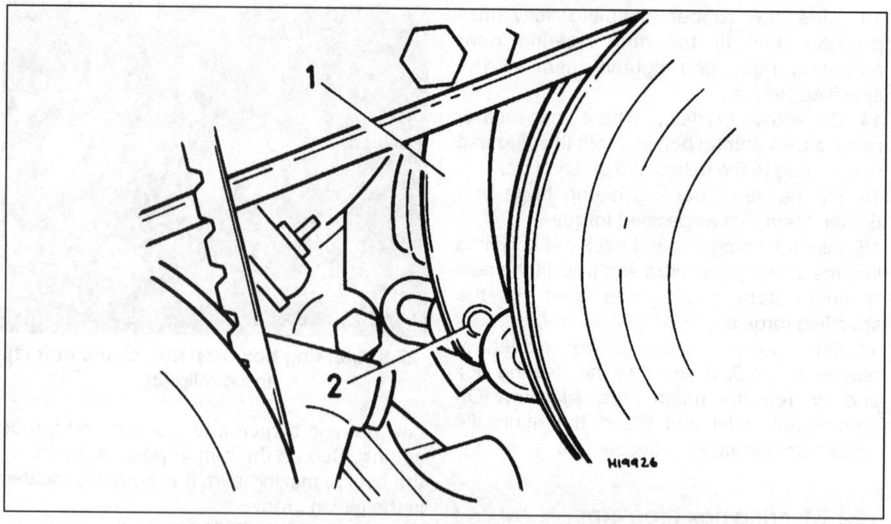

24.9 Threaded retaining plate (1) and mounting bolt (2)

10 Undo and remove the adjuster lockbolt from the rear of the pump, then recover the locking nut and toothed adjuster.

11 Remove the pump from the engine.

Refitting

12 Refit the pump by following the removal procedure in reverse, noting the following points:

- *a) With the drivebelt in position, adjust the tension as described in Chapter 1A or 1B.*
- *b) When refitting the filter cartridge pressure spring and nut, tighten the nut just sufficiently to pre-load the spring.*
- *c) On completion of refitting, fill the reservoir with the specified quantity and grade of fluid, then start the engine and turn the steering from full left lock to full right lock several times. Check the fluid level and top up if required. Repeat the procedure until the fluid level remains constant. Finally, refit the cover and cap nut.*

Models from October 1984 onwards

Removal

13 Firmly apply the parking brake then jack up the front of the vehicle and support it on axle stands (see "*Jacking and vehicle support*").

14 Working as described in Chapter 1, release the drivebelt tension and unhook the drivebelt from the pump pulley, noting that the pulley retaining bolts should be slackened prior to releasing the tension.

15 Where necessary, remove the air inlet hose to improve access to the pump (see Chapter 4).

16 Unscrew the retaining bolts and remove the pulley from the power steering pump, noting which way around it is fitted.

17 Wipe clean the area around the pump unions and make identification marks between the hydraulic pipes and hoses and the pump.

18 Slacken the union nuts and disconnect the hoses from the pump. Be prepared for fluid spillage, and position a suitable container beneath the hoses whilst unscrewing the nuts. Plug the hose ends and steering pump orifices, to prevent fluid leakage and to keep dirt out of the hydraulic system.

19 Where necessary, unbolt the support bracket from the rear of the pump.

20 Slacken and remove the power steering pump mounting bolts and remove the pump assembly from the engine compartment.

21 If the power steering pump is faulty, seek the advice of your Mercedes-Benz dealer as to the availability of spare parts. If spares are available it maybe possible to have the pump overhauled by a suitable specialist or alternately obtain an exchange unit. If not the pump must be renewed.

Refitting

22 Refit the pump and tighten the mounting bolts to the specified torque. Where necessary, refit the support strut to the rear of the pump.

23 Using the marks made on removal, reconnect the hoses to the pump and tighten the union nuts securely.

24 Refit the pulley to the pump, making sure it is fitted the correct way around, and tighten its retaining bolts to the specified torque.

25 Fit the drivebelt and tension as described in Chapter 1.

26 On completion, refill the pump and bleed the hydraulic system as described in Section 25.

25 Power steering system - bleeding

1 With the engine stopped, fill the fluid reservoir up to the upper level marking on the plastic tube which is fitted to the reservoir cover stud. Use only the specified type of fluid.

2 With the engine stopped, slowly move the steering from lock-to-lock several times to purge out the trapped air, then top-up the level in the fluid reservoir. Repeat this procedure until the fluid level in the reservoir does not drop any further.

3 Have an assistant start the engine, whilst you keep watch on the fluid level. Be prepared to add more fluid as the engine starts as the fluid level is likely to drop quickly. The fluid level must be kept above the lower mark on the plastic tube at all times.

4 With the engine running at idle speed, turn the steering wheel slowly two or three times approximately 45° to the left and right of the centre, then turn the wheel twice from lock to lock. Do not hold the wheel on either lock, as this imposes strain on the hydraulic system. Repeat this procedure until bubbles cease to appear in fluid reservoir.

5 If, when turning the steering, an abnormal noise is heard from the fluid lines, it indicates that there is still air in the system. Check this by turning the wheels to the straight-ahead position and switching off the engine. If the fluid level in the reservoir rises, then air is present in the system and further bleeding is necessary.

6 Once all traces of air have been removed from the power steering hydraulic system, turn the engine off and allow the system to cool. Once cool, check that fluid level is up to the maximum mark, topping-up if necessary (see "*Weekly checks*").

26 Steering damper - removal and refitting

Note: *New steering damper bolt nuts will be required on refitting.*

Removal

1 Firmly apply the parking brake then jack up the front of the vehicle and support it on axle stands (see "*Jacking and vehicle support*").

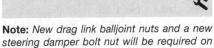

26.2a Slacken and remove the left-hand . . .

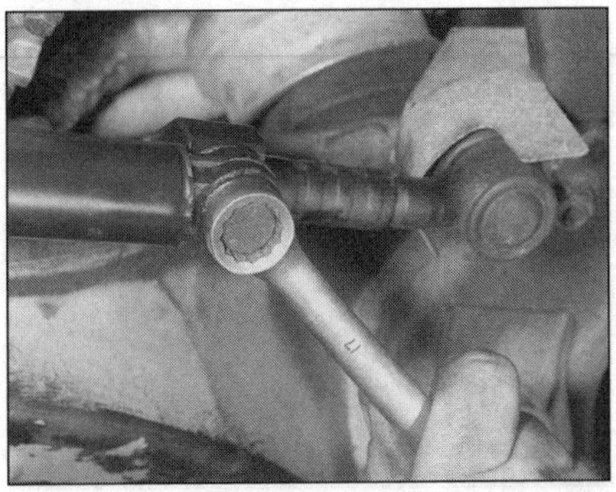

26.2b . . . and right-hand mounting bolts and remove the steering damper

2 Slacken and remove the damper retaining nuts and bolts and remove the damper, noting which way around it is fitted **(see illustrations)**.

3 Inspect the damper assembly for signs of wear or damage and renew if necessary. Inspect the rubber mountings for signs of damage and deterioration and renew if necessary.

Refitting

4 Refitting is the reverse of removal ensuring that the damper is fitted the correct way around. Fit new nuts to the retaining bolts and tighten them to the specified torque setting.

27 Steering drag link - removal and refitting

Note: *New drag link balljoint nuts and a new steering damper bolt nut will be required on refitting.*

Removal

1 Firmly apply the parking brake then jack up the front of the vehicle and support it on axle stands (see "*Jacking and vehicle support*").

2 Slacken and remove the retaining nut and bolt and detach the steering damper from the drag link.

3 Slacken and remove the nuts securing the drag link balljoints to the steering box and intermediate arm. Free the balljoints, if necessary using a balljoint separator, and remove the drag link from underneath the vehicle.

4 Check that the link balljoints move freely without any sign of roughness and that the balljoint gaiters show no sign of deterioration and are free from cracks and splits. If the balljoints are worn or damaged the drag link assembly must be renewed. If only the gaiter appears to be damaged, renew it and pack the balljoint with fresh grease.

Refitting

5 Ensure that the balljoint shanks are clean and dry, then refit the drag link. Fit the new retaining nuts and tighten them to the specified torque.

6 Reconnect the steering damper to the drag link and insert the retaining bolt. Fit a new nut to the bolt and tighten it to the specified torque setting. Lower the vehicle to the ground.

28 Steering intermediate arm - removal and refitting

Note: *A new intermediate arm pivot bolt nut will be required on refitting. New drag link and track rod balljoint nuts will also be required.*

Removal

1 Firmly apply the parking brake then jack up the front of the vehicle and support it on axle stands (see "*Jacking and vehicle support*").

2 Slacken and remove the securing nuts and detach the drag link and track rod balljoints from the intermediate arm. If necessary, free the balljoints using a balljoint separator **(see illustration)**.

3 Unscrew the retaining bolt(s) and remove the heatshield from the arm pivot.

4 Unscrew the intermediate arm pivot bolt nut and remove the washer. Withdraw the pivot bolt then remove the intermediate arm along with the spacer which is fitted between the arm and pivot.

5 Inspect the intermediate arm for signs of damage and renew as necessary. Check the arm pivot bushes for signs of wear or deterioration and renew if necessary. The original bushes can be tapped or pulled out of position and the new bushes drawn into position using a suitable nut and bolt fitted with large washers, having first lubricated them with soapy water.

Refitting

6 Offer up the intermediate arm, positioning the spacer between the arm and upper pivot bush, and insert the pivot bolt. Fit the washer and new nut to the pivot bolt, tightening it to the specified torque, then refit the heatshield.

7 Ensure that the balljoint shanks are clean and dry and locate them in the intermediate arm. Fit the new balljoint nuts and tighten them to the specified toque setting then lower the vehicle to the ground.

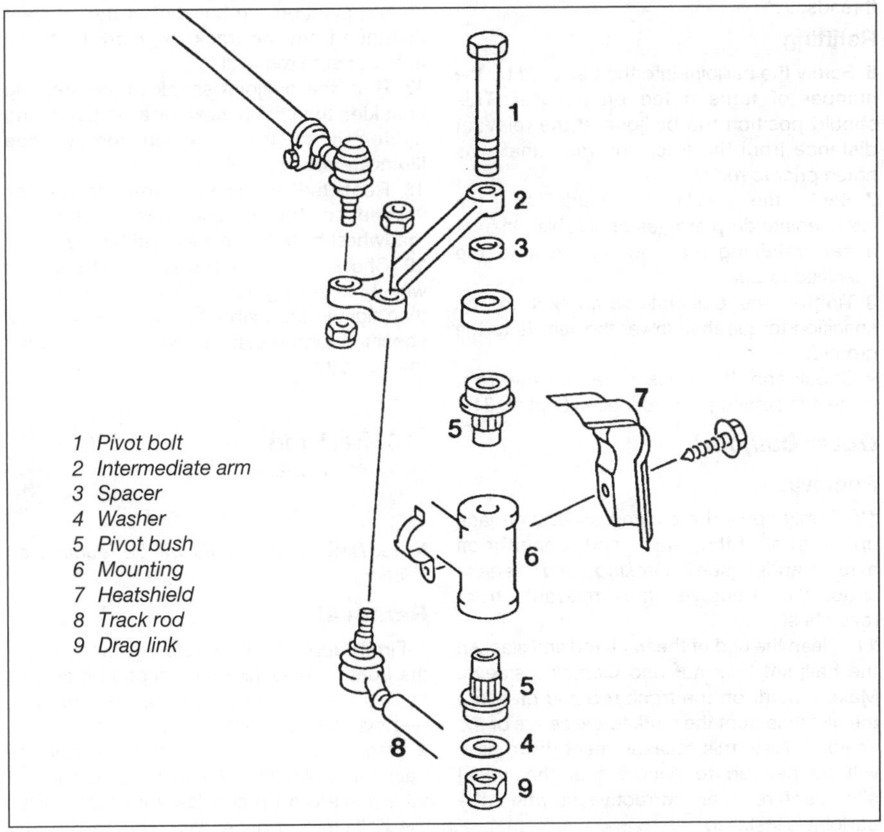

28.2 Steering intermediate arm components

29 Track rod balljoint - removal and refitting

Note: *A new balljoint nut will be required on refitting.*

Inner balljoint

Removal

1 Firmly apply the parking brake then jack up the front of the vehicle and support it on axle stands (see *"Jacking and vehicle support"*).

2 Clean the inner end of the track rod and slacken the balljoint clamp bolt. Make a mark on the track rod and measure the distance from the mark to the centre of the balljoint. Note this measurement down as it will be needed to ensure that the wheel alignment remains correctly set when the balljoint is installed.

3 Slacken and remove the balljoint nut and free the balljoint from the intermediate/drop arm (as applicable). If necessary, free the balljoint tapered shank using a universal balljoint separator.

4 Counting the **exact** number of turns necessary to do so, unscrew the balljoint from the track rod end.

5 Carefully clean the balljoint and the threads. Renew the balljoint if its movement is sloppy or too stiff, if excessively worn, or if damaged in any way; carefully check the stud taper and threads.

Refitting

6 Screw the balljoint into the track rod by the number of turns noted on removal. This should position the balljoint at the relevant distance from the track rod mark that was noted prior to removal.

7 Refit the balljoint shank to the intermediate/drop arm (as applicable), then fit a new retaining nut and tighten it to the specified torque.

8 Tighten the balljoint clamp bolt to the specified torque then lower the vehicle to the ground.

9 Check and, if necessary, adjust the front wheel toe setting as described in Section 31.

Outer balljoint

Removal

10 Firmly apply the parking brake then jack up the front of the vehicle and support it on axle stands (see *"Jacking and vehicle support"*). Remove the relevant front roadwheel.

11 Clean the end of the track rod and slacken the balljoint lock nut and clamping sleeve. Make a mark on the track rod and measure the distance from the mark to the centre of the balljoint. Note this measurement down as it will be needed to ensure that the wheel alignment remains correctly set when the balljoint is installed.

12 Slacken and remove the balljoint nut and free the balljoint from the steering knuckle. If necessary, free the balljoint tapered shank using a universal balljoint separator **(see illustration)**.

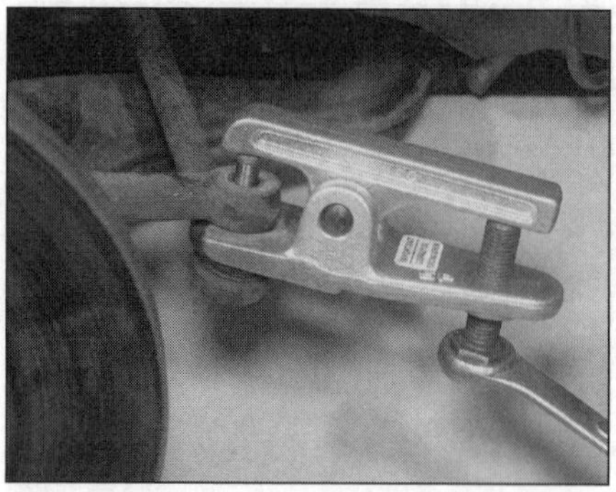

29.12 Using a balljoint separator to free the track rod from the steering knuckle

13 Counting the **exact** number of turns necessary to do so, unscrew the balljoint from the track rod end.

14 Carefully clean the balljoint and the threads. Renew the balljoint if its movement is sloppy or too stiff, if excessively worn, or if damaged in any way; carefully check the stud taper and threads.

Refitting

15 If necessary, transfer the locknut onto the new track rod balljoint.

16 Screw the balljoint into the track rod by the number of turns noted on removal. This should position the balljoint at the relevant distance from the track rod mark that was noted prior to removal.

17 Refit the balljoint shank to the steering knuckle, then fit a new retaining nut and tighten it to the specified torque **(see illustration)**.

29.17 On refitting, fit a new retaining nut and tighten it to the specified torque

18 Refit the roadwheel, then lower the vehicle to the ground and tighten the roadwheel bolts to the specified torque.

19 Check and, if necessary, adjust the front wheel toe setting as described in Section 31, then tighten the balljoint clamping ring to the specified torque setting and securely tighten the locknut.

30 Track rod - removal and refitting

Note: *New balljoint nuts will be required on refitting.*

Removal

1 Firmly apply the parking brake then jack up the front of the vehicle and support it on axle stands (see *"Jacking and vehicle support"*). Remove the relevant front roadwheel.

2 Slacken and remove the nuts securing the track rod balljoints to the steering knuckle and intermediate/drop arm (as applicable). Free the balljoints, if necessary using a balljoint separator to release their tapered shanks, and remove the track rod from underneath the vehicle.

3 Check that the track rod balljoints move freely without any sign of roughness and that the balljoint gaiters show no sign of deterioration and are free from cracks and splits. If the balljoints are worn or damaged they must be renewed as described in Section 29. If just the gaiters appear to be damaged, renew and pack the balljoint(s) with fresh grease.

Refitting

4 Ensure that the balljoint shanks are clean and dry. If a new track rod assembly is being fitted, check that the length of the rod is correctly set prior to installation; the distance between the balljoint centres should be 337 ± 12 mm.

5 Manoeuvre the track rod into position, ensuring it is the correct way around (the inner balljoint is the one secured in position with the clamp and the outer balljoint by a locknut and clamping ring), and engage the balljoint shanks in the steering knuckle and arm.

6 Fit the new retaining nuts to the balljoints and tighten them to the specified torque.

7 Lower the vehicle to the ground and check the front wheel toe setting as described in Section 31.

31 Wheel alignment and steering angles - general information

Definitions

A car's steering and suspension geometry is defined in four basic settings - all angles are expressed in degrees (toe settings are also expressed as a measurement); the steering axis is defined as an imaginary line drawn through the axis of the suspension strut, extended where necessary to contact the ground.

Camber is the angle between each roadwheel and a vertical line drawn through its centre and tyre contact patch, when viewed from the front or rear of the car. Positive camber is when the roadwheels are tilted outwards from the vertical at the top;

negative camber is when they are tilted inwards.

The front camber angle is adjusted by slackening and rotating the lower arm front pivot bolt and can be adjusted using a camber angle gauge. The rear wheel camber is not adjustable and is given for reference only; while it can be checked using a castor checking gauge, if the figure obtained is significantly different from that specified, the vehicle must be taken for careful checking by a professional, as the fault can only be caused by wear or damage to the body or suspension components.

Castor is the angle between the steering axis and a vertical line drawn through each roadwheel's centre and tyre contact patch, when viewed from the side of the car. Positive castor is when the steering axis is tilted so that it contacts the ground ahead of the vertical; negative castor is when it contacts the ground behind the vertical.

The front castor angle is adjusted by slackening and rotating the lower arm rear pivot bolt and can be adjusted using a castor angle gauge. The rear wheel castor is not adjustable and is given for reference only; while it can be checked using a castor checking gauge, if the figure obtained is significantly different from that specified, the vehicle must be taken for careful checking by a professional, as the fault can only be caused by wear or damage to the body or suspension components.

Toe is the difference, viewed from above, between lines drawn through the roadwheel centres and the car's centre-line. "Toe-in" is when the roadwheels point inwards, towards each other at the front, while "toe-out" is when they splay outwards from each other at the front.

The front wheel toe setting is adjusted by screwing the track rod in or out of its balljoints, to alter the effective length of the track rod assembly.

Rear wheel toe setting is also adjustable. The toe setting is adjusted by slackening and rotating the lower rear (track) control arm inner pivot bolt.

Checking and adjustment

Due to the special measuring equipment necessary to check the wheel alignment and steering angles, and the skill required to use it properly, the checking and adjustment of these settings is best left to a Mercedes-Benz dealer or similar expert. Note that most tyre-fitting shops now possess sophisticated checking equipment.

Front wheel toe setting

To check the toe setting, a tracking gauge must first be obtained. Two types of gauge are available, and can be obtained from motor accessory shops. The first type measures the distance between the front and rear inside edges of the roadwheels, as previously described, with the vehicle stationary. The second type, known as a 'scuff plate', measures the actual position of the contact surface of the tyre, in relation to the road surface, with the vehicle in motion. This is achieved by pushing or driving the front tyre over a plate, which then moves slightly according to the scuff of the tyre, and shows this movement on a scale. Both types have their advantages and disadvantages, but either can give satisfactory results if used correctly and carefully.

Make sure that the steering is in the straight-ahead position when making measurements.

If adjustment is necessary, apply the parking brake then jack up the front of the vehicle and support it securely on axle stands (see "*Jacking and vehicle support*").

First clean the track rod threads; if they are corroded, apply penetrating fluid before starting adjustment. Slacken the inner balljoint clamp bolt and outer balljoint locknut and clamping ring.

Alter the length of the track rod, by screwing it into or out of the balljoints by rotating the track rod using a pair of grips; shortening the track rod length will reduce toe-in/increase toe-out.

When the setting is correct, hold the track rod and tighten the inner balljoint clamp bolt to the specified torque setting. Tighten the outer balljoint clamping ring to the specified torque and securely tighten the locknut.

If after adjustment, the steering wheel spokes are no longer horizontal when the wheels are in the straight-ahead position, remove the steering wheel and reposition it (see Section 17).

Check that the toe setting has been correctly adjusted by lowering the vehicle to the ground and re-checking the toe setting; re-adjust if necessary.

Front wheel camber and castor setting

If access to camber and castor angle measuring equipment can be gained, the camber and castor angles can be checked as follows. Both camber and castor angles should be adjusted simultaneously, since any alteration to the camber also affects the castor and vice versa.

Attach the gauges to the vehicle and check the camber and castor angles are within the specified limits.

If adjustment is necessary, slacken the mounting clamps securing the anti-roll bar to both front suspension lower arms. Also slacken the lower arm pivot bolt nuts.

Rotate the pivot bolts until both camber and castor angles are correctly set then hold the bolt stationary and tighten the pivot bolt nuts to the specified torque.

Check that both the camber and castor angles are correctly set then tighten the anti-roll bar mounting clamp nuts to the specified torque and remove the gauges.

Rear wheel toe setting

The procedure for checking the rear toe setting is same as described for the front wheel toe setting.

To adjust the setting, slacken the lower track control arm inner pivot bolt nut. Rotate the pivot bolt until the toe setting is correctly set then hold the pivot bolt stationary and tighten the pivot bolt nut to the specified torque.

Check that the toe setting has been correctly adjusted by lowering the vehicle to the ground and re-checking the toe setting; re-adjust if necessary.

Notes

Chapter 11
Bodywork

Contents

Bonnet - adjustment 7
Bonnet - removal and refitting 6
Bonnet emblem - removal and refitting 13
Bonnet hinge - removal and refitting 8
Bonnet lock - removal and refitting 11
Bonnet release cable - removal and refitting 10
Bonnet support strut - removal and refitting 9
Boot lid - removal and refitting 14
Boot lid lock - removal and refitting 15
Bumpers - dismantling and reassembly 17
Central locking system vacuum pump - removal and refitting 39
Centre console - removal and refitting 40
Door inner trim panel - removal and refitting 18
Door lock solenoids (central locking system) - removal and refitting 28
Door mirror assembly (electrically-operated mirror) - removal and refitting 34
Door mirror assembly (manual mirrors) - removal and refitting 32
Door mirror glass (electrically-operated mirror) - renewal 33
Door mirror glass (manual mirror) - renewal 31
Facia - removal and refitting 42
Front and rear bumpers - removal and refitting 16
Front and rear doors - removal and refitting 29
Front door exterior handle - removal and refitting 24
Front door lock - removal and refitting 25
Front door window glass - removal and refitting 20
Front door window regulator - removal and refitting 19
Front seats - removal and refitting 35
General description 1
Glovebox - removal and refitting 41
Maintenance - bodywork and underframe 2
Maintenance - upholstery and carpets 3
Major body damage - repair 5
Minor body damage - repair 4
Radiator grille - removal and refitting 12
Rear door exterior handle - removal and refitting 26
Rear door fixed quarter-light - removal and refitting 23
Rear door lock - removal and refitting 27
Rear door window glass - removal and refitting 22
Rear door window regulator - removal and refitting 21
Rear seat - removal and refitting 36
Seat belts - removal and refitting 37
Sunroof - general 38
Windscreen and rear window - removal and refitting 30

Degrees of difficulty

Easy, suitable for novice with little experience	**Fairly easy,** suitable for beginner with some experience	**Fairly difficult,** suitable for competent DIY mechanic	**Difficult,** suitable for experienced DIY mechanic	**Very difficult,** suitable for expert DIY or professional

1 General description

The body is of unitary all-steel construction, and incorporates computer-calculated impact crumple zones at the front and rear, with a central safety cell passenger compartment. During manufacture the body is dip-primed, fully sealed and undercoated then painted with multi-layered base and top-coats.

The bodyshell on all models covered by this manual is of four-door saloon configuration.

2 Maintenance - bodywork and underframe

The general condition of a vehicle's bodywork is the one thing that significantly affects its value. Maintenance is easy but needs to be regular. Neglect, particularly after minor damage, can lead quickly to further deterioration and costly repair bills. It is important also to keep watch on those parts of the vehicle not immediately visible, for instance the underside, inside all the wheelarches and the lower pan of the engine compartment.

The basic maintenance routine for the bodywork is washing - preferably with a lot of water, from a hose. This will remove all the loose solids which may have stuck to the vehicle. It is important to flush these off in such a way as to prevent grit from scratching the finish. The wheelarches and underframe need washing in the same way to remove any accumulated mud which will retain moisture and tend to encourage rust. Paradoxically, the best time to clean the underframe and wheelarches is in wet weather when the mud is thoroughly wet and soft. In very wet weather the underframe is usually cleaned of large accumulations automatically and this is a good time for inspection.

Periodically, except on vehicles with a wax-based underbody protective coating, it is a good idea to have the whole of the underframe of the vehicle steam cleaned, engine compartment included, so that a thorough inspection can be carried out to see what minor repairs and renovations are necessary. Steam cleaning is available at many garages and is necessary for removal of the accumulation of oily grime which sometimes is allowed to become thick in certain areas. If steam cleaning facilities are not available, there are one or two excellent grease solvents available which can be brush applied. The dirt can then be simply hosed off. Note that these methods should not be used on vehicles with wax-based underbody protective coating or the coating will be removed. Such vehicles should be inspected annually, preferably just prior to winter, when the underbody should be washed down and any damage to the wax coating repaired. Ideally, a completely fresh coat should be applied. It would also be worth considering the use of such wax-based protection for injection into door panels, sills, box sections, etc, as an additional safeguard against rust damage where such protection is not provided by the vehicle manufacturer.

After washing paintwork, wipe off with a chamois leather to give an unspotted clear finish. A coat of clear protective wax polish will give added protection against chemical pollutants in the air. If the paintwork sheen has dulled or oxidised, use a cleaner/polisher combination to restore the brilliance of the shine. This requires a little effort, but such dulling is usually caused because regular washing has been neglected. Care needs to be taken with metallic paintwork, as special non-abrasive cleaner/polisher is required to avoid damage to the finish. Always check that the door and ventilator opening drain holes and pipes are completely clear so that water can be drained out. Bright work should be treated in the same way as paint work. Windscreens and windows can be kept clear of the smeary film which often appears by the use of a proprietary glass cleaner. Never use any form of wax or other body or chromium polish on glass.

3 Maintenance - upholstery and carpets

Mats and carpets should be brushed or vacuum cleaned regularly to keep them free of grit. If they are badly stained remove them from the vehicle for scrubbing or sponging and make quite sure they are dry before refitting. Seats and interior trim panels can be kept clean by wiping with a damp cloth. If they do become stained (which can be more apparent on light coloured upholstery) use a little liquid detergent and a soft nail brush to scour the grime out of the grain of the material. Do not forget to keep the headlining clean in the same way as the upholstery. When using liquid cleaners inside the vehicle do not over-wet the surfaces being cleaned. Excessive damp could get into the seams and padded interior causing stains, offensive odours or even rot. If the inside of the vehicle gets wet accidentally it is worthwhile taking some trouble to dry it out properly, particularly where carpets are involved. *Do not leave oil or electric heaters inside the vehicle for this purpose.*

4 Minor body damage - repair

Repair of minor scratches in bodywork

If the scratch is very superficial, and does not penetrate to the metal of the bodywork, repair is very simple. Lightly rub the area of the scratch with a paintwork renovator, or a very fine cutting paste, to remove loose paint from the scratch and to clear the surrounding bodywork of wax polish. Rinse the area with clean water.

Apply touch-up paint to the scratch using a fine paint brush; continue to apply fine layers of paint until the surface of the paint in the scratch is level with the surrounding paintwork. Allow the new paint at least two weeks to harden: then blend it into the surrounding paintwork by rubbing the scratch area with a paintwork renovator or a very fine cutting paste. Finally, apply wax polish.

Where the scratch has penetrated right through to the metal of the bodywork, causing the metal to rust, a different repair technique is required. Remove any loose rust from the bottom of the scratch with a penknife, then apply rust inhibiting paint to prevent the formation of rust in the future. Using a rubber or nylon applicator fill the scratch with bodystopper paste. If required, this paste can be mixed with cellulose thinners to provide a very thin paste which is ideal for filling narrow scratches. Before the stopper-paste in the scratch hardens, wrap a piece of smooth cotton rag around the top of a finger. Dip the finger in cellulose thinners and then quickly sweep it across the surface of the stopper-paste in the scratch; this will ensure that the surface of the stopper-paste is slightly hollowed. The scratch can now be painted over as described earlier in this Section.

Repair of dents in bodywork

When deep denting of the vehicle's bodywork has taken place, the first task is to pull the dent out, until the affected bodywork almost attains its original shape. There is little point in trying to restore the original shape completely, as the metal in the damaged area will have stretched on impact and cannot be reshaped fully to its original contour. It is better to bring the level of the dent up to a point which is about 3 mm below the level of the surrounding bodywork. In cases where the dent is very shallow anyway, it is not worth trying to pull it out at all. If the underside of the dent is accessible, it can be hammered out gently from behind, using a mallet with a wooden or plastic head. Whilst doing this, hold a suitable block of wood firmly against the outside of the panel to absorb the impact from the hammer blows and thus prevent a large area of the bodywork from being 'belled -out'.

Should the dent be in a section of the bodywork which has a double skin or some other factor making it inaccessible from behind, a different technique is called for. Drill several small holes through the metal inside the area - particularly in the deeper section. Then screw long self-tapping screws into the holes just sufficiently for them to gain a good purchase in the metal. Now the dent can be pulled out by pulling on the protruding heads of the screws with a pair of pliers.

The next stage of the repair is the removal of the paint from the damaged area, and from an inch or so of the surrounding 'sound' bodywork. This is accomplished most easily by using a wire brush or abrasive pad on a power drill. although it can be done just as effectively by hand using sheets of abrasive paper. To complete the preparation for filling, score the surface of the bare metal with a screwdriver or the tang of a file, or alternatively, drill small holes in the affected area. This will provide a really good 'key' for the filler paste.

To complete the repair see the Section on filling and re-spraying.

Repair of rust holes or gashes in bodywork

Remove all paint from the affected area and from an inch or so of the surrounding 'sound' bodywork, using an abrasive pad or a wire brush on a power drill. If these are not available a few sheets of abrasive paper will do the job just as effectively. With the paint removed you will be able to gauge the severity of the corrosion and therefore decide whether to renew the whole panel (if this is possible) or to repair the affected area. New body panels are not as expensive as most people think and it is often quicker and more satisfactory to fit a new panel than to attempt to repair large areas of corrosion.

Remove all fittings from the affected area except those which will act as a guide to the original shape of the damaged bodywork (eg: headlamp shells etc). Then, using tin snips or a hacksaw blade, remove all loose metal and any other metal badly affected by corrosion. Hammer the edges of the hole inwards in order to create a slight depression for the filler paste.

Wire brush the affected area to remove the powdery rust from the surface of the remaining metal. Paint the affected area with rust inhibiting paint; if the back of the rusted area is accessible treat this also.

Before filling can take place it will be necessary to block the hole in some way. This can be achieved by the use of aluminium or plastic mesh, or aluminium tape.

Aluminium or plastic mesh is probably the best material to use for a large hole. Cut a piece to the approximate size and shape of the hole to be filled, then position it in the hole so that its edges are below the level of the surrounding bodywork. It can be retained in position by several blobs of filler paste around its periphery.

Aluminium tape should be used for small or very narrow holes. Pull a piece off the roll and trim it to the approximate size and shape required, then pull off the backing paper (if used) and stick the tape over the hole; it can be overlapped if the thickness of one piece is insufficient. Burnish down the edges of the tape with the handle of a screwdriver or similar, to ensure that the tape is securely attached to the metal underneath.

Bodywork repairs - filling and re-spraying

Before using this Section, see the Sections on dent, deep scratch, rust holes and gash repairs.

Many types of bodyfiller are available, but generally speaking those proprietary kits which contain a tin of filler paste and a tube of resin hardener are best for this type of repair. A wide, flexible plastic or nylon applicator will be found invaluable for imparting a smooth and well contoured finish to the surface of the filler.

Mix up a little filler on a clean piece of card or board - measure the hardener carefully (follow the maker's instructions on the pack) otherwise the filler will set too rapidly or too slowly. Using the applicator apply the filler paste to the prepared area; draw the applicator across the surface of the filler to achieve the correct contour and to level the filler surface. As soon as a contour that approximates to the correct one is achieved, stop working the paste - if you carry on too long the paste will become sticky and begin to 'pick up' on the applicator. Continue to add thin layers of filler paste at twenty-minute intervals until the level of the filler is just proud of the surrounding bodywork.

Once the filler has hardened, excess can be removed using a metal plane or file. From then on, progressively finer grades of abrasive paper should be used, starting with a 40 grade production paper and finishing with 400 grade wet-and-dry paper. Always wrap the abrasive paper around a fiat rubber, cork, or wooden block - otherwise the surface of the filler will not be completely feat. During the smoothing of the filler surface the wet-and-dry paper should be periodically rinsed in water. This will ensure that a very smooth finish is imparted to the filler at the final stage.

At this stage the 'dent' should be surrounded by a ring of bare metal, which in turn should be encircled by the finely 'feathered' edge of the good paintwork. Rinse the repair area with clean water, until all of the dust produced by the rubbing-down operation has gone.

Spray the whole repair area with a light coat of primer - this will show up any imperfections in the surface of the filler. Repair these imperfections with fresh filler paste or bodystopper, and once more smooth the surface with abrasive paper. If bodystopper is used, it can be mixed with cellulose thinners to form a really thin paste which is ideal for filling small holes. Repeat this spray and repair procedure until you are satisfied that the surface of the filler, and the feathered edge of the paintwork are perfect. Clean the repair area with clean water and allow to dry fully.

The repair area is now ready for final spraying. Paint spraying must be carried out in a warm, dry, windless and dust free atmosphere. This condition can be created artificially if you have access to a large indoor working area, but if you are forced to work in the open, you will have to pick your day very carefully. If you are working indoors, dousing the floor in the work area with water will help to settle the dust which would otherwise be in the atmosphere. If the repair area is confined to one body panel, mask off the surrounding panels; this will help to minimise the effects of a slight mix-match in paint colours. Bodywork fittings (eg: chrome strips, door handles etc) will also need to be masked off. Use genuine masking tape and several thicknesses of newspaper for the masking operations.

Before commencing to spray, agitate the aerosol can thoroughly, then spray a test area (an old tin, or similar) until the technique is mastered. Cover the repair area with a thick coat of primer; the thickness should be built up using several thin layers of paint rather than one thick one. Using 400 grade wet-and-dry paper, rub down the surface of the primer until it is really smooth. While doing this, the work area should be thoroughly doused with water, and the wet-and-dry paper periodically rinsed in water. Allow to dry before spraying on more paint.

Spray on the top coat, again building up the thickness by using several thin layers of paint. Start spraying in the centre of the repair area and then, using a circular motion, work outwards until the whole repair area and about 2 inches of the surrounding original paintwork is covered. Remove all masking material 10 to 15 minutes after spraying on the final coat of paint.

Allow the new paint at least two weeks to harden, then, using a paintwork renovator or a very fine cutting paste, blend the edges of the paint into the existing paintwork. Finally, apply wax polish.

Plastic components

With the use of more and more plastic body components by the vehicle manufacturers (eg: bumpers, spoilers, and in some cases major body panels), rectification of more serious damage to such items has become a matter of either entrusting repair work to a specialist in this field, or renewing complete components. Repair of such damage by the DIY owner is not really feasible owing to the cost of the equipment and materials required for effecting such repairs. The basic technique involves making a groove along the line of the crack in the plastic using a rotary burr in a power drill. The damaged part is then welded back together by using a hot air gun to heat up and fuse a plastic filler rod into the groove. Any excess plastic is then removed and the area rubbed down to a smooth finish. It is important that a filler rod of the correct plastic is used, as body components can be made of a variety of different types (eg: polycarbonate, ABS, polypropylene).

Damage of a less serious nature (abrasions, minor cracks etc) can be repaired by the DIY owner using a two-part epoxy filler repair material. Once mixed in equal proportions, this is used in similar fashion to the bodywork filler used on metal panels. The filler is usually cured in twenty to thirty minutes, ready for sanding and painting.

If the owner is renewing a complete component himself, or if he has repaired it with epoxy filler, he will be left with the problem of finding a suitable paint for finishing which is compatible with the type of plastic used. At one time the use of a universal paint was not possible owing to the complex range of plastics encountered in body component applications. Standard paints, generally speaking, will not bond to plastic or rubber satisfactorily. However, it is now possible to obtain a plastic body parts finishing kit which consists of a preprimer treatment, a primer and coloured top coat. Full instructions are normally supplied with a kit, but basically the method of use is to first apply the pre-primer to the component concerned and allow it to dry for up to 30 minutes. Then the primer is applied and left to dry for about an hour before finally applying the special coloured top coat. The result is a correctly coloured component where the paint will flex with the plastic or rubber, a property that standard paint does not normally possess.

5 Major body damage - repair

Where serious damage has occurred, or large areas need renewal due to neglect, it means that complete new panels will need welding in, and this is best left to professionals. If the damage is due to impact, it will also be necessary to completely check the alignment of the bodyshell, and this can only be carried out accurately by a Mercedes-Benz dealer using special jigs. If the body is left misaligned, it is primarily dangerous as the car will not handle properly, and secondly, uneven stresses will be imposed on the steering, suspension and possibly transmission, causing abnormal wear, or complete failure, particularly to such items as the tyres.

6 Bonnet - removal and refitting

Removal

1 Raise the bonnet to the vertical position by pressing the catch on the left-hand hinge, releasing the retaining wire clip on the support strut, and pushing upwards.
2 Extract the retaining clip and withdraw the support strut from its lower mounting stud **(see illustration)**.
3 Disconnect the windscreen washer hose(s) at the check valve on the right-hand side and release the hose clips on the bonnet hinge.
4 Pull the wiring for the heated washer jets out of the bonnet cavity adjacent to the jet(s) and disconnect the wiring plug connections.
5 Tie a length of string to the main feed cable and pull the wiring out of the bonnet cavity from the hinge end. As soon as the end of the string appears, untie it and remove the wire. When refitting, tie the cable to the string to draw it back into position.
6 Remove the hinge retaining straps by releasing the upper bent-over locking portion from the hinge pin, then withdrawing the straps upwards **(see illustration)**.
7 Mark the position of the lower threaded hinge bolts on both sides so that the bonnet can be refitted in its original position.
8 With the help of an assistant to support the bonnet, undo the lower retaining nut each side, withdraw the hinge bolts and hinge pins and carefully lift off the bonnet.

Refitting

9 To refit the bonnet, push the hinge pin and hinge bolt bushes into the hinges, if these came out during removal.
10 Place the bonnet in position and insert the lower hinge bolt. Turn the bolt until the square collar engages with the rectangular hole in the hinge lever.
11 Insert the upper hinge pin and turn it until the slot in the hinge pin head is horizontal.
12 Refit the hinge nut, position the bonnet so that the previously made marks are aligned, then tighten the nut. Refit the hinge retaining strap, then repeat these operations for the hinge on the other side.
13 Tie the washer jet wiring to the drawstring and pull the wires through the bonnet into place. Reconnect the wiring plug(s).
14 Reconnect the washer hose(s) at the check valve, and secure with new hose clips to the bonnet hinge.
15 Locate the support strut on the mounting stud and secure with the retaining clip.
16 Lower the bonnet and check its fit and alignment. If necessary adjust the bonnet position as described in Section 7.

7 Bonnet - adjustment

1 With the bonnet closed, check the gap between the bonnet and front wings on both sides (transverse adjustment), the alignment of the front edge of the bonnet with the front edge of the wing when looking down, (longitudinal adjustment), and the height of the bonnet front edge and top edge in relation to the wing (height adjustment).

Transverse adjustment

2 Open the bonnet and slacken the two bolts securing the lock upper plate to the bonnet **(see illustration)**
3 By trial and error, move the upper plate until a gap of approximately 5.0 mm (0.2 in) exists between the bonnet and the front wings on each side.

Longitudinal adjustment

4 Remove the bonnet support strut as described in Section 9.
5 Remove the plastic covering from under the wheelarch, on the side being adjusted, for access to the bonnet hinge retaining nuts.
6 From within the engine compartment, slacken the locknut and screw down the bonnet rubber buffer behind the hinge.
7 Slacken the four bonnet hinge retaining bolts from under the wheelarch.
8 With the bonnet closed, position it in such a way that when viewed from the front looking down, the edge of the bonnet and the edge of the front wing are in alignment.
9 Tighten the hinge nuts with the bonnet closed and correctly aligned.
10 Refit the wheelarch covering and bonnet support strut, then check the height adjustment.

Height adjustment

11 From within the engine compartment, slacken the locknut and screw down the bonnet rubber buffer behind the hinge.
12 Slacken the nut on the bonnet-to-hinge lower retaining bolt.
13 By trial and error, move the bonnet as necessary, tightening the hinge bolt each time until the bonnet upper edge and front wing edge are aligned.
14 Now raise the rubber buffer a few turns at a time until the front edge of the bonnet and the edge of the wing, when viewed from the front, are aligned. Tighten the buffer locknut when adjustment is correct.

8 Bonnet hinge - removal and refitting

Removal

1 Remove the bonnet as described in Section 6.
2 Remove the plastic wheelarch covering from under the wheelarch for access to the hinge retaining nuts.
3 Undo the four hinge retaining nuts and remove the hinge.

Refitting

4 Refitting is the reverse sequence to removal. Adjust the bonnet as described in Section 7 after fitting.

9 Bonnet support strut - removal and refitting

Removal

1 Open the bonnet to the vertical position by pressing the catch on the left-hand hinge, releasing the retaining wire clip on the support

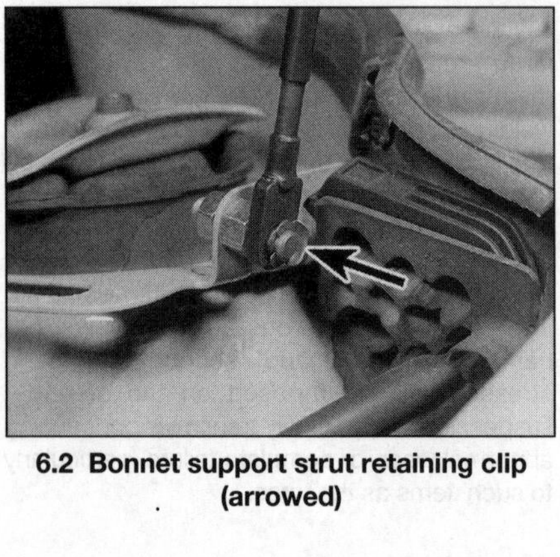

6.2 Bonnet support strut retaining clip (arrowed)

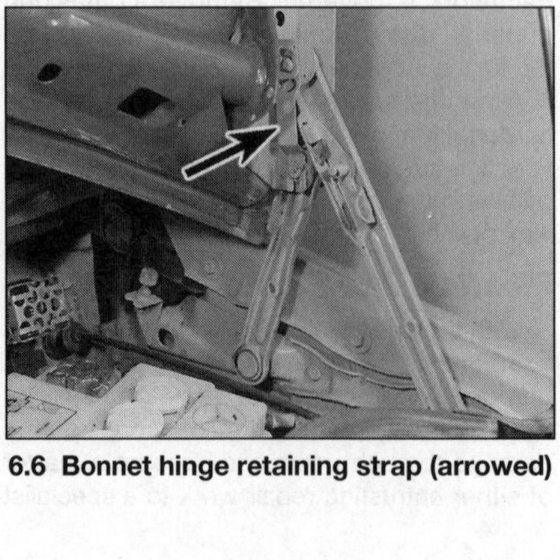

6.6 Bonnet hinge retaining strap (arrowed)

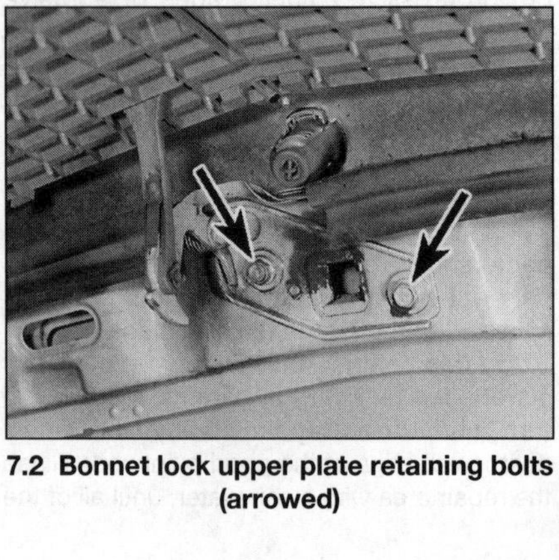

7.2 Bonnet lock upper plate retaining bolts (arrowed)

strut and pushing the bonnet upwards until the hinge locks.

2 Extract the strut lower retaining clip, undo the upper retaining nut and remove the strut.

Refitting

3 Refitting is the reverse sequence to removal.

10 Bonnet release cable - removal and refitting

Removal

1 Release the locking stud on the front panel adjacent to the support strut and remove the cover under the lock. **Note**: *On cars with air conditioning. undo the two screws and move the fan. then release the four upper clips and move the radiator rearwards for access*

2 Disconnect the release cable at the lock lever and support bracket.

3 From inside the car, remove the cover under the facia on the left-hand side.

4 Undo the screw and remove the release handle, then disconnect the cable.

5 Push out the rubber grommet at the cable entry point on the bulkhead.

6 Tie string to the release cable so that as the cable is pulled through the bulkhead it will pull the string with it.

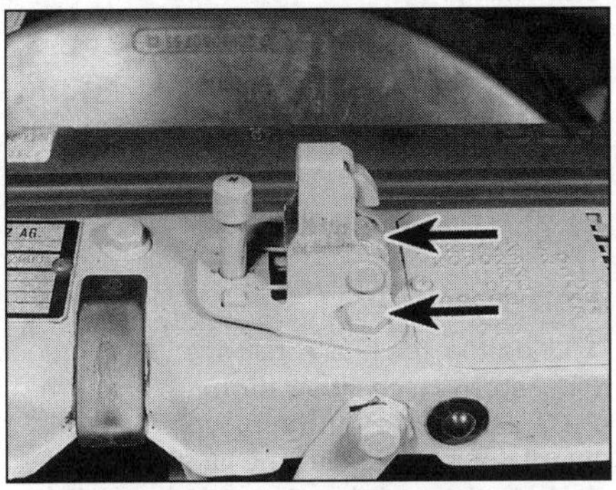

11.3 Bonnet lock retaining bolts (arrowed)

7 Pull out the cable in a forward direction. When the drawstring appears, untie it and remove the cable from the car.

Refitting

8 Refitting is the reverse sequence to removal - use the string to draw the new cable through the bulkhead into the car.

11 Bonnet lock - removal and refitting

Removal

1 Release the locking stud on the front panel adjacent to the support strut and remove the cover under the lock. **Note**: *On cars with air conditioning, undo the two screws and move the fan. then release the four upper clips and move the radiator rearwards for access*

2 Disconnect the release cable at the lock lever and support bracket.

3 Undo the two retaining bolts and remove the lock from the front panel **(see illustration)**.

Refitting

4 Refitting is the reverse sequence to removal. Minor adjustment of the closing action can be carried out by slackening the front panel support strut lower mounting bolt, and moving the strut and panel up or down slightly as necessary.

12 Radiator grille - removal and refitting

Removal

1 Open the bonnet, and from the inside at the front, undo the six retaining bolts.

2 Remove the grille surround and grille from the bonnet.

3 Release the pin clamps securing the grille to the grille surround on both sides.

4 Undo the lower screw and the upper nut that also retains the Mercedes badge. Remove the badge, then lift the grille out of the grille surround.

Refitting

5 Refitting is the reverse sequence to removal.

13 Bonnet emblem - removal and refitting

Removal

1 From the underside of the bonnet, pull the spring clip down using heavy duty pliers, against considerable spring tension, and turn the clip 90° to the left. Make sure that the spring clip enters into the grooves of the rosette.

2 Pull the star upwards out of the grille surround to remove.

Refitting

3 Refitting is the reverse sequence to removal.

14 Boot lid - removal and refitting

Removal

1 Disconnect the battery negative terminal.

2 Prise out the luggage compartment lamp, disconnect the wiring and remove the lamp.

3 Withdraw the wiring harness from the boot lid cavity.

4 Mark the outline of the hinges on the boot lid using a pencil.

5 Place some rags beneath the lower corners of the boot lid and, with the help of an assistant, undo the hinge retaining bolts **(see illustration)**. Remove the boot lid from the car.

Refitting

6 Refitting is the reverse sequence to removal, but align the hinges with the outline marks made prior to removal before tightening the bolts. Adjust the lock striker plate as necessary to achieve satisfactory opening and closing of the boot lid **(see illustration)**.

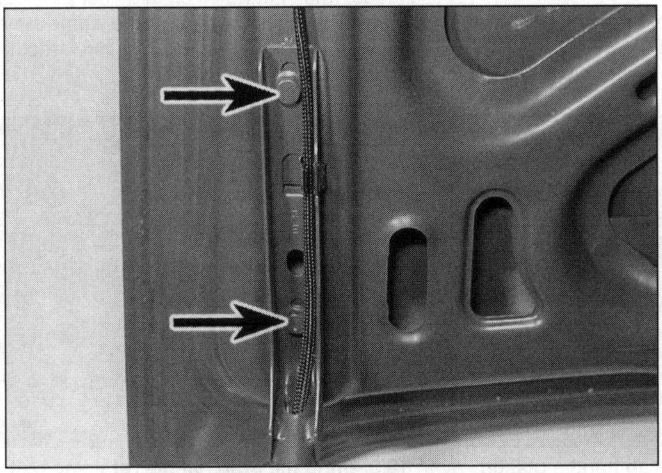

14.5 Boot lid-to-hinge retaining bolts (arrowed)

14.6 Boot lid striker plate retaining bolts (arrowed)

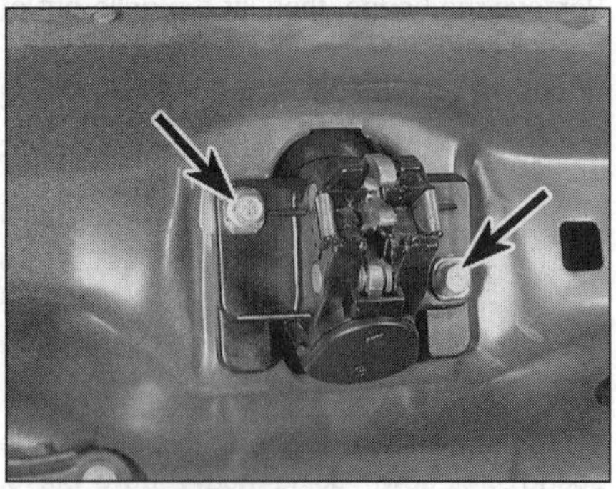
15.1 Undo the bolts (arrowed) and withdraw the boot lock

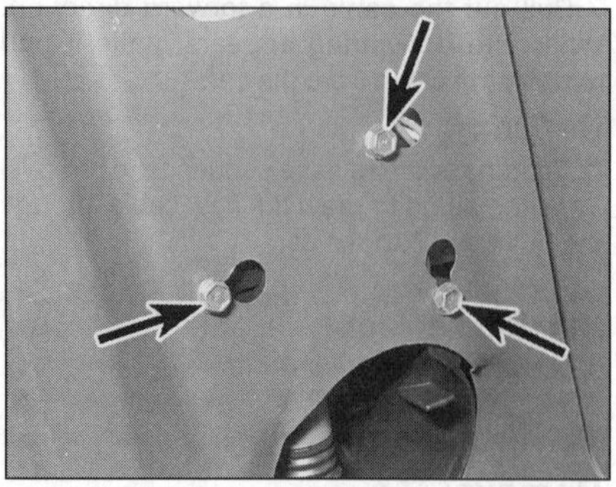
15.2 Central locking solenoid retaining bolts (arrowed)

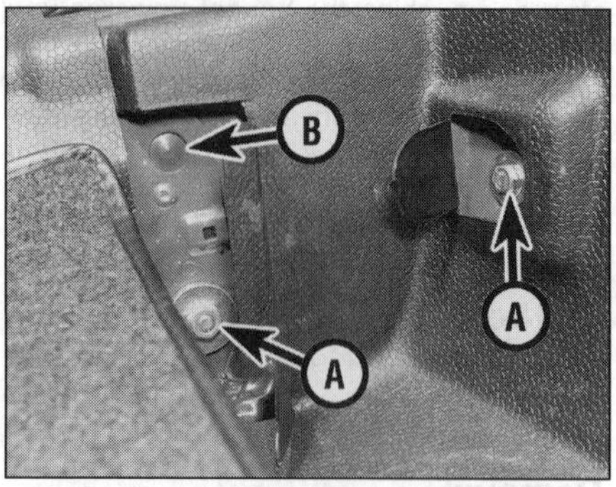

16.6 Rear bumper retaining bolts (A). Additional bolt may be fitted at (B)

15 Boot lid lock - removal and refitting

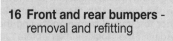

Removal

1 Open the boot lid, undo the two bolts and withdraw the lock **(see illustration)**.

2 If central locking is fitted, undo the three solenoid retaining screws **(see illustration)** and disconnect the operating rod from the lock prior to removal.

3 To remove the solenoid, disconnect the vacuum hose and withdraw the unit from the boot lid aperture.

Refitting

4 Refitting is the reverse sequence to removal. Adjust the lock striker plate as necessary to achieve satisfactory opening and closing of the boot lid.

16 Front and rear bumpers - removal and refitting

Front bumper

1 Undo the single bolt each side securing the bumper laterally to the side support members.

2 Undo the two nuts and remove the washers on each side at the front securing the bumper to the chassis members.

3 Push out the clips along the top edge of the bumper in front of the radiator.

4 Carefully pull the bumper forwards and remove it from the car.

5 Refitting is the reverse sequence to removal.

Rear bumper

6 From inside the luggage compartment, open the flaps in the trim panels and undo the bumper retaining bolts on each side **(see illustration)**.

7 Carefully pull the bumper rearwards and remove it from the car.

8 Refitting is the reverse sequence to removal.

17 Bumpers - dismantling and reassembly

1 The front and rear bumpers comprise a protective strip, foam member, trim covering and stiffener sandwiched together to form an assembly. Dismantling of both front and rear bumpers is as follows.

2 Undo the side retaining screws at the extreme ends on both sides.

3 Push back the holding straps, top and bottom, in pairs starting from the outside and working towards the centre.

4 Remove the protective strip and the foam member.

5 Push back the clips and remove the trim from the stiffener.

6 Push back the detent on the threaded holders on both sides, while at the same time sliding the holder down to remove.

7 Undo the nuts and bolts securing the front holders, and remove the holders.

8 Reassembly is the reverse sequence to dismantling.

18 Door inner trim panel - removal and refitting

Removal

1 Undo the screw and remove the door lock trim capping **(see illustration)**.

2 Carefully prise off the plastic cover at the top of the grab handle **(see illustration)**.

3 Undo the grab handle retaining bolt **(see illustration)**.

4 Ease the interior release handle out of the trim panel, while at the same time sliding the complete housing forwards to

18.1 Remove the door lock trim capping

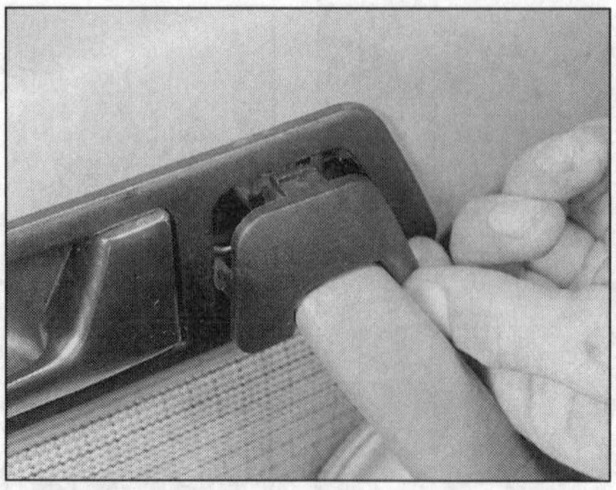
18.2 Prise off the grab handle plastic cover

18.3 Undo the grab handle retaining bolt

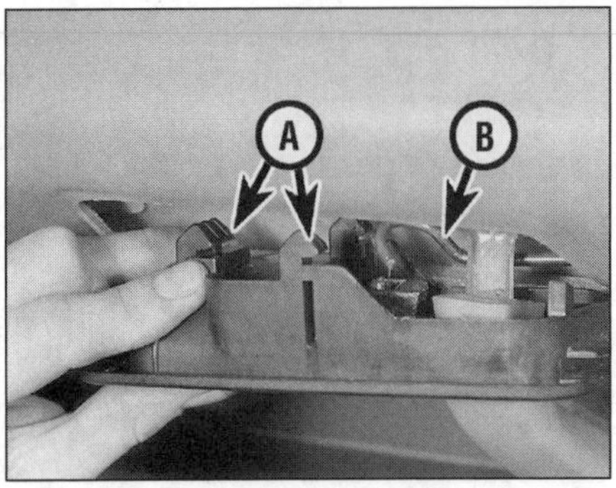

18.4 Release the interior handle hooks (A) and disengage the operating rod (B)

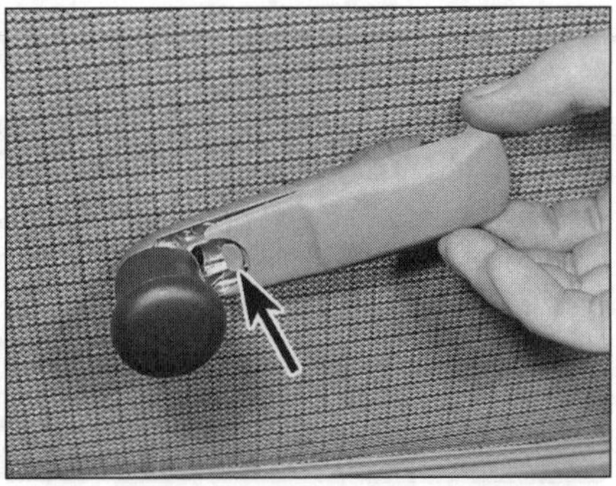

18.6 Remove the regulator handle trim after pressing down the detent (arrowed)

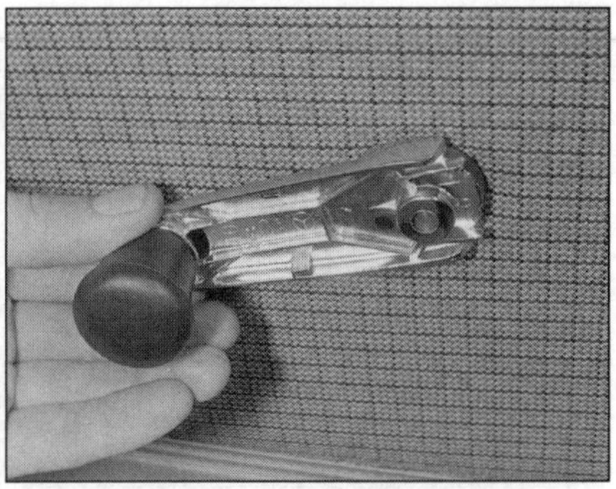

18.7a Withdraw the regulator handle . . .

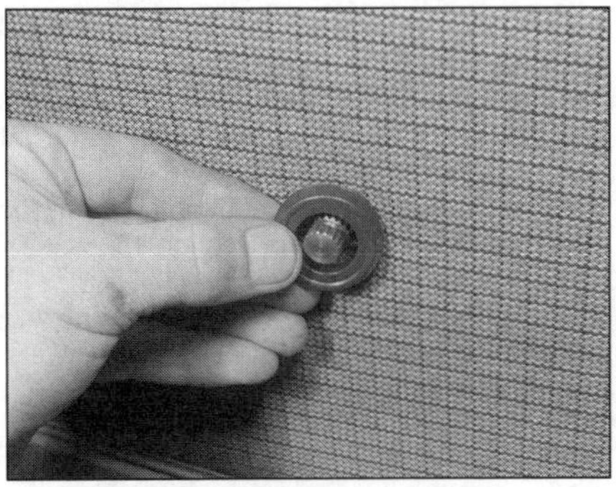

18.7b . . . and the trim disc

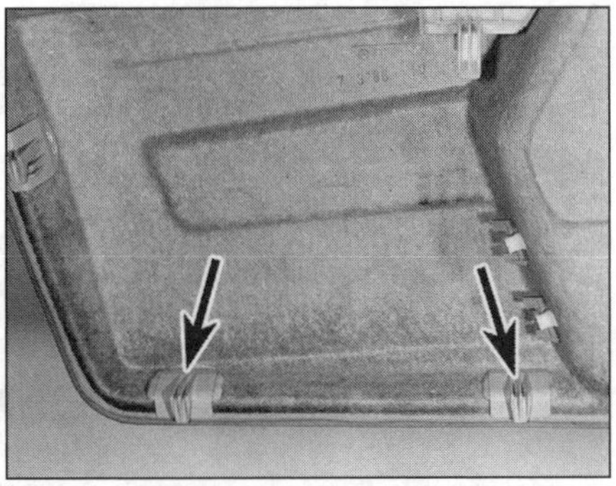

18.8 Door trim panel lower rear hooked retainers (arrowed)

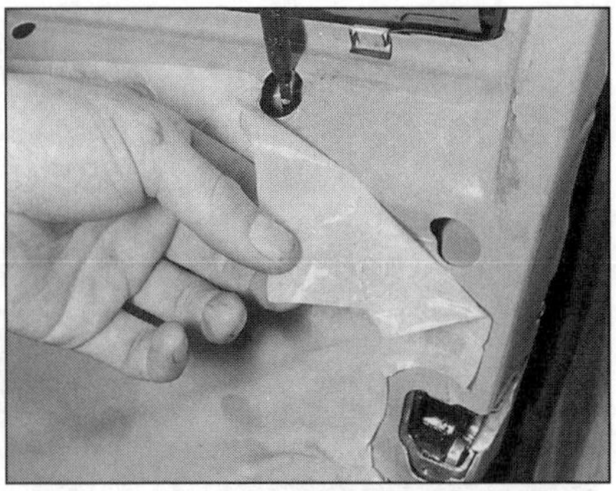

18.9 Carefully peel back the waterproof sheet

release the internal retaining hooks **(see illustration)**.

5 Disengage the lock operating rod from the rear of the interior release handle, and remove the handle and housing from the door.

6 On cars with manually-operated window regulators, slide the regulator handle trim off the handle, after releasing the detent by pressing down with a small screwdriver **(see illustration)**.

7 Withdraw the regulator handle and the trim disc **(see illustrations)**.

8 Lift the trim panel upwards to release the hooked retainers at the rear of the panel at the centre, bottom and sides **(see illustration)**. When the panel is free, lift it over the interior lock button and remove it from the door.

9 For access to the door internal components, carefully peel back the waterproof sheet and remove it from the door **(see illustration)**.

Refitting

10 Refitting is the reverse sequence to removal. When engaging the panel hooked retainers, first engage the longer one at the centre of the panel **(see illustration)**, then lift the panel just sufficiently to engage the rest without disengaging the centre one.

19 Front door window regulator - removal and refitting

Removal

1 Remove the door inner trim panel as described in Section 18.

2 Lower the window until the nut securing the regulator arm to the window regulator channel is accessible through the small aperture at the front of the door **(see illustration)**.

3 Support the window in this position either by using a wooden wedge between the window and door, or by using masking tape over the top of the door frame **(see illustration)**.

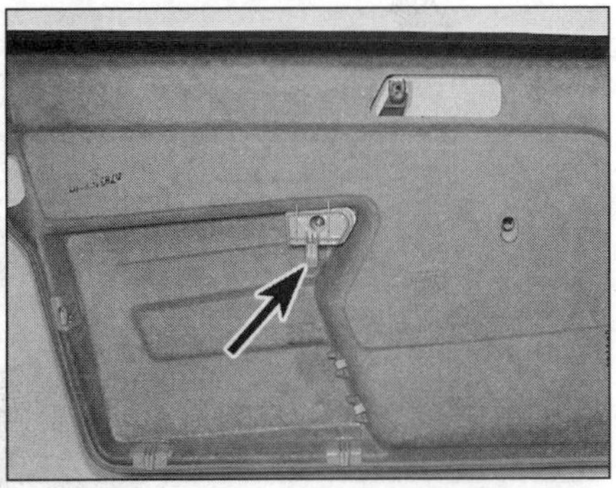

18.10 Engage the panel centre hooked retainer first (arrowed) when refitting

19.2 Undo the regulator arm-to-regulator channel nut

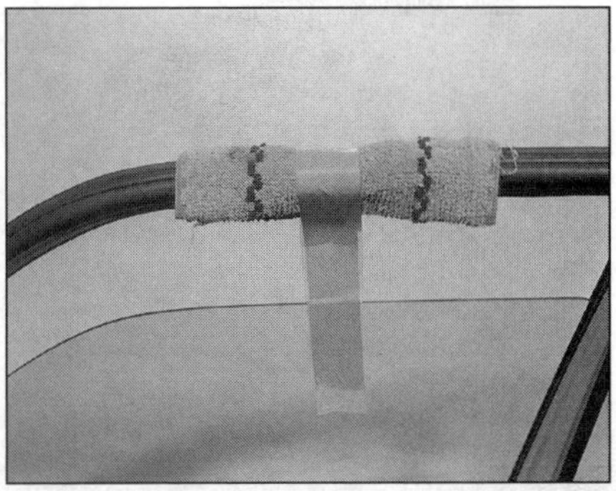

19.3 Using masking tape to support the window

19.6 Undo the guide rail retaining nuts (arrowed)

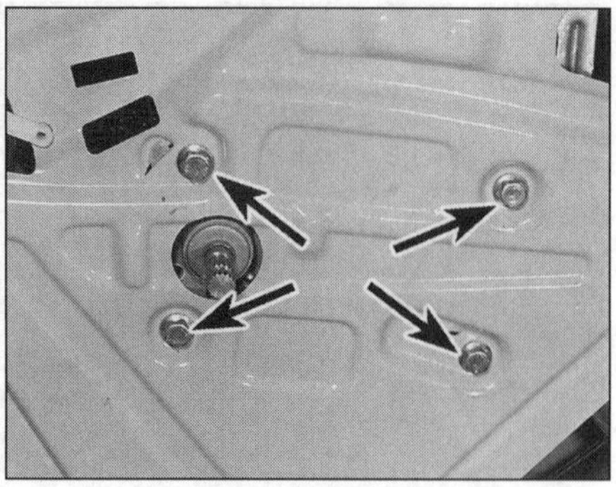

19.7 Undo the four regulator retaining bolts (arrowed)

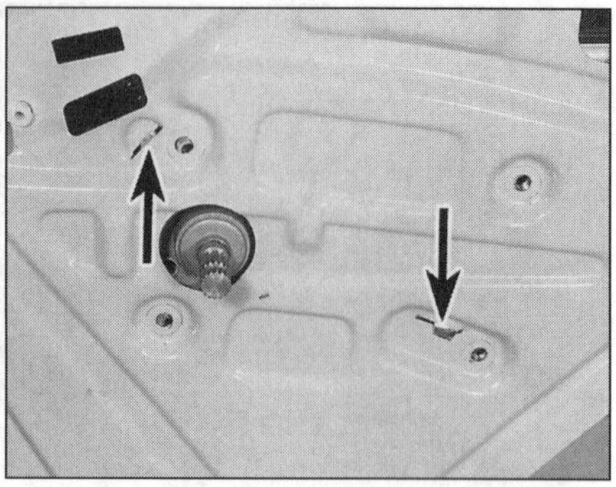

19.8 Release the detents (arrowed)

19.9a Disengage the regulator rear arm . . .

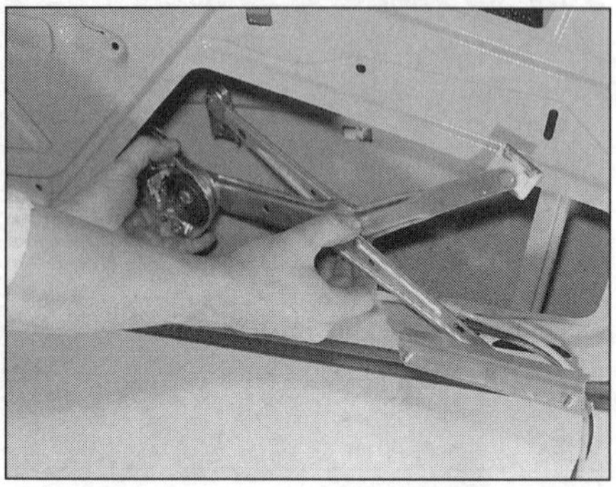

19.9b . . . and remove the regulator

4 With the window supported. undo the regulator arm to channel retaining nut.

5 On cars with electric windows, disconnect the wiring at the cable connector terminals.

6 Undo the two nuts securing the guide rail to the door panel **(see illustration)** and release the rail from the panel.

7 Undo the four bolts **(see illustration)** on cars with manual windows, or three bolts on cars with electric windows, securing the regulator assembly to the door.

8 On cars with manual windows, temporarily refit the regulator handle, and turn it as if to lower the window until the two detents **(see illustration)** are swivelled out of their location. Remove the regulator handle.

9 Disengage the regulator rear arm from the regulator channel, and withdraw the regulator assembly out through the door lower aperture **(see illustrations)**.

Refitting

10 Refitting is the reverse sequence to removal, but only tighten the regulator arm-to-regulator channel nut, and the two guide rail nuts finger-tight initially, then adjust the window operation as follows, before refitting the trim panel.

11 Wind the window down to the fully-open position.

12 Push the window down and forwards at the front, into the front guide channel, and rearwards at the top into the rear guide channel.

13 With the window held in this position, tighten the regulator arm to regulator channel retaining nut.

14 Push the guide rail rear nut downwards and tighten, then tighten the guide rail front nut.

15 Check the window operation and refit the trim panel as described in Section 18.

20 Front door window glass - removal and refitting

Removal

1 Remove the door inner trim panel as described in Section 18.

2 Lower the window fully, and undo the nut securing the regulator arm to the regulator channel at the front **(see illustration)**.

3 Undo the two nuts securing the guide rail to the door panel.

4 Disengage the regulator rear arm from the regulator channel, and the guide member from the guide rail **(see illustration)**.

5 Remove the guide member from the regulator channel, then lift the glass upwards and out on the inside of the door frame **(see illustration)**.

Refitting

6 Refitting is the reverse sequence to removal, and adjust the regulator as described in Section 19.

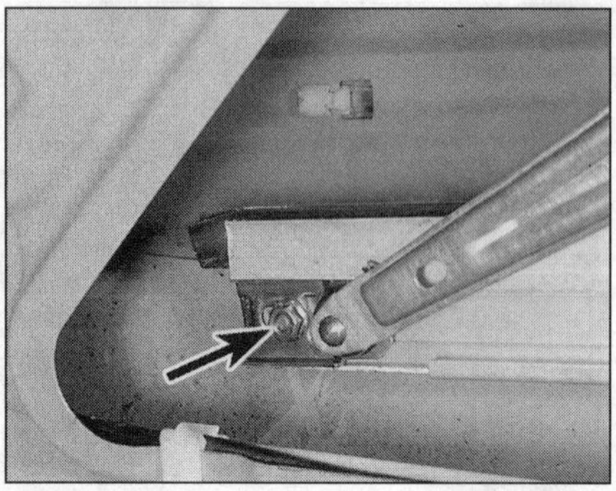

20.2 Undo the regulator arm nut (arrowed)

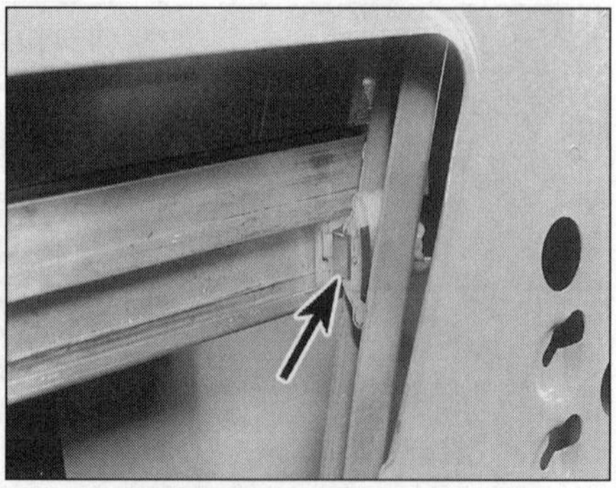

20.4 Disengage the guide member (arrowed) from the guide rail

20.5 Remove the glass on the inside of the door frame

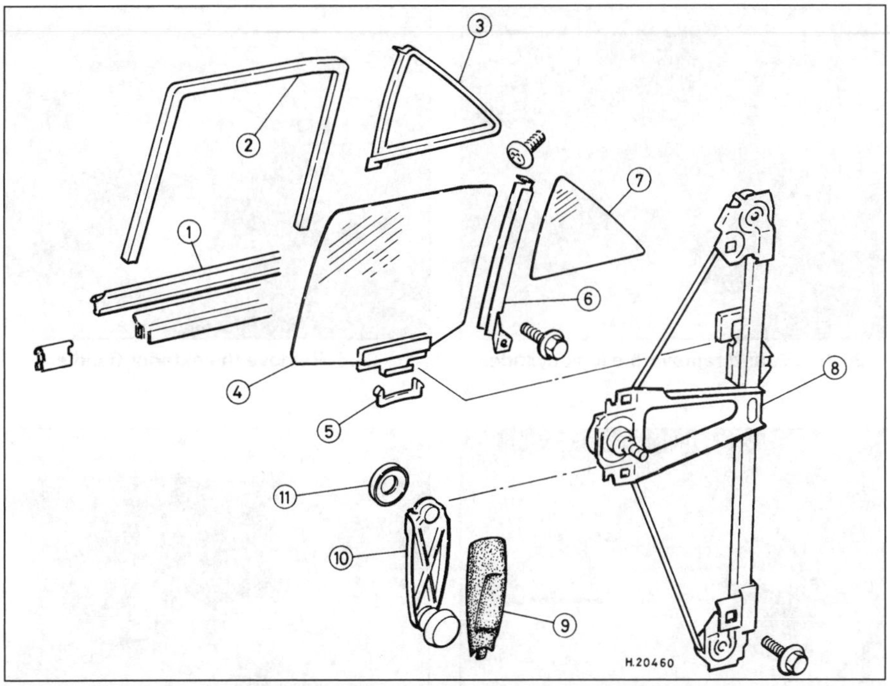

21.02 Rear door window glass and regulator

1 Waist rail inner and outer sealing strips
2 Glass channel
3 Quarter-light frame
4 Window glass
5 Locking clip
6 Rear guide rail
7 Quarter-light glass
8 Regulator
9 Regulator handle trim
10 Regulator handle
11 Trim disc

21 Rear door window regulator - removal and refitting

Removal

1 Remove the door inner trim panel as described in Section 18.

2 Open the window until the guide member of the regulator guide rail is accessible through the aperture in the top centre of the door panel **(see illustration)**.

3 Support the window in this position either by using a wooden wedge between the window and the door, or by using masking tape over the top of the door frame and onto the glass on the inside and outside.

4 On cars with electric windows, open the wiring plug connection and release the two wires for the window lift motor.

5 Remove the locking clip securing the window glass to the guide member of the regulator guide rail.

6 Undo the two regulator retaining bolts on manual windows, or the three regulator nuts on electric windows.

7 Undo the regulator guide rail lower retaining bolt.

8 Swivel the regulator rearwards to release the guide member from the channel at the bottom of the window glass.

9 On cars with electric windows, remove the motor wiring cable connector from the door panel.

10 Manipulate the regulator assembly out of the large aperture in the door panel.

Refitting

11 Refitting is the reverse sequence to removal.

22 Rear door window glass - removal and refitting

Removal

1 Remove the door inner trim panel as described in Section 18.

2 Lower the window fully.

3 Using a plastic wedge or similar tool, carefully prise up the inner and outer sealing strips at the top of the door panel.

4 Remove the locking clip securing the window glass to the guide member of the regulator guide rail.

5 Move the window glass to the rear to release the channel at the bottom of the glass from the guide member.

6 Pull the flexible guide channel out of the rear guide rail, then undo the lower bolt securing the rail to the door panel and the upper screw securing the rail to the door frame.

7 Slide the guide rail downwards and remove it from one of the door panel apertures.

8 Lift the window glass upwards and remove it on the inside of the door frame.

Refitting

9 Refitting is the reverse sequence to removal.

23 Rear door fixed quarter-light - removal and refitting

Removal

1 Refer to Section 22 and carry out the operations listed in paragraphs 1 to 7 inclusive.

2 Pull the quarter-light forwards and remove it from the door.

Refitting

3 Refitting is the reverse sequence to removal, but lubricate the quarter-light sealing channels with a soapy solution to ease insertion.

24 Front door exterior handle - removal and refitting

Removal

1 Remove the door inner trim panel as described in Section 18.

2 Remove the closing plug from the rear edge of the door **(see illustration)**.

3 Using an Allen key inserted through the closing plug hole, undo the lock cylinder retaining grub screw **(see illustration)**.

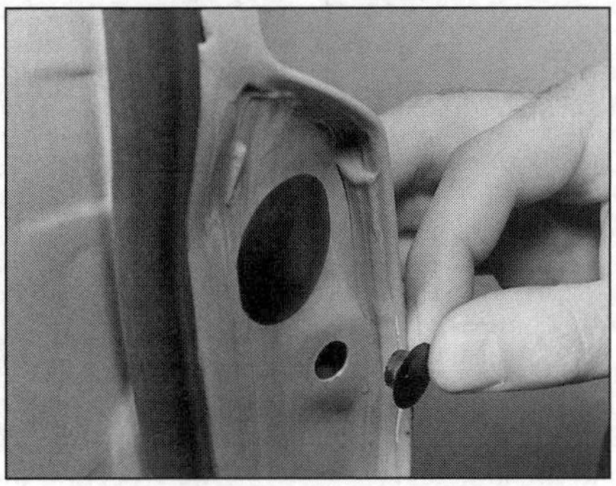

24.2 Remove the closing plug

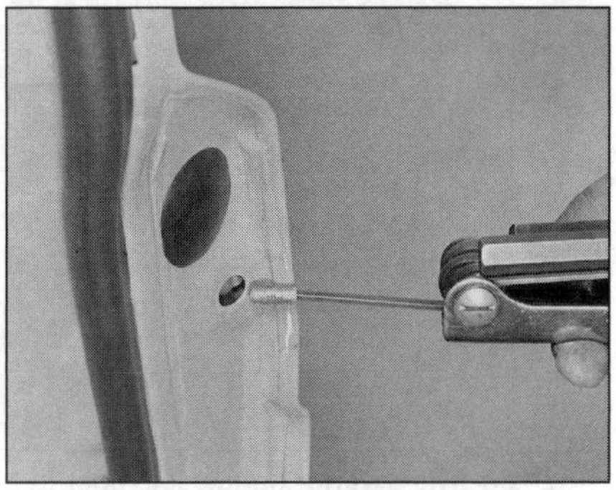

24.3 Undo the grub screw

24.4a Turn the key 60° to the rear . . .

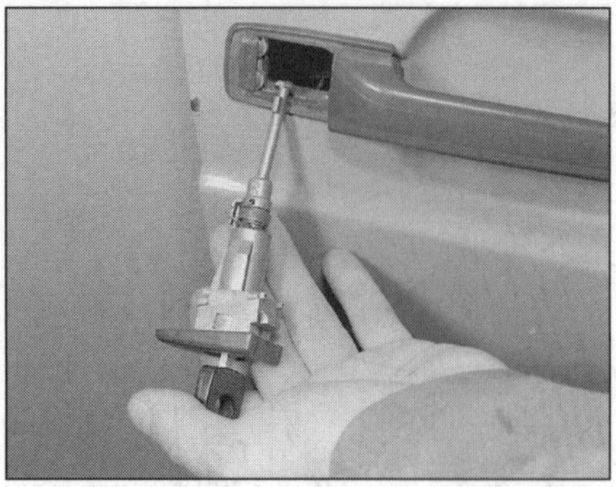

24.4b . . . and remove the lock cylinder

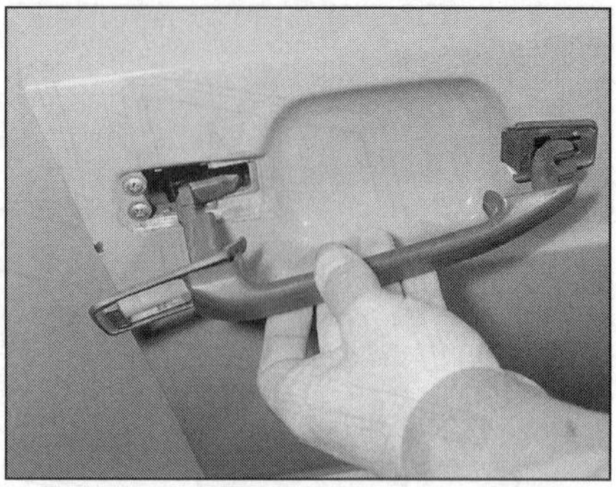

24.5 Remove the exterior handle

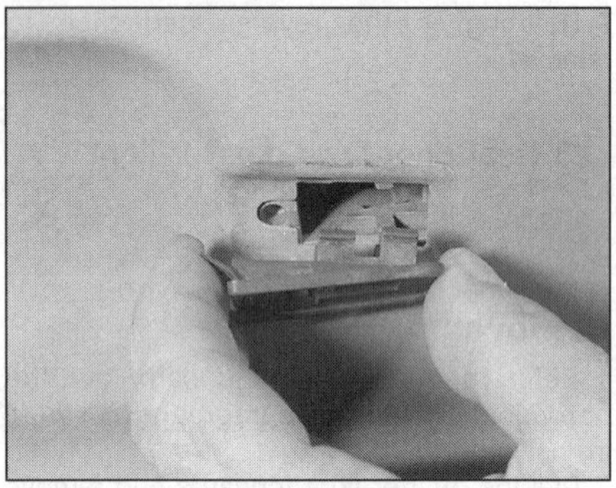

24.6 Remove the rubber escutcheon

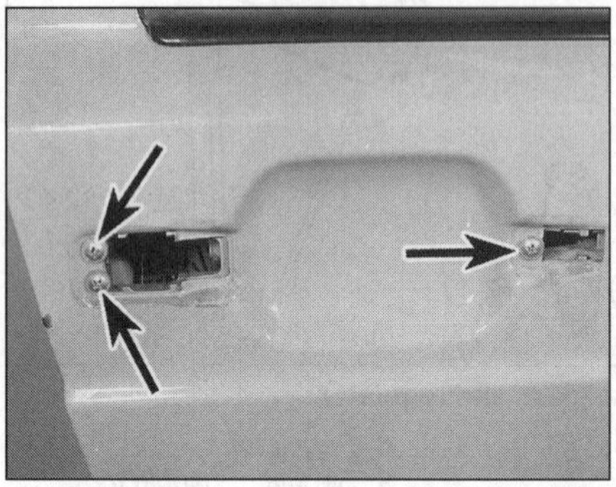

24.7a Undo the mounting bracket screws (arrowed) . . .

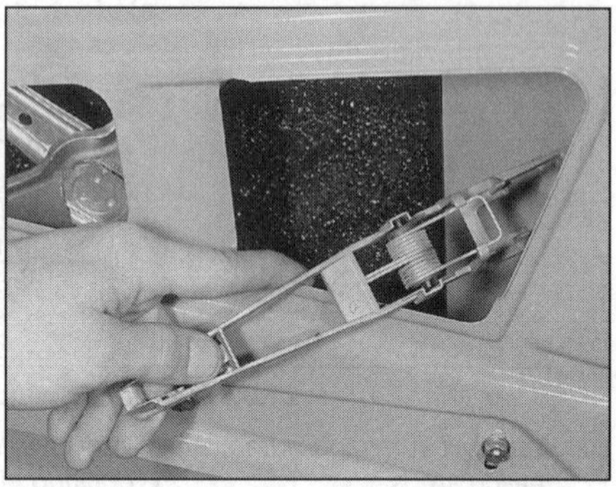

24.7b . . . and remove the mounting bracket

4 Insert the key into the door lock cylinder and turn it approximately 60° to the rear **(see illustration)**. At the same time, push the lock cylinder rearwards to disengage the internal tang, and withdraw it from the door handle **(see illustration)**.

5 Push the door exterior handle to the rear, while at the same time pulling outwards, then disengage the tangs at the front from the mounting bracket **(see illustration)**.

6 Remove the rubber escutcheon from the handle front location **(see illustration)**.

7 Undo the three mounting bracket retaining screws and remove the mounting bracket from the aperture in the inner door panel **(see illustrations)**.

Refitting

8 Refitting is the reverse sequence to removal. When inserting the handle, ensure that the rear operating leg slides behind the wire spring of the mounting bracket as well as the lock lever **(see illustration),** then slide the handle forwards to secure. The tag on the handle rear rubber escutcheon fits between the door panel and the mounting bracket **(see illustration)**.

25 Front door lock - removal and refitting

Removal

1 Remove the front door exterior handle as described in Section 24.

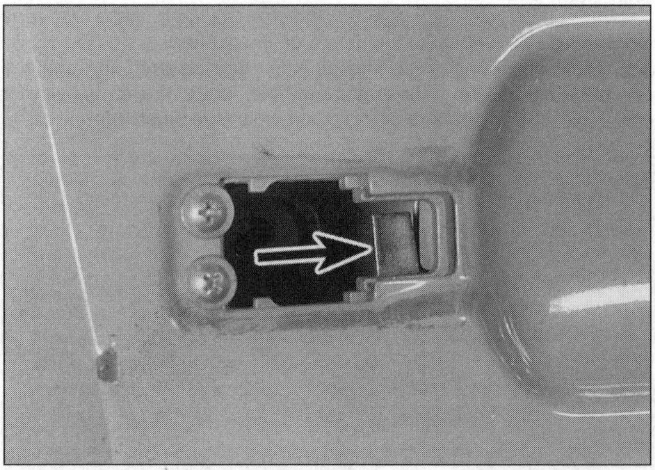

24.8a The exterior handle leg must fit behind the lock lever (arrowed) when refitting . . .

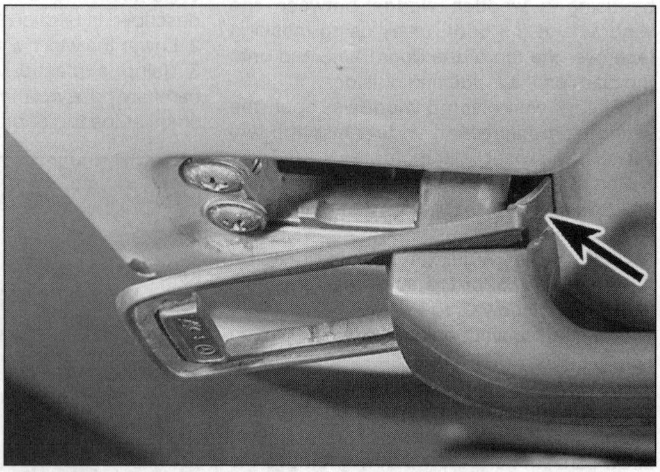

24.8b . . . and the handle escutcheon tag (arrowed) locates between the door and bracket

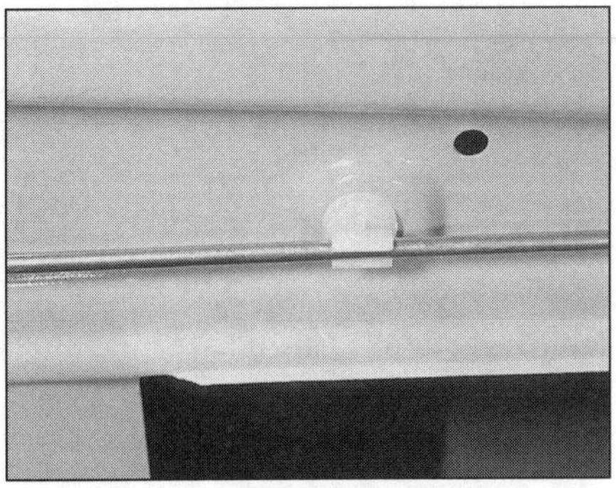

25.2a Release the connecting rod at the guide . . .

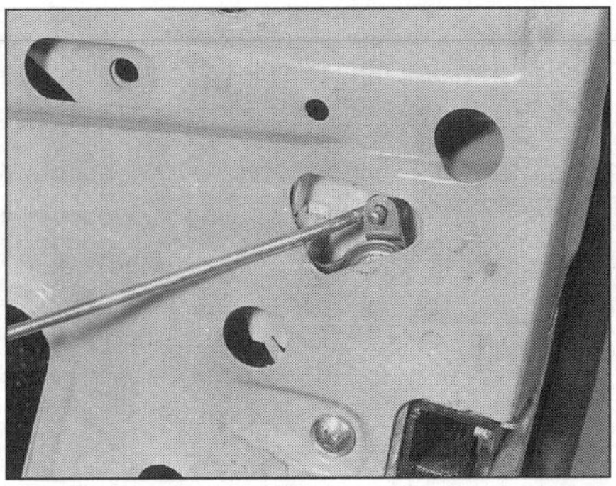

25.2b . . . and lock lever

25.3a Release the clip arrowed . . .

25.3b . . . and remove the water deflector

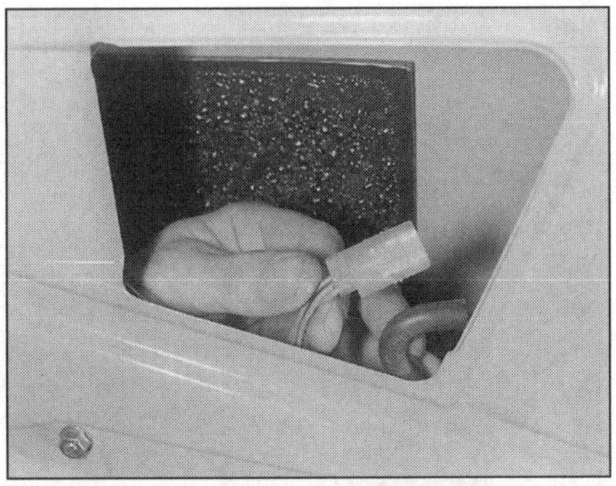

25.3C Disconnect the wiring and vacuum hose at the solenoid

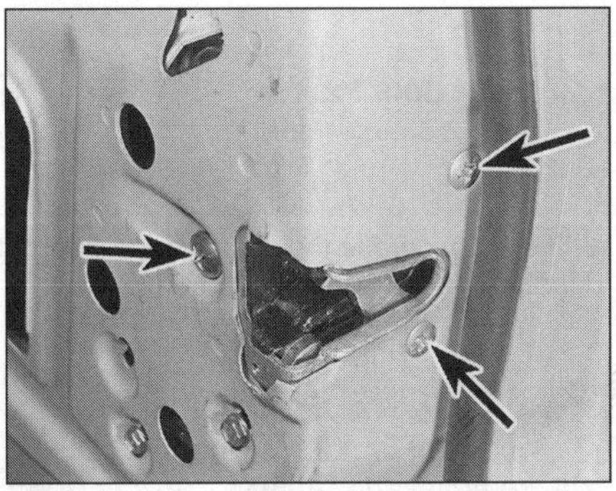

25.4 Undo the door lock retaining screws (arrowed) . . .

2 Release the inner door handle connecting rod from the door guide **(see illustration)** then disengage it from the lock lever **(see illustration)**.

3 On cars equipped with central locking, release the retaining clip on the top edge of the door and remove the plastic water deflector from the door aperture **(see illustrations)**. Disconnect the wiring and vacuum connections at the central locking solenoid **(see illustration)**.

4 Undo the screws securing the door lock to the door **(see illustration)**.

5 On cars equipped with central locking, undo the screws securing the central locking solenoid to the door **(see illustration)**.

6 Lower the door lock and remove it, complete with central locking solenoid (where fitted), through the door panel aperture **(see illustration)**.

Refitting

7 Refitting is the reverse sequence to removal. When fitting the water deflector on cars with central locking, the deflector must slide up behind the window guide channel before clipping onto the top edge of the door.

26 Rear door exterior handle - removal and refitting

1 The procedure is the same as for the front door handle as described in Section 24, except that there is no lock cylinder to remove. Instead, remove the plastic trim covering by pushing it to the rear.

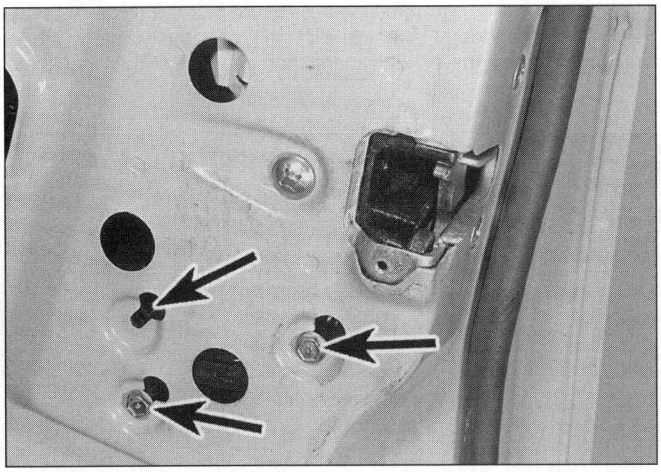

25.5 . . . and central locking solenoid screws (arrowed)

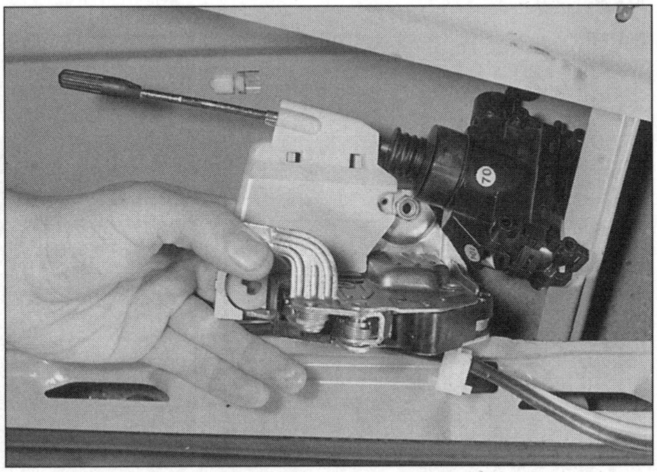

25.6 Remove the lock and solenoid from the door

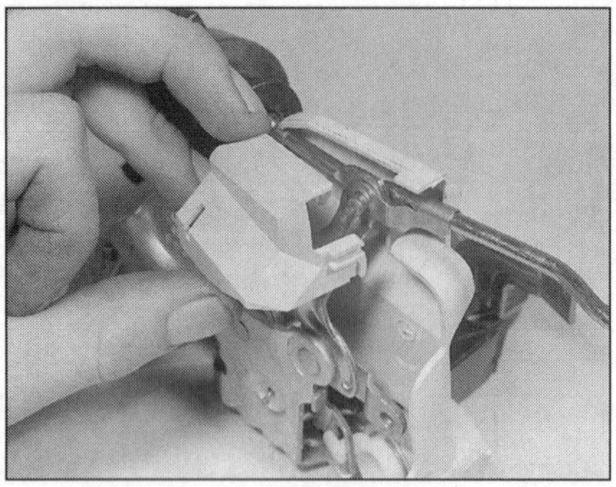

28.2 Prise off the plastic cover

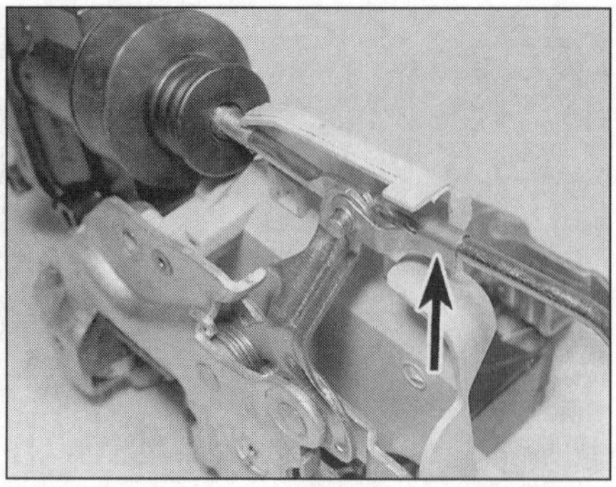

28.3 Remove the retaining clip (arrowed)

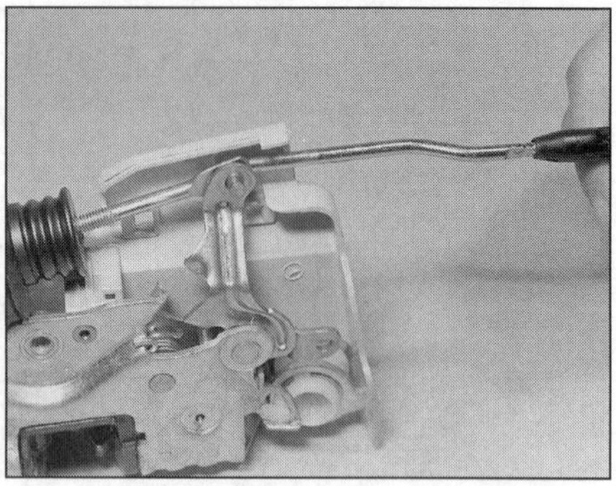

28.4a Withdraw the lock button rod . . .

27 Rear door lock - removal and refitting

1 The procedure is the same as for the front door lock as described in Section 25.

28 Door lock solenoids (central locking system) - removal and refitting

Removal

1 Remove the door lock, complete with solenoid, from the front or rear doors as applicable, as described in Section 25 or 27.

2 Carefully prise off the plastic cover over the solenoid and lock connecting levers **(see illustration)**.

3 Push the retaining clip end upwards, then remove it from the interior lock button rod **(see illustration)**.

4 Withdraw the interior lock button rod to release the solenoid operating rod, and withdraw the solenoid **(see illustrations)**.

Refitting

5 Refitting is the reverse sequence to removal.

28.4b . . . release the solenoid operating rod . . .

28.4c . . . and withdraw the solenoid

29 Front and rear doors - removal and refitting

Removal

1 On cars equipped with central locking or electric windows, remove the inner trim panel as described in Section 18 and disconnect the applicable wiring or vacuum hose connections. Release the convoluted hose between the door and pillar, and pull the wiring and hoses out of the door.

2 Remove the rubber seal from the door check strap **(see illustration)**, extract the retaining clip and washer, and drive out the check strap pin upwards using a punch.

3 Accurately mark the outline of the upper and lower hinge plates on the pillar using a pencil.

4 With an assistant supporting the door, undo the two upper and two lower bolts securing the hinge plates to the body pillar **(see illustrations)**.

5 Withdraw the door rearwards from the car.

Refitting

6 Refitting is the reverse sequence to removal, but ensure that the hinge plates are aligned with the previously made marks. Adjustments can be made at the hinge plates

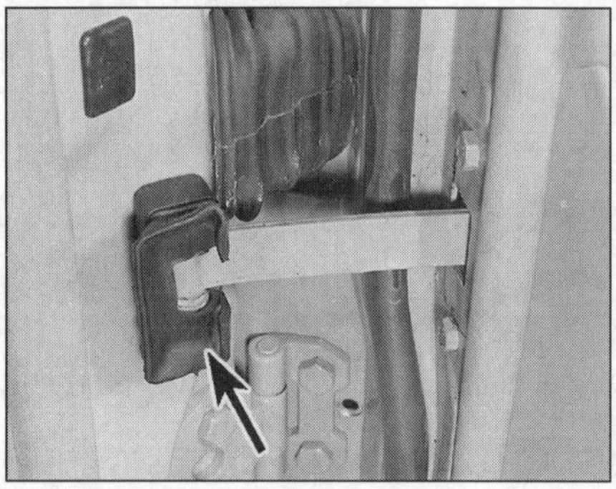

29.2 Remove the rubber seal from the check strap (arrowed)

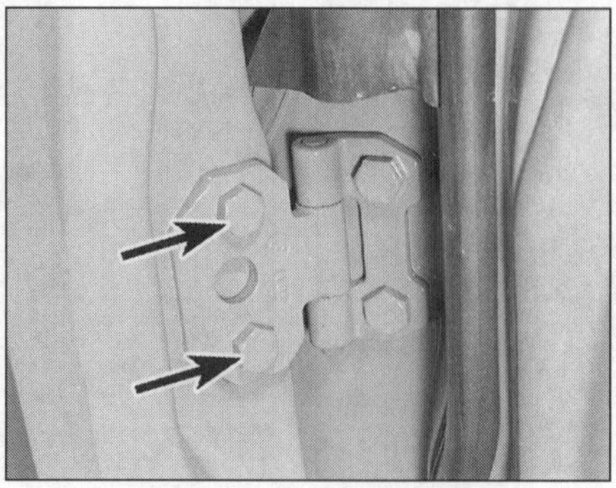

29.4a Hinge plate-to-door pillar bolts for the front door (arrowed) . . .

29.4b . . . and rear door

29.6 Front door striker plate

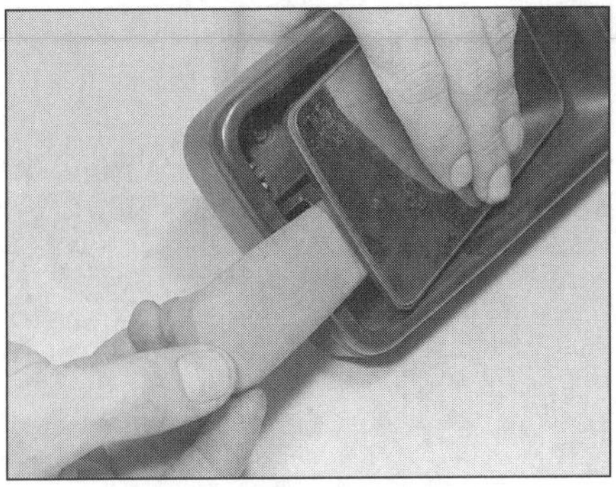

31.1a Prise out the mirror glass using a plastic wedge . . .

31.1b . . . to release the ball from the socket (arrowed)

and at the door striker **(see illustration)** to provide an equal gap all round the door, and to align the contour of the door panel with that of the front wing.

30 Windscreen and rear window - removal and refitting

1 Due to the methods of attachment, and the special equipment required to complete the task successfully, removal and refitting of the windscreen and rear window should be entrusted to a dealer or an automotive glass replacement specialist.

31 Door mirror glass (manual mirror) - renewal

Removal

1 Using a plastic wedge, very carefully prise the ball on the rear face of the mirror glass out of the plastic socket on the mirror body **(see illustrations)**,

2 If the mirror is electrically heated, disconnect the wiring plug at the rear of the mirror glass **(see illustration)**.

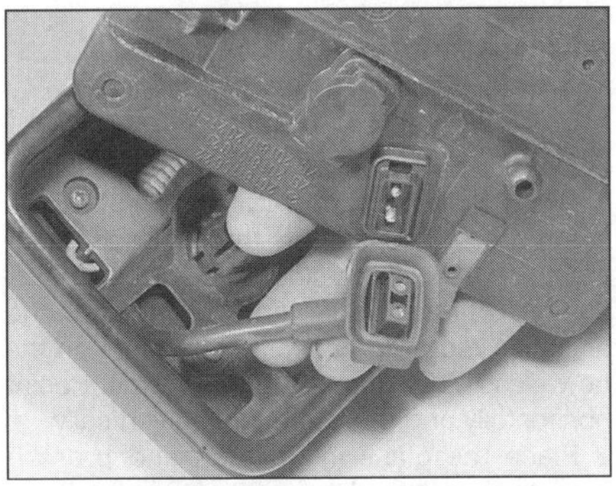

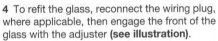

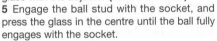

31.2 Disconnect the wiring plug on electrically-heated mirrors

3 Pull the mirror rearwards to disengage the adjuster at the front and remove it from the mirror body.

Refitting

4 To refit the glass, reconnect the wiring plug, where applicable, then engage the front of the glass with the adjuster **(see illustration)**.

5 Engage the ball stud with the socket, and press the glass in the centre until the ball fully engages with the socket.

31.4 Engage the front of the glass with the adjuster when refitting

32 Door mirror assembly (manual mirror) - removal and refitting

Removal

1 Extract the small plastic clip from the adjustment lever by carefully prising it out with a screwdriver **(see illustration)**.

2 Withdraw the adjustment lever cover **(see illustration)**.

3 Prise off the trim panel at the top,

32.1 Extract the small plastic clip

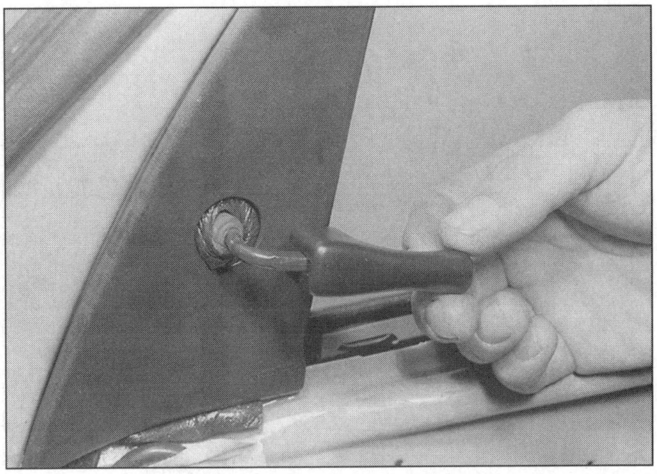

32.2 Withdraw the lever cover

11

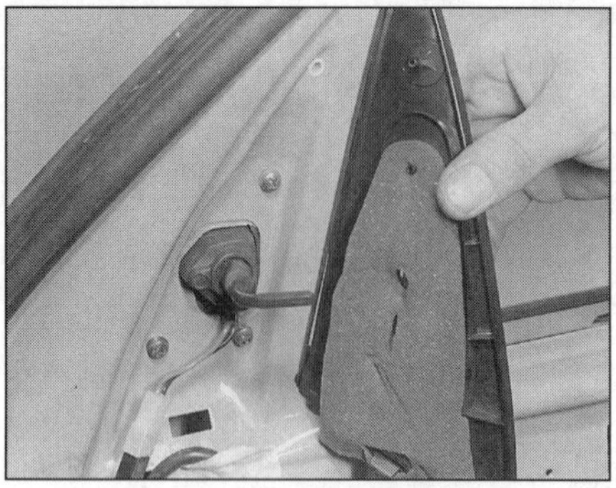
32.3 Remove the trim panel

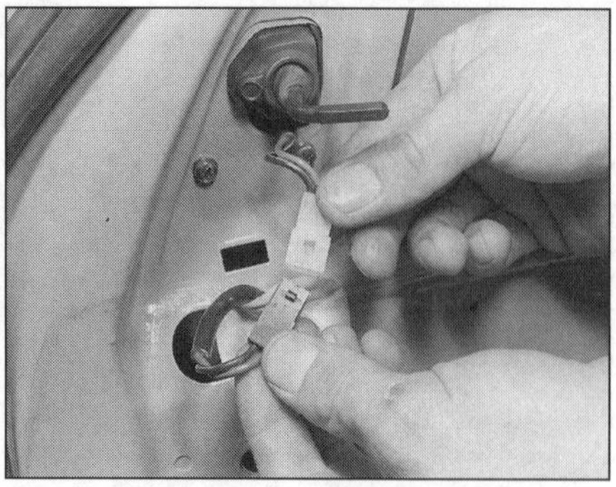
32.4 Disconnect the wiring connector

32.5a Undo the three screws . . .

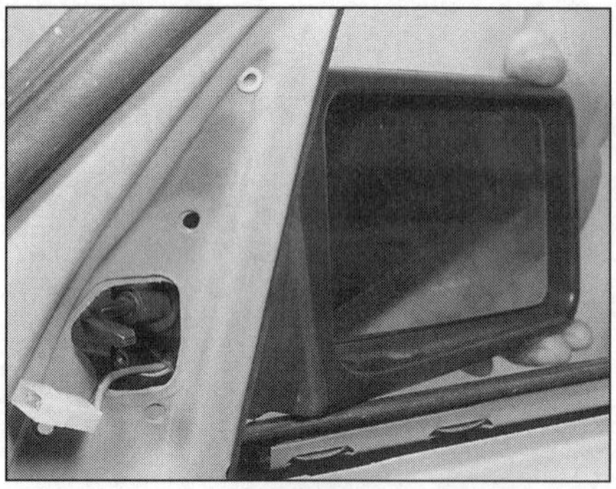
32.5b . . . and remove the mirror assembly

disengage its bottom edge from the door trim panel and remove it **(see illustration)**.

4 If the mirror glass is electrically heated, separate the wiring at the connector **(see illustration)**.

5 Undo the three screws **(see illustration)** and remove the mirror assembly from the door **(see illustration)**.

Refitting

6 Refitting is the reverse sequence to removal.

33 Door mirror glass (electrically-operated mirror) - renewal

1 Using a plastic wedge, very carefully prise the mirror glass off the three engagement points on the reverse side of the glass.

2 Align the engagement points on the adjusting motor to accept the sockets on the new glass. Align the upper engagement point horizontally and the lateral points vertically.

3 Place the glass in position and press it in until it is heard to engage in the three places.

34 Door mirror assembly (electrically-operated mirror) - removal and refitting

Removal

1 Prise off the trim panel for the mirror attachment at the top, disengage its bottom edge from the door trim panel and remove. Remove the foam fabric shim.

2 Unscrew the wiring plug retaining screw and disconnect the plug.

3 Undo the three screws and remove the mirror from the door.

4 To remove the adjustment motor, remove the mirror glass as described in Section 33, then undo the three motor retaining screws.

5 Hinge the mirror back and hold it in this position with a suitable distance piece.

6 Turn the wiring socket in a clockwise direction and remove the motor and wiring from the mirror body.

Refitting

7 Refitting is the reverse sequence to removal.

35 Front seats - removal and refitting

Driver's seat

1 Move the seat to the rear and set the height adjuster to its lowest position.

2 Undo the two bolts at the front securing the guide rails to the floor **(see illustration)**.

3 Move the seat forwards and set the height adjuster to its highest position.

4 Undo the two bolts at the rear securing the guide rails to the floor **(see illustration)**.

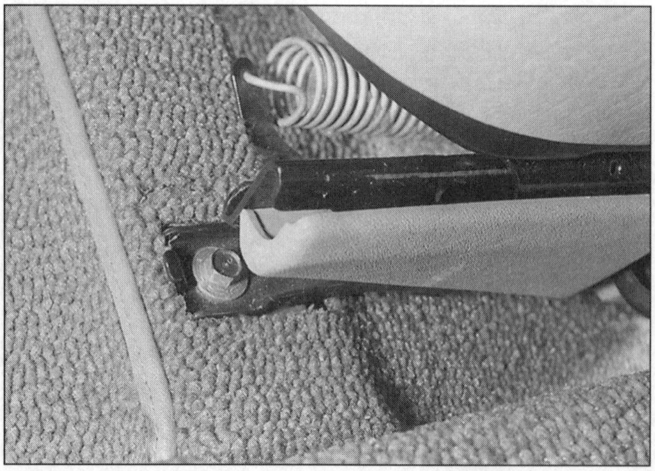
35.2 Undo the seat front guide rail bolts . . .

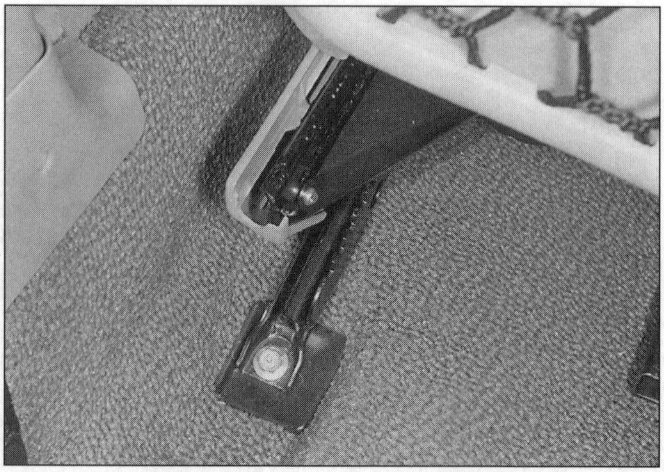
35.4 . . . and the rear guide rail bolts

5 Slightly raise the seat and pull it forwards out of the slide rail.
6 Refitting is the reverse sequence to removal.

Passenger's seat

7 Move the seat to the rear and undo both front guide rail retaining bolts.
8 Slide the seat forwards and remove the covers on the guide rails at the rear.
9 Undo the guide rail rear retaining bolts, then pull the seat forwards out of the slide rail.
10 Refitting is the reverse sequence to removal.

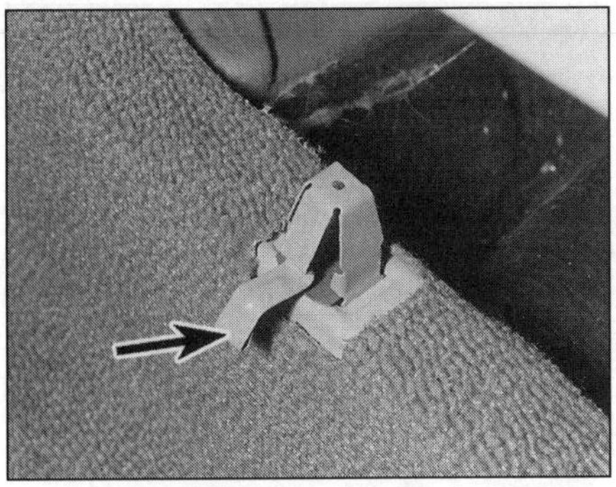

36.1 Push in the detent clip (arrowed) to release the rear seat bench

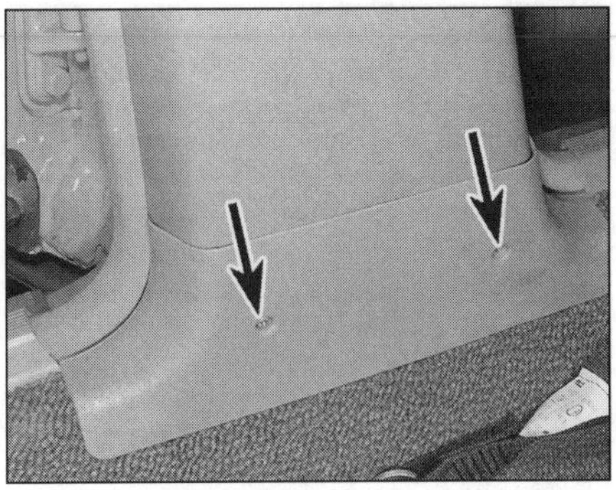

37.1 Centre pillar trim panel screws (arrowed)

36 Rear seat - removal and refitting

Seat bench

1 Push in the detent clip on the left- and right-hand sides of the seat bench at the bottom **(see illustration)**, while at the same time lifting up the seat bench.
2 Withdraw the seat bench and remove it from the car.
3 Refitting is the reverse sequence to removal.

Seat back rest

4 Remove the seat bench.
5 Undo the three retaining screws at the bottom of the back seat.
6 Push the back rest upwards to disengage the four upper tags, then remove the back rest from the car.
7 Refitting is the reverse sequence to removal, but ensure that the upper tags engage with their holders.

37 Seat belts - removal and refitting

Warning: Models equipped with an SRS (airbag) system have automatic tensioning devices fitted to the front seat belts. For safety reasons, no attempt should be made to disturb, remove or repair any of the front seat belt components - work of this nature must be entrusted to a Mercedes-Benz dealer.

Front belt

1 Undo the two centre pillar trim panel lower retaining screws **(see illustration)**.
2 Swivel the seat belt rearwards, remove the cap over the lower mounting bolt by sliding it off the bottom of the belt (ie: forwards), then undo the seat belt lower mounting bolt.
3 Pull off the door rubber sealing weatherstrip around the centre pillar.
4 Move the centre pillar trim downwards to release the upper retaining clip, and remove the trim.
5 Undo the seat belt upper guide retaining bolt and the inertia reel retaining bolt, then remove the belt.
6 If the seat belt stalk is also to be removed, first remove the driver's or passenger's seat as applicable as described in Section 35.
7 Hold the stalk and undo the retaining bolt on the side of the seat. Remove the stalk.
8 Refitting is the reverse sequence to removal.

Rear belt

9 Remove the rear seat bench as described in Section 36.
10 Undo the bolt securing the seat belt mounting to the floor **(see illustration)**.
11 Pull off the door rubber sealing weatherstrip around the trim panel on the rear pillar.
12 Carefully push off the trim panel clips at the front towards the centre of the car by means of a wedge.
13 Push the trim panel upwards and remove it from the rear pillar.
14 Remove the rear seat back rest as described in Section 36.
15 Undo the belt upper guide retaining bolt on the rear pillar.
16 Unclip the sound-deadening material around the rear inertial reel.
17 Undo the inertia reel retaining bolt and remove the seat belt from the car.
18 If the stalk(s) are to be renewed, undo the single bolt, remove the separating plate and remove the relevant stalk **(see illustration)**.
19 Refitting is the reverse sequence to removal.

38 Sunroof - general

1 A sliding sunroof, either mechanically- or electrically-operated, is available as a factory-fitted option.
2 Adjustment or repair of the sunroof or its component parts should be left to a dealer, as the complexity of the unit and the need for special tools and equipment renders these operations beyond the scope of the average owner.

39 Central locking system vacuum pump - removal and refitting

Removal

1 Disconnect the battery negative terminal.

37.10 Rear seat belt mounting bolt

37.18 Rear seat belt stalk retaining bolt

39.3a Lift up the sound proofing box cover . . .

39.3b . . . and take out the vacuum pump

39.4 Disconnect the vacuum hoses and wiring plug

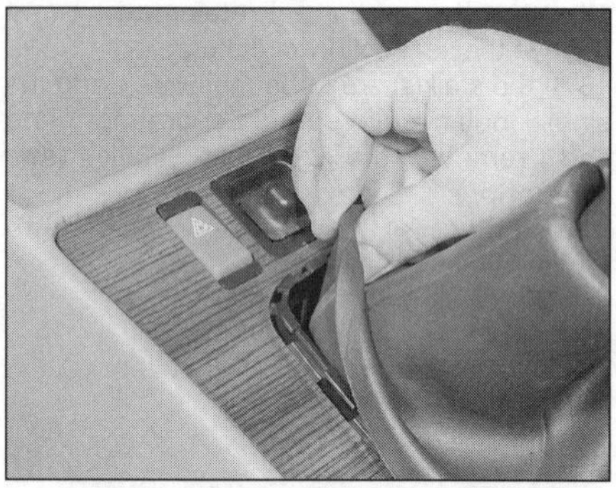

40.1a Release the gear lever boot . . .

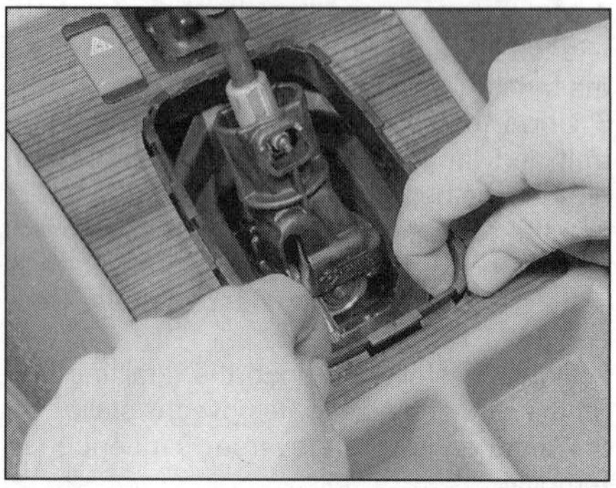

40.1b . . . lift the console cover at the rear . . .

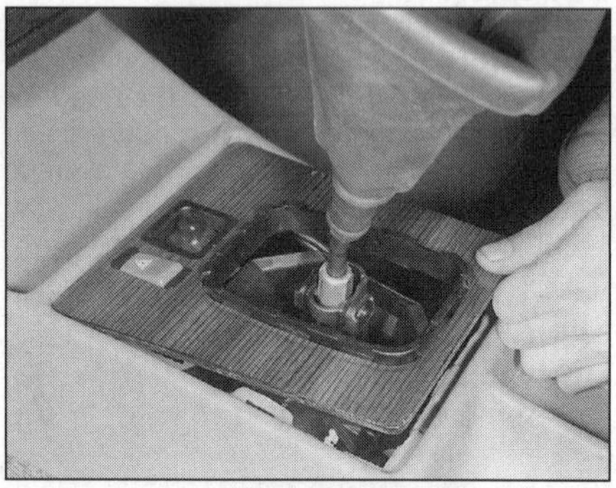

40.1c . . . then slide it rearwards to remove

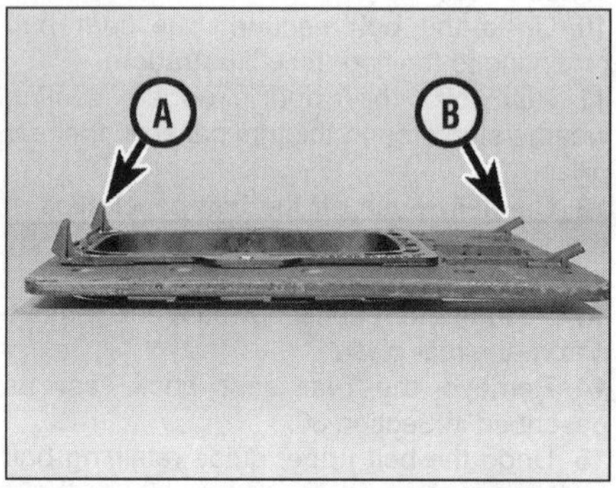

40.1d Console cover rear tags (A) and front lugs (B)

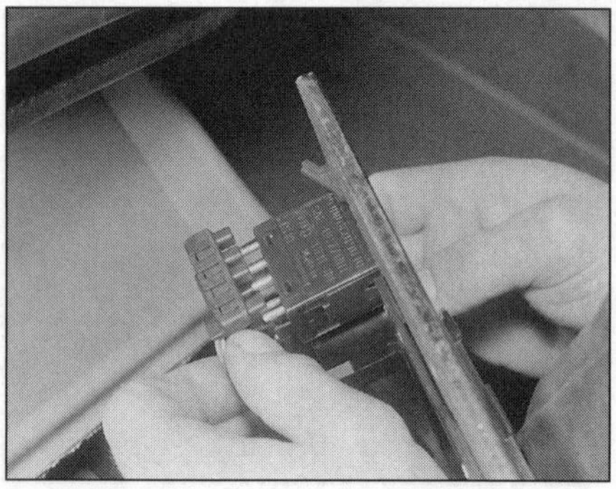

40.3 Disconnect the wiring at the console cover switches

40.5 Undo the front ashtray housing screws

2 Remove the rear seat bench as described in Section 36.

3 Lift up the cover on the sound proofing box and lift the unit out of its location **(see illustrations)**.

4 Disconnect the vacuum hoses and wiring plug, and remove the unit from the car **(see illustration)**.

Refitting

5 Refitting is the reverse sequence to removal.

40 Centre console - removal and refitting

Removal

1 On manual gearbox models, release the gear lever boot from the console cover and slide the boot up the lever **(see illustration)**. Using the fingers at the rear of the plastic centre part of the console cover, lift the cover at the rear, then slide it to the rear and lift off **(see illustrations)**. Note that the cover is secured by two extremely tight rear tags and two lugs at the front **(see illustration)**.

2 On automatic transmission models, lift the console cover at the rear by means of a plastic wedge inserted in the gap between the selector position plate and the cover. Move the cover to the rear to disengage the two front lugs and lift off.

3 Disconnect the wiring plugs at the console cover switches, after identifying their locations, and remove the cover **(see illustration)**.

4 Refer to Chapter 9 and slacken the parking brake adjuster under the car so that the lever can be pulled up to the nearly-vertical position.

5 Remove the front ashtray, then undo the two upper screws securing the ashtray housing to the facia **(see illustration)**.

6 Withdraw the ashtray housing, disconnect

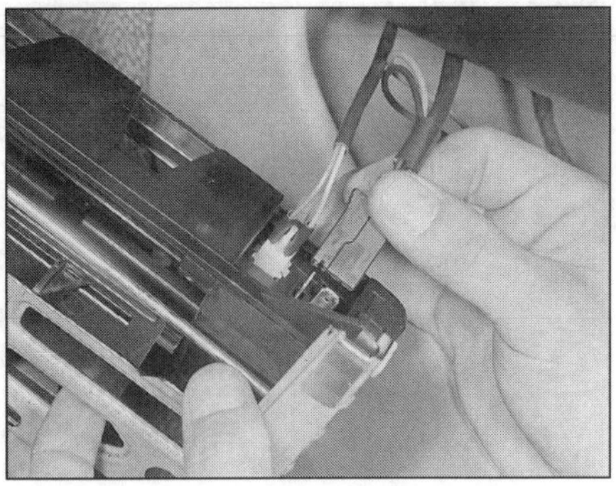

40.6a Disconnect the wiring . . .

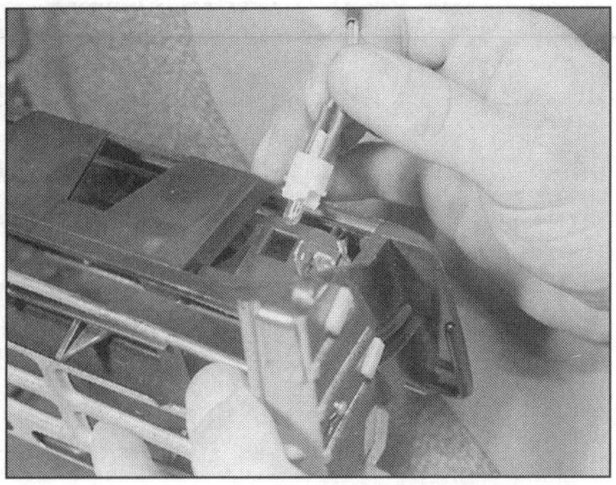

40.6b . . . and illumination bulbholder at the ashtray housing

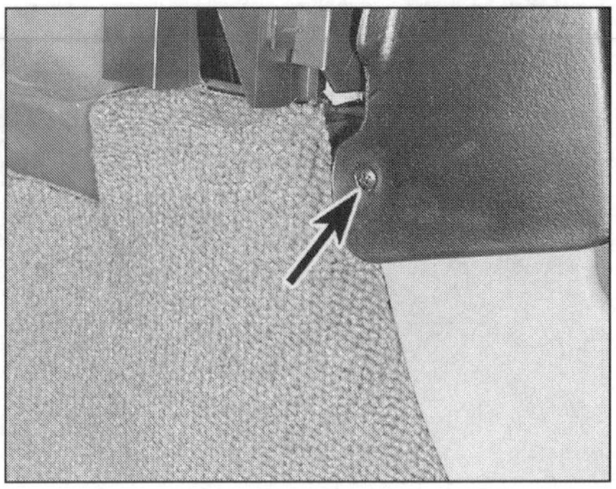

40.8 Undo the side retaining screw (arrowed)

the wiring and illumination bulb and remove the housing **(see illustrations)**.

7 Remove the floor mats on both sides from the footwells.

8 Undo the retaining screw each side securing the facia and console edges **(see illustration)**.

9 Release the spire clip and retaining screw (where fitted) and remove the footrest on the driver's side **(see illustration)**.

10 Remove the front carpets on both sides.

11 On the passenger's side undo the lower retaining screw and remove the front kick panel **(see illustrations)**.

12 Undo the central retaining screw and remove the console side cover carpet on both sides **(see illustration)**. On the driver's side the cover carpet is also secured by an additional spire clip.

13 With extreme effort, pull off the grip on the parking brake lever and slide it off the front of the lever **(see illustrations)**.

14 Pull the parking brake lever up and remove the lower lever lining **(see illustration)**.

15 Undo the console retaining bolt in front of the gear lever or selector housing **(see illustration)**.

16 Remove the rear ashtray, then remove the ashtray holder by prising up the lower holding clip **(see illustrations)**.

17 Working through the ashtray aperture, undo the console rear retaining bolt.

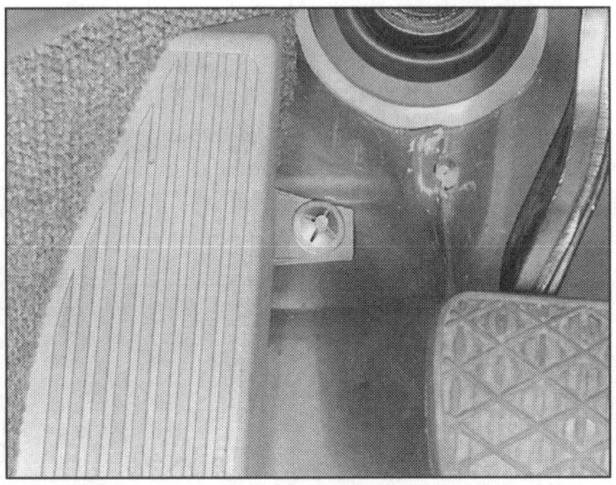

40.9 Release the footrest retaining spire clip

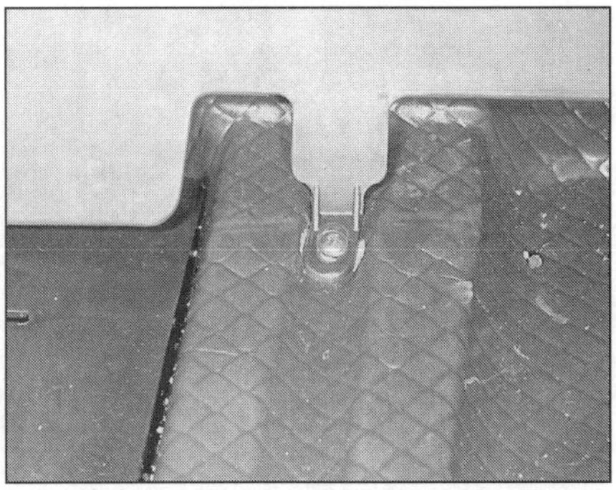

40.11a Undo the kick panel retaining screw . . .

40.11b . . . and remove the panel

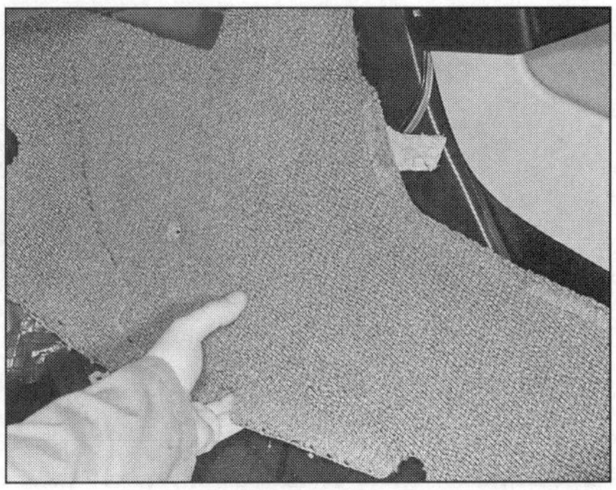

40.12 Remove the console side cover carpets

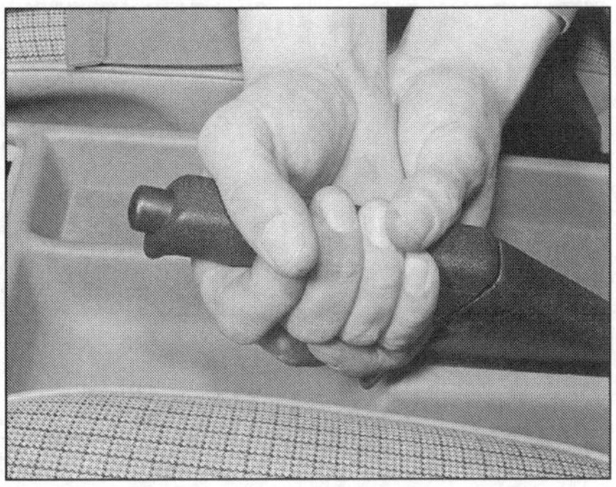

40.13a Pull off the handbrake lever grip . . .

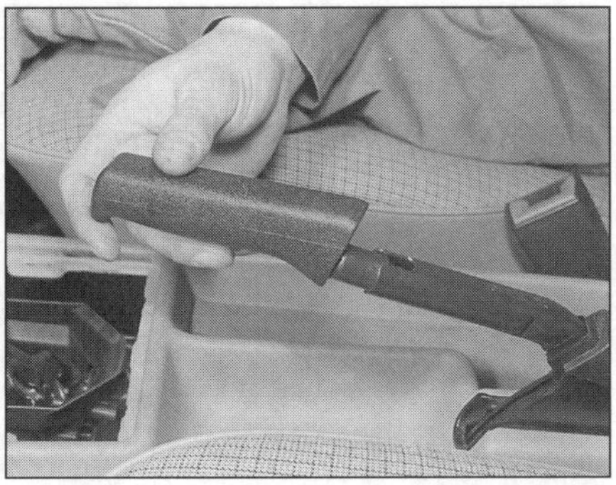

40.13b . . . and remove it from the lever

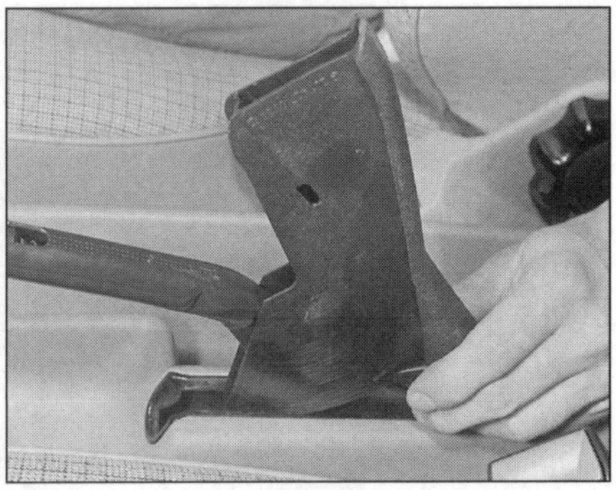

40.14 Remove the handbrake lever lower lining

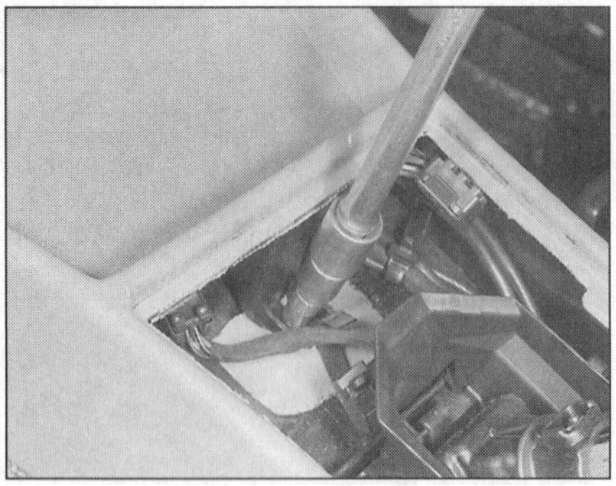

40.15 Undo the front retaining bolt

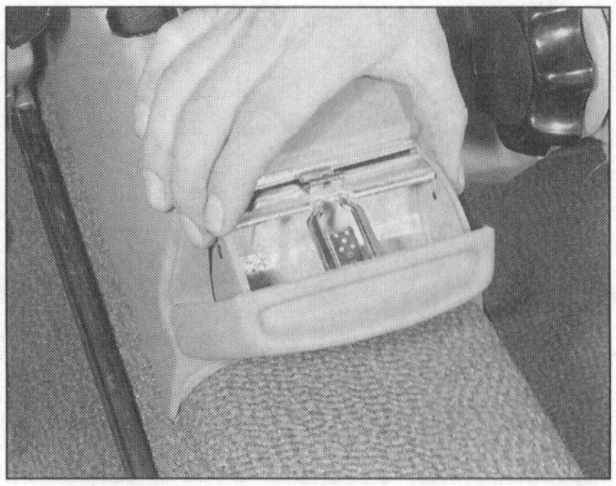

40.16a Remove the rear ashtray . . .

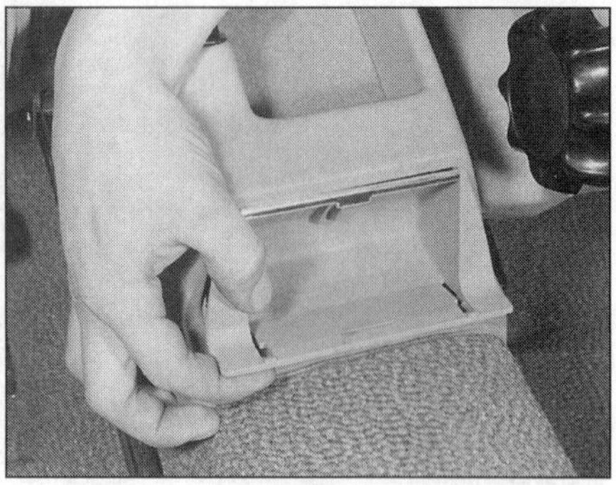

40.16b . . . and the ashtray housing

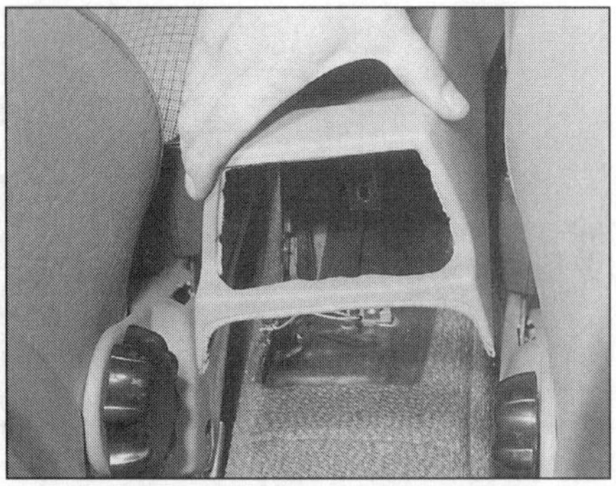

40.19a Lift up the console at the rear . . .

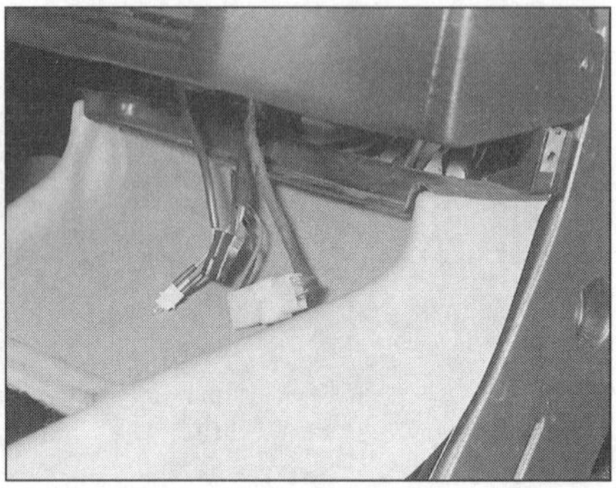

40.19b . . . and disengage it at the front

18 Move both front seats towards the rear, and pull the parking brake lever up as far as it will go.

19 Lift the console at the rear, and disengage it from the facia at the front **(see illustrations)**.

20 Lift the console up over the parking brake lever and remove it from the car.

Refitting

21 Refitting is the reverse sequence to removal. Adjust the parking brake as described in Chapter 9 on completion.

41 Glovebox - removal and refitting

Removal

1 Disconnect the battery negative terminal.

2 Prise out the glovebox lamp, disconnect the wiring and remove the lamp **(see illustration)**.

3 Undo the two screws and remove the latch bracket **(see illustration)**.

4 Remove the expanding rivets by prising out the rivet expander with a screwdriver, then remove the expander and rivet body **(see illustrations)**.

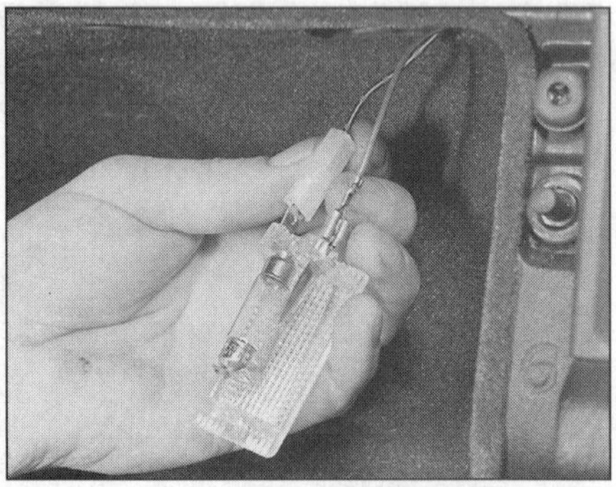

41.2 Remove the glovebox lamp

41.3 Undo the latch bracket screws

41.4a Prise out the rivet expander . . .

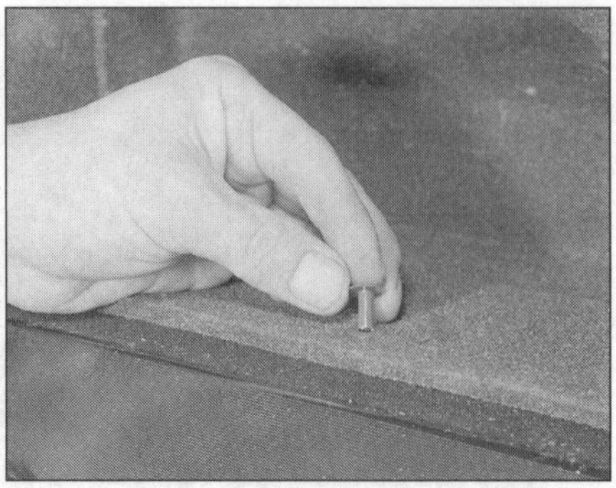

41.4b . . . then remove the rivet expander . . .

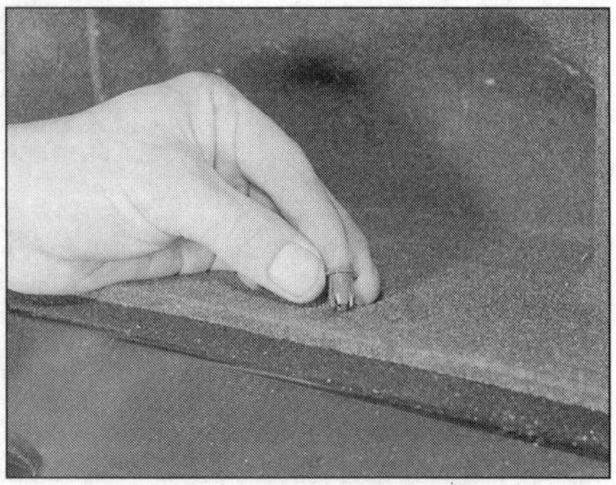

41.4c . . . and rivet body

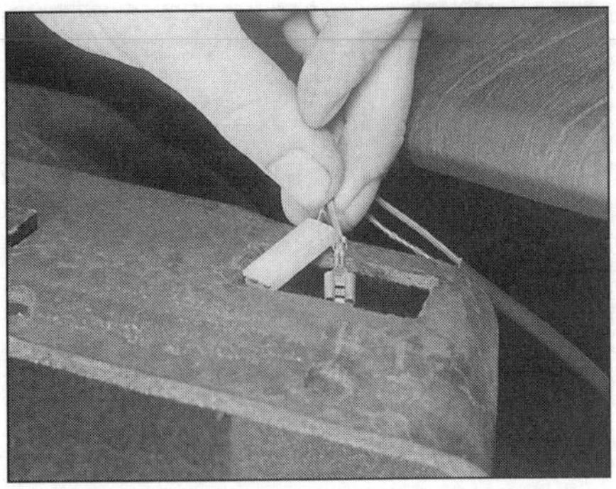
41.5 Withdraw the wires as the glovebox is removed

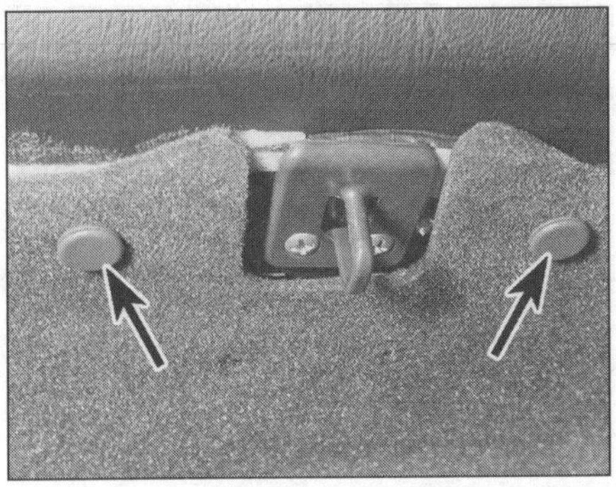
42.3 Prise off the trim caps (arrowed) and undo the screws

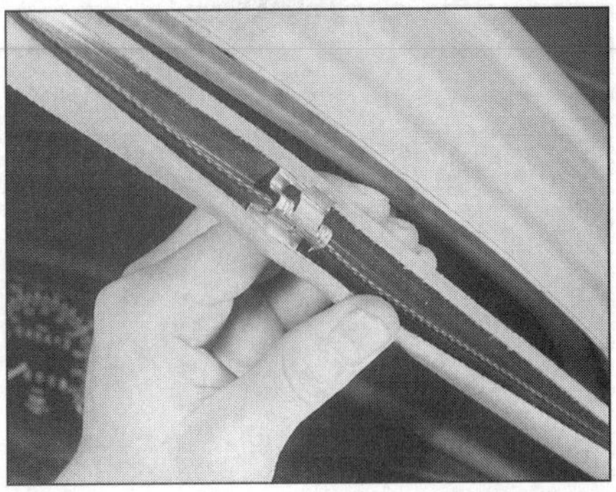
42.4 Pull away the door seal weatherstrip

5 Withdraw the glovebox, pull the lamp wiring through the aperture and remove the glovebox from the facia **(see illustration)**.

Refitting

6 Refitting is the reverse sequence to removal.

42 Facia - removal and refitting

Removal

1 Remove the instrument panel as described in Chapter 12.

2 Remove the glovebox as described in Section 41.

3 Remove the covers under the facia on both sides. On the driver's side, the cover is retained by four screws and a spire clip, and on the passenger's side, by three screws. Prise off the trim caps for access to the screws **(see illustration)**.

4 Pull away the door seal weatherstrip on the front body pillar on both sides **(see illustration)**.

5 Remove both front pillar trim panels by pushing the panel in the area of the retaining clips away from the pillar using a plastic wedge **(see illustration)**.

6 Undo the retaining screw and remove the speaker grille from the top of the facia on both sides.

7 Undo the upper retaining bolt on each side adjacent to the speakers **(see illustration)**.

8 Using pliers and a protective cloth, pull off the knob on the light switch, then undo the switch retaining nut **(see illustration)**. Disconnect the wiring and remove the switch.

9 Prise out the headlamp beam adjustment rotary switch, disconnect the wiring and vacuum hoses and remove the switch. Note that the hose attachments are lilac at the top and lilac/yellow at the bottom.

10 Prise out the facia upper switches, or push them out from behind, identify the wiring plug connections and disconnect the wiring plugs. Remove the switches.

11 Undo the two side retaining bolts, left and right, securing the facia to the body stiffener **(see illustration)**.

12 Pull off the air ducts on the left and right outer air nozzles **(see illustration)**.

13 Identify their locations. then disconnect the wires at the glovebox lamp switch **(see illustration)**.

42.5 Remove the front pillar trim panels

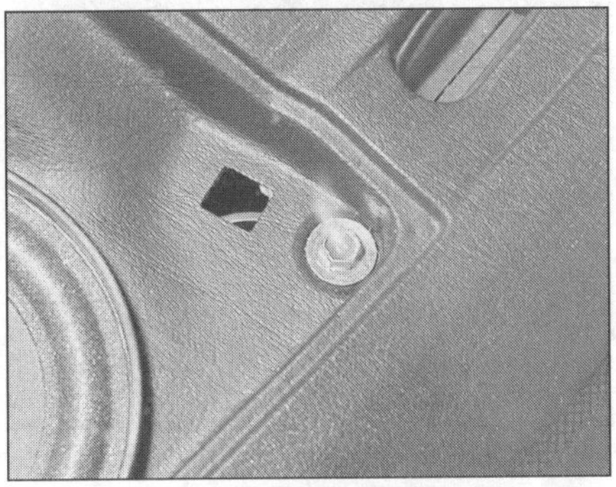
42.7 Undo the upper bolt by the speaker each side

42.8 Undo the light switch retaining nut (arrowed)

42.11 Undo the facia side retaining bolts (arrowed)

42.12 Pull off the air ducts on the outer nozzles

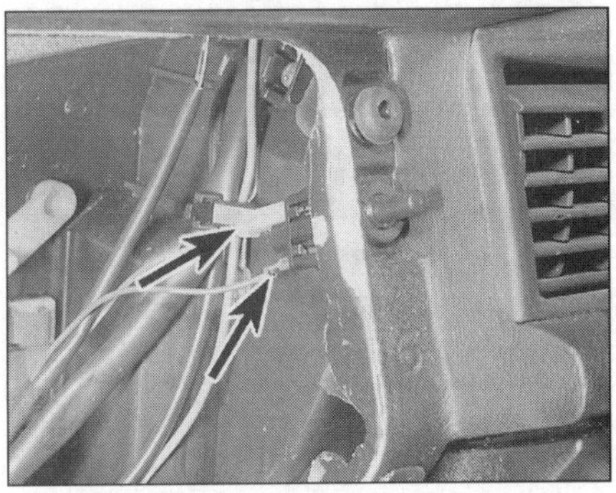
42.13 Disconnect the glovebox lamp switch wires (arrowed)

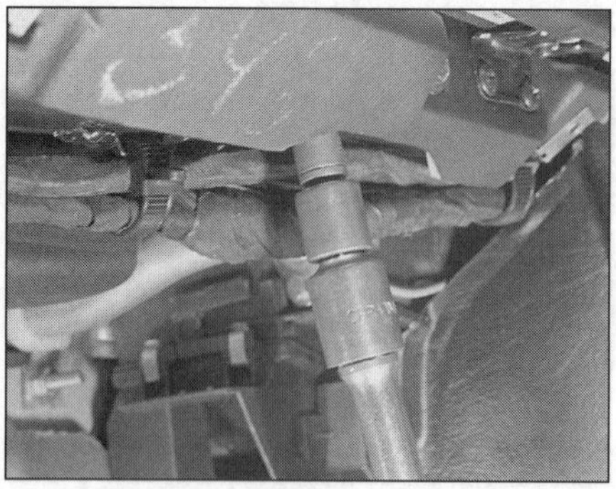

42.14 Undo the facia-to-stiffener lower bolt

42.18 Undo the heater control retaining nuts

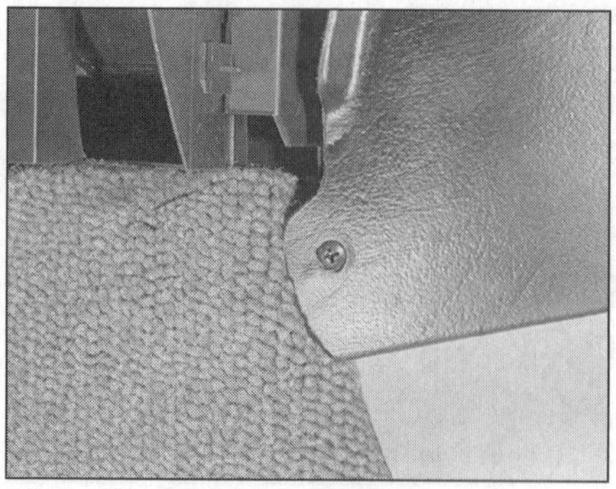

42.15 Undo the side retaining screws

14 Undo the bolt securing the underside of the facia to the body stiffener **(see illustration)**.
15 Undo the screw securing the facia to the centre console on both sides **(see illustration)**.
16 Using pliers and a protective cloth, pull off the three heater control knobs.
17 Pull off the blower control switch knob **(see illustration)**.
18 Undo the three heater control retaining nuts **(see illustration)**.
19 Using pliers and a protective cloth, pull out the centre vent grilles **(see illustration)**.
20 Undo the screws on each side of the centre vent grille apertures **(see illustration)**.

42.17 Pull off the blower control switch knob

21 Carefully prise off the ignition switch trim surround **(see illustration)**.
22 Close the fresh air flap and undo the bolt, working through the lever slot **(see illustration)**.
23 Pull the air hose off the rear of the centre vent nozzles **(see illustration)**.
24 Undo the retaining bolt behind the glovebox cover **(see illustration)**, and the inner nut at the bottom right-hand side.
25 Pull out the demister nozzles on the heater box and withdraw the facia from the car.

Refitting

26 Refitting is the reverse of removal.

42.19 Pull out the centre vent grilles

42.20 Undo the screws in the centre vent aperture (arrowed)

42.21 Prise off the ignition switch trim surround

42.22 Undo the bolt (arrowed) through the lever slot

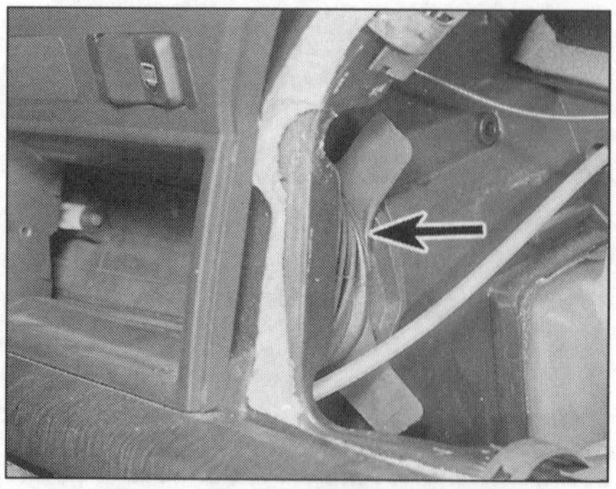

42.23 Pull off the centre vent air hose (arrowed)

42.24 Undo the bolt behind the glovebox cover (arrowed)

Chapter 12
Body electrical system

Contents

Airbag system - general information and precautions 27
Airbag system components - removal and refitting 28
Anti-theft alarm system - general information 26
Audio equipment - removal and refitting 22
Bulbs (exterior lamps) - renewal 11
Bulbs (interior lamps) - renewal 12
Central electrics unit - removal and refitting 4
Cruise control system components - removal and refitting 25
Door courtesy light switches - removal and refitting 7
Electrical fault finding - general information 2
Exterior lamps - removal and refitting 13
Facia and centre console switches - removal and refitting 6
Front and rear speakers - removal and refitting 23
Fuses and relays - general information 3
General information and precautions 1
Headlamp glass - removal and refitting 14
Headlamp height adjustment system - description 16
Headlamps - alignment 15
Horns - removal and refitting 21
Instrument panel - removal and refitting 8
Instrument panel components - removal and refitting 9
Radio aerial - removal and refitting 24
Speedometer cable - removal and refitting 10
Steering column combination switch - removal and refitting 5
Windscreen washer system - removal, refitting and adjustment ... 20
Windscreen wiper blades and arms - removal and refitting 17
Windscreen wiper motor - removal and refitting 19
Windscreen wiper motor and linkage - removal and refitting 18

Degrees of difficulty

Easy, suitable for novice with little experience	**Fairly easy,** suitable for beginner with some experience	**Fairly difficult,** suitable for competent DIY mechanic	**Difficult,** suitable for experienced DIY mechanic	**Very difficult,** suitable for expert DIY or professional

Specifications

System type	12 volt, negative earth	
Battery		
Type	12 volt lead-acid, 54 to 100 Ah depending on market	
Bulbs	**Wattage**	
Exterior lights		
Headlight (dipped and main beam)	55 (H4 type)	
Front foglight	55 (H3 type)	
Front sidelight	4	
Direction indicator	21	
Direction indicator side repeater	5	
Stoplight	21	
Taillight	10	
Reversing light	21	
Rear foglight	21	
Number plate light	5	
Interior light		
Front courtesy lights	10	
Rear courtesy lights	10	
Luggage compartment light	10	
Instrument panel:		
Illumination bulbs	3	
Warning light bulbs	1.5	
Torque wrench settings	**Nm**	**lbf ft**
Windscreen wiper motor:		
Mounting bolts	5	4
Spindle nut	25	18
Driver's side airbag screws	6	4

12

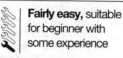

1 General information and precautions

Warning: Before carrying out any work on the electrical system, read through the precautions given in Safety First! at the beginning of this manual and in Chapter 5A.

The electrical system is of the 12 volt negative earth type. Power for the lights and all electrical accessories is supplied by a lead/acid type battery, which is charged by the alternator.

This Chapter covers repair and service procedures for the various electrical components not associated with engine. Information on the battery, alternator and starter motor can be found in Chapter 5A.

It should be noted that prior to working on any component in the electrical system, the battery negative terminal should first be disconnected to prevent the possibility of electrical short circuits and/or fires.

2 Electrical fault finding - general information

Note: *Refer to the precautions given in 'Safety first!' and in Chapter 5A before starting work. The following tests relate to testing of the main electrical circuits, and should not be used to test delicate electronic circuits (such as anti-lock braking systems), particularly where an electronic control module (ECU) is used.*

General

1 A typical electrical circuit consists of an electrical component, any switches, relays, motors, fuses, fusible links or circuit breakers related to that component, and the wiring and connectors which link the component to both the battery and the chassis. To help to pinpoint a problem in an electrical circuit, wiring diagrams are included at the end of this Manual.

2 Before attempting to diagnose an electrical fault, first study the appropriate wiring diagram to obtain a complete understanding of the components included in the particular circuit concerned. The possible sources of a fault can be narrowed down by noting if other components related to the circuit are operating properly. If several components or circuits fail at one time, the problem is likely to be related to a shared fuse or earth connection.

3 Electrical problems usually stem from simple causes, such as loose or corroded connections, a faulty earth connection, a blown fuse, a melted fusible link, or a faulty relay (refer to Section 3 for details of testing relays). Visually inspect the condition of all fuses, wires and connections in a problem circuit before testing the components. Use the wiring diagrams to determine which terminal connections will need to be checked in order to pinpoint the trouble spot.

4 The basic tools required for electrical fault-finding include a circuit tester or voltmeter (a 12-volt bulb with a set of test leads can also be used for certain tests); a self-powered test light (sometimes known as a continuity tester); an ohmmeter (to measure resistance); a battery and set of test leads; and a jumper wire, preferably with a circuit breaker or fuse incorporated, which can be used to bypass suspect wires or electrical components. Before attempting to locate a problem with test instruments, use the wiring diagram to determine where to make the connections.

5 To find the source of an intermittent wiring fault (usually due to a poor or dirty connection, or damaged wiring insulation), a 'wiggle' test can be performed on the wiring. This involves wiggling the wiring by hand to see if the fault occurs as the wiring is moved. It should be possible to narrow down the source of the fault to a particular section of wiring. This method of testing can be used in conjunction with any of the tests described in the following sub-Sections.

6 Apart from problems due to poor connections, two basic types of fault can occur in an electrical circuit - open circuit, or short circuit.

7 Open circuit faults are caused by a break somewhere in the circuit, which prevents current from flowing. An open circuit fault will prevent a component from working, but will not cause the relevant circuit fuse to blow.

8 Short circuit faults are caused by a `short' somewhere in the circuit, which allows the current flowing in the circuit to 'escape' along an alternative route, usually to earth. Short circuit faults are normally caused by a breakdown in wiring insulation, which allows a feed wire to touch either another wire, or an earthed component such as the bodyshell. A short circuit fault will normally cause the relevant circuit fuse to blow.

Finding an open circuit

9 To check for an open circuit, connect one lead of a circuit tester or voltmeter to either the negative battery terminal or a known good earth.

10 Connect the other lead to a connector in the circuit being tested, preferably nearest to the battery or fuse.

11 Switch on the circuit, bearing in mind that some circuits are live only when the ignition switch is moved to a particular position.

12 If voltage is present (indicated either by the tester bulb lighting or a voltmeter reading, as applicable), this means that the section of the circuit between the relevant connector and the battery is problem-free.

13 Continue to check the remainder of the circuit in the same fashion.

14 When a point is reached at which no voltage is present, the problem must lie between that point and the previous test point with voltage. Most problems can be traced to a broken, corroded or loose connection.

Finding a short circuit

15 To check for a short circuit, first disconnect the load(s) from the circuit (loads are the components which draw current from a circuit, such as bulbs, motors, heating elements, etc).

16 Remove the relevant fuse from the circuit, and connect a circuit tester or voltmeter to the fuse connections.

17 Switch on the circuit, bearing in mind that some circuits are live only when the ignition switch is moved to a particular position.

18 If voltage is present (indicated either by the tester bulb lighting or a voltmeter reading, as applicable), this means that there is a short circuit.

19 If no voltage is present, but the fuse still blows with the load(s) connected, this indicates an internal fault in the load(s).

Finding an earth fault

20 The battery negative terminal is connected to `earth'- the metal of the engine/transmission and the car body - and most systems are wired so that they only receive a positive feed, the current returning through the metal of the car body. This means that the component mounting and the body form part of that circuit. Loose or corroded mountings can therefore cause a range of electrical faults, ranging from total failure of a circuit, to a puzzling partial fault. In particular, lights may shine dimly (especially when another circuit sharing the same earth point is in operation), motors (eg. wiper motors or the radiator cooling fan motor) may run slowly, and the operation of one circuit may have an apparently unrelated effect on another. Note that on many vehicles, earth straps are used between certain components, such as the engine/transmission and the body, usually where there is no metal-to-metal contact between components due to flexible rubber mountings, etc.

21 To check whether a component is properly earthed, disconnect the battery and connect one lead of an ohmmeter to a known good earth point. Connect the other lead to the wire or earth connection being tested. The resistance reading should be zero; if not, check the connection as follows.

22 If an earth connection is thought to be faulty, dismantle the connection and clean back to bare metal both the bodyshell and the wire terminal or the component earth connection mating surface. Be careful to remove all traces of dirt and corrosion, then use a knife to trim away any paint, so that a clean metal-to-metal joint is made. On reassembly, tighten the joint fasteners securely; if a wire terminal is being refitted, use serrated washers between the terminal

3.1 Central electrics unit location in engine compartment

3.2 Lift off the central electrics unit cover

and the bodyshell to ensure a clean and secure connection. When the connection is remade, prevent the onset of corrosion in the future by applying a coat of petroleum jelly or silicone-based grease or by spraying on (at regular intervals) a proprietary ignition sealer or a water dispersant lubricant.

3 Fuses and relays - general information

Main fuses

1 The fuses are situated in the central electrics unit, located at the rear of the engine compartment on the right-hand side **(see illustration)**. On some models there may also be a few additional fuses located in the auxiliary fusebox, which is situated next to the main fusebox.

2 To gain access to the fuses, release the fuse cover front retaining clip then unclip and remove the cover **(see illustration)**.

3 A list of the circuits each fuse protects is given on the label attached to the inside of the fusebox cover.

4 To remove a fuse, first switch off the circuit concerned (or the ignition), then pull the fuse out of its terminals. The wire within the fuse should be visible; if the fuse is blown it will be broken or melted **(see illustration)**.

5 Always renew a fuse with one of an identical rating; never use a fuse with a different rating from the original or substitute anything else. Never renew a fuse more than once without tracing the source of the trouble. The fuse rating is stamped on top of the fuse; note that the fuses are also colour-coded for easy recognition.

6 If a new fuse blows immediately, find the cause before renewing it again; a short to earth as a result of faulty insulation is most likely. Where a fuse protects more than one circuit, try to isolate the defect by switching on each circuit in turn (if possible) until the fuse blows again. Always carry a supply of spare fuses of each relevant rating on the vehicle, a spare of each rating should be clipped into the base of the fusebox.

Relays

7 The relays are also located in the central electrics unit behind the fuses, and also in an additional holder situated just to the front of the main unit **(see illustration)**.

8 If a circuit or system controlled by a relay develops a fault and the relay is suspect, operate the system; if the relay is functioning it should be possible to hear it click as it is energised. If this is the case the fault lies with the components or wiring of the system. If the relay is not being energised then either the relay is not receiving a main supply or a switching voltage or the relay itself is faulty. Testing is by the substitution of a known good unit but be careful; while some relays are identical in appearance and in operation, others look similar but perform different functions.

9 To renew a relay first ensure that the ignition switch is off. The relay can then simply be pulled out from the socket and the new relay pressed in.

4 Central electrics unit - removal and refitting

Caution: The Central Electrics Unit contains components that are sensitive to the levels of static electricity generated by a person during normal activity. Once the multiway harness connector has been unplugged, the exposed connector pins can freely conduct stray static electricity to these components, damaging or even destroying them - the damage will be invisible and may not manifest itself immediately. Expensive repairs can be avoided by observing the following basic handling rules:

a) Handle the disconnected unit by its case only; do not allow fingers or tools to come into contact with the pins.

b) When carrying the unit around, "ground" yourself from time to time, by touching a metal object such as an unpainted water pipe, this will discharge any potentially damaging static that may have built up.

c) Do not leave the unit unplugged from its connector for any longer than is absolutely necessary.

Removal

1 Disconnect the battery negative terminal.

2 Remove the cover under the facia on the driver's side for access to the connections on the underside of the unit.

3 Disconnect all the wiring multi-plugs from the underside of the central electrics unit. Each multi-plug is a different shape so they can only be fitted one way round into one particular socket. However it is advisable to label each plug as to its approximate location as they are removed. If a small hooked piece of wire is used to engage in the tag of each plug, this will make removal easier.

4 Undo the bolts securing the main earth connections to the bulkhead behind the instrument panel. Make a note of each of the earth lead locations.

5 From within the engine compartment, undo the screws and remove the additional relay holder.

6 Remove the cover over the fuses on the central electrics unit.

7 Undo the two screws and two nuts securing the unit to the bulkhead.

8 Pull the unit forwards and upwards, then unscrew the wiring terminals and disconnect the wiring plugs. Make a note of their locations as each wire is removed.

9 Remove the central electric unit from the engine compartment.

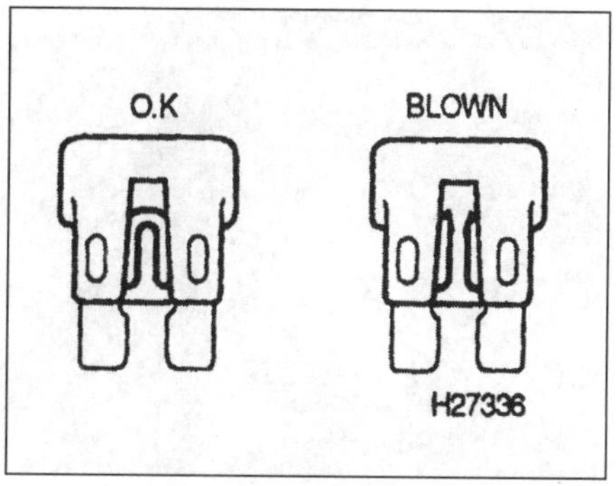

3.4 A 'blown' fuse can be recognised by its melted/broken wire

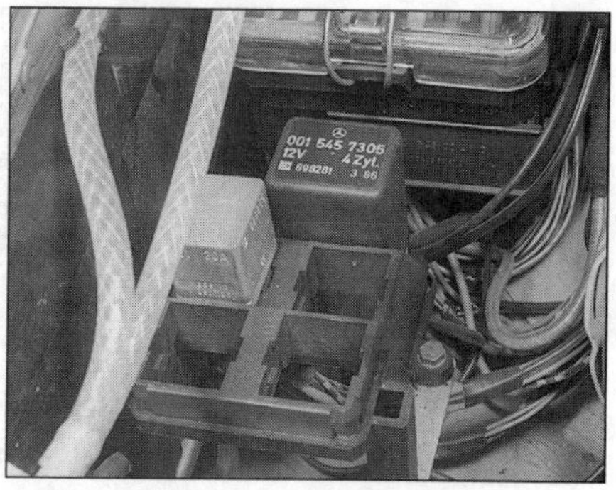

3.7 Additional relay holder location

5.4 Combination switch retaining screws (arrowed)

Refitting

10 Refitting is the reverse sequence to removal.

5 Steering column combination switch - removal and refitting

Removal

1 Disconnect the battery negative terminal.
2 Remove the cover under the facia on the driver's side.
3 Remove the steering wheel as described in Chapter 10.
4 Undo the three screws securing the combination switch to the steering column **(see illustration)**.

6.6b . . . then withdraw the knob

6.3 Prise out the switch and disconnect the wiring plug

5 Disconnect the combination switch wiring multi-plug from the central electrics unit under the facia. To do this, use a small hooked piece of wire to engage in the tag of the wiring plug, and pull the plug out using the wire.
6 Withdraw the combination switch and steering column shroud from the column, then remove the switch and cable from the shroud.

Refitting

7 Refitting is the reverse sequence to removal.

6 Facia and centre console switches - removal and refitting

1 Before removing any switches, disconnect the battery negative terminal, and reconnect on completion.

Facia switches

2 To remove the switches on either side of the instrument panel, carefully prise one end of the relevant switch out of its location using a knife blade or thin screwdriver. Protect the facia face as you do this.
3 Withdraw the complete switch and disconnect the wiring plug at the rear **(see illustration)**.
4 To refit, connect the wiring plug and push the switch into position, one end at a time.

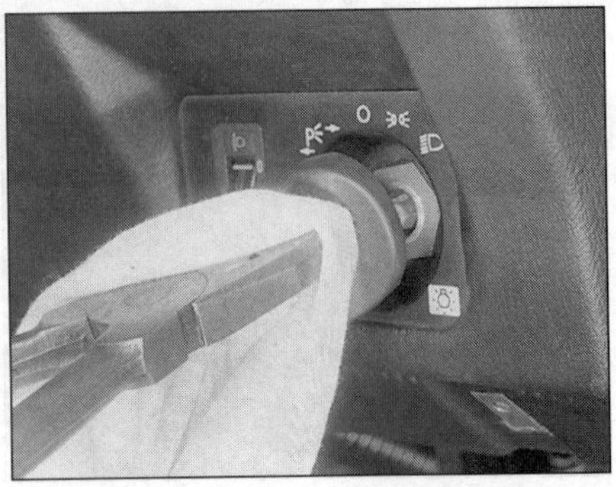
6.6a Use pliers and a protective cloth to release the switch knob . . .

Headlamp switch

5 Remove the cover under the facia on the driver's side.
6 Using pliers and a protective cloth, carefully pull off the switch knob **(see illustrations)**.
7 Using a small screwdriver, prise out the beam control rotary switch **(see illustration)**. Disconnect the vacuum hoses, pull out the illumination bulbholder and remove the switch.
8 Undo the main lighting switch retaining nut **(see illustration)** and withdraw the switch from behind the facia. Disconnect the wiring plug and remove the switch.
9 Refitting is the reverse sequence to removal.

Centre console switches

10 Using a small screwdriver, carefully prise the relevant switch from its location **(see illustration)**.
11 Disconnect the wiring multi-plug and remove the switch.
12 Refitting is the reverse sequence to removal.

7 Door courtesy light switches - removal and refitting

Removal

1 Disconnect the battery negative terminal.

6.7 Headlamp beam control switch removal

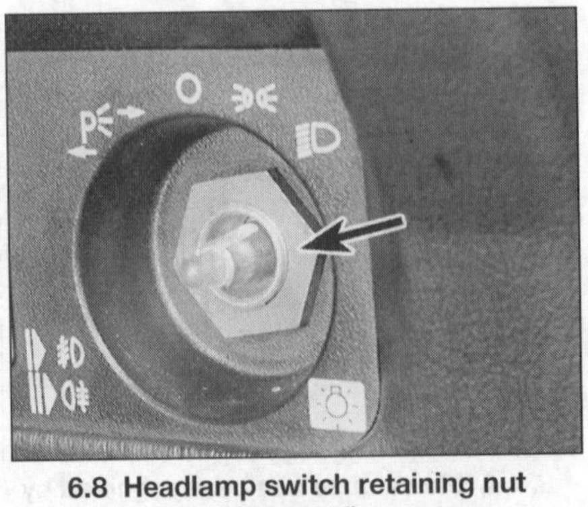
6.8 Headlamp switch retaining nut (arrowed)

6.10 Centre console switch removal

7.2 Door courtesy light switch location

2 Carefully prise out the switch **(see illustration)**, disconnect the wiring and remove the switch.

Refitting

3 Refitting is the reverse sequence to removal.

8 Instrument panel - removal and refitting

Removal

1 Disconnect the battery negative terminal.

2 Remove the steering wheel as described in Chapter 10.

3 Remove the cover under the facia on the driver's side.

4 Working under the facia from below, detach the air duct to the right-hand vent for access to the rear of the instrument panel.

5 Unscrew the speedometer cable retaining nut and withdraw the cable.

6 Push out the instrument panel from the rear to release it from the five retaining spring clips.

7 Make a note of the wiring plugs and connections on the rear of the panel and disconnect them **(see illustrations)**.

8 Remove the panel from the car.

Refitting

9 Refitting is the reverse sequence to removal.

8.7a Disconnect the wiring on the left-hand side . . .

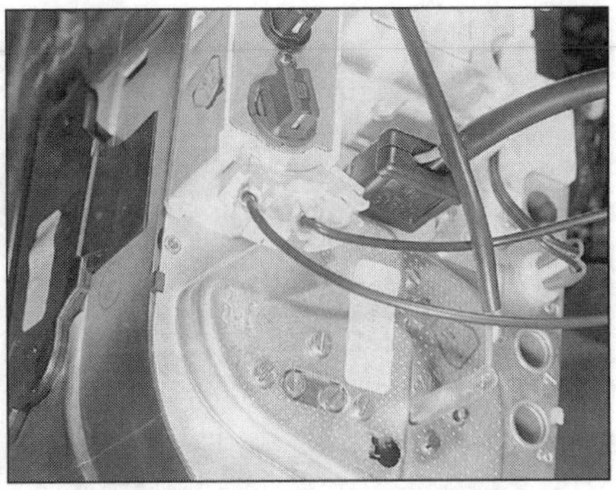

8.7b . . . and right-hand side of the instrument panel

9 Instrument panel components - removal and refitting

1 Remove the instrument panel as described in the previous Section.

Panel illumination and warning lamp bulbs

2 Turn the bulb holders anti-clockwise and remove them from the rear of the instrument panel **(see illustration)**.

3 Remove the illumination bulbs by pulling them out of their holders. The warning lamp bulbs (except for the alternator warning lamp) are renewed complete with their holders.

4 Refit the bulbholders by pushing down and turning clockwise.

Speedometer

5 Remove the resistance pack adjacent to the rear of the speedometer by pulling it upwards **(see illustration)**. If it is secured by two screws, undo these first.

6 Undo the four screws securing the speedometer to the rear of the instrument panel.

7 Undo the two screws, or release the two clips and pull off the lamp carrier above the speedometer.

8 Where fitted, remove the water level indicator bulb and release the wiring adjacent to the speedometer.

9 Withdraw the speedometer from the instrument panel.

10 Refitting is the reverse sequence to removal.

Tachometer

11 Remove the speedometer as previously described.

12 Undo the two additional screws **(see illustration)** and remove the unit.

13 Refitting is the reverse sequence to removal.

Gauge cluster

14 Remove the speedometer as previously described.

15 Undo the two additional screws **(see illustration)** and remove the gauge cluster.

16 Refitting is the reverse sequence to removal.

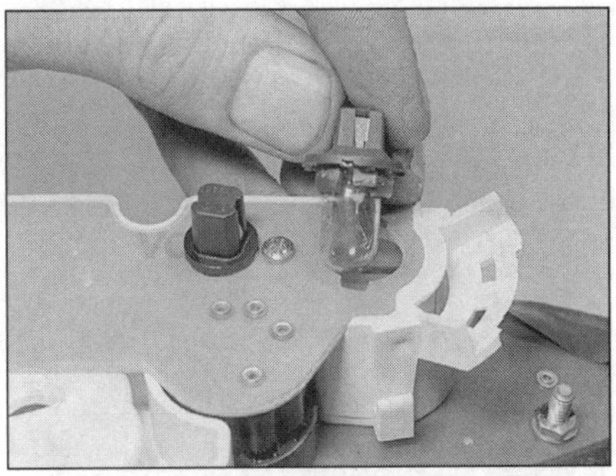

9.2 Instrument panel illumination bulb renewal

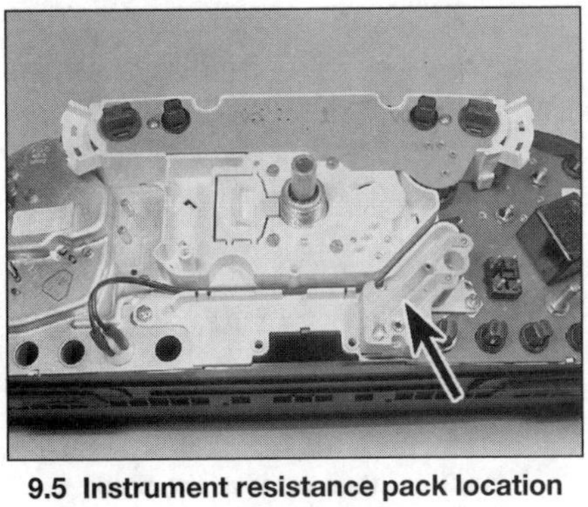

9.5 Instrument resistance pack location (arrowed)

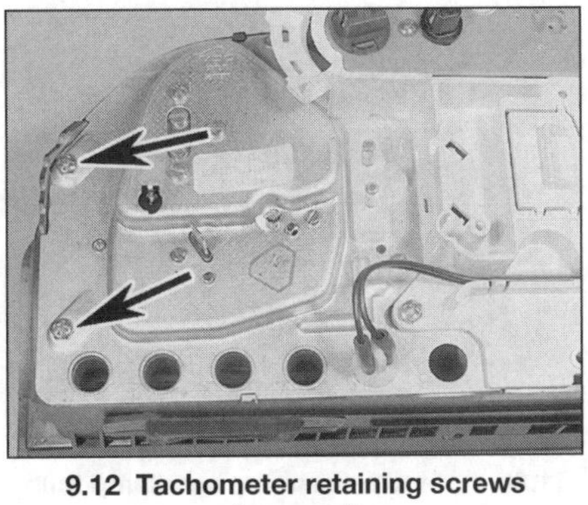

9.12 Tachometer retaining screws (arrowed)

9.15 Gauge cluster retaining screws (arrowed)

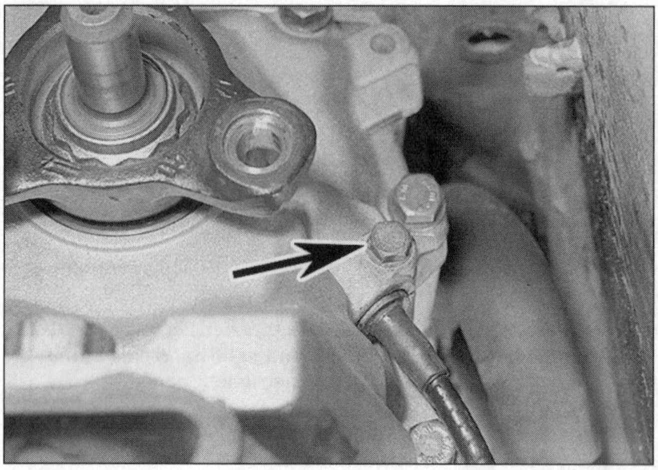

10.7 Undo the speedometer cable retaining bolt (arrowed)

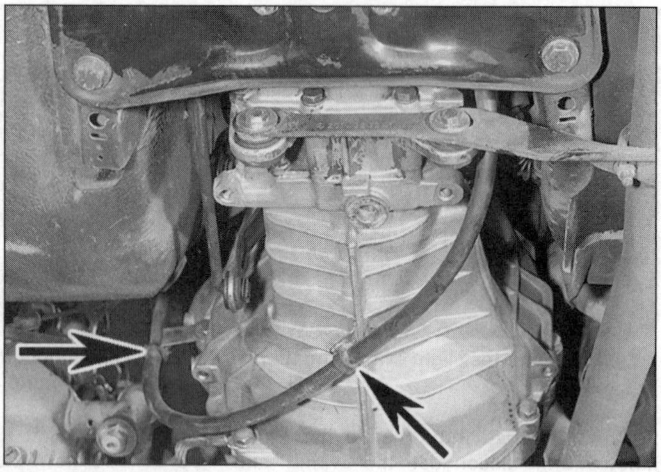

10.8 Release the cable from the transmission support clips (arrowed)

10 Speedometer cable - removal and refitting

Removal

1 Disconnect the battery negative terminal.

2 Remove the cover under the facia on the driver's side.

3 Working under the facia, detach the air duct to the right-hand vent for access to the rear of the instrument panel.

4 Unscrew the speedometer cable retaining nut and withdraw the cable.

5 Pull the cable into the engine compartment and release it from any brackets or support clips.

6 Jack up the front of the car and support it on axle stands (see "*Jacking and vehicle support*").

7 From under the car, undo the cable retaining bolt on the side of the gearbox or automatic transmission and withdraw the cable **(see illustration)**.

8 Release the cable from the support clips below and to the side of the transmission **(see illustration)** then remove the cable from the car.

Refitting

9 Refitting is the reverse sequence to removal.

11 Bulbs (exterior lamps) - renewal

Headlamp

1 From within the engine compartment, spring up the two lamp unit cover clips, tip the cover back and lift it up to remove **(see illustrations)**.

2 Disconnect the wiring plug **(see illustration)** and release the bulb retaining clip by squeezing the clip arms together and swinging outward **(see illustration)**.

3 Withdraw the bulb from the lamp unit **(see illustration)**. Take care not to touch the glass with your fingers.

> HAYNES HiNT *If the glass is touched, wipe the bulb with a rag moistened with methylated spirit.*

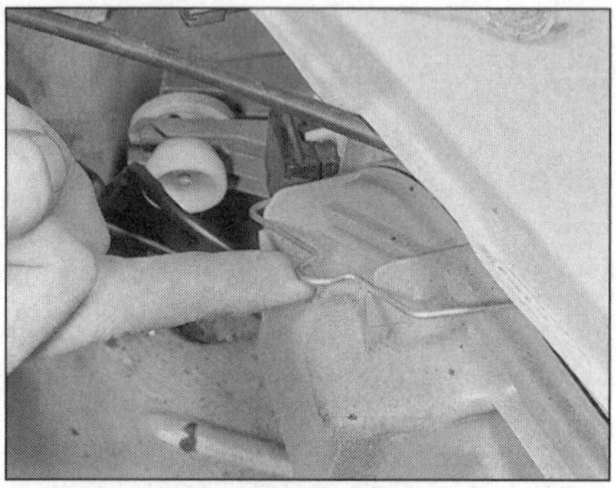

11.1a Spring up the headlamp cover clips . . .

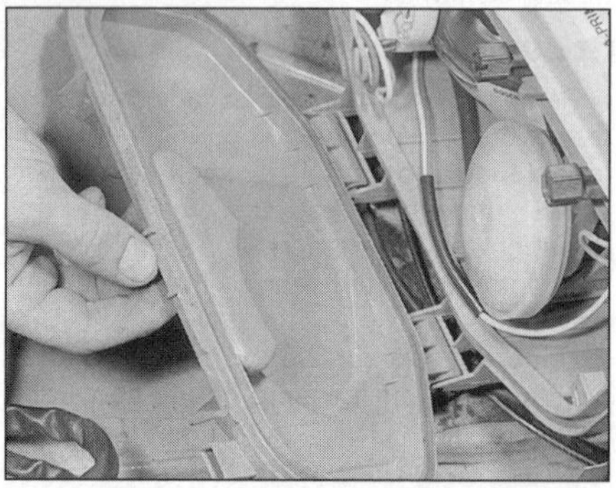

11.1b . . . and remove the cover

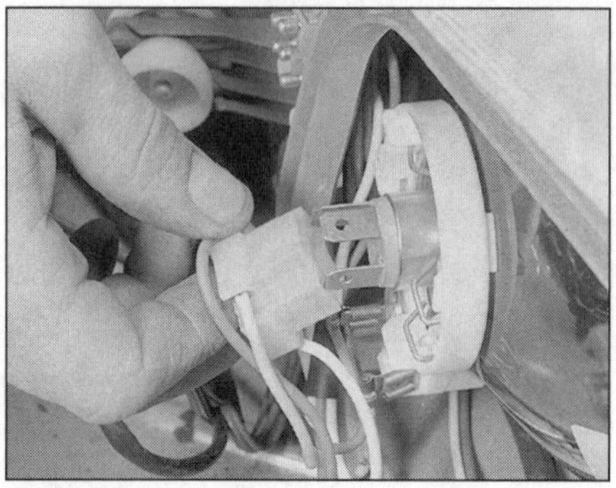

11.2a Disconnect the wiring plug . . .

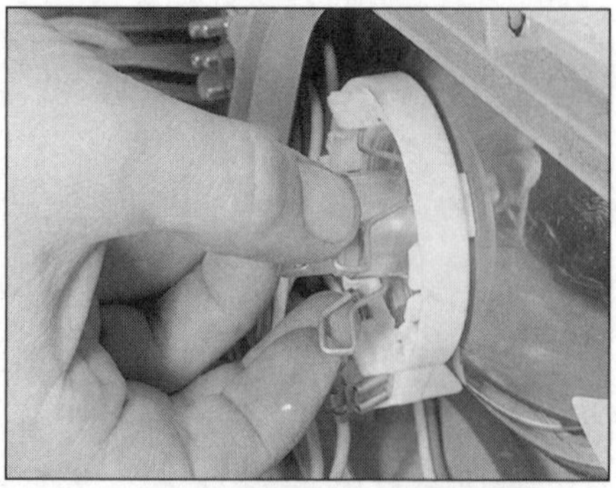

11.2b . . . and release the headlamp bulb retaining clip . . .

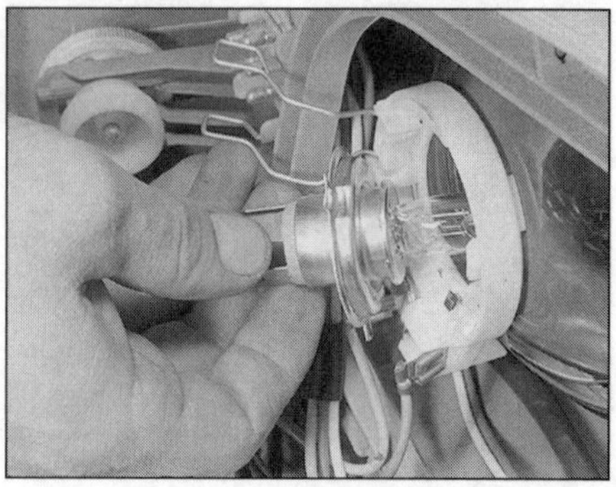

11.3 . . . then remove the bulb

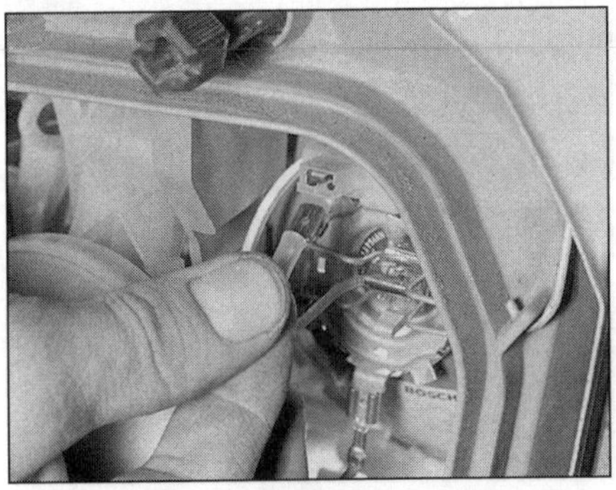

11.10 Disconnect the electrical lead at the foglamp

11.11 Release the retaining clip to remove the foglamp bulb

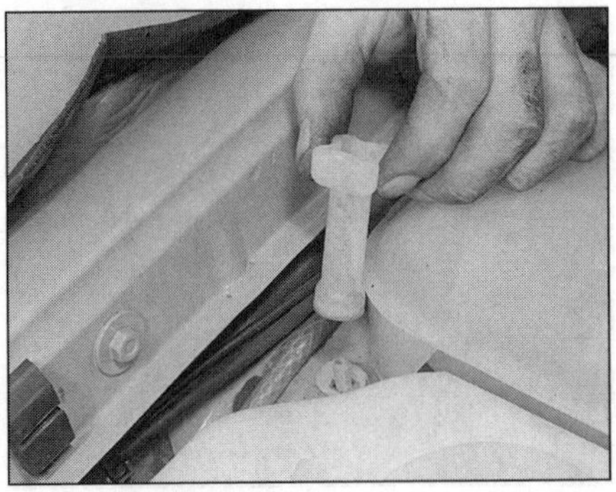

11.14 Washer reservoir cap nut removal

4 Refitting is the reverse sequence to removal, but ensure that the tags on the bulb plate engage with the recesses in the lamp unit.

Sidelamp

5 Remove the headlamp unit cover as described in paragraph 1.

6 Pull out the sidelamp bulbholder, located beneath the headlamp bulb.

7 Remove the bulb by turning it slightly anti-clockwise.

8 Refitting is the reverse sequence to removal.

Foglamp

9 Remove the headlamp unit cover as described in paragraph 1.

10 Disconnect the bulb electrical lead at the connector **(see illustration)**.

11 Compress the retaining clip arms and swing the clip outwards **(see illustration)**.

12 Withdraw the bulb from the lamp unit, taking care not to touch the glass. Wipe the glass with a rag moistened with methylated spirit if the glass is touched.

13 Refitting is the reverse sequence to removal.

Front direction indicator

14 If working on the right-hand bulb, disconnect the wiring on the washer reservoir level sensor, unscrew the large plastic cap nut **(see illustration)** and move the reservoir slightly to provide access to the bulb.

15 Disconnect the wiring at the bulbholder, then turn the holder slightly anti-clockwise to remove **(see illustrations)**.

16 Turn the bulb slightly anti-clockwise to remove it from the holder.

17 Refitting is the reverse sequence to removal.

Front direction indicator side repeater

18 Carefully prise the side repeater lens unit out of the body side panel, using a screwdriver inserted under the front edge of the unit.

19 Withdraw the bulb holder from the lens unit and remove the bulb from the holder **(see illustration)**.

20 Refitting is the reverse sequence to removal.

Rear lamp cluster bulbs

21 From inside the luggage compartment, turn the two lock catches as far as they will go to the left and withdraw the bulb carrier from the lamp unit **(see illustrations)**.

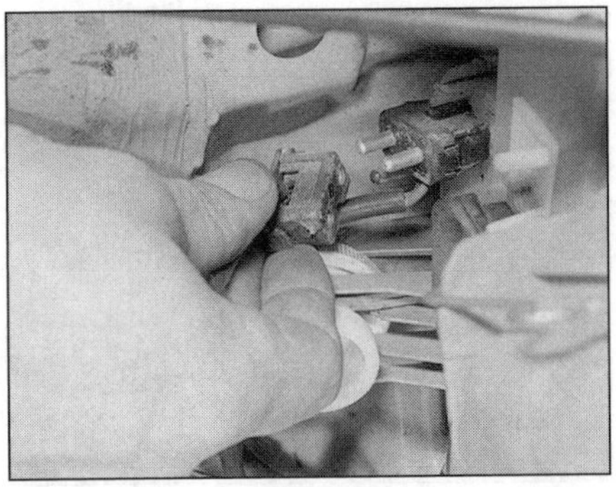

11.15a Disconnect the direction indicator bulb wiring . . .

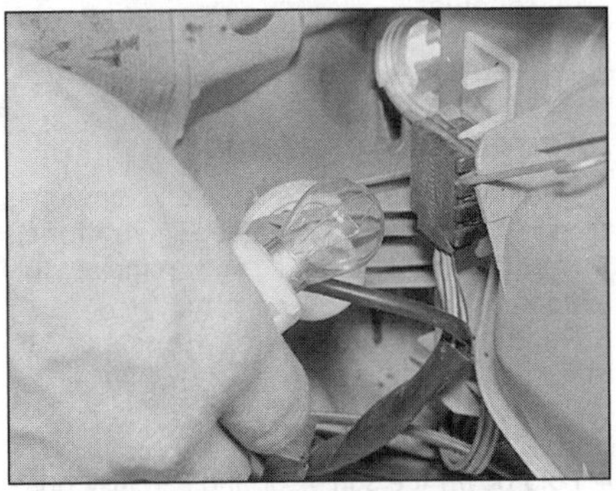

11.15b . . . and remove the bulbholder

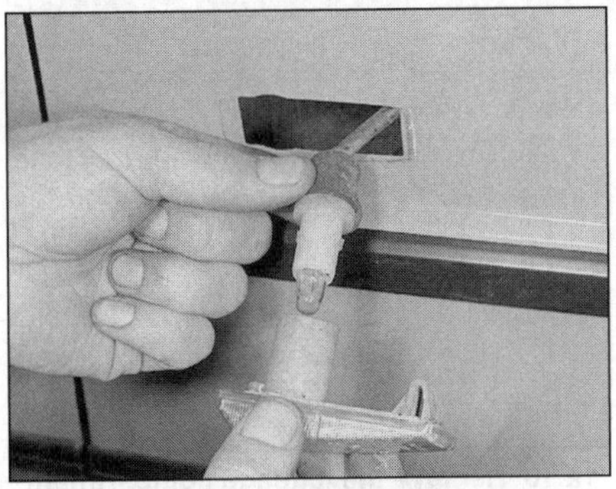

11.19 Renewing the direction indicator side repeater bulb

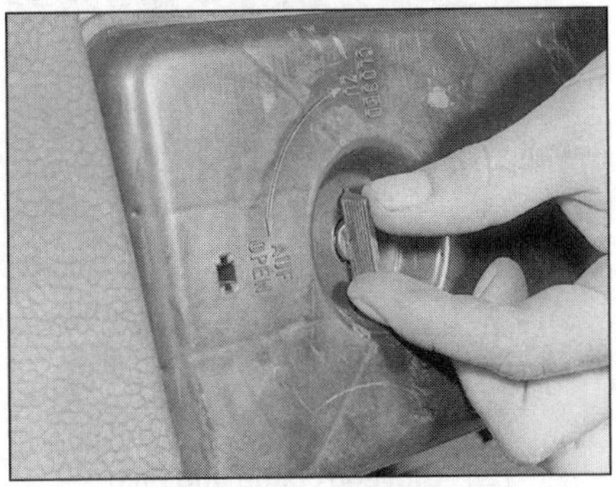

11.21a Release the lock catches . . .

11.21b . . . and withdraw the rear lamp bulb carrier

11.22 Remove the relevant bulb from the carrier

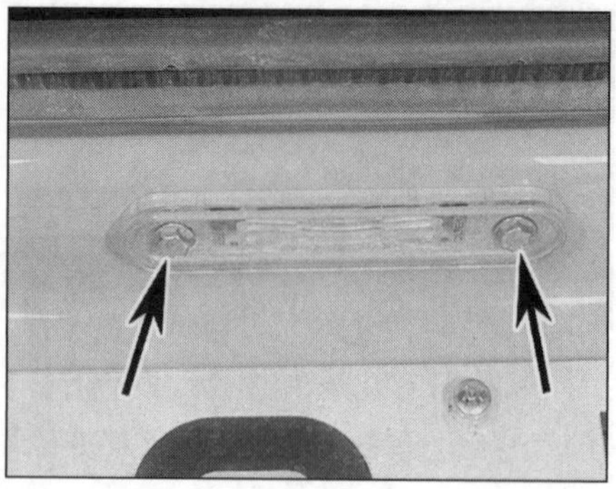

11.24a Undo the two screws (arrowed) . . .

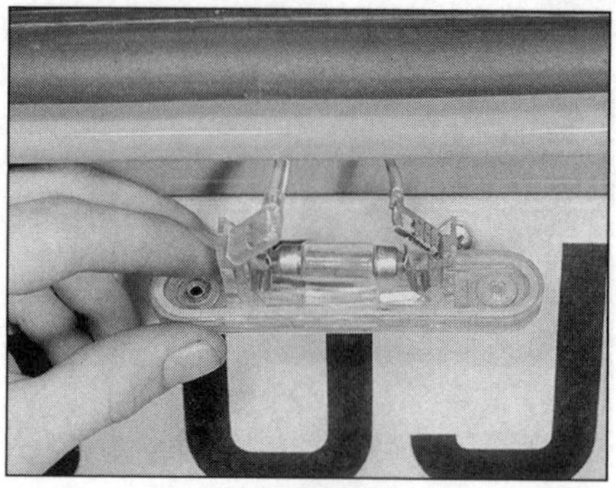

11.24b . . . and withdraw the number plate lamp

22 Remove the relevant bulb by turning anti-clockwise slightly **(see illustration)**. The bulb numbers and their wattages are shown adjacent to each bulb location.

23 Refitting is the reverse sequence to removal.

Number plate lamp

24 Undo the two retaining bolts and withdraw the lens unit **(see illustrations)**.

25 Spread the contacts and remove the festoon type bulb.

26 Refitting is the reverse sequence to removal.

12 Bulbs (interior lamps) - renewal

Interior courtesy lamp

1 Carefully prise out the lamp and lens unit, then fold back the reflector **(see illustrations)**.

2 Spread the contacts and remove the festoon type bulb.

3 Refitting is the reverse sequence to removal.

Sun visor illumination

4 Fold down the sun visor and carefully prise off the cover on the left-hand and right-hand recesses.

5 Spread the contacts and remove the festoon type bulb.

6 Refitting is the reverse sequence to removal.

Glovebox lamp

7 Prise the lamp lens unit out of its location and spread the contacts to remove the festoon type bulb **(see illustration)**.

8 Refitting is the reverse sequence to removal.

Luggage compartment lamp

9 Working through the boot lid aperture, spread the contacts and remove the festoon type bulb.

10 For increased working clearance, withdraw the switch and bulbholder then remove the bulb **(see illustration)**.

13 Exterior lamps - removal and refitting

Front direction indicator lamp

1 If working on the right-hand unit, disconnect the wiring on the washer reservoir level sensor, unscrew the large plastic cap nut and move the reservoir slightly to provide access.

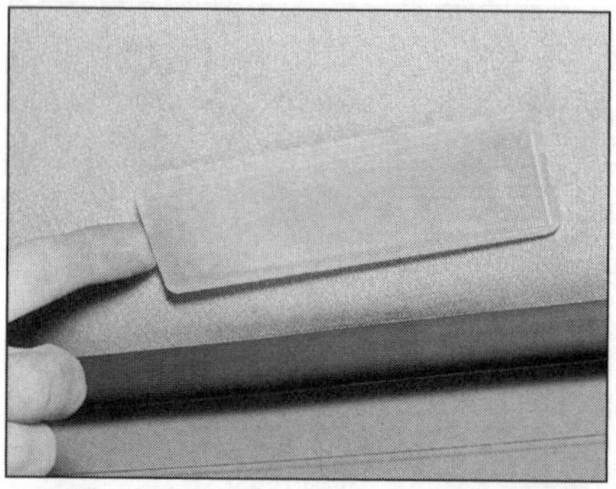

12.1a Prise out the interior lamp and lens unit . . .

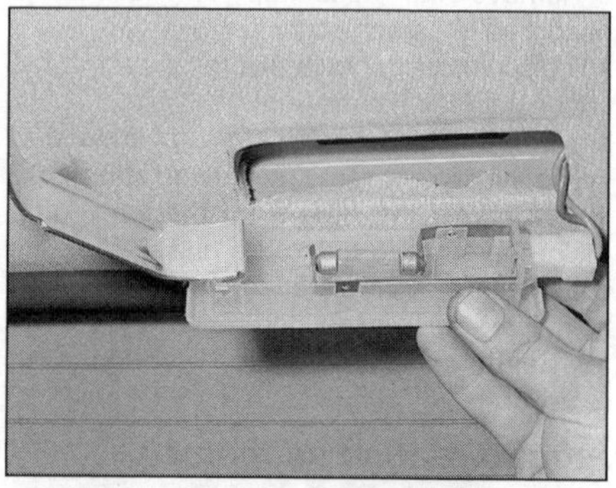

12.1b . . . then fold back the lens and remove the bulb from the rear . . .

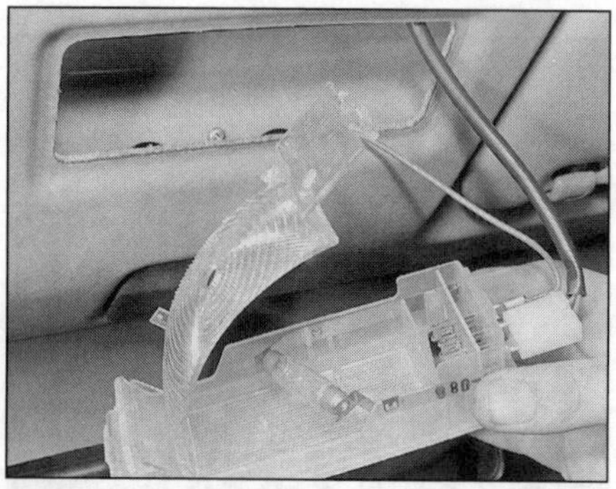

12.1c . . . or from the front interior lamp

12.7 Glovebox lamp and bulb

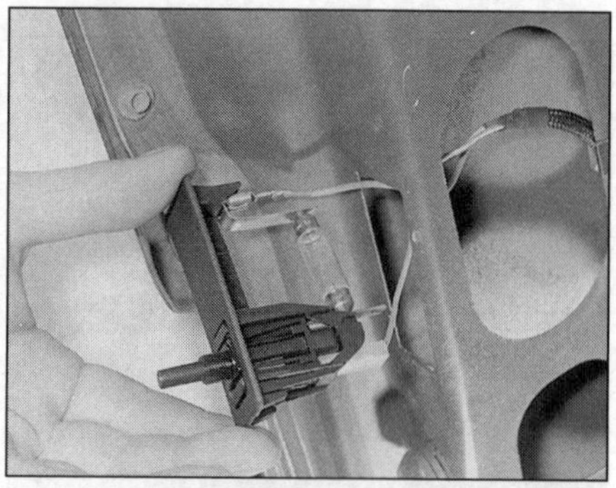

12.10 Remove the luggage compartment lamp switch and bulbholder for increased clearance

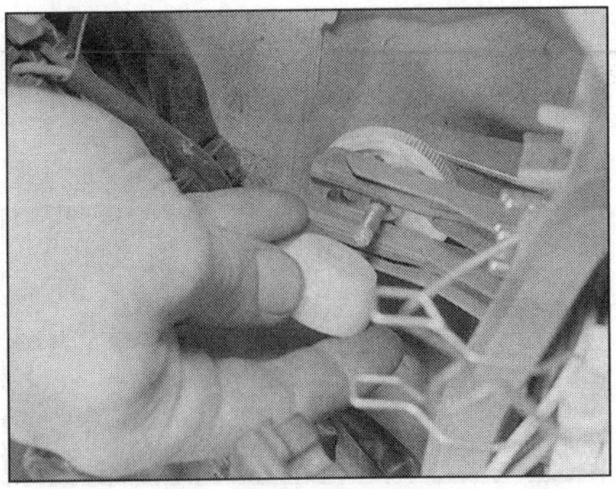

13.3 Unscrew the direction indicator lamp knurled nut

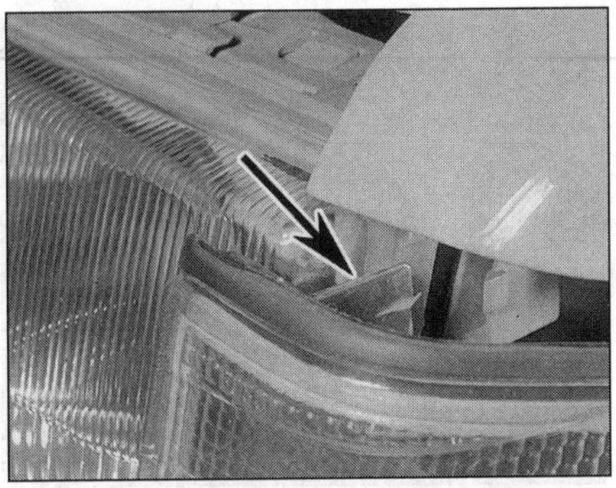

13.4 Direction indicator lamp upper retaining lug (arrowed)

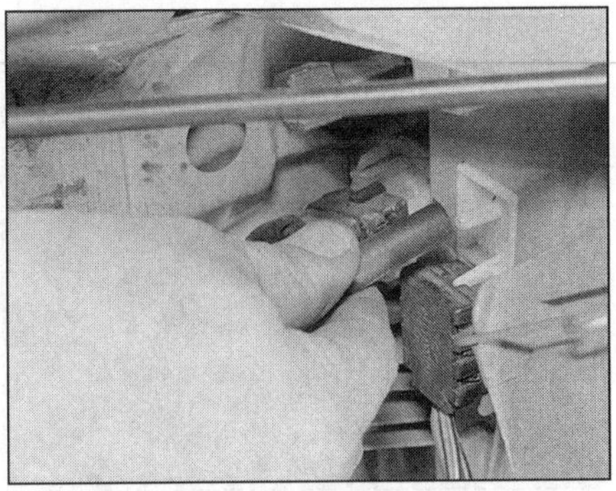

13.6a Disconnect the headlamp unit vacuum hose. . .

2 Disconnect the wiring at the rear of the bulbholder.

3 Unscrew the knurled retaining nut **(see illustration)** and pull the lamp out in a forward direction.

4 Refitting is the reverse sequence to removal, but ensure that the two lugs engage with the guides in the headlamp unit **(see illustration)**.

Headlamp unit

5 Remove the front direction indicator lamp as described previously.

6 Disconnect the vacuum hose and the wiring multi-plug at the rear of the lamp unit **(see illustrations)**.

7 Undo the inner end retaining bolt then disengage the finishing strip outer end by sliding it toward the centre of the car **(see illustrations)**. Remove the strip.

8 Undo the two upper retaining bolts and the single lower bolt **(see illustrations)**, then withdraw the unit from its location.

9 Refitting is the reverse sequence to removal, but ensure that the lower retaining lug engages with the slot in the bodywork **(see illustration)** before fitting the lower retaining screw. Tighten the mountings initially finger-tight and make any small corrections to the unit fitted position by turning the upper retaining nuts as necessary. Tighten the mountings securely after positioning.

Rear lamp cluster

10 From inside the luggage compartment, turn the two lock catches as far as they will go to the left and withdraw the bulb carrier from the lamp unit.

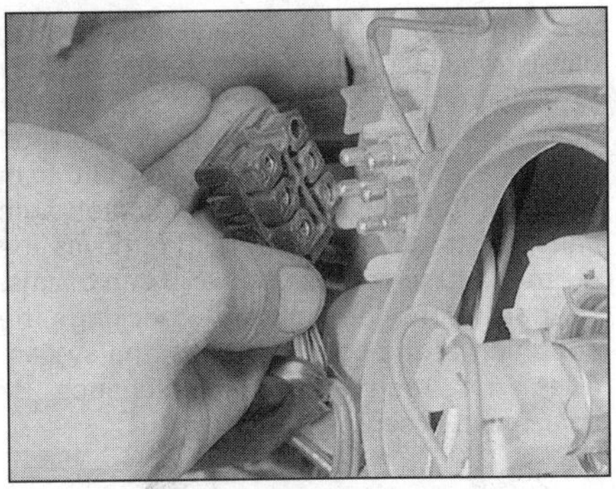

13.6b . . . and multi-plug

13.7a Undo the finishing strip retaining bolt . . .

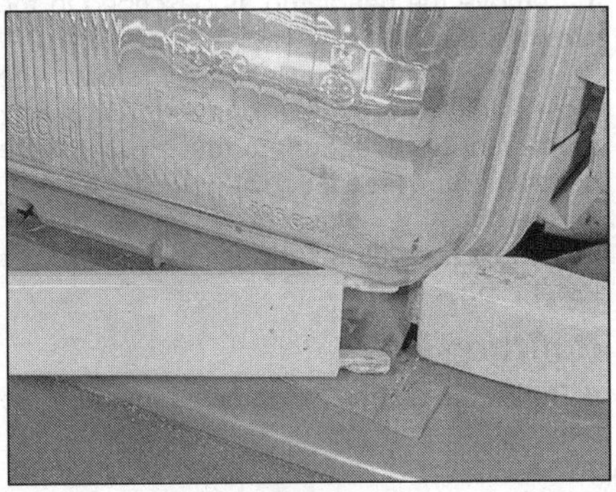

13.7b . . . and disengage the outer end tags

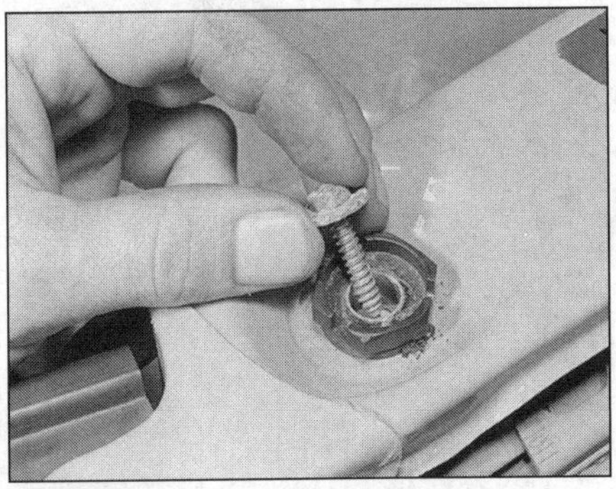

13.8a Undo the upper retaining bolts . . .

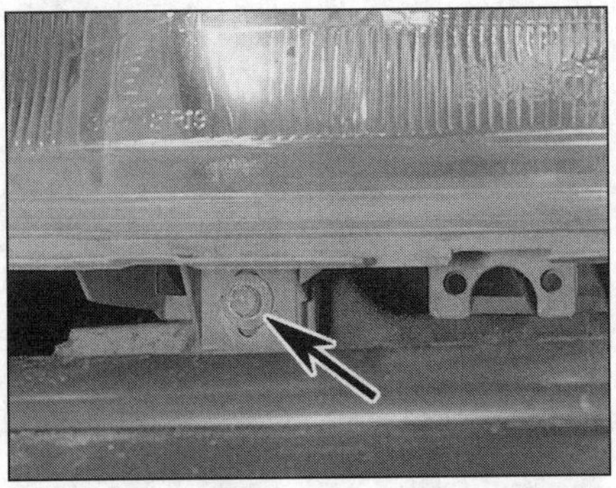

13.8b . . . and single lower bolt (arrowed)

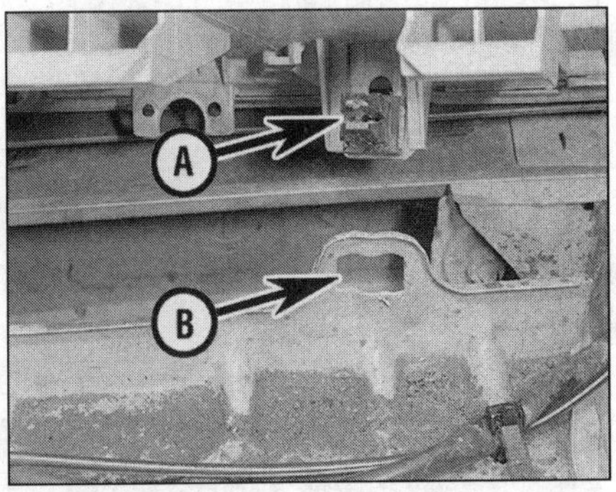

13.9 Ensure that the lower lug (A) enters the slot (B) when refitting

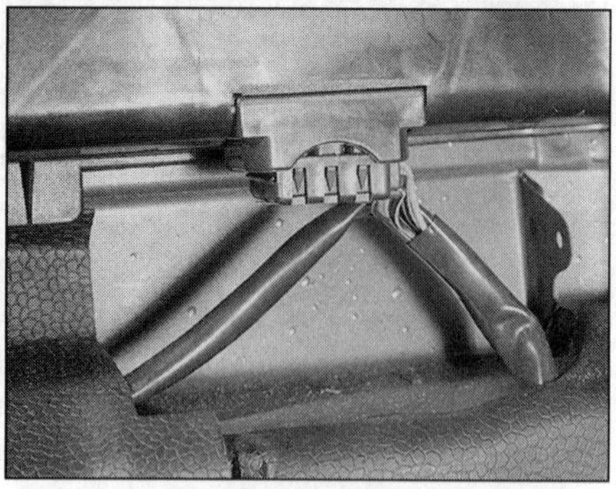

13.11a Disconnect the rear lamp cluster wiring multi-plug . . .

13.11b . . . undo the six nuts . . .

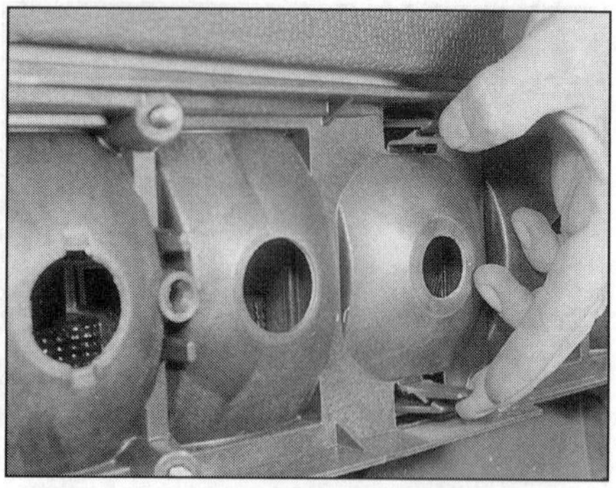

13.12a . . . depress the two catches . . .

11 Disconnect the wiring multi-plug, then undo the six lamp cluster retaining nuts **(see illustrations)**.

12 Depress the two catches and remove the unit from the outside of the car **(see illustrations)**.

13 Refitting is the reverse sequence to removal.

14 Headlamp glass - removal and refitting

Removal

1 Remove the headlamp as described in the previous Section.

2 Using a screwdriver carefully release the eight retaining tags, four on the top and four on the bottom securing the glass to the headlamp unit **(see illustration)**.

3 Remove the glass and frame as an assembly **(see illustration)** then pull off the lower rubber seal.

Refitting

4 Refitting is the reverse sequence to removal.

15 Headlamps - alignment

1 At periodic intervals the headlamp aim should be checked and if necessary adjusted.

2 Due to the light pattern of the lenses, optical beam setting equipment must be used to achieve satisfactory aim of the headlamps. It is recommended therefore that this work is carried out by a Mercedes-Benz dealer.

16 Headlamp height adjustment system - description

The headlamps are provided with a beam height adjustment system to enable the driver to regulate the beam height from inside the car to cater for different vehicle loading.

The system is operated by vacuum supplied by the inlet manifold and stored in a vacuum reservoir under the left-hand front wheel arch.

Control of the system is by a three position switch adjacent to the lighting switch on the facia. According to switch position, the vacuum supplied to the headlamp adjusting unit is regulated. The adjusting unit consists of a diaphragm which is connected to the movable headlamp lens by means of a pullrod having a stroke of approximately 3.0 mm (0.12 in). Vacuum applied to the diaphragm causes it to deflect which in turn moves the pullrod to raise or lower the headlamp beams.

Apart from periodically checking the condition of the vacuum hoses, the system does not require any maintenance or adjustment in service.

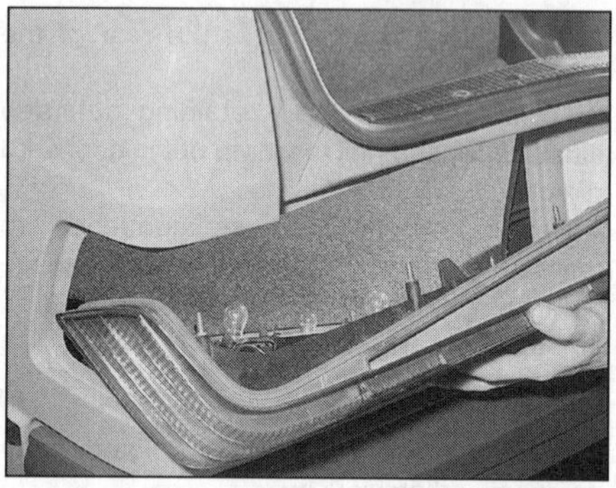

13.12b . . . and remove the lamp unit

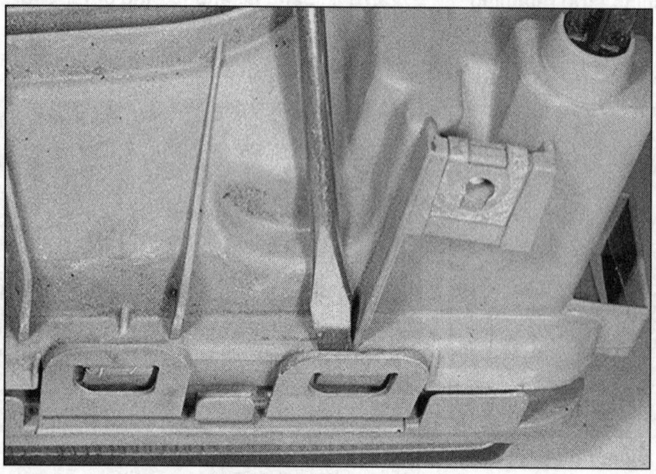

14.2 Release the retaining tags . . .

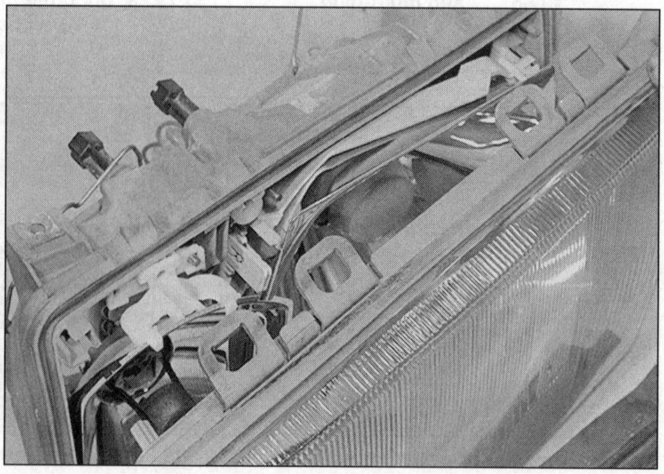

14.3 . . . and remove the headlamp glass

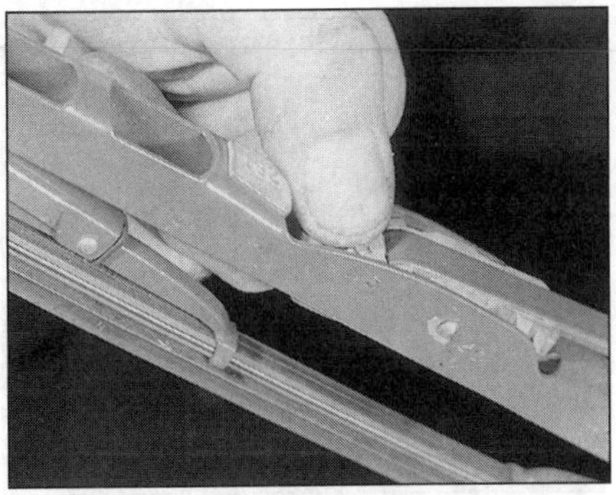

17.6a Depress the plastic clip . . .

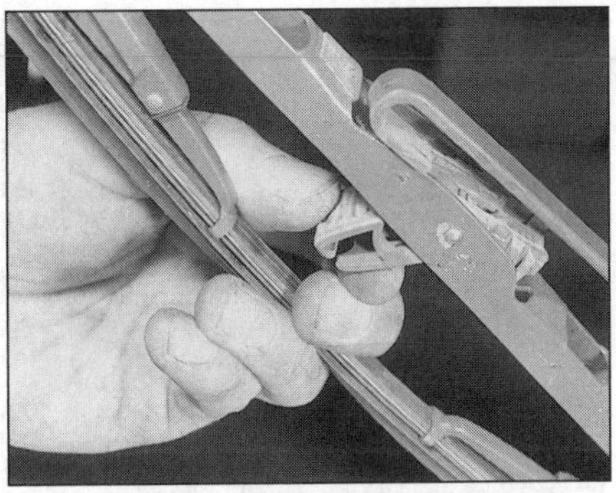

17.6b . . . and lift the blade from the hooked part of the arm

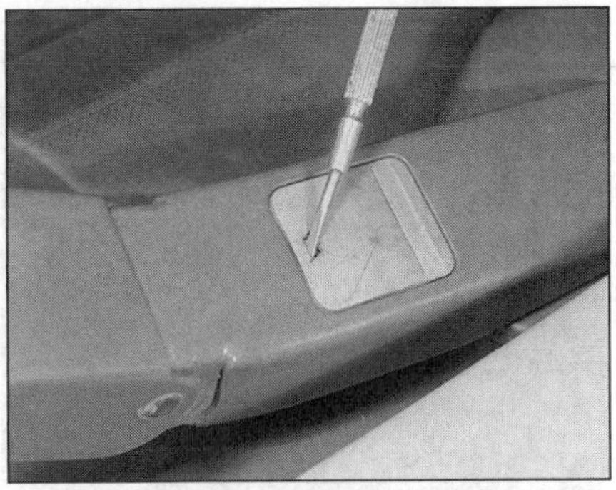

17.11 Release the cover with a thin screwdriver

17 Windscreen wiper blades and arms - removal and refitting

Wiper blades (up to January 1985)

1 Lift the wiper blade and arm from the windscreen.

2 Depress the catch on the blade and withdraw the blade from the end of the arm.

3 Where an auxiliary blade is fitted at the base of the arm, extract the retaining clip and washer and remove the auxiliary blade.

4 Refitting is the reverse sequence to removal.

Wiper blades (January 1985 onwards)

5 Lift the wiper blade and arm from the windscreen.

6 Depress the plastic clip and lift the blade from the hooked part of the arm **(see illustrations)**.

7 Insert the blade, then move the clip up to lock. Release the wiper arm from the raised position by prising the spring catch on the underside of the arm and lower the blade onto the screen.

Wiper arm (up to January 1985)

8 Raise the bonnet to its vertical position by depressing the catch on the left-hand hinge and releasing the spring clip on the support strut.

9 Hinge back the plastic cover, then unscrew the nut securing the arm to the spindle. Remove the washer and pull off the arm.

10 Refitting is the reverse sequence to removal, but ensure that the blade rests on the windscreen in the parked position before pushing the arm onto the spindle.

Wiper arm (January 1985 onwards)

11 To remove the arm on the panoramic wiper assembly, release the wiper arm cover using a thin screwdriver and open the cover **(see illustration)**.

12 Undo the wiper arm retaining bolt and withdraw the arm from the drive mechanism **(see illustration)**.

13 Refit the arm onto the drive mechanism and push it up until the arm bolt hole is aligned with the machined slot in the pumping shaft **(see illustration)**.

14 Refit the retaining bolt and close the cover.

18 Windscreen wiper motor and linkage - removal and refitting

Pre- January 1985 models

Removal

1 Disconnect the battery negative terminal.

2 Remove the wiper arm as described in the previous Section.

3 Prise off the closing cover on the top of the wiper arm spindle.

4 Push out the two clips, one each side at the front, securing the air inlet cover over the plenum chamber.

5 Lift up the rubber seal to release the front part of the air inlet cover.

6 Lift up the rear rubber seal on both sides then undo the two screws, one each side, securing the air inlet cover to the bulkhead.

7 Withdraw the air inlet cover from the plenum chamber.

8 Undo the three rear bolts and one front bolt securing the motor and linkage assembly to the bulkhead.

9 Remove the cover over the central electrics unit (fusebox) and undo the two retaining nuts and two screws.

17.12 Undo the wiper arm retaining bolt

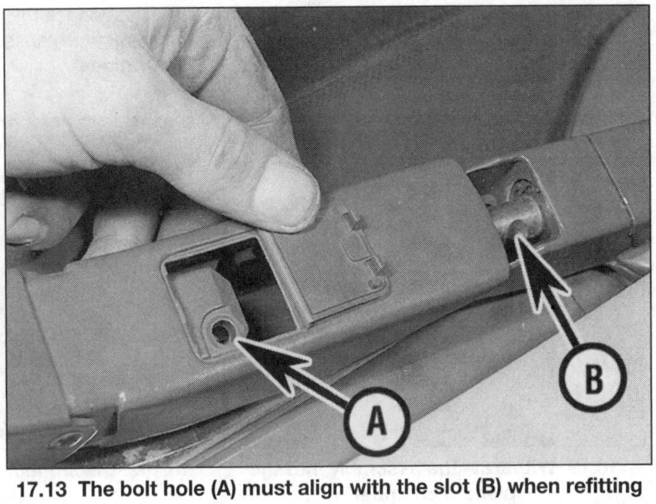

17.13 The bolt hole (A) must align with the slot (B) when refitting

18.14 Undo the air inlet cover front screws

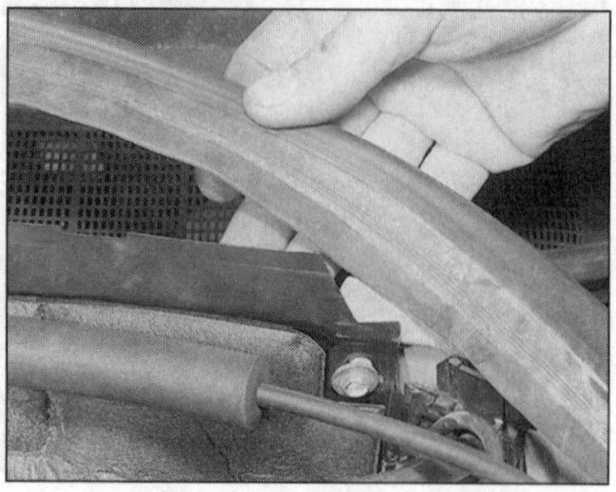
18.15 Lift up the rubber seal

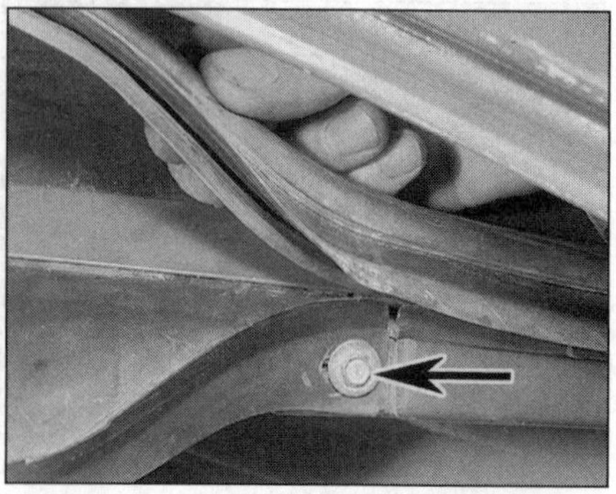
18.16 Lift up the rear rubber seal and undo the screw (arrowed) on both sides

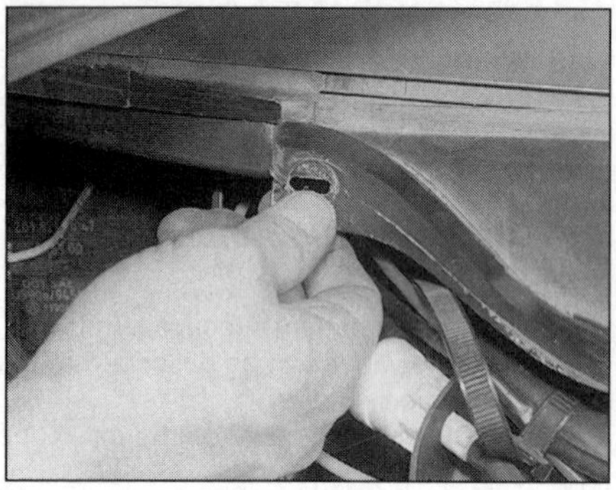
18.17 Withdraw the air inlet cover

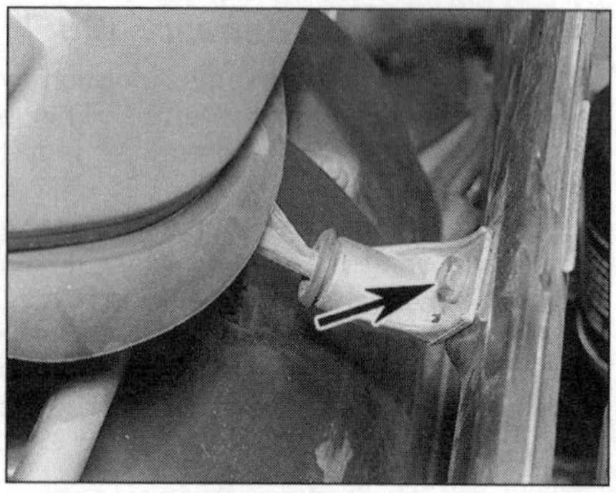
18.18a Undo the bolt (arrowed) . . .

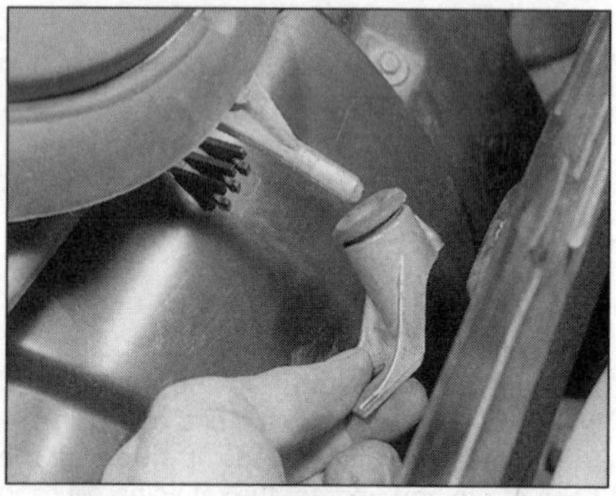
18.18b . . . and remove the support bracket

10 Lift the central electrics unit up and forward, then disconnect the wiper motor wiring multi-plug from the unit base.

11 Manipulate the motor and linkage assembly out of its location.

Refitting

12 Refitting is the reverse sequence to removal.

January 1985 models onwards

Removal

13 Remove the panoramic wiper arm as described in the previous Section.

14 Undo the two screws and clips, one each side at the front, securing the air inlet cover over the plenum chamber **(see illustration)**.

15 Lift up the rubber seal to release the front part of the air inlet cover **(see illustration)**.

16 Lift up the rear rubber seal on both sides, then undo the two screws, one each side, securing the air inlet cover to the bulkhead **(see illustration)**.

17 Withdraw the air inlet cover from the plenum chamber **(see illustration)**.

18 Undo the bolt and pull the front support bracket off the linkage stud **(see illustrations)**.

19 Undo the bolts securing the linkage to the bulkhead and withdraw it forward into the plenum chamber **(see illustration)**.

20 Disconnect the motor wiring multi-plug and remove the assembly from the car **(see illustrations)**.

Refitting

21 Refitting is the reverse sequence to removal.

19 Windscreen wiper motor - removal and refitting

Removal

1 Remove the wiper motor and linkage assembly from the car as described in the previous Section.

2 Unscrew the retaining nut and remove the

18.19 Withdraw the assembly into the plenum chamber

18.20a Disconnect the motor wiring multi-plug . . .

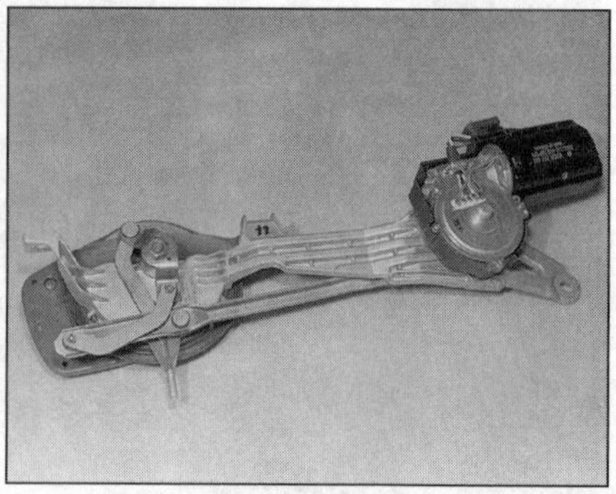
18.20b . . . and remove the motor and linkage assembly

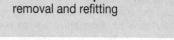

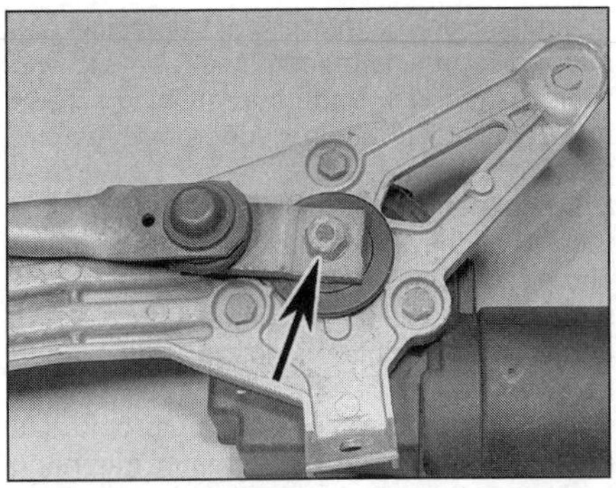

19.2 Undo the bellcrank arm retaining nut (arrowed)

bellcrank arm from the motor spindle **(see illustration)**.

3 Undo the three bolts and remove the motor from the linkage bracket.

4 Additionally, on the panoramic wiper assembly, the linkage arm can be removed from the wiper arm assembly after undoing the nut at the other end **(see illustration)**.

Refitting

5 Refitting is the reverse sequence to removal, but with the linkage and motor in the parked position, the bellcrank and linkage must be parallel with each other as the bellcrank is fitted to the motor spindle **(see illustration)**.

20 Windscreen washer system - removal, refitting and adjustment

1 The windscreen washer system consists of a water reservoir located at the front right-hand side of the engine compartment, an electric pump attached to the reservoir and an electrically heated triple nozzle jet located in the centre of the bonnet, or two double nozzle jets located on each side of the bonnet, on cars equipped with the panoramic windscreen wiper. A water level indicator is also fitted to the reservoir on later models to inform the driver of low water supply in the reservoir.

Removal

2 To remove the reservoir, disconnect the wiring and water hoses at the pump and also the wiring plug at the water level indicator, if fitted.

3 Unscrew the large plastic cap nut, then lift the reservoir up and out of its location.

4 The pump is a push fit in the reservoir and can be removed by carefully prising it out. The pump is a sealed unit and cannot be repaired.

5 A check valve is located in the water hose alongside the right-hand front suspension strut turret. The valve can be removed after detaching the hoses.

6 To remove the jets, disconnect the water hose and electrical connection from within the aperture on the inside of the bonnet.

7 Push the jet upwards and withdraw it from the bonnet.

Refitting and adjustment

8 Refitting all the components is the reverse sequence to removal.

9 Adjust the nozzles using a pin, so that the water contacts the windscreen centrally - allow for the downforce created by the airflow over the bonnet and windscreen, when the car is in forward motion.

21 Horns - removal and refitting

Removal

1 The twin horns are attached to the support strut in front of the radiator, accessible with the bonnet open.

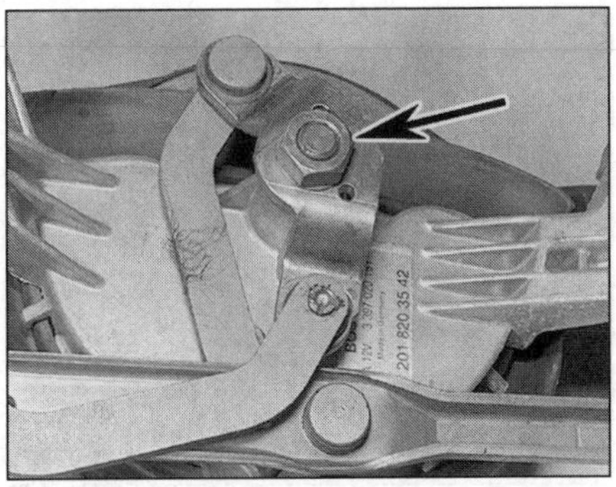

19.4 Linkage arm retaining nut (arrowed)

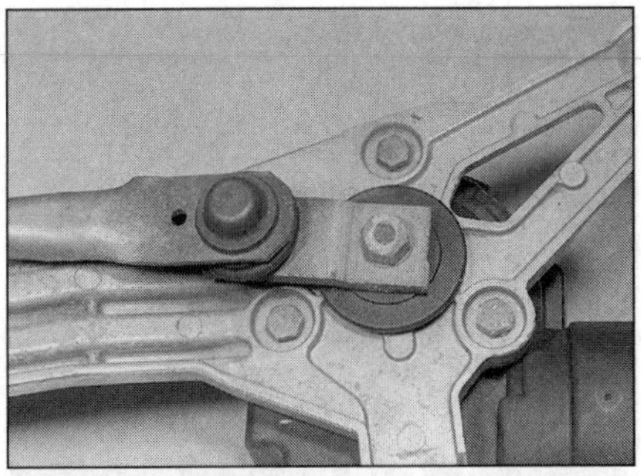

19.5 The bellcrank arm and linkage arm must be parallel and in line when refitting the bellcrank arm

21.2 Horn wiring terminal screws (arrowed)

2 To remove the horns, disconnect the battery negative terminal, then unscrew the wiring terminal screws on each horn. Make a note of the wiring locations on each terminal **(see illustration)**.

3 Undo the horn bracket attachments and remove the horns.

Refitting

4 Refitting is the reverse sequence to removal.

22 Audio equipment - removal and refitting

Removal

1 Disconnect the battery negative terminal.

2 According to the type of equipment fitted, the method of removal varies slightly. If there are two small holes vertically in line on each side of the radio faceplate, then the unit has a DIN standard attachment and is removed by inserting two special hooked removal tools into these holes to release the internal catches. These special tools may. be purchased from radio accessory outlets, or can be made up from suitable wire rod such as welding rod.

3 Insert the removal tools into the slots until they can be felt to engage with the catches. Now pull the unit forward out of its aperture **(see illustration)**.

4 Disconnect the electrical connections and aerial lead at the rear of the radio **(see illustration)** and push the retaining clips

22.3 Removing the radio with the removal tools

22.4 Disconnect the wiring at the rear of the radio

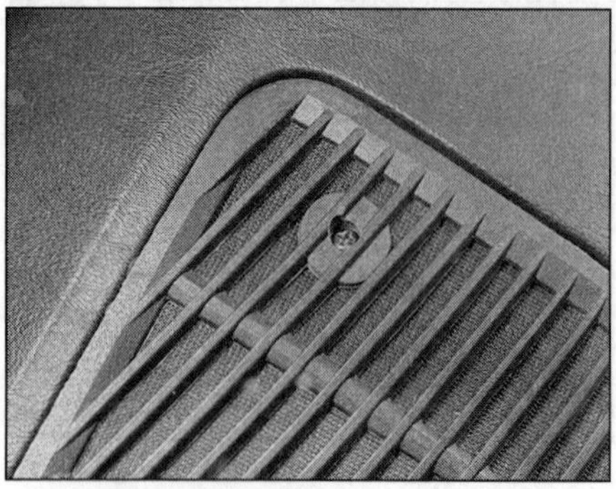

23.2 Speaker grille retaining screw

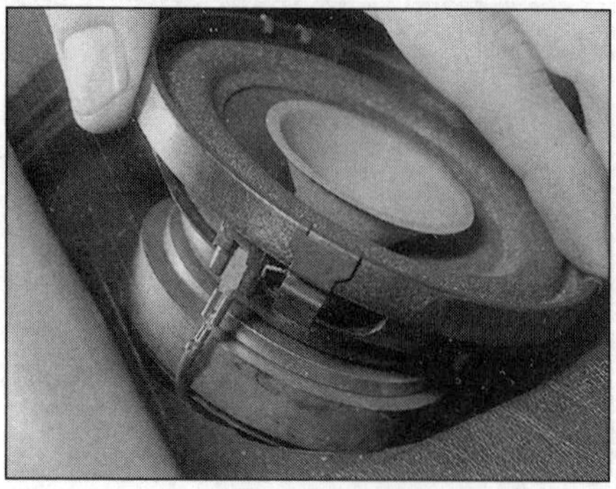

23.3 Speaker removal

inward to release the removal tools. Remove the unit from the car.

5 To refit, push the radio cassette player back into its aperture until the clips engage.

6 If the radio faceplate does not have holes for removal tools, then the unit is secured in position by means of the ashtray holder mountings.

7 Open the ashtray and undo the screws at the top of the ashtray holder.

8 Lower the ashtray and push the radio out of its aperture.

9 Disconnect the electrical connections and aerial lead at the rear and remove the radio from the car.

Refitting

10 Refitting is the reverse sequence to removal.

23 Front and rear speakers - removal and refitting

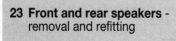

Front speakers

1 The front speakers are located at each side of the facia at the top.

2 Undo the two screws and remove the speaker grille **(see illustration)**.

3 Using a plastic wedge, carefully ease the speaker out of its location **(see illustration)**.

4 Disconnect the wiring and remove the speaker.

5 Refitting is the reverse sequence to removal. If two colour marks are visible on the speaker rim, these should point towards the rear of the car when the speaker is fitted.

Rear speakers

6 The rear speakers are located on each side of the rear parcel shelf.

7 Using a short screwdriver, undo the four screws and remove the speaker grille.

8 Undo the speaker retaining screws and withdraw the speaker from the parcel shelf.

9 Disconnect the wiring and remove the speaker.

10 Refitting is the reverse sequence to removal.

24 Radio aerial - removal and refitting

Removal

1 Disconnect the battery negative terminal.

2 Remove the inner trim covering on the left-hand side of the luggage compartment.

3 Disconnect the aerial lead, wiring connections and earth strap from the aerial motor.

4 Undo the retaining bolts and withdraw the unit from inside the luggage compartment.

Refitting

5 Refitting is the reverse sequence to removal.

25 Cruise control system components - removal and refitting

Electronic control unit (ECU)

Removal

1 The cruise control ECU is located behind the driver's side lower facia panel.

2 Remove the headlight beam adjustment switch, as described earlier in this Chapter.

3 Remove the driver's side lower facia panel as described in Chapter 11.

4 Disconnect the wiring connector(s) then undo the retaining screws and remove the ECU from underneath the facia.

Refitting

5 Refitting is the reverse of removal. On completion check the operation of the cruise control system.

Cruise control actuator

Removal

6 The cruise control actuator is mounted onto the side of the cylinder block.

7 On most models it will be necessary to remove the air cleaner housing to gain access to the actuator. If necessary, to further improve access, firmly apply the parking brake then jack up the front of the vehicle and support it on axle stands (see "*Jacking and vehicle support*"). Undo the retaining screws and remove the engine undercover (where fitted).

8 Disconnect the battery negative terminal then trace the wiring back from the actuator and disconnect it at the wiring connector.

9 Carefully unclip the link rod from the actuator balljoint using a flat-bladed screwdriver.

10 Slacken and remove the nuts/bolts (as applicable) securing the actuator mounting bracket to the cylinder block and remove the assembly from the engine compartment.

11 If necessary, undo the bolts securing the actuator to its mounting bracket noting the correct fitted locations of the rubber mountings and spacers.

Refitting

12 Refitting is the reverse of removal ensuring that the actuator mounting rubbers are in good condition. If necessary, the length of the link rod can be adjusted by slackening the locknut and screwing the balljoint onto/off the rod. Once the length of the rod is correct connect it to the actuator and securely tighten the locknut.

System operating switch

13 The switch is part of the steering column combination switch. Refer to Section 5 for removal and refitting details The cruise control switch can be unclipped from the main switch once it has been removed.

Speed sensor

Removal

14 The speed sensor is mounted onto the rear of the speedometer.

15 To gain access to the sensor remove the instrument panel as described in Section 8.

16 Undo the retaining screw and remove the sensor from the rear of the speedometer.

Refitting

17 Refitting is the reverse of removal.

26 Anti-theft alarm system - general information

Note: *This information is applicable only to the anti-theft alarm system fitted by Mercedes-Benz as standard equipment.*

Some models in the range are fitted with an anti-theft alarm system as standard equipment. The alarm has switches on all the doors (including the boot lid/tailgate), the bonnet, the audio unit and the ignition switch and also a tilt switch which is sensitive to shocks. If the boot lid/tailgate, bonnet or either of the doors are opened or the ignition switch or audio unit are switched on whilst the alarm is set, or if the tilt switch senses the vehicle is being tampered with, the alarm horn will sound and the hazard warning lights/headlights will flash. The alarm also has an immobiliser function which makes the ignition/starter (as applicable) system inoperable whilst the alarm is triggered.

The alarm is set using the key in the front door lock or boot/tailgate lock; on later models the alarm is also set when the doors are locked using the remote central locking device. The LED on the centre console will flash to indicate that the alarm system is operational. **Note:** *On early (pre September 1987) models, the alarm will only be set if the main (rectangular) key is used, if the secondary (circular) key is used the doors will be locked but the alarm will not be set.*

Should the alarm system become faulty the vehicle should be taken to a Mercedes-Benz dealer for examination. They will have access to a special diagnostic tester which will quickly trace any fault present in the system.

27 Airbag system - general information and precautions

A driver's airbag was fitted as standard to some models in the range; on other models they were available as an optional extra. Models fitted with a driver's side airbag have the word AIRBAG or SRS-AIRBAG stamped on the airbag unit, which is fitted to the centre of the steering wheel. The airbag system comprises of the airbag unit (complete with a gas generator), the control unit (with an integral impact sensor) and a warning light in the instrument panel. On early models the system also incorporates a reserve power source and a voltage transformer.

The airbag system is triggered in the event of a heavy frontal impact above a predetermined force; depending on the point of impact. The airbag is inflated within milliseconds and forms a safety cushion between the driver and steering wheel. This prevents contact between the upper body and wheel/facia and therefore greatly reduces the risk of injury. The airbag then deflates almost immediately. The control unit also operates the front seat belt tensioner mechanisms at the same time as the airbag (see Chapter 11).

Every time the ignition is switched on, the airbag control unit performs a self-test. The self-test takes approximately 4 seconds and during this time the airbag warning light in the instrument panel is illuminated. After the self-test has been completed the warning light should go out. If the warning light fails to come on, remains illuminated after the initial period or comes on at any time when the vehicle is being driven, there is a fault in the airbag system. The vehicle should be taken to a Mercedes-Benz dealer for examination at the earliest possible opportunity.

Warning: Before carrying out any operations on the airbag system, disconnect the battery negative terminal. Peel back the carpet in the front passenger footwell then undo the retaining screws and remove the footrest panel from the floor. Locate the airbag system wiring test connector which is red in colour and disconnect it; this will disable the airbag system. When operations are complete, reconnect the test connector and make sure no one is inside the vehicle when the battery is reconnected.

Warning: Note that the airbag(s) must not be subjected to temperatures in excess of 100°C. When the airbag is removed, ensure that it is stored the correct way up to prevent possible inflation.

Warning: Do not allow any solvents or cleaning agents to contact the airbag assemblies. They must be cleaned using only a damp cloth.

Warning: The airbags and control unit are both sensitive to impact. If either is dropped or damaged they should be renewed.

Warning: Disconnect the airbag control unit wiring plug prior to using arc-welding equipment on the vehicle.

28 Airbag system components - removal and refitting

Note: *Refer to the warnings given in Section 27 before carrying out the following operations.*

1 Turn the ignition key to position '0', then disconnect the battery negative cable, and position it away from the terminal. Peel back the carpet in the front passenger footwell then undo the retaining screws and remove the footrest panel from the floor. Locate the airbag system wiring test connector which is red in colour and disconnect it; this will disable the airbag system.

Driver's side airbag

Removal

2 Slacken and remove the two airbag retaining screws from the rear of the steering wheel, rotating the wheel as necessary to gain access to the screws.

3 Return the steering wheel to the straight-ahead position then carefully lift the airbag assembly away from the steering wheel and disconnect the wiring connector from the rear of the unit. Note that the airbag must not be knocked or dropped and should be stored the correct way up with its padded surface uppermost.

Refitting

4 Ensure that the wiring connector is securely reconnected and seat the airbag unit centrally in the steering wheel, making sure the wire does not become trapped. Fit the retaining screws and tighten them to the specified torque setting, noting the left-hand retaining screw should be tightened first.

5 Reconnect the red test connector and refit the passenger footrest panel and fold down the carpet. Ensure no one is inside the vehicle and reconnect the battery. Turn on the ignition switch and check the operation of the airbag warning light, whilst turning the steering wheel from full left lock to full right lock.

Airbag control unit

6 Removal and refitting of the control unit should be entrusted to a Mercedes-Benz dealer. On refitting the control unit must be tested using special Mercedes-Benz diagnostic equipment to ensure that the system is operating correctly. For reference, the control unit is mounted underneath the front of the centre console.

Airbag wiring contact unit

Removal

7 Remove the steering wheel as described in Chapter 10.

8 Remove the headlight beam adjustment switch as described earlier in this Chapter.

9 Remove the driver's side lower facia panel as described in Chapter 11.

10 Trace the wiring back from the contact unit, freeing it from all the relevant retaining clips, and disconnect it from the main wiring harness.

11 Loosen the contact unit screws just sufficiently so that the unit is freed from the top of the steering column and can be removed; this will lock the contact unit in position and prevent it from being rotated whilst it is removed. **Note:** *Do not fully remove the retaining screws and dismantle the contact unit.*

Refitting

12 Prior to refitting, ensure that the contact unit is correctly centralised. This shouldn't be a problem if the retaining screws have not been disturbed. If there is any doubt about the unit position, screw the retaining screws fully into position in the contact unit and rotate the contact unit insert in a clockwise direction until resistance is felt. From this point, rotate the insert back through two to two and a half rotations until the fixing screws are aligned with the holes then unscrew the screws slightly to lock the unit in position.

13 Slide the contact ring into position, making sure its wiring is correctly routed, and engage the recess at the centre of the contact ring with the corresponding lug on the steering column. Ensure that the contact ring is correctly engaged with the column and securely tighten its retaining screws.

14 Reconnect the wiring connectors and refit the remaining components by reversing the removal sequence.

Key to symbols

- Bulb
- Switch
- Multiple contact switch (ganged)
- Fuse (F10)
- Resistor
- Variable resistor
- Connecting wires
- Item no. (7)
- Pump/motor
- Earth
- Gauge/meter
- Diode
- Line connector
- Solenoid actuator

Cross sectional area wire colour (0.75mm² black/yellow) — 0.75sw/ge —

Connections to other circuits (e.g. diagram 3/grid location B2. Direction of arrow denotes current flow. (3/B2)

Wire - permanent positive supply (double line)

Wire - permanent direct earth (thick line)

Wire - interconnecting (thin line)

Denote examples of standard terminal designation or connector contact no. (30, E3)

Earth locations

E1	Main earth (behind instrument cluster)
E2	Front right (at light unit)
E3	Front left wheel arch (ignition coil)
E4	Front roof light
E6	Rear left boot wheel arch
E7	Rear right boot wheel arch
E9	Front left (at light unit)
E10	Battery
E11	Engine
E12	Centre console
E14	Hydraulic unit bracket

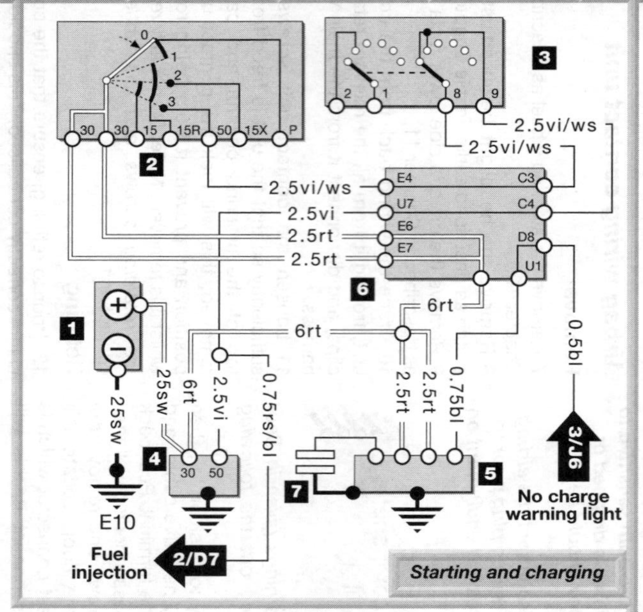

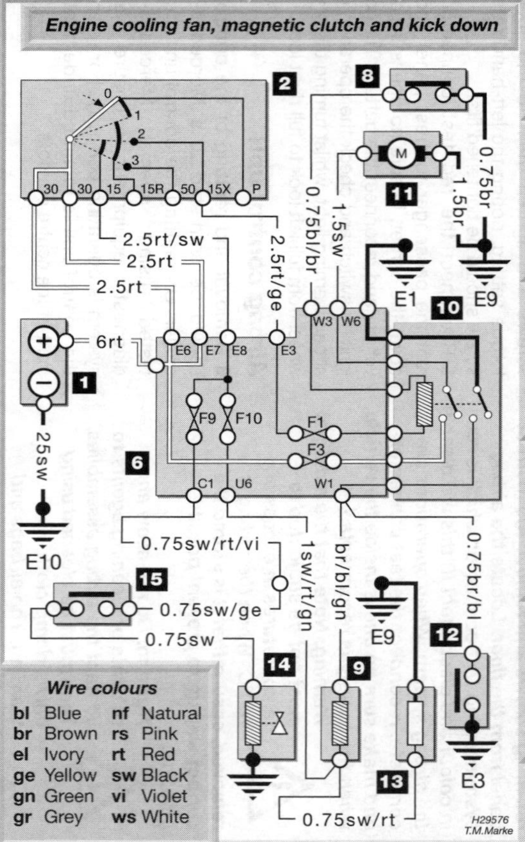

Wire colours

bl	Blue	nf	Natural
br	Brown	rs	Pink
el	Ivory	rt	Red
ge	Yellow	sw	Black
gn	Green	vi	Violet
gr	Grey	ws	White

Fuses

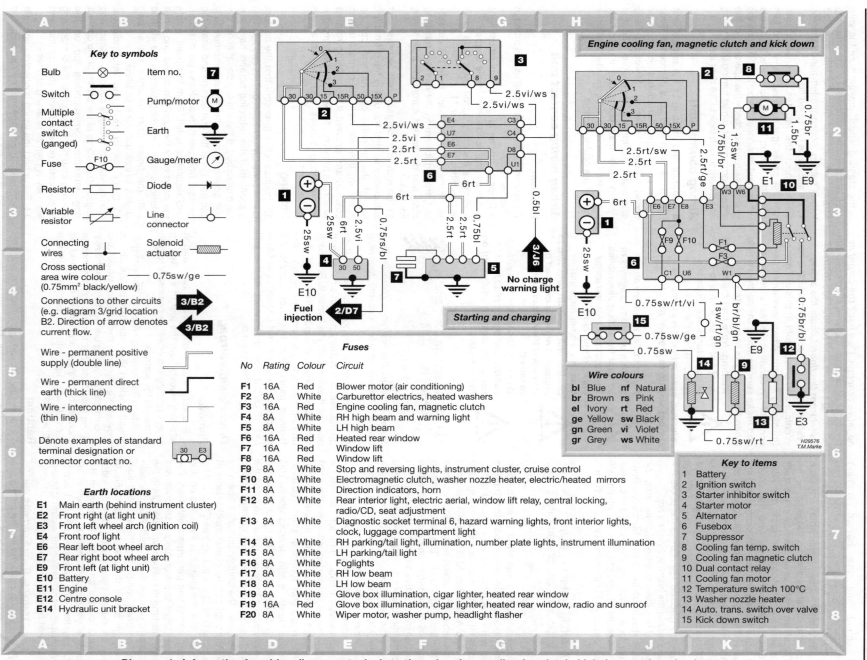

No	Rating	Colour	Circuit
F1	16A	Red	Blower motor (air conditioning)
F2	8A	White	Carburettor electrics, heated washers
F3	16A	Red	Engine cooling fan, magnetic clutch
F4	8A	White	RH high beam and warning light
F5	8A	White	LH high beam
F6	16A	Red	Heated rear window
F7	16A	Red	Window lift
F8	16A	Red	Window lift
F9	8A	White	Stop and reversing lights, instrument cluster, cruise control
F10	8A	White	Electromagnetic clutch, washer nozzle heater, electric/heated mirrors
F11	8A	White	Direction indicators, horn
F12	8A	White	Rear interior light, electric aerial, window lift relay, central locking, radio/CD, seat adjustment
F13	8A	White	Diagnostic socket terminal 6, hazard warning lights, front interior lights, clock, luggage compartment light
F14	8A	White	RH parking/tail light, illumination, number plate lights, instrument illumination
F15	8A	White	LH parking/tail light
F16	8A	White	Foglights
F17	8A	White	RH low beam
F18	8A	White	LH low beam
F19	8A	White	Glove box illumination, cigar lighter, heated rear window
F19	16A	Red	Glove box illumination, cigar lighter, heated rear window, radio and sunroof
F20	8A	White	Wiper motor, washer pump, headlight flasher

Key to items

1. Battery
2. Ignition switch
3. Starter inhibitor switch
4. Starter motor
5. Alternator
6. Fusebox
7. Suppressor
8. Cooling fan temp. switch
9. Cooling fan magnetic clutch
10. Dual contact relay
11. Cooling fan motor
12. Temperature switch 100°C
13. Washer nozzle heater
14. Auto. trans. switch over valve
15. Kick down switch

Diagram 1 : Information for wiring diagrams, typical starting, charging, cooling fan clutch, kick down and washer heater

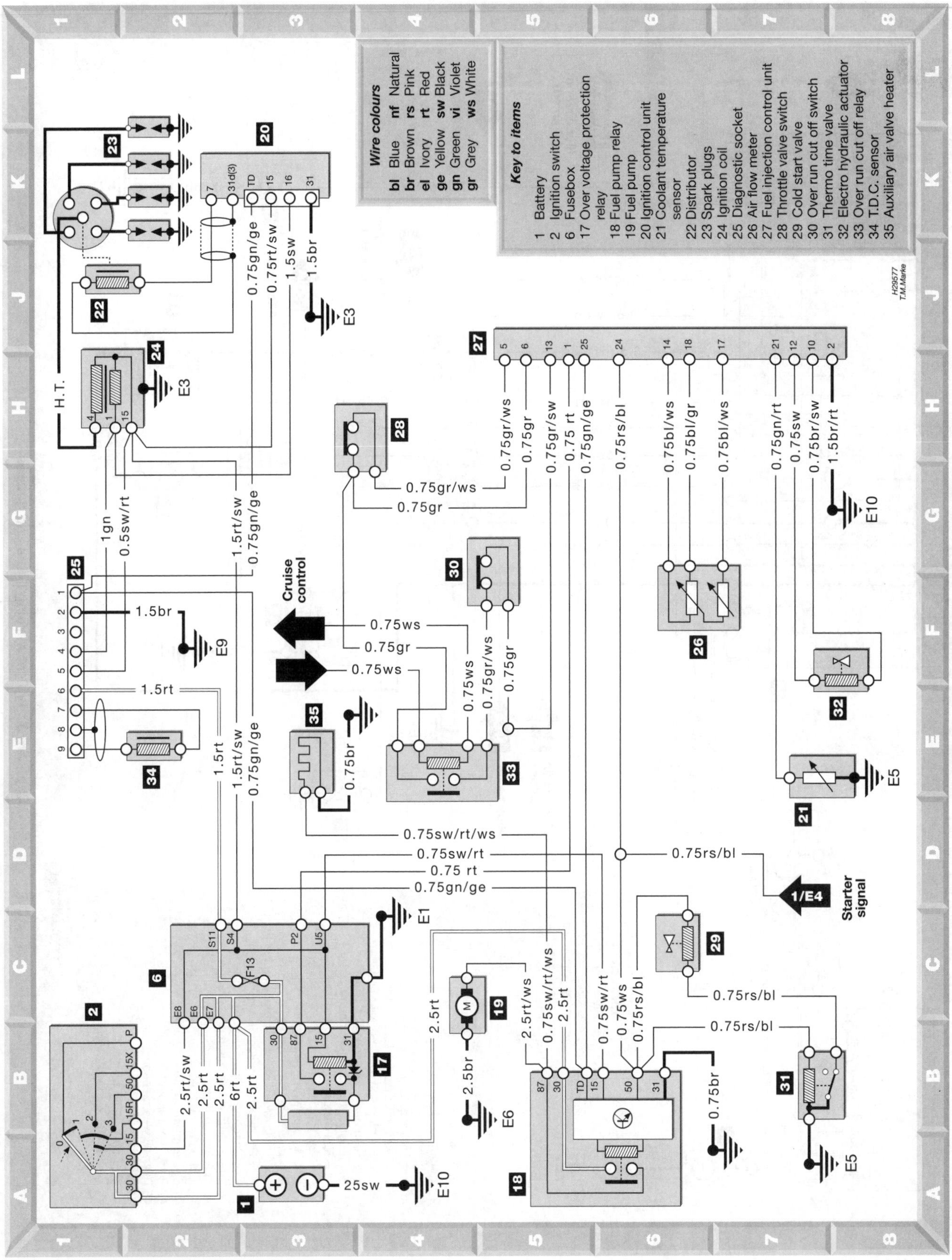

Wire colours
bl Blue
br Brown
el Ivory
ge Yellow
gn Green
gr Grey
nf Natural
rs Pink
rt Red
sw Black
vi Violet
ws White
Key to items
1 Battery
2 Ignition switch
6 Fusebox
17 Over voltage protection relay
18 Fuel pump relay
19 Fuel pump
20 Ignition control unit
21 Coolant temperature sensor
22 Distributor
23 Spark plugs
24 Ignition coil
25 Diagnostic socket
26 Air flow meter
27 Fuel injection control unit
28 Throttle valve switch
29 Cold start valve
30 Over run cut off switch
31 Thermo time valve
32 Electro hydraulic actuator
33 Over run cut off relay
34 T.D.C. sensor
35 Auxiliary air valve heater
Cruise control
Starter signal
1/E4
H.T.
H29577
T.M.Marke

Diagram 2 : Typical engine management system

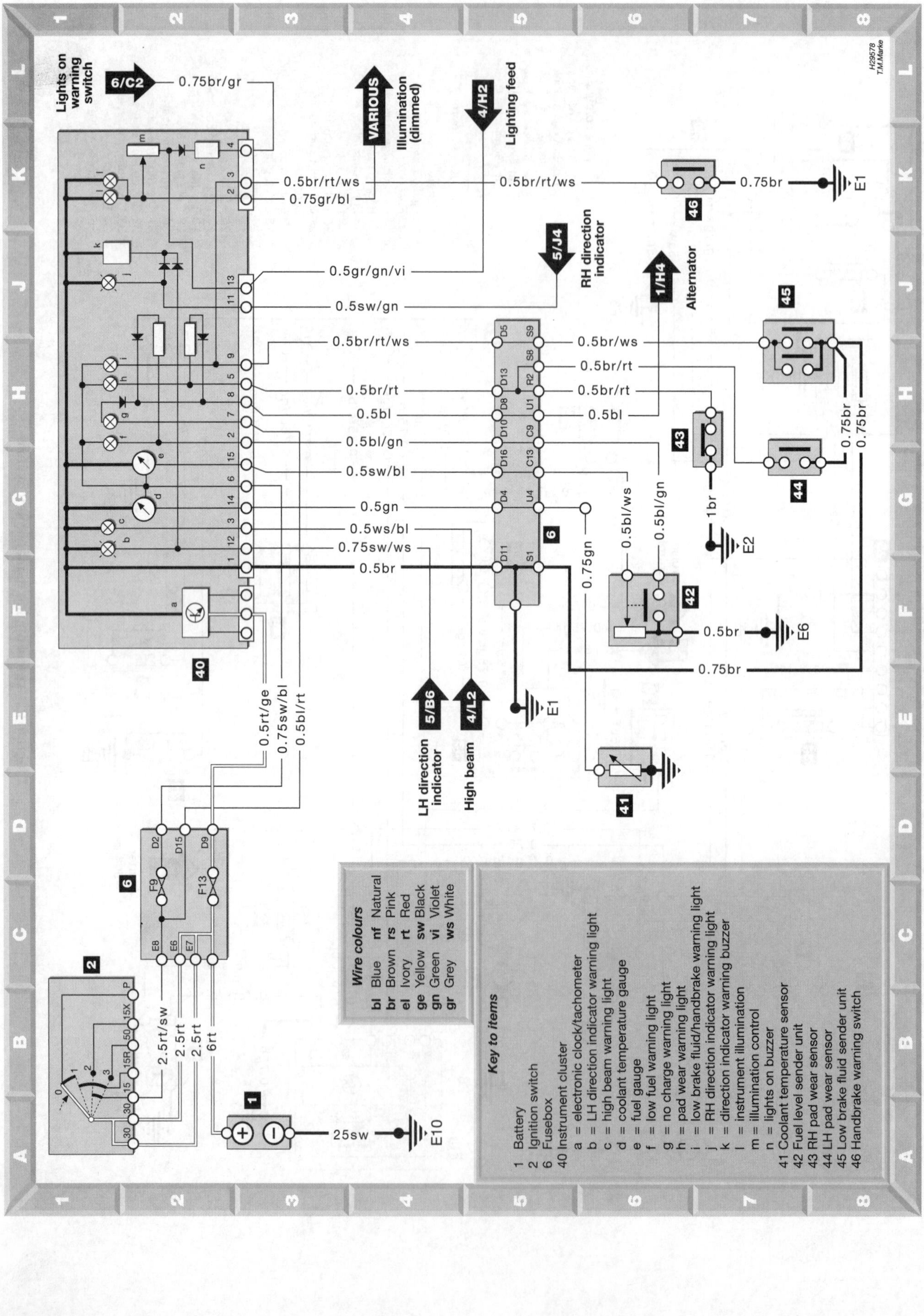
Lights on warning switch
6/C2
0.75br/gr
VARIOUS
Illumination (dimmed)
4/H2
Lighting feed
5/J4
RH direction indicator
1/H4
Alternator
H29578
T.M.Marke
0.5br/rt/ws
0.75gr/bl
0.5br/rt/ws
0.75br
E1
0.5gr/gn/vi
0.5sw/gn
0.5br/rt/ws
0.5br/ws
0.5br/rt
0.5br/rt
0.5br/rt
0.5bl
0.5bl
0.5bl/gn
0.5sw/bl
0.5gn
0.5ws/bl
0.75sw/ws
0.5br
0.75gn
0.5bl/ws
0.5bl/gn
1br
E2
0.75br
0.75br
0.5br
E6
0.75br
E1
0.5rt/ge
0.75sw/bl
0.5bl/rt
5/B6
LH direction indicator
4/L2
High beam
2.5rt/sw
2.5rt
2.5rt
6rt
25sw
E10
Wire colours
bl Blue
br Brown
el Ivory
ge Yellow
gn Green
gr Grey
nf Natural
rs Pink
rt Red
sw Black
vi Violet
ws White
Key to items
1 Battery
2 Ignition switch
6 Fusebox
40 Instrument cluster
a = electronic clock/tachometer
b = LH direction indicator warning light
c = high beam warning light
d = coolant temperature gauge
e = fuel gauge
f = low fuel warning light
g = no charge warning light
h = pad wear warning light
i = low brake fluid/handbrake warning light
j = RH direction indicator warning light
k = direction indicator warning buzzer
l = instrument illumination
m = illumination control
n = lights on buzzer
41 Coolant temperature sensor
42 Fuel level sender unit
43 RH pad wear sensor
44 LH pad wear sensor
45 Low brake fluid sender unit
46 Handbrake warning switch

Diagram 3 : Typical warning lights and gauges

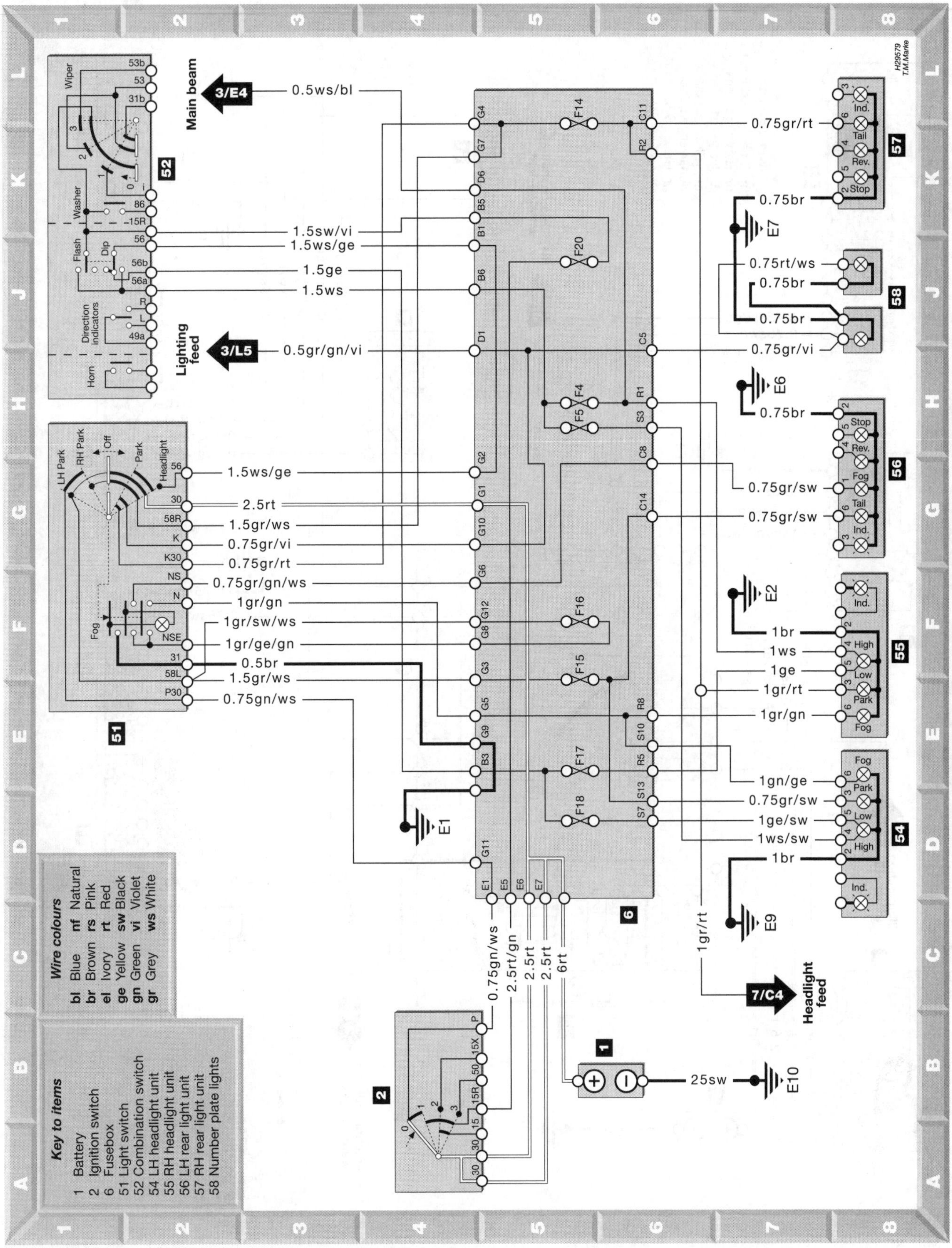

Diagram 4 : Typical exterior lighting - side, tail, fog and headlights

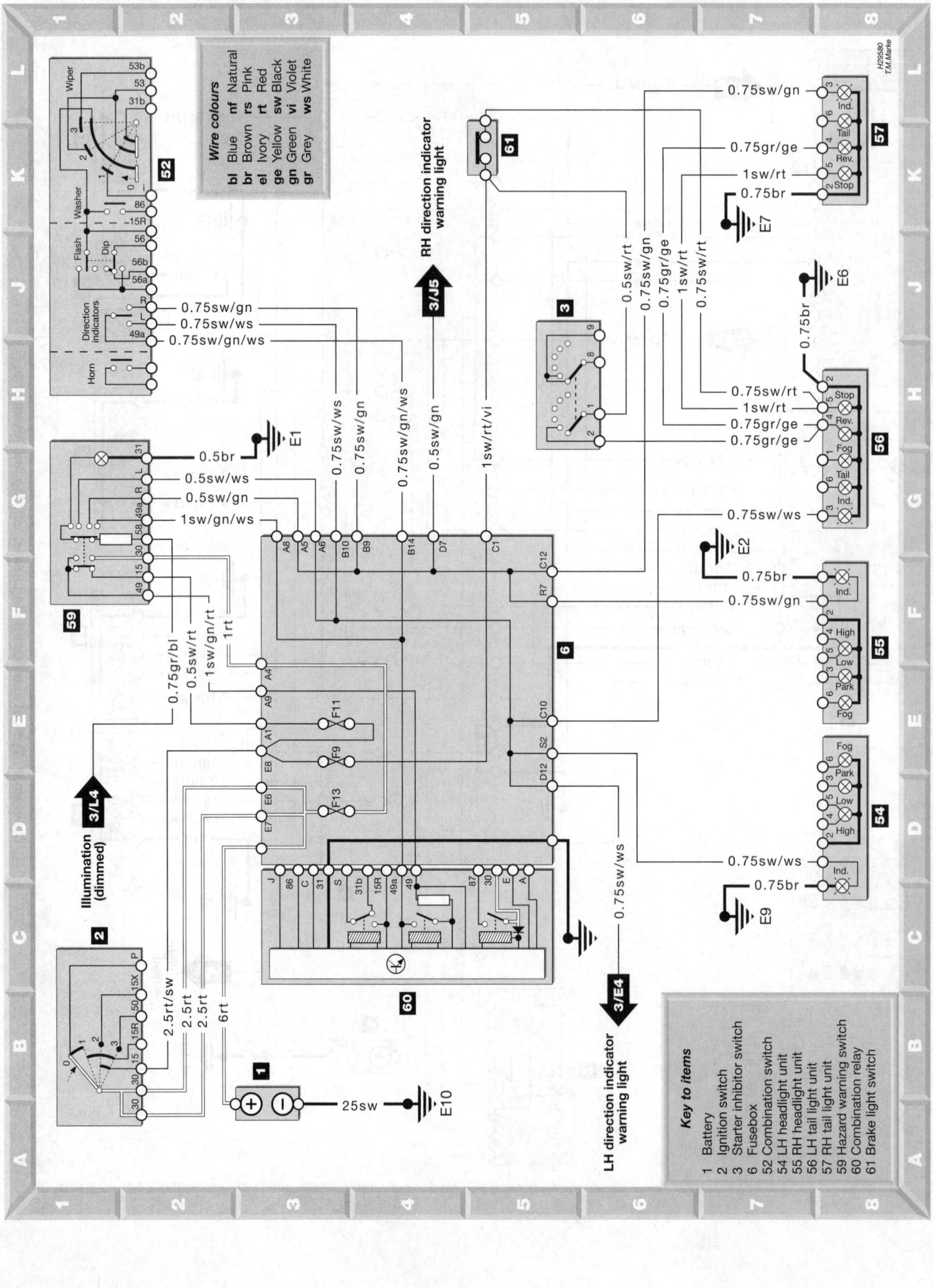

Diagram 5 : Typical exterior lighting continued - direction indicators, hazard warning, stop and reversing lights

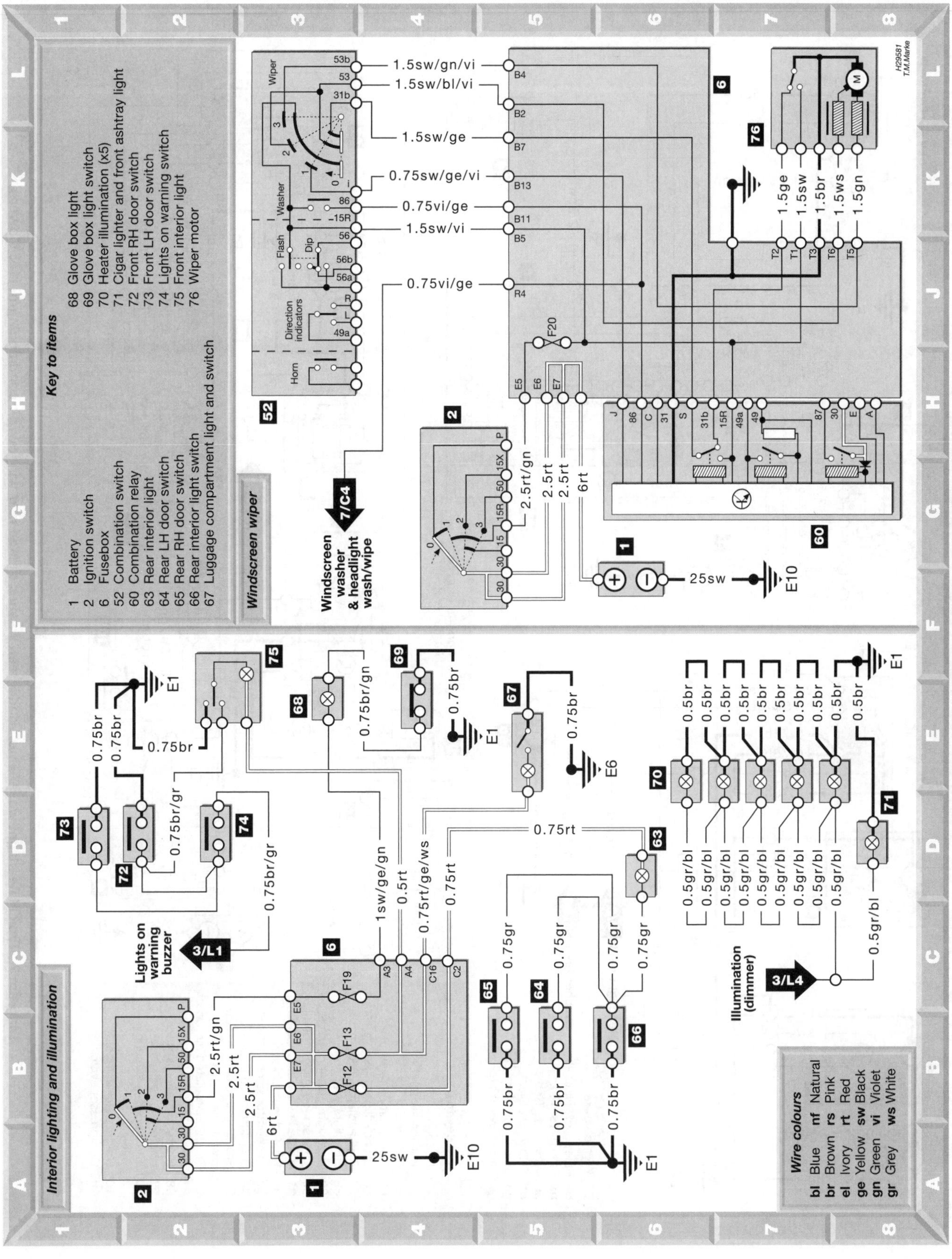

Diagram 6 : Typical interior lighting and windscreen wiper

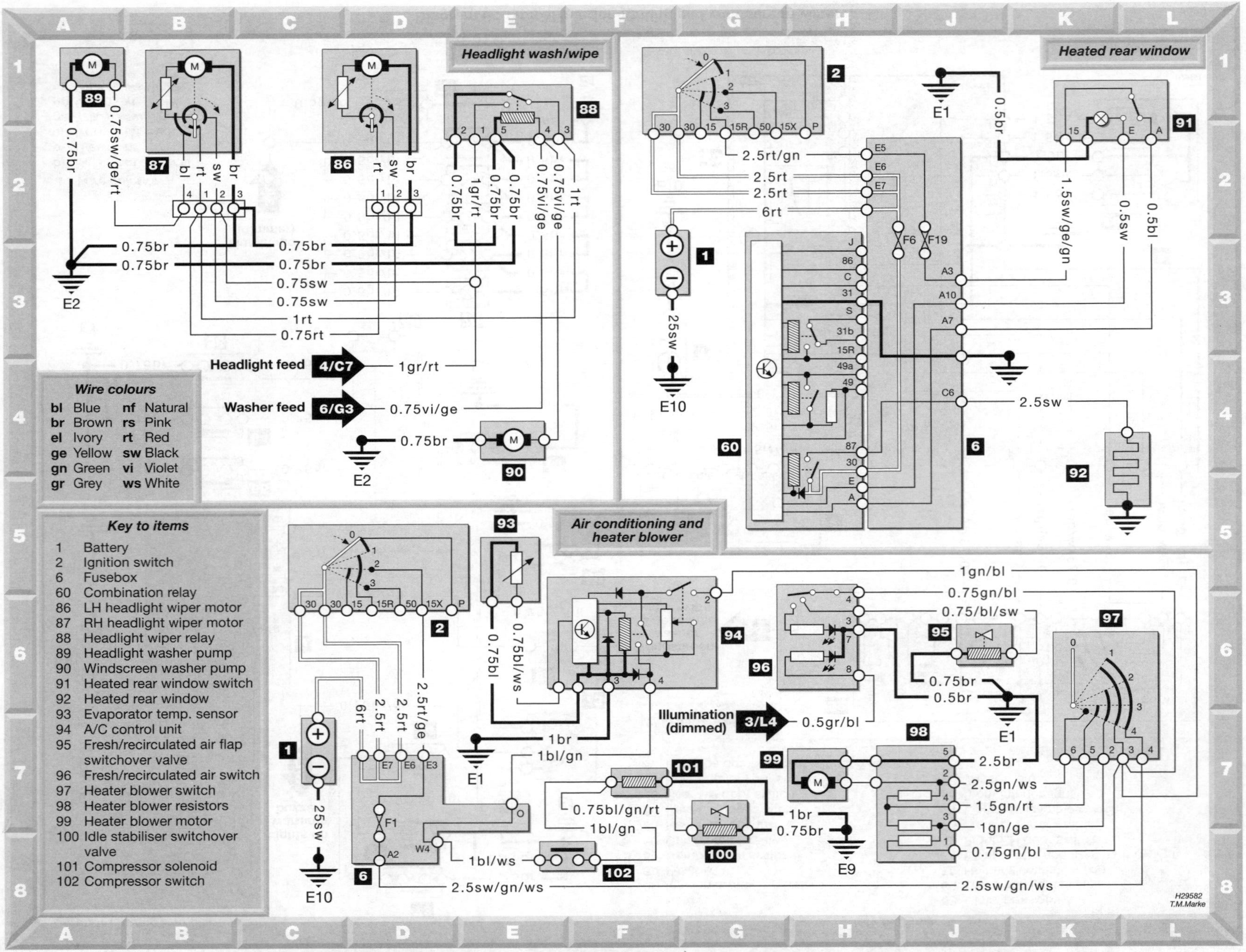

Wire colours

bl	Blue	nf	Natural
br	Brown	rs	Pink
el	Ivory	rt	Red
ge	Yellow	sw	Black
gn	Green	vi	Violet
gr	Grey	ws	White

Key to items

1 Battery
2 Ignition switch
6 Fusebox
60 Combination relay
86 LH headlight wiper motor
87 RH headlight wiper motor
88 Headlight wiper relay
89 Headlight washer pump
90 Windscreen washer pump
91 Heated rear window switch
92 Heated rear window
93 Evaporator temp. sensor
94 A/C control unit
95 Fresh/recirculated air flap switchover valve
96 Fresh/recirculated air switch
97 Heater blower switch
98 Heater blower resistors
99 Heater blower motor
100 Idle stabiliser switchover valve
101 Compressor solenoid
102 Compressor switch

Diagram 7 : Typical headlight wash/wipe, windscreen washer, heated rear window, air conditioning/heater blower

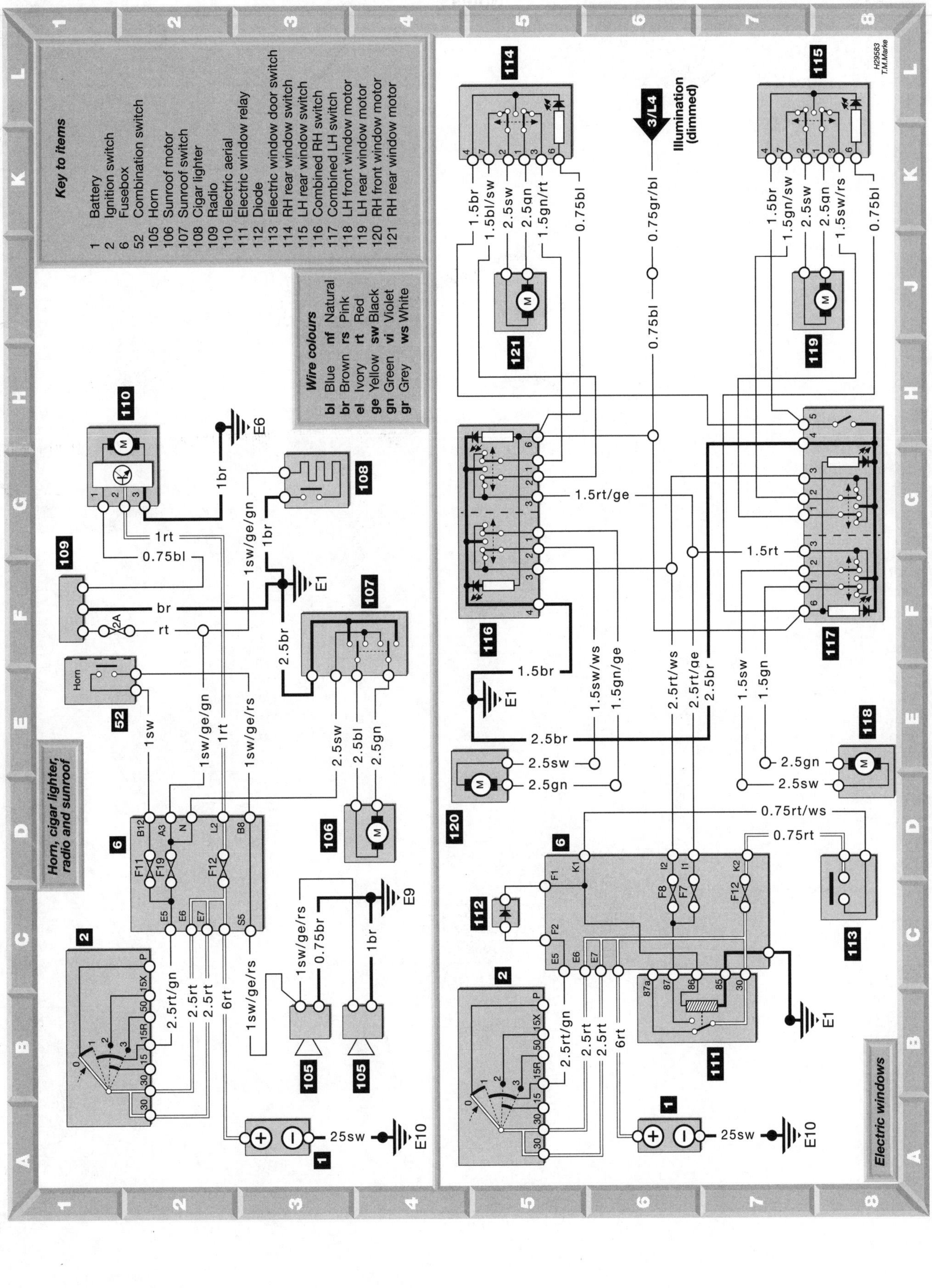

Diagram 8 : Typical horn, cigar lighter, radio, sunroof and electric windows

Notes

Dimensions and Weights .... REF•1
Conversion Factors .... REF•2
Buying Spare Parts .... REF•3
Vehicle Identification .... REF•3
General Repair Procedures .... REF•4
Jacking and Vehicle Support .... REF•5
Radio/cassette unit Anti-theft System .... REF•5
Tools and Working Facilities .... REF•6
MOT Test Checks .... REF•8
Fault Finding .... REF•12
Glossary of Technical Terms .... REF•20
Index .... REF•24

Dimensions and weights

Note: *All figures are approximate, and may vary according to model. Refer to manufacturer's data for exact figures.*

Dimensions

Overall length .... 4448 mm
Overall width .... 1690 mm
Overall height (unladen) .... 1375 mm
Wheelbase .... 2665 mm
Turning circle .... 10.6 m

Weights

Kerb weight:*
Petrol engine models:
1.8 litre models .... 1170 kg
2.0 litre models .... 1180 kg
2.3 litre models .... 1240 kg
2.6 litre modes .... 1290 kg
Diesel engine models:
2.0 litre models .... 1180 kg
2.5 litre non-turbo models .... 1250 kg
2.5 litre turbo models .... 1300 kg
Maximum gross vehicle weight:*
Petrol engine models:
1.8 litre models .... 1670 kg
2.0 litre models .... 1680 kg
2.3 litre models .... 1730 kg
2.6 litre modes .... 1740 kg
Diesel engine models:
2.0 litre models .... 1680 kg
2.5 litre non-turbo models .... 1750 kg
2.5 litre turbo models .... 1800 kg
**Depending on model and specification*

Length (distance)

Inches (in)	x 25.4	= Millimetres (mm)	x 0.0394	=	Inches (in)
Feet (ft)	x 0.305	= Metres (m)	x 3.281	=	Feet (ft)
Miles	x 1.609	= Kilometres (km)	x 0.621	=	Miles

Volume (capacity)

Cubic inches (cu in; in^3)	x 16.387	= Cubic centimetres (cc; cm^3)	x 0.061	=	Cubic inches (cu in; in^3)
Imperial pints (Imp pt)	x 0.568	= Litres (l)	x 1.76	=	Imperial pints (Imp pt)
Imperial quarts (Imp qt)	x 1.137	= Litres (l)	x 0.88	=	Imperial quarts (Imp qt)
Imperial quarts (Imp qt)	x 1.201	= US quarts (US qt)	x 0.833	=	Imperial quarts (Imp qt)
US quarts (US qt)	x 0.946	= Litres (l)	x 1.057	=	US quarts (US qt)
Imperial gallons (Imp gal)	x 4.546	= Litres (l)	x 0.22	=	Imperial gallons (Imp gal)
Imperial gallons (Imp gal)	x 1.201	= US gallons (US gal)	x 0.833	=	Imperial gallons (Imp gal)
US gallons (US gal)	x 3.785	= Litres (l)	x 0.264	=	US gallons (US gal)

Mass (weight)

Ounces (oz)	x 28.35	= Grams (g)	x 0.035	=	Ounces (oz)
Pounds (lb)	x 0.454	= Kilograms (kg)	x 2.205	=	Pounds (lb)

Force

Ounces-force (ozf; oz)	x 0.278	= Newtons (N)	x 3.6	=	Ounces-force (ozf; oz)
Pounds-force (lbf; lb)	x 4.448	= Newtons (N)	x 0.225	=	Pounds-force (lbf; lb)
Newtons (N)	x 0.1	= Kilograms-force (kgf; kg)	x 9.81	=	Newtons (N)

Pressure

Pounds-force per square inch (psi; lbf/in^2; lb/in^2)	x 0.070	= Kilograms-force per square centimetre (kgf/cm^2; kg/cm^2)	x 14.223	=	Pounds-force per square inch (psi; lbf/in^2; lb/in^2)
Pounds-force per square inch (psi; lbf/in^2; lb/in^2)	x 0.068	= Atmospheres (atm)	x 14.696	=	Pounds-force per square inch (psi; lbf/in^2; lb/in^2)
Pounds-force per square inch (psi; lbf/in^2; lb/in^2)	x 0.069	= Bars	x 14.5	=	Pounds-force per square inch (psi; lbf/in^2; lb/in^2)
Pounds-force per square inch (psi; lbf/in^2; lb/in^2)	x 6.895	= Kilopascals (kPa)	x 0.145	=	Pounds-force per square inch (psi; lbf/in^2; lb/in^2)
Kilopascals (kPa)	x 0.01	= Kilograms-force per square centimetre (kgf/cm^2; kg/cm^2)	x 98.1	=	Kilopascals (kPa)
Millibar (mbar)	x 100	= Pascals (Pa)	x 0.01	=	Millibar (mbar)
Millibar (mbar)	x 0.0145	= Pounds-force per square inch (psi; lbf/in^2; lb/in^2)	x 68.947	=	Millibar (mbar)
Millibar (mbar)	x 0.75	= Millimetres of mercury (mmHg)	x 1.333	=	Millibar (mbar)
Millibar (mbar)	x 0.401	= Inches of water (inH_2O)	x 2.491	=	Millibar (mbar)
Millimetres of mercury (mmHg)	x 0.535	= Inches of water (inH_2O)	x 1.868	=	Millimetres of mercury (mmHg)
Inches of water (inH_2O)	x 0.036	= Pounds-force per square inch (psi; lbf/in^2; lb/in^2)	x 27.68	=	Inches of water (inH_2O)

Torque (moment of force)

Pounds-force inches (lbf in; lb in)	x 1.152	= Kilograms-force centimetre (kgf cm; kg cm)	x 0.868	=	Pounds-force inches (lbf in; lb in)
Pounds-force inches (lbf in; lb in)	x 0.113	= Newton metres (Nm)	x 8.85	=	Pounds-force inches (lbf in; lb in)
Pounds-force inches (lbf in; lb in)	x 0.083	= Pounds-force feet (lbf ft; lb ft)	x 12	=	Pounds-force inches (lbf in; lb in)
Pounds-force feet (lbf ft; lb ft)	x 0.138	= Kilograms-force metres (kgf m; kg m)	x 7.233	=	Pounds-force feet (lbf ft; lb ft)
Pounds-force feet (lbf ft; lb ft)	x 1.356	= Newton metres (Nm)	x 0.738	=	Pounds-force feet (lbf ft; lb ft)
Newton metres (Nm)	x 0.102	= Kilograms-force metres (kgf m; kg m)	x 9.804	=	Newton metres (Nm)

Power

Horsepower (hp)	x 745.7	= Watts (W)	x 0.0013	=	Horsepower (hp)

Velocity (speed)

Miles per hour (miles/hr; mph)	x 1.609	= Kilometres per hour (km/hr; kph)	x 0.621	=	Miles per hour (miles/hr; mph)

Fuel consumption*

Miles per gallon (mpg)	x 0.354	= Kilometres per litre (km/l)	x 2.825	=	Miles per gallon (mpg)

Temperature

Degrees Fahrenheit = (°C x 1.8) + 32

Degrees Celsius (Degrees Centigrade; °C) = (°F - 32) x 0.56

** It is common practice to convert from miles per gallon (mpg) to litres/100 kilometres (l/100km), where mpg x l/100 km = 282*

Buying spare parts

Spare parts are available from many sources, including maker's appointed garages, accessory shops, and motor factors. To be sure of obtaining the correct parts, it will sometimes be necessary to quote the vehicle identification number. If possible, it can also be useful to take the old parts along for positive identification. Items such as starter motors and alternators may be available under a service exchange scheme - any parts returned should be clean.

Our advice regarding spare parts is as follows.

Officially appointed garages

This is the best source of parts which are peculiar to your car, and which are not otherwise generally available (eg, badges, interior trim, certain body panels, etc). It is also the only place at which you should buy parts if the vehicle is still under warranty.

Accessory shops

These are very good places to buy materials and components needed for the maintenance of your car (oil, air and fuel filters, light bulbs, drivebelts, greases, brake pads, touch-up paint, etc). Components of this nature sold by a reputable shop are usually of the same standard as those used by the car manufacturer.

Besides components, these shops also sell tools and general accessories, usually have convenient opening hours, charge lower prices, and can often be found close to home. Some accessory shops have parts counters where components needed for almost any repair job can be purchased or ordered.

Motor factors

Good factors will stock all the more important components which wear out comparatively quickly, and can sometimes supply individual components needed for the overhaul of a larger assembly (eg, brake seals and hydraulic parts, bearing shells, pistons, valves). They may also handle work such as cylinder block reboring, crankshaft regrinding, etc.

Tyre and exhaust specialists

These outlets may be independent, or members of a local or national chain. They frequently offer competitive prices when compared with a main dealer or local garage, but it will pay to obtain several quotes before making a decision. When researching prices, also ask what "extras" may be added - for instance fitting a new valve and balancing the wheel are both commonly charged on top of the price of a new tyre.

Other sources

Beware of parts or materials obtained from market stalls, car boot sales or similar outlets. Such items are not invariably sub-standard, but there is little chance of compensation if they do prove unsatisfactory. in the case of safety-critical components such as brake pads, there is the risk not only of financial loss, but also of an accident causing injury or death.

Second-hand components or assemblies obtained from a car breaker can be a good buy in some circumstances, but this sort of purchase is best made by the experienced DIY mechanic.

Vehicle identification

Modifications are a continuing and unpublicised process in vehicle manufacture, quite apart from major model changes. Spare parts manuals and lists are compiled upon a numerical basis, the individual vehicle identification numbers being essential to correct identification of the component concerned.

When ordering spare parts, always give as much information as possible. Quote the car model, year of manufacture and registration, chassis and engine numbers as appropriate.

The *Vehicle Identification Number (VIN)* plate is riveted to the bonnet crossmember and is visible once the bonnet has been opened. The vehicle identification (chassis) number is also stamped onto the top of the right-hand front suspension mounting turret **(see illustration)**.

The *body number and paint code* are marked on a coloured plate which is also attached to the bonnet crossmember where it is situated next to the VIN plate **(see illustration)**.

The *engine number* is either stamped onto the rear of the right-hand face of the cylinder block or onto the front of the left-hand face of the cylinder block, depending on engine type.

The chassis number is stamped on the right hand suspension strut turret

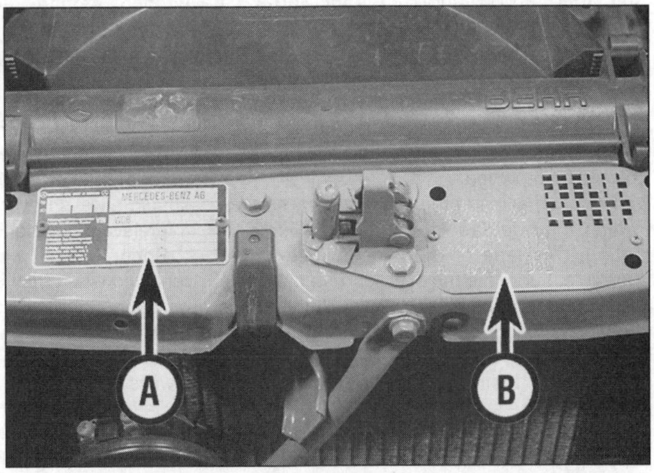

Vehicle Identification Number (VIN) plate (A) and body number and paint code (B)

General repair procedures

Whenever servicing, repair or overhaul work is carried out on the car or its components, it is necessary to observe the following procedures and instructions. This will assist in carrying out the operation efficiently and to a professional standard of workmanship.

Joint mating faces and gaskets

When separating components at their mating faces, never insert screwdrivers or similar implements into the joint between the faces in order to prise them apart. This can cause severe damage which results in oil leaks, coolant leaks, etc upon reassembly. Separation is usually achieved by tapping along the joint with a soft-faced hammer in order to break the seal. However, note that this method may not be suitable where dowels are used for component location.

Where a gasket is used between the mating faces of two components, ensure that it is renewed on reassembly, and fit it dry unless otherwise stated in the repair procedure. Make sure that the mating faces are clean and dry, with all traces of old gasket removed. When cleaning a joint face, use a tool which is not likely to score or damage the face, and remove any burrs or nicks with an oilstone or fine file.

Make sure that tapped holes are cleaned with a pipe cleaner, and keep them free of jointing compound, if this is being used, unless specifically instructed otherwise.

Ensure that all orifices, channels or pipes are clear, and blow through them, preferably using compressed air.

Oil seals

Oil seals can be removed by levering them out with a wide flat-bladed screwdriver or similar tool. Alternatively, a number of self-tapping screws may be screwed into the seal, and these used as a purchase for pliers or similar in order to pull the seal free.

Whenever an oil seal is removed from its working location, either individually or as part of an assembly, it should be renewed.

The very fine sealing lip of the seal is easily damaged, and will not seal if the surface it contacts is not completely clean and free from scratches, nicks or grooves. If the original sealing surface of the component cannot be restored, and the manufacturer has not made provision for slight relocation of the seal relative to the sealing surface, the component should be renewed.

Protect the lips of the seal from any surface which may damage them in the course of fitting. Use tape or a conical sleeve where possible. Lubricate the seal lips with oil before fitting and, on dual-lipped seals, fill the space between the lips with grease.

Unless otherwise stated, oil seals must be fitted with their sealing lips toward the lubricant to be sealed.

Use a tubular drift or block of wood of the appropriate size to install the seal and, if the seal housing is shouldered, drive the seal down to the shoulder. If the seal housing is unshouldered, the seal should be fitted with its face flush with the housing top face (unless otherwise instructed).

Screw threads and fastenings

Seized nuts, bolts and screws are quite a common occurrence where corrosion has set in, and the use of penetrating oil or releasing fluid will often overcome this problem if the offending item is soaked for a while before attempting to release it. The use of an impact driver may also provide a means of releasing such stubborn fastening devices, when used in conjunction with the appropriate screwdriver bit or socket. If none of these methods works, it may be necessary to resort to the careful application of heat, or the use of a hacksaw or nut splitter device.

Studs are usually removed by locking two nuts together on the threaded part, and then using a spanner on the lower nut to unscrew the stud. Studs or bolts which have broken off below the surface of the component in which they are mounted can sometimes be removed using a stud extractor. Always ensure that a blind tapped hole is completely free from oil, grease, water or other fluid before installing the bolt or stud. Failure to do this could cause the housing to crack due to the hydraulic action of the bolt or stud as it is screwed in.

When tightening a castellated nut to accept a split pin, tighten the nut to the specified torque, where applicable, and then tighten further to the next split pin hole. Never slacken the nut to align the split pin hole, unless stated in the repair procedure.

When checking or retightening a nut or bolt to a specified torque setting, slacken the nut or bolt by a quarter of a turn, and then retighten to the specified setting. However, this should not be attempted where angular tightening has been used.

For some screw fastenings, notably cylinder head bolts or nuts, torque wrench settings are no longer specified for the latter stages of tightening, "angle-tightening" being called up instead. Typically, a fairly low torque wrench setting will be applied to the bolts/nuts in the correct sequence, followed by one or more stages of tightening through specified angles.

Locknuts, locktabs and washers

Any fastening which will rotate against a component or housing during tightening should always have a washer between it and the relevant component or housing.

Spring or split washers should always be renewed when they are used to lock a critical component such as a big-end bearing retaining bolt or nut. Locktabs which are folded over to retain a nut or bolt should always be renewed.

Self-locking nuts can be re-used in non-critical areas, providing resistance can be felt when the locking portion passes over the bolt or stud thread. However, it should be noted that self-locking stiffnuts tend to lose their effectiveness after long periods of use, and should be renewed as a matter of course.

Split pins must always be replaced with new ones of the correct size for the hole.

When thread-locking compound is found on the threads of a fastener which is to be re-used, it should be cleaned off with a wire brush and solvent, and fresh compound applied on reassembly.

Special tools

Some repair procedures in this manual entail the use of special tools such as a press, two or three-legged pullers, spring compressors, etc. Wherever possible, suitable readily-available alternatives to the manufacturer's special tools are described, and are shown in use. In some instances, where no alternative is possible, it has been necessary to resort to the use of a manufacturer's tool, and this has been done for reasons of safety as well as the efficient completion of the repair operation. Unless you are highly-skilled and have a thorough understanding of the procedures described, never attempt to bypass the use of any special tool when the procedure described specifies its use. Not only is there a very great risk of personal injury, but expensive damage could be caused to the components involved.

Environmental considerations

When disposing of used engine oil, brake fluid, antifreeze, etc, give due consideration to any detrimental environmental effects. Do not, for instance, pour any of the above liquids down drains into the general sewage system, or onto the ground to soak away. Many local council refuse tips provide a facility for waste oil disposal, as do some garages. If none of these facilities are available, consult your local Environmental Health Department, or the National Rivers Authority, for further advice.

With the universal tightening-up of legislation regarding the emission of environmentally-harmful substances from motor vehicles, most current vehicles have tamperproof devices fitted to the main adjustment points of the fuel system. These devices are primarily designed to prevent unqualified persons from adjusting the fuel/air mixture, with the chance of a consequent increase in toxic emissions. If such devices are encountered during servicing or overhaul, they should, wherever possible, be renewed or refitted in accordance with the vehicle manufacturer's requirements or current legislation.

OIL CARE

FOLLOW THE CODE

OIL BANK LINE

0800 66 33 66

Note: It is antisocial and illegal to dump oil down the drain. To find the location of your local oil recycling bank, call this number free.

The jack supplied with the vehicle tool kit should only be used for changing the roadwheels - see *"Wheel changing"* at the front of this manual. When carrying out any other kind of work, raise the vehicle using a hydraulic (or "trolley") jack, and always supplement the jack with axle stands positioned under the vehicle jacking points.

To raise the front of the vehicle, position a block of wood on the jack head and position the jack underneath the centre of the front suspension subframe crossmember. Lift the vehicle to the required height and support it on axle stands positioned underneath the front rubber support blocks, which are located directly underneath the vehicle jack location holes in the sill **(see illustration)**.

To raise the rear of the vehicle, position a block of wood on the jack head and position the jack underneath the final drive unit. Lift the vehicle to the required height and support it on axle stands positioned underneath the rear rubber support blocks, which are located directly underneath the vehicle jack location holes in the sill.

The jack supplied with the vehicle locates in the holes provided in the sill. Unscrew the access plug and insert the jack fully into the hole in the sill. Ensure that the jack head is correctly engaged before attempting to raise the vehicle.

Never work under, around, or near a raised vehicle, unless it is adequately supported in at least two places.

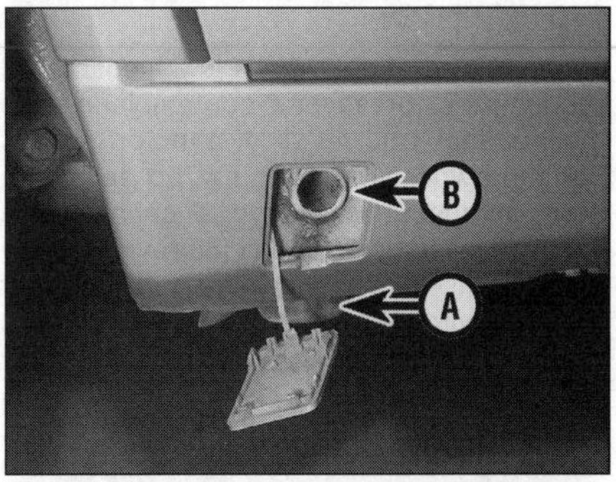

The vehicle can be raised using the rubber blocks (A) which are located directly underneath the vehicle jack location holes (B)

Radio/cassette unit anti-theft system - precaution

The radio/cassette/CD player/autochanger unit fitted as standard equipment by Mercedes-Benz is equipped with a built-in security code, to deter thieves. If the power source to the unit is cut, the anti-theft system will activate. Even if the power source is immediately reconnected, the radio/cassette unit will not function until the correct security code has been entered. Therefore, if you do not know the correct security code for the unit, **do not** disconnect the battery negative lead, or remove the radio/cassette unit from the vehicle.

The procedure for reprogramming a unit that has been disconnected from its power supply varies from model to model - consult the handbook supplied with the unit for specific details or refer to your Mercedes-Benz dealer.

Introduction

A selection of good tools is a fundamental requirement for anyone contemplating the maintenance and repair of a motor vehicle. For the owner who does not possess any, their purchase will prove a considerable expense, offsetting some of the savings made by doing-it-yourself. However, provided that the tools purchased meet the relevant national safety standards and are of good quality, they will last for many years and prove an extremely worthwhile investment.

To help the average owner to decide which tools are needed to carry out the various tasks detailed in this manual, we have compiled three lists of tools under the following headings: *Maintenance and minor repair*, *Repair and overhaul*, and *Special*. Newcomers to practical mechanics should start off with the *Maintenance and minor repair* tool kit, and confine themselves to the simpler jobs around the vehicle. Then, as confidence and experience grow, more difficult tasks can be undertaken, with extra tools being purchased as, and when, they are needed. In this way, a *Maintenance and minor repair* tool kit can be built up into a *Repair and overhaul* tool kit over a considerable period of time, without any major cash outlays. The experienced do-it-yourselfer will have a tool kit good enough for most repair and overhaul procedures, and will add tools from the *Special* category when it is felt that the expense is justified by the amount of use to which these tools will be put.

Maintenance and minor repair tool kit

The tools given in this list should be considered as a minimum requirement if routine maintenance, servicing and minor repair operations are to be undertaken. We recommend the purchase of combination spanners (ring one end, open-ended the other); although more expensive than open-ended ones, they do give the advantages of both types of spanner.

- ☐ *Combination spanners:*
  Metric - 8 to 19 mm inclusive
- ☐ *Adjustable spanner - 35 mm jaw (approx.)*
- ☐ *Spark plug spanner (with rubber insert) - petrol models*
- ☐ *Spark plug gap adjustment tool - petrol models*
- ☐ *Set of feeler blades*
- ☐ *Brake bleed nipple spanner*
- ☐ *Screwdrivers:*
  Flat blade - 100 mm long x 6 mm dia
  Cross blade - 100 mm long x 6 mm dia
- ☐ *Combination pliers*
- ☐ *Hacksaw (junior)*
- ☐ *Tyre pump*
- ☐ *Tyre pressure gauge*
- ☐ *Oil can*
- ☐ *Oil filter removal tool*
- ☐ *Fine emery cloth*
- ☐ *Wire brush (small)*
- ☐ *Funnel (medium size)*

Repair and overhaul tool kit

These tools are virtually essential for anyone undertaking any major repairs to a motor vehicle, and are additional to those given in the *Maintenance and minor repair* list. Included in this list is a comprehensive set of sockets. Although these are expensive, they will be found invaluable as they are so versatile - particularly if various drives are included in the set. We recommend the half-inch square-drive type, as this can be used with most proprietary torque wrenches.

The tools in this list will sometimes need to be supplemented by tools from the *Special* list:

- ☐ *Sockets (or box spanners) to cover range in previous list (including Torx sockets)*
- ☐ *Reversible ratchet drive (for use with sockets)*
- ☐ *Extension piece, 250 mm (for use with sockets)*
- ☐ *Universal joint (for use with sockets)*
- ☐ *Torque wrench (for use with sockets)*
- ☐ *Self-locking grips*
- ☐ *Ball pein hammer*
- ☐ *Soft-faced mallet (plastic/aluminium or rubber)*
- ☐ *Screwdrivers:*
  Flat blade - long & sturdy, short (chubby), and narrow (electrician's) types
  Cross blade – Long & sturdy, and short (chubby) types
- ☐ *Pliers:*
  Long-nosed
  Side cutters (electrician's)
  Circlip (internal and external)
- ☐ *Cold chisel - 25 mm*
- ☐ *Scriber*
- ☐ *Scraper*
- ☐ *Centre-punch*
- ☐ *Pin punch*
- ☐ *Hacksaw*
- ☐ *Brake hose clamp*
- ☐ *Brake/clutch bleeding kit*
- ☐ *Selection of twist drills*
- ☐ *Steel rule/straight-edge*
- ☐ *Allen keys (inc. splined/Torx type)*
- ☐ *Selection of files*
- ☐ *Wire brush*
- ☐ *Axle stands*
- ☐ *Jack (strong trolley or hydraulic type)*
- ☐ *Light with extension lead*

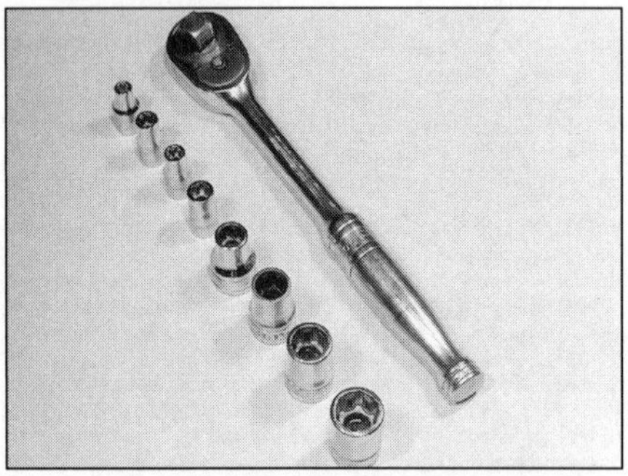

Sockets and reversible ratchet drive

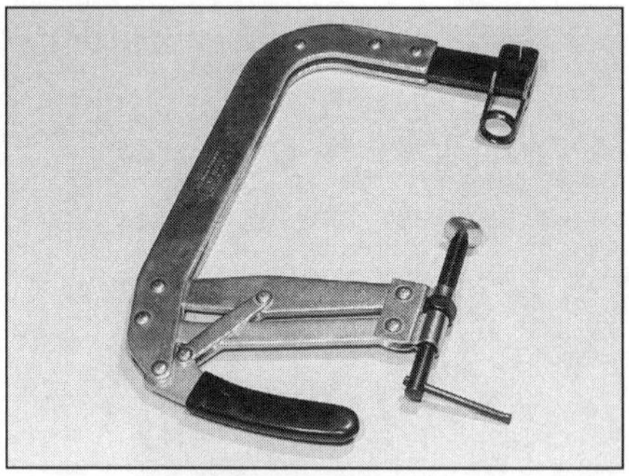

Valve spring compressor

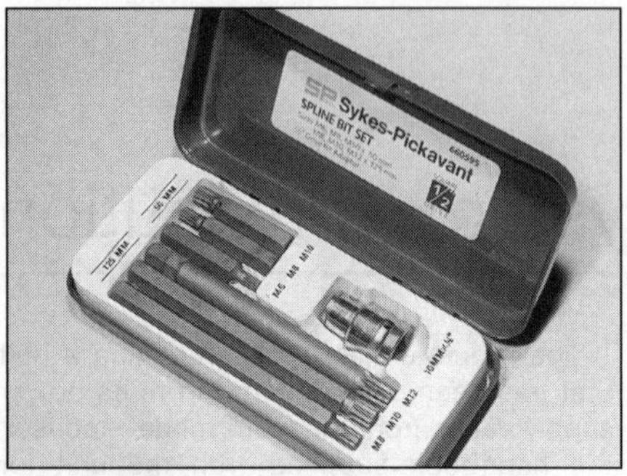

Spline bit set

Piston ring compressor

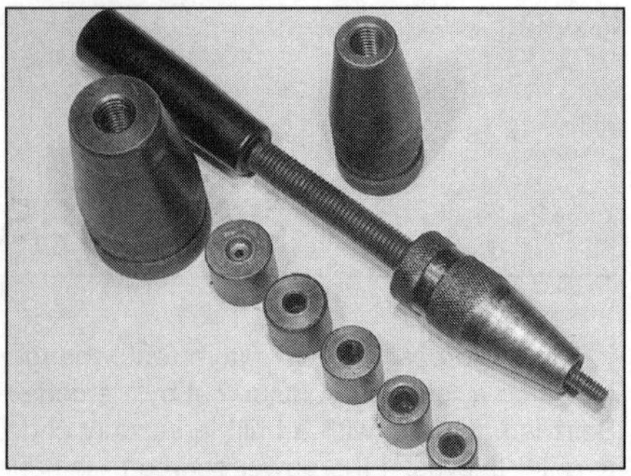

Clutch plate alignment set

Special tools

The tools in this list are those which are not used regularly, are expensive to buy, or which need to be used in accordance with their manufacturers' instructions. Unless relatively difficult mechanical jobs are undertaken frequently, it will not be economic to buy many of these tools. Where this is the case, you could consider clubbing together with friends (or joining a motorists' club) to make a joint purchase, or borrowing the tools against a deposit from a local garage or tool hire specialist. It is worth noting that many of the larger DIY superstores now carry a large range of special tools for hire at modest rates.

The following list contains only those tools and instruments freely available to the public, and not those special tools produced by the vehicle manufacturer specifically for its dealer network. You will find occasional references to these manufacturers' special tools in the text of this manual. Generally, an alternative method of doing the job without the vehicle manufacturers' special tool is given. However, sometimes there is no alternative to using them. Where this is the case and the relevant tool cannot be bought or borrowed, you will have to entrust the work to a dealer.

- ☐ *Valve spring compressor*
- ☐ *Valve grinding tool*
- ☐ *Piston ring compressor*
- ☐ *Piston ring removal/installation tool*
- ☐ *Cylinder bore hone*
- ☐ *Balljoint separator*
- ☐ *Coil spring compressors (where applicable)*
- ☐ *Two/three-legged hub and bearing puller*
- ☐ *Impact screwdriver*
- ☐ *Micrometer and/or vernier calipers*
- ☐ *Dial gauge*
- ☐ *Stroboscopic timing light*
- ☐ *Dwell angle meter/tachometer*
- ☐ *Universal electrical multi-meter*
- ☐ *Cylinder compression gauge*
- ☐ *Hand-operated vacuum pump and gauge*
- ☐ *Clutch plate alignment set*
- ☐ *Brake shoe steady spring cup removal tool*
- ☐ *Bush and bearing removal/installation set*
- ☐ *Stud extractors*
- ☐ *Tap and die set*
- ☐ *Lifting tackle*
- ☐ *Trolley jack*

Buying tools

Reputable motor accessory shops and superstores often offer excellent quality tools at discount prices, so it pays to shop around.

Remember, you don't have to buy the most expensive items on the shelf, but it is always advisable to steer clear of the very cheap tools. Beware of 'bargains' offered on market stalls or at car boot sales. There are plenty of good tools around at reasonable prices, but always aim to purchase items which meet the relevant national safety standards. If in doubt, ask the proprietor or manager of the shop for advice before making a purchase.

Care and maintenance of tools

Having purchased a reasonable tool kit, it is necessary to keep the tools in a clean and serviceable condition. After use, always wipe off any dirt, grease and metal particles using a clean, dry cloth, before putting the tools away. Never leave them lying around after they have been used. A simple tool rack on the garage or workshop wall for items such as screwdrivers and pliers is a good idea. Store all normal spanners and sockets in a metal box. Any measuring instruments, gauges, meters, etc, must be carefully stored where they cannot be damaged or become rusty.

Take a little care when tools are used. Hammer heads inevitably become marked, and screwdrivers lose the keen edge on their blades from time to time. A little timely attention with emery cloth or a file will soon restore items like this to a good finish.

Working facilities

Not to be forgotten when discussing tools is the workshop itself. If anything more than routine maintenance is to be carried out, a suitable working area becomes essential.

It is appreciated that many an owner-mechanic is forced by circumstances to remove an engine or similar item without the benefit of a garage or workshop. Having done this, any repairs should always be done under the cover of a roof.

Wherever possible, any dismantling should be done on a clean, flat workbench or table at a suitable working height.

Any workbench needs a vice; one with a jaw opening of 100 mm is suitable for most jobs. As mentioned previously, some clean dry storage space is also required for tools, as well as for any lubricants, cleaning fluids, touch-up paints etc, which become necessary.

Another item which may be required, and which has a much more general usage, is an electric drill with a chuck capacity of at least 8 mm. This, together with a good range of twist drills, is virtually essential for fitting accessories.

Last, but not least, always keep a supply of old newspapers and clean, lint-free rags available, and try to keep any working area as clean as possible.

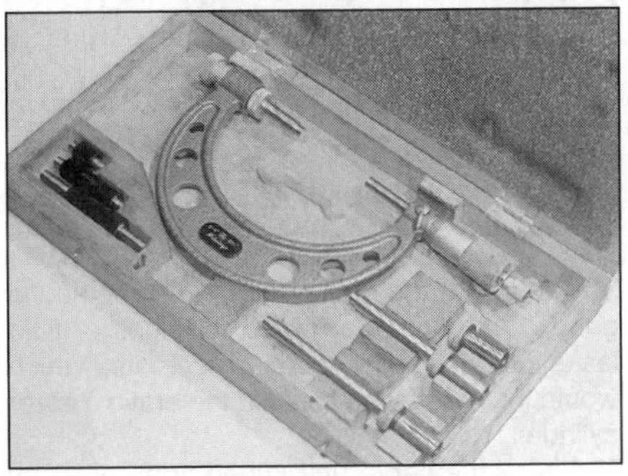

Micrometer set

Dial test indicator ("dial gauge")

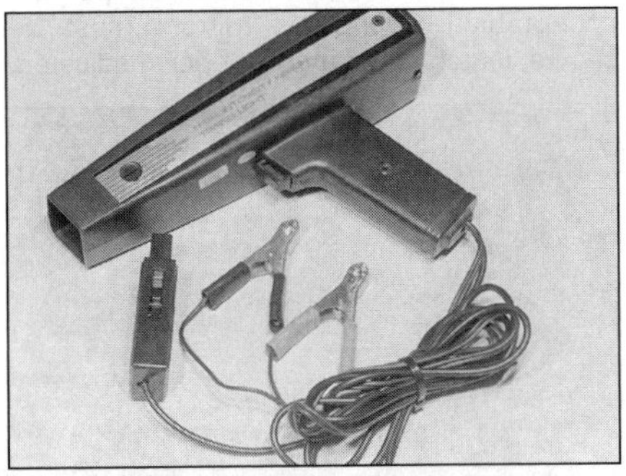

Stroboscopic timing light

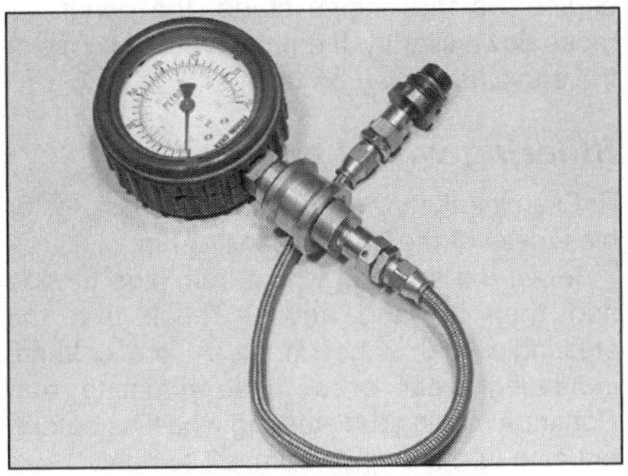

Compression tester

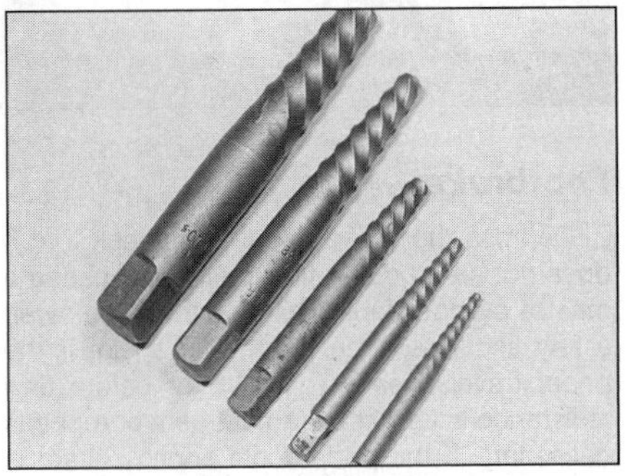

Stud extractor set

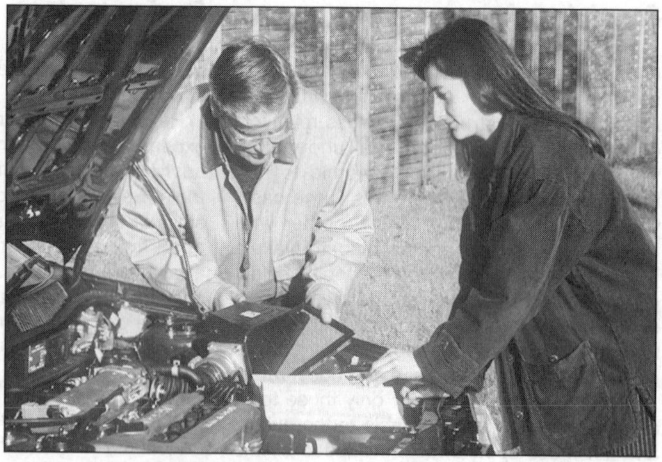

This is a guide to getting your vehicle through the MOT test. Obviously it will not be possible to examine the vehicle to the same standard as the professional MOT tester. However, working through the following checks will enable you to identify any problem areas before submitting the vehicle for the test.

Where a testable component is in borderline condition, the tester has discretion in deciding whether to pass or fail it. The basis of such discretion is whether the tester would be happy for a close relative or friend to use the vehicle with the component in that condition. If the vehicle presented is clean and evidently well cared for, the tester may be more inclined to pass a borderline component than if the vehicle is scruffy and apparently neglected.

It has only been possible to summarise the test requirements here, based on the regulations in force at the time of printing. Test standards are becoming increasingly stringent, although there are some exemptions for older vehicles. For full details obtain a copy of the Haynes publication Pass the MOT! (available from stockists of Haynes manuals).

An assistant will be needed to help carry out some of these checks.

The checks have been sub-divided into four categories, as follows:

1 Checks carried out **FROM THE DRIVER'S SEAT**

2 Checks carried out **WITH THE VEHICLE ON THE GROUND**

3 Checks carried out **WITH THE VEHICLE RAISED AND THE WHEELS FREE TO TURN**

4 Checks carried out on **YOUR VEHICLE'S EXHAUST EMISSION SYSTEM**

1 Checks carried out FROM THE DRIVER'S SEAT

Handbrake

☐ Test the operation of the handbrake. Excessive travel (too many clicks) indicates incorrect brake or cable adjustment.

☐ Check that the handbrake cannot be released by tapping the lever sideways. Check the security of the lever mountings.

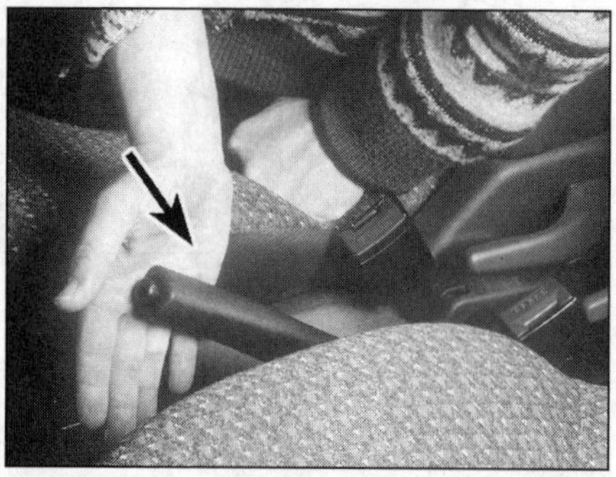

Footbrake

☐ Depress the brake pedal and check that it does not creep down to the floor, indicating a master cylinder fault. Release the pedal, wait a few seconds, then depress it again. If the pedal travels nearly to the floor before firm resistance is felt, brake adjustment or repair is necessary. If the pedal feels spongy, there is air in the hydraulic system which must be removed by bleeding.

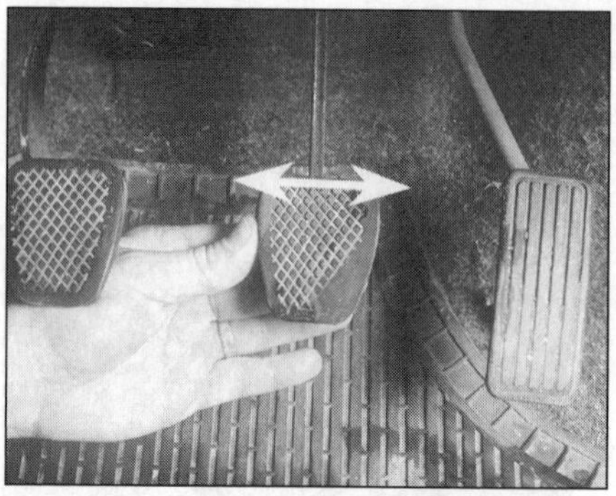

☐ Check that the brake pedal is secure and in good condition. Check also for signs of fluid leaks on the pedal, floor or carpets, which would indicate failed seals in the brake master cylinder.

☐ Check the servo unit (when applicable) by operating the brake pedal several times, then keeping the pedal depressed and starting the engine. As the engine starts, the pedal will move down slightly. If not, the vacuum hose or the servo itself may be faulty.

Steering wheel and column

☐ Examine the steering wheel for fractures or looseness of the hub, spokes or rim.

☐ Move the steering wheel from side to side and then up and down. Check that the steering wheel is not loose on the column, indicating wear or a loose retaining nut. Continue moving the steering wheel as before, but also turn it slightly from left to right.

☐ Check that the steering wheel is not loose on the column, and that there is no abnormal

movement of the steering wheel, indicating wear in the column support bearings or couplings.

Windscreen and mirrors

☐ The windscreen must be free of cracks or other significant damage within the driver's field of view. (Small stone chips are acceptable.) Rear view mirrors must be secure, intact, and capable of being adjusted.

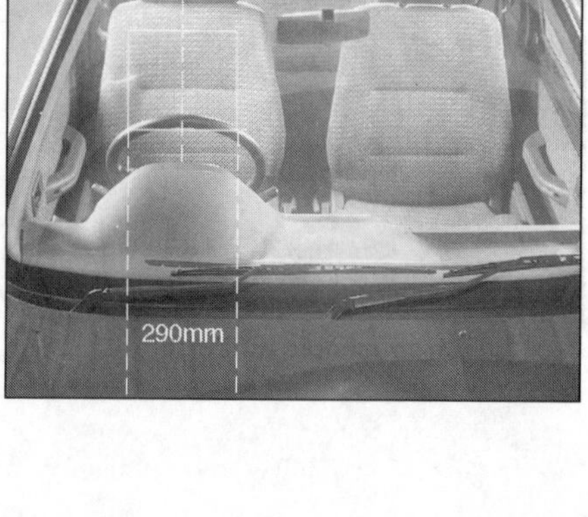

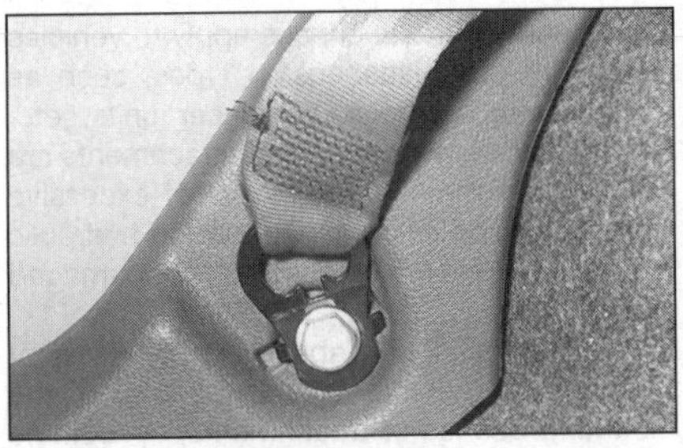

Seat belts and seats

Note: *The following checks are applicable to all seat belts, front and rear.*

☐ Examine the webbing of all the belts (including rear belts if fitted) for cuts, serious fraying or deterioration. Fasten and unfasten each belt to check the buckles. If applicable, check the retracting mechanism. Check the security of all seat belt mountings accessible from inside the vehicle.

☐ The front seats themselves must be securely attached and the backrests must lock in the upright position.

Doors

☐ Both front doors must be able to be opened and closed from outside and inside, and must latch securely when closed.

2 Checks carried out **WITH THE VEHICLE ON THE GROUND**

Vehicle identification

☐ Number plates must be in good condition, secure and legible, with letters and numbers correctly spaced – spacing at (A) should be twice that at (B).

☐ The VIN plate and/or homologation plate must be legible.

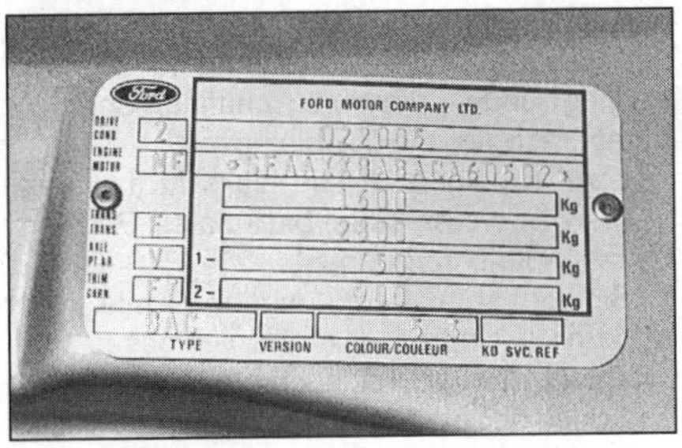

Electrical equipment

☐ Switch on the ignition and check the operation of the horn.

☐ Check the windscreen washers and wipers, examining the wiper blades; renew damaged or perished blades. Also check the operation of the stop-lights.

☐ Check the operation of the sidelights and number plate lights. The lenses and reflectors must be secure, clean and undamaged.

☐ Check the operation and alignment of the headlights. The headlight reflectors must not be tarnished and the lenses must be undamaged.

☐ Switch on the ignition and check the operation of the direction indicators (including the instrument panel tell-tale) and the hazard warning lights. Operation of the sidelights and stop-lights must not affect the indicators - if it does, the cause is usually a bad earth at the rear light cluster.

☐ Check the operation of the rear foglight(s), including the warning light on the instrument panel or in the switch.

Footbrake

☐ Examine the master cylinder, brake pipes and servo unit for leaks, loose mountings, corrosion or other damage.

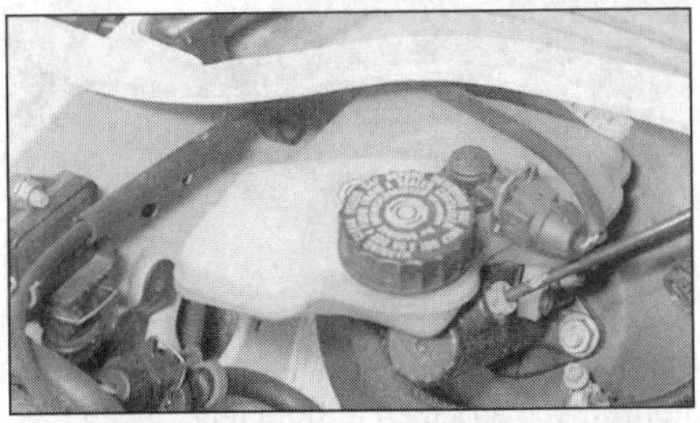

☐ The fluid reservoir must be secure and the fluid level must be between the upper (**A**) and lower (**B**) markings.

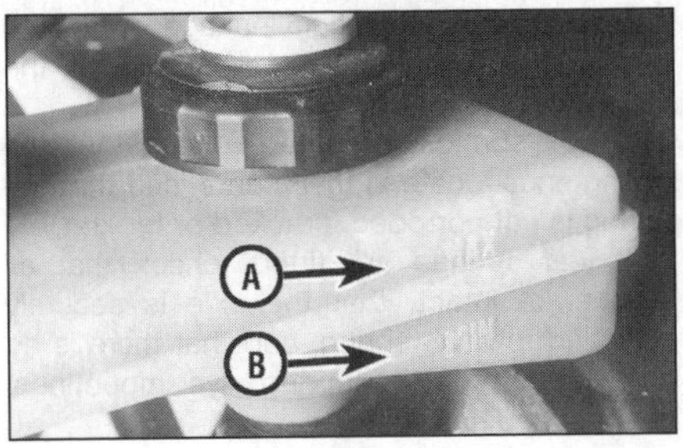

☐ Inspect both front brake flexible hoses for cracks or deterioration of the rubber. Turn the steering from lock to lock, and ensure that the hoses do not contact the wheel, tyre, or any part of the steering or suspension mechanism. With the brake pedal firmly depressed, check the hoses for bulges or leaks under pressure.

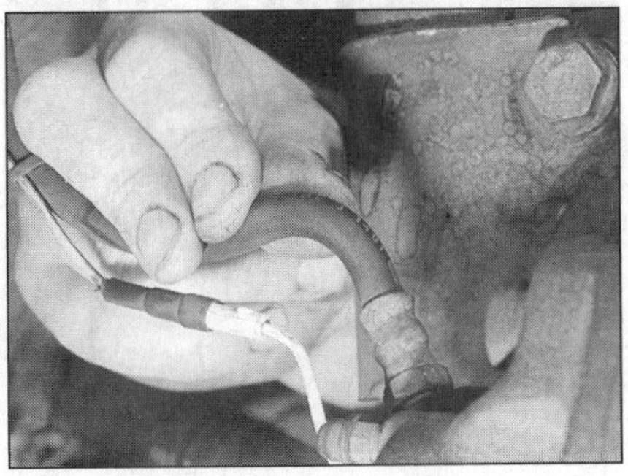

Steering and suspension

☐ Have your assistant turn the steering wheel from side to side slightly, up to the point where the steering gear just begins to transmit this movement to the roadwheels. Check for excessive free play between the steering wheel and the steering gear, indicating wear or insecurity of the steering column joints, the column-to-steering gear coupling, or the steering gear itself.

☐ Have your assistant turn the steering wheel more vigorously in each direction, so that the roadwheels just begin to turn. As this is done, examine all the steering joints, linkages, fittings and attachments. Renew any component that shows signs of wear or damage. On vehicles with power steering, check the security and condition of the steering pump, drivebelt and hoses.

☐ Check that the vehicle is standing level, and at approximately the correct ride height.

Shock absorbers

☐ Depress each corner of the vehicle in turn, then release it. The vehicle should rise and then settle in its normal position. If the vehicle continues to rise and fall, the shock absorber is defective. A shock absorber which has seized will also cause the vehicle to fail.

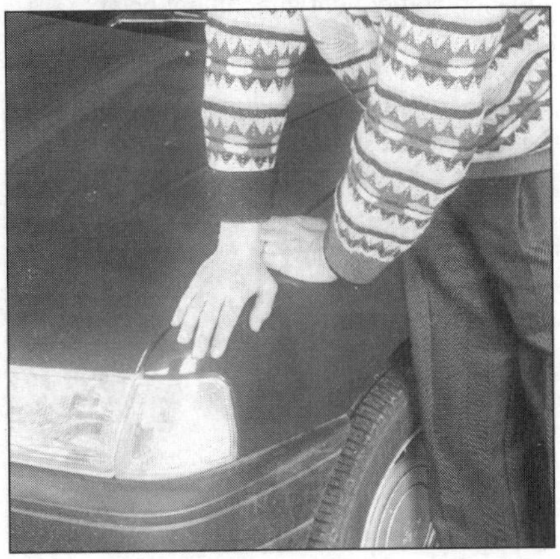

Exhaust system

☐ Start the engine. With your assistant holding a rag over the tailpipe, check the entire system for leaks. Repair or renew leaking sections.

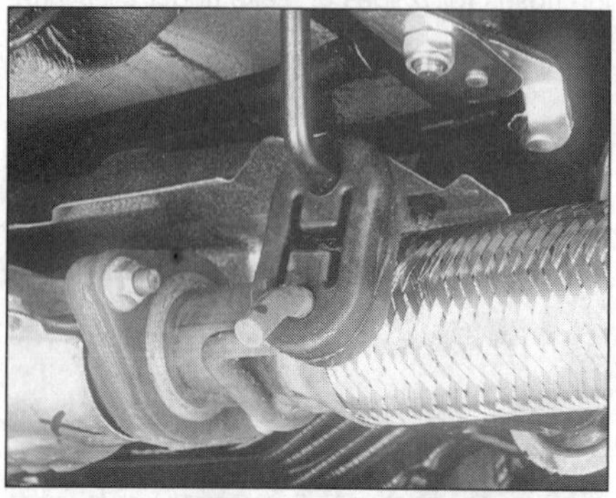

3 Checks carried out WITH THE VEHICLE RAISED AND THE WHEELS FREE TO TURN

Jack up the front and rear of the vehicle, and securely support it on axle stands. Position the stands clear of the suspension assemblies. Ensure that the wheels are clear of the ground and that the steering can be turned from lock to lock.

Steering mechanism

☐ Have your assistant turn the steering from lock to lock. Check that the steering turns smoothly, and that no part of the steering mechanism, including a wheel or tyre, fouls any brake hose or pipe or any part of the body structure.

☐ Examine the steering rack rubber gaiters for damage or insecurity of the retaining clips. If power steering is fitted, check for signs of damage or leakage of the fluid hoses, pipes or connections. Also check for excessive stiffness or binding of the steering, a missing split pin or locking device, or severe corrosion of the body structure within 30 cm of any steering component attachment point.

Front and rear suspension and wheel bearings

☐ Starting at the front right-hand side, grasp the roadwheel at the 3 o'clock and 9 o'clock positions and shake it vigorously. Check for free play or insecurity at the wheel bearings, suspension balljoints, or suspension mountings, pivots and attachments.

☐ Now grasp the wheel at the 12 o'clock and 6 o'clock positions and repeat the previous inspection. Spin the wheel, and check for roughness or tightness of the front wheel bearing.

☐ If excess free play is suspected at a component pivot point, this can be confirmed by using a large screwdriver or similar tool and levering between the mounting and the component attachment. This will confirm whether the wear is in the pivot bush, its retaining bolt, or in the mounting itself (the bolt holes can often become elongated).

☐ Carry out all the above checks at the other front wheel, and then at both rear wheels.

Springs and shock absorbers

☐ Examine the suspension struts (when applicable) for serious fluid leakage, corrosion, or damage to the casing. Also check the security of the mounting points.

☐ If coil springs are fitted, check that the spring ends locate in their seats, and that the spring is not corroded, cracked or broken.

☐ If leaf springs are fitted, check that all leaves are intact, that the axle is securely attached to each spring, and that there is no deterioration of the spring eye mountings, bushes, and shackles.

☐ The same general checks apply to vehicles fitted with other suspension types, such as torsion bars, hydraulic displacer units, etc. Ensure that all mountings and attachments are secure, that there are no signs of excessive wear, corrosion or damage, and (on hydraulic types) that there are no fluid leaks or damaged pipes.

☐ Inspect the shock absorbers for signs of serious fluid leakage. Check for wear of the mounting bushes or attachments, or damage to the body of the unit.

Driveshafts (fwd vehicles only)

☐ Rotate each front wheel in turn and inspect the constant velocity joint gaiters for splits or damage. Also check that each driveshaft is straight and undamaged.

Braking system

☐ If possible without dismantling, check brake pad wear and disc condition. Ensure that the friction lining material has not worn excessively, (A) and that the discs are not fractured, pitted, scored or badly worn (B).

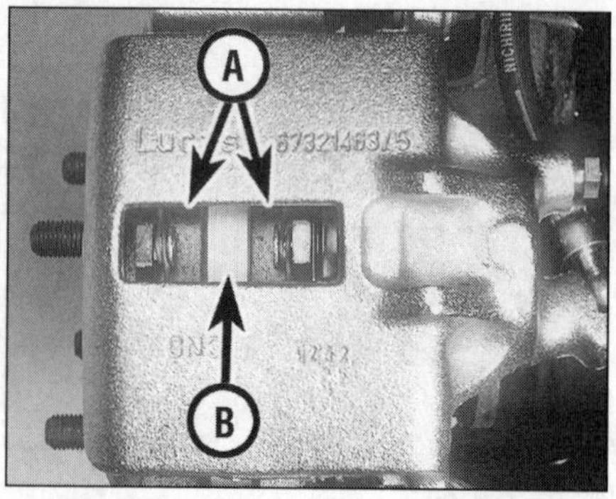

☐ Examine all the rigid brake pipes underneath the vehicle, and the flexible hose(s) at the rear. Look for corrosion, chafing or insecurity of the pipes, and for signs of bulging under pressure, chafing, splits or deterioration of the flexible hoses.

☐ Look for signs of fluid leaks at the brake calipers or on the brake backplates. Repair or renew leaking components.

☐ Slowly spin each wheel, while your assistant depresses and releases the footbrake. Ensure that each brake is operating and does not bind when the pedal is released.

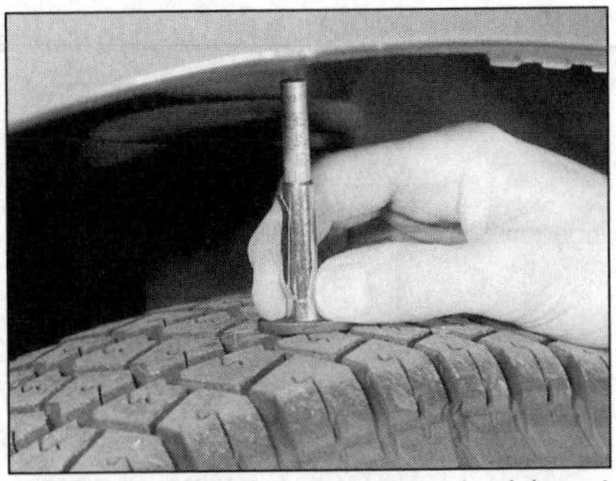

☐ Examine the handbrake mechanism, checking for frayed or broken cables, excessive corrosion, or wear or insecurity of the linkage. Check that the mechanism works on each relevant wheel, and releases fully, without binding.

☐ It is not possible to test brake efficiency without special equipment, but a road test can be carried out later to check that the vehicle pulls up in a straight line.

Fuel and exhaust systems

☐ Inspect the fuel tank (including the filler cap), fuel pipes, hoses and unions. All components must be secure and free from leaks.

☐ Examine the exhaust system over its entire length, checking for any damaged, broken or missing mountings, security of the retaining clamps and rust or corrosion.

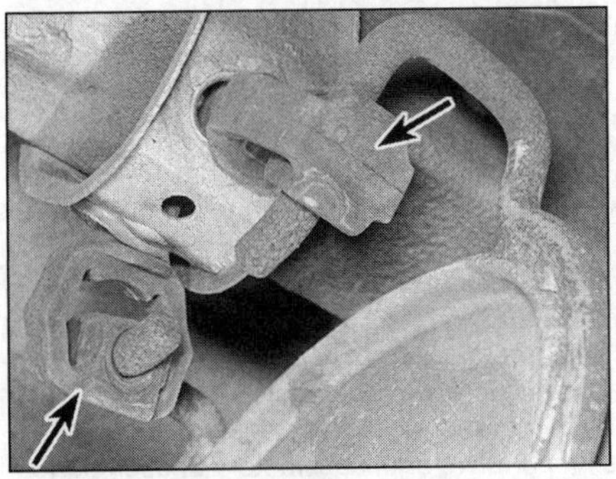

Wheels and tyres

☐ Examine the sidewalls and tread area of each tyre in turn. Check for cuts, tears, lumps, bulges, separation of the tread, and exposure of the ply or cord due to wear or damage. Check that the tyre bead is correctly seated on the wheel rim, that the valve is sound and properly seated, and that the wheel is not distorted or damaged.

☐ Check that the tyres are of the correct size for the vehicle, that they are of the same size and type on each axle, and that the pressures are correct.

☐ Check the tyre tread depth. The legal minimum at the time of writing is 1.6 mm over at least three-quarters of the tread width. Abnormal tread wear may indicate incorrect front wheel alignment.

Body corrosion

☐ Check the condition of the entire vehicle structure for signs of corrosion in load-bearing areas. (These include chassis box sections, side sills, cross-members, pillars, and all suspension, steering, braking system and seat belt mountings and anchorages.) Any corrosion which has seriously reduced the thickness of a load-bearing area is likely to cause the vehicle to fail. In this case professional repairs are likely to be needed.

☐ Damage or corrosion which causes sharp or otherwise dangerous edges to be exposed will also cause the vehicle to fail.

4 Checks carried out on **YOUR VEHICLE'S EXHAUST EMISSION SYSTEM**

Petrol models

☐ Have the engine at normal operating temperature, and make sure that it is in good tune (ignition system in good order, air filter element clean, etc).

☐ Before any measurements are carried out, raise the engine speed to around 2500 rpm, and hold it at this speed for 20 seconds. Allow the engine speed to return to idle, and watch for smoke emissions from the exhaust tailpipe. If the idle speed is obviously much too high, or if dense blue or clearly-visible black smoke comes from the tailpipe for more than 5 seconds, the vehicle will fail. As a rule of thumb, blue smoke signifies oil being burnt (engine wear) while black smoke signifies unburnt fuel (dirty air cleaner element, or other carburettor or fuel system fault).

☐ An exhaust gas analyser capable of measuring carbon monoxide (CO) and hydrocarbons (HC) is now needed. If such an instrument cannot be hired or borrowed, a local garage may agree to perform the check for a small fee.

CO emissions (mixture)

☐ At the time of writing, the maximum CO level at idle is 3.5% for vehicles first used after August 1986 and 4.5% for older vehicles. From January 1996 a much tighter limit (around 0.5%) applies to catalyst-equipped vehicles first used from August 1992. If the CO level cannot be reduced far enough to pass the test (and the fuel and ignition systems are otherwise in good condition) then the carburettor is badly worn, or there is some problem in the fuel injection system or catalytic converter (as applicable).

HC emissions

☐ With the CO emissions within limits, HC emissions must be no more than 1200 ppm (parts per million). If the vehicle fails this test at idle, it can be re-tested at around 2000 rpm; if the HC level is then 1200 ppm or less, this counts as a pass.

☐ Excessive HC emissions can be caused by oil being burnt, but they are more likely to be due to unburnt fuel.

Diesel models

☐ The only emission test applicable to Diesel engines is the measuring of exhaust smoke density. The test involves accelerating the engine several times to its maximum unloaded speed.

Note: *It is of the utmost importance that the engine timing belt is in good condition before the test is carried out.*

☐ Excessive smoke can be caused by a dirty air cleaner element. Otherwise, professional advice may be needed to find the cause.

Engine

- ☐ Engine fails to rotate when attempting to start
- ☐ Engine rotates, but will not start
- ☐ Engine difficult to start when cold
- ☐ Engine difficult to start when hot
- ☐ Starter motor noisy or excessively-rough in engagement
- ☐ Engine starts, but stops immediately
- ☐ Engine idles erratically
- ☐ Engine misfires at idle speed
- ☐ Engine misfires throughout the driving speed range
- ☐ Engine hesitates on acceleration
- ☐ Engine stalls
- ☐ Engine lacks power
- ☐ Engine backfires
- ☐ Oil pressure warning light illuminated with engine running
- ☐ Engine runs-on after switching off
- ☐ Engine noises

Cooling system

- ☐ Overheating
- ☐ Overcooling
- ☐ External coolant leakage
- ☐ Internal coolant leakage
- ☐ Corrosion

Fuel and exhaust systems

- ☐ Excessive fuel consumption
- ☐ Fuel leakage and/or fuel odour
- ☐ Excessive noise or fumes from exhaust system

Clutch

- ☐ Pedal travels to floor - no pressure or very little resistance
- ☐ Clutch fails to disengage (unable to select gears)
- ☐ Clutch slips (engine speed increases, with no increase in vehicle speed)
- ☐ Judder as clutch is engaged
- ☐ Noise when depressing or releasing clutch pedal

Manual transmission

- ☐ Noisy in neutral with engine running
- ☐ Noisy in one particular gear
- ☐ Difficulty engaging gears
- ☐ Jumps out of gear
- ☐ Vibration
- ☐ Lubricant leaks

Automatic transmission

- ☐ Fluid leakage
- ☐ Transmission fluid brown, or has burned smell
- ☐ General gear selection problems
- ☐ Transmission will not downshift (kickdown) with accelerator pedal fully depressed
- ☐ Engine will not start in any gear, or starts in gears other than Park or Neutral
- ☐ Transmission slips, shifts roughly, is noisy, or has no drive in forward or reverse gears

Differential and propeller shaft

- ☐ Vibration when accelerating or decelerating
- ☐ Low pitched whining; increasing with road speed

Braking system

- ☐ Vehicle pulls to one side under braking
- ☐ Noise (grinding or high-pitched squeal) when brakes applied
- ☐ Excessive brake pedal travel
- ☐ Brake pedal feels spongy when depressed
- ☐ Excessive brake pedal effort required to stop vehicle
- ☐ Judder felt through brake pedal or steering wheel when braking
- ☐ Brakes binding
- ☐ Rear wheels locking under normal braking

Suspension and steering

- ☐ Vehicle pulls to one side
- ☐ Wheel wobble and vibration
- ☐ Excessive pitching and/or rolling around corners, or during braking
- ☐ Wandering or general instability
- ☐ Excessively-stiff steering
- ☐ Excessive play in steering
- ☐ Lack of power assistance
- ☐ Tyre wear excessive

Electrical system

- ☐ Battery will not hold a charge for more than a few days
- ☐ Ignition/no-charge warning light remains illuminated with engine running
- ☐ Ignition/no-charge warning light fails to come on
- ☐ Lights inoperative
- ☐ Instrument readings inaccurate or erratic
- ☐ Horn inoperative, or unsatisfactory in operation
- ☐ Windscreen wipers inoperative, or unsatisfactory in operation
- ☐ Windscreen washers inoperative, or unsatisfactory in operation
- ☐ Electric windows inoperative, or unsatisfactory in operation
- ☐ Central locking system inoperative, or unsatisfactory in operation

Introduction

The vehicle owner who does his or her own maintenance according to the recommended service schedules should not have to use this section of the manual very often. Modern component reliability is such that, provided those items subject to wear or deterioration are inspected or renewed at the specified intervals, sudden failure is comparatively rare. Faults do not usually just happen as a result of sudden failure, but develop over a period of time. Major mechanical failures in particular are usually preceded by characteristic symptoms over hundreds or even thousands of miles. Those components which do occasionally fail without warning are often small and easily carried in the vehicle.

With any fault-finding, the first step is to decide where to begin investigations. Sometimes this is obvious, but on other occasions, a little detective work will be necessary. The owner who makes half a dozen haphazard adjustments or replacements may be successful in curing a fault (or its symptoms), but will be none the wiser if the fault recurs, and ultimately may have spent more time and money than was necessary. A calm and logical approach will be found to be more satisfactory in the long run. Always take into account any warning signs or abnormalities that may have been noticed in the period preceding the fault - power loss, high or low gauge readings, unusual smells, etc - and remember that failure of components such as fuses or spark plugs may only be pointers to some underlying fault.

The pages which follow provide an easy-reference guide to the more common problems which may occur during the operation of the vehicle. These problems and their possible causes are grouped under headings denoting various components or systems, such as Engine, Cooling system, etc. The Chapter and/or Section which deals with the problem is also shown in brackets. Whatever the fault, certain basic principles apply. These are as follows:

Verify the fault. This is simply a matter of being sure that you know what the symptoms are before starting work. This is particularly important if you are investigating a fault for someone else, who may not have described it very accurately.

Don't overlook the obvious. For example, if the vehicle won't start, is there fuel in the tank? (Don't take anyone else's word on this particular point, and don't trust the fuel gauge either!) If an electrical fault is indicated, look for loose or broken wires before digging out the test gear.

Cure the disease, not the symptom. Substituting a flat battery with a fully-charged one will get you off the hard shoulder, but if the underlying cause is not attended to, the new battery will go the same way. Similarly, changing oil-fouled spark plugs for a new set will get you moving again, but remember that the reason for the fouling (if it wasn't simply an incorrect grade of plug) will have to be established and corrected.

Don't take anything for granted. Particularly, don't forget that a "new" component may itself be defective (especially if it's been rattling around in the boot for months), and don't leave components out of a fault diagnosis sequence just because they are new or recently-fitted. When you do finally diagnose a difficult fault, you'll probably realise that all the evidence was there from the start.

Engine

Engine fails to rotate when attempting to start

- ☐ Battery terminal connections loose or corroded (*"Weekly checks"*)
- ☐ Battery discharged or faulty (Chapter 5A)
- ☐ Broken, loose or disconnected wiring in the starting circuit (Chapter 5A)
- ☐ Defective starter solenoid or switch (Chapter 5A)
- ☐ Defective starter motor (Chapter 5A)
- ☐ Starter pinion or flywheel ring gear teeth loose or broken (Chapters 2 and 5A)
- ☐ Engine earth strap broken or disconnected (Chapter 5A)

Engine rotates, but will not start

- ☐ Fuel tank empty
- ☐ Battery discharged (engine rotates slowly) (Chapter 5A)
- ☐ Battery terminal connections loose or corroded (*"Weekly checks"*)
- ☐ Ignition components damp or damaged - petrol models (Chapters 1 and 5)
- ☐ Broken, loose or disconnected wiring in the ignition circuit - petrol models (Chapters 1 and 5)
- ☐ Worn, faulty or incorrectly-gapped spark plugs - petrol models (Chapter 1A)
- ☐ Preheating system faulty - diesel models (Chapter 5D)
- ☐ Choke mechanism incorrectly adjusted, worn or sticking - carburettor petrol models (Chapter 4A)
- ☐ Faulty fuel cut-off solenoid - carburettor petrol models (Chapter 4A)
- ☐ Fuel injection system faulty - fuel-injected petrol models (Chapter 4B)
- ☐ Stop solenoid faulty - diesel models (Chapter 4C)
- ☐ Air in fuel system - diesel models (Chapter 4C)
- ☐ Major mechanical failure (eg camshaft drive) (Chapter 2)

Engine difficult to start when cold

- ☐ Battery discharged (Chapter 5A)
- ☐ Battery terminal connections loose or corroded (*"Weekly checks"*)
- ☐ Worn, faulty or incorrectly-gapped spark plugs - petrol models (Chapter 1A)
- ☐ Preheating system faulty - diesel models (Chapter 5D)
- ☐ Choke mechanism incorrectly adjusted, worn or sticking - carburettor petrol models (Chapter 4A)
- ☐ Fuel injection system faulty - fuel-injected petrol models (Chapter 4B)
- ☐ Other ignition system fault - petrol models (Chapters 1 and 5)
- ☐ Fast idle valve incorrectly adjusted - diesel models (Chapter 4C)
- ☐ Low cylinder compressions (Chapter 2)

Engine difficult to start when hot

- ☐ Air filter element dirty or clogged (Chapter 1)
- ☐ Choke mechanism incorrectly adjusted, worn or sticking - carburettor petrol models (Chapter 4A)
- ☐ Fuel injection system faulty - fuel-injected petrol models (Chapter 4B)
- ☐ Low cylinder compressions (Chapter 2)

Starter motor noisy or excessively-rough in engagement

- ☐ Starter pinion or flywheel ring gear teeth loose or broken (Chapters 2 and 5A)
- ☐ Starter motor mounting bolts loose or missing (Chapter 5A)
- ☐ Starter motor internal components worn or damaged (Chapter 5A)

Engine starts, but stops immediately

- ☐ Loose or faulty electrical connections in the ignition circuit - petrol models (Chapters 1 and 5)
- ☐ Vacuum leak at the carburettor/throttle body or inlet manifold - petrol models (Chapter 4)
- ☐ Blocked carburettor jet(s) or internal passages - carburettor petrol models (Chapter 4A)
- ☐ Blocked injector/fuel injection system faulty - fuel-injected petrol models (Chapter 4B)

Engine idles erratically

- ☐ Air filter element clogged (Chapter 1)
- ☐ Vacuum leak at the carburettor/throttle body, inlet manifold or associated hoses - petrol models (Chapter 4A)
- ☐ Worn, faulty or incorrectly-gapped spark plugs - petrol models (Chapter 1A)
- ☐ Uneven or low cylinder compressions (Chapter 2)
- ☐ Camshaft lobes worn (Chapter 2)
- ☐ Timing chain incorrectly fitted (Chapter 2)
- ☐ Blocked carburettor jet(s) or internal passages - carburettor petrol models (Chapter 4A)
- ☐ Blocked injector/fuel injection system faulty - fuel-injected petrol models (Chapter 4B)
- ☐ Faulty injector(s) - diesel models (Chapter 4C)

Engine misfires at idle speed

- ☐ Worn, faulty or incorrectly-gapped spark plugs - petrol models (Chapter 1A)
- ☐ Faulty spark plug HT leads - petrol models (Chapter 1A)
- ☐ Vacuum leak at the carburettor/throttle body, inlet manifold or associated hoses - petrol models (Chapter 4A)
- ☐ Blocked carburettor jet(s) or internal passages - carburettor petrol models (Chapter 4A)
- ☐ Blocked injector/fuel injection system faulty - fuel-injected petrol models (Chapter 4B)
- ☐ Faulty injector(s) - diesel models (Chapter 4C)
- ☐ Distributor cap cracked or tracking internally - petrol models (where applicable) (Chapter 5).
- ☐ Uneven or low cylinder compressions (Chapter 2)
- ☐ Disconnected, leaking, or perished crankcase ventilation hoses (Chapter 4)

Engine (continued)

Engine misfires throughout the driving speed range

- ☐ Fuel filter choked (Chapter 1)
- ☐ Fuel pump faulty, or delivery pressure low (Chapter 4)
- ☐ Fuel tank vent blocked, or fuel pipes restricted (Chapter 4)
- ☐ Vacuum leak at the carburettor/throttle body, inlet manifold or associated hoses - petrol models (Chapter 4A)
- ☐ Worn, faulty or incorrectly-gapped spark plugs - petrol models (Chapter 1A)
- ☐ Faulty spark plug HT leads - petrol models (Chapter 1A)
- ☐ Faulty injector(s) - diesel models (Chapter 4C)
- ☐ Distributor cap cracked or tracking internally - petrol models (where applicable) (Chapter 5)
- ☐ Faulty ignition coil - petrol models (Chapter 5)
- ☐ Uneven or low cylinder compressions (Chapter 2)
- ☐ Blocked carburettor jet(s) or internal passages - carburettor petrol models (Chapter 4A)
- ☐ Blocked injector/fuel injection system fault - fuel-injected petrol models (Chapter 4B)

Engine hesitates on acceleration

- ☐ Worn, faulty or incorrectly-gapped spark plugs - petrol models (Chapter 1A)
- ☐ Vacuum leak at the carburettor/throttle body, inlet manifold or associated hoses (Chapter 4)
- ☐ Blocked carburettor jet(s) or internal passages - carburettor petrol models (Chapter 4A)
- ☐ Blocked injector/fuel injection system fault - fuel-injected petrol models (Chapter 4B)
- ☐ Faulty injector(s) - diesel models (Chapter 4C)

Engine stalls

- ☐ Vacuum leak at the carburettor/throttle body, inlet manifold or associated hoses - petrol models (Chapter 4A)
- ☐ Fuel filter choked (Chapter 1)
- ☐ Fuel pump faulty, or delivery pressure low - petrol models (Chapter 4)
- ☐ Fuel tank vent blocked, or fuel pipes restricted (Chapter 4)
- ☐ Blocked carburettor jet(s) or internal passages - carburettor petrol models (Chapter 4A)
- ☐ Blocked injector/fuel injection system fault - fuel-injected petrol models (Chapter 4B)
- ☐ Faulty injector(s) - diesel models (Chapter 4C)

Engine lacks power

- ☐ Timing chain incorrectly fitted (Chapter 2)
- ☐ Fuel filter choked (Chapter 1)
- ☐ Fuel pump faulty, or delivery pressure low (Chapter 4)
- ☐ Uneven or low cylinder compressions (Chapter 2)
- ☐ Worn, faulty or incorrectly-gapped spark plugs - petrol models (Chapter 1A)
- ☐ Vacuum leak at the carburettor/throttle body, inlet manifold or associated hoses - petrol models (Chapter 4A)
- ☐ Blocked carburettor jet(s) or internal passages - carburettor petrol models (Chapter 4A)
- ☐ Blocked injector/fuel injection system fault - fuel-injected petrol models (Chapter 4B)
- ☐ Faulty injector(s) - diesel models (Chapter 4C)
- ☐ Injection pump timing incorrect - diesel models (Chapter 4C)
- ☐ Brakes binding (Chapters 1 and 9)
- ☐ Clutch slipping (Chapter 6)

Engine backfires

- ☐ Timing chain incorrectly fitted (Chapter 2)
- ☐ Vacuum leak at the carburettor/throttle body, inlet manifold or associated hoses - petrol models (Chapter 4A)
- ☐ Blocked carburettor jet(s) or internal passages - carburettor petrol models (Chapter 4A)
- ☐ Blocked injector/fuel injection system fault - fuel-injected petrol models (Chapter 4B)

Oil pressure warning light illuminated with engine running

- ☐ Low oil level, or incorrect oil grade (*"Weekly checks"*)
- ☐ Faulty oil pressure sensor (Chapter 5)
- ☐ Worn engine bearings and/or oil pump (Chapter 2)
- ☐ High engine operating temperature (Chapter 3)
- ☐ Oil pressure relief valve defective (Chapter 2)
- ☐ Oil pick-up strainer clogged (Chapter 2)

Engine runs-on after switching off

- ☐ Excessive carbon build-up in engine (Chapter 2)
- ☐ High engine operating temperature (Chapter 3)
- ☐ Faulty fuel cut-off solenoid - carburettor petrol models (Chapter 4A)
- ☐ Fuel injection system fault - fuel-injected petrol models (Chapter 4B)
- ☐ Faulty stop solenoid - diesel models (Chapter 4C)

Engine noises

Pre-ignition (pinking) or knocking during acceleration or under load

- ☐ Ignition timing incorrect/ignition system fault - petrol models (Chapters 1 and 5A)
- ☐ Incorrect grade of spark plug - petrol models (Chapter 1A)
- ☐ Incorrect grade of fuel (Chapter 1)
- ☐ Vacuum leak at the carburettor/throttle body, inlet manifold or associated hoses - petrol models (Chapter 4A)
- ☐ Excessive carbon build-up in engine (Chapter 2)
- ☐ Blocked carburettor jet(s) or internal passages - carburettor petrol models (Chapter 4A)
- ☐ Blocked injector/fuel injection system fault - fuel-injected petrol models (Chapter 4B)

Whistling or wheezing noises

- ☐ Leaking inlet manifold or carburettor/throttle body gasket - petrol models (Chapter 4A)
- ☐ Leaking exhaust manifold gasket or pipe-to-manifold joint (Chapter 4)
- ☐ Leaking vacuum hose (Chapters 4, 5 and 9)
- ☐ Blowing cylinder head gasket (Chapter 2)

Tapping or rattling noises

- ☐ Worn valve gear or camshaft (Chapter 2)
- ☐ Ancillary component fault (water pump, alternator, etc) (Chapters 3, 5, etc)

Knocking or thumping noises

- ☐ Worn big-end bearings (regular heavy knocking, perhaps less under load) (Chapter 2)
- ☐ Worn main bearings (rumbling and knocking, perhaps worsening under load) (Chapter 2)
- ☐ Piston slap (most noticeable when cold) (Chapter 2)
- ☐ Ancillary component fault (water pump, alternator, etc) (Chapters 3, 5, etc)

Cooling system

Overheating

- ☐ Insufficient coolant in system (*"Weekly checks"*)
- ☐ Thermostat faulty (Chapter 3)
- ☐ Radiator core blocked, or grille restricted (Chapter 3)
- ☐ Cooling fan or viscous coupling faulty (Chapter 3)
- ☐ Inaccurate temperature gauge sender unit (Chapter 3)
- ☐ Airlock in cooling system (Chapter 3)
- ☐ Pressure cap faulty (Chapter 3)

Overcooling

- ☐ Thermostat faulty (Chapter 3)
- ☐ Inaccurate temperature gauge sender unit (Chapter 3)
- ☐ Viscous coupling faulty (Chapter 3)

External coolant leakage

- ☐ Deteriorated or damaged hoses or hose clips (Chapter 1)
- ☐ Radiator core or heater matrix leaking (Chapter 3)
- ☐ Pressure cap faulty (Chapter 3)
- ☐ Coolant pump internal seal leaking (Chapter 3)
- ☐ Coolant pump-to-block seal leaking (Chapter 3)
- ☐ Boiling due to overheating (Chapter 3)
- ☐ Core plug leaking (Chapter 2)

Internal coolant leakage

- ☐ Leaking cylinder head gasket (Chapter 2)
- ☐ Cracked cylinder head or cylinder block (Chapter 2)

Corrosion

- ☐ Infrequent draining and flushing (Chapter 1)
- ☐ Incorrect coolant mixture or inappropriate coolant type (*"Weekly checks"*)

Fuel and exhaust systems

Excessive fuel consumption

- ☐ Air filter element dirty or clogged (Chapter 1)
- ☐ Choke mechanism incorrectly adjusted, or choke sticking - carburettor petrol models (Chapter 4A)
- ☐ Fuel injection system fault - fuel injected petrol models (Chapter 4B)
- ☐ Faulty injector(s) - diesel models (Chapter 4C)
- ☐ Ignition timing incorrect/ignition system fault - petrol models (Chapters 1 and 5)
- ☐ Tyres under-inflated (*"Weekly checks"*)

Fuel leakage and/or fuel odour

- ☐ Damaged or corroded fuel tank, pipes or connections (Chapter 4)

Excessive noise or fumes from exhaust system

- ☐ Leaking exhaust system or manifold joints (Chapters 1 and 4)
- ☐ Leaking, corroded or damaged silencers or pipe (Chapters 1 and 4)
- ☐ Broken mountings causing body or suspension contact (Chap0 ter 1)

Clutch

Pedal travels to floor - no pressure or very little resistance

- ☐ Hydraulic fluid level low/air in the hydraulic system (Chapter 6)
- ☐ Broken clutch release bearing or fork (Chapter 6)
- ☐ Broken diaphragm spring in clutch pressure plate (Chapter 6)

Clutch fails to disengage (unable to select gears)

- ☐ Hydraulic fluid level too high
- ☐ Clutch disc sticking on gearbox input shaft splines (Chapter 6)
- ☐ Clutch disc sticking to flywheel or pressure plate (Chapter 6)
- ☐ Faulty pressure plate assembly (Chapter 6)
- ☐ Clutch release mechanism worn or incorrectly assembled (Chapter 6)

Clutch slips (engine speed increases, with no increase in vehicle speed)

- ☐ Hydraulic fluid level too high
- ☐ Clutch disc linings excessively worn (Chapter 6)
- ☐ Clutch disc linings contaminated with oil or grease (Chapter 6)
- ☐ Faulty pressure plate or weak diaphragm spring (Chapter 6)

Judder as clutch is engaged

- ☐ Clutch disc linings contaminated with oil or grease (Chapter 6)
- ☐ Clutch disc linings excessively worn (Chapter 6)
- ☐ Faulty or distorted pressure plate or diaphragm spring (Chapter 6)
- ☐ Worn or loose engine or gearbox mountings (Chapter 2)
- ☐ Clutch disc hub or gearbox input shaft splines worn (Chapter 6)

Noise when depressing or releasing clutch pedal

- ☐ Worn clutch release bearing (Chapter 6)
- ☐ Worn or dry clutch pedal bushes (Chapter 6)
- ☐ Faulty pressure plate assembly (Chapter 6)
- ☐ Pressure plate diaphragm spring broken (Chapter 6)
- ☐ Broken clutch disc cushioning springs (Chapter 6)

Manual transmission

Noisy in neutral with engine running

- ☐ Input shaft bearings worn (noise apparent with clutch pedal released, but not when depressed) (Chapter 7A)*
- ☐ Clutch release bearing worn (noise apparent with clutch pedal depressed, possibly less when released) (Chapter 6)

Noisy in one particular gear

- ☐ Worn, damaged or chipped gear teeth (Chapter 7A)*

Difficulty engaging gears

- ☐ Clutch fault (Chapter 6)
- ☐ Worn or damaged gearchange linkage/cable (Chapter 7A)
- ☐ Incorrectly-adjusted gearchange linkage/cable (Chapter 7A)
- ☐ Worn synchroniser units (Chapter 7A)*

Vibration

- ☐ Lack of oil (Chapter 1)
- ☐ Worn bearings (Chapter 7A)*

Jumps out of gear

- ☐ Worn or damaged gearchange linkage/cable (Chapter 7A)
- ☐ Incorrectly-adjusted gearchange linkage/cable (Chapter 7A)
- ☐ Worn synchroniser units (Chapter 7A)*
- ☐ Worn selector forks (Chapter 7A)*

Lubricant leaks

- ☐ Leaking differential output oil seal (Chapter 7A)
- ☐ Leaking housing joint (Chapter 7A)*
- ☐ Leaking input shaft oil seal (Chapter 7A)*

**Although the corrective action necessary to remedy the symptoms described is beyond the scope of the home mechanic, the above information should be helpful in isolating the cause of the condition, so that the owner can communicate clearly with a professional mechanic.*

Automatic transmission

Note: *Due to the complexity of the automatic transmission, it is difficult for the home mechanic to properly diagnose and service this unit. For problems other than the following, the vehicle should be taken to a dealer service department or automatic transmission specialist. Do not be too hasty in removing the transmission if a fault is suspected, as most of the testing is carried out with the unit still fitted.*

Fluid leakage

- ☐ Automatic transmission fluid is usually dark in colour. Fluid leaks should not be confused with engine oil, which can easily be blown onto the transmission by airflow.
- ☐ To determine the source of a leak, first remove all built-up dirt and grime from the transmission housing and surrounding areas using a degreasing agent, or by steam-cleaning. Drive the vehicle at low speed, so airflow will not blow the leak far from its source. Raise and support the vehicle, and determine where the leak is coming from. The following are common areas of leakage:

  a) *Oil pan (Chapter 1 and 7B)*
  b) *Dipstick tube (Chapter 1 and 7B)*
  c) *Transmission-to-fluid cooler pipes/unions (Chapter 7B)*

Transmission fluid brown, or has burned smell

- ☐ Transmission fluid level low, or fluid in need of renewal (Chapter 1)

Transmission will not downshift (kickdown) with accelerator pedal fully depressed

- ☐ Low transmission fluid level (Chapter 1)
- ☐ Incorrect selector cable adjustment (Chapter 7B)

General gear selection problems

- ☐ Chapter 7B deals with checking and adjusting the selector cable on automatic transmissions. The following are common problems which may be caused by a poorly-adjusted cable:

  a) *Engine starting in gears other than Park or Neutral.*
  b) *Indicator panel indicating a gear other than the one actually being used.*
  c) *Vehicle moves when in Park or Neutral.*
  d) *Poor gear shift quality or erratic gear changes.*

- ☐ Refer to Chapter 7B for the selector cable adjustment procedure.

Engine will not start in any gear, or starts in gears other than Park or Neutral

- ☐ Incorrect starter/inhibitor switch adjustment (Chapter 7B)
- ☐ Incorrect selector cable adjustment (Chapter 7B)

Transmission slips, shifts roughly, is noisy, or has no drive in forward or reverse gears

- ☐ There are many probable causes for the above problems, but the home mechanic should be concerned with only one possibility - fluid level. Before taking the vehicle to a dealer or transmission specialist, check the fluid level and condition of the fluid as described in Chapter 1. Correct the fluid level as necessary, or change the fluid and filter if needed. If the problem persists, professional help will be necessary.

Differential and propeller shaft

Vibration when accelerating or decelerating

- ☐ Worn universal joint (Chapter 8)
- ☐ Bent, distorted or unbalanced propeller shaft (Chapter 8)

Low pitched whining; increasing with road speed

- ☐ Worn differential (Chapter 8)

Braking system

Note: *Before assuming that a brake problem exists, make sure that the tyres are in good condition and correctly inflated, that the front wheel alignment is correct, and that the vehicle's load is distributed evenly. Apart from checking the condition of all pipe and hose connections, any faults occurring on the anti-lock braking system should be referred to a Mercedes-Benz dealer for diagnosis.*

Vehicle pulls to one side under braking

- ☐ Worn, defective, damaged or contaminated brake pads on one side (Chapters 1 and 9)
- ☐ Seized or partially-seized brake caliper piston (Chapters 1 and 9)
- ☐ A mixture of brake pad lining materials fitted between sides (Chapters 1 and 9)
- ☐ Brake caliper mounting bolts loose (Chapter 9)
- ☐ Worn or damaged steering or suspension components (Chapters 1 and 10)

Noise (grinding or high-pitched squeal) when brakes applied

- ☐ Brake pad friction lining material worn down to metal backing (Chapters 1 and 9)
- ☐ Excessive corrosion of brake disc (may be apparent after the vehicle has been standing for some time (Chapters 1 and 9)
- ☐ Foreign object (stone chipping, etc) trapped between brake disc and shield (Chapters 1 and 9)

Brake pedal feels spongy when depressed

- ☐ Air in hydraulic system (Chapters 1 and 9)
- ☐ Deteriorated flexible rubber brake hoses (Chapters 1 and 9)
- ☐ Master cylinder mounting nuts loose (Chapter 9)
- ☐ Faulty master cylinder (Chapter 9)

Excessive brake pedal travel

- ☐ Faulty master cylinder (Chapter 9)
- ☐ Air in hydraulic system (Chapters 1 and 9)
- ☐ Faulty vacuum servo unit (Chapter 9)

Excessive brake pedal effort required to stop vehicle

- ☐ Faulty vacuum servo unit (Chapter 9)
- ☐ Disconnected, damaged or insecure brake servo vacuum hose (Chapter 9)
- ☐ Primary or secondary hydraulic circuit failure (Chapter 9)
- ☐ Seized brake caliper piston (Chapter 9)
- ☐ Brake pads incorrectly fitted (Chapters 1 and 9)
- ☐ Incorrect grade of brake pads fitted (Chapters 1 and 9)
- ☐ Brake pad linings contaminated (Chapters 1 and 9)
- ☐ Faulty vacuum pump - diesel models (Chapter 9)

Judder felt through brake pedal or steering wheel when braking

- ☐ Excessive run-out or distortion of discs (Chapters 1 and 9)
- ☐ Brake pad linings worn (Chapters 1 and 9)
- ☐ Brake caliper mounting bolts loose (Chapter 9)
- ☐ Wear in suspension or steering components or mountings (Chapters 1 and 10)

Brakes binding

- ☐ Seized brake caliper piston (Chapter 9)
- ☐ Incorrectly-adjusted parking brake mechanism (Chapter 9)
- ☐ Faulty master cylinder (Chapter 9)

Rear wheels locking under normal braking

- ☐ Rear brake pad linings contaminated (Chapters 1 and 9)
- ☐ Rear brake discs warped (Chapters 1 and 9)

Suspension and steering

Note: *Before diagnosing suspension or steering faults, be sure that the trouble is not due to incorrect tyre pressures, mixtures of tyre types, or binding brakes.*

Vehicle pulls to one side

- ☐ Defective tyre (*"Weekly checks"*)
- ☐ Excessive wear in suspension or steering components (Chapters 1 and 10)
- ☐ Incorrect front wheel alignment (Chapter 10)
- ☐ Accident damage to steering or suspension components (Chapter 1)

Wheel wobble and vibration

- ☐ Front roadwheels out of balance (vibration felt mainly through the steering wheel) (Chapters 1 and 10)
- ☐ Rear roadwheels out of balance (vibration felt throughout the vehicle) (Chapters 1 and 10)
- ☐ Roadwheels damaged or distorted (Chapters 1 and 10)
- ☐ Faulty or damaged tyre (*"Weekly checks"*)
- ☐ Worn steering or suspension joints, bushes or components (Chapters 1 and 10)
- ☐ Wheel bolts loose (Chapters 1 and 10)

Excessive pitching and/or rolling around corners, or during braking

- ☐ Defective shock absorbers (Chapters 1 and 10)
- ☐ Broken or weak spring and/or suspension component (Chapters 1 and 10)
- ☐ Worn or damaged anti-roll bar or mountings (Chapter 10)

Wandering or general instability

- ☐ Incorrect front wheel alignment (Chapter 10)
- ☐ Worn steering or suspension joints, bushes or components (Chapters 1 and 10)
- ☐ Roadwheels out of balance (Chapters 1 and 10)
- ☐ Faulty or damaged tyre (*"Weekly checks"*)
- ☐ Wheel bolts loose (Chapters 1 and 10)
- ☐ Defective shock absorbers (Chapters 1 and 10)

Excessively-stiff steering

- ☐ Seized steering linkage balljoint or suspension balljoint (Chapters 1 and 10)
- ☐ Broken or incorrectly-adjusted auxiliary drivebelt - power steering (Chapter 1)
- ☐ Incorrect front wheel alignment (Chapter 10)
- ☐ Steering box or linkage damaged (Chapter 10)

Suspension and steering (continued)

Excessive play in steering

- ☐ Worn steering column intermediate shaft coupling joint (Chapter 10)
- ☐ Worn steering linkage balljoints (Chapters 1 and 10)
- ☐ Worn steering box (Chapter 10)
- ☐ Worn steering or suspension joints, bushes or components (Chapters 1 and 10)

Lack of power assistance

- ☐ Broken or incorrectly-adjusted auxiliary drivebelt (Chapter 1)
- ☐ Incorrect power steering fluid level ("*Weekly checks*")
- ☐ Restriction in power steering fluid hoses (Chapter 1)
- ☐ Faulty power steering pump (Chapter 10)
- ☐ Faulty steering box (Chapter 10)

Tyre wear excessive

Tyres worn on inside or outside edges

- ☐ Tyres under-inflated (wear on both edges) ("*Weekly checks*")
- ☐ Incorrect camber or castor angles (wear on one edge only) (Chapter 10)
- ☐ Worn steering or suspension joints, bushes or components (Chapters 1 and 10)
- ☐ Excessively-hard cornering
- ☐ Accident damage

Tyre treads exhibit feathered edges

- ☐ Incorrect toe setting (Chapter 10)

Tyres worn in centre of tread

- ☐ Tyres over-inflated ("*Weekly checks*")

Tyres worn on inside and outside edges

- ☐ Tyres under-inflated ("*Weekly checks*")

Tyres worn unevenly

- ☐ Tyres/wheels out of balance (Chapter 1)
- ☐ Excessive wheel or tyre run-out (Chapter 1)
- ☐ Worn shock absorbers (Chapters 1 and 10)
- ☐ Faulty tyre ("*Weekly checks*")

Electrical system

Note: *For problems associated with the starting system, refer to the faults listed under "Engine" earlier in this Section.*

Battery will not hold a charge for more than a few days

- ☐ Battery defective internally (Chapter 5A)
- ☐ Battery terminal connections loose or corroded ("*Weekly checks*")
- ☐ Auxiliary drivebelt worn or incorrectly adjusted (Chapter 1)
- ☐ Alternator not charging at correct output (Chapter 5A)
- ☐ Alternator or voltage regulator faulty (Chapter 5A)
- ☐ Short-circuit causing continual battery drain (Chapters 5A and 12)

Ignition/no-charge warning light remains illuminated with engine running

- ☐ Auxiliary drivebelt broken, worn, or incorrectly adjusted (Chapter 1)
- ☐ Alternator brushes worn, sticking, or dirty (Chapter 5A)
- ☐ Alternator brush springs weak or broken (Chapter 5A)
- ☐ Internal fault in alternator or voltage regulator (Chapter 5A)
- ☐ Broken, disconnected, or loose wiring in charging circuit (Chapter 5A)

Ignition/no-charge warning light fails to come on

- ☐ Warning light bulb blown (Chapter 12)
- ☐ Broken, disconnected, or loose wiring in warning light circuit (Chapter 12)
- ☐ Alternator faulty (Chapter 5A)

Lights inoperative

- ☐ Bulb blown (Chapter 12)
- ☐ Corrosion of bulb or bulbholder contacts (Chapter 12)
- ☐ Blown fuse (Chapter 12)
- ☐ Faulty relay (Chapter 12)
- ☐ Broken, loose, or disconnected wiring (Chapter 12)
- ☐ Faulty switch (Chapter 12)

Instrument readings inaccurate or erratic

Instrument readings increase with engine speed

- ☐ Faulty voltage regulator (Chapter 12)

Fuel or temperature gauges give no reading

- ☐ Faulty gauge sender unit (Chapters 3 and 4)
- ☐ Wiring open-circuit (Chapter 12)
- ☐ Faulty gauge (Chapter 12)

Fuel or temperature gauges give continuous maximum reading

- ☐ Faulty gauge sender unit (Chapters 3 and 4)
- ☐ Wiring short-circuit (Chapter 12)
- ☐ Faulty gauge (Chapter 12)

Horn inoperative, or unsatisfactory in operation

Horn operates all the time

- ☐ Horn push either earthed or stuck down (Chapter 12)
- ☐ Horn cable-to-horn push earthed (Chapter 12)

Horn fails to operate

- ☐ Blown fuse (Chapter 12)
- ☐ Cable or cable connections loose, broken or disconnected (Chapter 12)
- ☐ Faulty horn (Chapter 12)

Horn emits intermittent or unsatisfactory sound

- ☐ Cable connections loose (Chapter 12)
- ☐ Horn mountings loose (Chapter 12)
- ☐ Faulty horn (Chapter 12)

Electrical system (continued)

Windscreen wipers inoperative, or unsatisfactory in operation

Wipers fail to operate, or operate very slowly

- ☐ Wiper blades stuck to screen, or linkage seized or binding (Chapters 1 and 12)
- ☐ Blown fuse (Chapter 12)
- ☐ Cable or cable connections loose, broken or disconnected (Chapter 12)
- ☐ Faulty relay (Chapter 12)
- ☐ Faulty wiper motor (Chapter 12)

Wiper blades sweep over too large or too small an area of the glass

- ☐ Wiper arms incorrectly positioned on spindles (Chapter 1)
- ☐ Excessive wear of wiper linkage (Chapter 12)
- ☐ Wiper motor or linkage mountings loose or insecure (Chapter 12)

Wiper blades fail to clean the glass effectively

- ☐ Wiper blade rubbers worn or perished ("*Weekly checks*")
- ☐ Wiper arm tension springs broken, or arm pivots seized (Chapter 12)
- ☐ Insufficient windscreen washer additive to adequately remove road film ("*Weekly checks*")

Windscreen washers inoperative, or unsatisfactory in operation

One or more washer jets inoperative

- ☐ Blocked washer jet (Chapter 1)
- ☐ Disconnected, kinked or restricted fluid hose (Chapter 12)
- ☐ Insufficient fluid in washer reservoir ("*Weekly checks*")

Washer pump fails to operate

- ☐ Broken or disconnected wiring or connections (Chapter 12)
- ☐ Blown fuse (Chapter 12)
- ☐ Faulty washer switch (Chapter 12)
- ☐ Faulty washer pump (Chapter 12)

Washer pump runs for some time before fluid is emitted from jets

- ☐ Faulty one-way valve in fluid supply hose (Chapter 12)

Electric windows inoperative, or unsatisfactory in operation

Window glass will only move in one direction

- ☐ Faulty switch (Chapter 12)

Window glass slow to move

- ☐ Regulator seized or damaged, or in need of lubrication (Chapter 11)
- ☐ Door internal components or trim fouling regulator (Chapter 11)
- ☐ Faulty motor (Chapter 11)

Window glass fails to move

- ☐ Blown fuse (Chapter 12)
- ☐ Faulty relay (Chapter 12)
- ☐ Broken or disconnected wiring or connections (Chapter 12)
- ☐ Faulty motor (Chapter 11)

Central locking system inoperative, or unsatisfactory in operation

Complete system failure

- ☐ Blown fuse (Chapter 12)
- ☐ Faulty relay (Chapter 12)
- ☐ Broken or disconnected wiring or connections (Chapter 12)
- ☐ Faulty motor (Chapter 11)

Latch locks but will not unlock, or unlocks but will not lock

- ☐ Faulty master switch (Chapter 12)
- ☐ Broken or disconnected latch operating rods or levers (Chapter 11)
- ☐ Faulty relay (Chapter 12)
- ☐ Faulty motor (Chapter 11)

One solenoid/motor fails to operate

- ☐ Broken or disconnected wiring or connections (Chapter 12)
- ☐ Faulty operating assembly (Chapter 11)
- ☐ Broken, binding or disconnected latch operating rods or levers (Chapter 11)
- ☐ Fault in door latch (Chapter 11)

A

ABS (Anti-lock brake system) A system, usually electronically controlled, that senses incipient wheel lockup during braking and relieves hydraulic pressure at wheels that are about to skid.

Air bag An inflatable bag hidden in the steering wheel (driver's side) or the dash or glovebox (passenger side). In a head-on collision, the bags inflate, preventing the driver and front passenger from being thrown forward into the steering wheel or windscreen.

Air cleaner A metal or plastic housing, containing a filter element, which removes dust and dirt from the air being drawn into the engine.

Air filter element The actual filter in an air cleaner system, usually manufactured from pleated paper and requiring renewal at regular intervals.

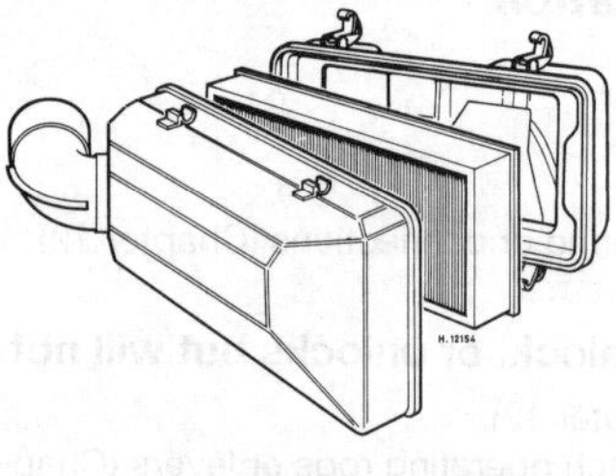

Air filter

Allen key A hexagonal wrench which fits into a recessed hexagonal hole.

Alligator clip A long-nosed spring-loaded metal clip with meshing teeth. Used to make temporary electrical connections.

Alternator A component in the electrical system which converts mechanical energy from a drivebelt into electrical energy to charge the battery and to operate the starting system, ignition system and electrical accessories.

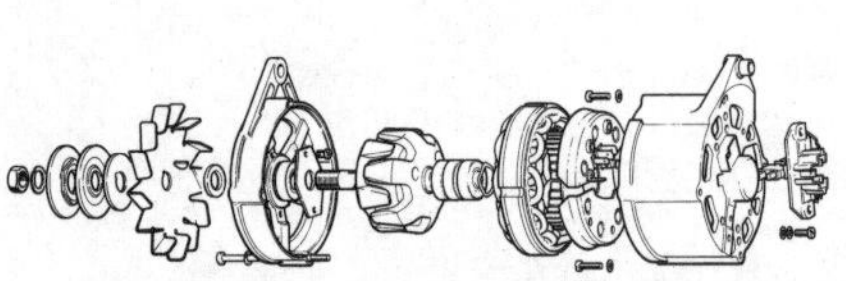

Alternator (exploded view)

Ampere (amp) A unit of measurement for the flow of electric current. One amp is the amount of current produced by one volt acting through a resistance of one ohm.

Anaerobic sealer A substance used to prevent bolts and screws from loosening. Anaerobic means that it does not require oxygen for activation. The Loctite brand is widely used.

Antifreeze A substance (usually ethylene glycol) mixed with water, and added to a vehicle's cooling system, to prevent freezing of the coolant in winter. Antifreeze also contains chemicals to inhibit corrosion and the formation of rust and other deposits that would tend to clog the radiator and coolant passages and reduce cooling efficiency.

Anti-seize compound A coating that reduces the risk of seizing on fasteners that are subjected to high temperatures, such as exhaust manifold bolts and nuts.

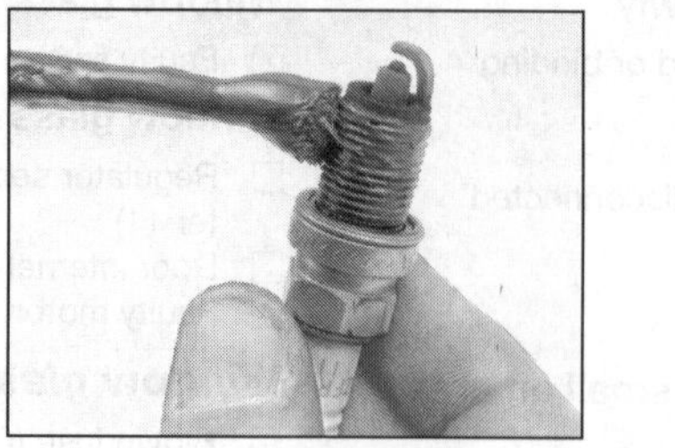

Anti-seize compound

Asbestos A natural fibrous mineral with great heat resistance, commonly used in the composition of brake friction materials. Asbestos is a health hazard and the dust created by brake systems should never be inhaled or ingested.

Axle A shaft on which a wheel revolves, or which revolves with a wheel. Also, a solid beam that connects the two wheels at one end of the vehicle. An axle which also transmits power to the wheels is known as a live axle.

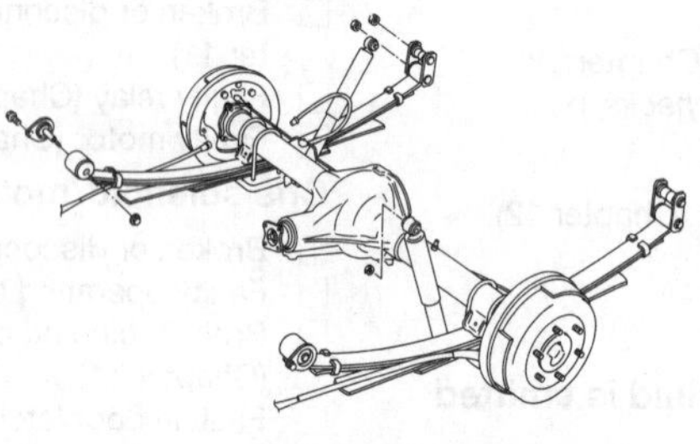

Axle assembly

Axleshaft A single rotating shaft, on either side of the differential, which delivers power from the final drive assembly to the drive wheels. Also called a driveshaft or a halfshaft.

B

Ball bearing An anti-friction bearing consisting of a hardened inner and outer race with hardened steel balls between two races.

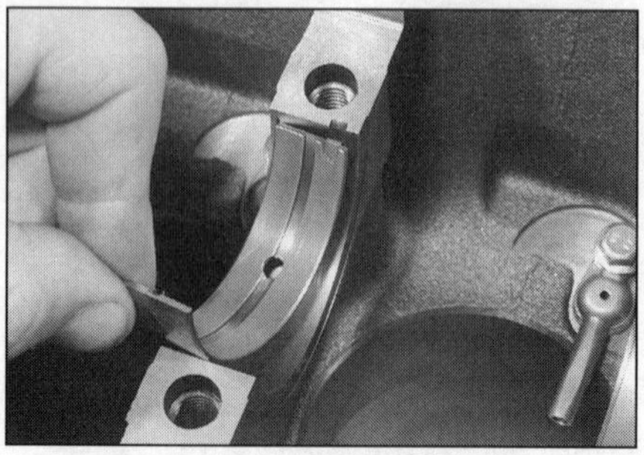

Bearing

Bearing The curved surface on a shaft or in a bore, or the part assembled into either, that permits relative motion between them with minimum wear and friction.

Big-end bearing The bearing in the end of the connecting rod that's attached to the crankshaft.

Bleed nipple A valve on a brake wheel cylinder, caliper or other hydraulic component that is opened to purge the hydraulic system of air. Also called a bleed screw.

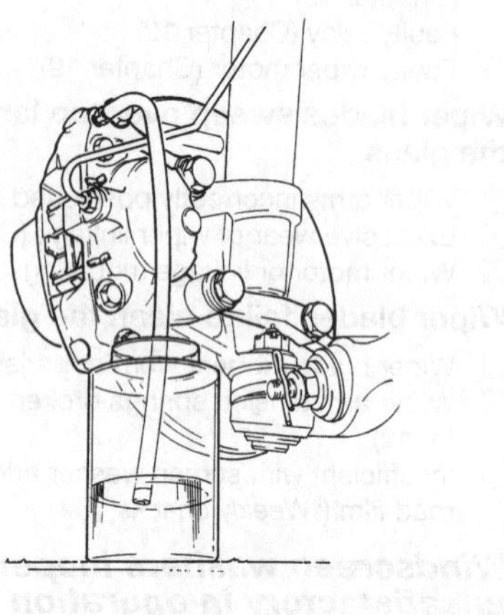

Brake bleeding

Brake bleeding Procedure for removing air from lines of a hydraulic brake system.

Brake disc The component of a disc brake that rotates with the wheels.

Brake drum The component of a drum brake that rotates with the wheels.

Brake linings The friction material which contacts the brake disc or drum to retard the vehicle's speed. The linings are bonded or riveted to the brake pads or shoes.

Brake pads The replaceable friction pads that pinch the brake disc when the brakes are applied. Brake pads consist of a friction material bonded or riveted to a rigid backing plate.

Brake shoe The crescent-shaped carrier to which the brake linings are mounted and which forces the lining against the rotating drum during braking.

Braking systems For more information on braking systems, consult the *Haynes Automotive Brake Manual*.

Breaker bar A long socket wrench handle providing greater leverage.

Bulkhead The insulated partition between the engine and the passenger compartment.

C

Caliper The non-rotating part of a disc-brake assembly that straddles the disc and carries the brake pads. The caliper also contains the hydraulic components that cause the pads to pinch the disc when the brakes are applied. A caliper is also a measuring tool that can be set to measure inside or outside dimensions of an object.

Camshaft A rotating shaft on which a series of cam lobes operate the valve mechanisms. The camshaft may be driven by gears, by sprockets and chain or by sprockets and a belt.

Canister A container in an evaporative emission control system; contains activated charcoal granules to trap vapours from the fuel system.

Canister

Carburettor A device which mixes fuel with air in the proper proportions to provide a desired power output from a spark ignition internal combustion engine.

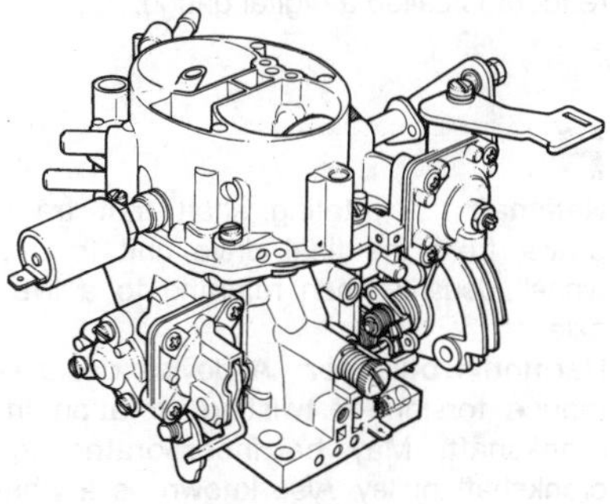

Carburettor

Castellated Resembling the parapets along the top of a castle wall. For example, a castellated balljoint stud nut.

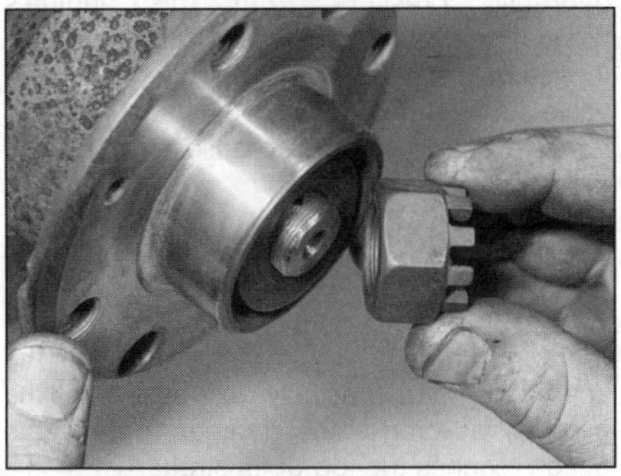

Castellated nut

Castor In wheel alignment, the backward or forward tilt of the steering axis. Castor is positive when the steering axis is inclined rearward at the top.

Catalytic converter A silencer-like device in the exhaust system which converts certain pollutants in the exhaust gases into less harmful substances.

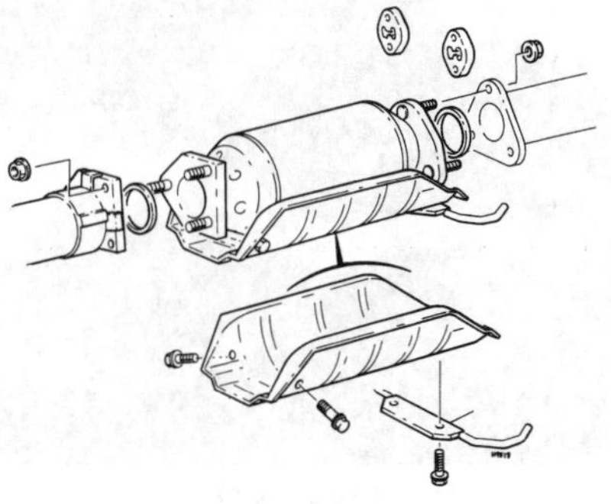

Catalytic converter

Circlip A ring-shaped clip used to prevent endwise movement of cylindrical parts and shafts. An internal circlip is installed in a groove in a housing; an external circlip fits into a groove on the outside of a cylindrical piece such as a shaft.

Clearance The amount of space between two parts. For example, between a piston and a cylinder, between a bearing and a journal, etc.

Coil spring A spiral of elastic steel found in various sizes throughout a vehicle, for example as a springing medium in the suspension and in the valve train.

Compression Reduction in volume, and increase in pressure and temperature, of a gas, caused by squeezing it into a smaller space.

Compression ratio The relationship between cylinder volume when the piston is at top dead centre and cylinder volume when the piston is at bottom dead centre.

Constant velocity (CV) joint A type of universal joint that cancels out vibrations caused by driving power being transmitted through an angle.

Core plug A disc or cup-shaped metal device inserted in a hole in a casting through which core was removed when the casting was formed. Also known as a freeze plug or expansion plug.

Crankcase The lower part of the engine block in which the crankshaft rotates.

Crankshaft The main rotating member, or shaft, running the length of the crankcase, with offset "throws" to which the connecting rods are attached.

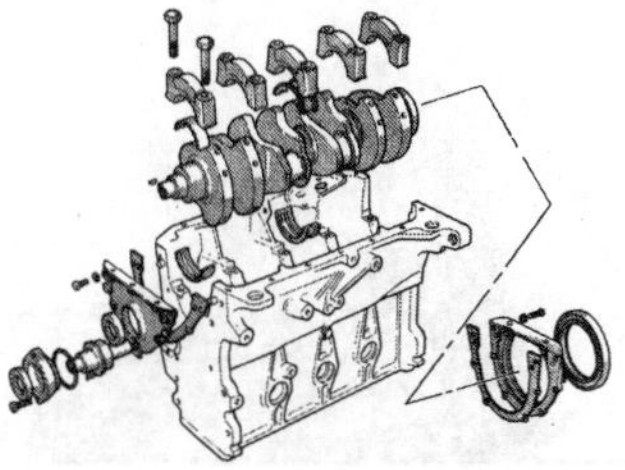

Crankshaft assembly

Crocodile clip See Alligator clip

D

Diagnostic code Code numbers obtained by accessing the diagnostic mode of an engine management computer. This code can be used to determine the area in the system where a malfunction may be located.

Disc brake A brake design incorporating a rotating disc onto which brake pads are squeezed. The resulting friction converts the energy of a moving vehicle into heat.

Double-overhead cam (DOHC) An engine that uses two overhead camshafts, usually one for the intake valves and one for the exhaust valves.

Drivebelt(s) The belt(s) used to drive accessories such as the alternator, water pump, power steering pump, air conditioning compressor, etc. off the crankshaft pulley.

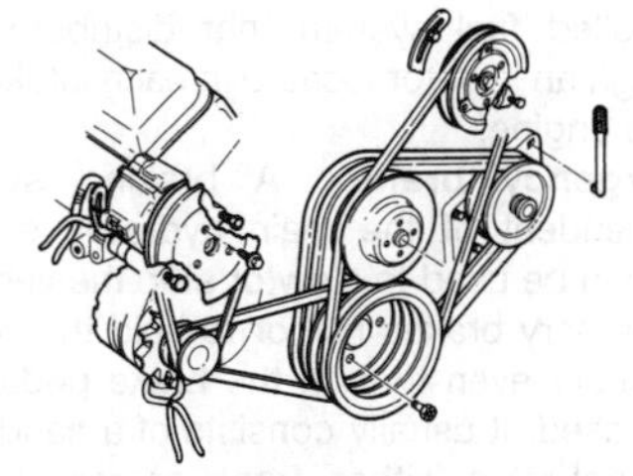

Accessory drivebelts

Driveshaft Any shaft used to transmit motion. Commonly used when referring to the axleshafts on a front wheel drive vehicle.

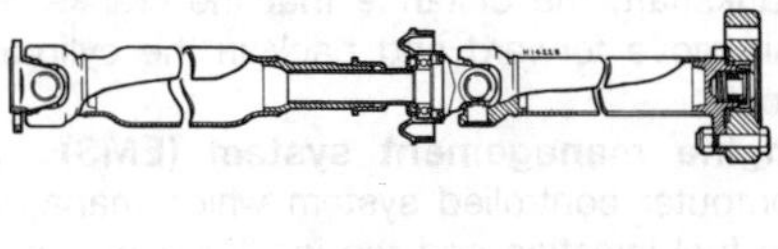

Driveshaft

Drum brake A type of brake using a drum-shaped metal cylinder attached to the inner surface of the wheel. When the brake pedal is pressed, curved brake shoes with friction linings press against the inside of the drum to slow or stop the vehicle.

Drum brake assembly

E

EGR valve A valve used to introduce exhaust gases into the intake air stream.

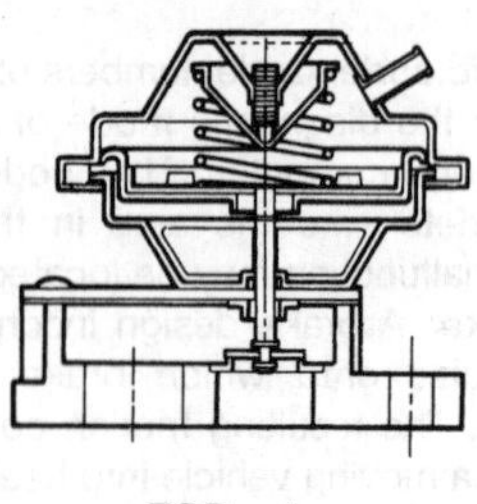

EGR valve

Electronic control unit (ECU) A computer which controls (for instance) ignition and fuel injection systems, or an anti-lock braking system. For more information refer to the *Haynes Automotive Electrical and Electronic Systems Manual.*

Electronic Fuel Injection (EFI) A computer controlled fuel system that distributes fuel through an injector located in each intake port of the engine.

Emergency brake A braking system, independent of the main hydraulic system, that can be used to slow or stop the vehicle if the primary brakes fail, or to hold the vehicle stationary even though the brake pedal isn't depressed. It usually consists of a hand lever that actuates either front or rear brakes mechanically through a series of cables and linkages. Also known as a handbrake or parking brake.

Endfloat The amount of lengthwise movement between two parts. As applied to a crankshaft, the distance that the crankshaft can move forward and back in the cylinder block.

Engine management system (EMS) A computer controlled system which manages the fuel injection and the ignition systems in an integrated fashion.

Exhaust manifold A part with several passages through which exhaust gases leave the engine combustion chambers and enter the exhaust pipe.

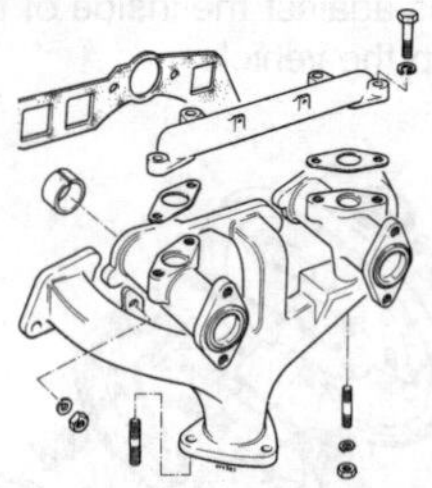

Exhaust manifold

F

Fan clutch A viscous (fluid) drive coupling device which permits variable engine fan speeds in relation to engine speeds.

Feeler blade A thin strip or blade of hardened steel, ground to an exact thickness, used to check or measure clearances between parts.

Feeler blade

Firing order The order in which the engine cylinders fire, or deliver their power strokes, beginning with the number one cylinder.

Flywheel A heavy spinning wheel in which energy is absorbed and stored by means of momentum. On cars, the flywheel is attached to the crankshaft to smooth out firing impulses.

Free play The amount of travel before any action takes place. The "looseness" in a linkage, or an assembly of parts, between the initial application of force and actual movement. For example, the distance the brake pedal moves before the pistons in the master cylinder are actuated.

Fuse An electrical device which protects a circuit against accidental overload. The typical fuse contains a soft piece of metal which is calibrated to melt at a predetermined current flow (expressed as amps) and break the circuit.

Fusible link A circuit protection device consisting of a conductor surrounded by heat-resistant insulation. The conductor is smaller than the wire it protects, so it acts as the weakest link in the circuit. Unlike a blown fuse, a failed fusible link must frequently be cut from the wire for replacement.

G

Gap The distance the spark must travel in jumping from the centre electrode to the side electrode in a spark plug. Also refers to the spacing between the points in a contact breaker assembly in a conventional points-type ignition, or to the distance between the reluctor or rotor and the pickup coil in an electronic ignition.

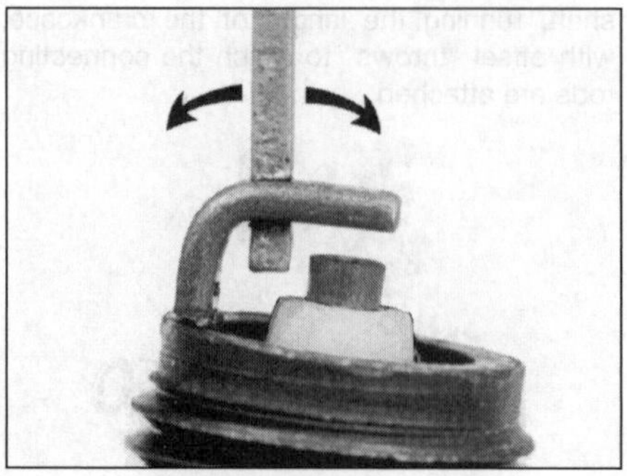

Adjusting spark plug gap

Gasket Any thin, soft material - usually cork, cardboard, asbestos or soft metal - installed between two metal surfaces to ensure a good seal. For instance, the cylinder head gasket seals the joint between the block and the cylinder head.

Gasket

Gauge An instrument panel display used to monitor engine conditions. A gauge with a movable pointer on a dial or a fixed scale is an analogue gauge. A gauge with a numerical readout is called a digital gauge.

H

Halfshaft A rotating shaft that transmits power from the final drive unit to a drive wheel, usually when referring to a live rear axle.

Harmonic balancer A device designed to reduce torsion or twisting vibration in the crankshaft. May be incorporated in the crankshaft pulley. Also known as a vibration damper.

Hone An abrasive tool for correcting small irregularities or differences in diameter in an engine cylinder, brake cylinder, etc.

Hydraulic tappet A tappet that utilises hydraulic pressure from the engine's lubrication system to maintain zero clearance (constant contact with both camshaft and valve stem). Automatically adjusts to variation in valve stem length. Hydraulic tappets also reduce valve noise.

I

Ignition timing The moment at which the spark plug fires, usually expressed in the number of crankshaft degrees before the piston reaches the top of its stroke.

Inlet manifold A tube or housing with passages through which flows the air-fuel mixture (carburettor vehicles and vehicles with throttle body injection) or air only (port fuel-injected vehicles) to the port openings in the cylinder head.

J

Jump start Starting the engine of a vehicle with a discharged or weak battery by attaching jump leads from the weak battery to a charged or helper battery.

L

Load Sensing Proportioning Valve (LSPV) A brake hydraulic system control valve that works like a proportioning valve, but also takes into consideration the amount of weight carried by the rear axle.
Locknut A nut used to lock an adjustment nut, or other threaded component, in place. For example, a locknut is employed to keep the adjusting nut on the rocker arm in position.
Lockwasher A form of washer designed to prevent an attaching nut from working loose.

M

MacPherson strut A type of front suspension system devised by Earle MacPherson at Ford of England. In its original form, a simple lateral link with the anti-roll bar creates the lower control arm. A long strut - an integral coil spring and shock absorber - is mounted between the body and the steering knuckle. Many modern so-called MacPherson strut systems use a conventional lower A-arm and don't rely on the anti-roll bar for location.
Multimeter An electrical test instrument with the capability to measure voltage, current and resistance.

N

NOx Oxides of Nitrogen. A common toxic pollutant emitted by petrol and diesel engines at higher temperatures.

O

Ohm The unit of electrical resistance. One volt applied to a resistance of one ohm will produce a current of one amp.
Ohmmeter An instrument for measuring electrical resistance.
O-ring A type of sealing ring made of a special rubber-like material; in use, the O-ring is compressed into a groove to provide the sealing action.

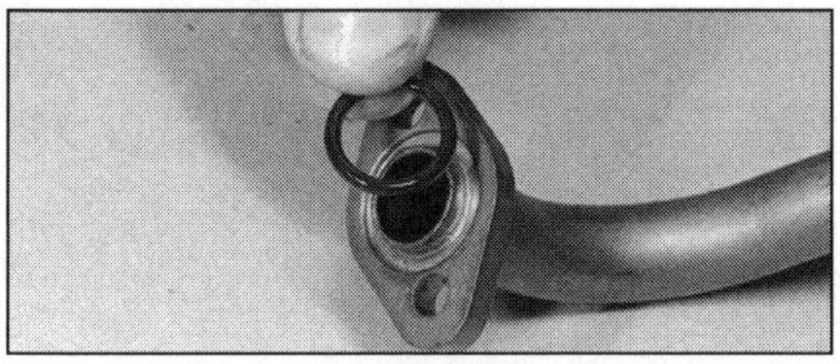

O-ring

Overhead cam (ohc) engine An engine with the camshaft(s) located on top of the cylinder head(s).
Overhead valve (ohv) engine An engine with the valves located in the cylinder head, but with the camshaft located in the engine block.
Oxygen sensor A device installed in the engine exhaust manifold, which senses the oxygen content in the exhaust and converts this information into an electric current. Also called a Lambda sensor.

P

Phillips screw A type of screw head having a cross instead of a slot for a corresponding type of screwdriver.
Plastigage A thin strip of plastic thread, available in different sizes, used for measuring clearances. For example, a strip of Plastigage is laid across a bearing journal. The parts are assembled and dismantled; the width of the crushed strip indicates the clearance between journal and bearing.

Plastigage

Propeller shaft The long hollow tube with universal joints at both ends that carries power from the transmission to the differential on front-engined rear wheel drive vehicles.
Proportioning valve A hydraulic control valve which limits the amount of pressure to the rear brakes during panic stops to prevent wheel lock-up.

R

Rack-and-pinion steering A steering system with a pinion gear on the end of the steering shaft that mates with a rack (think of a geared wheel opened up and laid flat). When the steering wheel is turned, the pinion turns, moving the rack to the left or right. This movement is transmitted through the track rods to the steering arms at the wheels.
Radiator A liquid-to-air heat transfer device designed to reduce the temperature of the coolant in an internal combustion engine cooling system.
Refrigerant Any substance used as a heat transfer agent in an air-conditioning system. R-12 has been the principle refrigerant for many years; recently, however, manufacturers have begun using R-134a, a non-CFC substance that is considered less harmful to the ozone in the upper atmosphere.
Rocker arm A lever arm that rocks on a shaft or pivots on a stud. In an overhead valve engine, the rocker arm converts the upward movement of the pushrod into a downward movement to open a valve.
Rotor In a distributor, the rotating device inside the cap that connects the centre electrode and the outer terminals as it turns, distributing the high voltage from the coil secondary winding to the proper spark plug. Also, that part of an alternator which rotates inside the stator. Also, the rotating assembly of a turbocharger, including the compressor wheel, shaft and turbine wheel.
Runout The amount of wobble (in-and-out movement) of a gear or wheel as it's rotated. The amount a shaft rotates "out-of-true." The out-of-round condition of a rotating part.

S

Sealant A liquid or paste used to prevent leakage at a joint. Sometimes used in conjunction with a gasket.
Sealed beam lamp An older headlight design which integrates the reflector, lens and filaments into a hermetically-sealed one-piece unit. When a filament burns out or the lens cracks, the entire unit is simply replaced.
Serpentine drivebelt A single, long, wide accessory drivebelt that's used on some newer vehicles to drive all the accessories, instead of a series of smaller, shorter belts. Serpentine drivebelts are usually tensioned by an automatic tensioner.

Serpentine drivebelt

Shim Thin spacer, commonly used to adjust the clearance or relative positions between two parts. For example, shims inserted into or under bucket tappets control valve clearances. Clearance is adjusted by changing the thickness of the shim.
Slide hammer A special puller that screws into or hooks onto a component such as a shaft or bearing; a heavy sliding handle on the shaft bottoms against the end of the shaft to knock the component free.
Sprocket A tooth or projection on the periphery of a wheel, shaped to engage with a chain or drivebelt. Commonly used to refer to the sprocket wheel itself.
Starter inhibitor switch On vehicles with an

automatic transmission, a switch that prevents starting if the vehicle is not in Neutral or Park.

Strut See MacPherson strut.

T

Tappet A cylindrical component which transmits motion from the cam to the valve stem, either directly or via a pushrod and rocker arm. Also called a cam follower.

Thermostat A heat-controlled valve that regulates the flow of coolant between the cylinder block and the radiator, so maintaining optimum engine operating temperature. A thermostat is also used in some air cleaners in which the temperature is regulated.

Thrust bearing The bearing in the clutch assembly that is moved in to the release levers by clutch pedal action to disengage the clutch. Also referred to as a release bearing.

Timing belt A toothed belt which drives the camshaft. Serious engine damage may result if it breaks in service.

Timing chain A chain which drives the camshaft.

Toe-in The amount the front wheels are closer together at the front than at the rear. On rear wheel drive vehicles, a slight amount of toe-in is usually specified to keep the front wheels running parallel on the road by offsetting other forces that tend to spread the wheels apart.

Toe-out The amount the front wheels are closer together at the rear than at the front. On front wheel drive vehicles, a slight amount of toe-out is usually specified.

Tools For full information on choosing and using tools, refer to the *Haynes Automotive Tools Manual.*

Tracer A stripe of a second colour applied to a wire insulator to distinguish that wire from another one with the same colour insulator.

Tune-up A process of accurate and careful adjustments and parts replacement to obtain the best possible engine performance.

Turbocharger A centrifugal device, driven by exhaust gases, that pressurises the intake air. Normally used to increase the power output from a given engine displacement, but can also be used primarily to reduce exhaust emissions (as on VW's "Umwelt" Diesel engine).

U

Universal joint or U-joint A double-pivoted connection for transmitting power from a driving to a driven shaft through an angle. A U-joint consists of two Y-shaped yokes and a cross-shaped member called the spider.

V

Valve A device through which the flow of liquid, gas, vacuum, or loose material in bulk may be started, stopped, or regulated by a movable part that opens, shuts, or partially obstructs one or more ports or passageways. A valve is also the movable part of such a device.

Valve clearance The clearance between the valve tip (the end of the valve stem) and the rocker arm or tappet. The valve clearance is measured when the valve is closed.

Vernier caliper A precision measuring instrument that measures inside and outside dimensions. Not quite as accurate as a micrometer, but more convenient.

Viscosity The thickness of a liquid or its resistance to flow.

Volt A unit for expressing electrical "pressure" in a circuit. One volt that will produce a current of one ampere through a resistance of one ohm.

W

Welding Various processes used to join metal items by heating the areas to be joined to a molten state and fusing them together. For more information refer to the *Haynes Automotive Welding Manual.*

Wiring diagram A drawing portraying the components and wires in a vehicle's electrical system, using standardised symbols. For more information refer to the *Haynes Automotive Electrical and Electronic Systems Manual.*

Note: *References throughout this index are in the form - "Chapter number" • "page number"*

A

Accelerator cable - 4A•5, 4B•5, 4C•3
Accessory shops - REF•3
Aerial - 1A•18, 1B•13, 12•14
Air bags - 0•5
Air cleaner - 1A•20, 1B•14, 4A•2, 4A•3, 4B•3, 4C•2
Air conditioning system - 1A•12, 1A•14, 1B•9, 3•12
Air injection system - 4D•6
Airbag system - 12•15
Alarm system - 12•14, REF•5
Alternator - 1A•12, 5A•3, 5A•4
Anti-jerk control system - 4C•9
Anti-lock braking system (ABS) - 9•15, 9•16
Anti-roll bar - 10•8, 10•13, 10•14
Anti-theft alarm system - 12•14
Antifreeze - 0•13, 0•16, 1A•2, 1A•3, 1A•24, 1B•2, 1B•16, 3•2
Asbestos - 0•5
ASR - 9•16, 9•18
ATF - 0•16, 1A•2, 1A•10, 1A•21, 1B•2, 1B•7, 1B•15, 7B•0
Audio equipment - 12•13, REF•5
Automatic transmission - 2A•19, 2B•16, 2C•16, 7B•0 *et seq*
Automatic transmission fault finding - REF•16
Automatic transmission fluid - 0•16, 1A•2, 1A•10, 1A•21, 1B•2, 1B•7, 1B•15, 7B•0
Automatic transmission fluid filter - 1A•21, 1B•15
Auxiliary drivebelts - 1A•11, 1B•8
Auxiliary shaft - 2A•10, 2A•12

B

Backfire - REF•14
Balljoint - 10•22
Battery - 0•5, 0•15, 5A•2, 5A•3
Battery fault - REF•18
Big-end bearings - 02D•17, 02D•20
Bleeding brakes - 9•2
Bleeding clutch - 6•6
Bleeding power steering - 10•20
Body corrosion - REF•11
Body electrical system - 12•1 *et seq*
Bodywork - 11•1 *et seq*
Bonnet - 11•4, 11•5
Boot lid - 11•5, 11•6
Bosch CIS-E (KE•Jetronic) fuel injection system - 4B•1 *et seq*
Brake fluid - 0•12, 0•16, 1A•23, 1B•16
Braking system - 1A•18, 1B•13, 9•1 *et seq*, REF•8, REF•9, REF•10
Braking system fault finding - REF•17
Bulbs - 0•15, 12•6, 12•8
Bumpers - 11•6
Burning - 0•5

C

Cables - 4A•5, 4B•5, 4C•3, 7B•1, 9•15, 11•5, 12•6
Calipers - 9•8, 9•9
Camber setting - 10•23
Camshaft - 2A•12, 2B•9, 2C•10
Camshaft cover - 2A•4, 2B•3, 2C•5
Camshaft front oil seal - 2B•15
Camshaft sprocket - 2A•9, 2B•8, 2C•8
Capacities - 1A•2, 1B•2
Carburettor damper oil - 0•16, 1A•14
Carburettor fuel system - 4A•1 *et seq*
Carpets - 11•2
Castor setting - 10•23
Catalytic converter - 4D•5
Central locking system - 11•12, 11•15
Central locking system fault - REF•19
Centre console - 11•16, 12•4
Charcoal canister - 1A•23, 4D•2
Charging system - 5A•3
Clutch - 1A•19, 1A•22, 1B•13, 1B•15, 6•1 *et seq*
Clutch fault finding - REF•15
CO emissions (mixture) - REF•11
Coil - 5B•3, 5C•2
Coil spring - 10•7, 10•11
Compression test - 2A•3, 2B•3, 2C•4
Connecting rods - 02D•12, 02D•14, 02D•20, 02D•21
Console - 11•16, 12•4
Contents - 0•2
Control arms - 10•11
Conversion factors - REF•2
Coolant - 0•13, 0•16, 1A•2, 1A•3, 1A•24, 1B•2, 1B•16, 3•2
Coolant level sensor - 3•7
Coolant pump drivebelt - 1A•12
Coolant temperature sensor - 5B•6, 5C•4, 5D•2
Cooling, heating and ventilation systems - 3•1 *et seq*
Cooling system fault finding - REF•15
Corrosion - REF•15
Courtesy light - 12•4, 12•8
Crankcase - 02D•13
Crankcase emission control - 4D•2, 4D•3
Crankshaft - 02D•12, 02D•15, 02D•18
Crankshaft oil seals - 2A•18, 2B•15, 2B•16, 2C•16
Crankshaft pulley - 2A•5, 2B•4, 2C•5
Crankshaft speed sensor - 5B•6, 5C•4
Crankshaft spigot bearing - 2A•18, 2B•16, 2C•16
Crankshaft sprocket - 2A•10, 2B•8, 2C•9
Cruise control system components - 12•14
Crushing - 0•5
Cylinder block - 02D•13
Cylinder head - 2A•14, 2B•11, 2C•11, 02D•9, 02D•10, 02D•11

D

Dents in bodywork - 11•2
Depressurisation - fuel injection system - 4B•3
Diesel engine in-car repair procedures - 2C•1 *et seq*
Diesel fuel injection system - 0•5, 4C•1 *et seq*
Differential fault finding - REF•16
Dimensions - REF•1
Direction indicator - 12•7, 12•8
Discs - 9•7, 9•8
Distributor - 5B•4, 5C•3
Doors - 11•6, 11•8, 11•9, 11•10, 11•11, 11•12, 11•13, 11•14, 12•4
Doors - REF•9
Drivebelts - 1A•11, 1B•8
Driveplate - 2A•18, 2B•15, 2C•15
Driveshafts - 1A•16, 1B•11, 8•3, 8•4
Drivetrain - 1A•18, 1B•13
Drop arm - 10•19

E

Earth fault - 12•2
EGR valve - 4D•4
Electric shock - 0•5
Electric windows fault - REF•19
Electrical equipment - 1A•18, 1B•1, REF•9
Electrical system - 12•1 *et seq*
Electrical system fault finding - 12•2, REF•18, REF•19
Electromagnetically coupled fan - 3•7
Electronic control unit (ECU) - 9•16, 9•19, 12•14
Electronic diesel engine control system (EDS) - 4C•10
Emblem - 11•5
Emission control systems - 4D•2
Engine fault finding - 5B•3, 5C•2, REF•13, REF•14
Engine oil - 0•11, 0•16, 1A•2, 1A•7, 1B•2, 1B•6
Engine overload protection system - 4C•10
Engine removal and general engine overhaul procedures - 02D•1 *et seq*
Environmental considerations - REF•4
Evaporative emission control - 4D•2
Evaporative loss emission control system - 4D•2
Exhaust and emission control systems - 4D•1 *et seq*
Exhaust emission checks - REF•11
Exhaust Gas Recirculation (EGR) system - 4D•3
Exhaust manifold - 4D•3
Exhaust specialists - REF•3
Exhaust system - 1A•17, 1B•12, 4D•2, 4D•5, REF•10

F

Facia - 11•19, 12•4
Fans - 3•6
Fast idle exhaust CO - 1A•15
Fast idle speed - 1A•15
Fault Finding - REF•12 *et seq*
Fault finding - automatic transmission - REF•16
Fault finding - braking system - REF•17
Fault finding - clutch - REF•15
Fault finding - cooling system - REF•15
Fault finding - differential - REF•16
Fault finding - electrical system - 12•2, REF•18, REF•19
Fault finding - engine - 5B•3, 5C•2, REF•13, REF•14
Fault finding - fuel and exhaust systems - REF•15
Fault finding - manual transmission - REF•16
Fault finding - propeller shaft - REF•16
Fault finding - steering - REF•17, REF•18
Fault finding - suspension - REF•17, REF•18
Filling - 11•3
Filter, air - 1A•20, 1B•14, 4A•2, 4B•3, 4C•2
Filter, automatic transmission fluid - 1A•21, 1B•15
Filter, fuel - 1A•20, 1B•14
Filter, oil - 1A•7, 1B•6
Final drive oil - 0•16, 1A•2, 1A•17, 1B•2, 1B•12
Final drive, driveshafts and propeller shaft - 8•1 *et seq*
Fire - 0•5
Fluids - 0•16
Flywheel - 2A•18, 2B•15, 2C•15
Foglamp - 12•7
Four-cylinder petrol engine in-car repair procedures - 2A•1 *et seq*
Fuel accumulator - 4B•6
Fuel and exhaust systems - REF•11
Fuel and exhaust systems fault finding - REF•15
Fuel consumption high - REF•15
Fuel filter - 1A•20, 1B•14
Fuel gauge - 4A•4, 4B•5, 4C•3
Fuel gauge fault - REF•18
Fuel injection pump - 2C•9, 4C•4, 4C•6, 4C•7
Fuel injectors - 4B•9, 4C•8
Fuel lift pump - 4C•3
Fuel pressure regulator - 4B•10
Fuel pump - 4A•4, 4B•4
Fuel tank - 4A•4, 4B•5, 4C•3
Fume or gas intoxication - 0•5
Fumes from exhaust system - REF•15
Fuses - 0•15, 12•3

G

Gaiters - 1A•16, 1B•11, 8•4
Gashes in bodywork - 11•2
Gaskets - REF•4
Gauges - 4A•4, 4B•5, 4C•3, 12•5, REF•18
Gear selector - 7B•1
Gearbox oil - 0•16, 1A•2, 1A•17, 1B•2, 1B•12, 7A•1, 7A•2
Gearchange components - 7A•2
Glossary of technical terms - REF•20 *et seq*
Glovebox - 11•18
Glovebox lamp - 12•8
Glow plugs - 5D•2
Grille - 11•5
Guide rails - 2A•11, 2B•9, 2C•9, 2C•10

H

Handbrake - See **Parking brake**
Handles - 11•9, 11•11
HC emissions - REF•11
Headlights - 1A•18, 1B•13, 12•6, 12•4, 12•9, 12•10
Heater - 3•10
Hinges - 1A•18, 1B•13, - 11•4
Horns - 12•13
Horn fault - REF•18
HT coil - 5B•3, 5C•2
Hub bearings - 1A•18, 1B•13, 10•3, 10•4, 10•9
Hub carrier - 10•8
Hydrofluoric acid - 0•5

I

Idle exhaust CO - 1A•14
Idle speed - 1A•14, 1B•10
Idle speed control system - 4C•9
Idling fault - REF•13
Ignition switch - 10•16
Ignition system: 4-cylinder petrol engine - 1A•19, 5B•1 *et seq*
Ignition system: 6-cylinder petrol engine - 1A•19, 5C•1 *et seq*
Ignition system fault - REF•18
Ignition timing - 5B•5, 5C•3
Indicators - 12•7, 12•8
Injectors - 4B•9, 4C•8
Inlet air temperature sensor - 5B•6
Inlet manifold - 4A•11, 4B•11, 4C•10
Input shaft oil seal - 7A•3
Instrument panel - 12•5
Instruments - 1A•18, 1B•13
Instrument fault - REF•18
Interior light - 12•4, 12•8
Introduction - 0•4

J2

Jacking and Vehicle Support - REF•5
Joint mating faces - REF•4
Jump starting - 0•7

K

Knuckle assembly - 10•5

L

Lambda sensor - 4B•10
Leakdown test - 2C•4
Leaks - 0•9, 1A•10, 1B•8, REF•15, REF•16
Lights inoperative - REF•18
Locknuts, locktabs and washers - REF•4
Locks - 1A•18, 1B•13, 10•16, 11•5, 11•6, 11•10, 11•12
Locks fault - REF•19
Lower arm - 10•7, 10•13
Lubricants - 0•16
Luggage compartment lamp - 12•8

M

Main bearings - 02D•17, 02D•18
Maintenance schedule - 1A•3, 1B•3
Manifolds - 4A•11, 4B•11, 4C•10, 4D•3
Manual transmission - 2A•19, 2B•16, 2C•16, 7A•1 *et seq*
Manual transmission fault finding - REF•16
Manual transmission oil - 0•16, 1A•2, 1A•17, 1B•2, 1B•12, 7A•1, 7A•2
Master cylinder - 6•4, 9•10
Mirrors - 11•13, 11•14, REF•8
Misfire - 5B•3, 5C•2, REF•14, REF•15
Mixture settings - 1A•14
MOT test checks - REF•8 *et seq*
Motor factors - REF•3
Mountings - 2A•19, 2B•16, 2C•16

N

Number plate lamp - 12•8

O

Oil cooler - 2C•16
Oil filter - 1A•7, 1B•6
Oil pressure fault - REF•14
Oil pump - 2A•17, 2B•14, 2C•14
Oil seals - 2A•18, 2B•15, 2C•16, 7A•3, 8•3, 10•19, REF•4
Oil, carburettor damper - 0•16
Oil, engine - 0•11, 0•16, 1A•2, 1A•7, 1B•2, 1B•6
Oil, final drive - 0•16, 1A•2, 1A•17, 1B•2, 1B•12
Oil, manual transmission - 0•16, 1A•2, 1A•17, 1B•2, 1B•12, 7A•1, 7A•2
Open circuit - 12•2
Output flange oil seal - 7A•3
Overcooling - REF•15
Overheating - REF•15

P

Pads - 1A•16, 1A•17, 1B•11, 9•4, 9•6
Parking brake - 1A•17, 1B•11, 9•12, 9•16, REF•8
Pedals - 6•6
Petrol engine in-car repair procedures - 2A•1 *et seq, 2B*•1 *et seq*
Pierburg 2E-E carburettor - 4A•9
Piston rings - 02D•17
Pistons - 02D•12, 02D•14, 02D•20, 02D•21
Plastic components - 11•3
Poisonous or irritant substances - 0•5
Power steering fluid - 0•12, 0•16, 1A•2, 1B•2
Power steering pump - 1A•12, 10•19
Pre-ignition (pinking) - REF•14
Preheating system: diesel engine - 5D•1 *et seq*
Propeller shaft - 1A•18, 1B•12, 8•5, 8•7, 8•8
Propeller shaft fault finding - REF•16

Q

Quarter-light - 11•9

R

Radiator - 1A•24, 1B•17, 3•3
Radiator grille - 11•5
Radio aerial - 1A•18, 1B•13, 12•14
Re-spraying - 11•3
Rear lamp cluster - 12•7, 12•9
Rear window - 11•13
Reference - REF•1 *et seq*
Relays - 9•18, 12•3
Release bearing - 6•2
Repair procedures - REF•4
Reversing light switch - 7A•3, 7B•2
Road test - 1A•18, 1B•13
Roadside Repairs - 0•6 *et seq*
Rocker gear - 2A•12, 2B•9, 02D•11
Rotor arm - 5B•5, 5C•3
Routine maintenance and servicing - diesel engine models - 1B•1 *et seq*
Routine maintenance and servicing - petrol engine models - 1A•1 *et seq*
Routine maintenance - bodywork and underframe - 11•1
Routine maintenance - upholstery and carpets - 11•2
Rust holes in bodywork - 11•2

S

Safety first - 0•5
Scalding - 0•5
Scratches in bodywork - 11•2
Screw threads and fastenings - REF•4
Seat belts - 1A•18, 1B•12, 11•15, REF•9
Seats - 11•14, 11•15, REF•9
Servo unit - 9•11, 9•12
Shock absorbers - 1A•16, 1B•11, 10•5, 10•9, REF•9, REF•10
Shoes - 9•12
Short circuit - 12•2
Sidelamp - 12•7
Six-cylinder petrol engine in-car repair procedures - 2B•1 *et seq*
Slave cylinder - 6•3
Spare Parts - REF•3
Spark plugs - 1A•9
Speakers - 12•14
Speed sensor - 12•14
Speedometer - 12•5, 12•6
Springs - 10•7, 10•11, REF•10
Start-up after overhaul - 02D•21
Starter inhibitor - 7B•2
Starter motor - 5A•5
Starter motor fault - REF•13
Starting and charging systems - 5A•1 *et seq*
Steering - 1A•15, 1A•18, 1B•10, 1B•13
Steering angles - 10•22
Steering box - 10•18, 10•19
Steering column - 10•15, 10•17, REF•8
Steering column combination switch - 12•4
Steering damper - 10•20
Steering drag link - 10•21
Steering fault finding - REF•17, REF•18
Steering intermediate arm - 10•21
Steering lock - 10•16
Steering mechanism - REF•10
Steering wheel - 10•14, REF•8
Stop-light switch - 9•15
Stromberg carburettor - 1A•14, 4A•7
Sump - 2A•16, 2B•13, 2C•14
Sun visor - 12•8
Sunroof - 11•15
Suspension and steering - 1A•15, 1A•18, 1B•10, 1B•13, 10•1 *et seq*, REF•9, REF•10
Suspension fault finding - REF•17, REF•18
Swirl chambers - 02D•10
Switches - 3•7, 7A•3, 7B•2, 9•15, 10•16, 12•4

T

Tachometer - 12•5
TDC sensor - 5B•6, 5C•4
Temperature coolant sensor - 3•8
Temperature gauge fault - REF•18
Tensioner rail - 2A•11, 2B•9, 2C•9
Thermo-valve/purge valve - 4D•2
Thermo-viscous coupled fan - 3•6
Thermostat - 3•5
Throttle body - 4B•7
Throttle cable - 4A•5, 4B•5, 4C•3
Throttle linkage lubrication - 1A•10, 1B•7
Timing - 5B•5, 5C•3
Timing chain - 2A•7, 2B•6, 2C•7
Timing chain cover - 2A•5, 2B•4, 2C•5
Timing chain tensioner - 2A•8, 2B•7, 2C•8
Toe setting - 10•23
Tools - REF•4, REF•6, REF•7
Towing - 0•9
Track rod - 10•22
Traction control (ASR) - 9•16, 9•18
Trim panels - 11•6
Turbocharger - 4D•4
Tyres - REF•11
Tyre condition - 0•14
Tyre pressures - 0•16
Tyre specialists - REF•3
Tyre wear excessive - REF•18

U

Underbonnet check points - 0•10, 0•11
Underframe - 11•1
Upholstery - 11•2

V

Vacuum pump - 9•19
Vacuum servo unit - 9•11, 9•12
Vacuum solenoid valve - 4D•3
Valve clearances - 1A•19
Valve lifters - 2A•12, 2B•9, 2C•10, 02D•11
Valve timing marks - 2A•3, 2B•3, 2C•4
Valves - 02D•10
Vehicle Identification - REF•3, REF•9
Ventilation components - 3•10
Vibration damper - 2A•5, 2B•4, 2C•5

W

Warning lamp bulbs - 12•5
Washer fluid - 0•13
Washer system - 1A•18, 1B•13, 12•13
Washers fault - REF•19
Water pump - 1A•12, 3•8
Weekly Checks - 0•10 *et seq*
Weights - REF•1
Wheel alignment - 10•22
Wheel bearings - 1A•18, 1B•13, 10•3, 10•4, 10•9, REF•10
Wheel changing - 0•8
Wheel sensors - 9•17, 9•19
Wheels - REF•11
Wheels locking under braking - REF•17
Window regulator - 11•7, 11•9
Windows - 11•8, 11•9
Windows fault - REF•19
Windscreen - 11•13, REF•8
Wiper blades - 0•13, 12•11
Wiper fault - REF•19
Wiper motor - 12•11, 12•12
Wiring diagrams - 12•16 et seq
Working facilities - REF•7

Haynes Manuals – The Complete List

Title	Book No.
ALFA ROMEO	
Alfa Romeo Alfasud/Sprint (74 - 88)	0292
Alfa Romeo Alfetta (73 - 87)	0531
AUDI	
Audi 80 (72 - Feb 79)	0207
Audi 80, 90 (79 - Oct 86) & Coupe (81 - Nov 88)	0605
Audi 80, 90 (Oct 86 - 90) & Coupe (Nov 88 - 90)	1491
Audi 100 (Oct 76 - Oct 82)	0428
Audi 100 (Oct 82 - 90) & 200 (Feb 84 - Oct 89)	0907
Audi 100/A6 (May 91 - May 97)	3504
AUSTIN	
Austin/MG Maestro 1.3 & 1.6 (83 - 95)	0922
Austin/MG Metro (80 - May 90)	0718
Austin Montego 1.3 & 1.6 (84 - 94)	1066
Austin/MG Montego 2.0 (84 - 95)	1067
Mini (59 - 69)	0527
Mini (69 - Oct 96)	0646
Austin/Rover 2.0 litre Diesel Engine (86 - 93)	1857
BEDFORD	
Bedford CF (69 - 87)	0163
Bedford Rascal (86 - 93)	3015
BMW	
BMW 316, 320 & 320i (4-cyl) (75 - Feb 83)	0276
BMW 320, 320i, 323i & 325i (6-cyl) (Oct 77 - Sept 87)	0815
BMW 3-Series (Apr 91 - 96)	3210
BMW 3-Series (sohc) (83 - 91)	1948
BMW 520i & 525e (Oct 81 - June 88)	1560
BMW 525, 528 & 528i (73 - Sept 81)	0632
BMW 5-Series (sohc) (81 - 91)	1948
BMW 1500, 1502, 1600, 1602, 2000 & 2002 (59 - 77)	0240
CITROEN	
Citroen 2CV, Ami & Dyane (67 - 90)	0196
Citroen AX Petrol & Diesel (87 - 94)	3014
Citroen BX (83 - 94)	0908
Citroen CX (75 - 88)	0528
Citroen Visa (79 - 88)	0620
Citroen Xantia Petrol & Diesel (93 - Oct 95)	3082
Citroen XM Petrol & Diesel (89 - 98)	3451
Citroen ZX Diesel (91 - 93)	1922
Citroen ZX Petrol (91 - 94)	1881
Citroen 1.7 & 1.9 litre Diesel Engine (84 - 96)	1379
COLT	
Colt 1200, 1250 & 1400 (79 - May 84)	0600
DAIMLER	
Daimler Sovereign (68 - Oct 86)	0242
Daimler Double Six (72 - 88)	0478
FIAT	
Fiat 126 (73 - 87)	0305
Fiat 127 (71 - 83)	0193
Fiat 500 (57 - 73)	0090
Fiat Cinquecento (June 93 - 98)	3501
Fiat Panda (81 - 95)	0793
Fiat Punto (94 - 96)	3251
Fiat Regata (84 - 88)	1167
Fiat Strada (79 - 88)	0479
Fiat Tipo (88 - 91)	1625

Title	Book No.
Fiat Uno (83 - 95)	0923
Fiat X1/9 (74 - 89)	0273
FORD	
Ford Capri II (& III) 1.6 & 2.0 (74 - 87)	0283
Ford Capri II (& III) 2.8 & 3.0 (74 - 87)	1309
Ford Cortina Mk IV (& V) 1.6 & 2.0 (76 - 83)	0343
Ford Escort (75 - Aug 80)	0280
Ford Escort (Sept 80 - Sept 90)	0686
Ford Escort (Sept 90 - 97)	1737
Ford Escort Mk II Mexico, RS 1600 & RS 2000 (75 - 80)	0735
Ford Fiesta (inc. XR2) (76 - Aug 83)	0334
Ford Fiesta (inc. XR2) (Aug 83 - Feb 89)	1030
Ford Fiesta (Feb 89 - Oct 95)	1595
Ford Fiesta Petrol & Diesel (Oct 95 - 97)	3397
Ford Granada (Sept 77 - Feb 85)	0481
Ford Granada (Mar 85 - 94)	1245
Ford Mondeo 4-cyl (93 - 96)	1923
Ford Mondeo Diesel (93 - 96)	3465
Ford Orion (83 - Sept 90)	1009
Ford Orion (Sept 90 - 93)	1737
Ford Sierra 1.3, 1.6, 1.8 & 2.0 (82 - 93)	0903
Ford Sierra 2.3, 2.8 & 2.9 (82 - 91)	0904
Ford Scorpio (Mar 85 - 94)	1245
Ford Transit Petrol (Mk 2) (78 - Jan 86)	0719
Ford Transit Petrol (Mk 3) (Feb 86 - 89)	1468
Ford Transit Diesel (Feb 86 - 95)	3019
Ford 1.6 & 1.8 litre Diesel Engine (84 - 96)	1172
Ford 2.1, 2.3 & 2.5 litre Diesel Engine (77 - 90)	1606
FREIGHT ROVER	
Freight Rover Sherpa (74 - 87)	0463
HILLMAN	
Hillman Avenger (70 - 82)	0037
HONDA	
Honda Accord (76 - Feb 84)	0351
Honda Accord (Feb 84 - Oct 85)	1177
Honda Civic (Feb 84 - Oct 87)	1226
Honda Civic (Nov 91 - 96)	3199
HYUNDAI	
Hyundai Pony (85 - 94)	3398
JAGUAR	
Jaguar E Type (61 - 72)	0140
Jaguar MkI & II, 240 & 340 (55 - 69)	0098
Jaguar XJ6, XJ & Sovereign (68 - Oct 86)	0242
Jaguar XJ6 & Sovereign (Oct 86 - Sept 94)	3261
Jaguar XJ12, XJS & Sovereign (72 - 88)	0478
JEEP	
Jeep Cherokee Petrol (93 - 96)	1943
LADA	
Lada 1200, 1300, 1500 & 1600 (74 - 91)	0413
Lada Samara (87 - 91)	1610
LAND ROVER	
Land Rover 90, 110 & Defender Diesel (83 - 95)	3017
Land Rover Discovery Diesel (89 - 95)	3016
Land Rover Series IIA & III Diesel (58 - 85)	0529
Land Rover Series II, IIA & III Petrol (58 - 85)	0314
MAZDA	
Mazda 323 fwd (Mar 81 - Oct 89)	1608

Title	Book No.
Mazda 323 (Oct 89 - 98)	3455
Mazda 626 fwd (May 83 - Sept 87)	0929
Mazda B-1600, B-1800 & B-2000 Pick-up (72 - 88)	0267
MERCEDES-BENZ	
Mercedes-Benz 190, 190E & 190D Petrol & Diesel (83 - 93)	3450
Mercedes-Benz 200, 240, 300 Diesel (Oct 76 - 85)	1114
Mercedes-Benz 250 & 280 (68 - 72)	0346
Mercedes-Benz 250 & 280 (123 Series) (Oct 76 - 84)	0677
Mercedes-Benz 124 Series (85 - Aug 93)	3253
MG	
MGB (62 - 80)	0111
MG Maestro 1.3 & 1.6 (83 - 95)	0922
MG Metro (80 - May 90)	0718
MG Midget & AH Sprite (58 - 80)	0265
MG Montego 2.0 (84 - 95)	1067
MITSUBISHI	
Mitsubishi 1200, 1250 & 1400 (79 - May 84)	0600
Mitsubishi Shogun & L200 Pick-Ups (83 - 94)	1944
MORRIS	
Morris Ital 1.3 (80 - 84)	0705
Morris Minor 1000 (56 - 71)	0024
NISSAN	
Nissan Bluebird fwd (May 84 - Mar 86)	1223
Nissan Bluebird (T12 & T72) (Mar 86 - 90)	1473
Nissan Cherry (N12) (Sept 82 - 86)	1031
Nissan Micra (K10) (83 - Jan 93)	0931
Nissan Micra (93 - 96)	3254
Nissan Primera (90 - Oct 96)	1851
Nissan Stanza (82 - 86)	0824
Nissan Sunny (B11) (May 82 - Oct 86)	0895
Nissan Sunny (Oct 86 - Mar 91)	1378
Nissan Sunny (Apr 91 - 95)	3219
OPEL	
Opel Ascona & Manta (B Series) (Sept 75 - 88)	0316
Opel Ascona (81 - 88) (Not available in UK see Vauxhall Cavalier 0812)	3215
Opel Astra (Oct 91 - 96) (Not available in UK see Vauxhall Astra 1832)	3156
Opel Calibra (90 - 98) (See Vauxhall/Opel Calibra Book No. 3502)	
Opel Corsa (83 - Mar 93) (Not available in UK see Vauxhall Nova 0909)	3160
Opel Corsa (Mar 93 - 94) (Not available in UK see Vauxhall Corsa 1985)	3159
Opel Frontera Petrol & Diesel (91 - 98) (See Vauxhall/Opel Frontera Book No. 1985)	
Opel Kadett (Nov 79 - Oct 84)	0634
Opel Kadett (Oct 84 - Oct 91) (Not available in UK see Vauxhall Astra & Belmont 1136)	3196
Opel Omega & Senator (86 - 94) (Not available in UK see Vauxhall Carlton & Senator 1469)	3157
Opel Rekord (Feb 78 - Oct 86)	0543
Opel Vectra (88 - Oct 95) (Not available in UK see Vauxhall Cavalier 1570)	3158

Title	Book No.
Opel Vectra Petrol & Diesel (95 - 98) (Not available in UK see Vauxhall Vectra 3396)	3523
PEUGEOT	
Peugeot 106 Petrol & Diesel (91 - June 96)	1882
Peugeot 205 (83 - 95)	0932
Peugeot 305 (78 - 89)	0538
Peugeot 306 Petrol & Diesel (93 - 95)	3073
Peugeot 309 (86 - 93)	1266
Peugeot 405 Petrol (88 - 96)	1559
Peugeot 405 Diesel (88 - 96)	3198
Peugeot 406 Petrol & Diesel (96 - 97)	3394
Peugeot 505 (79 - 89)	0762
Peugeot 1.7/1.8 & 1.9 litre Diesel Engines (82 - 96)	0950
Peugeot 2.0, 2.1, 2.3 & 2.5 litre Diesel Engines (74 - 90)	1607
PORSCHE	
Porsche 911 (65 - 85)	0264
Porsche 924 & 924 Turbo (76 - 85)	0397
PROTON	
Proton (89 - 97)	3255
RANGE ROVER	
Range Rover V8 (70 - Oct 92)	0606
RELIANT	
Reliant Robin & Kitten (73 - 83)	0436
RENAULT	
Renault 5 (72 - Feb 85)	0141
Renault 5 (Feb 85 - 96)	1219
Renault 9 & 11 (82 - 89)	0822
Renault 18 (79 - 86)	0598
Renault 19 Petrol (89 - 94)	1646
Renault 19 Diesel (89 - 95)	1946
Renault 21 (86 - 94)	1397
Renault 25 (84 - 92)	1228
Renault Clio Petrol (91 - 93)	1853
Renault Clio Diesel (91 - June 96)	3031
Renault Espace (85 - 96)	3197
Renault Laguna (94 - 96)	3252
Renault Mégane Petrol & Diesel (96 - 97)	3395
ROVER	
Rover 111 & 114 (95 - 96)	1711
Rover 213 & 216 (84 - 89)	1116
Rover 214 & 414 (89 - 96)	1689
Rover 216 & 416 (89 - 96)	1830
Rover 200 Series Petrol & Diesel (95 - 98)	3399
Rover 400 Series Petrol & Diesel (95 - 98)	3453
Rover 618, 620 & 623 (93 - 97)	3257
Rover 820, 825 & 827 (86 - 95)	1380
Rover 2000, 2300 & 2600 (77 - 87)	0468
Rover 3500 (SD1) (76 - 87)	0365
Rover Metro (May 90 - 94)	1711
SAAB	
Saab 90, 99 & 900 (79 - Oct 93)	0765
Saab 9000 (4-cyl) (85 - 95)	1686
SEAT	
Seat Ibiza & Malaga (85 - 92)	1609

Title	Book No.
SKODA	
Skoda Estelle 105, 120, 130 & 136 (77 - 89)	0604
Skoda Favorit (89 - 92)	1801
SUBARU	
Subaru 1600 & 1800 (Nov 79 - 90)	0995
SUZUKI	
Suzuki SJ Series, Samurai & Vitara (82 - 97)	1942
Suzuki Supercarry (86 - Oct 94)	3015
TALBOT	
Talbot Alpine, Solara, Minx & Rapier (75 - 86)	0337
Talbot Horizon (78 - 86)	0473
Talbot Samba (82 - 86)	0823
TOYOTA	
Toyota Carina E (May 92 - 97)	3256
Toyota Corolla (fwd) (Sept 83 - Sept 87)	1024
Toyota Corolla (rwd) (80 - 85)	0683
Toyota Corolla (Sept 87 - 92)	1683
Toyota Corolla (Aug 92 - 97)	3259
Toyota Hi-Ace & Hi-Lux (69 - Oct 83)	0304
Toyota Starlet (78 - Jan 85)	0462
TRIUMPH	
Triumph Acclaim (81 - 84)	0792
Triumph GT6 & Vitesse (62 - 74)	0112
Triumph Herald (59 - 71)	0010
Triumph Spitfire (62 - 81)	0113
Triumph Stag (70 - 78)	0441
Triumph TR7 (75 - 82)	0322
VAUXHALL	
Vauxhall Astra (80 - Oct 84)	0635
Vauxhall Astra & Belmont (Oct 84 - Oct 91)	1136
Vauxhall Astra (Oct 91 - 96)	1832
Vauxhall/Opel Calibra (90 - 98)	3502
Vauxhall Carlton (Oct 78 - Oct 86)	0480
Vauxhall Carlton (Nov 86 - 94)	1469
Vauxhall Cavalier 1600, 1900 & 2000 (75 - July 81)	0315
Vauxhall Cavalier (81 - Oct 88)	0812
Vauxhall Cavalier (Oct 88 - Oct 95)	1570
Vauxhall Chevette (75 - 84)	0285
Vauxhall Corsa (93 - 97)	1985
Vauxhall/Opel Frontera Petrol & Diesel (91 - 98)	3454
Vauxhall Nova (83 - 93)	0909
Vauxhall Rascal (86 - 93)	3015
Vauxhall Senator (Sept 87 - 94)	1469
Vauxhall Vectra Petrol & Diesel (95 - 98)	3396
Vauxhall/Opel 1.5, 1.6 & 1.7 litre Diesel Engines (82 - 96)	1222
VOLKSWAGEN	
VW Beetle 1200 (54 - 77)	0036
VW Beetle 1300 & 1500 (65 - 75)	0039
VW Beetle 1302 & 1302S (70 - 72)	0110
VW Beetle 1303, 1303S & GT (72 - 75)	0159
VW Golf Mk 1 1.1 & 1.3 (74 - Feb 84)	0716
VW Golf Mk 1 1.5, 1.6 & 1.8 (74 - 85)	0726
VW Golf Mk 1 Diesel (78 - Feb 84)	0451
VW Golf Mk 2 (Mar 84 - Feb 92)	1081
VW Golf Mk 3 Petrol & Diesel (Feb 92 - 96)	3097

Title	Book No.
VW Jetta Mk 1 1.1 & 1.3 (80 - June 84)	0716
VW Jetta Mk 1 1.5, 1.6 & 1.8 (80 - June 84)	0726
VW Jetta Mk 1 Diesel (81 - June 84)	0451
VW Jetta Mk 2 (July 84 - 92)	1081
VW LT vans & light trucks (76 - 87)	0637
VW Passat (Sept 81 - May 88)	0814
VW Passat (May 88 - 91)	1647
VW Polo & Derby (76 - Jan 82)	0335
VW Polo (82 - Oct 90)	0813
VW Polo (Nov 90 - Aug 94)	3245
VW Polo Hatchback (95 - 98)	3500
VW Santana (Sept 82 - 85)	0814
VW Scirocco Mk 1 1.5, 1.6 & 1.8 (74 - 82)	0726
VW Scirocco (82 - 90)	1224
VW Transporter 1600 (68 - 79)	0082
VW Transporter 1700, 1800 & 2000 (72 - 79)	0226
VW Transporter with air-cooled engine (79 - 82)	0638
VW Transporter water-cooled (82 - 90)	3452
VW Vento Petrol & Diesel (Feb 92 - 96)	3097
VOLVO	
Volvo 142, 144 & 145 (66 - 74)	0129
Volvo 240 Series (74 - 93)	0270
Volvo 262, 264 & 260/265 (75 - 85)	0400
Volvo 340, 343, 345 & 360 (76 - 91)	0715
Volvo 440, 460 & 480 (87 - 92)	1691
Volvo 740 & 760 (82 - 91)	1258
Volvo 850 (92 - 96)	3260
Volvo 940 (90 - 96)	3249
YUGO/ZASTAVA	
Yugo/Zastava (81 - 90)	1453
TECH BOOKS	
Automotive Brake Manual	3050
Automotive Carburettor Manual	3288
Automotive Diagnostic Fault Codes Manual	3472
Automotive Diesel Engine Service Guide	3286
Automotive Electrical and Electronic Systems Manual	3049
Automotive Engine Management and Fuel Injection Systems Manual	3344
Automotive Gearbox Overhaul Manual	3473
Automotive Service Summaries Manual	3475
Automotive Timing Belt Manual - Ford	3474
Automotive Welding Manual	3053
In-Car Entertainment Manual (3rd Edition)	3363
CAR BOOKS	
Automotive Fuel Injection Systems	9755
Car Bodywork Repair Manual	9864
Caravan Manual (2nd Edition)	9894
Haynes Technical Data Book (89 - 98)	1998
How to Keep Your Car Alive	9868
Japanese Vehicle Carburettors	1786
Motorcaravan Manual, The	L7322
Small Engine Repair Manual	1755
SU Carburettors	0299
Weber Carburettors (to 79)	0393

CL06.07/98

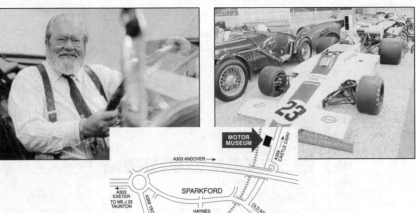

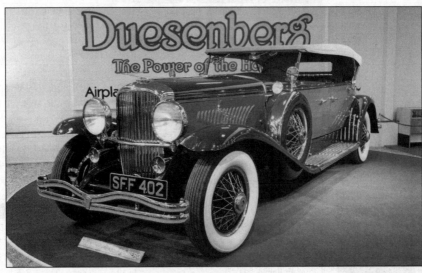